DICTIONARY OF
American History

Third Edition

EDITORIAL BOARD

DICTIONARY OF
American History

Third Edition

Stanley I. Kutler, *Editor in Chief*

Volume 1
Aachen to Butler

CHARLES SCRIBNER'S SONS

New York • Detroit • San Diego • San Francisco • Cleveland • New Haven, Conn. • Waterville, Maine • London • Munich

THOMSON
™
GALE

Dictionary of American History, Third Edition
Stanley I. Kutler, *Editor*

© 2003 by Charles Scribner's Sons
Charles Scribner's Sons is an imprint
of The Gale Group, Inc., a division of
Thomson Learning, Inc.

Charles Scribner's Sons® and Thomson
Learning™ are trademarks used herein
under license.

For more information, contact
Charles Scribner's Sons
An imprint of the Gale Group
300 Park Avenue South
New York, NY 10010

For permission to use material from this
product, submit your request via Web at
http://www.gale-edit.com/permissions, or you
may download our Permissions Request form
and submit your request by fax or mail to:

Permissions Department
The Gale Group, Inc.
27500 Drake Rd.
Farmington Hills, MI 48331-3535
Permissions Hotline:
248-699-8006 or 800-877-4253, ext. 8006
Fax: 248-699-8074 or 800-762-4058

LIBRARY OF CONGRESS CATALOGING-IN-PUBLICATION DATA

Dictionary of American history / Stanley I. Kutler.—3rd ed.
    p.   cm.
Includes bibliographical references and index.
    ISBN 0-684-80533-2 (set : alk. paper)
    1. United States—History—Dictionaries.   I. Kutler, Stanley I.
E174 .D52   2003
973'.03—dc21

Printed in United States of America
10 9 8 7 6 5 4 3 2 1

EDITORIAL AND PRODUCTION STAFF

(continued on next page)

Captions
Richard Slovak

Primary Source Document Selection
Mark D. Baumann   Cynthia R. Poe   Honor Sachs   Christopher Wells

Cartography
Donald S. Frazier
Robert F. Pace

Tina Bertrand   Robert Wettemann

McMurry University
Abilene, Texas

Line Art
Argosy Publishing

Index
Coughlin Indexing Services, Inc.

Page Design
Pamela Galbreath

Cover Design
Jennifer Wahi

Imaging
Robert Duncan   Leitha Etheridge-Sims   Mary Grimes   Lezlie Light
Dan Newell   David G. Oblender   Chris O'Bryan   Kelly A. Quin
Luke Rademacher   Robyn Young

Permissions
Margaret Chamberlain

Compositor
Impressions Book and Journal Services, Inc.

Manufacturing
Wendy Blurton

Publisher
Frank Menchaca

ARTICLE REVIEW
AND UPDATING

CONTENTS

LIST OF MAPS

PREFACE

The *Dictionary of American History* has been the leading reference work in United States history for more than six decades. This third edition builds on the original, edited by James Truslow Adams (six volumes, 1940), the 1976 revision in eight volumes, and the two-volume supplement edited by Robert H. Ferrell and Joan Hoff in 1996. As promised in 1940, the *Dictionary* is committed to making the voluminous record of the past readily available in one convenient source, where the interested reader can locate the facts, events, trends, or policies of American history. Once again, we have contributions from a wide array of authorities, representing varied professions, occupations, and regions.

For this edition, we have been especially mindful that as new generations of Americans examine their history, the priorities, importance, and interpretations of this history evolve. History changes—and it does not. The facts historians choose to emphasize, and the manner in which they render certain events, mirror the way society views itself and its past. Those who study U.S. history will find that these volumes retain the original edition's thorough coverage of political, military, and economic developments. But the scope of the historical profession's interest has significantly expanded during the past quarter century, as historians increasingly have emphasized social, cultural, personal, and demographic considerations—all of which contribute to our ever-expanding knowledge of the American experience.

Diversity always has been a major theme of American history. But in recent years, American historical writing has reflected a heightened search for inclusiveness to better acknowledge and comprehend that diversity. The *Dictionary* originally focused on political and military history, reflecting the discipline's chief concerns at the time. But today we talk about "political culture," not just politics. Political history is not just about compiling electoral results or noting the passage of laws or programs. The social, cultural, and economic forces that propel political agendas are very much within its scope. The new *Dictionary of American History* therefore devotes proper attention to the roles of women, blacks, Indians, and various ethnic groups and socioeconomic classes. We recognize that we cannot discuss slavery, the struggle for civil rights, or poverty without noting the agency of blacks themselves, as instigators of change. And we cannot discuss industrialization and labor in America without considering the women—New England mill girls, immigrant workers in the needle trades, "career girl" clerks—whose actions and experiences are vital to understanding these processes.

This new edition significantly expands the *Dictionary* to over three million words, roughly 20 percent more than the previous edition. Bibliographies have been greatly increased and brought up to date. For the first time, the *Dictionary* is illustrated. This edition features more than 1,200 photographs and 252 maps. Cross-referencing has been greatly enhanced by the use of both internal highlighting (MANIFEST DESTINY) and copious *see also* references. The cross-references also direct the reader to an entirely new resource: the whole of volume 9 is a major archive of primary source documents and original period maps. This collection will enable the student to advance beyond narrative summary to the sine qua non of historical research: examination of the original materials. Finally, the index volume is now supplemented by a guide to historical writing, with pedagogical examples drawn from the *Dictionary* itself, as well as a section correlating hundreds of entries to widely adopted American history textbooks.

In one respect, however, the contents have been simplified. The total number of articles has been reduced. When the editors first convened in November 1996, they faced the question that confronts all encyclopedists—whether to lump subjects together for the sake of comparative analysis or atomize them for easy look-up. Previous editions had tended in the latter direction. There were 6,425 separate entries in the second edition, supplemented by 757 more in 1996. The editors felt that readers would be better served by a degree of consolidation. The present edition contains 4,434 entries. Instead of detailing dozens of separate colonial explorations, for example, the subject is treated in five major essays on explorations and expeditions (British, Dutch, French, Russian, and Spanish). The related topic of U.S.-sponsored expeditions is treated in this same complex of articles. This editorial change is one of degree. No one suggested omitting de Soto or Coronado or Lewis and Clark. Individual entries on those major expeditions remain. But many others no longer claim their own subject headings. Instead they are treated contextually and comparatively in the essays noted above. Of course, readers in search of specific details can still access them in the full-length index of the present set and in the several forthcoming electronic versions of the *Dictionary*.

Because the original *Dictionary of American History* is itself a valuable cross-section of American historiography, Scribners has preserved the old material in digital form (presently available as *Scribner's American History and Culture on CD-ROM* and as a prime component of the Gale Group's *History Resource Center*, a massive online compilation of history reference materials accessible via major public and research libraries). We have deleted old entries and added new ones. Nearly 2,500 of the old *Dictionary* entries, mostly brief, have been consigned to the archives: Adams Express Company; Battle of Adobe Walls; Anti–Horse Thief Association; *Bank of the U.S. v. Planter's Bank of Georgia*; Camp Butler; Immunity Bath; Fort Mifflin; Old Fuss and Feathers; Raisin River Massacre; Society of Colonial Wars; Visible Admixture Law; and Zoar Society, to name a few. These writings, primarily from 1940, will remain available as a fascinating tool for those who study the profession of history.

To consolidate the *Dictionary*'s wealth of material and bring it up to date, the editors decided on a four-part approach. In the making of the present edition, each article was classified as retained, revised, replaced, or brand new.

- *Retained* (1,785 articles). Where the original material was judged sound and the original contributor particularly distinguished (Allan Nevins on Standard Oil, Perry Ellis on the Antinomian Controversy, or even General John J. Pershing on American Expeditionary Forces), the core of the old entry has been retained. A team based at the University of Wisconsin under the direction of Andrew Rieser was assigned to check the old material for accuracy in the light of new scholarship and to bring the bibliographies up to date. These articles are generally signed by the original authors, with the reviser's initials following (*Allan Nevins* / A. R.).

- *Revised* (448 articles). Some articles were deemed to be essentially valid but in need of significant addition or change of emphasis. All such articles were assigned to contemporary scholars, who were given a flexible mandate to revise to a greater or lesser degree. Many different judgments were rendered by the contemporary scholarly community. Some experts decided to retain the bulk of the old material and supply only a silent emendation. More often the rewriting was extensive and appears over a joint signature or that of the new author alone.

- *Replaced* (1,360 articles). For the entries judged unsatisfactory in the light of present knowledge, entirely new scholarly treatments have been commissioned.

- *New* (841 articles). Events like the contested presidential election of 2000 and the 9/11 attacks obviously demanded articles of their own. Likewise such concepts as African American Studies, Creationism, Sexual Orientation, and Zionism are treated here for the first time.

While radically refashioning the contents of the *Dictionary*, the editors did adhere to one of its original distinguishing traits. Unlike other U.S. history compendiums, the *Dictionary* does not include biographies. This decision stems from the work's origin as a complement to Scribner's *Dictionary of American Biography* (1927–1995). Today the *Dictionary of American Biography*, supplemented by the newer *Scribner Encyclopedia of American Lives* and many other biographical reference works, remains a prime source for the lives of famous Americans. We found that by omitting the standard short lives, the *Dictionary of American History* would have room for far more substantial treatments of other subjects. Of course, countless individuals who have influenced American life can still be traced in the *Dictionary*'s index.

The cumulative result of the editors' work is the most thorough reworking in the history of historical reference books. "Sandusky" has been archived, while "San Diego," now one of the nation's ten largest cities, has been substantially expanded. We also have shifted our emphasis. In 1940, the *Dictionary* had an entry on Archangel, a Russian port, occupied and used by Allied Expeditionary Forces who went to the Soviet Union to contain the Bolshevik Revolution. But the old *Dictionary* had no essay on the larger scope of the Russian intervention in 1918, and obviously, if students need to know about that intervention, it is unlikely that they would simply search for a piece on Archangel. The new edition includes an entry on the intervention and a larger one on the whole course of Russian-American relations.

Time obviously adds to the body of facts. But altered circumstances force us to change emphasis or focus, and our interpretations of events and historical processes are constantly evolving. Consider:

The South.   For more than 350 years, the South represented a major component of American colonial and national history. The region played a large role in the settlement and development of the nation, but the central historical concern was riveted on its economic system of slavery, and the political and social implications of the "peculiar institution." That system, of course, resulted in the Civil War, an event of transcendent importance in American history. The impact of the war—whether in the events of Reconstruction, the continued subjugation of the large African American minority, or the region's semicolonial status in the American economic system—offered standard fare for historical narrative until well past the midpoint of the twentieth century. But the South's "Lost Cause" eventually became just that, and the history of the South in the past forty to fifty years has become something substantially different. The civil rights movement eventually liberated white and black people alike, as President Jimmy Carter famously said. The entrenched power of the region's congressmen provided a substantial flow of federal money for military and economic spending in the region. The area's resistance to unionization made it a magnet for the migration of northern industry. Technological change, such as air conditioning, substantially contributed to making the area habitable and attracting new population from the northern and midwestern parts of the country.

Today, "the South" is a vastly different place, with a drastically altered political, economic, and social standing within the American nation. All these considerations can be found in the new volumes, under such varied headings as the South, Civil Rights Laws, Discrimination, Right-to-Work Laws, and Air Conditioning. And yet we have retained (and revised) the historical description of the slave economy and the social system it sustained (Plantation System; Slave Trade; Slavery), for such institutions remain essential to understanding the historical and evolving nature of the South, and indeed of the nation as a whole.

The West. The 1940s perception of the American West also was vastly different from today's. The image of the "Wild West," romanticized and exaggerated in such popular works as *The Virginian* and *Stagecoach*, now has been replaced by one of a vibrant economy, a leader in technological development, and an innovator of unique lifestyles. Again, we must examine a major population shift, migrations of peoples and industries, the growth of new cities, and the role of vast outlays of federal money. Yet such key concepts of more traditional American historiography as transportation, public lands, and mining still must be addressed in order to understand the region's history. Furthermore, the role of water—and the lack of it—remains essential for interpreting the development of what essentially remains the "Great American Desert."

African American life today is vastly different than it was sixty years ago, when segregation, by law in the South and by informal custom elsewhere, retained a firm grip on American life. World War II and its aftermath brought important changes, fueled in part by population exchange and migration. In the decades since, African American history and its relationship to the history of the nation as a whole have changed greatly as well. In 1940, the "Negro" generally was discussed in a passive sense; now we examine African American life and culture for their dynamic contributions to American life. Today, diversity, race, and ethnicity are celebrated as integral components of American culture, not ignored or swept aside. In this edition of the *Dictionary of American History*, the student will find a broad range of topics illustrating the experience and cultural life of a group that now constitutes approximately 13 percent of the population. These topics include African American Religions and Sects, and African American Studies. Elsewhere there are integrated treatments of the black experience in higher education, literature, the military, and the polling place (Suffrage). Readers may also consult such topics as Black Cavalry in the West, Black Nationalism, Black Panthers, Black Power, the Civil Rights Movement, the Harlem Renaissance, Race Relations, and many others.

The World Trade Center, of course, was not included in the 1940 or 1976 editions. But in this revision, we include it as representative and symbolic of U.S. preeminence in world economic affairs. In the past decade, the Trade Center has become, too, a symbol of American vulnerability to a new threat of terrorism. Both the bombing of 1993 and the events of 11 September 2001 are treated in the new work.

Producing the *Dictionary of American History* has been a cooperative effort. Charles Scribner's Sons sponsored the project from its outset in the 1930s. The inevitable corporate changes have not altered its commitment. Publisher Karen Day inaugurated this revision in 1996. She and Frank Menchaca, her successor, consistently offered the necessary leadership and material support. Managing Editor John Fitzpatrick and Associate Editor Anna Grojec provided the direction and daily attention to keep things going. Their fine staff of assistants and copy editors has been superb. Valued and respected friends and colleagues contributed mightily to the completion of this task. Lizabeth Cohen, Pauline Maier, and Louis Masur participated in the formulation and conception of the volumes. Andrew Rieser directed a team of enthusiastic, hardworking graduate students in updating many hundreds of entries. Frederick Hoxie provided his unrivaled knowledge of Native American history and completely revamped the editorial content for that area. Last but hardly least, Associate Editors Michael Bernstein, Hasia Diner, David Hollinger, and Graham Hodges supplied the bulk of editorial direction and substantive criticism of the work, supplemented by the expertise of Philip Pauly in the life sciences and Rolf Achilles in the visual arts. I am grateful to all who joined me in this venture.

Stanley I. Kutler
Madison, Wis.
10 August 2002

DICTIONARY OF
American History

Third Edition

A

AACHEN. An important, if costly, symbolic victory for the Allies during World War II, Aachen was the first German city captured and held by Allied troops. Sitting along a system of German defensive works known as the West Wall, the city was taken by the American First Army, commanded by General Courtney Hodges, after a bitter series of street-to-street battles in September and October 1944.

The original American advance toward Aachen in September came as a result of General Dwight Eisenhower's decision on 10 September 1944 to support the ill-fated British and U.S. airborne operation code-named Market Garden, which occurred west of Aachen in Belgium and Holland from 17 September to 26 September 1944. Even after Market Garden's failure, Hodges kept up the fight for Aachen. The bitterest fighting occurred from 15 to 21 October, with the Americans using heavy air and artillery bombardments to support infantry slowly advancing from house to house. The German Seventh Army, having delayed the Americans by five weeks, withdrew to more defensible positions on the 21st. Aachen demonstrated that despite its defeat in France, the German army was far from beaten. The optimistic claims of some officers that the Allies would be in Berlin by Christmas were laid bare. Much hard fighting remained.

BIBLIOGRAPHY

Doubler, Michael. *Closing with the Enemy: How GIs Fought the War in Europe.* Lawrence: University Press of Kansas, 1994.

Michael S. Neiberg

ABC CONFERENCE. In May 1914 Argentina, Brazil, and Chile convened a conference in Niagara Falls to mediate a conflict between the United States and the Victoriano Huerta regime in Mexico. The conflict had arisen when President Woodrow Wilson ordered American forces to land in Veracruz. The battle that ensued dragged the United States directly into the Mexican Revolution and threatened war between the two nations. The conference failed because Venustiano Carranza, a rival of Huerta's, rejected its proposal for a provisional government. Huerta's resignation in July 1914, however, temporarily eased the crisis. In March 1916 the conflict erupted with renewed intensity when Pancho Villa launched a raid on Columbus, New Mexico.

BIBLIOGRAPHY

Gilderhus, Mark T. *Diplomacy and Revolution: U.S.–Mexican Relations under Wilson and Carranza.* Tucson: University of Arizona Press, 1977.

Quirk, Robert E. *An Affair of Honor: Woodrow Wilson and the Occupation of Veracruz.* Lexington: University of Kentucky Press, 1962.

Dana G. Munro/A. G.

See also **Veracruz Incident.**

ABENAKI. At first contact with Europeans, Abenaki peoples occupied most of northern New England. The Abenakis included the Penobscots, Norridgewocks, Kennebecs, and Androscoggins in Maine; Pennacooks and Pigwackets in the Merrimack Valley and White Mountains of New Hampshire; Sokokis and Cowasucks in the upper Connecticut Valley; and the Missisquois and other groups on the shores of Lake Champlain in Vermont. Abenakis were primarily hunters, but their subsistence economy also included fishing, gathering, and corn agriculture.

English expansion northward after King Philip's War in 1675–1676 drove many Abenakis to seek refuge at French mission villages like Odanak on the St. Lawrence. In the imperial wars between 1689 and 1763, most Abenakis made common cause with the French against the English. The English retaliated with bounties on Abenaki scalps and raids on Abenaki villages, most notably the Rogers' Rangers attack on Odanak in 1759. The fall of New France opened Abenaki country to English settlement. Although many Abenakis supported their colonial neighbors in the American Revolution, encroachment on Abenaki lands continued.

After European diseases, the fur trade, and invasion disrupted their subsistence patterns, many Abenakis continued traditional ways of living in the more remote areas of their homelands. Others found work as farm laborers, basket makers, trappers, loggers, and mill workers. Some served as guides for travelers and tourists. Many married non-Indians. Most lived in poverty. By the nineteenth century, most New Englanders assumed the Abenakis had effectively "disappeared."

But Abenaki people "resurfaced" in the late twentieth century. In 1980 the Penobscots and Passamaquoddies won $81.5 million in compensation for lands taken illegally by Maine and Massachusetts. Abenakis in Vermont promoted awareness of Native issues as they fought to protect human remains, preserve the Abenaki language, and revive traditional dances and crafts. They challenged the state on issues of sovereignty and petitioned the Bureau of Indian Affairs for federal recognition, which remained undecided at the beginning of the twenty-first century.

BIBLIOGRAPHY

Calloway, Colin G. *The Western Abenakis of Vermont, 1600–1800: War, Migration, and the Survival of an Indian People.* Norman: University of Oklahoma Press, 1990.

Haviland, William A., and Marjory W. Power. *The Original Vermonters: Native Inhabitants Past and Present.* Rev. ed. Hanover, N.H.: University Press of New England, 1994.

Wiseman, Frederick Matthew. *The Voice of the Dawn: An Autohistory of the Abenaki Nation.* Hanover, N.H.: University Press of New England, 2001.

Colin G. Calloway

See also **King Philip's War; Tribes: Northeastern.**

ABILENE, an early cattle town in Kansas, was established by Illinois cattle buyer Joseph G. McCoy in 1867 as a depot to which drovers might bring Texas livestock for rail shipment to Kansas City. Trail drivers' attempts to reach market in 1866 had failed largely because of the hostility of settlers in Missouri and eastern Kansas. Residents there feared the spread of Texas fever, which prevailed among longhorn cattle and could infect their domesticated cattle. Located on the Kansas Pacific Railway, Abilene was a popular shipping point for several years, until the westward advance of settlers forced the drovers to new cattle towns farther west.

BIBLIOGRAPHY

Dykstra, Robert R. *The Cattle Towns.* New York: Knopf, 1968.

Edward Everett Dale / s. b.

See also **Cattle Drives; Cow Towns; Railroads.**

ABILENE TRAIL was a cattle trail from northern Texas to the railway terminal in Abilene, Kansas. Its exact route is disputed owing to its many offshoots. The trail crossed the Red River a little east of Henrietta, Texas, and continued north across Indian Territory (present-day Oklahoma) to Caldwell, Kansas, and then on past Wichita and Newton to Abilene. The first herds were probably driven along its path in 1866, although the trail was not named until the city of Abilene was established in 1867.

BIBLIOGRAPHY

Haywood, C. Robert. *Trails South: The Wagon-Road Economy in the Dodge City–Panhandle Region.* Norman: University of Oklahoma Press, 1986.

Skaggs, Jimmy M. *The Cattle-Trailing Industry: Between Supply and Demand, 1866–1890.* Lawrence: University Press of Kansas, 1973.

Edward Everett Dale / h. s.

See also **Cattle Drives.**

ABLEMAN V. BOOTH, 62 U.S. 506 (1859). In 1854, a United States deputy marshal, acting on behalf of the Missouri slave owner Benjamin S. Garland, seized Joshua Glover, a fugitive slave, living in Racine, Wisconsin, and took him to Milwaukee. The mayor of Racine quickly issued an arrest warrant for Garland, while abolitionists in Racine obtained a writ of habeas corpus from a county judge ordering U.S. Marshal Stephen V. Ableman to bring Glover before him. Before these could be served, the abolitionist activist and newspaper publisher Sherman Booth led a mob that rescued Glover, who soon disappeared, presumably going to Canada.

Marshal Ableman then arrested Booth and John Rycraft for violating the Fugitive Slave Law of 1850, but in *In re Booth* (1854), the Wisconsin Supreme Court released the men. Ableman then rearrested both men, who were subsequently convicted in federal court. However, in *In re Booth and Rycraft* (1854), the Wisconsin Supreme Court again issued a writ of habeas corpus, forcing Ableman to release Booth and Rycraft.

With Booth out of jail, Ableman turned to the U.S. Supreme Court, but the Wisconsin Supreme Court ignored the national court and refused to forward the record of the case to Washington. The case remained suspended until the Wisconsin Supreme Court published its opinions. The U.S. Supreme Court then used these opinions as the basis for overturning the state supreme court in *Ableman v. Booth.*

In a powerful opinion, Chief Justice Roger Taney condemned the Wisconsin court's actions, emphatically denying that any state courts could interfere with the federal courts. With some irony, Taney declared that the states' rights position of the Wisconsin court was "preposterous" and "new in the jurisprudence of the United States, as well as the States." Taney emphatically asserted national power and state subordination to the Constitution and to the Supreme Court, writing that each state is obligated "to support this Constitution. And no power is more clearly conferred than the power of this court to decide ultimately and finally, all cases arising under such Constitution and laws."

After the decision, Ableman once again arrested Booth, who was soon rescued from custody and remained at large for about two months, giving speeches in Wisconsin and challenging Ableman to arrest him. Ableman ultimately did arrest him, and he remained in jail for another six months, until President James Buchanan pardoned him in March 1861.

BIBLIOGRAPHY

Finkelman, Paul. *An Imperfect Union: Slavery, Federalism, and Comity.* Chapel Hill: University of North Carolina Press, 1981.

Hyman Harold M., and William M. Wiecek. *Equal Justice Under Law: Constitutional Development, 1835–1875.* New York: HarperCollins, 1982.

Paul Finkelman

See also **Fugitive Slave Acts.**

ABOLITION. *See* **Antislavery.**

ABORTION

To 1800

Records of abortions exist from throughout the American colonies in the seventeenth and eighteenth centuries. A variety of herbs and other plant products, including tansy, savin, pennyroyal, seneca snakeroot, and rue were used as abortifacients, some available from physicians but many attainable through herb gardens. Historians have had difficulty determining which were effective, which were not, and which were fatal to the mother, but they conclude that many of the concoctions taken were poisonous. Some have been determined so toxic it seems unlikely that women ingested them voluntarily, unless attempting suicide. It is possible that another person—often the man who impregnated her—would persuade the woman to ingest it. However, intense reactions to medication were viewed as proof of effectiveness, so vomiting and blistering were considered necessary side effects.

Because abortions were often performed at home and detailed records were rare, it is difficult to make precise estimations of abortion rates. However, it appears that rates in the colonial era were relatively low. Surgical abortions were rare. Lack of medical knowledge, particularly regarding infection, almost guaranteed the death of the mother if surgery were performed. Cases of infanticide were more common than surgical abortions, as pregnancies might be hidden until term under loose clothing and infanticide would at least protect the life of the mother.

The tendency toward abortion depended largely on community attitudes toward nonmarital pregnancy and childbearing in general, but it was also closely tied to economics. In a developing colonial society with a land-based economy, children were generally welcomed. Economic desperation was comparatively rare, resulting in relatively low rates of abortion and infanticide. In the case of nonmarital pregnancy, social pressure to name the father and demands on him to pay support eased the burden on

women of even the lowest means. Paternity suits were common, the vast majority of which ended in financial support or marriage or both. The rates of premarital pregnancy in the colonies increased dramatically in the late eighteenth century, with up to 30 percent of births occurring before nine months of marriage. There was generally much more pressure on men to take responsibility for pregnancy than chastisement of women for becoming pregnant.

Conception and "Quickening"

New scientific notions of pregnancy and fetal development arose during the Age of Enlightenment as scientists and religious leaders debated the origins of life. Calvinists and Anglicans argued against abortion, citing numerous biblical passages stating that human life begins at conception. But the battle lines were not drawn simply between religion and science, as scientists disagreed among themselves about the origins of human life. Anton van Leewenhoek, famous for his development of the microscope, argued in the late seventeenth century that an entire human was contained in each male sperm, and was simply implanted in a woman. Other scientists, concerned about the waste of human lives if that held true, argued that an entire human life existed in a woman's egg, and was simply "activated" by male sperm.

Some historians have argued that until the mid-nineteenth century, human life was widely understood to begin at "quickening," the moment when a pregnant woman could first feel the fetus move—generally in the late fourth or early fifth month of pregnancy. Colonial common law instituted punishment for abortion only after quickening. Evidence shows that the scientific community, the religious community, and the community at large all believed that human life in some form began before quickening, but under common law, abortions before quickening were legal. After quickening, however, the fetus—although by no means "viable" (able to survive outside the uterus)—was considered a separate being. Until quickening, the best evidence of pregnancy was the absence of menses, which could have been a symptom of various other conditions. Until the mid-nineteenth century, women were often provided with abortifacients to remove a "blockage," and once menses resumed, she was considered treated. The cause of the blockage was not an issue of legal concern.

Women often had access to abortifacient plant products and the knowledge necessary to use them to "resume menses." Once experiencing quickening, however, she was more or less obligated to carry the fetus to term. Quickening offered better proof of pregnancy, and usually marked a pivotal point after which terminating a pregnancy was unquestionably more dangerous. Until the early nineteenth century, the power of deciding to terminate an early pregnancy essentially lay with the woman. However, by the late colonial period, others were becoming increasingly involved in the practice, as physicians and apothecaries were marketing and selling abortifacients.

Even under the regulation of "experts," they were often deadly.

Restrictions on Abortion

The first legal restrictions on abortion in the United States were aimed at the sale of abortifacients. State laws of the 1820s and 1830s listed abortifacients as poisons and made their sale illegal. In some states, laws also regulated practitioners who performed surgical abortions. All of these laws were intended to protect the life of the mother, and domestic use of abortifacients before quickening was not a crime. By 1840, ten of the nation's twenty-six states had passed abortion regulations.

Widespread attempts at criminalization of abortion began in the 1850s. The American Medical Association (AMA), founded in 1847, played a major role here. For a number of reasons, its members promoted legislation to restrict abortion in various states. The AMA reflected a trend in the field of medicine that valued accreditation and expertise. Members of the AMA attacked physicians of an older generation, as well as homeopaths and midwives, as ill-trained and incompetent, and in its attempt to improve medicine it took control of the practice of abortion. Many of the new generation of physicians also viewed themselves as moral leaders, and in their crusades aimed at preserving and protecting human life, they attacked abortion on moral grounds. One element of this crusade lessened the significance of quickening, considering it simply one stage in fetal development. This laid the groundwork for prohibiting abortion at any stage.

To some extent, abortion regulation through the mid-nineteenth century might be considered in the larger context of social reform movements in America. However, in later decades the anti-abortion crusades reflected the increasing influence of the Victorian Era. Then, pregnancy—or at least illicit pregnancy—was considered a woman's punishment for immoral behavior. Abortion would allow a woman to go unpunished. Even access to methods to prevent such a pregnancy would facilitate such immoral behavior. A result was the passage of legislation to prohibit the practice of abortion and the sale and distribution of contraceptives and contraceptive information. The Comstock Law of 1873—named for the purity crusader Anthony Comstock—categorized abortion and birth control as obscenity, prohibiting them under federal anti-obscenity legislation.

Various states also criminalized abortion, except for cases in which the mother's life was endangered by pregnancy or childbirth. This gave physicians the authority to determine when an abortion could be permitted. In addition, state regulations prohibiting the sale or distribution of abortifacients were reworked to allow physicians to prescribe them.

In many cases, middle- and upper-class women who had personal physicians maintained comparatively easy access to abortion. However, abortion rates increased among the poor and ethnic minorities. By midcentury, national concerns over shifting demographics drew attention to birth rates among the "proper stock" as opposed to those among the "lesser stock." The growing trend among white middle- and upper-class women to seek abortions was an influential factor in criminalizing the procedure. Mass immigration resulted in a growing working class that was perceived as a threat to the dominant Anglo-Protestant culture. Many physicians commonly conducted abortions among the poor and minorities, some publicly declaring that white Protestant women should have more children.

Abortion and Women's Roles

The development of anti-abortion legislation not only reflected ideas of race and class, but also affected gender roles. Before the mid-nineteenth century, women held a stronger position in realm of pregnancy, childbearing, and abortion than afterward. Childbirth took place at home, often with the assistance of a midwife; pregnant women were looked after by other women; and individuals had access to natural herbs that were known abortifacients. In addition, only a pregnant woman knew when quickening took place. The devaluation of quickening by the medical community had already weakened a woman's authority in her own pregnancy. Criminalizing abortion, except under a doctor's recommendation, and abortifacients without a doctor's prescription, further weakened her authority.

Anti-abortion movements generally grew when women demanded more rights. From the mid- to the late nineteenth century, public condemnation of abortion paralleled the women's movement for political rights. Fears that women would forsake their proper social roles and the responsibility of motherhood if they had the right to abortion helped to shape the debate, and ultimately the success, of anti-abortion legislation. Equal opportunity in politics and in higher education appeared to reduce family size and some hoped that the prohibition of abortion and birth control might offset this trend. At the turn of the twentieth century, the women's movement included new demands for sexual freedom, and anti-abortion activists worked to limit abortions. Although widely criminalized, physicians still performed some abortions and illegal abortions were common. The separation of sexuality and procreation allowed greater sexual freedom for women, spurring new attacks on abortion.

Abortion and Contraception

In the 1910s, a powerful birth control movement took hold in America. Leaders of the movement, particularly Margaret Sanger, did not equate birth control with abortion. Rather, they argued that legalizing contraceptives would reduce abortion rates. Public opinion still accepted early-term abortions, and abortion was often the preferred method of birth control. With little access to contraceptives because of the Comstock Law, couples had few choices. Proponents of legal contraceptives reported graphic details of numerous self-induced abortions performed by desperate women, who often died as a result.

Clinics were established to provide contraceptives and contraceptive information. Medical professionals who opened clinics bypassed Comstock laws that barred contraceptives and contraceptive information from importation and from the U.S. mails. Critics feared that such information encouraged "free sex" among single women, when in fact it was primarily intended for married working-class couples who had no access to personal physicians. Critics of abortion similarly feared that single women were having abortions to facilitate an uninhibited sexual lifestyle. In fact, most women having abortions were married. Working-class women generally had children early, ending later pregnancies through abortion. Upper-class women generally delayed childbearing and often ended early pregnancies through abortion. In either case, they saw it as a form of birth control, although birth control advocates drew clear distinctions between contraception and abortion.

At first glance, the criminalization of abortion appeared to have a significant effect on abortion rates. In the mid-nineteenth century, some records show that as many as one out of five or six pregnancies ended in abortion, while some report that in 1900 only one in twenty did. However, the fact that abortions were a crime made it less likely that women would report them. Drawing from case reports of hospital personnel who treated women bleeding as the result of apparent abortion, scholars estimate as many as 2 million abortions per year at the end of the nineteenth century. One doctor estimated between six to ten thousand abortions were performed (many by the women themselves) in 1904 in Chicago alone. Because of criminalization, and because the abortion issue has been so politicized, it is difficult to determine accurate abortion rates. However, it is clear that criminalization did not prevent it.

The birth control movement's eventual success was linked to its alliance with the American Medical Association, which—as the movement gained strength—began to support the legalization of contraceptives. Sanger and the AMA worked hand in hand into the 1930s in efforts to condone birth control and to secure legislation to protect doctors from prosecution for prescribing contraceptives. Again, physicians gave themselves control of the distribution of contraceptives, with the support of the courts and legislative bodies. In 1936, the AMA officially abandoned its official opposition to birth control.

Black Market Abortions
The Great Depression of the 1930s created an environment in which birth control became an acceptable response to social ills because more families were economically desperate and unable to care for additional children. At the same time, however, the number of abortions performed was on the rise—so quickly that many considered it an epidemic. Scholars generally estimate that more than 500,000 took place each year in the United States during the depression. The cost of a "black market" abortion was usually under seventy-five dollars, far below

the cost of feeding another child. In addition, women often lost their jobs to men during the depression, and a pregnant woman was almost certain to lose her job.

A few doctors began to support publicly the repeal of anti-abortion laws during the 1930s. However, the opposition was strong. First, Pope Pius XI's 1930 encyclical, Casti Connubii, pronounced that a developing fetus had a soul. Although America was not a Catholic nation, its largest denomination by then was Roman Catholicism, and the issue of abortion had taken on a new character in the international religious-political realm. The Soviet Union had legalized abortion in the 1920s and the procedure was viewed as tightly tied to a brand of socialist feminism in western Europe. Any connection between feminism and socialism that was tied to abortion would force legalization to confront considerable obstacles in the United States.

The demands on physicians to perform abortions were great and many received additional training in the procedure. The procedure most often used was dilation and curettage, but the injection of potassium soap solution was common by the 1930s. Physicians were legally protected as they were granted the right to conduct therapeutic abortions. Physician-abortionists were considered specialists in the medical community and general practitioners referred their patients to them. The profession officially condemned abortion, but doctors were widely involved, if not directly, then through making referrals. In essence, they could ensure their patients had access to abortion without actually performing them.

To perform an abortion except with the intent to save the life of the mother meant possible arrest. Physician-abortionists who devoted their practice exclusively to abortion risked police raids and prosecution. Raids were especially common in the 1940s and 1950s and served to expose publicly abortionists and their patients. Patients were commonly interrogated in police stations and courtrooms. Police and prosecutors went after patients rather than the referring physicians, who possessed more incriminating evidence than the women did. Because of the raids, many hospitals stopped conducting therapeutic abortions. Advances in medicine, particularly in the development of antibiotics and antiseptics, made hospitals the safest and cleanest places to have an abortion. However, hospital administrators were unwilling to face the publicity resulting from continual raids on clinics and arrests of physicians.

Medical advances also affected the ways in which the fetus was perceived. Imaging techniques allowed physicians to focus on the fetus as a developing human and they increasingly considered the uterus as the space in which the fetus developed. In the 1950s, a culture of family and children encouraged women to embrace motherhood and they were chastised for considering abortion. Other medical advances made pregnancy-related illnesses, complications, and deaths comparatively rare. Therefore, hospitals became less likely to offer therapeutic abortions.

Abortion Supporters. Adele Thomas, Mary Higgins, and C. Starr (*left to right*) picket at City Hall in St. Louis to allow municipal hospitals to perform abortions. © UPI/CORBIS-BETTMANN

In addition, improvements were made in sterilization procedures. In the 1950s, approximately half of the nation's hospitals offered women abortions if they agreed to simultaneous sterilization. Hospitals established therapeutic abortion committees not only to develop such regulations, but to decide in individual cases when an abortion would be permitted.

Calls for Reform and Repeal

In the mid-1950s, a small group of physicians and public health workers began a movement to reform abortion laws. They had seen the disastrous effects of criminalization on women and the medical profession that had developed in recent decades. In 1955, Planned Parenthood organized a small conference of health care professionals to organize against the existing laws. But they did not gain the momentum necessary to overturn legislation until the birth of the women's movement in the 1960s. An integral part of that movement was the demand for reproductive rights. The demand began at the grassroots level with one of the most influential organizations, Citizens for Humane Abortion Laws, founded in 1962 in California. That same year, Sherri Finkbine, a television celebrity, attracted the nation's attention when she traveled to Sweden to have an abortion after finding out that she had taken a drug containing thalidomide early in her pregnancy. In 1961, researchers discovered that thalidomide—which was commonly prescribed to pregnant women to combat sleeplessness and morning sickness—caused severe birth defects, primarily the stunting of fetal limb development.

In *Griswold v. Connecticut* (1965), the U.S. Supreme Court ruled in favor of Planned Parenthood staffers who had violated Connecticut state law in dispensing a contraceptive device to a married woman. The Court ruled on the grounds that their 1961 convictions were violations of the right to privacy. The case brought national attention to birth control laws that were considered repressive, and the right-to-privacy decision paved the way for privacy considerations in the issue of abortion. The public chastisement of women caught during clinic raids in the 1950s was often claimed to violate the right to privacy, but there was no strong legal precedent to turn to in those cases. The year 1966 marked the founding of the National Organization for Women (NOW), which would strengthen the attack on abortion laws. By the 1960s, the focus of abortion rights activists was shifting from a call for reform to a call for repeal of anti-abortion laws, and various women's groups addressed abortion at the national level. In 1969, abortion rights leaders held the first National Conference on Abortion Laws and formed the National Association for Repeal of Abortion Laws (NARAL). However, grassroots organizations remained instrumental as abortion was prohibited at the state level, and although banned in every state, it was regulated on different terms.

The landmark case in abortion history was *Roe v. Wade* (1973). In that case (which was supported by other cases), a twenty-three-year-old pregnant woman challenged Texas's abortion law, which the Supreme Court ultimately found unconstitutional. The decision, written by Justice Harry Blackmun and based on the residual right to privacy, overturned numerous statutes that had been in place for more than one hundred years. Restrictions on abortions during the first trimester of pregnancy were lifted and abortions in the second trimester were allowed with few restrictions. States were given the right to intervene during the second and third trimesters to protect the life of the woman and the potential life of the fetus.

The reaction to *Roe v. Wade* was swift and far-reaching. As a result of the case, NARAL changed its name to the National Abortion Rights Action League, preparing for opposition. The Catholic Church quickly professed its opposition and fundamentalist Protestants

Abortion Opponents. Demonstrators march in front of the White House in opposition to abortion rights—an annual event in Washington, D.C. LIBRARY OF CONGRESS

hastened their efforts to support a pro-life movement. In 1977, Congress prohibited the use of Medicaid funds for abortion except for therapeutic reasons, and in a few other cases. The religious right gained political momentum with the election of conservatives to Congress and Ronald Reagan and George Bush Sr. to the presidency during the 1980s. This resulted in the creation of an abortion "litmus test" for Supreme Court nominees, who were considered on the basis of their stand on abortion, regardless of their experience or positions on other issues. In *Webster v. Reproductive Health Services* (1989) the Supreme Court limited the scope of *Roe v. Wade*, and in *Planned Parenthood of Southeastern Pennsylvania v. Casey* (1992) it reaffirmed abortion rights while permitting further restrictions.

The 1990s saw a rise in extreme measures on the pro-life side, including the harassment of women entering clinics, the bombing of clinics, and attacks on physicians known to perform abortions. In the second half of the decade, Congress repeatedly passed a bill that would ban "partial-birth abortion," but President William Jefferson Clinton vetoed it.

Partial-birth abortions are conducted in the third trimester of pregnancy when a fetus is viable, and involve the dilation of the cervix and extraction of the fetus while puncturing the skull. Although very rare, accounting for 0.04 percent of all abortions, the procedure was used extensively in the public debate by anti-abortion activists. At the end of the decade, extremists continued to attract attention to the issue and the litmus test was predicted to be a factor under George W. Bush's administration. But the nation saw groups such as right-to-life feminists calling for better options for pregnant women and rising to provide alternative solutions such as better wages for women, pregnancy and child-care employment leave, and better support for young, unwed mothers. Recent studies have shown a decrease in abortion rates and an increase in births out of marriage, demonstrating a significant shift in social mores.

BIBLIOGRAPHY

Baird-Windle, Patricia, and Eleanor J. Bader. *Targets of Hatred: Anti-Abortion Terrorism.* New York: St. Martin's Press, 2001.

Blanchard, Dallas A. *The Anti-Abortion Movement and the Rise of the Religious Right: From Polite to Fiery Protest.* New York: Twayne, 1994.

Craig, Barbara Hinkson, and David M. O'Brien. *Abortion and American Politics.* Chatham, N.J.: Chatham House, 1993.

Hull, N. E. H., and Peter Charles Hoffer. *Roe v. Wade: The Abortion Rights Controversy in American History.* Lawrence: University Press of Kansas, 2001.

Jacoby, Kerry N. *Souls, Bodies, Spirits: The Drive to Abolish Abortion since 1973.* Westport, Conn.: Praeger, 1998.

Jaffe, Frederick S., Barbara L. Lindheim, and Philip R. Lee. *Abortion Politics: Private Morality and Public Policy.* New York: McGraw-Hill, 1981.

Mohr, James C. *Abortion in America: The Origins and Evolutions of National Policy, 1800–1900.* New York: Oxford University Press, 1978.

Olansky, Marvin. *Abortion Rites: A Social History of Abortion in America.* Wheaton, Ill.: Crossways Books, 1992.

Reagan, Leslie J. *When Abortion Was a Crime: Women, Medicine, and Law in the United States, 1867–1973.* Berkeley: University of California Press, 1997.

Solinger, Rickie, ed. *Abortion Wars: A Half Century of Struggle, 1950–2000.* Berkeley: University of California Press, 1998.

Kathleen A. Tobin

See also **American Medical Association; Birth Control; *Griswold v. Connecticut*; National Organization for Women (NOW); *Planned Parenthood of Southeastern Pennsylvania v. Casey*; *Roe v. Wade*; Sexuality; *Webster v. Reproductive Health Services*.**

ABRAHAM, PLAINS OF,

on the west side of the city of Quebec, were named after Abraham Martin, a Quebec pilot, who once owned part of the land. They were the scene, in 1759, of the battle for the heavily fortressed and seemingly impregnable city of Quebec, which, when it fell, brought an end to the dream of French empire in North America. In addition, the battle resulted in the death of two great generals, James Wolfe of Great Britain and Louis Joseph de Montcalm of France. The site is now a Canadian national park.

BIBLIOGRAPHY

Lloyd, Christopher. *The Capture of Quebec.* London: Batsford, 1959.

Donaldson, Gordon. *Battle for a Continent: Quebec 1759.* Garden City, N.Y.: Doubleday, 1973.

Lawrence J. Burpee / c. w.

See also **French and Indian War; New France; Quebec, Capture of.**

ABRAHAM LINCOLN BRIGADE.

Americans comprised about 2,800 of the approximately 40,000 international volunteers who responded to the Spanish Republican government's 1936 plea for help against a revolt by right-wing military officers. In this conflict, called the Spanish Civil War, the rebels gained the military assistance of Nazi Germany and Fascist Italy, while the Republican side had far less extensive aid from the Soviet Union. Communist parties operated worldwide to recruit and send volunteer brigades to fight against the Spanish fascist forces. Nearly one hundred African Americans signed up, their antifascist fervor augmented by the recent Italian fascist invasion of Ethiopia. Communists and non-Communists, the volunteers began to arrive in early 1937. Few had prior military experience. Most made their precarious way through blockaded France and across the Pyrenees to join the Spanish Republican Army.

Before going into battle with minimal training, the volunteer units were divided into linguistic combat battalions often named after national heroes. The Americans chose to call their units the Abraham Lincoln and George Washington Battalions of the Fifteenth Brigade. Some also served as doctors and nurses with the medical units, or as ambulance and truck drivers. Initially thrown into the Jarama Valley sector of the battle for Madrid, the volunteers suffered heavy casualties but Madrid did not fall. A costly Republican offensive followed in the Brunete region, west of the capital, in July 1937. Later in the summer, the much-reduced Lincoln Battalion absorbed much of what was left of the Washington Battalion. Other Americans joined the Canadian Mackenzie-Papineau Brigade and fought on. The fighting then shifted to the Aragon-Ebro front in the northeast to prevent the fascist forces from cutting the Republican territory in two. The shrinking Lincoln contingent participated in the bitter winter campaign at Teruel, and in the unsuccessful Republican offensive in the Ebro region. By that time one-third of the Lincolns had been killed, and most of the remainder had sustained injuries.

To pressure the Germans and Italians to withdraw their forces, the Republican government in 1938 ordered the demobilization of all International Brigades. But Hitler and Mussolini kept their troops fighting alongside Franco's forces until Madrid fell the following March, leaving the fascist forces victorious. Still, the surviving Lincolns returned home heroes and heroines to the left, but suspect "premature antifascists" to government officials and conservatives. The support by many Lincoln veterans of the Nazi-Soviet Pact from 1939 to 1941 seemed even to liberals to contradict the veterans' professed antifascism, but once the United States and the Soviet Union entered the war, many of them enlisted in the armed forces to again pursue victory over fascism. As leftists in the postwar McCarthy era, the Veterans of the Abraham Lincoln Brigade faced and survived U.S. government repression. When in 1956 Soviet premier Nikita Khrushchev publicly admitted the crimes of his predecessor, Joseph Stalin, many prominent Lincoln veterans left the Communist Party but remained eager to uphold the legitimacy and rectitude of their antifascist activity in the 1930s, and also supported the peace and civil rights movements of later decades. With the number of Lincoln veterans shrinking, a sister organization, the Abraham Lincoln Brigade Archives, came into existence in 1979 to carry on by educational activity the memory of the brigade.

BIBLIOGRAPHY

Abraham Lincoln Brigade Archives. Home page at http://www.alba-valb.org/.

Bruckner, Noel, Mary Dore, and Sam Sills. *The Good Fight.* New York: KINO International, 1984. Videotape.

Carroll, Peter N. *The Odyssey of the Abraham Lincoln Brigade.* Stanford, Calif.: Stanford University Press, 1994.

Nelson, Cary, and Jefferson Hendricks. *Madrid 1937: Letters of the Abraham Lincoln Brigade from the Spanish Civil War.* New York: Routledge, 1996.

Landis, Arthur H. *The Abraham Lincoln Brigade.* New York: Citadel, 1967.

Marvin E. Gettleman

See also **Communist Party, United States of America; Spain, Relations with.**

ABSCAM SCANDAL. A Federal Bureau of Investigation (FBI) sting operation stemming from a 1978 investigation of stolen paintings and organized crime uncovered corruption among elected officials on the local, state, and national levels. Because a U.S. senator and several congressmen were implicated, Abscam (short for "Arab Scam") further promoted widespread public cynicism about the integrity of federal lawmakers. Conversely, the operation led to severe criticism of the FBI for targeting members of Congress and otherwise engaging in entrapment. FBI undercover agents masqueraded as wealthy Arab sheiks and offered bribes for assistance with such matters as obtaining gambling licenses. Videotape caught politicians accepting large amounts of cash or stock. Department of Justice officials approved Abscam in 1978 and terminated it in early 1980 after the news media became aware of the program. Congressional leaders charged that the department had in fact prematurely leaked the names of suspects to television and print reporters. While promising a thorough investigation of any such leaks, Attorney General Benjamin R. Civiletti nevertheless refused to cooperate with the parallel congressional investigations. Instead, the attorney general had prosecutors concentrate on the cases to be presented before grand juries in Washington, D.C., and elsewhere. Those efforts resulted in the bribery convictions of former New Jersey senator Harrison A. Williams and six former members of the House of Representatives. The Abscam scandal marked the first of several major corruption scandals in Congress in the 1980s, the most notorious of which was the "Keating Five" savings and loan scandal, which implicated prominent senators.

BIBLIOGRAPHY

Greene, Robert W. *The Sting Man: Inside Abscam.* New York: Dutton, 1981.

U.S. Congress, Senate, Select Committee to Study Law Enforcement Undercover Activities of Components of the Department of Justice. *Final Report.* Washington, D.C.: United States Government Printing Office, 1983.

*Kenneth O'Reilly/*A. G.

See also **Corruption, Political; Political Scandals.**

ABSTRACT EXPRESSIONISM, often known as "the New York School" or "American action painting,"

Jackson Pollock. The most widely known abstract expressionist, especially for his "drip" technique, in front of one of his other works. Artists Rights Society

describes the works of a loose community of painters in New York from the mid-1940s to the mid-1950s. Initially influenced by surrealism and cubism, abstract expressionists rejected the social realism, regionalism, and geometric abstraction so popular with American painters of the 1930s. Instead, they turned first to mythology and then to their own experiences and insights as subject matter for their bold, at times dizzying, abstract compositions.

The term "abstract expressionism" dates from 1946, when Robert Coates of the *New Yorker* first used it to describe the works of several American abstractionists.

Because works of abstract expressionism can diverge wildly in terms of structure and technique, art historian Irving Sandler divides abstract expressionists into two categories: gesture painters and color-field painters. Jackson Pollock remains the preeminent gesture painter; in such paintings as *Cathedral* (1947) and *Autumn Rhythm* (1950), Pollock eschewed recognizable symbols entirely, composing delicate webs of interpenetrating shapes. Color-field painters, on the other hand, suppressed all references to the past by painting unified fields of varying color. Unlike their counterparts, who often valued the act of painting as much as the finished product, Mark Rothko, Barnett Newman, and other color-field painters strove to reproduce the metaphysical experience of the sublime.

Because each artist emphasized his or her own absolute individuality, abstract expressionists continually rejected the notion that they had coalesced into a school. Nevertheless, by 1943, Jackson Pollock, Lee Krasner, Willem de Kooning, Elaine de Kooning, Robert Motherwell, William Baziotes, and other future abstract expressionists were becoming increasingly familiar with each other's work. From 1943 to 1945, Peggy Guggenheim exhibited many early works of abstract expressionism in her Art of This Century Gallery. During the late 1940s, many abstract expressionists also congregated in the Subjects of the Artist School, the Cedar Tavern, and the infamous Eighth Street Club to socialize and engage in intellectual debate. Critics Clement Greenberg and Harold Rosenberg emerged as abstract expressionism's most articulate champions.

Set against a backdrop of Cold War conformity, abstract expressionists often saw their work as the ultimate statement of romantic individuality and artistic freedom. By the early 1950s, however, abstract expressionism was losing much of its initial appeal. Although some abstract expressionists continued to experiment with pure abstraction, others began to reintroduce recognizable subject matter into their canvases. By mid-decade, abstract expressionism was finding a frequent home in major museums and private collections. The United States Information Agency (USIA) even organized exhibitions of abstract expressionism in response to accusations of American "philistinism."

BIBLIOGRAPHY

Gibson, Ann Eden. *Abstract Expressionism: Other Politics*. New Haven, Conn.: Yale University Press, 1997.

Sandler, Irving. *The Triumph of American Painting: A History of Abstract Expressionism*. New York: Praeger, 1970.

John M. Kinder

See also **Cubism.**

ACADEMIC FREEDOM describes a group of rights claimed by teachers—the right to study, to communicate ideas, and to publish the results of reflection and research without external restraints—in short, to assert the truth as they perceive it. Academic freedom developed in the universities of western Europe in the seventeenth and eighteenth centuries. It emerged in a period of growing tolerance nurtured by the spread of scientific inquiry, reaction to the fiercely destructive religious conflicts that had for so long plagued Europe, the growth of commerce, and the evolution of the liberal state with its general bias toward liberty. Academic freedom is now recognized in most countries.

The principal justification of academic freedom is that through the unhampered interplay of ideas, the world's stock of usable knowledge is enlarged. Thus, while academic freedom directly benefits the teacher or institution, in a larger and much more significant sense, it serves vital public interests. American professors have fought for academic freedom since the nineteenth century, but the U.S. Supreme Court did not endorse the concept until the mid-twentieth century. The first case in which a majority of the Court's justices ruled that academic freedom is protected by the Constitution was *Sweezy v. New Hampshire* (1957). Today, the concept of academic freedom is well established in Supreme Court jurisprudence. In most countries, academic freedom refers to the autonomy of the institution and its independence from external restraints; in the United States, in accordance with the individualistic bent of its constitutional law, the claim to academic freedom is usually associated with an individual teacher's freedom from interference with the free play of the intellect.

Academic freedom is invariably tied to the concept of tenure (status granted after a trial period, protecting a teacher from summary dismissal), since without security of employment, teachers cannot safely exercise their intellectual freedom. Tenure does not mean, however, that teachers can never be dismissed. Rather, it means they can be dismissed only for adequate cause, established according to the exacting requirements of due process, and including at some stage a judgment by professional peers. Academic freedom does not protect teachers from dismissal for causes not related to the exercise of their intellectual rights.

There are many associations throughout the world that are concerned with the defense of academic freedom and tenure; one of the most vigorous defenders in the United States is the AMERICAN ASSOCIATION OF UNIVERSITY PROFESSORS (AAUP). Such defense is needed because academic freedom is often under great pressure from a wide variety of sources: political parties, politicians, economic interests, religious and racial groups, alumni, donors, and members of governing boards. When the Supreme Court decided *Sweezy*, professors were under attack by politicians trying to ferret out communists. Today, critics of academia accuse professors of politically indoctrinating students, of presenting only a single point of view, of irrelevant discussions, and occasionally of deliberately misrepresenting course content in course catalog descriptions. The increased involvement of professors in off-campus business and government affairs has also generated scrutiny of academic research. Topics of concern include limits on research as a result of industrial-academic collaboration; influence by companies that employ researchers as consultants, thereby creating a conflict of interest; money rather than scientific inquiry being the propellant for research; and limits of academic disclosure dictated by corporate sponsors.

BIBLIOGRAPHY

De George, Richard T. *Academic Freedom and Tenure: Ethical Issues*. Lanham, Md: Rowman and Littlefield, 1997.

Hofstadter, Richard, and Walter P. Metzger. *The Development of Academic Freedom in the United States.* New York: Columbia University Press, 1955.

Kahn, Sharon E., and Dennis Pavlich. *Academic Freedom and the Inclusive University.* Vancouver: University of British Columbia Press, 2000.

Sowell, Thomas. *Inside American Education: The Decline, the Deception, the Dogmas.* New York: Free Press, 1993.

David Fellman
Myrna W. Merron / c. p.

See also **Education; Education, Higher: Colleges and Universities; First Amendment; Political Correctness.**

ACADIA. The history of Acadia, long an exposed borderland where New France and New England overlapped, is indissociable from the deportation of much of its French-speaking population from 1755 to 1763. This tragedy overshadows another, the later marginalization of the region's aboriginal inhabitants.

There have been several Acadias. To begin with, in 1524 explorer Giovanni da Verrazzano baptized as Arcadia a lush, probably Virginian coastal landscape. He named it in honor of the ancient Greeks' earthly paradise. On later sixteenth-century maps, the name reappeared near the Gulf of St. Lawrence. Both the new location and the ensuing loss of the letter "r" suggest that cartographers had learned of Native Micmac place-names containing, in European renderings, the suffix *acadie.* French negotiators were apt to label Acadia the entire swath of territory extending from the Gaspé Peninsula to the Kennebec River. Indeed, northern Maine, Abenaki territory that would long remain a disputed fur-trading frontier, was the scene of the first French settlement in the region over the winter of 1604–1605 on St. Croix Island. But increasingly during the seventeenth century, the toponym "Acadia" would refer to peninsular Nova Scotia and the Chignecto Isthmus, where the Micmacs already accepted the presence of French traders and missionaries.

It was here, and more precisely at Port Royal (later Annapolis Royal, Nova Scotia)—initially founded by the survivors of that first Maine winter and briefly (1629–1632) inhabited by Scots (hence Nova Scotia)—that French settlement began in earnest in the late 1630s. Numbering fourteen hundred by 1701, the Acadians, as the French settlers were soon known, spread northwestward from Port Royal, converting the marshlands of the Bay of Fundy into dike-protected grain fields. Before 1755, a minority would scatter along other coastlines of the Maritime Provinces. Periods of English rule (1654–1667 and 1690–1697) and regular visits from New England merchants had made the Nova Scotia Acadians familiar with the costs and benefits of their borderland existence well before the 1710 British conquest, confirmed by the 1713 treaty ending Queen Anne's War, of peninsular Nova Scotia.

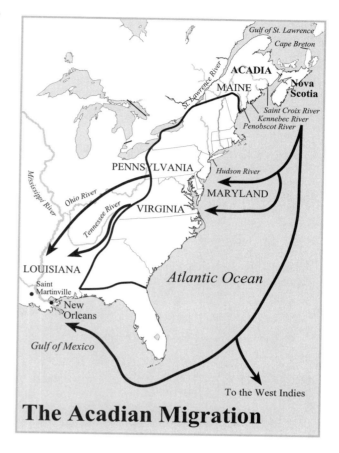

The Acadian Migration

Over the next four decades, they understandably resisted pressure from the missionaries acting for their former king to give up their farmsteads and move to French territory and from the British to swear an oath of allegiance to George II. Upon the outbreak of the French and Indian War in 1754, British authorities feared invasion by the French with Micmac support. They regarded the Acadians as hostile, even though most of the latter were neutral and themselves feared Micmac attacks. In 1755, Nova Scotia governor Charles Lawrence ordered their dispersal. From then until 1763, upwards of ten thousand Acadians were deported or fled; many of those who did not perish ended up in France, Canada, and Louisiana, where they came to be called Cajuns. Some refugees eventually returned to join those who had remained in the region as fugitives to found a new Acadia under British rule. Most of these survivors settled in eastern or northern New Brunswick and a few elsewhere in the Maritimes, but not on the ancestral marshlands now occupied by New Englanders. Relegated for the most part to marginal land, many turned to fishing or lumbering. The second half of the nineteenth century saw both socioeconomic and institutional diversification as a middle class emerged and towns grew. Five-sixths of the 300,000 Maritimers whose mother tongue is French live in New

Brunswick, an officially bilingual province since 1969 and the center of Acadia.

BIBLIOGRAPHY

Griffiths, N. E. S. *The Contexts of Acadian History, 1686–1784.* Montreal: McGill-Queen's University Press, 1992.

Harris, R. Cole, ed. *Historical Atlas of Canada.* Vol. 1, *From the Beginning to 1800.* Toronto: University of Toronto Press, 1987.

Chiasson, Anselme, and Nicolas Landry. "Acadia, Contemporary." *Canadian Encyclopedia.* Toronto: McClelland and Stewart, 1999.

Reid, John G. *Acadia, Maine, and New Scotland: Marginal Colonies in the Seventeenth Century.* Toronto: University of Toronto Press, 1981.

———. "An International Region of the Northeast: Rise and Decline, 1635–1762." In *The Northeastern Borderlands: Four Centuries of Interaction.* Edited by Stephen J. Hornsby, Victor A. Conrad, and James J. Herlan. Fredericton, New Brunswick, Canada: Acadiensis Press, 1989.

Thomas Wien

See also **Colonial Wars; French and Indian War; Maine.**

ACCIDENTS. The United States saw a substantial decrease in accident-related deaths in the twentieth century. Despite a greater number and variety of motor vehicles, firearms, poisonous products, and dangerous pastimes and leisure activities, the nation achieved a 55 percent reduction in deaths from unintentional injuries from 1912 to 2000.

The National Safety Council, a federally chartered nonprofit organization, attributes the decline in accidental deaths to a number of factors, including improvements in technology such as seat belts and air bags, which have helped curb the number of road fatalities. Evolving legislation and proactive safety education has also contributed to safer living, as have broad social changes: the shift from agriculture and manufacturing to an information-based economy has lowered the number of hazardous jobs.

Everyday Accidents

Motor vehicle accidents were by far the largest source of unintentional-injury deaths, claiming 43,501 lives in 1998—roughly 2.5 times more than falls, the second most common cause. Males were twice as likely to die in a car crash as females, but the gender gap was almost nonexistent for falling victims, with twice as many men and women over the age of 75 falling to their deaths as all other age groups combined. Men were nearly three times more likely to die of the third most common accident, poisonings, and four times more likely to drown. The fifth leading cause of accidental death, choking, was fairly evenly distributed between men and women, and, like falls, increased dramatically with age.

Road fatalities in the United States decreased by 17 percent between 1990 and 2000; however, the number of people who died of accidental death in the home rose. Deadly falls, more than half of which happened at home, were up by nearly 40 percent; and poisonings, led by pharmaceutical and narcotics overdoses, more than doubled. The most accident-prone states in 2000 were Alabama, Kentucky, Mississippi, and Tennessee; the least accident-prone, with approximately half as many unintentional-injury deaths per capita, were Connecticut, Maine, Massachusetts, New Hampshire, Rhode Island, and Vermont.

Other National Safety Council findings reveal an interesting snapshot of America at the end of the twentieth century. Between 1998 and 2000, light delivery vehicles for the U.S. Postal Service had the highest number of accidents per mile for all truck fleets. In 1999, basketball accounted for the greatest number of sports injuries, followed by bicycle riding and football. In 1999, more hospital emergency room visits were related to people using their beds (455,027) than handling knives (446,225).

National Tragedies and Blunders

The most notorious accidents in American history have accounted for relatively few deaths compared to the lives lost from everyday injuries.

Great Chicago Fire (8–10 October 1871). An unusual autumn drought and heat wave, combined with high winds, allowed a small barn blaze to grow into a conflagration that ravaged much of Chicago. As the inferno spread, flames leapt over rivers; firefighters dynamited entire buildings in a vain attempt to slow the fire's progress. The blaze, which only died down when rain began to fall on 10 October, killed between two and three hundred people, destroyed approximately 18,000 buildings, and caused $200 million in damages. Increased fire safety awareness and fire-fighting capabilities, along with a revolution in building materials—from wood to brick and steel—helped decrease fire-related deaths by almost two thirds between 1913 and 2000, even as the population nearly tripled.

Triangle Shirtwaist Company Fire (25 March 1911). Just minutes before quitting time, employees of a Manhattan clothing manufacturer were trapped by a flash fire that began in a pile of oil-soaked rags. Due to cramped conditions and a lack of adequate exits, 146 workers, mostly young immigrant women, either died in the blaze or leapt to their deaths from windows eight to ten stories above the street. The scope of the tragedy prompted sweeping reforms in factory safety regulations, aided in part by the efforts of the National Safety Council, formed two years after the tragedy. In 2000, workplace accidents were the smallest category of unintentional-injury deaths, showing a decrease of 90 percent since 1912, despite a quadrupling of the workforce and a ninefold increase in productivity.

Three Mile Island Nuclear Accident (28 March 1979). A dangerous combination of mechanical and human failures brought a Pennsylvania nuclear power plant to the brink of catastrophic meltdown. The crisis was quickly and successfully addressed and no one was killed, but the accident sparked a major public outcry. While energy officials insisted that the surrounding area was not contaminated, scientists still disagree on whether people living near the plant suffered adverse effects from radiation vented during the crisis. According to the Nuclear Regulatory Commission, no health problems or deaths have been directly related to nuclear power in the United States, but no new nuclear plants have been built in the country since the THREE MILE ISLAND event.

American Airlines Flight 191 (25 May 1979). Shortly after taking off from Chicago's O'Hare airport, a DC-10 lost its left wing engine, causing it to veer out of control and crash to the ground, killing all aboard. The deadliest commercial airliner crash in American history claimed 272 lives and prompted the grounding of all DC-10s in the United States pending investigation of, among other issues, maintenance procedures. Although airline accidents are major headline grabbers, the number of lives lost in such accidents does not equal even 1 percent of the deaths caused by passenger automobile accidents between 1997 and 1999.

Exxon Valdez Oil Spill (24 March 1988). A reportedly inebriated and fatigued crew ran an oil tanker, the EXXON VALDEZ aground in Alaska's Prince William Sound, dumping 11 million gallons of oil into the water and devastating local wildlife. Exxon spent $2.2 billion on the cleanup effort and twelve years later declared the environment "healthy and robust." The National Oceanic and Atmospheric Administration reported that the area had made a remarkable recovery but remained an "ecosystem in transition." While the accident was the worst of its kind in American history, it has since dropped off the list of the world's 50 largest oil spills.

BIBLIOGRAPHY

Flexner, Stuart, and Doris Flexner. *The Pessimist's Guide to History: From the Big Bang to the New Millennium.* Updated ed. New York, Harper Perennial, 2000.

National Safety Council. *Injury Facts, 2000.* Itasca, Ill.: The Council, 2000.

Paul Bacon

See also **Disasters; Triangle Shirtwaist Fire.**

ACHILLE LAURO, an Italian cruise ship hijacked en route from Alexandria to Port Said, Egypt, in October 1985 by four members of the Palestine Liberation Front (PLF), an Arab extremist group. Holding 438 hostages, the hijackers sailed to Tartus, Syria, and demanded that Israel release fifty PLF prisoners. Denied entry at Tartus, the terrorists executed a wheelchair-bound American passenger. They surrendered after fifty-two hours and were taken to Cairo. When Egyptian President Hosni Mubarak allowed the hijackers to fly to Tunisia, American

navy jets forced the flight to land in Sicily. U.S. investigations linked the hijacking to Palestine Liberation Organization leader Yasir Arafat and PLF president Mohammed Abul Abbas Zaidan.

BIBLIOGRAPHY

Cassese, Antonio. *Terrorism, Politics, and Law: The "Achille Lauro" Affair.* Princeton, N.J.: Princeton University Press, 1989.

Carolyn Bronstein / c. w.

See also **Arab Nations, Relations with; Hostage Crises; Terrorism.**

ACID RAIN, precipitation whose acidity has increased on account of some human activity. Dust storms, volcanic eruptions, and biological decay can affect the acid level of rain or snow, but industrial pollutants may raise the acidity of a region's precipitation more than tenfold. Certain pollutants mix with atmospheric water vapor to form acids, which may then fall to the ground in a process called dry disposition, or fall in combination with rain or snow, called wet disposition.

The term "acid rain" was coined in 1872 by Robert Angus Smith, an English chemist who studied the chemical content of rain near Manchester, England. In retrospect it is clear that U.S. cities such as Chicago, Pittsburgh, and St. Louis, heavy consumers of bituminous coal, also suffered from acid precipitation. Nevertheless the first large-scale effort to monitor the chemistry of precipitation did not occur until the late 1940s with the work of Hans Egner of Sweden. In the 1960s, European researchers began publicizing the effects of acidic precipitation on soils, vegetation, aquatic ecology, and human-made structures. In the 1970s, the discovery that several Canadian lakes had high acid levels (pH levels between 4 and 5) increased public awareness of the issue. By that time problems as diverse as crumbling monuments, fish kills, and dying forests were linked to acid precipitation.

The acid rain issue transcends political boundaries. Power plants in the Midwest of the United States, for example, may create acid rain that falls to the ground in eastern Canada. Indeed pressure from Canada, Sweden, and Norway, net receivers of atmospheric sulfur dioxide, led to a series of international acid rain conferences beginning in 1979. Acid rain debates seriously strained relations between the United States and Canada in the 1980s. The Canadian government expressed anger when the Ronald Reagan administration deferred action pending further study of the issue.

Efforts to abate acid rain have focused on two pollutants, sulfur dioxide, a by-product of burning coal or fuel oil, and nitrogen oxides generated largely by automobiles and power plants. In the United States the federal CLEAN AIR ACT (CAA) of 1970 restricted both pollutants. However, acid rain was not the motivating factor behind the CAA, and studies later suggested the law may have worsened the problem. When monitoring devices were

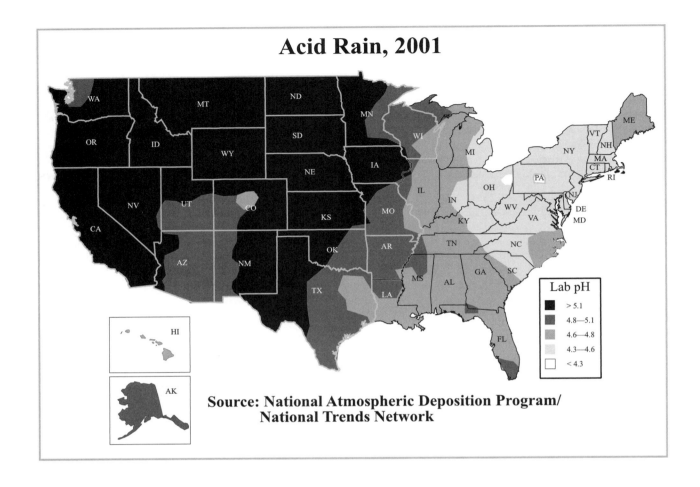

Acid Rain, 2001

Lab pH
- > 5.1
- 4.8—5.1
- 4.6—4.8
- 4.3—4.6
- < 4.3

**Source: National Atmospheric Deposition Program/
National Trends Network**

placed near factories, many firms simply built taller smoke-stacks to disperse pollutants higher into the atmosphere, away from the monitors. Consequently acid rain spread even wider. In 1977 amendments to the CAA required that utilities install scrubbers in each new coal-fired power plant. Implementation of these and additional amendments in the 1980s are credited for decreasing annual sulfur dioxide emissions in the United States from 26 to 21 million metric tons by 1989. Similarly nitrogen oxide emissions, which peaked at 22 million metric tons in 1981, fell to 19 million tons by 1990.

In 1990 additional amendments to the CAA imposed stricter AIR POLLUTION standards on vehicles and set a cap on national sulfur emissions governed by a market-based system of emission allowances. These regulations, along with a provision allowing eastern utilities to use more low-sulfur western coal, apparently helped reduce acid precipitation in the Northeast by up to 25 percent. But acidified water and soil continued to imperil lake and forest ecosystems. A major study sponsored by the U.S. ENVIRONMENTAL PROTECTION AGENCY released in late 1999 found that sulfate levels had fallen sharply in most lakes of the Northeast and the Midwest, but that acidity levels had not fallen along with them, perhaps because pro-

longed acid precipitation had weakened the lakes' natural buffering capacity.

BIBLIOGRAPHY

Bryner, Gary C. *Blue Skies, Green Politics: The Clean Air Act of 1990.* Washington, D.C.: CQ Press, 1993.

Schmandt, Jurgen, Judith Clarkson, and Hilliard Roderick, eds. *Acid Rain and Friendly Neighbors: The Policy Dispute Between Canada and the United States.* Rev. ed. Durham, N.C.: Duke University Press, 1988.

Regens, James L., and Robert W. Rycroft. *The Acid Rain Controversy.* Pittsburgh, Pa.: University of Pittsburgh Press, 1988.

Hugh Gorman / w. p.

See also **Canada, Relations with; Conservation; Electric Power and Light Industry; Energy Industry; Energy, Renewable; Water Pollution.**

ACQUIRED IMMUNE DEFICIENCY SYNDROME (AIDS), an infectious disease that fatally depresses the human immune system, was recognized in the United States in 1980. By 1982 the disease had appeared in 24 states, 471 cases had been diagnosed, 184 people had died, and the Centers for Disease Control (CDC) in Atlanta had termed the outbreak an epidemic. AIDS has challenged the authority and integrity of respected medical institutions, strained the capacity of the health care system, forced the reevaluation of sexual mores, and tapped reservoirs of fear, prejudice, and compassion within individuals and communities.

On 5 June 1981, the CDC's *Morbidity and Mortality Weekly Report* (*MMWR*) published an article by Dr. Michael Gottlieb of the University of California at Los Angeles School of Medicine, describing five cases of *Pneumocystis carinii* pneumonia (PCP) in young homosexual men. A second *MMWR* article on 4 July documented ten additional cases of PCP, as well as twenty-six cases of Kaposi's sarcoma (KS), a rare skin cancer, in young homosexual males in New York City and San Francisco. PCP is normally seen only in patients with immune dysfunction and KS in elderly men. Under the direction of James Curran, the CDC began to investigate, hypothesizing that the young men were suffering from an immune-system deficiency related to their lifestyle. In early August, however, CDC staff identified the strange "gay plague" in heterosexual intravenous drug users in New York City.

In the first six months of 1982, cases were reported among hemophiliacs receiving blood components, Haitian refugees, and infants born to drug-using mothers. Transmission through blood transfusion was documented in June. Although physicians had named the outbreak gay-related immune deficiency (GRID), many suspected a viral infection transmissible through sexual contact or blood transfusion rather than a lifestyle-related disease; some proposed a multifactor etiology. At a meeting in July, the CDC coined the term "AIDS," which became accepted usage for the several related disorders.

More than 1,000 Americans had been diagnosed with AIDS by early 1983; of those, 394 had died. Although the CDC had identified instances in which the infection had been transmitted through blood transfusion, the Red Cross and major blood banks refused to institute rigorous screening, which was costly and might discourage donors. In March 1983, the CDC and the Public Health Service, concerned about the risk of infection, issued a statement naming four "high-risk" groups of donors, advising them not to give blood and to avoid sexual contact. This warning, together with a May article in the *Journal of the American Medical Association* suggesting the possibility of infection through casual contact, heightened media and public awareness, intensified fears, and prompted ostracism of people with AIDS (PWAs). Some health care workers refused to treat PWAs. In many areas, moral objections blocked inexpensive control measures, such as condom distribution and sterile-needle exchanges for drug users.

Researchers, including Robert Gallo at the National Cancer Institute in Bethesda, Maryland, and Luc Montagnier at the Pasteur Institute in Paris, attempted to identify and characterize the viral agent that caused AIDS. By January 1984, Gallo's laboratory had cultured twenty samples of a virus he named HTLV-III, believing it related to the human T-cell leukemia virus he had isolated in 1980. In February 1984, Montagnier's group reported their discovery of lymphadenopathy-associated virus (LAV), which they asserted was the AIDS virus. Their work was confirmed by Donald Francis at the CDC. Genetic testing established that LAV and HTLV-III were nearly identical. Gallo and Margaret Heckler, Secretary of Health and Human Services, announced on 23 April 1984, however, that the National Cancer Institute had found the AIDS virus and had developed an antibody test for blood screening, clinical testing, and diagnosis. An international committee renamed the virus HIV (human immunodeficiency virus) in late 1986. Shortly thereafter, President Ronald Reagan and France's President Jacques Chirac announced that the Pasteur Institute and the National Cancer Institute would share credit for the discovery and royalties from the patented blood test. (Later probes of possible misappropriation of the French virus by Gallo and his lab assistant Mikulas Popovic were dropped in 1993.)

Isolation of the virus confirmed AIDS as an acute infectious disease, encouraging research into vaccines and therapeutic drugs. Lack of money hampered work, however. The Reagan administration was unwilling to initiate expensive programs to control a disease associated with homosexuality and drug use. Individual congressmen, including Phillip Burton of San Francisco and Henry A. Waxman of Los Angeles, together with Assistant Secretary for Health Edward Brandt, pushed for supplemental AIDS funding in 1983 and 1984, with limited success. Organizations such as the Gay Men's Health Crisis in New York and Mathilde Krim's AIDS Medical Foundation (AMF) provided funds, but support for research remained inadequate.

The burden of care for AIDS patients, many without private insurance, fell on state and local governments and on volunteers largely drawn from the gay community. Many gay men and lesbians initially resisted involvement with the "gay plague," which threatened to deepen the stigma attached to homosexuality. Others resented public-health warnings to alter sexual practices. Gay organizations fought both universal antibody-screening and the closing of public bathhouses in New York and San Francisco, which authorities saw as reservoirs of infection. At the same time gay groups provided support, patient care, and money to PWAs, including those who were not gay. Gay men volunteered as research subjects in community-based drug trials organized by local physicians and developed patient networks that circulated experimental and imported drugs to treat PWAs suffering from opportunistic infections such as PCP and cytomegalovirus. Gay leaders lobbied for more money. A few risked community ostracism by becoming public advocates for safer sexual practices.

Although hampered by lack of money from the federal government, research into therapeutic drugs did produce results. In early 1985, Samuel Broder at the National

AIDS Protest. Activists in Rockville, Md., protest federal Food and Drug Administration policies, 1988. PATSY LYNCH

Cancer Institute and other researchers confirmed that the compound azidothymidine (AZT), developed by the pharmaceutical firm Burroughs-Wellcome, appeared active against the AIDS virus in laboratory cultures. The FOOD AND DRUG ADMINISTRATION (FDA) quickly approved the manufacturer's plan for clinical trials and facilitated release to the market in 1987, although the efficacy trial lasted only seven months. The AIDS Clinical Trial Network, established by the National Institute for Allergy and Infectious Diseases (NIAID), developed protocols to test AZT in patient groups at hospitals across the country. Burroughs-Wellcome put AZT on the market in February 1987, at the price of $188 per 10,000 milligrams; the annual cost of the drug for some patients was reported to be $8,000 or higher. Although harshly criticized, the company waited until December before dropping the price 20 percent.

While NIAID pursued AZT trials, physicians and patients were trying other compounds to slow the disease or treat opportunistic infections. The FDA gave low priority to several compounds, such as AL721 and HPA23. In the case of others, such as the Syntex compound ganciclovir, PWAs received the drug at cost for several years under a compassionate use protocol. The FDA then required a blind comparison with a placebo before ganciclovir could be marketed, but few PWAs were willing to

enroll in a placebo trial after they already had used an experimental compound or if they feared rapid progression of their disease. Investigators in the NIAID-endorsed AZT trials experienced difficulty recruiting subjects.

Gay AIDS activists sought access to more drugs, access to information about trials, trial protocols that recognized patient needs and risks, inclusion of minority PWAs in trials, and PWA participation in development and testing. The AIDS Coalition to Unleash Power (ACT UP) captured media attention with demonstrations and street theater; the group soon acquired a radical image that alienated researchers, the public, and more conservative gay groups. The small group Treatment and Data Subcommittee (later the Treatment Action Group), led by Iris Long, James Eigo, and Mark Harrington, created a registry of clinical trials and gave testimony to the President's Commission and at congressional hearings. At the request of President George H. W. Bush, the clinical-trial authority Louis Lasagna held hearings in 1989 on new drug approval procedures. The hearings accentuated lack of progress by the FDA and NIAID and provided a forum for Eigo and Harrington to present their program. Anthony Fauci, director of NIAID and a target of ACT UP criticism, met with activists and backed a new parallel track for community-based, nonplacebo drug trials. The parallel track system was in operation by early 1990, but the concept remained controversial as it competed for money and trial subjects with conventional controlled trials. President Bush in 1990 appointed David Kessler as FDA commissioner, who quickly gained a reputation for activism and endorsed parallel track.

By 1991, the character of AIDS in the United States had changed again. Although incidence was increasing in all population groups, rates were most rapid among the poor, African Americans, Hispanic Americans, and women and children. Health care providers, researchers, and PWAs no longer defined the epidemic as an acute infectious disease responsive to early aggressive intervention. They recognized AIDS as a chronic disease characterized by a lengthy virus incubation (up to eleven years); onset of active infection possibly related to medical or lifestyle cofactors; an extended course involving multiple infectious episodes; and the need for flexible treatment with a variety of drugs as well as long-term supportive services. Despite this progress, however, at the beginning of the twenty-first century, AIDS still remained a fatal disease and an effective vaccine was still years away.

As of 31 December 1984, 7,699 PWAs had been diagnosed and almost half of them were dead. Although the disease was taking a heavy toll among gay white males, more than half the cases now were nonwhite persons, including many women and children. The First International AIDS Conference, held in Atlanta in April 1985, made public much new clinical information. Participants debated screening programs advocated by the Reagan administration and public-health experts but opposed by gays and other potentially stigmatized groups. Confer-

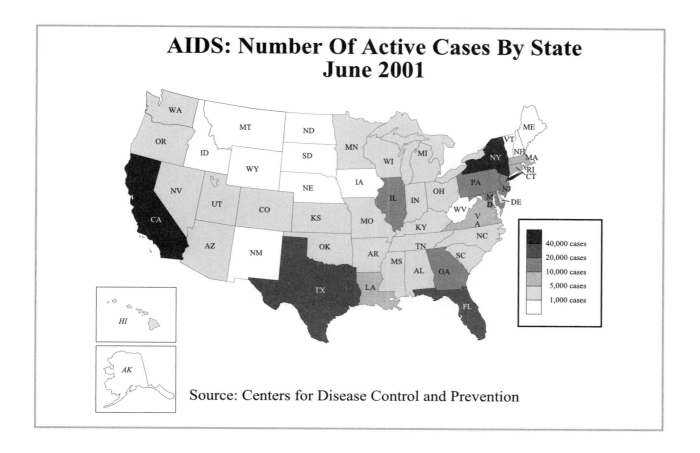

AIDS: Number Of Active Cases By State
June 2001

40,000 cases
20,000 cases
10,000 cases
5,000 cases
1,000 cases

Source: Centers for Disease Control and Prevention

ence reports contributed to increased fear and concern in 1985, which intensified when the country learned that the actor Rock Hudson was dying of AIDS. Shortly thereafter, the news that a school in Kokomo, Indiana, had denied a young PWA named Ryan White the right to attend school with his classmates epitomized Americans' fear of and aversion to the disease.

Attitudes were changing, however. Hudson's death in October shocked Hollywood, which was heavily affected by the disease. The American Foundation for AIDS Research, supported by a Hudson bequest, merged with Krim's AMF to form AmFAR, which attracted support from such celebrities as Elizabeth Taylor. Ryan White was accepted by another Indiana school and became a national symbol of courage before his death in 1990. In October 1986, Surgeon General C. Everett Koop broke with the Reagan administration with a bluntly worded report on the epidemic, calling for sex education in schools, widespread use of condoms, and voluntary antibody testing. Koop's report followed statements from the Public Health Service and the National Academy of Sciences Institute of Medicine that described the administration's response to AIDS as inadequate. President Reagan in 1987 created the President's Commission on the Human Immunodeficiency Virus Epidemic and shortly afterward spoke at the Third International AIDS Conference in Washington, D.C. Basketball player Magic Johnson's November 1991 announcement that he had contracted HIV through unprotected heterosexual sex, followed by the tennis player Arthur Ashe's disclosure five months later that he had AIDS as a result of a blood transfussion during bypass surgery, helped transform the public image of AIDS to a disease that reached beyond the gay community. In late 1993, public concern for PWAs was reflected in critical acclaim for the film *Philadelphia* and the stage play *Angels in America*, both of which examined the personal and social consequences of AIDS.

Public attitudes toward PWAs had gradually shifted from discrimination and fear to compassion and acceptance, but the burdensome costs of treatment and services were a challenge to the national will. In one example, the Comprehensive AIDS Resource Emergency Act of 1990, often called the Ryan White Act, authorized $2.9 billion for areas of high incidence. It passed both houses of Congress with enthusiastic bipartisan support but a few months later budget negotiations reduced the money drastically. Nevertheless, federal efforts to control the epidemic increased. On 5 October 1993, Congress approved an increase of $227 million in support, bringing the 1994 total to $1.3 billion. Fulfilling a campaign promise, President

Bill Clinton created the position of national AIDS policy coordinator and appointed Kristine Gebbie to the post. In 1994, after lobbying by PWAs and researchers, he appointed the NIAID immunobiologist William Paul to head the Office of AIDS Research, with full budgetary authority. As of January 1996, *The AmFAR HIV/AIDS Treatment Directory* listed 77 clinical trial protocols for HIV infection and 141 protocols for opportunistic infections and related disorders. Twenty-one drugs were available to patients through compassionate use or expanded access protocols. Researchers held out hope that the disease would prove susceptible to new agents used in combination with AZT and its relatives, ddl and ddo. Many trials, however, continued to have difficulty recruiting patients and some community-based trials were threatened by budget cuts.

By the end of the twentieth century, more than 774,000 AIDS cases had been diagnosed in the United States, and almost 450,000 people had died of the disease. New treatments had lengthened lives and education had slowed transmission of the disease; nevertheless an estimated 110 people were being infected with HIV each day. And even though a remedy remained elusive, the sense of urgency in the fight against AIDS had waned. President George W. Bush appointed Scott Evertz as director of the Office of National AIDS Policy, but was slow to fill other key appointments to offices in the CDC and the Department of Health and Human Services that dealt with AIDS research and policy. Bush created a White House Task Force on HIV/AIDS but in his first budget proposal did not recommend funding increases for domestic AIDS programs.

By the beginning of the twenty-first century, AIDS had been brought under control in the United States through political action, intensive education, and expensive drug therapy. But the disease continued to ravage other parts of the world. By the end of 2001, 40 million people were living with HIV/AIDS, 95 percent of whom were in developing countries. The hardest hit area was Sub-Saharan Africa where 2.5 million people were dying each year. The Bush Administration's response to this global crisis was as mixed as its response to the domestic one. Secretary of State Colin Powell made global AIDS issues a priority, but Bush refused to sign a United Nations declaration on children's rights that supported sex education for teenagers. The United States joined several international efforts to halt the spread of the epidemic, including the International Partnership Against HIV/AIDS in Africa (IPAA), but its initial contribution to the UN Global Fund to finance responses to AIDS and other deadly infectious diseases was only $200 million. The Fund, created in 2001, sought $7–10 billion per year from all donors. U.S. AIDS activists now fight on two fronts. On the domestic front, they push the federal government to provide more funding for research and the care of PWAs, and they push researchers to develop a vaccine and treatments with fewer side effects. Most important they continue to impress upon young people who do not re-

member the AIDS epidemic before AZT that they should use "safe sex" practices, because AIDS is still a fatal disease. On the global front, activists seek to encourage the U.S. government to increase aid for global AIDS programs, to support debt cancellation for developing countries ravaged by the disease, and to take steps to ensure access to treatment in foreign countries.

BIBLIOGRAPHY

Altman, Dennis. *AIDS in the Mind of America*. Garden City, N.Y.: Anchor Press/Doubleday, 1986.

Fee, Elizabeth, and Daniel M. Fox, eds. *AIDS: The Making of a Chronic Disease*. Berkeley: University of California Press, 1992.

Goldstein, Nancy, and Jennifer L. Manlowe, eds. *The Gender Politcs of HIV/AIDS in Women: Perspectives on the Pandemic in the United States*. New York: New York University Press, 1997.

Grmek, Mirko D. *History of AIDS: Emergence and Origin of a Modern Pandemic*. Princeton, N.J.: Princeton University Press, 1990.

Hannaway, Caroline, Victoria A. Harden, and John Parascondola, eds. *AIDS and the Public Debate: Historical and Contemporary Perspectives*. Washington, D.C.: IOS Press, 1995.

Murphy, Timothy F. *Ethics in an Epidemic: AIDS, Morality, and Culture*. Berkeley: University of California Press, 1994.

Roiphe, Katie. *Last Night in Paradise: Sex and Morals at the Century's End*. Boston: Little, Brown, 1997.

Shilts, Randy. *And the Band Played On: Politics, People, and the AIDS Epidemic*. New York: St. Martin's Press, 1987.

Daniel M. Fox
Marcia L. Meldru
Cynthia R. Poe

See also **ACT UP; Centers for Disease Control and Prevention; Clinical Research; Epidemics and Public Health; Gay and Lesbian Movement; National Institutes of Health; Sexuality; Sexually Transmitted Diseases.**

ACT FOR THE IMPARTIAL ADMINISTRATION OF JUSTICE. *See* Intolerable Acts.

ACT UP, the AIDS Coalition to Unleash Power, was founded in 1987 by the homosexual author and activist Larry Kramer as a grassroots organization "united in anger" to end the AIDS crisis. Through aggressive nonviolent protests and civil disobedience, ACT UP became the standard-bearer for AIDS activism in the late 1980s and the early 1990s. Organizations in major U.S. cities effectively increased public understanding of AIDS, pressed the federal Food and Drug Administration to release new treatments for AIDS, demanded that the government establish a national policy on AIDS and prohibit discrimination against AIDS patients, and urged pharmaceutical companies to make AIDS treatments more

ACT UP. Playwright Larry Kramer founded the aggressively activist organization in 1987 to counter widespread official neglect and discrimination regarding AIDS. AP/WIDE WORLD PHOTOS

affordable. Numerous activist groups later sprouted from ACT UP to address the changing concerns of AIDS and discrimination against homosexuals.

BIBLIOGRAPHY

Andriote, John-Manuel. *Victory Deferred: How AIDS Changed Gay Life in America.* Chicago: University of Chicago Press, 1999.

Epstein, Steven. *Impure Science: AIDS, Activism, and the Politics of Knowledge.* Berkeley: University of California Press, 1996.

Kramer, Larry. *Reports from the Holocaust: The Making of an AIDS Activist.* New York: St. Martin's, 1989.

Kristen L. Rouse

See also **Acquired Immune Deficiency Syndrome (AIDS); Sexual Orientation.**

ACTION was a federal agency established by President Richard Nixon on 1 July 1971. Its intention was to make the service organizations established during the 1960s operate more efficiently. The programs absorbed were the Active Corps of Executives, the PEACE CORPS, the Retired Senior Volunteer Program, the Service Corps of Retired Executives, the National Student Volunteer Program, and Volunteers in Service to America (VISTA). In the 1980s, the Reagan administration urged private groups to take some of the load borne by VISTA, and VISTA itself was cut in personnel, thereby diminishing the power and influence of ACTION. In 1990, the National and Community Service Act further weakened ACTION's administrative role, and in 1993, the National and Community Service Trust Act absorbed ACTION into the Corporation for National and Community Service.

BIBLIOGRAPHY

"The National and Community Service Act of 1990." Available from http://www.cns.gov/about/ogc/legislation.html.

United States Congress, Senate Committee on Labor and Public Welfare, Special Subcommittee on Human Resources. Action Act of 1972 and Action Domestic Programs. Joint hearing before the Special Subcommittee on Human Resources and the Subcommittee on Aging of the Committee on Labor and Public Welfare, United States Senate, 92nd Congress, Second session on S. 3450 . . . and related bills, Older Americans Action Programs. Washinton, D.C.: Government Printing Office, 1972.

Kirk H. Beetz

ADAMSON ACT, enacted on 3 September 1916 at President Woodrow Wilson's behest in response to a pending strike by the major brotherhoods of railway workers. It established an eight-hour day for interstate railway workers and time and a half for overtime. The railroads challenged the law before the Supreme Court, claiming that it raised wages rather than regulated hours. In March 1917, impatient with the Court's inaction, the brotherhoods demanded immediate institution of the eight-hour day and scheduled a strike. Wilson again intervened, postponing the strike and then securing from the railroads a promise to grant the eight-hour day regardless of the Court's decision. One day after the settlement was announced, the Court upheld the law in *Wilson v. New,* 243 U.S. 332 (1917).

BIBLIOGRAPHY

Kerr, K. Austin. *American Railroad Politics, 1914–1920: Rates, Wages, and Efficiency.* Pittsburgh, Pa.: University of Pittsburgh Press, 1968.

Kolko, Gabriel. *Railroads and Regulation.* Westport, Conn.: Greenwood Press, 1976.

Link, Arthur Stanley. *Woodrow Wilson and the Progressive Era, 1910–1917.* New York: HarperCollins, 1963.

James D. Magee / T. M.

See also **Labor Legislation and Administration; Railroad Brotherhoods; Railroad Mediation Acts.**

ADDRESS OF THE SOUTHERN DELEGATES. In response to a series of antislavery resolutions, southern delegates called a caucus for 23 December 1848. John C. Calhoun of South Carolina submitted an address "moderate in manner" but calculated to unite the South. The proposal was adopted on 22 January 1849. Calhoun's address recounted acts of northern "aggression," including the nullification of constitutional guarantees for the return of fugitive slaves and the exclusion of slavery and Southerners from the common territories. Calhoun concluded that the abolitionist movement intended to overthrow white supremacy in the South. Fewer than half of the southern delegates signed the address, however, and it only intensified sectional rancor.

BIBLIOGRAPHY

Ford, Lacy K., Jr. *Origins of Southern Radicalism: The South Carolina Upcountry, 1800–1860.* New York: Oxford University Press, 1988.

Niven, John. *John C. Calhoun and the Price of Union: A Biography.* Baton Rouge: Louisiana State University Press, 1988.

Wiltse, Charles M. *John C. Calhoun.* 3 vols. Indianapolis: Bobbs-Merrill, 1944–1951.

Fletcher M. Green / A. G.

See also **Sectionalism; Wilmot Proviso.**

ADDYSTON PIPE COMPANY CASE, 175 U.S. 211 (1899). The Supreme Court, by a unanimous decision based on the SHERMAN ANTITRUST ACT, permanently enjoined six producers of cast-iron pipe from continuing an agreement that eliminated competition among themselves. Justice Rufus Peckham, speaking for the Court, denied that the *United States v. E. C. Knight Company* decision should prevail in this case. He argued that here was a definite conspiracy to interfere with the flow of interstate commerce and a positive scheme to limit competition and fix prices. This decision, which gave teeth to the Sherman Antitrust Act, encouraged increased federal antitrust actions after 1900.

BIBLIOGRAPHY

Sklar, Martin J. *The Corporate Reconstruction of American Capitalism, 1890–1916.* New York: Cambridge University Press, 1988.

Sullivan, E. Thomas, ed. *The Political Economy of the Sherman Act.* New York: Oxford University Press, 1991.

Allen E. Ragan / A. R.

See also **Antitrust Laws;** *United States v. E. C. Knight Company.*

ADENA is the name given to what is now recognized as a diverse set of precontact archaeological cultures that occupied the watershed of the Upper Ohio Valley in West Virginia, Kentucky, and Ohio. The Adena cultural expression flourished between around 500 B.C. to A.D. 1, although some authorities would extend its time span to A.D. 200.

The Grave Creek mound at Moundsville, West Virginia, was the first of the Adena type to have been accorded attention by travelers and is the largest known example, having originally been measured at sixty-seven feet in height. However, the name for this cultural tradition is taken from a mound that was located on the Adena estate of Governor Worthington, near Chillicothe, Ohio. Throughout the eastern woodlands, Adena mounds took the form of pointed conicals, in contrast to the dome shapes of the Middle Woodland Period (see HOPEWELL). Evidence at Adena mounds usually reveals repeated use over extended periods and includes remains from cremations and bundles of human bone placed under a thin blanket of soil, sometimes accompanied by pipes, polished stone artifacts, and other objects. A distinctive Adena burial facility was a large house with a circular ground plan. Burials were placed in its floor and covered with small individual mounds. After the structure was deliberately decommissioned, the location was covered by a large mound of soil as part of a ritual practice of completion.

Adena mounds stood in isolation from domestic living areas. Presumably they served a nearby scattering of people. The population was highly dispersed in small settlements of one to two structures. Their subsistence was achieved through foraging and the cultivation of native plants, such as squash, sunflower, and goosefoot (*chenopodium*).

Art motifs that became important later can already be seen at Adena archeological sites. Imagery on artwork features the shamanic transformation of humans into animals—particularly birds—and back to human form.

Objects made of special rocks and minerals gathered from some distance through trade have been found interred with the dead in Adena mounds. Of particular importance are objects of native copper. Shaped and polished stonework took a number of distinctive shapes, particularly that of a breastpiece (quadraconcave gorget) with cut-away sides. Distinctive tubular smoking pipes testify to the offering of smoke to the spirits. It is possible that the objective of pipe smoking was altered states of consciousness achieved through the use of the hallucinogenic plant *Nicotiana rustica*. Such a practice would have supported the work of shamans. All told, Adena was a manifestation of a broad regional increase in the number and kind of artifacts devoted to spiritual needs.

BIBLIOGRAPHY

Dragoo, Don W. *Mounds for the Dead: An Analysis of the Adena Culture.* Pittsburgh, Pa.: Carnegie Museum, 1963.

Fagan, Brian M. *Ancient North America: The Archaeology of a Continent.* London: Thames and Hudson, 1991.

James A. Brown

See also **Indian Mounds.**

ADKINS V. CHILDREN'S HOSPITAL, 261 U.S. 525 (1923), is a major precedent in the development of liberty of contract and substantive due process. In 1897, the United States Supreme Court held that the due process clauses of the Fourteenth and Fifth Amendments protect the rights of persons to enter into contracts (*Allgeyer v. Louisiana*). *Lochner v. New York* (1905) extended this to contracts of employment, and restricted the states' police powers to regulate hours of employment previously acknowledged in *Holden v. Hardy* (1898). But in *Muller v. Oregon* (1908), the court accepted state regulation of female employees' hours, and in *Bunting v. Oregon* (1917) it upheld state regulation of both hours and overtime wages, for both men and women. Knowledgeable observers concluded that *Bunting* had implicitly overruled *Lochner*.

Adkins nevertheless held a District of Columbia minimum-wage statute unconstitutional. In his first major opinion, Justice George Sutherland held that "freedom of contract is . . . the general rule and restraint the exception." Regulation of women's wages fit none of the hitherto recognized categories of permissible state regulation, and violated "the moral requirement implicit in every contract of employment" that wages reflect exactly the value of the worker's contribution. Sutherland stated that ratification of the Nineteenth Amendment in 1920 put women and men on a footing of equality, thereby implicitly condemning *Muller*. He denounced the policy of minimum-wage laws for forcing employers to shoulder welfare responsibilities. In dissents, Chief Justice William Howard Taft and Oliver Wendell Holmes criticized the majority for substituting their policy preferences for the legislatures'. Holmes ridiculed the notion that the Nineteenth Amendment had eliminated differences between men and women, and questioned the idea of liberty of contract itself as a constraint on the police power.

Adkins inhibited regulation of women's hours and wages until it was overruled by *West Coast Hotel Co. v. Parrish*, 300 U.S. 379 (1937).

BIBLIOGRAPHY

Arkes, Hadley. *The Return of George Sutherland: Restoring a Jurisprudence of Natural Rights.* Princeton, N.J.: Princeton University Press, 1994. Warmly supportive of the decision and its author.

Powell, Thomas Reed. "The Judiciality of Minimum-Wage Legislation." *Harvard Law Review* 37 (1924): 545–573. A now classic contemporary condemnation of the decision.

William M. Wiecek

See also **Lochner v. New York; Muller v. Oregon.**

ADMINISTRATIVE DISCRETION, DELEGATION OF.

Article I of the Constitution provides that "all legislative Powers herein granted shall be vested in a Congress of the United States." Congress thus holds the supreme legislative power and is the primary policy-making body in the U.S. government. Before the New Deal, it was widely believed that Congress could not delegate the power to make national policy to non-elected bodies such as administrative agencies. This so-called nondelegation doctrine kept administrative agencies small and weak. They could enforce laws established by Congress but were unable to develop policy themselves.

The non-delegation doctrine was thought to have a number of benefits. First, it kept the policy-making power of the federal government in the hands of elected officials, who arguably would be attuned to the interests of the citizenry. Second, keeping the legislative authority within Congress helped ensure that the policy-making process was deliberative. Moreover, the bicameral nature of the legislature coupled with the executive veto power ensured that only those decisions reaching a level of consensus would be adopted.

The doctrine had costs as well, and these became more obvious during the Great Depression. The economic and social upheaval created by the Depression convinced many that the federal government needed to be much more proactive in crafting economic policy, protecting those hurt by the Depression, and fashioning social and economic regulations. The greatest danger, some thought, was not government action but rather government inaction. Also, there was rising concern that the problems facing the nation were too complex and immediate for Congress to address effectively.

In the NEW DEAL, Congress created a number of administrative agencies to regulate and set policy in their areas of jurisdiction. In order to maximize the benefits of expertise and regulatory flexibility, Congress generally created administrative agencies with the authority to regulate a given economic activity.

In 1935, however, the Supreme Court in two cases struck down congressional delegations of power. In *Panama Refining Co. v. Ryan* (1935), the Court struck down portions of the National Industrial Recovery Act of 1933 as too broadly delegating authority to the National Recovery Administration to establish a code of fair competition for various industries. In *Schechter Poultry Corp. v. United States* (1935), the Court considered the Act again and struck it down in its entirety. One key defect in the Act was Congress's delegation of policy-making power to private groups that themselves were subject to the competition codes. These cases established the legal rule that in order for a delegation to be constitutional, Congress must define an intelligible principle to guide administrative regulation and to limit administrative discretion.

Once the Court announced this intelligible principle rule, however, it became more relaxed in authorizing congressional delegations. In fact, the Supreme Court has not struck down a congressional statute on non-delegation grounds since 1935. The Court does, however, occasionally cite the non-delegation doctrine as a reason to interpret a regulatory statute narrowly.

The principles of accountability and deliberation that provided the foundation of the non-delegation doctrine continue to be important for administrative agencies, though they are bolstered through other mechanisms. The norm of accountability is protected with the use of internal procedures, for example with the use of notice and comment periods in the drafting of regulations, which gives interested parties the right to participate in the regulatory process. Accountability is also protected because the president appoints the heads of most agencies and can thus hold them accountable for the policy decisions they make. Congress can also oversee agencies through congressional hearings, budgetary oversight, and statute.

The principle of agency deliberation is bolstered by the requirement of considered decision-making in both rulemaking and adjudication. Courts enforce this requirement by reviewing agency actions to ensure they are not arbitrary, capricious, an abuse of discretion, or contrary to law.

A vigorous non-delegation doctrine is also a principle in many state constitutions. This makes sense, in that state legislatures govern smaller jurisdictions than Congress, tend to regulate less complex matters, and can be more flexible than Congress.

BIBLIOGRAPHY

Aman, Alfred C., Jr., and William T. Mayton. *Administrative Law*. 2d ed. St. Paul, Minn.: West, 2001.

Schwartz, Bernard, *Administrative Law*. 3d ed. Boston: Little, Brown, 1991.

Kent Greenfield

See also **Administrative Justice.**

ADMINISTRATIVE JUSTICE, or, more commonly, administrative adjudication, is the exercise by an administrative agency of judicial powers delegated to the agency by a legislative body. Agencies typically possess both legislative and judicial powers in their area of authority. The legislative power gives the agency the authority to issue regulations, and the judicial power gives the agency the authority to adjudicate contested cases within its area of jurisdiction. This article focuses on the latter power.

The current distinction between adjudication within administrative agencies and adjudication in courts of law was not made historically. For example, the English Court of Exchequer evolved from the administrative Exchequer, a tax-assessing and collecting agency. American usage derives from the separation of powers in the U.S. Constitution and from its limitation of the "judicial power of the United States" to certain types of "cases . . . and controversies." Administrative adjudication was once criticized as being contrary to the reservation of judicial power to courts as set down in Article III of the Constitution. The Supreme Court held in *Crowell v. Benson* (1932), however, that agencies could adjudicate cases as long as provision was made for ultimate judicial review.

Administrative courts are not ordinarily engaged in determining the rights and duties of individuals as against other individuals. Rather, they typically deal with individuals in relation to government in terms of benefits sought or disabilities incurred from government action. It is this function that chiefly distinguishes administrative tribunals from civil courts. In contrast to the criminal courts, administrative tribunals are typically empowered to assess various penalties, such as forfeiture of licenses for the violation of a statutory or administrative regulation. Some administrative agencies, however, are not vested with adjudicative powers and must proceed through the regular courts for civil or criminal punishment of violations.

Another fundamental difference between administrative tribunals and courts is the nature of subject matter jurisdiction. The subject matter of an agency's administrative regulation and adjudication is normally a single economic activity, a set of closely related economic activities, or specific benefits conferred by government. The concern of the National Labor Relations Board with labor relations is an example of the first; the jurisdiction of the FEDERAL COMMUNICATIONS COMMISSION over radio, television, and telephone exemplifies the second; and adjudication of the validity of benefit claims by such agencies as the Veterans Administration represent the third. In contrast, the subject matter jurisdiction of courts embraces a broad spectrum of civil and criminal law.

The Administrative Procedure Act of 1946 (APA) imposes uniform procedural requirements on most U.S. agencies and requires the judicial function to be separated from the legislative and executive aspects within the agencies. Some agencies not covered by this act have alternate provisions in their organizational statutes; some have had additional procedural requirements imposed.

The APA specifies the requirements for notification and hearings of agencies under its jurisdiction. When Congress has specified that the administrative adjudication must be formal, the APA requires that the agency's decision be made upon a record established in a trial-type hearing, and that an initial decision be made by the officer who hears the evidence. This hearing examiner, known as an "administrative law judge," makes an initial decision based on reasoned analysis, written findings of fact, and conclusions of law. The initial decision is frequently subject to appeal to intra-agency boards or to the commission or board that is the highest administrative authority of the agency. The act further provides for a broad right of review of agency adjudication by the courts. In general, judicial review of formal agency adjudication is limited to questions of law, and administrative findings of fact are binding on the courts unless unsupported by substantial evidence. Questions of law include allegations that constitutional or statutory rights have been denied, failure to observe required procedures, and the agency's scope of authority. If Congress has not specified that the administrative adjudication must be formal, the APA is silent with regard to the procedures to be used. The requirements in such informal adjudications spring from constitutional requirements of procedural due process and from the right of courts to overturn agency action that is arbitrary, capricious, an abuse of discretion, or in violation of law.

Administrative regulation and adjudication is not limited to the national governmental level. It has become widespread in the states and municipalities, embracing such subjects as public utilities, natural resources, banking, securities, worker's compensation, unemployment insurance, employment discrimination, rents, automobile operation and inspection, corporations, elections, welfare, commercial insurance, land use, and environmental and consumer protection. Some states have administrative procedure acts comparable to the federal act of 1946; but in the states, judicial review is characteristically broader than under the federal act.

BIBLIOGRAPHY

Aman, Alfred C., Jr., and William T. Mayton. *Administrative Law*. 2d ed. St. Paul, Minn.: West Group, 2001.

Schwartz, Bernard. *Administrative Law*. 3d ed. Boston: Little, Brown, 1991.

Robert S. Goostree
Kent Greenfield

See also **Federal Agencies.**

ADMIRALTY LAW AND COURTS. Admiralty law covers disputes resulting from maritime casualties and private transactions related to ships and the transport of cargoes and passengers by sea. It is a unique body of law, based on centuries of tradition emerging from the seafaring traditions of the ancient Mediterranean world and enriched in recent years by international agreements and national statutes. The word "admiral" comes from the Arabic *amir-al-bahr*, meaning "commander of the sea." "Admiralty" or "maritime law" covers private commercial disputes and is distinct from "the law of the sea" or "ocean law," which covers public-law relations among governments, including maritime boundaries, navigational freedoms, resource exploitation, and environmental protection.

The earliest admiralty principle is traced to the island of Rhodes more than 2,000 years ago: "if, for the sake of lightening a ship, a jettison of goods has been made, what has been given for all will be made up by the contribution of all." This notion has evolved into the principle of the "general average," which is central to admiralty, and to the modern law of insurance. Codes of admiralty principles were promulgated by the major maritime cities and countries during the medieval period, and these codifications continue to provide important historical anchors for modern admiralty codes. Some countries, including Britain, established separate "admiralty courts." Today, admiralty disputes are resolved by courts of general jurisdiction, but they still look to a distinct body of law based

on the ancient codes of the maritime world to decide such controversies. The United States has never had separate admiralty courts, but separate rules governed admiralty disputes until 1966, when these rules were merged with the general procedural rules governing civil litigation.

Article III, section 2 of the U.S. Constitution gives federal courts authority over "all cases of admiralty and maritime jurisdiction," and the 1789 Judiciary Act assigned these cases to the federal district courts it created. In the United States, therefore, admiralty disputes are almost always resolved in the federal courts rather than the courts of the fifty states. Among the topics currently included within the domain of admiralty law are insurance of ships and cargoes, bills of lading, charters, towage, pilotage, sailors' rights (in the event, for instance, of injury or death), collision, salvage, maritime liens, ships' mortgages, liability limitations, piracy, and the effect of warfare on commercial transports.

The substantive law that U.S. federal courts apply in admiralty disputes is the general customary law that judges find from the ancient codifications and earlier judicial decisions. In his dissenting opinion in *Mitchell v. Trawler Racer* (1960), Justice Felix Frankfurter said that "no area of federal law is judge-made at its source to such an extent as is the law of admiralty." But some U.S. statutes are important in clarifying and resolving disputed areas, including the 1927 Longshore and Harbor Workers' Compensation Act (establishing a detailed workers' compensation regime), the 1920 Jones Act (relating to injury or death of sailors), the 1920 Death on the High Seas Act, the 1851 Limited Liability Act (concerning cargoes), the 1893 Harter Act (regulating cargo liability issues), the 1936 Carriage of Goods by Sea Act (COGSA; the central statute in commercial maritime law today and one of the most frequently litigated statutes involving international trade), and the 1912 Salvage Act.

The key international agreements regulating maritime disputes today are the 1910 Brussels Convention for the Unification of Certain Rules of Law with Respect to Collision Between Vessels, the 1972 International Regulations for Preventing Collisions at Sea (COLREGS), and the 1994 York-Antwerp Rules regulating the general average. The 1910 Collision Convention entered into force in 1913, but is not in force in the United States because U.S. cargo interests objected to its failure to require joint and several liability (which would make each party contributing to the accident liable for the full loss if the other parties could not pay). The 1972 collision regulations were adopted through the International Maritime Organization (IMO), the London-based United Nations agency in charge of shipping, and came into force in 1977. The York-Antwerp Rules emerged from an 1864 conference in York, United Kingdom, followed by an 1877 meeting in Antwerp, Belgium, and they have been revised every twenty to twenty-five years. These rules are not a formal treaty subject to ratification but rather a set of principles governing liability that are included almost automatically in every private cargo contract.

Admiralty law is rich with its unique history and tradition, and court cases adjudicating issues relating to the rights of crewmembers or the duties of companies providing marine insurance typically employ the colorful, salty language that is associated with maritime adventures. Although the principles applied do not differ dramatically from those that apply to land-based disputes, court decisions nonetheless draw upon the heritage that has formed this special area of the law, and it remains an independent discipline with its own language and its own distinctive governing treaties and statutes.

BIBLIOGRAPHY

Gilmore, Grant, and Charles L. Black Jr. *The Law of Admiralty.* 2d ed. Mineola, N.Y.: Foundation Press, 1975.

Robertson, David W., Steven F. Friedell, and Michael F. Sturley. *Admiralty and Maritime Law in the United States.* Durham, N.C.: Carolina Academic Press, 2001.

Jon M. Van Dyke

See also **Jones Act.**

ADOBE (corrupted to "dobie" by Anglo-Americans), a type of construction used principally in the Rocky Mountain plateau and the southwestern United States. The method came from North Africa via Spain and was introduced into the Southwest by the Spanish conquerors in the sixteenth century. Most of the Spanish mission buildings were made of this material. Wet clay and chopped hay or other fibrous material were mixed together and then tramped with bare feet. This was molded into bricks and sun dried. Mud was used as mortar. Adobe was widely used to build forts and trading posts as far east

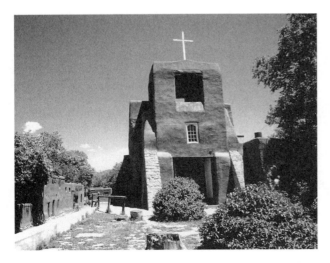

San Miguel Mission. This adobe church in Santa Fe, N. Mex., dates from 1626. JAMES BLANK

and north as Nebraska. In the twentieth century, the adobe look emerged as a popular residential building style in southwestern cities and suburbs.

BIBLIOGRAPHY

Spears, Beverly. *American Adobes: Rural Houses of Northern New Mexico.* Albuquerque: University of New Mexico Press, 1986.

Everett Dick / A. R.

See also **Building Materials; New Mexico; Pueblo.**

ADOLESCENCE. Adolescence emerged as a concept in the 1890s, when psychologists began investigating the abilities, behaviors, problems, and attitudes of young people between the onset of puberty and marriage. G. Stanley Hall, a pioneer in the study of children and their learning processes, is credited with giving adolescence its first full definition in his text *Adolescence: Its Psychology and Its Relations to Physiology, Anthropology, Sociology, Sex, Crime, Religion and Education*, published in 1904. Hall thought that the stresses and misbehavior of young people were normal to their particular time of life, because he believed human development recapitulated that of human society. For Hall, just as the human race had evolved from "savagery" to "civilization," so too did each individual develop from a primitive to an advanced condition. Adolescence corresponded to, or recapitulated, the period of prehistory when upheaval characterized society and logical thinking began to replace instinct.

A year after Hall's book appeared, the psychoanalyst Sigmund Freud published an essay in which he identified adolescence as a period of emotional upheaval, inconsistent behavior, and vulnerability to deviant and criminal activity caused by psychosexual conflicts. For the past century, the qualities of anxiety and awkwardness resulting from physiological development and sexual awareness that Hall and Freud emphasized have pervaded popular as well as scientific definitions of adolescence.

Puberty had been a subject of medical and psychological discussion for centuries, but social, economic, and biological changes in late-nineteenth-century Western society focused new attention on the status and roles of young people. The development of industrial capitalism reduced the participation of children in the workforce, while advances in nutrition and the control of disease lowered the age of sexual maturation. As a result, individuals were isolated for a more extended period in a state of semidependency between childhood and adulthood. In the United States, as well as in Europe, researchers and writers in various fields began using the term "adolescence" to apply to the particular era of life when a new order of events and behavior occurred, thereby making it a formal biological, psychological, and even legal category. Terms such as "youth" and, later, "teenager" were used synonymously but less precisely to describe the status of individuals in adolescence. Because adolescence occurred when persons were presumably preparing to enter adult roles in family, work, and community, their needs and guidance assumed increasing importance. Consequently, educators, social workers, and psychologists constructed theories and institutions geared toward influencing the process of growing up.

Rise of a Youth Peer Culture

The age consciousness of American society that intensified in the early twentieth century sharpened the distinctiveness of adolescence. By the 1920s, especially, the age grading and the nearly universal experience of schooling pressed children into peer groups, creating lifestyles and institutions that were not only separate from but also occasionally in opposition to adult power. Compulsory attendance laws, which kept children in school until they were fourteen or older, had a strong impact in the United States, where by 1930 nearly half of all youths aged fourteen to twenty were high school students. Enrollment of rural youths and African Americans remained relatively low (only one-sixth of American blacks attended high school in the 1920s). But large proportions of immigrants and native-born whites of foreign parents attended high school. Educational reformers developed curricula to prepare young people for adult life, and an expanding set of extracurricular organizations and activities, such as clubs, dances, and sports, heightened the socialization of youths in peer groups. As a result, secondary school and adolescence became increasingly coincident.

As high school attendance became more common (in 1928 two-thirds of white and 40 percent of nonwhite children had completed at least one year of high school), increasing numbers of adolescents spent more time with peers than with family. This extended time away from parents, combined with new commercial entertainments such as dance halls, amusement parks, and movies, helped create a unique youth culture. Ironically—though perhaps understandably—the spread of this culture caused conflict with adults, who fretted over adolescents' independence in dress, sexual behavior, and other characteristics that eluded adult supervision. The practice of dating, which by the 1920s had replaced adult-supervised forms of courtship and which was linked to both high school and new commercial amusements, was just one obvious new type of independent adolescent behavior.

Adults expressed concern over the supposed problems of adolescents, particularly their awakening sexuality and penchant for getting into trouble. Indeed, in the adult mind, sexuality stood at the center of adolescence. Male youths especially were seen as having appetites and temptations that lured them into masturbation and homosexuality. Young women's sexuality could allegedly lead to promiscuity and prostitution. As a result, according to psychologists and physicians in the 1920s, adolescence was a time of life that necessitated control, not only by the self but also by parents, doctors, educators, social workers, and the police. Moreover, they believed that peer association—sometimes in street gangs—in combination with the stresses and rebelliousness natural to adolescence, contributed to the rise of juvenile delinquency; in this conception, adolescence made every girl and boy a potential delinquent. Thus, juvenile courts, reform schools, and other "child-saving" institutions were created to remedy the problems that adolescents allegedly experienced and caused.

Adolescence in the Depression and World War II

During the depression years of the 1930s, the potential for intergenerational conflict increased as the scarcity of jobs and low pay for those who were employed thwarted young people's personal ambitions and delayed their ability to attain adult independence. Economic pressures forced many young people to stay in school longer than had been the case in previous generations. By 1940, 49 percent of American youths were graduating from high school, up from 30 percent in 1930. Although adolescents in the 1930s had less disposable income than those in the 1920s, they still influenced popular culture with their tastes in music, dance, and movies.

The expanding economy during World War II brought three million youths between the ages of fourteen and seventeen, about one-third of the people in this age category, into full or part-time employment by 1945. The incomes that adolescents earned helped support a renewed youth culture, one that idolized musical stars such as Glenn Miller and Frank Sinatra and created new clothing styles such as that of the bobby-soxer. Their roles in the national economy and mass culture complicated the status of adolescents, trapping them between the personal independence that war responsibilities provided them and the dependence on family and adult restrictions that the larger society still imposed on them.

Postwar Teen Culture

After the war, the proportion of adolescents in the population in Western countries temporarily declined. Children reaching teen years just after World War II had been born during the depression, when a brief fall in the birth rate resulted in a smaller cohort of people reaching adolescence. Furthermore, a marriage boom followed the war, drastically reducing the age at which young people were entering wedlock; in the United States, the median age at marriage for women declined from twenty-three to twenty-one. By 1960, 40 percent of American nineteen-year-olds were already married.

The marriage boom soon translated into the baby boom, which eventually combined with material prosperity to foster a more extensive teen culture. By 1960, the first cohort of baby boomers was reaching teen age, and goods such as soft drinks, clothing, cars, sports equipment, recorded music, magazines, and toiletries, all heavily and specifically promoted by advertisers to young people with expanding personal incomes, comprised a flourishing youth market that soon spread overseas. At the same time, radio, television, movies, and mass-market publications directed much of their content to this segment of the population. Marketing experts utilized long-standing theories about the insecurities of adolescence, along with surveys that showed adolescents tending toward conformist attitudes, to sell goods that catered to teenagers' desires to dress, buy, and act like their peers.

As in earlier years, parents and other adults fretted over children who they believed were maturing too rapidly, as adolescents began manifesting independent behavior in their tastes and buying habits. Even before the baby boomers entered their teen years, social scientists, educators, and government officials were reaching a near-panic state over premarital pregnancy and juvenile delinquency. The U.S. rate of premarital pregnancy among white women aged fifteen to nineteen doubled from under 10 percent in the 1940s to 19 percent in the 1950s. The rock-and-roll generation signified a type of rebellion that often included antisocial behavior that in turn garnered heavy media attention. Newspapers eagerly publicized gang wars and other sensational cases of juvenile crime, and police departments created juvenile units to deal with a presumed teenage crime wave.

While many of the postwar trends in adolescence, especially their influence on the consumer economy, continued past the twentieth century, by the late 1960s and early 1970s new attitudes about gender equality and birth control, stimulated in part by increased access to automobiles and generally higher material well-being, helped fashion new sexual values among adolescents. Increasingly, peer groups in high schools and colleges (in 1970, three-fourths of Americans were graduating from high school and one-third were enrolled in college) replaced dating with informal, mixed-gender "going out" and "parties." In addition, looser attitudes toward marriage, for which a date was seen as a first step, and greater acceptance (among adults as well as youths) of nonmarital sex, arose among adolescents and heightened concern over society's ability to control adolescents' sexual behavior.

By 1976, U.S. surveys showed that nearly one-fourth of sixteen-year-old white females and one-half of sixteen-year-old black females had had premarital intercourse; there were also nearly twenty-five illegitimate births for every thousand white females aged fifteen to nineteen and more than ninety such births for black females in that age group. By 1990, 55 percent of women aged fifteen to nineteen had experienced intercourse. Although this figure declined to slightly below half by century's end, the seeming sexual abandon practiced by many young people prompted some analysts to conclude that marriage was losing its special meaning. A sharp rise in average age of marriage, for men from twenty-three to over twenty-six and for women from twenty-one to over twenty-three between 1970 and 1990, reinforced such a conclusion.

In the 1960s a well-publicized and vocal minority of youths began to infuse adolescence with a new brand of political consciousness that seemed to widen the "generation gap." Much of the youth activism flourished on college campuses but enough of it filtered down to high schools that educators and other public authorities faced challenges they had not previously encountered. The civil rights movement and the assassination of President John F. Kennedy caused American teenagers to question the values of adult society, but the Vietnam War ignited them. Although the majority of youths did not oppose the war, a number of them participated in protests that upset traditional assumptions about the nonpolitical quality of high school life. In 1969, the Supreme Court declared in *Tinker v. Des Moines Independent School System* that the right of free speech applied to high school students who wished to wear black armbands in protest of the war.

After the Vietnam War ended, the alienation of adolescents from society—as well as, in adolescent minds, the alienation of society from adolescents—seemed to intensify rather than abate. Anger over the deployment of nuclear weapons and dangers to the ecosystem worldwide sparked student protests on both sides of the Atlantic. Moreover, a spreading drug culture, the attraction by teens to the intentionally provocative lyrics of punk rock and rap music, the rise of body art and piercing, the increase in single- (and no-) parent households, and the high number of families with two parents employed and out of the home for most of the day all further elevated the power of adolescent peer associations.

Juvenile crime continued to capture attention, as surveys in the 1980s estimated that between 12 and 18 percent of American males and 3 to 4 percent of females had been arrested prior to age twenty-one. To the frustration of public officials, crime-prevention programs ranging from incarceration to aversion to job placement and counseling failed to stem teen violence and recidivism.

As identity politics pervaded adult society, youths also sought havens within groups that expressed themselves through some behavioral or visual (although only occasionally ideological) manner. American high school populations contained dizzying varieties of identity groups such as "Goths," "jocks," "nerds," "Jesus freaks," "preppies," "druggies," and many more. All the while, commercial interests in the new global economy, from sneaker and sportswear manufacturers to music producers and snack-food makers, stayed hot on the teenage trail.

Questions about Adolescence as a Universal Concept

At the beginning of the twenty-first century, multiple models of American adolescence brought into question whether or not the historical concept had as much uniformity as some twentieth-century experts implied it had. Certainly almost all adolescents, regardless of race or class, undergo similar biological changes, though characteristics such as the age of menarche have shifted over time. But the social and psychological parameters appeared to have become increasingly complex and diverse. Although the most common images of adolescents set them inside the youth-oriented consumer culture of clothes, music, and movies, the darker side of growing up had captured increasing attention. Poverty, sexual abuse, substance abuse, learning disabilities, depression, eating disorders, and violence had come to characterize youthful experiences as much as the qualities of fun- and freedom-seeking depicted by the media and marketers. Popular theory still accepted that almost all adolescents confront similar psychological challenges of stress and anxiety, but the processes involved in growing up display complexities that confound attempts to characterize them. A continuing rise in age at marriage, which approached the late twenties for males and mid-twenties for females, made family formation less of an end point for adolescence, and the assumption by preteens of qualities and habits once exclusive to teenagers challenged the cultural definition of the age at which adolescence begins. The trend of young people assuming adult sexual, family, social, and economic behavior—and their attendant problems—blurred many of the qualities that previously gave adolescence its distinctiveness.

BIBLIOGRAPHY

Aries, Philippe. *Centuries of Childhood.* New York: Knopf, 1962.

Bailey, Beth L. *From Front Porch to Back Seat: Courtship in Twentieth-Century America.* Baltimore: Johns Hopkins University Press, 1988.

Chudacoff, Howard P. *How Old Are You?: Age Consciousness in American Culture.* Princeton, N.J.: Princeton University Press, 1989.

Coleman, James S. *The Adolescent Society.* New York: Free Press, 1961.

Fass, Paul F., and Mary Ann Mason, eds. *Childhood in America.* New York: New York University Press, 2000.

Graff, Harvey J., ed. *Growing Up in America: Historical Experiences.* Detroit, Mich.: Wayne State University Press, 1987.

Hine, Thomas. *The Rise and Fall of the American Teenager.* New York: Avon Books, 1999.

Jones, Kathleen W. *Taming the Troublesome Child: American Families, Child Guidance, and the Limits of Psychiatric Authority.* Cambridge, Mass.: Harvard University Press, 1999.

Kett, Joseph F. *Rites of Passage: Adolescence in America, 1790 to the Present.* New York: Basic Books, 1977.

Modell, John. *Into One's Own: From Youth to Adulthood in the United States, 1920–1975.* Berkeley: University of California Press, 1989.

Howard P. Chudacoff

See also **Childhood; Juvenile Courts; Sexuality.**

ADOPTION, the process of legally transferring parental rights and obligations from a child's biological parent or parents to one or more adults, is an age-old practice. The Code of Hammurabi in ancient Babylonia provided for such a transfer. Adoption was also practiced in ancient Egypt, Greece, and Rome. These adoptions focused on the needs of adults with regard to issues such as inheritance and religion. In 1851, Massachusetts passed the first modern adoption law, signaling a profound change in the meaning of adoption—the needs of the child, not the adult, would be paramount.

The Road to Legalized Adoption

Before 1851, legal adoption in the United States was extremely rare. English common law, on which American laws were based, did not recognize adoption because it jeopardized the inheritance rights of blood relatives. However, informal adoption (raising a child as one's own without any legal tie) was not uncommon. Beginning in the colonial era, dependent children were cared for in the homes of relatives, neighbors, or strangers, with the relationship often being formalized through indenture. Although indenture represented an economic relationship—providing for a child's basic needs in return for his or her labor—these arrangements could also be of a more familial nature. Childless couples often took these children, who were abandoned or orphaned, or whose parents were, for some reason, unable to care for them, sometimes using their wills to provide for their future. In addition, state legislatures occasionally passed private bills that changed a child's name and implicitly acknowledged its adoption.

By the mid-nineteenth century, a number of social and cultural transformations had occurred that set the stage for the passage of the Massachusetts Adoption Act of 1851. As the United States became more industrialized with the accompanying growth in cities and immigration, the number of orphaned, homeless, or neglected children rapidly grew as a result of the dislocations and uncertainties caused by these dramatic changes. Orphanages were opened to care for these children, but by midcentury some reformers began to argue that children needed the natural environment of a family, a setting that, not incidentally, was less expensive. In addition, affectionate child nurture and the belief in childhood innocence became more important, especially among the middle class, as homes lost many of their productive functions and became private havens presided over by a loving wife and mother.

Efforts to find homes for children intensified over the last half of the nineteenth century, with New York City reformer Charles Loring Brace leading the way. In 1853, Brace founded the New York Children's Aid Society, which "placed-out" poor and homeless urban youths into rural homes. In 1854, Brace loaded up 138 children and sent them west to Pennsylvania by train. In the ensuing decades, dozens of similar societies were created, and by 1930, "orphan trains" had relocated as many as 200,000 children to western states. Relatively few of these children were legally adopted, since the majority had at least one living parent or were older than adopters preferred.

Nevertheless, the placing-out movement contributed to the development of adoption laws and the growing acceptance of adoption. As more people took in unrelated children and raised them as their own, the need for a standardized legal means to formalize and protect that relationship grew. Meanwhile, courts had begun in the early nineteenth century to consider "the best interests of the child" when making decisions about custody. Under this doctrine, affection and nurturance could be viewed as equally significant as paternal rights or blood ties. Together, these changes led the Massachusetts legislature to pass the 1851 adoption act. The statute made the adoption procedure clear. The measure required the written consent of the biological parents or of a child's guardian if its parents were dead, severed all legal bonds between the biological parents and the child, created legal ties between the adoptive parents and the child as if it had been born to them, and required the judge to determine that the adoptive parents were "fit and proper" before issuing the adoption decree. By the end of the nineteenth century, most states had passed adoption statutes that, like the Massachusetts law, focused on the welfare of the child.

Social Workers, Stricter Adoption Laws, and Issues of Background

During the Progressive Era, some reformers began to focus specifically on adoption and to develop placement standards that emphasized investigation to ensure that a child's biological family was not unnecessarily broken up. The policy of keeping birth families together, which was widely accepted by 1910, coupled with social workers' efforts to encourage unwed mothers to keep their children, meant that relatively few children were available for adoption. Some of the few who were available were placed through private adoption agencies, which were first opened during this period. Unlike social welfare professionals, these volunteer-staffed agencies did not insist that unmarried mothers keep their infants.

Meanwhile, adoption was gradually gaining acceptance. From 1907 to 1911, the *Delineator*, a popular women's magazine, ran a child-rescue campaign that urged its largely white and middle-class readers to adopt a dependent child as part of their patriotic duty. Since Americans understood all women to be essentially maternal, the magazine even encouraged single women to adopt. The campaign led to the adoption of at least two thousand children. It also contributed to the acceptance of adoption by downplaying the significance of a child's heredity—a primary fear of many prospective adopters—and emphasizing the power of a nurturing, Christian environment to overcome any genetic taint.

Heredity was a controversial issue in adoption, as were questions of race, ethnicity, and religion. Very few child welfare agencies existed to serve the needs of African American children, and blacks continued the tradition of informally adopting needy children in their communities. Concerns about race mixing also meant that any child whose race was not crystal clear would not be placed. The focus on racial matching, however, could conflict with efforts to preserve a dependent child's natal religion. In 1904, whites in Arizona kidnapped forty Irish orphans that Catholic nuns had placed with Mexican Catholic families and placed them in white families. The courts allowed the white families to keep the children over the vigorous objections of the Catholic Church.

In the 1920s, social workers continued to work for stricter adoption laws that stressed investigation and professional oversight. One goal was to revise state adoption statutes along the lines of the Children's Code of Minnesota, passed in 1917. Although the 1851 Massachusetts Adoption Act required a judge to determine an adoptive home's suitability, those investigations were notoriously superficial. By contrast, the Children's Code required a thorough investigation into the adoptive home by a state agency before the adoption could be approved, as well as a six-month probationary period before the adoption could be finalized. The code also closed adoption records to public inspection. By the end of the 1930s, most states had passed new adoption laws or updated old ones, and many contained the principles of the Children's Code. Nevertheless, almost half of all adoption placements were still made without the initial oversight of social welfare professionals. In these independent or private agency adoptions, lawyers, physicians, and volunteers placed children largely based on their intuition.

Adoption as the "Perfect Solution"

The 1940s saw significant changes in social workers' views toward illegitimacy and an explosion in the number of adoptions. Social welfare professionals began to argue that unwed mothers did not make the best parents and that their children would forever suffer from the stigma of illegitimacy. Psychological theory buttressed this position, suggesting that unwed mothers were neurotic young women whose pregnancies signaled a more deep-seated problem; by placing her child for adoption, the woman would gain a second chance to solve her problem and live a normal life. This view was especially appealing given that the war had seen a dramatic rise in the number of illegitimate births, including those to white, middle-class teens.

At the same time as the supply of adoptable infants increased, so did the demand. Already by the 1930s, concerns about a dependent child's heredity had lessened and the number of adoptions had grown. During the war and the postwar period, the number of legal adoptions swelled, as childless couples scrambled for a child with whom they could take their place in the postwar baby boom. In the mid-1930s, estimates put the number of adoptions at about 17,000 annually. By 1945, estimates had it at 50,000 a year; by 1965, the number had increased to 142,000. Adoption had became the "perfect solution" for all three parties to it.

Problems with the "Perfect Solution"

Although the numbers of adoptable children had increased, the supply could in no way meet the growing demand. In response, social workers in the late 1940s began to redefine the concept of "adoptability" to include minority, older, disabled, and foreign-born children.

Most significantly, professionals began to focus for the first time on the needs of African American children. When efforts to find African American homes fell short, social workers in the 1960s began to place black children in white homes for adoption. By the early 1970s, approximately fifteen thousand transracial adoptions had occurred. In 1972, however, the National Association of Black Social Workers (NABSW) issued a statement that rejected transracial adoptions as a form of cultural genocide. In the wake of this pronouncement, many states required same-race placements. In the 1980s, the issue resurfaced because of the large percentage of black children in foster care who needed permanent homes. In the 1990s, a number of white foster parents filed antidiscrimination suits in order to adopt African American children. Despite the NABSW's continued resistance, Congress passed the Multiethnic Placement Act of 1994, which prohibited agencies from delaying or denying the adoption of a child in order to find racially matched parents. Any agency that did so risked the loss of federal aid.

The postwar shortage of white, American-born children also led to an interest in intercountry adoption. Orphaned and abandoned children from Germany and Japan were adopted in the years immediately after World War II. The adoption of Asian children increased dramatically after the Korean War; between 1966 and 1976, Americans adopted 32,000 foreign-born, primarily Korean, children. In 2000, Americans adopted more than 18,000 foreign children, over half from Russia and China. Girls comprised the overwhelming majority of Chinese adoptees, because Chinese families prize male children, whose value has increased since China began its one-family-one-child policy to curb population growth. In 2001, foreign-born children made up about 20 percent of all American adoptions. To combat the confusion and corruption that often marred these adoptions, such as exorbitant last-minute fees and failure to disclose a child's health problems, the Hague Convention on Intercountry Adoptions was written in 1993. This multinational treaty, which the United States ratified in 2000, establishes, among other things, accreditation standards for agencies; it remains to be seen if nations will abide by the treaty.

The shortage of white infants intensified in the early 1970s. Feminism and the cultural acceptance of premarital sex created a climate in which unmarried mothers no longer felt compelled to place their children. The legalization of abortion in 1973 also seems to have reduced the number of available children. The result was a rapid decline in the number of unrelated adoptions in the early 1970s, from almost ninety thousand in 1970 to fewer than fifty thousand in 1975. And for many of the mothers who still wished to place their children, a new attitude prevailed. These women now often took a role in choosing their child's parents, sometimes maintaining ongoing contact after placement. Although the trend at the start of the twenty-first century was clearly toward more openness, there was considerable opposition to these "open adoptions," with a concern that children would be confused as to who their "real parents" are.

Meanwhile, birth mothers and adoptees who had been part of the "perfect solution" began to critique the secrecy surrounding adoption. Although laws had closed records from the public, birth parents and adopted persons often had access to their case histories before World War II, since many children had been placed at an age when they could remember their biological families. With more unwed mothers giving up their children after the war, agencies sealed case files to protect all parties from the stigma of illegitimacy. In 1971, an adoptee, Florence Fisher, founded the Adoptees' Liberty Movement Association with the goal of unsealing records once an adoptee reached the age of eighteen. The adoption rights movement also included birth parents, primarily mothers, some of whom founded Concerned United Birthparents in 1976. Unsealing adoption records has proved to be an extremely contentious issue; as a compromise, many states have established state adoption registries and passed "search and consent" laws that assign a confidential intermediary to locate the birth parents to ensure that they desire contact.

More recently, adoptions by gays and lesbians became a hotly contested issue. Although by the end of the twentieth century a number of states routinely accepted gay parents, restrictive legislation still existed. In 2001, a federal judge upheld Florida's 1977 law that automatically disqualified gays and lesbians. Gay activists, in addition to contesting such laws, also challenged legislation that prevented homosexual couples from adopting together.

BIBLIOGRAPHY

Ashby, LeRoy. *Endangered Children: Dependency, Neglect, and Abuse in American History.* New York: Twayne, 1997.

Bartholet, Elizabeth. *Family Bonds: Adoption and the Politics of Parenting.* Boston: Houghton Mifflin, 1993.

Berebitsky, Julie. *Like Our Very Own: Adoption and the Changing Culture of Motherhood, 1851–1950.* Lawrence: University Press of Kansas, 2000.

Carp, E. Wayne. *Family Matters: Secrecy and Disclosure in the History of Adoption.* Cambridge, Mass.: Harvard University Press, 1998.

Gordon, Linda. *The Great Arizona Orphan Abduction.* Cambridge, Mass.: Harvard University Press, 1999.

Grossberg, Michael. *Governing the Hearth: Law and the Family in Nineteenth-Century America.* Chapel Hill: University of North Carolina Press, 1985.

Holt, Marilyn Irvin. *The Orphan Trains: Placing Out in America.* Lincoln: University of Nebraska Press, 1992.

Kunzel, Regina. *Fallen Women, Problem Girls: Unmarried Mothers and the Professionalization of Social Work, 1890–1945.* New Haven, Conn.: Yale University Press, 1993.

Marsh, Margaret, and Wanda Ronner. *The Empty Cradle: Infertility in America from Colonial Times to the Present.* Baltimore: Johns Hopkins University Press, 1996.

Rappaport, Bruce M. *The Open Adoption Book: A Guide to Adoption Without Tears.* New York: Macmillan, 1992.

Wadia-Ells, Susan, ed. *The Adoption Reader: Birth Mothers, Adoptive Mothers, and Adopted Daughters Tell Their Stories.* Seattle, Wash.: Seal Press, 1995.

Julie Berebitsky

See also **Childbirth and Reproduction; Childhood; Children's Rights; Foster Care.**

ADVENTIST CHURCHES. The Seventh-day Adventist Church traces its roots to the early-nineteenth-century endeavors of William Miller (1782–1849). A captain in the War of 1812, Miller farmed in Low Hampton, New York. An ardent Jeffersonian democrat and a deist, Miller was converted to the evangelical Christian faith in a Baptist revival. Driven by gnawing concern about what happened after death, Miller devoted his spare time to careful study of a Bible annotated with Anglican Archbishop James Ussher's famous chronology. Like Ussher, Miller was fascinated by dates. His close reading of the Old Testament book of Daniel, enhanced by other biblical passages, prompted Miller to plot a calendar for the "end times." By 1818, his reading and Ussher's dates convinced Miller that Christ would return in 1843. He kept the news to himself for the next thirteen years, but his conviction about the inexorable approach of the end ultimately drove him to tell others.

Miller began preaching in 1831 and received a Baptist preaching license in 1833. He published his lectures about Christ's second advent in 1835. His unusually specific interpretations of biblical prophecies regarding Christ's second coming and his diligence in disseminating his view, won him a local following. He plodded on throughout the northeast, preaching in more than 800 venues before 1840. In 1840 his fortunes changed, thanks to a noted Boston publicist, Joshua V. Himes. The pastor of Boston's Chardon Street Chapel, Himes thrived amid causes and crowds. He promoted Miller and envisioned a national crusade. Soon two millennialist papers, a hymnal called *The Millennial Harp*, and a lecture tour that brought Miller to hundreds of audiences in an ever-expanding circle whipped up considerable millennial fervor. Some 200 preachers of the end as well as hundreds of public lecturers eventually enlisted perhaps 50,000 Americans to await with certainty Christ's imminent return.

These Millerites encouraged one another and recruited skeptics in revival and camp meetings, where they used charts and illustrations to hammer home their message. Some were profoundly impressed and used words like "terror" and "conviction" to describe the public response to the proclamation of the end of the world, set rather vaguely by Miller for sometime between 21 March 1843 and 21 March 1844. Others proved more willing to identify precise likely dates. As each passed quietly by, desertions depleted the ranks of the faithful. Miller revisited his calculations but professed still to expect Christ's return. Doctrinal conflict with local congregations intensified as the Millerite furor grew. After 22 October 1844

Adventist Prophetess. In December 1844, seventeen-year-old Ellen Harmon experienced a series of visions that thrust her to the forefront of the Adventist movement while helping to heal divisive rifts between factions in the church. She remained a church leader until her death in 1915. AP/WIDE WORLD PHOTOS

(a date advanced by the Millerite preacher Samuel Snow) passed uneventfully, the movement disbanded. The passage of time dimmed millennial hopes. Christ's failure to materialize became known as the Great Disappointment, and the mass movement Himes had skillfully manipulated collapsed. Miller retreated to Vermont, where he lived out his days as the leader of a small Adventist church.

The few Adventists who clung to the hope of an imminent end of time, meanwhile, disagreed among themselves about how to proceed. Some advocated observing the Seventh Day rather than the "popish" Sunday. They argued, too, about Satan, the millennium, the atonement, and the state of the dead. The disunity provided the stage on which the Adventist Prophetess, Ellen Harmon White, emerged. Just seventeen years old in 1844, Ellen Harmon had a vision that reassured her that the date, 22 October 1844, had been correct, but the faithful had awaited the wrong event. This remarkable rationale was followed by a series of visions that helped negotiate some of the differences among Adventist factions. Prone to visions and other forms of religious enthusiasm, White (Ellen Harmon married the Adventist elder James White in 1846) addressed all aspects of Adventism in a steady stream of prophetic utterances that quickly found their way into print. All Adventists did not immediately fall under her spell, but White professed a divine commission as God's messenger to the scattered Millerites, and she pursued this calling. An expanding core of Adventists accepted her spiritual teaching and her particular views on health. White urged Adventists to shun liquor and tobacco and to take care in what they ate. In 1863, she became an enthusiastic (and lifelong) advocate of hydropathy.

Ellen and James White moved to Battle Creek, Michigan, in 1855, and they made the town an Adventist hub. In 1860, the group assumed the name Seventh-day Adventists and incorporated a publishing house. In 1863, Adventists convened their first general conference. Ellen White's nine-volume *Testimonies* now provided direction and inspiration to a stable and growing religious community. Her protégé, John Kellogg, a vegetarian, contributed to the dietary focus that came to characterize Adventist health causes and gave Battle Creek a reputation as a cereal capital. Adventism's global outreach promoted hospitals and health services wherever missionaries traveled.

In 1903, again following Ellen White, the offices of the church moved to the outskirts of Washington, D.C. She died in 1915. The church grew steadily—but apart from the mainstream of American Protestantism—throughout the twentieth century. During the 1980s and 1990s, influential Adventists showed an inclination to identify more closely with evangelical Protestants. This caused considerable turmoil and some separations, and it initiated a period of historical reflection on Adventist distinctives. Especially difficult was the issue of the special authority that the denomination has historically conceded to the writings of Ellen White. Also troubling to evangelicals was the Adventist doctrine of "soul sleep," which maintained that those who died did not immediately enter heaven or hell. Adventists also held strongly to specific interpretations of prophecies about heaven that differed from the generally accepted range of eschatologies that animated American Protestantism. Adventist churches expect their members to tithe, and—following Miller's early Baptist sympathies—they baptize by immersion.

Active in more than 200 countries, in 2000 the Seventh-day Adventist Church counted well over 900,000 members in the United States and more than 11 million worldwide. Adventist Churches have fared especially well in Mexico and Latin America and in Southern Asia. Nearly 400 clinics and dispensaries extend the medical care offered in more than 170 hospitals. In North America, the tiny, scattered, ridiculed band that persisted after the Great Disappointment of 1844 observes its Sabbath in more than 4,800 churches, and it counts nearly 49,600 more meeting places worldwide. Around the world, Adventist Sabbath schools enroll some 14,500,000 students, and 56 publishing houses support their global endeavors. The headquarters boasts that there is one Seventh-day Adventist for every 510 people. It also acknowledges some concern that, at the turn of the century, more than 20 people left for every 100 who joined an Adventist church.

BIBLIOGRAPHY

Gaustad, Edwin S., ed. *The Rise of Adventism: Religion and Society in Mid-Nineteenth-Century America*. New York: Harper and Row, 1974.

Numbers, Ronald L. *Prophetess of Health: Ellen G. White and the Origins of Seventh-day Adventist Health Reform*. Knoxville: University of Tennessee Press, 1992.

Edith L. Blumhofer

See also **Religion and Religious Affiliation.**

ADVENTURERS. *See* **Merchant Adventurers.**

ADVERTISING.
Whether trying to alter spending patterns or simply alert buyers to a firm's existence, business has for centuries turned to advertising. As the type of media has changed, so too has advertising's form. But aside from a fundamental post–World War I shift in the perception of advertising's power, its function is the same today as it was in 1700: Advertising aims to boost sales.

Buyers purchase a product presumably because they perceive a need or desire for it. They decide from whom and what brand to purchase. Awareness of their choices and an evaluation of which option is "best" influences their decisions. Until the twentieth century, advertising sought only to convey information. But modern advertising seeks to "create demand" by influencing buyers' perceived needs or desires.

Before "Modern" Advertising
In the American colonial period, advertisements were primarily signboards on inns, taverns, coffeehouses, and the like. Travelers needed information about inns, but locals did not need advertisements in order to find the blacksmith.

The first newspaper to appear continuously, the Boston *News-Letter*, was established in 1704. It contained sporadic advertisements. Real estate advertisements, rewards for runaway apprentices, and notices of slaves for sale were all common, as were announcements of sale of cordage, wine, and cloth. These advertisements were limited to text; they contained no photographs or drawings.

Benjamin Franklin founded the *Pennsylvania Gazette* in 1728. The *Gazette* included more advertisements than did any other colonial newspaper, with up to half the pages devoted to advertising. Franklin is credited with introducing the use of large-point headings, using white space to separate the advertisements from the text, and, after 1750, including illustrations.

Over the next century, there was little subsequent change in advertising. Advertisements provided information about goods for sale, arrivals and departures of ships, and stagecoach schedules. Print advertisements were confined primarily within column rules; advertisements spanning more than one column were yet to come.

In the 1860s, newspaper circulation increased, and magazine and periodical advertising began. Advertising volume increased markedly. Multicolumn display advertisements were designed; their first use was to call attention to the transcontinental railroad bonds that were being sold to the public. By the 1870s, multicolumn advertisements were common.

Along with advertising, publicity also works when it comes to boosting sales. The similar effects of advertising and free publicity were illustrated in the 1870s by American showman P. T. Barnum, who sought new patrons for his circus show. Barnum owned a field near railroad tracks over which passenger trains passed. To attract the attention of train passengers, he put an elephant to work plowing the field. Newspapers ran articles about the elephant. The publicity generated such enthusiasm for his show that others sought to emulate his free-publicity-as-unpaid-advertising success.

Industrialization and Advertising

Diffusion of steam power in the 1850s paved the way for a wave of technological change in the 1870s and 1880s. The American system of mass production characterized much of American manufacturing by 1890. Increased mechanization generated increased fixed costs, creating an economic incentive to build large factories that could enjoy economies of scale in production but which were dependent on mass demand. The transcontinental railroad allowed relatively low-cost shipment of goods, making regional or national markets economically feasible. Telegraph wires allowed low-cost and fast nationwide transmission of information. Manufacturers created brand names and sought to familiarize buyers nationally with their product. Where a housewife had once ordered a pound of generic baking powder, now she was encouraged to insist on known quality by requesting only Royal Baking Powder. Similar national advertising campaigns were undertaken in the 1880s and early 1890s by, among others, Corticelli Best Twist Silk Thread, Quaker Oats Company, and Procter & Gamble's Ivory soap.

Manufacturers believed that buyers were primarily interested in the quality of the product; competition by price was uncommon. National firms included drawings of sprawling factories and factory owners in their advertisements; the larger the factory and thus the more successful the firm, the higher quality the merchandise could be presumed to be. Singer Sewing Machines, Steinway Pianos, and McCormick Harvesters and Reapers all produced advertisements of this sort.

Following industrialization, seasonal or cyclical declines in demand could drive firms to bankruptcy because the now high fixed costs continued unabated even when sales and production dropped. The need to maintain demand became especially apparent during the 1893–1897 economic depression. Many businesses failed; many more came close. Businesses needed methods to insulate themselves from cyclical downturns in sales and production. Advertising was one tactic they employed.

The U.S. population increased from 31 million in 1860 to 76 million in 1900. Only 20 percent of the population lived in urban areas in 1860, increasing to nearly 40 percent by 1900. The need for easy provision of consumer goods increased as more people therefore lived divorced from the land. Standardized production and transportation improvements further contributed to the development of the department store. Stores such as R. H. Macy and Company of New York City, John Wanamaker's of Philadelphia, and Marshall Field of Chicago, all established by 1870, advertised regularly in newspapers. Rural families turned to mail-order catalogs—in essence, large books filled cover-to-cover with advertisements. Montgomery Ward's first catalog was issued in 1872; Sears, Roebuck and Co. entered the field in 1893.

By 1900, advertising in newspapers was supplemented by advertising on streetcars, on billboards, and in magazines. Full-page advertisements, especially in women's magazines, sought to influence women's choices. *Ladies' Home Journal*, established in 1883 by Cyrus H. K. Curtis, led the way. The Crowell Publishing Company founded *Women's Home Companion*. William Randolph Hearst began *Cosmopolitan*, *Good Housekeeping*, and *Harper's BAZAAR*. Between 1890 and 1905 the monthly circulation of periodicals increased from 18 million to 64 million.

Development of Advertising Agencies

Advertising agents were middlemen in 1850: they bought advertising space from newspapers and resold it at a profit to a company seeking to place an advertisement. Beginning in about 1880, N. W. Ayer and Son of Philadelphia offered its customers an "open contract" under which Ayer would be the company's sole advertising agent and, in exchange, would price advertising space at cost plus a fixed-rate commission. The idea caught on. Manufacturers were soon blocked from buying advertising space without an agent. In 1893, the American Newspaper Publishers Association agreed to not allow discounts on space sold to direct advertisers. Curtis Publishing Company, publishers of *Ladies' Home Journal*, inaugurated the same practice in 1901, and other magazine publishers soon followed suit. The cost-plus-commission basis for the agency was accepted industry wide in 1919, with the commission standardized at 15 percent.

Until the 1890s, conceptualization and preparation of advertising copy were the responsibility of the firm placing the advertisement. But as companies followed N. W. Ayer & Son's cost-plus-commission pricing policy, agents could no longer compete with each other on price; they needed some other means of distinguishing their services from those of competing agents. Advertising agents—soon to be known as advertising agencies—took on their modern form: writing copy; creating trademarks, logos, and slogans; and overseeing preparation of artwork. Ayer hired a full-time copywriter in 1892; Procter and Collier of Cincinnati did so by 1896; Lord & Thomas of Chicago did so by 1898. By 1910, advertising agencies were universally characterized by the presence of full-time copywriters and artists.

Advertising slogans that lasted nearly 100 years came from these advertising specialists. Ivory soap's slogan "99-44/100% Pure" appeared in 1885; Prudential's "Rock of Gibraltar" started in 1896; and N. W. Ayer and Son suggested the brand name "Uneeda" to the National Biscuit Company (later Nabisco) in 1900. Trademarks such as the Morton Umbrella Girl made famous by Morton Salt did not become common until after 1905, when federal legislation allowed the registration of trademarks for a period of 20 years with provision for renewal.

Advertising men were widely seen as no better than P. T. Barnum's sideshow barkers falsely hawking two-headed freaks rather than professionals presenting dignified, honest, and compelling images of bath soap. One step in convincing others that advertising was a profession to be taken seriously was the 1917 formation of the American Association of Advertising Agencies. The Association crafted broadly defined industry standards. Thereafter, the industry was quickly afforded the respect it desired. In 1926, President Calvin Coolidge addressed the Association's annual convention. For its ability to create mass demand, he credited advertising with the success of the American industrial system.

Modern Advertising

Modern advertising—advertising with the goal of creating desire for a product where none previously existed—began in the early twentieth century. With the blessing of leaders in the advertising industry, academic psychologists had begun applying principles of psychology to advertising content in the late 1890s. In 1901, psychologist Walter Dill Scott, speaking on the psychology of advertising, addressed a gathering of businessmen. His book *The Theory of Advertising* appeared in 1903. Advertisers were initially skeptical of Scott's thesis that psychological principles, especially the concept of suggestion, could be effectively applied to advertising.

An ongoing conflict thus arose in the early twentieth century between two types of advertising: "reason-why" and "atmosphere" advertising. Dominant in the late nineteenth century, reason-why advertising consisted of long, detailed discourses on the features of a product. Atmosphere advertising reflected psychology's influence; it emphasized visual imagery that evoked emotions. The conflict between the two types of advertising was especially intense in the decade before World War I (1914–1918). In 1909, the advertisers of Colgate toothpaste took the conflict directly to consumers, giving them the opportunity to decide "Which Is the Better Ad?"—the one that offered a detailed explanation of the health advantages of Colgate toothpaste, or the one that used illustrations to associate the use of Colgate with a happy family life.

Most practitioners and advertisers were won over by about 1910. Psychologists were judged correct; advertising could change needs and desires. After 1910, most advertising copy emphasized buyers' needs and desires rather than the product's objectively described characteristics. Advertising's success during World War I fully settled the issue. American advertisements sounded a patriotic pitch as they sought to sell Liberty and Victory Bonds, raise money for the Red Cross, and more. Some advertising historians even credited the industry with shortening the war.

By the mid-1920s, the two types of advertising peacefully coexisted. Reason-why copy was deemed appropriate for industrial advertising where decision-making rested on a "rational" profit motive. Atmosphere advertising dominated consumer goods advertising; with increasing standardization of consumer products eliminating many of the real differences between brands, the emphasis of advertising shifted to the "imagined" advantages.

A number of advertising textbooks appeared in the 1920s, authored by professors of psychology whose academic affiliations were often with schools of business. Surveys sought to ascertain the fundamental wants or desires of human beings. A typical list would include appetite, love, sexual attraction, vanity, and approval by others. Atmosphere advertisements emphasized how a product could satisfy these desires.

Advertisers increasingly looked upon themselves as quite set apart from the consumers who saw their ads. Copywriters were male. Consumers were female. Roland Marchand, author of *Advertising the American Dream* (1985), found that advertisers in the 1920s and 1930s were predominantly male, white, Christian, upper-class, well-educated New Yorkers who frequently employed servants and even chauffeurs, and whose cultural tastes ran to modern art, opera, and symphonies. They saw their audience as female, fickle, debased, emotional, possessing a natural inferiority complex, having inarticulate longings, low intelligence, and bad taste, and being culturally backward. The copy and visual imagery created by these advertising men often emphasized the woman's desire to be loved or her desire to be a good mother.

Ironically, just at the time advertisers sought increased respect through formation of their own professional association, the advertisements they were writing conveyed ever more disrespect for their readers. Many advertising historians note the post–World War I change in advertising's tone. Frederick Lewis Allen, author of the renowned history of the 1920s *Only Yesterday* (1931) wrote:

> "[In the 1920s], no longer was it considered enough to recommend one's goods in modest and explicit terms and to place them on the counter in the hope that the ultimate consumer would make up his or her mind to purchase. . . . [T]he copywriter was learning to pay less attention to the special qualities and advantages of his product, and more to the study of what the mass of unregenerate mankind wanted—to be young and desirable, to be rich, to keep up with

the Joneses, to be envied. The winning method was to associate the product with one or more of these ends, logically or illogically, truthfully or cynically. . . ." (pp. 141–2)

Advertising is often charged with creating a culture of consumerism in which people define themselves by the goods they buy. Certainly the first big boom in advertising volume and the rise of consumerism are coincidental: Consumerism first characterized the United States in the early twentieth century; advertising volume increased at an annual rate of nearly 9 percent between 1900 and 1920. Moreover, it was in this period that advertising first began emphasizing the ability of goods to meet emotional needs and, more to the point, first began its efforts to create needs where none had previously been felt.

Television and Beyond

The function of advertising has remained constant since the advent of modern advertising but its form has evolved as new forms of media have appeared. Radio broadcasting began in 1922 and with it, radio advertising. By 1930, 40 percent of households owned a radio; more than 80 percent owned one by 1940. Radio advertising expenditures doubled between 1935 and 1940 to $216 million in 1940.

Television began in the 1950s and quickly found its way into almost everyone's living room: 11 percent of households owned a television in 1950 but 88 percent owned one just a decade later. Television advertising expenditures increased nearly tenfold between 1950 and 1960, reaching $1.6 billion by 1960.

Outdoor advertising increased with paved mileage. In the decade after World War II (1939–1945), outdoor advertising expenditures, adjusted for inflation, increased 5 percent annually as paved mileage in the United States increased 3 percent annually. One of the more famous billboard campaigns, begun in 1925, was for Burma-Shave, a brushless shaving cream manufactured by the American Safety Razor Company. Their jingles appeared one line per sign over the course of a mile or more, always ending with the name of the product:

> If you think
> She likes
> Your bristles
> Walk bare-footed
> Through some thistles
> Burma-Shave

The introduction of the videocassette recorder (VCR) led to more changes in advertising. New in 1980, by 1990 over two-thirds of U.S. households owned a VCR. Viewers could fast-forward through commercials when watching taped shows, presenting a new challenge to advertisers. "Product placement" was the result. Firms now paid to have their products used in television shows and films. The practice was spurred by one phenomenal success: the use of Reese's Pieces candy in the 1982 film *E. T. The Extra-Terrestrial* had increased candy sales by over 65 percent. By 2000, product placement was pervasive.

TABLE 1

Advertising Volume

	Amount (billions of dollars)	Average rate of growth (percent)
1900	0.5	—
1920	2.9	8.8
1929	3.4	1.7
1946	3.3	− 0.1
1960	11.9	9.5
1970	19.6	5.1
1990	129.6	9.9
2000	236.3	6.2

SOURCE: 1900–1970, U.S. Bureau of the Census, *Historical Statistics of the United States: Colonial Times to 1970,* Series T444. 1990, 2000, U.S. Census Bureau, *Statistical Abstract of the United States: 2001,* Table 1271.

The most recent media development, the Internet, was advertisement-free until the first banner advertisements were sold in 1994. Ownership of computers and use of the Internet are both increasing rapidly; by 1999, 34 percent of adults nationwide claimed access to the Internet or an online service. Internet advertising increases apace.

Consumer objections to advertising and its tactics have resulted in legislation, lawsuits, and voluntary restraint. The 1914 Federal Trade Commission Act empowered the Federal Trade Commission (FTC) with the authority to regulate "unfair methods of competition." The 1938 Wheeler-Lea Amendment extended the FTC's powers to "unfair or deceptive acts or practices." The detrimental effects of billboards on the countryside inspired the federal Highway Beautification Act in 1965, which regulated placement of billboards near interstate highways. The "Joe Camel" campaign for Camel cigarettes introduced by R. J. Reynolds in the 1970s resulted in a 1990s federal lawsuit because of the campaign's alleged attempt to hook kids on smoking. A voluntary ban on television advertising by the Distilled Spirits Council of the United States was just one part of its Code of Good Practice regarding marketing and advertising, first adopted in 1934. Political advertising, with the goal of swaying voters rather than consumers, enjoys First Amendment protection but does face some constraints under state laws and under the Federal Communications Commission's Equal Access Law as well as the Federal Election Campaign Act.

Advertising Statistics

Data on advertising expenditure and employment in the industry is summarized in the annual *Statistical Abstract of the United States,* available online and in any reference library. As seen in Table 1, advertising expenditure has had several periods of rapid growth: the 1910s, 1950s, and 1980s. Advertising volume in 2000 was just over 2 percent of gross domestic product. Over 400,000 people worked in advertising in 2000, a nearly threefold increase since 1980. Approximately 40,000 establishments provided advertising and related services in 2000, about one-third of which had paid employees.

What constitutes an advertisement has changed over time: a name on a wooden signboard; an information-packed display in a newspaper; a full-color glossy advertisement in a magazine; a beautiful blonde singing about a new Chevrolet; candy scattered in a wood for an extraterrestrial alien; logos on the side of coffee mugs; Nike swooshes on professional sports team uniforms; pop-up advertisements on the Internet. The changes will continue as media opportunities develop.

BIBLIOGRAPHY

Fox, Stephen. *The Mirror Makers: A History of American Advertising and Its Creators.* New York: Morrow, 1984.

Laird, Pamela Walker. *Advertising Progress: American Business and the Rise of Consumer Marketing.* Baltimore: Johns Hopkins University Press, 1998.

Marchand, Roland. *Advertising the American Dream: Making Way for Modernity, 1920–1940.* Berkeley: University of California Press, 1985.

Norris, James D. *Advertising and the Transformation of American Society, 1865–1920.* New York: Greenwood Press, 1990.

Pope, Daniel. *The Making of Modern Advertising.* New York: Basic Books, 1983.

Presbrey, Frank. *The History and Development of Advertising.* Garden City, N.Y: Doubleday, 1929.

Scott, Walter Dill. *The Theory of Advertising: A Simple Exposition of the Principles of Psychology in Their Relation to Successful Advertising.* Boston: Small, Maynard and Company, 1903.

Martha L. Olney

AEROBICS, meaning "with oxygen," refers to physical exercise to improve cardiorespiratory endurance. Aerobic movement is rhythmic and repetitive, engaging the large muscle groups in the arms and legs for at least twenty minutes at each session. The ensuing demand for a continuous supply of oxygen creates the aerobic training effect, physiological changes that enhance the ability of the lungs, heart, and blood vessels to transport oxygen throughout the body. The most beneficial aerobic exercises include cross-country skiing, swimming, running, cycling, walking, and aerobic dance. Activities that rely on brief or discontinuous bursts of energy, such as weight lifting, are anaerobic ("without oxygen").

An early proponent of aerobics was Kenneth H. Cooper, a medical doctor whose 1968 book *Aerobics* introduced the first exercise program for cardiorespiratory improvement. Cooper also founded the Institute for Aerobics Research in Dallas, Texas. The Aerobics and Fitness Association of America certifies aerobics instructors and sets equipment and training standards.

Aerobic movement as a formal exercise has been popular since the late 1960s. The correlation between optimum physical activity and lowered incidence of cardiovascular disease gained wide medical acceptance. Exercise also appears to strengthen the immune system and ameliorate depression. Aerobic workout innovations from the 1980s to the early 2000s included such equipment as steps, weights, and elastic bands; cross-training programs, which involve two or more types of exercise; aerobic dances that combine yoga, martial arts, and other forms of movement with music, including African, Caribbean, salsa, hip-hop, rock, and jazz; and adaptations of such traditional activities as bicycling and boxing into aerobic routines such as spinning and cardio-kickboxing.

BIBLIOGRAPHY

White, Timothy P., and the editors of the "University of California at Berkeley Wellness Letter." *The Wellness Guide to Lifelong Fitness.* New York: Rebus, 1993.

Carol Gaskin/D. B.

See also **Recreation; Sports.**

AFFIRMATIVE ACTION is the network of law and public policy developed in the post–World War II era to allocate resources such as jobs, educational opportunities, procurement and construction contracts, and voting strength to African Americans and, beginning in the late 1960s, to women and other minorities. The purpose of affirmative action, to remedy the underrepresentation of women and minorities in workplaces, business ownership, and educational institutions, has been articulated through a variety of formal and informal approaches, including presidential executive orders, administrative guidelines, judicial decisions, and personnel practices, that apply to the nation's public and private institutions.

Affirmative action had precedents in racial and labor policies that sought to compensate for past injustices, such as the Reconstruction-era plans to redistribute former slaveholders' lands to the freedmen. The National Labor Relations Act (1935) required employers to "take affirmative action" to reinstate employees fired for union activity. In 1941, President Franklin Roosevelt issued Executive Order 8802, prohibiting racial discrimination in war-related industries. He drew upon the notion of affirmative action by bringing the power of the federal government to bear on war-related industries that had excluded African Americans in the past. President Harry Truman broadened Roosevelt's executive order to require that any company that was a government contractor in peacetime formally agree not to discriminate on the basis of race, creed, color, or national origin. While these gestures were not compensatory, their major thrust mandated the equitable treatment of minorities by bringing them into formerly segregated fields of employment.

For the next two decades, civil rights activists and their congressional allies attempted to pass stronger and more comprehensive laws to diminish employment discrimination. Local, state, and federal antidiscrimination statutes enacted during the late 1940s and the 1950s did little to rectify discriminatory employment patterns because they relied upon individual complainants and exhaustive investigations rather than proactive employment policies. In 1961, President John F. Kennedy issued Executive Order 10925, which reiterated features of earlier executive orders requiring contractors not to discriminate. This order explicitly directed contractors to take "affirmative action to ensure that applicants are employed without regard to race." The affirmative action clause provoked scant comment upon its release. While employers expressed certainty about what it meant to discriminate, they were pensive and skeptical about what affirmative action would require. To the President's Committee on Equal Employment Opportunity, which enforced the executive order, affirmative action meant that nondiscrimination was not enough to satisfy the contract's obligations. Government contractors now were required to recruit and promote minority employees, although hiring goals for minorities remained vague. Activists from the National Association for the Advancement of Colored People and other civil rights groups believed these statutes were inadequate, and as early as the late 1940s, they pressed for a stronger federal antidiscrimination law.

The passage of the equal employment section (Title VII) of the Civil Rights Act of 1964 heralded a new phase in the fight against discrimination by expanding the concept of employment discrimination and its remedy, affirmative action. Title VII deemed it unlawful for an employer to refuse to hire an individual because of his or her race, color, religion, sex, or national origin. No section of the legislation explicitly mentioned affirmative action, but political and judicial actions eventually used this law to rationalize vigorous remedies for discrimination and exclusion, such as preferential treatment and racial proportionalism in hiring, promoting, voting, and admitting to college. Congressional opponents of Title VII were concerned that the legislation would force an employer to hire on the basis of race rather than merit, but they compromised with the inclusion of provisos intended to prevent quotas and racial proportionalism. The act established the Equal Employment Opportunity Commission (EEOC) to investigate and conciliate complaints of discrimination and to recommend cases for the Justice Department to bring before federal courts. The Equal Employment Opportunity Act of 1972 extended Title VII coverage to state and local government employees and to private workplaces with as few as fifteen employees. In this act Congress also authorized the EEOC to sue in federal district court.

In the 1960s, federal contracting guidelines articulated affirmative action to its fullest in large part because President Lyndon Johnson in 1965 issued Executive Order 11246, which created the Office of Federal Contract Compliance (OFCC). Congressional proscriptions did not bind the OFCC, unlike the EEOC, and as a result, the OFCC could require any variety of methods to increase the representation of minorities in the workplace. The construction industry, which had low rates of nonwhite workers, was one of the first to use the new tools of affirmative action under this executive order. The OFCC concentrated on results by setting goals and timetables to achieve a more equitable racial balance in workplaces.

After 1970, the national discussion of affirmative action turned to the judiciary, and the U.S. Supreme Court attempted to clarify the possibilities and limitations for affirmative action delineated in the Constitution. In *Griggs v. Duke Power Company* (1971), the Court examined concepts of merit as well as selection and promotion procedures in light of the results they produced, thereby destroying the employer's defense that discriminatory procedures stemmed from "business necessity." In its decision, the Court ruled that the company's intelligence test had no bearing on workers' performance and adversely affected the promotion possibilities of nonwhites. *Griggs* is notable because the Court upheld the notion that the underrepresentation of minorities in a given workforce might serve as statistical proof that a company discriminated. In the wake of this decision, the lower courts began to require affirmative action, or preferences for minority employees for promotion and transfer, as necessary to remedy past discrimination and to achieve equity in the workplace.

The Supreme Court's most comprehensive review of affirmative action affected employment, and, as a result, lower courts, government agencies, private businesses, and labor unions turned to voluntary and involuntary race- and gender-conscious remedies to comply with Title VII. These affirmative remedies, which modify hiring qualifications, alter seniority systems, institute programs to train and upgrade minority employees, and set aside percentages of business contracts, came to define "affirmative action." The Court gave qualified support to early affirmative action programs with *Fullilove v. Klutznick* (1980) and *United Steelworkers of America v. Weber* (1979), in which the Court upheld minority set-asides in contracting and the constitutionality of voluntary affirmative action plans. After the late 1980s, however, the Supreme Court became less approving of racially conscious measures that promoted racial balance or diversity in awarding government contracts or in decisions regarding tenure and layoffs.

Title VII also prohibited discrimination against women, but this provision was not fully articulated until the 1970s, when federal agencies began to include hiring goals for women. In 1973, a landmark consent decree signed by AT&T, the EEOC, and the Departments of Justice and Labor banned discriminatory practices against women and minorities and provided for employee upgrades and millions of dollars in salary increases. In *Johnson v. Transportation Agency of Santa Clara County* (1987), the Supreme Court made it clear that affirmative action plans for hiring and promoting underrepresented workers should take into account gender as well as race. Female employees subject to intentional discrimination and sexual harassment received some of the largest settlements as a result of the 1991 Civil Rights Act, which allowed plaintiffs who were victims of racial or sexual discrimination to recover compensatory and punitive damages.

The Supreme Court also gave considerable attention to affirmative action in higher education. *Bakke v. Regents of the University of California* (1978), one of the Court's best-known affirmative action decisions, both limited and preserved the use of racial set-asides in admissions. A judicial majority agreed that racial preferences were constitutionally permissible to promote a diverse student body but that racial classifications should be subjected to greater scrutiny. The Court equivocated on the diversity justification by allowing a lower court's decision to stand in *Hopwood v. Texas* (1996), in which a federal district court ruled that affirmative action is permissible solely to remedy past discrimination.

The Supreme Court's increasing conservatism regarding affirmative action mirrored a growing popular rejection of race-conscious remedies, such as preferential treatment, set-asides, and quotas. The Court further scrutinized the race-based assumptions of federal contracting programs just as the administration of President Bill Clinton announced its "mend it, don't end it" stance on affirmative action policy. Throughout the 1990s, affirmative action persisted as a controversial flashpoint. Basic definitions of the policy and the necessity for racial classifications remained unresolved, and statewide and municipal referenda tested the popularity of preferential treatment. California voters approved a referendum in November 1996 to end the state's affirmative action programs, and voters in several states of the South and the West organized ballot initiatives. While government programs and educational institutions were most vulnerable to court interpretation and voter referenda, affirmative action was embraced most fully by some private corporations in the wake of discrimination settlements that called for the payment of back wages, punitive damages, and the development of programs to hire and upgrade women and minority employees.

BIBLIOGRAPHY

Graham, Hugh Davis. *The Civil Rights Era: Origins and Development of National Policy 1960–1972.* New York: Oxford University Press, 1990.

Moreno, Paul D. *From Direct Action to Affirmative Action: Fair Employment Law and Policy in America, 1933–1972.* Baton Rouge: Louisiana State University Press, 1997.

Skrentny, John David. *The Ironies of Affirmative Action: Politics, Culture, and Justice in America.* Chicago: University of Chicago Press, 1996.

Spann, Girardeau A. *The Law of Affirmative Action: Twenty-five Years of Supreme Court Decisions on Race and Remedies.* New York: New York University Press, 2000.

Stacy Kinlock Sewell

See also **Bakke v. Regents of the University of California; Civil Rights Act of 1964; Civil Rights Act of 1991; Discrimination: Race, Religion, Sex; Equal Employment Opportunity Commission; Griggs v. Duke Power Company; Minority Business; Set-Asides.**

AFGHANISTAN, SOVIET INVASION OF. At the end of December 1979, Soviet troops moved into Afghanistan, setting off an international crisis. The situation had been building since April 1978, when a coup led by the pro-Soviet Armed Forces Military Council installed a Marxist government under the leadership of Noor Mohammed Taraki. Rebel groups resisted, and fighting intensified. In February 1979, rebel forces kidnapped U.S. ambassador Adolph Dubs, who died in a shoot-out between the rebels and government forces. In September 1979, Taraki resigned after a bitter power struggle, and the government passed into the hands of Hafizullah Amin. After barely two months in office, Amin was replaced by Babrak Karmal, who had invited the intervention of Soviet troops and who was supported by Moscow. The Soviet government insisted that it was sending in a "limited military contingent" to repel aggression from abroad.

The U.S. government denounced the Soviet invasion. While aiding the rebels with advisers and arms, the administration of President Jimmy Carter curtailed U.S. grain shipments to the Soviet Union, cut off sales of high-technology equipment, and imposed limits on Soviet fishing privileges in U.S. waters. Carter's most publicized action was to forbid participation by U.S. athletes in the Olympic Games held in Moscow during the summer of 1980. In what is known as his "Evil Empire" speech, President Ronald Reagan in 1982 noted that it was not democratic nations that had invaded Afghanistan. He referred to forces seeking conflict in the world as "totalitarian evil." The Reagan administration supplied the Afghan rebels with Stinger surface-to-air missiles, which substantially reduced the effectiveness of Soviet airpower in the war.

The Afghan war was a great drain on the Soviet military, and it cost the Soviet regime significant international prestige. Soviet leader Mikhail Gorbachev withdrew the last Soviet troops in February 1989. After the Cold War ended in 1990, the United States turned its interest away from Afghanistan, and the increasingly fundamentalist Islamic nation slid into the second phase of a civil war that had begun in 1978.

BIBLIOGRAPHY

Arnold, Anthony. *Afghanistan: The Soviet Invasion in Perspective.* Rev. and enl. ed. Stanford, Calif.: Hoover Institution Press, 1985.

Demonstration for Afghanistan. Muslims kneel in prayer at Lafayette Park in Washington, D.C., across from the White House, during a protest against the Soviet occupation of Afghanistan. AP/ WIDE WORLD PHOTOS

Gaddis, John Lewis. *We Now Know: Rethinking Cold War History.* New York: Oxford University Press, 1997.

Alfred E. Senn / A. G.

See also **Cold War; Olympic Games, American Participation in.**

AFRICA, RELATIONS WITH. Despite its fascinating cultures and great needs, Africa has rarely interested U.S. policymakers for its own sake. Throughout the 1970s and 1980s they continued to view Africa primarily as a setting for U.S.-Soviet rivalries. Policies therefore were frequently superficial and clumsy, with little attention paid to their long-term effects on Africans. Four factors have been instrumental in shaping U.S. policies in Africa. First and most important was the COLD WAR, which drove U.S. policymakers to resist what they believed was Soviet expansion. The Central Intelligence Agency often emerged as a principal executor and, some have argued, maker of U.S. policy, conveying military aid, sometimes secretly, to African groups believed to be anticommunist. A second factor is the nearly thirty million Americans of African descent in the United States, enabled by the Civil Rights Movement of the 1960s to elect increasing numbers of African Americans to Congress. African American politicians focused more government attention on African affairs than had been the case in the past. Third, the decades since 1970 have been marked by economic and political crises in many African states. Mass media widely publicized some of the more severe cases of destitution and starvation, inducing the U.S. government to pay attention to these areas, especially in Ethiopia, Sudan, Somalia, and Rwanda. Fourth, the black African struggle against apartheid in South Africa often claimed center stage in U.S. policy, largely because South Africa's race relations were thought to resemble those of the United States.

Southern Africa (countries south of the Democratic Republic of the Congo and Tanzania) concerned U.S. policymakers in the 1970s and 1980s, because it was there that white minority rule continued the longest, despite efforts of blacks to end it. U.S. opposition to white rule, however, was complicated by Cold War considerations. Henry A. Kissinger, secretary of state during the presidencies of Richard M. Nixon (1969–1974) and Gerald R. Ford (1974–1977), concluded that white minority rulers deserved support because they were sympathetic to U.S. interests and, despite violent opposition, would hold on to power for the foreseeable future.

In the Portuguese colonies of Angola and Mozambique, for example, guerrilla campaigns against Portuguese rule had been going on since the early 1960s. Although the United States was unsympathetic to Portuguese colonialism, it secretly supported the status quo because Portugal was a North Atlantic Treaty Organization (NATO) ally against the Soviet- and Cuban-backed Popular Movement for the Liberation of Angola (MPLA) and Front for the Liberation of Mozambique (FRELIMO). When losses in the war induced the Portuguese army to overthrow its own government in 1974, all Portuguese colonies in Africa were freed. FRELIMO and the MPLA established new governments in their respective countries. Immediately, however, the United States supported such pro-Western opposition movements as the National Union for the Total Independence of Angola (UNITA), led by Jonas Savimbi. Because the Republic of South Africa ultimately supported Savimbi's UNITA, the United States found itself in an embarrassing alliance with the apartheid state. Congress ended support for the Angolan rebels in late 1975, but a civil war covertly financed by the United States and the Soviet Union raged for another twenty years. Even after the first national election in 1990 the fighting continued because Savimbi refused to accept the results. Decades of war left tens of thousands of land mines strewn across the region, maiming villagers, slowing economic recovery, and hampering relief efforts. War between UNITA and the Angola government flared again in 1998. By 2002, UNITA controlled valuable diamond mines and one-third of the countryside.

In Zimbabwe (formerly Southern Rhodesia), a white minority defied British rule in 1965 and seized power to prevent a transfer of authority to black Africans. Blacks launched a guerrilla war led by the Marxist teacher Robert Mugabe, backed by the communist bloc; again the Nixon administration supported different nonsocialist black groups despite the fact that they had little popular support. The United States broke United Nations–sponsored sanctions against the white government by purchasing Rhodesian chromium, thereby improving the economic position of whites. The Democratic administration of President Jimmy Carter (1977–1981) did little to change these policies. Nonetheless, Mugabe's forces came to power in 1980, ending white rule in Zimbabwe. Mugabe's notoriously corrupt and brutal regime was still in power in 2002.

In South Africa, the United States opposed apartheid but did little of substance about it. U.S. leaders believed the main opposition group, the African National Congress, was dominated by communists, and therefore assumed that black majority rule would bring increased influence for the Soviet Union. The United States maintained economic and political ties with the white minority as it gently tried to persuade the South African government to moderate its racism, a tactic that was continued despite little evidence it was working. The U.S. government did nothing to persuade businesses to "disinvest" from the South African economy, a move that many thought would have a real effect. In fact, during the Nixon years, U.S. private investment in South Africa more than doubled.

The Carter administration owed its existence in part to black voters and initially stressed human rights in its foreign policy to a greater degree than did its Republican predecessors. Led by UN delegate Andrew Young, a civil rights veteran, the Carter administration increased its public condemnation of apartheid, although this policy did not materially undermine its existence. The election of Ronald Reagan in 1980 saw a return to the more tolerant policies of the Nixon years. Known as "constructive

engagement," Reagan's approach stressed increased interaction between U.S. and South African interests, assuming that without economic cooperation, the United States would have no leverage to promote changes in South African society. The vigorously anticommunist Reagan also saw the opposition to apartheid as Soviet-dominated. Further, U.S. diplomats tended to see the situation in South Africa as similar to that of the American South of the 1950s, leading to faulty assumptions about the possibilities for peaceful change. In fact, most U.S. administrations made this same misjudgment to a certain extent. The increased power of blacks in Congress and activities of private organizations, especially the lobbying group TransAfrica, helped force a change in policy. Congress voted economic sanctions against South Africa in 1986, which Reagan reluctantly accepted. Worldwide sanctions and the increased violent resistance by black South Africans were important in bringing about the end of apartheid and the first free election in South Africa in 1994. The fall of the Soviet Union in the late 1980s was also crucial, because thereafter the argument that the apartheid government was anticommunist lost its force.

The end of the Cold War had important implications for U.S. policy outside southern Africa. American policy had supported Mobutu Sese Seko, the military dictator of Zaire, because of his anticommunism and despite the brutalities of his rule. With the fall of the Soviet Union, U.S. support gradually declined, although Mobutu still clung to power and to his $6 billion in European banks, while Zairian society disintegrated around him. In 1996, rebel leader Laurent-Désiré Kabila, supported by foreign Tutsi soldiers, swept Mobutu from power and—consistent with his promise to reform and democratize the country—renamed it the Demcratic Republic of the Congo. But Kabila ousted the Tutsis from his fledgling government, souring his relations with neighboring Uganda and Rwanda. The sporadic fighting that ensued threatened to expand into a regional war. Kabila was assassinated in 2001; his son Joseph, who was named head of state, initiated attempts to alleviate the conflict.

A similar situation existed in the northeast African state of Somalia, but there the United States intervened with troops. Another military man, Siad Barre, had seized power in 1969 and played the United States against the Soviet Union, managing at times to gain the support of each. As the Cold War ended, Siad Barre was overthrown, but the massive weaponry brought by Cold War politics remained. Siad Barre's collapse led to bloody civil war. The war and a drought in 1992 produced mass starvation that was broadcast nightly on the world's television screens. U.S. and other troops under the auspices of the UN were successful in seeing that food reached destitute Somalis. When those troops tried to end the civil war, however, they failed spectacularly. The U.S. contingent withdrew in 1994 after the release of video footage showing the bodies of U.S. Marines, killed in a firefight after

Clinton in Africa. The president speaks at the former West African slave-trading center on Gorée Island, Senegal, on 2 April 1998, at the end of an eleven-day, six-nation visit to Africa, during which he expressed regret over American slavery and more recent U.S. neglect of the continent. AP/WIDE WORLD PHOTOS

their Blackhawk helicopter crashed, being dragged through the streets of Mogadishu.

The Somalia humiliation probably affected U.S. policy toward Rwanda, in central Africa, where drought and ethnic tension produced a volatile situation. In early 1994, a small group of politicians and their supporters began murdering opponents. This group lost control of the situation, and as the death toll reached the hundreds of thousands, the United States and UN, undoubtedly remembering Somalia, did little to stop it. It was not until the government was overthrown and mass media coverage began to have an effect that the United States and other nations intervened to alleviate the suffering of the half million refugees created by the strife.

In an unusual case, the United States bombed the north African state of Libya in 1986 to punish it for terrorist acts it was alleged to have sponsored and attempted to kill its leader, Mu'ammar al-Gadhafi, who survived, although some members of his family and entourage died. The United States kept a cautious eye on Gadhafi during the 1990s. After the devastating terrorist attacks of 11 September 2001, President George W. Bush included Libya in his "Axis of Evil," countries suspected by the U.S. of actively supporting terrorists. Also in north Africa, the United States provided Egypt with economic and military aid to support Egyptian moves for peace in the Middle East.

U.S. activity in much of the rest of Africa was less obviously political. The Agency for International Development, the government's principal means of promoting economic development in poorer parts of the world, worked diligently in many areas of Africa. Although its projects have not always been well conceived, some succeeded in establishing better water supplies, halting soil erosion, and improving transportation. U.S. governmental and private agencies collaborated with the World Health Organization to control such diseases as smallpox and river blindness. Some U.S. activity in Africa focused on efforts to understand and cope with AIDS, which some theorize began in Africa. In any case, the disease spread quickly throughout the continent, threatening to decimate the populations of some nations in the twenty-first century. The U.S. has also given its tacit support to the Southern African Development Community (SADC). Although criticized for its failures to address human rights concerns or deal with corruption, SADC remained the continent's best hope for coping with the civil strife and cross-border wars that threatened to destabilize the region.

Despite successes, U.S. aid to Africa has been controversial. Some observers argued that there was too much stress on military aid, which until the late 1980s exceeded economic aid. The effect, they charged, was to prolong dictatorial "anticommunist" regimes with little popular support. Economic aid was criticized because it was misused by recipients, either to enrich themselves or to promote apparently socialist policies. Many of the same critics argued that the United States gained no advantage from this aid. With control of Congress passing to Republicans in 1995, whose numbers included many of these critics, African nations worried that U.S. aid to Africa would decrease considerably. The issue of U.S. support became especially crucial during the AIDS epidemic of the 1990s. AIDS emerged as the leading cause of death among African youth. Doctors feared that one-third of the population, including millions of children, were infected with the HIV virus. The administration of George W. Bush in 2002 pledged a half billion dollars to combat the epidemic. But some feared that a much greater commitment from industrialized nations would be needed to stave off a humanitarian crisis of unprecedented scale.

In the summer of 2002, U.S. Treasury Secretary Paul O'Neill teamed with the popular singer Bono in a highly publicized ten-day tour of Africa. As this oddball pairing made clear, the renewed economic interest in Africa, combined with the continued civil strife and health concerns plaguing the region, ensures that Africa's role in U.S. foreign policy will continue to grow.

BIBLIOGRAPHY

Diawara, Manthia. *In Search of Africa.* Cambridge, Mass.: Harvard University Press, 1998.

El-Khawas, Mohamed A., and Barry Cohen, eds. *The Kissinger Study of Southern Africa.* Westport, Conn.: L. Hill, 1976.

Lemarchand, René, ed. *American Policy in Southern Africa: The Stakes and the Stance.* Washington, D.C.: University Press of America, 1981.

Meriwether, James Hunter. *Proudly We Can Be Africans: Black Americans and Africa, 1935–1961.* Chapel Hill: University of North Carolina Press, 2002.

Minter, William. *King Solomon's Mines Revisited: Western Interests and the Burdened History of Southern Africa.* New York: Basic Books, 1986.

Nwaubani, Ebere. *The United States and Decolonization in West Africa, 1950–1960.* Rochester, N.Y.: University of Rochester Press, 2001.

R. L. Watson / A. R.

See also **Acquired Immune Deficiency Syndrome (AIDS); Atrocities in War; Foreign Aid; Somalia, Relations with; South Africa, Relations with; Terrorism.**

AFRICAN AMERICAN RELIGIONS AND SECTS.

When the first Africans landed in North America during the Spanish explorations of the fifteenth century, their spiritual backgrounds included Christianity, Islam, and a number of ancient African religions. Similar to Christianity and Islam, these traditional African religions explained the world and the reason for human existence. In addition, these religions gave Africans various rituals for celebrating important life events and predicting potential misfortunes.

A rather large group of Africans believed in a plurality of powers, including the forces of nature and a legion of magical spirits. However, most tribes believed in a Supreme Being as the creator and giver, and considered life itself sacred. The deeply spiritual Africans believed strongly that there was no separation between life on earth and the afterlife, since all life took place on a continuum, where every part directly affected every other part. Those who lived good lives would please the spirits and reap rewards, but those who did evil risked angering the spirits and losing their protection.

Africans' belief in one Supreme Being, the distinction between good and evil, and the belief in creation as the work of one God were similar to the viewpoints of Christianity's and Islam's origins. This similarity and the prior exposure many Africans had experienced with Christian and Muslim missionaries in Africa did much to lessen the cultural shock of white evangelicalism.

The Religion of Slaves

During the early history of slavery in America, European church and state officials ordered colonists to instruct slaves in the ways of Catholicism. But these early American missionaries faced a number of obstacles in undertaking this task. Language barriers still existed, slave owners opposed the efforts, and many slaves lacked any desire to learn the religion of those who had enslaved them. In addition, those who accepted Christianity incorporated it into their multideistic beliefs and rituals. African practices, rituals, and dogmas were preserved in the new African American religions of Candomblê, Santería, and Vodou, commonly referred to as Voodoo, Hoodoo, or witchcraft.

Partially due to their beliefs in multiple powers and spirits, as well as their various dogmas and ritual traditions, African Americans were considered heathens who practiced a loathsome form of pagan idolatry. White Americans were threatened by such practices and put forth substantial effort to eradicate them. These attempts to obliterate Africans' religion were quite successful, with many of the practices and rituals being destroyed within a single generation.

Many scholars have attacked these eradication efforts, calling slavery so demeaning that it stripped African Americans of their dignity, humanity, and basis for religion. Others argue that African Americans never completely lost their religion and, in fact, held on to it purposely as a form of resistance or rebellion.

For a majority of whites, their mission to the slaves was part of God's grand plan to convert the entire continent of Africa. Others, however, sought to exploit religion as a way to pacify and comfort the slaves, using religion to show that they could still enjoy happiness and gratification in their eternal spiritual lives. While the views and opinions of whites at that time were decidedly mixed, it was rare for members of the "ruling race" to overlook the unfortunate caste and economic status of black people, which made racially inclusive Christianity virtually impossible.

Proselytizing the Slaves

The first major effort to Christianize African slaves came in 1701 when the British Society for the Propagation of the Gospel in Foreign Parts sent forty missionaries to America. The society's primary goal was to revive Anglicans (now known as Episcopalians) and Indian tribes. In their related efforts to convert slaves, however, the organization ran into a great deal of resistance from plantation owners and other slaveholders.

In the 1780s, Methodists formulated strong rules against slavery, calling it contrary to the laws of God and damaging to society as a whole. In fact, by 1784, Methodists issued an intent to excommunicate Methodists who did not free their slaves within two years. In time, attitudes began to shift regarding slavery, and changes in southern religious hierarchies began to take place. Planters eventually granted permission to proselytize household slaves. But the mood again changed in the early 1800s when a large number of whites feared slave rebellion and the impact it would have on the general way of life. Thus, Christianity was not preached to slaves because many whites were afraid that becoming Christian could raise slaves' self-esteem, convince them of their equality to whites, and encourage them to take literally such parables as the exodus from Egypt.

Furthermore, whites feared that allowing slaves to assemble would give them an opportunity to plan rebellions, and teaching them to read the Bible would have the unwanted effect of slave literacy. This fear of insurrection was the very reason slave owners originally dispersed slaves who spoke the same language. It was for this same reason that many southern state legislatures passed laws preventing African Americans from assembling and worshipping, except under white supervision and in highly controlled circumstances.

However, another line of thought concluded that making Christians of the slaves would teach them to turn the other cheek, accept their lives, and pray for redemption and eternal happiness in the afterlife. As this notion spread, increased efforts to proselytize to African Americans began to take hold. Congregations invited African Americans and set aside segregated seating for them. A small number of slave owners even erected churches and recruited African American preachers to spread the word. Others, particularly those with large slave populations, such as Reverend Charles Colcock Jones, developed a Christian lesson plan designed specifically to prevent insurrection and rebellion.

Soon, a biblical justification of slavery based on the Old Testament account of the curse of Ham also developed. Promoters of this theory claimed that Ham, the son of Noah, was the father of dark-skinned people and cursed to be a slave forever. This story, however, is surrounded by debate since the curse was actually placed on Canaan, the oldest of Ham's four sons. The Canaanites, descendants of Canaan, became slaves of the Hebrews who were once slaves of the Egyptians, fulfilling the prophecy that Canaan would be a "servant of servants." Despite contrary evidence, slaveholders told the story to convince African Americans that they were forever condemned to do menial labor for white overseers. Another frequently advanced belief depicted Africans as beings of a lower social order who lacked souls and were therefore incapable of committing to the Christian faith or being rewarded with its promise of salvation. Most Africans and African Americans refused to accept either of these postulates and became highly critical of white preaching that attempted to rationalize slavery and keep them in their place. Scholars theorize that the life-affirming nature of many African spiritual practices may have helped slaves to reject notions of themselves as inherently evil or lacking souls.

The Religious Revival

As Christianity began to take hold in a majority of slaves, African Americans were fairly quick to adopt the prevailing evangelical culture. But denominations that stressed an ordered religious service, such as those held by Episcopalians and Presbyterians, did not attract the slaves. Most African Americans gravitated to the emotionalism of the Methodists and Baptists. In fact, the religion of the South's African American population shared much in common with the evangelical Protestantism of the region's whites. These evangelical southern whites, who were some of the first to convert slaves to the Christian faith, imparted many of their forms and practices to African American churches.

Because household slaves were normally the only African Americans allowed to attend white churches, a large majority of field slaves formed their own clandestine church meetings—called "hush harbors" and "praying grounds"—that took place secretly and in remote areas. These meeting places later became stops on the Underground Railroad. Though African American evangelicalism had a great deal in common with white evangelicalism, the safety provided by late-hour meetings and secluded locales allowed African Americans to express themselves differently and to interpret their faith freely in any way they desired.

One major way that African Americans distinguished themselves from their white counterparts was in the expressiveness and zeal with which they celebrated their spirituality. For African American Christians, the message of God's gifts, forgiveness, and sacrifice of love effected exuberant shouts of joy and praise. Thus, African Americans attending the more sedate services in white churches were not only segregated, but also inhibited in their ability to praise God.

Baptist Church. African American Baptist churches began to hold services—if whites were present—a few years before this church was founded in Savannah, Ga., in 1779. GETTY IMAGES

African American preachers, though often illiterate, frequently earned praise from whites for their ministry abilities and rhythmic, chanted sermons. Unbeknownst to some of the white listeners, however, revolutionary themes were often implicit in the preaching and spiritual music of African Americans. The proposition that God could intervene to alter natural order—which is what many whites considered slavery—was one such recurring proclamation in African American sermons. Songs such as "Steal Away to Jesus" and "Swing Low, Sweet Chariot" conveyed a message that was clear to African Americans: Jesus died for everyone, including African Americans, and this fundamental equality meant that everyone could be saved in a spiritual and literal sense.

African American Denominations

The first independent African American church was a Baptist church founded at Silver Bluff, South Carolina, around 1773 on the plantation of George Galphin. Other African American Baptist churches went up all along the South Atlantic seaboard, including ones in Williamsburg and Petersburg, Virginia, during 1776. However, these independent churches were allowed to hold worship services only when white persons were present, and were usually completely prohibited from meeting at night.

By the beginning of the nineteenth century, due to continued segregation in white Methodist churches, a handful of independent African American Methodist churches cropped up in Delaware, Maryland, New Jersey, New York, and Pennsylvania. The first two African American denominations originated as the result of discrimination-based contentions between the Methodist Church and its African American members. Since the two denominations did not break away for doctrinal reasons, their theology and doctrines remain similar to other Methodist churches. The basis of that theology comes from two primary theological documents: Apostle's Creed and the Twenty-Five Articles of Religion, which is based on the Thirty-Nine Articles of Religion of the Church of England that John Wesley sent to the United States as a guide for the newly forming Methodist Societies.

Though many believe the first African American Methodist church was the African Methodist Episcopal Church (AME) formed in Philadelphia in 1816, the truth is that the first was formed nine years earlier. The African Union Church was incorporated in Wilmington, Delaware in 1807, claiming the honor as the first Methodist church organized by African Americans. It was not until nine years later that the former slave Richard Allen, along with representatives from five independent African American Methodist churches, founded the AME Church, creating the first African American denomination.

The auspicious beginnings of the AME Church—Allen and two other African Americans were removed from Saint George's Methodist Church after sitting in a newly

African Methodist Episcopal Church. Mother Bethel AME Church in Philadelphia; its minister, Richard Allen, was the leading founder of the first black denomination. GETTY IMAGES

ordained all-white section—resulted in the development of the most well-known African American denomination. Allen, who had led his congregation out of the segregated Saint George Church in 1787, faced a great deal of hostility from his former church home, including threats to be permanently expelled. However, tensions later cooled and Allen led a new congregation into the Bethel African Methodist Church, and in 1799, Bishop Francis Asbury of the Methodist Episcopal Church (MEC) ordained Allen minister of Bethel AME Church, now known as Mother Bethel. In less than forty years, the AME Church, which began with eight clergy members and five churches, would grow to include 176 clergy, 296 churches, and 17,375 members. By the end of the twentieth century, the AME Church had 8,000 clergy, 6,200 congregations, and a membership of more than 2.5 million.

The second black denomination originated under similar circumstances. In 1796, James Varick and other members of the John Street Methodist Church in New York City petitioned Bishop Asbury for permission to hold separate church meetings. These separate services occurred until 1801, when the African American congregation built its own church. However, they continued to be led by the white minister of the John Street Church. In 1820, the congregation voted to leave and establish the African Methodist Episcopal Zion Church (AMEZ). The AMEZ Church became famous as the "freedom church" because of its strong stance against slavery and the large number of black abolitionists, including Harriet Tubman and Frederick Douglass, who were members. The AMEZ Church also acquired the distinction of being the first Methodist church to ordain a woman when, in 1894, it ordained Julia A. J. Foote as a deacon and, in 1898,

ordained Mary J. Small as an elder. Over the next hundred years, the church's membership increased to 1.2 million, comprising 3,125 congregations and 3,002 clergy members.

The third major African American Methodist denomination is the Christian Methodist Episcopal (CME) Church. It began following the Civil War (1861–1865) when African Americans in the Methodist Episcopal Church, South, which had broken away from the MEC because of disagreements on slavery, asked for permission to form a separate body. This group of African American congregations formed the Colored Methodist Episcopal Church in Jackson, Tennessee, in 1870. The members adopted the Methodist South's Book of Discipline and elected William H. Miles and Richard H. Vanderhorst as their bishops. In 1954, the organization changed its name to the Christian Methodist Episcopal Church. Records show that the CME church in the late twentieth century had a membership of approximately 1 million.

After the Civil War ended, free African Americans made formation of independent church congregations one of their first priorities. The autonomy emphasized by Baptist ideals and the complementary rejection of complex hierarchy and governance structures fit well with this goal and helped ensure that Baptist theology would become the leading denomination among freed slaves. Ironically, the same desire for autonomy that made Baptist traditions appealing to African Americans, who had no power in white churches, also made the formation of a national organization somewhat difficult. Though state and local organizations formed quickly, it was not until the late 1800s that national organizations began to take shape.

In 1895, the National Baptist Convention, USA, Incorporated (NBC), was established in Atlanta. This new African American denomination was the result of the unification of three separate Baptist groups: the Foreign Mission Baptist Convention, the American National Baptist Convention, and the Baptist National Education Convention. Although the beliefs of the NBC were identical to the beliefs espoused by white Baptist denominations, the NBC placed a great deal of emphasis on activism, promoting Christian missions abroad, and providing leadership and spiritual growth opportunities for African Americans. Their activism was rooted in the goal of transcending the evil of slavery and preaching for civil rights and equal citizenship. The denomination grew to be the largest African American church in the United States with a membership of approximately 7 million and 30,000 congregations by the early twenty-first century.

In 1915, a disagreement over the NBC publishing house and adoption of a charter created a sizable rift within the organization. Reverend R. Boyd, who organized the publishing house, left the congregation and took a sizable number of its members with him. The group went on to form the National Baptist Convention of America (NBCA), with a membership that grew to about 2.4 million by the end of the century.

Black Muslim National Convention. This offshoot of Islam has split into two groups: the orthodox American Muslim Mission and the separatist Nation of Islam. © UPI/CORBIS-BETTMANN

Another schism within the NBC resulted in the creation of a third African American Baptist denomination. The Progressive National Baptist Convention (PNBC) was organized in Cincinnati, Ohio in 1961. This group, which included Martin Luther King Jr., broke away from the NBC due to a split regarding succession to the presidency of the convention and differing approaches to the burgeoning Civil Rights movement. The PNBC church hosted its first convention in 1962 and proceeded over the next forty years to develop a membership tally totaling around 1.2 million.

During the late nineteenth century, a movement emerged from the Methodist churches, proposing that a second spiritual experience, called sanctification, occurred after conversion. Baptist ministers Charles H. Mason and Charles P. Jones began preaching this doctrine to their congregations and were soon expelled from the Baptist church. In 1897, Mason and sixty-two members who followed him went on to form the Church of God in Christ (COGIC) in Lexington, Mississippi. Mason believed that the Lord had revealed this name to him as he walked down a street in Little Rock, Arkansas. The COGIC is a Pentecostal body that is considered the only major black denomination originating with African Americans. The denomination's membership in the 1990s has been cited by various sources as between 3.5 and 7 million.

During slavery, Muslim African Americans were few in number, making up less than 20 percent of the slave population, and isolated in a country intent on converting them to Christianity. The first organized Muslim movement began in 1913 when Timothy Drew, also known as the Noble Drew Ali, established the first Moorish Science Temple in Newark, New Jersey. Seventeen years later in Detroit, a group with similar beliefs formed and became known as the Nation of Islam. The Nation of Islam quickly expanded and began spreading a message that included an account of the white race's origins. The story claimed that the entire human race was black until a scientist created white people, who turned out to be devils. Orthodox Muslims considered these beliefs heretical and denounced them. Following a leadership change in the 1980s, the Nation of Islam broke into two sects: one returning to the original teachings, and the other abandoning separatist notions and adopting the beliefs held by Muslims across the globe. The latter group, which became the largest African American Islamic movement of the late twentieth century, is known as the American Muslim Mission. Approximately 1 million African Americans followed the Islamic religion by the year 2000.

The African American church has been an inseparable part of African American life since the early days of slavery. It manifests a certain uniqueness in form and status, both of which were born from the peculiar history of African Americans. From the pervasive images of freedom that dominate African American spirituals to the expressiveness demonstrated in so many African American worship services, religion, particularly Christianity, has played a tremendous role in the emergence and ongoing transformation of African American culture. When Frederick Douglass frequently sang the line, "I am bound for Canaan," he meant not only that he was headed for a spiritual promised land, but also that he was going to the American North to experience a physical freedom. This dual sense of "freedom" has put economic and political empowerment at the forefront of African American religion since its beginnings in the United States.

BIBLIOGRAPHY

Maffly-Kipp, Laurie. "African-American Religion in the Nineteenth Century." National Humanities Center. Updated October 2000. Available from http://www.nhc.rtp.nc.us.

Mays, Benjamin Elijah, and Joseph William Nicholson. *The Negro's Church*. New York: Institute of Social and Religious Research, 1933.

Raboteau, Albert J. *Canaan Land: a Religious History of African Americans*. New York: Oxford University Press, 2001.

Wilmore, Gayraud S. *Black Religion and Black Radicalism: an Interpretation of the Religious History of African Americans*. 3rd ed., rev. and enl. Maryknoll, N.Y.: Orbis Books, 1998. The original edition was published in 1972.

James T. Scott

See also **African Americans; African Methodist Episcopal Church; Baptist Churches; Church of God in Christ; Islam; Nation of Islam.**

AFRICAN AMERICAN STUDIES, a field of academic and intellectual endeavors—variously labeled Africana Studies, Afro-American Studies, Black Studies, Pan-African Studies—that was a direct product of the social movements of the 1950s and 1960s. The quests for African liberation, the civil rights movements, and the black power and black arts movements had created an ambience in which activist members of the faculties at colleges and universities and black students who had come of age during the late 1960s sought to foster revolutionary changes in the traditional curricula. In search of relevance—to use a word that became a cliché during that period—the students wanted a curriculum that forthrightly addressed their particular history and the social problems that adversely affected the lives of the vast majority of African Americans, not only at predominantly white colleges and universities but also the masses in African American communities as well. Consequently, all-black organizations sprang up on most major campuses around the nation and demanded courses in black history and culture. In so doing, black students shunned traditional European and European American courses in hopes of not only establishing blacks' contributions to history

and society but also of engendering robustly ecumenical perspectives in the curricula.

The first African American Studies units were founded as a response to student protests at San Francisco State College (now University), Merritt College in Oakland, California, and Cornell University. With the support of the Black Student Union, and many students from other racial groups, Nathan Hare, a sociologist who had written an exposé of the black middle class while teaching at predominantly black Howard University, compelled San Francisco State's administration in 1968 to create the first African American Studies department in the United States. One year later, James E. Turner, a doctoral student, was appointed the head of the African Studies and Research Center unit at Cornell University, after widely publicized pictures of gun-toting black students were circulated by the mass media. Although there were no strictly operational definitions of what constituted the field of African American Studies in the early years, most of its practitioners concurred in the opinion that it was the study of African peoples and their brethren the world over—with emphases on history, cultures, and social problems. The purpose of the field was not only to ameliorate the conditions under which black people lived but also to enhance their self-image and self-esteem, and build their character.

Despite the idealistic goals of the founders, the economic crisis that lasted from the mid-1970s until the early 1980s wreaked havoc with the budgets of most institutions of higher learning. As a result, African American Studies came under the scrutiny and criticism of both the administrations at those institutions attempting to trim their budgets and the prominent black academics who were critical of what they perceived as the units' lax academic standards, unqualified faculties, and poor leadership. Although administrators slashed the budgets of many fields in the humanities, African American Studies units were especially vulnerable—primarily because they were still in a fledgling stage.

Martin Kilson, a distinguished political scientist at Harvard University who refused to join his institution's unit, and the Duke University scholar of English, Kenny Williams, raised serious questions about the intellectual integrity and validity of African American Studies. Critical of the instability and the hyper-politicization of African American Studies in the 1970s, the aforementioned scholars compelled a reassessment and fostered a reconceptualization of its curriculum and position in the academy. As a result, in the 1980s, such leading black academics as Ron Karenga, the author of a popular textbook entitled *Introduction to Black Studies* (1982), sought to provide a theoretical base for African American Studies with his concept of Kawaida, which provided an holistic cultural nationalist approach to black history, religion, social organization, politics, economics, psychology, and the creative arts. During this same period, Molefi Kete Asante was appointed the head of African American Studies at

Temple University. That institution nurtured the department, and in 1988, it became the first institution in the country to award the doctorate in the comparatively new field.

Asante's theoretical conceptualizations were significant, for he attempted to center his work and that of his students and colleagues on the examination of African and African American culture, which he labeled "Afrocentrism." This brand of cultural nationalism deconstructs "Eurocentrism" and seeks to reclaim his peoples' "pre-American heritage."

In recent years, Asante and other Afrocentrists have been criticized for presenting a static view of history and culture, and thereby ignoring the dynamic interaction between blacks and European and European American cultural, economic, and political structures. Despite the futility of his attempt to conceptualize the field, Asante, like Karenga, made a heroic effort to set up some parameters for the focus of African American Studies.

The goal of standardization and definition of African American Studies has become increasingly difficult—especially with the emergence of other notable scholars in the field who have an ideological orientation that differs from those of the founders. Manning Marable, the political scientist, historian, journalist, and director of the Institute for African American Studies at Columbia University, for example, purveys the social democratic ideology; the sociologist Abdul Alkalimat and his heroes—Langston Hughes, Paul Robeson, W. E. B. Du Bois—were socialists. In short, as the 1980s came to a close there was no single theoretical orientation in the curriculum of African American Studies that most scholars concurred in.

As the twentieth century came to a close, the most vocal and visible African American Studies unit emerged at Harvard University, under the direction of literary critic and historian Henry Louis Gates Jr. The program, which at one time included the noted philosopher, orator, and theologian, Cornell West; the philosopher, Anthony Appiah; and the distinguished sociologist, William Julius Wilson, was what Arthur Lewin, an associate professor of Black and Hispanic Studies at Baruch College, call "inclusionist." In other words, Gates and his colleagues sought to foster a great appreciation and tolerance of African Americans by the American public by dispassionately informing them of black peoples' history and culture. *Africana: The Encyclopedia African and African American Studies* (1999) is just one example of their endeavors.

African American Studies units have been in existence for over thirty years. Nonetheless, they continue to maintain varying identities, which militates against the development of the status of the discipline. The field has made persons aware of the contradictions and paradoxes that mire both European American and African American thought on race.

BIBLIOGRAPHY

Aldridge, Delores P. "Status of Africana/Black Studies in Higher Education in the U.S." *In Out of the Revolution: The Development of Africana Studies*, edited by Delores P. Aldridge and Carlene Young. Landham, Md.: Lexington Books, 2000.

Exum, William H. *Paradoxes of Protest: Black Student Activism in a White University*. Philadelphia: Temple University Press, 1985.

Harris, Robert, Jr. "The Intellectual and Institutional Development of African Studies." In *Three Essays: Black Studies in the United State*, edited by Robert L. Harris Jr., Darlene Clark Hine, and Nellie McKay. New York: The Ford Foundation, 1990.

Hayes, Floyd W., III. "Preface To the Instructor." In *A Turbulent Voyage: Readings in African American Studies*, edited by Floyd W. Hayes III. San Diego: Collegiate Press, 2000.

Vernon J. Williams Jr.

See also **Civil Rights Movement; Education, Higher: African-American Colleges.**

AFRICAN AMERICANS. African American history lies at the foundation of United States history. The story of African Americans began in Africa, where ethnic groups such as the Ashanti, Bantu, Congolese, and Yoruba began their chaotic and protracted journey to what would become the United States.

The First African Americans

The arrival of Africans in America began almost five hundred years ago in 1528, with the arrival of the Moroccan Esteban de Dorantes in Texas. He was the first of many Spanish-speaking Africans who were populating western America. Between the fifteenth and nineteenth centuries, Africans were imported as property to the "New World" for slave plantations via the transatlantic SLAVE TRADE. Conservative estimates place the number at 8 to 12 million, but the total may be as high as 20 million. The trade in African men, women, and children exploded into one of the most massive and despotic extractions of a people from their land and way of life in history. These migrants became unwilling participants in a system of enslavement that gave rise to the African diaspora and African Americans. Of the total number of Africans sold into slavery, 600,000 to 1,000,000, or about 6 percent, were brought to the British North American colonies.

The first English-speaking Africans arrived in Jamestown, Virginia, in 1619. Initially British colonists and Africans coexisted, but developments in colonial America precipitated the enslavement of black people. By the late sixteenth century, it became clear to white colonists that Indians would not be a viable source of forced labor. Increasingly, white and black indentured servants became targets of the New World's economic development. Eventually, the labor of indentured servants became problematic and scarce. The number of indentured white servants who made the journey to America began to dwindle, and those already in America started to demand an equal share of the wealth, while life expectancies rose sufficiently to make the purchase of slaves financially sensible. Colonists, therefore, turned to the African slave trade to meet their labor needs.

Initially, some European indentured servants and laborers joined with Africans to oppose the exploitation of white and black laborers, but when attitudes and laws changed and as black skin became commensurate with slavery, whites understood that being white—no matter how poor—exempted them from outright slavery. White slave owners came to understand the value of their investments in black human property. White wealth and dreams of prosperity became tied to the survival of black slavery as an institution. As a result, whites began to support statutes that strengthened the chains of black slavery. As the eighteenth century came to a close, Africans were generally considered capital. Black people resisted enslavement, however, and often worked to undermine the institution. They ran away or feigned ignorance and illness, for example, to undermine the commercial success of the farms for which they labored. Slaves such as Nat Turner and Gabriel Prosser physically confronted their masters and overseers in both individual clashes and collective rebellion.

Africans in America, despite their subordinate status, were able to forge a strong sense of community. They learned to speak English and, in the process, expanded and enhanced the language through new words and pronunciations. Many Africans also embraced Christianity and reconstructed it, while some continued to follow their original religions, including Islam. Usually, black people merged their faith with that of the ruling class. From their earliest arrival in America, many blacks also endeavored to give meaning to America's professed belief in freedom by calling upon colonial officials to recognize their right to liberty. In 1791, for example, Benjamin Banneker, an astronomer and publisher of almanacs, and perhaps the most accomplished black person in early America, wrote to Thomas Jefferson to argue for the respect and inclusion of black people in America's experiment in democracy. Most Africans in America, however, could not rely on petitions or whites to recognize their "unalienable" right to secure their freedom. Rather, they articulated belief in their own inherent worth through ongoing resistance to white supremacy and racial slavery.

By the eighteenth century, black acculturation gave rise to a stable, identifiable, and diverse African American culture, both in slave societies and in free black communities. This black culture was anchored in an expanded, flexible family structure and an emerging black church that found the means to survive under difficult circumstances. During this period, nothing exposed the contradiction between slavery and freedom for Africans as much as the American fight for independence from Great Britain. Some black people such as Crispus Attucks, one of the first casualties of the American Revolution, demonstrated their desire to be free from British rule, both as people of African descent and as Americans. On the other hand, having been promised liberation by the royal governor, Lord Dunmore, in 1775, some black people were loyal to the English monarchy only to witness its demise at the hands of tenacious American colonists. But whether in the poems of Phillis Wheatley, the legal action of Quok Walker, or the efforts of Paul Cuffee, Americans of African descent helped define what it meant to be revolutionary citizens. For black slaves in particular, independence was not simply a philosophical debate; it stood as an essential alternative to permanent bondage.

As blacks fought for freedom from both American slavery and British colonial rule, the debate over slavery intensified. As the United States emerged from the crucible of war, black slavery endured and expanded, especially in the South. Between the mid-1600s and 1865, most blacks were considered possessions. They were examined, marketed, sold, purchased, exchanged, and treated as chattel. Black people were ridiculed as aberrant and inferior, and most were denied the freedoms set forth in the Declaration of Independence. Out of this ordeal, Africans in America became a new people. They were no longer Ashanti, Bantu, Kongolese, and Yoruba; they constructed new identities rooted in their African past, yet inextricably linked to a burgeoning American culture.

By 1789, despite America's proclamation that "all men are created equal," slavery as an institution was still legal in eleven of the thirteen States. Moreover, the Atlantic slave trade, which was officially banned in 1808 but continued extralegally until the 1850s, continued to bring thousands of enslaved Africans to America. The primary destinations of black slaves were the rice plantations of low-country South Carolina and the tobacco farms of Piedmont, Virginia. Although there were, as there had always been, "free" blacks in the United States, by 1789, there were fewer than 60,000 of them out of a total black population of 700,000.

By 1831, slavery had emerged as an even more powerful and "peculiar institution." It existed, for example, in twelve southern states, but was almost nonexistent in the twelve northern states. Moreover, although the slave trade had not existed as a legally sanctioned enterprise in almost twenty-five years, cotton plantations from Georgia to Mississippi that depended upon slave labor became inextricably linked to the "Southern way of life." The invention of the cotton gin in 1793 made cotton cultivation a lucrative business. Between 1811 and 1821 it fueled the expansion of slavery from the Atlantic coastal states to Texas. Slave labor also emptied swamps and cleared land for settlement and agriculture. This territorial expansion in turn stimulated an enormous surge in the slave population. By 1831, there were over two million black slaves in the United States, primarily in the deep South. By 1860 the number had risen to 3,953,760. In 1831 the United States was also home to 300,000 free black people, primarily located in the North and upper South; by 1860 there were 488,070.

Major social and cultural changes had taken place among black people in America by 1831. Resistance to slavery intensified as black communities and slaves watched their hopes of freedom continually dissolve and began to learn the ideology behind the American and French revolutions and gain knowledge of the successful slave revolt in Saint Domingue (Haiti). Despite the odds, some blacks continued to gain their freedom from bondage; most of those who succeeded had to struggle to survive the transition from slavery to freedom. Like their enslaved counterparts, free black people were relegated to the bottom of the American racial hierarchy, dominated by the theory of white supremacy. Despite being the objects of white racism, "free" blacks often set themselves apart from black slaves. This class—small, sometimes prosperous, and often literate—usually considered themselves superior to their enslaved counterparts.

Many "free" black people, however, in the North and upper South, expanded their concept of the black community to include those blacks still held in bondage. Many in this group, including celebrated abolitionist Frederick Douglass, championed black equality and freedom in all quarters. By 1831, Africans in America understood that only by destroying slavery could true freedom and equality be secured. Many believed—as did Nat Turner, who initiated a large-scale slave uprising in the fall of 1831—that it would take a devastating event such as a sustained revolt to abolish the institution. By 1840, slavery and its expansion became the most controversial and divisive issue in the nation. By 1860, northern and southern leaders could not avoid the problem of slavery and its expansion, thanks to pressure from a small but influential band of abolitionists—including Maria W. Stewart, David Walker, and William Lloyd Garrison.

Emancipation and the Illusion of Freedom

The end of slavery as an institution in American life can be tied to the election of Abraham Lincoln in 1860. Lincoln, a Republican, believed that the Constitution protected slavery in the states, but was opposed to its extension. He objected to the spread of slavery into Kansas and other territories. Southerners believed the Constitution protected slavery and saw Lincoln's resolve as a threat to their political standing in Congress and to their "way of life." Lincoln was elected in 1860, and following his inaugural address in March 1861, South Carolina seceded from the Union in retaliation. By February 1861, it was followed by six more southern states. Lincoln's calls for healing were unsuccessful. The Confederacy launched an artillery attack on Fort Sumter in South Carolina on 12 April, and Lincoln called for volunteers to put down the rebellion. America's divided house fell, and the sectional conflict exploded into Civil War. After five years of fighting, the Southern Confederacy was forced to surrender to Northern troops on 9 April 1865. Four million African Americans emerged from the conflict legally free. Rati-

World War II. During the war American industries, especially those in the West, employed African Americans such as this woman in jobs that had previously been closed to them. The migration to urban areas to find those jobs helped spur the growth of the civil rights movement, as African Americans gained majority status in many cities. NATIONAL ARCHIVES AND RECORDS ADMINISTRATION

fication of the Thirteenth Amendment in December 1865 abolished slavery. The Confederate defeat, however, did not end white supremacy or black subjugation. As one nineteenth-century observer noted, "cannons conquer, but they do not necessarily convert." Former slaveholders faced emancipation with despair and fury and immediately embarked upon a crusade to "redeem" the South and force blacks into a state of virtual slavery.

Emancipated blacks set out to make the best of their new status. Millions of former slaves searched the South for loved ones from whom they had been separated. Women like the writer Harriet Jacobs attempted to reconstruct their shattered lives and families, while creating a space for themselves to enjoy their freedom. To gain control over their labor, black washerwomen and domestic workers in Atlanta organized to raise their wages through strikes and demonstrations. In South Carolina, black women took a leading role in negotiating labor arrangements with their former masters. Black men sought

Percy L. Julian. Despite facing enormous obstacles due to his race, Percy L. Julian, shown here at Fisk University, became one of the leading chemists in the world in the 1940s and 1950s. Among his accomplishments was discovering a treatment for glaucoma and uncovering a method to cheaply synthesize the "wonder drug" cortisone, making it available to the masses. FISK UNIVERSITY LIBRARY

wage labor, worked to acquire land, and made use of the ballot. Out of this movement to reclaim themselves and their families, black communities in the postwar South grew, while organizing schools and health care services. Legally, black people benefited from the enactment of several Constitutional amendments during the subsequent "Reconstruction" period. The ratification of the Fourteenth Amendment on 28 July 1868 affirmed state and federal citizenship rights for African Americans, and the Fifteenth Amendment, ratified on 30 March 1870, guaranteed that no American would be denied the right to vote on the basis of race. Radical Republicans also pushed through the CIVIL RIGHTS ACT OF 1875, which was supposed to prohibit discrimination in public accommodations throughout the South.

Abraham Lincoln's Proclamation of Amnesty and Reconstruction on 8 December 1863 allowed blacks to secure fleeting political success. Blacks seized this opportunity to elect state and national Congressmen. Six hundred blacks, most of them former slaves, served as state legislators. During RECONSTRUCTION, there were two black senators in Congress—Hiram Revels and Blanche K. Bruce, both Mississippi natives who were educated in the North—and fourteen black members of the House. African Americans also sought to improve their lives by carving out spaces where they could congregate and build community away from the watchful eyes of whites. Reestablished, primarily Protestant, black churches emerged as spiritual havens for African Americans. Education was extremely important to African Americans as well. With the assistance of philanthropic northern whites, blacks established primary and secondary schools, as well as predominantly black colleges, across the South in the postwar period. Tuskegee Institute (1881) in Alabama and Howard University (1867) in Washington, D.C., represent two of the more celebrated examples of historically black colleges and universities founded during this era.

For African Americans, however, the ability to exercise their new rights was short-lived. Southern whites created laws and practices to circumscribe and oppress the lives of blacks. They created BLACK CODES, which limited the areas in which blacks could purchase or rent property, and vagrancy laws that forced African Americans to return to work on the plantations from which they were recently liberated. These measures helped force blacks into a state of peonage that would last well into the second half of the twentieth century. Blacks were not permitted to testify in court, except in cases involving other blacks, and fines were levied against them for alleged seditious speeches, insulting gestures and acts, absence from work, violating curfews, and the possession of firearms. Blacks had their freedom assaulted by white terrorist organizations as well. The prototype of these groups was the KU KLUX KLAN, organized in 1866 in Pulaski, Tennessee, as a "social club." The Klan was responsible for whippings, mutilations, burnings, and murders of men, women, and children. Violence emerged as one of the most effective ways of keeping blacks politically powerless.

Politically, whites used quasi-legal measures to oppress blacks. Polling places were often erected far from black communities and changed without warning, ballot boxes were stuffed, votes were manipulated, poll taxes were levied, and gerrymandering ran rampant. Black people were separated from whites on trains and ships and were banned from white hotels, barbershops, restaurants, and theaters. By 1885, most Southern states had laws requiring separate schools, and in 1896, the Supreme Court upheld SEGREGATION in its landmark "separate but equal" doctrine set forth in PLESSY V. FERGUSON. The rights of blacks had been neutralized. By 1900, the "New South" was free to conduct its affairs as it saw fit. The New South, however, looked very much like the old. The new century, in fact, opened tragically with 214 lynchings in the first two years. The law, the courts, the schools, and almost every institution in the South favored whites. In the face of this opposition, African Americans and their supporters had few answers. This was an era of white supremacy.

African Americans in the South began to vote with their feet. Between 1900 and 1910, black people tried to escape the South by migrating to the northern and western United States in relatively modest numbers. When wartime industrial needs and labor demands increased between World Wars I and II, however, more than two million black southerners were motivated to migrate north and west to urban areas like Chicago, Detroit, New York, Philadelphia, and San Francisco. This flight erupted into the largest African American migration in history. These migrants sought refuge and opportunity, and many found what they were looking for, while others found social isolation, political marginalization, and economic oppression.

All African Americans, whether they remained in the South or migrated to the North, experienced fundamental changes in their lives during the first decades of the twentieth century. African American men returned home from World War I—a war fought to make the world safe for democracy—prepared and determined to demand democracy for themselves and their community. Their militancy was rewarded with violence. African American men were lynched in their military uniforms, black institutions were attacked by white mobs, and African American workers, who were often the last hired, were the first to be fired during demobilization. On the other hand, many African Americans worked to "uplift the race" in northern and western urban areas by organizing groups such as the NATIONAL ASSOCIATION FOR THE ADVANCEMENT OF COLORED PEOPLE. Even though the 1920s witnessed ongoing race-related social, economic, and political problems, many black artists experienced "renaissances" in African American art, literature, and music in Harlem and Chicago. Some African American leaders became political agents, and others became successful in business.

When the Great Depression struck America in 1929, African Americans were among the hardest hit. The years between 1929 and 1940 were marked by both progress and persistent problems for black people. At a time when a black leader like Mary McLeod Bethune could hold an influential appointment in the Franklin D. Roosevelt administration, African American workers had the highest unemployment rate in the nation. Moreover, while New Deal legislation displaced black sharecroppers in the South, the federal government also offered unprecedented opportunities for African American artists and writers such as Aaron Douglass and Zora Neale Hurston. However, discrimination and racial violence, unemployment, and housing shortages remained complicated and dispiriting issues for African Americans. As the United States entered World War II in 1941, blacks seized this opportunity to demand full inclusion in American society. African Americans were critical of the United States for fighting for democracy overseas while blacks lived in a segregated and unjust society in America. Black people fought fascism in Europe and white supremacy in the United States, which they christened the "Double-V": victory abroad and victory at home.

Mother of the Civil Rights Movement. On 1 December 1955, seamstress Rosa Parks changed history and inspired millions when she refused to give up her seat on a Montgomery, Ala., bus to a white man, as the law required. Among the honors she has since received is the Eleanor Roosevelt Woman of Courage Award, given to her in 1984 by the Wonder Woman Foundation. AP/WIDE WORLD PHOTOS

The Civil Rights Movement and Beyond

World War II and the industries that arose to support it also improved the prospect of good jobs and a freer life for African Americans, particularly in the West. As a result, a huge migration ensued that increased black populations in those urban areas. In the western region, some black populations grew tenfold. This migration gave rise to the nation's CIVIL RIGHTS MOVEMENT during the 1950s and 1960s, and ignited the careers of local black leaders such as Dr. Lincoln J. Ragsdale Sr. in Phoenix, Arizona, and Dr. Martin Luther King Jr. and Malcolm X at the national level. The black American freedom struggle quickly became a more inclusive beacon in the global fight for human rights, the defeat of European colonialism, and the destruction of racism. It ushered in profound and positive changes.

The Civil Rights Movement produced several pieces of legislation, which reaffirmed the rights of African Americans. The most effective were the CIVIL RIGHTS ACT OF 1964 and the VOTING RIGHTS ACT OF 1965. The Civil Rights Act prohibited discrimination in public places, and discrimination by employers of labor unions on the basis of color, race, religion, national origin, and sex. The Voting Rights Act re-enfranchised blacks by outlawing obstructionist educational requirements for voting and by

The Leader. Martin Luther King Jr. was the most prominent figure in the national civil rights movement of the 1960s. A founder of the influential Southern Christian Leadership Conference, Dr. King was the chief proponent of using nonviolent protests to combat racism. King was assassinated by James Earl Ray in Memphis, Tenn., on 4 April 1968. Fisk University Library

can organizations continued to work for the advancement of the community as a whole.

By 1970, most black people were optimistic about the future of race relations and the black community. Many black people believed that the BLACK POWER movement would instill a new confidence and independence in African Americans. Furthermore, a rash of victories in electoral politics gave hope to millions of African Americans. By the 1970s, in fact, several blacks, such Carl Stokes in Cleveland and Richard Hatcher in Gary, Indiana, were elected mayors of major urban centers. In 1972, Shirley Chisholm became the first African American to make a serious bid for a major-party presidential nomination; Jesse Jackson, a protégé of Dr. Martin Luther King Jr.'s did it again in 1984. By the end of the twentieth century an influential and growing black middle class had emerged. Multimillionaires such as the journalist, actor, talk show host, producer, and entrepreneur Oprah Winfrey and the athlete and businessman Michael Jordan stood as symbols of the ability of blacks to achieve against overwhelming odds. Despite persistent problems such as joblessness, police brutality, and economic and political inequality, African Americans—whose population stood at thirty million, or slightly over 10 percent of the population, by 2000—continued to make substantial gains. Indeed, the poverty, economic isolation, political marginalization, and racism in African American history are really aspects of a larger history of black progress through struggle, a history of survival and achievement.

empowering the attorney general to have the Civil Rights Commission assign federal registrars to uphold the voting rights of African Americans.

The impact of the Civil Rights Movement was monumental. Although their tremendous accomplishments did not end racial inequality or usher in true socioeconomic integration, black Americans did enjoy some major gains. However, jobs, infrastructure, and opportunity moved to predominantly white suburbs; unemployment remained disproportionately high among African Americans; and dislocations in black family structures, drug use, gang violence, police brutality, and urban poverty all emerged as disheartening and complex issues for black communities. Although African Americans had ended de jure segregation, they quickly realized that de facto segregation and racial socioeconomic inequality were just as debilitating and often more difficult to combat. Despite these problems, the black middle class continued to grow, most black families remained intact, and African Ameri-

Pied Piper of Dance. After the assassination of Martin Luther King in 1968, Arthur Mitchell felt obligated to found the Dance Theater of Harlem a year later to give African American dancers a chance to perform classical ballet. The first African American to perform with the prestigious New York City Ballet, Mitchell said his goal was "to build better human beings."

BIBLIOGRAPHY

Hine, Darlene Clark, William C. Hine, and Stanley Harrold. *The African American Odyssey.* 2d ed. Upper Saddle River, N.J.: Prentice Hall, 2002.

Kelley, Robin D. G., and Earl Lewis, eds. *To Make Our World Anew: A History of African Americans.* New York: Oxford University Press, 2000.

Marable, Manning. *Race, Reform, and Rebellion: The Second Reconstruction in Black America, 1945–1990.* 2d ed. Jackson: University Press of Mississippi, 1991.

Taylor, Quintard, Jr. *In Search of the Racial Frontier: African Americans in the American West, 1528–1990.* New York: Norton, 1998.

White, Deborah G. *Too Heavy a Load: Black Women in Defense of Themselves, 1894–1994.* New York: Norton, 1999.

Matthew Whitaker

See also **Discrimination: Race; Harlem Renaissance; Lynching; Migration, African American; South, the; Suffrage: African American; Tuskegee University.**

AFRICAN METHODIST EPISCOPAL CHURCH

(AMEC), the first separatist African American denomination. Many Methodist churches, especially in Philadelphia, had large numbers of black members whose growing hostility to racial discrimination within the church prompted Richard Allen, a licensed Methodist preacher, to lead a mass withdrawal from St. George's Methodist Episcopal Church, Philadelphia, in 1787. Allen subsequently helped to organize the Bethel African Methodist Episcopal Church of Philadelphia. In 1816, five black congregations came together to create the African Methodist Episcopal Church, with Allen as its first bishop.

The AMEC's strength resided in its benevolent associations—the Free African Societies—which concerned themselves with racial solidarity and abolitionism. Bethel Church was a station on the Underground Railroad and many members of First AME Church in Charleston, South Carolina, were involved in the Denmark Vesey slave uprising of 1822. AME churches sought to provide both social services and education. Bishop Daniel Payne spearheaded the campaign to establish Wilberforce University, the first institution of higher education founded by African Americans, in 1856. The AMEC grew from 20,000 members in 1861 to 400,000 in 1896, a process aided by expansion into the Caribbean and Africa.

Church structures and doctrines were modeled after the original Methodist Episcopal Church. AME bishops tend to have greater power than among the United Methodists, and the Church places a great emphasis on social service, for which congregations have a host of auxiliary organizations to accomplish their objectives. The Church is run by a General Conference that meets every four years, but has no established national headquarters. It supports five colleges and two seminaries and began to ordain women in 1948.

Richard Allen. An engraving of the former slave, the first African American ordained in a Methodist church, and the founder and first bishop of the African Methodist Episcopal Church.

Associated with the AMEC, though a separate denomination, is the African Methodist Episcopal Zion Church (AMEZC). In 1796, Peter Williams led a group of black Methodists out of the John Street Methodist Episcopal Church in New York City. This group established Zion Church, which was incorporated as an African Methodist Episcopal Church in 1801, with the provision that membership be limited to those of African descent. Zion Church retained a close relationship with the African Methodist Episcopal Church until 1820, when a conflict arose over AMEC preachers sent to New York by Richard Allen. The first bishop of the AMEZC was James Varick, who had helped establish *Freedom's Journal*, the first black newspaper in the United States. The AMEZC grew to 350,000 members by 1896. Two of its more prominent members were Harriet Tubman and Frederick Douglass. Like the AMEC, the AMEZC is run by a General Conference, but its bishops have considerable autonomy in interpreting Church regulations. There is no court of appeal for episcopal decisions and the traditions of a local church may override aspects of church teaching. The Church maintains one college and one seminary, both in Livingston, North Carolina. In 1891, it became the first black denomination to permit the ordination of women.

In the twentieth century, the AMEC showed an increasing interest in black liberation theology, pentecostalism, and political activism. Floyd Flake, pastor of Allen AME Church in Queens, New York, won several terms in the U.S. House of Representatives. In 1999, the African Methodist Episcopal Church had 2,500,000 members and the African Methodist Episcopal Zion Church had 1,276,000 members.

BIBLIOGRAPHY

Gregg, Howard D. *History of the African Methodist Episcopal Church: The Black Church in Action.* Nashville, Tenn.: AMEC, 1980.

Lincoln, C. Eric, and Lawrence H. Mamiya. *The Black Church in the African American Experience.* Durham, N.C.: Duke University Press, 1990.

Little, Lawrence S. *Disciples of Liberty: The African Methodist Episcopal Church in the Age of Imperialism, 1884–1916.* Knoxville: University of Tennessee Press, 2000.

Walls, William J. *The African Methodist Episcopal Zion Church: Reality of the Black Church.* Charlotte, N.C.: A.M.E. Zion Publishing House, 1974.

Jeremy Bonner

See also **African American Religions and Sects; Denominationalism; Religion and Religious Affiliation.**

AGENCY FOR INTERNATIONAL DEVELOPMENT.

In 1961, the U.S. Agency for International Development (USAID) was created to coordinate bilateral nonmilitary assistance to foreign countries as part of a global campaign to counter the appeal of communism. At first, USAID focused on large-scale infrastructure projects. During the 1970s, however, emphasis shifted to addressing the basic needs of the poorest members of society by promoting health, nutrition, rural development, and family planning programs. In the 1980s and 1990s, the agency turned many of its operations over to private, for-profit contractors, and channeled aid programs into development of the private sector.

Throughout its existence USAID had to respond to critics from the right, who complained that foreign aid was a waste of taxpayers' money, and those from the left, who argued that the agency was guided more by ideological anti-communism than by the need to alleviate poverty. USAID officials responded by pointing out that four-fifths of the agency's funds for foreign assistance were spent on goods and services provided by American businesses, and that the total amount of U.S. foreign aid was low, falling below 0.2 percent of the gross national product in the 1990s, placing the United States last among major donor countries. Ideological concerns were often apparent in the selection of recipients. For example, South Vietnam alone absorbed more than 25% of USAID's worldwide budget in the 1960s.

BIBLIOGRAPHY

Berríos, Rubén. *Contracting for Development: The Role of For-Profit Contractors in U.S. Foreign Development Assistance.* Westport, Conn.: Praeger, 2000.

Porter, David. *U.S. Economic Foreign Aid: A Case Study of the United States Agency for International Development.* New York: Garland, 1990.

Ruttan, Vernon W. *United States Development Assistance Policy: The Domestic Politics of Foreign Economic Aid.* Baltimore: Johns Hopkins University Press, 1996.

Max Paul Friedman

See also **Foreign Aid.**

AGENT ORANGE was an herbicide used by the United States during the Vietnam War (1955–1975; U.S. involvement 1964–1975) to deprive Viet Cong and North Vietnamese soldiers of forest cover and food crops. "Operation Ranch Hand" was the code name for the application of Agent Orange, as well as other defoliants such as Agent White and Agent Blue, by specially equipped Air Force cargo planes. More than forty-six percent of South Vietnam's territory was sprayed with herbicide under Operation Ranch Hand between 1962 and 1970. Agent Orange proved to be the most effective of the herbicides, as it contained dioxin, an extremely toxic chemical agent. Within a few weeks after its application, Agent Orange would turn lush, green forests brown and barren. It also had a detrimental effect on humans.

In 1966, the North Vietnamese charged that herbicides such as Agent Orange were responsible for causing congenital deformities in infants. Three years later, a report in a South Vietnamese newspaper made the same allegation. That same year, a study by the National Institutes of Health presented evidence that the dioxin found in Agent Orange caused deformities in babies. The United States suspended the use of Agent Orange in 1970, and ended Operation Ranch Hand in 1971.

After the war, studies continued to probe the impact that the dioxin found in Agent Orange could have on people. Americans who served in South Vietnam and were exposed to Agent Orange reported high incidences of skin rashes, breathing problems, various types of cancer, and birth defects in their children. A class action suit brought by affected veterans against the Veterans Administration was settled out of court in 1985. As part of the settlement, the chemical companies responsible for Agent Orange established a $180 million fund to assist veterans with legitimate claims, as well as the families of veterans who died from Agent Orange exposure.

BIBLIOGRAPHY

Moss, George Donelson. *Vietnam: An American Ordeal.* 3d ed. Upper Saddle River, N.J.: Prentice Hall, 1998.

Olson, James S., ed. *Dictionary of the Vietnam War.* New York: Greenwood Press, 1988.

John A. Morello

See also **Chemical and Biological Warfare; Insecticides and Herbicides; Vietnam War.**

AGING. *See* **Old Age.**

AGNOSTICISM, denying that human beings can know if God exists, emerged in the 1860s and 1870s as the opinion of a small but influential minority of religiously serious, well-read Americans. Many belonged to the class of writers, academics, and scientists soon labeled "intellectuals." They commonly enjoyed relatively high economic and social status. The word "agnosticism" itself was coined in 1869 (from Greek roots denoting "unknown") by the English scientist Thomas Huxley, and American agnosticism closely tracked similar, somewhat earlier tendencies among British bourgeois intelligentsia. Several of the most prominent early American agnostics—such as the scholar and cultural critic Charles Eliot Norton, the journalist E. L. Godkin, the historian Henry Adams, and the jurist Oliver Wendell Holmes Jr.—were deeply entwined in transatlantic webs of friendships that linked the two countries' intellectual life. And as these names suggest, agnosticism first developed in the United States among urban northeasterners.

Agnosticism was not so much a positive belief as a negative conclusion. Victorian agnostics wished to apply to all questions of knowledge what they took to be the criteria of the natural and human sciences. To decide matters of fact by any other standard they characteristically regarded as immoral—a credo classically articulated in the 1870s by the English mathematician William Clifford: "It is wrong always, everywhere, and for every one, to believe anything upon insufficient evidence." That agnostics readily carried this principle into religious issues can be explained not only by widespread faith in science but more specifically by the fact that for two centuries theological writers had enlisted science to prove religious belief. That this hoary scientific apologetic foundered after 1860 owed much to contraction by scientists of what counted as scientific evidence, a restriction associated especially with Darwinism. In ensuing decades, a growing number of Americans weighed the evidence for the existence of God and concluded that nothing approaching scientific evidence existed to prove a God.

Typically, agnostics bore no grudge against those who did retain faith in God. Although agnostics tended to see themselves as clearer thinkers and more rigorous moralists, they rarely trumpeted their unbelief or publicly attacked the churches. In this, agnosticism was unlike atheism, actively denying God. Atheism in both the United States and Europe flowed from dislike of organized religion, and atheists—their outrage at "priestcraft" often stoked by class resentment—were usually anticlericals. Lacking powerful established churches to resent, the United States proved much less fertile ground for atheism than did Europe, and agnosticism became the more common form of unbelief.

Agnosticism was entrenched in American culture by 1900, although the vast majority of Americans have continued to believe in God. Unbelief has probably remained chiefly an opinion of intellectual elites, especially academic ones. Unlike atheists, agnostics have rarely felt any need to institutionalize their views (the Ethical Culture movement was a rare exception, founded in 1876 by Felix Adler). To invent a structure to house a *lack* of beliefs perhaps seemed oxymoronic. Hence, agnosticism did not really evolve intellectually after establishing itself (except among academic philosophers) but rather in the twentieth century blended into low-key religious indifferentism.

BIBLIOGRAPHY

Turner, James. *Without God, Without Creed: The Origins of Unbelief in America.* Baltimore: Johns Hopkins University Press, 1985.

James Turner

See also **Atheism; Science and Religion, Relations of.**

AGRARIANISM. Thomas Jefferson, the patron of American agrarianism, wrote in his *Notes on Virginia* (1785), "Those who labor in the earth are the chosen people of God, if He ever had a chosen people, whose breasts He has made His peculiar deposit for substantial and genuine virtue. It is the focus in which He keeps alive that sacred fire, which otherwise might escape from the face of the earth." The origins of this sentiment are traceable to Virgil's *Arcadia* (first century B.C.) about an idealized pastoral society, and it reappears constantly in both secular and sacred Western literature. Jefferson's conviction placed it at the center of U.S. history.

The Elements of Agrarianism

Agrarianism expresses a number of political and cultural perspectives. The creed can be summed up in four parts. First, farming has a spiritual dimension that generates many virtues, among them self-reliance, moral integrity, and honor, because direct contact with nature leads to a meaningful relationship with God. Accordingly, like God, the cultivator creates order out of chaos. Second, farming is the only occupation offering total self-sufficiency and independence, primarily because it is the only occupation that creates genuine wealth. (This physiocratic assumption has loomed large in American history.) Third, the farmer, through his work, gains a sense of place and identity. The reason for this psychological wholeness is simple: the farmer does not live and work in the city, an artifice of mankind's hubris. He is an alien in the hostile, man-made environment that is the city. Since ancient Rome, the city has been the traditional home of the pro-

George Washington. This 1853 lithograph shows the president and general in his preferred role, as an eighteenth-century farmer (holding the reins of his horse) pursuing the agrarian ideal. GRANGER COLLECTION, LTD.

letariat, the landless, propertyless rabble. Fourth, with its fellowship of cooperation and labor, the agricultural landscape features the model society. These characteristics and values of agrarianism have long been a constant in the nation's history.

As a basis for reform, agrarianism—like many other ideals—contains both a forward-looking element, a brave new world, and a desire to return the country to an earlier condition of individual innocence and social purity. Generally, the "backward" agrarian denounced what he saw as the corrupting influence of the modern world, while the "forward" agrarian saw social justice in the integration of technology into American agriculture. In addition, agrarians oppose monopoly and privilege, and desire the liberation of the individual from dependencies of all kinds and their related corruptions.

The agrarian ideal turns on the cultivation of virtue and abundance. Jefferson and countless other writers linked the two. Recent historical scholarship regarding republicanism in American history illustrates the connection. Land was abundant in Jefferson's America. It provided the means to a virtuous and independent life, the essence of agrarianism. The American environment and westward expansion turned classical republicanism into an expression of democracy. Old World classical republicanism was an ideology of leisure restricted to men of landed property. The frontier, however, created a New

World version of republicanism that allowed a material stake in society for every man who transformed the wilderness into his private property, thereby becoming a middle-class citizen. It permitted every man the means for political and economic independence. The classical polis was now the family farmhouse.

Agrarianism in American History

This ideological context, the fate of the agrarian ideal, illustrated the chronology of American history. After the War of Independence in 1776, home rule became the American Revolution—who rules at home. Agrarianism became a part of the cultural and political struggles for a middle-class utopia. The political conflict between Thomas Jefferson and the Democrats against Alexander Hamilton and the Federalists was a dispute between agrarian-minded men and men of commerce. At different times, both sides were nervous about the rise of the city. Hamilton's vision of a national commercial society differed from Jefferson's agrarianism, particularly in its social conservatism and the use of the federal government in the advancement of commerce and industry. Hamilton worried about landless men living in such a place as New York City.

Agriculture, of course, was never free of the need for overseas and domestic markets, and particularly not after the market revolution of Jacksonian America. The emerging commercial order always included the yeoman farmer. In fact, as the United States became an urban, industrial society, the family farmer, a potent political icon, maintained a strong presence in the value system.

Jefferson's use of the federalist approach to the Constitution in the purchase of the Louisiana Territory was neither the first nor the last irony in the history of American agrarianism. The United States experienced the antebellum market revolution in which farmers and workers involved in the transportation of goods looked to the government for help in realizing the agrarian ideal. Up to a point, everyone wanted the advancement of the individual; moving west was the means, the central myth, in American history. Unfortunately racism was a part of agrarianism. As Jacksonian Democrats defended the *herronvolk* doctrine, "it's a white man's country," slavery reached far into agrarianism when the sanctity of private property extended to the ownership of African Americans.

The causes, course, and consequences of the Civil War were complex. In a real sense the split in agrarianism contributed mightily to its origin. As the ideology of "free soil, free men, free land" developed, the notion that freedom was colorblind began its long and painful process through American history. The theme of yeoman agrarianism now was the threat of slavery to the farmer's political and economic freedom. For many Americans, Jefferson's Monticello had become Simon Legree's plantation. Yet slavery, too, appealed to the agrarian ideal as the plantation became the defining image of the rebel South.

During the war the Homestead Act of 1862 indicated the political and cultural strength of agrarianism. The creation of the Department of Agriculture in 1889 also reflected agrarian concerns as the debates over land policy continued. The Department of Agriculture was an institutional recognition of agrarianism's effect on public policy. After the war, Thaddeus Stevens's campaign for the freedman to have "forty acres and a mule" again suggested the agrarian influence, as did the Dawes Act of 1883, which sought to turn the Plains Indians into yeoman farmers.

In the Gilded Age, the agrarian ideal became the suburbs, the country place, and the gentleman-farmer estate as more of the population became city dwellers. Populists believed that the family farmer must be saved from economic ruin and cultural irrelevance. The influx of a new wave of immigrants gave a reactionary twist to turn-of-the-century agrarianism, fueling anti-urbanism, as illustrated by the eugenicists and other advocates of the pastoral life. On the other hand, Liberty Hyde Bailey's Country Life Movement blended agrarianism with an urban existence. Bailey's reform was a genteel claim for the simple, rural life.

By the 1920s the yeoman farmer had a modified image. Agrarian interests were strong in Congress and were heard with increased vigor during the Great Depression. The New Deal objective was the preservation of the fam-

Calvin Coolidge. The president uses a scythe at his family farm in Plymouth, Vt., in the 1920s, when agrarian interests remained strong despite the growing pull of the cities. LIBRARY OF CONGRESS

ily farmer, but the results were problematic during the remainder of the twentieth century as many moved to the cities. As the squire of Hyde Park, Franklin Delano Roosevelt understood the complex problems of farm life in modern America. The New Deal and its legacies recognized the political power of the agrarian ideal with its emotional appeal for family life.

Ideologically, the twentieth century modified the cultural expressions of agrarianism. As the crabgrass frontier replaced the farming frontier, Americans still enjoyed outdoor recreation, national parks, camping, conservation, and so on. The homestead of previous times became ownership of a freestanding house. Owning a weekend place in the country is an example of Americans' desire to "have it both ways," or to participate in the city life for one's livelihood and hold on to one's agrarian roots. Some reactionary advocates of agrarianism, particularly in the South, rejected twentieth-century America with scorn; others, such as those associated with Dorothy Day's Catholic Worker movement, adopted a left-wing perspective, deriving their ideas from the Distributism of G. K. Chesterton and Hilary Belloc, twentieth-century British advocates of agrarianism who favored a more egalitarian distribution of land.

Symbolically, agrarianism's strength remains strong in the American idiom. After all, James Earl Carter became president as a peanut farmer and George W. Bush moved into his Texas ranch when he became the chief executive. In one form or another, agrarianism endures in American life and thought.

BIBLIOGRAPHY

Foner, Eric. *Free Soil, Free Labor, Free Men: The Ideology of the Republican Party Before the Civil War.* New York: Oxford University Press, 1970. An account of the most successful expression of agrarianism.

Peterson, Merrill D. *The Jefferson Image in the American Mind.* New York: Oxford University Press, 1960. A brilliant treatment of Jefferson as icon of agrarianism and a host of other creeds.

Pickens, Donald K. "The Expanding Economy: An Overview of United States As an Exercise in Middle Class Utopianism." *Journal of the American Studies Association of Texas* 4 (1973): 30–37.

———. "The Republican Synthesis and Thaddeus Stevens." *Civil War History* 31 (March 1985): 57–73. The relationship between agrarianism and the agitation for forty acres and a mule.

———. "The Turner Thesis and Republicanism: A Historiographical Commentary." *Pacific Historical Review* 61 (1992): 319–340. Explores the connections among agrarianism, westward expansion, and political theory.

White, Morton. *The Intellectual Versus the City.* New York: Mentor Books, 1964. An old but handy summary of why many American thinkers were inclined toward agrarianism.

Donald K. Pickens

See also **Dawes General Allotment Act; Frontier; Homestead Movement; Jeffersonian Democracy; Land Policy; Populism; Slavery; Suburbanization; Urbanization.**

AGRICULTURAL MACHINERY. Before the late eighteenth century, farmers tilled their fields with wooden moldboard plows. In order to prevent the moldboard from wearing out quickly, plowrights or blacksmiths plated it with thin iron strips. Wooden moldboard plows could not be mass-produced or repaired easily because they did not have standardized designs or parts. Only iron, which could be cast, wrought, or molded, would enable consistent duplication of plows specifically designed for a variety of soils. In 1807, David Peacock, a New Jersey inventor, patented the first successful plow with a cast-iron moldboard and a wrought-iron, steel-edged share that made the plow easy to repair. The concept of standardized, replaceable parts for the manufacturing of plows, however, is usually credited to Jethro Wood of Scipio, New York. In 1814, Wood patented a plow with replaceable parts. Wood's plow probably did more to replace the wooden moldboard plows than any other design, and farmers quickly adopted it. After Wood's invention, plow

technology, design, and manufacturing changed little until 1837, when John Deere of Grand Detour, Illinois, made a plow to cut through the thick sod and heavy prairie soil. Deere's plow had a highly polished wrought-iron moldboard and a steel share, and it required only half the draft power of other plows. Deere's plow became known as the "singing plow," because it produced a whine or hum as it cut through the soil. During the late 1870s, large-scale wheat farmers in California and the Red River Valley of North Dakota began using two-bottom sulky or riding plows. These plows enabled a farmer to turn from five to seven acres per day, compared to one acre per day with a one-horse walking plow, but four or five horses were required for draft power. Plows with more than four moldboards remained impractical until the late nineteenth and early twentieth centuries, when steam- or gasoline-powered tractors could provide the necessary force to pull them through the soil.

Farmers usually seeded their crops by hand. In 1841, however, Moses and Samuel Pennock of Chester, County Pennsylvania, designed a grain drill that deposited seeds through tubes attached to a box. By the mid-1860s, farmers that raised small grains commonly used the grain drill. Farmers typically used a dibble stick or hoe to plant their corn crop by hand. In 1864, however, John Thompson and John Ramsay of Aledo, Illinois, developed a corn planter that dropped seeds at designated spots in the furrows through a tube that extended to a hopper. This implement became known as a check-row planter, because it planted evenly spaced seed that permitted cultivation of the crop from four directions. The check-row planter became the standard corn-planting implement until it was replaced by drills in the twentieth century.

Until the development of the reaper, farmers cut their small grain crops with a sickle or scythe, permitting them to harvest just three acres per day. In 1831, Cyrus Hall McCormick tested a reaper in Rockbridge County, Virginia. McCormick improved his reaper by adding a reel to collect the stalks uniformly before the cutter bar, but he did not market it until 1840. In 1833, Obed Hussey tested his reaper in Hamilton County, Ohio. Instead of a reel, Hussey's machine used a reciprocating sickle with large triangular teeth that cut through the stalks. Hussey and McCormick continued to improve their reapers while other inventors developed similar implements. By 1855, wheat farmers commonly used the reaper to harvest grain. By the mid-1860s, reapers had a self-raking mechanism to clear the cut grain from the platform for the oncoming binders.

During the 1850s, inventors worked to develop a machine that would bind sheaves of small grains into bundles. In 1856, C. A. McPhitridge of St. Louis, Missouri, patented the first machine to bind grain with wire. This machine had a mechanism that wrapped wire around the gavel of cut grain and deposited the bundle of the ground ready for shocking. By the mid-1870s, the binder had become popular among grain farmers, but the wire was expensive, heavy, and difficult to dispose. During the mid-1870s John Appleby gave his attention to developing a twine binder. As early as 1857 he worked on a device that wrapped twine around a bundle of grain and tied a knot. He solved this technical problem about 1874 or 1875 and, in 1878, Parker & Stone of Beloit, Wisconsin, built four binders with Appleby's knotter. By 1880, the twine binders were rapidly replacing wire binders. Twine binders would remain the primary implement for harvesting small grain crops until farmers began replacing these machines with combines during the 1920s. Reapers and binders enabled farmers to harvest from twelve to fifteen acres per day.

Threshing machines date from 1791, when Samuel Mulliken, a Philadelphia inventor, patented the first implement. Yet, it was not until the 1820s that workable, hand- and horse-powered threshing machines were developed. Jacob Pope, a Boston inventor, built the most popular threshing machine. This hand-powered machine only separated the grain from the heads as the operator fed the stalks into the revolving threshing cylinder. Pope's threshing machine did not remove the straw or winnow the chaff. By the early 1830s, horse-powered sweeps and treadmills drove the working parts of threshing machines and enabled farmers to thresh more grain with less labor. In 1837, Hiram A. and John A. Pitts of Winthrop, Maine, patented a threshing machine that separated the grain, removed the straw, and winnowed the chaff in one operation. This machine could thresh about 100 bushels per day. By the 1850s, farmers who raised small grains commonly used threshing machines.

In 1831, Hiram Moore, with the aid of John Hascall in Kalamazoo County, Michigan, tested the first successful machine to harvest and thresh small grain crops in one operation. By 1843, Moore believed that he had developed a practical combined harvesting and threshing machine, but it was too large and expensive for small-scale grain farmers. The development of the combine came during the 1870s at the hands of David Young and John C. Holt of Stockton, California. Although one day it would become a major improvement, no one produced the combine on a large scale until the organization of the Stockton Combined Harvester and Agricultural Works in 1884. The large-scale wheat farms and dry conditions in California proved ideal for combine harvesting. The working parts of the combine were powered by steam, oil, and, by 1904, gasoline engines, while teams of twenty or more horses or mules pulled it through the fields. The largest of these machines could cut 100 acres and thresh 2,500 bushels of wheat per day. Smaller combines pulled by gasoline-powered tractors with power-take-off mechanisms that drove the machine's gears helped make this implement popular in the Midwest by the late 1930s.

Prior to the mid-nineteenth century, horses, mules, or oxen provided the power to operate the tillage, planting, harvesting, and threshing machinery. In 1849, A. L. Archambault of Philadelphia manufactured the first mo-

bile or portable steam engine. By the Civil War several dozen agricultural manufacturing companies built steam engines, all designed for belt work, that is, to power farm implements such as threshing machines, but steam engines were not used on a widespread basis until the 1870s. These steam engines, however, were not self-propelled and farmers used horses to pull them from place to place. In 1873, the firm of Merritt and Kellogg of Battle Creek, Michigan, marketed the first traction steam engine. During the late 1870s, manufacturers also began producing steam traction engines that could pull a plow. By the 1890s, large traction steam engines easily plowed forty-five acres per day in the wheat lands of the West. These steam engines, however, were too large and expensive for the small-scale farmers, and their popularity peaked about 1915, when gasoline-powered tractors began replacing them for plowing and threshing.

During the early twentieth century, farm machinery companies began building gasoline tractors. The Hart-Parr Company of Charles City, Iowa, built a popular tractor, but the early designs were too large, heavy, and expensive for small-scale farmers. Gasoline-powered tractors did not become practical until Henry Ford offered the Fordson for sale in 1918. Farmers could use this lightweight, low-cost, two-plow tractor for tillage and threshing, but its four-wheel design made the cultivation of row crops difficult. In 1924, the International Harvester Company produced a small, low-priced tractor with a tricycle design, the Farmall, which enabled farmers to cultivate row crops without crushing the plants. By the mid-1920s, the Fordson and Farmall had relegated the steam tractors to the past. By the late 1930s, a farmer could plow an acre in about thirty minutes, but it took nearly two hours with a horse and plow. By 1955, tractors exceeded the number of horses on farms.

While the tractor became the most important agricultural machine nationwide, the mechanical cotton picker became the most important farm machine on a regional basis during the twentieth century. Although the first mechanical cotton picker received a patent in 1850, the International Harvester Company did not develop a successful mechanical picker until 1942, and quantity production did not begin until 1948. The success of this spindle picker, however, required changes in the cotton plant so that it would ripen uniformly and produce bolls in clusters for easier picking by the machine. By 1975, the mechanical picker had mechanized the cotton harvest.

Agricultural machinery has enabled farmers to conduct more work with less labor, and convert fields used to feed horses to cropland for food and fiber for human consumption. Agricultural machines also enabled farmers to work more land and contributed to the consolidation of farms and the decline of the agricultural population. The tractor and the cotton picker helped end sharecropping in the South, while the threshing machine and combine, used for both wheat and corn, let farmers expand their operations. Although agricultural machines helped

Agricultural Machinery. A motorized farm plow in operation, 1981. © GUNTER MARX/CORBIS

remove many farm men, women, and children from the land because they were not needed for agricultural production or could not afford the implements or the land to operate them efficiently, overall, agricultural machines have helped farmers increase production, eased their labor, and improved the quality of farm life.

BIBLIOGRAPHY

Holley, Donald. *The Second Great Emancipation: The Mechanical Cotton Picker, Black Migration, and How They Shaped the Modern South.* Fayetteville: University of Arkansas Press, 2000.

Hurt, R. Douglas. *American Agriculture: A Brief History.* Ames: Iowa State University Press, 1994. Revised edition, West Lafayette, Ind.: Purdue University Press, 2002.

McClelland, Peter D. *Sowing Modernity: America's First Agricultural Revolution.* Ithaca, N.Y.: Cornell University Press, 1997.

Williams, Robert C. *Fordson, Farmall, and Poppin' Johnny: A History of the Farm Tractor and Its Impact on America.* Urbana: University of Illinois Press, 1987.

R. Douglas Hurt

See also **Cotton Gin; McCormick Reaper; Steam Power and Engines.**

AGRICULTURAL PRICE SUPPORTS. Introduced to meet the emergency of the Great Depression, agricultural price supports have persisted as a critical, if controversial, element of farm regulation. The Commodity Credit Corporation (CCC) was incorporated on 17 October 1933 to administer the system of price supports. Farmers received short-term loans, typically lasting twelve or eighteen months, of an amount that was determined by multiplying a fixed price per unit (such as a bushel of corn or a bale of cotton) by the quantity of crop they put up for collateral. The loans also carried a nonrecourse clause. If at any time the market price rose above the fixed price used to calculate the loan, a farmer could pay off the loan and sell the crop on the open market. If the market price dropped below the fixed price, then once the loan expired, farmers could pay off their debt by forfeiting their crop to the CCC. This meant farmers had no reason to accept a lower market price; thus, the fixed price acted as a minimum price on the market.

In 1933, policymakers intended the CCC to provide immediate relief, as prices of cash crops, such as corn, cotton, and wheat, had fallen by more than half their 1929 levels. The CCC, in trying to raise prices and farmers' incomes, worked alongside two other regulatory agencies. The Agricultural Adjustment Administration (AAA) paid farmers to replace cash crops with soil-conserving crops. This reduced the supply of cash crops reaching the markets and helped bolster prices. The Farm Credit Administration (FCA) refinanced thousands of farm mortgages in 1934 and 1935, thereby reducing the burden of farmers' debts relative to their incomes. Together these three agencies provided a measure of relief, but their initiatives did not help those families most in need of aid. In the 1930s, some one to two million farmers earned less than $500 a year. The impact of this trio of regulatory agencies was felt instead among financially secure farmers, but even then, the regulatory agencies proved controversial for their effect on markets.

The controversy surrounding price supports turned on the distinction between their short-term (static) effect as compared to their long-term (dynamic) impact. Viewed in the short term, price supports interfered with markets by raising prices above their equilibrium. The artificially high prices resulted in vast surpluses at government warehouses and worked to sustain farmers who otherwise would not have been able to compete with their more efficient rivals. Viewed from a long-term perspective, prior to the coming of New Deal regulation, farmers had faced the possibility of wide swings in prices for their cash crops. Price supports stabilized the long-term trend in prices and this altered farmers' investment climate. Farmers had always labored in highly competitive markets and this continued with the coming of New Deal regulation. With prices stable, though, farmers showed a new willingness to invest in land and expensive machinery. The competitiveness had not changed, but farmers' responses to it had. Whereas gains in labor productivity in the farm sector had been small prior to 1930, from the 1930s through the 1970s, labor productivity rose more than 4 percent annually—a rate that exceeded almost all other parts of the U.S. economy.

Price supports also conditioned which farmers survived and on what terms. Ironically, as long as prices eluded the goal of New Deal policymakers and tended to fall, price supports and credit programs created conditions that fostered farmers' investments in land and technology. Further, those farmers who could not survive the new terms of competition sold out in the face of rising land prices. Foreclosure came to just a few. Conversely, when prices met the intent of policymakers and rose above the CCC's price support levels in the 1970s, farmers who had accumulated debt found themselves at risk to failure when prices suddenly retreated, and by the mid-1980s foreclosures were concentrated among commercial, debt-ridden operators. During the 1980s, political sentiment swung sharply against price regulation in a variety of industries. Members of Congress debated whether to eliminate price supports, and despite calls for a return to the free market, in 2002 farmers could still count on the CCC's loans.

BIBLIOGRAPHY

Clarke, Sally H. *Regulation and the Revolution in United States Farm Productivity.* New York: Cambridge University Press, 1994.

Cochrane, Willard W., and Mary E. Ryan. *American Farm Policy, 1948–1973.* Minneapolis: University of Minnesota Press, 1976.

Johnson, D. Gale, ed. *Food and Agricultural Policy for the 1980s.* Washington, D.C.: American Enterprise Institute, 1981.

Schultz, Theodore W. *Agriculture in an Unstable Economy.* New York: McGraw-Hill, 1945.

U.S. Department of Agriculture. *Agricultural Statistics, 2001.* Washington, D.C.: Government Printing Office, 2001.

———. "Financial Characteristics of U.S. Farmers, January 1985." *Agricultural Information Bulletin No. 495* (July 1985).

———. The USDA Web site for its price support division. Available at http://www.fsa.usda.gov/dafp/psd/default.htm.

Sally Clarke

See also **New Deal; Price and Wage Controls.**

AGRICULTURE. The decreased role of agriculture in American life at the beginning of the twenty-first century masks the extent to which farming has often shaped the national experience. Agriculture, at the very least, features an impressively lengthy heritage. The first American farmers were Native Americans who cultivated indigenous and Mesoamerican plants in excess of seven thousand years ago. AmerIndian agriculture evolved according to environmental, technological, and cultural imperatives. In the South, river valleys and floodplains attracted early farming endeavors. Squash was planted in the Lower Tennessee River valley over four thousand years ago. In subsequent years, southern tribes developed sophisticated intercropping skills based around complementing one crop with another. Beans and corn proved an ideal mix, beans providing valuable soil nutrients (such as nitrogen) required by corn, while cornstalks served as convenient climbing vehicles for beans.

Agricultural pursuits varied by region. In the Upper Great Lakes, Ojibwa and Assiniboine nations sowed wild rice in fertile marshlands. The slight interest in horticulture on the Great Plains reflected the dominance of hunting pursuits. From the eighth century onwards, corn represented the most widespread agricultural product in the aboriginal economy. In the Southwest, Anasazi farmers developed their own hybrid corn from chapalote and maize de ocho. Native Americans also pioneered irrigated agriculture. In the Salt and Gila Valleys, the Hohokam dug (and successfully maintained) irrigation canals up to seventy-five feet across. Two canals measuring over ten miles in length watered fields near today's Phoenix.

Colonial Agriculture

The first European farmers drew on indigenous wisdom in order to survive. Prepared for gold-searching rather than subsistence farming, early residents of Jamestown, Virginia, relied on local Indian knowledge of planting to circumvent starvation. Settlers learned how to cultivate corn and tobacco. The pilgrims of the fledgling Plymouth Colony similarly discovered the wonders of maize. As the Massachusetts Bay Colony expanded, pioneers introduced cows, horses, and sheep to the eastern landscape. With few sheds and little fencing, livestock initially ran wild. Most early colonists were city gentry, religious dissenters, or indentured servants—all with little experience of farming. Tools proved basic, with the hoe, axe, and scythe the most common implements. Those who were fortunate enough to own plows made money by working the fields of their neighbors. Fresh immigrants sought out Indian clearings for crop cultivation rather than expend significant time on tree felling and heavy brush clearance. While a few regions, such as the Connecticut River valley and the Hudson River area, proved ideal for agriculture, thin and rocky soil compromised crop productivity on the eastern seaboard. Most farmers migrated to fresh terrain when soils became depleted rather than develop sustainable agricultural systems. The sheer abundance of land lent itself to this practice, with more territory always available for cultivation. The taking of Indian land occasionally provoked violent confrontation. In 1676, tormented by Indian attacks and crop failures, Nathaniel Bacon led a vigilante group of servants and small farmers to exact revenge on local Native American communities. Governor William Berkeley, who challenged the rebellion, was placed under house arrest.

Easily grown and requiring no machinery to process, corn served as the staple food crop in the fledgling colonial economy. Meanwhile, tobacco emerged as a key trade commodity. The first English tobacco was grown in Virginia in 1613. A smoking craze in western Europe encouraged colonists to continually increase their production of tobacco for export. Virginia farmers so focused on the weed that colonial governors issued regulations warning residents to plant some food crops for subsistence. In 1628, production surpassed 550,000 pounds. In the absence of harvesting machinery, tobacco, along with other crops, depended on ample manual labor. At first, indentured servants filled the niche in the fast-expanding tobacco fields of Virginia and Maryland, as well as in the rice fields of South Carolina. However, servitude gave way to slavery. By 1700, southern agriculture was already dependent on a slave economy.

During the 1700s, established New England agriculturalists experimented with more specialized forms of production. Animal husbandry developed in response to needs for draft horses to pull wagons and quality meat for town dwellers. German American farmers bred the much-lauded Conestoga breed of draft horse. By furnishing all manner of grains for consumption in the fast-expanding cities of the Atlantic seaboard, as well as for export abroad, New Jersey and Pennsylvania farmers earned their colonies the reputation of breadbasket kingdoms. Meanwhile, in the South, plantation owners reaped successive financial harvests from a single-crop economy based on exploitative labor. In 1708, tobacco exports reached 30 million pounds. On the eve of the American Revolution, the figure surpassed 100 million.

Farming in the New Republic

During the American Revolution, agriculture proved essential in keeping both armies fighting. Farmers responded to war by increasing their production of cattle, fruit, and crops. A female labor force filled roles previously occupied by men. Shortages usually came about as a result of troop movements and transportation problems rather than agricultural shortfalls. Both sides drew on the lofty image of owning one's own farm to recruit men for war duties, offering acres of land to those who volunteered.

The victorious United States was, first and foremost, an agricultural nation. Having procured a farm in New York, French commentator J. Hector St. John de Crèvecoeur, writing immediately after the Revolution, explained how "this formerly rude soil has been converted by my father into a pleasant farm, and in return, it has established all our rights; on it is founded our rank, our freedom, our power as citizens, our importance as inhabitants of such a district" (*Letters from an American Farmer* [1782]). In *Notes on the State of Virginia* (1787), Thomas Jefferson expounded his idea of a virtuous agrarian nation by claiming that "those who labor in the earth are the chosen people of God." Agriculture united men of differing classes and persuasions, appealing to both the rugged frontiersman and the dignified gentleman—the latter finding outlet in the Philadelphia Society for Promoting Agriculture (1785) and the South Carolina Society for Promoting and Improving Agriculture and Other Rural Concerns (1785). Farming was a way of life. The 1810 census recorded a total population of 7.2 million Americans, 90 percent of whom lived on farms.

Successive land acts—most notably the Land Survey Ordinance of 1785 and the Land Act of 1796—set in motion the transfer of the public domain to private hands. Land was surveyed, parceled into townships, and auctioned. However, a minimum purchase of 640 acres, at first priced at one dollar, then increased to two, proved beyond the reach of the average farmer. Land speculators benefited most from the distribution system, while squatting on unclaimed tracts became popular with poorer farmers. Geometric parcels, the infamous grid system, hardly abided by landscape topography or suited river access. When sales proved disappointing, the government instituted credit reforms and reduced the minimum acreage to 160 acres.

Farming expanded west of the Appalachians during the late 1700s. The Ohio River valley, with its rich soil and timber resources, invited settlement. However, frontier farming proved far from easy. Migrant families arrived at their wilderness purchase with few animals, tools, or financial resources. Densely forested land required extensive clearing. Agricultural technology remained primitive, with the time-honored plough, the sickle, the hoe, and the axe physically testing the endurance and the resolve of the agrarian pioneer. The transporting of goods was limited by dirt roads and changeable weather conditions. When it rained, roadways disappeared beneath mud and surface water. Farmers set their sights on quick improvements to properties before selling out to purchase a larger acreage. Successful frontier farming depended on good soil and a dedicated family. From an early age, children contributed to the home economy from milking to harvesting. Country stores proved important suppliers of all manner of items from tea and coffee to gunpowder and pottery.

Having exhausted soils in Georgia and the Carolinas, southern plantation owners joined small-scale farmers in moving into Alabama, Mississippi, and western Georgia in the early 1800s. The wealthiest plantation holders purchased vast swathes of land; poorer farmers were often left with marginal plots. Cotton became a staple crop of the South with the invention of the mechanized cotton gin by Eli Whitney in 1793. The machine separated valuable cotton fiber from unwanted seed. In 1811, output of cotton in the South exceeded 80 million pounds.

The antebellum period was marked by new technologies, increasing commercialization and specialization, geographical expansion, and transportation innovation. Much-improved transport routes aided New England farmers. The opening of the Erie Canal in 1825 allowed grain to be moved at far cheaper cost. While initially charging twenty-two dollars per ton for travel, by 1835 the cost of canal transport had dropped to just four dollars. The Cumberland or National Road, starting at Cumberland, Maryland, reached Vandalia, Illinois, in 1841. Westerly migration continued unabated, with the farming frontier extending to Indiana, Illinois, and Iowa in the north and Texas in the south. Pioneers took to raising cattle for beef in Ohio and parts of Kentucky. As industrializing cities attracted many rural migrants, northern farmers welcomed developments in labor-saving agricultural machinery. John Deere engineered the steel moldboard plow in 1837 (dubbed the "singing plow" for the whining noise it produced when cutting), a tool much valued on the midwestern prairie with its rough sod. Agricultural societies and fairs proliferated. Nonetheless, farming endeavors in the United States were divided according to two types of agricultural system: small-scale farming in the North and the plantation in the South.

Postbellum Agriculture in the South and the North

The testing climate of the Civil War highlighted inadequacies in southern agriculture. Not only was farmland wrecked by conflict and slash-and-burn techniques, but structural deficiencies came to the fore. Transport systems were shown to be deficient and southern agriculture lacked a diversity of products. White planters suddenly found themselves without a labor force. The reconstruction of southern agriculture proved difficult. Freed slaves relished the idea of having their own farm, a project taken up by the government under the auspices of the Southern Homestead Act (1866). However, available public land was generally of poor quality, while freedmen lacked the money necessary for forest clearance, housing, and planting. Only four thousand claimants applied for plots under the act and the measure was repealed ten years later. Systems of tenancy gradually emerged in the postbellum South. Sharecropping involved the lease of typically twenty to forty acres (along with tools and housing) by a landowner to a working family. In return, the family forfeited a proportion (usually half) of its crop. Merchants and landowners loaned cash or supplies to sharecroppers who had little money to pay for basic living expenses. In prac-

tice, revenue from the harvest frequently failed to cover repayments, and many sharecroppers found themselves with spiraling debts. White landowners grew to exercise levels of control similar to the pre–Civil War era. Cotton production dominated the southern landscape, aided by high prices (rising to forty-three cents a pound) in the late 1860s. Even when prices dropped to ten cents a pound in the mid-1870s, output continued to rise. By 1890, production had reached 8 million bales a year.

In the North, increased markets and the absence of significant wartime disruption allowed farmers to repay debts and improve their landholdings. Land prices soared, rising in Iowa from twelve dollars an acre in 1860 to twenty-five dollars ten years later. Agriculture became more mechanized, with new plows and reapers taking advantage of farm horses. Regional specialization proceeded apace as farmers were forced to become more competitive and efficient. Facing foreign and domestic competition, many sheep raisers abandoned marginal lands to take up jobs in the swelling cities. Dairying and fruit growing became increasingly popular in New England, aided by high prices, urban demand, and innovations in refrigeration technology.

The government maintained a keen interest in the agricultural sector during this period. After lobbying from the U.S. Agricultural Society (1852), Congress established the Department of Agriculture in 1862 (raised to cabinet level in 1889). Isaac Newton, who had previously served the agricultural division of the Patent Office, assumed the mantle of first commissioner. During the same year, the Land-Grant College Act (or MORRILL ACT) allotted public land to individual states for the purpose of establishing agricultural colleges. Federal and state agencies became involved in information gathering, regulation, and scientific research. In 1884, the Bureau of Animal Industry was established to curb imports of diseased animals and to work towards the eradication of Texas fever, a cattle affliction spread by ticks. The HATCH ACT of 1887 offered federal support to agricultural experiment stations linked to land grant colleges. (The first station had been established in 1875 at Wesleyan University in Middletown, Connecticut.) Scientists studied insect disease, dairy production techniques, and plant breeding and hybridization. The late 1800s also saw the strengthening of farmers associations, who sought to influence state and federal policy in matters of animal health as well as price subsidies and credit payments. Formed in 1867, the National Grange of the Patrons of Husbandry explored cooperative ventures, demanded lower railroad tariffs and banking rates, and lobbied for gender equality. The Farmers' Alliance exerted an influence over federal agricultural policies in the 1880s, but it was largely subsumed under the People's Party's 1892 platform of economic intervention, nationalization of railroads, and agricultural assistance. After a lackluster performance in the 1896 election, the populist movement dissipated, though farmers' associations continued to draw support. In 1902, Texan Isaac

Newton Gresham established the Farmer's Educational and Cooperative Union. Later known as the National Farmers' Union, the organization gained popularity on the Great Plains and in the Midwest.

The Conquest of the West

The first government agents and army scouts to cross the Mississippi spoke of a barren area entirely unfit for agriculture. In 1810, Zebulon Pike defined the Great Plains—the undulating sea of grass that stretched from longitude 100° west to the Rocky Mountains—by its aridity. The report accompanying Major Stephen Long's 1820 expedition described the region as "a dreary plain, wholly unfit for cultivation, and of course uninhabitable by a people depending upon agriculture for their subsistence." Long's famous phrase, the "Great American Desert," passed into the popular vernacular and was featured on maps of the United States for many years after. Accustomed to temperate eastern climes, travelers to the High Plains appeared shocked by its lack of trees, sparse vegetation, and seasonal extremes. Traditional agriculture did not seem possible in this semi-arid environment.

However, another image took hold in the American mind, one that rendered agriculture instrumental to the settlement of the West in the 1800s. Inspired by Jefferson's agrarian vision for the United States, and informed by the ideology of Manifest Destiny, citizens began to regard the West as a garden, a pastoral paradise for the taking. One of the first to publicize this idea was explorer John Frémont, who insisted that agriculture could flourish on the plains. Similar advertisements abounded in railroad publications from the 1860s. Many believed that bringing the plains under cultivation would encourage moisture; in the famous expression of the time, "rain would follow the plow."

Interest in the West following the Louisiana Purchase of 1803 focused on its valuable fur trade, other trading opportunities, and minerals. In the 1830s, emigrants established farms in Oregon's fertile Willamette Valley. The Mormons pioneered irrigated agriculture by diverting streams and building canals in Salt Lake City from the late 1840s. In California, a produce economy grew up around San Francisco and the Central Valley servicing Gold Rush mining towns with wheat, wine, and fruit. However, these represented localized pockets of agricultural activity. Of a total 1.5 million American farmers in 1850, only 119,000 tended lands west of the Mississippi.

It was the passing of attractive land laws that enticed Americans and Europeans to the West in number. Land and prosperity were connected under the Homestead Act of 1862, legislation allotting 160 acres of "free land" to citizens over the age of twenty-one who had never fought against the United States. (The latter provision was dropped in 1866 to allow ex-Confederates to file claims.) Title was granted after five years of cultivation or payment could be commuted after six months at $1.25 an acre. Fifty-seven percent of farms on the frontier were established under the Homestead Act. Settlers also purchased plots at auction or from land speculators.

Beginning in the late 1860s, families stacked their belongings into wagons and headed west in droves. Kansas, the Dakotas, and Nebraska attracted more than 430,000 land claims before 1895. Between 1896 and 1920, the homestead boom spanned Montana, the Dakotas, Colorado, Oklahoma, and New Mexico. The first homesteads were built in streambeds and along rivers. After these prized lots were taken, settlers staked claims on the prairie. Faced with a dearth of wood and water, farmers built houses from sod and dug wells. Many settlers planted corn or wheat as cash crops and kept a small vegetable plot or garden. However, customary agricultural practices proved ill suited to western terrain. Less corn grew on 160 acres in west Kansas than on 40 acres in Illinois. Contending with a lack of tools, limited labor, and occasional plagues of grasshoppers, many first-generation farmers elected to go back east or push on to the Pacific. The agrarian dream nonetheless had a powerful allure, and there were always sod busters willing to try their luck on the prairie.

Great Plains farmers learned to adapt. Many remedied the lack of timber for fencing by planting Osage orange hedges. Mennonites from Germany introduced Turkey Red Wheat, a hardy variety that withstood harsh prairie winters. In the 1870s, Colorado landowners led by George Washington Swink tapped water from the Arkansas River to grow cantaloupes and sugar beets. Technological advances aided the western farmer. Wind pumps, barbed wire, grain drills, sulky plows, and mechanical reapers improved productivity and labor efficiency. The railroad brought a revolution in transportation, allowing farmers to gain supplies and ship their products to market swiftly and easily. Some even believed that the steel wires of the railroad encouraged rain. Heavy rains indeed fell west of longitude 97° west between 1878 and 1887, bringing with them a flood of hopeful farmers.

Although cattle had been raised at Spanish missions since the 1700s and pioneers such as William Sublette had brought steers to Wyoming in the 1830s, the cattle kingdom rose to dominance in the western economy only after the Civil War. The industry began in Texas, where enterprising outfits such as the XIT Ranch capitalized on the availability of grassland and the abundance of longhorn cattle (some 5 million by 1866) to build a successful ranching economy. Cattle freely roamed the range until the spring and fall roundups, when cowpunchers drove herds to railheads, bound for the Chicago stockyards. Some 10 million animals were driven out of Texas between 1865 and 1890. By the 1870s, the cattle industry had spread across the Central and Northern Plains. As demand for higher quality meat increased, shorthorns and herefords replaced the scrawny but resilient longhorns. The open range gave way to closed pasture in the 1880s following the invention of barbed wire and escalating land feuds between homesteaders and cattlemen.

The late 1800s brought a time of depression for the agricultural economy of the West. Homesteaders faced problems of overproduction and falling market prices. Between 1866 and 1894 wheat prices fell from $2.06 a bushel to just 49 cents. The summers of 1886 and 1894 were among the driest on record. Many farmers faced starvation and destitution. Between 1890 and 1900, the number of farms in western Kansas declined from 14,300 to 8,900. Life was equally desperate for ranchers. Overstocking of the open range caused prices to plummet, and when the blizzards of 1887 hit, up to 85 percent of the cattle perished. Writing in 1901, William D. Johnson of the U.S. Geological Survey called the settlement of the Great Plains an "experiment in agriculture on a vast scale. It nevertheless ended in total failure."

Much of the trans-Mississippi region had been brought into cultivation by 1900. Wheat proliferated east of the Rockies, cattle and sheep grazed the intermountain West, and speciality crops grew on Pacific slopes. With the majority of western lands receiving less than twenty inches of rainfall a year, successful agriculture remained dependent on irrigation. The federal government played a crucial role in making the environment more suitable for farming. The TIMBER CULTURE ACT of 1873 allotted free title to 160 acres if one quarter of that area was planted with trees, while the Desert Land Act of 1877 gave 640 acres to settlers who agreed to water their land, although such measures were sometimes rendered ineffective by fraud. Recognizing a need for the federal government to help organize water projects, Congress passed the Newlands Reclamation Act of 1902, a landmark scheme that assigned the Reclamation Service (later the Bureau of Reclamation) the task of overseeing reclamation projects. Seen as second only in significance to the Homestead Act, the Newlands Act irrigated the West through a series of dams along watercourses including the Salt River in Arizona and the Truckee and Carson Rivers in Nevada. By 1924, federal projects had watered 1.2 million acres in the region.

From Golden Age to Disaster
Government irrigation programs, technological innovation, a strong export economy, and a growing urban population delivered a golden age to American farmers in the early years of the twentieth century. Public confidence ran high, as did prices for agricultural products. World War I provided a further boost to grain, stock, and cotton markets. Land became a valuable commodity, the price of farm lots doubling in Iowa between 1914 and 1920. Meanwhile, Congress sought to address the limitations of the original Homestead Act, increasing allotments for western crop and animal producers to 640 acres under the Kinkaid Act of 1904, the Enlarged Homestead Act of 1909, and the Stock Raising Homestead Act of 1916.

The early 1900s witnessed a commercial revolution in American agriculture. Technological improvements increased efficiency and productivity. Some 17,000 tractors were produced annually by 1917. That year, Henry Ford unveiled the Fordson, a maneuverable tractor affordable to the small farmer at $750. Farmers became increasingly adept at managing crops and animals to maximize output. Scientists genetically altered corn to breed a more productive hybrid seed. Advances in veterinary science resulted in the near elimination of tick fever in cattle by 1914. The American landscape increasingly bore the hallmarks of commercial agriculture. Farmers in Connecticut and New York concentrated on fruit production; Minnesota, Wisconsin, and Michigan were renowned for dairy; the midwestern farmer favored corn and soybeans; wheat and alfalfa grew on the Great Plains; and cotton and tobacco remained staples in the South. The tendency towards rationalization reached its apogee in California, where Central Valley farmers developed a lucrative fruit-and-vegetable enterprise based on commodity exchanges and supply controls. Large-scale industrialized producers came to dominate the market in the Far West based on capital investment, vertical integration, and cheap migrant workers lacking union representation.

The period of agricultural prosperity that marked the early 1900s came to an end in the 1920s. Crop prices decreased as war demand and relief programs faltered. Many small farmers had overextended themselves to meet wartime exigencies. Mechanization, increased acreage under cultivation, a declining birthrate, and protectionism created a surfeit of agricultural products. Prices plummeted, with gross income from agriculture declining from nearly $17 billion in 1919 to less than $12 billion ten years later. The situation became more acute after the Wall Street Crash of 1929, which caused a massive fall in the domestic produce market as a consequence of mass unemployment. In 1932, grain prices ran at twelve cents per bushel; hogs rated at three cents a pound. In 1933, the index of farm prices stood at 70, from a figure of 148 four years earlier.

Farmers in the Midwest faced environmental as well as economic catastrophe. A dry spell beginning in 1931 brought parched crops, cracked earth, and dust storms. Many farmers abandoned their plots, leaving more loose topsoil to be whipped up by strong winds. Historians continue to debate the cause of the Dust Bowl, positing drought, inappropriate agricultural practices, and an exaggerated belief in human ingenuity as contributory factors.

On 14 April 1935, a day known as Black Sunday, dust storms darkened the sky from the eastern seaboard to the Rockies, an area of some 100 million acres. In the worst-affected regions—Oklahoma, Kansas, Texas, Colorado, and New Mexico—the "Dirty Thirties" caused crop failures, livestock die-offs, and a bout of respiratory ailments. One eyewitness recalled how "all we could do about it was just sit in our dusty chairs, gaze at each other through the fog that filled the room and watch that fog settle slowly and silently, covering everything—including ourselves—in a thick, brownish gray blanket." Around 500,000 people

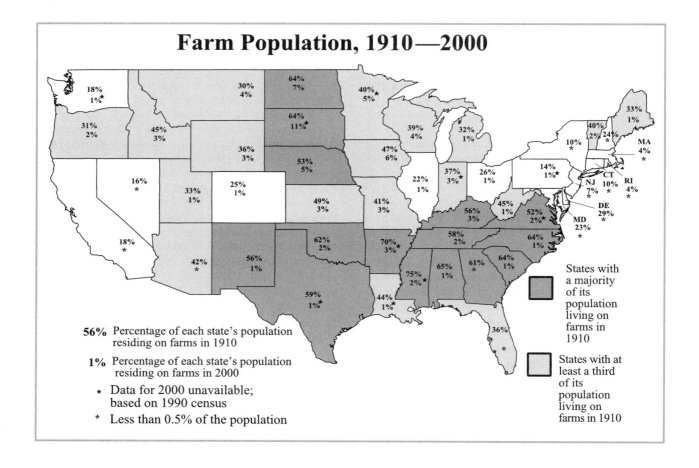

Farm Population, 1910—2000

56% Percentage of each state's population residing on farms in 1910

1% Percentage of each state's population residing on farms in 2000

★ Data for 2000 unavailable; based on 1990 census

* Less than 0.5% of the population

States with a majority of its population living on farms in 1910

States with at least a third of its population living on farms in 1910

chose to leave the Midwest during the 1930s, a migration epitomized by the flight of the Okies to California.

The New Deal

Having pledged a "New Deal for the American People" at the Democratic National Convention in July 1932, Franklin Delano Roosevelt took office in March 1933, determined to tackle the social and economic malaise wrought by the Great Depression. Judging it imperative to keep the country farming, New Deal reforms were quick to focus on agriculture. Agrarian communities received crop subsidies, credit relief, and soil conservation programs to the tune of $1 billion. Such measures continued a historic involvement of the federal government in promoting agriculture. However, FDR's activist program inaugurated a new level of intervention. Where the Hoover administration had previously advocated voluntary crop supply restrictions and limited help for cooperatives, Roosevelt committed the government to agricultural planning, production, distribution, and financial subsidy on an unprecedented scale.

The centerpiece of legislation for the American farmer was the Agricultural Adjustment Act (AAA) of May 1933. The AAA sought to stabilize crop prices and farmers' incomes by controlling the production of seven basic

commodities. The federal government was authorized to negotiate with producers to reduce acres under cultivation, while a tax on processors further discouraged production. Farmers received compensatory checks for leaving land fallow, a handout that the government hoped would prevent loan foreclosures. Between 1934 and 1935, the AAA successfully reduced the amount of land given over to tobacco and cotton, but it failed to have a discernible impact on staples such as wheat, hogs, corn, and dairy. Critics pointed out that the AAA favored large and efficient producers (with more land to put aside) over tenants and sharecroppers. In 1936, the U.S. Supreme Court ruled the tax on processors unconstitutional, resulting two years later in a revised act that compensated producers who instituted soil conservation measures.

The Commodity Credit Corporation (CCC) of October 1933 allowed the government to purchase crops and distribute them in such a way as to prevent price rises. Commodities that could be stored were withheld from sale, while perishable goods were given to charitable organizations and schools or were exported. The CCC paid more than the market value, providing an important safety valve for farmers in need of support. Other measures designed to shore up the agricultural sector by providing financial aid included the Farm Credit Act of 1933, the Resettlement Administration of 1935, and the FARM SECURITY ADMINISTRATION (1937).

New Dealers prized rural electrification as a way of modernizing American agriculture. As of 1930, only 571,000 of the 6.3 million farms in the country featured electrical lighting. Regional disparities existed. California, Utah, and Washington were well catered for, not least because of the preponderance of irrigation programs requiring considerable power to run. In Arkansas and Louisiana, by contrast, only one in one hundred farms had electricity. A public scheme providing loans for power lines and generating stations was established under the TENNESSEE VALLEY AUTHORITY (TVA) in 1933. Created by executive order the same year, the Electric Home and Farm Authority (EHFA) forwarded low-cost loans to farmers for electrical equipment. Inspired by the success of the TVA in bringing power to agrarian communities in Alabama, Georgia, Mississippi, and Tennessee, Roosevelt inaugurated a countrywide Rural Electrification Administration (REA) in May 1935. Improvements in production techniques, mechanization, rural education, and domestic life marked the REA as an outstanding success.

The REA's motto, "if you put a light on every farm, you put a light in every heart," nonetheless failed to stem the flow of families leaving the land for the city. In New England, the number of farms dropped from 103,255 in 1930 to 21,670 in 1950. The three million African American tenants and sharecroppers who worked in the South faced poverty, unemployment, and racial discrimination. The New Deal brought benefits in the form of loans, price support, and soil restoration, yet it proved of limited effectiveness in improving the overall lot of the farmer. It was only with World War II and increased demand for foodstuffs, increases in industrial employment, and buoyant prices that the agricultural sector fully recovered. That said, FDR's New Deal remained immensely important for American agriculture, as programs enacted in the 1930s set a pattern of government regulation that persisted for the rest of the twentieth century.

Agriculture since 1945

The post-1945 period saw American agriculture become more industrialized and capital intensive. Acreage under cultivation increased with advances in technology, irrigation, and genetic engineering. The number of individual farm units declined markedly. At the time of the Civil War, 60 percent of the American population was involved in agriculture. By 1972, this figure stood at 4.6 percent. At the beginning of the twenty-first century, less than 2 percent of Americans were engaged in farming.

The commercialization of agriculture ensured that the small family farm lost out to large, efficient, and mechanized producers able to benefit from economies of scale. In 1955 John H. Davis, former assistant secretary of agriculture, coined the phrase "agribusiness" to describe the new breed of corporations that controlled the entire agricultural process from production to marketing,

making deals with individual producers to deliver crops at fixed prices. The modernization of American agriculture brought significant regional changes. As consolidated agribusiness took hold of the modern plantation in the South, cattle, hogs, peanuts, and soybeans became as important as cotton. Meanwhile, the tenure system that had dominated southern agriculture since the late 1800s was replaced by owner or part-owned farms. By 1974, only 12 percent of farms in South Carolina were operated by tenants.

A single American farmer produced enough food to sustain ninety-seven other people by the 1990s (compared to five in 1800), a level of extremely high productivity facilitated by technology. Irrigated farming dominated the Great Plains after technicians in the 1950s developed machinery capable of siphoning water from the Ogallala Aquifer, a vast underground supply buried from fifty to three hundred feet below the prairie. From the 1940s onwards, chemicals, pesticides, and herbicides (many of which, including DDT, were developed for use in World War II and converted for peacetime use) further raised output. Crop duster planes scattered chemical supplements over the land in order to combat pests and aid seed growth. The use of such additives greatly increased production, although critics, notably the biologist Rachel Carson in her 1962 best-seller, *Silent Spring*, warned of dangerous ecological side effects. Citizen lobbying and scientific research led to a domestic ban on DDT in 1969. Since the late twentieth century, the agricultural sector has looked to biotechnology and genetic modification as ways to maximize crop resilience, productivity, and consumer appeal.

American agriculture continued to rely on government assistance. Federal programs centered on keeping farmers on the land by taking acreage out of cultivation and offering price supports, as with the Soil Bank Program of 1956 and the Food and Agriculture Act of 1965. Federal policy also encouraged production under subsidy for export to the developing world. With urban dwellers demanding high-quality, low-cost food, the rural sector faced considerable pressures in the post-1945 period. Boycotts and tractor convoys were among the tools employed by the National Farmers Organization, organized in 1955, and the National Farm Workers Association, founded in 1962, to lobby for improvements in rural standards of living. In the twenty-first century, prosperity for the farmer remains dependent on land, weather, market prices, capital investment, and government aid. As of 2000, federal spending on the agricultural sector ran at $71.1 billion, perhaps a testament to the special place of the farmer in American life.

BIBLIOGRAPHY

Berry, Wendell. *The Unsettling of America: Culture and Agriculture.* San Francisco: Sierra Club Books, 1986.

Cochrane, Willard W. *The Development of American Agriculture: A Historical Analysis.* 2d ed. Minneapolis: University of Minnesota Press, 1993.

Cowdrey, Albert E. *This Land, This South: An Environmental History.* Lexington: University Press of Kentucky, 1996.

Cronon, William. *Changes in the Land: Indians, Colonists, and the Ecology of New England.* New York: Hill and Wang, 1983.

Fite, Gilbert C. *Cotton Fields No More: Southern Agriculture, 1865–1980.* Lexington: University Press of Kentucky, 1984.

Hart, John Fraser. *The Land That Feeds Us.* New York: Norton, 1991.

Hurt, R. Douglas. *American Agriculture: A Brief History.* Ames: Iowa State University Press, 1994. A good introductory work that offers suggested readings at the end of each chapter.

Knobloch, Frieda. *The Culture of Wilderness: Agriculture as Colonization in the American West.* Chapel Hill: University of North Carolina Press, 1996.

MacDonnell, Lawrence J. *From Reclamation to Sustainability: Water, Agriculture, and the Environment in the American West.* Niwot: University Press of Colorado, 1999. A study of irrigation in western agriculture through four case studies.

Meinig, Donald, *The Shaping of America: A Geographical Perspective on 500 Years of History.* 3 vols. New Haven, Conn.: Yale University Press, 1986–1998. Includes Atlantic, continental, and transcontinental America.

Opie, John. *The Law of the Land: Two Hundred Years of American Farmland Policy.* Lincoln: University of Nebraska Press, 1987. A critical review highlighting the problematic assumptions behind American agriculture.

Saloutos, Theodore. *The American Farmer and the New Deal.* Ames: Iowa State University Press, 1982.

Starrs, Paul. *Let the Cowboy Ride: Cattle Ranching in the American West.* Baltimore: Johns Hopkins University Press, 1998.

Worster, Donald. *The Dust Bowl: The Southern Plains in the 1930s.* New York: Oxford University Press, 1979. A seminal account of the "Dirty Thirties" by one of the West's foremost environmental historians.

John Wills

See also **Agrarianism; Cattle; Dust Bowl; Farmers' Alliance; Granger Movement; Great Plains; Homestead Movement; Insecticides and Herbicides; Irrigation; Livestock Industry; New Deal; Plantation System of the South; Reclamation; Sharecroppers; Tobacco Industry.**

AGRICULTURE, AMERICAN INDIAN. The American Indians began farming on the North American continent approximately 7,000 years ago, when Native people in the area of present-day Illinois raised squash. During the next several thousand years, Indians east of the Mississippi River domesticated and cultivated sunflowers, goosefoot, and sump weed or marsh elder. Ancient farmers in Mesoamerica domesticated corn, or *Zea mays,* the cultivation of which spread northward after 3,400 B.C. and reached eastern North America about 2,000 years ago. By A.D. 800, many Indian groups had adopted maize agriculture, and by A.D. 1000, they had developed a complex agriculture based on three major crops—corn, beans, and squash—with a host of other plants providing supplemental crops. By the time of European contact they

Winnowing Wheat. This photograph by Edward S. Curtis, c. 1905, shows a Tewa woman working on part of a harvest in San Juan Pueblo, N. Mex. LIBRARY OF CONGRESS

were raising all types of corn known today: flint, flour, pop, dent, and sweet.

Agricultural Practices

Indian agriculture in the Southwest began as early as 4,000 years ago, when traders brought cultigens into this region from Mexico. By the beginning of the common era, the Indian farmers of the Southwest had made the seed selections and developed plant varieties best suited for the climate conditions in the region, from the cool, moist mountains to the hot, dry desert. Indian farmers in the Southwest began raising corn about 500 B.C. Southwestern farmers also cultivated several varieties of squash and beans. In contrast to eastern farmers, the southwestern agriculturists did not cultivate beans among the corn plants. Instead, they developed bush varieties that were self-supporting rather than vining. The development of bush beans was important because in the Southwest closely planted cultigens could not compete successfully for the limited soil moisture without irrigation. Besides corn, squash, and beans, southwestern farmers also cultivated cotton. Cotton probably reached the Southwest from Mexico about 300 B.C. The southwestern Indians valued the cotton fiber for weaving and the seed both for eating and for vegetable oil.

East of the Mississippi River, the men traditionally prepared the soil, but the women had the responsibility of planting, weeding, and harvesting the crops. Outside of the Southwest, Indian women had the major responsibility for domesticating plants, cultivating crops, and controlling the use of the land. They cleared the land for garden plots along streambeds or floodplains, where they could till the soil with their bone and stone hoes and plant with wooden dibble or digging sticks. Indian women domesticated and bred plants to the requirements of specific geographical locations. They bred corn plants to mature in a growing season that averaged from 200 days in Mesoamerica to 60 days in the northern Great Plains. They also bred corn to withstand the heat and desert conditions of the Southwest as well as the cool, moist areas of the present-day northern and eastern United States. Indian women maintained relatively pure corn varieties by planting seeds, such as blue, yellow, or red, sufficiently far apart in fields to prevent cross-pollination. Indian farmers used similar selection and planting techniques for beans, squash, and cotton.

Indian farmers did not fertilize their fields with organic matter. East of the Rocky Mountains they maintained soil fertility by planting beans in the same hills with their maize to add nitrogen to the soil. Indian agriculturists also used fire to control weeds and brush and to mineralize nutrients. Although burning depletes nitrogen and sulfur, it recycles organic-bound nutrients such as phosphorous, calcium, potassium, and magnesium. Contrary to popular belief, the Indians did not fertilize their corn with fish or teach the European immigrants to do so. Squanto apparently showed the Pilgrims how to use fish for fertilizer in 1621, but no evidence proves the Indians customarily followed this practice. Instead, Indian farmers abandoned exhausted croplands and cleared new areas for cultivation. Squanto knew about fertilization, but he probably gained that knowledge while a captive in Europe. The Indians preferred to rotate their fields instead of fertilizing to maintain crop productivity.

Land Tenure
In the present-day northern United States, the Indians adopted two forms of land tenure. Villages claimed sovereignty or exclusive ownership over an area, which other bands recognized. Within this general area of communal ownership, they recognized individual control of the gardens and fields. Family lineage usually determined who controlled and cultivated the land. The eldest woman of each lineage exerted overall control of the land. Each lineage retained the right to use those lands as long as the village remained on the site and the women cultivated the fields. Thus, ultimate land tenure depended upon village sovereignty over a particular area, and immediate, individual control of a field depended upon actual occupation and use. If a plot was cleared of trees and brush and planted with crops, it was automatically removed from the communal domain as long as the family continued to use it.

In the desert Southwest, land tenure differed slightly from that east of the Mississippi River. In contrast to eastern farmers, the women in the Southwest usually did not control the land. Their labor in the fields, however, gave them a right to a portion of the crop and the freedom to dispose of it without the permission of their husbands. Hopi women, however, controlled the land, inheriting it through a matrilineal system.

Several generalizations, then, can be made concerning the nature of Indian land tenure for agriculture. Title to a general territory was a group right, not an individual right. Usually, the Indians of North America did not think of private property as an absolute individual right or consider farmland a commodity that could be bought, sold, or permanently transferred in some fashion. The community owned the land, and the individual created a control or use claim by cultivating a specific plot. If arable land was plentiful, the individual's claim lapsed whenever the land became exhausted or abandoned. This characteristic of tenure was common in the present eastern United States. In the Southwest, where the climate limited arable land, an individual's claim to the fields remained valid even when they lay fallow. Tenure or control was not vested in an individual but with the lineage or household. This control unit could be either patrilineal or matrilineal, depending upon the particular Indian culture. Although a family or individual could claim additional land by clearing wasteland for cultivation, clan lineage determined the paramount right to it.

U.S. Government Policies
During the late eighteenth and early nineteenth centuries, some Indian groups, such as the Cherokees, adopted the Anglo-American practice of raising cattle, but they did not practice extensive agriculture, in part because whites often seized their lands. With the removal of many of the eastern nations west of the Mississippi River during the 1830s, the federal government attempted to teach these and other western nations the white man's methods of agriculture. The nomadic Indians of the Great Plains, however, rejected agriculture because the government attempted to remake their culture by insisting that the males learn to farm, whereas in the past only the women tended garden plots. Moreover, the federal government never provided adequate lands, instruction, technology, or financial support for the western nations to become self-supporting agriculturists. In 1887, the Dawes General Allotment Act enabled the federal government to begin the process of breaking up reservations by giving land to individuals, such as heads of households, to encourage farming. This legislation also opened Indian lands for white settlement, and it proved disastrous for Indian farmers. Many allotted Indians soon lost their lands to unscrupulous whites. At the same time, if an Indian landowner died without a will, federal policy mandated the division of all property equally among all the heirs. By the early twentieth century, many private Indian lands had been divided into sections too small to support farming operations. Heirship policy had removed approximately 7 million acres of Indian lands from cultivation by the mid-twentieth century. Heirship lands so fragmented reservations on the Great Plains that cattle raising proved impossible, and a lack of credit for seed, implements, and livestock prevented even subsistence agriculture. Consequently, the Bureau of Indian Affairs often leased Indian heirship and allotted land to white cattlemen because the Indian owners could not afford to use it for agriculture.

Witchitaw Village on Rush Creek. James Ackerman's lithograph, from an 1854 book on an exploration of the Red River in Louisiana in 1852, shows Wichita dwellings and fields. LIBRARY OF CONGRESS

During the twentieth century, environmental limitations in the West and federal Indian policy designed to assimilate and acculturate the Indians into white American society prevented the development of commercial agriculture on most reservations. In the Southwest, insufficient rangeland hindered agricultural development. Inadequate technical and financial support by the federal government also prevented the development of irrigation and further limited Indian agriculture. Many Indians in the Southwest, however, relied on stock raising for their income, and the San Carlos Apaches ranked among the most successful Indian cattlemen.

By 1950, however, Indian farmers averaged only $500 of income annually compared to white farmers, who earned $2,500 annually. At midcentury, most Indians still lived in rural areas, but they were not an agricultural people. By 1960, less than 10 percent of the Indian people farmed, down from 45 percent in 1940. Indian farmers could not meet their own basic economic and nutritional needs by farming because they did not have the necessary capital, technology, and expertise to practice successful agriculture. Indian farmers could not qualify for loans, and their farming operations prevented them from acquiring the capital to make improvements. Without land reform, few Indians had sufficient acreage to become commercial farmers. As a result, most Indians continued to lease their lands to white farmers and cattlemen. The continuation of these problems prevented the development of a viable Indian agriculture, and the matters of insufficient capital, inadequate credit, and heirship policy remained unsolved. By

the late twentieth century, although Indians controlled 52 million acres, including 10 million under private ownership, few Indians had any opportunity to become farmers. By 1997, only 10,638 Indian farmers remained and only 3,543 farmers earned $10,000 or more from agriculture. By the turn of the twenty-first century, Indian agriculture in the United States was insignificant and federal Indian agricultural policy had failed to help make the Indians successful small-scale farmers capable of meeting their needs for both subsistence and an adequate standard of living.

BIBLIOGRAPHY

Hurt, R. Douglas. *Indian Agriculture in America: Prehistory to the Present.* Lawrence: University Press of Kansas, 1987.

Matson, R. G. *The Origins of Southwestern Agriculture.* Tucson: University of Arizona Press, 1991.

Nabhan, Gary Paul. *Enduring Seeds: Native American Agriculture and Wild Plant Cultivation.* San Francisco: North Point Press, 1989.

Perdue, Theda. *Cherokee Women, Gender, and Culture Change, 1700–1835.* Lincoln: University of Nebraska Press, 1998.

Scarry, C. Margaret, ed. *Foraging and Farming in the Eastern Woodlands.* Gainesville: University of Florida Press, 1993.

Smith, Bruce D. *Rivers of Change: Essays on Early Agriculture in Eastern North America.* Washington, D.C.: Smithsonian Institution Press, 1992.

Wills, W. H. *Early Prehistoric Agriculture in the American South-west.* Santa Fe, N.Mex.: School of American Research Press, 1988.

R. Douglas Hurt

See also **Dawes General Allotment Act; Indian Economic Life; Indian Land Cessions; Indians and Tobacco.**

AGRICULTURE, DEPARTMENT OF.

In 1796 George Washington recommended creating a national board of agriculture to disseminate information on agricultural practices and award prizes for innovations. This goal was not realized until more than half a century later, but by the early 1820s Congress and most state legislatures had established agricultural committees. Agricultural societies and fairs in the same period attested to the widespread interest in improving farm techniques in a nation still overwhelmingly rural.

The Department of Agriculture originated in a roundabout way through the interest of Patent Office Commissioner Henry L. Ellsworth in farm machinery. In the late 1830s Ellsworth began collecting agricultural information and distributing to farmers seeds gathered overseas by embassy and military personnel. Starting in the 1840s, Patent Office annual reports began to include large sections related to agriculture, and in the 1850s the office initiated a modest research program. When the Civil War erupted, Southern Congressmen—who had questioned the constitutionality of a federal agricultural agency—left Washington. This allowed Congress to create a small Department of Agriculture (USDA) in 1862, which was given a broad mandate "to acquire and to diffuse . . . information on subjects connected with agriculture in the most general and comprehensive sense of that word. . . ." Shortly after President Abraham Lincoln signed the act on 15 May 1862, he appointed a successful Pennsylvania dairy farmer, Isaac Newton, to be the first commissioner of agriculture.

Soon the Department of Agriculture began hiring scientists and publishing regular statistics about commodity production and prices. Early research focused on improving plant and animal varieties. The passage of the Hatch Experiment Station Act in 1887 set up state agricultural experiment stations in the land-grant colleges that, with the cooperation and leadership of the Department's own investigators, rapidly propelled the United States to the forefront of scientific research in agriculture. In 1889 USDA attained the status of a cabinet department, and farm journalist Norman Jay Colman became the first secretary of agriculture.

Over the next thirty years, USDA steadily acquired new functions as Americans began asking the government to take on new roles. The Meat Inspection Act of 1890 gave USDA the job of inspecting exported meat, a function soon expanded to give the Department an extensive role in insuring the safety of domestic and exported foods. Also in the 1890s, the Department began to study nutri-tion, promote farm exports, and manage forestlands set aside for timber and recreation. It created two major agencies it later lost to other departments—the Weather Bureau (1890) and the Office of Road Inquiry (1893)—the latter of which evolved into the massive federal road-building program.

In 1914 the Smith-Lever Act set up an extension service to bring agricultural research directly to farmers. Like the experiment stations, extension was an early example of federal cooperation with the states. The 1914 Cotton Futures Act was the first of many laws putting USDA in the business of market regulation, while the Federal Farm Loan Act of 1916 launched the Department's first credit program for farmers. USDA also played an important role in increasing food production during World War I.

Following the collapse of wartime farm commodity prices in 1920, agriculture entered a new era in which surplus production would depress farm income and create demands for new forms of assistance. The Department's fledgling economics work was bolstered by the 1922 establishment of the Bureau of Agricultural Economics, whose analyses were designed to help farmers make better management decisions. The Capper Volstead Act of 1922 encouraged farmers to form cooperatives that would give them more control of supply purchases and marketing. The main interest, however, was in finding a way to restore farm prices to their previous levels. Bills setting up innovative farm programs were vetoed in the 1920s, but the onset of a general depression after 1929 made the government more willing to act.

The New Deal under Franklin D. Roosevelt and secretary of agriculture Henry A. Wallace transformed USDA into its modern form with a sweeping string of initiatives that greatly enlarged the scope of government action. The Agricultural Adjustment Act of 1933 attacked the surplus problem through both price supports and acreage reductions. While farm programs have been much modified since then, most of the subsequent tools for price support and adjustment were first used under the 1933 act. Soil conservation, which aimed to stop erosion on farmland, complemented the government's effort to remove marginal land from cultivation. Excess farm commodities were also reduced through school lunch and food stamp programs. The Department gave special attention to poor farmers through credit, education, tenant, and resettlement programs. It also made a substantial commitment to bringing the quality of rural life closer to urban standards through electrification and farm-to-market roads. Most of these new functions brought new agencies with them, and by 1940 USDA's employment had reached a peak of close to 100,000. Overall, USDA programs helped mitigate the worst effects of the Depression.

With the advent of World War II, farm surpluses became an advantage rather than a liability. USDA quickly shifted gears to encourage maximum production and to get all citizens involved in growing gardens and saving essential products like fats. Price controls and rationing, while not under USDA administration, kept food affordable while permitting as much as possible to be diverted to military use.

The postwar era began a period of rapid change for agriculture. Years of research came to fruition in an unprecedented technological revolution that resulted in the most rapid productivity increases in agricultural history. New farm machinery, better seeds, new animal breeds, and the rapid adoption of new chemical fertilizers and pesticides modernized agriculture. Farms became larger, more specialized, and more highly capitalized. Undercapitalized producers who could not compete left their farms, often for big cities. This created problems for rural areas losing population. In the mid-1950s USDA began planning rural development programs to find nonagricultural solutions to rural economic problems. Meanwhile, the productivity revolution had brought a return of surplus production and sent many commodity prices down to their minimum support levels. New conservation programs took some land out of cultivation.

Orville L. Freeman, secretary under President Kennedy, set about expanding USDA's non-farm programs. Seeking to turn surplus production to an advantage, he obtained greatly enlarged food stamp, food distribution, school lunch, and rural development programs to combat poverty and did much to increase donations to poor countries overseas, which had become significant under the Food for Peace (PL 480) program of 1954. The Department also began its first serious efforts to desegregate under Freeman and began to regulate pesticides more stringently because of environmental concerns about their effects on wildlife and human health.

The 1970s were a time of expanding farm exports and strong prices. At the same time, food programs grew to become over half the Department's budget. When exports tumbled in the early 1980s, many farmers were plunged into financial crisis. Congress responded with the Food Security Act (1985), which strengthened export promotion and conservation programs and gave farmers more flexibility to respond to market conditions. These trends continued with new legislation in 1990 and 1996. Free trade agreements in 1993 (North American Free Trade Agreement) and 1994 (Uruguay Round of the General Agreement on Tariffs and Trade) put American agriculture more than ever in a global context.

USDA went through a substantial reorganization beginning in 1994 that reduced the number of agencies and consolidated most farm programs. At the beginning of the twenty-first century, USDA remains one of the largest federal agencies. While still putting agriculture first, it serves all Americans through a wide range of programs covering food safety, nutrition, food subsidies, rural development, and forestry.

BIBLIOGRAPHY

Baker, Gladys L., et al. *Century of Service: The First 100 Years of the United States Department of Agriculture.* Washington, D.C.: U.S. Department of Agriculture, 1963.

Gaus, John M. *Public Administration and the United States Department of Agriculture.* Chicago: Public Administration Service, 1940.

Kerr, Norwood A. *The Legacy: A Centennial History of the State Agricultural Experiment Stations, 1887–1987.* Columbia: Missouri Agricultural Experiment Station, University of Missouri, 1987.

Rasmussen, Wayne D. "90 Years of Rural Development Programs." *Rural Development Perspectives* 2, no. 1 (October 1985): 2–9.

Douglas E. Bowers

See also **Agricultural Price Support; Agriculture; Hatch Act; Meat Inspection Laws; Smith-Lever Act.**

AGUE, a malarial disease transmitted by mosquitoes and characterized by intermittent fevers and chills, was a leading cause of chronic illness across America from the colonial period until 1900. While malaria is most often found in tropical and subtropical climates, American settlers were plagued by ague near wetlands, even in the temperate north. Because the disease originated in Europe and Africa, its effects on Native American populations were often devastating. By 1900, draining wetlands for agriculture and development led to a dramatic decline in malarial disease in all regions but the South; there, eradication required extensive public health campaigns during the first half of the twentieth century.

BIBLIOGRAPHY

Cassedy, James H. *Medicine in America: A Short History.* Baltimore: Johns Hopkins University Press, 1991.

Leavitt, Judith Walzer and Ronald L. Numbers, eds. *Sickness and Health in America: Readings in the History of Medicine and Public Health.* Madison: University of Wisconsin Press, 1997.

Loren Butler Feffer

See also **Epidemics and Public Health; Malaria; Wetlands.**

AIDS. *See* **Acquired Immune Deficiency Syndrome.**

AIDS QUILT displays, sponsored by the NAMES Project, have appeared across the nation since 1987 as a memorial to individuals who have died of AIDS-related causes. First created by the homosexual activist Cleve Jones, each panel of the quilt measures three by six feet, decorated with mementos or special items put together by loved ones of the deceased to commemorate his or her life. By 2000, the quilt contained more than 44,000 panels and was displayed for the sixth time in full on the Capitol

AIDS Quilt. Thousands of panels, each one commemorating a life and a death, are displayed on the Mall in front of the Capitol. PAUL MARGOLIES

Mall in Washington, D.C. Displays of portions of the quilt throughout the country help to convey the personal as well as the quantitative impact of the disease.

BIBLIOGRAPHY

Jones, Cleve, and Jeff Dawson. *Stitching a Revolution: The Making of an Activist.* New York: HarperCollins, 2000.

Ruskin, Cindy. *The Quilt: Stories from the NAMES Project.* New York: Pocket Books, 1998.

Kristen L. Rouse

See also **Acquired Immune Deficiency Syndrome (AIDS).**

AIR CAVALRY was formed on 16 June 1965, when the U.S. Army received Department of Defense authorization to organize the First Cavalry Division (Airmobile). The First Cavalry was designed to increase troop mobility and included more than four times the number of aircraft in a standard army division. Although the intensifying war in Vietnam provided the immediate impetus, the army had been contemplating such a division for several years. Army planners believed the military could have fought more effectively during the Korean War if American tech-

nology had been better exploited to provide superior mobility. Moreover, lack of mobility had been fatal to the French at Dien Bien Phu in 1954. In Vietnam the landscape and climate impeded American ground mobility, yet the army needed to move swiftly to offset the enemy's initiative and familiarity with the country.

The air mobility concept involved airborne maneuvers during an engagement, long-distance moves, airborne logistical and medical support, flexible and informed command through aerial command posts, and superior firepower. In a theater such as Vietnam, where American control of the air afforded protection from enemy fighter aircraft, helicopter and propeller-driven gunships could offer ground troops the sustained gunnery support that jet-powered airplanes could not. Transports bearing side-firing weapons could circle a ground target while maintaining extended fire at a constant altitude and range. By the spring of 1966 the C-47, the military version of the Douglas DC-3 transport, was armed with three 7.62 mm miniguns, electrically powered versions of the Gatling gun, each capable of firing six thousand rounds per minute. The appearance of its tracers earned this gunship the moniker "Puff the Magic Dragon." Other types of gunships were progressively more heavily armed.

The usual gunship, however, was a helicopter. During the American ground buildup in Vietnam, the standard helicopter gunship was a heavily armed version of the UH-1B Huey carrying fourteen rockets and door-mounted M60, 7.62 mm machine guns. Later, the AH-1G Cobra helicopter gunship appeared, carrying seventy-six air-to-ground rockets, a 7.62 mm minigun, and a 40 mm grenade launcher capable of firing four hundred rounds a minute. With this weaponry the Cobra gunship in the early 1970s figured heavily in army tests of the First Cavalry Division. Later reorganized, the unit added tank battalions to challenge Soviet armored superiority in Europe.

The airmobile concept proved to be one of the more successful American military innovations of the Vietnam War. In late 1965 the First Cavalry Division entered the Ia Drang Valley in a campaign to destroy North Vietnamese troops in the Central Highlands, who threatened to cut South Vietnam in two. In the battle of Plei Me, units of the division, uplifted to new positions at least forty times, helped drive Vietnamese soldiers into Cambodia. Thereafter, the army increasingly sought enough helicopters to give all infantry units air mobility whenever operations made it desirable. The success of American airpower in Vietnam opened a new era in the history of land warfare, as evidenced in U.S. tactics in subsequent conflicts, such as the PERSIAN GULF WAR OF 1991 and the KOSOVO BOMBING in 1999.

BIBLIOGRAPHY

Johnson, Lawrence W., III. *Winged Sabers.* Harrisburg, Pa.: Stackpole Books, 1990.

Krohn, Charles A. *The Lost Battalion*. Westport, Conn.: Praeger, 1993.

Moore, Harold G., and Joseph L. Galloway. *We Were Soldiers Once—and Young*. New York: Random House, 1992.

Young, Marilyn B. *The Vietnam Wars 1945–1990*. New York: HarperCollins, 1991.

Russell F. Weigley / E. M.

See also **Helicopters; Korean War; Vietnam War.**

AIR CONDITIONING. Mechanical air conditioning made its first appearance at the turn of the twentieth century. Defined as the control of temperature, humidity, cleanliness, and distribution of air, it largely grew out of successful efforts to control humidity levels indoors. Systems were custom designed for each installation and were used to either add moisture to the air or remove the excess depending upon the application. Two basic types of air conditioning were marketed: comfort air conditioning for establishing the optimum conditions for human comfort, and process air conditioning for setting the most favorable atmospheric conditions for industrial processing.

One of the first comfort air conditioning systems was designed by Alfred Wolff for the trading room of the New York Stock Exchange in 1902, while Willis Carrier installed a process air conditioning system in the Sacketts-Wilhems Printing Company the same year. Carrier has long been air conditioning's most famous engineer due in part to his pioneering status and in part to the visibility of his company, which established a dominant place in the industry first through its engineering expertise and then through its strong patent position.

For decades mechanical air conditioning systems were used primarily to correct the atmospheric conditions created by deleterious man-made environments such as crowded auditoriums and schools or dry, overheated factories. Process air conditioning far outstripped comfort air conditioning as the most lucrative market for the first fifteen years after its invention. Air conditioning systems were installed in various processing facilities such as munitions, candy, pasta, film, and textile factories to stabilize the handling properties of hygroscopic materials which absorbed moisture from the air. In fact, the term "air conditioning" was coined in 1904 by the textile engineer Stuart Cramer, who advocated the new technology over the old-fashioned practice of "yarn conditioning," which relied on adding moisture to the materials themselves rather than the air.

Comfort air conditioning eventually blossomed as an outgrowth of the mechanical ventilation systems required by state law in schools, theaters, and auditoriums. Large crowds of people in a single room invariably created unpleasant atmospheric conditions that early public health officials believed to be unhealthy as well. However, it was not until builders became more concerned with comfort than with health that air conditioning thrived. One of the

first film exhibition companies to exploit the appeal of comfort air conditioning was Balaban and Katz, which in 1917 equipped the Central Park Theater in Chicago with a system that was widely imitated. Operating expenses for these systems were kept low by recirculating a portion of the air from the theater, and the new patent pool, Auditorium Conditioning Corporation (anchored by Carrier Engineering Corporation and four partner companies), controlled that technology, receiving royalties on an estimated 90 percent of new air conditioning installations until the company was dissolved in 1945.

With the onset of the Great Depression, manufacturers of household appliances joined traditional air conditioning companies in pursuit of the residential market. Older air conditioning systems relied upon a water supply to cool either the machinery or the air, but around 1932 engineers at the De La Vergne Machine Company developed the air-cooled compressor, which freed air conditioning from its plumbing connections and accelerated the development of the air conditioner as a discrete plug-in appliance. Residential air conditioning now came in two basic types: a central air conditioning system, tied to the house with plumbing connections and air distribution ducts, and a window air conditioner that the consumer could install anywhere there was an electrical outlet.

Widespread adoption of air conditioning in homes and office buildings waited until the post–World War II building boom. The appearance of new designs, such as the block office building with extensive interior space that had no access to windows, meant that mechanical ventilation was a necessity. Air conditioning, with its provision for cooling, was an advantageous choice to counter the heat of large glass windows, high levels of interior lighting, numerous occupants, and increasing use of office machines. This combination of design and use of modern office buildings meant that nearly all required cooling no matter how moderate the local climate. In the home, the decision whether or not to buy air conditioning was often made by speculative builders rather than the individual consumer. Beginning around 1953, builders of tract homes routinely included air conditioning in their developments, underwriting the cost of the equipment by eliminating traditional design features such as high ceilings, overhanging eaves, and cross ventilation, which had originally helped homeowners cope with hot weather. This conscious substitution of air conditioning for passive cooling techniques made modern homes, like modern office buildings, dependent upon their mechanical systems. By 1957, the use of air conditioning in homes and offices shifted peak usage of electricity from the traditional high mark of December to August's cooling season.

The widespread adoption of air conditioning was accompanied by changes in the public's standard for comfort. Before air conditioning, consumers planned food, clothes, work, and entertainment around ways to mitigate the impact of hot weather. With a technological alternative, those hot-weather rituals declined, and their usefulness has been supplanted by a greater concern with privacy, efficiency, and unconstrained choice which makes them seem poor alternatives. Air conditioning has not only underwritten modern architectural design in the postwar era but also a modern lifestyle.

BIBLIOGRAPHY

Ackermann, Marsha E. *Cool Comfort: America's Romance with Air Conditioning.* Washington, D.C.: Smithsonian Institution Press, 2002.

Arsenault, Raymond. "The End of the Long Hot Summer: The Air Conditioner and Southern Comfort." *Journal of Southern History* 50 (1984): 587–628.

Cooper, Gail. *Air Conditioning America: Engineers and the Controlled Environment, 1900–1960.* Baltimore: Johns Hopkins University Press, 1998.

Ingels, Margaret. *Willis Haviland Carrier: Father of Air Conditioning.* Garden City, N.J.: Country Life Press, 1952. Reprint, New York: Arno Press, 1972.

Gail Cooper

AIR DEFENSE. Although American cities were not in danger of attack by air during World War I (1914–1918), American military planners did not overlook the ordeal of Great Britain under such attacks. Remote as the possibility was of bombing raids against the United States during the interwar period, war studies contemplated guarding against them through the use of fighter aircraft, antiaircraft artillery (AAA), and ground observers. In 1935, the United States War Department established regional air defense systems, incorporating radar by the end of the decade. By 7 December 1941, air defense systems—including radar, fighters, AAA, ground observers, and control centers—had been established along both continental coasts, in Panama, and in Hawaii. After the Japanese attack on Pearl Harbor, and the failure of the base's primitive radar system, air defense nationwide was greatly expanded. However, by 1943 it was evident that neither Germany nor Japan was capable of inflicting serious damage on American cities, so the air defenses were demobilized by the war's end.

After World War II (1939–1945), the tensions of the Cold War stimulated rapid development of air defenses throughout the continental United States, beginning with the 1946 establishment of the Air Defense Command (renamed Aerospace Defense Command in 1968). By 1950, construction of an improved radar network had begun, and several hundred modern radar stations would blanket the country a decade later. Until the electronic network came into full operation, a Ground Observer Corps of about 500,000 civilian volunteers provided backup warning capability. Radar surveillance extended northward into Canada, as well as seaward, by way of patrol ships and radar platforms. Intensive research and development in the application of electronic computers to air defense culminated in the early 1960s in the deployment of about twenty Semi-Automatic Ground Environment (SAGE) comput-

erized combat operation centers networked throughout the country. In 1958, the United States and Canada pooled their air defense resources for the common defense of their territories and established the North American Air Defense Command (NORAD). NORAD headquarters was established in a cavern under Cheyenne Mountain near Colorado Springs, Colorado.

With the coming of the space age, the world powers focused on developing inter-continental ballistic missiles (ICBMs). To counter this new threat, a Ballistic Missile Early Warning System was established, with special radar stations in Alaska, Greenland, and the United Kingdom. By the early 1960s, the ICBM had replaced the manned bomber as the chief instrument of intercontinental air warfare. Consequently, air defense priorities were readjusted to meet the new threat. In the early days of anti-ICBM defense, the system relied on the deterrent of overwhelming ICBM retaliation in the event of an attack—a concept known as "mutually assured destruction." The 1970s saw the construction of a Ballistic Missile Defense System, code-named "Safeguard." The system included radar, short- and long-range missiles, and supporting automatic data-processing equipment. Original plans called for large-scale deployment throughout the United States; but the Strategic Arms Limitation Talks (SALT I) between the United States and the Soviet Union resulted in a treaty, ratified by the U.S. Senate in July 1972, limiting each country to only two antiballistic missile (ABM) defenses. The United States constructed only one Safeguard missile site, in North Dakota, in 1974.

In March 1983, President Ronald Reagan called for the Strategic Defense Initiative (SDI), an advanced ground- and-space-based anti-ballistic missile system that would change the nature of the Cold War and hasten the demise of the Soviet Union. Western critics charged that SDI was too complex and expensive, but to Reagan, that was the whole idea. He foresaw that the Soviets could not compete with the United States in the race for SDI, not only with the vast amounts of money required for research and development, but also with the cutting-edge technology required. Even as American critics mocked the potential of SDI, attempting to trivialize it with the derisive name "Star Wars," the Soviets themselves gave the greatest credence to it by actually walking out of the October 1986 summit in Reykjavik, Iceland, when President Reagan refused their demands to give it up. Rejecting the doctrine of mutually assured destruction, President Reagan even offered to share SDI, when completed, with the Soviets. While research on SDI continued into the twenty-first century, and the system remained undeployed, it is recognized as a turning point not only in the technology of air defense, but in the Cold War that it helped to end with Western victory.

The Persian Gulf War (1991) saw the use of the Patriot Air-Defense Missile. Placed around Allied troop bivouacs, ports, and airbases in the Persian Gulf region, the fully automated Patriot tracked incoming Iraqi SCUD missiles with sophisticated radar, giving roughly six minutes of warning and launching automatically when the probability of an interception and kill was highest.

The Patriot system was originally intended as an anti-aircraft defense, but the needs of the war led the Army to improvise its new anti-missile role. While the military and White House hailed it as a success, critics claimed the effectiveness of the Patriot was overrated. Overall the system served as a valuable asset, not only militarily, but also politically, in reassuring Israel of American protection from Iraqi attacks.

The terrorist attacks on the United States that occurred on 11 September 2001 brought the difficulties of air defense to national attention once again. While the unconventional nature of the attacks made them difficult to counter, the tragedies certainly illuminated the ongoing desire for, as well as the complexities of, what General Dwight D. Eisenhower described in 1946 as a weapon that could "hit a bullet with another bullet."

BIBLIOGRAPHY

Atkinson, Rick. *Crusade: The Untold Story of the Persian Gulf War.* Boston: Houghton Mifflin, 1993.

Boyne, Walter J. *Beyond the Wild Blue: A History of the U.S. Air Force, 1947–1997.* New York: St. Martin's Press, 1997.

Craven, Wesley F. and James L. Cate, eds. *The Army Air Forces in World War II. Volume 1, Plans and Early Operations. Volume 6, Men and Planes.* Chicago: University of Chicago Press, 1948–58.

Goldberg, Alfred, ed. *A History of the United States Air Force, 1907–1957.* Princeton, N.J.: Van Nostrand, 1957.

Leyden, Andrew. *Gulf War Debriefing Book: An After Action Report.* Grants Pass, Oreg.: Hellgate Press, 1997.

Walker, Martin. *The Cold War: A History.* New York: Henry Holt, 1994.

Christian Mark DeJohn
Denys Volan

See also **Cold War; Defense Policy; Defense, National; 9/11 Attack; Nuclear Weapons; Persian Gulf War; Radar; Strategic Defense Initiative.**

AIR FORCE, UNITED STATES. The National Security Act of 1947 created the United States Air Force (USAF) after nearly three decades of debate within the government and the military about how best to integrate airpower into an overarching national defense structure. With its ability to project power rapidly across the globe, the air service also reflected greater U.S. involvement in the geopolitical arena. Several themes framed airpower's development and employment. First, technology permeates airpower history. Regardless of the vehicle—airplane, spacecraft, guided missile, or satellite—U.S. airmen consistently sought to expand existing technological boundaries. Second, organization and doctrine fueled debates regarding how best to employ airpower to achieve national policy goals. Third, the expanding nuclear inven-

tory thrust airpower to the forefront of strategy calculations. Finally, dramatically changing diplomatic contexts compelled airmen to adapt to shifts in strategy, operations, and tactics. Thus USAF history is more than an account of a series of wars and operations; it reflects a fundamental transformation in the U.S. conception of war fighting.

Early Cold War

In the aftermath of World War II, USAF leaders believed airpower had proven decisive. The large bomber formations that devastated German and Japanese cities appeared to confirm interwar theories proposed by such individuals as the Italian theorist Giulio Douhet, the Royal Air Force leader Sir Hugh Trenchard, the maverick American airman Brigadier General William "Billy" Mitchell, and the instructors at the U.S. Army's Air Corps Tactical School. The new service's leaders framed their institutional identity in terms that emphasized airpower's strategic role. This produced a force structure that favored long-range heavy bombers and nuclear weaponry at the expense of tactical platforms. Airpower enthusiasts argued that the nuclear bomber's "city-busting" capability rendered traditional armies and navies obsolete as long as the United States maintained a nuclear monopoly. In the early postwar years, this perspective engendered animosity among air, land, and sea service leaders. Tensions peaked in 1949 over the decision to procure the intercontinental B-36 bomber. In what became known as the "Revolt of the Admirals," sea service leaders argued vehemently against the B-36 program because it threatened navy plans for a supercarrier with expanded naval aviation roles.

In the early Cold War years, geopolitical crises intensified debates regarding the air force's role in national defense. In 1948, the Berlin crisis signaled increasing tensions between the Soviet Union and the West. The USAF launched Operation Vittles to supply Soviet-blockaded Berlin, thus offering wider possibilities for employing military forces in conflicts short of war. When the Soviet Union exploded its first atomic device in 1949, U.S statesmen realized they could no longer rely on nuclear monopoly and strategic bombing to protect the nation and its allies. On 25 June 1950, North Korean forces attacked South Korea and ushered in a new era of limited war, one operating below the Cold War's nuclear threshold. USAF forces applied the full range of conventional airpower—strategic bombing, interdiction, close air support, reconnaissance and surveillance, and search and rescue—to support United Nations operations on the Korean peninsula. In Korea, airpower proved less decisive than the strategic bombing campaigns of World War II, although in many ways it kept U.S. forces from being overrun at the outset of the war. In this war along the periphery of great power conflict, U.S. leaders refused to introduce nuclear weapons for fear of provoking a general war with the Soviet Union and China. The Korean War also witnessed a technological shift as jet aircraft revolutionized the quest to dominate the skies.

Technological developments characterized the remainder of the 1950s as the USAF sponsored research into new airframe designs, engine technologies, and guided missile systems. The Eisenhower administration's "New Look" strategy shaped an aviation force structure that employed both long-range bomber aircraft and nuclear weapons. The Strategic Air Command (SAC), equipped with weapons systems like the B-47 Stratojet, the B-58 Hustler, and the B-52 Stratofortress, formed the nuclear deterrent force's backbone, giving the USAF a true "global strike" capability. Later in the decade, research into missile technology promised to add medium-range and intercontinental missiles to the arsenal. Following SAC's lead, tactical forces mirrored the strategic fleet's nuclear emphasis. Fighter and fighter-bomber designs, including the F-100, F-104, and F-105, represented attempts to reconcile tactical and theater needs with nuclear battlefield requirements. The emphasis on deterrence and nuclear operations, however, created a void in the USAF's conventional war-fighting capability.

Vietnam

The VIETNAM WAR shaped a generation of American airmen's views about how to employ airpower. USAF leaders entered the conflict convinced that airpower could be most effective when employed against strategic industrial targets. In 1964, when President Lyndon B. Johnson committed U.S. forces to support the South Vietnamese government, USAF planners proposed attacks against ninety-four strategic targets in the North. Johnson opted for a more limited campaign—Operation Rolling Thunder—designed to coerce communist leaders to the negotiating table while simultaneously confining the war to Southeast Asia. Johnson and his defense secretary, Robert S. McNamara, envisioned a gradually escalating airpower campaign that increased the pressure on North Vietnamese leaders. U.S. leaders expended the bulk of American air strikes in vain attempts to interdict men and materiel destined for the battlefields of the South along the Ho Chi Minh trail. In the South, General William Westmoreland used airpower, including B-52 strikes, in concert with land forces in large-scale "search and destroy" sweeps designed to eradicate Viet Cong guerrilla units. The twin culminating points—the siege at Khe Sanh and the Tet Offensive—that signaled the failure of the Johnson administration's strategy occurred in 1968. Airpower, working in close cooperation with ground forces, ended a siege by 40,000 North Vietnamese soldiers of the Marine firebase at Khe Sanh. The strength of the Khe Sanh siege coupled with the general uprising during Tet, the Vietnamese New Year, convinced the American public that Johnson's gradualist strategy had failed. Republican Richard M. Nixon rose to the presidency with a mandate to extract the United States from the Vietnam quagmire.

In 1971 and 1972 Nixon took advantage of improved relations with the Soviet Union and the People's Republic of China to unleash airpower first against North Vietnamese conventional forces moving south in Operation Linebacker I, and later against communist industrial centers of gravity in Operation Linebacker II. New technologies including precision-guided munitions and more capable airframes combined with traditional bombing raids in short, violent campaigns that apparently helped bring the North Vietnamese back to the peace talks in Paris, although they did not prevent the North from achieving its overall goals in the war. USAF leaders argued that the Linebacker campaigns confirmed strategic bombing doctrine despite the U.S. failure in Vietnam and the dramatic changes in the international political context.

Desert Storm and the End of the Cold War

For the remainder of the 1970s and into the 1980s the USAF honed its tactical proficiency. The Vietnam experience indicated that a pilot or aircrew's chances of surviving aerial combat increased dramatically after the first ten missions. Red Flag, centered at Nellis Air Force Base, Nevada, emerged as the USAF's aerial combat training center to simulate those first ten combat missions. Its value became apparent in 1990–1991.

In August 1990, Iraq's dictator Saddam Hussein occupied the Persian Gulf nation of Kuwait. The UN provided a mandate for coalition action to restore Kuwait's sovereignty and to reduce the Iraqi military threat. In the largest airlift since Operation Vittles, Military Airlift Command's (MAC) C-5, C-141, and C-130 and SAC's KC-135 and KC-10 fleets created an air bridge that deployed materiel to bases in Saudi Arabia and neighboring countries. The USAF's complete offensive airpower capability—B-52, F-117 Stealth, F-111, F-15, F-16, EF-111, F-4, and Special Operations forces—also deployed to support the coalition. A robust support fleet, including KC-135 and KC-10 refueling tankers, E-3A airborne warning and control aircraft, and intelligence-gathering and command and control assets, bolstered the offensive capabilities brought to bear against Iraq. United States Central Command's joint force air component commander, Lieutenant General Charles Horner, led efforts to create an air strategy to isolate Iraqi ground forces, defeat Iraqi air defense networks, destroy nuclear, chemical, and biological weapons facilities, and reduce Iraqi ground forces' combat effectiveness. Although Desert Storm left Saddam Hussein's regime intact and his weapons programs still dangerous enough to necessitate UN weapons inspections, its success showcased USAF planning, command and control, precision weaponry, and space support, and above all it vindicated post-Vietnam investments in training and exercises. Many observers concluded that Desert Storm represented the first wave of a revolution in military affairs.

The end of the Cold War and the Soviet Union's collapse ushered in a host of changes for the USAF. Nuclear weapons no longer provided the air service's raison d'être. While nuclear deterrence remained vital to U.S. national security, the Defense Department leaders aligned the strategic forces under a separate unified command in 1992. The organizational scheme that had served the service since its inception also changed as SAC, MAC, and Tactical Air Command (TAC) stood down. The twenty-first century's streamlined air force integrated all combat forces under a single command, Air Combat Command (ACC). All airlift and air refueling assets came under the command of Air Mobility Command (AMC). Paradoxically, the Cold War victory did not decrease the USAF's operations tempo or its deployment commitments. Since 1991, USAF personnel served around the globe to keep the peace, offer humanitarian assistance, deter aggression, and enforce UN resolutions. The hallmarks of USAF airpower reside in the service's core competencies—air and space superiority, global attack, rapid global mobility, precision engagement, information superiority, and agile combat support. These six competencies reflect more than fifty years of institutional continuity and development.

BIBLIOGRAPHY

Clodfelter, Mark. *The Limits of Air Power: The American Bombing of North Vietnam.* New York: Free Press, 1989.

Futrell, Robert Frank. *Ideas, Concepts, Doctrine: Basic Thinking in the United States Air Force.* 2d ed. 2 vols. Maxwell Air Force Base, Ala.: Air University Press, 1989.

———. *The United States Air Force in Korea. 1950–1953.* Rev. ed. Washington, D.C.: Office of Air Force History, 2000.

Hallion, Richard P. *Storm over Iraq: Air Power and the Gulf War.* Washington, D.C.: Smithsonian Institution Press, 1992.

Lambeth, Benjamin S. *The Transformation of American Air Power.* Ithaca, N.Y.: Cornell University Press, 2000.

Melinger, Phillip S., ed. *The Paths of Heaven: The Evolution of Airpower Theory.* Maxwell Air Force Base, Ala.: Air University Press, 1997.

Thompson, Wayne. *To Hanoi and Back: The United States Air Force and North Vietam, 1966–1973.* Washington, D.C.: Air Force History and Museums Program, 2000.

Anthony Christopher Cain

See also **Air Force Academy; Air Power, Strategic; Aircraft, Bomber; Aircraft, Fighter; Berlin Airlift; Bombing; Korean War, Air Combat in; Persian Gulf War.**

AIR FORCE ACADEMY. President Dwight D. Eisenhower signed legislation creating the U.S. Air Force Academy on 1 April 1954, fulfilling recommendations that had been made by air-minded leaders since World War I. The academy was conceived as a four-year undergraduate institution, leading to the B.S. degree and a regular air force commission. The first class entered in the summer of 1955, using facilities at Denver, Colorado, prior to occupation of the permanent site at Colorado Springs three years later. The group, numbering 207, graduated on 3 June 1959. The academy reached its full authorized enrollment of 2,500 in 1962, and in 1964 legislation set the authorizations for the Military and Air Force Academies at 4,417, the same as the Naval Academy's. Each congressman was authorized five appointments to each academy at any one time and could nominate several individuals to compete for each vacancy. The 1964 legislation also increased the period of obligatory service after graduation from three to five years, beginning with the class of 1968.

From its start, the Air Force Academy departed from service academy tradition by providing advanced and accelerated studies beyond the prescribed curriculum. In 1964 the academy instituted a system of specialized-majors programs whereby every cadet elected a substantial part of his course work in one of several dozen areas. For its first forty years, the academy retained an all-military faculty, subsidizing graduate work for line officers at civilian institutions prior to faculty tours of about four years. A severe cheating incident in 1965 received national attention and resulted in more than 100 cadets leaving the academy. Reassessment of the academy's academic, athletic, and military systems left the traditional honor code unchanged—all cadets pledge, "We will not lie, steal, or cheat, nor tolerate among us anyone who does"—although certain rigidities in cadet life were reduced.

More than two-thirds of all graduates (including 85 percent of those physically qualified) have entered pilot training. The academy instituted an optional thirty-six-hour flying program in light aircraft for upperclassmen in 1968, and cadets could participate in glider and parachute activities. The academy has vigorously recruited minority youths. In 1973 it ended compulsory chapel attendance. Graduates received numerous decorations in Southeast Asia, where 90 lost their lives. Academy graduates through 1973 numbered 6,942, including 16 Rhodes scholars.

On 7 October 1975 President Gerald R. Ford signed legislation that allowed women to enroll for the first time in all of the nation's service academies, including the Air Force Academy. Despite a storm of protest and criticism from certain quarters, the first women enrolled at the academy on 28 June 1976, and the first class of women graduated in 1980. In 1993 the academy changed another of its long-standing policies and began to hire civilian instructors as members of the faculty, so that by the end of the century civilians composed about 20 percent of the faculty. Academy graduates through the end of the century numbered 34,065 cadets (more than half of whom were still on active duty), including 31 Rhodes scholars.

BIBLIOGRAPHY

Bruegmann, Robert, ed. *Modernism at Mid-century: The Architecture of the United States Air Force Academy.* Chicago: University of Chicago Press, 1994.

Ray L. Bowers / c. w.

See also **Military Academy; Naval Academy.**

AIR POLLUTION became a matter of concern in the United States in the nineteenth century, when population growth and industrialization increased the number of wood and coal furnaces, which generated enough smoke to overwhelm natural air-filtering processes and threaten human health. Coal-burning facilities in industrial centers like Pittsburgh, Pennsylvania, and smelter towns like Butte, Montana, spewed tons of smoke, soot, ash, and gases into the atmosphere. Boosters often applauded the smoke as a sign of prosperity. But by the late nineteenth century the hazards of smoke were better understood. Airborne pollutants became especially dangerous when a so-called thermal inversion occurred, trapping the pollutants and allowing them to build up for days in warm air overlaid by a cold air mass. In these cases, human exposure could and did cause respiratory illnesses and deaths. As early as 1815 some local governments required that manufacturers control emissions, and during the Progressive Era most major cities passed ordinances to control the "smoke nuisance." However, events such as the Donora smog of 1948, a thermal inversion in which twenty residents of Donora, Pennsylvania, died and more than five thousand fell ill, suggested that local efforts to abate air pollution were not sufficiently safeguarding public health.

In 1955, Congress enacted the first federal air-quality legislation, providing research and technical assistance to states. States and localities remained responsible for regulating factory emissions and the brown automobile-induced "photochemical smog" over urban basins, but this act expanded federal authority over air-quality control. With the CLEAN AIR ACT of 1963 Congress increased aid to states and for the first time allowed federal control over automobile emissions. In 1965 Congress enacted a law requiring automakers to install emissions-reducing devices on all cars built and sold in the United States after 1967.

The Air Quality Act of 1967 dramatically expanded federal control. It authorized federal regulation of stationary as well as mobile pollution sources, required states to impose air-quality standards in problem regions, and allowed federal controls where states failed to act. The Clean Air Act of 1970, a centerpiece of the burgeoning environmental movement, directed the ENVIRONMENTAL PROTECTION AGENCY (EPA), established the previous year, to set National Ambient Air Quality Standards (NAAQS). Under this law the EPA identified the principal air pollutants (particulates, sulfur dioxide, carbon monoxide, hydrocarbons, nitrogen dioxide, ozone, and, after 1978, lead), set maximum allowable levels for each, and required that states draft plans for meeting the federal standards. The act also required that stationary polluters secure federal permits contingent on their use of "best available" abatement technology and mandated that automakers achieve a 90 percent decrease in vehicle emissions by 1985 (a timetable relaxed somewhat by amendments in 1977).

In general these laws set maximum pollutant levels but left it to the polluters to find ways to meet them. This tactic, called "technology forcing," spurred automakers to adopt catalytic converters in the 1970s and compelled the

Air Pollution. Smog blankets New York City skyscrapers in May 1973. NATIONAL ARCHIVES AND RECORDS ADMINISTRATION

"big three" automakers (GM, Ford, and Chrysler) in 1993 to launch their Clean Car Initiative, a joint pledge to develop vehicles averaging ninety miles per gallon by 2003. When California insisted that zero-emission vehicles account for 10 percent of all new cars in the state by 2003, setting a precedent that other large states like New York were likely to follow, automakers stepped up efforts to develop new emissions technology. Much research focused on the "hybrid," an electric car with a small, supplementary fuel-burning motor that could radically cut emissions and reduce gasoline consumption. The first mass-produced hybrid, a Honda, was available in the United States in 1999. Other research focused on hydrogen-fed fuel cells, whose only exhaust is water vapor.

Industrial interests pleaded for less-stringent standards, claiming air-pollution control is expensive and economically damaging. Industries blamed the soaring inflation of the 1970s on environmental-protection legislation. In response the EPA delayed requirements and devised strategies for reducing pollution without placing undue burdens on manufacturers. For example, the "bubble" concept, formally adopted in a 1979 amendment to

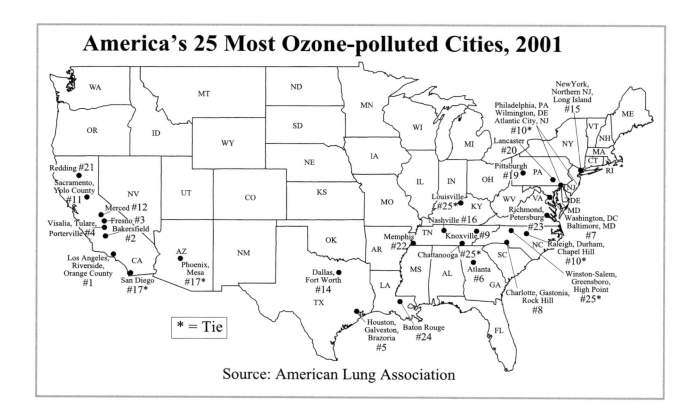

America's 25 Most Ozone-polluted Cities, 2001

New York, Northern NJ, Long Island #15

Philadelphia, PA Wilmington, DE Atlantic City, NJ #10*

Lancaster #20

Pittsburgh #19

Redding #21

Sacramento, Yolo County #11

Merced #12

Fresno #3

Visalia, Tulare, Porterville #4

Bakersfield #2

Los Angeles, Riverside, Orange County #1

San Diego #17*

Phoenix, Mesa #17*

Dallas, Fort Worth #14

Louisville #25*

Nashville #16

Richmond, Petersburg #23

Washington, DC Baltimore, MD #7

Memphis #22

Knoxville #9

Chattanooga #25*

Atlanta #6

Raleigh, Durham, Chapel Hill #10*

Winston-Salem, Greensboro, High Point #25*

Charlotte, Gastonia, Rock Hill #8

Houston, Galveston, Brazoria #5

Baton Rouge #24

* = Tie

Source: American Lung Association

the Clean Air Act, placed an imaginary bubble over an entire region and required the air in the bubble to meet NAAQS levels. Firms in the same bubble could trade pollution rights with each other, allowing excess pollution at one source as long as it was offset by lower emissions at another. (The previous approach had forced each individual "stack" to meet national standards.) By defining each factory as part of a larger air shed, the bubble concept was a step toward an ecosystem-oriented approach. Along these lines, the Clean Air Act of 1990 capped the nation's total sulfur oxide emissions and allowed firms to set up a nationwide market in pollution permits.

By the late 1990s, such measures had significantly reduced major air pollutants in most metropolitan areas. However, haze in scenic nonurban areas such as the Grand Canyon caused by nearby urban areas and power plants had emerged as a growing problem. Moreover, as environmentalists adopted an increasingly global perspective, they identified new air pollution issues. Among the issues was acid precipitation, sulfur dioxide and other chemicals that originate in industrial areas, drift across political borders, and wash out of the atmosphere with rain, snow, or fog, causing acid deposits in lakes and forests. Another new issue, especially following the discovery in 1985 of an "ozone hole" over Antarctica, was depletion of the Earth's ozone layer caused by chlorofluorocarbons (CFCs) used in aerosol propellants, foam plastics, refrigerants, and industrial processes. A third issue that entered environmental debates in the 1980s concerned the emission of "greenhouse gases," especially carbon dioxide, that trap heat in the Earth's atmosphere and, according to many scientists, cause global-scale climate changes. These transnational and global air-quality issues stoked the fears of the industrial interests regarding greater government intervention in their affairs. Such reactions reflect the "out of sight, out of mind" axiom that long characterized responses to air pollution. Efforts to control visible pollution, like smoke or smog, traditionally won widespread support. But the less visible and more theoretical problems attracted detractors, who questioned the scientific methods of pollution-control proponents and raised the specter of economic stagnation to forestall stricter regulations.

Along with global air quality, attention focused on indoor air quality. Radon, a naturally occurring radioactive gas that collects in basements across much of the nation, was identified as a significant carcinogen. Secondary tobacco smoke raised substantial alarm in the 1990s, when many businesses, municipalities, and even states (notably California in 1994) banned SMOKING in indoor workplaces. Mold spores, chemical fumes, and other invisible pollutants that circulate indoors were identified as health hazards in the 1980s, giving rise to the term "sick building syndrome" and forcing businesses to listen more carefully when employees complained of "bad air" in the workplace. Thus despite massive government intervention and the hopes of some environmentalists, air pollution did not disappear. The most visible pollutants generally lessened, but research revealed that air pollution was more complex, widespread, and intimate than previously thought.

BIBLIOGRAPHY

Andrews, Richard N. L. *Managing the Environment, Managing Ourselves: A History of American Environmental Policy.* New Haven, Conn.: Yale University Press, 1999.

Bailey, Christopher J. *Congress and Air Pollution: Environmental Policies in the USA.* Manchester, U.K., New York: Manchester University Press, 1998.

Grant, Wyn. *Autos, Smog, and Pollution Control: The Politics of Air Quality Management in California.* Aldershot, U.K., Brookfield, Vt.: Edward Elgar, 1995.

Hays, Samuel P. *Beauty, Health, and Permanence: Environmental Politics in the United States, 1955–1985.* New York: Cambridge University Press, 1987.

Miller, E. Willard, and Ruby M. Miller. *Indoor Pollution: A Reference Handbook.* Santa Barbara, Calif.: ABC–CLIO, 1998.

Stradling, David. *Smokestacks and Progressives: Environmentalists, Engineers, and Air Quality in America, 1881–1951.* Baltimore: Johns Hopkins University Press, 1999.

Switzer, Jacqueline Vaughn. *Environmental Politics: Domestic and Global Dimensions.* New York: St. Martin's Press, 1994.

Dennis Williams / w. p.

See also **Acid Rain; Automobile Industry; Electric Power and Light Industry; Energy Industry; Global Warming; Ozone Depletion.**

AIR POWER, STRATEGIC. Strategic air power employs aerial weapons to bypass the surface battlefield and to strike at key wartime industries. Typical targets are the transportation network, including railroads, bridges, marshaling yards, and harbors; the petroleum industry, including refineries and tank farms; the electrical generating system; and the aerospace industry. Intensive strategic bombardment campaigns, such as those conducted against Germany and Japan in World War II, embrace many target systems and compare to traditional sieges, in which all elements of a nation's economy and military strength—including its means of sustenance and its civilian labor force—come under attack.

Because the industrial strength of a nation lies principally in its cities, cities themselves are targets in an all-out strategic bombardment campaign. Heavy air attacks such as those in World War II against London, Hamburg, and Tokyo caused much criticism because of the great loss of life among civilians. Opponents claimed that bombardments strengthened opponents' will to resist and were inconclusive militarily; proponents argued that they shortened wars and obviated land invasions.

Strategic bombardment, first attempted by Germany in World War I with zeppelin and Gotha raids on London, did little more than terrify the population. However, the British people visualized the future development of air power and in 1917 established an air force independent of the army and navy, with a section under Gen. Hugh Trenchard charged with bombing industrial and rail targets far behind the enemy lines.

Seeking answers to the riddle of the stabilized western front in France that had taken such a heavy toll of lives, the then Maj. William (Billy) Mitchell, an aviator with the advance echelon of the U.S. Army, visited Trenchard and became an exponent of the new doctrine. But American air power developed slowly and achieved no significant bombing capability before the war's end.

Despite Mitchell's advocacy, after World War I the concept of strategic air power all but vanished in the United States, with American military aviation confined to an observation role. A small group of Billy Mitchell disciples maintained his enthusiasm through the 1930s, however, and by extending the theory and strategy of air power later became the American air leaders of World War II.

The early years of World War II shocked traditionalists who had disparaged the wartime role of air power. The Battle of Britain demonstrated the possibility of losing a war through air action alone, and Japanese air attacks in 1941 sank or immobilized most of America's Pacific fleet at Pearl Harbor and, two hours later, sank Britain's battleship *Prince of Wales* and battle cruiser *Repulse* in the western Pacific. The age of the battleship ended, giving place to air power.

After winning the Battle of Britain, the only force the British could bring to bear against the Axis powers on the continent was through strategic bombardment. At first merely diversionary, the RAF Bomber Command grew in size and its raids began to cripple the German economy. When the RAF turned to night operations to minimize losses, with a consequent degradation of bombing accuracy, it adopted "area" bombing to destroy civilian morale.

In January 1943, President Franklin D. Roosevelt met with Prime Minister Winston Churchill at Casablanca and agreed to the round-the-clock Combined Bomber Offensive against Germany. Although the tempo of the offensive increased steadily, Germany held out—despite an economy in complete collapse. The results of strategic air power seemed more conclusive in the Pacific war, where the Japanese were seeking channels for surrender even before the United States dropped atomic bombs on Hiroshima and Nagasaki.

With the advent of nuclear weapons and rocket missiles, many believed that air power alone would win total wars of the future. While rocketry was being developed, the United States organized the Strategic Air Command (SAC) with aircraft of intercontinental capabilities. Gen. Curtis E. LeMay is credited with creating the global nuclear force of SAC. By 1973 SAC was composed primarily of B-52 jet bombers and Minuteman intercontinental ballistic missiles (ICBMs). Although Russia forged ahead of the United States in numbers of ICBMs and warhead yield, the United States still held a slight lead in missile-launching submarines (see AIR DEFENSE).

The end of the Cold War brought an end to the arm's race, and with it the apparent likeliness of nuclear war. The creation of Air Combat Command (ACC) in 1992 grew out of the need to reevaluate the role of strategic air power in the post–Cold War world, unifying SAC, which had become identified almost entirely with nuclear deterrence, and the Tactical Air Command (TAC), which had overseen cooperative missions between the Air Force and ground and naval forces. The end of the Cold War also sparked the old debate about the ability of strategic air power alone to win wars, with an increasing number of analysts suggesting that aerial bombardment campaigns—from those in Korea and Vietnam to those in Iraq and Serbia—had increasingly become a panacea for politicians unwilling to commit the ground troops that appeared to be necessary to achieve their objectives. Incontestibly a cornerstone of the American military's *tactical* repertoire, strategic air power came under attack in the 1990s for being given too central a place in the country's *strategic* thinking.

BIBLIOGRAPHY

Borowski, Harry R. *A Hollow Threat: Strategic Air Power and Containment before Korea.* Westport, Conn.: Greenwood Press, 1982.

Fredette, R. H. *The Sky on Fire.* New York: Holt, Rinehart and Winston, 1966.

LeMay, Curtis E. *America Is in Danger.* New York: Funk and Wagnalls, 1968.

Eric J. Morser
Dale O. Smith

See also **World War II, Air War against Germany; World War II, Air War against Japan.**

AIR TRAFFIC CONTROLLERS STRIKE (1981).

The Professional Air Traffic Controllers Organization, the union representing the controllers employed by the FEDERAL AVIATION ADMINISTRATION, called a strike in August 1981 to press the government for salary increases, reduced hours, and better retirement benefits. When the more than eleven thousand striking members disobeyed President Ronald Reagan's ultimatum to return to their posts, they were fired. The government decertified the union as the controllers' bargaining agent and imposed severe fines and criminal charges against some union officials. Despite President Bill Clinton's reinstatement of the dismissed air traffic controllers in 1993, many observers believed Reagan's success in breaking this strike demonstrated the growing weakness of organized labor in the United States.

BIBLIOGRAPHY

Nordlund, Willis J. *Silent Skies: The Air Traffic Controllers' Strike.* Westport, Conn.: Praeger, 1998.

Shostak, Arthur B., and David Skocik. *The Air Controllers' Controversy.* New York: Human Sciences Press, 1986.

Andrew Feldman / A. R.

See also **Strikes.**

AIR TRANSPORTATION AND TRAVEL pro-

gressed slowly in the early years of powered flight. Few revenue-generating applications were developed before World War I (1914–1918), but capabilities advanced rapidly thereafter. Using army aircraft, the U.S. Army began airmail service in 1918 with a route from Washington to New York. Under auspices of the post office, service expanded steadily, with coast-to-coast routes attained by 1924. Growth led to the development of specialized mail planes. Aeromarine Airways, which operated flying boats between Key West, Florida, and Havana, Cuba, and between Miami, Florida, and the Bahamas, began the first significant passenger service in 1919. Operations were too limited to ensure profitability, however, and they ended in 1923. The eighteen-seat LawsonL-4 of 1920, perhaps the first true airliner, was tested experimentally. Major progress came in 1924 with the Stout corrugated metal aircraft. Ford acquired the aircraft in 1925 and produced it as the famous AT-4 trimotor, the first multiplace (having the ability to transport passengers) airliner in service.

Between the World Wars

Air travel struggled through most of the postwar decade, and infrastructure development lagged. Airfields were few, as were navigational aids and pilot certifications necessary for safe long-range operation. Pilots flew under visual flight rules, although airmail led to both light and radio beacons. But air travel still was not an option for the general public. In addition to safety concerns, long-distance air journeys could be an ordeal with numerous stops, weather delays, and slow, noisy, uncomfortable aircraft. Only 6,000 air passengers were carried in 1926, and coast-to-coast service could cost $400.

Passage of the Airmail Act of 1925 (Kelly Act) and the Air Commerce Act of 1926 led to major changes. Airmail service was contracted to private firms, and payments were lucrative. The Bureau of Air Commerce was formed under the Department of Commerce, and it established programs for pilot licensing and airways development. But the United States still trailed Europe in scheduled service, primarily due to the distances between American cities. A major difference was that airlines remained private enterprises, whereas in most countries airlines were government owned. Some small carriers were also manufacturers. Ryan Air Lines of San Diego, which built the *Spirit of St. Louis* for Charles Lindbergh, was not untypical. The single-engine Boeing 40A of 1927 was the first combined passenger- and mail-carrying aircraft, offering coast-to-coast service in twenty-seven hours with two passengers. The Ford AT-4 was joined by the Stinson 6000, Fokker F-10, and Boeing 80 trimotors, which expanded passenger service although carriers still required the subsidy of airmail. The Lockheed Vega, an advanced single-engine design, also enjoyed success from 1928 on.

Few investors showed interest in airlines before the Lindbergh flight from New York to Paris in May 1927, which suddenly impressed upon the public the potential of long-range air transportation. Equally noteworthy, another single-engine airplane piloted by Clarence Chamberlin and carrying his wealthy backer Charles Levine flew nonstop from New York to Germany only two weeks later. Levine thus became the first transatlantic air passenger. The "Lindbergh boom" resulted in, among other things, the formation of some forty-four airlines by 1929. Pan American, founded in 1927 by Juan Trippe as an East Coast airmail contractor, became the "chosen instrument" for international passenger service. With Wall Street backing, large, complex aviation holding companies formed, generally through acquisitions that combined manufacturing with passenger and mail carriers. The most notable were Curtiss-Wright, United Aircraft and Transport (UATC), the Aviation Corporation (AVCO), and North American Aviation (NAA), largely financed by General Motors.

Business flying and limited cargo service also began in the 1920s. Corporations and wealthy executives used the Stinson Detroiter, a comfortable cabin monoplane, and the amphibian Loening Air Yacht. The potential of air cargo, especially for low-bulk, high-value, time-sensitive goods, such as fresh fruit, film, repair parts, and medicines, had already been recognized, and many airlines, including predecessors of later major carriers, were originally formed for cargo. Almost from the beginning, cargo planes were used for illicit purposes. Some individuals used air cargo to transport liquor during Prohibition. A somewhat comparable twenty-first century counterpart is the use of small aircraft and old airliners for covert transportation of drugs from Latin and South America.

In 1930, more than 40,000 passengers were carried per month, and airmail approached 800,000 pounds per month. But the fleet still was small, with only about 640 aircraft, of which 400 were single-engine. The Airmail Act of 1930 made the postmaster general the de facto head of commercial aviation. Mail rates were established by volume rather than weight, providing incentives for the development of larger aircraft and the growth of passenger service. Three transcontinental routes were awarded to Transcontinental and Western Air (TWA), United Airlines (part of UATC), and American Airways (part of AVCO). But increasing allegations of a near-monopoly in airmail, with three companies, UATC, AVCO, and GM/NAA holding 90 percent of the market, led to the suspension of all contracts in 1934. The resulting legislation required true competitive bidding on contracts. New competitors entered the business, but

lower prices led to losses for all. Air transportation was in crisis, exacerbated by the Great Depression.

In another reform, holding companies were required to separate their manufacturing and transport operations. United Airlines became independent from UATC, American Airways (later American Airlines) from AVCO, and finally Eastern Air Lines from NAA. In 1929, Pitcairn Aviation of Philadelphia, which operated airmail and passenger services as well as flying schools, sold those operations to NAA (GM), who renamed it Eastern Air Transport in 1930. In 1938, Eastern Air Transport was incorporated as an independent company under the name Eastern Airlines. Western Air Express (WAE), formed in 1925, gained the distinction of being the oldest continuously operating airline in the United States. Transcontinental Air Transport (TAT), formed in 1929, merged with Western in 1930 to form Transcontinental and Western Air (TWA), also held by NAA. Western became independent again in 1934, and TWA was acquired by Howard Hughes in 1939. Northwest Airways (later Northwest Airlines) was founded in 1926 for cargo and added passenger service in 1927. Delta began as a crop-dusting operation in 1924 and added passenger service in 1929.

Airlines, aided by technical advances in airliners, survived the depression reasonably well. American operated a sleeper version of the biplane Curtiss Condor, the first successful overnight service, beginning in 1933. Later that year the Boeing 247, a powerful ten-passenger craft incorporating retractable landing gear, controllable pitch propellers, wing flaps, and soundproofing, was an almost revolutionary advance. The design was at the request of United, and orders followed. Rival TWA then issued a specification for a new trimotor, then the favored configuration, but the manufacturer Douglas responded with a new twin-engine design, the DC-1, with a stressed-skin structure and greater streamlining. The fourteen-passenger production model, the DC-2, quickly displaced the 247. American asked Douglas for a larger sleeper version to replace the Condor. The result was the 1935 Douglas Sleeper Transport (DST), soon designated the DC-3. Although in the DC-3 served the sleeper role only briefly, its efficiency made it the industry standard both domestically and internationally, carrying 75 percent of U.S. passenger traffic by 1939. It was the first transport with which airlines could earn a profit on passenger carrying alone.

Transoceanic air travel was a long-held dream, but Americans never showed the interest Germans did in the potential of Zeppelins or dirigibles. Loss of the navy *Akron* and *Macon* airships further diminished interest, then the *Hindenberg* disaster in 1939 ended all consideration. The dream was realized with large flying boats, the feeling being that water-landing capability in an emergency was necessary for safety. Pan American's 1931 specification led to the development of the Martin M-130 for Pacific service by 1935. Sikorsky also built a series of long-range flying boats. The most advanced, the Boeing 314 of 1939, pioneered luxury transatlantic service. Low volume led to losses for both manufacturers and airlines, however, despite airmail subsidies. The disruption of service during World War II (1939–1945) and the subsequent demonstrated superiority of land planes for overseas transportation ended the romantic flying boat era.

Aviation infrastructure progressed in the prewar years. Airport construction was speeded under the National Recovery Administration (NRA) from 1933, and air traffic control (ATC), represented by the opening of the Newark ATC center in 1935, was an important step. The Air Commerce Act of 1938 created the Civil Aeronautics Authority (CAA), which regulated the sixteen domestic carriers in routes and fares as well as the airways system. Another regulatory advance divided the authority into the Civil Aeronautics Administration (CAA) and the Civil Aeronautics Board (CAB) in 1940. The CAB, which regulated routes and fares, spurred development of long-range airways, further encouraging large airliners. Airmail remained important, but revenues were at market rates, effectively eliminating the passenger subsidy. The new category of feeder airlines serving smaller markets appeared in 1938. Small airlines also were formed in Alaska and Hawaii to serve the special needs of those territories, where surface transport was limited.

American air carriers recorded 3 million passengers in 1941, but the war ended commercial growth. The Air Transport Association (ATA), formed in 1936 to advance the interests of scheduled carriers, facilitated the industry-wide pooling of aircraft, pilots, and technicians into a worldwide transport system for the armed forces. Such cooperation precluded a direct government takeover. Boeing, Douglas, and Lockheed designed large four-engine land airliners in the 1930s. Only the pressurized Boeing 307 entered service before the war, but the Douglas DC-4 served widely as the military C-54. The Lockheed Constellation first flew as the military C-69, but along with the DC-4 it led to a long series of postwar airliners.

After World War II

Victory was accompanied by high optimism for the future. Many felt the age of mass air travel had arrived and that air cargo held great potential. The National Airport Act of 1946 promoted development of airports, and ground-controlled approach was developed in 1946. Local service airlines, principally equipped with the DC-3, expanded. But local service, with frequent stops and small passenger loads, could not operate profitably and received subsidies through the CAB to promote development. The eleven "trunk" airlines served a truly national air network, with Northwest becoming the fourth transcontinental carrier in 1946. Internationally, Atlantic service resumed in January 1945, followed by Pacific service in November. Pan American still led the Atlantic service but was joined by TWA (Trans World Airlines from 1950). Braniff, Eastern, and Panagra served Latin America, and United and Northwest served the Pacific. Postwar optimism soon declined as airline finances, always shaky, suffered in the

1947 downturn. Most suffered massive losses, and many airliner orders were cancelled. But in 1948, the fleet totaled 1,023 aircraft for both domestic and international service, with Douglas dominating.

Profit difficulties led to several manufacturer withdrawals from the field. Curtiss-Wright decided not to enter the postwar market, and orders for the advanced Republic Rainbow, the fastest airliner developed to that time, were cancelled in the recession. Martin, after losses on its new models, withdrew in 1953. Boeing also lost on the large, uneconomical 377 Stratocruiser, developed from the B-29 bomber. Lockheed and Douglas prospered with their four-engine airliners, however, as did Convair with its successful 240/240/440 twin-engine series. All received major export orders as the United States dominated world airliner markets.

After the Korean War (1950–1953), prosperity finally came, accompanied by the formation of numerous non-scheduled carriers and charter services outside the regulation of the CAB. Cargo airlines, such as Slick, Seaboard, and Flying Tiger, were established. Many surplus military transports and retired airliners were converted into freighters. Scheduled air freight was difficult to manage, however, and route structures were often inefficient, leading to profitability problems and the eventual decline of all-cargo service. Airlines also prospered from contract transportation of military personnel and the formation in 1953 of the Civil Reserve Air Fleet, in which certain airliners were designated for military duty in an emergency. Airmail remained important but became an adjunct to passenger service. Carriers frequently protested, however, that they did not receive an adequate share of postage revenues. Air travel effectively drove passenger rail service out of the market and also posed a threat to railroads in certain freight services. Local service still enjoyed growth, but some carriers disappeared through mergers. For instance, Chicago and Southern merged into Delta in 1953. In 1956, scheduled carriers recorded 46 million passengers and 1.2 million air freight shipments.

The Jet Age

The major influence on the future of air travel was the jet airliner. Aided by military aircraft and engine technology, the jet airliner made long-distance travel faster and more comfortable than ever. The transformation involved major risks to both manufacturers and airlines, but prospects were so bright that four major firms, Boeing, Douglas, Convair, and Lockheed, entered the competition. Losses later forced Lockheed and Convair out. Boeing, with its brilliant gamble in developing the 707 for both commercial and military uses, established leadership. Jets were far more expensive than piston-engine airliners, and they were far more fuel hungry. They were financially viable only with markedly higher productivity. Airlines disputed the CAB's reluctance to grant fare increases, which the airlines felt were necessary to finance the new generation, but they still rushed to order. Production of piston-engine airliners ended in 1958, and passengers rapidly accepted the new jets. Fairchild produced, under license, a Dutch turboprop airliner for local service. But orders were few, as it simply was too costly for small airlines despite the greater passenger appeal and the efficiency of a new design. The Federal Aviation Authority (FAA), established in 1958, succeeded the CAA as an independent agency supporting technical development, safety and pilot standards, airways development, and implementation of jet services.

In another sector, the use of helicopters for city center and airport connections was felt to have great potential. Large turbine-powered models appeared beginning in the late 1950s, and helicopter airlines were established in Los Angeles, Chicago, and New York. But high fares and operating expenses made profitability impossible, and such services slowly faded. Helicopter use expanded, however, in such roles as executive transport, oil service operations, and bush operations.

Air travel continued to grow rapidly in the 1960s both in business and leisure travel, and the transition to jets was virtually complete by the middle of the decade. Yet the potential market remained largely untapped; as late as 1962, two-thirds of the American population had never flown. In 1961, Eastern inaugurated an hourly, unreserved shuttle service connecting New York, Washington, D.C., and Boston. There were major safety advances, although traffic growth strained the ATC system, and there was a growing conflict between increasing volume and safety. Busy airports experienced conflicts between scheduled and business aircraft operations. Noise pollution near major airports also became an issue, leading to engine "hush kits." In 1967, the renamed FEDERAL AVIATION ADMINISTRATION (FAA) came under the auspices of the new Department of Transportation. New commuter airlines formed, reflecting growing demand, but they further strained the capacities of both the ATC and the airports. Former local service or feeder airlines continued to merge into regional carriers, and airmail subsidies largely ended by 1974.

In the late 1960s, the new generation of "jumbo" airliners, led by the Boeing 747, promised major advances in every aspect of air travel, including capacity, range, comfort, operating efficiency, safety, and costs. While the airliners were technical successes, their introduction was troubled, and manufacturers lost heavily. An American supersonic airliner did not proceed, as massive development expenses requiring government assistance, soaring fuel costs, and the sonic boom problem led the FAA to end the program. Only the heavily subsidized Anglo-French Concorde entered sustained service. Airline deregulation in 1978 was a landmark event. The CAB was abolished, easing market entry and acquisition of routes, and airlines were free to establish fares and schedules. Southwest Airlines, initially a Texas intrastate carrier stressing low fares, grew rapidly and profitably with deregulation, providing competition to major carriers. New discount airlines, most notably PeopleExpress, served the largely untapped market for no-frills service. In an interesting sidelight, rare in American business, major airlines enjoyed extraordinary management stability. Such pioneers as Trippe of Pan Am, Donald W. Nyrop of Northwest, C. R. Smith of American, W. A. "Pat" Patterson of United, Edward V. Rickenbacker of Eastern, Robert Forman Six of Continental, and C. E. Woolman of Delta led their companies for decades.

By the 1970s, cargo was some 20 percent of airline payload by weight. New cargo carriers appeared but in a far different form than previously. Federal Express, operating with high efficiency from a single hub at night, when passenger traffic was low, enabled economical shipment of even small parcels, providing major competition to the postal service. Emery Worldwide, United Parcel Service, and DHL Worldwide Express also competed.

Air travel growth continued into the 1980s, but financial stability remained elusive. Airlines were highly cyclical, vulnerable to sharp losses in any economic downturn. Most notably, during the three calendar years of 1990 to 1992, airlines suffered total losses of some $3 billion, more than the cumulative earnings of the industry in its history. A recession and vicious price cutting were major factors. But the proportion of the public flying rose steadily, and development of advanced airliners proceeded. Range had increased to the point that Australia and Japan could be reached nonstop from the West Coast, and twin-engine airliners served Atlantic routes. Regional growth led to a new category of jetliners with fifty to one hundred seats as efficiency increased to the point that smaller jets could be operated profitably on short-range routes.

In the Twenty-First Century
The total assets of U.S. carriers rose from $12 billion in 1969 to $117 billion in 1998. In 1998, the fleet totaled 8,111, of which 5,412 were turbine powered. Despite the greater productivity of airliners, the price of new ones rose relentlessly. The latest version of the Boeing 747 approached $200 million. No airline could afford to be left behind competitively, and large leasing firms, such as the International Lease Finance Corporation (ILFC), facilitated modernization. Early jets were so durable that some operated for thirty years or more, and the fleet aged steadily. Concerns over airframe fatigue and high fuel consumption compelled modernization, further pressing airline finances. Competition and the need for cost cutting led to a wave of bankruptcies and consolidations in the 1990s. Such famous names as Pan American, Eastern, Braniff, and TWA disappeared, and several smaller freight carriers declared bankruptcy. Some forecasts predicted that no more than three major airlines would survive. Similarly only two producers, Boeing and Airbus, remained. Regional airlines were numerous and were generally affiliated with major carriers, such as Comair's affiliation with Delta.

Despite financial pressures, air transportation was a critical component of the economy at the end of the twentieth century. Domestic traffic, 321 million passengers in 1984, rose to 561 million by 1998. United had a fleet of more than seven hundred airliners, and American and Delta had more than six hundred each by 2000. Perhaps the strongest indicator of the importance of the industry came after the hijacking of four airliners on 11 September 2001 in the terrorist attacks on the United States. Air travel was suspended for several days. Even after resumption, traffic dropped sharply, as much of the public was reluctant to fly again. Congress immediately appropriated some $15 billion in direct grants and loan guarantees to scheduled carriers, as many were in danger of financial collapse. The manufacturers also suffered, as many airlines postponed or cancelled orders in response to the drop in passenger traffic and reduced schedules. Nevertheless, long-term growth looked favorable.

BIBLIOGRAPHY

Aerospace Facts and Figures. Annual of the Aerospace Industries Association.

Bilstein, Roger E. *Flight in America.* 3d ed. Baltimore, Md.: Johns Hopkins University Press, 2001.

Davies, R. E. G. *Airlines of the United States since 1914.* London: Putnam, 1972.

Heppenheimer, T. A. *Turbulent Skies: The History of Commercial Aviation.* New York: John Wiley, 1995.

Pattillo, Donald M. *Pushing the Envelope: The American Aircraft Industry.* Ann Arbor, University of Michigan Press, 1998.

Donald M. Pattillo

See also **Aircraft Armament; Aircraft Industry; Airline Deregulation Act; Airmail; Terrorism.**

AIRBORNE UNITS. *See* **Paratroops.**

AIRCRAFT, BOMBER.

The first bomber developed by the United States, the Martin MB-1, first flown in August 1918, was developed too late for use in World War I. In the 1920s the United States had only a few British DH-4 and Martin NBS-1 bombers, which the celebrated general William (Billy) Mitchell used to sink retired battleships to prove his theory that a separate air force could successfully defend the U.S. coastline. The twin-engine, 107 mph Keystone biplane was standard until 1932. The Boeing Y1B-9 twin-engine all-metal 188 mph monoplane replaced the Keystone but was eclipsed by the Martin B-10, which, at 210 mph, was faster than any other American pursuit plane. Its replacements were the Douglas twin-engine 218 mph B-18 and the Boeing four-engine B-17.

World War II was fought with bombers developed during the late 1930s and early 1940s. They were designed for strategic bombardment or for tactical and supplemental strategic tasks. The main strategic bombers were the Boeing B-17 Flying Fortress and the Consolidated twin-tailed B-24 Liberator. Both were used in Eu-

rope, but the B-24's greater range made it more valuable in the Pacific arena. The B-17F and the B-17G, armed with twelve .50 caliber guns, carried 4,000 pounds of bombs over 2,000 miles at 300 mph; the B-24H and the B-24J, similarly armed, carried a 2,500-pound payload about 1,925 miles at 300 mph. The Boeing B-29 Superfortress, the war's largest bomber, carried twelve .50 caliber guns. Both the B-29A and the B-29B carried 20,000 pounds of bombs and had a range of 5,000 miles.

Medium and attack bombers carried out tactical and supplemental strategic tasks. The medium bombers included the North American B-25 Mitchell, used in Lieutenant Colonel Jimmy Doolittle's famous Tokyo Raid in 1942, and the Martin B-26 Marauder. Both were heavily armed, twin-engine, midwing planes capable of 285 mph flight speeds, with a range of 1,100 miles. Quick and highly maneuverable, attack bombers operated at low altitudes. The Douglas A-26 Invader (1944) was the war's most advanced medium—a 360 mph twin-engine midwing carrying eighteen .50 caliber guns, 6,000 pounds of bombs, and fourteen rockets and ranging over 1,000 miles.

The first intercontinental bomber, the Consolidated-Vultee B-36 (1946), attained a maximum speed of 383 mph and carried 10,000 pounds of bombs 7,500 miles. Fully jet powered bombers were developed late because of the jet engine's high fuel consumption. The first was the North American B-45 Tornado (1948), powered by four jets, with a maximum speed of 579 mph, a 10,000-pound payload, and a 1,910-mile range. The second fully jet powered bomber, the Boeing B-47 Stratojet, came armed with twin radar-aimed .50 caliber tailguns. The B-47 replaced the B-29 and the B-50 as a medium bomber until it was retired during the 1960s.

Bombing Raid. B-24s strike at the rail yards in Salzburg, Austria, December 1944. NATIONAL ARCHIVES AND RECORDS ADMINISTRATION

B-25s. Bombers pack the flight deck of the aircraft carrier *Hornet*. NATIONAL ARCHIVES AND RECORDS ADMINISTRATION

In 1954 the Boeing B-52 Stratofortress began replacing the B-36 as the mainstay of the Strategic Air Command. Powered by eight jets, the B-52G attained a maximum speed of 650 mph and carried 65,000 pounds of bombs. Refitted for low-altitude flight, the B-52 served remarkably into the twenty-first century. General Dynamics's B-58 Hustler served the Strategic Air Command through 1970. Powered by four jets, its maximum speed was 1,324 mph with a 1,200-mile combat radius. It carried "mission pods" under the fuselage, or four nuclear weapons underwing, as it had no internal bomb bay.

The U.S. Air Force's mid-1970s bomber force included the B-52G, the B-52H, the B-56G, and a few General Dynamics FB-111A bombers. Derived from the F-111 fighter-bomber, the FB-111A carries 37,000 pounds externally and internally at subsonic speeds; once the ordnance is dropped, the maximum speed is Mach 2.2. The FB-111A remained operational until the development of the B-1 class of bomber in the 1980s. Intended as a successor to the B-52 Stratofortress, Rockwell International's B-1 was a variable-wing strategic bomber that could fly low to penetrate radar defenses. The prototype B-1A, which first flew in 1974, could reach twice the speed of sound at high altitudes while carrying nuclear bombs to their targets.

The development of stealth technology removed the only glaring weakness of the bomber as a tool of mass destruction: its vulnerability to radar detection. The B-1B, airborne by 1984, incorporated some stealth features, including contoured exteriors built of radar-absorbing materials. Despite the prohibitive cost, research and development into stealth planes—aircraft that would be invisible to enemy radar—culminated in the Northrop Grumman B-2 advanced technology bomber, first flown in 1989. Like the single-seat fighter Lockheed F-117A, which debuted in 1981, the B-2 uses a pyramid-shaped

fuselage and swept wings made of carbon-fiber composites and high-strength plastics to reduce its radar signature. Engine intakes and exhausts are set low to the surface to avoid leaving a heat trace. Although the B-2 is slow, hard to maneuver, and can carry only limited munitions, it proved devastatingly effective during NATO's extended bombing campaign against the Serbian regime in Kosovo, Yugoslavia, in 1999 and in Operation Enduring Freedom in Afghanistan in 2001 and 2002.

BIBLIOGRAPHY

Craven, Wesley F., and James L. Cate, eds. *The Army Air Forces in World War II.* Volume 6: *Men and Planes.* Washington, D.C.: Office of Air Force History, 1983.

Gunston, Bill. *American Warplanes: A Full-Color Technical Directory of 200 of the Most Important Combat Aircraft to Serve the United States.* New York: Crescent Books, 1986.

Wagner, Ray. *American Combat Planes.* Garden City, N.Y.: Doubleday, 1981.

Warner Stark/c. w.

See also **Air Force, United States; Aircraft Armament; Aircraft Carriers and Naval Aircraft.**

AIRCRAFT, FIGHTER. The first American-built fighter, the Thomas-Morse MB-1 Scout, appeared in 1919. The U.S. Army relied on the Curtiss Hawk series until 1930, when the army switched to the Boeing P-26. As world tension generated technical advances, the army switched to the Republic P-35 and the Curtiss P-36 (Hawk 75), all-metal, low-wing monoplanes with enclosed cockpits, retractable landing gear, and heavier armament.

The Army Air Corps's interest in aircraft with close-support and coast defense roles retarded development of U.S. fighters, so that the standard fighters—the Curtiss P-40 Warhawk (1940) and the Bell P-39 Airacobra (1941)—were obsolescent when the United States entered World War II. The first advanced U.S. fighter (ordered 1939) was the Lockheed P-38 Lightning, a twin-engine, 414 mph, twin-tailed plane. The Republic P-47 Thunderbolt (1943), used in the ground-support role, was the only radial-engined fighter of the Army Air Force (AAF). Perhaps the war's best fighter, the North American P-51 Mustang, was in British service, where it excelled in a variety of roles before the AAF's need for bomber escorts brought widespread American use. The Northrop P-61 Black Widow (1943) was the first American plane specifically designed as a night fighter.

Unlike Britain and Germany, the United States used no jet aircraft during World War II, although it had begun jet development. The first U.S. jet, the Bell XP-59 Airacomet (1943), was capable of only 418 mph and was soon relegated to a training role. The Lockheed P-80 Shooting Star (553 mph) was the AAF's fastest World War II fighter, but it arrived too late for combat. The last AAF propeller fighter, the P-82 Twin Mustang, saw service in Korea.

The Republic F-84 Thunderjet, the first postwar fighter, evolved into the 693 mph F-84F Thunderstreak, which the Strategic Air Command (SAC) used for escort groups until 1957 and which served as the main fighter-bomber of the Tactical Air Command (TAC) until the F-100C. The North American F-86 Sabre, the Lockheed F-94, and the Northrop F-89 Scorpion overcame the effects of compressibility, used an afterburner, and added night and all-weather capability, respectively.

The Air Force ordered its first supersonic aircraft in the early 1950s. The Century series consisted of the North American F-100 Super Sabre, McDonnell Douglas F-101A Voodoo, Convair F-102 Delta Dagger, and the Lockheed F-104 Starfighter. The TAC's first fighter with a bomb bay—the Republic F-105 Thunderchief—was delivered in 1956. Other attack aircraft included the Vought A-7D Corsair II; the Northrop F-5 series; and the Cessna A-37. The Convair 1,526 mph F-106 Delta Dart, an almost fully automatic fighter, appeared in 1956.

A new generation of aircraft began to appear in the 1960s. The first, the McDonnell Douglas F-4 Phantom II series (1963), performed both as interceptor and attack plane. Two additional fighters, the General Dynamics F-111, an all-weather fighter-bomber, and the McDonnell Douglas F-15 Eagle, replaced the Phantom II. The Eagle (1974) entered service as the air force's frontline fighter. The F-14 Tomcat (1974) entered service as the navy's leading carrier-based, multirole fighter. The versatile General Dynamics (Lockheed Martin after 1992) F-16 Fighting Falcon (1979), designed for air superiority, gradually adopted air support and tactical strike roles. The versatile all-weather F/A-18 Hornet, the nation's first strike-fighter, primarily provided fleet air defense and fighter escort. The F/A-18E/F Super Hornet, introduced in 1995, added a new long-range, all-weather, multimission strike-fighter to the navy's arsenal.

BIBLIOGRAPHY

Craven, Wesley F., and James L. Cate, eds. *The Army Air Forces in World War II*. Volume 6, *Men and Planes*. Chicago: University of Chicago Press, 1955.

Wagner, Ray. *American Combat Planes*. 3d enl. ed. Garden City, N.Y.: Doubleday, 1968.

Waters, Andrew W. *All the U.S. Air Force Airplanes*. New York: Hippocrene Books, 1983.

Warner Stark / c. w.

See also **Air Force, United States; Air Power, Strategic; Aircraft Carriers and Naval Aircraft; Aircraft, Bomber; Aircraft Industry; Navy, United States.**

AIRCRAFT ARMAMENT, the weapons carried on a plane for offensive attack or for defense against enemy aircraft and ground targets. Early warplanes tended to carry either a small-caliber weapon capable of a high number of strikes per second or a larger, slower-firing weapon capable of high penetration and destruction. As technology advanced, aircraft often began to be outfitted with both.

The early, low-powered American fighter aircraft of World War I carried a single drum-fed Lewis gun, which was difficult for the pilot to reload single-handedly. With the development of more powerful aircraft engines and synchronized guns, planes began to be outfitted with twin belt-fed machine guns such as the British Vickers .303 Mk 1. Between the world wars, American fighters carried either two Browning air-cooled .30 caliber machine guns or one .30 and one .50 caliber machine gun. Although aircraft on both sides employed aerial cannon in World War I, the first models that proved to be practical in combat appeared during World War II. The P-39 Airacobra, for example, carried a 37 mm coaxial cannon. The most widely used was the Swiss 20 mm Oerlikon, as carried by the P-38 Lightning. Some B-25 bombers used primarily for attacking ground targets adopted the much larger 75 mm M4 cannon.

Flexible guns mounted to defend heavier aircraft had to remain small and light until engineers developed a new mount that allowed the gunner to overcome slip-stream interference. During and immediately following World War I, standard armament consisted of one or two Lewis guns mounted on a Scarff ring. Enclosed turrets first appeared in 1932 on the B-10 bomber, followed by American adoption of the British power turret, usually mounting twin .50 caliber guns. Remote-controlled turrets came in 1942 and became standard after World War II, as in the retractable twin turrets with 20 mm cannon on the B-36.

By the 1940s, radar-aimed 20 mm cannon had become standard equipment on bombers such as the B-52, while fighter aircraft carried radar-guided and computer-fired air-to-air rockets. The earliest of these was the Folding Fin Aircraft Rocket ("Mighty Mouse") carried by a modified F-86 and heavily used during World War II and the Korean War. Rockets generally replaced guns as the primary fighter weapon, although most fighters continued to carry at least one gun.

Developments in air-to-air ordnance during the 1950s included the infrared-homing Sidewinder missile, the heat-seeking Falcon missiles, and the MB-1 Genie, equipped with a nuclear warhead capable of destroying any aircraft within 1,000 feet of detonation. Gunnery developments included the 20 mm T-171 Vulcan multibarreled cannon capable of firing up to 6,000 rounds per minute. The radar-guided Sparrow missiles and the Phoenix missile, carried by the U.S. Navy's F-14 fighter, were developed during the 1970s.

BIBLIOGRAPHY

Wagner, Ray. *American Combat Planes*. Garden City, N.Y.: Doubleday, 1968.

Waters, Andrew W. *All the U. S. Air Force Airplanes, 1907–1983*. New York: Hippocrene Books, 1983.

Whitehouse, Arthur G. *The Military Airplane*. Garden City, N.Y.: Doubleday, 1971.

Warner Stark / c. w.

See also **Aircraft, Bomber; Aircraft, Fighter; Machine Guns; Missiles, Military; Munitions.**

AIRCRAFT CARRIERS AND NAVAL AIRCRAFT

Carriers

The first airplane launched from a ship flew from a jury-rigged platform on the bow of the American light cruiser *Birmingham* on 10 November 1910. The civilian pilot, Eugene B. Ely, made the first shipboard landing on 18 January 1911, on a platform over the stern guns of the cruiser *Pennsylvania*. It remained until World War I, however, for the British Royal Navy to take the steps essential to the development of a true aircraft carrier. The Royal Navy succeeded in taking fighter aircraft to sea that scored kills on German zeppelins over the sea approaches to Britain.

The first U.S. carrier was *Langley*, converted in 1922 from the collier *Jupiter*. *Langley* could operate thirty-four aircraft and steam at 15 knots. Japanese planes sank the *Langley* on 27 February 1942 as it was ferrying U.S. Army Air Force planes to Java.

The Washington Naval Conference of 1922, which limited construction of capital warships, laid the foundation of American carrier air power. Two U.S. battle cruisers—*Lexington* and *Saratoga*—were big and fast, at 33,000 tons and 33 knots, and carried a normal complement of nearly one hundred planes. They enabled U.S. naval strategists to develop the doctrine and tactics that projected American air power across oceans. The competition of carrier aviation with land-based aviation brought the United States into World War II with a broadly based aviation industry.

Lexington and *Saratoga*, classic attack carriers (CVs), extended the fleet's striking power while protecting it from enemy action. During the early months of World War II they both took the war to the southwest Pacific. *Lexington* was sunk 8 May 1942 in the Battle of the Coral Sea, and *Saratoga* served through the war, only to become a target vessel for the Bikini atomic bomb evaluations of 1946. The fleet began adding CVs with *Ranger* in 1934, *Yorktown* in 1937, *Enterprise* in 1938, *Wasp* in 1940, and *Hornet* in 1941.

Essex defined a class of twenty-four 27,000-ton vessels completed from 1942 to 1946, most of which served in the Pacific. None was ever sunk. The last on active duty, *Ticonderoga*, was retired in 1973.

Wartime conversions from light cruiser hulls added nine light carriers (CVLs) to the fleet in 1943. These 15,000-ton ships operated at 31 knots or more but only had complements of forty-five airplanes—half those of *Essex*. Concurrently, a class of escort carriers (CVEs)—112 in all—sprang from converted merchant hulls. The CVEs made less than 20 knots, carried fewer than thirty planes, and served primarily as submarine hunter-killers. Their presence compelled the German undersea force to play defense, rendering it increasingly ineffective. The support role of CVEs in amphibious landings put some in harm's way; five were sunk, variously by submarine, kamikaze, or cruiser gunfire.

Aircraft

The development of naval carrier aircraft before World War II produced three basic types of planes: the fighter (VF), the scout bomber (VSB), and the torpedo plane (VT). Fighters tended to become fighter-bombers (VBFs) near the end of the war as the skies became clear of enemy fighter opposition.

By 1929 a typical carrier complement included Boeing F2B-1 or F3B-1 fighters, Martin T4M-1 torpedo planes, and Chance Vought O2U-1 scout bombers. All were fabric-covered biplanes.

The early 1930s produced the first of the Grumman biplane fighter series—FF-1, F2F, and F3F—to break the 200 mph barrier. The Douglas TBD torpedo plane, whose 850-horsepower engine still could not reach 200 mph in level flight, began the trend to low-wing monoplanes in 1935. Scout dive-bombers of the 1930s in the 200 mph class included the Chance Vought SBU biplane and the SB2U low-wing, the last of the fabric-covered combat planes. The Curtiss SBC biplane also saw limited service.

World War II spurred aircraft engine development. Horsepower doubled, reaching 2,000 for fighters, and maximum speeds finally reached 300 mph and above. Biplanes passed into history.

Prewar fighters like the F2A Brewster Buffalo (hopelessly mismatched against Japanese fighters) and the F4F Grumman Wildcat, which attained a 7:1 kill ratio over seemingly better Japanese planes, evolved quickly during the war. The F6F Grumman Hellcat, with a kill ratio of 19:1, destroyed 75 percent of all enemy planes shot down by navy pilots in World War II. The F4U Chance Vought Corsair, flown chiefly by U.S. Marine pilots from advanced island bases, attained a kill ratio of 11:1.

Scout bombers progressed from the fabric-covered SB2U Vought Vindicator, last in action at Midway; through the SBD Douglas Dauntless, which turned the tide at Midway and in many of the battles for the southwest Pacific; to the SB2C Curtiss Helldiver, a problem from its introduction on the first *Essex* carriers in 1943 until the end of the war. All were 60-degree dive-bombers, a navy specialty for accuracy.

Torpedo planes entered the war with the inadequate TBD Douglas Devastator, which carried Torpedo Squadron 8 to extinction at Midway. Its replacement, the TBF

Headed for Tokyo. A B-25 bomber takes off from the aircraft carrier *Hornet* for the first U.S. attack on Japan in World War II (18 April 1942). NATIONAL ARCHIVES AND RECORDS ADMINISTRATION

Grumman Avenger, performed notably, seeing postwar service as an interim antisubmarine warfare (ASW) platform.

Patrol planes (VPs), operating from land or water, supplemented carrier aircraft chiefly for search, ASW patrols, and antishipping attacks. Among these, the PBY Consolidated Catalinas—the famed Black Cats of the southwest Pacific—performed particularly well. The PBM Martin Mariner provided better performance after 1943, and the PB4Y Consolidated Privateer, a navy version of the Consolidated Liberator, gave improved radar periscope detection.

Scout observation aircraft (VSO–VOS) contributed a minor but unique role in naval operations, from the first days of aviation to the advent of helicopters, which replaced them after World War II. Catapulted from battleships, cruisers, and (rarely) destroyers and retrieved at sea, they provided spotting capability for naval shore gunfire and rescued downed pilots, even under the guns of enemy-held atolls. Two types of these planes served throughout the war: the venerable biplane SOC Curtiss Seagull and the newer OS2U Vought Kingfisher.

Carrier Battles of World War II

The three major carrier battles of World War II were those of the Coral Sea, Midway, and the Philippine Sea. In addition, the deadly three-month campaign for Okinawa resulted in major damage to nine CVs, one CVL, and three CVEs as well as the destruction of more than two thousand enemy aircraft by carrier-based planes. Carrier raids against Japanese positions commenced early in 1942, the most notable being Colonel James Doolittle's "Shangri-La" raid on Tokyo on 18 April 1942. Equally important, air strikes from carriers spearheaded the North African landings in 1942 as well as every Pacific assault.

The Battle of the Coral Sea, 4–8 May 1942, kept Japan from landing forces at Port Moresby, New Guinea, and marked the end of southward expansion. U.S. forces lost the CV *Lexington* in exchange for the Japanese CVL *Shoho*. The Battle of Midway, 3–7 June 1942, reversed the offensive-defensive roles and frustrated Japanese strategic plans. The United States lost *Yorktown*, but Japan lost all four of its CVs in the operation, with all planes, pilots, and mechanics aboard. The Battle of the Philippine Sea, 19–21 June 1944, was the largest carrier battle in history.

The Japanese defeat in this battle marked the end of Japanese carrier intervention. Japan lost three carriers, two to U.S. submarines; the United States lost no ships. Japanese aircraft losses totaled five hundred to some one hundred for the United States. Only sixteen American pilots and thirty-three aircrewmen were lost, whereas Japan lost almost all of its remaining carrier pilots.

After World War II

U.S. carrier air power has had no real foreign counterpart since World War II; nonetheless, carrier forces have remained an active, major arm of U.S. foreign policy. The western Pacific has not been without a carrier task force since V-J Day. The Truman Doctrine, enunciated in 1947, immediately resulted in the assignment of carriers to the Mediterranean, and they have been an integral part of the Sixth Fleet since that time.

Four larger classes of carrier have evolved since the war: *Midway*, 45,000 tons (1945); *Forrestal*, 60,000 tons (1955); and the nuclear-powered *Enterprise*, 75,000 tons (1961), and *Nimitz* (97,000 tons). With them have come jet aircraft (1948), nuclear-bomb delivery capability (1951), and true all-weather operational capability (late 1960s). Further technological progress came in the 1950s with the adoption of the angled deck, which permits simultaneous launch and recovery and power-on landings, and the steam catapult, which provides the greater launch capability needed for jets. Early optical landing systems have evolved from the mirror to the Fresnel lens, encompassing a closed-circuit television monitor and advancing toward an automatic landing system. The Tactical Air Navigational System (TACAN) rose from specific needs of carriers. The Navy Tactical Data System arrived during Vietnam, utilizing many ancillary electronic, computerized command, and control features.

Antisubmarine warfare (ASW) carriers, the CVSs, entered the postwar fleet as replacements for the CVEs. The ASW carrier mission began to take on renewed importance with the growth of the Soviet submarine fleet. ASW operations used some CVEs and CVLs, but after the early 1950s converted Essex class ships replaced them. The CVS became the nucleus of a carrier-destroyer force used to clear the operating area for a carrier strike force, to search out and destroy enemy submarines, or to close off potential routes to enemy submarines. Aircraft complements aboard CVSs began to stabilize with S2F Grumman Tracker twin-engine aircraft (introduced in 1954), helicopters, and an early-warning detachment of specially configured electronic S2Fs. More advanced versions, redesignated S-2D and S-2E, began to reach the fleet in 1962.

Helicopters became operational aboard carriers with the first helicopter ASW squadron in 1952, although the XOP-1 autogiro was tested on *Langley* in 1931. The first ASW squadron was equipped with the Piasecki HUP-1, succeeded by the Sikorsky HSS-1 piston engine Seabat and then the HSS-2 turbine-powered Sea King. Most major vessels carry utility helicopters for such chores as stores movement and replenishment, personnel transfers, and lifeguard missions.

The development of nuclear-bomb delivery capability for carriers in the 1950s marked a period of international significance in carrier history. With attack planes on board available for nuclear missions, the carriers could cover the European peninsula, including the Ukraine and Caucasus, most of China, and eastern Siberia. Naval aircraft shared the national nuclear deterrent responsibility with the Strategic Air Command through the 1950s and into the 1960s, when the Polaris fleet and intercontinental ballistic missiles (ICBMs) took over the major burden. Nuclear power proved to be the most significant technological development for carriers after World War II, but Secretary of Defense Robert S. McNamara's decisions of 1962 delayed its exploitation. With the commissioning of Nimitz (1972) and Eisenhower (1974) classes, however, proponents of a nuclear-powered carrier force won part of their struggle.

Naval aircraft since World War II have been predominantly jet powered, but the propeller dive-bomber AD Douglas Skyraider persisted as the world's best attack airplane from the late 1940s into the 1970s, excelling in both Korea and Vietnam. With a single piston engine, the AD carries a bigger bomb load than the famous B-17 Flying Fortress.

Three attack planes and two outstanding fighters emerged from the many naval jet aircraft tested in high-accident-rate programs during the 1950s. The A4 McDonnell Douglas Skyhawk, designed as an atomic-delivery vehicle, gained substantial modifications for effective conventional weapons delivery. The twin-engine A-6 Grumman Intruder, an all-weather plane with several unique electronic countermeasure versions, was introduced in 1963. The A-7 Vought Corsair II, a single-engine day-attack jet designed to carry either nuclear or conventional weapons, first saw combat in 1967 in the Tonkin Gulf. In the fighter field, the F8U-1 Vought Crusader, a day fighter gun platform with missile capability, became operational in 1957. The F4 McDonnell Douglas Phantom II, an all-weather missile fighter first produced in 1961, became the U.S. Air Force's primary fighter.

Carrier participation in Korea resembled that in Vietnam. Both were peninsular wars characterized by a lack of land bases. As a result, U.S. carriers held responsibility for a major part of the air fighting over enemy territory, exploiting their quick and self-contained reaction capability, mobility, and wide choice of launch areas. Because they could get in and out of target areas more easily, carrier planes rather than land-based planes took out the Yalu River bridges and Hwachon Reservoir Dam in 1951 and the Haiphong and Hanoi power plants in 1965. In both conflicts, carriers operated free from enemy damage.

Carrier force levels fluctuate with need. V-J Day found ninety-nine carriers in commission. When war broke out in Korea (1950), fifteen carriers, but only seven CVs, were left. By 1953 thirty-nine carriers were in commission, of which seventeen were of Essex or Midway class. On-station commitments in Southeast Asia went from three CVAs to five CVAs in the first months of the air war in Vietnam, but Department of Defense analysts successfully kept the attack carrier level at fifteen. Meanwhile, ASW carrier strength declined from nine in 1965 to three in 1972. By century's end the United States was still the world's principal user of carriers, with a fleet of twelve active carriers and one on operational reserve. Carriers saw action in most of the country's post–Cold War global conflicts. During the Persian Gulf War, aircraft launched from carriers ran thousands of devastating sorties and ensured complete control of the skies above Iraq.

The carrier remained central to the navy's strategic planning for the twenty-first century. By 2008 the navy hoped to introduce a tenth and final *Nimitz*-class carrier, the CVN 77. The CVN 77 would be the first of a new generation of "smart" ships, incorporating new intelligence, communication, and targeting technologies. The navy also envisioned that a more fully automated and less expensive ship, the CVX, would be operational by 2013.

BIBLIOGRAPHY

Friedman, Norman. *U.S. Aircraft Carriers: An Illustrated Design History.* Annapolis, Md.: Naval Institute Press, 1983.

Melhorn, Charles M. *Two-Block Fox: The Rise of the Aircraft Carrier, 1911–1929.* Annapolis, Md.: Naval Institute Press, 1974.

Mooney, James L., ed. *Dictionary of American Naval Fighting Ships.* Volume 2. Washington, D.C.: Naval Historical Center, 1991.

Pawlowski, Gareth L. *Flat-Tops and Fledglings: A History of American Aircraft Carriers.* South Brunswick, N.J.: A. S. Barnes, 1971.

Reynolds, Clark G. *The Fast Carriers: The Forging of an Air Navy.* Huntington, N.Y.: R. E. Krieger, 1978.

William C. Chapman / C. W.; A. R.

See also **Air Force, United States; Aircraft Armament; Aircraft, Bomber; Aircraft, Fighter; Boeing Company; Helicopters; Navy, United States; Torpedo Warfare; World War II, Navy in.**

AIRCRAFT INDUSTRY. The Wright brothers' successful flights on 17 December 1903 were the culmination of a century of experimentation on both sides of the Atlantic. The reality of powered, controlled flight was not recognized for almost five more years, however. The U.S. Army ordered a Wright flyer in 1908, and in 1909 Glenn Curtiss and his associates made the first commercial sale of a flyer, an act that led the Wright brothers to sue Curtiss for patent infringement. The formation of the Curtiss-Herring and Wright Companies (both in 1909) for series production followed. Other aspirants, most significantly Glenn Martin in California, formed companies

in 1911, and the military services ordered flyers for observation and training. Combat roles for aircraft were not yet envisaged, and scheduled passenger service was undeveloped since early aircraft were not capable of carrying substantial loads.

World War I

Aviation remained little more than a curiosity until World War I (1914–1918) but progressed rapidly in Europe as combat roles developed. Concerns about the European lead in aviation prompted Congress to establish the National Advisory Committee for Aeronautics (NACA) in 1915 to support aviation research and development. When the United States entered the war in 1917, few manufacturers were active, and none had experience with mass production. The government left production in private hands during the war buildup rather than establishing state ownership, as was sometimes proposed, although the Naval Aircraft Factory was established. The small industry received major support as Congress appropriated large sums for aircraft, and several new firms were formed to fulfill war orders. Several European aircraft were selected for production in preference to domestic designs, and the automobile industry became heavily involved with both aircraft and engines. However, the war ended before American production could have a major impact. Nagging problems cast the fledgling industry in a bad light, but investigation concluded that most problems were due to inexperience and overambitious goals.

Between the Wars

Peace brought massive contract cancellations and the failure of many firms. The remaining active firms were also stressed. Despite the depressed state of the industry—only 263 new aircraft were built in 1922—technical development continued, and aircraft capabilities increased. Notable military designs included the Martin MB-2 bomber and the first fighters by such firms as Thomas-Morse, Chance-Vought, and Boeing. Most civil flying was recreational, facilitated by cheap military surplus trainers, such as the Curtiss JN-4 Jenny. Airmail began in 1918 and grew steadily, attaining coast-to-coast routes by 1924. Aeromarine Airways began limited passenger service in 1919 between Florida and Cuba in flying boats, but losses forced an end to the service in 1923.

The Manufacturers Aircraft Association and the Aeronautical Chamber of Commerce were formed in 1917 and 1922, respectively, to represent the industry's interests. The U.S. Army Engineering Division and the U.S. Navy Bureau of Aeronautics began to support development and testing. Exciting new records set by Americans, such as a new world altitude record of 34,508 feet in 1921 and a speed record of 223 miles per hour in 1922, spurred interest in the industry. The National Air Races, which began in 1920, enhanced public interest, and experiments with oxygen, parachutes, and aerial refueling added to aviation's potential. The first nonstop coast-to-coast flight in 1923 and the first global flight in 1924 by an army team were impressive achievements. Efficient air-cooled radial engines, such as the Wright Whirlwind, were also significant. The Lawson L-4 of 1920, with a capacity of eighteen passengers, was probably the first airliner, although it was only experimental.

Few could afford new private aircraft, but several firms, notably Travel Air, Stearman, Weaver (WACO), and Laird (Swallow), entered the field. Beyond sport flying and barnstorming exhibitions, practical private roles included aerial photography and surveying, crop dusting, bush flying in remote areas, and, to a small extent, business flying by large corporations.

National aviation policy developed slowly, but several investigative boards led to the Airmail Act of 1925 and the Air Commerce Act of 1926. Commercial airmail led to the formation of several carriers, and the Bureau of Air Commerce under the Department of Commerce undertook airways and airport development and licensing, maintenance, and training standards. Military aviation gained greater autonomy with the establishment of the Army Air Corps in 1926, and the military services started five-year aircraft procurement programs. The epic solo flight across the Atlantic by Charles Lindbergh in 1927 spurred a major aviation boom. The possibilities of aviation appeared unlimited, and both military and civil aircraft output expanded. More people wanted to learn to fly, and new aircraft firms entered the field. Another major development during the boom was the formation of large aviation holding companies with Wall Street financing as aviation appeared to become a major industry. The largest companies were United Aircraft and Transport Corporation (UATC), Curtiss-Wright, Detroit Aircraft, Aviation Corporation (AVCO), and North American Aviation, originally an investment firm in which General Motors held a major holding. The new giants acquired many existing firms and integrated most sectors of aviation, including aircraft production, airmail and passenger services, flying schools, and engine, propeller, and instrument production.

With the boom, scheduled commercial service, largely subsidized by airmail, grew rapidly. Passenger aircraft, such as the legendary Ford trimotor, the Boeing 80, and the Fokker series, led the way. But all were slow, uncomfortable, and noisy, and a coast-to-coast trip was a major and expensive undertaking requiring numerous stops.

The Great Depression ended the boom, and many firms failed. Stock prices of the holding companies fell farther than most. Military orders slowed as the five-year plans were completed, and private aircraft demand virtually disappeared. Yet advances during this otherwise grim period resulted in nothing less than a design revolution. The NACA reduced drag with airfoils and streamlined engine cowlings faired into the nose and wings. Monocoque fuselages, enclosed cockpits, replacement of biplanes with more efficient monoplanes, sophisticated instruments, refined aviation gasoline, increased engine power, retractable landing gear, and wider use of aluminum structures enabled greater performance and safety

advances. The Martin B-10, the first modern bomber, and the Boeing 247, the first modern airliner, appeared in the early 1930s, followed in 1935 by the Seversky P-35 fighter, the Boeing B-17 bomber, the Consolidated XP3Y flying boat, and the Douglas DC-3 airliner, which led their categories.

With the DC-3, airlines could operate profitably on passenger services without airmail subsidies, and this type became the world standard. Transoceanic air transportation also began in 1935 with large, luxurious Martin, Sikorsky, and Boeing flying boats, as water-landing capability in an emergency was required for safety. Production was small, however, and World War II (1939–1945) and the eventual proven superiority of large land planes ended this brief romantic era. Despite impressive technical advances, the industry struggled for profitability. Exports became critical, although such efforts frequently conflicted with American neutrality.

The personal flying sector also advanced. The market for light, two-seat models, such as the Taylor (later Piper) Cub and the Aeronca C-3 began to grow after 1935. The fast, powerful Beech Model 17 biplane and such cabin monoplanes as the Stinson Detroiter and Reliant, the Cessna Skymaster, and the Spartan Executive were significant business models, but many companies simply could not survive in a small market. Concurrently, the rotating-wing autogiro was widely anticipated as the solution to mass airplane ownership. The first American model was tested in 1928 by Harold Pitcairn, but a substantial market never developed.

A more modern industry structure gradually evolved. The ambitious Detroit Aircraft Corporation suffered bankruptcy in 1932, and antitrust concerns led to the breakup of the remaining holding companies by 1934, largely separating manufacturing and transport. Boeing again became independent from UATC, and North American transformed into a manufacturer, moved to southern California, and sought scarce military contracts. Despite the otherwise gloomy outlook, such important firms as Grumman, a revived Lockheed (from Detroit Aircraft), Bell, Vultee (originally part of AVCO), Northrop, Republic, and McDonnell were established in the 1929 to 1939 period, and production was increasingly located in southern California.

By 1938, as war approached, U.S. military forces were weak by world standards, and military aircraft orders remained low. Industry employment was only 36,000 workers, and over the thirty years of its history the industry had produced only about 50,000 aircraft, both military and civil, with one-third of that total produced between 1917 and 1918. Sound designs led to increased foreign demand, however, and military exports, always controversial, helped the industry survive until domestic demand rose. British orders in 1938 provided a major boost to industry finances and production capacity. With the onset of war, British and French purchasing commissions placed massive orders. Civil aviation benefited from

Boeing B-17F. This photograph by Andreas Feininger shows the fuselage section of the bombers called the "Flying Fortresses," being assembled at the Boeing plant in Seattle during World War II. LIBRARY OF CONGRESS

the establishment of the autonomous Civil Aeronautics Authority (CAA) in 1938 to succeed the Bureau of Air Commerce. The CAA promoted development of more advanced airliners among other activities.

World War II

The industry reached its greatest heights during World War II, when it produced some 300,000 aircraft over four years. Massive government assistance, including construction of giant defense plants, several of which survived into the twenty-first century, and large-scale transformation of the automobile and other industries into aircraft and engine production contributed to the achievement. The buildup was not free of production and contract problems, but a small number of labor disputes or shortages of critical supplies and wide employment of women workers aided the production success. Light aircraft companies produced their models for military roles and subcontracted to larger firms. Manufacturing, largely situated on the east and west coasts before the war, spread throughout the country.

The war spurred rapid technological advances, and aircraft companies cooperated to an unprecedented degree on technical matters. Pressurization, radar, further engine advances, and flush riveting extended aircraft capabilities. Two wartime developments led aviation's future: the helicopter and the jet engine. Both had been envisaged since the beginning of flight, but they did not reach practical application until the war. Igor Sikorsky tested the first American helicopter in 1939, and it en-

tered into active service during the last year of the war. The United States acquired British jet technology, and contracts for further development were awarded to such firms as Allison (a division of General Motors), Pratt and Whitney, General Electric, and Westinghouse, which soon gained the capability to develop new jet engines. The United States also benefited from captured German technology in delta and swept wings, rocket engines, and missiles. The Aircraft Industries Association (later the Aerospace Industries Association) succeeded the Aeronautical Chamber of Commerce as the chief industry trade association in 1945.

After World War II

Victory resulted in massive contract cancellations and a severe industry contraction, but business recovered with the Cold War buildup. The United States strengthened its domination of world airliner markets with the four-engine Lockheed Constellation and the Douglas DC-4, which originally served as wartime military transports, and their successors. Progress was not without problems, however, as airliner demand expanded and contracted according to business conditions with repercussions for manufacturers.

A wide though unrealistic expectation of mass private airplane ownership in the postwar era was fueled by prosperity and large numbers of military-trained pilots who desired their own planes. Production, mostly of small two-seat trainers, reached record levels in 1946, but the boom soon ended. Several manufacturers went into bankruptcy, and established companies such as Piper were imperiled. Orders for military variants of light aircraft during the Korean War (1950–1953) buildup helped, but private and utility aviation did not regain growth until the mid-1950s. Agricultural aviation, originally involving conversions of such types as the Stearman biplane trainer, became a growth market from 1953 on. Piper, Cessna, Grumman, Call, and others produced specialized agricultural aircraft.

Military-supported research and development led to impressive progress in the 1950s. Jet and rocket power, area-ruled fuselages, advanced wing platforms, and titanium in structures enabled supersonic flight, even from aircraft carriers. By 1954, the aircraft industry had become the largest American industrial employer, the preeminent technological industry, and the linchpin of national security in a nuclear world. All companies enjoyed busy factories with Cold War demands, exemplified by the licensing of the high-priority Boeing B-47 to Douglas and Lockheed. Despite the American companies' world leadership in military and commercial aircraft, light aircraft, missiles, and helicopters, the future of the industry looked bleak in many respects by the end of the decade. Production never again approached wartime levels, and each succeeding aircraft generation was far more complex and expensive than the last, making development beyond the capabilities of smaller firms. Several major firms incurred large financial losses. Mergers were regarded as

Lockheed P-80 (later renamed the F-80). The assembly line keeps production of the "Shooting Star," the first U.S. jet fighter in combat (starting in 1945), at two per day at Lockheed's plant in Burbank, Calif. NATIONAL ARCHIVES AND RECORDS ADMINISTRATION

both inevitable and essential, yet most companies were still dominated by the founders or by long-serving executives, who were reluctant to exit aircraft production or to merge.

The industry structure in 1960 remained similar to that at the end of the World War II. Merger proposals additionally were subject not only to military influence but to antitrust review. The number of firms slowly declined with the dearth of new programs, falling production, cost overruns, and management difficulties. Such renowned companies as Douglas, North American, Convair, Chance-Vought, and Republic eventually disappeared through merger after 1960. Bell transformed entirely to helicopters and the pioneer firm Martin exited aircraft development. Such changes raised concerns about the declining competitive environment.

The British had pioneered jet airliners, but U.S. military technology directly benefited airliner development. American airliners soon dominated the world market, equipping some 90 percent of the world fleet outside the Soviet bloc. Foreign designs were simply uncompetitive. Profitability remained elusive, however, and Convair, Lockheed, and finally Douglas abandoned the field. Business or executive flying grew steadily with twin-engine models, led by the prewar Beech Model 18, becoming significant factors. Piper, Cessna, and the new Aero Design firm also developed business twins. Even larger transports were used by corporations, although most were conversions of smaller wartime bombers and transports.

Progress with efficient smaller engines led to new executive models, such as the Grumman Gulfstream turboprop and the Lockheed and North American business jets. The growing market also aided diversification efforts of primarily military contractors. The Learjet, whose development began in Switzerland, flew in 1963 and spurred further growth in that sector. Single-engine light aircraft, numerically the most important segment, made steady progress with more comfortable, all-metal, tricycle-gear models, some with turbo-charged engines. Private flying remained too expensive for the public, however, and business flying dominated general aviation, the term used for all aviation outside military and scheduled commercial operations.

The industry was further transformed by the growing space and missile programs supported by the National Aeronautics and Space Administration (NASA), formed in 1958 to succeed NACA. Such programs involved not only the aircraft industry but also other technology companies, including the "big three" automakers. The aircraft industry became known as the aerospace industry, and guided missiles and the manned space program assumed large portions of total business. Martin, Douglas, North American, Grumman, and Boeing led the Mercury, Gemini, and triumphant Apollo programs.

The Vietnam War (U.S. involvement 1964–1975) spurred strong demand for helicopters in armed combat, and civil applications increased as well. Turbine power increased capabilities markedly. American fighters, led by the McConnell F-4 Phantom, were widely exported. General aviation manufacturers prospered, and the leading firms of Piper, Cessna, and Beech eventually became subsidiaries of large conglomerates. Demand for small business jets was highly cyclical, but long-term growth attracted new competitors, including the significant Cessna Citation series.

The aircraft industry was consistently the leading American industrial exporter. Composite structural materials, stealth technology, supersonic turbofan engines, and increasing computer use for design and in the cockpit were all impressive, but the number of prime contractors still declined as aircraft service lives were extended and new programs became more rare in the post-Vietnam era. Total aircraft production had declined from some 18,000 in 1969 to under 3,000 in 1987. General aviation production suffered the sharpest drop. Fairchild exited aircraft in 1986, and in the 1990s Grumman merged with Northrop, General Dynamics sold its military aircraft division to Lockheed, Martin and Lockheed merged, and Boeing acquired McDonnell Douglas and the remaining North American aerospace operations from Rockwell. Only two major military contractors, Lockheed Martin and Boeing, remained. With plant closings, southern California was no longer the center of the industry.

The end of the Cold War led to a decline in defense spending as a percentage of the GDP. New aircraft and missile programs declined in urgency. The space program also declined over time. The aerospace industry was no longer the leading industrial employer, as employment dropped below 1 million in 1993 and continued to fall. Concerns rose that technical capability would be lost and that aging aircraft would increase maintenance difficulties and would endanger military readiness. Commercial business displaced military as the largest sector of the industry, but the European Airbus consortium gained strength in the 1980s, posing a credible threat to American dominance.

Out-of-control product liability costs almost destroyed small aircraft production from the early 1980s un-

til legislation eased the problem in 1994. At that time single-engine aircraft production began to recover. Innovative new firms, such as Lancair and Cirrus Design, became significant. Earlier rising aircraft prices had created strong growth in the kit or homebuilt segment, which provided opportunities for entrepreneurs in the field. General aviation remained vulnerable, however, because it was the first sector hurt in a recession and the slowest to recover. Even the respected Mooney firm suffered bankruptcy in the 2001 slowdown.

The aerospace industry became increasingly globalized, as components for many aircraft were constructed in other countries. Great Britain became a partner in the important Joint Strike Fighter (JSF) program awarded to Lockheed Martin in 2001. Several general aviation and helicopter programs were developed multinationally or received foreign financing. Despite its long decline, aerospace was still critical to national security and global competitiveness but could survive only with highly diversified technology companies with lessened dependence on military contracts.

BIBLIOGRAPHY

Bilstein, Roger E. *The American Aerospace Industry: From Workshop to Global Enterprise.* New York: Twayne, 1996.

Pattillo, Donald M. *A History in the Making: 80 Turbulent Years in the American General Aviation Industry.* New York: McGraw-Hill, 1998.

———. *Pushing the Envelope: The American Aircraft Industry.* Ann Arbor: University of Michigan Press, 1998.

Vander Meulen, Jacob A. *The Politics of Aircraft: Building an American Military Industry.* Lawrence: University Press of Kansas, 1991.

Donald M. Pattillo

See also **Air Transportation and Travel.**

AIRLINE DEREGULATION ACT (1978). For forty years, the domestic commercial airline industry was extensively regulated by the Civil Aeronautics Board (CAB). Among other things, the CAB governed which airlines could serve which routes, determined which airlines were certified to enter the market, and restricted mergers among airline companies. In addition, the CAB set the fare structure for the industry: it established rates that tended to subsidize low-cost fares on shorter flights by imposing above-cost fares on longer flights.

Believing that such strict regulation made the industry inefficient and inhibited its growth, Congress in 1978 adopted the Airline Deregulation Act. Championed by Congressional Democrats and signed into law by President Jimmy Carter, the Act represented a fundamental shift away from regulation and toward an air transportation system that relied on competitive market forces to determine the quality, variety, and price of air services. Congress, in the words of the statute, determined that "maximum reliance on competitive market forces" would best further "efficiency, innovation, and low prices" as well as "variety [and] quality . . . of air transportation services." The Act phased out the regulatory power of the CAB, eliminating the agency in 1984. The Act did not, however, change the government's role in overseeing and regulating air safety through the Federal Aviation Administration.

Deregulation had a number of effects. In most markets, fares per passenger mile fell. The key factor contributing to the lower fares was the increased competition brought about by the entry of low-fare airlines into popular markets. In some markets, however, where there was less competition, fares rose above where they had been under the rate structure established by the CAB. Owing to the generally lower prices, air travel increased. In 1978, approximately 250 million passengers traveled by air. About 600 million people traveled by air in 1997.

Another of the more lasting changes was the greater use of airline "hubs,"—major airports where many of an airline's flights originate or terminate—by airline companies. The hub system emphasizes greater frequency of service by smaller aircraft and reduces the number of cities directly connected by any single carrier. This system virtually eliminates the need for wide-body aircraft in domestic air travel. Another effect of deregulation was the transfer of shorter routes from major carriers to smaller, regional airline companies. In the twenty years following the passage of the Act, regional and commuter passenger traffic grew at almost twice the rate of larger air carriers.

BIBLIOGRAPHY

Morrison, Steven A., and Clifford Winston. *The Evolution of the Airline Industry.* Washington, D.C.: Brookings, 1995.

Kent Greenfield

See also **Air Transportation and Travel; Civil Aeronautics Board; Federal Aviation Administration.**

AIRLINE INDUSTRY. *See* **Air Transportation and Travel.**

AIRMAIL. Following fifty-two experimental flights by the Post Office Department in 1911 and 1912, the first extended test of airmail service was made in May 1918, when the U.S. Army and the Post Office Department together set up an experimental line between New York and Washington, D.C., using army pilots. After three months, the department assumed entire control of the line and employed civilian aviators. This route was too short to give the plane much advantage over the railway and did not continue long. Other disconnected lines were tried, between New York and Cleveland, Cleveland and Chicago, and Chicago and Omaha, but all had the same fault—they were too short to attract mail at high rates. In 1920 the department installed a service between New York and San Francisco, with the planes flying only by

daylight and the mail being transferred at dusk to railway trains and rushed on, to take to the air again early next morning. On 1 July 1924 a continuous, day-and-night service across the continent began operations. In 1926 the department began to contract entirely with private corporations to handle all airmail. Branch lines and north-and-south lines were rapidly added. In 1930, when the postal service designated two new routes—New York to Los Angeles via St. Louis and Los Angeles to Atlanta—there were only two bids for the former contract and one for the latter. Charging that there had been collusion among airline owners in the bidding, Postmaster General James A. Farley on 9 February 1934 canceled all airmail contracts, and for four months army planes carried the mail while an official investigation was conducted. There were several fatal accidents by army fliers. New contracts were signed in June, and the service, which by this time covered most of the United States and connected with lines to Canada, the West Indies, Mexico, and Central and South America, was returned to private planes.

In 1935 regular mail service was established across the Pacific, between San Francisco and Manila, along with transatlantic service between New York and London beginning in 1939. In 1948 the postal service began to offer both domestic and international parcel post air service. In 1953 a private company—United Parcel Service (UPS)—began to compete directly with the United States Postal Service as a "common carrier," offering two-day airmail delivery service to major urban areas on the East and West coasts. It expanded its service steadily, so that it operated in all fifty states by 1978. Federal Express, which soon grew to be UPS's major private competitor, began operations in 1973 and expanded rapidly, along with UPS, after the federal government deregulated air cargo in 1977—the same year that the U.S. Postal Service abolished airmail as a separate rate category and established "express mail" as its new category of rush delivery. In the 1980s both private carriers expanded their fleets of airplanes and added both overnight and international delivery service, and in the 1990s they began to offer computerized tracking services while continuing to expand their delivery areas.

BIBLIOGRAPHY

Glines, Carroll. *Airmail: How It All Began.* Blue Ridge Summit, Penn.: Aero, 1990.

Harlow, Alvin F. *Old Post Bags.* New York: D. Appleton, 1928.

Holmes, Donald B. *Air Mail: An Illustrated History.* New York: Clarkson Potter, 1981.

Leary, William M., ed. *Pilots' Directions: The Transcontinental Airway and Its History.* Iowa City: University of Iowa Press, 1990.

Wisniewski, Stanley. "Multinational Enterprises in the Courier Service Industry." International Labour Organization Multilateral Enterprises Programme, working paper no. 1, Geneva 1997.

Alvin F. Harlow / A. R.; C. W.

See also **Air Transportation and Travel; Courier Services; Postal Service, U.S.**

AIRPORTS. *See* **Air Transportation and Travel.**

AIRPORTS, SITING AND FINANCING OF.

Airport development in the United States involves federal, state, regional, and local governments. No single jurisdiction has complete control. Early airport development was predominantly private, but cities and counties became dominant after World War I. As of 1919, airports were limited to military fields plus private strips and a few basic municipal strips. Most were no more than waterways or short grass strips.

Aircraft technology quickly outpaced airport development. This became clear with the DC-2, the larger DC-3, and the Boeing-247, which made a passenger industry viable. Such aircraft required both longer and surfaced runways. Higher passenger loads also necessitated functional airport terminals. These needs, in turn, required more complex engineering, more land, and more money.

By the early 1930s, municipalities had built new airports in Atlanta, Baltimore, Boston, Buffalo, Detroit, Los Angeles, and San Francisco. Other large cities, though, remained far behind, including New York with its infamous Hadley Field, a small airport located in a New Jersey suburb and with no amenities. Still, the Air Commerce Act of 1926 expressly prohibited the federal government from establishing, operating, or maintaining civilian airports. It did, however, establish a basic licensing procedure and a system of lighted federal airways that enabled a pilot to fly at night from one light to the next. The 1926 legislation limited the federal airport role to "encouraging" construction and improvement and giving advice and assistance on design and engineering, if requested. Yet this gave the federal government a significant role, as the Aeronautics Branch in the Department of Commerce performed much of the engineering and design work for early airports.

The Great Depression spurred airport development. The Works Progress Administration financed new airports, including New York City's La Guardia, which opened in 1939. World War II, however, slowed the development of civil airports. But, after the war, civilian aircraft under development just before the war entered service; these included the DC-4 and the Boeing-247. The DC-6, DC-7, and Boeing 347 soon followed them. Then, in the late 1950s and early 1960s, came the jet age with Boeing's 707 and DC-8.

Wartime disruption followed by new, larger aircraft made airports obsolete once again. Cities and counties responded with major expansion of existing airports and the replacement of some older, in-town airports, including Chicago's O'Hare in 1955. Congress responded in 1946 with new federal aid for airport construction. Congressional funding was erratic for the first two decades, but it accelerated after 1970 and became a significant influence on the construction of new runways, taxiways, lighting, gates, and other improvements. After about 1960, most federally supported construction was done at existing airports. The United States built just three large airports in the four subsequent decades: Dulles International (1962); Dallas–Fort Worth International (1974); and Denver International (1995).

By the 1950s, airports were recognized as regional economic assets, but they also posed regional problems, including noise and road congestion. These issues led to complex planning requirements, environmental requirements, and new governing structures.

At the end of the twentieth century, many of the largest airports were owned and operated by special purpose agencies created by state legislatures. Some agencies were responsible for several airports and even several modes of transport, as with the Massachusetts Port Authority. The Port Authority of New York and New Jersey illustrates an even more complex structure. The two states jointly created this multimodal authority, which owned and operated JFK International, La Guardia, Newark International, and Teterboro airports, plus bridges, tunnels, and the Port of New York. More commonly, however, special purpose authorities were limited to one or more airports, with no role in other modes of transport. Finally, cities and counties owned major airports, as in Chicago, Kansas City, Los Angeles, Miami, and elsewhere.

The federal government owns and operates no civilian airports. It once owned and operated Washington National Airport and, later, Dulles International Airport in northern Virginia. However, in 1986, Congress determined that those airports were regional assets and that federal ownership was inappropriate. Consequently, Congress leased their operation to the Metropolitan Washington Airports Authority, a new multistate authority with board members appointed by Virginia, the District of Columbia, and the president of the United States. The federal government also plays no role in initiating airport construction or expansion, which is done by airport sponsors. Washington's role in aviation focuses on the design and production of safe aircraft, safe operation, proper maintenance, and operation of the air traffic control system and air navigation facilities. But the federal presence in airport development remained strong. Although airports rely mostly on landing fees and concessions (restaurants, bars, and other retail activities) to finance capital improvements and operating expenses, the Federal Aviation Administration (FAA) provides significant financial assistance to airport "sponsors" for air-side construction. In addition, Federal Airport Improvement Program (AIP) projects entail comprehensive planning requirements that involve all jurisdictions in an urban region. The FAA also establishes and enforces minimal safety and environmental standards at airports that have scheduled airline traffic. Furthermore, it establishes criteria for relocation assistance. In each case, states may impose additional requirements.

If AIP funds are involved, as they usually are in major projects, airport sponsors must meet federal safety requirements for such things as fuel handling, signage, and fire and rescue. Projects also must pass environmental assessments made under the Environmental Protection Act of 1970 and must meet federal planning requirements, complete with public hearings and eventual project approval by regional planning bodies. Again, additional state requirements may have to be met.

Airport projects in the twenty-first century faced technical and political hurdles at all stages. Most political barriers were at the local level, where government is especially sensitive to public concerns about such matters as noise and congestion. However, airport development faced complex public demands at all levels of government. Constituencies could demand frequent and conveniently scheduled flights, fewer delays, less noise, safety at any cost, and low fares, stipulations that are often mutually exclusive. Given such competing public demands, securing approval for airport design, location, and operation was a monumental task.

BIBLIOGRAPHY

Komos, Nick. *Bonfires to Beacons: Federal Civil Aviation Policy under the Air Commerce Act, 1926–1938.* Washington, D.C.: Smithsonian Institution Press, 1989.

———. *The Cutting Air Crash: Case Study in Early Federal Aviation Policy.* Washington, D.C.: Department of Transportation, Government Printing Office, 1984.

Robert Matthews

See also **Air Transportation and Travel; Aircraft Industry; Federal Aviation Administration; Noise Pollution; Port Authority of New York and New Jersey.**

AISNE-MARNE OPERATION,

a French and American counteroffensive against the German army during World War I. In the spring of 1918, Germany launched a desperate effort to knock France out of the war before American forces arrived to support the French. The effort failed. By midsummer the German attack ground to a halt, and the arrival of thousands of fresh American troops made possible a major counterassault. The French Tenth Army opened the attack in mid-July, striking eastward into the salient just south of Soissons, France. The main attack was made by the Twentieth Corps, with three divisions on the front line, two American and one Moroccan. The attack took the Germans by surprise, and their outpost line made little resistance, but the line soon stiffened and the fighting was severe. It was not until 21 July that control of the Soissons-Château-Thierry highway was gained. The total penetration was eight miles.

From 21 July on, the armies farther east joined in the advance—the Sixth and the Fifth, along both faces of the salient. With the Sixth Army there were two U.S. corps headquarters—the First and the Third—and eight American divisions. The Germans conducted their retreat skillfully, making an especially strong stand on the Ourcq River on 28 July. But early in August they were back behind the Vesle River, which they would not cross again.

The Aisne-Marne Operation changed the complexion of the war. A German offensive had been stopped suddenly in mid-onslaught, and the advance changed to a retreat. The Marne salient had ceased to exist, and the Germans were never again able to undertake a serious offensive. The addition of hundreds of thousands of American troops to the Allied cause made further German resistance futile. In November, facing economic collapse at home and the combined forces of Britain, France, and the United States on the battlefield, Germany finally surrendered.

BIBLIOGRAPHY

Coffman, Edward M. *The War to End All Wars: The American Military Experience in World War I.* New York: Oxford University Press, 1968.

Fussell, Paul. *The Great War and Modern Memory.* New York: Oxford University Press, 1975.

Keegan, John. *The First World War.* New York: Knopf, 1999.

Oliver Lyman Spaulding / A. G.

See also **American Expeditionary Forces; Artillery; Chemical and Biological Warfare; Doughboy; Machine Guns; World War I, Navy in.**

AIX-LA-CHAPELLE, TREATY OF

(18 October 1748). Also called the Peace of Aix-la-Chapelle, this treaty ended the War of Austrian Succession (1740–1748), which in Britain's North American colonies was known as KING GEORGE'S WAR (1744–1748). The signatories were Great Britain, France, the Habsburg Empire, the United Provinces of the Low Countries (Netherlands), Prussia, Spain, Modena, Genoa, and Sardinia. The treaty basically returned the world situation to the status quo of 1744, with Prussia keeping the former Austrian province of Silesia and France regaining the fortress of Louisbourg on Cape Breton Island, Nova Scotia. This greatly surprised the New England colonists, who had put forth a major effort in 1745 to capture the fort for the British Empire. This disappointment damaged relations between London and the New England colonists. The treaty settled nothing with regard to British and French colonial and commercial rivalries in North America, particularly in the regions along the Ohio and Mississippi Rivers, and provided only a respite before the more significant French and Indian War (1754–1763), which was known as the Seven Years' War in Europe. Aix-la-Chapelle was a part of France when the treaty was signed there; it is now known as Aachen, Germany.

BIBLIOGRAPHY

Lodge, Richard. *Studies in Eighteenth-Century Diplomacy, 1740–1748.* London: J. Murray, 1930.

Phillips, Charles L., and Alan Axelrod. "Treaty of Aix-la-Chapelle." In *Encyclopedia of Historical Treaties and Alliances.* Volume 1. New York: Facts on File, 2001.

Sosin, Jack M. "Louisbourg and the Peace of Aix-la-Chapelle, 1748." *William and Mary Quarterly* 3d ser., 14 (October 1957): 516–535.

Daniel K. Blewett

AKIMEL O'ODHAM AND TOHONO O'OD-HAM.

The Akimel O'odham (River People, formerly known as Pima) and Tohono O'odham (Desert People, previously known as Papago) are the quintessential inhabitants of the Sonoran Desert of Arizona and Sonora. They speak closely related dialects of the Tepiman branch of the Uto-Aztecan language family. When Jesuit missionaries established missions among them beginning in 1687, the so-called Upper Pima inhabited autonomous villages along the river valleys of northern Sonora and south-central Arizona. The Papago moved from winter villages near springs to summer field camps along arroyos in the vast basin-and-range desert west of the Santa Cruz River. The Akimel and Tohono O'odham were the northernmost Tepiman speakers in a long, broken linguistic chain that included the Lower Pima (O'odham) of central and southern Sonora, the northern and southern Tepe-

Pima Matron. This 1907 photograph by Edward S. Curtis shows an Akimel O'odham (Pima) woman with a traditional basket. Photograph by Edward S. Curtis. © CORBIS

huane (Odami) of Chihuahua and Durango, and the Tepecano of northern Jalisco.

Many archaeologists believe the O'odham are descendants of the Hohokam, who occupied central and southern Arizona from A.D. 200 to 1450 and constructed the largest pre-Columbian irrigation canal systems north of coastal Peru. The Akimel O'odham cultivated irrigated plots of corn, beans, squash, and cotton. Jesuit missionaries introduced Old World animals—sheep, goats, cattle, and horses—and Old World plants, especially winter wheat. Because it was frost tolerant, wheat filled an empty niche in their agricultural cycle and allowed the Akimel O'odham to plant their fields year-round. Agricultural intensification also enabled the Akimel O'odham to live in larger settlements, an important adaptation as Apache livestock raiding grew more frequent during the 1700s and 1800s. By the mid-nineteenth century, O'odham along the Gila River became the greatest agricultural entrepreneurs in Arizona. They fed thousands of forty-niners during the California Gold Rush, supplied the Butterfield Stage, and sold produce to both Confederate and Union troops during the Civil War. By the 1870s, however, non-Indian settlers upstream were diverting most of the Gila's flow, withering Akimel O'odham fields. Akimel O'odham and their Yuman-speaking neighbors—the Maricopa, who share the Gila River Indian Community (1859), Salt River Indian Reservation (1879), and Ak-Chin Reservation (1912)—were still trying to recover Gila waters in the early twenty-first century.

The Tohono O'odham have fought their own water wars. Prior to the drilling of deep wells in the early twentieth century, they harvested desert plants like mesquite, agaves, and cactus fruit and planted summer crops of corn, squash, devil's claw, and pinto and tepary beans in fields along arroyos that filled with runoff after summer rains. Mission San Xavier del Bac, south of Tucson, where Jesuit and Franciscan missionaries resettled Tohono O'odham along the Santa Cruz River, was the only community on the reservation where irrigation agriculture was possible. Once surface flow along the Santa Cruz disappeared because of down cutting and groundwater pumping, however, O'odham agriculture at San Xavier died as well. In 1975 the Tohono O'odham pressured the federal government to file suit against agribusinessmen, copper mines, and the city of Tucson, who were sucking water from the aquifer beneath the San Xavier District, a part of the much larger Tohono O'odham Reservation (1911) to the west. To avert a legal Armageddon over water in the Tucson Basin, Congress passed the Southern Arizona Water Rights Settlement Act in 1982, granting the O'odham 76,000 acre-feet of water a year. In 2001, that settlement was only beginning to be implemented.

Approximately 24,000 Tohono O'odham and more than 16,000 Akimel O'odham live on and off four Arizona reservations. They largely make their living in the service and manufacturing sectors, although the four tribes operate farms as well. Casinos provide an important source

Tohono O'odham. Singers perform in the multitribal Fiesta de Tumacácori, held annually on the first weekend in December at the ruins of the old Franciscan Mission San José de Tumacácori in southern Arizona. Photograph by Tom Bean. © CORBIS

Rea, Amadeo M. *At the Desert's Green Edge: An Ethnobotany of the Gila River Pima*. Tucson: University of Arizona Press, 1997.

Russell, Frank. *The Pima Indians*. Tucson: University of Arizona Press, 1975. Originally published in 1904 and 1905.

Shaul, David Leedom, and Jane H. Hill. "Tepimans, Yumans, and Other Hohokam." *American Antiquity* 63 (1998): 375–396.

Sheridan, Thomas E. "The O'odham (Pimas and Papagos): The World Would Burn without Rain." In *Paths of Life: American Indians of the Southwest and Northern Mexico*. Edited by Thomas E. Sheridan and Nancy Parezo. Tucson: University of Arizona Press, 1996.

Spicer, Edward H. *Cycles of Conquest: The Impact of Spain, Mexico, and the United States on the Indians of the Southwest, 1533–1960*. Tucson: University of Arizona Press, 1962.

Underhill, Ruth M. *Papago Indian Religion*. New York: Columbia University Press, 1946.

Thomas E. Sheridan

See also **Tribes: Southwestern.**

ALABAMA. Geography has had a great influence on the history of Alabama. The state is bound by Tennessee on the north, Georgia on the east, Florida and the Gulf of Mexico on the south, and Mississippi on the west. Alabama is a state of contrasts, with mountainous regions in the north, the prairie lowlands called the Black Belt in the middle of the state, and coastal plain regions in the south. Cheaha Mountain is the highest point in the state, with an elevation of 2,407 feet.

The thirteen major rivers of Alabama construct a framework for intense agricultural production, transportation, and hydroelectric power. The Tallapoosa and Coosa Rivers run southeast through the state, the Tennessee River loops through the northeastern part of the state, the Tombigbee and Black Warrior Rivers merge in the west-central part of Alabama, and the Chattahoochee marks a portion of the eastern border with Georgia. Early on, rivers were central to the lives of the native inhabitants for accessing food supplies and for transportation. Early European settlers followed the Native Americans' pattern, establishing communities near water sources first.

Early Inhabitants

Archaeologists estimate that the first human settlements in Alabama date from around 9000 B.C. The first inhabitants lived in communities located near cave and bluff sites around the state, such as Russell Cave in Jackson County. Moundville, situated in Hale and Tuscaloosa counties on the Black Warrior River, is one of the largest prehistoric communities north of Mexico. By the 1600s, most of the Native Americans living in what would become Alabama belonged to four major nations: Creek, Cherokee, Choctaw, and Chickasaw. These nations (which included the Alabama, Apalache, Coushatta, and Mobile tribes) were related through a common language, Muskogean, and

of income, funding social services, education, and health care, which is particularly important since the O'odham suffer the highest incidence of Type 2 diabetes in the world. The legal recognition of their water rights has made the O'odham major players in the Arizona economy, giving them the clout they need to pursue tribal economic and political sovereignty in the twenty-first century.

BIBLIOGRAPHY

Bahr, Donald et al. *The Short Swift Time of Gods on Earth: The Hohokam Chronicles*. Berkeley: University of California Press, 1994.

Haury, Emil W. *The Hohokam: Desert Farmers and Craftsmen: Excavations at Snaketown, 1964–1965*. Tucson: University of Arizona Press, 1976.

many shared traditions. The Native Americans primarily lived in villages located on water sources, such as the Coosa and Tallapoosa Rivers. The largest group was the Creek Confederation, numbering about 22,000 when the Europeans first landed, but the effects of European communicable diseases were devastating to the Native Americans.

The state's name probably comes from the name of a Native American tribe that lived primarily in central Alabama. A major river in the state was named for this group, and the state was named for the river. Some experts believe that the name has roots in the Choctaw tongue; it is commonly translated as "thicket clearers."

European Contact

According to available documents, the first Europeans to reach Alabama were Spanish explorers Alonzo Alvares de Piñeda in 1519 and Pánfilo de Narváez in 1528. However, a 1507 German New World map depicts Mobile Bay in great detail, suggesting that an unknown individual charted the Alabama coast prior to the first Spanish explorers. Sometime in the 1540s Hernando de Soto entered the region. The treasurer from that expedition, Cabeza de Vaca, offered the first written account of the Alabama land, including the first description of the native inhabitants. A significant battle was fought at the village of Maubila between de Soto's Spaniards and Chief Tuscaloosa's (or Tascaluza's) warriors.

Don Tristán de Luna made the first attempt to establish a Spanish colony on the Alabama-Florida coast, but his efforts failed in 1561. The first permanent European settlement, Fort Louis de la Mobile, was established by Jean-Baptiste le Moyne de Bienville in 1702 at Mobile Bay (then part of Louisiana, ruled by the French). In 1717, Fort Toulouse was established on the Coosa River for trading purposes. The first African slaves arrived in Alabama in 1721, aboard the slave ship the *Africane*.

In 1780, during the Revolutionary War, Alabama was taken by Spain. The United States took back the Mobile area, considered the center of Spanish power, during the War of 1812. The Alabama Territory was created from Mississippi Territory land, and settlers disputed over rights to the land and fought to gain favor with the Creek Nation. The Creek War of 1813–1814 ended with the defeat of the Creeks at Horseshoe Bend. On 9 August 1814, Creek leader William Wetherford surrendered to General Andrew Jackson at Fort Jackson, where he signed a treaty that ceded the Creek lands to the federal government.

Becoming a State

After the defeat of the Creek nation, "Alabama Fever" swept the land. Thousands of settlers flocked to the state, seeking the temperate climate and rich soil that proved perfect for the production of cotton. Small farmers, planters, and professionals brought families from other Piedmont regions of the Southeast. The majority of newcomers to the state were farming-class families who brought with them few slaves and limited supplies. Most settled as squatters prior to land being made available for sale by the government.

William Wyatt Bibb, a former Georgia senator, was appointed the new territorial governor of Alabama in 1817. There have been five state capitals since the 1817 Congressional act that created Alabama: St. Stephens, Huntsville, Cahaba (at the juncture of the Cahaba and Alabama Rivers), Tuscaloosa, and finally Montgomery, on the Alabama River. The state's founders felt that a river location was important for the capital. The first steamboat, *The Alabama*, was built in St. Stephens in 1818.

Alabama was admitted to the Union on 14 December 1819 as the twenty-second state. The first Alabama Constitution was written in 1819, and William Wyatt Bibb was publicly elected that year as the first governor of the state. The 1830 Federal Census lists Alabama's population as 309,527; 190,406 were white and 119,121 were African American (with 117,549 designated as slaves and 1,572 as free blacks).

The Plantation and War

Alabama's cotton kingdom was built by the hands, minds, and spirits of slaves brought primarily from West Africa. Slavery, called the "peculiar institution," caused complicated social and cultural patterns to evolve in the state, the effects of which are still felt in Alabama. Plantations varied in size and aimed to be self-sufficient, but most farmers in the state worked small farms and owned no slaves.

In the 1830s, Alabama politicians aligned with President Andrew Jackson and his criticisms of the Bank of America and the idea of centralized wealth and power. European settlement continued to expand, and during Clement C. Clay's tenure as governor, the Creeks were exiled from the state. In 1832 the state's first railroad, the Tuscumbia Railway, opened. Its two miles of track ran from the Tennessee River to Tuscumbia. In 1854 the Alabama Public School Act was passed, creating a statewide education system.

As an agriculturally centered state, Alabama's politics were tied to the land. The dominant political parties were the Democrats and the Whigs, with the Democratic Party generally predominating. A fundamentally Jeffersonian and proslavery philosophy guided the Alabama government in the prewar years.

The debate over states' rights became more heated through the 1850s and early 1860s, and Alabama's leading advocate was William L. Yancy. Henry W. Hilliard and supporters of sectional reconciliation could not dissuade those advocating secession. On 11 January 1861, the Alabama Secession Convention passed an Ordinance of Secession, making Alabama the fourth state to secede from the Union. The influence of Jacksonian democracy on the state was profound. Alabamians generally supported individualism and a steadfast perseverance for independence, combined with perceptions that hard work was a virtue and that education and wealth lead to corruption.

After the formation of the Confederate States, a government was built in Montgomery in central Alabama, creating the "Cradle of the Confederacy" (and the "Heart of Dixie"). Jefferson Davis was inaugurated as president of the Confederate States of America there on 18 February 1861.

During the Civil War, 202 land and naval events occurred within Alabama's borders and Alabama civilian involvement was great. Not only did 90,000 to 100,000 white men fight for the Confederacy, an estimated 2,700 white men from north Alabama and as many as 10,000 blacks from the Tennessee Valley area enlisted in the Union army. During the war, as in most other Southern states, women and children assisted the Confederacy by supplying as many goods as possible, even as they maintained homes and farms while a significant portion of the working white male population was gone. Women also established clinics in communities and on the battlefield to care for wounded soldiers all across the state.

Beyond the Civil War
After the war, Alabama rewrote its constitution. In February 1868, the constitution was ratified and Alabama was readmitted to the Union. The state was put under Federal control as congressionally warranted, and the new constitution allowed blacks suffrage for the first time.

When the political and social order of the Confederacy fell in spring 1865, Alabama entered a period of upheaval and was forced to redefine itself. Tensions grew between the planter class and the small farmers, between the races, and between political factions. Alabama was riddled with losses from the war—political, financial, and social loss, as well as loss of human life. Alabamians resented the Federal troops that came into the state under President Andrew Johnson's plan of Reconstruction. The state was politically split: the anti-Confederacy contingency in northern Alabama opposed the conservatives in the south, and the racial divide created a great chasm in the state. No group in the state wanted to lose power or status. There was a period of accommodation by white southerners toward blacks, but reactions against the Civil Rights Act of 1866—granting equal rights to people of every race and color—were violent. The freed black population complicated the political structure of the state, and the acts of violence and terror reflected whites' fear that blacks and a federal presence in the state would crumble the old Alabama power. The Ku Klux Klan (KKK) moved into north Alabama after its birth in Tennessee and gradually moved through the state. Although federal response to Klan actions effectively stopped the group's activity for a while, the KKK would reappear later in Alabama's history.

Bourbon Democrats, claiming to have redeemed the people of Alabama from federal Reconstructionist rule by carpetbaggers and scalawags, passed a new constitution on 16 November 1875. Political dissension and corruption, along with animosity toward federal involvement in

the welfare and control of the state, made Alabama a hotbed for trouble. While slavery had been abolished, sharecropping and farm tenancy systems—established to continue the state's agricultural production—were forms of legalized slavery. After the Civil War came the first movement of blacks away from Alabama: while some former slaves chose to stay where there was work, many immediately left the land and people that had held them in bondage.

Industry emerged in Alabama in the early 1870s. The textile industry made its start in the Chattahoochee River Valley and near Huntsville. North Alabama, especially around Birmingham, was dotted with an ever-growing expanse of coal and iron mines. Birmingham would for many years be the industrial center of the state. All the resources needed to make steel were available within twenty miles of the city, drawing investors like Henry DeBardeleben and James Sloss to the area. The Tennessee Coal and Iron Company (TCI) moved its headquarters to Birmingham.

With the boom in industry, Alabama needed to strike a balance between the long-established agricultural constituency and the new industrial one. The level of poverty was intense, especially for farmers: it cost more to produce agricultural goods than they were worth. The Farmers' Alliance quickly gained ground in Alabama, creating cooperatives and becoming a voice of reform. Interest in the Populist Party grew along with reformist sentiments. The established Bourbon hegemony was threatened by the Populists' appeals to the working classes, including blacks.

The Democrats even used legal means to step around the Fifteenth Amendment, disenfranchising blacks and poor whites—thus setting in motion the widely accepted practice of legalized discrimination and violence toward blacks and, to a much lesser extent, other minority groups. In 1901 delegates from across the state met at the Constitutional Convention. They established suffrage requirements of residency, literacy, land ownership, and taxation that disenfranchised most black voters, as well many poor whites. The new Constitution of the State of Alabama was adopted on 3 September 1901.

War and the Great Depression
Alabamians rallied to the World War I effort. The state sent 86,000 men to combat; 6,400 of these were casualties. Military bases throughout the state offered training facilities to prepare soldiers for war.

As in the rest of the country, black and white women in Alabama were seriously advocating for their right to vote in the 1910s. When Tennessee ratified the Nineteenth Amendment in 1920, it was made law. Alabama ratified after that point, even though it was unnecessary. Women played a significant role in Alabama during the Progressive Era, leading education reforms, prohibition, child welfare, and prison reform. Both black and white women fought to improve the social and moral well-being of the state's inhabitants. Julia S. Tutwiler was one such reformer; she is remembered for advancing the educational opportunities for women and girls.

Although the early 1920s postwar era offered riches for some, most of the state remained poor. The boll weevil had come to Alabama in 1909, eventually forcing farmers to diversify crop production because of its devastating effects on cotton. While industry was a definite presence in the state, agriculture still reigned in the years between the World Wars. Because of poor conditions for crop production, the 1920s were a stark time for farmers all across the south. These conditions were echoed throughout the country during the Great Depression.

During the depression, some Alabama politicians played a significant role in the administration of President Franklin D. Roosevelt, including the New Deal. Alabama's Senator Hugo C. Black, a former member of the Ku Klux Klan, was appointed to the United States Supreme Court in 1937. One New Deal program in particular had an enormous effect on the state: the Tennessee Valley Authority (TVA).

The Great Depression was a time of such upheaval for families that many relocated to try to find work and stability. There was a mass migration of blacks leaving the state during this time and into the 1940s, when World War II's production demands offered work opportunities. New York, Chicago, Detroit, and other industrial cities offered blacks an opportunity for a better life.

World War II brought a measure of prosperity to the state. Most folks who wanted a job could find one. The Mobile Bay housed companies that built ships, and Childersburg was the home of the Alabama Ordnance Works, one of the nation's largest producers of smokeless gunpowder. Alabama sent 250,000 enlisted men to the war effort, with over 6,000 casualties.

Civil Rights

A shift occurred in Alabama's political allegiance to the Democratic Party starting in the 1940s, resulting mostly from questions and conflicts over civil rights.

As soon as federal troops left Alabama after Reconstruction, racial segregation was the understood, and eventually written, law of the state. In 1896, the U.S. Supreme Court ruled in Plessy v. Ferguson that "separate but equal" facilities for blacks and whites were legal. But separate was not equal in Alabama, and the modern history of the state would be formed by the black struggle for equality.

When the KKK returned to Alabama in 1915, its actions were not solely directed toward blacks. Reacting to the heavy influx of immigrants into the state and the Progressive social movement, the Klan struck out against anyone that seemed to threaten "traditional American values." By 1924, around 18,000 of Birmingham's 32,000 registered voters were Klan members, making the group a formidable presence.

The 1931 Scottsboro Boys incident placed Alabama and its politics in the international spotlight, raising questions about civil rights, the presence of the Communist Party, and northern political and social influence on the state. The incident started in March, when two white teenage girls riding a freight train near Scottsboro told police they had been raped by some black men on the train. Within fifteen days, nine young black men were arrested, charged, tried, convicted, and sentenced to die for the alleged rapes. The sentences met with international outrage over the mob atmosphere, and many activists called for a reversal of the rulings. This incident started a social and racial revolution in Alabama that would affect the racial dynamics of the entire country.

In 1954, the U.S. Supreme Court ruled in Brown v. Board of Education that separate but equal schools were illegal. Alabama's officials chose not to enforce or even recognize this mandate. In 1955 the U.S. Supreme Court ordered the University of Alabama to admit two black women who had been denied admission.

Dr. Martin Luther King Jr.'s presence in the state started when he began preaching at the Dexter Avenue Baptist Church in Montgomery. He later wrote "Letter from the Birmingham Jail" after being arrested for his involvement in nonviolent protests. On 1 December 1955, Rosa Parks refused to give up her seat in the middle of a public bus to a white man. Her action sparked the Montgomery Bus Boycott, which crippled the city of Montgomery economically. The boycott was the first significant civil rights victory in Alabama. Black voter registration became an intense focus in the state, bringing Freedom Riders from all over the country to help with the cause.

Violence erupted in response to the civil rights movement, including bombings directed toward King and other prominent nonviolent leaders. In 1963, a bomb killed four girls at the Sixteenth Street Baptist Church in downtown Birmingham, possibly the most infamous act of violence during the civil rights movement. That same year, police commissioner Eugene "Bull" Connor turned his intimidation tactics, fire hoses, and attack dogs on the peaceful protesters in Birmingham.

Forced federal integration was ordered in 1963. Governor George C. Wallace stood on the stairs at the University of Alabama and professed, "Segregation now; segregation tomorrow; segregation forever." Driven by what he thought people in the state wanted to hear, Wallace was vocally racist for most of his political career. He was first elected as governor of Alabama in 1962 and served four terms in that position over the next twenty years, with several unsuccessful bids at the White House.

The Selma to Montgomery March, led by King and other civil rights leaders, began in Selma on 21 March 1965 and ended four days later at the state capital. After the conclusion of the march and the speeches, Klansmen murdered a Detroit housewife as she helped take members of the march back home. This act, and others associated with voter registration drives, created a constellation of activism and violence.

The time was one of conflict, but black Alabamians and thousands of their supporters successfully birthed the movement that instigated change. The Civil Rights Acts of 1964 and 1968, and other federal interventions, made discrimination based on race illegal.

After the Civil Rights Movement

Divided into sixty-seven counties, the land area of Alabama is 32.5 million acres. In 2000, 28 percent was used as farmland. Although cotton was no longer the dominant crop in Alabama at the end of the twentieth century, it still figured prominently. Cotton is predominantly grown in the Tennessee Valley area, and some is grown in the Black Belt, Mountain, and Plateau regions. Peanuts, soybeans, corn, peaches, and pecans are also important crops. Cattle and poultry are major agricultural assets as well.

Forests are one of Alabama's most important agricultural resources. The timber industry is influential throughout all regions of the state, and it is vital to the state's economy. Other natural resources that figure into the state's economy are natural gas, sand and gravel, lime, clay, and coal.

Alabama has also made historic contributions to space exploration. The first U.S. satellite, *Explorer I* (launched on 31 January 1958), was developed in Huntsville. The George C. Marshall Space Flight Center, established in 1960, has played a significant role in the development of the space shuttle program and the space station.

At the end of the twentieth century, Alabama's rich resources made the state attractive to new industry. Tuscaloosa is known for electronics manufacturing, and Birmingham is home to cutting-edge biomedical research and engineering, and to telecommunications firms. New car manufacturing industries continued to come to the state. In 1989, the manufacturing sector of the state's economy employed 24 percent of Alabama's total workforce.

Alabama's rivers continue to be important to the state, especially for waterborne commerce. Alabama has more than 1,500 miles of navigable inland waterways. The Port of Mobile is a point of international shipping.

Alabama's population grew throughout the last thirty years of the century: 1970's population was 3,444,165, and 1990's population was 4,040,587. According to the 2000 Federal Census, there were 4,447,100 people living in Alabama, with the largest portion of the population aged 35 to 44 years old (685,512). There were 3,162,808 Alabamians who identified as white, 1,155,930 as black, 75,830 as Hispanic or Latino, 31,346 as Asian, 22,430 as American Indian and Alaska Native, and 1,409 as Native Hawaiian and other Pacific Islanders.

BIBLIOGRAPHY

Flynt, J. Wayne. *Poor but Proud: Alabama's Poor Whites.* Tuscaloosa: University of Alabama Press, 1989.

Jackson, Harvey H., III. *Rivers of History: Life on the Coosa, Tallapoosa, Cahaba, and Alabama.* Tuscaloosa: University of Alabama Press, 1995.

Kelley, Robin D. G. *Hammer and Hoe: Alabama Communists during the Great Depression.* Chapel Hill: University of North Carolina Press, 1990.

Letwin, Daniel. *The Challenge of Interracial Unionism: Alabama Coal Miners, 1878–1921.* Chapel Hill: University of North Carolina Press, 1998.

Litwack, Leon F. *Trouble in Mind: Black Southerners in the Age of Jim Crow.* New York: Knopf, 1998.

McKiven, Henry M., Jr. *Iron and Steel: Class, Race, and Community in Birmingham, Alabama, 1875–1920.* Chapel Hill: University of North Carolina Press, 1995.

Rogers, William Warren, Robert David Ward, Leah Rawls Atkins, and Wayne Flynt. *Alabama: The History of a Deep South State.* Tuscaloosa: University of Alabama Press, 1994.

Kyes Stevens

See also **Bourbons; Civil Rights Movement; Desegregation; Ku Klux Klan; Reconstruction; Scottsboro Case; South, the; Tribes: Southeastern.**

ALABAMA. In August 1861, James D. Bulloch, a Confederate naval agent, contracted with the Laird shipyard of Liverpool, England, to build a steam sloop-of-war. Known only as "number 290," in order to conceal its true identity, the vessel slipped away on its first shakedown cruise in July 1862, never returning to port. After, traveling to the Azores, the ship was armed and commissioned the Confederate commerce raider C.S.S. *Alabama.* Commanded by Captain Raphael Semmes, the *Alabama* left a path of destruction from the Atlantic to the Indian Ocean, sinking over sixty U.S. merchant vessels and one Union warship, the U.S.S. *Hatteras.* After twenty consecutive months at sea, and in need of extensive repairs, the *Alabama* set sail for France to secure dry-dock facilities where the ship could be overhauled. When the ship dropped anchor at the port of Cherbourg on 10 June 1864, news of the *Alabama*'s arrival in France spread quickly across Europe. Just four days later, the U.S.S. *Kearsarge*, commanded by Captain John S. Winslow, reached Cherbourg and took up post outside of the harbor in neutral waters. With no avenue of escape, and in spite of its poor condition, the *Alabama* sailed out to give battle to the *Kearsarge* on 19 June. As the two vessels closed on one another at a high speed, the *Alabama* opened fire first with no effect. The return salvo of the *Kearsarge* forced the *Alabama* to turn hard to port, resulting in both vessels exchanging broadsides as they steamed in a series of circles around one another. One hour later, with massive holes opened in its sides at the waterline, the *Alabama* sank. Captain Semmes and forty-one members of the crew were able to escape to England aboard the British yacht *Deerhound.* During the course of her brief career the *Alabama* had wreaked havoc on the American merchant marine.

BIBLIOGRAPHY
Official Records of the Union and Confederate Navies in the War of the Rebellion. Washington, D.C.: U.S. Government Printing Office, 1894–1922. Ser. 1, v. 1–27; ser. 2, v. 1–3.

Robinson, Charles M. *Shark of the Confederacy: The Story of the C.S.S.* Alabama. Annapolis, Md.: Naval Institute Press, 1995.

Semmes, Raphael. *Memoirs of Service Afloat During the War Between the States.* Secaucus, N.J.: Blue and Grey Press, 1987.

Gene Barnett

See also **Civil War; Navy, Confederate; Warships.**

ALABAMA **CLAIMS.** American grievances against Great Britain during and just after the Civil War clustered about this generic phrase, but they filled a broad category. Most Northerners regarded Queen Victoria's proclamation of neutrality, giving the South belligerent rights, as hasty and unfriendly. Confederate cruisers, built or armed by Britons, destroyed Northern shipping, drove insurance rates high, and forced many Northern ships under foreign flags. The Confederates raised large sums of money in Great Britain and outfitted blockade runners there.

Early in the war, Secretary of State William H. Seward instructed Minister C. F. Adams to lay the losses caused by the *Alabama* before the British government, with a demand for redress. In April 1863 British authorities halted the *Alexandra* when Adams proved it was intended for the Confederacy; in September, they detained two armored rams under construction. One other Confederate ship, the *Shenandoah*, clearly violated British neutrality laws, but only after refitting at Melbourne. Ultimately, the United States claimed damages totaling $19,021,000.

The United States occasionally repeated its claims but met no response until 1868. The Johnson-Clarendon Convention, signed that year, made no mention of the *Alabama* damages but provided for a settlement of all Anglo-American claims since 1853. Partly because of the unpopularity of the Andrew Johnson administration, the Senate overwhelmingly defeated the convention (13 April 1869). Senator Charles Sumner seized the opportunity to review the whole case against Great Britain. Not only had the *Alabama* and other cruisers done heavy damage, he declared, but British moral and material support for the South had doubled the war's duration. Sumner set the total U.S. bill at $2.1 billion, a demand that could be met only by the cession of Canada. Hamilton Fish, who became secretary of state in March 1869, took a saner position, announcing that Britain could satisfy the *Alabama* Claims with a moderate lump sum, an apology, and a revised definition of maritime international law.

The impasse between the two nations was brief. The two countries soon formed a joint commission to settle the whole nexus of disputes—Canadian fisheries, northwestern boundary, and *Alabama* Claims. The commission drew up the Treaty of Washington (signed 8 May 1871), which expressed British regret for the escape of the *Alabama* and other cruisers, established three rules of maritime neutrality, and submitted the *Alabama* Claims to a board of five arbitrators. On 14 September 1872 this tribunal awarded the United States $15.5 million in gold to meet its direct damages, all indirect claims having been excluded. American opinion accepted the award as adequate.

BIBLIOGRAPHY
Cook, Adrian. *The "Alabama" Claims.* Ithaca, N.Y.: Cornell University Press, 1975.

Davis, Bancroft. *Mr. Fish and the "Alabama" Claims.* Manchester, N.H.: Ayer, 1977.

Nevins, Allan. *Hamilton Fish.* New York: Ungar, 1957.

Allan Nevins/c. w.

See also **Blockade Runners, Confederate; Navy, Confederate; Washington, Treaty of.**

ALABAMA PLATFORM, adopted by the Alabama Democratic state convention in 1848 and approved by other Southern groups, was William L. Yancey's answer to the Wilmot Proviso and squatter sovereignty principles. It demanded congressional protection of slavery in the Mexican Cession. Rejected by the Democratic National Convention in 1848, the principle was adopted by a majority of the Democratic National Convention at Charleston in 1860. When the convention splintered into factions supporting rival candidates, the Alabama Platform emerged as a rallying cry for the Southern secessionists.

BIBLIOGRAPHY
Channing, Steven A. *Crisis of Fear: Secession in South Carolina.* New York: Simon and Schuster, 1970.

Freehling, William W. *The Road to Disunion.* New York: Oxford University Press, 1990.

Wendell H. Stephenson/A. R.

See also **Secession; Wilmot Proviso.**

ALAMO, SIEGE OF THE, a standoff between the Mexican army and a small band of Texan forces between 23 February and 6 March 1836 at the Alamo, a fort established in 1793 at a former Franciscan mission in San Antonio. The siege took place during the revolt of the Texas province to gain independence from Mexico.

In 1835 the Texan government dismissed its commander in chief, General Sam Houston, for recommending that the fort at San Antonio be abandoned. Lieutenant Colonel William Barret Travis and James Bowie were placed in command of about 155 men at the Alamo.

On 23 February 1836 General Antonio López de Santa Anna arrived at San Antonio with a Mexican force

The Alamo. The Mexican army lays siege to the small fort before its final assaults on 6 March 1836. © Bettmann/corbis

of 3,000–4,000 men. Travis and Bowie could have retreated to safety. Instead, they moved into the stout-walled Alamo mission, answered a demand for surrender with a cannon shot, sent couriers for reinforcements, and vowed not to surrender. A message signed by Travis read, "I have sustained a continual Bombardment and a cannondale for 24 hours and have not lost a man. . . . Our flag still proudly waves from the wall. I shall never surrender or retreat. . . . VICTORY OR DEATH." On the eighth day of battle, 32 recruits crept through the Mexican lines, the last reinforcements the garrison was to receive. This brought their number to about 187. Although suffering from want of sleep, and with ammunition running low, the Texans had lost only Bowie, who was ill and disabled by a fall.

At 4 A.M. on 6 March, Santa Anna stormed the Alamo on all sides. The first and second assaults were broken up. At dawn the Mexicans attacked again. The Texans' guns were hot from heavy firing in the two assaults, their ammunition was nearly gone, and men were dropping from exhaustion. When the walls were breached, the defenders fought by clubbing with rifles and drawing knives. The last point taken was the chapel, where casualties included David Crockett and twelve volunteers from Tennessee. That evening, the last of the 187 defenders was dead, but the Mexicans spared about 30 noncombatants. Mexican casualties numbered about 600.

The fall of the Alamo sowed panic throughout Texas, precipitating a flight of the civilian population and government leaders toward U.S. soil. Enraged over Travis's disastrous stand, Houston gathered an army to meet Santa Anna. The Texan general paraded his men and in an impassioned address rallied them to the battle cry, "Remember the Alamo!" With that cry they vanquished the Mexicans at San Jacinto, establishing the independence of the Texas Republic.

BIBLIOGRAPHY

Davis, William C. *Three Roads to the Alamo: The Lives and Fortunes of David Crockett, James Bowie, and William Barret Travis.* New York: HarperCollins, 1998.

Matovina, Timothy M. *The Alamo Remembered: Tejano Accounts and Perspectives.* Austin: University of Texas Press, 1995.

Nofi, Albert A. *The Alamo and the Texas War of Independence, September 30, 1835, to April 21, 1836: Heroes, Myths, and History.* Conshohocken, Pa.: Combined Books, 1992.

Marquis James
Honor Sachs

See also **Mexican-American War; San Antonio; San Jacinto, Battle of;** *and vol. 9:* **The Story of Enrique Esparza.**

ALASKA. For most of its history as a U.S. possession, Alaska was known as the "last frontier," the last part of the country where would-be pioneers could go to live out the American dream of freedom and self-sufficiency through hard work and ingenuity. But with the rise of environmental consciousness in the 1960s and 1970s, that notion subsided. Alaska became America's "last wilderness," the last place in America with vast stretches of undeveloped, unpopulated land. In 1980 Congress designated 50 million acres of the state as wilderness, doubling the size of the national wilderness system.

Few Americans knew much about the region when the United States purchased Alaska from Russia in 1867. Newspaper cartoons ridiculed the purchase as "Seward's Folly," "Icebergia," and "Walrussia." But informed Americans emphasized Alaska's resource potential in furbearers and minerals, and the U.S. Senate approved Secretary of State William H. Seward's purchase treaty in the summer of 1867 by a vote of 37–2.

At that time about thirty thousand indigenous people lived in the region, pursuing traditional subsistence. These people included the INUIT (northern Eskimos) who are culturally related to all Arctic indigenes; Yupik speakers (southern Eskimos) of the Yukon River and Kuskokwim River delta area; ALEUT PEOPLE living in the Aleutian Islands who are related to Alutiq-speaking people on the south shore of the Alaska Peninsula and on Kodiak Island; Dene-speaking Athabaskan Indians who live along the interior rivers; and the Dene-speaking Tlingit and Haida people (Pacific Northwest Coast Indians) of the Southeast Alaska Panhandle (Alexander Archipelago) who are related culturally to the coastal Indians of British Columbia, Washington, and Oregon.

Russian Interest
The Russians were the first outsiders to establish sustained contact with Alaska Native peoples, initially in the Aleutian Islands and later in the southeastern coastal islands. In 1725 Peter the Great commissioned an expedition to search east of Siberia for lands with economic resources useful to the Russian state. The expedition commander Vitus Bering failed to find America on his first attempt in 1728, but returning in 1741 he made a landfall on the Alaskan coast near Cape Suckling. Bering shipwrecked on a North Pacific island on his return voyage and died there on 8 December.

Bering's voyages did not provide a comprehensive picture of the geography of Northwest North America. That would await the third round-the-world voyage of Captain James Cook in 1778. But more than half of Bering's crew survived the shipwreck and returned to Kamchatka bringing pelts of various furbearers, including sea otter. Siberian fur trappers recognized the sea otter as the most valuable pelt in the world at the time, setting off a rush to the ALEUTIAN ISLANDS. Over the next half century, Russian trappers made one hundred individual voyages to the American islands to hunt sea otters, fur seals, and walrus, drawing Alaska's indigenous population into the world mercantilist economy.

American furs and walrus ivory were profitable for private investors who financed the voyages and for the Russian tsarist government, which took 10 percent of each voyage's profit. But the exploitation was costly to Alaska Natives. The Russians relied on Aleut Natives to hunt furbearers and held women and children hostage in the villages while Russian overseers traveled with the hunters. The entire Aleut population was brutalized and decimated by this practice, and new diseases the Russians introduced reduced the Aleut population from twenty thousand to two thousand by 1800.

Ranging relentlessly eastward, Russian trappers in 1759 discovered the Alaska Peninsula and Kodiak Island. In 1784 Grigory Shelekhov established the first permanent Russian post in North America on Kodiak Island. Returning to Russia, Shelekhov attempted to persuade Empress Catherine II to invest in the exploitation of North America, but concerned about Spanish and English interest in the region, she declined.

In 1799, however, Paul III chartered a government-sponsored private monopoly, the Russian American Company. Over the next sixty years the company systematically exploited Alaska's resources, primarily furs, returning handsome profits to the stockholders and the government. During the company's first twenty-year charter, Aleksandr Baranov extended Russian activities into the Alexander Archipelago, and in 1824 and 1825 the United States and Britain signed treaties formalizing Russia's occupation there but claiming the area to the south, the Oregon Country, as their own. The 1825 treaty established permanent boundaries for Alaska. In 1812 Baranov also established a Russian agricultural post on the California coast, eighty miles north of San Francisco, but failed in an attempt to establish a similar post in Hawaii in 1815.

Russia did not attempt to establish a new society in North America. The largest number of Russians ever in the colony at one time was 823. They sought only the efficient exploitation of the easily accessible resources. Yet despite the participation of the Russian navy, the company and the government could not keep the enterprise adequately supplied. By midcentury the colony depended on the fiercely independent Tlingit Indians for food. When the Crimean War (1854–1856) demonstrated that Russian America could not be defended, critics began to advocate relinquishing the colony, the profitability of which was becoming a problem.

American Interest
Sale to the United States was the only alternative, as England was Russia's principal European antagonist. In the aftermath of the American Civil War, negotiations proceeded quickly. The United States purchased the colony for $7.2 million. The formal transfer was conducted at Sitka on 18 October 1867, which became a state holiday in Alaska.

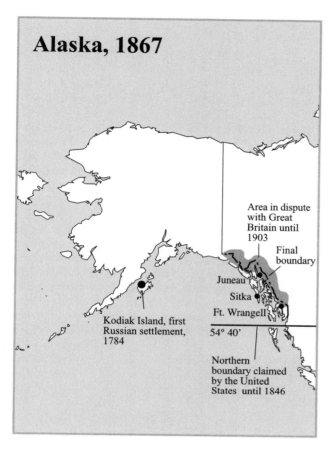

Alaska, 1867

Area in dispute with Great Britain until 1903

Final boundary

Juneau

Sitka

Ft. Wrangell

Kodiak Island, first Russian settlement, 1784

54° 40'

Northern boundary claimed by the United States until 1846

sive understanding of Alaska's geography and physiography by the end of the century.

By 1890 the census counted over five thousand non-Natives, most in Juneau, Sitka, and Wrangell in the southeastern panhandle. A few hundred non-Native prospector-traders worked along the interior rivers, trapping and trading furs among the Athabaskan Indians. Two hundred ships annually worked the lucrative Bering Sea and Arctic whale fishery and traded with the coastal Inuit.

Prospectors discovered gold on the Fortymile River near the Canadian border in 1886 and on Birch Creek near Fort Yukon in 1891, generating increasing interest in Alaska's mineral prospects. In 1896 George Carmacks and his Indian companions discovered placer deposits of unprecedented extent on tributaries of the Klondike River in the Yukon Territory, setting off the gold rush of 1897–1898. Forty thousand argonauts crossed the mountain passes from the tidewater to the upper Yukon River en route to the gold fields. The rush was short-lived but intense. Four thousand people found gold, but only four hundred found it in quantities that might be considered a "fortune."

Many gold trekkers continued into Alaska and searched virtually every river system for minerals. Gold was found in the creeks of the Seward Peninsula in the fall of 1898, sparking a major rush there and the founding of Nome. Another find in the Tanana River drainage in 1902 led to the founding of Fairbanks. Other discoveries generated minor rushes in a score of places, but most played out quickly. New settlers established a large number of small communities, however, and the 1900 census showed thirty thousand non-Natives in the territory, a figure that stayed virtually the same until 1940.

Although Alaskan gold production peaked in 1906, the federal government adopted substantial legislation in response to the gold rush to nurture economic development and to sustain new settlement, including construction of a telegraph line that connected the territory to Seattle, a system of license fees to generate territorial government revenue, civil and criminal legal codes, and a federally owned and operated railroad, the last a unique feature of government support of western settlement. In 1906 Congress authorized the biennial election of a non-voting territorial delegate to the U.S. House of Representatives and in 1914 a bicameral territorial legislature. At the same time Progressive Era conservation consciousness led to a number of federal conservation withdrawals, including the Tongass National Forest in 1905, the Chugach National Forest in 1907, Mount McKinley National Park in 1917, Katmai National Park in 1918, and Glacier Bay National Park in 1925.

The gold rush and government support also attracted corporate investors interested in developing Alaska's natural resources. By 1890 thirty-seven Pacific salmon canneries operated in Alaska, and by the end of the century more than twice that number operated. The invention of the fish trap, a system of surface to seafloor netting that

Secretary Seward wanted Alaska primarily as a gateway to new markets in Asia for American agricultural and manufactured products. Others recognized Alaska's resource potential. But until those resources were actually discovered and developed, Americans showed little interest in the region. The 1880 census revealed 30,000 Natives and a mere 435 non-Natives. Congress waited to implement legislation organizing the territory until it was warranted by the immigration of more pioneer settlers.

These settlers arrived quickly after 1880, when gold was discovered and investors began development of the Treadwell Mines at Juneau to exploit large lode deposits. By 1884 Treadwell boasted the largest gold stamp mill in North America, prompting Congress to pass the first organic legislation for the region that authorized the appointment of a governor, a judge, and other civil officials. Sitka was named the capital. The act provided for acculturation of Alaska Natives at the direction of a "general agent of education" who was to establish schools in Native villages and in the few white towns.

At the same time the U.S. Army began a systematic reconnaissance of Alaska's interior, which was largely unmapped. Explorations by Henry Allen, William Abercrombie, John Cantwell, George Stoney, J. C. Castner, Edwin Fitch Glenn, and others produced a comprehen-

led fish to a central enclosure, made fishing extremely efficient and produced high profits. By the 1920s moderate taxation of the salmon industry supplied three-fourths of territorial revenue.

The Guggenheim mining family also became interested in Alaska and early in the twentieth century developed a plan to coordinate development of gold, copper, coal, and oil deposits. Drawing the financier J. P. Morgan into a partnership, they created the Alaska Syndicate, which owned the Alaska Steamship Company; built, owned, and operated the Copper River and Northwestern Railway from Cordova at the tidewater to the Wrangell Mountains; owned the Kennecott Copper Mines; and developed oil deposits at Katalla. Their plans to develop coal deposits near Katalla were stopped when President Theodore Roosevelt closed access to Alaska coal lands in 1906 as a strategic measure. Deprived of the cheap, local source of coal, the syndicate scrapped plans to build their railroad to the Yukon River to link it to the internal river system. Having extracted $300 million worth of copper by 1939, the syndicate attempted to sell the railway to the federal government, but when negotiations collapsed, the partners dismantled the road and transferred the rails and rolling stock to operations in Arizona and Utah.

Aviation had a significant impact on Alaska and from the formation of the first companies in the mid-1920s developed rapidly. Perhaps more than in any other part of the country, the airplane in roadless Alaska permitted access to otherwise inaccessible areas, provided hope in times of medical emergency, and greatly speeded mail delivery. Bush pilots quickly became genuine heroes wherever in the territory they flew.

Federal aid helped Alaska weather the Great Depression. Public Works Administration (PWA) and the Civil Works Administration (CWA) loans for heavy public construction projects provided jobs, as did Civilian Conservation Corps (CCC) camps in every section of the territory. Also Native leaders worked with the federal government to extend the Indian Reorganization Act to Alaska in 1936 and to authorize a broad land claims suit by the Tlingit and Haida Indians in 1935. In an unusual rural rehabilitation project, two hundred families from the upper Midwest were transported to the Matanuska Valley near Anchorage in 1935 to start farms. But the experiment failed, for construction jobs created by the remilitarization of Alaska beginning in 1940 promised faster economic advance for the new settlers.

World War II transformed Alaska economically as the government invested $3 billion in three hundred new military installations in the territory. The military personnel in the territory numbered 300,000, five times the 1940 population. Attempting to divert American Pacific forces away from Midway Island in June 1942, Japanese forces captured two Aleutian Islands. In a dramatic battle on American soil in May 1943, a combined American and Canadian force of fourteen thousand retook Attu Island, suffering five hundred killed and nine hundred wounded.

The Japanese abandoned Kiska before the American invasion there.

Alaska gained population quickly during World War II. Afterward Cold War strategic defenses in the territory included airfields for long-range bombers and the Distant Early Warning radar net across the Arctic. The Atomic Energy Commission used Amchitka Island in the Aleutians for large-scale nuclear tests and contemplated using nuclear explosions to create a new harbor on Alaska's Arctic coast. Federal spending became the basis of the regional economy that supported a still-expanding population.

Statehood

Shortly after the war territorial leaders began a campaign to achieve statehood for Alaska. They were opposed by the canned salmon industry, which feared additional regulation and taxation. In addition the U.S. military was unenthusiastic because of the increased bureaucracy. But territorial leaders conducted an aggressive, national campaign based on the moral right of all American citizens to have all the rights of other citizens, and following a convention in 1955–1956, they presented Congress with a progressive, uncomplicated state constitution. When polls showed Americans overwhelmingly in support of

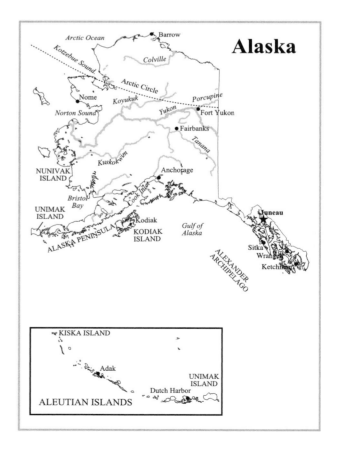

Alaskan statehood in 1958, Congress passed the enabling act. Statehood became official on 3 January 1959.

The statehood act entitled the new state to select 104 million acres of unoccupied, unreserved land from Alaska's 375 million acres. Federal reserves already claimed 54 million acres. But the act also prohibited the state from selecting any land that might be subject to Native title. The United States had never executed any Native treaties in Alaska, and the question of Native land title had not been settled. When the state began to select its land, Native groups protested the selections. By 1965, despite Native protests, the Bureau of Land Management (BLM) had transferred 12 million acres to the state, including, fortuitously as it developed, land at Prudhoe Bay on the North (Arctic) Slope. By then, however, Native claims blanketed the entire state. Secretary of the Interior Steward Udall halted all further transfers to the state until Native land claims could be sorted out.

That process had just begun when, in December 1967, Richfield Oil Company discovered North America's largest oil field at Prudhoe Bay. A 789–mile hot oil pipeline would be necessary to transport the oil from the Arctic Coast to Prince William Sound, crossing many miles of land that eventually was titled to Natives. Natives worked with state and industry leaders and the U.S. Congress to craft the ALASKA NATIVE CLAIMS SETTLEMENT ACT (ANCSA) OF 1971. By that act Natives obtained title to 44 million acres of traditionally utilized land, and the United States paid $962.5 million in compensation for extinguishments of Native title to Alaska's remaining 331 million acres. In an unprecedented provision, the money was used to capitalize profit-making Native regional and village economic development corporations. All Alaska Natives became stockholders in one or another of the corporations. Natives would thereby earn stock dividends from their corporations in perpetuity.

The act transformed the status of Alaska Natives, making their corporations an immediate major economic factor in Alaska. Despite early difficulties, most corporations were able to pay stock dividends by the 1990s. Natives adapted well to the roles of corporation leaders and stockholders, though lack of economic sustainability threatened the future of many of the remote villages. Of 100,000 Alaska Natives in a state population of 620,000 in 2000, 30,000 were permanent urban residents.

ANCSA did not guarantee construction of the Alaska pipeline, however, because national environmental groups sued to halt the project to preserve Alaska wilderness. When OPEC placed an embargo on oil exports to the United States following the 1973 Arab-Israeli War, Congress passed the Alaska Pipeline Authorization Act, and construction began.

The state established a comprehensive tax structure for oil production, and by the 1980s oil taxes produced 85 percent of public state revenue. By the 1990s most public sector material infrastructure in the state had been paid for by oil taxation. So dependent was the state on oil money that a contraction of the price per barrel from $40 in 1981 to $15 in 1986 eliminated thousands of jobs and led to the outmigration of 600,000 residents from the state in 1985 and 1986.

In 1976 Alaska voters approved the creation of a publicly owned state investment fund, the Alaska Permanent Fund, made up of 10 percent of all state oil revenue. In 1982 the state legislature mandated that about half of the earnings on the fund be paid per capita annually to all state residents. In 2000 the dividend payment was near $2,000 for each Alaska citizen.

Reflecting the raised environmental consciousness in the United States, ANCSA also included a provision for Congress to establish new federal conservation units in Alaska within eight years. Fearing the loss of opportunities for economic development, state leaders and residents opposed the provision, but Congress proceeded. The battle over the Alaska lands act was bitter and protracted, but in 1980 Congress passed the Alaska National Interest Lands Conservation Act (ANILCA), which reserved 104 additional Alaska acres in new conservation units, half of which were designated wilderness. Natives were guaranteed access to traditional subsistence resources across the new conservation areas. Mount McKinley Park was renamed Denali National Park.

Americans' new embrace of wilderness values generated both horror and anger when the fully loaded oil tanker *EXXON VALDEZ* went aground on Bligh Reef in Prince William Sound in March 1989, spilling 10.8 million gallons of oil in an area considered pristine wilderness. Thousands of seabirds and uncounted fish died, along with lesser numbers of seals, sea otters, and other bird and animal species, including killer whales. Native villagers in the sound feared the contamination of subsistence resources. Exxon Corporation spent three summers cleaning up the spill at a cost of $2 billion, and the corporation was fined $1 billion by the state and federal governments.

Alaska mirrors a long-standing debate in the United States over the proper balance between natural resource extraction and resource preservation. The coastal plain of Alaska's Arctic National Wildlife Refuge (ANWR) is presumed to contain significant oil deposits, which most Alaskans wish to see developed. But the area is considered wilderness by most Americans. The future of the refuge rests with Congress, where at the twentieth century's end vigorous debate continued.

BIBLIOGRAPHY

Gibson, James R. *Otter Skins, Boston Ships, and China Goods: The Maritime Fur Trade of the Northwest Coast, 1785–1841.* Seattle: University of Washington Press, 1992.

Haycox, Stephen. *Alaska—An American Colony.* Seattle: University of Washington Press, 2002.

———. *Frigid Embrace: Politics, Economics and Environment in Alaska.* Corvallis: Oregon State University Press, 2002.

————, and Mary Mangusso, eds. *An Alaska Anthology: Interpreting the Past.* Seattle: University of Washington Press, 1996.

Kollin, Susan. *Nature's State: Imagining Alaska as the Last Frontier.* Chapel Hill: University of North Carolina Press, 2001.

Mitchell, Donald Craig. *Sold American: The Story of Alaska Natives and Their Land, 1867–1959.* Hanover, N.H.: University Press of New England, 1997; Fairbanks: University of Alaska Press, 2000.

Sherwood, Morgan. *Exploration of Alaska, 1865–1900.* New Haven, Conn.: Yale University Press, 1965; Fairbanks: University of Alaska Press, 1992.

Stephen Haycox

See also **Explorations and Expeditions: Russian; Fur Trade and Trapping; Klondike Rush; Oil Fields; Petroleum Industry; Russia, Relations with; Tribes: Alaskan; Yukon Region.**

ALASKA NATIVE CLAIMS SETTLEMENT ACT

(1971). President Richard Nixon signed the Alaska Native Claims Settlement Act (ANCSA) into law on 18 December 1971, granting title to 44 million of Alaska's 375 million acres to various groups of Alaska Native people. At the time, most of Alaska's land was undistributed.

In 1958 Congress passed the Alaska Statehood Act, authorizing the new state to select 104 million acres of unappropriated and unoccupied land in the state. But the statehood act also included a disclaimer of title or right by Alaska to lands that might be held by Alaska Natives. As the state began to make selections of the lands it desired, Natives began to protest the selections on the grounds of prior use, and therefore, potential Native title. By 1966 the federal Bureau of Land Management had approved state title to 12 million acres, but by that time, Native protests blanketed the entire state. Secretary of the Interior Stewart Udall sought to resolve the confusion by issuing an injunction halting further conveyances to the state until Native claims could be dealt with fairly and comprehensively. Given the history of Native land claims in Congress and the courts, people in Alaska wondered how long it would take to resolve the conflict.

The discovery of America's largest single petroleum deposit, 15 billion barrels, at Prudhoe Bay on state-selected land on Alaska's North Slope in December 1967 immensely complicated the process. The only practical way to take the oil to market was via a trans-Alaska pipeline to the port of Valdez on the Gulf of Alaska, which meant building the pipeline across much Native-claimed land.

The statewide Alaska Federation of Natives, representing all Native groups, produced a bill, which, with modification, settled the Native claims (ANCSA). In exchange for clear title to 44 million acres in traditionally utilized areas, the U.S. extinguished Native title to the remaining land in Alaska, paying Native people $962.5 million in compensation. To make the money work in perpetuity for Alaska Natives, it was used to capitalize 12 (later 13) regional Native economic development corporations and as many as 211 village corporations, in one or another of which all Alaska Natives became preferred stockholders. The corporations were chartered under the laws of the State of Alaska and were free from paternalistic oversight. This settlement was monumental and unprecedented. Many Native leaders of talent and insight helped write the plan, lobby the bill through Congress, and explain its operation to Alaskan villagers. Among these leaders were Willie Hensley from Unalakleet, John Borbridge and Byron Mallot from the Alaskan Southeast, and Emil Notti from Koyukuk.

Though some analysts criticized the act as a vehicle for cultural genocide, forcing the alien concepts and structures of capitalism and modern for-profit corporations on Alaska Natives, Native leaders largely welcomed the measure. Some Native corporations experienced early financial stresses, but most weathered the start-up period and by the mid-1980s were stable. Amendments to the act in 1989 protected the land from foreclosure in bankruptcy and authorized new stock issues for persons born after 1971. In the early 2000s most corporations were financially successful, due in part to an opportunity to sell tax losses in the 1990s. Several corporations began to pay substantial dividends to their stockholders, and many had real estate and operating company holdings across America. Native leaders credit the act with protecting the Native land base in Alaska and establishing Native equality and legitimacy in the state.

BIBLIOGRAPHY

Berger, Thomas R. *Village Journey: The Report of the Alaska Native Review Commission.* New York: Hill and Wang, 1985.

Berry, Mary Clay. *The Alaska Pipeline: The Politics of Oil and Native Land Claims.* Bloomington: Indiana University Press, 1975.

Coates, Peter A. *The Trans-Alaska Pipeline Controversy: Technology, Conservation, and the Frontier.* Bethlehem, Pa.: Lehigh University Press, 1991.

Colt, Steve. *Two Views of the 'New Harpoon': Economic Performance of the ANCSA Regional Corporations.* Anchorage, Alaska: Institute of Social and Economic Research, 2001.

Mitchell, Donald Craig. *Sold American: The Story of Alaska Natives and Their Land, 1867–1959.* Hanover, N.H.: University Press of New England, 1997.

————. *Take My Land, Take My Life: The Story of Congress's Historic Settlement of Alaska's Native Land Claims, 1960–1971.* Fairbanks: University of Alaska Press, 2001.

Oswalt, Wendell. *Bashful No Longer: An Alaska Eskimo Ethnohistory, 1778–1988.* Norman: University of Oklahoma Press, 1990.

Stephen Haycox

See also **Alaskan Pipeline; Tribes: Alaskan.**

ALASKAN INDIANS. See **Tribes: Alaskan.**

ALASKAN PIPELINE. The Trans-Alaska Pipeline carries freshly pumped crude oil from America's largest oil deposit at Prudhoe Bay on Alaska's North (Arctic) Slope, 789 miles south to the ice-free port of Valdez on Prince William Sound. Richfield Oil Co. (later merged with Atlantic Oil Co. to form ARCO, Inc.) discovered the Prudhoe deposit in December 1967. Settlement by Congress of Alaska Native lands claims and environmental challenges cleared the way for construction, which began in March 1975. The pipeline required the labor of 28,000 personnel, cost $7.7 billion, and was completed in May 1977.

The 48-inch steel pipeline, partly buried and partly elevated, had by 2001 carried 13 billion barrels of oil, about 17 percent of America's daily supply. The line is owned and operated by Alyeska Pipeline Service Co., a consortium of North Slope oil producers including British Petroleum-Amoco-ARCO, ExxonMobil, Phillips Petroleum, Unocal, Amerada Hess, and Williams Alaska.

After the initial Prudhoe Bay discovery, subsequent exploration by a number of oil companies located more, though smaller, deposits. Production from these is carried in the line as well. Through the injection of seawater and re-injection of natural gas, more oil had been recovered than initially anticipated. Production peaked in 1988 with 2.1 million barrels daily. In 2001 the line carried 1 million barrels daily.

At Valdez the oil is pumped into ocean tankers that carry it to refineries in Washington and California. Some is exported to Asia. By 2001 more than 16,000 tankers had been loaded at Valdez. In March 1989 the tanker Exxon Valdez struck a reef in Prince William Sound, spilling 10.8 million barrels, the largest oil spill in North America. In September 2001, an individual shot a hole in the pipeline north of Fairbanks, spilling 6,800 barrels, the first such puncture.

BIBLIOGRAPHY

Coates, Peter A. *The Trans-Alaska Pipeline Controversy.* Bethlehem, Penn.: Lehigh University Press, 1991; Fairbanks: University of Alaska Press, 1998.

Roderick, Jack. *Crude Dreams: A Personal History of Oil and Politics in Alaska.* Fairbanks, Alaska: Epicenter Press, 1997.

Strohmeyer, John. *Extreme Conditions: Big Oil and the Transformation of Alaska.* New York: Simon and Schuster, 1993.

Stephen Haycox

See also **Petroleum Industry.**

ALBANY. Located along the upper Hudson River, Albany is best known as the capital of New York State. The city once had an important role as a transportation crossroads and manufacturing center.

In 1624, the Dutch West India Company established Fort Orange, the first permanent European settlement in the area, as the company's fur trading outpost. In 1664, British forces seized the fort and the surrounding village of Beverwyck, and changed the latter's name to Albany. In 1686 Albany received its first city charter. In 1797 it became the state capital. The Erie Canal connected Albany to the West in 1825, and the nation's first functioning railroad linked Albany and Schenectady in 1831. In 1830, Albany had a population of 24,209. A center of Irish and German immigration and a much smaller African American migration, Albany's major industries included iron casting, apparel, brewing, tobacco processing, publishing, and shipping. A powerful Democratic machine, built by Dan O'Connell and maintained by Mayor Erastus Corning, dominated Albany politics between the 1920s and the 1980s. After World War II, Albany lost much of its port traffic and industry, and its population declined from its 1950 peak of 135,000. Major highway and urban renewal projects, such as the Empire State Plaza, helped create a new service economy but displaced thousands of residents. In 2000 Albany's population was 95,658.

BIBLIOGRAPHY

Grondahl, Paul. *Mayor Corning: Albany Icon, Albany Enigma.* Albany, N.Y.: Washington Park Press, 1997.

Kennedy, William. *O Albany! Improbable City of Political Wizards, Fearless Ethnics, Spectacular Aristocrats, Splendid Nobodies, and Underrated Scoundrels.* New York: Viking, 1983.

Roberts, Anne F., and Judith A. Van Dyk, eds. *Experiencing Albany: Perspectives on a Grand City's Past.* Albany: Nelson A. Rockefeller Institute of Government, 1986.

Guian McKee

See also **Erie Canal; Hudson River; New York Colony; New York State.**

ALBANY CONVENTION. *See* **Leisler Rebellion.**

ALBANY PLAN. Albany Congress (1754), called by order of the British government for the purpose of conciliating the Iroquois and securing their support in the war against France, was more notable for the plans that it made than for its actual accomplishments. In June commissioners from New York, Massachusetts, Rhode Island, Connecticut, Pennsylvania, New Hampshire, and Maryland met with the chiefs of the Six Nations. The Iroquois were justifiably upset with the continued encroachment on their lands, the trading of Albany with Canada, and the removal of the well-considered Johnson (later Sir William Johnson) from the management of their affairs. Gifts and promises were bestowed and the alliance renewed, but the Iroquois went away only half satisfied.

For the better defense of the colonies and control of Indian affairs it had long been felt that occasional meetings of governors or commissioners was not enough, and that circumstances required a closer union. Discussion of such a union now became one of the principal subjects of the congress. Massachusetts indeed had granted its delegates authority to "enter into articles of union . . . for the general defense of his majesty's subjects." The plan adopted was one proposed by Benjamin Franklin and frequently referred to at the time as the Albany Plan. It provided for a voluntary union of the colonies with "one general government," each colony to retain its own separate existence and government. The new government was to be administered by a president general appointed by the Crown and a grand council of delegates from the several colonial assemblies, members of the council to hold office for three years. This federal government was given exclusive control of Indian affairs, including the power to make peace and declare war, regulate Indian trade, purchase Indian lands for the Crown, raise and pay soldiers, build forts, equip vessels, levy taxes, and appropriate funds. The home government rejected this plan because it was felt that it encroached on the royal prerogative. The colonies disapproved of it because it did not allow them sufficient independence. Nevertheless this Albany Plan was to have far-reaching results. It paved the way for the Stamp Act Congress of 1765 and the Continental Congress of 1774, and when the need of a closer union arose, it served as a guide in the deliberations of the representatives of the colonies.

BIBLIOGRAPHY

Newbold, Robert C. *The Albany Congress and Plan of Union of 1754.* New York: Vantage Press, 1955.

Shannon, Timothy J. *Indians and Colonists at the Crossroads of Empire: The Albany Congress of 1754.* Ithaca, N.Y.: Cornell University Press, 2000.

A. C. Flick / A. R.

See also **Continental Congress; Iroquois; Plans of Union, Colonial; Revolution, American: Political History; Stamp Act; Stamp Act Congress.**

ALBANY REGENCY. In the early 1820s, New York "Bucktail" Republicans led by Martin Van Buren fashioned an organization to impose discipline on their faction-ridden, personality-dominated state party. Dubbed the "Albany Regency," their apparatus became famous, and notorious, as the prototypical political machine, using caucuses and patronage to control its ranks and rewarding loyalty with political promotion. The organization backed Andrew Jackson for president in 1828 and affiliated with the Jackson-led national Democratic Party. It elevated Van Buren to national stature along with New York senators William L. Marcy (spokesman for the political SPOILS SYSTEM) and Silas Wright. It lost its dominance in state politics with the rise of the Whigs and dissolved into factions in the 1840s.

BIBLIOGRAPHY

Remini, Robert V. *Martin Van Buren and the Making of the Democratic Party.* New York: Columbia University Press, 1959.

Daniel Feller

ALBATROSS, the Yankee-owned ship that brought news of the outbreak of the War of 1812 to William Price Hunt, partner of the Pacific Fur Company, at its Astoria post in the disputed Oregon Territory. Hunt chartered the ship and removed the furs from Astoria to avoid possible British capture, thus abandoning the first American fur post on the Columbia River.

BIBLIOGRAPHY

Ronda, James P. *Astoria and Empire.* Lincoln: University of Nebraska Press, 1990.

Carl L. Cannon / A. R.

See also **Astoria; Fur Trade and Trapping; Pacific Fur Company.**

ALBEMARLE SETTLEMENTS. North Carolina's first permanent settlers, Virginians seeking good lands and Indian trade, arrived in the Albemarle Sound region in the middle of the seventeenth century. Led by Nathaniel Batts in 1655, settlement proceeded at such a rate that soon a new charter was granted to include the settlements in the Carolina proprietary grant, from which they were originally excluded. In 1664 a government was instituted with the appointment of William Drummond as governor of the county of Albemarle. Sir William Berkeley, governor of Virginia, issued land grants, attracting settlers to the region in large numbers. Quaker missionaries immigrated, and their converts soon prevailed in many areas. By 1689 the settled portion of Carolina had expanded beyond the original Albemarle section, and the county of Albemarle was abolished as a unit of government.

BIBLIOGRAPHY

Powell, William S., ed. *Ye Countie of Albemarle in Carolina.* Raleigh, N.C.: State Department of Archives and History, 1958.

William S. Powell / A. R.

See also **Land Grants; North Carolina; Quakers.**

ALBUQUERQUE, founded as an outpost of Mexico in 1598 and named for the Spanish Duke of Alburquerque (the first 'r' was later dropped), lies in the center of NEW MEXICO's high plateau (altitude 5,314 feet) on the east bank of the south-flowing Rio Grande. The region was part of the territory acquired by the United States in the 1848 settlement of the Mexican-American War and in many ways has retained its Hispanic character, particu-

Albuquerque, New Mexico. Founded as a Mexican outpost in 1598, Albuquerque experienced rapid growth during and after World War II, leading to a twenty-fold population increase (to 700,000) by 1990. This shot of a typical downtown street was taken in 1943. LIBRARY OF CONGRESS

lation multiplied twenty times—to over 700,000 in 1990—while the national population merely doubled. In part, this growth was fueled by influxes of Hispanics moving from agricultural areas to urban Albuquerque, increasing their proportion of the city's population to 34 percent in 1990 and thus aggravating political friction. This, in turn, brought a government reorganization in 1972, and the expansion of education and employment opportunities.

BIBLIOGRAPHY

Hodge, William H. *The Albuquerque Navajos.* Tucson: University of Arizona Press, 1969.

Logan, Michael F. *Fighting Sprawl and City Hall: Resistance to Urban Growth in the Southwest.* Tucson: University of Arizona Press, 1995.

Luckingham, Bradford. *The Urban Southwest: A Profile History of Albuquerque, El Paso, Phoenix, and Tucson.* El Paso: Texas Western Press, 1982.

Simmons, Marc. *Albuquerque: A Narrative History.* Albuquerque: University of New Mexico Press, 1982.

Michael Carew

ALCALDES. Under Mexican government, alcaldes were mayors of towns; they tried criminal and civil cases, presided over the town council, or *ayuntamiento*, and executed its decisions, kept order, issued licenses, and even inspected hides going to market. After the U.S. takeover of California in 1848, the military governors left the alcalde system intact. At that point, the alcaldes of the principal towns formed the only functioning civil structure. Well suited for a thinly populated frontier, the alcalde system collapsed in the flood of immigration in 1849, and the office was superseded by the new constitution when California became a state in 1850.

BIBLIOGRAPHY

Beck, Warren A., and David A. Williams. *California: A History of the Golden State.* Garden City, N.Y.: Doubleday, 1972.

Rolle, Andrew F. *California: A History.* Rev. 5th ed. Wheeling, Ill.: Harlan Davidson, 1998.

Cecelia Holland

See also **California.**

larly in the Old Town area of Albuquerque. For most of the remainder of the nineteenth century, the city served as a base for the army in the campaigns to constrain the Comanche and Apache peoples. The arrival of the railroad in the early 1880s brought new commercial activities and economic opportunities. But population growth was slow, increasing from 2,315 in 1880 to only 35,449 in 1940. This growth was prompted by the warm climate, a growing military presence, and opportunities in the mining, cotton, and cattle industries. Major New Deal public works projects in dam building and irrigation eased a scarcity of water.

Substantial regional and city development came during World War II (1939–1945) and the Cold War. Kirtland Air Force Base and the Sandia National Laboratories complex provided greatly increased economic opportunities. The resultant prosperity had the effect of widening the economic gap between the poorer Hispanic population, which comprised 25 percent of the city's population in 1940, and the dominant Anglo population, mostly professionals and retirees. The impetus of growth intensified in the five decades after World War II. The city's popu-

ALCATRAZ, an island in San Francisco Bay, California, was discovered by Spanish explorers in the sixteenth century. The United States took possession of the island in 1850 and fortified it, using it first as a military prison and later as a federal prison, beginning in 1933. Because of the strong, cold currents surrounding the island, most authorities considered it escape proof. Of the twenty-six prisoners who attempted escapes, five remain unaccounted for. The prison closed in 1963.

In November 1969 Native American activists occupied the island for over nineteen months, taking a stand

Alcatraz. An aerial view of the island and its famous federal prison, under the watch of four ships. © UPI/CORBIS-BETTMANN

that marked a turning point in the AMERICAN INDIAN MOVEMENT, which had begun earlier in 1969 and remained active into the late 1970s. Because the occupation brought together activists (and their broader base of supporters) from many different tribes, historians generally credit the occupation with breaking down the tribal nature of pre-1969 protests and helping to create a more unified fight for autonomy, self-determination, and appreciation of Native American cultures, even though the occupation did not achieve its initial goal of laying claim to title of the island. The island was opened to the public as part of the Golden Gate National Recreation Area in 1972.

BIBLIOGRAPHY

Eagle, Adam Fortunate. *Heart of the Rock: The Indian Invasion of Alcatraz.* Norman: University of Oklahoma Press, 2002.

Odier, Pierre. *The Rock: A History of Alcatraz.* Eagle Rock, Calif.: L'Image Odier, 1982.

Paul S. Voakes/c. w.

See also **Prisons and Prison Reform; San Francisco.**

ALCOHOL, REGULATION OF. Throughout their history as colonies and as a nation, Americans have tried through various means to regulate the use of alcoholic beverages. Indeed, no other item of personal use, not even weapons, has been subject to so much, so varied, and so persistent regulation as alcohol. The means used fall into two broad and not always perfectly distinct categories—persuasion and coercion. The balance between persuasive and coercive approaches has changed from time to time, and within each category new forms of regulation have appeared and disappeared. Regulation has targeted nearly every aspect of alcohol use: whether beverage alcohol is to be produced; what its various forms are to contain; whether it is to be sold; who is to sell it, where and when it is to be sold, and at what price; who shall be allowed to drink, and under what conditions; and how intoxicated

persons shall conduct themselves. The fundamental issue has never been whether alcohol use is to be regulated, but rather how.

Formative Years

Colonial governments followed English precedents in regulating alcohol. They set prices and fixed measures. The English tavern licensing system was maintained, and through it officials controlled the number of outlets, designated their functions, and monitored the character of publicans. Tavern keepers were sometimes enjoined to refuse service to classes of customers, such as slaves, apprentices, Native Americans, and habitual drunkards. Other laws punished excessive drinking, although such strictures were generally applied only to control threats to public order. The founders of Georgia went even further, attempting during the colony's first years to prohibit the use of distilled spirits altogether. Thus, although no organized temperance movement appeared, colonial Americans pioneered nearly every form of legal regulation that would later be employed.

While European Americans were establishing a framework for legal regulation, Native Americans led in the use of moral suasion. Native revitalization movements, such as those led by the Seneca Handsome Lake and by the Shawnee Tenskatawa ("the Prophet"), preached abstinence from the white man's liquor. In 1802 the federal government enacted a prohibitory law for "Indian Country" west of the Mississippi River, but the enactment failed to halt the process of tribal disorganization to which alcohol abundantly contributed.

By the early nineteenth century, Native Americans were not the only American society at risk of alcohol-induced disorganization. European American consumption reached historic highs by the 1820s, and the threat of widespread alcoholic damage to individuals and society produced the first mass temperance movement, headed by the American Temperance Society (ATS), founded in 1826. Through moral suasion, the ATS induced hundreds of thousands of temperate drinkers to abstain from distilled spirits. Bitter experience in attempting to rescue compulsive drinkers led reformers to reconceive their goal as total abstinence from all intoxicating beverages ("teetotalism"). By the late 1830s, temperance reformers were also seeking additional legislative curbs on the sale of liquor. Massachusetts's short-lived Fifteen-Gallon Law (1838), which prohibited purchases of hard liquor in quantities less than fifteen gallons, was a product of this movement, and other states passed similarly restrictive, though less draconian, laws. The transition from a suasionist approach to a coercive model set a pattern later temperance movements would follow again and again. As each new cycle of reform began by building on the legal foundation constructed by its predecessor, alcohol regulation gradually became more coercive.

Moral suasion experienced a resurgence in the early 1840s through a movement of reformed drunkards, the

Washingtonians, but by the end of that decade reformers began to consider statewide prohibition of alcohol a promising approach. After a campaign spearheaded by the Portland mayor Neal Dow, Maine in 1851 adopted a law banning the manufacture of liquor and restricting its sale to designated municipal agents and only for medicinal and mechanical purposes. Searches and seizures were authorized in enforcing the law, and heavy fines and jail sentences were prescribed for offenders. These strict measures were necessary, reformers believed, because local restrictions, such as raising the cost of licenses to sell liquor ("high license") and refusing to issue licenses ("no license") had failed to halt alcohol abuse. In addition to Maine, twelve northeastern and midwestern states and territories enacted statewide prohibition laws by 1855. While most of these were soon repealed or judicially overruled, the Civil War brought new restrictive measures to the previously laggard southern states. Four Confederate states banned distilling in order to conserve grain. By the end of the Civil War, states in all regions had gained experience in using state power to control alcohol production and use.

Use of State Power

During the years between the Civil War and World War I, the question of how to use local and state governmental power to control alcohol use became a perennial political issue. By 1890, six states were under statewide prohibition. Legally dry territory also spread through the use of local option, through which a minor political unit (a ward, township, municipality, or county) voted on the question of permitting liquor sales. Annual elections or referenda regularly embroiled many localities in heated conflict over the liquor issue. Southern prohibitionists made especially good use of local option, drying up most areas of the region by 1907. Both local and state prohibition laws, while outlawing the manufacture or sale of liquor, sometimes allowed personal importation of alcoholic beverages into the affected area. This leeway created considerable opportunity for the legal sale of liquor by mail order, and mail-order businesses also hastened to exploit profit opportunities created by thirsty drinkers marooned in states that forbade possession of beverage alcohol.

Alongside these coercive measures, moral suasionist or quasi-suasionist efforts to regulate alcohol use also continued to flourish. Three new initiatives emerged during the 1870s. In the winter of 1873–1874, tens of thousands of women conducted nonviolent marches on the liquor dealers of local communities across the Midwest and Northeast. Their actions closed many outlets, pledged many drinkers to sobriety, and stimulated formation of the Woman's Christian Temperance Union (1874), which thereafter conducted a multipronged campaign for personal abstinence and legal prohibition. "Reform clubs" for working-class and middle-class men appeared, offering mutual support for drinkers who wished to quit. A national organization for work among the rapidly grow-

ing Roman Catholic population, the Catholic Total Abstinence Union, was created in 1872 to promote temperance while eschewing legal means of restriction. Most Protestant evangelical churches also preached temperance, and some supported prohibition. Meanwhile, growing medical interest in habitual drunkards led to the founding of more than 100 inebriety asylums and other institutions, whose founders hoped that by confining chronic drinkers their pattern of recurring binges could be broken. This combination of legal and suasionist means helped to produce a historically low level of per capita consumption during the last decades of the nineteenth century.

The federal government became involved in alcohol regulation in two ways. First, the Pure Food and Drug Act (1906) included alcoholic beverages among the consumables whose quality Washington took on the job of monitoring. Second, the mail-order liquor business involved the federal government in the enforcement of state prohibition statutes because of its jurisdiction over interstate commerce. In 1890, the Wilson Act forbade shipment of liquor into prohibition states, but its effect was weakened by subsequent judicial decisions. When the number of prohibition states began to increase after 1907, and drinkers in states that forbade possession or consumption of liquor continued to import bottles, the federal government had to choose sides. The Webb-Kenyon Act (1913) banned importation of liquor into a state when state law forbade such shipments.

National Prohibition through the Eighteenth Amendment to the Constitution (in force 16 January 1920) capped the temperance movement's century-long campaign to regulate alcohol use. It rode on the crest of a wave made up of dry victories in state prohibition campaigns, a wartime federal ban on the use of grain in distilling (to conserve food supplies), and wartime prohibition. Among its manifold effects, national Prohibition led to the closing of the inebriety asylums and produced a shift in consumer preferences from beer to the more easily transported and more cost-effective distilled liquors. Although estimates of per capita consumption during the 1920s are problematic, Prohibition does seem to have succeeded in lowering intake from the relatively high level that had been reached during the 1910s. In concert with the Great Depression, the temperate attitudes inculcated during Prohibition helped to keep per capita consumption below the pre-Prohibition standard for a quarter of a century after the Eighteenth Amendment was repealed in 1933.

Since Prohibition's Repeal

Prohibition's impact on American drinking patterns was reinforced during the post-Prohibition years by a new web of regulations woven around alcohol use by the states. A few states retained prohibition; the last, Mississippi, repealed its dry law in 1966. Most, however, created either state agencies to issue licenses for retail sales, state monopolies on liquor sales, or hybrid blends of the two systems. State liquor agencies exercised a broad range of powers over the conditions under which alcohol was advertised, sold, and consumed. In the beginning, state officials used their powers to favor off-premises over on-premises consumption. As Prohibition faded further into the background, however, this policy was gradually relaxed.

In the aftermath of Prohibition's repeal, a new suasionist initiative emerged. In 1935, two habitual drunkards created a grassroots movement, Alcoholics Anonymous (AA), to provide mutual support to those who wished to stop drinking but could not do so alone. A publicity organization, the National Council on Alcoholism, formed to propagate AA's basic principle, that chronic drunkenness, which was now called "alcoholism," was addictive and a disease. The disease concept of alcoholism was also furthered by the work of an academic research institute, the Yale Center of Alcohol Studies. Such arguments, together with a rising level of per capita alcohol consumption during the 1960s, led the federal government to involve itself for the first time in alcohol research, through creation in 1970 of the National Institute of Alcohol Abuse and Alcoholism. This initiative, however, followed the lead of many states, which had previously mandated their own state alcoholism agencies, some of which took on treatment as well as research functions. Alcoholism treatment also flourished as many corporations and governments created "occupational alcoholism" programs, which often became "employee assistance" programs devoted to dealing with a broad range of personal problems.

At the end of the twentieth century, legal regulation of alcohol use focused upon two issues: the drinking age and drinking and driving. During the 1980s, the federal government briefly attempted to withhold highway funding from states that mandated a lower age than twenty-one years as the legal drinking age. Wider and deeper concern was manifested over drunken driving as automobile use became pervasive. New organizations such as Mothers Against Drunk Driving (founded 1980) organized at the grass roots, while state governments manipulated criminal laws in an effort to reduce highway carnage.

BIBLIOGRAPHY

Blocker, Jack S., Jr. *American Temperance Movements: Cycles of Reform.* Boston: Twayne, 1989.

Duis, Perry. *The Saloon: Public Drinking in Chicago and Boston, 1880–1920.* Urbana: University of Illinois Press, 1983.

Hamm, Richard F. *Shaping the Eighteenth Amendment: Temperance Reform, Legal Culture, and the Polity, 1880–1920.* Chapel Hill: University of North Carolina Press, 1995.

Kurtz, Ernest. *A.A.: The Story.* San Francisco: Harper and Row, 1988.

Pegram, Thomas R. *Battling Demon Rum: The Struggle for a Dry America, 1800–1933.* Chicago: Ivan R. Dee, 1998.

Tyrrell, Ian R. *Sobering Up: From Temperance to Prohibition in Antebellum America, 1800–1860.* Westport, Conn.: Greenwood Press, 1979.

Jack S. Blocker Jr.

See also **Indians and Alcohol; Prohibition; Temperance Movement; Volstead Act; Woman's Christian Temperance Union.**

ALCOHOLICS ANONYMOUS.

The modern manifestation of the self-help theme in temperance reform, Alcoholics Anonymous (AA) since its founding in 1935 has become the world's most visible and influential temperance movement. Founded by the New York businessman William Wilson and the Akron, Ohio, surgeon Robert Smith, AA bases its approach on the concepts of addiction, individual powerlessness over drink, secrecy, mutual assistance, total abstinence, and the incompleteness of recovery. A response to the dearth of self-help organizations after the repeal of national Prohibition, AA spread rapidly, first throughout the United States and then the world. AA is a highly decentralized, independent, and nonpolitical organization in which local groups, open to any alcoholic who wishes to recover, retain autonomy. By the early 2000s, AA claimed more than two million members worldwide, although the principle of anonymity makes its claims of membership and therapeutic success unverifiable. In cooperation with other agencies, AA succeeded in popularizing the concept of alcoholism as a disease. Success in this endeavor was crucial in the creation of the modern network of treatment programs supported by corporate, state, and federal funding. In addition, AA's twelve-step model for recovery has been widely adopted to treat a broad range of habits and afflictions.

BIBLIOGRAPHY

Kurtz, Ernest. *A.A.: The Story.* San Francisco: Harper and Row, 1988.

Jack S. Blocker Jr.

See also **Alcohol, Regulation of; Alcoholism; Temperance Movement.**

ALCOHOLISM.

The term "alcoholism" is a noun and concept suggesting both a destructively and chronically excessive beverage alcohol consumption and a medical-style conception of the source, character, explanation, and social and medical handling of the purported condition. The word's introduction is often attributed to Swedish physician Magnus Huss in 1849. The same two broad ideas have been conveyed in a changing parade of terminology since 1800—including, for example, "dipsomania," "inebriety," "habitual drunkenness," "alcohol addiction," "problem drinker," and others. Ordinary language has many words for the excessive drinker, too—including "drunkard," "boozehound," "sot," "lush," "wino," etc.—although these do not necessarily connote medico-scientific causation. Slang words or phrases for drunkenness are most numerous of all—for example, "blitzed," "bombed," "blasted," "three sheets to the wind," "wiped out," and a great many more—one scholar counted hundreds. Beginning in the late 1970s, "alcohol dependence," or the "alcohol dependence syndrome," became the preferred medico-psychiatric terms for the condition. However, the word "alcoholism" has persisted in popular thought and common usage.

An American preoccupation with alcohol-related excess dates back to the beginnings of the republic and beyond. Dr. Benjamin Rush—a physician, signer of the Declaration of Independence, and often regarded as father to both American psychiatry and the American temperance movement—authored a treatise in 1784 titled *An Inquiry into the Effects of Ardent Spirits*, in which the disease character of chronic drunkenness was asserted. Establishment of an inebriate's asylum was proposed as early as 1830 in Connecticut, and such an institution given form in a widely read paper by Dr. Samuel Woodward in 1838. The Washingtonian Movement, a lay self- and mutual-help movement, gained wide fame in the 1840s and occasioned the rise of special homes for inebriates. This short-lived movement in turn gave way to the development of larger asylums in the 1850s and 1860s—the first such state-run institution opened in Binghamton, New York in 1864. Dr. Leslie Keeley opened the first of his private treatment sanatoriums in 1880, and by 1901 was reported to have thirty-nine facilities nationwide. National Prohibition (1919–1933) did little, however, to advance alcoholism treatment in the nation.

A "modern alcoholism movement," ostensibly aimed at rescuing the alcoholic from the ignorance and maltreatment of the past, had its beginnings very soon after the repeal of Prohibition on 5 December 1933. The Fellowship of Alcoholics Anonymous (AA) often dates its origins to a chance meeting between its two founders, "Bill W." (William G. Wilson) and "Dr. Bob" (Robert H. Smith) in May 1935. Soon afterward, the American scientific community began a push to unravel the mystery of alcoholism and other alcohol-related problems. Although the two post-Prohibition enterprises—AA and modern science—were remarkably different from each other in character and approach, a loose coalition of the two was fashioned in the mid-1940s by Marty Mann and E. M. Jellinek.

Marty Mann was the daughter of a well-to-do socialite family that fell on hard times in the Great Depression, and was herself brought low by heavy drinking in the mid-1930s. Mann was hired by E. M. Jellinek of the Yale Center on Alcohol Studies, the chief center for new alcohol science at the time, to persuade the American public that alcoholism was a disease, that the alcoholic required and deserved treatment, and that such care was a public responsibility. Mann's organization—originally named the National Committee for Education on Alcoholism (NCEA); later (and in its heyday), the National Council on Alcoholism (NCA); and eventually, the National Council on Alcoholism and Drug Dependence (NCADD)—was launched in October 1944. Behind the scenes, Jellinek and the leadership of Yale's alcohol science enterprise were hoping that Mann's new campaign would provide grassroots support for the expansion of alcoholism treatment and the promotion of scientific research—in much the same way that the American Cancer Society had served that function for cancer researchers. Jellinek doubtless looked forward to the expansion of AA as an ever growing source of members interested in scientific inquiry into alcoholism.

Perhaps the crowning achievement of the modern alcoholism movement was the creation of the U.S. National Institute on Alcohol Abuse and Alcoholism (NIAAA), signed into law by President Richard M. Nixon on New Year's Eve, 1970. Along with the success of the modern alcoholism movement, however, came more than a few challenges and changes. New research, sponsored by NIAAA, undermined some of the tenets of the movement's traditional beliefs about alcoholism—seeming to show, for example, that some alcoholics could safely return to controlled drinking. The availability of new and significantly increased government funding for alcoholism research and treatment tended both to professionalize the field and to bring in competing conceptual models and institutions. Moreover, popular attention began to shift its focus to other alcohol-related problems: a new emphasis on fetal alcohol syndrome in the mid-1970s; the rise around 1980 of the Mothers Against Drunk Driving (MADD) campaigns; and a growing concern with college and underage drinking in the 1990s. These issues tended to dilute societal attention paid to the alcoholic, though a thriving alcoholism research enterprise continued apace at NIAAA.

Alcoholism, once the province of a determined post-Prohibition and post-World War II (1939–1945) movement, has become parent to a wider preoccupation with addictions. Through it all, however, AA has continued to sustain its central place in the alcoholism topic arena—despite the growth of a diffuse and vocal chorus of critics and providers of would-be alternatives. Illicit drugs—and the so-called "War on Drugs"—and tobacco have eclipsed alcohol in popular attention, and also to an extent reshaped and recontextualized alcohol as "a drug," or one among several "substance abuse" or "chemical dependency" problems.

BIBLIOGRAPHY

Baumohl, Jim, and Robin Room. "Inebriety, Doctors, and the State: Alcoholism Treatment Institutions Before 1940." In *Recent Developments in Alcoholism*. Edited by Marc Galanter. Vol. 5. New York: Plenum Publishing, 1987. Essential reading on pre-1940 alcoholism treatment and conceptualization.

Blocker, Jack S., Jr. *American Temperance Movements: Cycles of Reform*. Boston: Twayne Publishers, 1989. This author sees the alcoholism movement period as the most recent chapter in an ongoing historical story of temperance cycles.

Brown, Sally, and David R. Brown. *A Biography of Mrs. Marty Mann: The First Lady of Alcoholics Anonymous*. Center City, Minn.: Hazelden Information and Educational Services, 2001. A praiseful account but nevertheless rich in biographical information.

Katcher, Brian S. "Benjamin Rush's educational campaign against hard drinking." *American Journal of Public Health* 83, no. 2 (1993): 273–281.

Kurtz, Ernest. *Not-God: A History of Alcoholics Anonymous.* Center City, Minn.: Hazelden Information & Educational Services, 1979. The classic history of AA's origins and earlier years.

Levine, Harry Gene. "The vocabulary of drunkenness." *Journal of Studies on Alcohol.* 42, no. 3 (1981): 1038–1051. More words for drunkenness than you ever imagined.

White, William L. *Slaying the Dragon: The History of Addiction Treatment and Recovery in America.* Bloomington, Ill.: Chestnut Health Systems/Lighthouse Institute, 1998. A valuable historical compendium.

Wiener, Carolyn L. *The Politics of Alcoholism: Building an Arena Around a Social Problem.* New Brunswick, N.J.: Transaction Books, 1981. How the U.S. National Institute on Alcohol Abuse and Alcoholism affected this country's alcohol problems social arena.

Ron Roizen

See also **Alcoholics Anonymous; Prohibition; Substance Abuse; Temperance Movement.**

ALDEN V. MAINE, 527 U.S. 706 (1999), one in a line of cases that expanded the concept of the states' sovereign immunity from suit and weakened Congress's power to subject states to federal regulatory authority.

When the U.S. Supreme Court held in *Chisholm v. Georgia* (1793) that federal courts could entertain damage suits against states by nonresidents, the states responded by securing ratification of the Eleventh Amendment, which prohibited such suits. Until the late-twentieth century, the Supreme Court respected Congress's power to subject states to suit for purposes of enforcing federal laws, as in *Fitzpatrick v. Bitzer* (1976), which upheld such power when exercised under section 5 of the Fourteenth Amendment.

In *Seminole Tribe v. Florida* (1996), the Supreme Court held that the Eleventh Amendment prohibited Congress from opening federal courts to suits by individuals against the states when the basis of Congress's authority was the commerce clause of Article I. (The Court distinguished *Fitzpatrick* because Congress there acted under the Fourteenth Amendment, deemed a modification of the Eleventh Amendment.)

It was in that context that *Alden* held that Congress could not subject states to suit under federal laws in their own courts, either. Conceding that this holding was not justified by the Eleventh Amendment, Justice Anthony Kennedy held that the "Constitution's structure" required this unprecedented expansion of traditional understandings of sovereign immunity. He extolled an antebellum concept of state sovereignty vis-à-vis the federal government. Justice David Souter in dissent denied that the five-judge majority's vision of sovereign immunity had any historical support.

BIBLIOGRAPHY

Braveman, Daan. "Enforcement of Federal Rights against States: Alden and Federalism Nonsense." *American University Law Review* 49 (2000): 611–657.

William M. Wiecek

See also *Seminole Tribe v. Florida*; **State Sovereignty.**

ALDRICH-VREELAND ACT, an emergency currency law enacted 30 May 1908, as a result of the bankers' panic of 1907. Its aim was to give elasticity to the currency by permitting national banks to issue additional currency on bonds of states, cities, towns, and counties, as well as commercial paper. The act also created the National Monetary Commission to investigate monetary systems and banking abroad and to advise Congress on reforms of the American banking system. The numerous reports of the commission contributed to the creation of the FEDERAL RESERVE SYSTEM by the Federal Reserve Act of 1913 (the Glass-Owen Act).

BIBLIOGRAPHY

Degen, Robert A. *The American Monetary System: A Concise Survey of Its Evolution Since 1896.* Lexington, Mass.: Lexington Books, 1987.

Friedman, Milton, and Anna Jacobson Schwartz. *A Monetary History of the United States, 1867–1960.* Princeton, N.J.: Princeton University Press, 1963.

Thomas J. Mertz
Jeannette P. Nichols

See also **Financial Panics; National Monetary Commission.**

ALEUT. The Aleuts (from the Russian word *Aleuty*) consist of Near Island Aleuts, Kodiak Island Alutiiq (or Sugpiak, the "real people"), and Unangan Inuit (including some Dillingham Yupik and Cook Island Athabascans). They are indigenous to southwest Alaska, from Prince William Sound in the east, across the Alaska Peninsula, and extending west through the Aleutian Islands. They traditionally speak the Aleutic language, which has common roots in Proto-Eskimo-Aleut with the Inuit languages spoken throughout arctic Alaska, Canada, Greenland, and Siberia. Historically their societies consisted of hereditary common, slave, and noble (from whom the leaders were chosen) classes. Men tended to hold positions of political power, while women retained power and influence as shamans and healers, and it is speculated that elite family lines were matriarchal. Living in partly subterranean sod houses, they built relatively populous settlements, and had an economy based on hunting sea mammals, including whales. They rarely ventured inland, but traded along the Alaskan coasts, and seem to have traveled regularly throughout the North Pacific, including coastal Siberia, possibly for more than ten millennia.

In 1741 the Aleuts came into contact with Europeans following the arrival of a Russian expedition led by the

Aleut Crafts. These elaborately patterned woven baskets were made by Aleuts and Inuits, c. 1899. LIBRARY OF CONGRESS

Dane Vitus Bering, who estimated their population to be 20,000 to 25,000. Immediately the Russians enslaved them largely for their ability to hunt sea otters. The early Russian fur hunters exhausted the resources of each place they landed, leaving after massacring villages and devastating wildlife populations; by 1825 the Aleut population was below 1,500. Many Aleuts were converted to the Russian Orthodox Church, which remained a dominant influence after the American purchase of Alaska in 1867.

In 1971 Congress passed the Alaska Native Settlement Claims Act (ANSCA) as a way of returning 40 million acres of land to Alaskan Natives and creating an infrastructure for economic development and the management of natural resources. While the political pursuit of ANSCA united Native people throughout Alaska, its passage caused the 23,797 Aleuts (according to the 1990 U.S. Census) and their traditional homelands to be divided among five Native corporations: Aleut Corporation, Bristol Bay Native Corporation, Chugach Alaska Corporation, Cook Inlet Region Incorporated, and Koniag Incorporated.

BIBLIOGRAPHY

Crowell, Aron L., Amy F. Steffian, and Gordon L. Pullar, eds. *Looking Both Ways: Heritage and Identity of the Altuiiq People.* Fairbanks: University of Alaska Press, 2001.

Fortescue, Michael, Steven Jacobson, and Lawrence Kaplan. *Comparative Eskimo Dictionary with Aleut Cognates.* Fairbanks: Alaska Native Language Center, University of Alaska, 1994.

Jefferson Faye Sina

See also **Alaska; Alaska Native Claims Settlement Act.**

ALEUTIAN ISLANDS. Formerly called the Catherine Archipelago, the Aleutian Islands comprise some 150 mostly volcanic islands extending twelve thousand miles west of the Alaskan Peninsula; the four island groups are a continuation of the continental Aleutian mountain range. They separate the Bering Sea from the Pacific Ocean and are the boundary between the Eurasian and Pacific tectonic plates. When sea levels were low, as during the various ice ages, the islands provided a land bridge between Asia and Alaska, although the first migrants to America probably crossed the then-dry Bering Strait. The native people, Aleuts, numbered around sixteen thousand when encountered by the Russian-sponsored expedition of Alexey Chirikov and Vitus Bering in 1741. From 1799 the Russian-American Fur Company controlled the region and encouraged the proliferation of fur trapping. Aleut populations declined as a consequence of slavery, disease, and massacres (as with the Carib peoples of the Caribbean Islands). Further exploitation by Britain and the United States followed the exploratory voyages of James Cook, George Vancouver, Alexander Mackenzie, Robert Gray, and John Kendrick. The United States purchased Alaska from Russia in 1867 and by 1900 Unalaska had become a shipping port for gold from mainland Nome during Alaska's gold rush. It was not until 1893 that an arbitration court in Paris reconciled controversial hunting rights claims in the Bering Sea by declaring it open. Intensive seal hunting continued until 1911, when the United States, Canada, Russia, and Japan agreed upon formal protection; the Japanese withdrew from the agreement in 1941.

The strategic value of these fog-bound, inhospitable islands for the United States lies in their proximity to Russia's Far East and Japan. Vulnerability to Japan was evident during World War II when it bombed the U.S. naval base at Dutch Harbor in 1942 and later occupied the undefended islands of Attu, Kiska, and Agattu. These actions were an unsuccessful ploy to deflect the U.S. Pacific Fleet from Japan's primary objective of capturing the Midway Islands in the mid-Pacific. Japan's reinforcement attempts in the Aleutians in 1943 were thwarted by U.S.

Aleutian Islands. About 10,000 Aleuts live on these mostly volcanic islands, which also house military bases and research stations. UNIVERSITY OF PENNSYLVANIA MUSEUM ARCHIVES

counterattacks from military bases on Adak and Amchitka. The recapture of Attu involved eighteen days of combat with many casualties; Kiska was regained after the Japanese had withdrawn 5,183 troops by surface ships.

After World War II a U.S. coastguard fleet was stationed at Unalaska Island to patrol the sealing grounds and, after 1956, to enforce a convention on seal protection agreed upon by the United States, Canada, Japan, and the Soviet Union. Amchitka, because of its remoteness, was used for underground nuclear tests in 1965, 1969, and 1971. The island is also part of the Distant Early Warning Network constructed between 1950 and 1961, and has sites associated with the Relocatable Over the Horizon Radar that was established between 1986 and 1993. In the early 2000s, the majority of the mostly treeless islands comprise the Aleutian National Wildlife Reserve; hunting and fishing remain the primary occupations of the approximately ten thousand Aleuts, although sheep and reindeer are also husbanded. The islands are home to research stations and military bases.

BIBLIOGRAPHY

"Aleutian Islands." Available at http://www.Encylopedia.com.

U.S. Department of Energy. Office of Environmental Management. "Amchitka Island." Available at http://www.em.doe.gov.

G. L. MacGarrigle
A. M. Mannion

See also **Alaska; Sealing; World War II.**

ALEXANDER V. HOLMES COUNTY BOARD OF EDUCATION,

396 U.S. 19 (1969). In this case the U.S. Supreme Court overturned a ruling by the United States Court of Appeals for the Fifth Circuit, which effectively would have postponed until September 1970 the date when thirty-three Mississippi school districts would be required to implement desegregation plans. In its opinion, the Court declared it to be the obligation of all districts to eliminate dual school systems immediately. This opinion also proclaimed "no longer constitutionally permissible" the "all deliberate speed" formula that the Supreme Court had adopted in 1955 to describe the pace at which the desegregation of southern schools must proceed.

BIBLIOGRAPHY

Tushnet, Mark V. *Making Constitutional Law: Thurgood Marshal and the Supreme Court, 1961–1991.* New York: Oxford University Press, 1997.

Woodward, Bob, and Scott Armstrong. *The Brethren: Inside the Supreme Court.* Reprint, New York: Avon Books, 1996.

Michal R. Belknap

See also **Desegregation.**

ALEXANDRIA, a city in Virginia on the Potomac River, below Washington, D.C., was an important trading center until early in the nineteenth century, particularly as a tobacco warehousing and deep-sea shipping port. First settled in 1695, it was established as a town in 1749 on an original grant of 6,000 acres awarded in 1669. For nearly a century, the Alexander family had owned the site. It lay on the main stage route, the King's Highway, which ran southward into Virginia. Gen. Edward Braddock departed from there on his fatal expedition in 1755. The Fairfax Resolves were signed in Alexandria, 18 July 1774. Alexandria was incorporated in 1779. From 1791 to 1847, the city was under federal jurisdiction as part of the District of Columbia. Thomas Jefferson's EMBARGO ACT of 1807 destroyed its tobacco trade. During the American Civil War, Union troops occupied it. Alexandria was the home of many prominent Virginia families. Alexandria's population greatly increased in the twentieth century and reached 128,283 in 2000. It has become an affluent and largely residential city noted for its colonial architecture. Many corporations in diverse fields, such as Time-Life, Inc., and the Public Broadcasting Service (PBS), have chosen to make Alexandria their headquarters.

BIBLIOGRAPHY

Dabney, Virginius. *Virginia: The New Dominion.* Charlottesville: University Press of Virginia, 1983.

Hurst, Harold W. *Alexandria on the Potomac: The Portrait of an Antebellum Community.* Lanham, Md.: University Press of America, 1991.

Kolp, John Gilman. *Gentlemen and Freeholders: Electoral Politics in Colonial Virginia.* Baltimore: Johns Hopkins University Press, 1998.

Ethel Armes / A. E.

See also **Braddock's Expedition; Potomac River; Red River Campaign; Virginia; Washington, D.C.**

ALEXANDRIA CONFERENCE (28 March 1785), between Maryland and Virginia, dealt with navigation and commerce in Chesapeake Bay and the Potomac and Pocomoke Rivers. Scheduled to be held at Alexandria on 21 March, it actually met at George Washington's invitation at Mount Vernon. Daniel of St. Thomas Jenifer, Thomas Stone, and Samuel Chase represented Maryland; George Mason and Alexander Henderson represented Virginia. In ratifying the agreement, Maryland urged the inclusion of Pennsylvania and Delaware, while Virginia urged a meeting of all the states to adopt uniform commercial regulations. This effort to promote colony-wide trade agreements produced the Annapolis Convention, the origin of the Convention of 1787.

BIBLIOGRAPHY

Risjord, Norman K. *Chesapeake Politics, 1781–1800.* New York: Columbia University Press, 1978.

Walter B. Norris / A. R.

See also **Annapolis Convention; Colonial Commerce.**

ALGECIRAS CONFERENCE.

In 1904 France made agreements with England and Spain that allowed France to increase its trading rights in Morocco. Germany, angered because it was not consulted, demanded a conference of the signatories to the Morocco Agreement negotiated in Madrid in 1880. Among the signatories was the United States, to whom the German government now appealed for an extension of the Open Door policy to Morocco. In private correspondence Kaiser William II warned President Theodore Roosevelt that the crisis might lead to war between France and Germany if left unresolved. Roosevelt, in an attempt to obtain a peaceful solution, persuaded England and France to attend a conference at Algeciras, Spain, in 1906. At the conference, however, the Germans appeared so uncompromising that Roosevelt supported France, which in the end won a privileged position in Morocco. Although resolved peacefully, the Moroccan crisis intensified German-French hostility, which boiled over eight years later with the coming of World War I. The U.S. Senate ratified the treaty that resulted from Algeciras but declared that this action was taken solely to protect American interests and should not be interpreted as an abandonment of its nonintervention policy toward Europe.

BIBLIOGRAPHY

Gould, Lewis L. *The Presidency of Theodore Roosevelt.* Lawrence: University Press of Kansas, 1991.

Harbaugh, William H. *The Life and Times of Theodore Roosevelt.* New York: Oxford University Press, 1975.

Lynn M. Case / A. G.

See also **France, Relations with; Germany, Relations with.**

ALGONQUIN ROUND TABLE

was a group of journalists, playwrights, actors, and writers who gathered daily at a special table in the Rose Room at the Algonquin Hotel on West Forty-fourth Street in New York City from 1919 to about 1929. Their witticisms and jokes appeared in Franklin P. Adams's column "The Conning Tower" in the *New York Tribune,* conveying an alluring "insider's" image of metropolitan literary and theatrical life to far-flung readers. Core members included Adams, Robert Benchley, Heywood Broun, Edna Ferber, George S. Kaufman, Harpo Marx, Dorothy Parker, Robert Sherwood, Alexander Woollcott, and Harold Ross, editor of *The New Yorker.*

BIBLIOGRAPHY

Bryan, J., 3d. *Merry Gentlemen (and One Lady).* New York: Atheneum, 1985.

Gaines, James R. *Wit's End: Days and Nights of the Algonquin Round Table.* New York: Harcourt Brace Jovanovich, 1977.

Mina Carson

See also **New Yorker, The.**

Dorothy Parker. A 1933 photograph of the poet, critic, short-story writer and Algonquin Round Table star, famed for her sardonic, sometimes grim wit. AP/WIDE WORLD PHOTOS

ALIEN AND SEDITION LAWS.

Designed to impede opposition to the Federalists, the four bills known as the Alien and Sedition Acts were passed in the summer of 1798, amid fears of French invasion. Skepticism of aliens and of their ability to be loyal to the nation permeated three of the laws. The Naturalization Act (18 June 1798) lengthened the residency requirement for naturalization from five years to fourteen, required the applicant to file a declaration of intent five years before the ultimate application, and made it mandatory for all aliens to register with the clerk of their district court. Congress repealed this law in 1802. The Alien Friends Act (25 June 1798) gave the president the power to deport aliens "dangerous to the peace and safety of the United States." Its terms were sweeping but limited to two years, and it was never enforced. The Alien Enemies Act (6 July 1798) was the only one of the four to gather strong Republican support as a clearly defensive measure in time of declared war. It gave the president the power to restrain, arrest, and deport male citizens or subjects of a hostile nation.

The most controversial of the four laws was the Act for the Punishment of Certain Crimes (14 July 1798), the nation's first sedition act. This law made it a crime "unlawfully to combine and conspire" in order to oppose legal measures of the government, or to "write, print, utter, or publish . . . any false, scandalous and malicious writing" with intent to bring the government, Congress, or the president "into contempt or disrepute, or to excite against them . . . the hatred of the good people of the United States." The vice president, who at the time was a Republican, was not protected against seditious writings, and the act provided for its own expiration at the end of President Adams's term. Federalists in Congress argued that they were only spelling out the details of the proper restraints on free speech and press implied by common law. In fact, the act did liberalize the common law, because it specified that truth might be admitted as a defense, that malicious intent had to be proved, and that the jury had the right to judge whether the matter was libelous.

Federalist secretary of state Timothy Pickering directed enforcement of the Act for the Punishment of Certain Crimes against critics of the administration. Ten Republicans were convicted, including Congressman Matthew Lyon, the political writer James T. Callender, the lawyer Thomas Cooper, and several newspaper editors. Because Federalist judges frequently conducted the trials in a partisan manner, and because the trials demonstrated that the act had failed to distinguish between malicious libel and the expression of political opinion, this law was the catalyst in prompting a broader definition of freedom of the press. This experience also taught that the power to suppress criticism of public officials or public policy must be narrowly confined if democracy is to flourish.

The protest against these laws received its most significant formulation in the Kentucky and Virginia resolutions, drafted by Vice President Thomas Jefferson and James Madison. The resolutions claimed for the states the right to nullify obnoxious federal legislation, but they did not seriously question the concept of seditious libel. Rather, they merely demanded that such prosecutions be undertaken in state courts, as indeed they were during Jefferson's own presidency.

BIBLIOGRAPHY

Costa, Gregg. "John Marshall, the Sedition Act, and Free Speech in the Early Republic." *Texas Law Review* 77 (1999): 1011–1047.

Curtis, Michael Kent. *Free Speech, "The People's Darling Privilege": Struggles for Freedom of Expression in American History.* Durham, N.C.: Duke University Press, 2000.

Levy, Leonard W. *Legacy of Suppression: Freedom of Speech and Press in Early America.* Cambridge, Mass.: Belknap Press, 1960.

Smith, James Morton. *Freedom's Fetters: The Alien and Sedition Laws and American Civil Liberties.* Ithaca, N.Y.: Cornell University Press, 1956.

Linda K. Kerber / c. p.

See also **Federalist Party; Loyalty Oaths; Sedition Acts.**

ALIEN LANDHOLDING.

The common-law disability of aliens to inherit lands in the United States has always been removable by statute and by treaty. The Treaty of Peace, 1783, for example, overturned laws against British landholding occasioned by the American Revolution and required Congress to recommend to the state legislatures restitution of confiscated estates. Jay's Treaty went a step further by guaranteeing existing titles wherever held and treatment of British subjects with respect as equal to citizens. But the guarantee held neither for lands acquired thereafter nor for aliens other than the British. The Convention of 1800 removed the disability of alienage for French citizens in all the states. A treaty with Switzerland (1850) similarly affected Swiss citizens. In the absence of such a treaty, however, state laws applied. For example, in Kansas the disability was expressed in the state constitution. In California the state constitution authorized aliens to acquire, transmit, and inherit property equally with citizens. The U.S. Supreme Court upheld California's provision and similar ones in other states.

A number of factors, including a vast increase in European immigration, an extensive flow of British capital into the purchase of land and cattle companies in western states, and, along with this capital, establishment of Old World systems of land tenure, produced a contrary sentiment. The Nimmo Report of 1885, on range and ranch cattle traffic in the West, included a table showing the purchase by foreign companies of some 20 million acres of land, mostly in the West. Although the table somewhat exaggerated actual ownership, it did reveal how the benevolent land system had enabled English and Scottish capitalists to take over large segments of the ranch and cattle business (*see* FOREIGN INVESTMENT IN THE UNITED STATES). Even more startling to many who worried about the way large owners of foreign capital were benefiting from American policies was the purchase by William Scully, a notorious Irish landlord, of 220,000 acres of prime agricultural land in Illinois, Kansas, Nebraska, and Missouri, much of which he purchased from the government at a cost of $1.25 or less an acre. Scully rented this huge acreage to twelve hundred tenants under a modification of the Irish land system, which required that the tenants make all improvements and pay both the taxes and a cash rent. These requirements kept the tenants in poverty and their improvements substandard while limiting the social amenities of the Scully districts. Leaders of the growing antimonopoly movement and others troubled about the large foreign ownerships in the Great Plains excoriated Scully and demanded legislation that would outlaw further acquisition of land by aliens. Illinois led in 1887, when it denied aliens the right to acquire land. Nine other states rapidly followed suit either by constitutional amendment or by legislation, and Congress banned further acquisition of land by aliens in the territories. Since the measures could not apply retroactively, they succeeded only in halting further expansion of alien ownership.

BIBLIOGRAPHY

Dick, Everett. *The Lure of the Land: A Social History of the Public Lands from the Articles of Confederation to the New Deal.* Lincoln: University of Nebraska Press, 1970.

Gates, Paul W. *Landlords and Tenants on the Prairie Frontier.* Ithaca, N.Y.: Cornell University Press, 1973.

Zaslowsky, Dyan, and T. H. Watkins. *These American Lands.* Washington, D.C.: Island Press, 1994.

Paul W. Gates / c. w.

See also **Aliens, Rights of; California Alien Land Law; Jay's Treaty.**

ALIEN REGISTRATION ACT. *See* **Smith Act.**

ALIENS, RIGHTS OF. For more than a century, the Supreme Court has distinguished between the rights of aliens to enter the United States and the rights that arise after entry or admission. The so-called plenary power doctrine of the Chinese Exclusion Case (1889) held that aliens seeking to enter the United States could claim no constitutional rights. Although more recent cases, such as *Landon v. Plasencia* (1982), have recognized a limited right to procedural due process for certain returning permanent-resident aliens, the basic principle is that aliens have no procedural or substantive constitutional right to enter the United States. The Court has also held that aliens may not challenge immigration categories on equal protection grounds—*Fiallo v. Bell* (1977)—or on First Amendment grounds—*Kleindienst v. Mandel* (1972). Yet recent challenges to citizenship laws, such as in *Miller v. Albright* (1998), have garnered closer scrutiny by the Court.

The legal aspects of deportation (now known formally as "removal") are considerably more complex. Once an alien enters the territory of the United States, even illegally, he or she accrues an array of constitutional protections. The Supreme Court has, for constitutional purposes, distinguished deportation from criminal prosecution or punishment. Thus, for example, specific rights under the ex post facto clause—the Fifth Amendment right to silence, the Sixth Amendment right to counsel, the Seventh Amendment right to jury trial, and the Eighth Amendment prohibition of cruel and unusual punishment—do not apply (*Fong Yue Ting v. United States*, 1893). Due process protections have applied in this context, however, since *Yamataya v. Fisher* (1903). Over the years, statutory, regulatory, and case law have conferred various procedural protections, such as a right to counsel (at no expense to the government), certain limited Fourth Amendment protections, and others. Two of the most contentious practices have been the mandatory detention of certain aliens pending removal proceedings and the potentially unlimited detention of persons whom no other country is willing to accept after they have been ordered removed from the United States. For the latter case, the Supreme Court upheld, in *Zadvydas v. Davis et al.* (2001), a habeas corpus challenge and imposed a constitutionally mandated limit to such detention.

Outside of the immigration law context, aliens have extensive rights in the United States. The text of the Constitution limits very few rights—such as the federal right to vote and to hold certain national elective offices—to "citizens." In *Yick Wo v. Hopkins* (1886), a seminal case that involved a constitutional challenge to the discriminatory enforcement of a San Francisco ordinance regulating laundries, the Supreme Court held that "the rights of the petitioners . . . are not less, because they are aliens. . . . The Fourteenth Amendment to the Constitution is not confined to the protection of citizens." In matters outside of the immigration context, therefore, aliens and citizens receive analogous, but not identical, constitutional protection. Thus, in the United States, an alien generally has the right to speak freely, to travel within the country, to earn a living, to own property, to receive government benefits, and to bring suit against another, although there are limitations restricting these rights. Similarly, after *Wong Wing v. United States* (1896), an alien subject to criminal proceedings is entitled to the same constitutional protections available to citizens.

The extent of First Amendment protection granted to aliens is more complex. The First Amendment generally protects aliens, but some court decisions have held that aliens may be deported for conduct that, if undertaken by citizens, would be protected. In *Harisiades v. Shaughnessy* (1952), for example, the Supreme Court upheld the deportation of several permanent resident aliens because of their former membership in the Communist Party. More recently, in *Reno v. American-Arab Anti-Discrimination Committee* (1999), the Court held that deportable aliens generally cannot raise a defense of selective prosecution.

Aliens, both immigrants and nonimmigrants, may be granted authorization to work in the United States pursuant to federal immigration laws. Once an alien has the right to work, various federal and state antidiscrimination and fair employment laws generally prohibit discrimination by private employers on the basis of race, gender, or alienage. Indeed, some antidiscrimination laws may also apply to undocumented aliens in certain circumstances. Discrimination on the basis of alienage by government employers, on the other hand, may be permissible. Despite the broad language of *Yick Wo* in support of aliens' constitutional rights, U.S. courts have upheld various state laws that discriminated against aliens on the grounds that a "special public interest" was being protected. In *Heim v. McCall* (1915), for example, the Court upheld the exclusion of aliens from certain types of public employment by the State of New York.

But this body of law has been complex and unstable. Indeed in *Truax v. Raich* (1915) the same Court that decided *Heim* invalidated an Arizona law that required private employers of more than five people to make certain that at least 80 percent of their employees were "qualified electors or native born citizens." In *Takahashi v. Fish and Game Commission* (1948), the Court overturned a California law that forbade the granting of fishing licenses to Japanese residents (all of whom were "ineligible to citizenship" simply because of their nationality). The decision held that state power to discriminate against aliens is "confined within narrow limits."

The constitutional protection of aliens against state laws was further developed in *Graham v. Richardson* (1971), which challenged discriminatory state welfare laws. The Court determined that such classifications based on alienage are "inherently suspect" and subject to "close judicial scrutiny." Thus, state statutes that denied welfare benefits to all resident aliens or to those who have not resided in the United States for a specified number of years were held to violate the equal protection clause. Part of the Court's reasoning in *Graham*, however, was that such state schemes interfere with the general federal control of aliens in the United States. Thus, in *Mathews v. Diaz* (1976) the Court upheld as constitutional Congress's decision to condition an alien's eligibility for participation in a federal medical insurance program on continuous residence in the United States for five years and admission for permanent residence.

In public employment cases the Court has ruled that it is constitutional for states to require citizenship as a qualification for certain positions if the classification is properly tailored and applies to "persons holding state elective or important nonelective executive, legislative or judicial positions" who "participate directly in the formulation, execution or review of broad public policy" and therefore "perform functions that go to the heart of representative government" (*Sugarman v. Dougall*, 1973). In *Sugarman*, the Court struck down a New York statute that limited state competitive civil service positions to U.S. citizens. Pursuant to this approach, the Court has also subsequently overturned state laws that bar aliens from being licensed to practice law, from obtaining engineering licenses, and from state financial educational assistance. It has, however, upheld state restrictions for state trooper employment (*Foley v. Connelie*, 1978), for permanent certification as public school teachers (*Ambach v. Norwick*, 1979), and for probation officer positions (*Cabell v. Chavez-Salido*, 1982). In the federal employment context, as with public benefits, the Court has tended to be more deferential to the government, as for example in *Hampton v. Mow Sun Wong* (1976), in which the Supreme Court overturned a U.S. Civil Service Commission regulation that excluded noncitizens from federal civil service employment, but did so in a way that allowed the federal government much more leeway than was granted to the states.

Although some specific restrictions exist in some states, aliens generally have the right to purchase and inherit real and personal property. The United States has treaties with many countries that grant their citizens the right to purchase and inherit property in the United States. There are some federal statutory restrictions on alien ownership of agricultural, grazing, mineral, or timber land, in addition to certain restrictions placed on alien enemies during times of war or national emergency.

Under the immigration laws, aliens generally must apply for specific nonimmigrant visa status to study in the United States. Undocumented alien children do, however, have the right under the Fourteenth Amendment to state-provided public education (*Plyler v. Doe*, 1982).

BIBLIOGRAPHY

Aleinikoff, Thomas Alexander, David A. Martin, and Hiroshi Motomura. *Immigration and Citizenship: Process and Policy.* 4th ed. St. Paul, Minn.: West, 1998.

Bosniak, Linda, "Membership, Equality, and the Difference that Alienage Makes." *New York University Law Review* 69 (1994): 1047.

Gordon, Charles, Stanley Mailman, and Stephen Yale-Loehr. *Immigration Law and Procedure.* New York: Matthew Bender, 2001.

Legomsky, Stephen H. *Immigration and Refugee Law and Policy.* Westbury, N.Y.: Foundation Press, 1997.

Tribe, Laurence. *American Constitutional Law.* Mineola, N.Y.: Foundation Press, 1978.

Daniel Kanstroom

See also **Alien Landholding; Citizenship; Due Process of Law; Equal Protection of the Law; Immigration.**

ALL IN THE FAMILY was an influential situation comedy that ran on the CBS network from 1971 through 1979. Norman Lear created, produced, and wrote for the show, which was based on the British series *'Til Death Us Do Part*. *All in the Family* was a dramatic departure from the traditions of fictional TV, which until that time had tended to avoid contemporary and controversial issues. Archie Bunker, strikingly portrayed by Carroll O'Connor, was an unrepentant bigot trying to come to grips with the social, political, and cultural transformations of the era. In his loud discussions with his wife, Edith (Jean Staple-

All in the Family. The hit comedy's cast in 1975 (*from left*): Sally Struthers, Rob Reiner, Jean Stapleton, and Carroll O'Connor. AP/WIDE WORLD PHOTOS

ton), daughter (Sally Struthers), and son-in-law (Rob Reiner), he regularly used mild profanity and racial slurs. The show explored a catalog of forbidden topics that included racism, the war in Vietnam, the women's movement, and sexually oriented issues. It started what became known as the "relevance era" of American television.

All in the Family was a hit among critics and audiences alike. The show spent five straight seasons at the top of the Neilsen ratings, and Lear went on to produce several more series. More importantly, however, other producers (as well as network executives) realized that television could reflect the "real world" without alienating viewers.

Carroll O'Connor also starred in a spin-off CBS series, *Archie Bunker's Place* (1979–1983).

BIBLIOGRAPHY
McCrohan, Donna. *Archie & Edith, Mike & Gloria: The Tumultuous History of* All in the Family. New York: Workman, 1987.

Robert Thompson

See also **Television: Programming and Influence.**

ALLEGHENY MOUNTAINS, ROUTES ACROSS.

The steep eastern escarpment of the Allegheny Mountains (3,000–5,000 feet high and extending from the Mohawk Valley to the Tennessee River) was a serious impediment to western conquest and settlement in the eighteenth and nineteenth centuries. Routes across the Alleghenies depended upon gaps and approaches along the tributaries of rivers. Probably buffalo first trod these routes. Later, Native Americans followed them as trails. In turn they were used by explorers and fur traders.

The West Branch of the Susquehanna, extending close to the Allegheny River, furnished a route used by Native Americans, though only fur traders made much use of it during the early period. The branches of the Juniata River led to two historic routes across the Alleghenies: one, the Frankstown Path, much used by Pennsylvania fur traders; and the other, the Traders Path, followed by the Pennsylvania Road and Gen. John Forbes's expedition (Forbes's Road). The route used by Christopher Gist, George Washington, and Edward Braddock ran from the Potomac River at Wills Creek over the Alleghenies. From the headwaters of the Potomac also ran a route over the mountains, which was used in later times as the Northwestern Pike. The headwaters of the James River determined a route overland to branches of the Great Kanawha, one branch of which, the New River, also provided a route from the headwaters of the Roanoke River. Farthest south, CUMBERLAND GAP offered easy passage from eastern Tennessee to central Kentucky, making possible the greatly used WILDERNESS ROAD. In light of the extensive use made of Forbes's Road, Braddock's Road, and the Wilderness Road in the westward movement of white Americans, probably no routes in the United States are more properly known as historic high-

ways. The transportation of the twentieth century follows closely the old routes across the Alleghenies.

BIBLIOGRAPHY
Hulbert, Archer Butler. *The Old Glade (Forbes's) Road, Pennsylvania State Road.* New York: AMS Press, 1971.

Alfred P. James / A. R.

See also **Braddock's Expedition; Roads.**

ALLEGHENY RIVER.

The Allegheny River rises in Potter County, Pennsylvania, and flows in an arc through New York then back into Pennsylvania for a total length of about 325 miles. It unites with the Monongahela River to form the Ohio River, and the early French and English explorers considered the Allegheny a part of the Ohio. The Delawares and Shawnees settled along the Allegheny's course soon after 1720. After 1790 the river became an important highway for American settlers and freight in the keelboat and flatboat era.

BIBLIOGRAPHY
Kussart, S. *The Allegheny River.* Pittsburgh, Pa.: Burgum Printing Company, 1938.
Way, Frederick, Jr. *The Allegheny.* New York: Farrar and Rinehart, 1942.

Leland D. Baldwin / A. R.

See also **Keelboat; Ohio River.**

ALLIANCE FOR PROGRESS.

Early in John F. Kennedy's presidential term—but not sufficiently early for critics worried by the specter of communism in Latin America, Fidel Castro's 1959 revolution in Cuba, and the growing popularity among Brazil's landless of the Peasant Leagues movement headed by Francisco Julião—the president, at a White House reception for the Latin American diplomatic corps on 13 March 1961, proposed an alliance for progress in the Western Hemisphere. Based in principle on the successful Marshall Plan that rescued western Europe after World War II, Kennedy's proposal called for a concentrated joint effort to accelerate the economic and social development of Latin America within a democratic political framework. "Those who make democracy impossible," Kennedy said, "will make revolution inevitable."

The alliance speech was a powerful political statement marking a definite shift in U.S. policy that began in the late 1950s, at least partially in response to the growing revolutionary activity epitomized by Castro's overthrow of Fulgencio Batista in Cuba. The speech, the Kennedy personality, and the positive response of popular Latin American leaders combined to produce a remarkable mass psychological impact throughout the hemisphere. Its immediate effect was to improve dramatically the political relations between the United States and Latin America, especially with the "democratic left." The speech electrified the masses and gave encouragement to progressive political and intellectual forces within Latin America, but it also engendered bitterness and obdurate opposition among those who, for selfish or ideological reasons, resisted strongly if not always publicly the fundamental changes called for.

Between 1961 and 1969, public economic assistance to the Latin American countries in the form of grants and loans from all external sources was about $18 billion, of which about $10 billion came directly from official U.S. sources. However, on a net basis, that is, after taking account of loan repayments and interest, official U.S. direct aid is estimated to have been about $4.8 billion in the same period. This relatively small net transfer of official capital is explained by the fact that public indebtedness in Latin America in 1960 was more than $10 billion, the servicing of which diverted resources away from new investment.

Although profound changes in the economic, social, and political structures in Latin America began to take place in 1961 under the impetus of the alliance, a variety of forces within Latin America and a major shift in U.S. energies and resources associated with the Vietnam War drained the alliance effort of its vitality. These factors, combined with the intrinsic difficulty of bringing about radical social change within a free and democratic framework, resulted in a failure to meet early expectations concerning performance. Depending on the site, some or most of the food supplies from the United States, for example, surplus powdered milk and eggs, cheese, tinned beef, and flour, found their way into private hands and were sold for profit.

Some Alliance for Progress projects were seen as arrogant, impractical, or both. Latin American educators, who traditionally preferred European models, resented being told by well-meaning American advisers that the U.S. system of middle and high schools should replace the more rigorous but less democratic Latin American school system. The Alliance for Progress spent millions of dollars to build communities of tract houses so working-class families could take out mortgages on the little houses and therefore become property owners. But the project overlooked the fact that these housing tracts were located so far from the city center, where the heads of families worked, that most residents abandoned the new housing as soon as they could to move closer to their work.

President Lyndon B. Johnson kept the Alliance for Progress alive, but President Richard M. Nixon ended it, substituting a new agency, Action for Progress. Like the dollar diplomacy advocates of the 1920s and 1930s, Nixon's approach argued that "prosperity makes contentment and contentment means repose." But all of these programs, including the Alliance for Progress, differed fundamentally from dollar diplomacy. Rather than relying on Wall Street bankers to bring repose to Latin America with loans, American taxpayers provided the money, most of it in concessional terms.

BIBLIOGRAPHY

Berger, Mark T. *Under Northern Eyes: Latin American Studies and U.S. Hegemony in the Americas, 1898–1990.* Bloomington: Indiana University Press, 1995.

Schoultz, Lars. *Beneath the United States: A History of U. S. Policy Toward Latin America.* Cambridge, Mass.: Harvard University Press, 1998.

Ralph A. Dungan
Robert M. Levine

See also **Dollar Diplomacy; Latin America, Relations with; Marshall Plan.**

ALLISON COMMISSION, a joint, bipartisan congressional committee that was among the first to explore the question of whether federal intervention politicizes scientific research. Chaired by Senator William B. Allison of Iowa, the commission investigated the activities of four federal scientific agencies from 1884 to 1886. In addition to examining a jurisdictional dispute between the Navy Hydrographic Office and the Coast and Geodetic Survey over the charting of offshore waters, the commission examined the charge that the Geological Survey, the Coast Survey, and the Weather Service, which was then part of the Army Signal Corps, were doing research for abstract, not strictly practical, purposes.

In testimony before the committee, the scientists employed by the government maintained that their work was wholly practical. Several scientists contended that the legitimacy of research could not be judged by laymen, and they called for a reorganization of federal science to keep its administration out of the hands of mere political functionaries.

Congressman Hilary A. Herbert, an Alabama Democrat on the commission, insisted on the principle of maintaining direct democratic control over the scientific agencies. A devotee of limited government, he proposed sharp reductions in the activities of the two surveys, the award of the Coast Survey's offshore work to the Hydrographic Office, and the transfer of the Weather Service from the Army Signal Corps to a civilian department. Despite Herbert's efforts to scale down the scope and extent of federal science projects, however, the majority of the commission favored retaining the status quo in federal research, and Congress upheld the majority report. The government's relationship to scientific research has remained controversial ever since.

BIBLIOGRAPHY

Bruce, Robert V. *The Launching of Modern American Science, 1846–1876.* New York: Knopf, 1987.

Guston, David H., and Kenneth Keniston, eds. *The Fragile Contract: University Science and the Federal Government.* Cambridge, Mass.: MIT Press, 1994.

Daniel J. Kevles / A. G.

See also **Geophysical Explorations; Marine Sanctuaries; National Academy of Sciences; Signal Corps, U.S. Army.**

ALMANACS. One of the first publications to issue from the press in British North America was *An Almanack for New England for 1639*, printed by Stephen Daye in Cambridge, Massachusetts. Almanacs have been part of American culture ever since, adapting themselves to changing times while preserving their essential character.

In addition to monthly calendars and tables of astronomical events, almanacs included advice for farmers, medical and domestic recipes, and miscellaneous literary fare. Unlike their English counterparts, which often emphasized astrology and necromancy, the earliest almanacs in America stressed practical instruction and improvement. This was due partly to the Puritans, and partly to the environment of the more enlightened eighteenth century. Even so, most almanacs featured the "man of signs" or "the Anatomy," a crude wood-cut of a human figure, with corresponding links to the signs of the zodiac governing various parts of the body.

As printing spread throughout the colonies, so too did almanacs, which became an essential aspect of the printing business in colonial America. Timothy Green, James Franklin (elder brother of Benjamin), Daniel Fowle, and William Bradford were among several printers who originated almanacs in the colonies. By their very nature almanacs had to be adapted for local conditions and could not be imported. Almanacs were also used effectively in the propaganda wars at the time of the American Revolution. Nathaniel Ames, Benjamin West, Isaiah Thomas, Benjamin Edes, John Gill, Sarah Goddard, and Nathan Daboll produced almanacs that supported the patriots' cause through verse, essays, and graphic illustrations. The most famous compiler of almanacs in the eighteenth century was unquestionably Benjamin Franklin. Assuming the mantle of Richard Saunders, Franklin issued his first *Poor Richard* in Philadelphia in 1733.

In the nineteenth century, almanacs moved west with the country and continued to guide their readers through the seasons of life. As a rule, almanacs came with an explanation of the calendar, a list of eclipses for the year, the common notes, the names and characters of planets, signs of the zodiac, and the anatomy. They also included such practical things as interest tables, courts and court days, lists of government officials, population tables, postal rates, bank officers, exchange rates, and times and places of religious meetings. For studying the development of local economies on the frontier, almanacs are useful sources. Beyond the statistical matters, almanacs entered the realm of literature, broadly defined. Epigram, ballad, song, satire, elegy, ode, epistle, essay, recipe, joke, legend, proverb, belief, and anecdote were present in abundance.

Given such a fixed form, almanacs were surprisingly fluid and adaptable. They were frequently put into the service of various mass movements of the nineteenth century, such as temperance, antislavery, politics, and evangelical Christianity. Their ubiquity made them the natural standard-bearers for many popular crusades. Both the American Tract Society and the American Temperance Union issued hundreds of thousands of almanacs suitable for use in families, while the major protestant denominations also issued their annual registers.

But other almanacs were not intended for the parlor. As political campaigns became more sophisticated in their use of print, readers were treated to a steady stream of titles, such as the *Jackson Almanac, Young Hickory Almanac, Hard Cider and Log Cabin Almanac*, and *Rough and Ready Almanac*. While most of the campaign almanacs were filled with cartoons and invective, the *Whig Almanac*, published by Horace Greeley in New York, had a quasi-official status and was looked to by all parties for its accurate election returns.

Comic almanacs were also in vogue in the nineteenth century. Some tried to imitate the polite *Comick Almanack* of the English caricaturist George Cruikshank, but the most popular were not concerned with being polite. Turner and Fisher in Philadelphia and Robert Elton in New York were specialists in this line. With puns like "all-my-nack" in their titles, these publications carried bawdy jokes, ethnic and racial slurs, and humorous tales and anecdotes. The *Davy Crockett* almanacs were a genre unto themselves, combining aspects of the political and comic almanacs in one package.

After the Civil War, advertising, especially for patent medicines, drove the sales of most almanacs. *Ayer's American Almanac*, published by Dr. J. C. Ayer and Co., "practical and analytical chemists" of Lowell, Massachusetts, used the almanac for testimonials from satisfied users of their cathartic pills, sarsaparilla, ague cure, hair vigor, cherry pectoral, and other nostrums. This commercial emphasis continued into the twenty-first century.

In the twentieth century American corporations embraced the almanac. Ford Motor Company, Bell Telephone, Kellogg's, Seagram's, and Magnolia Petroleum are prominent examples. By sponsoring an almanac, corporations could find new audiences for their products and hope to induce brand loyalty through association. Almanacs also gained in popularity as reference tools. The *World Almanac* and the *New York Times Almanac* were well respected and frequently consulted for their accurate information. Regional publications, such as the *Texas Almanac*, published by the *Dallas Morning News*, reached targeted audiences. Religious sponsorship of almanacs continued to flourish; the *Deseret News Church Almanac*, published by the Latter-Day Saints in Salt Lake City, is a notable example. The *Sports Illustrated Almanac* appealed both to sports fans and barroom wagerers.

While specialized almanacs were abundant in the early twenty-first century, some almanacs continued much as they always had. The *Agricultural Almanac* of Lancaster, Pennsylvania, began publication in 1817. The *Hagers-Town Town and Country Almanack*, of Hagerstown, Maryland, was established in 1797. Both would be recognizable to their founders. The *Old Farmer's Almanac*, of Dublin, New Hampshire, became a bit glossier and thicker than its predecessors, but even Robert Bailey Thomas, the "old farmer" who founded the series in 1792, would find in its pages much that would be familiar to him.

Andrew Ellicott wrote in the *Maryland Almanack* for 1783: "One year passeth away and another cometh—so likewise 'tis with Almanacks—they are annual productions, whose destination and usefulness is temporary, and afterwards are thrown by and consigned to oblivion . . . it is no wonder, when they become old almanacks, that we frequently see them made use of by the pastry-cooks, or flying in the tail of the school-boy's kite." Historians, as well as cooks and kite fliers, can make good use of old almanacs, which reflect the passing years through the lens of popular culture. No other publication has been present on the American scene as long. Intended to be temporary, almanacs remain enduring sources for many lines of inquiry, from the colonial period to the modern era.

BIBLIOGRAPHY

Drake, Milton. *Almanacs of the United States.* New York: Scarecrow, 1962.

Kittredge, George Lyman. *The Old Farmer and His Almanac: Being Some Observations on Life and Manners in New England a Hundred Years Ago.* Boston: Ware, 1904.

Sagendorph, Robb. *America and Her Almanacs: Wit, Wisdom, and Weather 1639–1970.* Dublin, N.H.: Yankee, 1970.

Stowell, Marion Barber. *Early American Almanacs: The Colonial Weekday Bible.* New York: B. Franklin, 1977.

Russell Martin

See also **Poor Richard's Almanac**; *and vol. 9:* **Maxims from Poor Richard's Almanack.**

ALUMINUM, the most useful of the nonferrous metals, was first isolated in metallic form in 1825 by Hans Christian Oersted in Denmark. The metal remained a laboratory curiosity until 1854, when Henri Sainte-Claire Deville discovered a process using metallic sodium as a reductant that led to the first commercial production of aluminum. The price of the metal fell from $545 per pound in 1852 to $8 in 1885, and uses for the lightweight metal began to increase greatly. Emperor Napoleon III of France, for example, considered outfitting his army with lightweight aluminum armor and equipment, but the price of the metal remained too high for widespread use.

In 1886, an American, Charles Martin Hall, and a Frenchman, Paul Héroult, independently discovered that aluminum could be produced by electrolyzing a solution of aluminum oxide in molten cryolite (sodium aluminum fluoride). The electrolytic process won immediate acceptance by the commercial industry and in 2002 remained the sole commercial method used for making aluminum.

Hall's invention led to the formation of the Pittsburgh Reduction Company in 1888. This company, now known as Alcoa (for Aluminum Company of America), initially produced fifty pounds of aluminum per day, be-

coming by the turn of the twentieth century the world's largest producer of aluminum, a position it still enjoys in 2002. A more diverse aluminum industry developed in Europe. Within ten years, firms operated in Switzerland, Germany, Austria, France, and Scotland—all having obtained rights to Héroult's patents to make the metal. By 1900 total world production was about 7,500 short tons; American production was 2,500 tons.

The advent of the airplane in World War I greatly increased demand for the lightweight metal. In 1918 the primary capacity in the United States had grown to 62,500 short tons; world production amounted to 143,900 tons. Steady growth of the aluminum industry continued, and in 1939 the United States produced 160,000 tons of the 774,000 tons produced worldwide. The airplane became a key factor in waging World War II, and aluminum production throughout the world tripled; in the United States it grew sixfold. Another major period of growth in the industry took place during the Korean War, when the United States produced almost half of the world total of 3,069,000 tons. In 1972 total world production of aluminum came to some 12 million tons, but the American share, produced by twelve companies, had dropped to 34 percent, or 4,122,000 tons. By 2000, the aluminum industry in the United States operated more than three hundred plants in thirty-five states, employed more than 145,000 people, and produced an average of 11.5 million tons of aluminum annually.

Aluminum is the most abundant metallic element in the earth's crust. It is made from the mineral bauxite (hydrated aluminum oxide), which is found in plentiful supply throughout the tropical areas of the world. Five countries, Jamaica, Surinam, Guyana, Guinea, and Australia, mined about 61 percent of the world's supplies in 1972, with the remainder coming from twenty-two other countries. At the end of the twentieth century, the U.S. aluminum industry relied to a roughly equivalent degree on production from domestic ore materials (34.3 percent of production in 2000), imported ingots and mill products (33.5 percent), and recycled scrap materials (32.2 percent).

The great growth in the use of aluminum metal indicates its versatility. It has a unique combination of useful properties: lightness, good thermal and electrical conductivity, high reflectivity, malleability, resistance to corrosion, and excellent tensile strength in alloyed form. It is extensively employed in building and construction, where each new house uses almost four hundred pounds of the metal for such items as windows, doors, and siding. Another major market is transportation: the average automobile uses almost eighty pounds of aluminum, and truck and railroad car bodies use aluminum extensively because each pound of weight saved permits an extra pound of revenue-producing payload. The aerospace industries are also large consumers of aluminum. There are many electrical applications because it is one-third as heavy and roughly two-thirds as conductive as copper. Applications for the metal are also growing rapidly for containers and packaging, where it is used in cans, foil, and frozen-food containers. Indeed, the metal's versatility suggests countless possible applications.

BIBLIOGRAPHY

Van Horn, Kent R., ed. Prepared by engineers, scientists, and metallurgists of Aluminum Company of America. *Aluminum*. Vol. 2, *Design and Application*. Metals Park, Ohio: American Society for Metals, 1967.

Kenneth B. Higbie / c. w.

See also **Aircraft Industry; Automobile Industry.**

ALVIN AILEY AMERICAN DANCE THEATER,

a modern ballet company that uses African American music and culture as the centerpiece of its performances, was founded by dancer and choreographer Alvin Ailey in 1958. The company is best known for the ballet *Revelations*, a stylized, elegant combination of ballet and modern dance set to the music of Negro spirituals.

Ailey spent his childhood in Texas and, at age eleven, moved to Los Angeles, where he discovered culture other than Saturday matinee cowboy movies. The black dancer Katherine Dunham especially impressed him. In Los Angeles, Ailey trained under and then danced and did cho-

Alvin Ailey American Dance Theater. Hope Clark performs in Ailey's *Blues Suite.* © JOHAN ELBERS

reography for Lester Horton. At twenty-four, Ailey moved to New York City to join the cast of the Broadway play *House of Flowers.* He began to teach dance and to act in plays and films. After performances at the 92nd Street YMHA and the Jacob's Pillow Festival in Massachusetts, Ailey founded his own company, which included dancers Carmen de Lavallade and James Truitte. Other featured dancers who remained with the company for many years were Don Martin, Gary DeLoatch, and Donna Wood. Ailey's work includes the secular *Blues Suite*, set in a brothel; a tribute to jazz musician Charlie Parker, *For Bird—With Love*; and the heart-rending *Cry*, a solo celebrating black women and originally performed by Judith Jamison, who was named artistic director of the company upon Ailey's death in 1989.

BIBLIOGRAPHY

Ailey, Alvin, with Peter A. Bailey. *Revelations: The Autobiography of Alvin Ailey.* Secaucus, N.J.: Birch Lane Press, 1995.

Dunning, Jennifer. *Alvin Ailey: A Life in Dance.* Reading, Mass.: Addison-Wesley, 1996.

Mosby, Rebekah Presson. Interview with Alvin Ailey. National Public Radio, 1988.

Rebekah Presson Mosby

See also **Ballet; Dance.**

ALZHEIMER'S DISEASE,

the most common cause of dementia in the United States, is characterized by a slowly progressive mental deterioration. It is named for Dr. Alois Alzheimer, a German doctor who, in 1906, noticed unusual patterns in the brain of a woman who had died of a perplexing mental illness. Alzheimer's disease is not only a problem for those afflicted but is also of great consequence for their families and society; since 1980 it has been the subject of intensive medical research. The first symptom is usually loss of ability to remember new information. The abilities to speak, dress, and be oriented to time, along with loss of old memories ensue, and ultimately even loss of memory of one's own identity occurs. The onset is usually after age sixty-five, and the disease can progress over a period of just a few years to up to two decades. Alzheimer's disease is extremely common, with conservative estimates of 5 percent of the population over age sixty-five affected. The incidence rises with increasing age, so that at least 15 to 20 percent of all individuals over age eighty are afflicted.

Changes in mental abilities are associated with three neuropathological changes in the brain: the formation of abnormal tangles within nerve cells; the widespread deposition of a characteristic protein (amyloid); and the death of nerve cells important for communicating between one brain area and another. A small percentage of individuals with Alzheimer's have inherited one of several mutant genes, each of which appears to be able to cause the disease. One such cause of Alzheimer's disease is a mutation in the gene responsible for making the amyloid protein, which accumulates in the brain of patients with Alzheimer's disease as senile plaques. Another gene partly responsible for the disease (whose specific identity is still unknown) has been found to be located on chromosome 14. Yet another genetic influence on risk of developing Alzheimer's disease, probably present in half of all cases, is inheritance of the E4 allele of apolipoprotein E. Scientists are also studying education, diet, environment, and viruses to learn what role they might play in the development of Alzheimer's disease.

A number of drugs have been used to treat Alzheimer's disease. The U.S. Food and Drug Administration (FDA) approved the first, Cognex (tacrine) in 1993. Aricept (donepezil) became available in 1996. The FDA approved Exelon (rivastigmine) in 2000 and Reminyl (galantamine) in 2001. Each of these drugs increases the amount of acetylcholine available in the brain. Of the four drugs, Cognex has the most adverse side effects.

Although treatment and knowledge of Alzheimer's disease has improved dramatically, the cause of the disease remained unknown at the beginning of the twenty-first century.

BIBLIOGRAPHY

Mace, Nancy L., and Peter V. Rabins. *The 36-Hour Day: A Family Guide to Caring for Persons with Alzheimer's Disease, Related Dementing Illnesses, and Memory Loss in Later Life.* Baltimore: Johns Hopkins University Press, 1981. 3d ed. 1999.

Schneider, Edward L., and John W. Rowe, eds. *Handbook of the Biology of Aging.* 3d ed. San Diego: Academic Press, 1990.

Whitehouse, Peter J., Konrad Maurer, and Jesse F. Ballenger, eds. *Concepts of Alzheimer Disease: Biological, Clinical, and Cultural Perspectives.* Baltimore: Johns Hopkins University Press, 2000.

Bradley Hyman / F. B.

See also **Human Genome Project; Mental Illness; Old Age.**

AMALGAMATED CLOTHING WORKERS OF AMERICA.

The Amalgamated Clothing Workers of America (ACWA) was founded in 1914 in revolt against the established men's clothing workers union. It went on to become one of the most important and powerful industrial unions in American history. The ACWA arose out of a need among workers in the men's clothing trade for an organization that would represent every worker in the industry, not just the minority of skilled craftsmen, whose numbers were decreasing as clothing production became increasingly segmented and de-skilled in the late nineteenth century.

The first successful union of men's clothing workers was the United Garment Workers (UGW), founded in 1891 by immigrant workers who chose native-born craftsmen to head the union. Within a couple of decades, this effort at acceptability backfired as the UGW's leadership became increasingly distant from the union's immigrant majority. During two of the most significant clothing workers' strikes—in New York City during 1910 and Chicago in 1911—the UGW leaders refused to support the striking workers.

The tension between the native-born overalls makers who dominated the UGW leadership and the foreign-born majority reached its height at the 1914 national convention in Nashville, Tennessee. The urban immigrant delegates who made it there were denied seating on trumped-up charges of unpaid dues. So those delegates bolted the convention and at a nearby hotel convened themselves as the "true" United Garment Workers. After the new organization was forced to surrender its claim to the UGW name by court order, the new union adopted the name Amalgamated Clothing Workers of America at a subsequent convention. Sidney Hillman, a Chicago clothing worker, became the ACWA's first president. Although denied recognition by the American Federation of Labor (AFL), its numbers quickly swelled to 177,000 clothing workers by 1920.

During World War I, the ACWA maintained and even improved wages, hours, and working conditions. By 1917, it had established the forty-eight hour week in the nation's two biggest centers of clothing manufacturing—New York City and Chicago. During the 1920s, however, the union had to struggle to stay alive in the face of depression and red scare without and organized crime infiltration and racketeering within. During the Great Depression of the 1930s the ACWA was finally admitted into the AFL, but because of continuing differences within the federation over whether to organize by industry or craft, the ACWA joined the new Committee for Industrial Organization (CIO) (later the Congress of Industrial Organizations) as a charter member in 1935. The ACWA also shored up its political respectability when Hillman, as president of the ACWA, served on the advisory board of the National Recovery Administration (NRA) during its brief existence from 1933 to 1935. As the ACWA grew in numbers between the 1920s and the 1950s, it also expanded its scope, pioneering social welfare programs for its members that included health insurance, a health center, banks, and even a housing cooperative. As a result of plant closings and declining memberships, in 1976 the ACWA merged with the Textile Workers Union of America (TWUA) to form the Amalgamated Clothing and Textile Workers Union (ACTWU). Then, in 1995, ACTWU merged with the International Ladies Garment Workers Union (ILGWU) to form the Union of Needletrades, Industrial, and Textile Employees (UNITE!).

BIBLIOGRAPHY

Fraser, Stephen. *Labor Will Rule: Sidney Hillman and the Rise of American Labor.* New York: The Free Press, 1991.

Strong, Earl D. *The Amalgamated Clothing Workers of America.* Grinnell, Ia.: Herald-Register Publishing Co., 1940.

"UNITE! History." Available from http://www.uniteunion.org.

Susan Roth Breitzer

See also **Clothing Industry; International Ladies Garment Workers Union; New Deal; Trade Unions.**

AMANA COMMUNITY, a society of German pietists whose founders immigrated to the United States in the mid-nineteenth century. The community had its roots in Germany, where a pietistic sect called the Inspirationists had established the Community of True Inspiration to protest the arbitrary rule of church and state. For mutual protection, the Inspirationists congregated on several large estates, but high rents and unfriendly governments forced them to seek a new home in America. Under the leadership of Christian Metz, the Inspirationists crossed the Atlantic in 1843 and founded Ebenezer, a settlement near Buffalo in Erie County, New York. Here, they formally adopted communism as a way of life and developed a complex of six villages with jointly owned mills, factories, and farms.

The rapid expansion of nearby Buffalo threatened the isolation that the Inspirationists had sought in North America, and in 1855 they moved to the frontier state of Iowa, an increasingly common destination for many nineteenth-century immigrant religious communities. They located in Iowa County, incorporated as the Amana Society, and once more built houses, churches, schools, stores, and mills, and continued their community life of "brothers all." Eventually, fifteen hundred people inhabited seven Amana villages and owned 26,000 acres of prime farming land.

By the early twentieth century, both neighboring communities and industrial capitalism had begun to encroach upon the Amana villages. As memories of the founding Inspirationists faded and the old idealism grew dim, the communities' characteristic spiritual enthusiasm waned. By unanimous vote, the community reorganized in 1932 on the basis of cooperative capitalism as a joint stock company in which both business owners and employees held stock. For nearly a century, the Amana Community conducted the most successful experiment in American communism and established itself as the nation's longest-lasting communal society.

BIBLIOGRAPHY

Barthel, Diane L. *Amana: From Pietist Sect to American Community.* Lincoln: University of Nebraska Press, 1984.

Ohrn, Steven G. *Remaining Faithful: Amana Folk Art in Transition.* Des Moines: Iowa Department of Cultural Affairs, 1988.

Bertha M. H. Shambaugh / s. b.

See also **Migration, Internal; Pietism; Utopian Communities.**

AMAZON.COM. *See* **Electronic Commerce.**

AMBASSADORS are the highest-ranking diplomats sent abroad to represent their country's interests. In the United States, the president appoints ambassadors to act as his representatives in other nations. Normally stationed in an embassy in the host nation's capital, an ambassador is responsible for overseeing all American government activities in that country to further foreign policy goals.

The men and women who serve as ambassadors for the United States are either "career" members of the Foreign Service or "noncareer" political appointees. Foreign Service officers who become ambassadors have risen through the ranks of the United States Foreign Service and have years of experience working as diplomats overseas and at the United States State Department headquarters in Washington, D.C.

Political appointees are chosen to serve by the president from a variety of backgrounds. Sometimes the president appoints a noncareer ambassador because that person brings a unique talent or expertise to the particular ambassadorial post. The president also selects ambassadors based on their contributions, financial and otherwise, to his political campaigns or to his political party. Until the latter half of the twentieth century, most ambassadors were political appointees. Controversy surrounding the appointment of amateur diplomats has limited the practice so that they now comprise about 30 percent of the corps of ambassadors. However, noncareer ambassadors have tended to dominate the highest profile posts in Western Europe, Canada, the People's Republic of China, and the Soviet Union.

An ambassador's main function is to advance the interests of the United States. These interests include promoting trade and security, maintaining access to resources, facilitating cultural ties, and protecting the lives of American citizens. Ambassadors must be able to convey the president's goals to representatives of the host nation's government. Sometimes they are called upon to negotiate agreements on behalf of the president. Ambassadors are responsible for assessing the political climate in their host country and analyzing important events. At one time, ambassadors worked quietly behind the scenes, but the explosion of media outlets around the world has meant ambassadors are frequently in the public eye.

When ambassadors arrive at their post, they are required to present their credentials to the head of state in the host country. After this ceremony, they can begin their service at the embassy. In a small embassy, an ambassador may oversee just a few lower-ranking officials. In an embassy where the United States has a major presence, the ambassador must manage the work of a large staff and coordinate the activities of other government officials stationed in the host country. The officials who report to the ambassador are lower-ranking Foreign Service officers with expertise in economic, political, consular, and administrative work. Other members of the embassy team include employees of United States agencies with foreign affairs responsibilities. These include the Agency for International Development (AID), Defense Department, Peace Corps, Commerce Department, the United States

Information Agency (USIA), and the Central Intelligence Agency (CIA).

At the Congress of Vienna (1814) and the Congress of Aix-la-Chapelle (1818), diplomatic titles and ranks were first established. Ambassadors ranked highest, followed by ministers plenipotentiary and envoys extraordinary, ministers resident, and chargés d'affaires. All the great powers of Europe exchanged ambassadors to each others' capitals but not the United States. Although the Constitution gave the president the power to appoint "Ambassadors, other public Ministers and Consuls," until the administration of Grover Cleveland no president chose to name a diplomat serving under the rank of ambassador. The title was considered a vestige of the aristocratic order Americans had overthrown in their revolution for independence. In addition, the United States had not reached the status of a great power, nor did it conceive of itself as having a major role in foreign affairs. Rather than naming ambassadors, the United States chose to send lower-ranking envoys abroad to the nation's missions and consular posts.

In 1893, the United States exchanged its first ambassadors with the world's dominant power at the time, Great Britain. The same year, the United States appointed ambassadors to France, Germany, and Italy. In 1898, Mexico and Russia received American ambassadors. In the twentieth century, President Franklin Roosevelt dramatically augmented the level of American representation abroad. By the end of his administration in 1945, the United States had forty ambassadors around the world. Roosevelt was responsible for raising the rank of U.S. diplomats to the ambassadorial level throughout Latin America, America's traditional sphere of influence, in most of the European countries allied with America during World War II, as well as in the countries that had been occupied by the Axis powers. The United States also exchanged ambassadors with Canada and China. America's rise to superpower status after World War II led successive presidents to name ambassadors to all countries with resident missions.

In the twentieth century, some of the United States' most distinguished career ambassadors have included George Kennan (Soviet Union and Yugoslavia), Charles Bohlen (Soviet Union, France), Loy Henderson (Iraq, India, Nepal, and Iran), and Walter Stoessel (Poland, Soviet Union, and the Federal Republic of Germany). Notable noncareer ambassadors were David K. E. Bruce (France, United Kingdom, Germany), William Bullitt (France), Henry Cabot Lodge (Germany, South Vietnam), and W. Averell Harriman (United Kingdom, Soviet Union).

Ambassadors, like other foreign envoys, are officially protected from harm by what is known as diplomatic immunity. The host government cannot detain or arrest ambassadors, but has the right to oust them from the country. Nevertheless, the job carries a certain degree of risk. Ambassadors sometimes find themselves in dangerous situations, either because the host country is hostile to the

United States or is undergoing some sort of political upheaval or war. For example, five American ambassadors were assassinated in third world hot spots during the 1970s, in Guatemala, Sudan, Cyprus, Lebanon, and Afghanistan. The U.S. ambassador to Brazil was kidnapped in 1969.

BIBLIOGRAPHY

Johnson, Richard A. *The Administration of United States Foreign Policy.* Austin: University of Texas Press, 1971.

Plischke, Elmer. *United States Diplomats and their Missions: A Profile of American Diplomatic Emissaries since 1778.* Washington, D.C.: American Enterprise Institute for Public Policy Research, 1975.

Ellen G. Rafshoon

See also **Diplomatic Missions; Embassies; Foreign Service; State, Department of.**

AMENDMENTS, CONSTITUTIONAL. *See* **Bill of Rights in U.S. Constitution; Constitution of the United States.**

AMERASIA CASE. The Amerasia Case was the first major COLD WAR event to suggest a communist infiltration of the State Department. That charge faded soon after the *Amerasia* story broke in 1945 because World War II (1939–1945) was still absorbing the public's attention. But within a few years, the case became a staple of partisan politics. This was particularly true after the several events: the agreements made at the World War II Yalta summit conference gradually becoming known, the fall of China to communism in 1949, the perjury conviction in 1950 of former State Department employee Alger Hiss, and the nearly concurrent emergence of Senator Joseph R. McCarthy.

The 26 January 1945 issue of the Asian-American journal *Amerasia* contained an article based on a highly classified report on British-American relations in southeast Asia. In June 1945, the Federal Bureau of Investigation (FBI) arrested *Amerasia* editor Philip Jaffe and five others associated with the journal. The charge, espionage on behalf of Chinese communists, did not hold. On the one hand, there was an inherent conflict between freedom of the press and government classification restrictions designed to protect wartime secrecy. On the other, the lack of clear and convincing evidence to support the charge of espionage was compounded by at least one break-in and other questionable FBI surveillance activities. Ultimately, there was no trial. Jaffe pleaded guilty and one other person pleaded no contest in 1945—on the relatively benign charge of unauthorized possession of government documents. Even the Justice Department admitted that all parties were merely guilty of "an excess of journalistic zeal."

BIBLIOGRAPHY
Klehr, Harvey, and Ronald Radosh. *The Amerasia Spy Case: Prelude to McCarthyism.* Chapel Hill: University of North Carolina Press, 1996.

Kenneth O'Reilly

See also **McCarthyism.**

AMERICA, DISCOVERY OF. *See* Exploration of America, Early.

AMERICA, NAMING OF.

The earliest explorers and historians designated America the Indies, the West Indies, or the New World, and these terms remained the favorites in Spain and Portugal for more than two centuries. Beyond the Pyrenees Mountains, the chief source of information on the discoveries was Amerigo Vespucci's account of his voyages, translated into Latin. In 1507, a coterie of scholars at Saint-Dié, in Lorraine (in present-day France), chiefly Martin Waldseemüller and Mathias Ringmann, printed this work in *Cosmographiae Introductio*, a small volume designed to accompany and explain a wall map and globe executed by Waldseemüller. They suggested two names for the new "fourth part" of the world, one Amerige (pronounced A-mer-i-gay, with the "-ge" from the Greek, meaning "earth"), and the other America (in the feminine form, parallel to Europa and Asia). The latter form appeared on Waldseemüller's maps of 1507, and their wide circulation brought about the gradual adoption of the name. Waldseemüller was aware of only South America as a continent, but in 1538 Gerhardus Mercator extended the designation to both continents.

Although Vespucci was not responsible for bestowing the name, since 1535 the injustice to Christopher Columbus has aroused protest. Various impossible origins of the name "America" have circulated, such as that it comes from a native Indian word or from a sheriff of Bristol, England, named Richard Ameryk. The etymology of "Amerigo" derives from the old Germanic, meaning "ruler of the home." Today, the name "America" is ambiguous, since it often refers to the United States alone.

BIBLIOGRAPHY
Masini, Giancarlo, with Iacopo Gori. *How Florence Invented America: Vespucci, Verrazzano, and Mazzei and Their Contribution to the Conception of the New World.* New York: Marsilio Publishers, 1998.
Miller, Roscoe R. *Amerigo and the Naming of America.* New York: Carlton Press, 1968.

Allen Walker Read / A. E.

See also **Cartography; Exploration of America, Early.**

AMERICA AS INTERPRETED BY FOREIGN OBSERVERS.

The United States has fascinated foreign travelers throughout its history. Influential commentaries left by foreign travelers generally have identified aspects of American politics, society, and culture that seemed unique to the United States. Individual foreign visitors will be discussed following an overview of the basic patterns of their observations.

Many foreign commentaries have applauded the unique aspects of America. Foreign travelers and Americans themselves have often used this praise as a basis for the idea of "American exceptionalism," which holds that the United States has followed a unique historical path rather than being enmeshed in the larger patterns and processes of world history.

In the eighteenth and early nineteenth centuries the Declaration of Independence appealed to the conscience of the world, and the American Revolution enlisted international support. Once the nation was established, what had been an obscure colonial backwater became a phenomenon to be investigated. Foreign visitors took up the challenge of satisfying their curiosity about the United States as the hope of the world and as the country of the future.

In the nineteenth century the idea of exceptionalism developed out of foreigners' observations about the development and nature of American democracy. These observations focused on the conservative nature of the Constitution and political system; the rapidity of industrial development in the absence of government regulation; and the opportunity for and tolerance of experiments in communal living, public education, and reform of derelict persons. During the early years of the Republic, the existence of a large country with a popular government, not a monarchy, was indeed unusual. Some foreign visitors consequently hoped that the American experiment would survive even though they predicted its downfall. Foreign observers correctly perceived that the greatest threat to the country was slavery and the sectional conflict that it precipitated. Most travelers who observed slavery considered it to be an aberration of American democracy, not an intrinsic problem.

In the twentieth century, the perception of American exceptionalism was perpetuated by two factors. The first was the telling military and diplomatic role of the United States during World Wars I and II. The second was the prosperity and power of the American economy in the decades following these conflicts, including the status of the United States after 1991 as the world's sole superpower.

Other foreign travelers' commentaries have disparaged the United States, taking the form of either humorous satire or serious criticism. Nineteenth-century foreign observers' criticisms typically involved America's national excesses. These included the rambunctiousness of the democratic political system; the restlessness to develop natural resources, owing to capitalistic ambition and opportunity; boastfulness, often expressed in vulgar ways; and the national emphasis on practicality over elegance. Foreigners attributed this last tendency to a lack of refined or high culture.

Serious criticism of the country leveled by foreign observers grew in the twentieth century. Twentieth-century observers seemed more analytical than their predecessors, who were more likely simply to describe the American scene. This change occurred of necessity as America became more complex and diverse, an evolution that invited more penetrating observation. Criticisms also grew as a by-product of the country's greater efforts to influence other nations. Foreign policy moved from the isolationism counseled by George Washington and Thomas Jefferson to the internationalism and interventionism of Theodore Roosevelt, Woodrow Wilson, Franklin Roosevelt, John Kennedy, Ronald Reagan, and others. America's cultural development moved from a regional to a national level during the nineteenth century and then to the internationalization of American culture during the twentieth century. Both of these trends met with foreign visitors' criticism.

Still, to the present day foreign observers who have taken a negative stance toward American politics, society, and culture typically have exercised little or no lasting influence. The same can be said of those who have failed to celebrate the unique, positive qualities of the United States.

Foreign Observers of the Eighteenth and Nineteenth Centuries

The most important foreigner to record impressions of the United States in its infancy was J. Hector St. John de Crèvecoeur, who composed his *Letters from an American Farmer* (1782) over the course of the 1770s and published his work in London. Crèvecoeur immigrated to America in 1754, and settled on a farm in New York State. He traveled extensively among both white and Indian peoples, and was adopted by the Oneida Indians after he met them while occupied as a surveyor in Vermont. In 1780 he was obliged to return to France, but came back to the United States in 1783 and was appointed the French consul in New York City. His *Letters*, quickly published in French and German as well as English, excited Europe about American uniqueness, especially its climate, fauna, and wildlife, and no doubt induced some to settle in the United States. Crèvecoeur posed the question, "What then is the American, this new man?" He described a person whose past prejudices and manners were obliterated and replaced by new ones formed by the person's allegiance to new government and new land and by his or her new sociopolitical rank. In effect, Crèvecoeur was describing an American melting pot, a country where a new kind of national allegiance, one based on civic identity and economic standing, would replace the old European allegiance, based on ethnic identity.

The number of foreign visitors increased substantially in the nineteenth century as travel became easier and curiosity about the American experiment grew. Most of the important observers came from the United Kingdom. Frances Trollope arrived in the United States in 1827. She traveled in this country with Frances (Fanny) Wright, another Englishwoman, who had established a utopian community near Memphis, Tennessee, and had written favorably about the country in her *Views of Society and Manners in America* (1821). She observed that even American generals and statesmen tended to be farmers and extolled the virtues of pride in the land, physical fitness, and an organic sense of liberty that an agrarian American society nourished. It is thus ironic that her friend Trollope is remembered as the author of perhaps the most ill-natured of all books of travel in the United States, her *Domestic Manners of the Americans* (1832). Trollope was the leading figure of what was known as the Tory generation of hypercritical English travelers in this country. The title of Trollope's work is misleading, for she charged that Americans had no manners; moreover, she complained, they were inquisitive, boring, humorless, and self-satisfied. American women were scrawny; the men hollow-chested and round-shouldered. Persons of neither sex, except for blacks, had an ear for music. The culprit for all of this was Thomas Jefferson, whose proclamation that all were equal set off mediocre people's ambitions to rise above their proper station. Trollope related a cross-examination she witnessed of President Andrew Jackson by a citizen who did not believe Jackson's affirmations that his wife Rachel was still alive. Although they detested "Dame Trollope" for her critique, what Americans detested even more was that foreign observers did not esteem the rough-and-tumble ways that Trollope, to be fair, probably exaggerated only slightly.

An even more famous English writer, Charles Dickens, visited the country in 1842. Because of his prior transatlantic fame he received a rabidly cordial reception by ordinary Americans as well as literati and statesmen, including President John Tyler. Thus, Americans were disappointed that Dickens's *American Notes* (1842) was mostly critical of American society. All the parties Americans threw for him did not charm Dickens. He joined Trollope in excoriating American incivility. He also found fault with slavery, the absence of copyright laws, and the ill-treatment of prison inmates. His work, like Trollope's, provoked an American backlash, although less severe in his case. An anonymous American pamphlet, *Change for the American Notes* (1843), drew attention to English workhouses, slums, and debtors' prisons.

Most foreign travelers did not focus on slavery in their accounts. One who did was Frances (Fanny) Kemble, a young London actress. Kemble moved to Darien, Georgia, in 1832, where she married a southern planter. She indicated that she did not know at the time that her husband was an extensive slaveholder. She decided to keep a journal of her daily experiences. This became her *Journal of a Residence on a Georgia Plantation in 1838–1839* (1863). The *Journal* relates the story of her growing awareness of the horror of slavery. Kemble especially sympathized with slave women and the elderly slaves, who suffered from their owners' abuse or negligence.

The most notable German observer of the United States was Francis Lieber, a refugee and correspondent of the liberal revolutions that flashed across Europe throughout the nineteenth century. He arrived in the United States in 1827, became a professor of law and philosophy at Columbia College (later the University of South Carolina) in Columbia, South Carolina, and then moved to Columbia College (later Columbia University) in New York City. Lieber offered several acute glimpses of the American landscape and legal system, including *Letters to a Gentleman in Germany: Written after a Trip from Philadelphia to Niagara* (1834) and *The Stranger in America; or, Letters to a Gentleman in Germany Comprising Sketches of the Manners, Society, and National Peculiarities of the United States* (1835). While Lieber was teaching in South Carolina, he—like the Englishwoman Fanny Kemble—grew to oppose slavery. His public opposition to the institution ultimately led to his relocation to the North.

The French aristocrat Alexis de Tocqueville shared his English counterparts' revulsion at the American tendency to "barbaric" behavior. But his *Democracy in America* (2 vols., 1835, 1840) offset—and in the long term, overwhelmed—the sting of English carping. *Democracy in America* was the result of Tocqueville's interest in assessing the impact of individual liberty, institutional pluralism, and mass society on the United States. He believed that democracy was inevitable, so he wished to learn and to an extent warn Europe about it before it made its way across the Atlantic. Tocqueville observed that its lack of aristocracy, its hunger for property, and its love of change made American democracy an entirely middle-class society. He was wrong about this. But he was right about much else. He detected that Americans resolved problems by resorting to laws, so lawyers were a natural aristocracy. He worried that slavery might cause a national conflict, which it eventually did. And he foresaw that the United States and Russia would be two great world powers. *Democracy in America* is fascinating because of its eclecticism and its inductive reasoning, developing general principles from careful observation of details. For all of these qualities it is considered the greatest of all foreigners' accounts of the United States.

The most important foreign observer of the United States in the late nineteenth century was James Bryce. A native of Ireland, Bryce went on to serve as the British ambassador to the United States from 1907 to 1913. He began to lay the groundwork for that position in 1870, when he commenced visits to the United States to study its constitutional government. At the time, the rising tide of republicanism in Europe was sparking a national debate in Britain on representative government. Moreover, destiny seemed to be with the American republic. Having passed the test of Civil War, it was forging ahead so irresistibly that European institutions seemed outmoded. The product of Bryce's study was his *American Common-wealth* (1888). In this work Bryce captured the enthusiasm of the age. He praised the informality of American manners, signaling a shift in British observers' attitudes from earlier Tory revulsion. He also praised the work ethic of the members of Congress, whose alacrity contrasted sharply for Bryce with the indolence of the House of Lords. He sensed that the great power in American society lay at the time with railway magnates, whose autonomy from government interference fascinated Bryce. Sympathetic to the Progressive movement, he sharply criticized the corrupt urban machine politics of the age, which he felt fell far short of America's democratic potential.

Bryce made friends with many American statesmen, including the jurist Oliver Wendell Holmes Jr. and politicians such as Theodore Roosevelt and Woodrow Wilson. Bryce actually advised Wilson during the post–World War I struggle over the League of Nations. Most of the people with whom Bryce corresponded were of Anglo-Saxon background, and disposed to favor a close connection with Britain. Bryce's speeches and writings helped create the idea of an Anglo-Saxon racial superiority and also helped forge close British-American cultural and diplomatic relations. Thus, Bryce shared Wilson's bitterness over the United States' refusal after the war to commit itself to protecting European safety.

A contemporary of Bryce, José Martí, was the first important Latin American observer of the United States. A journalist, Martí arrived in New York City from Cuba in 1881. He began writing about his impressions of the United States for the newspaper *La Nación* of Buenos Aires, Argentina. Charles A. Dana, member of a famous New York City newspaper family, discovered Martí and hired him to write also for his newspaper, the *New York Sun*. Martí gave voice to a growing Latin American ambivalence about the power of the United States. Martí urged Latin Americans to adopt U.S. constitutional doctrines and practices. Commenting on the new immigration patterns of his time, he saw America as a vast melting pot in which "luckless Irishmen, Poles, Italians, Bohemians, Germans [are] redeemed from oppression or misery." He championed the writings of Ralph Waldo Emerson as a literature for all the Americas. On the other hand, Martí feared that U.S. imperialism would manifest itself in an expansion into Latin America, and especially in an annexation of Cuba. He died in 1895, fighting in the first stage of the Cuban revolution against Spain, and so did not live to see U.S. occupation of Cuba as a result of the Spanish-American War of 1898.

Foreign Observers of the Twentieth Century
Latin American writers in the twentieth century have seen José Martí as a prophet of both Latin American nationalism and North American hegemony. Important among these was Carlos G. Dávila, Chile's ambassador to the United States from 1927 to 1931 and later a New York City journalist, and Daniel Cosío Villegas, a leading Mexican intellectual and businessman familiar with the United States through both work and residence. Dávila's *We of*

137

the Americas was published in 1949. Villegas's works also include *The United States versus Porfirio Díaz* (1963) and *American Extremes* (1964). Both of these observers called for greater economic cooperation between the United States and its Latin American neighbors, not subjugation by the former of the latter. They also advocated Latin American resistance to the spread of North American culture.

John Alfred Spender and Herbert George (H. G.) Wells, English observers of the United States in the early twentieth century, addressed the tension the United States felt at the time between remaining isolated from world affairs and acknowledging its position and duties as a world power. The editor of the prestigious *Westminster Gazette*, Spender visited the United States in 1921 and in 1927. He recounted his impressions of America in the post–World War I period in his *Through English Eyes* (1928). Spender attempted to explain to Europeans the American reaction against continuing involvement in European affairs after the war. He urged patience with the American position, and predicted that once Americans realized the strength of the country they would accept their important part in world affairs and break with their historic neutrality.

Wells joined Spender in predicting a more activist U.S. foreign policy. He made six visits to the United States from 1906 to 1940, and it was his experiences on the first of these that prompted his *The Future in America: A Search after Realities* (1906). Wells, a socialist, spent time on his visit with Jane Addams, Booker T. Washington, and W. E. B. Du Bois. He was also a famous science fiction writer, and so was invited to lunch by Theodore Roosevelt. In his book Wells lamented the status of black Americans. He also expressed concern about the fact that ambitious Americans cared little about the long-term consequences of their capitalistic striving. Yet Roosevelt impressed Wells as "a very symbol of the creative will in man." Overall, *The Future in America* was an optimistic account of the overwhelming potential for American economic development in the form of "acquisitive successes, the striving failures, [and] the multitudes of those rising and falling who come between." At the end of *The Future in America*, Wells predicted a major Anglo-American role in the eventual emergence of an international government, a prediction vindicated in the formation of the United Nations in 1945, a year before Wells's death.

The most important foreign observer of American race relations was the Swedish economist, Gunnar Myrdal. In 1944, Myrdal published his two-volume study of black-white relations, *An American Dilemma: The Negro Problem and Modern Democracy*. He asserted that white Americans experience a troubling dilemma because of the discrepancy between the hallowed "American Creed," whereby they think, talk, and act under the influence of egalitarian and Christian precepts, and the oppressive way they treat black Americans. Myrdal, who was later awarded a Nobel Prize in economics, predicted that this

moral dilemma, heightened by the democratic rhetoric of World War II, would force changes in American race relations and end the country's greatest scandal. In the quarter century of civil rights activism and achievement that followed Myrdal's publication, "dilemma" served as a common metaphor for American race relations. Although Myrdal would eventually be seen as overly optimistic, in 1964 American intellectuals ranked his book one of the most significant works in the twentieth century for changing the direction of society.

The civil rights movement gained strength through the 1960s. This coincided with a time when many African nations moved out from under European colonization to independence. Black Americans and Africans, each group battling racism, shared political strategies and explored new cultural alliances. Tom Mboya was a leader of the independence movement of Kenya. He visited the United States in the 1950s and 1960s, and assessed his experience in several newspaper articles, which were collected in his *The Challenge of Nationhood* (1970). In this work Mboya discouraged black Americans' plans for expatriation to Africa. Instead, he called for patient efforts to realize their full potential as American citizens and encouraged Africans to support black Americans' efforts to achieve political and, more important to Mboya, economic equality in the United States. Like his American counterparts Martin Luther King Jr. and Malcolm X before him, in 1969 Tom Mboya was assassinated.

The most important Asian observer of the United States was Francis L. K. Hsu, who was was born in Manchuria in 1909 and immigrated to the United States shortly before World War II. A distinguished anthropologist at Northwestern University, he wrote extensively on the interaction between Chinese and American cultures. His *Americans and Chinese: Passages to Differences* (1953) confirmed a change in foreigners' observations about the spread of American power and influence from enthusiasm to anxiety. Hsu recognized that American influence had extended beyond the West and was in the process of spreading into Asia. For him, Americanization—the global spread of American corporate interests, based on assumptions of individual achievement, competitiveness, and exploitation of natural resources—was a pejorative term.

Finally, the most important contemporary foreign observer of American culture is Rob Kroes, who is associated with the Netherlands Institute for Advanced Studies and the European Association for American Studies. Kroes is a well-known authority on the impact of American popular culture on the rest of the world as well as on the United States itself. Perhaps the most memorable title of his some dozen works on the subject was *If You've Seen One, You've Seen the Mall: Europeans and American Mass Culture* (1996). A later work is titled *Them and Us: Questions of Citizenship in a Globalizing World* (2000).

BIBLIOGRAPHY

The works listed below are included because they describe the impact of the interpretations of the United States discussed above. In the cases of works written by the foreign observers themselves, the editions selected include helpful introductions that provide the context and significance of the work, as well as in some cases the responses of Americans to the work.

Allen, Gay Wilson, and Roger Asselineau. *St. John de Crèvecoeur: The Life of an American Farmer.* New York: Viking Press, 1987.

Belnap, Jeffrey, and Raúl Fernández, eds. *José Martí's "Our America": From National to Hemispheric Cultural Studies.* Durham, N.C.: Duke University Press, 1998. A collection of essays that assess the significance of Martí's writings. Originally collected and published in Cuba as *Nuestra América* in 1909.

Freidel, Frank. *Francis Lieber, Nineteenth-Century Liberal.* 1947. Gloucester, Mass.: Peter Smith, 1968.

Greenfield, Gerald Michael, and John D. Buenker. *Those United States: International Perspectives on American History.* 2 vols. New York: Harcourt Brace, 2000. A valuable textbook.

Hsu, Francis L. K. *Americans and Chinese: Passage to Differences.* 1953. Honolulu: University Press of Hawaii, 1981.

Nevins, Allan, ed. *American Social History As Recorded by British Travellers.* 1923. New York: Augustus M. Kelley, 1969.

Pachter, Marc, ed. *Abroad in America: Visitors to the New Nation, 1776–1914.* Reading, Mass.: Addison-Wesley, 1976. Includes paintings and photographs of contemporary American scenes and the visitors themselves.

Pierson, George Wilson. *Tocqueville in America.* 1938. Baltimore: Johns Hopkins University Press, 1996.

Regis, Pamela. *Describing Early America: Bartram, Jefferson, Crèvecoeur, and the Rhetoric of Natural History.* DeKalb: Northern Illinois University Press, 1992.

Southern, David W. *Gunnar Myrdal and Black-White Relations: The Use and Abuse of* An American Dilemma, *1944–1969.* Baton Rouge: Louisiana State University Press, 1987.

Tocqueville, Alexis de. *Democracy in America.* Translated and edited by Harvey C. Mansfield and Delba Winthrop. Chicago: University of Chicago Press, 2000. Replaces the previous standard edition, the 1954 text edited by Phillips Bradley.

Tuckerman, Henry T. *America and Her Commentators.* 1864. New York: Antiquarian Press, 1961.

Tulloch, Hugh. *James Bryce's* American Commonwealth: *The Anglo-American Background.* Woodbridge, N.H.: Boydell Press, 1988.

Timothy M. Roberts

See also **American Dilemma, An; Democracy in America.**

AMERICA FIRST COMMITTEE

(AFC). Founded in 1940 to fight against U.S. participation in World War II, the AFC initially enjoyed the backing of Henry Ford and the historian Charles A. Beard. Isolationists in all parts of the United States were involved, but the committee was especially active in Chicago. Indeed, the entire American Midwest stood as one of the strongholds of isolationist feeling. After Charles Lindbergh, an AFC leader, made what was widely considered an anti-Semitic speech in September 1941, the organization began to decline. The Japanese bombing of Pearl Harbor on 7 December 1941 only further eroded support for the America First Committee and similar isolationist pressure groups.

BIBLIOGRAPHY

Doenecke, Justus D., ed. *In Danger Undaunted: The Anti-Interventionist Movement of 1940–1941 As Revealed in the Papers of the America First Committee.* Stanford, Calif.: Hoover Institution Press, 1990.

Wayne Andrews/A. E.

See also **Isolationism;** *and vol. 9:* **America First.**

AMERICA THE BEAUTIFUL

is a patriotic hymn that originated as a poem written by Katharine Lee Bates in the summer of 1893 after a trip to Colorado Springs. The poem first appeared in *The Congregationalist* in 1895 and was set to music months later. Bates simplified the text in 1904 and made changes to the third stanza years later to create the words that are known today. From over seventy musical settings, the one now best known was written by S. A. Ward. Many citizens have lobbied Congress to make it the national anthem. The beloved hymn was performed frequently following the terrorist attacks of 11 September 2001.

BIBLIOGRAPHY

Bates, Katharine Lee. *Selected Poems.* Boston: Houghton Mifflin, 1930.

Sherr, Lynn. *"America the Beautiful": The Stirring True Story behind Our Nation's Favorite Song.* New York: Public Affairs, 2001.

Connie Ann Kirk

AMERICAN ACADEMY OF ARTS AND SCIENCES.

The Massachusetts legislature established the American Academy of Arts and Sciences on 4 May 1780. Following the broad vision of John Adams, the Academy's founder, the charter directed the Academy's programs toward both the development of knowledge—historical, natural, physical, and medical—and its applications for the improvement of society. The sixty-two incorporating fellows, all from Massachusetts, represented varying interests and high standing in the political, professional, and commercial sectors of the state. The first new members, chosen by the Academy in 1781, included Benjamin Franklin and George Washington as American fellows, as well as several foreign honorary members.

The initial volume of Academy *Memoirs* appeared in 1785, and the *Proceedings* followed in 1846. The early publications reveal the important place that science and technology held in the Academy from the outset, reflecting an era when the learned population could comprehend and even contribute to the development of scientific knowledge. By the last quarter of the nineteenth century, the professional scientists had largely come to represent the public face of the institution. Presentations on historical or other general interest topics at the meetings of the Academy, however, helped to sustain the founding concept of a broader learned culture, and this practice began to accelerate early in the twentieth century. The linkage of specialized and general knowledge in the Academy's history is exemplified by the important debates over Darwin's *Origin of Species* in the early months of 1860. Though viewed retrospectively as a clash between Harvard naturalists Asa Gray and Louis Agassiz—pro and con, respectively—a number of other Academy members participated as well. Much of the debate was summarized in the *Proceedings*, the publication of which continued for more than a hundred years; the content of the *Proceedings* now appears in the annual *Records*. In the 1950s the Academy launched its journal *Daedalus*, reflecting a postwar commitment to a broader intellectual and socially-oriented program.

The Academy has sponsored a number of awards throughout its history. Its first award, established in 1796 by Benjamin Thompson (Count Rumford), honored distinguished work on "heat and light" and provided support for research activities. Additional prizes recognized important contributions in the sciences, social sciences, and humanities. In 2000, a scholar-patriot award was inaugurated to honor individuals who have made significant contributions to the work of the Academy and whose lives exemplify the founders' vision of service to society.

During most of the nineteenth century, the Academy shared the headquarters of the Boston Athenaeum. Its first home was acquired in Boston in 1904. In the 1950s the Academy moved to Brookline, Massachusetts, and in 1981 the society moved into a new house in Cambridge, built with funds provided by former Academy president Edwin Land.

In the second half of the twentieth century, the Academy took significant steps to strengthen its ability to promote service and study. Projects became a central focus of the Academy, and a full-time professional staff was engaged. In an age of specialization, the multidisciplinary character of the Academy was seen as an important asset in dealing with the array of new problems that characterized the post–World War II era. In the late 1950s, arms control emerged as a signature concern of the Academy as scientists, social scientists, and humanists grappled with the social and political dimensions of scientific change. The Academy also engaged in collaborative institution-building, serving, for example, as the catalyst in establishing the national humanities center in North Carolina.

A new strategic plan, developed in the late 1990s, focused the Academy's efforts in three major areas: science, technology, and global security; social policy and education; and humanities and culture. In 2002, the Academy established a new visiting scholars program to support younger scholars.

Since its founding, 10,000 fellows and foreign honorary members have been elected to the Academy, with over 4,000 currently on the roster. From the beginning, the membership has included not only scientists and scholars but also an increasing number of writers and artists as well as representatives from the political and business sectors. Academy fellows have included such notables as John Adams, Thomas Jefferson, John James Audubon, Joseph Henry, Washington Irving, Josiah Willard Gibbs, Augustus Saint-Gaudens, J. Robert Oppenheimer, Willa Cather, T. S. Eliot, Edward R. Murrow, Jonas Salk, Eudora Welty, and Edward K. (Duke) Ellington. Foreign honorary members have included Leonhard Euler, Marquis de Lafayette, Alexander von Humboldt, Leopold von Ranke, Charles Darwin, Jawaharlal Nehru, Werner Heisenberg, and Alec Guinness. Astronomer Maria Mitchell was the first woman to be elected to the Academy, in 1848.

Until the 1930s the privilege of voting and holding office in the Academy was effectively reserved to those resident in Massachusetts. The postwar years saw a significant change. With a larger number of members elected from across the country, the Western Center was established in the late 1960s and the Midwest Center several years later. In 2000, the first international meeting was held in Paris. Now in its third century, the Academy is an active national and international learned society whose independence enables it to help shape public policy, contribute to intellectual debate, and advance the life of the mind.

BIBLIOGRAPHY

American Academy of Arts and Sciences. Home page at http://www.amacad.org.

Whitehill, Walter Muir. "Early Learned Societies in Boston and Vicinity." In *The Pursuit of Knowledge in the Early American Republic: American Scientific and Learned Societies from Colonial Times to the Civil War.* Edited by Alexandra Oleson and Sanborn C. Brown. Baltimore: Johns Hopkins University Press, 1976.

Leslie Berlowitz

See also **Learned Societies.**

AMERICAN ASSOCIATION FOR THE ADVANCEMENT OF SCIENCE.

The AAAS grew on the base of the small but successful Association of Geologists and Naturalists, founded in 1840, which met annually, shared research findings, pondered theoretical explanations for phenomena like mountain building, and skillfully advocated for scientific projects on the state and federal level. Under the leadership of the geologist brothers Henry Darwin Rogers and William Barton Rogers, among others, the AAAS was voted into existence in 1847 and held its first meeting in Philadelphia in 1848. Using British and German organizations as models, the AAAS held peripatetic annual meetings, gave reports on current research in specific fields, and opened sessions to the general public as part of their goal of "advancing science."

Until the National Academy of Sciences was formed in 1863, the AAAS served as a national forum and symbol of a growing scientific community. Nearly all active scientists joined, including the geologist Benjamin Silliman, the meteorologist William Redfield, the zoologist and geologist Louis Agassiz, the botanist Asa Gray, the geophysicist Alexander Dallas Bache, and the physicist Joseph Henry. The younger members were particularly insistent that the new association establish high standards for the published annual *Proceedings* and monitor public presentations at the meetings, and the sometimes stringent application of such standards led to antagonism toward a clique who privately called themselves the Lazzaroni. Perhaps because of tensions between amateurs and professionals, natural and physical scientists, and even regions—tensions not all directly related to the AAAS itself—membership began to decline at the end of the 1850s. When the members reconvened after a hiatus during the Civil War in 1866, the AAAS faced a challenge from the new National Academy of Sciences and later from a growing number of scientific societies organizing in specializing fields.

Under the long management of the AAAS secretary and anthropologist Frederick Ward Putnam, the AAAS continued to be a public forum for the sciences. Presidential addresses (rotating between the natural and physical sciences) and committee initiatives offered opportunities to debate major issues, including response to Darwinian evolution, the shaping of a new conception of "pure science," and the reformulation of nomenclature in entomology and other natural science fields. The membership numbers recovered as the scientific community grew and fellowships acknowledged outstanding scientific work and the new Ph.D. credential. As new specialized societies grew out of the sectional meetings of the AAAS, many of them would meet annually at the same time under the umbrella of the senior organization. When the psychologist James McKeen Cattell offered an arrangement that allowed the AAAS to publish the weekly *Science* as its official journal in 1900, the AAAS was able to achieve its dual goals, to promote (popularize) and advance (sponsor research) science through a regular publication.

With Cattell as editor for nearly the next half century, the AAAS remained a highly visible forum for science and in 1907 accepted the Smithsonian Institution's offer of free space in Washington, D.C. The organization sought to be representative of the large community of scientists and had never kept women, minorities, or physically handicapped scientists from membership. The astronomer Maria Mitchell had joined in the 1850s, for example, and W. E. B. Du Bois at the turn of the century—but they were a minority in the organization, as in the sciences more generally. During the 1930s, the association lacked leadership with initiative, and in 1944, Cattell sold *Science* to the AAAS. A postwar generation of leaders

One of the most controversial decisions of the AAAS involved the Atlanta meeting in 1955, which some members thought ought to be held outside the segregated South. When Margaret Mead, newly elected member of the AAAS board, mediated the question, she suggested that northern white scientists' experience with segregation would solidify their opposition to segregation. Certainly it affected Detlev Bronk, then a recent president of the AAAS, who was furious because he could not attend a session at black Atlanta University because white taxicab drivers could not take him to a black neighborhood and black taxicab drivers could not pick up a white man. The AAAS did not again meet in a southern city until 1990 in New Orleans.

Maria Mitchell, who had won a prize for her discovery of a comet and became professor of astronomy when Vassar College opened, attended an AAAS meeting in the 1850s and was fascinated by the politics of science. The discerning Quaker wrote: "For a few days Science reigns supreme—we are feted and complimented to the top of our bent, and although complimenters and complimented must feel that it is only a sort of theatrical performance for a few days and over, one does enjoy acting the part of greatness for a while."

moved toward a more systematic set of programs run by professional staff.

In the exhilarating 1950s and 1960s, membership grew and the organization turned to questions about the relationships among the sciences and between the sciences and society. The AAAS sponsored a conference at Arden House at Columbia University in 1951 that stressed public understanding of science, essential in a democratic society that was also striding forward in the sciences. Dael Wolfle became the executive officer in 1954 and helped formulate programs on the quality of science education and on political issues that were important to the scientists themselves. Some were concerns about financial resources for "big science," but many related to issues of personal autonomy as many scientists grew concerned about the implications of their research in the context of the Cold War. The AAAS provided a place for discussion, if not always a resolution, of these issues and enhanced scientific journalism through a fellowship program.

At the end of the twentieth century, the AAAS had about 150,000 members and served an international community of scientists through its journal and a number of Internet sites, experimenting with new modes of communication. Its widely publicized reports on scientific policy and funding in the federal government added to the important news in *Science* and the presentations at an-

141

nual meetings that regularly attracted more than 5,000 participants. Housed in an award-winning new building on New York Avenue in Washington, D.C., the AAAS had a large staff engaged in policy studies, projects on scientific ethics and religion, education and minority issues, and international programs.

BIBLIOGRAPHY

Abelson, Philip H., and Ruth Kulstad, eds. *The "Science" Centennial Review*. Washington, D.C.: AAAS, 1980.

Bruce, Robert V. *The Launching of Modern American Science, 1846–1876*. New York: Knopf, 1987.

Kohlstedt, Sally Gregory, Michael M. Sokal, and Bruce V. Lewenstein. *The Establishment of Science in America: 150 Years of the American Association for the Advancement of Science*. New Brunswick, N.J.: Rutgers University Press, 1999.

Sally Gregory Kohlstedt

See also **National Academy of Sciences; National Science Foundation.**

AMERICAN ASSOCIATION OF RETIRED PERSONS

(AARP) is a nonpartisan organization for persons fifty years old or over. It is the second largest membership organization in the United States, behind only the Catholic Church, and offers members a major voice in the political process, as well as a variety of services.

Ethel Percy Andrus, a seventy-two-year-old retired high school principal, founded AARP in 1958 as an outgrowth of the National Retired Teachers Association, which she had founded in 1947 to confront the tax and pension problems of retired teachers. Andrus envisioned AARP as an organization to serve members by providing assistance with such needs as health insurance and travel services and, more generally, to promote "independence, dignity, and purpose" among older Americans. The organization grew quickly from 50,000 members in 1958, to 750,000 in 1963, to 10 million in 1975, and to some 35 million in 2002, or about 46 percent of all Americans age fifty or older. More than half of all AARP members work, either full- or part-time. AARP attracts people with a low membership fee that entitles members to a variety of educational and community services, volunteer opportunities, and discounts on products and services ranging from health insurance and prescription drugs to rental cars.

AARP's organizational structure enables it to make the maximum use of its membership. At its national headquarters in Washington, D.C., most of the fifteen hundred paid staff members are federal and state lobbyists and analysts in an in-house think tank. AARP has offices in every state and the District of Columbia, Puerto Rico, and the Virgin Islands that administer community service and education programs and "reach out" to local policy makers. AARP uses sophisticated direct-mail marketing to attract new members and to communicate with current members; in one year AARP mailings accounted for 1.5 percent of all nonprofit third-class mail sent in the United States. Two radio series and a Web site offer information on current topics, but the centerpiece of AARP's communications with its membership is *Modern Maturity*, a magazine that ranks among the nation's leading publications in circulation. In 2001, AARP launched *My Generation*, a new magazine for members age 50–55 that addresses concerns of the "baby boom" generation.

Some have said that AARP's membership is more interested in discounts on products and services than on the association's legislative agenda. Nevertheless, the fact that its membership equals a substantial portion of the electorate, about one-third in 1992, prompts politicians to listen to AARP, especially regarding SOCIAL SECURITY and HEALTH CARE issues. For example, in the early 1980s, the administration of President Ronald Reagan proposed cuts in entitlements, including social security and Medicare. In response, AARP mobilized the grassroots support that helped Democrats take from Republicans twenty-six seats in the House of Representatives.

In 2000, AARP launched an aggressive voter education effort that included events in thirty-six states, the distribution of more than 20 million issue guides, presidential candidate forums, and the creation of an online voter registration site. At the end of the twentieth century, AARP was putting its political muscle behind a number of issues, including protecting social security benefits, assuring pension benefits for older employees, nursing home reform, low-income prescription drug coverage, assistance to victims of telemarketing fraud, and increased funding for home and community-based long-term care.

BIBLIOGRAPHY

Morris, Charles R. *The AARP: America's Most Powerful Lobby and the Clash of Generations*. New York: Times Books, 1996.

Price, Matthew C. *Justice between Generations: The Growing Power of the Elderly in America*. Westport, Conn.: Praeger, 1997.

Schurenberg, Eric, and Lani Luciano. "The Empire Called AARP." *Money* (October 1988): 128–138.

Scott T. Schutte/c. p.

See also **Generational Conflict; Medicare and Medicaid; Old Age.**

AMERICAN ASSOCIATION OF UNIVERSITY PROFESSORS,

a nonprofit organization committed to preserving ACADEMIC FREEDOM and maintaining high standards of academic and moral excellence in American universities. Its membership, now exceeding 45,000, comprises faculty and professional staff from accredited American universities and colleges. The American Association of University Professors has played a major role in the shaping of American academe in the twentieth century.

In 1900 sociologist Edward Ross was fired from his job at Stanford University over a disagreement with Mrs.

Leland Stanford. This alarmed academics across the country, including Johns Hopkins philosopher Arthur O. Lovejoy. In 1915 he and John Dewey held a meeting at Johns Hopkins in order to establish an organization dedicated to protecting the rights of university professors and others in academia. The American Association of University Professors was founded at that meeting.

In 1940 the American Association of University Professors left their greatest mark on the landscape of American academia when they released their "Statement of Principles on Academic Freedom and Tenure," which served as the blueprint for academic freedom and faculty standards throughout the country. The statement claims that academic freedom, in both teaching and research, is essential to the quest for truth, the true purpose of academia. The statement asserts that tenure is a necessary means for ensuring academic freedom as well as providing economic security and lays out a tenure system practically identical to that still used in the majority of American universities at the beginning of the twenty-first century. This was reinforced by the Supreme Court's 1957 ruling in *Sweezy v. New Hampshire*, which stated that the essentiality of academic freedom was almost self-evident and argued that teachers and students must "remain free to inquire." The association's statement was reevaluated and amended in 1970 and again in 1990, when all gender-specific language was removed.

The national headquarters of the American Association of University Professors is in Washington, D.C. They serve as a unifying force between the state and local chapters and as a congressional lobby. The legal division deals with a variety of issues, such as discrimination, intellectual property, and faculty contracts; it also submits amicus briefs before the Supreme Court and appellate courts.

Any institution with seven or more national members can form a campus chapter. These campus chapters together form state conferences to deal with legal and legislative issues on the state level. In 2000, the American Association of University Professors had members at more than 2,000 institutions, with 500 campus chapters and 39 state conferences. Six times a year they publish *Academe*, a journal for higher education. Their other major publication is the *Annual Report on the Economic Status of the Profession*, which is a comprehensive analysis of salaries in the field.

BIBLIOGRAPHY

Lucas, Christopher J. *American Higher Education: A History*. New York: St. Martin's Press, 1994.

Rudolph, Frederick. *The American College and University: A History*. Athens: University of Georgia Press, 1990.

Eli Moses Diner

AMERICAN ASSOCIATION OF UNIVERSITY WOMEN,

a national nonprofit organization that promotes education and equality for women. The organization is divided into three components: the Association, the Educational Foundation, and the Legal Advocacy Fund. With 150,000 members at more than 1,500 branches across the country, the Association has long been a powerful lobbying voice on such issues as education, social security, sex discrimination, reproductive rights, affirmative action, pay equity, and health-care reform. The Educational Foundation funds community action projects, grants, and fellowships for exceptional women scholars and scientists and research into girls and education. The Legal Advocacy Fund provides economic support and advice for women involved in lawsuits regarding sex discrimination in higher education.

The American Association of University Women grew out of the 1921 merger of two preexisting organizations, the Association of Collegiate Alumnae and the Southern Association of College Women. The former was founded in 1882 to augment opportunities for women in the workplace and in higher education. In 1885 they published their first research report debunking the popular myth that higher education impairs the health of women. In 1919 they helped form the International Federation of University Women, with organizations from Canada and Britain.

After the formation of the American Association of University Women, they set up their offices in Washington, D.C., ushering in a new era of political influence and activity. One of their earlier initiatives was to promote the appointment of women to foreign service. In the 1930s they strongly supported the right of doctors to provide information on contraceptives. In 1938 they published "The Living Wage for College Women," documenting sex discrimination in higher education.

The organization supported the formation of the United Nations and was accorded permanent observer status in 1946. In 1948 they strongly backed the Marshall Plan for economic redevelopment in Europe and as a result were awarded the Federal Republic of Germany's Order of Merit in 1953. The Association supported the passage of the CIVIL RIGHTS ACT OF 1964 and the VOTING RIGHTS ACT OF 1965.

BIBLIOGRAPHY

Solomon, Barbara Miller. *In the Company of Educated Women: A History of Women and Higher Education in America*. New Haven, Conn.: Yale University Press, 1985.

Eli Moses Diner

AMERICAN AUTOMOBILE ASSOCIATION

(AAA), a federation of state and local automobile clubs, has been the principal advocate for American motorists since its formation in 1902. Until that time, the automobile club movement in the United States was dominated by the Automobile Club of America (ACA), an elite group of New York City automobilists who organized in

1899 with the intention of exerting national influence. Early clubs in other cities also followed the ACA pattern of restricted memberships, elaborate clubhouse and garage facilities, and an emphasis on social functions—along with making significant efforts to secure improved roads and national regulation of the motor vehicle. AAA, popularly known as Triple A, formed when nine local clubs recognized the need for a national federation to coordinate their efforts on the many matters of concern to motorists that transcended municipal and state boundaries. (Many states, for example, refused to recognize the licenses and registrations of out-of-state motorists, making interstate travel by automobile difficult.) By its 1909 annual meeting, AAA represented thirty state associations with 225 affiliated clubs and claimed 25,759 members.

With the burgeoning use of the automobile after 1910, the clubs constituting AAA increasingly became mass membership organizations, offering special services to members in addition to concerning themselves with the wide range of matters affecting all motorists. The Automobile Club of Missouri inaugurated emergency road service for its members in 1915, a service soon offered by all AAA clubs. Reflecting the increasing popularity of "motor touring" of the time, AAA issued its first domestic tour book in 1917 and in 1926 published its first series of tour books, issued the first modern-style AAA road maps, and began rating tourist accommodations.

The club has been active in lobbying for motorist-friendly road facilities from its inception. From the 1916 Federal Aid Highway Act through the Interstate Highway Act of 1956, to the present, AAA has pushed hard for toll-free improved highways and for highway beautification programs. It has also been a vocal critic of national highway policy at times, arguing against the diversion of motor-vehicle-use taxes into nonhighway expenditures.

Over the years, AAA has been one of the nation's leading advocates of highway safety. In the 1930s it published *Sportsmanlike Driving*, a forerunner of modern driver-safety textbooks, and helped pioneer traffic safety education classes in elementary and junior high schools. In 1955, AAA discontinued its long-standing sanction and supervision of all automobile racing as being inconsistent with the organization's many highway safety activities. During the late twentieth century, it devoted significant resources to a campaign against drunk driving.

In 1972, AAA had 875 clubs and branches throughout the United States and Canada, and membership passed the 15 million mark. By 2002 the organization had some 35 million members, and its emergency road service program required contracts with nearly 13,000 local providers.

James J. Flink / c. w.

See also **Automobile; Automobile Industry; Automobile Racing; Automobile Safety; Roads.**

AMERICAN BALLET THEATRE, famous for its use of various ballet techniques, including Imperial Russian, American folk, and hi-tech contemporary, was founded in 1937 as the Mordkin Ballet, and reorganized as the Ballet Theatre in 1940 under the direction of Lucia Chase. Headed by Chase until her replacement by Mikhail Baryshnikov in 1980, the company became the American Ballet Theatre (ABT) in 1956. In 1960 the ABT was the first American ballet company to dance in the Soviet Union. Unlike the New York City Ballet Company, the ABT brought in foreign stars as compliments to its American corps. It also featured the work of such choreographers as Agnes de Mille, Jerome Robbins, and Twyla Tharp.

BIBLIOGRAPHY

Jacobs, Laura. "The ABT at Fifty." *The New Leader* 73, no. 4 (1990): 21–23.

Kaye, Elizabeth. *American Ballet Theatre: A 25-Year Retrospective.* New York: Columbia University Press, 1999.

Jennifer Harrison

See also **Ballet; Dance; New York City Ballet.**

AMERICAN BAR ASSOCIATION. Founded in 1878 at a gathering of seventy-five lawyers from twenty-one states and the District of Columbia, the American Bar Association (ABA) in 2002 includes nearly 410,000 members and stands as the legal profession's preeminent organization. Its twenty-three sections, five divisions, and scores of committees and commissions address a broad range of legal issues and specialty areas; produce hundreds of books, newsletters, and journals annually; and convene even greater numbers of meetings and conferences, all part of its mission to serve the needs of the profession and the public.

Simeon Eben Baldwin, a young Connecticut lawyer and Yale law professor who later become that state's governor and state supreme court chief justice, was the driving force behind the ABA's formation. Baldwin was joined in this effort by other prominent lawyers such as Benjamin Bristow of Kentucky, the first U.S. solicitor general, and William Evarts of New York, President Rutherford B. Hayes's secretary of state and defense attorney in President Andrew Johnson's impeachment trial. The goals of the ABA's founding constitution remain substantially the same today: "to advance the science of jurisprudence; promote the administration of justice and uniformity of legislation throughout the Union; uphold the honor of the profession of the law; and encourage cordial intercourse among the members of the American Bar."

During the ABA's first twenty-five years, "the membership was small, the policy selective, the air rather social." With membership by invitation only, the original roster of 289 grew to a mere 1,718 lawyers by 1903. Some of its early accomplishments, however, were significant, including legislation creating federal circuit courts of appeal to relieve the U.S. Supreme Court's substantial and backlogged caseload. During this period the ABA spawned groups such as the Association of American Law Schools and the National Conference of Commissioners on Uniform State Laws.

The turn of the twentieth century saw dramatic changes in the organization. Major initiatives over the next thirty to thirty-five years included codes of ethics for lawyers and judges, membership campaigns, publication of the *American Bar Association Journal*, law school standards, and legal services for those who could not afford to pay for them. In addition to holding its first public hearings (on issues of commercial law), the ABA took a prominent role in publicly opposing the judicial recall movement of the period. Its efforts on behalf of an independent judiciary would continue to be a hallmark of the organization, most prominently during the "court-packing" controversy of 1937.

In 1926 the ABA established its first permanent headquarters in Chicago and hired its first executive secretary. Ten years later there was a major change in governance, with the formerly small and exclusive Executive Council replaced by a larger, more representative House of Delegates and Board of Governors (these continue to the present day, with respective memberships of 536 and 37). The ABA had a significant number of distinguished presidents during this period, including U.S. President and Chief Justice William Howard Taft, Chief Justice Charles Evans Hughes, and Nobel Peace Prize recipients Frank Kellogg and Elihu Root.

By 1936 ABA membership exceeded 28,000, but its composition was neither diverse nor free from controversy. In 1911 three African American lawyers had been recommended and approved for membership without knowledge of their race. Though the ABA did not seek their resignations, a section was added to the membership form inquiring about a candidate's race and ethnicity. It was not until the early 1940s that a House of Delegates resolution affirmed that ABA membership was "not dependent on race, creed or color."

During the first part of the century, women, like African Americans, had little prominence in either the profession or the ABA. In 1918 Mary Frances Lathrop became the ABA's first woman member—and in fact went on to serve in its highest councils—but she was among a limited number of women in the organization.

From 1936 to 1969 ABA membership grew to nearly 140,000. The period began with the organization's strong opposition to President Franklin D. Roosevelt's proposals to reorganize the federal judiciary, and concluded with the passage of comprehensive Standards for Criminal Justice and a new, expanded Code of Professional Responsibility. In the intervening years the ABA assumed a formal role in reviewing the qualifications of federal judicial nominees, supported expanded legal services and civil rights programs, and spawned organizations addressing priorities in legal research, international law, minority legal education, and judicial education.

The most recent era began with the ABA taking a strong "rule of law" stance throughout the Watergate saga, in which former ABA President Leon Jaworski played a major role as special prosecutor. During this period the organization faced other significant issues such as lawyer advertising, tort reform, abortion, high-profile trials, and the rapidly changing nature of law practice. Internationally the ABA began providing extensive guidance to emerging democracies in the former Soviet Union and other countries seeking to strengthen their law schools, justice systems, and law reform efforts. As in earlier periods the ABA has continued its strong support of legal services and judicial independence.

At the beginning of the twenty-first century, the ABA is a far more diverse organization, reflecting the growing number of women and minorities entering the profession. This diversity has reached the highest offices of the organization, with women and minorities chairing the House of Delegates and two women having served as ABA president. Most recently the ABA elected the first African American to its presidency. In 2003 former Michigan supreme court justice and Detroit mayor Dennis Archer will lead an organization that could not have been imagined by Simeon Baldwin and his colleagues in 1878.

BIBLIOGRAPHY

American Bar Association. Home page at http://www.abanet .org/.

Sunderland, Edison. *History of the American Bar Association and its Work*. Ann Arbor, Mich.: American Bar Association, 1953.

Norman Gross

See also **Legal Profession.**

AMERICAN BIBLE SOCIETY

AMERICAN BIBLE SOCIETY was organized in 1816 by Elias Boudinot, who also served as its first president, to distribute the BIBLE through a nondenominational and nonprofit vehicle. In its first year, forty-three state, county, regional, and local Bible societies already in existence associated with the American Bible Society. As auxiliary organizations, these local groups helped to publish and distribute the Scriptures in English and other European languages, as well as in American Indian languages. The American Bible Society was part of a growing evangelical press, which blanketed the expanding nation with printings of the Bible, denominational newspapers, and religious tracts throughout the nineteenth century.

The program's emphasis gradually shifted from national to worldwide distribution. The American Bible Society has drawn upon scholarly expertise to translate the Bible (in its entirety or in part) into over 1,500 languages, representing over 97 percent of the world's population. To meet the challenge of presenting the biblical message

William Strong. The associate justice of the U.S. Supreme Court was vice president of the American Bible Society from 1871 to 1895. Wood engraving, c. 1877. GRANGER COLLECTION, LTD.

to new generations unfamiliar with traditional expressions, translators also prepare new popular-language biblical translations. New production techniques enabled the American Bible Society to reproduce the Scriptures on records, cassettes, and compact discs, as well as in braille. In the early 2000s the American Bible Society cooperated with the United Bible Societies in a global coordination of Scripture translation, production, and distribution on every continent.

The society's headquarters is in New York City, with regional offices in Chicago, Atlanta, and Los Angeles. This interconfessional organization is governed by its own elected officers, managers, and committees, and is supported by churches and individual donors.

BIBLIOGRAPHY

Gutjahr, Paul C. *An American Bible: A History of the Good Book in the United States, 1777–1880.* Stanford, Calif.: Stanford University Press, 1999.

Wosh, Peter J. *Spreading the Word: The Bible Business in Nineteenth-Century America.* Ithaca, N.Y.: Cornell University Press, 1994.

Shelby Balik

See also **Missionary Societies, Home; Missions, Foreign; Religious Thought and Writings.**

AMERICAN CIVIL LIBERTIES UNION. In 1920, the Boston Brahmin Roger Baldwin, Socialist Party leader Norman Thomas, social worker Jane Addams, and a small band of colleagues established the American Civil Liberties Union (ACLU). Avowedly pro-labor, the ACLU followed in the path laid by the National Civil Liberties Bureau, which had been created during World War I to safeguard the rights of political dissidents and conscientious objectors. Operating out of a ramshackle office on the outskirts of Greenwich Village, the ACLU's executive committee, headed by Baldwin, discussed the "Report on the Civil Liberty Situation for the Week." Encouraged by Baldwin, the ACLU championed the First Amendment rights of some of the least-liked groups and individuals in the United States, including the American Communist Party and the Ku Klux Klan. The ACLU relied on lawyers throughout the country to volunteer their services involving test cases. Among those heeding the call were the Harvard law professor Felix Frankfurter and Clarence Darrow, perhaps the best-known litigator in the United States during the early twentieth century.

Still in its infancy, the ACLU participated in several cases that became celebrated causes for liberals and radicals throughout the United States. These included the SACCO-VANZETTI CASE, in which two Italian-born anarchists were accused of having committed a murder involving a paymaster; the SCOPES TRIAL, in which John T. Scopes, a part-time biology teacher in Dayton, Tennessee, deliberately violated a state statute that proscribed the teaching of evolution in public schools; and the SCOTTSBORO CASE, in which eight indigent African-American youths, dubbed the "Scottsboro Boys," were accused of raping two white women near a small Alabama town. The ACLU's association with the cases—particularly the Scopes "Monkey Trial"—garnered considerable attention for the organization, as did its establishment of a national committee to bring about the release of the labor radicals Tom Mooney and Warren Billings, who had been convicted of planting a bomb that killed ten people during a "Preparedness Parade" in San Francisco in 1916, prior to America's entry into World War I. Baldwin referred to the case as "the most scandalous of any frame-up of labor leaders in our history." In contrast, the ACLU initially displayed little interest in contesting Prohibition, and ACLU leaders like Baldwin, Thomas, and John Haynes Holmes demonstrated a puritanical attitude regarding such controversial writings as D. H. Lawrence's *Lady Chatterley's Lover* (1928), despite having earlier challenged censorship in cities like Boston. Nevertheless, by the early 1930s, the ACLU, through its attorneys or amici curiae briefs, had helped to establish the principle that the rights articulated in the First Amendment were "preferred" ones, entitled to considerable protection against government encroachments.

Baldwin's directorship and his involvement with a series of united front and Popular Front groups identified the ACLU with the American left. In 1938, critics called for an investigation of the ACLU by the newly formed House Committee on Un-American Activities. Concerns about such a possibility, coupled with the announcement of the Nazi-Soviet Nonaggression Pact later that year, produced a decision that proved far-reaching for both the ACLU and American politics in general. In early 1940, the national office of the ACLU adopted an exclusionary policy that precluded board members from belonging to totalitarian organizations. This resulted in the infamous "trial" of longtime ACLU activist and Communist Party member Elizabeth Gurley Flynn before her fellow ACLU board members and her removal from the board. During the postwar red scare, an increasing number of organizations adopted similar anticommunist provisions.

The ACLU's stellar reputation for protecting the rights of all was called into question during World War II when the ACLU national leadership, despite Baldwin's opposition, failed to contest the internment of Japanese-Americans and aliens. In the early Cold War era, as red-baiting intensified, the organization provided little support for leftists who were coming under attack. Following Baldwin's retirement in early 1950, the ACLU, in keeping with its recently acquired respectability, became more of a mass organization. It also began to focus less exclusively on First Amendment issues. It supported the legal action by the NAACP that eventually culminated in the monumental ruling by the U.S. Supreme Court in BROWN v. BOARD OF EDUCATION OF TOPEKA (1954), which declared that segregation in public schools violated the Fourteenth Amendment. By the 1960s, the ACLU was concentrating more regularly on the right to privacy, equal protection, and criminal procedural rights.

Not all were pleased with the expanded operations of the ACLU, particularly a decision in 1977 to back the right of American Nazis to march in Skokie, Illinois, where many Holocaust survivors from Hitler's Europe resided. Thousands resigned their ACLU memberships, and financial pressures mounted. The organization again proved to be something of a political lightning rod when Republican Party presidential candidate George H. W. Bush, in the midst of a nationally televised debate in 1988, attacked his Democratic Party opponent, Michael Dukakis, as "a card-carrying member of the ACLU." Spearheaded by Executive Director Ira Glasser, the ACLU continued to be involved in such controversial issues as creationism and prayer in the school, which it opposed, and abortion and gay rights, which it championed. As of 2001, the ACLU had approximately 300,000 members.

BIBLIOGRAPHY

Cottrell, Robert C. *Roger Nash Baldwin and the American Civil Liberties Union.* New York: Columbia University Press, 2000.

Walker, Samuel. *In Defense of American Liberties: A History of the American Civil Liberties Union.* New York: Oxford University Press, 1990.

Robert C. Cottrell

See also **Civil Rights and Liberties; First Amendment.**

AMERICAN COLONIZATION SOCIETY.

In an effort to resolve the debate over slavery in the United States, a diverse group of antislavery activists founded the American Colonization Society (ACS) in 1817. The organization's goal was to remove both free and enslaved African Americans from the United States and transport them to Africa. The members of the ACS believed that only after implementation of such a drastic solution could racial conflict in the United States be brought to an end. Although society members claimed to have good intentions, the extreme nature of their proposals undermined the society's popular appeal. ACS members could not conceive of a biracial society in the United States, a limitation that brought them into direct conflict with other antislavery groups, particularly abolitionists, Radical Republicans, and African American leaders such as Frederick Douglass.

The notion of forcibly returning African Americans to Africa first appeared in the late eighteenth century. These plans, increasingly centered in the Upper South, emphasized what many whites and some blacks felt to be the untenable nature of a biracial society. They believed that racial conflict was inevitable when whites and blacks lived in close proximity to one another, and thus they turned to colonization as a solution to America's race problem. Although colonization supporters presented themselves as humanitarian opponents of slavery's evils, many white advocates of colonization objected to the presence of free blacks in American society. The racial underpinnings of white support for colonization thus could not be separated from genuine humanitarian opposition to slavery.

A deep-seated concern for American political unity also informed the growth of the colonization idea. Free labor in the North contrasted sharply with the chattel slavery foundation of the South, a distinction that bred political and economic conflict between the two regions in the nineteenth century. Supporters of African colonization believed that it would both preserve racial harmony and avert a major sectional crisis.

Following the War of 1812 the African colonization idea received impetus from the actions of Paul Cuffe, a black shipowner, who in 1815 transported thirty-eight American blacks to Africa at his own expense. One year later, a New Jersey Presbyterian minister, Robert Finley, convened a series of meetings that led to the formation of the ACS the following year. As one of the benevolent societies that appeared after the War of 1812, the ACS gained the support of Congregational and Presbyterian clergy, along with that of many of the most prominent

147

politicians from the Upper South and border states. Among its early members were Supreme Court Justice Bushrod Washington of Virginia and Senator Henry Clay of Kentucky. Official recognition was given to the society by several state legislatures, among them Virginia, Maryland, and Kentucky. The society's concentration in the Upper South and border states would prove a serious limitation, however, for it would never gain comparable strength in the North or the Deep South.

Notwithstanding its limited base of support in domestic politics, the society established the colony of Liberia on the west coast of Africa in 1822. In the following decade the number of auxiliary societies increased yearly; receipts grew; and although a total of only 2,638 blacks migrated to Liberia, the number jumped every year. Yet efforts to secure federal support were rebuffed and the triumph of Jacksonian democracy blocked the support necessary for a successful program. At the same time, opposition to the society from both abolitionists and proslavery forces combined with mounting debts and internal strife to undermine the organization. Although abolitionists shared the ACS's antislavery sentiments, they believed strongly in the possibility of a biracial society and adamantly rejected the notion that racial conflict could end only if African Americans left the United States. Nevertheless, the society made significant headway on the eve of the Civil War. The independence of Liberia after 1846 lifted a great financial burden, and in the 1850s, under the leadership of William McLain, the fortunes of the society revived. Prominent politicians once again endorsed colonization, and for the first time there was growing support for the idea from blacks.

The eruption of war between North and South, however, brought the society's influence in American politics to an end. President Abraham Lincoln's Emancipation Proclamation, which outlawed slavery in Confederate territory and laid the foundations for slavery's eventual abolition everywhere in the United States, inadvertently dealt the society a blow. Lincoln had once supported colonization, but his actions and speeches as president inspired the supporters of racial egalitarianism. In the wake of the Emancipation Proclamation, the Republican Party hoped to establish a biracial society in the South and saw colonization as anathema to their goals. Likewise, Frederick Douglass and other leading African Americans saw abolition as but the first step in establishing racial equality in the United States. The idea of freeing the slaves only to remove them to Africa struck Douglass and his compatriots as an outrageous injustice. Indeed, the tremendous sacrifices made by African American soldiers, nearly 200,000 of whom served in the Union army during the Civil War, on behalf of the nation made the idea of transporting them to Africa unthinkable.

In the war's aftermath the society clung to life. Under the leadership of its secretary, William Coppinger, the society stressed its educational and missionary activities, sending fewer than 2,000 blacks to Liberia in the 1880s.

In the 1890s, when rising racial tensions gave voice to back-to-Africa sentiments among southern blacks, the society, which was constantly plagued by lack of funds and in 1892 was deprived of the services of both the resourceful Coppinger and its longtime president, J. H. B. Latrobe, found itself unequal to the task. Lacking both leadership and a sense of purpose, the already emaciated organization shrunk further. After a brief period during which the society focused on an unsuccessful attempt to remodel the educational system of Liberia, the organization began to collapse, and by 1910 it had all but ceased to exist.

BIBLIOGRAPHY

Beyan, Amos Jones. *The American Colonization Society and the Creation of the Liberian State: A Historical Perspective, 1822–1900.* Lanham, Md.: University Press of America, 1991.

Elkins, Stanley. *Slavery: A Problem in American Institutional and Intellectual Life.* Chicago: University of Chicago Press, 1959.

Finkelman, Paul. *An Imperfect Union: Slavery, Federalism, and Comity.* Chapel Hill, N.C.: University of North Carolina Press, 1981.

Frederickson, George M. *The Black Image in the White Mind: The Debate on Afro-American Character and Destiny, 1817–1914.* New York: Harper and Row, 1971.

William G. Shade / A. G.

See also **Antislavery; Emancipation Proclamation; Freedmen's Bureau; House Divided; Liberia, Relations with; Nat Turner's Rebellion; Peculiar Institution; Slave Insurrections; Slavery.**

AMERICAN DILEMMA, AN. Gunnar Myrdal (1898–1987), a Swedish sociologist, was chosen by the Carnegie Corporation in 1938 to make a large-scale study of American race relations. After a five-year research effort, which involved the hiring of seventy-five assistants, Myrdal published the two meaty, densely documented volumes of *An American Dilemma* in 1944. The "dilemma" of the title was that white Americans said they believed in human freedom and equality—were actually fighting for these principles at the time in World War II—yet systematically denied freedom and equality to their own African American population.

The book became a classic as the most thorough study of American racism undertaken up to that time; it was something of a bible to the early civil rights movement in the 1950s. Myrdal was impressed by Americans' idealism and felt confident that if they fully understood their racial situation they would revolt against its injustice and reform it. He emphasized that as black Americans were released from segregation and given greater opportunities, they would demonstrate that their subordination had been environmental, not hereditary or intrinsic.

After 1960, however, as the civil rights movement became more militant and as racial issues underwent more intensive study, the reputation of *An American Dilemma* declined rapidly for its relative neglect of economic-power and social-class issues.

BIBLIOGRAPHY

Jackson, Walter A. *Gunnar Myrdal and America's Conscience: Social Engineering and Racial Liberalism, 1937–1987*. Chapel Hill: University of North Carolina Press, 1990.

Southern, David. *Gunnar Myrdal and Black-White Relations: The Use and Abuse of "An American Dilemma," 1944–1969*. Baton Rouge: Louisiana State University Press, 1987.

Patrick Allitt

See also **Civil Rights Movement; Race Relations.**

AMERICAN EXPEDITIONARY FORCES,

the American troops serving in Europe during World War I. When the United States declared war on Germany following President Woodrow Wilson's ringing address to Congress, the country found itself without plans for organizing a force that would be capable of offensive action in modern warfare. On 26 May 1917, Major General John J. Pershing, whom Wilson had selected to command American land forces abroad, received orders to proceed with his staff to France. Shortly after his arrival, convinced that military assistance on a vast scale would be necessary to Allied success, Pershing cabled the War Department that it should consider sending at least one million men to France by the following May and that war plans should be based on a force ultimately amounting to three million. By the time of the armistice in November 1918, approximately two million men had been transported to Europe, where they took a decisive part in bringing the war to a successful conclusion. To do this, the United States had to create its own supply system to train, equip, and provide for the subsistence of a large and rapidly mobilized army.

In the spring and early summer of 1918, a series of powerful German offensives threatened to defeat the Allies. In the crisis, Pershing placed the entire resources of the American Expeditionary Forces at the disposal of the Allied High Command, postponing until 24 July 1918 the formation of the American First Army.

The assistance that the United States gave the Allies in combat began in May with the capture of Cantigny by an American division in the first independent American offensive operation of the war. This was followed early in June by the entrance into battle of two divisions that stopped the German advance on Paris near Château-Thierry. In July, two American divisions, with one Moroccan division, formed the spearhead of the counterattack against the Château-Thierry salient, which marked the turning point of the war. Approximately 300,000 American troops fought in this second Battle of the Marne. In mid-September, the American First Army of 550,000 men reduced the Saint-Mihiel salient. The MEUSE-ARGONNE OFFENSIVE began in the latter part of

September. After forty-seven days of intense fighting, this great battle ended brilliantly for the First and Second Armies, with the signing of the armistice on 11 November 1918. More than 1,200,000 American soldiers had participated.

With the cessation of hostilities, Congress and the American public immediately turned their attention to repatriating the troops. By the end of August 1919, the last American division had embarked for home, leaving only a small force in occupied Germany, and on 1 September 1919, Pershing and his staff sailed for the United States.

BIBLIOGRAPHY

Hallas, James H. *Doughboy War: The American Expeditionary Force in World War I*. Boulder, Colo.: Lynne Rienner Publishers, 2000.

John J. Pershing / c. w.

See also **Armistice of November 1918; Demobilization; Mobilization.**

AMERICAN EXPEDITIONARY FORCES IN ITALY.

As proof of U.S. cooperation in World War I, the Italian minister of war urged that American units be sent to Italy. The United States complied by dispatching the 332d Infantry Regiment, the 331st Field Hospital, and the 102d Base Hospital. With headquarters at Treviso, the 332d Infantry made numerous marches to the front line, where Austrian and Italian soldiers could observe them. The regiment participated in the attack to force a crossing of the Piave River (26 October 1918) and in the Battle of the Tagliamento River (4 November 1918). American troops sailed from Italy in March 1919, following the German Armistice of 11 November 1918.

BIBLIOGRAPHY

Hallas, James H., ed. *Doughboy War: The American Expeditionary Force in World War I*. Boulder, Colo.: Rienner, 2000.

Robert S. Thomas / c. w.

AMERICAN FEDERATION OF LABOR–CONGRESS OF INDUSTRIAL ORGANIZATIONS

(AFL-CIO) is the product of a 1955 merger between the two labor federations that represented most trade unions in the United States. The AFL-CIO is not itself a union. Rather, it is an umbrella organization with which some eighty-five national unions affiliate. It rarely bargains with an employer, organizes a worker demonstration, or calls a strike. But it nevertheless constitutes the institutional voice of the labor movement, adjudicating disputes between affiliated unions, coordinating electoral and lobby activities at both the national and state levels, assisting the organizing work of constituent unions, and representing American labor abroad. Appropriately, the AFL-CIO maintains a large headquarters in Washington, D.C., across Lafayette Park from the White House.

Samuel Gompers. The head of the American Federation of Labor for nearly forty years *(center)*, with other union officials in 1918.

The American Federation of Labor

The parent of the AFL-CIO was the American Federation of Labor, founded in 1886. The AFL long considered itself the authentic "house of labor" to which all workers and unions should adhere. Each affiliate therefore would have an "exclusive jurisdiction" within which to organize a given trade or occupation. Under Samuel Gompers, who led the union federation during its formative era (1886–1894, 1896–1924), the AFL developed into the most politically and organizationally conservative trade union center in the industrial world. Gompers and many of his associates had been schooled in the Marxist tradition, and from it Gompers took a firm commitment to working-class, that is, trade union, autonomy; a hostility to middle-class social reform movements; and a fear of the state. The latter was justifiably reinforced by the exceptional hostility of the courts and corporations to strikes, social legislation, and trade unionism in the sixty years that followed the great railroad strike of 1877.

Gompers and most other officers therefore characterized AFL practices as favoring "voluntarism" or "PURE AND SIMPLE UNIONISM." In practice, this meant hostility to socialists, indifference or outright opposition to social reform, and a commitment to an organization largely representing skilled, male craftsmen. AFL affiliates, especially those of seamen, brewers, miners, and metal workers, could be exceptionally militant, but insularity and parochialism proved dominant strands. Although the United Mine Workers (UMW) and the International Longshoremen's Association represented thousands of African Americans, many in the AFL leadership thought of blacks, Mexicans, Asians, and other immigrants as a vast lumpen proletariat, dangerous and unorganizable.

With its membership concentrated in the building trades, on the railroads, in the mines, and in the garment shops, the AFL grew steadily in the years before World War I. Most AFL leaders cooperated with Woodrow Wilson's administration in World War I. The support, bitterly opposed by socialists and by some of Irish or German extraction, seemed to pay off as union membership soared to 5 million. For the first time, AFL affiliates, like the Machinists and the Amalgamated Meat Cutters and Butcher Workmen, organized large numbers of immigrant industrial workers. But disaster soon followed. When the Wilson administration abandoned its wartime effort to advance a cooperative "industrial democracy," the corporations sought to enforce a nonunion "open shop" once again. Millions of workers therefore participated in the 1919 strike wave, the largest in the nation's history. The strikes ended in defeat, disorganization, and substantial membership losses. By the time the Great Depression struck, AFL affiliates enrolled only 3 million workers.

Most AFL leaders were not prepared to take advantage of the labor law reforms enacted during the administration of Franklin Roosevelt. Although President William Green (1924–1952) had been a leader of the UMW, a union organized along inclusive, "industrial" lines, he sided with the craft unionists in the AFL hierarchy who insisted that skill-based union jurisdictions must remain inviolate. This put the AFL in opposition to the New Deal's National Labor Relations Board, which initially favored industrial unions and companywide collective bargaining. Moreover, craft unionism seemed dysfunctional to the effort to organize the great mass-production industries of that era, steel, automobiles, rubber, and electrical products, where semiskilled labor was predominant.

The Congress of Industrial Organizations

Late in 1935, under the leadership of John L. Lewis of the UMW and Sidney Hillman of the AMALGAMATED CLOTHING WORKERS OF AMERICA, dissidents in the AFL founded the Committee for Industrial Organization, which in 1938 became the fully independent Congress of Industrial Organizations (CIO) after dramatic organizing victories in steel, automobiles, and rubber. Under the presidencies of Lewis (1938–1940) and Philip Murray (1940–1952), the CIO pushed the entire trade union movement to the left and gave American politics something of a social democratic flavor. In contrast with the AFL, the CIO sought to organize factories, mills, and offices, where men and women from European immigrant, Appalachian white, or southern African American backgrounds were plentiful. Socialists and communists were initially welcomed as organizers and union sparkplugs. The radicals Walter Reuther, Harry Bridges, and Mike Quill quickly rose to top posts in the auto workers, longshoremen, and New York transport workers unions. The CIO linked its fortunes closely to the Democrats, especially the New Dealers, who became a more identifiable, labor-liberal faction after 1938. Unlike the Gompers-era leaders of the AFL, CIO leaders fought for social legislation of the most comprehensive sort.

Although the CIO was a more dynamic and in its first decade a more politically potent federation than its rival, the AFL remained the largest union group. By the time of the 1955 merger, the AFL enrolled about 8 million workers, 3 million more than the CIO. AFL growth was a product of the 1935 Wagner Act, which made organizing easier; employer preference for unions thought to be less radical or disruptive than those in the CIO; and the postwar boom in trucking, utilities, construction, and retail sales, where AFL unions predominated.

The Merger

The AFL-CIO merger was made possible by a political and organizational alignment of the two federations that began with World War II. Both union groups offered the government a no-strike pledge, and both participated on the War Labor Board that set wages and pushed forward a system of grievance arbitration inside many war plants. The AFL now supported Democrats almost as much as the CIO did. And both groups were frightened by a postwar shift in the political wind, most notably the 1946 failure to unionize the southern textile industry (Operation Dixie); passage of the 1947 TAFT-HARTLEY ACT, which made organizing more difficult; and the 1952 election of Dwight Eisenhower, the first Republican to occupy the White House in twenty years. Equally important, the CIO expelled or defeated its sizable communist wing, so

both federations now supported U.S. foreign policy during the Cold War. The CIO withdrew from the World Federation of Trade Unions, in which Soviet bloc "unions" participated, and in 1949 joined with the AFL in founding the anticommunist International Confederation of Free Trade Unions (ICFTU).

AFL president George Meany, whose union roots lay in the New York building trades, took the top post in the merged organization, while Reuther, who had served as president of the CIO (1952–1955), became head of the AFL-CIO Industrial Union Department. The new AFL-CIO eliminated much of the jurisdictional warfare that had irritated the public and marred union politics for more than a generation. It expelled the huge INTERNATIONAL BROTHERHOOD OF TEAMSTERS when a high profile congressional investigation revealed an embarrassing pattern of corruption among top Teamsters officials. And the AFL-CIO developed a powerful and well-focused voter-mobilization apparatus, which backstopped Democratic victories in 1958, 1960, and 1964, and which in 1968 almost turned the tide for the Democratic presidential candidate Hubert Humphrey.

But the AFL-CIO was a "sleepy monopoly," to use a phrase coined by the *New York Times* labor reporter A. H. Raskin. Union resources devoted to organizing new workers declined steadily in the 1950s and 1960s. The surge in public employee unionism that began in the 1960s was offset by an erosion of labor's strength in manufacturing and construction. Although some unionists, notably Reuther of the UNITED AUTOMOBILE WORKERS (UAW), wanted the AFL-CIO to play a more active role, complacency characterized the outlook of many on the federation's executive board. Thus, AFL-CIO membership hovered at about 13 million during the entire second half of the twentieth century, even as union density shrank from 33 percent of all wage earners in 1953 to about 14 percent at the beginning of the twenty-first century. "Why should we worry about organizing groups of people who do not want to be organized?" Meany told an interviewer in 1972.

Domestic Affairs

In domestic politics the AFL-CIO moved from the liberal wing of the Democratic Party in the mid–1950s to the center-right in the years after 1968. On issues of fiscal policy and New Deal–style social regulation, the AFL-CIO remained steadfastly liberal. It favored social spending on jobs, infrastructure, and education as well as Keynesian-inspired deficits during the series of sharp recessions that began in the late 1950s and extended through the early 1990s. Rejecting the "voluntarism" of the Gompers era, the AFL-CIO lobbied for a higher minimum wage, more plentiful unemployment insurance, generous welfare and old-age retirement benefits, health and safety regulations at work, and a national system of health insurance. Because many industrial unions had negotiated health care benefits under their collective bargaining contracts, the AFL-CIO concentrated its efforts on winning health provisions for retirees and the indigent, enacted as MEDICARE AND MEDICAID in 1965.

The AFL-CIO attitude toward racial discrimination and the civil rights movement proved far more equivocal. As the civil rights movement reached a climax early in the 1960s, thousands of union locals still discriminated against African Americans, Hispanics, and women whose skin was black, white, or brown. AFL-CIO leaders wanted to abolish the most overt forms of such discrimination but without a radical transformation of union politics, personnel, or bargaining relationships. During the 1950s, the AFL-CIO therefore defended union officials in the South who fought segregation and other forms of de jure discrimination. The AFL-CIO lobbied for the 1964 Civil Rights Act, in particular Title VII, which forbade the most egregious forms of employment discrimination.

But the AFL-CIO was wary of the civil rights movement itself, as it was of any popular mobilization that outflanked it on the left. The federation did not officially endorse the 1963 MARCH ON WASHINGTON, although several individual unions provided logistical support and thousands of union participants. By the late 1960s, when it became clear that patterns of workplace discrimination, many embedded within union seniority and apprentice systems, could not be eliminated without some form of "AFFIRMATIVE ACTION," the AFL-CIO threw its weight against most efforts to establish hiring and promotion quotas or to strengthen the new EQUAL EMPLOYMENT OPPORTUNITY COMMISSION. After the divisive 1968 New York City teachers strike, which put the interests of a heavily Jewish teaching corps against that of African American community control advocates, AFL-CIO political culture acquired a definite neoconservative flavor.

Foreign Affairs
The AFL-CIO played an even more conservative role in foreign affairs, where federation policy was long controlled by a small coterie that aligned labor's outlook with that of the most inflexible Cold Warriors. Aside from Meany, the key architects of AFL-CIO foreign policy included David Dubinsky, a former socialist who had fought the communists to near extinction in the New York needle trades; Jay Lovestone, once a secretary of the American COMMUNIST PARTY but after 1938 an anticommunist ideologue of highly sectarian views; and Lane Kirkland, a Meany aide who succeeded him in the AFL-CIO presidency (1979–1995).

In the ICFTU, the growing influence of European and Asian social democrats, who sought some sort of détente with the communist bloc, induced AFL-CIO leaders to sharply downplay their participation in such transnational labor bodies, including the Geneva-based International Labor Organization. Instead, the AFL-CIO set up its own network of government-funded "free labor" institutes in the 1960s. The Central Intelligence Agency and the U.S. State Department had a working relationship with Lovestone, who was in charge of the AFL-CIO

International Affairs Department from 1955 to 1974. In Africa, Latin America, and Asia, the AFL-CIO sought to build anticommunist unions aligned with U.S. foreign policy interests. The AFL-CIO was particularly active in Brazil, Guyana, Kenya, South Africa, the Philippines, and South Korea. In South Vietnam, the AFL-CIO, working closely with the U.S. mission, built an anticommunist labor movement, and in El Salvador it attempted to organize unions that supported the military's war against leftwing insurgents. The AFL-CIO considered communist bloc trade unions mere government-controlled fronts. Thus, when the genuinely independent union federation known as Solidarity burst forward on the Polish political scene in 1980, the AFL-CIO offered much moral and material aid.

The AFL-CIO staunchly backed U.S. policy throughout the Vietnam War. Dovish unionists had no impact on AFL-CIO policy, a circumstance that helped precipitate UAW withdrawal from the federation in 1968. Throughout the 1970s, the AFL-CIO backed the hawkish wing of the Democratic Party identified with the leadership of Senator Henry "Scoop" Jackson and fought the liberal, profeminist, multiracial "new politics" forces within the party. During the 1972 presidential campaign, Meany enforced a pro-Nixon neutrality on the AFL-CIO because he considered the Democratic candidate, Senator George McGovern, a man who "advocates surrender." In 1976, Lane Kirkland cofounded the Committee on the Present Danger, which advocated a new arms buildup and an aggressive posture toward both the Soviet Union and the Euro-American nuclear disarmament movement.

Refocusing the Federation
When Kirkland assumed leadership of the AFL-CIO in 1979, the federation faced a crisis. Economically, it was reeling from the RUST BELT recessions of the 1970s, which slashed membership in the construction trades and manufacturing. Politically, the AFL-CIO soon confronted a Republican administration that was the most overtly antiunion administration in half a century. After President Ronald Reagan broke a strike of federal air traffic controllers in the summer of 1981 (see AIR TRAFFIC CONTROLLERS STRIKE), many in management adopted a much tougher line against AFL-CIO affiliates, demanding wage concessions, fighting union organization, and seeking cutbacks in pensions and health benefits.

AFL-CIO steps to confront this crisis were modest. For the first time in its history, the federation actually sponsored a mass demonstration, Solidarity Day, that brought hundreds of thousands of unionists to the Washington Mall in September 1981. Kirkland even called out the troops a second time, albeit a full decade later. The AFL-CIO established a study commission whose report, "The Changing Situation of Workers and Their Unions," realistically assessed the failure of the nation's labor laws, the potency of employer opposition, and the fragmentary nature of union power. The AFL-CIO also downplayed its war with the "new politics" forces inside the Democratic Party and mobilized effectively if futilely on behalf of Democratic presidential candidates in 1984 and 1988.

If the AFL-CIO could do little to stem the antilabor tide, Kirkland did manage the union retreat with a certain organizational tidiness. By the early 1990s, the AFL-CIO was once again an inclusive "house of labor." Although the NATIONAL EDUCATION ASSOCIATION remained independent, the UAW rejoined the AFL-CIO in 1981 after a thirteen-year absence. The UMW, isolated even before the merger, joined under a new reform leadership, and the Teamsters again began paying dues in the late 1980s, albeit in a vain effort to win some institutional shelter against the government's racketeering probe of the union's corrupt top leadership. An important element of this AFL-CIO regrouping encouraged union mergers designed to streamline the leadership apparatus, avoid costly jurisdictional disputes, and generate a sufficient flow of dues to service the membership and organize new workers. By the end of the twentieth century, the AFL-CIO had one-third fewer affiliates than in 1955.

Kirkland and most of his backers believed that the revitalization of the labor movement depended on political and legal forces largely outside AFL-CIO control. His leadership therefore was plunged into crisis late in 1994, when conservative Republicans swept to power in the House of Representatives, sealing the fate of initiatives backed by the AFL-CIO that would have facilitated both organizing and collective bargaining. The most important element of this debacle was the collapse of the Bill Clinton administration's health care plan, whose enactment would have lifted from the bargaining table many of the health benefit conflicts that had generated strikes in the late 1980s. The AFL-CIO also saw a labor law reform commission chaired by the former secretary of labor John Dunlop end in stalemate, and the federation failed to win enactment of a law prohibiting the "striker replacements" that management deployed with increasing frequency to break strikes.

Although no incumbent president of the AFL, the CIO, or the AFL-CIO had been ousted from power in a century, an insurgent faction led by John Sweeney of the Service Employees International Union (SEIU) forced Kirkland to resign in 1995 and then handily defeated the election of his heir apparent, Tom Donahue. Like Lewis, who had challenged the AFL hierarchs sixty years before, Sweeney was not a radical. He was a middle-aged Irish Catholic from the Bronx, New York, who sought to forge a social compact with the corporations and the state. Thus, he helped torpedo AFL-CIO adherence to single-payer health insurance and backed the Clinton plan, which favored employer mandates. The SEIU was not a model of internal union democracy. Many of its older, urban affiliates, like New York City's big hotel and apartment house Local 32B–32J, were classic fiefdoms ruled in an autocratic fashion.

But Sweeney represented a wing of the trade union leadership, largely composed of the old industrial unions and those institutions organizing service and government workers, whose most clear-sighted elements had come to understand that labor's capacity to actually make a social contract required that the unions once again demonstrate their willingness to play a disruptive, insurgent role in society. The SEIU had grown to more than a million members because it poured a quarter of all dues income into organizing (5 percent was the union norm). Consequently, the union deployed hundreds of organizers, who used direct action and communitywide mobilizations to unionize janitors, health care workers, and private sector clericals.

The agenda of the Sweenyite AFL-CIO leadership was not far different from that of those who revived the labor movement in the 1930s: open the door to students and radicals, welcome the new immigrants, carve out a distinctive political presence somewhat independent of the Democrats, and above all "organize the unorganized." Some skeptics labeled the Sweenyite strategy "bureaucratic militancy," but whatever its limitations, it was a clear step to the left. For the first time in two generations, America's top trade union leadership stood, in fact and in imagination, on the progressive side of the nation's political culture.

The new AFL-CIO executive board finally expanded to include a substantial number of women and people of color. And the AFL-CIO staff was marbled with New Left veterans long frozen out of responsible posts by the Cold War culture that had lingered within the AFL-CIO even after the fall of the Berlin Wall. Thus, the AFL-CIO endorsed demonstrations seeking to make the World Trade Organization and the International Monetary Fund democratically accountable, and it encouraged a sometimes disruptive student movement that fought against sweatshop labor abroad and in favor of living wages at home. By the start of the twenty-first century, the new AFL-CIO leadership had been unable to make the organizational breakthrough it so desperately sought, but the labor federation was a more politically potent force both within the liberal community and in the electoral arena.

BIBLIOGRAPHY

Buhle, Paul. *Taking Care of Business: Samuel Gompers, George Meany, Lane Kirkland, and the Tragedy of American Labor.* New York: Monthly Review Press, 1999.

Carew, Anthony. "The American Labor Movement in Fizzland: The Free Trade Union Committee and the CIA." *Labor History* 39 (February 1998): 25–42.

Dark, Taylor E. *The Unions and the Democrats: An Enduring Alliance.* Ithaca, N.Y.: IRL Press, 1999.

Dubofsky, Melvyn, and Warren Van Tine. *John L. Lewis: A Biography.* New York: Quadrangle Books, 1977.

Gall, Gilbert J. *The Politics of Right to Work: The Labor Federations as Special Interests, 1943–1979.* New York: Greenwood Press, 1988.

Gottschalk, Marie. *The Shadow Welfare State: Labor, Business, and the Politics of Health Care in the United States.* Ithaca, N.Y.: ILR Press, 2000.

Goulden, Joseph C. *Meany*. New York: Atheneum, 1972.

Greene, Julie. *Pure and Simple Politics: The American Federation of Labor and Political Activism, 1881–1917*. New York: Cambridge University Press, 1998.

Kaufman, Stuart Bruce. *Samuel Gompers and the Origins of the American Federation of Labor, 1848–1896*. Westport, Conn.: Greenwood Press, 1973.

Lichtenstein, Nelson. *State of the Union: A Century of American Labor*. Princeton, N.J.: Princeton University Press, 2001.

McCartin, Joseph A. *Labor's Great War: The Struggle for Industrial Democracy and the Origins of Modern American Labor Relations, 1912–1921*. Chapel Hill: University of North Carolina Press, 1997.

Phelan, Craig. *William Green: A Biography of a Labor Leader*. Albany: State University of New York Press, 1989.

Tomlins, Christopher L. *The State and the Unions: Labor Relations, Law, and the Organized Labor Movement in America, 1880–1960*. New York: Cambridge University Press, 1985.

Zieger, Robert H. *The CIO, 1935–1955*. Chapel Hill: University of North Carolina Press, 1995.

Nelson Lichtenstein

See also **Labor; Labor Legislation and Administration; Strikes; Trade Unions;** *and vol. 9:* **Ford Men Beat and Rout Lewis.**

AMERICAN FEDERATION OF STATE, COUNTY, AND MUNICIPAL EMPLOYEES.

Primarily a labor union for workers in the public sector, the American Federation of State, County, and Municipal Employees (AFSCME) evolved from the Wisconsin State Administrative, Clerical, Fiscal, and Technical Employees Association, the first such statewide organization. Formed under the leadership of A. E. Garey in 1932 to lobby for civil service protection for public employees in Wisconsin, the union led the drive for a national union of public employees under the guidance of Arnold Zander, a Wisconsin state-personnel examiner. In December 1935 the Wisconsin Association combined with fourteen other public employee unions to become AFSCME and was organized as a department of the American Federation of Labor (AFL). The following September, AFSCME was chartered as an independent union within the AFL, and Zander was elected as the international union's first president.

With 10,000 members by the end of 1936, AFSCME used its clout to lobby at the state level for better civil service laws to protect its members from arbitrary dismissals and ensure fair hiring practices in public agencies. By 1955, AFSCME's membership had climbed to more than 100,000 workers, and the union began to demand the right to collective bargaining over wages, benefits, and working conditions, a precedent that had no clear basis in existing labor law. By executive order in 1958, New York City Mayor Robert Wagner granted collective bargaining rights to unions representing city employees, the first such recognition by a government entity. AFSCME

secured another key victory in 1962, when President John F. Kennedy recognized the right of federal employees to enter into collective bargaining. By 1965, AFSCME had more than 250,000 members.

In 1964 Jerry Wurf, director of New York City's powerful District Council 37, succeeded Zander as international president, a post he held until his death in 1981. Under Wurf's leadership, AFSCME continued to pressure government entities to grant collective bargaining rights and expanded its agenda to include civil rights issues. Tragically, when Dr. Martin Luther King Jr. was assassinated in 1968, he was in Memphis in support of an AFSCME garbage collectors' strike over union recognition and antidiscrimination employment policies. With a rising proportion of its membership drawn from diverse minority groups, AFSCME continued to take an active role in civil rights matters in succeeding years. The union also created one of the largest labor political-action committees in the United States to lobby for legislation and offer campaign support for political candidates, typically from the Democratic Party.

While industrial unions faced declining membership in the 1970s and 1980s, AFSCME continued to grow as it organized office and professional staffs along with hospital employees, custodians, drivers, and laborers at every level of government service. With AFSCME membership reaching 1.3 million in 2000, the union was active in opposing efforts to privatize government services, which it viewed as a significant threat to its members' job security, wages, and benefits. The union was also instrumental in securing a Supreme Court ruling in 1991 that recognized the right to organize workers at private hospitals. After Jerry Wurf's death in 1981, Gerald W. McEntee, only the third international president to lead the union, was elected AFSCME's top official.

BIBLIOGRAPHY

Goulden, Joseph. *Jerry Wurf: Labor's Last Angry Man*. New York: Atheneum, 1982. Biography of AFSCME's longtime international president.

LeBeau, Josephine, and Kevin Lynch. "Successful Organizing at the Local Level: The Experience of AFSCME District Council 1707." In *A New Labor Movement for the New Century*. Edited by Gregory Mantsios. New York: Monthly Review Press, 1998. Summary of AFSCME's contemporary organizing strategies.

Stieber, Jack. *Public Employee Unionism: Structure, Growth, Policy*. Washington, D.C.: Brookings Institution, 1973. Although dated, provides the best summary of AFSCME's bureaucratic structure.

Timothy G. Borden

See also **Labor.**

AMERICAN FEDERATION OF TEACHERS

(AFT) is a national union headquartered in Washington, D.C., and is affiliated with the American Federation of

Labor–Congress of Industrial Organizations (AFL-CIO). The AFT was founded in April 1916 by teachers in Winnetka, Illinois, and chartered by the AFL on 9 May 1916. While formed as a teachers' craft union, the AFT's base broadened in the late twentieth century to incorporate educational support staff and health professionals. Membership approximates 1 million. Sandra Feldman was the national AFT president in 2002, having been elected in 1997. In October 2001, the AFL formed a collaborative partnership with the 2.6-million-member National Education Association (NEA), a non-AFL-CIO teachers' association. The NEAFT Partnership promotes the common interests of members. The AFT has a nationwide presence, but membership is most concentrated in California, New York, and Illinois.

AFT Origins

Philosophical, strategic, and tactical conflicts historically divided the two organizations. Most members of the NEA, founded in 1857, were female teachers, but male administrators dominated the leadership to the mid-1960s. The NEA was a top-down national organization; state affiliates were formed only in the 1920s and local chapters in the late 1960s. The public school teachers who established the AFT, many of immigrant and working-class backgrounds, rejected the NEA for its anti-union bias, its emphasis on middle-class professionalism, and its advocacy for a centralized administrative system that would insulate individual schools from their neighborhoods. Dissatisfied with the NEA and resistant to the Chicago Board of Education's 1915 action barring teachers from union membership, teacher activists from greater Chicago and Gary, Indiana—with support from local teachers' unions elsewhere—organized the AFT as a national union with local affiliates. Although many of the Chicago activists were female elementary school teachers, male high school teachers predominated at the founding meeting and selected Charles Stillman, a supporter of the AFL president, Samuel Gompers, as AFT president. The then-Chicago-based AFT began nationwide organizing, but membership growth was slow. The AFT's first decades were marked by internal contentiousness, adversarial relations with the AFL, and public skepticism in a world polarized between wartime patriotism, anti-radical ethnocentrism, liberalism, and various socialist and communist ideologies. Functioning before public employee collective bargaining laws existed was a test of the AFT's mettle.

Organizing on the Home Front: The World War I Era, the Red Scare, and the 1920s

Controversies regarding World War I consumed the AFT. Discontent over gender relations and the onslaught of 100 percent Americanism divided its ranks. The female teacher activists in Chicago had recoiled at Stillman's election as AFT president and at Gompers's patriarchal AFL leadership. When Gompers and Stillman embraced U.S. entry into World War I, moreover, pacifists and so-cialists, including some women teachers, opposed the union leadership. Consequently, the AFT organized few elementary school teachers before 1930. Meanwhile, the NEA urged school boards to induce teachers to join their association, linking teacher membership in the NEA with patriotism and anti-union radicalism. The success of the NEA's school administrator leadership in promoting the association's anti-union, anti–collective bargaining posture hampered the AFT locals.

From World War I through the Red Scare and the 1920s, the AFT—sometimes in alliance with the American Civil Liberties Union and the American Association of University Professors—defended the academic freedom of teachers under attack for their political views. Together, they affirmed teachers' rights of free speech and association and fought to uphold teachers' due process rights, as when teachers' loyalty oaths were imposed. The AFT's reform agenda prompted some members to withdraw. Confrontation with Gompers over public employee strikes also divided the AFT.

During the 1920s, union loyalists broke new ground by electing two successive women national presidents. Florence Rood and Mary Barker were feminist activists and supporters of academic freedom. They worked with the ACLU in the defense of John Scopes, a Tennessee public school teacher tried for teaching Darwinian evolutionary theory. They also laid groundwork for state laws establishing tenure for teachers. Yet after Barker's retirement, no woman followed until Sandra Feldman's election in 1997.

The AFT also challenged the racial exclusivism of the craft union tradition. Beginning in 1916, the AFT established "colored" locals in segregated school districts. In 1918, the AFT demanded pay equalization for teachers, without racial distinction. Then, steadily by the 1930s, the AFT eliminated color barriers in most locals. During the 1930s, the AFT—in alliance with the National Association for the Advancement of Colored People—sought equal rights and accommodations for all students in the South. The NEA, meanwhile, was apathetic about racial segregation in education until the mid-1960s.

Depression Years

The depression forced budget cuts on schools, colleges, and universities, which prompted growing numbers to join the AFT. A turn by AFT leaders from philosophical issues to more pragmatic concerns during the early 1930s produced a membership approaching 32,000 by 1940.

Leadership struggles during the mid-1930s, however, revealed generational and ideological fissures. In Chicago young, college-educated teachers with bleak job prospects were pitted against entrenched older union leaders. In New York City, Philadelphia, and Los Angeles, rival liberal, socialist, and sectarian Marxist factions battled for control of the local and national union organizations. The more conservative factions had secured control of the national AFT leadership by 1940. Soon after, the national

AFL ousted the New York City and Philadelphia locals for succumbing to communist control. Later, new AFT locals were formed there.

Despite the internecine fighting, the AFT coordinated its local and state affiliates and worked with other labor organizations to enact tenure laws and to improve faculty retirement benefits. It also continued to defend academic freedom.

World War II Fallout and the Cold War

While teachers demonstrated wartime loyalty to the United States, inflation eroded their earnings. Because public employees were exempted from the NATIONAL LABOR RELATIONS ACT (1935) giving workers the right to bargain collectively, postwar teachers could not regain lost earning power. Also, funding for teachers and new schools in the postwar setting was insufficient and lobbying for state and federal legislative relief faltered. Consequently, frustrated teachers across the nation disregarded the AFT's own no-strike policy and walked out. Some teachers won favorable settlements; others faced jail.

Responding to rank-and-file defiance, the AFT Executive Council investigated allegations of communist subversion and collaboration with the Congress of Industrial Organizations (CIO) in defiance of AFT rules. Many suspect leaders in San Francisco and Los Angeles lost their jobs for disloyalty after they invoked their Fifth Amendment rights against self-incrimination before the House Un-American Activities Committee. Leaders of the successor AFT local in New York City refused to assist fellow teachers of the banned predecessor (reorganized as a rival CIO local), who were subjected to investigations for subversion. Not until 1953 did the AFT leadership reassess how the anticommunist investigations compromised the accused teachers' academic freedom and civil liberties.

Meanwhile, the AFT joined with civil rights activists to defeat segregation in public education. The goals of the AFT leadership were to advance social justice and to build union membership. To this end, the AFT filed amicus briefs for the plaintiffs in the desegregation cases *Briggs v. Elliot* (1952) and *BROWN V. BOARD OF EDUCATION* (1954), advocated the broadening of educational opportunities for all students, and supported the 1963 March on Washington and the mid-1960s voter registration drives. In 1957, the AFT revoked the charters of its few remaining segregated southern locals.

The Campaign for Collective Bargaining Laws

Without collective bargaining rights, teachers were left with low pay, without due process rights, and with no-strike clauses in their individual contracts. During the mid-1950s, the AFT took the offensive on collective bargaining, reversing its 1919 no-strike policy and educating both its members and the public about collective bargaining. State and local affiliates, allied with other public employee unions, lobbied for state and federal legislation re-

forming management–labor relations. AFT teachers in New York City staged one-day strikes in 1960 and 1962 to dramatize their demands. The pressure led to President John Kennedy's 1962 Executive Order 10988, extending collective bargaining rights to federal employees, and to enactment of state collective bargaining laws for teachers. Beginning in New York City, and then in urban centers across the nation, AFT locals won exclusive representation rights. Membership grew significantly. In 1965, the NEA had 943,000 members, although the union bargained for only 21,000 teachers. In this changing environment, the NEA democratized and gradually began functioning as a union. The AFT bargained for 74,000 teachers out of 110,000 members.

AFT's Tilt Rightward

In the late 1960s and the 1970s, the AFT moved rightward, although affiliates did not follow uniformly. Ethnic identity and community-based politics, U.S. military intervention in Southeast Asia, and a resurgent women's movement engaged teachers, while the AFT's focus on collective bargaining and ideological anticommunism nudged it towards the political right.

The 1968 clash over the establishment of New York City's Ocean Hill–Brownsville local school board polarized the membership and altered the relationship of the AFT to the civil rights movement. Previously, the AFT had opposed the NEA's centralized school administration concept. In 1968, however, Albert Shanker and the United Federation of Teachers (UFT), the New York City AFT local, resisted when city officials decentralized the Board of Education, establishing community councils to oversee local school boards. Many parents and neighborhood leaders supported community empowerment. Shanker,

Albert Shanker. The powerful and controversial longtime head of the United Federation of Teachers in New York and then the national American Federation of Teachers. GETTY IMAGES

however, called two strikes to defend a contract just negotiated with the central board and to reverse involuntary faculty transfers imposed, without due process, by the Ocean Hill–Brownsville Board. Some local teachers, disagreeing with Shanker about bureaucratic centralization and the propriety of military engagement in Southeast Asia, crossed picket lines. Detroit, Newark, Washington, D.C., and Chicago locals opposed Shanker on community control. Civil rights groups and black power activists, some embracing anti-Semitism, denounced Shanker as racist. The historic ties between the AFT and the civil rights movement weakened further while Shanker was the union's national president (1974–1997), especially when the AFT supported the plaintiff in the 1978 *Bakke* case, overturning racial quotas in university admissions. The California Federation of Teachers' (CFT) opposition to this action exemplified internal union division on affirmative action policy.

Meanwhile, however, the AFT advanced goals of the women's movement from the early 1970s. The CFT spurred the national AFT to organize the Women's Rights Committee. State affiliates launched legislative campaigns against gender discrimination and promoted pay equity and maternity leave contract provisions. During the 1980s and 1990s, women once again assumed leadership roles in the local, state, and national AFT organizations.

Organizing and Negotiating Contracts in a New Collective Bargaining Environment

Numerous states enacted public employee collective bargaining laws during the 1960s and 1970s. With good contracts linked to the availability of state and federal funds, the national AFT and its state affiliates intensified lobbying for public education allocations, especially when the effects of the 1980s taxpayer revolt decreased state revenue. While New York teachers statewide took the lead in unionizing throughout the 1960s, California took center stage from the mid-1970s and into the early 1980s. There, certification elections gave the AFT exclusive rights to represent a minority of K-12 teachers, as well as community college faculty in many districts. In 1983 the AFT also won representation rights for nontenure-track lecturers and librarians in the University of California system. Meanwhile, beginning in 1977, the CFT organized K-12 and community college paraprofessionals and won certification in some school and community college districts. Similar patterns occurred in other states.

AFT-NEA Merger

The potential for a merger of the AFT and the NEA to pool resources and defuse counterproductive rivalries was first raised in 1965 by AFT president David Selden. The NEA, however, rejected the merger bid in 1968. As AFT president later on, Albert Shanker was skeptical about the advantages of a merger. Throughout the 1990s, the sticking point was whether the NEA members in a merged organization would accept AFL-CIO affiliation. The new

NEAFT Partnership of 2001 makes AFL-CIO affiliation optional for them. The AFT and NEA collaboration was charted to strengthen the organizations' abilities to influence legislative outcomes and to negotiate favorable contracts in the twenty-first century.

BIBLIOGRAPHY

American Federation of Teachers. "About AFT." Available from http://www.aft.org/about.

———. "NEAFT Partnership Document." Available from http://www.aft.org/neaft_partdoc.html.

———. "NEAFT Partnership Joint Council Communique, October 24, 2001." Available from http://www.aft.org/neaft/102401.html.

Fraser, James W. "Agents of Democracy: Urban Elementary-School Teachers and the Conditions of Teaching." In *American Teachers: Histories of a Profession at Work*. Edited by Donald Warren. New York: Macmillan, 1989.

Glass, Fred, ed. *A History of the California Federation of Teachers, 1919–1989*. San Francisco: California Federation of Teachers, 1989.

Keck, Donald J. "NEA and Academe through the Years." Available from http://www.nea.org/he/roots.html.

Murphy, Marjorie. *Blackboard Unions: The AFT and the NEA, 1900–1980*. Ithaca: Cornell University Press, 1990.

O'Connor, Paula. "AFT History: Grade School Teachers Become Labor Leaders." Available from http://www.aft.org/history/afthist/oconnor/oconnor/index.html.

Jonathan W. McLeod

See also **American Federation of Labor–Congress of Industrial Organizations;** *Bakke v. Regents of the University of California;* **Collective Bargaining; National Education Association; Teachers' Loyalty Oath.**

AMERICAN FUR COMPANY. The American Fur Company represented John Jacob Astor's bid to challenge the dominant Canadian fur companies operating within the boundaries of the United States, namely the North West Company and the Michilimackinac Company. A poor German immigrant, Astor became involved in the fur trade in 1784 in New York. By the end of the century, Astor had gained dominance of the fur trade in the Northeast by transshipping American furs through Montreal to England, bypassing British tariffs on American furs. Astor then sought to gain control of the Mississippi-Missouri trade through St. Louis, but found his attempts blocked by Auguste Chouteau, one of the founders of St. Louis and its fur trade. In light of the Louisiana Purchase (1803) and the success of Lewis and Clark's explorations (1804–1806), Astor met with President Thomas Jefferson to discuss establishing a Pacific-based fur company. On 6 April 1808 the American Fur Company was incorporated in New York with $1 million capital stock and with Astor as the sole stockholder. In 1811 agents of the American Fur Company established Fort Astoria in Oregon.

The War of 1812 forced Astor to sell Astoria to the British and reassess his efforts along the Canadian border.

On 28 January 1811 Astor had created the Southwest Fur Company to coordinate his American Fur Company with the North West Company and the Michilimackinac Company as partners and joint stockholders. He then attempted to buy into the Missouri Fur Company of Manuel Lisa. Again the war interfered, but this time Astor was able to take advantage of it. By 1817 Astor had bought out his partners and gained control of the Mississippi Valley posts. He restructured the Southwest Fur Company as the Northern Department of the American Fur Company. He was well on his way to monopolizing the western fur trade.

In 1823 Astor used the fur brokerage firm of Stone, Bostwick and Company of St. Louis as his agents for the American Fur Company's Western Department in that city, giving him his long desired foothold there. Three years later, Astor negotiated with Bernard Pratte and Company to take over control of the Western Department. Pratte did so after entering into an agreement with William Ashley and the Rocky Mountain Fur Company, Astor's closest competitor in the United States. This agreement made Astor an equal participant with Ashley in a trapping and trading expedition into the Rocky Mountains.

Astor viewed the American government's Indian factory system as a major obstacle to the spread of his fur empire. The factory system regulated trade with the Indians and sharply curtailed the amount of liquor offered them in barter. Using interested men such as Lewis Cass, governor of the Territory of Michigan, and Thomas Hart Benton, U.S. senator from Missouri, Astor got the factory system abolished in 1822. Liquor then began to flow in large quantities up the Missouri to the Indians as the Western Department expanded. Astor stifled competition by fair and foul means. Under pressure from Astor's lobbying, Congress excluded foreigners from the trade in 1816 and, eight years later, designated specific places where trade could be conducted, greatly hampering the American Fur Company's competitors.

When the Hudson's Bay Company merged with the old North West Company in 1821, some nine hundred employees were dismissed. They formed the Columbia Fur Company, operating between the upper Mississippi and the upper Missouri Rivers. In the summer of 1827 Astor bought out the Columbia Fur Company and reorganized it as the Upper Missouri Outfit, centered at the Mandan villages on the northern Missouri River. Kenneth McKenzie was put in charge, and he immediately established Fort Floyd at the mouth of the Yellowstone River. Soon renamed Fort Union, it was one of the greatest American posts in the region. The combination of the Upper Missouri Outfit and the Western Department gave Astor near total control of the Missouri River fur trade.

McKenzie focused on a series of trading posts and forts where the Indians might come to trade. He and the American Fur Company were startled when the Rocky Mountain Fur Company took its trade to the Indians and the independent fur trappers, establishing the rendezvous system. For six years the Rocky Mountain organization and the American Fur Company struggled for dominance in the rich Rocky Mountain trade. In 1831 McKenzie won a coveted trade agreement with the Assiniboins and Blackfeet that opened up the Marias-Missouri River region. In 1832 Fort McKenzie was established near the mouth of the Marias River. The Rocky Mountain Fur Company countered with Fort Cass at the mouth of the Bighorn River as a center of the Crow trade, but shortly it was taken over by the American Fur Company. McKenzie then pushed for and succeeded in getting the steamboat *Yellowstone* built and then navigating it on the upper Missouri-Yellowstone watershed in 1832.

However, the days of the fur trade were numbered. In 1834, John Jacob Astor withdrew from the American Fur Company as it became clear that it would have to withdraw from the Rocky Mountains. Astor sold out at a time when the company had made, in its previous decade, profits and dividends of over $1 million. The Western Department went to Bernard Pratte, Pierre Chouteau and Company. The Northern Department was purchased by Ramsay Crooks and nine others who retained the name American Fur Company. Crooks and his associates confined the company's operations to the area between Detroit, the Ohio River, and the Red River of the North. They operated vessels on the Great Lakes and established fisheries on Lake Superior. They marketed the furs of Pratte, Chouteau and Company and tried to establish a banking business in the area. The American Fur Company failed in 1842, however, and was reconstituted in 1846 as a commission house before finally being dissolved in 1845.

BIBLIOGRAPHY

Berry, Don. *A Majority of Scoundrels: An Informal History of the Rocky Mountain Fur Company.* New York: Harper, 1961.

Blevins, Winfred. *Give Your Heart to the Hawks: A Tribute to the Mountain Men.* New York: Avon, 1973.

De Voto, Bernard. *Across the Wide Missouri.* Boston: Houghton Mifflin Company, 1947.

Jerry L. Parker

See also **Astoria; Fur Companies; Fur Trade and Trapping; Missouri River Fur Trade; North West Company.**

AMERICAN HISTORICAL ASSOCIATION

(AHA), founded in 1884 to establish high professional standards for training and research in the newly distinct academic discipline of history. At the 1884 meeting of the American Social Science Association (ASSA), "professors, teachers, specialists, and others interested in the advancement of history" voted to found the American Historical Association, independent from the ASSA. Herbert Baxter Adams, an associate professor in history at Johns Hopkins University, became the first secretary of the AHA, and

Andrew Dickson White, a historian and president of Cornell University, served as the first president.

In 1889, an act of Congress incorporated the association "for the promotion of historical studies, the collection and preservation of historical manuscripts and for kindred purposes in the interest of American history and of history in America." The act stipulated that the association should submit reports on "historical matters" to the secretary of the Smithsonian Institution, who should then "transmit to Congress such reports as he or she saw fit."

In 1895 two AHA members, George Burton Adams and John Franklin Jameson, began publishing a journal, the *American Historical Review* (AHR), which the association soon began to subsidize, eventually assuming formal control in 1915. Since then, the AHA has expanded its publishing program to include a monthly newsletter, *Perspectives*, and a wide variety of publications, including directories, bibliographies, resource guides, and professional and teaching pamphlets.

The association works both to publish documentary records and to preserve historical records, often working with the government. The National Archives, for instance, were established in large part through the efforts of the AHA. The teaching of history has also been a concern of the association from its start. When the secondary school curriculum was being created at the end of the nineteenth century, the AHA ensured history's important place in that curriculum and continued to work to improve history education through committees and commissions. At the graduate level, the AHA has developed teaching programs and has been instrumental in cultivating high standards for scholarship and training.

By the beginning of the twenty-first century, the AHA was the largest and oldest membership-based historical association in the United States, with over 15,000 individual members and 3,000 institutional members. Governed by a twelve-member elected council, the AHA is composed of three divisions: the Professional Division, which collects and disseminates information about employment and professional issues for all historians; the Research Division, which promotes historical scholarship, encourages the collection and preservation of historical documents and artifacts, works to ensure equal access to government records and information, and fosters the dissemination of information about historical records and research; and the Teaching Division, which collects and disseminates information about the training of teachers and about instructional techniques and materials and encourages excellence in the teaching of history in schools, colleges, and universities.

BIBLIOGRAPHY

Higham, John. *History: Professional Scholarship in America.* 2d ed. Baltimore: Johns Hopkins University Press, 1989.

Novick, Peter. *That Noble Dream: The Objectivity Question and the American Historical Profession.* New York: Cambridge University Press, 1988.

Ross, Dorothy. *The Origins of American Social Science.* New York: Cambridge University Press, 1991.

Miriam Hauss

See also **National Archives.**

AMERICAN INDEPENDENT PARTY, organized by George C. Wallace, governor of Alabama (1963–1967; 1971–1979; 1983–1987), in support of his 1968 presidential candidacy. Wallace and his running mate, General Curtis E. LeMay, opposed racial integration, supported states' rights, and called for a dramatically intensified American bombing campaign in North Vietnam. The party was popular in the South and among working-class whites in the industrial Midwest and Northeast. Wallace won 13.5 percent of the popular vote and forty-six electoral votes, carrying Alabama, Arkansas, Georgia, Louisiana, and Mississippi. After Wallace decided to enter the 1972 Democratic presidential primaries rather than run again as an independent candidate, the party declined rapidly.

BIBLIOGRAPHY

Carter, Dan T. *The Politics of Rage: George Wallace, the Origins of the New Conservatism, and the Transformation of American Politics.* New York: Simon and Schuster, 1995.

Jacob E. Cooke / A. G.

See also **States' Rights; Third Parties.**

AMERICAN INDIAN DEFENSE ASSOCIATION. In 1923, Richard E. Ely and other writers and social scientists interested in helping American Indians formed the American Indian Defense Association (AIDA). Ely named John Collier as executive secretary. The AIDA succeeded in defeating legislation harmful to Indians such as the Bursum Bill of 1922 and the Leavitt Bill of 1926, which would have taken land away from Pueblo Indians and curtailed American Indian civil and religious rights. Promoting American Indian cultural autonomy, it proposed a full reform agenda that included legislation on education, land rights, and arts and crafts. The Bureau of Indian Affairs did not, however, implement many of the proposed reforms until Collier's appointment as commissioner of Indian Affairs in 1933. Shortly thereafter, the AIDA merged with the Eastern Association on Indian Affairs to become the ASSOCIATION ON AMERICAN INDIAN AFFAIRS headed by writer and anthropologist Oliver La Farge.

BIBLIOGRAPHY

Collier, John. *From Every Zenith: A Memoir and Some Essays on Life and Thought.* Denver, Colo.: Sage Books, 1963.

Philip, Kenneth. "John Collier and the Crusade to Protect Indian Religious Freedom, 1920–1926." *Journal of Ethnic Studies* 1, no. 1 (1973): 22–38.

Rebecca McNulty

AMERICAN INDIAN GAMING REGULATORY ACT

(1988), an attempt by Congress to find a compromise between the rights of tribes to engage in gaming activities and the ability of the states to control gambling within their borders. Neither group was pleased with the act, and several lawsuits have been filed over statutory interpretation. Many tribes want the definition of tribal land to include any property under control of the tribe; many states feel tribal land should be restricted to mean historic reservation land. Many tribes assert that they are federally recognized, self-governing units that can decide their own gaming policies; many states believe gaming policy should be defined in a state's constitution.

The act defines three categories of gaming: Class I encompasses social and traditional games solely within the Indian tribe's jurisdiction; Class II includes bingo and similar games authorized by tribal resolution in states where private gambling is not prohibited by law; Class III includes casinos and operates under the same restrictions as Class II, but in addition, a compact between the state and the Indian tribe must define how the gaming will be conducted and must be approved by the Secretary of the Department of the Interior. In the early twenty-first century over half the states had some form of Indian gambling.

Unlike profits from non-Indian gambling activities, tribal gambling profits, as stipulated by the act, must be used for the welfare of the tribe, such as for education and housing. A loophole in the law allows individuals to profit after the social issues have been addressed.

As the number of Indian casinos has grown, problems have arisen. Some casinos are successful and raise a tribe's standard of living, while others have gone bankrupt. In their search for investors to bankroll startup costs, tribes have become targets for organized crime. Additionally, states cannot regulate whether jackpots are awarded or if low-payout machines are used. In some cases where compacts negotiated in good faith have not been reached, tribes have operated casinos without signed compacts. The National Indian Gaming Commission acts as a watchdog for the act.

BIBLIOGRAPHY

Riconda, Andrew, ed. *Gambling*. New York: H. W. Wilson Company, 1995.

Veda Boyd Jones

See also **Gambling; Indian Economic Life.**

AMERICAN INDIAN MOVEMENT

(AIM), an activist organization that came to national prominence in

Dennis Banks. One of the founders of the American Indian Movement appears at a protest in 1976, three years after his arrest at Wounded Knee, S. Dak. HARTMANN, ILKA

the 1970s, emerged during July 1968 in Minneapolis, Minnesota, in response to police brutality committed against urban Indians in the Twin Cities. AIM's three primary founders were Clyde Bellecourt (Ojibwa), Dennis Banks (Ojibwa), and George Mitchell (Ojibwa). According to Bellecourt, 120 American Indians of an estimated 20,000 living in the Twin Cities at this time began to hold regular meetings in the area of Franklin Avenue and initially called themselves the Concerned Indian American Coalition. Later, two Indian women elders suggested the name "AIM" since the leadership of the organization was "aiming" to take action on several fronts to correct past injustices against Indian people.

AIM leaders organized Indian patrols to scrutinize police actions. The patrols located drunken Indians in bars before the police found them. The patrols carried citizens band radios to intercept police calls so that they could witness arrests and make sure that the arrested Indians were not abused. The patrol members wore red jackets with a black thunderbird emblem and became known as "shock troops" in the Indian neighborhood. Within a few months, the coalition structured itself as a nonprofit corporation with an Indian board and staff.

Among its other community activities in the Twin Cities, AIM started culturally oriented schools for Indian youths called the Little Red Schoolhouse and Heart of the Earth. These efforts were a response to the fact that at the junior high level, Ojibwa youths had a dropout rate of 65 percent in public schools. As more American Indians arrived in the Twin Cities via relocation, AIM provided temporary shelter and meals and developed an Indian elders program.

AIM became a national organization as widespread frustration over the urban conditions caused by the relocation of many Indians to cities led more Indian people to join the fight for Indian justice. Within four years of its founding, AIM had established forty chapters in U.S. cities, on reservations, and in Canada. Active chapters were in San Francisco, Los Angeles, Denver, Milwaukee, and Cleveland. Among the individuals in AIM who became national leaders were Eddie Benton-Banai (Ojibwa) and Mary Jane Wilson (Ojibwa), who were instrumental in the early formation of the movement; Vernon Bellecourt (Ojibwa), Russell Means (Oglala), Richard Oakes (Mohawk), and Lehman Brightman (Lakota), who became director of Native American Studies at the University of California at Berkeley; John Trudell (Santee Dakota), who served as AIM national chairperson from 1974 to 1979; and Leonard Peltier (Metis), Anna Mae Aquash (Micmac), and Carter Camp (Ponca).

At the political level, AIM activists sought to bring attention to American Indian issues through a series of public protests, beginning with their participation in the nineteen-month occupation of Alcatraz that began in 1969. AIM activists protested at Mount Rushmore on 4 July 1971; at the Mayflower replica at Plymouth, Massachusetts, on Thanksgiving Day in 1971; and in Gordon, Nebraska, in February 1972, in response to the murder of Raymond Yellow Thunder. AIM members occupied the Bureau of Indian Affairs building in Washington, D.C., in November 1972 and initiated the nationwide Longest Walk in 1978, ending in Washington, D.C. Local chapters took over buildings in Wisconsin, California, and other states.

National attention peaked with two events, the first being AIM members' ten-week occupation of Wounded Knee, South Dakota (see WOUNDED KNEE, 1973). Authorities charged Dennis Banks and Russell Means and put them on trial for their actions at Wounded Knee, while other AIM members were arrested and released. Following an eight-month trial in 1974, a federal judge dismissed charges against Means and Banks.

The second event, known as the Oglala Firefight of 1975, grew out of heightened tensions between Indian activists and the Federal Bureau of Investigation after the events at Wounded Knee. The FBI was involved with surveillance of all major Indian protests, working to subvert such protests and challenging AIM leaders. The firefight broke out on 26 June 1975 between AIM members and the FBI at the Jumping Bull family compound on the Pine Ridge Reservation in South Dakota. The deaths of two FBI agents in the conflict led to a nationwide FBI effort to find the killer, and Leonard Peltier was ultimately convicted of the crime. (Two alleged accomplices were ac-

quitted in a separate proceeding.) Despite protests over many years that Peltier did not receive a fair trial, and international calls for his release, in 2002 he was still serving a prison sentence at Leavenworth, Kansas.

By the late 1970s, AIM no longer occupied national headlines, although it served an important purpose in altering federal Indian policy. During the 1970s, AIM split into two groups that put Clyde and Vernon Bellecourt on one side and Russell Means and his supporters on the other. This division remained unhealed, and AIM's politics were subdued due to conflict over leadership. Nevertheless, in the early twenty-first century it remained as one of the longest-lived national organizations representing American Indian issues.

BIBLIOGRAPHY

Johnson, Troy, et al., eds. *American Indian Activism: Alcatraz to the Longest Walk.* Urbana and Chicago: University of Illinois Press, 1997.

Nagel, Joane. *American Indian Ethnic Renewal: Red Power and the Resurgence of Identity and Culture.* New York: Oxford University Press, 1996.

Smith, Paul Chatt, and Robert Warrior, eds. *Like a Hurricane: The Indian Movement from Alcatraz to Wounded Knee.* New York: New Press, 1996.

Donald L. Fixico

See also **Indian Policy, U.S., 1900–2000; Indian Political Life; Indian Reservations.**

AMERICAN INDIAN RELIGIOUS FREEDOM ACT.

Passed in 1978 by both houses of Congress, the American Indian Religious Freedom Act (AIRFA), recognized the "inherent right" of American citizens to religious freedom; admitted that in the past the U.S. government had not protected the religious freedom of American Indians; proclaimed the "indispensable and irreplaceable" role of religion "as an integral part of Indian life"; and called upon governmental agencies to "protect and preserve for American Indians their inherent right of freedom to believe, express, and exercise the traditional religions." The resolution referred specifically to Indians' access to sacred sites, the use of natural resources normally protected by conservation laws, and participation in traditional Indian ceremonies.

AIRFA was enacted at a high-water mark of federal concern for American Indians, a time when U.S. policymakers were recognizing the validity of Indian claims to land and sovereignty and were acknowledging the history of U.S. mistreatment of Indian tribes. Progressives, who saw government as an instrument for assisting the disadvantaged, passed AIRFA as a corrective measure.

Observers have noted that AIRFA was construed too broadly and thus had "no teeth," and several court cases seemed to bear out this assessment. In a California case, *Lyng v. Northwest Indian Cemetery Protective Association* (1988), the Supreme Court ruled that Indian tribes' "practice of religion" would not be endangered by building a road through heavily forested public lands used for vision questing. In addition, AIRFA did not protect the Navajo sacred sites Chimney Rock and Rainbow Arch in Utah from disruptive tourist boats, the Hopi sacred site San Francisco Peaks in Arizona from the construction of ski resorts, or the Apache sacred site Mount Graham in Arizona from an astronomical observatory. In an Oregon case, *Employment Division v. Smith* (1990), the Supreme Court ruled that minority religions like the Native American Church, the peyote religion, cannot expect special protection from general laws, for example, against controlled substances, passed by the states, and the states do not have to defend their need for such laws, even when they infringe upon Indian religious practices. Following the unpopular *Smith* decision, a number of states enacted legislative exemptions for peyote use. In 1993, Congress tried to overturn *Smith* by passing the Religious Freedom Restoration Act, but the Supreme Court struck down the act in 1997, saying Congress lacks the authority to engage in judicial review.

Failures notwithstanding, AIRFA encouraged Indian tribes to press for their religious prerogatives, for example, at Bighorn Medicine Wheel and Devils Tower, Wyoming, in both cases enlisting the assistance of federal agencies in the protection of Indian religious practices on public lands. When Coast Salish tribes harvested cedars on public land to conduct their Paddle to Seattle (1989) and when the Makah tribe carried out its historic whale hunt (1999), they cited AIRFA as inspiration for their culturally restorative activities. AIRFA led also to the passage of other, more effective resolutions, such as the National Museum of the American Indian Act (1989), the Native American Graves Protection and Repatriation Act (1990), the Native American Language Act (1992), and President William Clinton's Executive Order No. 13007 (1996), which aims to protect Native American religious practices on public lands by ordering federal agencies, including the Bureau of Land Management, the U.S. Forest Service, and the National Park Service, to consult Indians in the management of their sacred sites.

BIBLIOGRAPHY

Gulliford, Andrew. *Sacred Objects and Sacred Places: Preserving Tribal Traditions.* Boulder: University Press of Colorado, 2000.

Vecsey, Christopher, ed. *Handbook of American Indian Religious Freedom.* New York: Crossroad Publishing, 1991.

Christopher Vecsey

See also **Dance, Indian; Indian Religious Life; Native American Graves Protection and Repatriation Act.**

AMERICAN LABOR PARTY (ALP), formed in July 1936 as the New York State branch of the Nonpartisan League. Circumstances specific to New York—a Tammany machine unsympathetic to President Franklin D. Roosevelt and the New Deal; a large pro-Socialist ethnic bloc; and a state law permitting dual nomination—dictated creation of a separate party rather than a Committee for Industrial Organization campaign body allied to the Democratic Party. The successful campaigns of Fiorello H. La Guardia for New York City mayor in 1937 and Herbert H. Lehman for governor in 1938 demonstrated that the ALP held the balance of power between the two major parties. Nevertheless, this potent position, displayed again in the elections of the next five years, eroded because of factional disputes and loss of union support and voter allegiance—the result primarily of Communist influence in the ALP. Furthermore, the election of Republican gubernatorial candidate Thomas Dewey in 1942 reflected a conservative resurgence in New York State. In 1944 the right wing split off to form the Liberal Party, and subsequently the ALP lost its swing position in New York politics. Although it recorded its highest vote in the national election in 1948 as the New York branch of the Progressive Party, the ALP thereafter declined rapidly and disbanded shortly after a poor showing in the 1954 governor's race. The New York pattern of third-party pressure politics that it had pioneered continued, however, through the activities of the Liberal Party and, from the opposite end of the political spectrum, of the Conservative Party, founded in 1962.

BIBLIOGRAPHY

Garrett, Charles. *The La Guardia Years: Machine and Reform Politics in New York City.* New Brunswick, N.J.: Rutgers University Press, 1961.

Kessner, Thomas. *Fiorello H. La Guardia and the Making of Modern New York.* New York: McGraw-Hill, 1989.

Moscow, Warren. *Politics in the Empire State.* New York: Knopf, 1948.

*David Brody/*A. G.

See also **New York State; Nonpartisan League, National; Political Parties.**

AMERICAN LEGION. The American Legion is the world's largest veterans' organization, with membership open to those holding an honorable discharge from active duty in the U.S. armed forces after 1914. Legionnaires dedicate themselves to perpetuating the principles for which they have fought, to inculcating civic responsibility in the nation, to preserving the history of their participation in American wars, and to binding together as comrades with all those who have fought. They also pledge to defend law and order, to develop "a one hundred percent Americanism," and to help the less fortunate through government and private programs.

Four Allied Expeditionary Forces officers-of-the-line informally started the Legion in February 1919 while still on active duty in Paris, France. These founders—Col. Theodore Roosevelt Jr., Lt. Col. George S. White, Maj. Eric Fisher Wood, and Lt. Col. William J. ("Wild Bill")

Donovan—sought both to bolster soldier morale during the post-armistice period and to provide an alternative to other veterans' groups being set up in the United States. A covert aim was to continue the political tenets of the "New Nationalism" of the defunct Bull Moose political party. They enunciated the organization's purposes at the Paris Caucus and saw them reaffirmed at the Continental Caucus, held three months later at St. Louis, Missouri. The Legion received its incorporation from the U.S. Congress on 16 September 1919. By 1925, the Legion achieved all the programs and policies it maintains today.

The Legion assumed the role of representative for all former doughboys even though its 1920 membership of 840,000 represented only about 18.5 percent of eligible veterans. At the onset of every war or military action since World War I (1914–1918), the Legion has persuaded Congress to amend its incorporation to allow veterans of those conflicts to join the Legion. Its membership fluctuated from a low of 610,000 in 1925 to a high of 3,325,000 in 1946, leveling off by 1972 to the 2,800,000 that was sustained through the end of the twentieth century.

Pursuit of its goal of "Americanism" led the Legion into many controversies. Legionnaires have striven to rid school textbooks and public libraries' shelves of perceived alien, Communist, syndicalist, or anarchist influences. During the "Red Scare" of 1919–20, four Legionnaires died in a shootout with Industrial Workers of the World organizers at Centralia, Washington. Legionnaires covertly spied on unsuspecting American citizens for the congressional House Un-American Activities Committee and the Federal Bureau of Investigation from the 1930s until the 1970s.

The American Legion's advocacy of military preparedness started in 1919. During the politically isolationist 1920s, this policy made the Legion unpopular with many, as did its continued support of universal military training into the 1970s. Similarly, its condemnation of U.S. participation in United Nations Economic and Social Council activities and its call for a total blockade of communist Cuba during the 1960s sparked debates. Representatives of the Legion spoke in support of a stronger military at every War/Defense department appropriation hearing from 1919 through 2002.

Through its strenuous efforts to obtain benefits for veterans, the American Legion earned the reputation by the late 1930s of being one of the nation's most effective interest groups. Its demand for a bonus for World War I veterans, finally met in 1936 over the objections of four successive Presidents, and its promotion of the GI Bill of Rights for World War II veterans, achieved in 1944, testify to its highly publicized dedication to all veterans—not just its members. The Legion practically created the U.S. Department of Veterans Affairs and its predecessors. Starting in 1978, the Legion demanded medical and monetary benefits for veterans exposed to Agent Orange in

Vietnam. The Legion works almost as hard to prevent similar beneficial programs for the nonveteran population.

Other, less controversial, activities project the Legion's preferred image. The local posts sponsor individual teams for the nationwide American Legion baseball league. Each state organization operates an annual hands-on political seminar for high school students. The Legion and the National Education Association began cosponsoring "American Education Week" in 1919 to foster local appreciation for good education opportunities for children. Legionnaires annually donate $20 million to charitable causes and 4 million work-hours to community service.

The Legion had five international groups, fifty U.S. state departments, and 14,500 local posts throughout the world as of 2002. The posts report to the departments who, in turn, send representatives to the annual national convention. The convention sets policy for the Legion and elects the National Commander and the National Executive Committee. The latter directs the Legion from national headquarters at Indianapolis, Indiana, between conventions. The Legion's charter forbids formal political activity by the organization or its elected officers. Nonetheless, the Legion does maintain a powerful liaison office in Washington, D.C., and every major contender for national office gives at least one speech to a Legion convention.

BIBLIOGRAPHY

"For God and Country: the American Legion, the World's Largest Veterans Association." Available from http://www.legion .org.

Moley, Raymond. *The American Legion Story*. New York: Duell, Sloan and Pearce, 1966.

Pencak, William. *For God and Country: The American Legion, 1919–1941*. Boston: Northeastern University Press, 1989.

Rumer, Thomas A. *The American Legion: An Official History, 1919–1989*. New York: M. Evans, 1990.

Bill Olbrich
Davis R. B. Ross

See also **Veterans Affairs, Department of; Veterans' Organizations.**

AMERICAN LIBERTY LEAGUE.

On 15 August 1934, after the onset of strikes that would last until 1938, the American Liberty League, funded largely by the Duponts and their corporate allies, was chartered in Washington. In its six years of existence, the Liberty League fought NEW DEAL labor and social legislation, rallied support for the conservative-dominated Supreme Court, and sought to build a bipartisan conservative coalition to defeat the Franklin D. Roosevelt administration and the trade union movement.

The Liberty League called upon businessmen to defy the NATIONAL LABOR RELATIONS ACT, hoping the Supreme Court would declare it unconstitutional, and led "educational campaigns" against social security, unemployment insurance, minimum wages, and other New Deal policies. After the New Deal's great victory in 1936, the Liberty League adopted a lower profile. Earlier, Franklin D. Roosevelt, in attacking the "economic loyalists," who were so visible in the leadership of the Liberty League, mocked the league's definition of "liberty" in his last speech of the 1936 presidential campaign, retelling a story, attributed to Abraham Lincoln, of a wolf, removed by a shepherd from the neck of a lamb, denouncing the shepherd for taking away its liberty. The league formally dissolved in September 1940.

Its influence on conservative politics in the United States was large. In the aftermath of the 1938 elections, conservative Democrats and Republicans in Congress stalemated New Deal legislation, using Liberty League themes of opposition to government spending, taxation, and communist influence in the administration and the labor movement to gain support. The Liberty League supported the early activities of the House Un-American Activities Committee and the National Lawyers Committee. The league's attempt to recruit and fund conservative scholarship and university forums on public policy issues prefigured the creation of corporate-funded conservative "THINK TANKS."

The issues raised by the Liberty League in the 1930s remain unresolved, as does its role in history. For those who see "big government," the regulation and taxation of business, and the redistribution of wealth to lower income groups as absolute evils, it has been vindicated by history and is posthumously triumphant. For those who see government as a shepherd or steward seeking to prevent society from reverting to a socioeconomic jungle where the strong devour the weak, it stands condemned as the champion of "free market" policies that today promote economic instability and social injustice, both in the United States and the world.

BIBLIOGRAPHY

Brinkley, Alan. "The Problem of American Conservatism." *American Historical Review* 99, no. 2 (April 1994): 409–429.

Leuchtenburg, William E. *The Supreme Court Reborn: The Constitutional Revolution in the Age of Roosevelt.* New York: Oxford University Press, 1995.

Rudolph, Frederick. "The American Liberty League, 1934–1940." *American Historical Review* 56, no. 1 (October 1950): 19–33. A useful early postwar critique that captures the New Deal generation's view of the league.

Wolfskill, George. *Revolt of the Conservatives: A History of the American Liberty League, 1934–1940.* Boston: Houghton Mifflin, 1962. The best introduction to the Liberty League.

Norman Markowitz

See also **Conservatism.**

AMERICAN MATHEMATICAL SOCIETY. *See* **Learned Societies.**

AMERICAN MEDICAL ASSOCIATION (AMA) was founded on 7 May 1847 as a response to the growing demands for reforms in medical education and practice. Dr. Nathan S. Davis (1817–1904), a delegate from the New York State Medical Society who later came to be known as the "founding father of the AMA," convened a national conference of physicians to address reforms in medical education, medical ethics, and public health. On 7 May 1847 more than 250 physicians from more than forty medical societies and twenty-eight medical colleges assembled in the Great Hall of the Academy of Natural Sciences in Philadelphia and established the American Medical Association. A Committee on Medical Education was appointed, and minimum standards of medical education were established. The first national code of American medical ethics, the cornerstone of professional self-regulation, was adopted. Written by Dr. John Bell (1796–1872) and Dr. Isaac Hays (1796–1879) and published in 1847, the Code of Medical Ethics of the American Medical Association provided guidelines for the behavior of physicians with respect to patients, society, and other medical professionals.

Throughout the nineteenth century the AMA worked to expose fraudulent and unethical practitioners and to limit licensure to allopathic physicians. In 1883 the *Journal of the American Medical Association* (*JAMA*) was established with Nathan Davis as the first editor. By 1901, *JAMA* was reporting a circulation of 22,049 copies per week, the largest of all medical journals in the world.

Membership, however, remained small, including only 10,000 of the 100,000 orthodox physicians. In 1901 the AMA underwent a major reorganization to become a more effective national body by providing proportional representation among state medical societies. The House of Delegates was established as the legislative body of the AMA. Each state society was allowed a specific number of delegates with voting rights. By 1906, membership in the AMA exceeded 50,000 physicians, and educational and licensing reforms began to take hold.

The newly established Council on Medical Education inspected 160 medical schools (1906–1907), and in 1910 the Flexner Report, *Medical Education in the United States and Canada*, was published. Funded by the Carnegie Foundation and supported by the AMA, the report exposed the poor conditions of many schools and recommended implementing rigorous standards of medical training. By 1923 the AMA had adopted standards for medical specialty training, and in 1927 the association published a list of hospitals approved for residency training.

By World War I, the AMA had become a powerful political lobby. Wary of governmental control, it fought proposals for national health insurance. The 1935 Social Security Act passed without compulsory health insurance due to AMA influence. Physician membership grew steadily to over 100,000 physicians by 1936. The AMA continued to fight government involvement in health care with a campaign against President Truman's initiatives in 1948.

In 1961 the American Medical Political Action Committee (AMPAC) was formed to represent physicians' and patients' interests in health care legislation.

The AMA continued to work on numerous public health initiatives, including declaring alcoholism to be an illness (1956), recommending nationwide polio vaccinations (1960), and adopting a report on the hazards of cigarette smoking (1964). AMA membership exceeded 200,000 physicians by 1965. From 1966 to 1973, the AMA coordinated the Volunteer Physicians in Vietnam program and in 1978 supported state legislation mandating use of seat belts for infants and children.

In 1983, membership included 250,000 physicians. As AIDS became an epidemic in the 1980s, the AMA passed a resolution opposing acts of discrimination against AIDS patients (1986) and established the office of HIV/AIDS (1988).

By 1990, health maintenance organizations (HMOs) and other third-party payers were involved extensively in health care delivery. Health care reform had become a political priority. In 1994 and 1995 the AMA drafted two Patient Protection Acts, and in 1998 the AMA supported the Patient's Bill of Rights.

In 2001, AMA membership included 300,000 physicians. As new threats to the nation's health, such as bioterrorism, began to emerge in the twenty-first century, the AMA continued to rely on the principles in the AMA Code of Medical Ethics (revised 2001) and the democratic process of the AMA House of Delegates to guide its actions and policies to fulfill its mission as "physicians dedicated to the health of America."

BIBLIOGRAPHY

Baker, Robert B., et al. *The American Medical Ethics Revolution: How the AMA's Code of Ethics Has Transformed Physicians' Relationships to Patients, Professionals, and Society.* Baltimore: Johns Hopkins University Press, 1999.

Duffy, John. *From Humors to Medical Science: A History of American Medicine.* Chicago: University of Illinois Press, 1993.

Starr, Paul. *The Social Transformation of American Medicine: The Rise of a Sovereign Profession and the Making of a Vast Industry.* New York: Basic Books, 1982.

Stevens, Rosemary. *American Medicine and the Public Interest: A History of Specialization.* Berkeley, Calif.: University of California Press, 1998.

Karen E. Geraghty

See also **Medical Profession; Medical Societies; Medicine and Surgery.**

AMERICAN MUSEUM OF NATURAL HISTORY

in New York City is the largest natural history museum in the world. It displays more than 30 million specimens from all branches of natural history along with a wealth of anthropological artifacts in a vast complex of interconnected buildings on the Upper West Side of Manhattan.

The museum was founded in 1869 by some of New York City's wealthiest men, who hoped a natural history museum would impart prestige to their city and educate the working classes about the laws of nature. As with the Metropolitan Museum of Art, which opened in 1870, the American Museum of Natural History soon became one of the pet philanthropies of the New York aristocracy. While the municipality funded the operation and maintenance of the facilities, the wealthy trustees, including the Dodge, Huntington, Morgan, Rockefeller, Schiff, Vanderbilt, and Whitney families, were responsible for acquiring and managing the collections. This method of financing has continued, supplemented by endowments, membership dues, and entrance fees.

The museum was originally situated in the Arsenal Building in Central Park. In 1874, President Ulysses S. Grant laid the cornerstone for the museum's permanent home, which opened in 1877. As the collections steadily grew in size, the museum pioneered in dioramas and other lifelike displays that presented large or striking specimens of flora and fauna in their natural habitats. Most famously, by the early 1900s the museum had acquired the world's largest collection of dinosaur bones, which subsequently were mounted in exhibits that corrected previous errors in interpretation and presentation.

The museum conducts a wide range of educational activities for the public and publishes the monthly magazine *Natural History.* It also sponsors hundreds of working scientists, who continue the legacy of the researchers Carl Akeley, Roy Chapman Andrews, Franz Boas, Margaret Mead, and Henry Fairfield Osborn.

BIBLIOGRAPHY

Hellman, Geoffrey. *Bankers, Bones, and Beetles: The First Century of the American Museum of Natural History.* Garden City, N.Y.: Natural History Press, 1969.

Kennedy, John Michael. "Philanthropy and Science in New York City: The American Museum of Natural History, 1868–1968." Ph.D. diss., Yale University, 1968.

Rainger, Ronald. *An Agenda for Antiquity: Henry Fairfield Osborn and Vertebrate Paleontology at the American Museum of Natural History, 1890–1935.* Tuscaloosa: University of Alabama Press, 1991.

Jonathan P. Spiro

See also **Philanthropy; Science Museums.**

AMERICAN PARTY

has been the name of several political parties in U.S. history. The first and most successful party of that name, popularly called the Know-Nothing Party because its members were instructed to answer all questions about their activities with "I know nothing," was founded in New York City in 1849. It was a coalition of several secret fraternal organizations, including the Order of United Mechanics, the Order of the Sons of America, the United Daughters of America, the Order of United Americans, and the Order of the Star

Spangled Banner. It was organized to oppose the great wave of immigrants who entered the United States after 1846. The Know-Nothings claimed that the immigrants, who were principally Irish and Roman Catholic, threatened to subvert the U.S. Constitution. Their state and national platforms demanded that immigration be limited, that officeholding be limited to native-born Americans, and that a twenty-one-year wait be imposed before an immigrant could become a citizen and vote.

The party won a number of offices at the state and congressional levels, and attracted many northern Whigs, along with a number of Democrats. Southern Whigs also joined because of growing sectional tensions caused by the reintroduction of the slavery issue into national politics in 1854. For a time, it seemed as if the Know-Nothings would be the main opposition party to the Democrats in the United States. With Millard Fillmore as its presidential candidate in 1856, the party won more than 21 percent of the popular vote and eight electoral votes. Differences over the slavery issue, however, led many members to join the Republican Party, and the American Party was spent as a national force before the election of 1860.

Among other parties so named was one organized in Philadelphia in 1887. The party platform advocated a fourteen-year residence for naturalization; the exclusion of socialists, anarchists, and other supposedly dangerous persons; free schools; a strong navy and coastal defense; continued separation of church and state; and enforcement of the Monroe Doctrine. At a convention held in Washington, D.C., on 14 August 1888, it nominated presidential candidate James L. Curtis of New York State, but he received only 1,591 votes at the November election.

Another American Party entered the 1924 election, and chose Gilbert O. Nations as its presidential candidate and C. H. Randall as its vice-presidential nominee. Despite its efforts to win support from the then-powerful Ku Klux Klan, the party received less than one percent of the vote.

In May 1969, at a gathering in Cincinnati, Ohio, yet another American Party was formed. Two years later it joined with the American Independent Party and in August 1972 the combined organization gathered in Louisville, Kentucky, to nominate U.S. representative John Schmitz for president and Thomas J. Anderson for vice president. The coalition party divided into its components in 1973, and since 1976 the American Party has run a presidential ticket in every election but has always received less than one percent of the vote.

BIBLIOGRAPHY

Anbinder, Tyler G. *Nativism and Slavery: The Northern Know Nothings and the Politics of the 1850's.* New York: Oxford University Press, 1994.

Overdyke, Darrell. *Know Nothing Party in the South.* Magnolia, Mass.: Peter Smith, 1968.

Jon Roland

See also **American Independent Party; Know-Nothing Party; Nativism;** *and vol. 9:* **American Party Platform.**

AMERICAN PHILOSOPHICAL SOCIETY

is the oldest learned society in America. The botanist John Bartram made the first proposal for a general scientific society in Philadelphia in 1739, but it was Benjamin Franklin who issued a public call to found a society of "Virtuosi or ingenious Men," offering his services as secretary. The new society held several meetings in 1743, elected members from neighboring colonies, and members read learned papers and made plans to publish them. However, Franklin complained, the members were "very idle"; consequently, the society languished and by 1746 it had died. In 1766, stimulated by the feelings of American nationalism engendered by the Stamp Act, some younger Philadelphians—many of Quaker background and belonging to the Assembly political party—formed the American Society for Promoting Useful Knowledge, which sought to develop and promote better agricultural methods, domestic manufactures, and internal improvements. In response, surviving members of the 1743 group and some others, Anglican and Proprietary in sentiment, then revived the "dormant" American Philosophical Society. Wisely, the rival societies merged in 1769 as the American Philosophical Society, Held at Philadelphia, for Promoting Useful Knowledge. In a contested election, the members chose Franklin, then in London, as the first president.

The society's first important scientific undertaking was to observe the transit of Venus (3 June 1769). Its reports were first published in the *Philosophical Transactions* of the Royal Society, then, in full, in its own *Transactions* (1771), which, distributed among European academies and philosophers, quickly established the society's reputation. Reorganized in 1784 and 1785 after wartime interruption, the society expanded its membership, erected a hall (still in use), and resumed publication of the *Transactions.* In the ensuing half-century it became the single most important scientific forum in the United States. Its tone was Jeffersonian, republican, deistic, and pro-French. By loaning its facilities, it encouraged such other learned bodies in Philadelphia as the College of Physicians, the Historical Society of Pennsylvania, the Academy of Natural Sciences, and the Agricultural Society.

Thomas Jefferson, president of the United States and the society simultaneously, used the society as a national library, museum, and academy of sciences, asking it to draft instructions for Meriwether Lewis and William Clark and, after the explorers' return, depositing their specimens and report in its museum and library. Materials on American Indian languages collected by Jefferson and another society president, Peter S. Du Ponceau, also went into the library. Joel R. Poinsett donated an impressive collection of ancient Mexican artifacts. During the nineteenth century, the *Transactions* carried many descriptive articles on American natural history, including those by Isaac Lea on malacology (the study of mollusks), Edward D. Cope on paleontology, F. V. Hayden on geology, Joseph Leidy on anatomy, and Leo Lesquereux on botany. The society's *Proceedings* also frequently reported Joseph Henry's experiments on electromagnetism.

The society lost preeminence during the mid-1830s to mid-1860s, when specialized learned societies arose. The federal government created its own learned institutions, such as the Smithsonian, and the *American Journal of Science* was founded. At midcentury the society seemed without imagination or energy—Henry Thoreau called it "a company of old women"—but it continued to meet, publish, and elect persons to membership, overlooking hardly any outstanding scientists.

The bicentennial of Franklin's birth in 1906 brought a renewal of activity, especially in historical publication. From 1927 to 1929 the society drafted plans to reorganize itself as a clearinghouse for scientific knowledge—with popular lectures, a newsletter, and a publications office designed to disseminate "authoritative news of forward steps in all branches of learning." Those plans collapsed with the onset of the Great Depression in 1929. Private bequests and gifts in the 1930s, particularly from R. A. F. Penrose and E. R. Johnson, produced striking changes, however. While retaining its old organization and traditional practices, the society extended its activities in several directions. It expanded its scholarly publications program, adding a book series, *The Memoirs*, and a year book to its highly respected monograph series, *Transactions of the American Philosophical Society*. In 1933 it inaugurated a program of research grants, including the gift of large amounts for some projects, such as for extensive archaeological work at Tikal, Guatemala, and a number of smaller grants to individuals (these totaled roughly $400,000 annually by the end of the twentieth century), primarily as a way of fostering scholarly publication. The society continued to develop its library, in 1959 opening its Library Hall, which houses one of the principal collections on the history of science in America, including rare first editions of Benjamin Franklin's *Experiments and Observations*, Sir Isaac Newton's *Principia*, and Charles Darwin's *Origin of Species*. In addition, the society sponsors three specific research programs in clinical medicine, North American Indians, and the history of the physical sciences. Since the late eighteenth century the society has also maintained an active awards program across a range of disciplines, from the arts and humanities to science and jurisprudence, including the Magellanic Premium (established in 1786), the Barzun prize, the Franklin and Jefferson Medals, the Lashley and Lewis awards, and the Moe and Phillips prizes.

A large percentage of the society's annual operating budget derives from its sizable endowment. The society's Annual Fund (launched in 1992) and foundation grants provide the remainder. Society membership is confined to those who are elected for "extraordinary accomplishment" in their professional fields; more than two hundred society members won the Nobel Prize for their work during the twentieth century. At the beginning of the twenty-first century, society membership stood at over seven hundred, 85 percent of whom resided within the United States.

BIBLIOGRAPHY

American Philosophical Society. *Year Book.* Philadelphia: The American Philosophical Society, published annually since 1937.

Bearn, Alexander G., ed. *Useful Knowledge: The American Philosophical Society Millenium Program.* Philadelphia: American Philosophical Society, 1999.

Hindle, Brooke. *The Pursuit of Science in Revolutionary America, 1735–1789.* Chapel Hill: University of North Carolina Press, 1956.

Whitfield J. Bell Jr. / c. w.

See also **Learned Societies; Lewis and Clark Expedition; Philanthropy.**

AMERICAN PROTECTIVE ASSOCIATION

(APA), founded at Clinton, Iowa, in 1887 by attorney Henry F. Bowers, represented anti-Catholic and anticapitalist sentiments during the 1890s. The APA movement grew slowly until the economic unrest of the panic of 1893 fueled its national growth. Unlike the Know-Nothing movement of the 1850s, the APA never formed a distinct political party and it invited foreign-born Americans to join its membership. However, its rapid expansion made it difficult to manage and, in an ill-fated move, the APA attempted to thwart the nomination of presidential candidate William McKinley in 1896. The attempt failed, and the APA's inefficacy became even more apparent when, in March 1897, McKinley's first cabinet appointment was a Catholic judge. Despite declining support, the APA lingered until the death of Henry Bowers in 1911.

BIBLIOGRAPHY

Desmond, Humphrey J. *The APA Movement.* 1912. Reprint, New York: Arno Press, 1969.

Manfra, Jo Ann. "Hometown Politics and the American Protective Association, 1887–1890." *The Annals of Iowa* 55 (Spring 1996): 138–166.

Jennifer Harrison

AMERICAN RAILWAY UNION.

In June 1893, Eugene V. Debs, secretary-treasurer of the Brotherhood of Locomotive Firemen, joined other brotherhood officers to found the American Railway Union (ARU), dedicated to uniting all rail workers "into one, compact working force for legislative as well as industrial action" (Salvatore, *Eugene V. Debs*, p. 115).

167

Prior to the formation of the ARU, labor organizing in the railroad industry had primarily been limited to craft unions, each admitting only workers belonging to a specific trade. The most powerful of these were brotherhoods of engineers, firemen, brakemen, and conductors, which strived to win decent wages and working conditions by stressing their members' good conduct and valuable skills. As an industrial union with a keen readiness to strike, the ARU represented a sharp departure from this conservative model of labor organizing.

The ARU was barely a year old when, in April 1894, it led a walkout by employees of the Great Northern Railroad who were protesting wage cuts and dismissals of men who joined the new union. Strikers showed impressive unity and gained the sympathy of communities from Minnesota to Washington State. Eventually Debs maneuvered the railroad's owner, James J. Hill, into agreeing to an arbitration that gave the strikers almost all of their wage demands. After this unprecedented victory, the ARU soon counted 150,000 members, far more than the combined membership of the craft brotherhoods.

Almost immediately, the new union was drawn into a greater struggle. After employees of the Pullman sleeping car company held a strike to protest wage cuts and firings in May 1894, the ARU committed itself to a nationwide boycott of all trains that included Pullman cars. Debs did not think his young union was ready for such an ambitious battle, and events soon proved him right. Arrayed against the ARU were the well-organized forces of the General Managers Association, a coalition of twenty-four railroads, acting in close collaboration with Attorney General Richard Olney. In July 1894, a week after the boycott began, government attorneys persuaded federal judges to grant an injunction prohibiting virtually all ARU activities in support of the action, because it interfered with interstate commerce and the U.S. mail. ARU officers were arrested, and when Samuel Gompers of the American Federation of Labor refused to call for a general strike to support the boycott, the ARU admitted defeat. Within a year, the union was defunct and Debs, convicted of contempt of court, was serving a short prison sentence.

The railroad brotherhoods soon patched themselves together and won a certain measure of success in bargaining with the railroad companies, which were eager to prevent a resurgence of the aggressive spirit represented by the ARU. Industrial unionism on the model of the ARU did not firmly establish itself in the United States until renewed labor militancy combined with new federal protections for organizing to spur the formation of the Congress of Industrial Organizations in 1936.

BIBLIOGRAPHY

Lindsey, Almont. *The Pullman Strike: The Story of a Unique Experiment and of a Great Labor Upheaval.* Chicago: University of Chicago Press, 1942.

Salvatore, Nick. *Eugene V. Debs: Citizen and Socialist.* Urbana: University of Illinois Press, 1982.

Stromquist, Shelton. *A Generation of Boomers: The Pattern of Railroad Labor Conflict in Nineteenth-Century America.* Urbana: University of Illinois Press, 1987.

Eugene E. Leach

See also **In Re Debs;** Injunctions, Labor; Labor Legislation and Administration; Pullman Strike; Railroad Brotherhoods; and vol. 9: **The Pullman Strike and Boycott, June 1894.**

AMERICAN REPUBLICAN PARTY.

The American Republican Party, an outgrowth of nativist sentiment against immigrant voting, began in New York in June 1843 as a ward-based third-party organization which pushed for poll watching as an anti-fraud precaution, direct election of city school officials, and the long-term goal of a twenty-one-year naturalization period for new immigrants. Largely drawn from craftsmen and small businessmen, who used their fraternal and trade organizations' symbolism in the party's campaigns, the group's constituency was deeply anti-Catholic and saw their primary foes as Irish immigrants.

Successful in city elections in 1844 in both Philadelphia and New York—its winning candidates included a mayor, city commissioners, a city auditor, and two congressmen—the party called a national convention in July 1845, when it also changed its name to the Native American Party. Although effective at the city level, the party was unable to get national support for changes in the naturalization process, and the continual ward-level campaigning of its candidates led to the perception by voters that the party was running political hacks. Fizzling quickly as war with Mexico captured the country's attention, the party collapsed by 1846, unable to make any substantial changes that would privilege native-born voters in the face of large-scale immigration and emigrant participation in city officeholding.

BIBLIOGRAPHY

Knobel, Dale T. *Paddy and the Republic: Ethnicity and Nationality in Antebellum America.* Middletown, Conn.: Wesleyan University Press, 1986.

———. *"America For the Americans": The Nativist Movement in the United States.* New York: Twayne, 1996.

Margaret D. Sankey

See also **Nativism.**

AMERICAN STUDIES

is the academic area of inquiry that seeks an integrated and interdisciplinary understanding of American culture. Rooted in the traditional disciplines of literature and history, the field has evolved from its establishment in the 1930s to include artifacts, methodologies, and practitioners drawn from a wide variety of disciplines within the humanities, including political science, sociology, theology, communications, anthropology, music, art history, film studies, architecture, geography, gender studies, ethnic studies, and other fields of inquiry.

Beginnings: The 1930s and 1940s

The self-reflective nature of some three hundred years of the American citizenry is the basis for the field of American Studies. The origins of a more formal and more organized field of inquiry within academia are to be found in the 1930s. Most of the founders of this movement were born between 1890 and 1910. Their collective coming of age and early intellectual careers were subject to a number of shared cultural and academic influences: the era of World War I (1914–1918) and its aftermath; the urbanization of America; the role of immigration in American society and culture; the Progressive era in politics; and the increasing professionalization of academia. Balanced against these markers of change, however, was the basic belief that John Winthrop referred to in 1620, that America was "a city on a hill," set forth as an example to all the world and under the direct protection of a benevolent God. This concept of a unique place called America had been echoed since the nation's founding, not only by Alexis de Tocqueville in the 1830s and Frederick Jackson Turner in the 1890s, but again in the 1920s and 1930s by modern American Studies scholars like Vernon Parrington and Constance Rourke.

During the 1930s, the Great Depression and resultant New Deal policies provided a fertile field for Americanists to observe and critique not only the national crisis and responses to it, but also the political and cultural history that had led to that particular historical moment. As did President Franklin D. Roosevelt and his advisors, this first generation of American Studies scholars took a pragmatic approach to history and tradition, enlarging their concept of what could constitute legitimate "texts" for study and approaching these with a critical eye. Many New Deal programs that employed intellectuals and artists provided extensive and exciting new collections of texts and artifacts for consideration: the WPA's productions of dramas, murals and other artwork; written, photographic and recorded oral history collections of shared American experience and memory; and the recordings of American folk music and folklore collected by Alan Lomax and others. Furthermore, the liberal thought and politics that dominated 1930s America were quite resonant with the interdisciplinary openness so integral to American Studies.

The liberalism of the 1930s persisted in the discipline, as the students of the 1940s were trained by the movement's founders. The willingness of American Studies scholars to continue to practice this liberalism and critical analysis during World War II (1939–1945) and, later, the Cold War, opened them up to charges of being unpatriotic or even un-American. However, these scholars argued that with the nation's increasing international profile, blind patriotism was no longer an option for Americans. Instead, it was crucial that Americans learn to honestly evaluate their own culture to be able to successfully and peacefully interact with the other nations of the world. The most influential institution in establishing this heyday of American Studies was the University of Minnesota where, in 1943, a number of outstanding scholars in the field came together. Headed by Tremain McDowell, Minnesota's American Studies faculty included Henry Nash Smith and Leo Marx; early graduate students included Allen Guttmann, Allen Trachtenberg and John William Ward. The World War II explosion of American Studies scholarship was concurrent with the emergence of the myth-symbol school, which would become virtually synonymous with the discipline from the 1940s through the mid-1960s.

The Myth-Symbol School

Many analysts of American Studies have argued that the so-called myth-symbol school is indeed the closest example approaching a systematized methodology that the field has ever known. Having its foundations in the crisis of American identity that emerged with the nation's involvement in World War II, this myth-symbol school sought to define what was essentially "American" about America. Practitioners sought the basis of Americanness in the country's bygone cultural grandeur; consequently, the most widely accepted vision came to be that of F. O. Matthiessen's *American Renaissance* (1941). In this landmark work, Matthiessen set forth the argument that it took the years from 1776 through 1830 for the new nation to escape the hold of European culture and to establish its own voice in the works of Ralph Waldo Emerson, Henry David Thoreau, Herman Melville, Nathaniel Hawthorne, and Walt Whitman. Playing on Matthiessen's sacralization of this period of America's reinvention of itself, the myth-symbol school sought to preserve and expand this myth as a means of retaining an American cultural identity in the post-World War II years of American global leadership and multiculturalism.

This concept of a national mythology has had far-reaching implications for the field of American Studies. Inherent in Matthiessen's ideas and in those of the entire myth-symbol school was a sacred stage on which an American cultural identity had been formed. The concept of America as a discrete, almost holy locale was paramount to the myth-symbol methodology; as the twentieth century progressed, however, the school's ability to retain the requisite isolation from corrupting outside influences was seriously eroded by the phenomenon of internationalism. Further, not only was America increasingly involved with countries and cultures outside its borders, but those countries' inhabitants and influences were increasingly coming into America and attempting to assimilate themselves into the American culture. America as melting pot was, effectively, destroying the uniqueness and cultural purity on which the myth-symbol school had been founded.

169

As many have been quick to point out, the flaw of the myth-symbol school as established in *American Renaissance* and extended in Henry Nash Smith's *Virgin Land* (1950) was precisely this reliance on the myth of a virgin landscape: Matthiessen, Smith, and others took as their starting point an uninhabited American wilderness that formed this pristine space. The denial of the existence of an "Other"—the Native Americans already here at the time of the first Europeans' arrival, the later immigrants of non-Anglo or non-Protestant background, or women—necessarily formed the critical flaw of the myth-symbol school.

Shifting Attitudes of the 1950s and 1960s

The 1950s and 1960s were decades of critical shifts in American life and culture, and academia was not immune to these changes. This period saw the field of American Studies struggle for and attain academic legitimacy, with a clear growth in the number of students in the field apparent by the early 1960s. Interestingly, this same period saw the resurgence of the earlier theory of "American exceptionalism"—that is, the notion that America, its citizens, and its culture were somehow unique among all the nations, citizens, and cultures on earth. Not coincidentally, by this time many of American Studies' highly influential founding scholars had taught or studied abroad, frequently as part of the Fulbright program; accordingly, they returned to America with broadened perceptions of life in America. Further, many students coming into an increasingly widespread and broadened American Studies curriculum brought new voices; the numbers of persons of Jewish, immigrant, working-class, or minority backgrounds within the field grew, as did the number of women entering the discourse.

This period is also notable for a return to the practical or "applied" notion of the field, reminiscent of its 1930s roots. The civil rights movement of the day drew academicians out of their classrooms and libraries and into a growing dialogue with their communities. The impact of the civil rights movement (and corollary increases in sensitivity to all types of "Others") upon the field of American Studies must not be underestimated. The heightened awareness of the need to avoid discrimination, whether against the new minority practitioners in the field or against various minority groups throughout American history, led to a corresponding increase in interest in the histories and voices of these minority groups.

American Studies in the Late Twentieth Century and Beyond

By the 1970s, American Studies had emerged as a strong voice for women and women's issues, primarily as a result of scholars' recognition that this segment of American culture had been largely ignored in the past. Similar recognition of past slights to other minority groups (African Americans, immigrant Americans, Native Americans, poor Americans, and so on) led to increased research into these areas of American experience. By the mid-1970s, scholars

began to move away from venerating certain categories of inquiry; that is, the heyday of the written literary text, the finely preserved government document, and the white Anglo-Saxon Protestant male was gone. These canonical subjects have since been supplanted by the recognition of the role of multiculturalism, an increased importance accorded to material artifacts and non-traditional "texts," and a growing emphasis on popular culture. Similarly, research and scholarship have continued to move away from traditional political and intellectual history and toward more inclusive areas of inquiry.

American Studies at the turn of the twenty-first century, then, had become concerned with several ongoing issues related to this new inclusiveness. First, defining the concept of "American" Studies had become increasingly complicated. The question was raised with growing frequency: "Who is an American?" Traditionally, the field had concerned itself with matters relating to the area within the boundaries of the United States of America; however, some critics insisted that Central and South American nations are just as legitimately included in the term, particularly in light of extensive Hispanic immigration to the United States. Others, interested in Canada, took a similar position, based on the geographical, political, and ideological similarities between Canada and the United States. Second, what exactly is it that scholars study about this arbitrarily defined "America"? Is "America" a geographic entity, or is it a cultural concept? Is it a political entity, or a personal one? Is there really an "America," or is what we call "America" merely a symbol, and thus not really a valid topic for study unless we propose a far more concrete definition? Thus, while American Studies no longer presumed "the American" necessarily to be the white male living in the United States, this very recognition raised yet another question: How much specialization and fragmentation can the field undergo and still retain any coherent identity?

Perhaps part of the answer to these questions lay in the fact that many late-twentieth-century American Studies scholars had returned to the roots of the discipline to examine past approaches. There was renewed interest in methodology and theory, including cultural anthropology, new historicism, and what Gene Wise has termed the search for "dense facts." However, only rarely would a modern scholar apply only one of these methods or examine only a limited scope of texts or actors. By 2002, the emphasis had truly shifted toward the combination of the most usable aspects of various methodologies and away from dogmatic reliance on narrow definitions of how American identity should be approached; with practitioners engaging in a celebration of diversity and disavowing the former myth of homogeneity. Obviously, the reductionism and certainty of the myth-symbol school no longer applied to modern American Studies, but this very inquiry and uncertainty are what have made the field one of the most interesting and dynamic areas within the humanities.

By the beginning of the twenty-first century, many American universities and a growing number of universities outside of the United States offered graduate degrees in American Studies. Many American schools also offered undergraduate degree programs in the field, and numerous overseas American Studies associations had been established. In the United States, the American Studies Association (ASA) was established in 1951 to serve as the scholarly organization of practitioners in the field. *American Quarterly* began publication in 1949 as a clearinghouse for scholarly research in American Studies. Those pursuing an education in American Studies can anticipate careers in traditional academic areas (either in a department of American Studies or in one of its contributing disciplines); careers in the public and private sector may also be pursued, in positions ranging from legal researcher to public history curator to media consultant and beyond.

BIBLIOGRAPHY

Gunn, Giles. *Thinking Across the American Grain: Ideology, Intellect, and the New Pragmatism.* Chicago: University of Chicago Press, 1992.

Kammen, Michael. *Mystic Chords of Memory: The Transformation of Tradition in American Culture.* New York: Knopf, 1991.

Lipsitz, George. *American Studies in a Moment of Danger.* Minneapolis: University of Minnesota Press, 2001.

Maddox, Lucy, ed. *Locating American Studies: The Evolution of a Discipline.* Baltimore: Johns Hopkins University Press, 1999.

Madsen, Deborah L. *American Exceptionalism.* Jackson: University Press of Mississippi, 1998.

Prown, Jules David, and Kenneth Haltman, eds. *American Artifacts: Essays in Material Culture.* East Lansing: Michigan State University Press, 2000.

Stearns, Peter N. *Meaning Over Memory: Recasting the Teaching of Culture and History.* Chapel Hill: University of North Carolina Press, 1993.

Tate, Cecil F. *The Search for a Method in American Studies.* Minneapolis: University of Minnesota Press, 1973.

Barbara Schwarz Wachal

See also **African American Studies.**

AMERICAN SYSTEM, a term invoked by Kentucky representative Henry Clay in his 30–31 March 1824 speech to Congress as part of his argument for a higher tariff. Clay, who went on to serve in the Senate and was the Whig Party presidential candidate in 1832 and 1844, believed the tariff would stimulate national manufacturing and agriculture by insulating the domestic market from foreign products. He based this approach at least in part on the economic strategy of the British, whose continued penetration into U.S. markets and protectionist policies against U.S. exports perpetuated a major trade imbalance between the two countries throughout the 1820s. Despite widespread resistance from antiprotectionists, who feared that high tariffs would prompt other countries to tax American exports, Congress in May 1824 narrowly approved a substantial raise in the rate.

The concept of the American System subsequently came to include a broader set of policies that Clay and his supporters propounded as the best means for strengthening the country's economy and restructuring the relationship between government and society. Clay's invocation of the term echoed the earlier economic nationalism of Alexander Hamilton who, in number 11 of the *Federalist Papers* in 1787, had also referred to an American System characterized by a powerful, activist federal government that would guarantee the sovereignty and prosperity of the United States. Clay's platform reflected a similar conviction that government intervention could stimulate domestic economic development more effectively than a reliance on market forces, and that a stronger economy would in turn make the country more resilient in dealing with foreign trade competition or military threats. By harmonizing the various economic interests within the United States, he maintained, such a policy would render American agricultural and manufacturing production more efficient than those of other nations. In addition to the tariff, Clay supported a strong central bank and federal funding for internal improvements to improve commodity circulation and make American producers more competitive. In particular, he called for increased construction of roads and canals, which he felt would unify the disparate regions of the United States, facilitate the transport of goods, and improve the country's ability to defend itself against invasion or rebellion.

The American System became the most coherent expression of economic nationalism propounded in the first half of the nineteenth century, and it enhanced Clay's already extensive influence in national politics. Yet during his political career, antinationalist forces centered in the Democratic Party managed to defeat many of the policies Clay proposed. Southern plantation owners, who depended on foreign markets to absorb much of their output, objected in particular to the protectionist slant of the American System. It was not until the 1860s and the administration of Abraham Lincoln, a longtime admirer of Clay and his policies, that the federal government began to implement many of the tenets embodied in the American System. In this sense, the American System prefigured the greater willingness of post–Civil War administrations to intervene more directly in the economic development of the United States.

BIBLIOGRAPHY

Baxter, Maurice G. *Henry Clay and the American System.* Lexington: University Press of Kentucky, 1995.

Shankman, Kimberly C. *Compromise and the Constitution: The Political Thought of Henry Clay.* Lanham, Md.: Lexington Books, 1999.

Watson, Harry L. *Andrew Jackson vs. Henry Clay: Democracy and Development in Antebellum America.* Boston: Bedford/St. Martin's, 1998.

Henry Mark Wild

See also **Hamilton's Economic Policies; Tariff; Transportation and Travel.**

AMERICAN TOBACCO CASE (*United States v. American Tobacco Company*, 221 U.S. 106, 1911). Buck Duke's American Tobacco Company was created in 1890 through the consolidation of five separate entities. By 1910, with the aid of a labyrinthine corporate holding structure, American Tobacco controlled an 86 percent share of the American cigarette market, 76 percent of pipe tobacco, and 84 percent of chewing tobacco. In 1907, the Roosevelt Administration initiated antitrust proceedings. Four years later, the U.S. Supreme Court, following the same reasoning used in another antitrust case—the Standard Oil case—found (with an 8-1 margin) that American Tobacco had attempted to restrain commerce and monopolize the tobacco business in violation of the Sherman Antitrust Act.

BIBLIOGRAPHY

Bickel, Alexander M. *History of the Supreme Court of the United States: The Judiciary and Responsible Government, 1910–21.* New York: Macmillan, 1984.

R. Volney Riser

See also **Sherman Antitrust Act; Standard Oil Company; Standard Oil Company of New Jersey v. United States.**

AMERICANS WITH DISABILITIES ACT (ADA) was passed in 1990 when Congress determined that the estimated 43 million disabled persons in the United States were a "minority . . . subjected to a history of purposeful unequal treatment." The ADA prohibited private employers from disability-based discrimination if an individual could do a job's "essential functions" with or without "reasonable accommodations." The act also mandated accessibility and reasonable accommodations and prohibited disability-based discrimination in state and local government services, public transit, telecommunications, and public places (restaurants, stores, theaters, private schools, hospitals, and other entities offering the public goods and services). The ADA allowed exemptions if compliance would cause "undue hardship" because of excessive cost. Because the act imported a tripartite definition of disability from the Rehabilitation Act without also adopting the existing agency regulations that explicated that definition, the scope of ADA coverage remains unclear. Since 1998 the Supreme Court has decided an increasing number of cases under the act, many of which focus on the question of who is "disabled" under the ADA. Despite these rulings being limited to individual claimants,

the court has curbed the scope of the ADA by holding that mitigating measures used to ameliorate functional limitations (for example, medication) also mitigate eligibility for disability status under the act. At the same time, the court has not yet articulated a standard for measuring the reasonableness of an accommodation.

BIBLIOGRAPHY

Burgdorf, R. L., Jr. "The Americans with Disabilities Act: Analysis and Implications of a Second-Generation Civil Rights Statute." *Harvard Civil Rights–Civil Liberties Law Review* 26 (summer 1991): 413–522.

Paul K. Longmore
Michael Stein

See also **Disability Rights Movement.**

AMERICA'S CUP, yachting's preeminent competitive event, is a quadrennial race dating back to 1851, when the *America* defeated the *Aurora* and a fleet of other British vessels in a race around the Isle of Wight. Britain, then the world's premier naval power, was stunned by the defeat. The cup itself was donated to the New York Yacht Club, where it remained for the next 132 years, as American defenders defeated no fewer than twenty-five challenges, five of them by Irish tea tycoon Sir Thomas Lipton.

In 1983, Alan Bond's *Australia II* of the Royal Perth Yacht Club, using a revolutionary winged keel, defeated the American defender Dennis Conner in a narrow 4–3 victory. Conner regained the cup for the San Diego Yacht

America's Cup. In this time trial in Newport, R.I., the *Columbia (background)*—the successful defender of the trophy in 1958—is already starting her run for home by the time the *Weatherly (foreground)*—which would go on to win in 1962— sails across the finish line. AP/WIDE WORLD PHOTOS

Club four years later. The cup then entered a bitter phase when Michael Fay of New Zealand challenged the Americans to an unusual rematch just one year later. Conner won using a sixty-foot catamaran, a design that Fay unsuccessfully challenged in court. Bill Koch's *America3* successfully defended the cup in 1992 using the new standard boat size. In 1995, Peter Blake's Team New Zealand soundly defeated Dennis Conner's *Young America* and brought the cup to the Royal New Zealand Yacht Squadron. In 1999, for the first time in the cup's history, no American boat was present in the final, when Team New Zealand beat Italy's *Prada*. While popular mostly with the well-to-do, the America's Cup race grew into one of the major international competitions, attracting challengers from eight different countries in the 1999 competition.

BIBLIOGRAPHY

Conner, Dennis, and Michael Levitt. *The America's Cup: The History of Sailing's Greatest Competition in the Twentieth Century.* New York: St. Martin's Press, 1998.

Lester, Gary, and Richard Sleeman. *The America's Cup, 1851–1987: Sailing for Supremacy.* Sydney, Australia: Lester-Townsend, 1986.

Kathleen B. Culver
Philippe R. Girard

See also **Sailing and Yacht Racing; Sports.**

AMERICORPS. Envisioned as a renewed commitment to national service programs, AmeriCorps harked back to the New Deal's CIVILIAN CONSERVATION CORPS and the Community Action Programs of the GREAT SOCIETY. The concept of a federally sponsored, community-oriented volunteer program originated in the 1992 platform of Democratic presidential candidate William J. Clinton, and proved one of the most popular proposals of the campaign. After Clinton's election, the creation of AmeriCorps became a priority for the incoming administration.

While some critics in the philanthropic community criticized the plan to pay volunteers—warning that it would demean the true nature of volunteerism—Congress approved the formation of AmeriCorps under the National and Community Service Trust Act of 1993. The act created the Corporation for National and Community Service to oversee AmeriCorps as well as two additional agencies, Learn and Serve America and the National Senior Service Corps. Within AmeriCorps, three departments carried out distinct programs: AmeriCorps*State and National, AmeriCorps*Volunteers in Service to America (VISTA), and AmeriCorps*National Civilian Community Corps (NCCC).

Administered through grant awards to state commissions, AmeriCorps*State and National programs matched volunteers in the areas of education, public health and safety, and the environment with existing local community programs. Typical AmeriCorps volunteers worked to reduce illiteracy, build housing, improve national park facilities, and provide assistance to physically and mentally challenged individuals. In return for a minimum of 1,700 hours of annual service, volunteers received a stipend for living expenses ($7,640 in 1998), health insurance, child-care assistance, and an educational award for tuition or outstanding student loans. In order to stem criticism of the program as a government intrusion into volunteer service, participants were limited to two years in the program and the stipend and health insurance benefits were kept at minimal levels. The AmeriCorps*VISTA program, a continuation of the original VISTA program begun in 1965, focused on poverty-related initiatives such as job training and public health programs, while NCCC participants worked to promote civic pride while learning leadership values in ten-month environmental and educational programs.

Although AmeriCorps was criticized for financial mismanagement during its initial phase, a strong commitment by President Clinton kept the program from being dismantled. Under the direction of Harris Wofford, the program improved its performance and reduced its expenses, a fact that helped it win approval from the incoming Republican administration of President George W. Bush in 2000. Although his move to include faith-based organizations in AmeriCorps programs raised controversy over issues of state funding for religious groups, the president's maintenance of a $237-million budget in 2001 ensured that an estimated 50,000 volunteers would continue to serve in AmeriCorps programs.

BIBLIOGRAPHY

Bandow, Doug. "AmeriCorps the Beautiful? National Service—or Government Service?" In *Volunteerism.* Edited by Frank McGuckin. New York: H. W. Wilson, 1998.

Hebel, Sara. "Bush Proposes Funds to Maintain AmeriCorps." *Chronicle of Higher Education* 46, no. 32 (April 2001): A42.

Waldman, Steven. *The Bill: How the Adventures of Clinton's National Service Bill Reveal What Is Corrupt, Comic, Cynical—and Noble—about Washington.* New York: Viking, 1995.

Wofford, Harris, and Steven Waldman. "AmeriCorps the Beautiful? Habitat for Conservative Values." In *Volunteerism.* Edited by Frank McGuckin. New York: H. W. Wilson, 1998.

Timothy G. Borden

See also **Volunteerism.**

AMES ESPIONAGE CASE. In one of the worst security breaches in American intelligence history, Aldrich Ames (1941–), a second-generation Central Intelligence Agency (CIA) employee, systematically destroyed the CIA's ability to monitor Soviet activities by betraying more than thirty double agents in the United States and the Soviet Union between 1985 and 1994. Of these individuals, at least ten were executed. During the same period, Ames also revealed the details of approximately one hundred covert operations to his Soviet handlers. For his treachery, Ames received more than $2 million. Ames's arrest and that of his second wife, Rosario, who aided him between 1992 and 1994, severely damaged the CIA's reputation, forced the retirement or resignation of several high-ranking CIA officials, including then-director R. James Woolsey, and resulted in stricter rules for Agency personnel.

Ames's treachery was all the more remarkable because his CIA career was so undistinguished. Despite consistently poor performance, he continued to be assigned to positions where he had access to top-secret information. At the same time, Ames's supervisors tolerated his drinking problem and never questioned his increasingly lavish lifestyle.

Ames, who began spying for the Soviets while he was head of the CIA's Soviet Counterintelligence Division, did so out of greed and contempt for the CIA. He attributed his success to his own cleverness and to his ability to pass routine lie detector tests, but he also benefited from sustained Soviet deception, bureaucratic ineptitude on the part of both the CIA and the Federal Bureau of Investigation (FBI), and from his superiors' unwillingness to believe that a CIA employee could be a traitor. Eventually, the CIA and the FBI cooperated in a massive investigation involving wiretaps, round-the-clock surveillance, and a house search that resulted in the couple's arrest and conviction. Both were imprisoned, Rosario for five years, and Ames for life.

BIBLIOGRAPHY

Adams, James. *Sellout: Aldrich Ames and the Corruption of the CIA.* New York: Viking, 1995. A British journalist's assessment of the impact of the Ames case.

Volkman, Ernest. *Espionage: The Greatest Spy Operations of the Twentieth Century.* New York: John Wiley, 1995. Case studies describing major clandestine efforts of the United States, its friends, and its enemies.

Weiner, Tim, David Johnston, and Neil A. Lewis. *Betrayal: The Story of Aldrich Ames, an American Spy.* New York: Random House, 1995.

Mary Jo Binker

See also **Spies.**

AMISH. Known widely for their distinctive dress and principled rejection of modernity, the Amish provide unending fascination to outsiders. In 1900 social scientists confidently predicted the early demise of the Amish, then numbering about 5,000 members. Instead, a century later they were among the fastest-growing churches in North America, with more than 1,400 congregations in thirty-three states (and Ontario), with adult membership approaching 90,000 and a total population of nearly 200,000.

The Amish are a continuation of the Anabaptist ("rebaptizer") movement of the sixteenth century. Although basically Protestant in doctrine, Anabaptists rejected in principle the church-state linkage hallowed by Catholic tradition and accepted by Protestant reformers. Instead, Anabaptists contended for a "gathered church" of committed believers, who sealed their conviction by adult baptism.

Anabaptists were among the first to urge religious liberty, condemning the use of force in religious matters; exclusion from church fellowship was the severest penalty they exacted in their congregations, which they sought to maintain in purity and unity. They based their specific beliefs and practices on the early church and on the New Testament, which they studied assiduously. They were mission-minded, extending their gospel over much of Europe despite ferocious persecution. Except for marginal groups who were militant, Anabaptists forbade any use of violence, instead practicing nonresistance to oppression.

Much of early Anabaptist activity took place in the Swiss cantons; to escape repeated pogroms, many Anabaptists sought refuge in more tolerant areas along the Rhine River, in the German Palatinate and the Alsace. By 1600 most Anabaptists were called Mennonites, after the former Dutch priest Menno Simons (c. 1496–1561).

The Amish movement took its name from an Alsatian convert named Jakob Ammann (1656?–1730?). Concerned that Mennonites were becoming lax in church discipline, Ammann sought church renewal by tightening discipline. He banned miscreants not only from church ordinances but also from all social encounters. Several Swiss elders thought this too harsh and rejected Ammann's actions, upon which Ammann placed *them* in the ban. Those Rhenish Mennonites who followed Ammann's lead were henceforth called the Amish. This took place in 1693, marking the emergence of the Amish as a separate Anabaptist body.

Amish began to emigrate to North America in major ways after 1736, first settling in Berks and Lancaster counties, Pennsylvania. Another large wave of Amish emigration (about 3,000 persons) took place between 1817 and 1860, with primary settlement in the Midwest, leaving perhaps 2,000 members in Europe. Migration continued in the twentieth century until 1937, when the last European Amish joined with Mennonites.

In the freer confines of the United States, many Amish families converted to more liberal Mennonite groups. This trend continued until the mid-nineteenth century, when two factions developed among American Amish. The more conservative were known as the Old Order Amish, wishing to preserve the old ways. The more progressive were known as the Amish Mennonites and merged over time with Mennonite conferences.

Old Order Amish

In the popular mind the Amish seem to be a fossilized body, blindly perpetuating the mind-set and lifestyle of early ages. In fact, they practice a highly rational selectivity in accepting or rejecting modern developments, always to perpetuate their faith and further family welfare. Nevertheless, their avoidance of high-school education, telephones in homes, radios and television, electricity from power lines, self-propelled farm implements, and motor vehicles evidence willful rejection of modern ways. Their plain style of dressing, with chin beards, broad-fall trousers, "soup-bowl" hair cuts, and broad-brimmed hats for men and nonpatterned, form-concealing caped dresses (but using some bright colors) and bonnets for women, also set them apart. (Children among the Amish are dressed much like adults.) Their insistence on the use of Pennsylvania-German in their families and German in their church services and their reference to non-Amish as "English" underscore their difference from general society. It is paradoxically these differences that have made the Amish so fascinating to outsiders.

Beliefs. The distinctive Amish lifestyle is based on their belief system, which has altered little since their formative years. Its formal foundation is the Dordrecht Confession of 1632, agreed upon by Dutch Mennonites and later accepted by German Mennonites. It is congruent with traditional Protestant creeds, except for its understanding of the Lord's Supper as commemoration rather than as sacrament and its emphasis on adult baptism, nonresistance, nonconformity, and shunning in church discipline.

Church membership through baptism (ordinarily of young adults) follows a class of instruction based upon the Dordrecht Confession. Applicants, when called before the congregation, respond affirmatively to questions of faith, promise obedience to church order (men agree to serve as ministers if chosen), and receive baptism by the pouring of water upon their heads.

The controlling concept of Amish belief is the *Ordnung.* This is the traditional order, an unwritten code upon which all of Amish life and practice is based. It is the code of conduct that governs all Amish actions, transmitted by tradition rather than by explicit rules. The bishop of each district is responsible for interpreting and perpetuating the Ordnung.

Another basic concept is *Gelassenheit.* Difficult to translate concisely, it has the meaning of yielding, self-surrender, and acceptance. It mandates giving up self-will and pride; instead, the believer accepts authority, bows to the common good, and defers to the traditions of the church and the decisions of its leaders. The welfare of the many is prior to the benefit of the individual. Restrictions on clothing, jewelry, and photographs make sure that vanity will be suppressed. The ultimate expression of *Gelassenheit* is martyrdom, yielding up one's life for one's faith, a tragic reality for thousands of Anabaptists. The Mennonite book of martyrs, *The Martyrs Mirror* (originally published in 1660), is, next to the Bible, the book found most often in Amish homes.

Worship. Amish meet every other Sunday on a rotating schedule at members' homes, usually in the residence but also in workshops or barns. Benches are taken from home

WHAT DOES IT MEAN TO BE AMISH?

Some time ago a group of fifty-two people chartered a bus and came to Holmes County to see the Amish. They had arranged to have an Amishman meet them and answer some of their questions.

The first question was: "We all go to church," and they named some of these churches, "so we know about Jesus, but what does it mean to be Amish?"

The Amishman thought a bit and then he asked a question of his own. "How many of you have TV in your homes?" Fifty-two hands went up. "Now, how many of you feel that perhaps you would be better off without TV in your homes?" Again fifty-two hands went up. "All right. Now, how many of you are going to go home and get rid of your TV?" Not one hand went up!

Now that is what it means to be Amish. As a church, if we see or experience something that is not good for us spiritually, we will discipline ourselves to do without. The world in general does not know what it is to do without!

Monroe L. Beachy

SOURCE: John A. Hostetler, ed. *Amish Roots: A Treasury of History, Wisdom, and Lore.* Baltimore: Johns Hopkins University Press, 1989, pp. 272–273.

to home in a specially built wagon. Members sit separately according to age and gender. The three-hour services are interspersed with hymns taken from the *Ausbund,* a sixteenth-century text-only hymnal. The singing is in unison, very slow, and without accompaniment. The preacher adopts a chanting style of speaking, the sermon consisting largely of biblical stories and strung-together scriptures. Following the service, the host family provides food for those in attendance. Meeting in homes encourages warm fellowship and also ensures that member families follow the *Ordnung* in every respect.

Church government. Amish are organized into districts of twenty to forty families. When a district grows too large to meet in homes, a new district is organized by redrawing boundary lines. All Amish living within the limits of a district must attend its worship services.

Each district ordinarily has a bishop, two ministers, and a deacon, known as *Diener* (servants). When an official is needed, members are called together to nominate the new leader from their ranks. Those nominated then draw lots to determine the one chosen. It is understood that this procedure ensures divine guidance. Ministry is for life and without payment. Those chosen accept the lot with deep emotion and a profound sense of unworthiness.

A Slower Pace. Automobiles wait as one of the Amish crosses the road in his horse and buggy in Lancaster, Pa., 1988.
ASSOCIATED PRESS/WORLD WIDE PHOTOS

Bishops meet periodically to discuss controversial issues, with the intent of preserving church unity. Nevertheless, many differences do emerge, especially in regard to the toleration of technology. There is no fixed organization above the districts, but an Amish National Steering Committee meets as needed to represent Amish concerns before government agencies.

Economics. Traditionally all Amish were farmers, and rural life is still the ideal. However, as the price of land burgeoned in areas of Amish concentration, it became difficult to provide new farms for the typically large families. Two major strategies emerged. The first is to seek affordable land elsewhere; this has led to new Amish colonies in the South, Midwest, and New York State. The second is to turn to nonfarm vocations. Many in Lancaster County have developed small businesses, such as cabinet and furniture making; other entrepreneurs cater to tourists, for example with bakeries or quilt making. In Elkhart County, Indiana, many Amish work in factories building recreational vehicles. In Holmes County, Ohio (the largest concentration of Amish anywhere), Amish have developed more than 700 microenterprises. Some Amish companies gross more than a million dollars per year.

Amish Bodies

In 2001 there were four distinct branches among the Amish: the Old Order Amish, the New Order Amish, the Beachy Amish, and the Amish Mennonites, in order of increasing liberalness. In addition, there are smaller groupings, in particular among the Old Order Amish, especially in Holmes County, Ohio (including the Swartzentruber, Troyer, and Andy Weaver subgroups), and in Mifflin County, Pennsylvania (the Byler, Renno, and "Nebraska" subgroups).

The Old Order Amish are by far the largest Amish branch, making up nearly 90 percent of the total, having 1,237 of the 1,439 congregations in the United States.

Like the Old Order Amish, the New Order Amish use horse-drawn transportation and meet for worship in homes, whereas the Beachy Amish and Amish Mennonites use motor vehicles and have meeting houses for worship.

BIBLIOGRAPHY

Hostetler, John A. *Amish Society.* 4th ed. Baltimore: Johns Hopkins University Press, 1993.

Kraybill, Donald B. *The Riddle of Amish Culture.* Rev. ed. Baltimore: Johns Hopkins University Press, 2001.

Kraybill, Donald B., and Carl F. Bowman. *On the Backroad to Heaven.* Baltimore: Johns Hopkins University Press, 2001.

Kraybill, Donald B., and C. Nelson Hostetter. *Anabaptist World USA.* Scottdale, Pa: Herald Press, 2001. Contains statistics.

Nolt, Steven M. *A History of the Amish.* Intercourse, Pa: Good Books, 1992.

Donald F. Durnbaugh

See also **Mennonites; Pennsylvania Germans.**

AMISTAD CASE. In 1839, fifty-three Africans, being illegally transferred on the Spanish schooner *La Amistad*, took control of the ship near Havana, Cuba, murdered part of the crew, and demanded transport back to Africa. Traveling toward the rising sun by day, as the Africans requested, and north by night, as the Spaniards wanted, the schooner was captured by the U.S.S. *Washington* off Long Island Sound as it was attempting to replenish supplies. The American vessel demanded one-third salvage claims for the value of the schooner and captives. After the U.S. circuit court in Hartford, Connecticut, refused to rule on the case, the U.S. district court in New London found the Africans not guilty of piracy charges since they were rising up against their illegal captors and upheld the salvage claim against the ship. Pressed by Spain to return the slaves and the ship, John Forsyth, secretary of state under Martin Van Buren, appealed the case to the Supreme Court after the U.S. circuit court in New London upheld the district court's decision.

Awaiting retrial, the thirty-three surviving male Africans were moved to private Connecticut homes and taught about Christianity and the English language while Yale students taught the three girls. Former president John Quincy Adams, citing natural law and the Declaration of Independence, defended the thirty-six Africans. The Supreme Court ruled that they were not pirates or robbers and that they were free Africans under international law, since the slave trade had been abolished in the United States and Spain. The United States was not responsible for their transportation back to Africa, so abolitionist societies such as the American Missionary Society and others gathered private donations to send the thirty-five survivors, their translator from the case, James Covey, and five white missionaries from New York on 27 November 1841 to Freetown, Sierra Leone, to help establish a Christian mission in Africa. The *Amistad* case was the

Joseph Cinque. An 1840 portrait of the leader of the *Amistad* mutiny, by the New Haven artist Nathaniel Jocelyn. NEW YORK PUBLIC LIBRARY PICTURE COLLECTION

first civil rights trial held before the Supreme Court and the first battle and victory of the abolitionists, for whom it symbolized the refusal to accept slavery.

BIBLIOGRAPHY

Cable, Mary. *Black Odyssey: The Case of the Slave Ship Amistad.* New York: Viking, 1971.

Jones, Howard. *Mutiny on the Amistad: The Saga of a Slave Revolt and Its Impact on American Abolition, Law, and Diplomacy.* New York: Oxford University Press, 1987.

Martin, B. Edmon. *All We Want Is Make Us Free: La Amistad and the Reform Abolitionists.* Lanham, Md.: University Press of America, 1986.

Martin, Christopher. *The Amistad Affair.* New York: Abelard-Schuman, 1970.

Michelle M. Mormul

See also **Antislavery; Slave Insurrections; Slave Trade.**

AMNESTY is the pardon of individuals or categories of people for the violation of law. Article II, Section 2 of the U.S. Constitution gives the president the power to "grant reprieves and pardons for offenses against the United States." In the last quarter of the twentieth century and into the twenty-first, categorical amnesty typically involved issues surrounding the Vietnam War (1946–1975, American involvement 1964–1975) or illegal immigration. During the 1970s, amnesty became a significant subject of debate, as the Vietnam War began to wind down and the domestic problems associated with that conflict required immediate attention. How would the United States deal with perhaps as many as fifty thousand military deserters and draft evaders? Actions taken after earlier wars set numerous precedents. In 1795, George Washington pardoned two participants in the Whiskey Rebellion. Abraham Lincoln and Andrew Johnson issued more than 200,000 such pardons in order to "bind up our nation's wounds" after the Civil War (1861–1865). More recently, Presidents Franklin D. Roosevelt and Harry Truman pardoned several thousand draft evaders from World War II (1939–1945). But at a time when political passions deeply divided the nation, would history offer helpful instruction for those involved in the heated political disputes of the present?

While participation in the Vietnam War continued, presidents refused to consider amnesty, but as soon as American soldiers were out of harm's way after 28 March 1973, the issue became less of a political hot potato. Thus, as the 1972 election approached, Democratic party nominee George McGovern was portrayed as the counterculture candidate who favored "amnesty, abortion and acid." But after Richard Nixon's resignation and Gerald Ford's pardon of the former president in September 1974, it became easier to broach the amnesty question. Still, when Ford offered conditional amnesty to military deserters and draft evaders, many combat veterans sent him their Vietnam medals in protest. Ford's program required unconvicted military deserters and draft evaders to turn themselves in to the government, reaffirm their allegiance to the United States, and then perform service jobs for two years. Those convicted of crimes associated with desertion and evasion would have their cases reviewed by a presidential clemency board. Jimmy Carter, in one of his first acts as president, granted a "full, complete, and unconditional pardon" to draft dodgers and deserters on 21 January 1977, thereby drawing to a close the legal, if not the political, antagonisms of the Vietnam War. A generation later, however, the issue of Vietnam service generated much less passion, as evidenced by Bill Clinton's election, even though he had legally (but perhaps irregularly) dodged military service during the Vietnam War, and by George W. Bush's election, even though he avoided Vietnam service by joining the Texas Air National Guard.

BIBLIOGRAPHY

Baskir, Lawrence M. and William A. Strauss. *Reconciliation After Vietnam: A Program of Relief for Vietnam Era Draft and Military Offenders.* Notre Dame, Ind.: University of Notre Dame Press, 1977.

Polner, Murray, ed. *When Can I Come Home? A Debate on Amnesty for Exiles, Antiwar Prisoners, and Others.* New York: Anchor Books, 1972.

Schardt, Arlie, William A. Rusher, and Mark O. Hatfield. *Amnesty? The Unsettled Question of Vietnam.* Croton-on-Hudson, N.Y.: Sun River Press, 1973.

Thomas Reins

AMTRAK.

On 1 May 1971, the U.S. government made Amtrak responsible for managing and operating all national passenger train service in the United States. Its name was derived from the words "America" and "track." Amtrak was created as a quasi-public corporation—a unique blend of government funding and oversight with private management and accountability.

By the late 1960s, a precipitous fifty-year decline in the quantity, quality, and profitability of American passenger rail service prompted high-level government debate over the need for some measure of public assistance. Between 1929 and 1966, passenger train routes—measured in miles—declined by nearly two-thirds. Technological improvements in the automobile, increased government funding for highway construction, and the growth of the commercial airline industry all contributed to the decline. Poor track conditions, outdated equipment, and unreliable service made train travel far less desirable than these other forms of transport. By 1967, the industry's first year without U.S. mail service business, the annual loss for the combined passenger train industry was $460 million. After that year, many companies considered terminating their passenger routes.

After two years of negotiations aimed at averting the loss of the entire passenger rail system, President Richard Nixon signed the Railpax bill on 30 October 1970. By April 1971, the entity's name was changed to Amtrak, and twenty of the twenty-six eligible private rail companies had signed the contract to join the new corporation. Despite Amtrak's efforts to consolidate passenger routes into a more manageable, efficient structure, the initial mandate from the Department of Transportation required the continuation of many marginal routes. It would be eight years until the corporation was given more flexibility in the design of its route structure. There were other obstacles as well. The initial federal grant of $40 million was less than 10 percent of the annual losses sustained by the private companies in their last pre-Amtrak years and not nearly enough to begin a process of rebuilding the industry. The new corporation was also required to operate under the existing labor contracts of the member companies, and management had little flexibility in reallocating workers in the new operational structure. Amtrak was also faced with the nearly impossible task of reversing the long-term public ambivalence to train travel while being able to provide only old, uncomfortable, and unreliable equipment.

While total passenger volume increased from 17 million in 1972 to 23 million by 2002, there had been no net increase in ridership since 1988. Yet during this stagnant decade of Amtrak passenger growth, commuter train pas-

Amtrak. The engine of a Turboliner passenger train, leased from the French in 1973 as part of an equipment upgrade in the nationwide rail system, undergoes a final check before departure from St. Louis, Mo., to Chicago. LIBRARY OF CONGRESS

senger volume jumped from 15.4 million to 58.2 million. This disparity indicated that Americans valued rail travel as a means to move to and from their occupations, or to move from suburb and countryside to large cities for shopping or entertainment, but as a means of transporting people from city to city, Amtrak faced stronger competition from the automobile and the airplane than it did in 1971.

Amtrak's most successful sector was the Northeast Corridor, the stretch of rails to and from Washington, New York, and Boston, and accounted for two-thirds of Amtrak's ridership and revenues. Ridership in the corridor went up after the introduction in 2001 of the Acela Express trains, which could achieve a top speed of 150 miles per hour, and after the terrorist attacks in New York and Washington on 11 September 2001. But the 1997 Amtrak Reform and Accountability Act set 2 December 2002 as an absolute deadline for Amtrak to reach operational self-sufficiency and the loss of federal support, and by the summer of that year, the Amtrak Reform Council was considering breaking off the Northeast Corridor as an independent entity and taking bids from private companies to finance long-distance trains elsewhere in the system.

BIBLIOGRAPHY

Bradley, Roger. *Amtrak.* Poole, U.K.: Blandford Press, 1985.

Edmondson, Harold A., ed. *Journey to Amtrak: The Year History Rode the Passenger Train.* Milwaukee, Wis.: Kalmbach, 1972.

Nice, David C. *Amtrak: The History and Politics of a National Railroad.* Boulder, Colo.: Lynne Rienner, 1998.

Wilner, Frank. *The Amtrak Story.* Omaha, Neb.: Simmons-Boardman, 1999.

Zimmerman, Karl. *Amtrak at Milepost 10.* Park Forest, Ill.: PTJ, 1981.

Patrick Amato

See also **Railroads; Railways, Interurban.**

AMUSEMENT PARKS.   Rooted in the European traditions of trade fairs (Bartholomew Fair, 1133–1855) and pleasure gardens (Vauxhall, 1661–1859), the modern American amusement park developed in the late nineteenth century. Young men and women were flocking to cities from rural America and eastern and southern Europe. Liberated from the discipline of community and family, they took control over their leisure. Moreover, workers enjoyed more free time and more discretionary income as labor unions won concessions on hours and wages. At the same time, engineers and entrepreneurs were learning to build better carousels, Ferris wheels, and roller coasters. The recreational needs of a new society intersected with the maturation of amusement technology, and parks took off.

Although not a park, the World's Columbian Exposition (Chicago, 1893)—which celebrated Columbus's journey to America specifically and Western progress in general—perfected the amusement formula that, more or less, still applies. First, it projected a coherent and controlled fantasy. The Court of Honor, a group of imposing neoclassical structures surrounding a giant basin and a hundred-foot gilt statue, transported visitors to a glistening, if illusory, ancient Greece, walled off from the hustle and bustle of the real city outside. Second, it marketed the exotic. The exposition's midway featured anthropologically inspired reproductions of foreign villages, freak shows, belly dancers, South Pacific islanders, and African

Coney Island. A long chute that plunges customers into an oval pool; one of the many rides at the world-famous resort in Brooklyn, 1900. © CORBIS-BETTMANN

Dahomey men in short grass skirts. Third, it was thrilling. The towering FERRIS WHEEL was the most popular attraction on the midway.

Coney Island, a beach resort in Brooklyn, New York, was home to the most famous amusement parks of the early twentieth century. Sea Lion Park (1895) was the first enclosed amusement park in the United States, but Steeplechase Park (1897) was the first truly popular one. Steeplechase Park catered to single men and women, offering such daring attractions as the "Barrel of Love," a revolving wheel that tended to make men and women collide; "blowholes" that lifted women's skirts; and "the Steeplechase," a horse-racing ride that accommodated two riders per animal. Luna Park (1903) relied on extravagance, not sexuality. The park created a permanent carnival atmosphere with pinwheels, hundreds of thousands of lights, and elaborate spires and turrets. Inspired by the Columbian Exposition, Luna Park had an Eskimo village and a Japanese garden. Its "Trip to the Moon" was a fantasy outer space populated with beautiful women, giants, and midgets, and its disaster shows recreated the Johnstown flood and the eruption of Mount Vesuvius.

Although Coney Island had some of the most creative amusement parks, by the turn of the century there were versions of Steeplechase or Luna Park in almost every city. Trolley companies built most of them to encourage more riders at night and on weekends, when business tended to be slow. A beach, a picnic area, and a few rides at the end of the trolley line attracted tens of thousands of passengers on a Sunday. Cleveland's Euclid Beach, Pittsburgh's Kennywood Park, and San Francisco's Chutes all started as trolley parks. By 1920, there were about two thousand amusement parks in the United States.

The "scream machine," a faster, scarier roller coaster, arrived in 1924, with the famous Bobs at Chicago's Riverview Park. Coney Island's Cyclone was built in 1927. But amusement parks were already beginning to decline. Cars gave people the option of spending leisure time wherever they wanted, not only where the trolley would take them. The Great Depression hurt parks badly, and when families started moving to the suburbs after World War II, city parks lost their clientele. By 1948, fewer than four hundred parks remained open, and almost none of the old urban parks would survive into the 1970s. Notable exceptions are Kennywood and Sandusky's Cedar Point.

Although suburbanization partly accounted for the failure of city parks, it also gave rise to a new kind of amusement park: the theme park. Walt Disney provided the model with Disneyland, which opened in Anaheim, outside of Los Angeles, in 1955. Built with corporate sponsorship money from firms including Pepsi, Monsanto, and ABC, Disneyland took the control and fantasy formula to new heights. The park was spotless. It was surrounded by a high wall with only one entrance. Its huge, friendly staff received training at "Disneyland University." Such measures, it was thought, enhanced the experience of Disneyland's five thematic areas: Adventureland, Fantasyland, Frontierland, Main Street U.S.A., and Tomorrowland. The suburban theme park was an instant success. During its first ten years, 50 million people visited Disneyland.

Walt Disney World opened in Orlando, Florida, in 1971 with the Disneyland-inspired Magic Kingdom, two resorts, and a resort community. Since then, the Disney empire has grown, with Tokyo Disneyland (1983) and Disneyland Paris (1992), and with the Disney World additions of EPCOT Center (1982), Disney-MGM Studios (1989), and Disney's Animal Kingdom Park (1998). EPCOT (Experimental Prototype Community of Tomorrow) was conceived as an experiment in fusing education and entertainment and bears a striking resemblance to the Columbian Exposition. It praises American business and technology and envisions continued progress and features stylized representations of foreign villages. Disney World and Disneyland are the two most visited theme parks in America.

In the wake of Disneyland's success, several corporate-owned theme parks gradually came into being, including Six Flags, Busch Gardens, Carowinds, Cypress Gardens, and Kings Dominion. Unlike Disney, however, these parks tend to focus on thrill rides in addition to the creation of fantasy. But even though each park is different and each one bigger and more elaborate, the general idea of what makes an amusement park remained basically unchanged throughout the twentieth century.

BIBLIOGRAPHY

Adams, Judith A. *The American Amusement Park Industry: A History of Technology and Thrills.* Boston: Twayne, 1991.

Fjellman, Stephen M. *Vinyl Leaves: Walt Disney World and America.* Boulder, Colo.: Westview Press, 1992.

Kasson, John F. *Amusing the Million: Coney Island at the Turn of the Century.* New York: Hill and Wang, 1978.

Peiss, Kathy Lee. *Cheap Amusements: Working Women and Leisure in Turn-of-the-Century New York.* Philadelphia: Temple University Press, 1986.

Jeremy Derfner

See also **Disney Corporation.**

ANABAPTISTS. *See* **Baptist Churches.**

ANACONDA COPPER was one of the largest copper-mining companies in the world and the principal producer of the Butte district of Montana. It was organized in 1881 as the Anaconda Silver Mining Company when entrepreneur Marcus Daly, having persuaded James B. Haggin, Lloyd Tevis, and George Hearst to purchase for $30,000 the small Anaconda silver mine, then only sixty feet deep. The ore contained just enough copper to facilitate the recovery of the silver for which it was being worked, but at greater depth, it became evident that the

mine's principal content was copper. A copper smelter was erected in 1884, and three thousand tons of ore were being treated daily by 1889. By 1887 the Montana mines became the leading copper-producing region in the nation, ahead of Michigan and Arizona. Continuing to expand through the purchase of other mines, the company was reorganized as the Anaconda Mining Company in 1891, with a capital of $25,000,000. The Hearst interests were sold to the Exploration Company, London, and the company was reorganized in 1895 as the Anaconda Copper Mining Company.

BIBLIOGRAPHY

Hyde, Charles K. *Copper for America: The United States Copper Industry from Colonial Times to the 1990s.* Tucson: University of Arizona Press, 1998.

Joralemon, Ira B. *Romantic Copper, Its Lure and Lore.* New York: D. Appleton-Century, 1935.

Murphy, Mary. *Mining Cultures: Men, Women, and Leisure in Butte, 1914–41.* Urbana: University of Illinois Press, 1997.

T. T. Read/ H. S.

See also **Copper Industry; Montana.**

ANARCHISTS. It is fitting that the word "anarchism" derives from *anarkhia,* the Greek word for "nonrule," for that is what anarchists essentially espouse: the eradication of government in favor of a natural social order. A libertarian variant of socialism, the ideals of anarchy date back at least as far as the eighteenth century. Elements of anarchic thought were evident in the seeds of the American Revolution and Thomas Jefferson's writings often hinted at anarchist thinking.

Nineteenth-Century Anarchism

During the nineteenth century, anarchism gained a wider following and branched out in two distinct directions: one pacifist and philosophical, the other violent and radical. Along the way, it helped inspired such diverse social changes as the Russian Revolution, unionization, and passive resistance techniques.

The modern stems of anarchy sprouted from philosopher Pierre-Joseph Proudhon's vision of a peaceful, anarchistic society of self-governing individuals, achieved through the erosion of artificial authoritarian government. His 1840 book, *What is Property?*, set the stage for international debate about the ownership of fruits of labor.

The term "anarchist" surfaced in Geneva at the initial congress of the First International (the International Workingmen's Association) in 1866 to describe the increasingly militant wing of the new Socialist Party emerging throughout western and central Europe. In 1872, following the sixth congress of the International, held at The Hague, the party leadership (including Karl Marx and Frederick Engels) ejected Russian revolutionary Michael Bakunin, who advocated the violent overthrow of capitalism in particular, and governments in general. The First International splintered as Bakunin and other extremists formed the aggressive far-left wing of a party devoted to anarchistic communism. As proponents of the "propaganda of action" (assassination as a tool of anarchy), Bakunin's followers blazed a bloody trail across Europe, slaying Russia's Tsar Alexander II, Italy's King Humberto, France's President Sadi Carnot, and Austria's Empress Elizabeth.

It was inevitable that violent anarchism would cross the Atlantic to the United States. For a nation still suffering from the aftermath of the Civil War, as well as the pains and progress of the Industrial Revolution and the overheated melting pot of mass immigration, the anarchists' ideas of self-governance were attractive to many disenfranchised Americans and newly arrived immigrants.

And so on 6 September 1901, Leon Czolgosz mortally wounded President William McKinley at the Pan-American Exposition in Buffalo, New York. After the shooting Czolgosz, a German-Pole who had resettled in Cleveland, Ohio, proudly confessed his crime and proclaimed himself a follower of Emma Goldman, the so-called mother of American anarchism. In 1902, the United States banned any immigrants identified as anarchists.

Emma Goldman, the Haymarket Riot, and Sacco and Vanzetti

A Russian-born émigré who arrived in the United States in 1885 at the age of seventeen, Goldman earned a following with her impassioned demands for women's rights (including access to birth control), better labor conditions, and the rights of the poor. She was jailed for a year after advocating that starving men steal bread to survive. She may also have assisted another Russian-born anarchist leader, Alexander Berkman, in the attempted assassination of industrialist Henry Clay Frick during the Homestead Strike in Pennsylvania during 1892. Goldman was also active in the early formation of labor unions and pro-union organizations, and supported the creation in 1905 of the radical Industrial Workers of the World (IWW), a leading force in the anarcho-syndicalist movement, also known as anarchist unionism.

But her greatest impact was probably as editor of the anarchist journal *Mother Earth* from 1906 to 1917. Government agents raided the journal's offices in 1917 and legend has it that a young J. Edgar Hoover poured over the confiscated materials to study the leftists he would battle throughout his career.

Goldman's revolutionary spirit was first sparked by the execution of four anarchists suspected in the bombing deaths of seven policemen during the infamous Haymarket Riot in Chicago on 4 May 1886. The riot and trial became a rallying point for nineteenth-century radicals and gave birth to the socialist holiday of May Day. When she died in 1940, Goldman's body was returned to the United States (she had been deported to Russia along with Berkman in 1919 for supporting draft evasion) and buried

Emma Goldman. The prominent anarchist, agitator, and editor of *Mother Earth*, who spent her last two decades in the Soviet Union after being deported. LIBRARY OF CONGRESS

near the gravesites of the executed Haymarket rioters. In 1920, the trial and execution of Nicola Sacco and Bartolomeo Vanzetti (a pair of anarchists accused of killing two men during a shoe company robbery in 1920) gained similar status as a watershed event among twentieth-century radicals.

Nonviolent Anarchism

While violent anarchism has seized most of the headlines over the years, a nonviolent wing of the anarchist movement, descending from Proudhon's ideals, also took root in America. Called individual anarchists, or radical pacifists, these believers in the peaceful overthrow of government had as one of their primary leaders Benjamin R. Tucker, the publisher of the individual anarchist journal *Liberty* from 1881 to 1908. Tucker's advocacy of passive resistance and other peaceful means of anti-establishment protest presaged the nonviolent twentieth-century freedom movements led by Mahatma Gandhi in India and the Reverend Dr. Martin Luther King Jr. in the United States.

ANCESTRAL PUEBLO (ANASAZI)

At the turn of the twentieth century, the softer, more philosophical side of anarchy is represented by thinkers and writers such as Noam Chomsky. He has helped redefine anarchy for a new era, moving away from revolutionary agitation and toward a more moderate, evolutionary socialism.

Vietnam and Afterward: Violence on the Left and Right

While the early twentieth century saw the greatest anarchist activity in American history, the Vietnam War era gave rise to a new generation of radicals. One of the most prominent antiwar organizations, Students for a Democratic Society (SDS), spun off a group of violent anarchists known as the Weathermen. Also called the Weather Underground, the group, led by Columbia University student Mark Rudd, was involved in at least five hundred bombings, as well as a four-day Days of Rage riot in Chicago in 1969. In the 1970s, the Weathermen organization essentially dissolved after several of its leaders were killed in a Greenwich Village explosion in 1970. But remnant members continued to wreak havoc throughout the decade.

The 1980s and 1990s saw an ideological shift among groups using anarchistic tactics, as right-wing extremist groups became the most active and violent antigovernment organizations in the nation. While true anarchism stems from leftist, socialist philosophy—ideals anathema to the far right—at least on the surface, both ends of the ideological spectrum have similarly anarchistic goals of individual self-rule obtained through the eradication of the government.

Individual survivalists and conspiracy theorists, drawn together by charismatic leaders and a shared hatred of the federal government, have often formed these right-wing organizations. They are frequently affiliated with hate groups such as the Ku Klux Klan or neo-Nazi organizations or with isolationist cults resistant to government intervention. Watershed events for these groups have included the deadly standoff between government agents and Randy Weaver's family in Ruby Ridge, Idaho, in 1992, and the FBI siege that ended in the destruction of the Branch Davidian compound (and the deaths of those inside) in Waco, Texas, in 1993. Both events fueled and reinforced the passion and fury of right-wing extremists.

The late twentieth century also witnessed several acts of violence by single perpetrators that some have called anarchic. But whether Timothy McVeigh's truck bombing of the Alfred P. Murrah Federal Office Building in Oklahoma City, Oklahoma, on 19 April 1995 (which took the lives of 168 people), or Ted Kaczynski's eighteen-year reign of mail-bomb terror as the Unabomber, were acts of violent anarchists or twisted madmen remains debatable. Both men were by driven to murder by their hatred of the establishment; but unlike most anarchists, neither was deeply involved in a political organization that supported their efforts.

BIBLIOGRAPHY

Arnold, Matthew. *Culture and Anarchy.* Edited by Samuel Lipman. New Haven, Conn.: Yale University Press, 1994. First published in 1869.

Avrich, Paul. *Sacco and Vanzetti.* Princeton, N.J.: Princeton University Press, 1991.

———. *Anarchist Voices: An Oral History of Anarchism in America.* Princeton, N.J.: Princeton University Press, 1996.

Chomsky, Noam. *Powers and Prospects: Reflections on Human Nature and the Social Order.* Boston: South End Press, 1996.

DeLeon, David, ed. *Leaders from the 1960s: A Biographical Sourcebook of American Activism.* Westport, Conn.: Greenwood, 1994.

Goldman, Emma. *Anarchism and Other Essays.* Mineola, N.Y.: Dover, 1977. First published in 1917.

———. *Anarchy! An Anthology of Emma Goldman's Mother Earth.* Washington, D.C.: Counterpoint, 2001.

Nozick, Robert. *Anarchy, State, and Utopia.* New York, N.Y.: Basic Books, 1974.

Proudhon, Pierre-Joseph. *What is Property?* Cambridge, U.K.: Cambridge University Press, 1994. First published in 1840.

Reichert, William O. *Partisans of Freedom: A Study in American Anarchism.* Bowling Green, Ohio: Bowling Green University Popular Press, 1996.

Zinn, Howard et. al., eds. *Talking about Revolution: Interviews with Michael Albert, Noam Chomsky, Barbara Ehrenreich, Bell Hooks, Peter Kwong, Winona Laduke, Manning Marable.* Cambridge, Mass.: South End Press, 1998.

Laura A. Bergheim

See also **Assassinations, Presidential; Assassinations and Political Violence, Other; Haymarket Riot; Homestead Strike; Industrial Workers of the World; Oklahoma City Bombing; Pacifism; Ruby Ridge; Sacco-Vanzetti Case; Students for a Democratic Society; Trade Unions; Unabomber; Waco Siege;** *and vol. 9:* **Bartolomeo Vanzetti's Last Statement.**

ANCESTRAL PUEBLO (ANASAZI).

The Colorado Plateau in southern Utah and Colorado and northern Arizona and New Mexico was home to prehistoric peoples termed "Anasazi" by early archaeologists. Today, the descendants of the "Anasazi" prefer the term "Ancestral Pueblo." These prehistoric farmers are well known for impressive masonry apartment houses or "pueblos," such as the great houses of Chaco Canyon, and for cliff dwellings, such as those found at Mesa Verde.

The Pecos classification, a basic chronological framework devised by archeologists, divides Ancestral Puebloan prehistory into the periods Basketmaker II (100 B.C.–A.D. 500), Basketmaker III (500–700), Pueblo I (700–900), Pueblo II (900–1100), Pueblo III (1100–1300), and Pueblo IV (1300–1500). During the Basketmaker II period, hunters and gatherers began to construct shallow pit house dwellings and to experiment with horticulture. Basketmaker III people lived in semisubterranean round or rectangular pit structures. Villages contained slab-lined

Ancestral Pueblo (Anasazi) Home. A cliff dwelling of the prehistoric Indians who inhabited what is now the southwestern United States. Photograph by Robert J. Huffman. FIELD MARK PUBLICATIONS

storage cists, two to forty domestic pit structures, and occasionally a much larger "great pit structure" used for community gatherings. By this period, Ancestral Puebloans were growing maize, beans, and squash and making grayware pottery. These activities continued throughout the Puebloan sequence. Other items of Basketmaker III material culture included elaborate basketry, reed and twig sandals, rabbit-fur robes, *manos* and *metates* (grinding stones) used to process corn, and the bow and arrow. Petroglyphs, or rock art, commonly depict maize, bighorn sheep, deer, birds, and anthropomorphic figures.

In most areas of the Colorado Plateau, the transition to aboveground dwellings occurred during the Pueblo I period. Ancestral Puebloans built early pueblos—arcs of connected jacal (mud and pole) surface rooms—and oriented them toward the south or southeast. Circular pit structures were built in front of the pueblos but were used as ceremonial meeting rooms, or "kivas." Cotton was grown in some areas. The Pueblo II and early Pueblo III periods were characterized by construction of masonry pueblos, agricultural intensification, escalating site density, and production of black-on-white and corrugated grayware ceramics. In Chaco Canyon and the surrounding area of northwest New Mexico, multistoried great houses were built in the midst of communities of smaller pueblo sites. These great houses were symmetrical structures built in a distinctive core-and-veneer masonry style and were often associated with masonry-lined great kivas. Pueblo Bonito, one of the largest, contained as many as eight hundred rooms and was four stories high. Irrigation agriculture was practiced in Chaco Canyon and some surrounding areas. Chaco Canyon was probably a center for periodic ritual gatherings attended by Ancestral Puebloans from a wide area. Prestige items found cached in Chaco Canyon include turquoise, shell beads, macaws, and wooden staffs. Cleared linear alignments extend from Chaco Canyon to the north and south. Rock art and building orientations indicate a concern with astronomical events.

During the Late Pueblo III period, Chaco Canyon was abandoned, and large, aggregated communities appeared in the Four Corners area. Some pueblos, such as Cliff Palace at Mesa Verde, were built in the shelter of sandstone overhangs. Cliff dwellings also were built across the Kayenta region of northwest Arizona and southeast Utah at this time. Evidence for violence at some Ancestral Puebloan sites in the Four Corners region suggests that cliff dwellings provided protection against real or imagined threats. Social instability was exacerbated by a great drought between A.D. 1275–1299.

By 1300, the Four Corners area was abandoned. Ancestral Puebloans moved to the Rio Grande Valley, the Zuni region, the Little Colorado River valley, and the Hopi Mesas, where they aggregated into large, plaza-oriented pueblos sometimes containing thousands of rooms. The katsina (or katchina) cult—an elaborate religious system including masked representations of deities—was adopted. Ceremonial cycles involved ritual performances in plazas and kivas. Glazeware and yellowware pottery were made. This Puebloan culture was encountered by the Spanish upon their arrival on the Colorado Plateau in 1540.

BIBLIOGRAPHY

Cassells, E. Steve. *The Archaeology of Colorado.* Boulder, Colo.: Johnson, 1983.

Plog, Stephen. *Ancient Peoples of the American Southwest.* London: Thames and Hudson, 1997.

Stuart, David E. *Anasazi America: Seventeen Centuries on the Road from Center Place.* Albuquerque: University of New Mexico Press, 2000.

Ruth M. Van Dyke

See also **Agriculture, American Indian; Architecture, American Indian; Indian Religious Life; Pueblo; Tribes: Southwestern.**

ANDERSONVILLE PRISON, established in February 1864 in Andersonville, Georgia, became a symbol of Southern brutality toward Northern prisoners of war. The breakdown of a military prisoner exchange system in the summer of 1863 resulted in an excess of war captives. A Confederate policy ordering the execution or reenslavement of black soldiers and arbitrary violations of the exchange agreement led to this collapse. Built to accommodate excess prisoners from Belle Isle in Virginia, Andersonville was intended to hold ten thousand prisoners on sixteen acres, but little preparation went into its establishment. The prison lacked barracks. It was a field surrounded by a log stockade and intersected by a stream, which served the prison both as a sanitation system and water supply. The dwindling economic state of the Confederacy, an ineffective railroad system, and military necessity prevented prison officials from supplying the captives with shelter, cooked food, clothing, medical care, or basic means of sanitation. The prison diet was inadequate, and captives were typically malnourished. Lack of nutrition and poor sanitary conditions led to the rapid spread of respiratory diseases, scurvy, and diarrhea.

As captives from the eastern and western theaters swelled the prison, it was expanded to twenty-six acres. By August 1864, 33,000 Union prisoners packed the camp, and more than a hundred prisoners died each day at Andersonville that summer. The advance of William T. Sherman's Union army in September 1864 forced the evacuation of Andersonville. Of the 45,000 men imprisoned in Andersonville, 13,000 died from disease, exposure, or malnutrition.

The Northern public regarded Andersonville as a Southern plot to murder prisoners of war. As such, the prison's commandant, Henry Wirz, was tried by a Northern war commission in August 1865. Sentenced to death and executed in November 1865, Wirz was the only Civil War participant tried for war crimes. Subsequent investigations and recent scholarship have cast doubt upon Wirz's guilt as a war criminal, but he provided the North with a scapegoat for the crimes of the South.

By the early 2000s, few historians viewed the South as deliberately mistreating prisoners of war. Instead, a lack of resources and the disintegration of the Confederate economy were the chief causes for the suffering of Northern prisoners. Unable to feed its own soldiers and citizens, the South certainly could not feed prisoners of war. The lack of an industrial base prohibited the South from producing barracks or even tents for shelter for prisoners. Poor planning and inefficient prison management also contributed to the mistreatment of Northern prisoners.

BIBLIOGRAPHY

McPherson, James M. *Battle Cry of Freedom: The Civil War Era.* New York: Oxford University Press, 1988.

W. Scott Thomason

See also **Prison Camps, Confederate; Prison Camps, Union;** *and vol. 9:* **Prisoner at Andersonville.**

ANESTHESIA, DISCOVERY OF. The discovery of surgical anesthesia in the early 1840s represented a unique American contribution to medicine. Between 1842 and 1846 four well-known attempts at applying surgical anesthesia were made, with varying success. The fourth attempt, in October 1846, sent news of anesthesia's discovery around the world. It was also, however, followed by an unseemly struggle between three of the men involved in the experimentation over credit for the discovery. William E. Clarke was a medical student at the Berkshire Medical College in Massachusetts. In January 1842 he returned to his hometown of Rochester, New York, during a break in the lecture schedule. Clarke discovered that the sister of one of his classmates, a Miss Hobbie, needed a tooth extracted. Using a towel, Clarke applied ether and the tooth was painlessly removed. However, Professor E. M. Moore, Clarke's preceptor, told him that the entire incident could be explained as the hysterical reaction of women to pain. At Moore's suggestion, Clarke discontinued his experimentation.

In March 1842 Crawford Long gave ether to James Venable for the removal of several sebaceous cysts in Venable's neck. Long continued to work with ether but as a country physician in rural Georgia he had few surgical opportunities. Also, being aware of claims that operations could be undertaken painlessly through the application of mesmerism, Long wanted to be sure that it was the ether that caused insensibility. As a result, Long did not publish his observations until 1849.

In December 1844 a traveling nitrous oxide show arrived in Hartford, Connecticut. Horace Wells, a dentist, observed one of his fellow citizens lacerate his leg while under the influence of the nitrous oxide gas. The wound did not cause pain. Wells concluded that nitrous oxide might have the capacity to abolish surgical discomfort. The following day, he had one of his own molars painlessly removed with the use of nitrous oxide. He continued to experiment with nitrous oxide and attempted a public demonstration of surgical anesthesia at the Massachusetts General Hospital. However, the patient moved and cried out (although later claiming he did not feel pain). Wells was publicly ridiculed as a failure.

A year and a half later another agent, sulfuric ether, was introduced as a possible anesthetic agent. William Thomas Green Morton, a dentist and medical student, was searching for a method of painless dentistry for his patients. At the suggestion of his chemistry professor, Charles Jackson, Morton began to experiment with ether. As with nitrous oxide, those seeking an experience of intoxication—especially medical students—had used ether for years. Morton anesthetized a dog and several other animals, and then did the same to his partner for removal of a molar. Having gained confidence from these experiments, Morton approached John Collins Warren, Harvard's professor of surgery, for the chance to anesthetize publicly a patient for an operation. Warren agreed.

On 16 October 1846, Morton's great opportunity came. He arrived fifteen minutes late, and Warren almost began the surgery without him. Through a glass inhaler, Morton administered what he called letheon to Gilbert Abbott for the removal of a jaw tumor. The patient was quiet during the operation, and upon awakening could not remember the procedure. Warren, the surgeon, exclaimed, "Gentlemen, this is no humbug."

Remarkably, the news of this event spread around the world in a matter of weeks. In late December 1846 anesthetics were being given in London, and by January 1847 in Paris and other European capitals. By June the news had reached Australia. Yet since Morton was seeking a patent for letheon, weeks would pass before it could be used routinely. While trying to hide the chemical nature of letheon, Morton was persuaded by early November to allow the Massachusetts General free and unrestricted use of the agent.

Morton, Wells, and Jackson fought over who should receive the credit for inventing ether. Several applications were made for compensation from the government, mostly as recompense for lost revenue as a result of patent infringement. The Academie des Sciences in Paris in 1848 awarded Wells the credit, much to the disgust of Jackson and Morton. During the long political battle, Jackson used Crawford Long's work to discredit Morton's claim. Eventually, the U.S. House of Representatives passed a bill granting Morton credit and money for the invention of anesthesia, but the Senate did not adopt it. Wells committed suicide in 1848, Morton died of a cerebral hemorrhage in 1868, and Jackson died in an insane asylum in 1880. Crawford Long died of a massive stroke in 1878 after delivering a baby, the only person linked to the ether controversy not to be beset by personal ruin.

BIBLIOGRAPHY

Bolton, Thomas B., and David J. Wilkinson. "The Origins of Modern Anesthesia." In *A Practice of Anaesthesia*. Edited by T. E. J. Healy and P. J. Cohen. London: Edward Arnold, 1995.

Fenster, Julie M. *Ether Day: The Strange Tale of America's Greatest Medical Discovery and the Haunted Men Who Made It*. New York: HarperCollins, 2001.

Nuland, Sherwin B. *Doctors: The Biography Medicine*. New York: Knopf, 1988.

Stetson, John B. "William E. Clarke and His 1842 Use of Ether." In *The History of Anesthesia: Third International Symposium Proceedings*. Edited by B. Raymond Fink. Park Ridge, Ill.: Wood-Library-Museum of Anesthesiology, 1992.

Toski, Judith A., Douglas R. Bacon, and Roderick K. Calverley. "The History of Anesthesiology." In *Clinical Anesthesia*. Edited by Paul G. Barash, Bruce F. Cullen, and Robert K. Stoelting. 4th ed. Philadelphia: Lippincott Williams and Wilkins, 2001.

Vandam, Leroy D. "The Introduction of Modern Anesthesia in the USA and the Spread of the Good News to the United Kingdom." In *The History of Anesthesia*. Edited by R. S. At-kinson and T. B. Boulton. Casterton Hall, U.K.: Parthenon, 1989.

Wilson, Gwen. *One Grand Chain: The History of Anaesthesia in Australia*. Melbourne, Australia: The Australian and New Zealand College of Anaesthetists, 1996.

Douglas Bacon

See also **Medicine and Surgery.**

ANGLO-AMERICAN RELATIONS. *See* **Great Britain, Relations with.**

ANIMAL PROTECTIVE SOCIETIES. Animal protective societies date from the late 1860s, when the first three were formed in New York City, Philadelphia, and Massachusetts. Most were organized by special charter at the state level and strengthened by contemporaneous legislation granting enforcement powers. These societies for the prevention of cruelty to animals (SPCAs) sought to prevent abuse in public conveyances, their transportation and slaughter for food, municipal animal control, military service, entertainment, hunting, shooting, trapping, and research and education. Animal protection groups enjoyed close ties with temperance and child rescue, as those working in all of these areas were concerned about the consequences of violence. The humane society, a variant on the SPCA model, incorporated children and senior citizens within the scope of its work in communities where government services were limited and philanthropy could not support separate organizations.

Eventually, animal rescue groups, workhorse associations, antivivisection and vivisection reform societies, sanctuaries and rest havens, and single-issue organizations augmented the field. By the early twentieth century, there were several hundred animal protection entities operating throughout North America. Despite the incorporation of a national umbrella organization, the American Humane Association, animal protection remained largely decentralized, with most societies operating independently of one another until the 1950s. The Twenty-Eight Hour Law (1873) regulating cattle transportation was the movement's single federal legislative success until the passage of the Humane Slaughter Act (1958).

The humane movement lost ground after World War I. Its decline in influence coincided with a broad-scale "industrialization" of animals in such contexts as food production and research, testing, and education. Animal protectionists won widespread support for elements of their program that targeted private, individual acts of cruelty, and kindness to animals became a cherished attribute of the modern personality. However, pressing humane standards forward against the influence of powerful interests in meatpacking, agriculture, transportation, and industrial and medical research proved more difficult. In many cases, whole categories of animal use were accorded explicit exemptions from statutes designed to prevent cruelty. Also, the assumption of municipal animal control duties by humane societies throughout the country—a serious practical and financial burden—made it difficult to sustain broader programs addressing mistreatment of animals in other contexts. The far-reaching agenda of the early animal protection societies atrophied.

After World War II, a convergence of trends in demographics, animal utilization, science, technology, moral philosophy, and popular culture brought certain forms of animal use under greater scrutiny, and several rounds of new group formation revitalized the movement. The first, between 1950 and 1975, saw the emergence of national organizations that avoided direct management of shelters or municipal animal control. These groups resurrected campaigns for humane slaughter, regulation of laboratory animal use, and abolition of the steel leghold trap. Between 1975 and 1990, grassroots organizations driven by the ideologies of animal rights and animal liberation recast concern for animals as a justice-based movement, and appropriated strategic thinking and mobilization methods characteristic of civil rights era causes. Dynamic competition spurred innovation on the part of older anti-cruelty societies, which began to develop greater consistency and progressive positions. Animal protection has gained credibility through professionalization, increased political sophistication, and the emergence of a science of animal welfare that now underpins most campaigns against cruelty.

BIBLIOGRAPHY

Bekoff, Marc, and Carron Meaney, ed. *Encyclopedia of Animal Rights and Animal Welfare*. Westwood, Conn.: Greenwood, 1998.

Finsen, Lawrence, and Susan Finsen. *The Animal Rights Movement in America: From Compassion to Respect*. New York: Twayne, 1994.

Unti, Bernard, and Andrew Rowan. "A Social History of Animal Protection in the Post-World War Two Period." In *State of the Animals 2001*, edited by Deborah J. Salem and Andrew N. Rowan. Washington, D.C.: Humane Society of the United States, 2001.

Unti, Bernard. "The Quality of Mercy: Organized Animal Protection in the United States, 1866–1930." Ph.D. diss., American University, 2002.

Bernard Unti

See also **Animal Rights Movement; Society for the Prevention of Cruelty to Animals.**

ANIMAL RIGHTS MOVEMENT aims to increase the quality of life of animals by preventing cruelty to animals or the killing of animals except to prevent their own suffering. The movement in America traces its roots to the first settlers. Massachusetts Bay Colony Puritans enacted the first animal protection laws in the Western world when they included two provisions prohibiting cruelty to animals in the colony's 1641 Body of Liberties.

New York State passed a law protecting animals in 1829, with Massachusetts passing a similar law seven years later.

Despite these measures, it was not until after the Civil War that animal rights became a major public issue. Henry Bergh organized the American SOCIETY FOR THE PREVENTION OF CRUELTY TO ANIMALS in 1866. Heir to a shipbuilding fortune, Bergh became a defender of abused carriage horses in New York City. He also prosecuted butchers, carters, carriage drivers, and organizers of dog-fights and cockfights. Bergh's efforts gained support from influential business and government leaders and inspired George Angell to form the Massachusetts Society for the Prevention of Cruelty to Animals and Caroline Earle White to start the American Anti-Vivisection Society. The early animal rights movement encountered strong resistance to its opposition to the use of dogs, cats, and other animals for medical experiments, but on other issues, animal rights advocates found themselves in successful alliance with conservationists, who saw animals as a resource that must be managed so that they remained in abundant supply.

By 1907, every state had an anticruelty statute in place, and over the course of the twentieth century, state governments enacted further laws prohibiting specific practices. Congress passed the Animal Welfare Act in 1966. Nevertheless, the use of animals in medical LABORATORIES, on factory farms, and for other business purposes increased, because judges saw in the prohibition of "unjustified" infliction of pain an effort to protect human morals, not animals, and generally did not find violations of the law where the purpose of the activity was to benefit human beings.

Support for the animal rights movement mushroomed over the last quarter of the twentieth century. In the 1970s, civil rights, feminist, environmental, and antiwar activists turned their attention to animal rights. Three highly publicized incidents changed animal rights into a national grassroots movement: (1) protests organized by Henry Spira against the American Museum of Natural History in New York City for its experiments on cats; (2) the arrest and conviction of Dr. Edward Taub in 1981 for abusive practices on monkeys at the federally funded Institute for Behavioral Research; and (3) the 1984 release of the Animal Liberation Front's documentary *Unnecessary Fuss*, which showed baboons at the University of Pennsylvania being bashed in the head for experiments on trauma. In 1990 an estimated 30,000 to 40,000 people took part in the March for the Animals in Washington, D.C. By the mid-1990s there were hundreds of local, regional, and national animal rights organizations—such as the People for Ethical Treatment of Animals and the National Anti-Vivisection Society—that devoted themselves to a variety of animal rights issues, including the ethical treatment of animals in laboratories, protection of endangered species, the humane treatment of farm animals, campaigns against killing animals for their furs, preventing the overpopulation of pets, and securing the rights of legal "personhood" for selected animal species.

BIBLIOGRAPHY

Finsen, Lawrence, and Susan Finsen. *The Animal Rights Movement in America: From Compassion to Respect.* New York: Twayne, 1994.

Price, Jennifer. "When Women Were Women, Men Were Men, and Birds Were Hats." In *Flight Maps: Adventures with Nature in Modern America.* New York: Basic Books, 1999.

Turner, James. *Reckoning with the Beast: Animals, Pain, and Humanity in the Victorian Mind.* Baltimore: Johns Hopkins University Press, 1980.

Wise, Steven M. *Rattling the Cage: Toward Legal Rights for Animals.* Cambridge, Mass.: Perseus Books, 2000.

Erik Bruun / c. p.

See also **Animal Protective Societies; Conservation.**

ANIMATION. *See* Cartoons.

ANNAPOLIS CONVENTION.

In January 1786, the Virginia legislature invited other states to send commissioners to a meeting where proposals granting the Continental Congress authority to regulate commerce would be discussed. Congress had previously sought similar authority, but its proposed amendment to the Articles of Confederation had failed to secure the required ratification by all thirteen states. The Virginia commissioners eventually fixed a mid-September meeting date at Annapolis, Maryland. Although eight states appointed commissioners, only a dozen delegates from five states appeared at Mann's Tavern in Annapolis by September 11. Those present included James Madison and Edmund Randolph from Virginia; John Dickinson, the principal author of the Articles of Confederation, from Delaware; and Alexander Hamilton from New York. With so few commissioners present, the convention could hardly act with any authority. Yet neither did its members want to disband empty handed, for doing so would concede another setback in their efforts to strengthen the Confederation. Seizing on a clause in the credentials of the New Jersey delegates, the commissioners endorsed a report, drafted primarily by Hamilton, calling for a general convention to assemble in Philadelphia the following May, for the purpose of considering the condition of the federal Union.

BIBLIOGRAPHY

Rakove, Jack N. *The Beginnings of National Politics: An Interpretive History of the Continental Congress.* New York: Alfred Knopf, 1979.

Jack Rakove

See also **Constitution of the United States;** *and vol. 9:* **From Annapolis to Philadelphia.**

ANNEXATION OF TERRITORY.

The United States originally comprised thirteen states hugging the Atlantic seacoast of North America. The Treaty of Paris (1783), ending the war of independence, provided the new nation with more land for continued westward settlement. The accord with Britain gave the republic all lands westward to the Mississippi River and north to the Great Lakes. Americans wanted the Floridas too, but Spain reclaimed that area, and the southern boundary was set at the thirty-first parallel.

Although American leaders had misgivings about the expansion of the union to the uncharted territory beyond the Mississippi, within half a century the nation's land holdings stretched across North America to the Pacific Coast. The question of whether slavery should be extended to the West was one of the central causes of the Civil War. During the three decades following the end of the war, the United States expanded no further. But by the turn of the twentieth century, America had joined the ranks of an imperial power with offshore territorial possessions as well.

Annexation of territory was accomplished by purchase, conquests from Native Americans, treaties with European powers, joint resolutions of annexation, and presidential proclamation.

Louisiana Purchase

The United States had gained trading rights along the Mississippi River and free access to the port of New Orleans when it signed PINCKNEY'S TREATY with Spain in 1795. The administration of President Thomas Jefferson believed the United States might lose these vital interests when Spain handed over its Louisiana territory to France in 1800. When France cut off river trade, Jefferson sent envoys to Europe who were instructed to offer to buy New Orleans and the Floridas for as much as $10 million. Meanwhile, the president built up army posts along the Mississippi in case war broke out against French forces.

Such a crisis was averted when Napoleon turned his imperial ambitions from the New World back to the Old World, for war against England. In 1803, Napoleon decided to sell the 828,000 acres comprising the Louisiana territory to the United States for $15 million. The resulting treaty (1803) guaranteed U.S. trade on the Mississippi and seemingly limitless space for future settlement and commerce. The annexation doubled the size of the country so that it now extended west to the Rocky Mountains, north to Canada, and south to the Gulf of Mexico.

Natural Dominion

President James Monroe's selection of John Quincy Adams to be his secretary of state made it possible for the United States to extend what Adams called America's "natural dominion" farther west and south. A brilliant diplomat, Adams was also an imperialist who believed that eventually all of North America would fall into American hands. In 1818, Adams succeeded in wrangling from England a joint occupation agreement for Oregon, opening the way for settlement in the Pacific Northwest. The forty-ninth parallel to the Rocky Mountains became the border between the U.S. and Canada.

A year later, Adams was able to gain diplomatic advantage over Spain, which was focused on repressing revolutionary struggles in South America. The secretary of state successfully negotiated the Transcontinental or ADAMS-ONÍS TREATY. In the deal, Spain agreed to cede the Floridas to the United States and give up its claims to Oregon north of the line of forty-two degrees latitude. In return, the United States relinquished any claims to Texas and agreed to pay Spain $5 million. Despite the favorable nature of the treaty, some segments of the American public were distressed by the "loss" of Texas. The persistent migration of Americans to Texas over the next two decades gave rise to expectations that Texas would one day be added to the union.

Tribal Lands

For over two centuries, white pioneers and Native Americans had been at war with one another for possession of North American land. In the late 1820s, under President Andrew Jackson, the U.S. government sought to force Indian tribes to surrender their tribal lands and move west beyond the Mississippi River to isolated western territory. Some tribes regretfully migrated but others resisted these efforts and ended up being killed in conflicts with U.S. militiamen. According to the historian Frederick Merk, in one five-year period, between 1832 and 1837, 2 million acres of land in the northern plains of the Great Lakes were ceded to the U.S. government by Native American tribes.

Texas and Manifest Destiny

In the mid-1840s, many Americans became convinced that it was America's "MANIFEST DESTINY" to expand across the continent and provide a haven to peoples willing to practice self-government and live in freedom. Thousands of U.S. settlers sought to fulfill the notion of manifest destiny by settling in Texas. Mexico initially encouraged the migration with offers of free land. After winning independence from Mexico under the leadership of General Sam Houston (1836), residents of the self-proclaimed Republic of Texas decided to request annexation by the United States. Their repeated requests to join the union were rejected until President John Tyler brought a formal annexation resolution before Congress in 1843. However, concerns about the spread of slavery to Texas and the risk of war with Mexico doomed the effort. The Senate rejected the original Texas annexation treaty.

The Texas issue was quickly revived. The presidential election of 1844 turned out to be a mandate on the issue of annexation. Because pro-Texas annexation candidate James K. Polk was victorious, lame-duck President Tyler felt justified in bringing the question of annexation back to Congress. On this occasion, Tyler asked the representatives to approve a joint resolution to annex Texas. After incoming president Polk allayed Congress's fears about the impact of the annexation on relations with Mexico, both houses approved the annexation resolution.

Congress's concerns about Mexico's negative reaction to annexation were confirmed. Mexico failed to accept the loss of Texas. Relations between the two countries deteriorated in light of Polk's efforts to purchase additional land from Mexico west of Texas as well as California. War erupted in 1846 when Polk sent General Zachary Taylor to occupy disputed territory between the Nueces and the Rio Grande. The Americans won the war with Mexico, and in the treaty of GUADALUPE HIDALGO (February 1848) Mexico surrendered not only California but also New Mexico and what is now Arizona, as well as parts of Colorado, Utah, and Nevada. Mexico was also forced to accept the Rio Grande as the border between the United States and Mexico. The United States paid Mexico $15 million for the land and assumed unpaid damage claims by American citizens against Mexico for up to $3.25 million.

Oregon

Since the Adams-Onís agreement, the British and the Americans had jointly occupied the Oregon territory. During the Polk administration, expansionists took up the battle cry "FIFTY-FOUR FORTY OR FIGHT." They wanted the United States to seek possession of the entire Oregon territory up to latitude 54° 40′, which would include what is now Washington State as well as present-day Idaho, Oregon, and British Columbia. Although Polk attempted to satisfy these expansionist aims, eventually he decided not to provoke war with England over Oregon. In 1846, the United States and Great Britain signed the Oregon Treaty that set the border between America and Canada at the current forty-ninth parallel. The Senate ratified the treaty.

Land for Transcontinental Railroad

In 1853, President Franklin Pierce gave authority to James Gadsden, a railroad developer, to purchase a 30,000-square-foot strip of Californian land south of the Gila River, today's southern New Mexico and the southern quarter of Arizona. The area was considered ideal as a gateway for a transcontinental railroad to the Pacific Coast. For $10 million, the United States also gained the right to pass across the Isthmus of Tehuantepec. In addition, the remaining border disputes were settled with Mexico.

Cuba Considered

In the 1850s, American expansionists looked south of America's borders for new territory to acquire. Mostly Southerners, they targeted Cuba, a slave-holding Caribbean island held by Spain located ninety miles from the Florida coast. In 1854, President Franklin Pierce instructed his minister to Spain, Pierre Soule, to try to buy Cuba from Spain. But Soule was a poor diplomat and outraged Spain by issuing threats. Afterwards, Pierce organized a conference in Ostend, Belgium, led by future president James Buchanan. Buchanan and pro-slavery diplomats produced the OSTEND MANIFESTO, which suggested the United States seize Cuba by force if Spain refused to sell it. When the manifesto became public, a national debate began over the South's efforts to extend slavery. The controversy led one of the manifesto's authors to repudiate it, and the U.S. government formally ended its pursuit of Cuba. Too many voices were raised over the wisdom of annexing a territory with so many inhabitants who were neither white nor Protestant.

While the United States failed to take Cuba, it did acquire a series of sparsely populated or uninhabited islands in the Caribbean and North Pacific in the 1850s. These possessions included Navassa Island, a tiny Caribbean island used for guano mining, and Baker Island, and the Johnston Atoll in Oceania. They were annexed through presidential proclamation.

Seward's Folly

After the Civil War, one of the few U.S. leaders who retained enthusiasm for continental expansion was Secretary of State William H. Seward. In 1867, the Russian tsar offered to sell Alaska to the United States. Russia had profited little from the 586,412 square miles of territory and preferred that Americans, rather than the British Navy, take possession of it. Few in the United States could see the wisdom of buying what appeared to be a barren chunk of ice, even if it was going cheap at the price of $7.2 million. After all, this was the era of Reconstruction. But Seward, a diehard believer in "manifest destiny," recognized that Alaska could be a useful outpost for the growing trade with the Far East as well as a wellspring of natural resources. The statesman hoped that the United States would subsequently seek territorial possessions in the Caribbean, such as Cuba and Puerto Rico. He found few supporters for these acquisitions. Yet Seward did succeed in obtaining what he believed were strategic posts in the Pacific: the tiny Midway Islands north of Hawaii. He predicted that the United States would someday be called on to aggressively defend its interests in Asia.

New Imperialism

In the 1890s, the United States began actively pursuing overseas expansion and risking conflict with European powers. A variety of factors drove the United States to become more assertive abroad. Advances in transportation and communication had shrunk the world, giving foreign events a heightened importance. More importantly, the growth in industrial production led to an increased demand for overseas markets. To protect its interests, the United States built up the nation's naval forces. According to historian Julius Pratt, officials came to think of the United States as a great power entitled to compete evenly with the other powers of the world for "naval and commercial supremacy of the Pacific Ocean and the Far East."

This new imperialism was plainly evident in America's war against Spain in 1898, the nation's first foreign conflict in over half a century. Although the 17,000 American troops were not well equipped, they easily defeated the Spanish in what diplomat John Hay called a "splendid little war." U.S. troops seized Cuba and Puerto Rico and Commodore George Dewey dramatically defeated the Spanish fleet at Manila in the Philippines. After the United States pretended to attack Spain itself, the Spanish agreed to an armistice. Under the terms of the peace treaty settling the war, the U.S. annexed Puerto Rico and Guam and purchased the Philippines for $25 million. Cuba became an American protectorate.

Also in 1898, the United States sought to finalize the annexation of Hawaii, a move that had been twice rejected by the Senate during the previous five years. Out of concern that the annexation treaty would once again be turned down, President William McKinley sought annexation through a joint resolution requiring only a majority vote by the Congress. McKinley's supporters argued that possession of Hawaii would help secure the West Coast and prevent foreign incursions in America's sphere of influence in the Pacific. Congress approved the annexation on a vote of 209 to 91.

Virgin Islands

The United States' last major land purchase was the 352 square miles comprising the Danish West Indies. On 27 March 1917, America acquired the "Virgin Islands" of St. Thomas, St. John, and St. Croix from Denmark.

BIBLIOGRAPHY

Beisner, Robert L. *From the Old Diplomacy to the New, 1865–1900.* Arlington Heights, Ill.: Harlan Davidson, Inc., 1986.

LaFeber, Walter. *The New Empire: An Interpretation of American Expansion, 1860–1898.* Ithaca, N.Y.: Cornell University Press, 1963.

Merk, Frederick. *Manifest Destiny and Mission in American History.* Cambridge, Mass.: Harvard University Press, 1995. The original edition was published in 1963.

Ellen G. Rafshoon

See also **Gadsden Purchase; Indian Land Cessions; Louisiana Purchase; Mexican-American War; Spanish-American War.**

ANSWERING MACHINES. The idea of devices to record telephone calls occurred simultaneously to several inventors, among them Thomas Edison, in the late nineteenth century. Edison's unsuccessful attempts to record a telephone call mechanically led to the invention of the phonograph, which achieved commercial success for entertainment purposes. In 1890, Valdemar Poulsen invented a telegraphone, the first magnetic recorder. Operating much like a modern tape recorder, the telegraphone was an automatic telephone answering machine, but it had no outgoing message. Following the advent of electronic tubes in the 1920s, several individuals and firms offered fully automatic answering machines that used magnetic tape and operated along the lines of the later, more familiar machines. These were used widely in Europe but were banned in the United States by AT&T, which saw them as a threat.

After World War II, new regulations made it possible to offer for sale answering machines such as one called the Electronic Secretary. Responding to demands from businesses, Bell Operating Companies began leasing answering machines in 1950. Reductions in cost stimulated demand for these machines by the mid-1970s, and they gained recognition as they were featured in motion pictures and television shows. With the dissolution of AT&T in 1984, most local operating companies ceased enforcing the remaining restrictions on answering machine use. Sales rose dramatically, exceeding one million units per year in the early 1980s. By the mid-1990s a majority of households owned a machine.

BIBLIOGRAPHY

Morton, David. *Off the Record: The Technology and Culture of Sound Recording in America.* New Brunswick, N.J.: Rutgers University Press, 2000.

David Morton

See also **Telephone.**

ANTELOPE CASE. The *Antelope* was originally a Spanish vessel that was taken by an American privateer in March 1820. Later, while carrying a cargo of slaves captured from Spanish and Portuguese ships, the *Antelope* was seized by a U.S. revenue cutter. The vessel and the Africans were claimed by Spanish and Portuguese viceconsuls on behalf of their citizens. Chief Justice John Marshall of the U.S. Supreme Court (10 Wheaton 66) ruled that the African slave trade was not contrary to the law of nations and that the American cutter had no right of search and seizure in peacetime. Marshall directed that the slaves be restored to the foreigner in possession at the time of the capture.

BIBLIOGRAPHY

Brandon, Mark E. *Free in the World: American Slavery and Constitutional Failure.* Princeton, N.J.: Princeton University Press, 1998.

Noonan, John T., Jr. *The "Antelope."* Berkeley: University of California Press, 1977.

Lionel H. Laing / A. R.

See also **Slave Trade.**

ANTHRACITE STRIKE. The anthracite coal strike of 1902 involved over 147,000 of the ethnically diverse miners of eastern Pennsylvania. Their goals were to gain operator recognition of the United Mine Workers (UMW), increased wages, and improved working conditions. When the mine operators rejected miners' demands, UMW president John Mitchell called the strike on 12 May 1902, and within several weeks the miners—including both established miners and newcomers from southern and eastern Europe—were joined by many engineers, firemen, and pumpmen in labor's greatest walkout to that time. By the fall of 1902, urban dwellers were in a near panic over what they feared was an imminent coal famine. This perception, along with clashes between strikers, nonstrikers, and management's private forces, resulted in the first federal intervention into a labor dispute that was not completely in support of management.

In October 1902, President Theodore Roosevelt invited representatives of both sides to meet with him in Washington, D.C., and asked them to compromise in the public interest. When the coal operators demurred, Roosevelt threatened federal seizure of the mines and sent his representative, Secretary of War Elihu Root, to negotiate with J. P. Morgan, whose firm had major interests in the railroads that owned the mines. Morgan and Root outlined the basis for arbitration while aboard Morgan's yacht, *The Corsair.* The Corsair Agreement was announced on 14 October 1902, with the coal operators forced to accept UMW head John Mitchell as the miners' representative on the Anthracite Coal Strike Commission. Ultimately, for the miners, the agreement was a defeat in one major respect: the document's preamble refused the UMW's primary objective: union recognition.

The results for miners and operators were mixed. An important union victory was the permanent establishment of the UMW in the anthracite coalfields, along with a nine-hour day, a 10 percent pay increase, and a structure for discussion and arbitration. But the anthracite commission had compromised on hours and wages, forced no changes in work rules, and decided that union recognition was beyond its jurisdiction. The labor-management boards that the commission established approximated collective bargaining, but in reality the power rested with federal judges. It was thirteen years more before the unions received actual recognition. Also, against the UMW's wishes, the commission recommended separate unions in bituminous and anthracite coal and condemned the union shop. The anthracite strike is noteworthy for making government the third party in labor disputes and earning Theodore Roosevelt recognition as the first president of the modern era not inextricably tied to business interests in labor-management matters.

BIBLIOGRAPHY

Cornell, Robert J. *The Anthracite Strike of 1902.* Washington, D.C.: Catholic University Press, 1957.

Harbaugh, William Henry. *Power and Responsibility: The Life and Times of Theodore Roosevelt.* New York: Octagon Books, 1975.

Morris, Edmund. *Theodore Rex.* New York: Random House, 2001.

Mowry, George Edwin. *The Era of Theodore Roosevelt, 1900–1912*. New York: Harper and Brothers, 1958.

Perlman, Seig, and Phillip Taft. *History of Labor in the United States, 1896–1932. Vol. 4, Labor Movements*. New York: Macmillan, 1935.

Wiebe, Robert H. "The Anthracite Strike of 1902: A Record of Confusion." *Mississippi Valley Historical Review: A Journal of American History* 48 (1961): 229–251.

Williams, John Alexander. *Appalachia: A History*. Chapel Hill: University of North Carolina Press, 2002.

Martha Avaleen Egan

See also **Coal Mining and Organized Labor; Strikes; Trade Unions; United Mine Workers of America.**

ANTHROPOLOGY AND ETHNOLOGY.

The history of the terms "anthropology" and "ethnology" tells much about the changing scope of the field and central debates within it. Today we assume that they are closely related—"ethnology" is the study of culture, a dominant part of the enterprise of "anthropology," the study of humankind—but this was not always the case. The two terms once had different, even opposed, meanings. In the eighteenth and nineteenth centuries, "anthropology" meant the science of the whole nature of man and emphasized the classification of physical characteristics, often to prove the fundamental differences among humans. "Ethnology" was the science of human races and included linguistics, physical measurements, and culture as evidence of human commonalities. That we now use the term "ethnic" to describe cultural difference and particularity indicates the sea change that has occurred. One central part of the history of anthropology, therefore, concerns a shift in emphasis from race to culture as a way to understand humanity. Although the answers have differed, the central questions of anthropology involve the unity and diversity of humankind: Are people alike? Are they different? Are commonalities more important than differences? Before the Enlightenment launched the scientific study of the human and natural world, the age of exploration and conquest provided the intellectual and political challenge for it. How to describe, explain, and control the peoples that Europeans encountered in the Americas, Africa, and Asia? Anthropology emerged as, and has largely remained, an enterprise in which "civilized" European and American observers study "primitive" non-European others. The changing scope of anthropology follows the history of European conquest of North America and the emerging national identity of the United States. The importation of slaves from Africa and the immigration of peoples from Europe and Asia intensified and complicated the process.

The Age of Exploration and Conquest

In the seventeenth century, European travelers, missionaries, colonizers, and naturalists asked questions about the peoples they encountered. Although not an organized endeavor with the name "anthropology," observers' efforts resembled those of later anthropologists. They too tried to explain the origin of native populations and their differences from Europeans. American "Indians," taking their name from Columbus's journey, already played a role in the colonial imagination of self and others, well before they would become the central focus of anthropology in the United States. Assuming a common origin, or monogenism, some speculated about the presence of the ten lost tribes who had wandered into this new Israel. Biblical references further explained the differences among Indian peoples and their differences from Europeans as the effects of the Tower of Babel and the proliferation of incommensurate dialects and ways of life. Environmental, especially climatic, theories were also thought to explain this offshoot of the human race, conveniently and increasingly seen as degenerate forms, destined for disappearance. As early as 1609, Richard Johnson's *Nova Brittania* described the strange and savage to the civilized as part of the self-defining process of conquest and settlement. One hundred years later, Robert Beverly's 1705 *History of the Present State of Virginia* provided the first descriptions of Indian religion, law, customs, dress, and family, to explain both native inhabitants and the condition of English settlement. Without a self-consciousness about an anthropological endeavor as such, these efforts demonstrated the foundational importance of the encounter of European colonizers with native peoples in the making of an American identity.

The Enlightenment

The eighteenth-century Enlightenment systematically analyzed what already existed through the necessity of conquest. Emphasizing scientific study of all of nature and a belief in progress, Enlightenment thinkers such as Jean Jacques Rousseau and Carolus Linnaeus defined the early anthropological tradition. This included Rousseau's use of travel accounts to query human similarities and differences and Linnaeus's classifications of species and varieties. Benjamin Franklin, George Washington, and Thomas Jefferson compiled Indian word lists for a larger linguistic classification project. As Jefferson embarked on unprecedented territorial acquisition, he asked Lewis and Clark to collect information on the natural and human life they encountered.

While the formation of the United States furnished both a laboratory and a political testing ground for knowledge about humanity, Enlightenment faith in progress also limited egalitarianism. The idea of the uncivilized savage, who could be "improved," was replaced by the primitive, a survivor of the past, whom progress had missed. Enlightenment efforts to classify varieties were certain of one thing: Indians were a vanishing species, outside of the progress of history. These studies also defined a central part of anthropology that would remain a source of controversy: the search for universal laws and the fact of human diversity.

Romanticism and Pre-Darwinian Developmentalism

Territorial expansion and the debates over slavery fueled arguments about racial differences in the pre-Darwinian period. In this context, developmentalism coexisted with the emerging Romantic view of the particularity of peoples, contributing to the early institutionalization of broad-based anthropological and ethnological endeavors and to the emergence of polygenist arguments stressing racial particularism and degeneracy. At the same time, ambitious efforts to institutionalize the knowledge of American peoples were under way.

From the 1830s into the 1850s, the Indian agent Henry Rowe Schoolcraft studied and published his findings on Indian myths and ways of life, with particular interest in what he called "savage mentality." Albert Gallatin and John Russell Bartlett founded the American Ethnological Society in 1842 to pursue linguistic and historical work, defining "ethnology" broadly. Similarly, the establishment of the Smithsonian Institution in 1846 formalized ambitious work on natural history and human and animal life.

In contrast to this catholic approach, another thread of research stressed comparative anatomy and polygenist arguments. This "American school" included Samuel George Morton, who published *Crania Americana* in 1839, Josiah Clark Nott, who co-authored *Types of Mankind: or, Ethnological Researches, Based upon the Ancient Monuments, Paintings, Sculptures, and Crania of Races* with George R. Gliddon in 1854, and the Swiss-born zoologist Louis Agassiz, who defended common human origins before he arrived in the United States, where black slaves and Indians and the arguments of polygenists convinced him otherwise. Instrumental in pro-slavery arguments in the antebellum period, this branch of work was one of the antecedents of the scientific racism popularized in the later nineteenth century. Anthropology in its various formations in the United States in the first half of the nineteenth century was part of a broader Euro-American enterprise that took the question of human diversity and unity as its central problem and the confrontation of "civilized" and "primitive" as its central context.

Darwinian Evolutionism

The response to Charles Darwin's theory of evolution in *On the Origin of Species* (1859) brought together earlier concerns with developmentalism, variation, and common origins with anatomical studies of racial difference and typologies. The idea of the common origin of humankind was compatible with human variation and stages and hierarchies of development. Using travelers' and naturalists' accounts and archaeological evidence to support theories of social evolution, Edward Burnett Tylor and John Lubbock in England and Lewis Henry Morgan, John Wesley Powell, and Daniel Garrison Brinton in the United States institutionalized an anthropology that focused broadly on human societies and cultures, defining an emerging "concept of culture" as something holistic and ranked in progressive hierarchies of development. Tylor is usually credited with developing these ideas in his 1871 *Primitive Culture*. Morgan's important studies—*League of the Iroquois* (1851) and *Ancient Society* (1877), which influenced Karl Marx and Friedrich Engels—provided detailed descriptions of governmental structures, property relations, and technological development to trace their relative place in the evolution from savagery to barbarism to civilization. These ambitious projects came to define "anthropology" and "ethnology" in Anglo-America. John Wesley Powell, the nominal "discoverer" of the Grand Canyon and an ardent evolutionist, headed the Bureau of Ethnology, a single institution founded in 1879 to organize "anthropologic" research in the United States. The doctor, linguist, and folklorist Daniel Brinton, who was the first professor of anthropology (with a chair in archaeology and linguistics at the University of Pennsylvania in 1886), published *Races and Peoples* in 1890, demonstrating the concerns of the emerging field. Scientific work in new government agencies and universities was compatible with wider endeavors that supported scientific racism. The world's fairs of 1893 and 1904, in Chicago and St. Louis respectively, included anthropological exhibits that became parts of museum collections and provided public, scientific, and popular support for ethnological work on polygenism and evolutionary anthropology. This was the time, after all, of legalized segregation and disfranchisement of African Americans, immigration restriction legislation, and removal of Indians to reservations.

Franz Boas and the American Historical School, 1890–1940

While he shared the commitment to salvage work among vanishing peoples, the German immigrant Franz Boas substantially challenged the reigning wisdom of anthropology in the United States. Conducting work among Indians, immigrants, and African Americans, Boas tried to alter the mandate of the Bureau of Ethnology to include all three groups. From his arrival in the 1880s until his death in 1942, he relentlessly criticized social evolutionism and scientific racism, arguing that race, language, and culture were separate, that historical diffusion, not evolutionary stages, accounted for similarities among peoples, that anthropometric evidence did not prove racial inferiority, and that cultures, in the plural, should be understood from the inside. The roots of cultural relativism were twofold: peoples were related (that is, connected), and values were dependent on the culture that produced them. This cultural approach was very different from the classificatory emphases that still dominated anthropological work. Anthropology, as Boas saw it, was the science of humankind, positioned to study connections and variations. Early in his career, Boas put forth his controversial views on cultural diffusion and contextualism. He argued that museum exhibits should not focus on objects ranked in evolutionary sequence but on "the phenomena called ethnological and anthropological in the widest sense of those words," in historical, geographical, physiological, and psychological contexts (Stocking, *Franz Boas Reader*,

p. 63). The purpose was to study "each ethnological specimen individually in its history and in its medium" (*Franz Boas Reader*, p. 62). Boas combined the projects of anthropology and ethnology in ways consistent with some earlier Anglo-American scholars, but he imported a German idea of culture as holistic, particularistic, and historical, without the German connotations of "anthropology" as concerned primarily with physical differences. Instead, he defined the four-fields approach to anthropology—linguistics, ethnology, biology, and archaeology—and looked to a time when they would be separate endeavors, "when anthropology pure and simple will deal with the customs and beliefs of the less civilized people only" (*Franz Boas Reader*, p. 35).

Boas was targeted because of his controversial views. He was censured by the American Anthropological Association for criticizing scientists who cooperated with the World War I effort, a move that was also a struggle between evolutionist, Washington-based anthropologists and antievolutionist, antiracialist New York Boasians. His vision succeeded because he peopled most of the emerging academic departments of anthropology with his students (Alfred Kroeber, Robert Lowie, Edward Sapir, Ruth Benedict, Margaret Mead, and Melville J. Herskovits among them) and because he succeeded in disseminating his views beyond the academy. *The Mind of Primitive Man* (1911) and *Anthropology and Modern Life* (1928) were popular renditions of his arguments against social evolutionism and scientific racism. All of his students continued work among Indian peoples and broadened the sphere of anthropological inquiry into regions of U.S. territorial domination. Margaret Mead's 1928 bestseller, *Coming of Age in Samoa*, disseminated the Boasian idea that culture dominated biology and that unique insight came from viewing a culture "from the inside." Ruth Benedict's popular *Patterns of Culture* (1934) advanced the ideas of cultural wholes and patterning, culture and personality, and cultural difference. The dominant meaning of anthropology in the United States was the broad-based endeavor focusing on culture rather than race as definitive of human life. By the beginning of World War II, when Boas died, his challenges to scientific racism were poised for broader acceptance, while the ideas of cultural relativism, advanced most forcefully by his students, generated new criticisms.

Cold War Anthropology

After World War II, the relativistic tolerance of the Boasian concept of culture seemed unsatisfactory, even dangerous, to those who saw the twin threats of Nazi fascism and Soviet totalitarianism. Did understanding cultures require acceptance? Were there no independent standards of judgment? Although the Boasians, Boas himself included, did not necessarily endorse such moral relativism, the consensus of the Cold War era increasingly characterized its work in this way. For instance, Ruth Benedict, who had worked for the Office of War Information and written *The Chrysanthemum and the Sword* (1946) about

Margaret Mead. The best-known disciple of Franz Boas in 1928, the year of her renowned study of Samoan culture. GETTY IMAGES

Japan, was criticized by Clyde Kluckhohn for suggesting that any and all cultural formations—slavery, cannibalism, Nazism, Communism—were immune from criticism.

If differences could not be uncritically celebrated, they were also no longer necessarily the primary focus of anthropological inquiry. In the wake of the war, and with the rise of anticommunism, universalism and a new scientism emerged as successful challengers to ideas of relativism and culture dominance. Scholars such as Ralph Linton at Columbia and Kluckhohn at Harvard pronounced the uniformity underlying diversity. This shift did not challenge some of the functionalism of the Boasian idea of culture and worked well with that orientation in other social scientific disciplines such as sociology. A renewed interest in biology and physical anthropology also redirected attention away from culture and toward the foundations of human nature that made people alike. Comparative studies of human and animal behavior sought to determine the uniformity of human need for survival, adaptation, and perpetuation of the species. From a different vantage point, Marvin Harris's *The Rise of Anthropological Theory*, originally published in 1968, argued against what he saw as the preoccupation with the idiosyncratic and irrational in favor of "cultural materialism"—adaptation to environmental, technological, and economic necessity—and the search for scientific laws. Another variant of the interest in biological over cultural determinism returned to the earlier thread of anthropology as the study of human differences and hierarchies. E. O. Wilson's 1975 *Sociobiology* and Richard Herrnstein and Charles Murray's 1994 *The Bell Curve*, about intelligence testing, generated controversy while refashioning arguments about biological and cultural differences. It was an example of the backlash against the egalitarianism of the social movements of the 1960s and 1970s. Similarly, Derek Freeman's 1983 exposé, *Margaret Mead and Samoa: The Making and Unmaking of an Anthropological Myth*, took on the most public figure of the old, cultural school to argue that her research had been flawed and her conclusions about the power of culture erroneous.

Crisis in Anthropology: Interpretive Anthropology and Post-Colonialism

Challenges also came from within the field of cultural anthropology. Interpretive anthropology developed as a rebuttal to both the universalism of sociocultural anthropology of the 1950s and 1960s and the biologism of the Darwinian revival. Clifford Geertz refocused attention on the particularities of individual cultures, combining the priorities of the Boasians with the functionalism of the sociologist Talcott Parsons. In Geertz's words, culture was "the webs of significance he [man] himself has spun" (*Interpretation of Cultures*, p. 5), and the task of the anthropologist was to untangle them and understand them from "the native's point of view" (*Local Knowledge*, p. 56). Geertz criticized the critics of relativism and reasserted the foundational significance of diversity to the anthropologist's charge.

Others read this fact of difference differently. The colonial struggles of the post–World War II era raised new questions about anthropology as the study of primitive "natives" by civilized "outsiders." Anthropology became deeply implicated as an imperialist project, a problem broached in the 1973 collection edited by Talal Asad, *Anthropology and the Colonial Encounter*. The criticisms were both epistemological—how can an outsider really "know" a native's point of view?—and political—what justified Euro-Americans' forays into Pueblo, Samoan, or Balinese societies? Fieldwork, required for anthropologists after Boas, became a fraught activity. Unlike the Boasians who used anthropology as a form of cultural critique of modern America, more recent scholars drew on feminism and post-colonialism to criticize anthropology itself.

One response to this criticism was the development of self-reflexive anthropology. Rather than assume a position of objectivity or authority, the anthropologist became the object of inquiry. James Clifford, George Marcus, and Clifford Geertz focused on the process of writing, constructing ethnographic knowledge through texts. George W. Stocking Jr., George Marcus, Michael Fischer, and Thomas Trautmann focused on the history of anthropology to understand the discipline itself. In both instances, anthropologists studied anthropologists. (Al-

though by training a historian, Stocking was a member of the University of Chicago anthropology department and received the Franz Boas Award for Exemplary Service to Anthropology from the American Anthropological Association in 1998.) Anthropology is probably unique among the social sciences for having developed a history of the discipline as a subfield. Retreating from the exotic as a locus of study, some directed the lens of anthropological understanding onto the complex, modern world to which they belonged. David M. Schneider studied American kinship, Michael Moffatt, college students. These works continued the tradition of cultural critique within twentieth-century anthropology, but they also reoriented the field away from its primitivist origins.

Another response to the dilemma of anthropology was to re-center it around "native ethnography." Related to the anthropology of modernity, this approach inverted the objects and their observers; "natives" could anthropologize themselves, avoiding the privileging of outsiders and providing superior understandings "from the inside." However, in a global world, where scholars are educated, work, and live away from their place of origin, in which cultural and other boundaries are permeable, the distinction between "native" and "non-native" is not always clear or fixed. Scholars such as Arjun Appadurai, Akhil Gupta, and James Ferguson have challenged the idea of culture as a bounded entity and called attention to globalization and diasporas.

Crisis and Reconfiguration: Anthropology in the Early Twenty-First Century

While the central questions of anthropology remain how to define and understand human unities and diversities, institutionally, a crisis persists. The problems that have divided and united anthropologists over the years—the relative significance of biology and culture, the centrality of culture to human experience—now extend well beyond the discipline. Boas's four-field program founders. Some major universities have abandoned it, and cultural and biological anthropologists occupy separate departments. How culture and biology interrelate no longer seems to be a live question. At the same time, "adjectival anthropologies"—the fragmentation into separate entities such as psychological, linguistic, economic, urban, or feminist anthropology—represent not only the specialization that has occurred throughout academic disciplines, but also particular debates within anthropology that challenge the coherence of the field. While anthropology's strength still comes from its history of studying and defining culture, it is no longer the sole way to approach the problem. Contemporary interest in postmodernism, globalism, and the cultural turn in a variety of fields, including cultural studies, have been influenced by, and have in turn influenced, anthropology's concern with ethnographic authority, the unity and diversity of cultures, and the very meaning of "culture." A pessimistic view is that the professional identity and purpose of anthropology are now much harder to define. An optimistic view is that the "blurring" of lines of intellectual inquiry shows anthropology's contribution and promise of future vitality.

BIBLIOGRAPHY

Berkhofer, Robert F., Jr. *The White Man's Indian: Images of the American Indian from Columbus to the Present.* New York: Knopf, 1978.

Clifford, James, and George E. Marcus, eds. *Writing Culture: The Poetics and Politics of Ethnography.* Berkeley: University of California Press, 1986.

Geertz, Clifford. *The Interpretation of Cultures.* New York: Basic Books, 1973.

———. *Local Knowledge: Further Essays in Interpretive Anthropology.* New York: Basic Books, 1983.

Harris, Marvin. *The Rise of Anthropological Theory: A History of Theories of Culture,* updated ed. Walnut Creek, Calif.: Alta-Mira Press, 2001. The original edition was published in 1968.

Hinsley, Curtis M., Jr. *The Smithsonian and the American Indian: Making a Moral Anthroplogy in Victorian America.* Washington, D.C.: Smithsonian Institution Press, 1994.

Pearce, Roy Harvey. *Savagism and Civilization: A Study of the Indian and the American Mind.* Baltimore: Johns Hopkins Press, 1965.

Stocking, George W., Jr. *Race, Culture, and Evolution: Essays in the History of Anthropology.* New York: Free Press, 1968. Reprint, Chicago: University of Chicago Press, 1982.

———. *Victorian Anthropology.* New York: Free Press, 1987.

———. *The Ethnographer's Magic and Other Essays in the History of Anthropology.* Madison: University of Wisconsin Press, 1992.

Stocking, George W., Jr., ed. *The Franz Boas Reader: The Shaping of American Anthropology, 1883–1911.* Chicago: University of Chicago Press, 1974.

Trautmann, Thomas R. *Lewis Henry Morgan and the Invention of Kinship.* Berkeley: University of California Press, 1987.

Julia E. Liss

ANTIBALLISTIC MISSILE TREATY. *See* Strategic Arms Limitation Talks.

ANTIBANK MOVEMENT.
President Andrew Jackson's 1830s destruction of the BANK OF THE UNITED STATES ignited an antibank movement directed against private banking corporations endowed by legislative charter with the right to issue circulating notes. The campaign spread to the states after the Panic of 1837, fed by popular resentment of a "moneyed aristocracy," disgust with an unsound paper currency, suspicion of the mysteries of finance and credit, frequent exposures of banking fraud and malfeasance, and long-standing Jeffersonian hostility to chartered corporations as fonts of privilege and corruption.

Democratic presidents Martin Van Buren and James K. Polk moved to sever all federal connection with banks through the Independent Treasury, finally established by Congress in 1846. In the states, Democrats battled to replace banknotes with gold and silver "hard money" and to outlaw banking corporations outright or extend full liability to stockholders. An alternative, embraced by many Whigs, was to check abuses by instituting "free banking" open to all comers under standardized safeguards. The antibank campaign went furthest in western states, where high demand for credit had fostered erratic banking practices. The movement subsided with the enactment of state reforms and the rise of the slavery issue, and was finally superseded by federal banking legislation during the Civil War. Resentment against bankers lingered, to resurface in the Populist movement and other insurgencies.

BIBLIOGRAPHY

Shade, William G. *Banks or No Banks: The Money Issue in Western Politics, 1832–1865.* Detroit, Mich.: Wayne State University Press, 1972.

Sharp, James Roger. *The Jacksonians versus the Banks: Politics in the States after the Panic of 1837.* New York: Columbia University Press, 1970.

Daniel Feller

See also **Banking: Bank Failures, State Banks; Free Banking System; Independent Treasury System.**

ANTI-CATHOLICISM.
Bigotry against Roman Catholics, as well as the ideas that have rationalized such bigotry, have long been elements in North American politics and popular culture. Like racism and anti-Semitism, anti-Catholicism is a fluid, international phenomenon buttressed by political, cultural, and intellectual justifications; like them, anti-Catholicism has served as a means of ostracizing a social group to consolidate political and cultural power in other groups. Additionally, just as historians trace the origins of racism to the early modern period, so too anti-Catholicism dates from this period—a legacy of Reformation-era disputes and of the European religious wars prior to 1648. (With origins in the ancient world, anti-Semitism dates much farther back.) A distinguishing mark of anti-Catholicism is that it developed in tandem with the modern papacy, a religio-political institution whose activities were widely perceived as threats to non-Catholic religious and secular authorities. Significantly, since Roman Catholics were the largest U.S. religious denomination after about 1870, anti-Catholicism was thereafter aimed at a religious plurality, not a religious minority, within the national population.

Frequently anti-Catholicism was voiced as opposition to the Roman papacy, particularly to papal influence in political affairs. It was carried to North America by seventeenth-century Puritan settlers of New England, where anti-Catholicism retained vitality despite the dearth of Catholics in that region until the nineteenth century. In the absence of a Catholic population, anti-Catholicism resulted from two notable sources, and it developed in context with repressive Penal Laws in early modern England and Ireland. First, demonstrated opposition to the papacy and to the European "Catholic countries" (especially Spain and France, which also held North American colonies) was a key indicator of English national identity in the seventeenth and eighteenth centuries; affirming the separation from Rome of the English government and of the Church of England served as a statement of "Englishness" and a mark of national pride. Second, early New England Puritans viewed their colonial enterprise as a "holy experiment" by which they would provide for the world a "modell of Christian charity" and God-centered government; they believed their experiment to be the beginning of a new order in religion and politics, purified of every hint of papal influence and of the historical accretions of Catholic doctrine that perverted true Christianity. As the widespread influence of the papacy persisted and even grew after the seventeenth century, expressions of autonomy from Catholic Rome continued to be active elements of political and cultural identity in England, its American colonies, and, later, in the United States. Anti-Catholicism notably reared itself the "New York Conspiracy," or "Negro Conspiracy," of 1741: after a series of New York City crimes, thirty-five people were executed, most of them African Americans accused of conspiring to overthrow the white gentry; included was a white man wrongly suspected to be a Jesuit priest and thought to have planned a revolt among blacks and poor whites. Significantly, the Maryland colony represented an exception to colonial anti-Catholicism: founded by English-Catholic George Calvert, Lord Baltimore, in 1633, it was the first British outpost to endorse freedom of religion, including legal toleration for Catholics and Jews.

Between 1830 and 1930—a century of massive immigration into the United States—anti-Catholicism was an active element in many debates around immigration, and it pervaded popular literature and political humor in the United States, occasionally fueling violence against Catholics. Frequently references to Rome's despotic influence over immigrant Catholics served as a backdrop to outbreaks of anti-Catholic activity. Among well-known events was the 1834 looting and burning of a Charlestown, Massachusetts, URSULINE CONVENT at the hands of anti-Catholic vandals. More representative, however, were nonviolent deployments of anti-Catholicism such as the proliferation in the 1830s and 1840s of popular "exposés" about the repressive influences and deviant sexual activities of Catholic clergy and nuns, and the 1884 presidential election, wherein Republicans decried the Democratic Party's association with "rum, Romanism, and rebellion" (references to the party's stance on Prohibition, its heavily immigrant-Catholic base, and its strength in the secessionist South). Other notable examples included the activities of the American Protective Association in the 1890s across the northern and midwestern United States, which endeavored "to place the political position of this [U.S.] government in the hands of Protestants to the entire exclusion of the Roman Catholics"; the anti-Catholic

rhetoric of the Ku Klux Klan in the early-twentieth-century South and Midwest; and the rhetoric used against New York governor Alfred E. Smith, an Irish-American Catholic, in his 1928 bid for the presidency. Later, during John F. Kennedy's 1960 presidential campaign, the same arguments used against Smith—particularly, the possibilities of political manipulation by Roman authorities—were resurrected.

After 1930, unabashed expressions of anti-Catholicism increasingly gave way to more reasoned debates, especially debates regarding Catholicism's relation to the autonomous individual. Concepts of American identity have long enshrined the notion that Americans are democratic by temperament and individual, autonomous actors free from undue pressures upon their moral choices. Given its history of definitive pronouncements upon moral issues and its connection to the papacy, Catholicism was thought by many to be antithetical to individual autonomy, thus antithetical to "being American"—a view fueled by the 1870 official proclamation of papal infallibility in certain matters of faith and morality. Prominent twentieth-century intellectuals like the philosophers John Dewey and Theodor Adorno commented on Catholicism's inherent authoritarianism and its potentially debilitating effects upon the human psyche and personal autonomy, suggesting that it weakened individual moral conviction and shaped the sort of "followers" suitable for totalitarian regimes. At the popular level, church teachings on matters of sexuality received much attention throughout the twentieth century, and American commentators on birth control, abortion, and homosexuality—including many Catholic commentators—criticized as repressive the prohibitive church teachings on these issues, emphasizing the centrality of personal choice in matters of sexuality and the church's disrespect for individual autonomy. Certainly not every expression of disagreement with official church teaching can be understood as "anti-Catholic"; nonetheless, many U.S. church leaders and lay Catholic commentators have noted the persistence in these debates of centuries-old distinctions between Catholicism and national identity, suggesting that modern anti-Catholic attitudes have assumed greater subtlety to conform to the norms of civil public debate.

Since the late eighteenth century, the majority of church leaders have responded to anti-Catholicism by appealing to American values of religious freedom and toleration and encouraging Catholics to affirm the compatibility of being both patriotic Americans and loyal Catholics. In consequence, Catholics sometimes have portrayed themselves as hyper-American, culminating in innumerable public affirmations of patriotism, especially during World War I and the early Cold War era, when suspicion of "un-American" activities reached high points.

BIBLIOGRAPHY

Billington, Ray Allen. *The Protestant Crusade, 1800–1860: A Study of the Origins of American Nativism*. New York: Macmillan, 1938.

Colley, Linda. "Britishness and Otherness: An Argument," *Journal of British Studies* 31 (1992): 309–329. Treats anti-Catholicism in early modern England.

Gleason, Philip. "American Identity and Americanization." In *The Harvard Encyclopedia of American Ethnic Groups*. Edited by Stephan Thernstrom. Cambridge, Mass.: Belknap Press, 1982.

Greeley, Andrew M. *An Ugly Little Secret: Anti-Catholicism in North America*. Kansas City, Mo.: Sheed Andrews and McMeel, 1977.

Kinzer, Donald L. *An Episode in Anti-Catholicism: The American Protective Association*. Seattle: University of Washington Press, 1964.

MacLean, Nancy. *Behind the Mask of Chivalry: The Making of the Second Ku Klux Klan*. New York: Oxford University Press, 1994.

McGreevy, John T. "Thinking on One's Own: Catholicism in the American Intellectual Imagination, 1928–1960." *Journal of American History* 84 (1997): 97–131.

James P. McCartin

See also **Catholicism; Discrimination; Know-Nothing Party; Nativism; Religion and Religious Affiliation.**

ANTICOMMUNISM was a stance rather than a movement. It did not revolve around a principal anticommunist organization or a core ideology. Anticommunists were defined by what they were against rather than what they were for. Rather than a single anticommunism, there were numerous varieties, and since the 1917 Bolshevik revolution in Russia a multitude of civil, political, and religious organizations incorporated anticommunism as a subsidiary part of their activities while countless single-purpose and usually short-lived anticommunist organizations sprang up. The various anticommunisms did not follow a common agenda aside from their shared opposition to communism or even approve of each other. At times government authorities prosecuted, persecuted, and harassed Communists; at other times the government was indifferent and nongovernment organizations spearheaded the anticommunist cause.

Varieties of Anticommunism

Conservative and patriotic anticommunism found expression through such private organizations as the AMERICAN LEGION, the American Chamber of Commerce, and the Veterans of Foreign Wars as well as through the Republican Party and the conservative wing of the Democratic Party. On the left, the American Federation of Labor and its leader, Samuel Gompers, were hostile to communism from 1917 onward, resenting Communist attempts to subordinate trade unions to party control and judging that independent unions could operate successfully only in a democratic polity. The smaller Congress of Industrial Organizations contained a number of Communist-aligned unions, but in 1950, headed by the United Steelworkers of America leader Philip Murray and the United Auto Workers chief Walter Reuther, it, too, concluded that American trade unionism and communism were incompatible and expelled its Communist faction.

Communism's militant atheism and the suppression of Christianity in the U.S.S.R. sparked strong religiously based anticommunism among both Protestants, particularly Evangelicals, and Roman Catholics. Roman Catholics were aroused in the 1930s by the violent suppression of the church in Spain by a government in which Communists were dominant. Catholics became further mobilized after 1945 by communist persecution of Catholics in Eastern Europe. Catholic lay organizations such as the Knights of Columbus, Catholic Daughters of America, Cardinal Mindszenty Foundation, Catholic War Veterans, and the Association of Catholic Trade Unionists became actively anticommunist. The Soviet takeover of Eastern Europe also aroused hostility among ethnic Americans with forebears from the region. Polish Americans through such organizations as the Polish American Congress played a significant role in shifting the Democratic Party to an anticommunist stance in the post–World War II period.

Political Anticommunism

In the 1940s and 1950s Republicans often used anticommunism as a partisan weapon against Democrats and liberals, seeking to link them to communism. Richard Nixon (R-Calif.) gained national prominence as a member of the HOUSE COMMITTEE ON UN-AMERICAN ACTIVITIES investigating Soviet espionage, while Senator Joseph McCarthy (R-Wis.) used anticommunism in a demagogic fashion to accuse prominent members of the Truman administration of treason. The conservative Democratic Senator Pat McCarran of Nevada authored the sweeping Internal Security Act of 1950 and chaired the Senate's Internal Security Subcommittee's investigations into communism. Anticommunism became ascendant among liberal Democrats after World War II when Communists and their allies, dissatisfied with President Truman's increasing hostility to Soviet foreign policy, made a bid for the leadership of liberalism. In 1948 left liberals hostile to Truman's Cold War policies joined with Communists to create the Progressive Party as an alternative to the Democratic Party and backed Henry Wallace as a left alternative to Truman's reelection. In the ensuing intraliberal civil war, anticommunist liberals, working though the Americans for Democratic Action, argued that liberal belief in political democracy and such fundamental liberties as freedom of speech, press, and association precluded cooperation with communism, which rejected those in theory and practice. Communists and their allies suffered a catastrophic political defeat when Wallace and the Progressives did very poorly, and the Democratic Party came under the firm control of Truman's Cold War Democrats and such anticommunist liberals as Senators Hubert Humphrey (D-Minn.), Paul Douglas (D-Ill.), and Henry Jackson (D-Wash.). Other left anticommunisms included that of the Socialist Party, particularly in the 1930s and 1940s under the leadership of Norman Thomas, which saw communism's rejection of political democracy as a betrayal of the basic values of socialism, and that of a number of intellectual figures grouped around the literary journal *Partisan Review*, who came out of the Trotskyist movement and regarded the Stalinist regime as a nightmarish distortion of their earlier idealistic hopes.

On the fringes of politics a variety of extremist anticommunist groups appeared that variously defined communism as a vast conspiratorial menace secretly manipulating the government or as the front for a Jewish or Masonic plot. Notable in the 1950s was the John Birch Society, which regarded the Republican President Dwight Eisenhower as part of the communist conspiracy, and the claim by the anti-Semitic demagogue Gerald L. K. Smith that fluoridating drinking water to prevent cavities was really a communist plot to poison the American public.

Government Anticommunism

President Woodrow Wilson welcomed Russia's March 1917 revolution that removed the tsar. The November Bolshevik revolution, however, threatened the United States and its World War I allies. Lenin withdrew Russia from the war, enabling Germany to shift troops to the western front and threatening to overwhelm French and British forces. The United States rushed hundreds of thousands of hastily trained soldiers to France. Linkage in the public mind of Bolshevism with the German enemy grew stronger when it became known that imperial Germany had transported Lenin to Russia from exile and provided financial aid in hope of destabilizing the Russian state. The first congressional inquiry into communism, the 1918–1919 hearings conducted by Senator Lee Overman (D-N.C.), began as investigations into "pro-Germanism" that evolved into a hostile exploration of Bolshevism. President Wilson sent troops to occupy Murmansk, Archangel, and Vladivostok to seize military supplies sent earlier to Russia and assist anti-Bolshevik forces, but withdrew them by early 1920 without serious clashes with Communist troops. The United States refused diplomatic recognition to the new Soviet government until 1933.

Domestically, in 1919–1920 anarchists were suspected in a series of bombings that killed at least thirty-five persons and injured hundreds. U.S. Attorney General A. Mitchell Palmer, in cooperation with local police and aided by citizen volunteers, rounded up several thousand radicals in the "PALMER RAIDS." More than a thousand alien radicals were deported and several hundred citizen radicals were imprisoned under state antisubversion laws. Anarchists bore the brunt of government prosecutions in the "red scare," but the newly organized Communist parties were driven underground. By 1921 fear of world revolution subsided when Soviet attempts to spread beyond Russia failed. The United States and most state governments ceased legal attacks on radicals, and the FBI ended most of its surveillance of revolutionaries. The Communist Party surfaced as a legal, aboveground organization.

Public hostility to communism remained pervasive but passive.

In 1930–1932 a House of Representatives committee chaired by Hamilton Fish (R-N.Y.) investigated reports of a vast Communist conspiracy but was discredited by reliance on forged documents that had been sold to the NATIONAL CIVIC FEDERATION, a business-led anticommunist group. In 1936, President Roosevelt, concerned about fascist subversion, authorized the FBI to reenter the internal security field, and it undertook surveillance of both fascists and Communists. In 1938 the House of Representatives created a Special Committee on Un-American Activities, chaired by Martin Dies (D-Tex.), to investigate domestic Nazis and Communists. Dies, a conservative Democrat who disapproved of Roosevelt's New Deal, emphasized linking Communists to Roosevelt's reforms.

The COMMUNIST PARTY, USA (CPUSA) supported the August 1939 Nazi-Soviet Pact and assailed Roosevelt's policies of assisting those nations fighting Germany. Fearing Communists would become a "fifth column" in time of war, the Roosevelt administration imprisoned Earl Browder, CPUSA chief, for using a false passport. Several states also prosecuted Communists under local antisubversion laws, but in most places Communists continued to work openly. After the Nazi attack on the U.S.S.R. in June 1941, the CPUSA shifted to support the war policies of the Roosevelt administration, federal attacks on the CPUSA ceased, and Roosevelt released Browder from prison in 1942.

In 1947 President Truman, concerned that Soviet espionage services had recruited American Communists as spies, established a security program for government employees that excluded Communists from government jobs. In 1948 the Truman administration indicted the top leadership of the CPUSA under the sedition sections of the SMITH ACT; they were convicted and imprisoned in 1950. Republicans, using the House Un-American Activities Committee (HUAC, successor to the Dies committee), began to attack the Truman administration as lax in regard to Communist espionage. HUAC hearings were often known for a circuslike atmosphere, but they were successful in beginning the process that led to the 1950 conviction of Alger Hiss for perjury regarding spying for the U.S.S.R. After the outbreak of the Korean War and with American troops fighting Communist soldiers, public anticommunism became heated, and Congress passed a series of stern anticommunist laws. American courts, however, rendered key sections of these laws inoperable, and the Communist Party continued to operate openly. A Supreme Court decision in *Yates v. United States* in 1957 rendered the Smith Act nearly unusable as a prosecutorial tool against seditious speech.

By the mid-1950s the CPUSA had become a tiny movement without significant influence. The CPUSA's marginalization, along with the death of Stalin in 1953, the end of the Korean War, and the stabilization of the

Aftermath of Antietam. Until long afterward, Alexander Gardner (and his associates) received little personal recognition for unprecedented stark battlefield photographs like this one of dead Confederates collected for burial. Initial credit went to his famous employer in New York, Mathew Brady—who took few photographs of the war himself. LIBRARY OF CONGRESS

COLD WAR, reduced the fervor of public anticommunism and its salience as a partisan political issue but not its pervasiveness. The Vietnam War of the 1960s, however, resulted in the discrediting of anticommunism in the eyes of those opposed to American involvement, and some liberals adopted the view, similar to that of Wallace and the 1948 Progressive Party, that cooperation with communism was acceptable and repudiated the Cold War policies begun by Truman. Public hostility to communism and the Soviet Union, nonetheless, remained strong, as demonstrated by the election to the presidency for two terms (1981–1989) of Ronald Reagan, a veteran anticommunist who called the U.S.S.R. an "evil empire" and challenged it to tear down the Berlin Wall, increased military expenditures, and sharpened America's Cold War policies.

BIBLIOGRAPHY

Fried, Richard M. *Nightmare in Red: The McCarthy Era in Perspective.* New York: Oxford University Press, 1990.

Haynes, John Earl. *Red Scare or Red Menace? American Communism and Anticommunism in the Cold War Era.* Chicago: Ivan R. Dee, 1996.

Latham, Earl. *The Communist Controversy in Washington: From the New Deal to McCarthy.* Cambridge, Mass.: Harvard University Press, 1966.

O'Neill, William L. *A Better World: Stalinism and the American Intellectuals.* New Brunswick, N.J.: Transaction, 1990.

Powers, Richard Gid. *Not Without Honor: The History of American Anticommunism.* New York: Free Press, 1995.

Schrecker, Ellen. *Many Are the Crimes: McCarthyism in America.* Boston: Little, Brown, 1998.

John Earl Haynes

See also **Blacklisting; McCarthyism; Progressive Party, 1948;** *and vol. 9:* **The Blue Book of the John Birch Society; Censure of Senator Joseph McCarthy; Senator Joseph McCarthy: The History of George Catlett Marshall, 1951; The Testimony of Walter E. Disney.**

ANTIETAM, BATTLE OF. The Battle of Antietam took place on 17 September 1862. With an estimated 23,100 total casualties, it was the bloodiest single-day battle of the American Civil War. As a result of the high number of casualties on each side, the battle was a tactical draw, although a strategic victory for the Union.

The battle was a result of the Confederate army's first attempt to wage war in the North. Early in September 1862 General Robert E. Lee's Army of Northern Virginia crossed the Potomac into Maryland. He concentrated at Frederick, then sent T. J. "Stonewall" Jackson's corps south to take Harpers Ferry and General James Longstreet's corps westward across the South Mountain. On 14 September, Union general George Brinton McClellan's Army of the Potomac forced the mountain passes.

Lee began to concentrate toward the Potomac and took position at Sharpsburg, on Antietam Creek. While Longstreet was assembling, Lee heard that Jackson had captured Harpers Ferry and made the bold decision to stand and fight behind the creek, with the Potomac at his back. Longstreet took the right of the line, and Jackson's troops, as they arrived, took the left. McClellan planned to strike Lee's left with three corps (commanded by Generals Joseph Hooker, Joseph Mansfield, and Edwin Sumner). He would follow this blow with an attack by General Ambrose E. Burnside's corps on the Confederate right and hold Fitz-John Porter's and W. B. Franklin's corps, with Alfred Pleasonton's cavalry, in reserve in the center. But Hooker, Mansfield, and Sumner attacked successively, not simultaneously, and each in turn was beaten. Burnside's attack on the other flank came still later.

On the Confederate side, Longstreet's line had been weakened to reinforce Jackson, for Lee had no real reserve. As a result, although Burnside made some progress at first, when fully engaged he was struck in flank by A. P. Hill's division, the last of Jackson's troops returning from Harpers Ferry. Burnside was driven back to the bridge by which he had crossed the creek, and darkness ended the fighting.

On 18 September, Lee stood fast and McClellan did not renew his attack. The following day, Lee withdrew his army across the Potomac. The numbers engaged are uncertain; perhaps a fair estimate is 50,000 Union, 40,000 Confederate. But this represented Lee's entire strength, and McClellan had 20,000 troops in reserve, never used. Losses for the Union army numbered about 12,000 casualties, including 2,108 killed. The Army of Northern Virginia lost almost 25 percent of its forces, including at least 1,500 killed. News of the carnage spread throughout the country after newspapers published photographer Alexander Gardner's vivid and disturbing photographs of the battlefield. As a strategic Northern victory, Antietam provided the positive news President Abraham Lincoln thought a prerequisite for issuing the Emancipation Proclamation. The victory also gave the impression that the North was doing better in the war, which may have helped elections for the Republican Party in 1862.

Antietam was designated a national battlefield by an act of Congress on 30 August 1890. Today the park is run by the National Park Service and receives approximately 280,000 visitors each year.

BIBLIOGRAPHY

Gallagher, Gary W., ed. *The Antietam Campaign.* Chapel Hill: University of North Carolina Press, 1999.

Harsh, Joseph L. *Sounding the Shallows: A Confederate Companion for the Maryland Campaign of 1862.* Kent, Ohio: Kent State University Press, 2000.

Johnson, Curt, and Richard C. Anderson Jr. *Artillery Hell: The Employment of Artillery at Antietam.* College Station: Texas A&M University Press, 1995.

Honor Sachs
Oliver Lyman Spaulding

See also **Civil War; Emancipation Proclamation; Maryland, Invasion of.**

ANTIFEDERALISTS. When those who sought ratification of the Constitution of the United States (1787–1788) coopted the name "Federalist," they forced onto their opponents the unfortunate label "Antifederalist." This reversal of names made the Antifederalists appear purely negative when they in fact stood for affirmative visions of government that were simply different from the framework advocated by the Constitution's defenders. The term also falsely projected unity onto a disparate group that to a significant extent was united mainly in its opposition to the proposed government. Perhaps most misleading of all, the designation "Antifederalist" applied to a group that generally supported a less centralized "federal" government in which the states would retain more power, while the term "Federalist" fell to those who advocated the more centralized national government that they believed the Constitution would guarantee. The Antifederalists, like many of history's losers, have been misunderstood and underappreciated.

Despite certain differences among them, the Antifederalists' opposition to the Constitution reflected several common themes. These more genuine "federalists" tended to retain a belief in majoritarian representative government as best implemented at the state or local level, with powers delegated to the national government only in matters in which the states would be unable or unlikely to act in a united fashion. Antifederalists generally believed that governmental power was best concentrated in the legislature as the most democratically responsive branch. They were also more likely than not to maintain that such local, legislatively oriented government offered the best protection for fundamental rights. Moreover, one way to insure each of these protective mechanisms was through the precise allocation of government power through specific texts. Antifederalists therefore feared that the dangerously vague Constitution delegated too much power to the federal government at the expense of the states, allocated excessive authority to the executive and judiciary to the detriment of Congress, and established a government that threatened the very freedoms Americans has just recently defended against Great Britain.

Amidst these general tendencies, opposition to the Constitution was hardly monolithic. To some Antifederalists, for example, the Senate represented a dangerous concentration of aristocratic power, while to others it was an inadequate check on a near-dictatorial presidency. Scholarship has also drawn a distinction between elite Antifederalists, who championed power at the state level specifically, and their more "middling" counterparts, who preferred greater authority at the local level on the ground that even the state governments were too distant and unrepresentative.

In making their cases, the Antifederalists failed to produce either leaders or writings to equal their antagonists. While the Federalists could rely on the power of names like George Washington and Benjamin Franklin, the opposition at best could muster either older revolutionary figures of less national stature, such as Patrick Henry, Richard Henry Lee, or George Mason, or younger advocates who had yet to establish their reputations fully, including George Clinton, James Monroe, and Melancton Smith. Likewise Antifederalists never produced a manifesto as compelling as James Wilson's widely reprinted "Speech at a Public Meeting in Philadelphia" or as coherent as *The Federalist*, though the latter had far less of an impact at the time than subsequently. Probably the closest comparable works from the Antifederalist side were Mason's "Objections to the Constitution," *Letters from the Federal Farmer*, most likely by Melancton Smith, and the essays of "Brutus."

The opposition that these writings reflected was substantial and widespread. Antifederalists commanded clear majorities in Rhode Island, New York, North Carolina, and South Carolina; outnumbered the Federalists by closer margins in Massachusetts and Virginia; and boasted significant strength in every other state except Delaware and New Jersey. Throughout the nation the Antifederalist cause tended to flourish more strongly in western regions than along the coast. At one time it was widely believed that the Federalists primarily drew their strength from social and economic elites, while the Antifederalists mainly drew from persons of more modest status and means. Research has shown that these broad generalizations do not withstand scrutiny and that the correlation between class and support for the Constitution is far more subtle and complex.

More straightforward are the traditions from which the Antifederalists drew. Many Antifederalist advocates saw themselves as defenders of a more genuine vision of republican self-government that was embodied in the early state constitutions drafted after independence as well as in the struggle for independence itself. This legacy in turn owed a large debt to English Whig thought, which had furnished an important basis for the colonies' struggle for greater autonomy from Britain. Invoking these understandings, Antifederalist rhetoric equated opposition to the distant, unrepresentative, and dangerous new federal government with the revolutionary struggle against the British Parliament and Crown. Federalist leaders such as James Madison and Wilson countered that the Constitution instead sought to guard against certain abuses of republican government the better to preserve it. Antifederalists nonetheless remained skeptical, viewing the Federalist project as nothing less than a betrayal of the principles of 1776.

Despite their advantage in numbers and reliance on familiar understandings, the Antifederalists proved no match for their Federalist counterparts. Among other things, they failed to organize as effectively, to counter the Federalists' superior command of the plan they proposed, or to offer an alternative of their own to address the widely perceived problems the nation faced. The Federalists outmaneuvered their adversaries in arguing that the special conventions in which the Constitution would be considered demonstrated a greater trust in the people than the state governments the Antifederalists defended. In Massachusetts, ratification stalled until Federalists agreed to forward recommended amendments that the new government would take up once the Constitution went into effect. This device successfully undermined Antifederalist opposition in each state thereafter. Pockets of strong opposition remained, however, and by the time the first Congress met in 1789, North Carolina had yet to overturn its initial rejection of the Constitution, and Rhode Island had still not voted in the first place.

Even in defeat the Antifederalists managed to score a number of lasting victories. Most notably they forced an extensive, wide-ranging, at times highly detailed debate over the proposed Constitution's underlying assumptions as well as over the meaning of its many specific and often terse provisions. The fears Antifederalists expressed in many instances forced Federalists to publicly retreat from positions they may otherwise have desired. When, for example, Antifederalist polemics charged that the necessary and proper clause would lead to a consolidated national government of limitless power, those who defended the Constitution typically countered by minimizing the authority the provision conveyed. One ironic result of this give and take is that some of the most expansive interpretations of federal power come from the Antifederalists who most abhorred it, while narrower constructions often come from the same Federalists who wanted broad national authority. Whether any of the competing interpretations that emerged as a result can be said to have yielded an "original understanding" is a question best treated with care and caution.

Another Antifederalist legacy is the BILL OF RIGHTS (1791). Few of the Constitution's features generated more persistent and widespread criticism than its failure to include a genuine enumeration of liberties, an omission that stood in stark contrast to the constitutions of the states. Certain Federalist leaders, notably Alexander Hamilton, Madison, and Wilson, replied that a bill of rights was irrelevant on the grounds of popular sovereignty. In this view the people at large, assembled in conventions, granted specific, enumerated powers to the new government, none of which authorized the infringement of rights they otherwise retained. This argument, however, did not mollify opposition as effectively as the strategy of recommended amendments, a significant portion of which called for the listing of traditional rights. Thanks partly to a change of heart by Madison, the First Congress made good on the Federalist pledge to propose such a list, which the states then ratified as the first ten amendments to the Constitution. The extent to which Antifederalist goals survived in the catalog fashioned by the Federalist-dominated Congress is debatable. To cite one instance, while numerous recommended amendments sought to make clear that the federal government received only those powers "expressly" granted, the Tenth Amendment offered the less restrictive formulation that the states and the people retained merely those powers not delegated to the new government.

The Antifederalist inheritance lingers in the idea of a loyal opposition. By engaging in the ratification process so fully, the Constitution's opponents paradoxically legitimated it, making it far more difficult to reject whatever outcome the final votes produced. Washington's election as president and Congress's approval of the Bill of Rights, however flawed, further set Antifederalist minds at ease. Rather than resist the new government, those who had argued against its adoption therefore chose to seek their goals within its framework. As a result a number of prominent former Antifederalists, including Elbridge Gerry, Lee, Luther Martin, and Monroe, took their seats in early Congresses or other government positions. None of these leaders attempted to create an "Antifederalist" party, and none emerged. Organized parties remained suspect, and new, unanticipated controversies forged new alliances that cut across the older Federalist-Antifederalist divide.

Instead, it was in their writings, understandings, and rhetoric that the Antifederalists endured—in certain respects, even into the twenty-first century. Historians generally agree that their views contributed heavily to Jeffersonian and Jacksonian thought. Antifederalist concerns also emerged in later dissenting traditions, including elements of the Progressive movement of the late nineteenth and early twentieth centuries. Since the New Deal (1933–1941), fears of a too-powerful, too-distant federal government have also echoed the Antifederalists' original concerns. Ironically, later advocates of state power and democratic accountability often invoked the Federalists rather than their true forebears. In this the Antifederalists continued to lose, even as they won.

BIBLIOGRAPHY

Cornell, Saul. *The Other Founders: Anti-Federalism and the Dissenting Tradition in America, 1788–1828.* Chapel Hill: University of North Carolina Press, 1999. A fresh and rigorous interpretation.

Hutson, James A. "Country, Court, and the Constitution: Antifederalism and the Historians." *William and Mary Quarterly* 38, no. 3 (July 1981): 337–368. Extremely useful.

Kenyon, Cecilia. "Men of Little Faith." *William and Mary Quarterly* 12, no. 1 (January 1955): 3–43. Continues to frame discourse.

Kramnick, Isaac. "The 'Great National Discussion': The Discourse of Politics in 1787." *William and Mary Quarterly* 45, no. 1 (January 1988): 3–32.

Main, Jackson Turner. *The Antifederalists: Critics of the Constitution, 1781–1788.* Chapel Hill: University of North Carolina Press, 1961. Important neoprogressive view.

McDonald, Forrest. "The Anti-Federalists." In *The Reinterpretation of the American Revolution, 1763–1789.* Edited by Jack P. Greene. New York: Harper and Row, 1968.

Murrin, John. "The Great Inversion, or Court versus Country: A Comparison of the Revolutionary Settlements in England (1688–1721) and America (1776–1816)." In *Three British Revolutions: 1641, 1688, 1776.* Edited by J. G. A. Pocock. Princeton, N.J.: Princeton University Press, 1980. Highly original overview.

Rakove, Jack N. *Original Meanings: Politics and Ideas in the Making of the Constitution.* New York: Knopf, 1996. Wide-ranging synthesis.

Storing, Herbert J. *What the Anti-Federalists Were For.* Chicago: University of Chicago Press, 1981.

Wood, Gordon S. *The Creation of the American Republic, 1776–1787.* New York: Norton, 1972. Germinal work.

———. "Interests and Disinterestedness in the Making of the Constitution." In *Beyond Confederation: Origins of the American Constitution and National Identity.* Edited by Richard Beeman, Stephen Botein, and Edward C. Carter II. Chapel Hill: University of North Carolina Press, 1987. Rethinking of earlier ideas.

Martin S. Flaherty

See also **Bill of Rights in United States Constitution; Constitution of the United States; *Federalist Papers*.**

ANTI-IMPERIALISTS. This term is used generally to connote those who resisted or disapproved of American colonialist impulses at various moments and especially those who opposed U.S. colonial expansion after the SPANISH-AMERICAN WAR. Although a number of anti-imperialists had first opposed the acquisition of island territories during the administration of Ulysses Grant, and others survived to proclaim the faith in the 1920s, anti-imperialism as a movement is limited to the years 1898–1900.

Many anti-imperialists rejected organizational activity, but a majority claimed membership in one of the branches of the Anti-Imperialist League, which was founded in Boston in November 1898. By 1900 the league claimed to have 30,000 members and more than half a million contributors. Its primary goal was the education of public opinion. The league published hundreds of pamphlets denouncing the acquisition of an island empire and the abandonment of America's unique "mission" to hold before the nations of the world the model of a free and self-governing society. Its members included reformers, educators, labor leaders, and Democratic politicians. George S. Boutwell, Erving Winslow, Edwin Burritt Smith, David Starr Jordan, and Carl Schurz were prominent leaders of the league, and its chief financial contributor was Andrew Carnegie. Other important anti-imperialists included William Jennings Bryan and ex-presidents Benjamin Harrison and Grover Cleveland.

Although diverse in motives and party affiliation, the anti-imperialists shared common fears and beliefs. They were convinced that imperialism threatened the ideals and institutions of their own country, and many believed that it was unjust to dictate the political goals and institutions of foreign peoples. Although many anti-imperialists shared the racial bias of their imperialist opponents and some urged the expansion of foreign markets as a solution to domestic surplus, for most, racial "difference" did not require racial subordination, nor did trade expansion demand GUNBOAT DIPLOMACY. The anti-imperialists typically insisted that it was as wrong for a republic to have colonies as it was for a representative government to have subject peoples. Tyranny abroad, they believed, could only undermine democracy at home. They offered arguments against the constitutionality, economic wisdom, and strategic safety of a policy of insular imperialism. Colonial expansion not only denied the practice of the past, it would waste American resources, undermine the Monroe Doctrine, and embroil the United States in the rivalries of the European powers. Although hampered by having to preach a doctrine of abnegation to a nation of optimists and weakened by a failure to agree on a single policy alternative for the disposition of the Philippine Islands, the anti-imperialists were participants in one of the most intelligently reasoned debates in American history.

Even though they were important as a moral and educational force, the anti-imperialists must be classified among the political failures of American history. Their labors, along with the heavy cost of the PHILIPPINE INSURRECTION, may have helped to check the territorial ambitions of the more zealous imperialists, but none of the anti-imperialists' immediate goals were secured. The new island territories were officially annexed; President William McKinley easily won reelection in 1900 despite the opposition of the Anti-Imperialist League, and the Philippine Insurrection was mercilessly crushed.

BIBLIOGRAPHY

Beisner, Robert L. *Twelve Against Empire: The Anti-Imperialists, 1898–1900.* New York: McGraw-Hill, 1968. Reprint, Chicago: Imprint, 1992.

Tompkins, E. Berkeley. *Anti-Imperialism in the United States: The Great Debate, 1890–1920.* Philadelphia: University of Pennsylvania Press, 1970.

Fraser Harbutt

See also **Imperialism**; *and* vol. 9: **Anti-Imperialist League Platform**.

ANTI-MASONIC MOVEMENTS.

Widespread anti-Masonry first developed in the 1790s with unsubstantiated charges that Masonic lodges in the United States imported and encouraged radical European revolutionary ideas. Nonetheless, after 1800 Freemasonry—a fraternal order originally brought to the colonies from Britain—flourished and included such distinguished members as George Washington, Andrew Jackson, and Henry Clay. Freemasonic lodges, offering mutual support and fellowship primarily to mobile, middle-class men who had time to participate and could afford to pay substantial dues, multiplied North and South. Masons uniformly swore oaths never to reveal the content of their elaborate, secret rituals and promised to defend fellow Masons. By the 1820s, most states had chartered grand lodges to oversee the many local lodges. Handsome new Masonic temples, together with Masonic participation in public parades and ceremonies, attracted attention in the North, particularly in western New York, sections of Ohio and Pennsylvania, and portions of the six New England states.

In March 1826 a disgruntled Mason, William Morgan of Batavia, New York, engaged a newspaper editor to help him publish a book exposing the content of Masonic rituals. On 12 September 1826 a group of outraged Masons from western New York kidnapped Morgan. Morgan's subsequent disappearance and suspected murder by Masons first ignited a series of New York trials, then fueled a concerted campaign by opponents of Masonry who wished to identify individual Masons, eliminate local lodges, outlaw Masonic oaths, and revoke the charters of Masonic state organizations. Between 1826 and 1836 anti-Masons from Vermont to the Michigan Territory forcefully argued that Freemasonry was inherently aristocratic, secular, and immoral—a danger to young men, families, Christianity, and the republic. The uncompromising program to eradicate Masonry split churches, divided communities, induced about two-thirds of Masons to desert their lodges, and created the a third party, the Antimasonic Party.

Anti-Masons established newspapers and tract societies and held mass meetings featuring the testimony of seceding Masons. Having discovered large numbers of Masons in public offices, anti-Masons drove state legislatures to investigate Masonry and turned to political action. From 1827 to 1833 in Morgan's Genesee County, New York, they captured every county office. Elsewhere, they gained local offices, won seats in state legislatures, and elected governors in Pennsylvania, Vermont, and Rhode Island. In September 1831 the anti-Mason convention at Baltimore, the first national party nominating convention, selected Maryland's William Wirt, former U.S. attorney general, as its presidential candidate for 1832. Unwilling to campaign, Wirt carried only Vermont. By 1836 the evolving Democratic and Whig parties had begun to absorb the anti-Masons.

Originally a grassroots social movement whose complex bases of support differed from place to place, antimasonry became a crusade in Northern communities buffeted by confusing social, economic, and religious changes, but it lacked appeal in the South. Anti-Mason agitators, often established or rising businessmen and lawyers who resembled their Masonic counterparts, drew new voters into politics, advanced the convention system of selecting political candidates, contributed to the voter realignment that produced the Whig and Democratic party system, and helped launch the careers of politicians such as William Seward and Millard Fillmore. After the Civil War the efforts by Wheaton College president Jonathan Blanchard and aged evangelist Charles G. Finney to attack secret societies and revive anti-Masonry fizzled.

BIBLIOGRAPHY

Goodman, Paul. *Towards a Christian Republic: Antimasonry and the Great Transition in New England, 1826–1836.* New York: Oxford University Press, 1988.

Kutolowski, Kathleen Smith. "Antimasonry Reexamined: Social Bases of the Grass-Roots Party." *Journal of American History* 71, no. 2 (September 1984): 269–293.

Vaughn, William P. *The Antimasonic Party in the United States, 1826–1843.* Lexington: University Press of Kentucky, 1983.

Vaughn, William Preston. "The Reverend Charles G. Finney and the Post Civil War Antimasonic Crusade." *The Social Science Journal* 27, no. 2 (April 1990): 209–221.

Julienne L. Wood

See also **Freemasons.**

ANTIMONOPOLY PARTIES (also known as Reform or Independent parties) appeared in the old northwest starting in 1873, and their short-lived influence as third parties ended after the presidential election of 1876. These parties appeared briefly in California, Indiana, Illinois, Iowa, Kansas, Michigan, Minnesota, Missouri, Nebraska, and Oregon. Forming in Republican-dominated states, these third parties scared the ruling party, although the long-term effect was to split the nascent agrarian movement so badly that it took years to recover.

Antimonopoly parties were organized by farmers, many of whom were members of the Grange (Patrons of Husbandry). Although the Grange began in 1868 as a secret society dedicated to cooperation instead of politics, many Grangers became involved in political movements. Women were recruited for membership and possessed the same right to vote and hold office as male members. As a result, the Grange in the west endorsed women's suffrage and temperance. Grange chapter bylaws forbade the endorsement of political candidates or running for office under the banner of the group; members, however, were encouraged to seek legislative solutions to agrarian problems.

By 1873, when a financial panic gripped Wall Street, antimonopoly parties had been formed in Illinois, Iowa, and Wisconsin by Grange members determined to involve the agrarian movement more directly in politics. In these three states, dissidents broke with their state leaders to help form third-party movements in their states. In Wisconsin, Grange members called for all members interested in a third party to meet at Milwaukee in August 1873. Although state Grange leaders thwarted this meeting, the third-party threat presented by Wisconsin agrarians created uncertainty for the state's Republicans in the 1874 election. Similarly, in Iowa, Grangers contributed to the formation of the state's Antimonopoly Party in 1873. Described by historian D. Sven Nordin as "an illegitimate son of the First Granger Movement" (*Rich Harvest*, p. 175), the Iowa party united more farmers under one banner than previous organizations, and framed their ideas into a compact of grievances promoting cooperation and denouncing monopolies. A huge drive in

Antimonopoly Battle. This cartoon from the *New York Graphic*, 14 August 1873, bears the caption "Which Will Win? The Farmer or the Railroad Monster?" © CORBIS

1873 attempted to commit the Illinois State Grange to the Farmers' and People's Antimonopoly Party.

Antimonopoly party platforms reflected farmers' concerns, demanding reduced taxation and governmental and economic reform; in some states, they also sought state regulation of corporations, particularly railroads. In 1874, antimonopolists in Iowa, Minnesota, and Wisconsin helped secure passage of railroad regulatory laws commonly known as the "Granger laws." Electoral victories came that year at the local level in Oregon and Illinois; by fusing with Democrats, antimonopolists elected their entire ticket in Wisconsin and some seats in Iowa.

The rise and fall of Minnesota's third party reflects the tension between Grangers and the antimonopoly movement. Minnesota Grange leader Ignatius Donnelly built grassroots support for a third party in 1873, and although his Antimonopoly Party was defeated that fall, he was elected to the state senate. Donnelly began publishing *The Anti-Monopolist* in 1874 and attempted to fuse the Grange with the antimonopolists. Although many Grange members joined him, the state's leadership refused to sanction overtly political activities, leading Donnelly to charge them with preserving the Republican Party (and by implication, monopolies) at the expense of farmers. When a farmers' coalition proved insufficient to elect Donnelly to Congress in 1875, he quit the agrarian movement and joined the growing Greenback Party. His career typifies the fragmentation of the agrarian movement and suggests reasons for the demise of antimonopoly parties in 1876.

BIBLIOGRAPHY

Edwards, Rebecca. *Angels in the Machinery: Gender in American Party Politics from the Civil War to the Progressive Era.* New York: Oxford University Press, 1997.

Nordin, D. Sven. *Rich Harvest: A History of the Grange, 1867–1900.* Jackson: University Press of Mississippi, 1974.

Summers, Mark Wahlgren. *The Gilded Age, or, The Hazard of New Functions.* Upper Saddle River, N.J.: Prentice-Hall, 1997.

Patricia Hagler Minter

See also **Granger Cases; Granger Movement; Greenback Movement.**

ANTINOMIAN CONTROVERSY,

a theological dispute begun in Boston by Anne Hutchinson in the fall of 1636. She had been a parishioner and devout admirer of John Cotton in Boston, England, and with her husband followed him to the new Boston, where they were admitted to membership in the First Church. She was exceptionally intelligent, learned, and eloquent and began innocently to repeat to small weekday gatherings the substance of Cotton's sermons. Soon, however, she commenced delivering opinions of her own. At the height of her influence, about eighty persons were attending lectures in her house.

She caused turmoil by reinterpreting the clerical doctrine of the covenant of grace. The standard view held that the elect entered a covenant with God on the condition of their believing in Christ, in return for which God contracted to give them salvation. Thereafter these "justified saints" devoted themselves to good works, not in order to merit redemption but as evidence of their having been called. Hutchinson declared that stating the matter in this way put too much emphasis upon works and denied the fundamental Protestant tenet of salvation by faith alone. Consequently she preached that the believer received into his soul the very substance of the Holy Ghost and that no value whatsoever adhered to conduct as a sign of justification.

This conclusion, feared the New England clergy, would hasten the decline of morality that Protestant theologians had everywhere endeavored to resist, and it could clearly lead to disastrous social consequences. They identified in Hutchinson's teachings a form of "Antinomianism," that is, a discarding of the moral law. She made matters worse by accusing all the clergy except Cotton of preaching a covenant of works, so that, in the words of John Winthrop, the governor of Massachusetts Bay Colony, it began to be as common in Massachusetts to distinguish the party of works and the party of grace "as in other countries between Protestants and papists." Thus she threatened to split the colony into factions, particularly when she was supported by her brother-in-law, the Reverend John Wheelwright, and the new young governor, Henry Vane.

The other clergy and magistrates believed that the existence of the whole colony was at stake; led by Winthrop, and employing consummately clever tactics, they regained control of the government in May 1637, then proceeded to disarm Hutchinson's partisans and suppress the movement. Hutchinson was examined by a synod of the ministers, which found her guilty of eighty erroneous opinions. John Cotton publicly repudiated her and Wheelwright was banished to New Hampshire. Hutchinson was arraigned before the general court, where she boasted of having received explicit revelations from the Holy Ghost, a possibility that no orthodox Protestant community could for a moment admit. She was excommunicated from the First Church in March 1638, John Cotton pronouncing sentence upon her, and banished from the colony by the court, whereupon she fled to Rhode Island.

BIBLIOGRAPHY

Battis, Emery. *Saints and Sectaries: Anne Hutchinson and the Antinomian Controversy in the Massachusetts Bay Colony.* Chapel Hill: University of North Carolina Press, 1962.

Hall, David D., ed. *The Antinomian Controversy, 1636–1638: A Documentary History.* 2d ed. Durham, N.C.: Duke University Press, 1990.

Lang, Amy Scrager. *Prophetic Woman: Anne Hutchinson and the Problem of Dissent in the Literature of New England.* Berkeley: University of California Press, 1987.

Miller, Perry. *Orthodoxy in Massachusetts, 1630–1650.* Cambridge, Mass.: Harvard University Press, 1933.

Perry Miller / A. R.

See also **Mysticism; Religious Liberty; Religious Thought and Writings; Women in Churches.**

ANTIQUITIES ACT

of 1906, officially, An Act for the Preservation of American Antiquities, was the first federal general historic preservation law. The act authorized the president to designate as national monuments "historic landmarks, historic and prehistoric structures, and other objects of historic or scientific interest" on federal lands. It also required permits for excavation on public lands and provided criminal penalties for unauthorized damage to or appropriation of objects of antiquity on those lands.

In 1906, the primary goal of Congress was to stop the decay and plundering of Native American ruins in the Southwest. Among the earliest monuments were Devils Tower in Wyoming, El Morro in New Mexico, and Montezuma Castle in Arizona. But presidents interpreted the act's language broadly and transformed the law into a conservation measure to protect large amounts of scenic or wilderness lands, some of which later became national parks. In the first such expansive use of the Antiquities Act, Theodore Roosevelt in 1908 designated 806,400 acres surrounding the Grand Canyon as a monument to protect structures of scientific interest. Subsequently, every president except Richard Nixon used the act to establish or expand national monuments. The power of presidents to unilaterally designate monuments often has created controversy. For example, President Bill Clinton created eight monuments in the final two months of his presidency, generating new calls to restrict presidential authority under the act.

BIBLIOGRAPHY

Cunningham, Richard B. *Archaeology, Relics, and the Law.* Durham, N.C.: Carolina Academic Press, 1999.

Lee, Ronald F. *The Antiquities Act of 1906.* Washington, D.C.: National Park Service, 1971.

Rothman, Hal. *Preserving Different Pasts: The American National Monuments.* Urbana: University of Illinois Press, 1989.

Cynthia R. Poe

See also **Conservation; National Park System.**

ANTI-RENT WAR. Centered in the Catskill counties of New York state, the Anti-Rent War of 1839–1846 was a rebellion against the old patroon system of estate landownership. Protest took the form of harassment of rent collectors by farmers disguised as "Indians," who shot seized livestock and broke up rent sales. In 1845, however, protesters killed a deputy sheriff, prompting a sheriff's posse, reinforced by state militia, to begin wreaking havoc in Delaware County while searching for the killers. Ninety-four anti-rent men were arrested and indicted for murder, while 148 were charged with other crimes, including arson, theft, and rioting.

However, this heavy-handed reaction against a system largely obsolete outside New York drew great sympathy for the anti-renters, and in the 1845 New York elections, a governor gained office on the promise of pardoning all the anti-renters, reforming the land system, and beginning the practice of electing the New York attorney general, all of which were done by 1846.

BIBLIOGRAPHY

Christman, Henry. *Tin Horns and Calico: A Decisive Episode in the Emergence of Democracy.* Cornwallville, N.Y.: Hope Farm Press, 1975.

Huston, Reeve. *Land and Freedom: Rural Society, Popular Protest, and Party Politics in Antebellum New York.* Oxford: Oxford University Press, 2000.

Margaret D. Sankey

ANTI-SALOON LEAGUE. An interdenominational Protestant organization dedicated to advancing prohibition through political means. Founded in 1893 by Rev. H. H. Russell at Oberlin College, the Ohio Anti-Saloon League is credited with being the first nonpartisan, single-

issue interest group in modern American politics. The multiplication of Russell's "Ohio plan" in other states led to the creation of a national body in 1895. Using modern techniques of organization and persuasion, the league pushed for local option and state prohibition laws through legislation and by supporting dry candidates for office. Beginning in 1913, it led the successful fight for a constitutional amendment. As the effects of national prohibition became felt in the 1920s, the league came under increasing criticism. Revocation of the Eighteenth Amendment in 1933 ended its influence in American politics.

BIBLIOGRAPHY

Kerr, K. Austin. *Organized for Prohibition: A New History of the Anti-Saloon League.* New Haven, Conn.: Yale University Press, 1985.

Odegard, Peter H. *Pressure Politics: The Story of the Anti-Saloon League.* New York: Columbia University Press, 1928. Reprint, New York: Octagon Books, 1966.

C. Wyatt Evans

See also **Prohibition; Social Legislation; Temperance Movement.**

ANTI-SEMITISM and the fight against it have played a small but significant role in American history. During the colonial period, the most serious incident of anti-Semitism occurred not in a British colony, but in the Dutch colony of New Amsterdam (later New York), where in 1654 Governor Peter Stuyvesant attempted to bar Jews from the city. In the British colonies, Jews generally faced no worse treatment than did Catholics or other Christian minorities. The main obstacles they faced were religious requirements for holding political office.

In the colonial and early confederation period, every one of the thirteen colonies except for New York required all office holders to take a Christian oath. Some went even further—in South Carolina, belief in Protestant Christianity was a voting requirement. But by 1877, the last Christian voting requirement had been eliminated, and the United States offered many attractive incentives to Jewish immigration.

The Early Twentieth Century

By the early twentieth century, the United States had become the immigration destination of choice for Jews from all over the world. Yet vestiges of anti-Semitism remained. In order to combat these, the American Jewish Committee (AJC) was formed in 1906. Their goal was to protect Jewish civil rights, not only in the United States, but also internationally. A few years later, in 1913, the Anti-Defamation League of B'nai B'rith was formed. This organization focused on combating negative media stereotypes of Jews and economic discrimination.

The strength of these Jewish defense groups demonstrated that although the United States had problems with anti-Semitism, these problems could be redressed by organization within the political system. These opportunities helped the United States remain the main destination for Jewish immigrants until the second decade of the twentieth century. Palestine was then only a distant second.

Between the 1910s and 1930s, the Jewish population of Palestine tripled to nearly 30 percent. This population explosion was directly connected to anti-Semitism and nativism in America. In 1921, the U.S. Congress clamped down on immigration from Eastern Europe, where a majority of European Jews lived. After the United States was closed off, more Jewish immigrants moved to Palestine than any other country. This would eventually have a profound impact on anti-Semitism in America. In the meantime, however, domestic American anti-Semitism was growing more visible.

During the 1920s, automaker Henry Ford, an early financial supporter of Hitler, was quite effective in promulgating anti-Semitic material, both at home and abroad. His anti-Semitic articles in his newspaper, *The Dearborn Independent*, were mainly for domestic consumption. But his anti-Semitic book, *The International Jew* (1922), found a wide readership not only in the United States, but in Germany as well. (Hitler kept Ford's book at his office, with a portrait of Ford above his desk.) Ford also disseminated an older anti-Semitic work, *The Protocols of the Elders of Zion*. This notorious and fraudulent work claimed to expose a secret Jewish conspiracy to rule the world.

In the 1930s, one of the places where people were most concerned with this mythical Jewish conspiracy was in Germany. The Nazi campaign against the Jews was an international development with links to American anti-Semitism. After *Kristallnacht*, many German Jews tried desperately to emigrate to the United States. They were kept away because of U.S. immigration quotas that the government refused to relax. The ostensible reason was fear of Nazi infiltrators hidden in a sudden flood of Jewish refugees. A more covert reason was the anti-Semitism of upper-level state department officials such as Breckenridge Long.

During this period, as fascism became a strong minority movement in America, anti-Semitism became more common. One of the most visible far-right anti-Semites was Charles Coughlin, the popular "radio priest" who referred to Franklin D. Roosevelt's New Deal as "The Jew Deal."

Although his administration was characterized by some of its enemies as "philo-Semitic," one aspect of Roosevelt's military policy during World War II (1939–1945) has since been labeled anti-Semitic: U.S. complicity in the joint allied decision not to bomb the railways leading into major concentration camps such as Auschwitz, even when the Allies had clear proof of the Holocaust.

After the Holocaust

It was postwar knowledge of the Holocaust, more than anything else, that made anti-Semitism socially and mor-

ally unacceptable in almost all parts of postwar America. This new sentiment was given concrete expression by a major Hollywood film of 1947, *Gentleman's Agreement*. A scathing indictment of anti-Semitism, it not only did well at the box office, but was given the Oscar that year for best picture.

Then, one year later, in 1948, the Jews in Palestine declared that they were an independent nation. Within fifteen minutes of their declaration, President Harry S. Truman made the United States the first nation to recognize the existence of Israel. From that moment on, the United States became the key supporter of Israel in the Middle East.

The international importance of Israel to America's interests in the Middle East, combined with the moral opprobrium attached to the Holocaust, made American Jewish defense groups such as the AJC even more ambitious in their aims. Essentially, they went from defensive strategies to offensive operations. More specifically, leaders of Jewish defense groups in the 1940s developed an ideology centered upon what they called a new "unitary theory of prejudice." This was the then-radical idea that prejudice itself, no matter what group it was directed at, was a major social problem. This allowed Jewish groups like the Anti-Defamation League to move beyond strictly Jewish issues to work with other minority groups, especially African Americans in the civil rights movement.

Their efforts came to a triumphal climax of sorts with the 1950 publication of the book *The Authoritarian Personality*, by Theodor Adorno and others. This widely read and tremendously influential work successfully attempted to present prejudice—prejudice against any minority—as a personality disorder.

Ironically enough, at the start of the new millennium one of the few American groups that still noticeably exhibited anti-Semitism was one that had previously been helped tremendously by the Jewish campaign against prejudice: African Americans. Certain African American leaders, notably the NATION OF ISLAM's Louis Farrakhan, revitalized old myths about a Jewish conspiracy to rule the world. In the process, these leaders not only reopened old wounds, but created new and bitter antagonisms between American minority groups that had once worked together as allies.

BIBLIOGRAPHY

Dinnerstein, Leonard. *Anti-Semitism in America.* New York: Oxford University Press, 1994.

Gurock, Jeffrey S., ed. *Anti-Semitism in America.* New York: Routledge, 1998.

Jaher, Frederic Cople. *A Scapegoat in the New Wilderness: The Origins and Rise of Anti-Semitism in America.* Cambridge, Mass: Harvard University Press, 1994.

Kaufman, Jonathan. *Broken Alliance: The Turbulent Times between Blacks and Jews in America.* New York: Touchstone, 1995.

Svonkin, Stuart. *Jews against Prejudice: American Jews and the Fight for Civil Liberties.* New York: Columbia University Press, 1997.

Richard Bradley

See also **Civil Rights Movement; Fascism, American; Jews; Jewish Defense League; Zionism.**

ANTISLAVERY sentiment and activity in the United States took several forms during its evolution from the quiet protest of the Germantown Quakers in 1688 through the tragic and violent American Civil War, which spawned the Thirteenth Amendment to the CONSTITUTION OF THE UNITED STATES. Response to slavery varied from adamant defense to mild doubts to militant hostility. The antislavery movement was a crucible for the white conscience in matters of race, because nearly all slaves in the United States were black. As a consequence, different elements within the society perceived the problem of slavery in radically different ways and proposed sometimes contradictory solutions.

In the U.S. the antislavery movement was a multifarious one that featured diverse and often clashing objectives and organizational forms. Throughout the history of antislavery activism in the United States, there was a small number of people who may with justice be called abolitionists, those who sought to abolish slavery throughout the country and to incorporate the freed blacks into American society. In the eighteenth century abolitionists generally supported plans for gradual emancipation, but a new generation of abolitionists who appeared in the 1830s demanded an immediate end to slavery and advocated the integration of American society. A much larger group among the opponents of slavery were those who feared that blacks neither could nor should integrate into American society as equals. These critics of slavery instead proposed the colonization of free blacks outside the United States. Increasingly, colonizationists shifted away from their early opposition to slavery to focus upon the removal of free blacks. The northern sectionalists came to be the largest element in the antislavery crusade; they opposed slavery as the basis of the social and political power of an aristocratic class that unfairly dominated the political process to the disadvantage of northern whites. The racial attitudes of this group covered a broad spectrum, and its main efforts centered upon restricting the expansion of slave territory.

Gradualism

The early history of antislavery in America consisted primarily of the agitation of certain British and American QUAKERS, but even in this group antislavery sentiments grew slowly because many wealthy Quakers were slaveholders. Only by the mid-1700s, when the Society of Friends faced a severe internal crisis brought on by the effects of the Great Awakening and the Seven Years War, did opposition to slavery increase measurably among Quakers. It was not until the 1780s that the major Quaker meetings could announce that their membership was free of slaveholders.

By the late eighteenth century the opposition to slavery had spread beyond the Society of Friends to other people whose response to slavery grew out of the secular thought of the Enlightenment. Because of its underlying republican ideology, emphasizing liberty and individual rights, the American Revolution encouraged antislavery sentiments. During the late eighteenth and early nineteenth centuries, all the states abolished the African slave trade, and most moved toward the ultimate eradication of slavery. This movement proceeded most rapidly in the states north of the MASON-DIXON LINE, where slavery was of minor economic importance. Moreover, the enactment of the Northwest Ordinance in 1787 had confined slavery to the area that increasingly became known as the South.

Gradual emancipation in the northern states did not take place without opposition, and the newly formed antislavery societies played a crucial role in these early achievements. Aside from supporting gradual emancipation, these early antislavery societies attacked the Fugitive Slave Law and the African slave trade, distributed antislavery literature, and encouraged education of blacks. Although the membership of these early organizations included such prominent political figures as Benjamin Franklin, John Jay, Alexander Hamilton, and Benjamin Rush, Quakers usually dominated them. Because of this narrow sectarian base and the ideological limitations of early antislavery sentiment, the movement rapidly waned following its victories in the northern states.

Colonization

During the three decades following 1800, opposition to slavery entered a new phase. Efforts at gradual emancipation gave way to proposals for the colonization of free blacks, and the center of antislavery activity shifted to the upper South. Although the most vocal opponents of slavery during these years were active in southern states, true abolitionism never gained a foothold anywhere in the South. In the two decades following the American Revolution, all the southern states except Georgia and South Carolina moved toward emancipation by easing the process of private manumission, and between 1800 and 1815 societies devoted to gradual emancipation sprouted in all the states of the upper South. After 1800 the tide turned and flowed in the opposite direction. By 1830 nearly all vocal abolitionists were forced to leave the South. As the crucial debate in the Virginia legislature in 1832 revealed, the only antislavery advocates remaining in the South by then were the rapidly dwindling supporters of the AMERICAN COLONIZATION SOCIETY (ACS).

The ACS had originated in response to fears that free blacks could not successfully incorporate into American society. Its activities typified the conservative reform emanating from a period of fairly modest social and economic change, but its early membership included, along with some of the South's leading politicians, such abolitionists as Benjamin Lundy, the Tappan brothers, Gerrit Smith, and the young William Lloyd Garrison. Abolitionists formed only a minor element in the ACS, however. In the early years, most advocates of colonization usually related the proposal to schemes for manumission and gradual emancipation, but most colonizationists cared little about the plight of the slave and hoped to rid the country of the troublesome presence of a race generally deemed inferior and degraded. The doctrine of gradualism based on a faith in the perfectibility of all people gave way to the racist perspectives that typified the nineteenth century. As the ACS became increasingly dominated by those whose main purpose was the deportation of free blacks and shedding its antislavery character, the abolitionists turned against the organization.

Immediatism

The appearance of Garrison's *Thoughts on African Colonization* in 1832 and the debates at Lane Seminary in 1834 signaled a major shift in American antislavery and the emergence of the movement for immediate abolition. One can trace the roots of the doctrine of immediatism to the basic elements of eighteenth-century antislavery thought and relate its appearance in the United States in the 1830s to such causes as British influence, increasing black militancy, and the failure of gradual emancipation in the South. Nevertheless, the new intensity and enthusiasm that characterized the drive for immediate, uncompensated abolition came about primarily from evangelical perfectionism. Although abolitionists were often ambivalent about their precise programs, their new approach connoted a direct response to the recognition of the sinfulness of slavery and epitomized the abolitionist movement of this period. In rejecting the detached eighteenth-century perspective that had governed the psychology of gradual emancipation, the advocates of immediate abolition "made a personal commitment to make no compromise with sin."

In the 1830s antislavery sentiments spread throughout the northern states, and a new network of abolition societies appeared. The New England Antislavery Society formed in 1831. Two years later at a meeting in Philadelphia, delegates from Massachusetts, New York, and Pennsylvania established a national organization, the American Anti-Slavery Society (AAS). In rapid order, auxiliaries appeared in all the eastern states, and members made an energetic effort to revive western abolitionism. Following the Lane debates, Theodore Dwight Weld served as an agent for the AAS by lecturing and organizing local groups throughout Ohio and the western portions of New York and Pennsylvania. In 1835 he founded the Ohio State Antislavery Society, which shortly became second only to the New York Society among the state auxiliaries of the AAS. His success prompted the AAS to extend the agency system by sending out a new host of agents, the "Seventy," to further expand the number of

Angelina Grimké. Like her sister Sarah, an activist against slavery and for women's rights; she delivered several important antislavery lectures and subsequently assisted her husband, the prominent abolitionist Theodore Dwight Weld.

local societies and advance the idea of immediate abolition of slavery.

As a result of such activities, the number of state and local societies multiplied rapidly. Historians, however, know little about the makeup of these societies except that they proliferated in rural Yankee areas "burned over" by the Great Revival and that a majority of their members were women. Abolitionist leaders were highly educated and moderately prosperous men of some importance in their communities. Their most significant characteristics were an intense religious commitment and Yankee origins. Nearly two-thirds were pastors, deacons, and elders of evangelical churches, and an even larger proportion of white abolitionist leaders traced their family origins to New England.

A distinctive group within the movement consisted of the free blacks who were prominent in the activities of the underground railroad and who provided a crucial element of abolitionist leadership. Unfortunately, whites generally denied blacks positions of power in these organizations, and blacks resented the racism and paternalism of the whites. During the 1830s and 1840s, a series of all-black National Negro Conventions focused the efforts of black abolitionists.

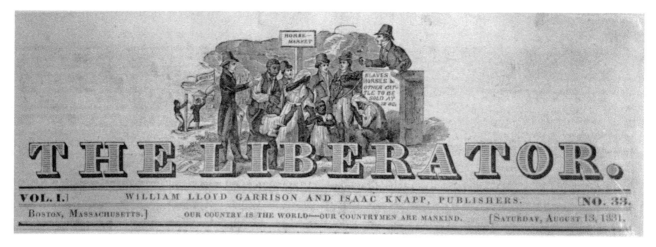

The Liberator. The masthead of the most famous antislavery newspaper, published from 1831 to 1865 by the uncompromising abolitionist William Lloyd Garrison. LIBRARY OF CONGRESS

The major activity of the abolitionists in the 1830s consisted of the dissemination of antislavery arguments in the hope that moral suasion would effect the end of slavery in the United States. They produced abolitionist newspapers, such as Garrison's *Liberator* and the *Emancipator*, which functioned as the major organ of the AAS. Aside from its newspaper, the AAS issued a quarterly, two monthlies, and a children's magazine. It also supported a yearly antislavery almanac and a series of pamphlets that included the classics of antislavery literature. While it was not until the 1840s and 1850s that slave narratives and sentimental antislavery novels appeared, the appeal to sentiment was central to the most powerful of the abolitionist attacks on slavery published in the 1830s, Weld's *Slavery As It Is.*

In 1835 the AAS launched its postal campaign under the direction of Lewis Tappan. The society hoped to inundate the South with publications and convince southerners to rid themselves of the evils of slavery. Although the intention of the literature was to sway the minds and sentiments of the slaveholders, critics immediately viewed it as incendiary. In July 1835, a mob attacked the Charleston, South Carolina, post office and burned a number of abolitionist newspapers. In the following year, a law excluding antislavery literature from the mails failed in Congress, but with the cooperation of the Jackson administration, local postmasters effectively eliminated the circulation of abolitionist material in the South.

When the postal campaign failed, the AAS shuffled its organizational structure and turned to a campaign to present Congress with petitions on a variety of subjects related to slavery. The petition was a traditional antislavery instrument, but in 1835, John C. Calhoun and his South Carolina colleague in the House, James Hammond, moved against hearing any antislavery pleas. In an effort to disassociate themselves from this attack on the civil rights of northern whites, northern Democrats accepted the more moderate gag rule that automatically tabled all antislavery petitions. Undaunted, the AAS flooded Congress with petitions. The largest number of these petitions opposed the annexation of Texas and called for the abolition of slavery in the District of Columbia. Yet by 1840 the gag rule had effectively stifled the petition campaign.

Political Antislavery

Although it had grown rapidly during the 1830s, at the end of the decade, the abolition movement remained unpopular and weak. The abolitionists had encountered mob violence in the North, no major politician dared associate himself with their cause, and the leading religious denominations rejected their teachings. Factional bickering and financial reverses further undermined the movement. The theoretical Seventy agents had never reached full strength, and after 1838 their numbers dwindled drastically. Because the panic of 1837 and the subsequent depression dried up their sources of funds, the local societies had to curtail numerous activities. Then, in 1840, after several years of bickering over the relation of abolitionism to the churches and to other reform movements, particularly women's rights, the AAS split into warring factions. In that year the radical followers of Garrison took over the AAS. The moderate element formed a new organization, the American and Foreign Anti-Slavery Society (AFAS). By this time, the Great Revival, which had fired the growth of abolitionism in the previous decade, had run its course, and neither of these organizations retained the vitality that had characterized the AAS in the first five years of its existence.

In 1839 the majority of American abolitionists, faced with the distinct possibility of failure and agreeing that their earlier tactics had not won support for abolition, decided to establish a political party devoted to their cause. After an unsuccessful attempt to get New York gubernatorial candidates to respond publicly to their inquiries, Alvan Stewart, Gerrit Smith, and Myron Holley moved to form the LIBERTY PARTY (or Human Rights party). The Liberty party devoted itself to bringing the slavery question into politics and hoped to keep the doctrine of immediatism alive by offering individuals an opportunity to go on record against slavery. Through 1844 the new party retained its abolitionist character by attacking the immorality of slavery and demanding equal justice for free blacks. During these years its support grew among the moderate abolitionists associated with the AFAS. While the Liberty party had induced most abolitionists to join its ranks, it is doubtful that abolition sentiment grew in the North during these years. At the height of its popularity, the party's votes came mainly from men who had earlier converted to abolitionism but had voted for the WHIG PARTY in 1840. It was strongest in the small, moderately prosperous Yankee farming communities that evangelical revivalism had earlier touched and that had been centers of organized abolition activities. After 1844 the Liberty party split over the question of broadening the party's appeal, and the majority of its members drifted into the FREE SOIL PARTY, which appeared in 1848.

The failure of both moral suasion and political activity led many blacks and a few whites to greater militancy. In 1843 the Buffalo National Convention nearly adopted Henry Highland Garnet's advocacy of self-defense and slave revolt. Within a decade, especially after the passage of the Fugitive Slave Law in 1850, numerous local conventions of blacks echoed his sentiments. In Christiana, Pennsylvania, Boston, and Syracuse, attempts by both blacks and whites to aid fugitive slaves became the focus of sporadic violence. It was not until 1859, however, that anyone connected with the abolition movement attempted to encourage rebellion among the slaves. After several years of planning, John Brown launched his unsuccessful Harpers Ferry raid.

Although individual abolitionists continued to agitate throughout the 1850s, organized abolitionism passed from the scene. As it emerged in the 1840s and 1850s, political antislavery compromised abolitionist goals in order to present a program moderate and broad-gauged enough to attract voters in the North whose opposition to slavery arose from their desire to keep blacks out of the territories and slaveholders out of positions of power in the federal government. The final phase of antislavery activity in the United States primarily emerged from hostility toward slaveholders and the values of the society in which they lived. Antisouthernism provided a vehicle through which the REPUBLICAN PARTY could unite all forms of northern antislavery feeling by 1860.

The growth of popular antagonism toward the South in the northern states began with the controversy over the gag rule. While the abolitionists had constantly attacked the excessive political power wielded by slaveholders, known as "slave power," Whig politicians in the

Increasing Militancy. Bostonians, including former moderates embittered by the Kansas-Nebraska Act, vociferously protest the return of fugitive slave Anthony Burns—under heavy guard after a violent earlier attempt to free him—to Virginia, 2 June 1854. (The dealer who bought Burns resold him, for a large profit, to an antislavery group, which gave him his freedom.) GETTY IMAGES

early 1840s made the most use of the issue to define a moderate pro-northern position between the abolitionists and the Democrats. The events associated with the Mexican-American War and actions of James Polk's administration caused a split in the DEMOCRATIC PARTY and the enunciation of the WILMOT PROVISO, which would have excluded slavery from the territory gained by the war. The followers of Martin Van Buren in New York, increasingly enraged by the power of slaveholders within their party, joined with the so-called Conscience Whigs of Massachusetts and the majority of the Liberty party to form the Free Soil party. While its members included many true abolitionists, its platform represented both a broadening of the appeal of antislavery and a turning away from the earlier goals of the abolitionists. The party focused almost entirely on limiting the expansion of slavery to keep the territories free for the migration of whites. Its platform avoided traditional abolitionist demands, and its followers spanned the wide spectrum of contemporary racist opinion.

During the years between 1850 and 1854, not only abolitionism but also antisouthernism seemed to fade. Yet, at that very moment, a surge of nativism and anti-Catholicism throughout the North shattered traditional party alignments. Then, in 1854 and 1855, the fights over the KANSAS-NEBRASKA ACT and the chaos in Kansas Territory revived antisouthernism and channeled it through the new Republican party. Although it deserves credit for ending slavery in the United States, the Republican party was by no means an abolitionist party nor one devoted solely to antislavery. Its platform touched on a wide variety of economic and social questions and appealed to a diverse group of northerners.

Ex-Whigs, with smaller but crucial groups of free-soil and nativist ex-Democrats and the remnants of the Free Democratic party, made up the new party. Consequently, it included both vicious racists and firm believers in racial justice. Although most Republicans had moderately liberal racial views for the day, many supported colonization schemes, and nearly all expressed reservations about the total integration of the society. The main focus of their antislavery sentiments was the southern slaveholder, and the only antislavery plank in their platform demanded the exclusion of slavery from the territories. In this limited form, a majority of northerners could embrace antislavery. Still, the party shied away from any direct attack on slavery. When secession threatened, many Republicans were willing to guarantee the existence of slavery in the southern states through a constitutional amendment.

The needs of war, as much as the constant agitation of the small abolitionist element within the Republican party, propelled the country toward emancipation. President Abraham Lincoln, who had long doubted the feasibility of social integration, prosecuted the war primarily to maintain the Union. Caught between the radical and conservative wings of his own party, the president moved cautiously toward the enunciation of the Emancipation Proclamation, the issuance of which on 1 January 1863 freed the slaves in areas still in rebellion. Later, with a good deal more forthrightness, he lent his support to the Thirteenth Amendment, which declared slavery unconstitutional anywhere in the United States.

BIBLIOGRAPHY

Ericson, David F. *The Debate over Slavery: Antislavery and Proslavery Liberalism in Antebellum America.* New York: New York University Press, 2001.

McPherson, James M. *The Struggle for Equality: Abolitionists and the Negro in the Civil War and Reconstruction.* Princeton, N.J.: Princeton University Press, 1964.

Newman, Richard S. *The Transformation of American Abolitionism: Fighting Slavery in the Early Republic.* Chapel Hill: University of North Carolina Press, 2002.

Quarles, Benjamin. *Black Abolitionists.* New York: Oxford University Press, 1969.

Stauffer, John. *The Black Hearts of Men: Radical Abolitionists and the Transformation of Race.* Cambridge, Mass.: Harvard University Press, 2002.

Wyatt-Brown, Bertram. *Lewis Tappan and the Evangelical War Against Slavery.* Cleveland, Ohio: Press of Case Western Reserve University, 1969.

William G. Shade/A. E.

See also **Civil War; Colonization Movement; Emancipation Movement; Emancipation Proclamation; Fugitive Slave Acts; Gag Rule, Antislavery; Harpers Ferry Raid; Immediatism; Kansas-Nebraska Act; New England Antislavery Society; Slavery;** *and vol. 9:* **Address to President Lincoln by the Working-Men of Manchester, England; Earliest American Protest against Slavery; A House Divided; John Brown's Last Speech; Notes Illustrative of the Wrong of Slavery; The Crime Against Kansas; The Impending Crisis of the South: How to Meet It.**

ANTITRUST LAWS aim to ensure the existence of competitive markets by sanctioning producers and suppliers of products and services when their conduct departs from that competitive ideal. Of course, what constitutes this ideal and what conduct betrays it have varied during the long history of antitrust law. Until the late nineteenth century, this regulatory enterprise belonged chiefly to the courts. Then, with the rise of large-scale industrial corporations, Congress entered the fray. Beginning in 1890, Congress has enacted three key antitrust statutes—the Sherman Act, the Clayton Act, and the Robinson-Patman Act—each responding to a moment of heightened public anxiety about monopolistic combinations and their anticompetitive business practices.

Long before the Sherman Act, Americans harbored a deep hostility toward monopolies. Several of the first state constitutions, written in the 1770s and 1780s, condemned monopolies as violations of the cherished principles of equal rights and equality before the law. Some of the founding generation, including Thomas Jefferson, sought to include a prohibition on monopolies in the federal Bill of Rights. Andrew Jackson helped make the second National Bank one of the most controversial "monopolies" of Antebellum America.

For a Jefferson or Jackson, "monopoly" meant state-granted authority over some economic activity, like a particular domain of banking or a trade or a means of transportation, in the hands of some politically privileged group at the expense of the majority. To possess a monopoly in this sense was to enjoy a legal right to exclude others from pursuing the same activity.

Gradually, this emphasis on state-created monopolies gave way to an emphasis on economic power in a given market and on the abuse of that power. At common law, to "monopolize" came to mean preventing others from entering or competing in a market or line of business by agreement or combination among erstwhile competitors. An agreement or combination to restrict competition by itself was not enough; unless it aimed to close the channels of trade to others, or unless it resulted in outrageous prices or the withholding of necessaries of life, it did not fall under this common law prohibition.

Nineteenth Century

By the late nineteenth century, general incorporation laws, enacted in Jackson's day to make the privilege of incorporation available to all, had helped make the corporation a common form of industrial enterprise. At the same time, booming technological development and industrial growth brought new wealth, new inequalities, and new concentrations of economic power.

The "rise of big business" began with the railroads in the 1850s; only in the 1880s and 1890s, however, did manufacturing firms follow suit. By 1900, John D. Rockefeller's Standard Oil Company, James B. Duke's American Tobacco Company, and dozens of other new nation-spanning giants had emerged, exerting substantial control over entire industries and their newly nationalized markets. In popular political discourse, firms like these were dubbed "trusts"; in fact, most did not take the legal form of a trust, but all shared centralized management and great size.

The search for profits and control motivated this great movement of expansion and consolidation. In many industries, new technologies and new ways of organizing production yielded economies of scale, which advantaged large firms. Bigness, however, magnified the costs of sharp increases in the cost of materials, market downturns, or "ruinous competition" brought on by new market entrants and the "overproduction" of goods. Some firms sought to manage these hazards through vertical integration; others through horizontal arrangements. The latter involved producers of a given good agreeing to limit production and/or maintain prices; it could take the simple form of a contract or the more complex and "tighter" form of a cartel or, finally, a merger among previously competing firms. Vertical integration, by contrast, involved the gathering of many functions into a single firm: from the extraction of raw materials, for example, to the transformation of those materials into finished products, to the wholesaling and retailing of those products. The leading example of this kind of corporation was Standard Oil, whose ruthless and predatory practices generated a public outcry against the "Trusts." So, too, did the horizontal mergers that resulted in "Trusts" like the gigantic American Sugar Refining and American Tobacco Companies. While the "Trusts" often brought down, or left unaffected, the costs of goods to consumers, their vast power over the nation's economy—as well as their exploitive labor practices and their penchant for buying and selling state and federal lawmakers—were ominous. The Trusts also seemed bent on destroying the nation's small- and medium-sized businesses and producers.

Before the passage of the Sherman Act in 1890, the states had responded to the Trusts with their own antitrust efforts, inscribing antimonopoly provisions in their state constitutions and enacting antitrust legislation of their own. State antitrust measures took various forms—many protecting against some combination of monopoly, restraint of trade, restraint of competition, pooling, price fixing, output limitations, territorial divisions, resale restraints, exclusive dealing, refusals to deal, local price discrimination, and predatory pricing—and often set forth more detailed prohibitions and provided for stricter sanctions than did federal legislation (including fines and prison terms). What is more, the states and not the federal government issued corporate charters. Accordingly, the power to regulate and limit corporate growth directly, through structural constraints, was a power widely viewed as belonging to the states; and where the states undertook to enforce such limits, the United States Supreme Court upheld them.

During the 1880s, a few state attorneys general undertook formidable suits under this body of law. In general, however, state prosecutors and state judges proved reluctant to invoke these restraints, out of fear that strict enforcement would result in factory closures and ultimately damage local economies. The giant corporations and the corporate bar also succeeded in lobbying through the New Jersey, Delaware, and New York state legislatures major revisions of those states' corporation laws, eliminating or weakening key restraints on corporate growth and consolidation. Corporations hobbled by other states' more traditional legal regimes easily reincorporated in the liberalized jurisdictions.

Despite these sharp practical limitations of state antitrust law, members of Congress and the federal bench would continue, during the formative era of federal antitrust, to view state government as a primary locus of authority over the Trusts. So, when Congress took up the matter in 1888–90, the division of federal versus state authority loomed large in debates. Senator John Sherman of Ohio, chair of the Senate Finance Committee and sponsor of the Sherman Act, saw clearly the inadequacies of state regulation. His first antitrust bill envisioned direct federal control over corporate structure, authorizing federal courts to dissolve all agreements or combinations "extending to two or more states," and "made with a view or which tend to prevent full and free competition" in goods "of growth, production, or manufacture," much as state officials could "apply for forfeiture of charters." Sherman's bill, however, ran afoul of the constitutional scruples of colleagues on the Judiciary Committee, who saw it as usurping power belonging to the states, not the national government. The latter redrafted Sherman's bill in terser terms, so the statute as enacted omitted reference to "growth, production, or manufacture" and simply condemned every combination in restraint of trade or commerce and also made monopolization and attempts to monopolize any part of interstate trade or commerce.

The 1890 Congress deliberately left to the courts the task of determining which specific forms of business conduct and business arrangements violated the general common-law-inspired language of the Act. As a procedural matter, the Act departed from the common law in two key respects. It made such restraints or monopolies not merely void (as they were at common law) but punishable as misdemeanors and also liable to private, civil suits for treble damages. As a substantive matter, however, for two decades, judges and commentators could not agree on whether the new statute simply codified the common law norms or enacted stricter prohibitions. The common law distinguished between "reasonable" and "unreasonable" restraints, condemning only the latter, but the statutory language contained no such language. As is often the case, it seems likely that Congress preferred ambiguous statutory language that could please many competing constituencies: in this case, both the agrarian and populist public demanding a restoration of proprietary forms of capitalism and the dismantling of the great trusts, and also the metropolitan business interests that favored the continued development and flourishing of the new large-scale corporations. To the latter constituency, Sherman offered assurances that the courts would carry forward the old common law distinction and leave alone the "useful" combinations, no matter how large. Likewise, the members of the Judiciary Committee, who drafted the language of the actual statute, affirmed that it did no more than authorize the federal courts to extend the "old doctrine of the common law" to interstate (and foreign) commerce.

Twentieth Century

The Supreme Court pursued a somewhat jarring course. Until 1911, a majority of the Court insisted that the Act went further than the common law, condemning all restraints of trade. Thus, the Court read the Act to outlaw cartel-like arrangements on the part of trade associations of railways or manufacturing firms, which, from participants' perspective, merely aimed to halt "ruinous competition" by establishing uniform rates or prices. By contrast, where such arrangements did not aim to foreclose competition from outsiders nor result in "unreasonable" costs to the public, but instead appeared to be "for the purpose of preventing strife and financial ruin," common law courts frequently had upheld them. Similarly, in respect of tighter consolidations, common law doctrine generally held that a corporation's buying out of former competitors was not, as such, an unlawful restraint or monopoly; unlawfulness demanded other showings, such as an effort to prevent the former owners from reentering, or to prevent outsiders from entering or remaining in the line of business.

The Supreme Court majority, however, interpreted the statute in light of the widely shared social and political vision of a market order composed of small producers and independent proprietors. On this account, "powerful combinations of capital" threatened the well-being of the republic because they tended to "drive out" the "small business man" and the "independent dealer," and this was wrong, irrespective of whether such "powerful combinations" lowered or raised the price of consumer goods. This outlook met ridicule from dissenters like Justices Oliver Wendell Holmes and Edward D. White, political leaders like Theodore Roosevelt, and the corporate bar. In 1911, in the Standard Oil and American Tobacco cases,

the Court, under now Chief Justice White, changed course and held that the common law's "rule of reason" was implicit in the Act. This tension between a vision of Antitrust that condemns the "curse of Bigness" and concentrated corporate power on broad social and political grounds, versus one that has no gripe with bigness and focuses more narrowly on some conception of consumer welfare and on the prevention of particularly abusive and predatory competitive tactics, would continue to run through the changing course of legal development for the next century.

During the same two decades, while Court doctrine seemed to affirm smallness, bigness proceeded apace. Most of the nation's two hundred largest corporations were formed during the decade bracketing the turn of the century. The great majority of these new corporations, the "big business" of the early twentieth century, controlled forty percent or more of the market shares of their products; and together, they held more than one-seventh of the nation's manufacturing capacity. Many observers insisted that antitrust doctrine actually encouraged this merger movement, because its strictures seemed to fall far more heavily on cartels and loose price-fixing agreements than on mergers. In any case, public confidence in the nation's antitrust laws had all but vanished by the 1912 presidential election, and candidates Theodore Roosevelt and Woodrow Wilson both promised to bring greater public authority to bear upon the giant new corporations. Roosevelt's solution lay in supplanting state corporate charters with federal ones. Bigness, Roosevelt candidly declared, was here to stay. He proposed creating a new body of federal corporation law to separate the "good Trusts" (with their greater efficiency and economies of scale) from the "bad" (with their predatory business practices and their purely opportunistic and anti-competitive welding together of firms). For his part, candidate Wilson echoed his advisor Louis Brandeis in decrying the "curse of Bigness"; bigness in this view was generally a bad thing in itself. The Brandeisian reform vision evoked the hope of restoring a more decentralized political economy in which smaller firms continued to flourish. So, for example, Brandeis thought trade associations among small businesses deserved substantial freedom from antitrust regulation, while industrial giants ought to be policed more harshly.

Two years later, President Wilson signed into law two new antitrust measures, the Federal Trade Commission (FTC) and the Clayton Acts of 1914. The FTC Act gave birth to a regulatory commission—the Federal Trade Commission—with the power to identify and proscribe a wide range of "unfair methods of competition" and "deceptive business practices." The Wheeler-Lea Amendments of 1938 broadened the FTC Act, adding "unfair or deceptive acts or practices in commerce" to the prohibition against "unfair methods of competition," in the hope of increasing the efficiency of the FTC by reducing the time and expense involved in proving that a violator's activities had a negative effect on competition. The Clayton Act, on the other hand, responded to the call for more explicit and detailed antitrust legislation. In contrast to the highly general language of the Sherman Act, the provisions of the Clayton Act outlawed specific business practices, such as price discrimination, tying and exclusive dealing contracts, and corporate stock acquisitions.

Congress amended the Clayton Act twice, once in 1936 by the Robinson-Patman Act, and again in 1950 by the Celler-Kefauver Antimerger Act. The Robinson-Patman Act revised the prohibition against price discrimination in Section 2 of the original Clayton Act; it is the only federal law that specifically bans discriminatory pricing practices. Enacted in response to new forms of anticompetitive price discrimination, the law had a Brandeisian inspiration. It aimed to prevent chain stores from exploiting their bulk purchasing power to gain discriminatory price concessions from suppliers that unfairly threatened the competitiveness of independent retailers. In its effort to maintain a fair and competitive balance between small merchants and large chain stores, the Robinson-Patman Act was an attempt to reestablish equality of opportunity in business.

The Celler-Kefauver Act proscribed certain types of corporate mergers achieved through asset or stock acquisition, disallowing mergers that significantly lessened overall competition in a market (as opposed to the original Clayton Act, which dealt only with the effects of mergers on competition between the two merging companies). It aimed to inhibit apparently unhealthy concentration by trying to maintain a substantial number of smaller, independent competitors. From 1950 to 1980, Republican and Democratic administrations, as well as the federal courts, vigorously enforced the antimerger laws. The courts also redefined "monopolization" under the Sherman Act, so that statutes outlawed all exclusionary, restrictive, or anticompetitive conduct. The executive branch and the courts also assailed any cartel-like activity, including restraints that limited the access of horizontal competitors to outlets or inputs. The world of antitrust regulation changed dramatically during the 1980s with the advent of the Reagan administration. Economic stagnation created a climate in which businesses pressed the government for aid, and the Reagan administration ushered in a new era of laissez-faire, loosening federal regulation in many arenas including antitrust.

The hands-off antitrust policies of the Reagan and Bush years opened space for a major increase in corporate mergers. The anti-anti-merger policy, together with the more general diminution in antitrust enforcement, found intellectual support in the Chicago School's neo-classical liberalism. The latter held that unfettered freedom of business consolidation and competition almost always enhanced overall efficiency in the economy; and that such efficiency, in turn, conduced to "consumer welfare." The Chicago School's antitrust theorists, and with them Republican executives and judges, spurned as sentimental and economically senseless the social and political considerations that animated earlier generations of antitrust policymakers.

The Clinton administration, 1993–2001, ushered in a reformed "consumer welfare" standard. Instead of protecting the freedom of firms to maximize efficiency by their own lights, new policies tried preserving competition for the benefit of consumers. At the same time, while the focus of past antitrust activism was on price competition and preventing business activities that could result in artificially high prices, the Clinton administration's focus was on encouraging innovation and preventing business activities or combinations that could stifle innovation.

As business became increasingly globalized, the need for international enforcement of antitrust laws became apparent. Attempts at establishing transnational antitrust laws at the end of the twentieth century came up short. During the Clinton years, the United States championed a system of international cooperation in the enforcement of national antitrust laws as an alternative to a more thoroughgoing international solution.

BIBLIOGRAPHY

Letwin, William. *Law and Economic Policy in America: The Evolution of the Sherman Antitrust Act*. New York: Random House, 1965.

Peritz, Rudolph J. R. *Competition Policy in America: History, Rhetoric, Law, 1888–1992*. New York: Oxford University Press, 2000.

Sklar, Martin. *The Corporate Reconstruction of American Capitalism, 1890–1916*. New York: Cambridge University Press, 1988.

William E. Forbath

See also **Clayton Act; Northern Securities** *Company v.* **United** *States;* **Sherman Antitrust Act.**

ANTIWAR MOVEMENTS.

Peace and antiwar movements provide a means to focus pacifist sentiment into organized, domestic expressions of dissent toward American foreign policy. Antiwar sentiment has usually been the attitude of the minority, and antiwar movements have traditionally struggled to be seen as representing a thoughtful and respectable critique of U.S. foreign policy rather than the radical fringe. Although peace movements have often existed in times of peace, it has been in times of military conflict or the increased risk of such conflict that the movements have thrived.

Antiwar sentiment dates back to the colonial period. Pacifism was one of the central tenets of the Quakers (Society of Friends). But in the early nineteenth century peace movements flourished as the result of two converging developments. First was an increasing disposition toward human development in a reform-oriented age when temperance, antislavery, and women's rights campaigns were also flourishing. More immediately, it was in reaction to the Napoleonic Wars at the beginning of the nineteenth century and most particularly to the unpopular War of 1812 against the British that the first organized movements dedicated specifically to pacifism came into being. Federalist opponents to the War of 1812 had labeled themselves "Friends of Peace" during the war's duration, and after it had finished, in 1815, the Massachusetts Peace Society and a New York equivalent were formed. Several other bodies were also formed; among them the American Peace Society (APS), founded in 1828 by William Ladd, proved one of the most enduring and influential even though it primarily campaigned for the abolition of slavery.

Early movements approached the challenge in different ways, some through legalistic arbitration, some through enforcement, some through military reductions, and some used an approach championed by the temperance movement, abstinence. The American movements' interaction with their European counterparts proved important, and a series of international peace congresses convened in Europe in the late 1840s and early 1850s provided the opportunity for reciprocal learning and exemplified the growing tendency toward arbitration as the means to ending military conflict.

The APS supported the North during the Civil War. It continued its activities after the war, walking a line between the public's apathy and the radical's dissatisfaction with its compromising tactics, a viewpoint that found expression in the Universal Peace Union (UPU). Led by Alfred Love, the UPU called for immediate disarmament, an international treaty substituting arbitration for war, and an end to imperialism. Toward the end of the nineteenth century organized religion began to voice its opposition to war. The Women's Christian Temperance Union and advocates of women's rights declared for peace. As the conflict with Spain over Cuba intensified, the APS felt that any attempt to resolve the crisis would be futile, while the UPU worked tirelessly to avert war. Peace found another ally in the Anti-Imperialist League, founded in 1898, which included some prominent American politicians and capitalists.

In the years immediately preceding World War I, over sixty peace societies were in existence. The American Society for the Judicial Settlement of International Disputes, the World Peace Foundation, the Carnegie Endowment for International Peace, and a series of peace congresses were paralleled by peace leagues and associations in secondary schools and colleges and the expression of peace sentiments in the business world and by the American Federation of Labor. The outbreak of war in Europe in 1914 triggered the formation of the Woman's Peace Party, feminist led; the American Union against Militarism, anti-interventionist and antipreparedness; and the League to Enforce Peace, an international organization. But few of these groups could withstand the surge of patriotism that came with the war years. During the 1930s pacifism received a surge of support that manifested itself in the formation of a myriad of peace-inclined

groups. In 1933 thirty-seven peace organizations formed the National Peace Conference, but within two years the movements were dividing into isolationists and collective security advocates.

Because few questioned the righteousness of the war against Nazism, Fascism, and the perpetrators of the attack on Pearl Harbor, and also because many subscribed to the view that the pacifism of the 1930s had led directly to the appeasement of Hitler, during and immediately after World War II the peace movement was small, disorganized, and largely silent. By mid-1954, however, that was changing as the campaign for nuclear disarmament propelled a resurgence of the peace movement. In the context of Cold War tensions, the nuclear arms race seemed a dire threat to human survival. Peace advocates now campaigned for disarmament and a reduction in United States–Soviet tensions, and more immediately for a ban on nuclear testing. Two groups that emerged in 1957, the National Committee for a Sane Nuclear Policy (SANE) and the Committee for Nonviolent Action (CNVA), provided the organizational focus of the peace movement until the emphasis shifted from nuclear weapons to Vietnam. Both organizations were loosely structured and their ranks were filled with people from varied backgrounds who came together under the general moniker of "nuclear pacifists." Their methods were varied, but most often they attempted to focus the public's attention through public discourse rather than action.

The most organized, politically powerful, and politically and socially divisive antiwar movement of the twentieth century was the campaign against U.S. involvement in the Vietnam War. Beginning as early as 1955, the anti-Vietnam War movement grew in parallel to the growth of U.S. involvement, reaching its peak in the mid-1960s to the early 1970s. Early dissent was focused on college campuses, where professors and students criticized U.S. policy publicly, staging teach-ins, and used the tools of the academic trade to articulate the dissent movement. By now two words were used to describe the spectrum of views on pacifism—"doves" described the pacifists and "hawks" described those inclined toward military solutions; both terms became labels of derision.

By the early 1960s the antiwar campaign received a major boost through its commonality of interests with the civil rights movement. As well as benefiting from mutual support, from the civil rights movement the antiwar movement learned the tactics of dissent, ranging from militant radicalism to nonviolent protest. Of common concern to both movements was the principle of self-determination, but more immediate and tangible concerns related to the racial inequities of the military draft and the disproportionate numbers of casualties suffered from among the ranks of African American men. Prominent civil rights leaders like Dr. Martin Luther King Jr. and Bayard Rustin were early critics of the war but ultimately the antiwar campaign split the civil rights movement into factions.

Antiwar Protest. Demonstrators gather outside the Justice Department in Washington, D.C., on 4 May 1971, during a nearly three-week period of extended rallies and marches against the Vietnam War.

President Johnson's 1965 escalation of the American involvement in Vietnam provoked many, who had previously harbored private concerns about American policy, to express themselves for the first time. The result was that the movement expanded beyond college campuses. Initially, the peace movement generally aimed at building public consensus, but by 1967 some activists were resorting to increasingly drastic methods and civil disobedience gave way to urban unrest punctuated by violence. Over the weekend of 21–22 October 1967 approximately over 55,000 antiwar protesters converged on Washington, D.C., threatening to escalate their expressions of opposition from dissent to resistance by disrupting the U.S. military machinery itself. For the first time since the 1932 Bonus March, U.S. troops and marshals were deployed in Washington, D.C., to protect against domestic protesters. Similar mass protests were staged in San Francisco and New York. After Richard Nixon's promise during the 1968 presidential election campaign to end American involvement in the conflict, the peace movement temporarily subsided. When, in the spring of 1970, Nixon announced that U.S. troops would fight in Cambodia, the antiwar movement became reinvigorated. The division of

the nation was graphically and violently demonstrated on 4 May 1970, when National Guard units opened fire on antiwar protesters at Kent State University in Ohio, killing four unarmed students. After 1975, following the U.S. withdrawal from Vietnam, the antiwar movement rapidly and drastically subsided.

During the 1980s the primary focus of the peace movement once again became nuclear disarmament. The resurgence began in Europe and quickly spread to the United States in reaction to the Reagan administration's defense policies. Sharing a commonality of interests with the growing environmentalist movement, the disarmament campaign became a powerful political force. In the wake of the Cold War, the peace movement for the most part lacked a coherent and sustained target and became largely subsumed by other movements such as environmentalism and antiglobalization.

BIBLIOGRAPHY

DeBenedetti, Charles. *An American Ordeal: The Antiwar Movement of the Vietnam Era.* Syracuse, N.Y.: Syracuse University Press, 1990.

Hixson, Walter L., ed. *The Vietnam Antiwar Movement.* New York: Garland, 2000.

Wittner, Lawrence. *The Struggle against the Bomb.* 2 vols. Stanford, Calif.: Stanford University Press, 1993.

David G. Coleman

See also **Doves; Pacifism; Peace Movements;** *and vol. 9:* **Peace and Bread in Time of War; Statement by Committee Seeking Peace with Freedom in Vietnam.**

ANZIO, a town on the west coast of Italy, thirty-three miles south of Rome, became a battleground in the spring of 1944 during the Italian campaign of World War II. The Germans under Field Marshal Albert Kesselring stubbornly defended southern Italy between Naples and Rome in the fall of 1943. General Mark Clark of the Fifth U.S. Army and General Sir Harold Alexander of the British army planned an Anglo-American amphibious invasion at Anzio to loosen the German grip on the mountainous terrain around Cassino, precipitate a battle for Rome, and compel the Germans to retreat to positions north of Rome.

The operation was risky because the Anzio forces would be isolated in German-held territory. Under pressure from Prime Minister Winston Churchill, who wished to capture Rome before the cross-Channel invasion into Normandy, the Sixth Corps under General John Lucas landed British and American troops at Anzio and neighboring Nettuno against virtually no opposition on 22 January 1944.

The Germans rallied quickly, penned the invaders into a small beachhead, and almost drove the Anglo-American force into the sea. The Allies held their precarious positions for four months, amassing forces for a spring offensive. On 11 May 1944 Alexander broke the Gustav Line, and Clark's units linked up with the beach-

Devil Dancers. Mescaleros participate in an Apache tribal ritual in which they portray mountain-dwelling spirits. AP/WIDE WORLD PHOTOS

head fourteen days later. The Sixth Corps, now under General Lucian Truscott Jr., joined the main forces, and Allied troops entered Rome on 4 June, two days before the cross-Channel attack.

BIBLIOGRAPHY

Blumenson, Martin. *Anzio: The Gamble That Failed.* Philadelphia: Lippincott, 1963.

D'Este, Carlo. *Fatal Decision: Anzio and the Battle for Rome.* New York: HarperCollins, 1991.

Vaughan-Thomas, Wynford. *Anzio.* New York: Holt, Rinehart and Winston, 1961.

Martin Blumenson / A. R.

See also **Gustav Line; Monte Cassino.**

APACHE. The ancestors of the American Indians known as the Apaches, who call themselves the Inde, are believed by scholars to have migrated south from western Canada around 1200 A.D. They left behind the forebears of such tribes as the Carrier and Chipewyan Indians, all of whom are classified in the Athapascan language family.

Traveling along the eastern slope of the Rocky Mountain cordillera, these Apache ancestors eventually settled on the western edge of the Great Plains. Living in skin tepees and hunting buffalo afoot, they composed one of the largest prehorse Plains Indian cultures. In 1541 Spanish explorers observed them in what is now eastern New Mexico and western Texas.

As the Plains population bulged westward, fed by the collapse of the prehistoric Cahokia culture of the Missis-

sippi River Valley and the advent of European settlement on the Atlantic coast, the Apaches also migrated west, though the band now known as the Kiowa Apaches stayed behind in territory later called Kansas. Known as the Tanima, or "liver eaters," the Kiowa Apaches became the bane of American settlers, fighting fiercely to defend their land. Their descendants live on the Kiowa-Apache reservation in Oklahoma.

The band known today as the Lipan Apaches also remained on the Plains. Early in the seventeenth century, as their fellow tribesmen migrated into New Mexico, the Lipans chose to remain in what is today south-central Texas. Primarily hunter-gatherers, the Lipans were accomplished BUFFALO hunters, seasonally breaking down into two subgroups to maximize their kill. Following the hunt, the Lipans reorganized into small extended family groups. Led by respected headmen, each matrilocal family functioned autonomously until the next buffalo hunt or until threatened by their traditional enemies, the Comanches. The Lipans were deeply tied to their homeland, and were known to roll on the ground in reverence upon returning to their own territory. Modern descendants of the Lipans can be found in Oklahoma, Texas, and New Mexico.

Closely related to the Lipans were the Jicarilla Apaches, "the little basket makers," who chose to push west into what is today northern New Mexico. Though extended matrilocal families formed the basic unit of social organization, the Jicarillas broke down into two subgroups for ceremonial purposes. Those living east of the Rio Grande were known as the Llaneros, or "Plains people." Those living west of the Rio Grande were known as the Olleros, or "potters." Contrary to the theories of modern anthropologists, the Jicarillas believe they originally emerged from beneath the earth at a sacred site thought to be near Taos, New Mexico, or San Juan, Colorado. The Pueblo culture of New Mexico heavily influenced the Jicarillas. It is believed that they adopted their ritual relay race from the Pueblos, and imitated the Pueblo agricultural complex. The Jicarillas cleared fields, cut irrigation ditches, built dams, and cultivated crops on family plots.

While the Kiowa Apaches and Lipans developed ceremonial curing rites to ensure their survival on the dangerous Plains, the Jicarillas' spirituality focused on hunt medicine, to guarantee success while hunting far to the east of their homeland. Unlike other Apaches, the Jicarillas caught and ate fish as part of their diet. But it was the women's labor in gathering edible food that provided the mainstay of the Jicarillas' diet. Jicarilla women found ample time to devote to food gathering because their social organization accented the grandparent-grandchild relationship, freeing middle-aged women from the day to day rigors of raising children.

Scholars classify the Kiowa-Apaches, the Lipans, and the Jicarilla Apaches as the eastern group of the southern Athapascans. The Mescaleros, Chiricahuas, and Western Apaches comprise the western group of southern Athapascans, along with the closely related Navajo tribe. While the Jicarillas migrated to northern New Mexico, to land they still maintain as a reservation, the Mescaleros settled in south-central New Mexico, where their reservation was still located in the early 2000s.

The Spanish first observed the Mescaleros in 1653, calling them the Faraones (pharaohs). Secure in permanent villages in the Sierra Blanca Mountains, the Mescaleros maintained close relations with the Jicarillas, sometimes intermarrying with them. Also at times they aided the Lipans in their struggle against the Comanches. With less access to the Plains than the Lipans and Jicarillas, the Mescalero food complex centered on venison and natural harvests, most especially the mescal cactus, for which they were later named. In relation to certain ceremonies, the Mescaleros occasionally ate mountain lion and bear. Though seasonal nomads, extended matrilocal families

SAN JUAN, HEAD CHIEF.　　　GORGONIO, MEDICINE-MAN.　　　NANTZILI, HEAD WAR CHIEF.

Mescaleros. This group of Apaches, shown in different modes of dress, lives in south-central New Mexico. ARCHIVE PHOTOS, INC.

regularly settled in wickiup villages to repair hunting and farming implements and sit out severe winter weather.

Southwest of the Mescaleros, the Chiricahuas inhabited the mountains of present-day southern Arizona and northern Mexico. Masters of their rugged mountain strongholds, the Chiricahuas scourged the Spanish to the south, and raided the Piman-speaking peoples to the west. By 1790, allied with the Lipan and Mescalero Apaches, the three Chiricahua subbands, the Chokonens, Chihennes, and Nednai, formed an impenetrable barrier to encroaching Spaniards. Despite their strength, Americans eventually defeated the Chiricahuas, exiling them to Florida. Not until the twentieth century did they find an adopted home with the Mescaleros.

North of the Chiricahuas lived the largest Apache band, the Western Apaches, composed of twenty subbands, of which the White Mountain Apaches were most numerous. An overarching matrilineal clan system linked the various subbands of the Western Apache, creating an enduring net of obligatory clan bonds and obligations. While they were the most agricultural of the Apache bands, the Western Apaches also raided deep into Mexico. They avoided the Chiricahuas, with whom they occasionally intermarried. The Western Apaches aided the Americans in their fight against the Chiricahuas, however, strengthening their hold on their own homeland, where they still lived in the early 2000s.

By the time Americans arrived in the Southwest, an estimated 5,000 to 10,000 Apaches controlled an area of the Southwest one thousand miles east to west and five hundred miles north to south, from mountaintops to the desert floor. It took the Americans almost forty years before they could be confident of their authority in what had previously been Apacheria.

BIBLIOGRAPHY

Basehart, Harry W. *Mescalero Apache Subsistence Patterns and Socio-Political Organization*. New York: Garland, 1974.

Basso, Keith H., ed. *Western Apache Raiding and Warfare, from the Notes of Grenville Goodwin*. Tucson: University of Arizona Press, 1971.

Bender, Averam Burton. *A Study of Western Apache Indians, 1846–1886*. New York: Garland, 1974.

———. *A Study of Jicarilla Apache Indians, 1846–1887*. New York: Garland, 1974.

Goodwin, Grenville. *The Social Organization of the Western Apache*. With a preface by Keith H. Basso. Tucson: University of Arizona Press, 1969.

Gordon, Burton Leroy. *Environment, Settlement and Land Use in the Jicarilla Apache Claim Area*. New York: Garland, 1974.

Opler, Morris E. *An Apache Life-Way: The Economic, Social, and Religious Institutions of the Chiricahua Indians*. Chicago: University of Chicago Press, 1941.

Ray, Verne Frederick. *Ethnohistorical Analysis of Documents Relating to the Apache Indians of Texas*. New York: Garland, 1974.

Schroeder, Albert H. *A Study of the Apache Indians*. New York: Garland, 1974.

Sonnichsen, C. L. *The Mescalero Apaches*. Norman: University of Oklahoma Press, 1958.

Thomas, Alfred Barnaby. *The Mescalero Apache, 1653–1874*. New York: Garland, 1974.

———. *The Jicarilla Apache Indians: A History, 1598–1888*. New York: Garland, 1974.

United States Indian Claims Commission. *Jicarilla Apache Tribe: Historical Materials, 1540–1887*. New York: Garland, 1974.

Victoria A. O. Smith

See also **Kiowa; Tribes: Great Plains, Southwestern.**

APACHE WARS. When Spaniards entered New Mexico in 1598 they unwittingly claimed a region in flux. The mysterious disappearance of the Anasazi culture in the twelfth century (see ANCESTRAL PUEBLO) had left communities of pueblo-dwellers scattered across the Rio Grande Valley and northern Arizona. The vanished HOHOKAMS had disbanded by 1500 A.D., survived only by the agricultural Piman-speaking peoples in scattered rancherias. The Athapascan-speaking Apaches had only recently emerged from the Rocky Mountains, pushed from behind by the numerous COMANCHES.

Forced by the Comanches into present-day Oklahoma, Texas, New Mexico, and Arizona, the Apaches alternately attacked and traded with the Pueblos. By the mid-seventeenth century Apaches had successfully raided the Spaniards' jealously guarded horse herds. When the Pueblos revolted from the Spaniards in 1680, Apaches aided them from horseback. When Spain reconquered New Mexico in 1692, Apache warriors controlled the region from the Gulf of California to west Texas, where they battled the powerful Comanches.

Faced with the fierce Comanches in Coahuilla and Texas, the Spaniards attempted to make peace with the Jicarilla Apaches, founding a short-lived mission for them near the Taos pueblo in 1733. The Spanish built a line of presidios to protect colonists from Apache and Comanche raiders, but as late as 1786 Apaches still raided deep into Mexico.

When Mexicans began their war for independence from Spain in 1811, they signed a peace treaty with the marauding Lipans, whose numbers had been devastated by smallpox in 1764. But even as Mexico negotiated with the Indians who prevented their northward expansion, American hunters and trappers invaded the southwest out of Santa Fe, crowding the Jicarillas' land. The invasion of Apacheria had begun.

In 1833 Charles Bent was issued a license to trade with several tribes on the Arkansas River. When these tribes, including the Kiowa Apaches, made peace among themselves in 1840, American troops were dispatched to the west to protect the Santa Fe wagon trail, which cut through Jicarilla territory. In Texas, now in the hands of Americans, peaceful relations with Apaches fell apart. In 1842 bands of Lipans and Mescaleros immigrated to

Mexico, free to raid on Texas settlements. Although the Comanches and remaining Mescaleros and Lipans signed a treaty with Texas in 1851, by 1855 Americans had erected a line of forts across the southern frontier for protection from Lipan raiders.

After the Mexican-American War, the Treaty of GUADALUPE HIDALGO forfeited much of the southwest to the Americans. In 1854–1855 General George Carlton, led by Kit Carson, waged war on the Jicarillas. Overwhelmed by the American presence, the Mescaleros signed a treaty in 1855, but the Jicarillas refused to surrender. The acquisition of the southwest territory in 1848 had placed the Chiricahuas and Western Apaches within the domain of the United States. By 1858 stage lines traversed Chiricahua territory in southern Arizona. Chokonen headman Cochise maintained peaceful relations with Americans until falsely accused of taking a young boy into captivity in 1861.

In the notorious Bascom Affair at Apache Pass in the Chiricahua mountains, an inexperienced lieutenant hanged several of Cochise's family members, leading the headman no choice but to seek revenge, as dictated by Apache custom. The merciless Chiricahuas attacked southern Arizona, emptying the region of American settlers.

Meanwhile, in 1864 the peaceful Mescaleros had been forced to move to the barren Bosque Redondo with the defeated Navajos. Unable to survive on meager rations, the Mescaleros slipped back to their mountain homes, hiding from American soldiers until finally they were issued a reservation on their own land in southern New Mexico in 1872. The starving Jicarillas refused to relocate to Mescalero, and continued raiding American settlements.

While war raged with the Chiricahuas in southern Arizona, the U.S. cavalry penetrated Western Apache territory further north where they found the White Mountain headmen eager to establish friendly relations. After the construction of Fort Apache, General George Crook used it in 1872 to stage a retaliatory expedition on the Tonto Apaches, who had been raiding the mineral-rich settlements around Prescott, Arizona. Accompanied by White Mountain and Cibecue scouts, Crook carried out the bloody defeat of the Tontos, the westernmost branch of the Western Apaches.

By 1872 Cochise had come to terms with the Americans, who granted the Chokonens a reservation on their homeland in southeastern Arizona. Following Cochise's death in 1874, the Chiricahuas were removed to the newly established San Carlos reservation east of Fort Apache. There they were joined by the White Mountain Apaches, who had been forced off their lands near Fort Apache following the Tonto campaign.

Although related culturally and linguistically, the Chiricahuas and White Mountain Apaches had never been friendly. Close confinement on the reservation aggravated their differences. In 1875 tensions grew more intense when the Chihenne band of Chiricahuas, led by Victorio, was forcibly removed from New Mexico to San Carlos. Finally, in 1880 the Chiricahuas fled the reservation to join the Nednai deep in Mexico. However, Mexicans annihilated Victorio and most of his band at Tres Castillos.

While Crook and the Apache scouts waged war in Arizona, American troops invaded Mexico in 1873 to punish the Lipan raiders. The survivors were deported to the Mescalero reservation. In 1875 the Kiowa Apaches agreed to a reservation in Oklahoma, ending the Apache menace on the southern Plains. In 1881 the U.S. government finally agreed to settle the Jicarillas on their homeland, but Anglo protests prevented them from settling there until 1888.

In 1883 Crook convinced the Chiricahuas, now led by Geronimo, to return to San Carlos, but in 1885 the disgruntled warriors fled the reservation again. Crook failed to remove them from Mexico, and in early 1886, frustrated by his failure, he resigned his command. His replacement, General Nelson Miles, fortified the region with 4,000 troops and in September 1886 finally convinced Geronimo to surrender.

The Chiricahua prisoners of war were exiled to Florida and Alabama, where they languished until the Comanches invited them to live at Fort Sill, Oklahoma, in 1894. Following the death of Geronimo in 1909, many Chiricahuas elected to move to the Mescalero reservation, while the remainder stayed at Fort Sill, where they still lived in the early 2000s. Some scholars believe descendants of the undefeated Nednai survive in Mexico today.

BIBLIOGRAPHY

Davis, Britton. *The Truth about Geronimo.* Foreword by Robert M. Utley. New Haven, Conn.: Yale University Press, 1929; Lincoln and London: University of Nebraska Press, 1976.

Debo, Angie. *Geronimo: The Man, His Time, His Place.* Norman: University of Oklahoma Press, 1976.

Sweeney, Edwin. *Cochise: Chiricahua Apache Chief.* Norman: University of Oklahoma Press, 1991.

Thrapp, Dan L. *The Conquest of Apacheria.* Norman: University of Oklahoma Press, 1967.

Victoria A. O. Smith

See also **Warfare, Indian; Wars with Indian Nations.**

APALACHEE MASSACRE (1704) was an episode in Queen Anne's War. Having failed to take St. Augustine, Florida, in 1702, former governor James Moore of Carolina invaded the Apalachee district in western Florida with fifty Englishmen and one thousand Creek Indians in 1704. Moore defeated Captain Mexia's force of thirty Spaniards and four hundred Apalachees. Moore's troops pillaged and destroyed all but one of the fourteen Franciscan mission settlements and captured about fourteen hundred Christian Indians.

BIBLIOGRAPHY

Boyd, Mark F., Hale G. Smith, and John W. Griffin. *Here They Once Stood: The Tragic End of the Apalachee Missions.* Gainesville: University of Florida Press, 1951.

Thomas, David Hurst, ed. *The Missions of Spanish Florida.* New York: Garland, 1991.

Francis Borgia Steck / A. R.

See also **Colonial Wars.**

APALACHIN CONFERENCE. On 14 November 1957 the New York State Police discovered a meeting of sixty-five to seventy ranking mobsters at the home of Joseph Barbara, outside Apalachin, New York. The gangsters were leaders from various parts of the country and from a number of organized crime families. The police became suspicious of criminal activity when they discovered that Barbara, the president of Canada Dry Bottling Company, was making a large number of hotel reservations and when they observed several well-known Mafia figures in the area. When the police approached the gathering, the participants fled into the woods, and the police set up roadblocks to stop them. Fifty-eight gangsters were stopped at the roadblocks or in the surrounding area, and taken to the police station for questioning. The subsequent investigations marked the beginnings of the U.S. government's war on organized crime. The conference revealed the world of organized crime to the public, which in return resulted in an increase in governmental response to addressing organized crime. Prior to the conference the Federal Bureau of Investigation, led by J. Edgar Hoover, had been resistant to investigating claims of organized crime. In response to the discovery, the Justice Department established the Special Group on Organized Crime in the spring of 1958, and both the New York State legislature and the U.S. Senate investigated the incident.

BIBLIOGRAPHY

Albanese, Jay S. *Organized Crime in America.* Cincinnati, Ohio: Anderson, 1989.

Wilker, Josh. *Organized Crime.* Philadelphia: Chelsea House, 1999.

Woodiwiss, Michael. *Organized Crime and American Power: A History.* Toronto: University of Toronto Press, 2001.

Shira M. Diner

See also **Conspiracy; Crime, Organized; Narcotics Trade and Legislation.**

APARTMENT HOUSES. Although the term "apartment" is an American invention from the late nineteenth century, Americans were slow to accept this style of multi-unit, horizontal living.

In Europe, the Industrial Revolution in the early nineteenth century boosted the popularity of multi-family buildings, by offering convenient, affordable, and fash-

Tenements. Apartment living initially had a bad reputation as a result of densely packed, often poorly constructed buildings such as these, inhabited by working-class and immigrant families. LIBRARY OF CONGRESS

ionable housing for the burgeoning urban middle and upper classes. This was particularly true in Paris and Vienna.

Parisians had embraced apartment living since the seventeenth century. In a multi-use pattern that would gain popularity in the U.S. in the 1950s and 1960s, a typical French apartment house included a street level with commercial tenants and residential apartments on the upper floors. In this pre-elevator era, wealthier tenants lived on the first floor level, or bel étage, above a mezzanine, or entresol, and the higher the level, the more modest the apartment. Attic space bedrooms were reserved for servants.

With the exception of Scotland, where private "flats" (from the Scottish word, "flaet" meaning "story" or "floor") for Edinburgh's wealthy classes dated back to the sixteenth century, Britain's middle and upper classes shunned multi-unit living until the early twentieth century.

"French Flats" in America

Nineteenth-century middle-class Americans preferred a private, multi-story, detached house to a one-level flat in a building shared with strangers. Until the late nineteenth century, multi-unit housing was also tinged by the image of "tenements," multi-unit residences for working class and immigrant families.

Rising costs for urban property after the Civil War prompted builders to market apartments as a respectable alternative to boarding houses. These early apartments were modeled after Parisian apartments and were referred to as "French flats" to distinguish them from tenements. One of the earliest was the 1869 Stuyvesant Apartments on East Eighteenth Street in Manhattan, designed by the Paris-trained American architect Richard Morris Hunt.

Architects adapted French flats to American middle-class requirements with modern plumbing, bedroom closets, storage space, and large, fully equipped kitchens. By the 1870s, the urban housing crunch created such a boom in apartment house construction that, in Manhattan, alone, 112 apartment houses were built in 1875.

By the 1880s, apartment living not only had shed its negative connotations, but also had become a fashionable choice for wealthy families in search of luxury living at prestigious urban addresses. The introduction of the first electric elevators in the late 1880s, along with fireproof steel frame construction, pushed apartment houses skyward from their previous six- and seven-story limits.

Manhattan's Central Park, opened to the public in 1859, created a boom in luxury apartment buildings along the park's western edge. The most famous was the Dakota at Seventy-second Street and Central Park West, completed in 1884. With its sixty-five suites, some with as many as twenty rooms, the Dakota came with a wine cellar, a gymnasium, and croquet and tennis courts, and included central heating, elevator service, and its own electric generator.

Apartments Come of Age

By 1900, more than 75 percent of urban Americans were living in apartments. Apartments served as a second residence for many wealthy Americans and offered a convenient, respectable, and safe residence near work for urban singles and middle-class families. San Francisco's Tenderloin district, then a middle-class neighborhood with residential hotels and apartment houses, was popularly known as "the apartment house district."

In the 1920s, when the majority of Americans were living in cities, architects were designing apartments for a variety of family sizes, needs, and budgets. These included one-room "efficiency" and "bachelor" apartments, walkup apartments, apartments with elevators, and apartment hotels, residential hotels offering meals for long-term tenants, an adaptation of London's "catering flats."

The 1920s also witnessed a boom in luxury, high-rise apartment buildings. Wealthy New Yorkers began buying luxury "cooperative" apartments, a concept first introduced in the early 1880s as "home clubs" by New Yorker Philip G. Hubert. New York was also home to the first combination loft living spaces, called "studio apartments," for artists. In the 1950s, loft living in lower Manhattan's SoHo neighborhood became the model for late-twentieth-century conversions.

As middle-class families began moving into the suburbs, developers followed with "garden apartments" that included landscaped courtyards. In the late 1920s and 1930s, architects also added "modern" decorative elements and tropical-inspired hues to apartment house exteriors, later coined "Art Deco." One of the most famous clusters was built in the new resort of Miami Beach. The city's Art Deco district is on the National Register of Historic Places.

When high-speed elevators were introduced in the 1950s, apartment towers brought apartment living to new levels. One of the earliest luxury residential towers in the

Deluxe Housing. A horse-drawn carriage passes a fifteen-story apartment building on Fifth Avenue in New York City, 1931. AP/WIDE WORLD PHOTOS

United States was Mies van der Rohe's project on Lake Shore Drive in Chicago. Constructed in 1950 and 1951, the twenty-six-story, twin, steel and glass towers set the tone for apartment building construction over the next two decades.

Self-contained cities, luxury residential towers included shops, banks, and restaurants on the lower levels. Apartment towers for middle-class tenants followed suit. One of the prime examples is Lefrak City in Queens, New York, built from 1960 to 1968. Advertised as having "unprecedented amenities for the era," the complex included 5,000 apartments in twenty eighteen-story towers and offered air-conditioning, tennis courts, a pool, a playground, and a post office.

Isolated apartment towers did not work for subsidized public housing, however, evidenced by the failed "urban renewal" projects of the 1950s. Envisioned as improvements over the decaying row houses and boarding houses they replaced, many have been torn down to be replaced by multi-use, low-level residences.

Recycling Older Models

Today, apartments continue to meet Americans' changing housing needs, as the numbers of singles, divorced, childless couples, and older Americans grow. Since the 1980s, condominiums have satisfied the need for maintenance-free homeownership. Commuter-weary suburbanites are moving into urban loft units in converted retail and industrial buildings. In Lowell, Massachusetts, textile mills have been turned into subsidized housing for low-income and senior tenants. In Richmond, Virginia, developers are converting tobacco warehouses and dairies into luxury rental units.

As Americans are living longer, the demand for retirement and independent living apartments has skyrocketed. This may inspire the next wave in innovative apartment design, as the post-World War II generation moves in.

BIBLIOGRAPHY

Cromley, Elizabeth C. *Alone Together: A History of New York's Early Apartments*. Ithaca, N.Y.: Cornell University Press, 1990.

Rybczynski, Witold. *City Life: Urban Expectations in a New World*. New York: Scribner, 1995.

Sandweiss, Eric. "Building for Downtown Living: The Residential Architecture of San Francisco's Tenderloin." In *Perspectives in Vernacular Architecture*. Edited by Thomas Carter and Bernard L. Herman. Vol. 3. Columbia: University of Missouri Press, 1989.

Schoenauer, Norbert. *6,000 Years of Housing*. Revised ed. New York: Norton, 2000.

Elizabeth Armstrong Hall

See also **Elevators; Industrial Revolution; Tenements; Urbanization.**

APPALACHIA. Appalachia is a region in the eastern United States that can be defined by its physical geography (centered on the Appalachian Mountains) as well as by its unique culture (folk traditions, dialect, foods, art, and music). There are no precise boundaries marking Appalachia. However, the Appalachian Regional Commission, established by the U.S. government in 1965, identifies Appalachia as a 200,000-square-mile region that encompasses all of West Virginia as well as parts of New York, Pennsylvania, Maryland, Ohio, Virginia, Kentucky, Tennessee, North Carolina, South Carolina, Georgia, Alabama, and Mississippi. In 2000, the population of this region was nearly 23 million.

Long before European settlement in the early 1790s by people of English, Scotch-Irish, and German descent, Appalachia was home to many Native American tribes, particularly the Cherokee and the Iroquois. Early European settlers were influenced by the rugged topography and relative isolation from the rest of the nation, which

Appalachia. A 1995 aerial view, photographed by Lyntha Scott Eiler, of mountaintop removal and subsequent reclamation efforts in the vicinity of Indian Creek, in the Appalachian coal country of southwestern West Virginia. LIBRARY OF CONGRESS

prompted a sense of self-sufficiency among the people of Appalachia.

Growing American industrialization at the beginning of the twentieth century brought attention to the region rich for its natural resources. The exploitation of the gas, oil, and, in particular, coal resources of Appalachia was initially beneficial to the region. However, unsafe working conditions and strip mining, which scarred the landscape, were costly to both the Appalachian people and their environment. Coal remains an important resource of the region, but it no longer represents a major source of employment.

The last half of the twentieth century brought greater national attention, often unwanted, to Appalachia. Part of President Lyndon Johnson's War on Poverty focused on the poor of Appalachia. Since the early 1970s, greater emphasis has been given to urban growth, education, health care, and protection of the environment there. There has also been an expanding movement among the people of Appalachia to protect and preserve their unique cultural traditions.

BIBLIOGRAPHY

Drake, Richard B. *A History of Appalachia*. Lexington: University Press of Kentucky, 2001.

Janet S. Smith

See also **Coal Mining and Organized Labor; Conservation; Mining Towns; Music: Folk Revival.**

APPALACHIAN TRAIL, a footpath from Springer Mountain in Georgia to Mount Kathadin in northern Maine. It was conceived in 1921 by Benton MacKaye as "a project in regional planning" and completed in 1937 by the volunteers of the Appalachian Trail Conference.

The National Trails System Act (1968) furthered efforts to protect the narrow and largely private corridor. By 2002, federal and state governments guaranteed public access to all but a hundred miles of the 2,168-mile trail. Although some "through hikers" attempt the entire distance in a season, the trail is mostly encountered in short segments accessible to much of the eastern population.

BIBLIOGRAPHY

Appalachian Trail Conference. Home page at http://www .appalachiantrail.org.

Emblidge, David, ed. *The Appalachian Trail Reader.* New York: Oxford University Press, 1996.

Marshall, Ian. *Story Line: Exploring the Literature of the Appalachian Trail.* Charlottesville: University Press of Virginia, 1998.

John Fitzpatrick

See also **National Park System.**

APPEALS FROM COLONIAL COURTS.

Starting in the late seventeenth century, new proprietary and royal colonial charters reserved for the British king-in-council the right to hear certain cases on appeal from provincial courts. Through this appellate procedure the British Privy Council sought to bring the American colonial legal systems into conformity with England's, particularly in such matters as the rules of evidence and the jury system. Pending appeals, executions of the colonial courts were suspended. Such appeals were both costly and protracted.

Major issues of colonial policy—such as Indian relations, currency law, and intestate succession—were reviewed in litigation brought on appeal. For example, the Virginia clergy appealed to English authorities to disallow the Two Penny Act, a colonial law that effectively reversed earlier statutes that guaranteed Anglican ministers' tenures and salaries. Although the Privy Council upheld the appeal and disallowed the law, the ministers had to sue to recover back salaries from the period when the Two Penny Act was in effect, and these suits proved unsuccessful.

In another case, *Winthrop v. Lechmere* (1728), the council invalidated the Connecticut custom of divisible descent of intestate estates. In appeals of later cases, however, the council reversed its ruling, allowing colonial property law and inheritance customs to stand. The New England colonies at best grudgingly conceded the appellate authority. The Connecticut and Rhode Island charters made no provision for judicial review, and at times the Massachusetts authorities deliberately ignored an order of the Privy Council.

BIBLIOGRAPHY

Greene, Jack P. *Peripheries and Center: Constitutional Development in the Extended Polities of the British Empire and the United States, 1607–1788.* Athens: University of Georgia Press, 1986.

Lovejoy, David S. *The Glorious Revolution in America.* New York: Harper and Row, 1972.

Richard B. Morris / s. b.

See also **Parson's Cause; Privy Council; Royal Disallowance.**

APPOINTING POWER.

The power of appointment of a dictator or absolute monarch is unlimited, but in a constitutional republic the power can be limited in complex ways. The U.S. Constitution provides that certain officers, such as federal judges, ambassadors, and senior cabinet officials, are appointed by the president with the "advice and consent" of the Senate. An issue soon arose, however, regarding whether an official thus appointed could be terminated by the president alone, or only with Senate approval. The Constitution is silent on the subject. Practice and precedent seem to have settled that the president does not need Senate consent to terminate executive branch appointees in the absence of legislation to the contrary, but that judicial appointees may be removed only through impeachment by the House of Representatives and trial by the Senate. However, Congress has also created positions with fixed terms, or has placed limits—such as civil service rules—on the ability of executive branch supervisors to terminate or reassign personnel, or even on how they can be supervised. It has created independent agencies and authorities with large independent budgets and their own powers to raise revenues.

Another issue that has arisen is whether and to what extent appointees can subdelegate their authority to their own appointees, or whether judges and legislators can appoint their own staffs. Practice and precedents seem to have settled that they may appoint assistants, but that judges may not delegate judicial powers and legislators may not delegate legislative powers. However, Congress has adopted legislation authorizing executive branch officials to issue regulations that effectively delegate legislative powers.

A key problem with government appointments has been whether and to what extent persons should be appointed or assigned on the basis of talent or seniority, or to reward party service and assist in implementing party policies. In his early appointments, President George Washington emphasized "fitness of character," selecting men of high reputation. As the party system developed, however, Washington and his successors sought men of their own political persuasion.

President Andrew Jackson argued in his first message to Congress in 1829 that "rotation" in office every few years was needed to keep officials sensitive to popular needs. During the next fifty years, federal and state appointments were largely based upon party service and personal connections. By the 1870s, this "spoils system" was widely condemned for resulting in a decline in competence and honesty in government service. In 1883, Congress approved the Pendleton Act, which established "open, competitive examinations" to qualify job applicants. Initially, only 10 percent of federal employees were covered by civil service rules, but the figure had risen to about 86 percent by 1950. Only a few thousand exempt positions remained at the top of each federal agency to permit discretionary appointment of persons to carry out administration policies, and a few other positions remained available to reward party loyalty and interest-group support. However, nonexempt employees were often unresponsive to administration policies, and could pursue policies of those who appointed or sponsored them.

BIBLIOGRAPHY

Morganston, Charles Emile. *The Appointing and Removal Power of the President of the United States: A Treatise on the Subject of the Appointing and Removal Power.* Westport, Conn.: Greenwood Press, 1976. Reprint of Senate document no. 172, published in 1929.

Sayre, Wallace S., ed. *The Federal Government Service.* 2d ed. Englewood Cliffs, N.J.: Prentice-Hall, 1965.

Jon Roland

See also **Civil Service; Patronage, Political; Pendleton Act; Rotation in Office; Spoils System.**

APPOMATTOX, former courthouse (county seat) of the county of the same name in Virginia, twenty miles east southeast of Lynchburg, and scene of the surrender of the Confederate Army of Northern Virginia to the Union Army of the Potomac on 9 April 1865. General Robert E. Lee, retreating from Petersburg and Richmond, Virginia, on the night of 2–3 April, planned to withdraw into North Carolina via Danville. However, the Federal troops across his front at Jetersville forced him westward to Farmville, where he hoped to procure rations for a march to Lynchburg. En route to Farmville, Lee came under heavy attack. On 6 April, at Sayler's Creek, he lost about six thousand men. By the time Lee reached Appomattox Courthouse on 8 April, long marches without food had depleted the Confederate ranks to two small corps. That night, the reflections of Federal campfires against the clouds showed that the surviving Confederates were surrounded on three sides. To continue fighting, Lee reasoned, would only carry a hopeless struggle into country that had escaped the ravages of war.

On 9 April, at about 1:00 P.M., Lee rode into the village and, at the house of Major Wilmer McLean, formally arranged the surrender of all forces then under arms in Virginia. When on 12 April the troops marched into an open field to lay down their weapons and their flags, the Federal guard presented arms. At Appomattox 7,892 Confederate infantrymen surrendered with arms in their hands. The total number of troops paroled was about 28,000. Union general Ulysses S. Grant tried to get the Confederate commander to advise all the remaining Confederate troops to cease resistance, but Lee insisted that this was a decision for the civil authorities. Appomattox became a national historic site in 1954.

BIBLIOGRAPHY

Davis, Burke. *To Appomattox: Nine April Days, 1865.* New York: Rinehart, 1959.

The Surrender of Lee. An 1892 representation of the scene at the McLean house. © CORBIS

Hattaway, Herman, and Archer Jones. *How the North Won.* Urbana: University of Illinois Press, 1983.

Wheeler, Richard. *Witness to Appomattox.* New York: Harper and Row, 1989.

Douglas Southall Freeman / A. R.

See also **Petersburg, Siege of; Virginia, Army of Northern.**

APPORTIONMENT is the decennial computation and assignment of seats in the House of Representatives to the individual states, or the allocation of legislative seats within a state. Article I, section 2, clause 3, of the U.S. Constitution as amended by the Fourteenth Amendment provides for the apportionment of seats in the U.S. House of Representatives every ten years on the basis of population, except for the rule that each state shall have at least one representative. However, this constitutional provision is silent on how the congressmen are to be elected. To remedy the common practice of at-large or "winner take all" elections, the Apportionment Act of 1842 required single-member congressional districts, composed of contiguous, or adjoining, territory. In 1872 Congress legislated that all districts should contain "as nearly as practicable an equal number of inhabitants," and in 1901 it passed a law requiring that districts should be of "compact territory."

Technically speaking, Congress apportions its House membership, and the states district themselves for the election of representatives. After the 1920 census, which showed for the first time that urban Americans outnumbered rural Americans, Congress was deadlocked on how to reapportion its House seats. To avoid future impasses, Congress in 1929 provided for a so-called permanent system of reapportionment that would discourage further growth in the size of the House and would obviate the necessity for further congressional action on the subject. Unfortunately, the 1929 reapportionment act did not specify that districts were to be contiguous, compact, and of equal size. The Supreme Court in *Wood v. Broom* (1932) ruled that those provisions were no longer in force. Thus, voters complaining of the inequity of districts of grossly unequal population and of gerrymandering could find no law in effect to prevent such practices. Not until *Baker v. Carr* in 1962 did the Court reverse itself and rule that federal courts could review apportionment cases. In 1964, in a six-to-three decision, the Supreme Court decided the case of *Wesberry v. Sanders,* ruling that congressional districts must be substantially equal in population. Departing from the precedent established in *Baker,* and also in *Reynolds v. Sims* earlier in the same year, the Court did not use the Fourteenth Amendment as its justification but based its decision on the history and wording of Article I, section 2, of the Constitution. The Court stated that this language means that "as nearly as is practicable, one man's vote in a congressional election is to be worth as much as another's."

The Supreme Court has also played a key role in the apportionment of state legislatures. Until the Supreme Court ruling in *Baker v. Carr,* constitutional standards by which apportionment should be measured were not established. In a group of six state legislative reapportionment cases—collectively known by the name of the first case, *Reynolds v. Sims* (1962)—the Supreme Court made these major points: the Fourteenth Amendment's equal protection clause "requires that the seats in both houses of a bicameral state legislature must be apportioned on a population basis"; "mathematical exactness of precision" in carving out legislative districts may be impossible, but apportionments must be "based substantially on population"; "the so-called federal analogy is inapplicable as a sustaining precedent for state legislative apportionments"; and deviation from the one man, one vote rule for both houses is unconstitutional even if endorsed in a statewide initiative process or referendum because "a citizen's constitutional rights can hardly be infringed upon because a majority of the people choose to do so."

The equal population (one man, one vote) principle enunciated in *Reynolds* brought relief from decades of malapportionment. In spite of what the 1920 census revealed about urban and rural population, many state legislatures had refused to reapportion either congressional districts or state legislatures to reflect the change in population, thus allowing the rural areas to continue to hold the reins of political power. Rural areas were also legally favored in those states in which the state constitutions provided apportionment based partly or wholly on counties or towns rather than on population. The majority opinion in *Reynolds* did not attempt to spell out precise state constitutional tests because "what is marginally permissible in one state may be unsatisfactory in another." It endorsed a case-by-case development of standards and seemed to be requiring a good-faith effort to achieve "precise mathematical equality." Left unresolved were requirements for compactness and contiguousness of districts, and the constitutionality of multimember districts. By the early 2000s, apportionment remained a highly contentious and partisan issue, one that neither the Supreme Court nor the Congress had completely resolved.

BIBLIOGRAPHY

Cain, Bruce E. *The Reapportionment Puzzle.* Berkeley: University of California Press, 1984.

Eagles, Charles W. *Democracy Delayed: Congressional Reapportionment and Urban-Rural Conflict in the 1920s.* Athens: University of Georgia Press, 1990.

Schwab, Larry M. *The Impact of Congressional Reapportionment and Redistricting.* Lanham, Md.: University Press of America, 1988.

Calvin B. T. Lee / A. G.

See also **Congress, United States; Connecticut Compromise; Preferential Voting; Primary, White; Suffrage: Exclusion from the Suffrage.**

APPRENTICESHIP

APPRENTICESHIP was a contractual agreement to prepare youth for labor in agriculture or the crafts. During the eighteenth century many occupations began the process of training new practitioners in their "art and mystery" through some form of apprenticeship. Naval officers and blacksmiths, carpenters and domestic servants, and sailors and yeoman farmers all might have begun as apprenticed, indentured laborers. By the end of the twentieth century the practice had become relegated mainly to building trades unions, such as the International Brotherhood of Electrical Workers and the United Steel Workers of America.

Craft apprenticeship began as a practice of European medieval guilds, which controlled prices and guaranteed the quality of products. Although commercial interests began to weaken the guilds during the sixteenth century, England's 1563 Statute of Artificers made some guild practices national law and ensured that craft apprenticeships would continue. The statute also required all parents to apprentice their children to a craft or to agriculture if they did not have the resources to bind their children to a profession. The 1601 English Poor Law further bolstered craft apprenticeship by requiring local authorities to bind children whose parents would not. Both of these laws also expanded the practice of indentured apprenticeship to agriculture partly as a response to the thousands of desperate commoners created by the elimination of traditional land rights, an early stage of capitalism. As a result craft and agricultural apprenticeships were both common during the seventeenth and eighteenth centuries.

Although the practice of apprenticeship survived immigration to North America, English enforcement measures, such as the guilds, did not. Consequently agricultural and craft apprenticeship indentures were widely used, but the laws governing them had to be enacted locally. Each colony had its own enforcement codes based on the English model. Craft apprenticeship was common in early American cities prior to industrialization, though less so in the South, where enslaved African Americans worked in the crafts more frequently. Indentured agricultural labor was more common in the southern staple crop economies, where it fueled Virginia's first tobacco boom. But even in the South agricultural indentures became less common after the 1670s, when plantation masters began the dramatic shift to enslaving African laborers. Agricultural apprenticeship of white youth ceased altogether after the American Revolution, as servitude became increasingly associated with slavery and blackness.

The craft apprentice's indenture bound master and apprentice to specific obligations and entitlements. Parents, guardians, the courts, and orphanages negotiated indentures on behalf of children, but the documents typically named the master and the child and were signed by both. The agreements entitled the master to full authority over the youth until he or she attained maturity, usually the teens for girls and age twenty-one for boys. Masters promised to teach their trades and to provide shelter and food, usually clothing, and basic education for their apprentices. Contracts stipulated that the child was bound to obey his or her master in all legal circumstances. Eventually boys could expect to become journeymen and, upon completion of their training, to set up a shop of their own. Girls, usually apprenticed to become domestics, seamstresses, or upholsterers, usually expected to marry.

During the eighteenth century North American apprenticeship was transformed by masters, who introduced cash wages and disciplinary measures, and apprentices, who increasingly fled. Benjamin Franklin exemplified both trends. Franklin broke his own apprenticeship to his brother, a printer, in the 1720s by fleeing to Philadelphia and finding work in a printing office as a manager, a specialization masters developed to increase the productivity of their journeymen. Beginning in the 1730s Franklin made his fortune in printing not only through his famous frugality and industry but also by expanding the specialization of tasks and building capital with which to seed other printing enterprises. Franklin's success and celebrity were rare examples, but nothing was unique about these changes, which tended to break up, simplify, and discipline labor rhythms. When Adam Smith, in *An Inquiry into the Nature and Causes of the Wealth of Nations* (1776), extolled the value of the division of labor as the greatest source of "improvement in the productive powers," he acknowledged a process already in motion in Great Britain and North America (*Wealth of Nations*, p. 7). Claiming that "long apprenticeships are altogether unnecessary," Smith evoked the emerging capitalist ethos Franklin exemplified, and he foreshadowed the final demise of those aspects of craft apprenticeship that had crossed the Atlantic (*Wealth of Nations*, p. 138).

During the nineteenth century industrialization brought an end to craft apprentices' expectation of becoming shop masters. Between 1820 and the Civil War small manufactories in cities such as New York and Philadelphia began to expand their operations. Many masters lost their shops through competition with others, including former master craftspeople, who became factory owners. The journeymen increasingly could expect a life of wage labor rather than small shop ownership, and apprenticed boys and girls could expect to supply cheap unskilled child labor. Some shops, particularly in trades such as printing, no longer trained novices and beginners to practice a trade. Printers who could write copy, set and ink type, work the press, and bind volumes began to disappear. Specialization reduced the skill-level of many jobs. Unskilled, nonapprenticed, low-wage labor was all many masters of the steam presses of the antebellum period felt they needed.

But industrialization never completely eliminated craft apprenticeship. In 1869 a Massachusetts charitable organization surveyed masters and found that forty-six out of fifty-two had served apprenticeships. Yet these men had served without indentures, the contracts that bound masters and apprentices for a term of years and with specific obligations such as education. Instead they had served for wages at their masters' pleasure. In the post–Civil War era trade unions became the principle defenders and promoters of the apprentice system, insisting on certain ratios of apprentices to journeymen. But the ratios continued to decline, even in the building trades, where apprenticeship persisted through the twentieth century.

BIBLIOGRAPHY

Franklin, Benjamin. *The Autobiography and Other Writings.* Edited by Ormond Seavey. Oxford: Oxford University Press, 1993.

Meldrum, Timothy. *Domestic Service and Gender, 1660–1750: Life and Work in the London Household.* New York: Longman, 2000.

Morgan, Edmund S. *American Slavery, American Freedom: The Ordeal of Virginia.* New York: Norton, 1975.

Rorabaugh, W. J. *The Craft Apprentice: From Franklin to the Machine Age in America.* New York: Oxford University Press, 1986.

Smith, Adam. *An Inquiry into the Nature and Causes of the Wealth of Nations,* Edwin Cannan, ed. Chicago: University of Chicago Press, 1976 [1904].

Stansell, Christine. *City of Women: Sex and Class in New York, 1789–1860.* Urbana: University of Illinois Press, 1987.

Wilentz, Sean. *Chants Democratic: New York City and the Rise of the American Working Class, 1788–1850.* New York: Oxford University Press, 1984.

James Spady

See also **Industrial Revolution; Labor; Trade Unions.**

APPROPRIATIONS BY CONGRESS.

The power to appropriate funds gives Congress influence over all activities of the federal government. Article 1, section 9 of the U.S. Constitution specifies that "No Money shall be drawn from the Treasury, but in Consequence of Appropriations made by Law." Through appropriations Congress can fund or frustrate a president's programs, dictate policy to government agencies, and reward members with federal projects in their home districts and states. Writing in the *FEDERALIST PAPERS,* James Madison described appropriations as Congress's "most complete and effective weapon . . . for carrying into effect every just and salutary measure."

Congress first enacted all appropriations in a single bill. As spending grew, it divided appropriations into bills with specific purposes. Until the Civil War, the House Committee on Ways and Means and the Senate Finance Committee both raised and appropriated federal funds. To establish better control over spending, the House of Representatives in 1865 and the Senate in 1867 created their own Appropriations Committees. Each has thirteen subcommittees to handle specific appropriations. The chairs of these subcommittees hold such authority that they are known as the "cardinals" of Capitol Hill.

At the beginning of each year the OFFICE OF MANAGEMENT AND THE BUDGET submits the president's proposed budget. The Budget Committees approve or amend that budget, setting overall revenue and spending targets. Other standing committees report legislation authorizing programs that will often exceed the budget's financial limits. The Appropriations Committees then determine which programs to fund and at what levels. They seek to complete their work before the start of the next fiscal year on 1 October.

Congress enacts appropriations on a single-year basis, although it authorizes some agencies to make long-term contractual agreements. Without approval of the annual appropriations, federal money cannot be spent and agencies cannot function. Since the 1980s, Congress has passed continuing resolutions whereby, if it does not complete action on an appropriation, the affected agencies can continue to operate under their previous year's budget. In a showdown with congressional Republicans in 1995, President Bill Clinton vetoed several appropriations, causing much of the federal government to shut down temporarily.

Presidents have generally been reluctant to veto an entire appropriations bill over objections to a particular item. Some presidents impounded—or did not spend—appropriated funds for unwanted programs, a practice voided by the Congressional Budget and Impoundment Act of 1974. In an effort to reduce soaring deficits, Congress in 1996 granted presidents an item veto. But in 1998 the U.S. Supreme Court declared the item veto an unconstitutional delegation of Congress's authority over federal spending.

The Constitution provides for revenue bills to originate in the House, and by extension the House claimed the right to originate appropriations. If the Senate votes for different amounts than what the House has appropriated, the two versions must be reconciled by a conference committee. Congress also enacts supplemental appropriations to meet additional or unexpected needs, such as disaster relief.

Reflecting their power and prestige, and the vast expansion of federal spending, the Appropriations Committees have the largest membership of any committee in either house. Despite protests from presidents over congressional "earmarking" of appropriations for specific purposes, and criticism over "pork barrel" legislation that funds members' desired projects, Congress has tenaciously preserved its power of the purse.

BIBLIOGRAPHY

Fenno, Richard F., Jr. *The Power of the Purse: Appropriations Politics in Congress.* Boston: Little, Brown, 1966.

Kiewiet, D. Roderick, and Mathew D. McCubbins. *The Logic of Delegation: Congressional Parties and the Appropriations Process.* Chicago: University of Chicago Press, 1991.

Munson, Richard. *The Cardinals of Capitol Hill: The Men and Women Who Control Government Spending.* New York: Grove Press, 1993.

Donald A. Ritchie

See also **Balanced Budget Amendment; Budget, Federal.**

ARAB AMERICANS come from many different nations in the Middle East and North Africa. Unified, to some extent, by common cultural traditions, language, and religion, the Arab American community in the United States includes peoples from Morocco, Tunisia, Egypt, Lebanon, Palestine, and Yemen. Today, Arab Americans live in all fifty states, with the heaviest concentrations in California, Florida, Illinois, Massachusetts, Michigan, New York, New Jersey, Ohio, Texas, and Virginia. More than half the Arab American population lives in large metropolitan areas such as New York City, Los Angeles, Detroit, Chicago, and Washington, D.C. Almost half are descended from immigrants who came to the United States between 1880 and 1940. According to 1990 census figures, approximately 940,000 Arab Americans reside in the United States. However studies show that Arab Americans have been significantly undercounted; more recent estimates put their numbers closer to 3.5 million.

Early Settlement and Immigration

The first significant wave of Arab immigration to the United States began in the late nineteenth century with the arrival of Syrians from what was then called Greater Syria. The area, which included the modern countries of Lebanon, Syria, Jordan, and Israel, as well as the region of Palestine, had been part of the Ottoman Empire. Approximately ninety percent of these new arrivals were Christian; most were farmers seeking better opportunities, while others left to avoid being drafted into the Turkish army. Between 1880 and 1914, approximately 100,000 Syrians came to the United States. Although not all the immigrants were of Syrian or Turkish origin, immigration officials tended to classify them as such.

At first, many intended only to stay in the United States for a short time, but they soon decided to remain permanently, because of better opportunities. Arab Americans were lured by the prospect of making money and being their own boss and many became peddlers. In time,

Syrian American Children. An early-twentieth-century photograph taken in New York. © CORBIS

some took their profits and opened dry goods businesses or other retail establishments. Others found work in the automobile plants in Detroit. Soon "Little Syrias," as they were called, began appearing in many large cities of the United States, each having its own grocery stores, newspapers, churches, and fraternal and religious organizations.

The second wave of immigrants came to the United States in the years following World War II, differing in important ways from those who came earlier. Unlike the previous arrivals who were often uneducated, the newer Arab immigrants were more likely to be professionals with college degrees. One other significant difference was religion. The majority of new Arab immigrants were members of the Islamic faith. Of the Arab Americans who came to the United States after World War II, the Palestinians are by far the largest group.

Many immigrants left to escape the political turmoil that continued to plague much of the Middle East. With the establishment of Israel as a state in 1948, thousands of Palestinians departed. The numbers of Arab immigrants to the United States rose again following the Israeli defeat of Egypt, Syria, and Jordan in the Six-Day War of 1967. Besides those fleeing political unrest and war, some Arab immigrants, such as the wealthy Egyptians, whose property and assets the government seized as part of a nationalization of Egyptian businesses, came to the United States in search of better economic and educational opportunities.

Unlike the first wave of Arab immigrants, who often struggled to master a language and new customs, many of this second wave have enjoyed a smoother transition to the American way of life. Many immigrants already spoke English and had skills that broadened their employment opportunities. Others have come on student visas to finish their educations in American colleges and universities. The immigration of educated men and women resulted in a severe "brain drain" in the Arab world, particularly between 1968 and 1971, as educated Arabs, seeing that there were few jobs to be had, elected to stay in the United States.

Culture and Tradition

One outcome of the Arab defeat in 1967 was the growth of Arab nationalism and ethnic pride among Arab Americans. As this consciousness grew, so did the vitality of the Arab American community. As a result, certain institutions such as Arab newspapers and magazines, which had been decreasing in popularity and readership, took on a new vitality. The second wave of immigrants also founded clubs and organizations such as the Association of Arab American University Graduates, formed in 1967, and the Arab American Institute, created in 1985 to influence United States foreign policy toward the Arab world. At the same time, Arab Americans have become more active in local, state, and national affairs.

The second wave of Arab immigration has also spurred other Americans to learn more about Arab cul-

Kahlil Gibran. An 1898 photograph of the influential Lebanese-born poet and novelist, who lived in New York beginning in 1912 and wrote in both Arabic and English on religious and mystical themes. ROYAL PHOTOGRAPHIC SOCIETY

ture and history. College campuses across the country developed programs that included the study of Arab languages, history, art, music, and religion. Among the most pervasive Arab American influences on American culture has been the cuisine. Thirty years ago, many Americans were unfamiliar with even the rudiments of Arab cooking. Today, scores of Middle Eastern restaurants and groceries have exposed many Americans to the multitude of Arab dishes. Perhaps one reason for the recent popularity of Arab food is that it is healthier than many traditional American dishes.

Notable Arab Americans

A number of individual Arab Americans have made important contributions to American culture, science, politics, literature, and sports. Some of the more noteworthy Arab Americans in politics include consumer activist and former presidential candidate Ralph Nader, former senator George Mitchell of Maine, Secretary of Heath and Human Services during the Clinton Administration, Donna Shalala, the former Governor of New Hampshire, John Sununu, and the noted White House reporter for United Press International, Helen Thomas. Frank Zappa, a musician and composer who rose to popularity during the 1960s and 1970s, was of Arab American descent. Other notable Arab Americans include Christa McAuliffe, the first teacher-astronaut who lost her life when the space shuttle Challenger exploded in 1986; NFL quarterback Doug Flutie, who also established the Doug Flutie Jr. Foundation for Autism, an organization dedicated to helping families of autistic children; and Candy Lightner, founder of Mothers Against Drunk Driving.

BIBLIOGRAPHY

Abraham, Sameer, ed. *Arabs in the New World: Studies on Arab-American Communities.* Detroit, Mich.: Wayne State University, 1983.

Ashabranner, Brent. *An Ancient Heritage: The Arab-American Minority.* New York: Harper Collins, 1991.

Jaafari, L. "The Brain Drain to the United States: The Migration of Jordanian and Palestinian Professionals and Students." *Journal of Palestine Studies* 3 (Autumn 1973): 119–131.

McCarus, Ernest N., ed. *The Development of Arab American Identity.* Ann Arbor: University of Michigan Press, 1994.

Naff, Alixa. *Becoming American: The Early Arab Immigrant Experience.* Carbondale: University of Southern Illinois Press, 1985.

Meg Greene Malvasi

See also **Immigration.**

ARAB NATIONS, RELATIONS WITH.

The Arab world is today divided into eighteen states plus a proto-state, the Palestinian Authority, but it is united in language, culture, and religion (more than 90 percent Muslim). All of the Arab world, except Morocco, Mauritania, and parts of the Arabian peninsula, was for centuries loosely united in the Ottoman Empire. All of the Arab world, except inner Arabia and northern Yemen, was subsequently divided by European imperial rule.

American relations with this vast Arab world fall into two periods of unequal duration:

1. From the late eighteenth century until World War II, marked by a few years of sporadic conflict with the Barbary states and then a long period of benign but limited trade and educational/cultural contact.

2. Slightly more than a half century of a powerful American presence in the area, bringing in its wake all the advantages and liabilities of that status.

With the outbreak of the American Revolution, American shipping no longer had the support of British treaties with the states of North Africa—Tripoli, Tunis, Algiers, and Morocco, all but the latter being juridically a part of the Ottoman Empire but independent in fact. American ships were thereafter exposed to Barbary piracy or, more accurately, privateering. Between the years 1776 and 1815, scores of American ships were seized and more than 450 Americans held captive in North Africa, often for many years.

Relations with Morocco were a happier story. Sultan Muhammad of Morocco recognized American independence de facto as early as 1777, and a treaty was signed between Morocco and the United States in 1786—the first ever with an Arab or Middle Eastern state. A few incidents in 1801–1802 aside, this treaty as renewed remains in effect to this day.

Relations with Algiers, Tunis, and Tripoli were, however, stormier, and the United States responded in multiple, often inconsistent ways. Congress appropriated money to ransom prisoners and offer tribute, and several different individuals were appointed as emissaries for this purpose. Yet some in the United States sensed that naval power would protect American shipping better than treaties and tribute (or at least insure reasonable treaties and tribute). In 1794, Congress authorized the building of several frigates and smaller ships, and this act marks the beginning of the U.S. Navy.

Warfare with the different Barbary states was interspersed with periods of peace. The line in the Marine Hymn "to the shores of Tripoli" marks the American conflict with Tripoli (Libya) during the years 1801–1805. Over the years the United States paid the Barbary states a total of about 1.5 million dollars (a huge sum in those days when the annual federal budget seldom exceeded 4 million) in cash and gifts (American-built ships were greatly prized). This era of U.S. relations had a more glorious ending for the young American republic: In 1815 a U.S. fleet under the command of Stephen Decatur forced treaties upon Algiers, Tunis, and Tripoli that ended privateering against the United States and even imposed indemnity payments.

American relations with the Arab world throughout the remainder of the nineteenth century were limited: American trade continued but at a very low level compared to other world areas. For example, one American ship called at Muscat in Oman between 1855 and 1913. Not surprisingly, that consulate was closed two years later, in 1915. Consulates existed in numerous other cities, but these were very low-pressure postings. Most of the consuls were foreign nationals selected in the absence of available Americans.

The impact of American missionaries on the Middle East throughout these years was greater than that of either American consuls or traders. Protestant missionaries began to arrive early in the nineteenth century. Their converts, with rare exceptions, were not the majority Muslims nor the Jews but members of the different Eastern Christian Churches and not too many of them, either. The missionary impact in education was, however, considerable, creating the American University of Beirut (originally Syrian Protestant College, founded in 1866) and the American University in Cairo, founded in 1919. Although the importance George Antonius in his classic *The Arab Awakening* (1938) attributed to these few Protestant missionaries in fostering Arab nationalism has been correctly downsized by later scholarship, theirs was a significant role.

Woodrow Wilson's diplomacy, stressing self-determination of nations, provided a great stimulus to nationalist aspirations in the Arab world and well beyond, but his initiatives, for example the fifth and twelfth of his celebrated Fourteen Points, or his sending the King-Crane Commission to Syria in 1919 to determine what kind of postwar settlement the people there wanted, came to naught as America turned to isolationism.

Thereafter, the significant American activity in the Arab world involved oil. The United States, adhering to its venerable Open Door policy, supported private American ventures to capture a share of Middle Eastern oil. Examples include American hard bargaining to secure a one-quarter holding in Iraqi oil in the 1920s, and the creation of the Kuwait Oil Company as a partnership between Gulf Oil and the Anglo-Persian Oil Company (later Anglo-Iranian, now British Petroleum).

The close American connection with Saudi Arabia may be traced back to the signing of an oil concession in May 1933 between King Ibn Saud and a consortium of American companies destined to become the Arabian-American Oil Company (ARAMCO).

World War II inaugurated an era of intensive American involvement in the Arab world continuing to this day. American troops first engaged Nazi forces not in Europe but in North Africa, landing in Morocco and Algeria in November 1942 (Operation Torch, commanded by General Dwight D. Eisenhower) and moving thereafter in a joint Anglo-American campaign that ended with the surrender of 400,000 Axis forces in Tunisia in May 1943. President Roosevelt's meetings with Morocco's King Muhammad V during the 1943 Casablanca Conference and with King ibn Saud in 1945 following the Cairo conference were emblematic of this new American presence, as was the wartime decision to extend lend-lease aid to Saudi Arabia. By the end of the 1940s the United States had become the preeminent Western power in the Middle East, confronting a very old player in Middle Eastern diplomacy, Russia, which had become, as the Soviet Union, the most powerful state ever ruled from Moscow. The 1947 Truman Doctrine was a response to Soviet probes in Greece, Turkey, and Iran. At that time the Arab world lying to the south was seen as securely within the Western camp, but also in turmoil and disaffected by continuing colonial rule. American policy makers viewed their task as simultaneously working toward a new regional order of independent Middle Eastern states that would freely join the Western security network against the Soviet Union.

Success was spotty. The several Arab states or nationalist movements solicited and obtained some American support for decolonization, but many, still fearing an overly heavy Western hand, resisted American-led defensive arrangements. This was especially the case in the 1950s and 1960s under the leadership of Egypt's Nasser. By this time the Soviet Union, in its 1955 arms deal with

Egypt, had jumped over the "northern tier" of Greece, Turkey, and Iran and had become directly involved in the Arab world.

Complicating U.S. ties with the Arab world has been American support for Israel, created in 1948. Since then, much American diplomacy in the Arab world can be told in terms of efforts to achieve an Israeli-Arab settlement, with crisis points being the many wars between Israel and its Arab neighbors—1948, the Suez War in 1956, the Six Day war of June 1967, the 1969–1970 war of attrition between Israel and Egypt, the Ramadan/Yom Kippur War of October 1973, the 1982 Israeli invasion of Lebanon, and the 2002 Al Aqsa Intifada.

Illustrative of American peace efforts over the entire past century are the Anglo-American efforts to orchestrate an Egyptian-Israeli settlement in the early 1950s, the July 1970 (Secretary of State) Rogers Initiative for an Egyptian-Israeli cease-fire, Secretary of State Kissinger's "shuttle diplomacy" following the October 1973 war, the sustained American diplomacy from 1977 until the Egyptian-Israeli peace treaty in 1979, and the ill-fated efforts by President Clinton in the last weeks of his administration in 2000 to achieve a definitive Israeli-Palestinian settlement. In 2001–2002, amid the vicious cycle of Palestinian suicide bombings and massive Israeli military responses, the assumption on all sides was that the American position would be the decisive factor.

The juxtaposition of the Cold War in the Middle East and the Arab-Israeli confrontation provides the larger framework for explaining American diplomacy in the Arab world between the 1940s and 1990. Two subsequent presidential "doctrines" following that of Truman in 1947 reveal as much. The Eisenhower Doctrine of January 1957 came after the United States had pressured the British, French, and Israelis to withdraw from their invasion of Egypt (the Suez War, 1956). Prompted by the belief that the resulting sharp decline of British and French standing in the area created a "power vacuum," the Eisenhower Doctrine offered support to countries in the area threatened by "international communism."

Most Arab states, however, either supporting or fearing Nasserist neutralism, refused to sign on. Years later, when the Soviet invasion of Afghanistan provoked fears that their next step might be toward the Persian Gulf, the January 1980 Carter Doctrine took a more unilateralist position: The Persian Gulf region was defined as an area of vital U.S. interest, and any outside intrusion would be resisted by force if necessary. Arab states that have maintained generally good relations with the United States over the past half century include Saudi Arabia and small Arab states of the Gulf along with Jordan, Tunisia, and Morocco. All of these, interestingly, have escaped military coups or revolutions.

Other states experiencing military coups offer a different history. Iraq and Libya were both pro-Western before military coups in 1958 and 1969, respectively, and anti-Western thereafter. Algeria started independence in

1962 with a strong Third World neutralist orientation. Syria was something of a shuttlecock in regional politics in the 1940s and 1950s, and then a Soviet client but an unstable state in the 1960s. Starting in 1970, Hafiz al Asad achieved internal stability and Syria thereafter combined close ties to the Soviet Union with a prickly regional independence.

The most significant switch in superpower patrons was in Egypt—from the Nasserist alliance with the Soviets beginning in 1955, and continuing with ups and downs until Sadat in the 1970s achieved a diplomatic revolution by moving Egypt from the Soviet to the American camp and signing a peace treaty with Israel.

America's post-1940s diplomacy in the Arab world has involved both "proxy wars" and direct U.S. military intervention. The former were an important part of all the Arab-Israeli wars, the most acute confrontation being in the October 1973 war, when the United States even issued a nuclear alert in response to the Soviet threat to intervene militarily to save Egypt from defeat. The United States intervened militarily twice in Lebanon, in 1958 and 1982–1983—and then in 1990–1991 sent roughly half a million American troops to lead an international coalition of forces (including Arab armies) mustered to liberate Kuwait from the Iraqi invasion.

Since at least the 1960s, internal and regional developments within the Arab world have resulted in the rise of fundamentalist Islamist groups opposed to their own governments, which are seen as corrupt, irreligious, and subservient to the imperialist and infidel United States. Moreover, since the end of the Cold War these diverse xenophobic impulses have been directed almost exclusively at the United States. Thus, to the fundamentalist "Afghan Arabs" (radicals from Arabia and many other Arab countries who fought and trained in Afghanistan from the 1980s on) organized in Al Qaeda led by Osama bin Laden, the terrorist attacks on New York and Washington on 11 September 2001 were but one step in their war against infidelity at home and abroad.

The United States at the beginning of the new millennium has pronounced interests in the Arab world, often expressed in the triptych "oil, the open door, and Israel." It has demonstrated the power and the will to intervene, including militarily (the 1990–1991 Gulf War plus bruited plans to move again against Saddam Hussein's Iraq). After the 11 September attacks, it sent troops to Afghanistan in a "War on Terror" to hunt down Al Qaeda extremists. It has adequate to good working relations with most Arab governments, but thereby shares in the often considerable hostility those governments face. All this makes the United States for the foreseeable future the principal outside player in the ongoing Arab and Middle Eastern diplomatic arena. As a result the United States, failing a most unlikely scaling down of U.S. commitments, is caught up in the many unresolved problems confronting this region.

BIBLIOGRAPHY

Badeau, John S. *The American Approach to the Arab World*. New York: Harper and Row, 1968.

Brands, H. W. *Into the Labyrinth: The United States and the Middle East, 1945–1993*. New York: McGraw-Hill, 1994.

Brown, L. Carl, "The United States and the Middle East." In Brown, ed., *Centerstage: American Diplomacy Since World War II*. New York: Holmes and Meier, 1990.

De Novo, John A. *American Interests and Policies in the Middle East: 1900–1939*. Minneapolis: University of Minnesota Press, 1963.

Field, Jr., James A. *America and the Mediterranean World, 1776–1882*. Princeton: Princeton University Press, 1969.

Finnie, David H. *Pioneers East: The Early American Experience in the Middle East*. Cambridge, Mass.: Harvard University Press, 1967.

Kaufman, Burton I. *The Arab Middle East and the United States: InterArab Rivalry and Superpower Diplomacy*. New York: Twayne Publishers, 1996.

Lesch, David, ed. *The Middle East and the United States: A Historical and Political Reassessment*. Boulder, Colo.: Westview, 1996.

Little, Douglas. "Gideon's Band: America and the Middle East since 1945," *Diplomatic History* 18/4 (Fall 1994), 513–540 (historiographical essay).

Quandt, William B. "America and the Middle East, A Fifty Year Overview." In L. Carl Brown, ed., *Diplomacy in the Middle East: The International Relations of Regional and Outside Powers*. New York: St. Martin's Press, 2001.

Stookey, Robert W. *America and the Arab States: An Uneasy Encounter*. New York: John Wiley and Sons, 1975.

Yergin, Daniel. *The Prize: The Epic Quest for Oil, Money, and Power*. New York: Simon and Schuster, 1991.

L. Carl Brown

See also **Iran, Relations with; Israel, Relations with; Israeli-Palestinian Peace Accord; Lebanon, U.S. Landing in; 9/11 Attack; Persian Gulf War.**

ARAPAHO. An American Indian ethnic group, whose members are found principally on the Wind River Indian Reservation in Wyoming and on allotments on the former Cheyenne-Arapaho Reservation in Oklahoma, Arapahos are descendents of Algonquian-speaking peoples who migrated from the Great Lakes onto the Great Plains in the distant past. By the eighteenth century, distinct northern and southern divisions occupied lands on the Plains, where, drawn by bison herds and horses acquired from Comanches, they embraced Plains Indian cultural traditions. These divisions should be understood as flexible residence groups rather than unified political or economic entities. The band remained the most important unit of organization, and Arapaho governance operated through a series of age-grade societies (societies organized by age) that provided stable leadership while facilitating interband cooperation.

By the middle nineteenth century, Arapahos found themselves in competition with waves of settlers, miners,

Ben Friday Sr. A Northern Arapaho spiritual leader (1904–1994). © SARA WILES

and military personnel for control of their lands and resources. Arapahos responded by endorsing the 1851 Fort Laramie Treaty, but while this agreement supposedly guaranteed peaceful relations with settlers, the 1864 massacre at Sand Creek convinced Southern Arapahos to surrender traditional lands to join Southern Cheyennes on a reservation in western Oklahoma. With a few exceptions, Northern Arapahos generally avoided engaging the United States Army, expecting to enjoy secure title to a reservation of their own in return. Instead, they settled on the Shoshone Reservation in 1878 (Wind River Indian Reservation after 1937), a "temporary" measure that eventually became permanent.

On reservations, Arapahos struggled to maintain their political, social, and religious institutions in the face of deepening poverty and aggressive government civilization programs. On the Cheyenne-Arapaho Reservation, implementation of Dawes Act allotment policies in 1891 replaced the tribal land base with individual homesteads. Land sales followed as did increased reliance on wage work and on quite minimal revenues from oil leases. Since 1935, a joint constitutional committee established under the auspices of the Indian Reorganization Act has governed affairs of the combined Cheyenne-Arapaho tribe.

Northern Arapahos also faced allotment and efforts by ranchers and farmers to gain control over valuable resources. Non-Indian farmers obtained title to irrigated lands within reservation boundaries, and water rights remain a bone of contention between Indians and the State of Wyoming. But the Wind River Reservation remains substantially intact, and Northern Arapaho age-grade societies' ceremonial organizations continue to operate. Though they rejected the Indian Reorganization Act, Arapahos govern themselves through a six-member business committee that meets with an Eastern Shoshone counterpart on matters of mutual interest. Since 1947, the two tribes have divided oil revenues, the Arapahos dedicating most of their share to per capita payments, with some funding community development projects. But unemployment remains high, with tribal economic development projects like the Arapaho Ranch unable to produce many jobs.

Nevertheless, Arapahos remain politically vital and active ceremonially. Their annual sun dance, held on the Wind River Reservation, affirms a sense of shared identity and is a focal point for ethnic identity and tribal self-determination.

BIBLIOGRAPHY

Berthrong, Donald. *The Cheyenne and Arapaho Ordeal: Reservation and Agency Life in the Indian Territory, 1875–1907.* Norman: University of Oklahoma Press, 1976.

Fowler, Loretta. *Arapahoe Politics, 1851–1978: Symbols in Crises of Authority.* Lincoln: University of Nebraska Press, 1982.

Stamm, Henry E., IV. *People of the Wind River: The Eastern Shoshones, 1825–1900.* Norman: University of Oklahoma Press, 1999.

Trenholm, Virginia Cole. *The Arapahoes, Our People.* Norman: University of Oklahoma Press, 1970.

Brian C. Hosmer

See also **Tribes: Great Plains.**

ARBITRATION is the use of an impartial third party to resolve a dispute. Unlike mediation or conciliation, in which a third party facilitates the end of a dispute by helping the negotiators find common ground, an arbitrator ends a dispute by issuing a binding settlement. Before submitting their dispute to arbitration, the parties to a dispute agree to abide by the arbitrator's ruling.

Arbitration has been used to resolve disputes for centuries. Examples from as far back as the sixth century B.C.E. affirm the use of arbitration to resolve disputes between individuals and between city-states in ancient Greece. In the Old Testament, King Solomon acted as an arbitrator to resolve a conflict between two women over the identity of a child (1 Kings 3:16–28). George Washington in 1799 provided for the use of arbitration should any disputes arise over his will.

In U.S. history, labor arbitration, to settle industrial disputes between labor unions and employers, and commercial arbitration, to settle disputes involving business and consumer transactions, have been the most extensive uses of arbitration. The development of labor arbitration stems from the government's desire to avoid strikes that threaten the public interest, while commercial arbitration results from a desire to avoid the court system.

Commercial arbitration has expanded to include international commercial arbitration and has become more widespread as participants in the legal system have explored the use of alternative dispute resolution (ADR) to reduce the costs and delays of court cases. ADR includes arbitration, mediation, and other forms of dispute resolution. A significant example is the growing trend to use arbitration instead of the courts to resolve employment disputes involving allegations of discrimination and other violations of federal and state employment laws.

The Arbitration Process

The central features of the arbitration process are generally similar regardless of the topic of the dispute. Except in some cases in which arbitration is required by law, the parties agree ahead of time, usually when drafting a contract, to submit any disputes to binding arbitration. Nearly every union contract between labor unions and employers specifies arbitration as the final step of the grievance procedure to resolve employee grievances. A typical clause in contracts between builders, architects, and owners in the construction industry might read as follows: "Any controversy or claim arising out of or relating to this contract, or the breach thereof, shall be settled by arbitration administered by the American Arbitration Association under its Construction Industry Arbitration Rules, and judgment on the award rendered by the arbitrator(s) may be entered in any court having jurisdiction thereof."

Once arbitration is initiated by one of the parties, an arbitrator must be selected. If the parties have not selected an arbitrator, agencies such as the American Arbitration Association and the Federal Mediation and Conciliation Service can provide a short list of qualified arbitrators. The parties then select an arbitrator from this list, for example, by alternately striking out names. Some arbitration processes may involve a panel of arbitrators, especially in complex commercial cases. When labor arbitration involves a panel, it is common to have an impartial chairperson, one member selected by labor, and one member selected by management.

Each party to the dispute then presents its case and argues its position at a hearing. It is of utmost importance that each party receives a full and fair hearing. Witnesses and exhibits often are presented to support a case, though the strict rules of evidence used by judges are not followed. The arbitrator decides the relevance and importance of the evidence. As with a traditional court case, opening and closing statements are made, and witnesses can be cross-examined. The parties frequently are represented by attorneys.

After the hearing, the arbitrator considers all of the material and issues a ruling. In commercial arbitration, it is common for the decision to simply provide the arbitrator's resolution to the disputed issues without providing details about the arbitrator's reasoning. In labor arbitration, however, it is common for the decision to be accompanied by an opinion indicating the reasons for the decision. The opinions are often used as precedents in subsequent cases.

The parties agree ahead of time to abide by the arbitrator's ruling or award. Laws such as the Federal Arbitration Act and judicial precedent have established the authority of arbitration awards, and the scope for challenging an award in court is limited to alleged problems in the process, such as arbitrator misconduct or disregard for the contract or law. The merits of an arbitrator's decision are not subject to judicial review, and awards can be enforced by the courts.

Labor Arbitration

Labor arbitration usually resolves disputes involving labor unions, employees, and employers. It is commonly divided into two distinct categories: interest arbitration and rights arbitration.

Interest arbitration resolves conflicts of interest over the establishment of the terms and conditions of employment, for example, the wage rate, working hours, and number of vacation days for each employee. In labor relations, these terms and conditions are negotiated through collective bargaining, and agreements are formalized in collective bargaining agreements or union contracts. A breakdown in these negotiations typically results in a strike. Interest arbitration avoids or ends strikes. In the United States the development of interest arbitration can be attributed to the government's desire to protect the public interest by preventing or ending strikes in key industries during the first part of the twentieth century. In 1902, President Theodore Roosevelt ended a five-month coal strike via arbitration, and several laws provided for voluntary arbitration in the railroad industry and the appointment of boards of inquiry if interstate commerce was affected.

Interest arbitration in the private sector is voluntary, and the parties can choose arbitration as an alternative to a strike if desired. Examples have involved the apparel and steel industries as well as Major League Baseball. Congress, however, has prevented railroad strikes through arbitration, and President Bill Clinton ended a flight attendants strike at American Airlines in 1993 by persuading the parties to submit their dispute to arbitration.

In the public sector, interest arbitration is often compulsory, that is, required by law, which echoes the rationale of preventing strikes that harm the public interest. At least twenty states and the federal government deny government employees the right to strike and instead require interest arbitration. These compulsory arbitration laws are especially prevalent among occupations deemed essential, such as police officers, firefighters, and prison guards. Most interest arbitration in the United States occurs in the public sector under these compulsory statutes; private sector negotiators are generally reluctant to give up their right to strike and to turn over their decision-making authority to a third party.

In contrast, rights arbitration is widely used in both private- and public-sector labor relations. Rights arbitration resolves conflicts of rights, more commonly referred to as grievances, which are disagreements over the application or implementation of an existing union contract. In other words, has a right that was granted by the contract to a specific party been violated? A common example involves the discipline and discharge of employees. Most union contracts specify that employees can only be disciplined and discharged with just cause, so grievances are frequently filed over whether or not a specific instance of discipline or discharge was consistent with the requirements of just cause. An arbitrator might rule that the discharge was consistent with just cause and therefore stands or that management violated a principle of just cause and therefore the grievant is entitled to be reinstated to his or her job, perhaps with back pay. Other examples include questions of whether or not the contractual provisions were followed in layoffs or promotions, whether or not a specific employee was eligible for vacation pay, or whether or not management has the right to subcontract work.

The widespread adoption of rights or grievance arbitration in the United States originated during World War II. This period was marked by significant growth in union membership and an obvious public interest in avoiding strikes that interrupted war production. The U.S. government, through the National War Labor Board, prompted organized labor to give up the right to strike over grievances in return for binding grievance arbitration as the final step of the grievance procedure. At the conclusion of the war, the only thing that labor and management could agree on was that grievances were best settled through a grievance procedure ending in binding arbitration rather than a strike.

Grievance arbitration was further institutionalized by the important Supreme Court decisions in *Textile Workers v. Lincoln Mills* (1957) and the Steelworkers Trilogy Cases (1960). In short, these decisions prohibit labor and management from ignoring an arbitration clause in their contract, provide significant legitimacy to the arbitration process, and restrict the scope of judicial review.

No-strike clauses are in 95 percent of union contracts, and clauses providing for binding arbitration to settle unresolved grievances are in nearly all contracts. Note carefully that these no-strike clauses pertain to grievances, rights disputes during the term of a collective bargaining agreement, not to interest disputes at the expiration of the agreement. This system of grievance arbitration, with its established body of precedents on just cause and other important issues, is widely recognized as a positive contribution to labor-management relations in the workplace.

However, the application of arbitration to employment disputes in the nonunion arena is contentious. A number of employment laws provide employees with rights pertaining to nondiscrimination, safety and health, family and medical leave, and other subjects. To avoid costly litigation, some employers require employees, as a condition of employment, to agree to arbitrate any future employment law disputes rather than take the employer to court.

The Supreme Court, in *Gilmer v. Interstate/Johnson Lane Corporation* (1991), upheld forcing an employee who agreed to binding arbitration in advance to submit his or her dispute to arbitration, but numerous legal and policy questions remained. In particular, it is central to the legitimacy of arbitration as a dispute resolution process that all parties receive due process. In light of the differences in resources between corporations and individual employees, it is debatable whether or not employees are provided with due process in this nonunion context, especially if they must waive their right to litigation as a condition of employment in advance of any dispute. This issue impacts significantly arbitration in the United States.

Commercial Arbitration

Commercial arbitration resolves disputes involving business transactions. Merchants and traders have used arbitration for centuries. The chambers of commerce of New York and other eastern cities used arbitration before 1800, though perhaps not frequently. Widespread acceptance of commercial arbitration, however, did not start until the 1920s. New York State passed a law in 1920 and Congress passed the Federal Arbitration Act in 1925, making contract clauses containing an agreement to arbitrate disputes legally binding. Also significant was the founding in 1926 of the American Arbitration Association, a not-for-profit organization that provides guidelines and assistance in using arbitration.

As a result, contracts in the United States between builders, architects, and owners in the construction industry or between cloth mills and garment manufacturers in the textile and apparel industry often have a clause specifying that disputes will be resolved through arbitration. Transactions in the real estate, financial securities, and publishing industries often include arbitration as the dispute resolution procedure. One of the largest commercial arbitration applications involves uninsured motorist claims, in which liability and damages are determined through arbitration.

While labor arbitration developed as a means for avoiding strikes, the rationale for commercial arbitration is to avoid the court system. Relative to court action, arbitration can be faster, less expensive, and more private. Moreover, arbitrators are experts in the subject matter of the dispute. Increased economic globalization and complex international business relationships combined with a reluctance to litigate disputes in a foreign court have increased adoption of arbitration to resolve international business disputes.

BIBLIOGRAPHY

Bales, Richard A. *Compulsory Arbitration: The Grand Experiment in Employment.* Ithaca, N.Y.: ILR Press, 1997. Overview of arbitration to settle employment law disputes. Includes historical and contemporary developments.

Bühring-Uhle, Christian. *Arbitration and Mediation in International Business: Designing Procedures for Effective Conflict Management.* The Hague and Boston: Kluwer Law International, 1996.

Devinatz, Victor G., and John W. Budd. "Third Party Dispute Resolution—Interest Disputes." In *The Human Resource Management Handbook,* part 2. Edited by David Lewin, Daniel J. B. Mitchell, and Mahmood A. Zaidi. Greenwich, Conn.: JAI Press, 1997. Reviews the extensive research literature on interest arbitration.

Dunlop, John T., and Arnold M. Zack. *Mediation and Arbitration of Employment Disputes.* San Francisco: Jossey-Bass, 1997.

Elkouri, Frank, and Edna Asper Elkouri. *How Arbitration Works.* 5th ed. Edited by Marlin M. Volz and Edward P. Goggin. Washington, D.C.: Bureau of National Affairs, 1997. The classic treatment of grievance arbitration.

Kheel, Theodore W. *The Keys to Conflict Resolution: Proven Methods of Settling Disputes Voluntarily.* New York: Four Walls Eight Windows, 1999. Wisdom and examples from an experienced arbitrator and mediator.

Ponte, Lucille M., and Thomas D. Cavenagh. *Alternative Dispute Resolution in Business.* Cincinnati, Ohio: West Educational, 1999.

John Budd

See also **Collective Bargaining; Labor Legislation and Administration; Strikes.**

ARBOR DAY. On the motion of the agriculturist J. Sterling Morton, the Nebraska State Board of Agriculture designated 10 April 1872 as a day to plant trees, naming it Arbor Day. Morton had moved to the Nebraska Territory in 1854, and he quickly tried to remedy the treeless conditions of the plains. In 1875 the state legislature changed Arbor Day to 22 April, Morton's birthday, and made it a legal holiday. It is now observed in every state except Alaska, usually on the last Friday in April. Arbor Day is also a legal holiday in Utah and Florida, although Floridians observe it in January.

BIBLIOGRAPHY

Olson, James C. *J. Sterling Morton.* Lincoln: University of Nebraska Press, 1942.

Schauffler, Robert Haven, ed. *Arbor Day: Its History, Observance, Spirit and Significance, with Practical Selections on Tree-Planting and Conservation, and a Nature Anthology.* New York: Moffat, Yard and Company, 1909.

Everett Dick/H. S.

See also **Conservation; Forestry; Holidays and Festivals; Nationalism.**

ARCHAEOLOGY is the scientific reconstruction and understanding of prehistoric and historic human behavior from the evidence of material remains. Although the theories archaeologists employ for framing their questions of the past have changed dramatically in the short one hundred years of its existence as an academic discipline, archaeology's primary goals—reconstructing and interpreting past human behavior and culture—have remained essentially unchanged. In the United States, archaeology has traditionally been viewed as one of the four classic subdisciplines of anthropology, along with cultural anthropology, physical anthropology, and linguistics.

While archaeology is also historical in certain aspects, it differs from the study of written and oral history—although it uses both—in two fundamental ways. First, the materials archaeologists generally find in the ground do not indicate directly what to think about them or about the ancient cultures that produced them. Therefore, archaeologists have to make sense of the material remains of the past through analogy to historic cultures, experimentation, inference, behavioral modeling, and good detective work. Second, archaeology is a humanistic discipline as well as a science. As humanists, archaeologists are concerned with how societies function, the evolution of cultural complexity, ethnicity, ideology, power, and a host of other universal questions about human behavior and organization. As scientists, archaeologists develop and construct pictures of the past from limited evidence, just as physicists develop and construct a coherent view of how the natural world works from a limited set of observations. This combination of humanism and sci-

Iroquois Longhouse. This communal dwelling is made of upright saplings and elm bark.

ence is one of archaeology's many fascinations and strengths as a discipline: it reflects the ingenuity of the modern scientist through its use of technology and rigorous methodology as well as the processes of the modern historian through its focus on reconstructing the past and giving it relevance to the present and future.

American archaeology as a discipline is divided into two types: prehistoric and historic. Prehistoric archaeology is concerned with testing anthropological theories of human behavior and cultural evolution against the archaeological record of societies that left no known written records. Historic archaeology uses archaeological data both to test hypotheses about the operation of historically known societies and to fill in the historical gaps concerning the more mundane, but crucially important, aspects of the day-to-day functioning of those societies.

The History of Archaeology in the United States

The first systematic, well-planned archaeological investigation in the United States was organized by Thomas Jefferson in 1784. Because Jefferson had decided to carefully excavate one of the prehistoric earthen mounds on his property in Virginia in the hope of finding out who built it, he is often considered to be the "father of American archaeology." The fact that he excavated was important, since few individuals in his day undertook such a step. His work was also so carefully done that he was able to observe how soil, refuse, and artifacts had built up over time, and he was thus able to link the known present to the unknown past. And, most important, his excavation was carried out not to find objects but to resolve an archaeological question: Were the Native Americans present in Virginia descendants of those who built the mounds? (Jefferson demonstrated that they were.)

While Jefferson's research was little known until the late nineteenth century, the "mound builder question" did continue to engage the interest of Americans. As a result, several organizations, such as the American Philosophical Society, the American Antiquarian Society, and the Smithsonian Institution, started to try to unravel the mystery. Findings were, however, sporadic and inconclusive. As a result, in 1884, Congress finally dedicated funds to solving the problem through a series of surveys and data collection to be carried out by Cyrus Thomas of the Bureau of American Ethnology (BAE), the first federally appointed archaeologist. The answer was determined within ten years: all of the mounds present in the United States were the products of the ancestors of current Native peoples. The bureau continued to explore the prehistory of the United States over the course of its eighty-seven year existence, culminating in the multivolume *Handbook of North American Indians* in the late 1970s. The BAE was incorporated into the Anthropology Department at the Smithsonian Institution in 1965.

The resolution of the question of who built the mounds led to a growing public recognition of the need for cooperation between government agencies, academic

Cliff Palace. A section of one of the prominent pre-Columbian Indian dwellings preserved at Mesa Verde National Park, Colo. NATIONAL ARCHIVES AND RECORDS ADMINISTRATION

institutions, and individual researchers to answer questions about America's past. This circumstance was one factor that helped lead to the formation of archaeology as a discipline. In addition, by 1906 the federal government saw the need to protect archaeological sites and artifacts and began creating national monuments and parks as well as passing legislation such as the Antiquities Act.

That archaeology was largely incorporated within anthropology by 1900 was a result of the work of Franz Boas, considered to be the founder of anthropology in the United States. Boas realized at the beginning of the twentieth century that no ethnographic study of the quickly vanishing New World peoples could be complete without a thorough understanding of their present culture, their past culture, their biology, and their language. This realization led to the formation of anthropology as a professional discipline with the creation of the American Anthropological Association in 1902 and to the rapid founding of departments of anthropology at universities like Columbia, Harvard, Yale, Chicago, Michigan, and California at Berkeley. The foundations of academic archaeology in the United States were laid well before Boas, however, with the creation of the Archaeological Institute of America in 1879, which mainly concerned itself with Old World archaeology. Anthropological archaeology focusing on America's past was not formalized as a discipline until the founding of the Society for American Archaeology in 1934.

Anthropological archaeology as a distinct discipline has gone through many phases in its efforts to understand the past. At first, scholars were mainly interested in finding rare and unique artifacts. Then, archaeologists focused on describing as much as possible about the past by recording the smallest details of many types of artifacts and architecture. Once accurate dating techniques became widely available, archaeologists began to ask more and more complex questions about the past.

The archaeologist who provided the first dating breakthrough was Alfred V. Kidder. Through his painstaking excavation work at Pecos Pueblo in New Mexico from 1918 to 1928, he was able to demonstrate that archaeologists could better understand chronology by carefully paying attention to two factors: how soil, refuse, and artifacts built up over time at a site, and how artifacts change through time at a site. Especially important was his discovery of the series of changes that the pottery in the northern Southwest had undergone. Once this series of changes was understood, a researcher could generally date a site in the region from the pottery found at it. Kidder's research set the standard for the discipline and is still widely used today.

The problems with exact dating were solved with the advent of dendrochronology (tree-ring dating) in the 1920s by Andrew E. Douglass and radiocarbon dating in the 1940s by Willard F. Libby. Tree-ring dating allowed researchers in the Southwest to obtain the exact dates when certain prehistoric structures were built, while radiocarbon analysis allowed exact dating in a wider variety of contexts and over much greater periods of time. The dating revolution enabled archaeologists to construct highly detailed descriptive temporal sequences for most of the known prehistoric cultures of America. It also opened the door to even bigger questions: When did the first Americans arrive? (The answer turned out to be much earlier than anyone had imagined.) When did certain cultures start to develop? When did Native Americans start practicing agriculture? Despite these technical dating advances, the focus of archaeology was still on description rather than explanation.

Nevertheless, the dating revolution signaled the beginning of archaeology as a truly multidisciplinary enterprise, for the new dating techniques were developed by chemists and astronomers, not archaeologists. At present, because researchers have become increasingly interested in how past peoples interacted with and were affected by their surroundings, many archaeological projects now also include biologists, geographers, geologists, and environmental scientists.

The Great Depression helped forge archaeology as a discipline because it generated some of the most massive archaeological projects the United States has ever seen. These projects, carried out by the Civilian Conservation Corps, the Works Projects Administration, and the Tennessee Valley Authority, were intended to keep extremely large numbers of people employed. Such projects required skilled archaeologists with incredible leadership and managerial abilities to run them. Many of the most influential archaeologists of the twentieth century, including James A. Ford, Roger E. Taylor, and Alex D. Krieger, got their start on these projects. Such massive undertakings also signaled the beginning of large-scale

government funding of archaeology, which continues to this day.

It was not until the 1960s that many archaeologists finally became frustrated with the discipline's focus on minute description over concrete explanation. No one was talking about *why* cultures developed in certain ways or *why* cultural change took place at all. The infusion of fresh anthropological and scientific thinking into archaeology by a new generation of researchers, such as Lewis Binford, Michael Schiffer, and others, catapulted archaeology into a new era, one that was centered on trying to discover the universal processes behind cultural complexity and change. Despite the postmodern, nonscientific leanings of some current researchers, American archaeology remains largely focused on these goals.

Archaeology and the Public

Archaeology, by discovering history firsthand through the welter of objects left behind from past human activity, has raised the consciousness of the American public with respect to this country's cultural heritage. Furthermore, the media in all its forms spends a great deal of time showcasing the discoveries of archaeologists, especially the controversial and exciting ones.

Since the 1970s, archaeologists have been embroiled in public debates about who owns the past and has the right to protect it and interpret it. Native Americans have protested that their histories were being written by other people, that their heritage was being sold in auction houses or put on display in museums, and that their ancestral sites were being destroyed. Ultimately, the historic preservation movement, along with the legal protection of unmarked graves, brought much of America's archaeological heritage under the auspices of the federal and state governments and helped address some Native American concerns. By the 1990s, it was increasingly common for tribes to have their own preservation officers and for archaeologists to plan investigations that addressed both archaeological and indigenous questions and needs.

Archaeology is still struggling with how best to meet the needs of the general public while maintaining its responsibility to preserve the past for the future.

BIBLIOGRAPHY

Fagan, Brian M., ed. *The Oxford Companion to Archaeology*. New York: Oxford University Press, 1996.

Meltzer, David J., Don D. Fowler, and Jeremy A. Sabloff, eds. *American Archaeology, Past and Future: A Celebration of the Society for American Archaeology, 1935–1985*. Washington, D.C: Smithsonian Institution Press, 1986.

Renfrew, Colin, and Paul Bahn. *Archaeology: Theories, Methods, and Practice*. New York: Thames and Hudson, 2000.

Sturtevant, William C., ed. *Handbook of North American Indians*. 20 vols. Washington, D.C.: Smithsonian Institution Press, 1978–1996.

Thomas, David Hurst. *Exploring Ancient Native America: An Archaeological Guide*. New York: Macmillan, 1994.

Trigger, Bruce G. *A History of Archaeological Thought.* Cambridge, U.K.: Cambridge University Press, 1989.

Willey, Gordon R., and Jeremy A. Sabloff. *A History of American Archaeology.* San Francisco: W. H. Freeman, 1980.

Devin Alan White

See also **Anthropology and Ethnology; Archaeology and Prehistory of North America; Indian Mounds; Radiocarbon Dating.**

ARCHAEOLOGY AND PREHISTORY OF NORTH AMERICA.

Settlement of the North American continent began at least 15,000 years ago, after the ocean level had dropped to expose a landmass beneath the modern-day Bering Strait. The people who first crossed from Asia into North America were probably small family groups or hunting parties, who came both by foot and in watercraft along the North American coastline. Over the next several thousand years, the descendents of these people developed unique societies across North America with complex political, economic, and religious systems and lifeways adapted to particular local environments.

Archaeologists refer to the earliest North Americans as Paleoindians. What is known about them comes largely from evidence found in caves, as caves offered both temporary shelter for these highly mobile groups and excellent conditions for archaeological preservation. The bones of butchered animals, flaked stone tools, and the remnants

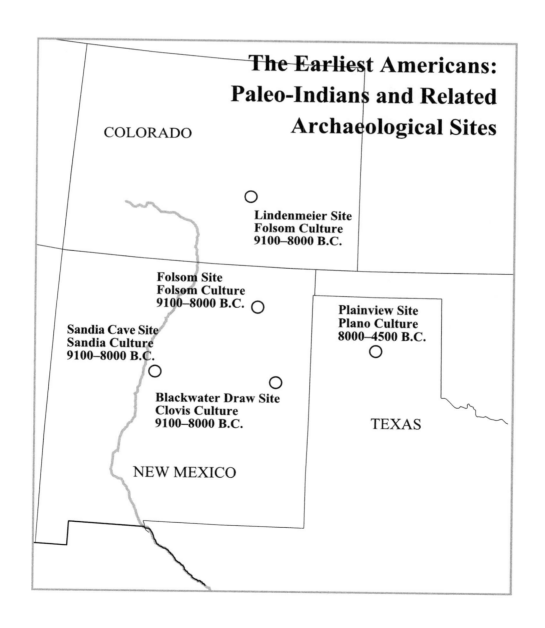

The Earliest Americans: Paleo-Indians and Related Archaeological Sites

COLORADO

Lindenmeier Site
Folsom Culture
9100–8000 B.C.

Folsom Site
Folsom Culture
9100–8000 B.C.

Sandia Cave Site
Sandia Culture
9100–8000 B.C.

Plainview Site
Plano Culture
8000–4500 B.C.

Blackwater Draw Site
Clovis Culture
9100–8000 B.C.

TEXAS

NEW MEXICO

Early Weapons. From 12,000 B.C. to 9,000 B.C., the Clovis civilization was the dominant Indian group in North America. They are perhaps most famous for the sharp, fluted stone points they made to attach to spears and other projectiles for hunting. The points, like the ones shown here, have been found in every mainland state in the United States. © WARREN MORGAN/CORBIS

of fire-hearths point to human habitation of the Bluefish Caves in the Yukon by 13,000 B.C., and of Meadowcroft Rockshelter in Pennsylvania by 12,500 B.C. Ten-thousand-year-old sagebrush bark sandals have been found at Fort Rock Cave in Oregon. The earliest known human remains in North America come from Santa Rosa Island in California and date to at least 11,000 B.C.

Paleoindian people across the North American continent focused on hunting megafauna (bison, mammoths, giant ground sloths), using a toolkit that included knives, scrapers, some bone tools, and fine projectile points—including the distinctive Clovis point. The Clovis points were "fluted" to allow attachment to a short shaft that could be mounted on a spear. Smaller mammals and collected vegetable foods were supplemental to the diet.

With the extinction of megafauna at the end of the Pleistocene (c. 10,000 years ago), Paleo-Indian peoples diversified, shifting away from big-game hunting to become more generalized hunter-gatherers. This change also marked the end of the use of the Clovis point and the adoption of a more generalized toolkit. People now followed an annual pattern of movement throughout a large geographic area, hunting and gathering seasonal foods. Favored sites were probably returned to year after year and bands formed in areas where food was abundant. What ensued was the flourishing across the continent of cultural groups that were increasingly reliant on both local environmental conditions and interaction with neighboring groups.

The Far West

The West Coast offers one of the richest natural environments on the planet. The environmental diversity found along the coast allowed for the development of some of the most complex hunter-gatherer societies in the

world. Resource availability greatly affected the people of this region, and at the time of European contact there was a great diversity of societies, from small mobile bands out toward the Great Basin, to large semi-permanent communities along the coast.

In the Pacific Northwest, fishing industries date to at least 5000 B.C. A Northwest Coast cultural tradition clearly emerges about 3500 B.C., with the rapid increase in the number of village sites, the intensification of shellfish collection, the development of specialized technologies for marine fisheries and specialized woodworking tools, and a general trend towards cultural homogeneity throughout the region. After 1000 B.C. people lived in wood-plank houses in increasingly larger and defensible villages and relied upon fish weirs, vegetable foods, and food storage for sustenance. The societies in the Pacific Northwest had different social classes, with elite and commoners distinguished by status markers and assigned religious tasks.

The basic California coastal lifestyle, which included shellfish collection, fishing, and sea mammal hunting, was in place at least 10,500 years ago. Around 5000 B.C., the marine lifestyle began to be augmented by a seasonal cycle in which fall nut and seed harvests alternated with shellfish collection. This way of life placed a greater reliance on vegetable foods, particularly the acorn of the oak tree. The focus on gathering many types of resources from many different natural environments helped spur the growth of complex hunter-gatherer societies. By A.D. 1000 the flow of trade goods like obsidian and shell beads was widespread throughout California and the Great Basin. Although material culture was broadly similar throughout California, local groups each developed unique stylistic traditions. Native people in California spoke over one hundred different languages, and by the time of European contact, there were more than 300,000 native people living in California.

The Great Basin does not have the abundant natural resources of the Pacific Northwest and California. Around 10,000 years ago, native peoples practiced big-game hunting around the remnants of Ice Age lakes in what archaeologists call the Western Pluvial Lakes Tradition. As the pluvial lakes dried up around five to seven thousand years ago, native peoples diversified their collection of foods, foraging year-round for many types of vegetable and animal foods, and storing goods at semi-permanent winter base camps. Piñon nuts become a critical part of the desert diet by about A.D. 500, around the same time that pottery and the bow-and-arrow were introduced. About A.D. 400, some groups in the south of the Great Basin developed ties with the Southwest, and cultivated maize, beans, and squash. However, these groups remain differentiated from Southwest cultures because of a continued reliance on hunter-gatherer lifeways to augment agriculture.

The Southwest

The Southwest is classically defined as extending from Durango, Colorado, in the north to Durango, Mexico, in

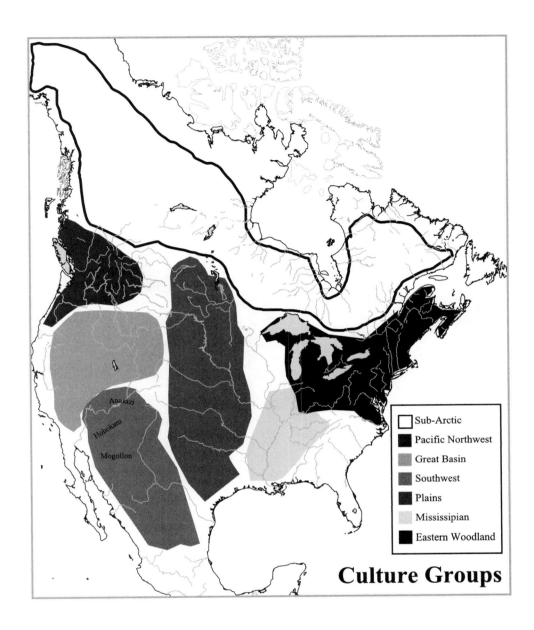

Sub-Arctic
Pacific Northwest
Great Basin
Southwest
Plains
Mississipian
Eastern Woodland

Culture Groups

the south and from Las Vegas, Nevada, in the east to Las Vegas, New Mexico, in the west. Although this area encompasses extremely diverse environments, it has a predominantly arid to semi-arid climate, and this aridity has conditioned the nature of human existence in the region for the past 11,000 years.

During what archaeologists refer to as the Archaic period (5500 B.C.–A.D. 200), the climate and vegetation of the Southwest came to assume their modern patterns. Economies were based on hunting modern game animals and gathering plants. Archaic stone tools were less specialized and less distinctive than those of the Paleoindian period, due to a more generalized subsistence base. While it is clear that Archaic peoples did obtain domesticated crops—such as maize, beans, and squash—from groups

farther south in Mesoamerica, these were not heavily relied upon. Instead, agriculture during this time period can mainly be viewed as an activity that native groups casually experimented with as a means to supplement their normal set of resources.

By A.D. 500 agriculture had begun to take root in the Southwest, bringing with it sedentism (the practice of establishing permanent, year-round settlements), ceramic traditions, and cultural complexity. From roughly A.D. 500 to A.D. 750, the foundations of the three main cultural groups found in the prehistoric Southwest were laid down, as people began to aggregate into larger and larger settlements and started to interact with each other across long distances through political, economic, and ideological means. By A.D. 1000 the Ancestral Puebloan (Anasazi),

Pueblo Bonito. Chaco Canyon, which is located in northwest New Mexico, was the center of the Anasazi culture in the eleventh century. Twelve separate towns were located within thirty-two square miles in the canyon, with the largest one being Pueblo Bonito, shown here. All of the towns featured aboveground, multiroom pueblos made of masonry blocks. © GEORGE H. H. HUEY/CORBIS

Hohokam, and Mogollon traditions were fairly well defined on the Colorado Plateau, in the Sonoran Desert, and in southern New Mexico, respectively.

Of the three traditions, the most complex are the Ancestral Puebloan and the Hohokam, which both "peaked" at roughly the same time (A.D. 1150), yet rarely interacted with one another despite their proximity. The height of Ancestral Puebloan culture can be seen at Chaco Canyon, New Mexico, which was the center of a regional system of sites spanning an area of approximately 100,000 square kilometers. A series of ceremonial roads connected most of these sites to one another. The height of Hohokam culture can be observed in the Phoenix Basin (at sites like Snaketown), which for all intents and purposes during this time period is one contiguous archaeological site composed of hundreds of communities interlinked by a massive irrigation canal network. Both regional systems carried on long-distance trade with Mesoamerica, although the Hohokam did so more frequently and directly.

While the accomplishments of both of these traditions are impressive, the environment of the Southwest is marginal and very fragile. Severe droughts, resource instability, and overexploitation of the environment, combined with competition, warfare, and a host of other factors, eventually caused the collapse of both regional systems. While it is not entirely clear what the fate of the

Hohokam people was, the history of the Ancestral Puebloan people is fairly well understood. By A.D. 1300 groups on the Colorado Plateau and elsewhere began to move south, and eventually reorganized themselves into the large Pueblos of New Mexico and Arizona that the Spanish encountered and that we are familiar with today, including the Zuni, Hopi, and Acoma.

Plains

The Plains area extends from the Canadian boreal forest in the north to central Texas in the south, and from the Rocky Mountains in the west to the Missouri River and the eastern boundaries of the states of Nebraska, Kansas, and Oklahoma in the east. Prior to settlement by European Americans, this region was almost continuous open grassland, interrupted by isolated mountainous areas, as well as forested regions located along major river valleys. The Plains climate is extremely unpredictable, but is generally characterized by heavy summer rains, a steep east-to-west decrease in precipitation, and cold winters. Bison dominated the landscape, although deer and elk could be found in the forests.

While the Paleoindian emphasis on big-game hunting may have persisted on the northwestern Plains, by the Archaic period native groups generally had broken up into smaller, more mobile social groups that diversified

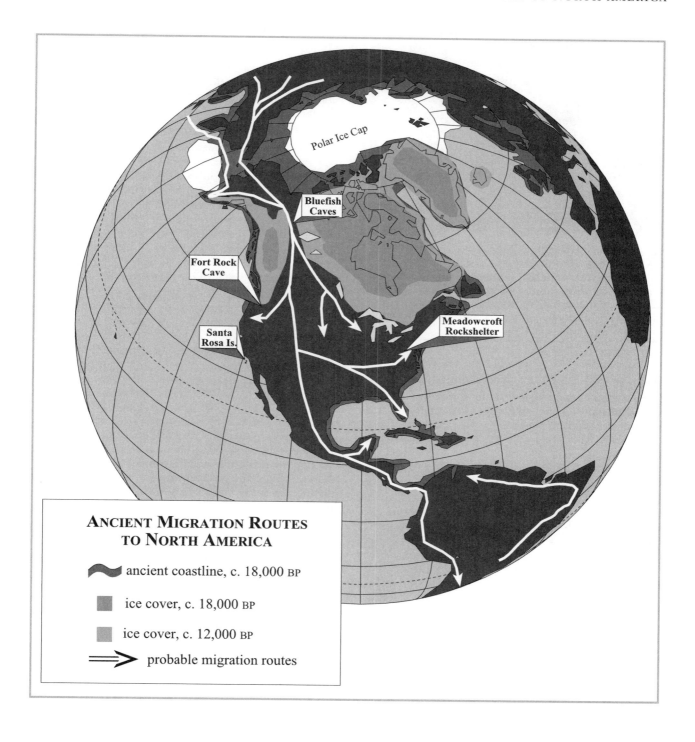

ANCIENT MIGRATION ROUTES TO NORTH AMERICA

~ ancient coastline, c. 18,000 BP

■ ice cover, c. 18,000 BP

■ ice cover, c. 12,000 BP

⟹ probable migration routes

their subsistence base. By A.D. 900 the Plains were populated by nomadic bison hunters in the north and west and semi-sedentary, incipient horticulturalists in most other areas. At this time, villages begin to appear throughout most of the Plains. While the exploitation of wild resources such as bison was still important, the inhabitants of these villages relied heavily upon cultivated corn, beans, squash, and sunflower. The development of these village complexes is most likely related to the rise of more complex societies in the Mississippian and Eastern Woodlands areas at the same time. Nomadic bison hunters continued their ways of life with little discernible change

Serpent Mound. Also called the Great Serpent Mound, the earthen structure is the largest "effigy" mound located in the United States. Three-feet high and nearly a quarter-mile long, when viewed from the air the mound resembles an uncoiling serpent. Undoubtedly built for religious or mythical purposes, the mound is located on a plateau near Brush Creek in Adams County, Ohio. © BETTMANN/CORBIS

throughout the Plains Village Period. Both groups were heavily and negatively impacted by European contact in the 1500s and the subsequent European American settlement of the Plains.

Mississippian

By Mississippian, archaeologists mean the hundreds of late precontact societies that thrived from roughly A.D. 750 to A.D. 1500 throughout the Tennessee, Cumberland, and Mississippian river valleys. These societies were once known collectively to Americans as the Moundbuilders, a "mysterious" group of people who apparently built all of the large earthen mounds found throughout the eastern United States and then vanished without a trace before Europeans arrived. As the eastern half of America was more thoroughly explored during the nineteenth century and as archaeologists began working at Moundbuilder sites, a more complex picture of these peoples developed, leading to a more appropriate name for their culture and the understanding that they never really disappeared at all.

The Mississippian emergence is characterized by a number of distinctive features: characteristic pottery (usually containing crushed mussel shell); village-based maize agriculture; construction of large flat-topped mounds, commonly situated near the town plaza; and a stratified social organization embodying permanent (and most likely hereditary) offices. Mississippian people also adopted the bow and arrow, explicitly connected their religion to agricultural productivity, often worshiped a fire-sun deity, and engaged in intensive long-distance trade.

During their heyday, the Mississippian elite presided over vast and complex ceremonial centers, sites that today are called Cahokia, Moundville, Spiro, and Etowah. The Mississippian aristocracy was invested with power by the

thousands upon thousands of farming people who lived in smaller palisaded hamlets and farmsteads and relied on the elites for protection and guidance. The locus of political power continually shifted, "cycling" between several large communities that lost and regained prominence depending on their population sizes, their ability to access important resources, and the charisma of their leaders.

One of the most fascinating windows into the ancient Mississippian world is the site of Cahokia, the largest city in precontact native North America. At its peak, Cahokia was home to at least 20,000 people, although some estimates are twice this number. The city contained a complex of 120 earthen mounds surrounded by a massive wooden palisade that reached fifteen feet in places. A few mounds were used to bury the dead, but most were devoted to ceremonies involving the living. The majority of the population lived outside of the complex.

Much of eastern North America did not participate in the complete elaboration of Mississippian culture. However, all were to some extent dependent upon Mississippian-style economics. Descendents of the great American Indian confederacies of the American South—including the "Five Civilized Tribes"—are deeply rooted in their Mississippian ancestry.

Eastern Woodlands

The prehistory of the Eastern Woodlands features the range of lifeways found throughout North America. The development of agriculture, the construction of large complexes of geometric and effigy earthworks, extensive long-distance trade, and rich aesthetic traditions reveal the complexity of native civilizations of the Eastern Woodlands.

Native people in the Northeast shifted from big-game hunting to generalized hunting and gathering about 8000–6000 B.C. Population density in resource-rich areas led to the elaboration of different material-culture styles, manifested in the development of various side-notched, corner-notched, and stemmed projectile points. The first burial mound was erected at L'Anse Amour in Labrador around 5600 B.C. The trend toward greater complexity, diversity, and population size began about 4000 B.C., and led to regional variation throughout the Northeast.

The development of visible burial centers and the intensification of local and regional exchange mark the shift into what archaeologists call the Woodland Period (1000 B.C.–A.D. 1). Trade brought crops like maize, gourds, and squashes to the Northeast from Mexico, and grit-tempered pottery containers became increasingly important as people started to rely upon the cultivation of both indigenous and introduced crops. A mortuary-centered system known as the Adena complex (c. 1000 B.C.–A.D. 100) was located in the central Ohio Valley and shared by many nearby cultural groups. Earlier Adena burial centers are marked by an essentially egalitarian burial program, utilitarian grave goods, and small, earthen burial mounds. Later Adena ceremonial centers featured elaborate buri-

Ceremonial mounds. The Cahokia region, which was near present-day Saint Louis, was the site of more than one hundred ceremonial mounds built between 1050 and 1250. The largest, shown here while being excavated in 1972, was called Monks Mound after the group of Trappist Monks who lived on a nearby mound. Monks Mound was the largest pre-Columbian construction north of Mexico. © RICHARD A. COOKE/CORBIS

als, with exotic grave goods and large earthen mounds with circular enclosures thought to be gathering places.

After A.D. 100 the cultural groups in the Northeast intensified gathering and agricultural techniques, fixed boundaries to legitimize a right to local resources, and developed a set of complex local and regional ties. The most spectacular archaeological evidence of the elaboration of Northeastern Woodland cultures is found in the Hopewell ceremonial sites in Ohio. These religious and political centers range from a few acres to a few hundred acres in size and typically contain a burial mound and a geometric earthwork complex. Mortuary structures underneath the mounds were often log tombs containing cremation or bundled burials and exotic grave goods like copper and meteoric iron from the Plains or alligator and shark teeth from the Southeast. The extent of the Hopewell interaction sphere underscores the growing sophistication and class stratification of Northeastern cultures over time and the importance of "powerful" exotic items in local, public display.

End of Prehistory
The end of prehistory was brought on by European settlement of the North American continent, which forever changed the way of life for native communities. Beginning from the 1500s onward, Native Americans were encroached upon by European powers seeking a toehold in the New World. In some regions, entire native communities were simply destroyed or subjugated, as in the Southwest and California. However, in all instances Native Americans interacted and traded with Europeans. Native trade was an important factor in colonial American

politics and economics in the Northeast and Southeast and for Russian expansion along the Pacific Coast.

The long-term impact of European contact was devastating to the Native American way of life. The introduction of disease, the relentlessness of European and eventually American expansionist aggression, and the breakdown of traditional cycles of agriculture and gathering all taken together brought widespread disruption. Nonetheless, at the beginning of the twenty-first century, the descendents of the "First Americans" continue to practice aspects of their traditional lifeways in communities across the continent.

BIBLIOGRAPHY
Fagan, Brian M. *Ancient North America: The Archaeology of a Continent.* New York: Thames and Hudson, 1995.
Fagan, Brian M., ed. *The Oxford Companion to Archaeology.* New York: Oxford University Press, 1996.
Sturtevant, William C., et al., eds. *Handbook of North American Indians.* Washington, D.C.: Smithsonian Institution Press, 1978–1996. Currently at twenty volumes.
Thomas, David Hurst. *Exploring Ancient Native America: An Archaeological Guide.* New York: Routledge, 1999.

Brian Isaac Daniels
Devin Alan White

See also **Adena; Ancestral Pueblo (Anasazi); Cahokia Mounds; Hohokam; Hopewell; Indian Mounds; Spiro.**

ARCHANGEL CAMPAIGN, an Allied operation that supported Russian forces during World War I. On 16 March 1918 Germany compelled the revolution-torn Russia to ratify the Treaty of Brest Litovsk. The Allies were concerned because the treaty gave the German army entry into Finland, thus positioning it for marches upon the Russian ports of Murmansk and Archangel, where military supplies from Allied ships had been stockpiled. The Allies also feared that U-boat bases might be established on the North Cape. The new Bolshevik government in Moscow welcomed Allied troop landings at Murmansk in March 1918 as support against further demands by Berlin. The Allies proposed to form a shield in desolate northern Russia behind which the Russians could build a new Red Army. On this premise British officers led a push nearly 400 miles southward and firmly secured the railroad approach to Murmansk.

By 3 August 1918 Allied relations with the Bolsheviks had deteriorated, and Archangel was seized by 1,500 British and French troops. The Allied force at Archangel was enlarged on 5 September by the addition of three American battalions from the 339th Infantry Regiment of Lieutenant Colonel George E. Stewart and was reinforced a few weeks later by two additional companies. Although constituting 40 percent of the Allied troops under the command of British major general Frederick C. Poole, Americans had little say in planning operations.

The original American mission as envisioned by President Woodrow Wilson was "to guard military stores which [might] subsequently be needed by Russian forces and to render such aid as [might] be acceptable to the Russians in the organization of their own self-defense." By September 1918, however, civil war was raging in Russia, and Britain and France favored the Whites. An Allied force of 10,000, including U.S. soldiers, pushed into Siberia, hoping to reach a Trans-Siberian Railroad link at Vyatka, 600 miles to the southeast.

In the summer the Bolshevik army had been too feeble to prevent the Allied seizure of Archangel, but by autumn Mikhail S. Kedrov had formed the Sixth Army around two understrength rifle divisions. The Reds had ample spaces for flanking maneuvers, and by mid-October the Allied advance was stalled about halfway to the objective of Vyatka. The U.S. 339th by then was responsible for a front of nearly 450 miles. The principal combats, trifles compared to the colossal battles in the main theaters of World War I, were at Tulgas and Kodish. (Trotsky was falsely rumored to have been present.)

The general armistice on the western front on 11 November 1918 removed the anti-German rationale for the campaign. Wilson was absorbed in his plans for Versailles, and the American public had little enthusiasm for a new commitment to restore order in Russia. Consequently, the 339th held place through a more or less peaceful winter and spring and began sailing for home on 2 June 1919 with the French. The British withdrew on 28 September. This ambiguous venture cost the United States 144 men killed in action and about 100 more dead from illness or accident. For generations some historians referred to the venture as American "imperialism."

BIBLIOGRAPHY

Goldhurst, Richard. *The Midnight War.* New York: McGraw-Hill, 1978.

Ironside, Sir Edmund. *Archangel, 1918–1919.* London: Constable, 1953.

Kettle, Michael. *The Road to Intervention, March–November 1918.* New York: Routledge, 1988.

Melton, Carol Kingsland Willcox. "Between War and Peace." Ph.D. diss., Duke University, 1991.

Strakhovsky, Leonid I. *Intervention at Archangel.* Princeton, N.J.: Princeton University Press, 1944.

R. W. Daly / A. R.

See also **Murmansk; Russia, Relations with; Siberian Expedition.**

ARCHITECTURE. Seventeenth- and eighteenth-century settlers able to erect or purchase buildings in what later became the United States arrived with knowledge of structure and design that in their places of origin was at once fixed and changing. Time-honored ideas about what and how to build were far more commonly agreed upon than commitment to particular architectural styles, an imbalance largely explained by social location. Town and country artisans and laborers building for themselves were bound by ancient construction and compositional conventions, whereas privileged groups and institutions—landed aristocracy, urban gentry, state, church, and university—hired master craftsmen or gentlemen amateurs to supply the latest fashions.

Colonial and Postcolonial (to 1810s)

Regardless of social location, however, European settlers in North America confronted unfamiliar conditions—climate, topographies, materials—that in some cases modified how they built. Rural New Englanders, for example, whose lands were as littered with rocks as dense with trees, seized upon wood as their primary building material, even though at home they had had more experience with stone: soft species of pine were easier to cut, peg, and haul than stones to haul, dress, and lay. Stone was more efficiently deployed to mark property lines, contain animals, and construct the large hearths necessary in a cold climate.

Settlers in New Netherlands, on the other hand, quickly built kilns for firing brick—the preferred material in the Low Countries, where trees could be scarce—and in short order began erecting gabled row houses, with narrow ends to the street or to the slips they dug in the manner of Continental canal cities. Kilns had been erected even earlier in Virginia during 1611, where clay for brick and oyster shells for lime were plentiful. Adam Thoroughgood arrived as an indentured servant in 1621, but by the time he built his residence (c. 1636–1640), he owned a 5,350-acre plantation. Befitting his new standing, his brick house—which survives and may be the oldest on the Atlantic Seaboard—made reference to late Tudor Gothic style, as did Bacon's Castle (c. 1655) in Surrey County, also in brick but on a much more generous scale for the even wealthier Surrey County planter, Arthur Allen. Like houses farther north, both displayed characteristically medieval oversized chimneys, asymmetric plans, and facades. Unlike the more northerly well-to-do, however, their owners consciously emulated what they mistakenly though had remained fashionable in England. But by the time of William Byrd II built Westover (1730–1734) in Charles City County, an elegant mansion that would have appealed to London admirers of Christopher Wren, English Georgian was showing signs of becoming the architectural preference of wealthy planters and merchants from New Hampshire to the Carolinas.

Very different was Spanish California, where the principal architectural embellishments were twenty-one mission complexes strung along El Camino Real from San Diego to Alcalá (1769) to San Francisco de Solano (1823). As in the East (before the 1780s), there were no architects in the West and few craftsmen except those summoned from Mexico. Priests were the designers and superintendents of construction and of impressed indigenous labor, creating in effect tiny urban cores awaiting urban surroundings. The San Juan Capistrano mission (1776) is representative. A plastered, brick and stone, single-aisled Romanesque church with red-tiled roof, a baptistry, sacristy, and apse is attached to the corner of a large, nearly rectangular court (into which residents could retreat if attacked) surrounded by an arched colonnade. The latter fronted guest and bedrooms; kitchen, pantry, parlor, and refectory; and facilities for making hats, candles, soap, wine, woolens, shoes, and olive oil, along with forge, metal and carpentry shops, and guardhouse. A covered walkway and thick walls provided cooling while broad, undecorated stretches of facade offered an aesthetic simplicity that would not be seen again on so large a scale in North America for over a century; except, that is, in the Spanish Southwest (and Florida).

In these other Spanish holdings, California's contradictory impulses were exaggerated. The Governor's Palace (1610–1614) in Santa Fe, New Mexico, is a long, low adobe rectangle, unornamented except by structural elements: rubble plinth, round projecting rafters, and regularly spaced posts supporting the colonnade roof. Similar simplicity characterizes Mission St. Francis of Assisi (1805–1815) at Ranchos de Taos, New Mexico, the apse end of which, though crude adobe, has all the solemnity and some of the power (if nowhere the grandeur and beauty) of the Cathedral (begun 1282) at Albi, France. By contrast, Pedro Huizar's portal to the Church of San Jose y Miguel de Aguayo (1720–1731) in San Antonio, Texas, is as lavish as Spanish Baroque could possible be. Nothing in English North America rivaled this display, although private and public architecture there was, ironically, moving closer to English splendor as American independence approached.

What is called Georgian, speaking dynastically, or Palladian (after Italian Renaissance architect Andrea Palladio), speaking architecturally, made great inroads after 1750. Whether ecclesiastical, residential, or commercial, it raised colonial standards of quality and elegance. Peter Harrison, a Newport, Rhode Island, ship captain and merchant, was not a professional architect if that means supervising construction and taking a stipulated fee, but as a gentleman amateur he kept current with the literature of his avocation. Buildings like the Redwood Library (1748–1750), Touro Synagogue (1759–1763), and the Brick Market (1761–1762) in Newport are squarely based on Renaissance and neo-Renaissance models depicted in the library he had assembled during his travels. Perfectly symmetrical, Doric or Ionic ordered, porticoed and pedimented, and built of brick and stone, his work—like that of William Buckland in the Chesapeake, Samuel McIntire in Salem, Massachusetts, and anonymous gentlemen builders elsewhere—interpreted English Georgian for traders and planters eager to announce their social prominence by architectural decree. Thomas Jefferson's Monticello (1768–1809), in Charlottesville, Virginia, one of the most famous creations by a self-taught amateur who mixed French, Roman, and Palladian sources, epitomized this

impulse. Born in Boston, Charles Bulfinch may qualify as America's first professional architect in that for a time he attempted to live off his earnings. His work (c. 1787–1830) has been included in the so-called Federalist Style, a modified English Georgian well represented by three Boston townhouses (1795–1796, 1800–1802, 1805–1808) for Federalist Party leader and merchant Harrison Gray Otis. Their three or four horizontally articulated stories, forming an unpretentious cube, flat or minimally sloping roof, piano nobiles, porticos opening directly to the sidewalk, and subdued decoration, yielded a quiet elegance strongly appealing to merchants in northeastern ports, where Bulfinch was much emulated. His broad range of buildings included university and market halls, banks, hospitals, prisons, numerous churches (like his exquisite 1816 Church of Christ in Lancaster, Massachusetts), state houses for Maine and Massachusetts, and alterations at Washington, D.C. (as Architect of the Capitol) from 1817 to 1829. Even before taking that post, Bulfinch more than any other architect had raised American design to a level of functional and artistic excellence few during the colonial period might have anticipated.

Eclecticism of Taste and Style

Eclecticism in architecture—selecting aspects of diverse historical styles to form new and acceptable compositions—characterized Europe and America throughout the nineteenth century. In 1929, historian Henry-Russell Hitchcock distinguished between eclecticism of taste—different styles employed contemporaneously but only one on a given building (as with Richard Norris Hunt's two versions of the Breakers in Newport, Rhode Island, for William Vanderbilt: Loire Valley Renaissance in 1892, Genovan Renaissance the next year)—and eclecticism of style, mixing different mannerisms in the same building (for example, Frank Furness's Pennsylvania Academy of Fine Arts in Philadelphia [1871–1876] with English, French, Greek, and Egyptian references). The two eclecticisms coexisted in space, time, and a given architect's work, but if eclecticism of taste dominated during the first half of the century, eclecticism of style—with some exceptions—surpassed it in the second.

Formal American independence in 1783 spurred the demand for public architecture on state and national levels, and since the new republic also considered itself in some ways democratic, its leaders looked for architectural guidance to what they understood as the wellsprings of both, namely, democratic Greece and republican Rome. But Greek and Roman architecture was available to most Americans in treatises written during and after the Renaissance, the result being that publicly funded structures—and by mimesis privately funded buildings of a public nature, such as banks, churches, and some universities—were only generically neoclassical, some more Greek (Benjamin Latrobe's Bank of Pennsylvania in Philadelphia [1799–1801]), some more Roman (Jefferson's Rotunda [1817–1826] at the University of Virginia in Charlottesville). In the end, Greek prevailed because Greek temples, pedimented and colonnaded boxes of straightforward post-and-beam construction, offered simple interior spaces adaptable to virtually any program and geometrically precise exteriors that appealed to Americans, who in 1785 had overlaid the Northwest Territory in a geometrically precise survey grid. The combination of adaptability and order resonated among those whose self-proclaimed mission was to tame the wilderness.

Beginning with public buildings like William Strickland's Second Bank of America of the United States in Philadelphia (1818, the first in the country based squarely on the Parthenon) and Ithiel Town's Connecticut State Capitol (1827) in Hartford (a generic Doric temple), what became known as Greek Revival was used for every conceivable purpose in every nook and cranny of the land until its popularity waned in the East shortly before the Civil War (1861–1865), a bit later in the West. In Hopkinton, New Hampshire, for example, one of the churches, the library, town offices, what are now the firehouse and the general store, and several main street residences are in the style, all painted white because when erected, conventional wisdom held that Greek architecture had been uniformly white. Despite corrective scholarship, no one has yet repainted, happily so, since towns like Hopkinton display a harmony of form and color seldom seen in North America.

Despite its ubiquity, Greek Revival was not unchallenged. Beginning in the 1790s and gathering momentum over the next decades until it reached a zenith of popularity in the 1840s and 1850s, the Gothic Revival (sometimes called Romantic or picturesque architecture) took hold at first with ecclesiastical structures. Prominent church architects included New Yorkers Richard Upjohn, whose work reached Texas and California, and James Renwick, whose St. Patrick's Cathedral (1858–1879) is the best-known example of the genre. Alexander Jackson Davis was as adept with neo-Greek as with neo-Gothic, but made his most singular mark with picturesque villas, the most impressive being Knoll (1838–1842), renamed Lyndhurst after its remodeling and expansion (1864–1867). But the most influential advocate for picturesque design was Andrew Jackson Downing, America's premier landscape architect, whose naturalistic gardens, widely read publications, and house designs with partner Calvert Vaux earned nationwide respect. Gothic Revival church architecture is characterized by pointed arches, steep roofs, pinnacles, and window tracery often supplemented by battlements and buttresses. Residential neo-Gothic might include these features plus steep gables, elaborately sawn trim, projecting windows, verandas, vertically siding frequently, and asymmetrical plans as often as not. (Greek Revival did not have verandas and was never asymmetrical.) Gothic Revival houses were intended to interpret site and to open to the outdoors, thus appealing to part-time gentry who purchased country estates with fortunes made in town and to those of lesser standing whose income limited them to modest lots on the city's edge. If their mo-

tives included escaping what they believed to be the gathering hordes of unruly immigrants, Downing's commitment to picturesque architecture and landscaping stemmed from the idealistic notion that individual integrity and independence was best cultivated in a natural setting. But his best intentions—publishing self-build plans for $400 working peoples' houses, for example—were heeded by those who needed them least.

The lesser appeal of Egyptian, Tuscan, and Romanesque styles had also waned by the 1860s, after which the eclecticism of taste became somewhat type-oriented: most universities in neo-Gothic, but some in neoclassical; government buildings, banks, urban railroad terminals, and exposition buildings in neoclassical, neo-Renaissance, and Beaux-Arts (after the classical- and Renaissance-oriented École des Beaux-Arts in Paris). Eclecticism of style was more common on commercial buildings and residences of the rising middle class and the very rich, although Florentine Renaissance and Loire Valley châteaux styles found acceptance with the latter.

American architects began to train in Europe, particularly at the École des Beaux-Arts, or in new architecture programs at home (the Massachusetts Institute of Technology's opened in 1868, Columbia University's in 1881). After their studies, they often toured Europe as they began to read national professional magazines (the first was launched in 1876) inevitably featuring woodcuts and, later, photographs of Continental masterpieces. They read the immensely influential John Ruskin, whose preferred style was Venetian Gothic, and translations of the authoritative Eugêne-Emmanuel Violet-le-Duc, whose ideal was French Gothic. Most importantly, as American architects began to design for an immensely wealthy social class—newly created by post-Civil War industrialization—composed of arrivistes unfamiliar with aesthetic niceties but unerringly aware, as European parvenus since at least the Renaissance had been, that architectural patronage, if interpreted as connoisseurship by established elites, might eventually lead to social acceptance and, if interpreted by the general public as social service, might temper their reputation as rapacious exploiters of the commonweal. As all this happened, expert knowledge of time-honored styles and archeological accuracy in their deployment became indispensable for American architects, whose own social standing rose in direct proportion to their ability to provide nouveaux riches with simulacra of the very architectural styles that bygone aristocrats had made their own. Hence the hegemonic eclecticism after the Civil War.

The Architecture of National Power (1880s to 1930s)

Toward the end of the nineteenth century, generic neoclassicism of lavishness not seen before began to dominate public and quasi-public architecture. State houses, city halls, courthouses, police headquarters, and other government structures no less than art museums, concert halls, libraries, and railroad terminals—sometimes grouped in City Beautiful civic centers—sprang up everywhere, not entirely as a result of the 1893 World's Columbian Exposition in Chicago. It is true that 21 million visitors, equivalent to one-third the national population, thrilled to its Courts of Honor, a water basin surrounded by nine neoclassical behemoths. But neoclassicism was already on the rise, most notably in works by McKim, Mead, and White, like the Boston Public Library (1887–1895) or the Rhode Island State Capitol (1891–1903) in Providence.

As it evolved, neoclassicism became ever more imperial. McKim, Mead, and White's Pennsylvania Station waiting room (1902–1910) in New York City was 25 percent larger in volume than the gigantic tepidarium in the Roman Baths of Caracella (A.D. 206–217) on which it was modeled, while George W. Post's Wisconsin State Capitol (1906–1917) in Madison, loosely based (its dome not so loosely) on Christopher Wren's St. Paul's Cathedral (1666–1710) in London, dominated the countryside for miles around its hilltop site. Neoclassicism had its appeal in Europe, but "nowhere outside the United States were the classical orders to be drawn up in so many parade formations," wrote Marcus Whiffen in his *American Architecture since 1890: A Guide to the Styles* (1969). "More marble was used in building in the United States in the years 1900–1917," he added, "than was used in the Roman Empire during its entire history."

The explanation for this explosion exemplifies how architecture is put to use outside the world of art. By 1900, the United States had successfully fulfilled its "manifest destiny" on the North American mainland and was constructing a territorial and economic empire overseas. Indigenous people there and in the American West, not to mention native- and foreign-born factory and farm laborers across the country, were increasingly attracted to Greenbackism, populism, socialism, unionization—to radical movements in their many forms—in unprecedented numbers. Memories of shattering disruptions like the 1886 Haymarket Massacre and the 1894 Pullman Strike—only the tip of the class-conflict iceberg, in any case—were made even more vivid by events like the 1911 death by fire of 146 women locked inside their Triangle Shirtwaist Company factory in lower Manhattan so that union organizers could not get to them. Political protest had never been more heated, class conflict more violent, and outright anticapitalist sentiment more widespread than during the "years of marble" from 1900 to 1917.

In this context, state authorities correctly understood that the social order was under serious attack, and for the same reasons that the National Guard armories with medieval crenellation were erected in wealthy urban neighborhoods, so was government at all levels drawn to the architecture of Rome, not of its republic but of its empire, the most enduring Western empire in fact and in collective memory. The seldom-stated but visually obvious implication was that physical assault against the state and the quasi-public institutional structure supporting it, that it in turn supported, as well as political assault on capitalist

arrangements and republican forms of government, would not prevail—that the objects of assault would endure forever. To face down social upheaval and to announce imperial objectives, government and quasi-government architecture referred to the "eternal city" as often as not.

Neoclassicism waned with state suppression and the decline of outspoken dissent during and after World War I (1914–1918) but revived in the Great Depression, and throughout Europe as well, particularly under authoritarian regimes in Italy, Germany, and the Soviet Union. In the United States, it was much simplified from its earlier incarnation by square columns and capitals, spare ornament, crisp rectilinearity, and reduced use of pediments, porticos, and domes (which, when present, resembled spires). Examples are the Gallatin County Courthouse (1936) in Bozeman, Montana, the Library of Congress Annex (1938) in Washington, D.C., and the Soldiers Memorial (1939) in St. Louis, all erected with Works Progress Administration assistance. Fascist and National Socialist architecture differed only in scale: grander in Italy, positively grandiose in Germany. In the Soviet Union it was fussily ornate, recalling the turn of the century.

With the absence or reduction of private investment during the 1930s, governments financed an even greater amount of architecture than before, which is to say that during two historical moments of unusually high demand for social justice or social spending, authorities were unusually concerned with maintaining social order. It mattered not whether order was sustained by increased policing or liberal reform, whether the state was dictatorial or democratic, or—in the United States—whether it was the Gilded Age, the Progressive Era, or the New Deal. Regardless of political ideology, governments buttressed legitimacy by appropriating classical architecture, which in times of crisis was the artistic court of last resort.

The Rise and Decline of Modernism (1880s to 1970s)

Three 1932 productions by Henry-Russell Hitchcock and the Museum of Modern Art curator Philip Johnson—the exhibit *Modern Architecture: International Exhibition*, its catalog of that title, and their book, *The International Style: Architecture since 1922*—had the effect of equating all that was new with a single mode of expression, the name of which they invented and the existence of which they had no doubt. The characteristics of the International Style, they contended, were the sublimation of mass to volume; continuous, horizontally organized, regular but not symmetrical monochrome surfaces of one material; and the subordination of discrete rooms to free-flowing continuous spaces in open floor plans. Form and composition were determined by structure and interior program, they implied, preferably clad in steel, concrete, glass, and if need be, brick. Sixty-five of the seventy-three projects depicted in their book were European.

Book, exhibition, and catalogue were as narrowly selective as they were hugely influential, omitting, for example, all "new architecture," as it was often called in Europe, that did not conform to their aesthetic preferences. But for at least three decades, the International Style was widely accepted as real, as a distinctive school of design constituting the entirety of the so-called modern movement. Architectural modernism, however, was never a unified entity. Although it is true that repudiation of historically based styles—albeit in myriad ways—was largely worked out in Europe during the 1920s and early 1930s, rumblings of discontent had been heard on both sides of the Atlantic since at least the 1880s.

In the United States, the work of Henry Hobson Richardson in the 1880s, although distantly rooted in Romanesque, featured simplified single masses beneath unified roofs, near monochrome and mono-material, reduced applied ornament, and sensitivity to site. The Ames Gate Lodge (1880–1881) in North Easton, Massachusetts, is a striking example. The so-called Chicago School—notably Holabird and Roche, Adler and Sullivan, Burnham and Root, William Le Baron Jenney, and Solon S. Bemen—specializing in commercial architecture, took Richardson's simplifications further. Bemen's Studebaker Building in Chicago (1895) and Holabird and Roche's Mandel Brothers Store Annex (1900–1905) were grids of masonry- or metal-clad steel columns and beams in-filled with glass. The full implication of dispensing with load-bearing walls was grasped in 1921–1922 when Ludwig Mies van der Rohe in Germany proposed free-form skyscrapers entirely encased in glass panels clipped to the edges of floor slabs.

In his Prairie Houses (1900–1910s)—so-called because erected in undeveloped Chicago suburbs—Frank Lloyd Wright accented broad stretches of unadorned facade with long runs of crisp contrasting trim and windows in strips; inside, public spaces were merged to form partially open plans. His clean-lined rectilinear exteriors, more textured than the black white surfaces of a minimalist like Vienna's Adolf Loos but less ebullient than contemporary Art Nouveau and the several European Secessions (from historically based academic architecture) made considerable impact abroad. The four giants of the new European architecture—Le Corbusier in France, J. J. P. Oud in The Netherlands, Mies and Walter Gropius in Germany—each acknowledged (Corbusier later recanted) his influence. Perhaps the most innovative American other than Wright was the Californian Irving Gill, whose sharp-edged, rectilinear, virtually unornamented white stucco buildings were stripped almost as clean as Adolf Loos's.

During the 1920s, Chicago-area architecture was more widely admired in Europe, where modernism was taking firm root, than at home, where it languished among continuing historical revivals. When modernism did appear it likely came from abroad. Rudolph Schindler and Richard Neutra emigrated from Vienna in 1914 and 1923, respectively, to work briefly with Wright before settling in Los Angeles, where their houses for Philip Lovell

(Schindler's, 1922–1926; Neutra's 1927–1929) in particular were closer in spirit to Corbusier's than to American contemporaries. Only two skyscrapers of the decade were truly modern: the McGraw-Hill Building (1929–1931) in New York City, by Raymond Hood and Andrè Fouilloux (from Paris), and the Philadelphia Savings and Fund Society (1929–1932), by George Howe and William Lescaze (from Zurich). Although a handful of Americans embraced the new architecture, its most conspicuous manifestations before the Wall Street Crash were by European émigrés.

The little that was erected during the depression occasionally flirted with modernism, as in the cases of New York City's Rockefeller Center (1931–1940), by a team of design firms in vertical Art Deco, or Wright's Johnson Wax Administration Building (1936–1939) at Racine, Wisconsin, in streamlined, horizontal "American moderne." But as the decade waned, the arrival of two German émigrés, Gropius in 1937 to direct Harvard's School of Design program and Mies in 1938 to assume the same position at the Illinois Institute of Technology, transformed architectural education and practice in the United States.

That was especially true with Mies, who later produced a master plan for his Chicago campus that in style and scale was revolutionary for this country. Nineteen low-rise structures (not all built) of welded steel frames painted black with glass walls or concrete in-filled with brick and glass were followed by three apartment towers on Lake Shore Drive. Even before his enormously influential Seagram Building (1954–1958) in New York City was announced, others were adopting his manner, particularly Skidmore, Owings, and Merrill at their 1952 glass and metal Lever House, among others in New York City. From high-rise buildings the Miesian model spread to virtually every design type during the next two decades. What had taken hold throughout Europe immediately after World War I (1914–1918), in quantity mostly social housing sponsored by socialist and social democratic governments, found favor in the United States after World War II (1939–1945), initially among corporate clients. With the transition, modern architecture changed fundamentally, from low-rise, amply fenestrated brick and concrete structures to high-rise, almost completely fenestrated flat-roof slabs.

As modernism spread to every design genre, stylistic variations appeared, of course. But within the variety there remained commonality: either bland sterility or aggressive anonymity, especially apparent when modern buildings clustered—along Park and Sixth Avenues in New York City, for example, or at the University of Illinois Chicago Circle Campus (1965–1987), mostly by Skidmore, Owings, and Merrill. As large chunks of city and suburb became virtually interchangeable and as it dawned on clients that architectural conformity compromised corporate and personal identity, the appeal of glass-box architecture began to wane, noticeably in the 1970s.

The New Eclecticism (1970s–)

In his book, *Complexity and Contradiction in Architecture* (1966), Robert Venturi condemned "the puritanically moral language of orthodox Modern[ism]." He favored "messy vitality over obvious unity," "the ugly and ordinary architecture" he soon embraced in *Learning from Las Vegas* (1972). Most architects were reluctant to fetishize "the vulgar" but were receptive to his notion that modernism's "forced simplicity" did not adequately reflect the "ambiguities of contemporary experience." Indeed, retreat from the Miesian model was already under way before Venturi wrote.

The New Formalism of the early 1960s—strictly symmetrical, smooth-skinned, flat-roofed buildings with screens and grilles—was associated with institutional work of Philip Johnson, Minuro Yamasaki, and Edward Durell Stone. The acknowledged master of neo-expressionism (said to have evolved from 1910s and 1920s German expressionism)—characterized by the sublimation of right angles to sensuously sweeping curves made possible by suspended steel cable roofs and concrete (gunite) sprayed over metal frames—was Eero Saarinen, whose TWA terminal (1956–1962) at Idlewild Airport (later Kennedy) in New York City is the most famous of its type. Brutalism referred to massive asymmetrical structures, usually in poured concrete left rough, with small openings, deep recesses, and aggressive projections emphasizing the play of light and shadow; Paul Rudolph's Art and Architecture Building (1958–1965) at Yale University was firmly brutalistic, more so than the Jonas Salk Institute for Biological Studies (1959–1965) in La Jolla, California, or other structures by Louis Kahn, whose masterly work could not easily be categorized but who was influenced nonetheless by the genre.

As if to vindicate him, postmodernism arose shortly after Venturi's second book appeared. A kind of umbrella term in architecture in general from the late 1970s the 1990s, Pomo involved the return of ornament, polychrome, mixed materials, and historical design elements like Palladian windows, gables, pediments, elaborate moldings, and the classical orders, as well as unprecedented experimentation with shapes, composition, and the juxtaposition of formerly incompatible features as seen in the works of Charles Moore, Michael Graves, Robert A. M. Stern, and many others, including Venturi.

As the 1990s opened, Pomo was surpassed in media attention by Decon—deconstructivist architecture—represented by prominent figures like Peter Eisenman and Frank Gehry. As with Pomo, Decon borrowed freely from literary studies: a building was a "text" with no intrinsic meaning other than what was brought to it by "readers"—observers, critics, architects themselves. History had little to offer because knowledge is subjective, noncumulative. The architect was therefore free to design any thing in any way. The resulted surpassed even Pomo in its radical disassembling and reconstructing of parts to form heretofore unimagined wholes, perhaps most famously represented by Gehry's Guggenheim Museum (1991–1997) in Bilbao, Spain.

With architects practicing globally, with new materials and technologies at hand, and with every incentive to experiment, expressive possibility is greater than ever before, resulting in a new eclecticism. To mannerisms already mentioned, pluralism adds several identifiable categories: "green" or sustainable energy conserving design; conscious reworking of vernacular and "populist"—that is, commercial—traditions; revived classicism; neomodernism with its "minimalist" or extremely simplified versions; and high-tech, making art of structural and mechanical systems.

These categories are porous. Some architects work exclusively in one while others combine two or more in a single building or in their work as a whole, borrowing freely from each other all the while, benefiting as well from an "anything goes" professional climate. Nor are the categories as mutually exclusive or as historically correct as in the eclecticisms of taste and style. Nevertheless, "selecting aspects of diverse [but no longer exclusively] historical styles in order to form new and acceptable compositions" is the norm. In the absence of stylistic consensus, compositional possibility in the twenty-first century is virtually unlimited.

BIBLIOGRAPHY

Curtis, William J. R. *Modern Architecture since 1900.* 3rd ed. Upper Saddle River, N.J.: Prentice Hall, 1996.

Goldberger, Paul. *The Skyscraper.* New York: Knopf, 1981.

Kirker, Harold. *The Architecture of Charles Bulfinch.* Cambridge, Mass.: Harvard University Press, 1969.

Lambert, Phyllis, ed. *Mies in America.* New York: Abrams, 2001.

Ochsner, Jeffrey Karl. *H. H. Richardson: Complete Architectural Works.* Cambridge, Mass.: MIT Press, 1983.

Pierson, William H., Jr., ed. *American Buildings and Their Architects.* Vols. 1, 2, 4, and 5. New York: Oxford University Press, 1970, 1972, 1976, 1978.

Riley, Terence. *The International Style: Exhibition 15 and the Museum of Modern Art.* Edited by Stephen Perrella. New York: Rizzoli, 1992.

Roth, Leland M. *A Concise History of American Architecture.* New York: Harper and Row, 1979.

———. *McKim, Mead and White, Architects.* New York: Harper and Row, 1983.

Saliga, Pauline, ed. *Fragments of Chicago's Past: The Collection of Architectural Fragments at The Art Institute of Chicago.* Chicago: The Art Institute, 1990.

Schuyler, David. *Apostle of Taste: Andrew Jackson Downing, 1815–1852.* Baltimore: Johns Hopkins University Press, 1996.

Short, C. W., and R. Stanley-Brown. *Public Buildings: Architecture under the Public Works Administration, 1933–39.* New York: Da Capo, 1986.

Twombly, Robert. *Frank Lloyd Wright: His Life and His Architecture.* New York: Wiley, 1979.

———. *Power and Style: A Critique of Twentieth-Century Architecture in the United States*. New York: Hill and Wang, 1996.

Robert Twombly

See also **Capitol at Washington; Monticello; University of Virginia.**

ARCHITECTURE, AMERICAN INDIAN.

The traditional architecture of American Indians was greatly influenced by the building materials available in a particular region of the country. There were other determining factors as well.

Technology imposed three basic structural types: the bent frame with covering, as used for the wigwam; the compression shell, as used for the igloo and tipi; and the post and beam wood frame, as used for the lean-to, the shed, and the plankhouse. Frequently the form of a dwelling utilized more than one technique. Construction practices required great skill, as workers had to steam a sapling until it bent without breaking, to down trees and split boards, to rainproof animal hides, to make fiber ties for binding building materials, or to manufacture adobe bricks.

To protect themselves against the elements, Indians built double-shelled walls of skins or wood that could be insulated with grass or moss. Walls of cane or reeds were erected around dwellings to serve as windbreaks. The sides of structures were covered with bark and animal skin that could be removed on hot summer days. Arbors were built with bough roofs and no walls so inhabitants could rest in the shade.

Social customs governed the size of a structure. If a man lived with his wife's family when he married or vice versa, then the dwelling would be enlarged to accommodate the spouse, and later, children. Many structures, such as the Iroquois's longhouse or the Pueblo's apartment-style buildings, were built in a modular fashion that allowed remodeling. Circular dwellings were often joined to nearby structures by passageways.

The economics of food gathering generally required that Indian tribes have more than one home. Many had summer quarters that allowed easy access to the food source. For example, the Northwest Coast Indians moved inland to collect berries and fish the salmon-laden rivers; and the Pueblo Indians moved closer to their fields to tend their crops. More sedentary Indians in the Northeast would move entire villages to harvest particular runs of fish or birds. They also moved their villages if the supply of saplings for building materials was used up or if the garden soil was exhausted. Many southeastern Indians had summer and winter houses next door to each other with unattached storage units.

Indian views of religion and myths often determined the placement of a dwelling. Prayers were said before construction and blessings asked for after the structure was complete. Different dwellings were needed for various religious ceremonies. Specific structures were designed for sweating, giving birth, cleansing, meditating, dancing, worshipping, and honoring the dead.

During the immediate precontact period, the styles of Indian architecture can be divided into broad geographic regions of ecological similarities. The basic structure in the Northeast woodlands and Great Lakes areas was a frame of bent saplings covered by bark sheets or reed mats. These wigwams, utilized by three major language groups, the Iroquoian, the Algonquian, and the Siouan, were usually round or oblong dome-shaped huts averaging twelve to fifteen feet in diameter. In some areas, the same basic structure was elongated to stretch 100 feet or more. These longhouses were year-round dwellings for extended families or were used as lodges for religious ceremonies.

In the Southeast, the Cherokees, Chickasaws, Choctaws, and Creeks lived in towns. Often the chief's house was built on a burial mound; other significant buildings, such as those used for town council or for worship, might also be situated on top of mounds. Houses were constructed of timber and wattle and daub, a clay and grass plaster placed over woven laths of rods or cane; roofs were normally made of thatch, bark, or palmetto leaves. Council houses, also made of wattle and daub, were built for special meetings and assemblies and could hold up to 500 Indians on tiers of raised platforms.

Many Plains agricultural groups lived in earthlodge villages. An earthlodge was usually forty to sixty feet in diameter, but could be larger. Typically, a twelve-post circular arrangement served to support the walls and roof, with a central four-post-and-beam structure used to support the 100 or so rafters. The roof was made of willow branches and prairie grass and topped with sod. These lodges were used during the agricultural season. During hunting season, the Indians would follow the game employing portable housing. Tipis, designed around a three- or four-pole foundation, were covered with buffalo hides. When Indians moved from place to place, dogs carried the poles and hides. Only with the advent of horses did many Plains Indians take up a nomadic existence with large tipis that could be moved by large pack animals.

In the far north, Eskimos survived the dark frigid artic in winter houses or igloos. Winter houses were partially sunk into the ground and their frames were made of whatever could be found nearby: walls were made of rocks or sod, roof supports, of whale bones or driftwood. Layers of seal or walrus skins were covered with dried moss or sod and used for roofs. A long entranceway that angled down and then back up was used to eliminate chilling windblasts and required inhabitants to climb through a trapdoor into the interior. Igloos were made of snow blocks angled and tilted to form a dome. They also featured a long entrance passage. In summer, Eskimos lived in tents of skins covering wooden frames with and without ridgepoles.

Along the Northwest Pacific Coast, Indians harvested planks for their homes from dense cedar forests. They used post and beam construction with rafters to build longhouses (averaging sixty-feet long) for multiple families. They grouped these houses in winter villages facing the shore. Shed roofs and gabled roofs were made with rocks to hold roof planks in position. In summer, many Indians took planks from their homes to use at salmon fishing camps, while others built temporary lean-to dwellings out of brush and cedar-bark mats.

In the Southwest, Indians built dwellings four or five stories high using stone or sun-dried adobe bricks and mortar. Towns were comprised of clustered multiroomed houses with connecting rooftops, interior passageways, underground religious chambers (kivas), public plazas, and work terraces. Steps and ladders led to upper floors. The probable ancestors of these Pueblo Indians were the Anasazis, who built cliff dwellings archeologists believe suggest the use of sophisticated architects and construction contractors.

BIBLIOGRAPHY

Ferguson, William M. *The Anasazi of Mesa Verde and the Four Corners.* Boulder: University Press of Colorado, 1996.

Morgan, William N. *Precolumbian Architecture in Eastern North America.* Gainesville: University Press of Florida, 1999.

Nabokov, Peter, and Robert Easton. *Native American Architecture.* New York: Oxford University Press, 1989.

Wedel, Waldo R. *Central Plains Prehistory: Holocene Environments and Cultural Change in the Republican River Basin.* Lincoln: University of Nebraska Press, 1986.

Veda Boyd Jones

See also **Adobe; Indian Technology; Tipi; Wigwam.**

ARCHIVES are the records of an institution or organization that are no longer current but are preserved because they contain information of permanent value. They are the recorded memory, preserved for those who might find them useful in the future. Those who handle archival materials carry out several functions to preserve materials and make them accessible to potential users: appraisal, arrangement, description, and reference.

The beginnings of archives in the United States can be attributed to the Massachusetts Historical Society, the first of its kind, formed in 1791 "to preserve the manuscripts of the present day to the remotest ages of posterity." Similar local and national organizations soon followed, many of which collected the private papers and memorabilia of famous individuals in addition to official documents.

Systematic archival practice began in the United States in 1899, when the American Historical Association created the Public Archives Commission to investigate and report upon the historical character, contents, and functions of public repositories of manuscript records.

This commission worked with thirty advisers across the United States to determine the character of the historical archives of the federal government and the individual states, as well as to report on the provisions made for their maintenance and accessibility. The purview of this commission did not include private and semipublic archives. The commission completed surveys for almost every state, resulting in Claude H. Van Tyne and Waldo G. Leland's *Guide to the Archives of the Government of the United States in Washington* (1904), a compilation of archival resources.

As more historical societies and archival repositories arose, there began to be even more concern about the most efficient ways of preserving historical materials. By the early 1800s, an Ohio historical society developed a method of protecting its holdings in airtight metallic cases that were numbered and indexed so that the holdings of each case could be identified without opening it. The various archives across the country had their own systems of organization and storage, with varying degrees of success. By the end of the nineteenth century, archival theories and practices were shared among many societies and associations. This collaboration led to the formation of a distinct archival profession in the United States and the founding of the AMERICAN HISTORICAL ASSOCIATION (AHA) in 1884. The AHA began with the development of standardized systems of archival organization. Various subgroups sprang from the AHA, including the Historical Manuscripts Commission, the Public Archives Commission, and, in 1909, the Conference of Archivists, which met annually to create new archives and to promote and improve archives already in existence. During the 1930s, President Franklin D. Roosevelt's Works Progress Administration created the Historical Records Survey and the Survey of Federal Archives. In 1934, Congress established the NATIONAL ARCHIVES as an independent federal agency.

In 1936, the Society of American Archivists (SAA) was founded "to promote sound principles of archival economy and to facilitate cooperation among archivists and archival agencies." The Conference of Archivists founded the SAA to differentiate between historians and scholars who use archival materials and archivists, who are responsible for the care, organization, and management of historical materials. A more democratic body than its predecessor, the SAA opened membership not just to directors of large archival institutions, but to all "who are or have been engaged in the custody or administration of archives or historical manuscripts," including archives of all sizes and orientation, from small private and business archives to large historical collections. The SAA was founded with 124 individual and four institutional members and doubled in size during its first year. A. R. Newsome was elected to serve as the SAA's first president; a board of directors was also elected. The newly formed SAA proposed an annual convention at which professional papers would be delivered, information exchanged, and philosophies of archival organization discussed. At the first annual convention in June 1937, Newsome outlined a course for the SAA that has continued to be its policy into the twenty-first century. The SAA was "to become the practical self-help agency of archivists for the solution of their complex problems" and "to strive to nationalize archival information and technique."

The evolving information society challenges archivists to reexamine what it is they do and how they do it. The mechanisms for preserving information are changing as new technologies are developed, and others are rendered obsolete. Most archivists proceed with caution in adapting various technologies for archiving. With issues such as access versus ownership, digital storage, in particular, presents challenges to archivists' preservation efforts. The U.S. legal system has also been drawn into the issue of digital preservation, as archival organizations dispute the mandate that federal agencies maintain electronic versions of word processing and E-mail documents, even after electronic, paper, or microform records have been made.

BIBLIOGRAPHY

Duranti, Luciana. "The Impact of Digital Technology on Archival Science." *Archival Science* 1, no. 1 (2001): 39–55.

Gracy, David B., II. *An Introduction to Archives and Manuscripts.* New York: Special Libraries Association, 1981.

Hodson, John Howard. *The Administration of Archives.* New York: Pergamon Press, 1972.

Menne-Haritz, Angelika. "Access—the Reformulation of an Archival Paradigm." *Archival Science* 1, no. 1 (2001): 57–82.

Posner, Ernst. *Archives and the Public Interest: Selected Essays.* Washington, D.C.: Public Affairs Press, 1967.

Riberiro, Fernanda. "Archival Science and Changes in the Paradigm." *Archival Science* 1, no. 3 (2001): 295–310.

Van Tyne, Claude H., and Waldo G. Leland. "Guide to the Archives of the Government of the United States in Washington." *Papers of the Bureau of Historical Research.* No. 14. Washington, D.C.: Carnegie Institution, 1904.

Mary Anne Hansen

ARIZONA. Situated on the western slope of the Rocky Mountains, the forty-eighth state covers 113,956 square miles of arid terrain divided into three geographical provinces. The Colorado Plateau province, bounded by Utah to the north and the Mogollon Rim to the south, is a scenic combination of extensive forests, open grasslands, spiraling mesas, and stunning canyons, including the Grand Canyon. Streams crisscrossing the eroded country feed into the Little Colorado River, which flows northeast to the Colorado River. Cutting diagonally from the White Mountains in the northeast to the Sierra Estrella range in the central southwest is the Central Mountain province, characterized by elongated mountains that join the Sonora Desert province, which stretches southward to the Mexican border. Both of the southern provinces claim watersheds that drain into the Gila River, which flows westward to the Colorado River.

Indigenous Roots

Evidence indicates human habitation of the region at approximately twelve thousand years ago, with the ancient Anasazi Indians occupying the Plateau region above the Rim and the more technologically advanced Hohokam residing in the Gila Valley, where they engineered an extensive system of canal networks that ultimately attracted the attention of Jack Swilling, who founded the capital city of Phoenix in 1867.

By the time of the official Spanish Entrada in 1540, the majority of the native population was living in essentially four areas: the Moqui or present-day Hopi (possibly descendants of the Anasazi) and the Navajo resided north of the Little Colorado; the Walapai, Havasupai, Mohave, and Yuma nations along the Colorado River; the Yavapai and Apache in the central and eastern mountains; and the Pima and Papago (possible descendants of the Hohokam) located in the central river valleys.

Spanish and Mexican Era (1539–1846)

A rumor floating around European cities about seven Catholic fathers founding seven golden cities spurred Spanish interest in the region, particularly in the aftermath of Álvar Núñez Cabeza de Vaca's colorful report on his trek from Florida to northern Sonora. In 1539, Viceroy Antonio de Mendoza dispatched Fray Marcos de Niza (Franciscan) and Esteban, a Moorish slave who had accompanied Cabeza de Vaca, to investigate the allegations. Following the course of the San Pedro River through eastern Arizona, the party eventually reached the Zuni villages in western New Mexico. After Esteban was slain by the natives, Fray Marcos returned to Mexico City, where he filed a report that led to the formation of a larger mission launched the following year and led by Francisco Vásquez de Coronado, who captured the Zuni pueblos, then sent exploration parties westward to the Moqui villages and canyon country. Hernando de Alarcón simultaneously sailed up the Colorado River with Coronado's supply ships and explored the regions around present-day Yuma.

By 1690, Father Eusebio Kino and other Jesuit missionaries had introduced Christianity and cattle raising to the Piman-speaking people, conducted extensive explorations of the Santa Cruz and San Pedro Valleys, and followed the Gila River to its juncture with the Colorado. The Jesuits planted three missions: San Xavier del Bac (1700), San Cayetano del Tumacacori (1701), and San Gabriel de Guevavi (1701).

Arizona was popularly accorded its name following a silver strike known as Real de Arizonac on a ranchero near present-day Nogales in 1736. The discovery evoked controversy when its founders failed to report it to the Crown. Rumors spread that the Jesuits were behind the secrecy, setting in motion a list of conflicts that would lead

Charles III to expel the order from the Spanish Empire entirely in 1767, following the Pima Revolt of 1751, which led to the founding of a presidio at Tubac as a means of quelling future uprisings. The first European American women arrived the following year, in 1752.

When Spanish ventures in southern Arizona fell under the threat of Apache attack, Charles III authorized the military to achieve by force what the missionaries had failed to accomplish with the Bible. Hugo O'Conor, an Irish mercenary under services to the Spanish Crown, was appointed Commandant-Inspector for the interior regions. In 1776, he relocated the Tubac presidio farther north on the Santa Cruz River, opposite the Pima village of Tucson.

Even that radical measure proved of little consequence in curbing Apache raids until Bernardo de Galvez became Viceroy of New Spain in 1786. Aware that the Apache were infinitely better schooled in the art of desert warfare than Spanish soldiers, he ordered that the raiders be persuaded to settle near the presidio, where they could be systematically debauched with alcohol.

In the midst of the newfound calm, the first cries for Mexican independence echoed across the south. The struggle, which lasted from 1810 to 1821, had virtually no impact on Arizona, since no resident participated in the fighting nor did the battlefields extend into the northern regions.

As a means of replenishing war-depleted coffers, the Mexican government opened the Santa Fe Trade in 1822. The first set of arrivals were mountain men and trappers like James Ohio Pattie, Jedediah S. Smith, William Sherley "Old Bill" Williams, Paulino Weaver, and others. Along with mapping most of the rivers, they systematically destroyed the ecological balance by their callous decimation of the beaver population.

The Mexico City government's hold over the area was so precarious that Colonel Stephen W. Kearny took Santa Fe on 18 August 1846 without firing a shot, before crossing Arizona en route to Mexico. The MORMON BATTALION played a critical role in isolating locations for settlements that Salt Lake City planted across the northern regions, through the White Mountains and as far south as Gilbert. When the new civil government was established, Arizona was opaquely made part of the New Mexico Territory. Those areas south of the Gila River were acquired through the 1853 GADSDEN PURCHASE.

Geographical proximity to California goldfields brought an estimated 60,000 hopefuls across Arizona during the next decade, many of whom retraced their steps after gold was discovered at the confluence of the Sacramento Wash and Colorado River in 1857. The previous year, the Sonora Exploring and Mining Company had reopened a number of old silver mines near Tubac. Miners and the entrepreneurs who came to mine them sparked a population increase that led to the founding of ferry services along the Colorado River and mercantile houses in most large settlements.

Beginning in 1856, residents began to petition Congress for a separate Arizona Territory under the rationale that the Santa Fe government was incapable of efficiently administering the western region. Four years of rejection led delegates from thirteen Arizona and New Mexico towns to form the Provisional Territory of Arizona. When the Southern states left the Union in 1861, a group of Southern sympathizers met at Mesilla and pledged loyalty to the Confederate States of America. Union forces arrived the following year and recaptured the area after minor clashes at Stanwix Station and Picacho Pass, the two westernmost battles of the Civil War (1861–1865). On 24 February 1863, President Abraham Lincoln affixed his signature to the Organic Act, which officially proclaimed the Territory of Arizona, with a north-south boundary line of 109 degrees latitude, as opposed to the east-west line of 34 degrees longitude stipulated in the original documents.

The Territory of Arizona (1863–1912)

Mining, military, railroad building, and agricultural activities dominated the economic landscape during the early decades of the territorial era. Rich gold and silver discoveries, including the legendary silver bonanza at Tombstone in 1877, drew eastern investors to the area, a trend that found renewed vigor when the discovery of electricity gave new value to copper during the 1870s.

By 1880, copper was king, with mines operating at Ray, Clifton-Morenci, Jerome, Globe-Miami, Ajo, and Bisbee. Copper companies such as Phelps Dodge and the Arizona Copper Company built towns, short-line railroads, and a modern business and banking network, and they claimed political dominance in the legislature, which shifted locations with the territorial capital from Prescott (1865–1866) to Tucson (1867–1888) and back to Prescott (1888), before the capital was permanently located in Phoenix in 1889.

The threat of Navajo and Apache raiders led to the building of an excess of two dozen camps, forts, and supply depots by 1870. In 1863, renowned Colonel Kit Carson led a contingent of U.S. soldiers and Ute warriors on a mission to round up the Navajo. In the grim finale, approximately 8,000 Navajo were forced to take the Long Walk to the Bosque Redondo Reservation in New Mexico. When they were finally allowed to return to Arizona in 1868, little headway had been made toward curbing the Apache, whose resistance continued until the Chiricahua were forcibly relocated to Florida in 1886.

Completion of the first transcontinental railroad occurred when the Southern Pacific reached Tucson in 1880, sparking a decade of railroad building that facilitated troops, mail, and the agricultural activities taking place in the Salt River Valley. Cattle ranching and citrus were nascent industries destined to assume dominance, particularly after the completion of the Roosevelt Dam in

1911 granted Salt River Valley Ranches a stable source of water.

People kept pace with the promise, including a steady stream of health seekers, which led to the founding of tent cites that transformed into hospitals and fancy resorts in both Tucson and Phoenix.

Population increases put new fire to the growing movement for statehood. In 1902, the statehood issue was debated in Congress. An enabling act passed in 1910, leading to a convention in Phoenix that drafted a constitution and submitted it to Washington. After a recall provision was eliminated, President William H. Taft signed Arizona into the union on 14 February 1912.

Since Statehood

As the last contiguous state, Arizona was uniquely poised by both geography and social temperament to evolve into its current status as a classroom for the cyber-age. By 1912, years of isolation and perceived federal indifference had given way to an insular form of capitalism kept honest by low-density settlement patterns and paperless business transactions sealed by a handshake. Moneymaking enjoyed the reverence of a secular religion, with chance, change, and experimentation its primary tenets. Because the majority of local leaders were either first-generation heirs to pioneer fortunes built subsequent to the California Gold Rush or recent affluent arrivals seeking relief from various respiratory ailments, the rights of the individual most often took precedence over the general welfare, reducing social reform efforts to little more than a dull roar throughout most of the century.

When it became a state, Arizona's growth pattern essentially mirrored that of the nation, albeit with the deviance common to the built-in perks and special privilege explicit in solicited development. Land was plentiful, taxes were low, labor cheap, crime virtually nonexistent, and governmental restraint on free enterprise minimal and never vigorously enforced. Local boosters touted potential and investors took notice, heralding a new era of prosperity that ranked Arizona ninth in the nation in per capita motor vehicle ownership by 1921, a consumer preference that proved critical to the development of a thoroughly modern road system by decade's end. These same years witnessed the introduction of air-cooled commercial buildings in both Phoenix and Tucson, adding a definitive brick to boosters' arguments that desert living was tantamount to "paradise on earth."

Although Arizona's prosperity was primarily based on copper, cotton, cattle, and citrus, tourism was fast adding a fifth arm to the economic equation, particularly after the advent of five-star resorts such as the $2 million Arizona Biltmore, which was opened in Phoenix in 1929 by a team of investors, including chewing gum magnet William Wrigley Jr., who built an opulent mansion adjacent to the hotel. Louis Swift, Cornelius Vanderbilt Jr., and other industrial giants soon followed suit, earning the capital city prestigious renown as the fashionable place for the wealthy to winter.

The new arrivals brought with them the political conservatism of their Midwestern roots, complete with the self-help doctrine that holds charitable giving a matter of private conscience rather than legal statute. Poverty, dislocation, and disease were remedied by private contributions and formal fundraising events, typically hosted by a prominent individual with a broad network of affluent friends. The success of these venues limited tax-based relief for human tragedies to the Insane Asylum of Arizona, which was informally renamed the Arizona State Hospital in 1922.

The Great Depression brought the winds of change and a new system of social recompense that never fell easy on the minds of leaders attuned to the notion of unfettered free enterprise and individual responsibility. Although the suffering was acute and widespread in rural areas, urban centers were immune to the hardships until 1932, when a downturn in world copper prices led to layoffs and mine closures. Out-of-work miners descended on Phoenix and Tucson, quickly outstripping charitable resources to the point that both cities vigorously petitioned for federal funds from the Reconstruction Finance Corporation during the final hours of the Herbert Hoover administration.

During the New Deal, over forty Civilian Conservation Corps camps were built in Arizona, opening the floodgates to massive federal spending regionwide during the years surrounding World War II (1939–1945). Motorola, AiResearch, and other semiconductor concerns sprang up, giving a boost to both aviation and population, as well as raising issues about the color line separation historically practiced in Arizona up to that time. Federal dollars meant federal rules, including ending segregation in the military and public schools. Renowned pilot Lincoln Ragsdale, one of the original Tuskegee airmen, was charged with integrating Luke Air Force Base in the aftermath of World War II. A fully integrated school system was not realized statewide until the mid-1960s. Housing integration was an even more exacting fight, with over 90 percent of the state's minority residents living in neighborhoods drawn along racial line as late as 1962. Three years later, Arizona passed its first civil rights law, but de facto segregation on the basis of economics continues.

Gender was less of an issue than race in determining social status, but antiquated notions of the "weaker sex" led to certain disparities in the body politic. For example, when Eva Dugan was tried, convicted, and sentenced to hang for the murder of a local farmer in 1926, a public outcry of special circumstance arose on the basis of gender. When the only woman to be hanged in Arizona received her punishment on 21 February 1930, misadjusted balance weights resulted in her decapitation as she dropped through the trap, launching a new round of arguments that prompted Arizona voters to select the lethal gas chamber as the official means of execution in 1933. That same year, the state sent its first woman to the national Congress, Isabella Selmes Greenway of Tucson, a childhood friend and bridesmaid of First Lady Eleanor Roosevelt.

The Democratic Party enjoyed nearly complete dominance statewide until the "free people, free speech, free enterprise" philosophies of Phoenix businessman Barry M. Goldwater gave rise to a renegade/conservative movement determined to quell the perceived excesses of the liberal temper of the times. Following Goldwater's election to the U.S. Senate in 1952, the Republican Party supplanted its Democratic rivals everywhere except southern Arizona, which has steadfastly remained the most liberal section of the state.

Throughout most of the twentieth century, Arizona enjoyed the prestige of two of the most powerful voices in the national Congress: Democratic Senator Carl Hayden and Republican Barry M. Goldwater, the first Arizonan to run for the office of President of the United States. The state claimed additional accolades when President Richard Nixon appointed Phoenix attorney William H. Rehnquist to the United States Supreme Court. President Ronald Reagan appointed him Chief Justice in 1986. Reagan also appointed the august body's first female jurist, Arizonan Sandra Day O'Connor, in 1981.

Politics were turbulent during the final half of the twentieth century. In 1988, Governor Evan Mecham was impeached and found guilty of two of the three counts cited in the original indictment. Secretary of State Rose Mofford was appointed Arizona's first female governor. On 7 September 1997, Governor Fife Symington resigned in the wake of fraud charges stemming from his years as a developer. He was subsequently tried, convicted on seven felony counts, and ordered to pay back his investors. On 9 September 1997, Justice Sandra Day O'Connor swore in Jane Hull as governor. She was elected to the office in her own right during the November elections, wherein Arizona made history by being the first state in the nation to elect women to the top five posts in state government.

Arizona's population of a half million in 1940 increased tenfold by 2000, earning the state two additional seats in the House of Representatives. Of the 5,130,632 residents listed in the 2000 federal census, 63.8 percent were of European American descent, 25.3 percent cited their heritage as Hispanic or Latino, 3.1 percent as African American, 5.0 percent as American Indian or Alaskan Native, 1.8 percent as Asian, and 0.1 percent as Native Hawaiian or other Pacific Islander, with the remainder claiming no specific heritage. The average household enjoyed an annual income of $34,751, with an estimated 15.5 percent of Arizona residents living beneath the federal poverty line. Of that number, 23.4 percent are children living in single-parent households. Roughly 68 percent of the population owns their own home, as opposed to 66.2 percent nationwide.

Approximately 85 percent of Arizona residents live in Maricopa County, with an estimated 1,500 new residents arriving daily. Growth has left Tucson with a groundwater shortage problem and raised environmental concerns statewide. During the 1990s alone, the gross state product jutted from $66 million in 1990 to over $140 million at the end of the century. Roughly 13.2 percent of resident firms are minority owned, with another 27 percent owned by women, a figure that is a full percentage point higher than the national average. In 2002, the Phoenix metropolitan area was ranked as the top manufacturing urban complex in the nation.

Less than 18 percent of Arizona land is in private hands, leaving vast stretches of wilderness available for recreation. The GRAND CANYON alone boasts an estimated 10 million tourists annually. Every sport from skydiving to golf is available in the state. Residents share the victory and defeats of three major league teams: the Phoenix Suns, the Arizona Cardinals, and the Arizona Diamondbacks (who won the 2001 World Series), as well as enjoy a broad slate of cultural activities and state-of-the-art institutions, including three state universities and numerous private colleges and specialty schools. Along with horse and dog racing, legalized gambling is available in one of the many Indian casinos that have sprung up over the past two decades.

Modern Arizona is best likened to the rest of the United States and several foreign countries combined. Less than a third of the residents are Arizona born, with the average tenure of white-collar executives less than four years. The majority of the latter transfer to the area to work in the highly mobile computer chip industry, a vital lynchpin in the state's economy since the 1980s. The lion's share of new arrivals continue to be lured to the area by climate, spectacular scenery, and the economic potential intrinsic to a high-growth setting, despite the fact that Arizona ranks in the bottom third of the nation with regard to tax dollars allocated for indigent care, mental health, and other social welfare programs.

The quality of public education is an ongoing concern without easy remedy. In 1998, the Arizona legislature allocated roughly $400 million in state funding to construct, equip, and maintain public schools at state-established minimum standards, leaving districts the option of passing capital overrides to pay for projects and facilities not included in the original plan. Recent trends toward vouchers have spurred a new round of debate similar to those occurring in other parts of the nation relative to the face and future of tax-supported education in the twenty-first century.

BIBLIOGRAPHY

"Arizona Land Ownership Status," adapted from Circular No. 2, Revised June 1995, by Ken A. Phillips, Chief Engineer, Salt River Project.

Department of Economic Security, Arizona State Data Center, 2001.

Faulk, Odie B. *Arizona: A Short History.* Norman: The University of Oklahoma Press, 1970.

Iverson, Peter. *Barry Goldwater: Native Arizonan*. Norman: University of Oklahoma Press, 1997.

Luckingham, Bradford. *Phoenix: The History of a Southwestern Metropolis*. Tucson: The University of Arizona Press, 1989.

Sheridan, Thomas E. *Los Tucsonenses: The Mexican Community in Tucson, 1854–1941*. Tucson: The University of Arizona Press, 1986.

Sonnichsen, C. L. *Tucson: The Life and Times of an American City*. Norman: University of Oklahoma Press, 1982.

U.S. Department of Commerce, Bureau of the Census, Arizona, 2000.

Wagoner, Jay J. *Early Arizona: Prehistory to Civil War*. Tucson: The University of Arizona Press, 1975.

———. *Arizona Territory, 1863–1912: A Political History*. Tucson: The University of Arizona Press, 1970.

Walker, Henry P., and Don Bufkin. *Historical Atlas of Arizona*. Norman: University of Oklahoma Press, 1979.

Evelyn S. Cooper

ARKANSAS. Arkansas, located just west of the Mississippi River, straddles a border between the South and the West and encompasses something of both those regions in its history and customs.

Throughout most of the eighteenth century, the small white population was concentrated at Arkansas Post, located on the Arkansas River just a few miles above where it feeds into the Mississippi River. Arkansas Post was established by Henri de Tonti in 1686, but it was a small and primitive affair that had a difficult time surviving. It was abandoned in 1699, founded again in 1721, and then moved several times between 1749 and 1780.

While Arkansas Post clearly had importance as a place for reprovisioning boats on the long journey on the Mississippi River, it had political and economic importance as well. Politically, it gave the French—and, after the Seven Years' War, the Spanish—a foothold in an otherwise undermanned region, and it provided them a means for establishing relations with Native Americans in the area, particularly the Quapaws.

Other native groups in Arkansas had less contact with whites at the post, but the Osages did make themselves known. While their home villages were in southwestern Missouri, the Osages claimed most of northern and western Arkansas as their hunting grounds and ferociously protected their prerogatives there, effectively inhibiting white settlement in western Arkansas until the early nineteenth century. When the Americans took over and began to resettle Cherokee and Choctaw Indians in west Arkansas, the Osages resisted and were themselves resettled to INDIAN TERRITORY (present-day Oklahoma).

The American Era in Arkansas

The LOUISIANA PURCHASE ushered in the American era in Arkansas, and it had implications for the Indians there, some of whom had moved to Arkansas voluntarily in the late eighteenth century to escape the Americans. Cherokees, for example, settled along the Black and St. Francis rivers in the 1780s and 1790s. Although some eastern Indians, particularly the Cherokees, were "removed" to Arkansas in the late 1810s, they were later resettled in Indian Territory. Native groups would find themselves at a distinct disadvantage as the Americans spread across the Mississippi River; established plantation agriculture, particularly on Quapaw lands in southeastern Arkansas; and placed the state on a certain economic trajectory and a collision course with the CIVIL WAR.

As white settlers swept into the region in the first three decades of the nineteenth century, they found ample fertile land to develop in Arkansas and secured the cooperation of the federal government in removing all Indians from the territory by the mid-1830s. By the time that Arkansas applied for separate territorial status in 1819—it had been part of Missouri Territory until then—slavery was firmly established, and it came as a shock when New York Representative John Taylor proposed effectively banning slavery. The debate that ensued became intertwined with Missouri's application for statehood, and, in fact, the idea of a dividing line (36 degrees, 30 minutes—the border between Missouri and Arkansas), which became one of the key features of the great MISSOURI COMPROMISE, was first articulated by Taylor in connection with the Arkansas bill. In the end, of course, slavery remained intact in Arkansas and became an important element in the delta's economy and in the state's political history.

Other differences existed between the southeast and northwest. While the southeast was given over to cotton cultivation, plantation agriculture, and a higher concentration of land ownership, a mixed agriculture of wheat, corn, livestock, and orchards predominated in the northwest, where land holdings tended to be much smaller. Part of the Arkansas Ozark Mountain range, northwest Arkansas was simply not suitable for plantation agriculture. The northwest was predominantly Whig in political orientation, and although some Whigs had interests in the delta, most planters there were Democrats.

A crucial factor in the ability of southeastern planters to control Arkansas politics was their influence upon the capital city. The first territorial capital, Arkansas Post, proved to be an inadequate location, and in 1820 a centrally located site farther up the Arkansas River, known as the "little rock," was chosen as the new territorial capital. LITTLE ROCK developed rapidly, and with significant ties to the southeastern Arkansas planters, Little Rock businessmen and politicians could be counted upon to support issues of importance to them.

Conflicts over Statehood

Its central role in the political struggle between the southeast and the northwest became manifest when Arkansas drafted its first state constitution in early 1836. The drive for statehood in Arkansas had been influenced by the desire to maintain a balance on the national level between slave and free states. When it became clear in 1834 that the territory of Michigan was preparing to apply for statehood in the near future, Arkansas territorial delegate Ambrose Sevier was determined that Arkansas would be paired with Michigan.

When delegates met in Little Rock to draft a state constitution, southeastern planters were defeated in their attempts to apply the three-fifths rule in counting slaves for purposes of representation, but they succeeded in carving out a three-district political structure: one made up of southeast counties, one of northwest counties, and one of three counties in the center of the state. The largest of those three counties in the central district was, of course, Pulaski, where Little Rock was located. Northwestern delegates largely opposed this arrangement because it was clear that this central district would support the southeast, but enough northwestern delegates voted in favor of it to secure its passage.

Arkansas in the Civil War

When the secession crisis of 1860 took place, some Southerners believed that President Abraham Lincoln's election to the presidency alone was sufficient to justify immediate SECESSION, but most Arkansans were willing to give Lincoln a chance to prove that he was not, as he insisted, opposed to slavery where it existed. Those most in favor of immediate secession were from the southeastern delta; those most opposed were from the northwest. A secession convention was called in March 1861, just as Lincoln was taking the oath of office. The northwestern delegates succeeded in defeating the immediate secessionists, but the convention scheduled an election to take place the following August that would allow voters to decide the issue. Before that election could be held, however, Confederate forces fired on Fort Sumter on April 12, and in response Lincoln put out a call for troops to all the states. Arkansas's moment of truth had arrived. The secession convention called itself back into session and voted 69 to 1 to secede and join the Confederate cause.

Although few important battles were fought in the state, the Civil War brought devastation to Arkansas. It was ill-positioned to fight a war. Due to banking problems, the state was in poor economic standing at the time the Civil War broke out. Meanwhile, state officials feared—with justification—that Arkansas troops would be transferred east of the river, leaving Arkansas relatively defenseless. Although the Confederate military never fully abandoned Arkansas, it remained a lower priority and suffered as a consequence.

Ironically, the largest battles fought in the state took place in northwest Arkansas, the area least in favor of secession. On March 7–8, 1862, Federal forces pushed into the state from Missouri, hoping to wipe out Confederate resistance in the northwest counties and possibly reach the Arkansas River valley. Confederate forces met the Union forces at Pea Ridge (or Elkhorn Tavern). After a see-saw battle with heavy losses on the Federal side, the Confederates were ultimately forced to retire south to the Boston Mountains, but the Federals failed to follow them. Neither side truly won the battle as neither achieved its objectives. Much of Arkansas was then embroiled in a relentless guerrilla war from which many civilians, particularly in northwest Arkansas, fled.

The Reconstruction Era

The Reconstruction history of Arkansas is similar to that of other southern states. Initially Confederates regained political office under President Andrew Johnson's mild Reconstruction policies, only to be removed and disfranchised under congressional (or radical) RECONSTRUCTION. The Republican Party of Arkansas, like that of other southern states, attempted to build railroads, founded an educational system, and fell victim to charges of corruption. Ultimately, Reconstruction was overturned and a Redeemer Democrat, Augustus Garland, took over as Democratic governor in 1874.

One major issue emanating from the Civil War was what to do about the freedmen. The FREEDMEN'S BUREAU functioned in Arkansas during its brief life, but planters soon regained the upper hand and reduced the Arkansas freedmen to a kind of peasantry through the sharecropping system. Meanwhile, the cotton economy sank into a long decline, although Arkansas planters remained locked into it through the system of advances they received from cotton factors, who demanded they grow cotton. The state legislature, now controlled by Democrats, forswore an activist role in addressing the economic problems facing farmers. By the early 1880s farmers in Arkansas were in such dire straits that they formed the Agricultural Wheel, an organization determined to influence the legislature to address their problems. By 1886 they mounted a candidate for governor who very nearly defeated the Democratic candidate.

The fact that blacks had voted for the "Wheel" candidate did not escape the attention of leading Democrats, and fearful of the threat from below, Democrats were motivated to conquer by dividing their enemies along racial lines. In 1891 the legislature enacted both segregation and disfranchising legislature. The Separate Coach law prohibited blacks from riding in first-class coaches within the state. The election law of 1891 discriminated against illiterate voters (by allowing only election officials to mark their ballots) and imposed a poll tax. A final disfranchising piece of legislation became effective in 1906 when the state Democratic Party declared a "white only" policy, whereby only whites could vote in the Democratic primary.

Industrial Development Emerges

The end of the nineteenth century also marked something of an economic renaissance in Arkansas, albeit of a very limited kind. Despite efforts on the part of Arkansas boosters to attract industry and development to the state, the only industries that emerged were extractive in nature. The lumber industry, for example, became extraordinarily important all over Arkansas, from the eastern delta to the Ouachita and Ozark mountains in the west. Northern financiers and entrepreneurs, eager to reach the wealth of the Arkansas forests, extended hundreds of miles of railroad into a state that on the eve of the Civil War had less than a hundred miles of rail line. Deforestation in eastern Arkansas led directly to the expansion of the plantation system there and an explosion of population growth in the early twentieth century. By the end of that century, coal mining had become important. In central Arkansas, meanwhile, bauxite mining emerged near Benton. But efforts to move beyond these extractive industries and broaden the economy past its dependence on agriculture failed.

Progressivism, Riots, and Flood

Just as the urge to reform and perfect swept across the rest of the country during the Progressive Era, it touched Arkansas as well. It was during the first decades of the twentieth century that the convict leasing system was eliminated, women got the right to vote, and the educational infrastructure was improved. Both the initiative and the referendum were adopted in Arkansas. Prohibition was implemented in 1916, three years before the national ban. As the automobile became a more important means of transportation, roads expanded. Unfortunately, many road improvement districts went bankrupt during the economic downturn following World War I. The governors of the 1920s and 1930s struggled with this legacy of debt.

But those two decades brought other significant problems that captured the attention of the state's governors and legislators. In 1919 a race riot in Phillips County brought unfavorable publicity. This was "red summer," when labor strife and race riots occurred across the country. In the Arkansas case, black SHARECROPPERS had formed a union and hired an attorney to represent them in suits they planned to file against planters for whom they worked. The planters learned of the union and purportedly concluded that the union was planning to murder them and appropriate their lands. After an incident outside a union meeting left a white man dead, a full-fledged race riot resulted, and Governor Charles Brough called on the president to dispatch troops from Camp Pike. Five whites and at least twenty-five blacks were killed, although unofficial reports suggest the number of blacks killed greatly exceeded that number.

While the Elaine Race Riot brought unfavorable publicity to the state, the sharp decline in prices paid for agricultural products that persisted throughout the 1920s brought ruin to farmers and many of the merchants and bankers who depended upon the agricultural economy. As if their economic woes were not problem enough, the great flood of 1927 inundated Arkansas. More than two million agricultural acres were flooded within the state. Arkansas had hardly recovered from this disaster and was reeling from the deteriorating economic conditions faced by Americans after the stock market crash of 1929 when the drought of 1930–1931 struck. Crops withered in the fields and livestock died while the Red Cross ruminated over whether a drought was the kind of natural disaster they should respond to. Finally, the Red Cross stepped in, but it was New Deal programs fostered under Franklin Roosevelt's presidency that began to improve the agricultural economy. The Agricultural Adjustment Administration (AAA) launched its crop reduction program in 1933 and secured the cooperation of planters and farmers throughout the state in "plowing up" up to 30 percent of the planted cotton acres. Farmers were given a check for "renting" the plowed-up acres to the government, although they were free to raise certain unrestricted crops on those lands.

As it worked out, the AAA greatly advantaged planters and large farmers and brought further devastation to tenant farmers. Planters who no longer needed the services of tenant farmers simply evicted them. Many planters refused to share the crop payments with the tenants remaining on their plantation.

Some historians have credited the AAA program with being largely responsible for the demise of the tenancy and sharecropping system and the emergence of capital-intensive agriculture. But World War II played an important role in pulling labor away from agricultural areas—sending them to the military or to work in defense industries—and, in any case, the transition from labor-intensive to capital-intensive agriculture in the Arkansas delta depended upon the creation of a marketable mechanical cotton harvester. Those were developed during the war and began to come off assembly lines in sufficient numbers by the late 1940s to begin a revolution in southern agriculture. As chemicals, some of them developed during the war for other purposes, were put to use on the delta plantations to keep weeds down, the shift was further augmented. By the end of the 1950s the transition was all but complete, leaving in its wake a massive depopulation of the Arkansas delta that wreaked havoc on small-town economies.

Attracting Industry to the State

The state was not quiescent in the face of the changes transforming the delta. At Governor Orval Faubus's suggestion, the legislature created the Arkansas Industrial Development Commission in 1955. Despite more than fifty years of efforts to expand industrial production in the state, no industrial base of any significance had been established. Faubus appointed Winthrop Rockefeller, scion of the famous New York Rockefellers, who had settled in Arkansas after World War II, as the first director of the AIDC. He served as director for nine years and pursued industrial development with zeal and energy. He had some successes, but the kinds of industries that ultimately settled in Arkansas were of a character that did not promote further development. In fact, with more than six hundred new industrial plants located in the state during his tenure, providing more than ninety thousand new jobs, those factories paid low wages to largely unskilled workers. By the mid-1960s, moreover, it was clear that Arkansas was serving as a way station for those industries on a trek south in search of lower wages. Towns that secured factories in 1955 would likely be looking for replacement factories a decade later.

Ironically, it was in part the fear of losing industrial development possibilities that influenced Little Rock businessmen to take a stand on the Central High School crisis that began in 1957. Governor Orval Faubus had taken an extreme segregationist position just when it seemed the Little Rock school board had worked out a reasonable plan of gradual integration. He called out the National Guard to prevent nine black children from entering the school in the fall of 1957, and President Dwight D. Eisenhower was ultimately forced to nationalize the state guard and send in troops to enforce integration. The next year, Faubus elected to close the schools rather than allow them to be integrated.

For their part, the businessmen recognized that the crisis had drawn national and international attention that threatened their efforts to encourage industrial development in the city. They wanted an end to the bad publicity. By the early 1960s, even Faubus was changing his tune. With black voters gaining strength, particularly in the Arkansas delta, he began courting them and forswearing his segregationist past. When he decided not to run for office in 1966, his former AIDC director, Winthrop Rockefeller, secured the Republican nomination and defeated Jim Johnson, an avid race baiter. Clearly, Arkansas had had enough of the politics of race.

The Republican Rise to Power

The last six decades of the twentieth century witnessed a dramatic economic and political transformation in Arkansas. The emergence of the Republican Party and an economic boom in northwest Arkansas, two events that were not entirely unrelated, changed the face of the Arkansas political and economic landscape. While the delta struggled economically in the wake of the transformation of the plantation system, it reinvented itself politically as black voters made themselves felt at the polls. For the first time since Reconstruction, blacks were elected to important political positions on the local level in Arkansas.

Meanwhile, the rise of four economic giants in northwest Arkansas put that region on a phenomenal growth trajectory. Sam Walton, a retail genius, founded Wal-Mart, with its headquarters in Bentonville. John Tyson began his chicken business in Springdale, and his son, Don Tyson, expanded it dramatically and made it a worldwide enterprise. J. B. Hunt, who began as a simple trucker, founded a trucking empire and moved his headquarters to northwest Arkansas. John A. Cooper, who had founded a successful retirement community known as Cherokee Village, worked his magic in Bella Vista beginning in the 1960s, at approximately the same time that Walton, Don Tyson, and Hunt were laying the foundation for their businesses. The three business enterprises attracted a number of vendors and allied industries, and the population growth that followed generated an unprecedented construction boom.

Most of those who moved into northwest Arkansas and crowded into the growing suburbs of Little Rock were conservative in orientation. Only the presence of three moderate Democrats who could speak the language of fiscal conservatism kept the state otherwise in the hands of the Democrats. Dale Leon Bumpers, David Pryor, and Bill Clinton all served as governor between 1972 and 1992 (with the exception of a two-year period when a maverick Republican, Frank White, occupied the state house). Bumpers and Pryor would go on to have distinguished careers in the Senate, and Clinton, of course, went to the White House. In fact, his departure may have played a significant role in the Republican resurgence in Arkansas. Not only did he take with him many young Democrats who might have positioned themselves for elective office had they remained in Arkansas, but he also left the state in the hands of his Democratic lieutenant governor, Jim Guy Tucker, who proved to be more vulnerable than anyone could have imagined. Within two years, Tucker faced serious charges arising from the Whitewater investigation and resigned, giving the seat over to Mike Huckabee, a popular Republican. Meanwhile, Republicans were experiencing a political renaissance elsewhere in the state, claiming a congressional seat in 1992 and a Senate seat in 1996. Clearly, by the end of the twentieth century, the Republican Party had become a force to be reckoned with, and the massive demographic changes that had occurred in the previous fifty years were a major factor in bringing that about.

BIBLIOGRAPHY

Bolton, S. Charles. *Arkansas: Remote and Restless, 1800–1860.* Fayetteville: University of Arkansas Press, 1998.

Donovan, Timothy P., Willard B. Gatewood, and Jeannie Whayne, eds. *Governors of Arkansas.* Fayetteville: University of Arkansas Press, 1995.

Dougan, Michael B. *Arkansas Odyssey: The Saga of Arkansas from Prehistoric Times to the Present.* Little Rock, Ark.: Rose, 1993.

Johnson, Ben F. III. *Arkansas in Modern America, 1930–1999.* Fayetteville: University of Arkansas Press, 2000.

Moneyhon, Carl. *Arkansas and the New South, 1874–1929.* Fayetteville: University of Arkansas Press, 1997.

Reed, Roy. *Faubus: The Life and Times of an American Prodigal.* Fayetteville: University of Arkansas Press, 1997.

Whayne, Jeannie, Tom DeBlack, George Sabo, and Morris S. Arnold. *Arkansas: A Narrative History.* Fayetteville: University of Arkansas Press, 2002.

Whayne, Jeannie, and Willard B. Gatewood, eds. *The Arkansas Delta: A Land of Paradox.* Fayetteville: University of Arkansas Press, 1993.

Jeannie Whayne

See also **Desegregation; Plantation System of the South.**

ARKANSAS RIVER emerges in central Colorado and flows southeast through Kansas, Oklahoma, and Arkansas to the Mississippi River. Known to the early French as Rivière des Ark or d'Ozark, the 1,450-mile river derived its present-day name from the Arkansas Indians who lived along its banks. Hernando de Soto became the first European to explore the river on his journey into the Southwest in 1541. The French explorers Louis Jolliet and Jacques Marquette reached its mouth in 1673, in their search for a river "coming in from California on the southern sea." The Arkansas Post (in present-day southeastern Arkansas), established in 1686 by Henry de Tonti, was the first permanent settlement in the Arkansas River region, and the early history of the river centers around the post.

During the eighteenth century, the headwaters of the Arkansas were in Spanish territory. In 1696, the Spanish explorer Uribarri applied the name "Rio Napestle" to the upper Arkansas, a name the Spanish continued to use until the nineteenth century. The 1819 Adams-Onís Treaty between the United States and Spain made the Arkansas River west of the 100th meridian a part of the western boundary of the United States. The name "Arkansas," which had applied only to lower reaches of the stream, was carried westward by American traders and trappers and succeeded in replacing the name "Rio Napestle," or "Napeste."

The Arkansas River was a highway for the French and Spanish. In the nineteenth century, it was navigable with keelboats as far west as Grand River. By the early twentieth century, it had also become a source of water for farms, industries, and cities and the subject of conflicts among the various users of the river's waters.

BIBLIOGRAPHY

Lecompte, Janet. *Pueblo, Hardscrabble, Greenhorn: The Upper Arkansas, 1832–1856.* Norman: University of Oklahoma Press, 1978.

Lewis, Anna. *Along the Arkansas.* Dallas, Tex.: The Southwest Press, 1932.

Sherow, James Earl. *Watering the Valley: Development along the High Plains Arkansas River, 1870–1950.* Lawrence: University Press of Kansas, 1990.

Anna Lewis / c. p.

See also **Louisiana Purchase; Treaties with Foreign Nations.**

ARLINGTON NATIONAL CEMETERY, originally part of George Washington's estate, has become one of the most important shrines that the United States maintains. In 1861 the United States seized the estate from its owner, Robert E. Lee, and by 1864 it had begun using the grounds as a cemetery. Following an 1882 Supreme Court decision, the government officially purchased the estate from Lee's heir. The dead of every war since the American Revolution and distinguished statesmen, including John F. Kennedy, rest in the cemetery.

The U.S. government has restored Arlington House and erected a Memorial Amphitheater. The Tomb of the Unknowns commemorates the dead of the two world wars and the Korean War.

BIBLIOGRAPHY

Holt, Dean W. *American Military Cemeteries: A Comprehensive Illustrated Guide to the Hallowed Grounds of the United States, Including Cemeteries Overseas.* Jefferson, N.C.: McFarland, 1992.

Angela Ellis

See also **Cemeteries, National;** *United States v. Lee;* **Unknown Soldier, Tomb of the;** *and vol. 9:* **Dedicating the Tomb of the Unknown Soldier.**

ARMINIANISM, a form of theological thought based on the 1608 *Declaration of Sentiments* of the Dutch theologian Jacobus Arminius (1559–1609). Often referred to as "anti-Calvinism," Arminianism holds the freedom of the human will as its basic tenet and thus denies one of John Calvin's foundational ideas: the irresistibility of the grace of God. Arminius states that God's grace is indeed resistible because all human beings are responsible for

Jacobus Arminius. A portrait of the Dutch theologian who broke with Calvinism over the issue of free will, and whose ideas especially shaped the rise of Methodism. LIBRARY OF CONGRESS

their own thoughts and actions. Accordingly, sin is actual because it is possible, in direct contrast to Calvin's treatment of sin as purely theoretical because of the inability of the elect to sin. Therefore, Arminianism states that salvation requires both willful repentance and willful acceptance of God's grace, not simply a helpless reliance on arbitrary election.

Arminianism's belief in the role of man's free will fueled the evangelical fervor of the nineteenth century, and its adoption by John Wesley was a driving force in the formation of the powerful Methodist denomination both in England and in America. Arminianism widely appeared in America during the early 1740s as an engagement of the Puritan and Presbyterian reliance on Calvin's principles; in doing so, ministers addressed the major focuses of Jonathan Edwards's preaching and of the entire Great Awakening (1734–c. 1745).

American Arminians combined Armenius's ideas with the Enlightenment's reliance on reason and rational thought to offer a theology that resonated with the beliefs of many of the nation's citizens. Some of these broader philosophies included a work ethic that valued honest and thoughtful toil, the sense that their work ultimately held some meaning and purpose, and the attitude of voluntarism and reform that became prevalent during the nineteenth century. These final attributes were fed by the Second Great Awakening and the general evangelicalism that pervaded American Methodist and Baptist churches during that same period. As a result, the inclusive doctrines of Arminianism passed from heresy into an orthodoxy that remains strong at the beginning of the twenty-first century.

BIBLIOGRAPHY

Sell, Alan P. F. *The Great Debate: Calvinism, Arminianism, and Salvation.* Grand Rapids, Mich.: Baker Book House, 1983.

Barbara Schwarz Wachal

See also **Great Awakening; Methodism.**

ARMISTICE OF NOVEMBER 1918.

German military leaders acknowledged in October 1918 that their country had been defeated and, seeking more favorable terms than they were likely to obtain from Britain or France, appealed to U.S. President Woodrow Wilson for an armistice based on the FOURTEEN POINTS. Wilson refused to negotiate with a government that did not represent the German people. He sent his top adviser, Colonel Edward M. House, to Paris to negotiate a common position with the French and the British. Neither European ally was willing to accept the Fourteen Points in toto. The British objected to the provision for freedom of the seas, and the French wanted no limitation to be put on German reparations payments.

On 9 November, Kaiser Wilhelm II abdicated the throne, clearing the way for an agreement. The armistice ending the war was signed in a railway carriage in the Compiègne Forest at 11 A.M. on 11 November. It called for immediate German withdrawal from Belgium, France, and Alsace-Lorraine; Allied occupation of German territory west of the Rhine; and the renunciation of the treaties of Brest-Litovsk and Bucharest. Germany was stripped of its navy and its East Africa colony. The armistice laid the framework for the final peace treaty worked out at the Paris Peace Conference in 1919.

BIBLIOGRAPHY

Goemans, H. E. *War and Punishment: The Causes of War Termination and the First World War.* Princeton, N.J.: Princeton University Press, 2000.

Lowry, Bullitt. *Armistice 1918.* Kent, Ohio: Kent State University, 1996.

Weintraub, Stanley. *A Stillness Heard Round the World: The End of the Great War, November 1918.* New York: E. P. Dutton, 1985.

Max Paul Friedman

See also **Versailles, Treaty of; World War I.**

ARMORED SHIPS,

first developed in Europe by the French and British navies, entered the U.S. Navy during the Civil War, where they made their combat debut. The Union navy, although generally associated with monitors, the low-freeboard, large-gun, turreted ironclads that captured the public's imagination during the war, contained a variety of designs suited for both riverine and coastal operations. The Confederate navy, whose paucity of industrial facilities limited experimentation, used fewer and simpler designs for the same purposes. Both sides employed several different armor schemes, depending on application, including thick wooden enclosures, cotton bales, sheets of tin on a wooden backing, layers of iron bolted to reinforced wooden hulls and superstructures, and laminated iron armor.

The period of naval retrenchment that followed the Civil War saw little innovation in the United States. Monitors remained the navy's only armored vessels until the late 1880s, when more modern battleships and armored cruisers were authorized and began joining the fleet. These vessels reflected the substantial changes in naval technology introduced in Europe since the Civil War: breechloading steel cannon, steel hulls, more powerful engines, and stronger armor. Armor, for example, evolved from iron plates to compound plates of iron and steel fused together to new steel alloys to steel plates tempered by the Harvey and Krupps processes. Initially introduced in small numbers, these armored warships grew in number as the United States began expanding its international presence.

The writings of the American naval theorist Alfred Thayer Mahan, which argued for the primacy of capital ships and were accepted worldwide, accelerated the navy's growth. Following Mahan's precepts, the navy reinvented

Armored Ship. During the Civil War, the *Casco* (seen here on the James River in Virginia) was one of the Union's turreted ironclads known as monitors, after the famous first ship of that class. NATIONAL ARCHIVES AND RECORDS ADMINISTRATION

itself, rejecting its traditional commerce-raiding mission for a strategy based on fleet actions by armored capital ships. Although armored warships existed in a variety of sizes and configurations, battleships became the measure of a nation's international standing by the turn of the century. The launching of H.M.S. *Dreadnought* in 1906 confirmed the battleship's dominance and set the standard for armored vessels. The first all-big-gun warship, it was quickly copied by Great Britain's competitors, including the United States. Another class of lightly armored big-gun warships that sacrificed some protection for speed, the battle cruisers, soon joined the world's leading navies.

Countries jealously compared numbers, types, and technical sophistication of armored capital ships, convinced that these massive weapons would play a vital role in future wars. But by the end of World War I, proponents had little direct evidence of their effectiveness. The Battle of Jutland, the only major fleet action of the war, proved inconclusive, while the greatest threat to the Allied war effort presented itself in the form of the commerce-raiding submarine, the antithesis of the armored capital ship. Still, the concept of fleet actions conducted by armored capital ships emerged from the war still enjoying strong support among the navy's planners. Subsequent American war plans, especially War Plan Orange (for war against Japan), still envisioned titanic fleet encounters between contending nations.

Even as navy planners continued to express their faith in battleships and cruisers, a potent challenge emerged. Airpower proponents argued that the armored ships' days were numbered because of their vulnerability to aerial attack. In an embarrassing publicity stunt, General William ("Billy") Mitchell successfully bombed and sank a stationary captured German battleship, the *Ostfriesland*, in 1921. Within the navy, Fleet Problem IX, conducted in 1929, demonstrated the unarmored aircraft carrier's potential to project force over great distances and sink armored war-

ships. Still, the battleship and its armored consorts remained supreme in the eyes of naval strategists.

The Japanese attack on Pearl Harbor in December 1941 shattered those illusions. With five of the navy's finest battleships destroyed or severely damaged, it had no choice but to use those ships that remained for offensive operations, including three aircraft carriers. Those carriers, and others that followed, became the core of the fast carrier task forces that spearheaded the war in the Pacific. Armored ships also played an important part in these campaigns, but lost their dominant role even as ship design peaked with the wartime introduction of the Iowa-class battleships. Postwar strategic thinking that saw future wars in terms of atomic conflict found little use for armored warships built to engage each other. Although they periodically reappeared during the Korean and Vietnam wars, as well as the late 1980s, their expense and lack of distinct mission made them anachronistic, each time leading to decommissioning.

BIBLIOGRAPHY

Baer, George W. *One Hundred Years of Sea Power: The U.S. Navy, 1890–1990.* Stanford, Calif.: Stanford University Press, 1994.

Baxter, James Phinney. *The Introduction of the Ironclad Warship.* 1933. Reprint, Hamden, Conn.: Archon, 1968.

Cooling, Benjamin Franklin. *Gray Steel and Blue Water Navy: The Formative Years of America's Military-Industrial Complex, 1881–1917.* Hamden, Conn: Archon, 1979.

Muir, Malcolm. *Black Shoes and Blue Water: Surface Warfare in the United States Navy, 1945–1975.* Washington, D.C.: Naval Historical Center, 1996.

O'Connell, Robert L. *Sacred Vessels: The Cult of the Battleship and the Rise of the U.S. Navy.* Boulder, Colo.: Westview Press, 1991.

Kurt Hackemer

See also **Dreadnought; Ironclad Warships; Navy, United States; Warships.**

ARMORED VEHICLES. Modern armored vehicles emerged from attempts to solve the unprecedented lethal challenges presented by WORLD WAR I battlefields. First Lord of the Admiralty Winston Churchill became an enthusiastic sponsor of British lieutenant colonels Ernest D. Swinton's and Maurice Hankey's proposals for vehicles with armor plating, caterpillar tracks, machine guns, and self-contained artillery. Tanks—a term used to preserve the weapon system's secrecy—made their first appearance on 15 September 1916 on the Somme battlefield near Flers. By 1918, British, French, and American units employed more than 500 tanks in the Allied counter to the German Michael offensive. Tanks afforded the Allies armored protection and mobility along with striking power that demoralized the German army in August, thus setting the stage for ultimate victory some three months later. British armor pioneer John Frederick Charles Fuller proposed an ambitious combined arms offensive for the following spring—Plan 1919—with nearly 5,000 tanks as the centerpiece of the action, but the armistice precluded its implementation. As the war closed, army leaders in Britain, France, and the United States understood the new weapon's potential but failed to create strong institutional components designed to advance the doctrinal and technological foundations laid in the Great War.

The U.S. Army's official doctrine during the interwar years emphasized the support and cooperation that tanks could provide infantry forces. The image of a deadlocked battlefield crisscrossed by trench networks and dominated by machine-gun emplacements and artillery dictated an auxiliary role for armored forces. According to army doctrine, tanks would protect infantry as they traversed the trenches to achieve tactical, rather than operational, breakthroughs. The U.S. Army's force structure reflected these self-imposed constraints until 1937. In that year, the Seventh Cavalry Brigade, commanded by Adna R. Chaffee, acquired new M1A1 light tanks, thus laying the foundation for the independent armored formations that would characterize WORLD WAR II. Despite Chaffee's new acquisition, however, the World War I–vintage technology, doctrine, and organization continued to rule the army until the service began expanding before World War II. The Louisiana Maneuvers held in May 1940, in which the Seventh Cavalry Brigade operated the bulk of the nation's 300 light tanks, represented the U.S. Army's most significant experiment with armored force employment of the interwar period.

The U.S. military learned harsh doctrinal lessons as German forces schooled in the operational breakthroughs achieved against Poland, France, and Russia became masters of armored warfare in the early years of World War II. German tank commanders including Generals Heinz Guderian and Erwin Rommel and Field Marshal Erich von Manstein achieved remarkable operational successes using tanks as the main combat arm. German armored forces aimed to thrust deep into the enemy rear to sow confusion and disorganization among operational headquarters. German armored-force dominance in the sweeping envelopments achieved against Russian forces in 1941 signaled a revolution in land warfare. The operational success of the German commanders appeared to confirm ideas expressed in the interwar years by armored-warfare proponents like Fuller, Basil H. Liddell Hart, and the maverick French general Charles de Gaulle.

By 1943, the U.S. Army counted sixteen armored divisions and sixty-five independent tank battalions in its ranks. From modest beginnings, the United States dramatically expanded tank production to produce nearly 90,000 tanks by 1945. After several harsh battlefield experiences, such as the defeat at KASSERINE PASS in North Africa, the U.S. Army reorganized its armored divisions for more operational flexibility. The breakout and dash across France executed by Lieutenant General George S. Patton's Third Army after the Normandy invasion illus-

Armored Vehicles. An American tank advances in Tunisia during the North African campaign of World War II. NATIONAL ARCHIVES AND RECORDS ADMINISTRATION

trated the army's mature approach to armored warfare in World War II. By the war's end, the army had adopted an armored division composed of infantry, self-propelled artillery, and tanks; mobility and firepower became the bywords of the American approach to land warfare.

The advantages armored forces provided in the European theater of World War II proved difficult to maintain. During the KOREAN WAR, U.S. forces were criticized for being "roadbound" and too dependent on armored vehicles that were ill-equipped to cope with the mountainous Korean terrain. Furthermore, M-26 Pershing and the World War II–vintage Sherman tanks could not compete on a par with the superb Soviet T-34 tank. Despite lackluster performance in the war, army leaders continued to emphasize the combined-arms approach to land warfare.

Cold War strategists anticipated a Warsaw Pact conventional thrust across northern and central Europe against nominally weaker NATO forces. U.S. tank doctrine relied on superior firepower, mobility, and prodigious amounts of air support to halt what was envisioned as Soviet-backed forces surging westward. In the later years of the Cold War, the United States relied on the massive Abrams tank to combat the numerically superior Warsaw Pact forces. The M1 Abrams fielded in the 1980s boasted the equivalent of nearly 18 inches of armor protection for its crews. Later Abrams models provided 31.5

inches of armor against kinetic energy rounds and considerably more protection against penetrating ordnance.

At the turn of the twenty-first century, army doctrine continued to rely on the pairing of armor and infantry, but the speed and lethality of modern battle dictated requirements for armored fighting vehicles that protected troops while allowing them to keep pace with fast-moving tank thrusts. The M2 Bradley fighting vehicle, equipped with a grenade launcher, machine gun, 25 mm canon, and antitank missile launcher, transported infantry squads to the fight. Armored personnel carriers, self-propelled artillery, Multiple Launch Rocket System, transport and attack aviation, and a host of maintenance and support systems rounded out the modern armored division. Nearly three decades of technological and doctrinal development came to fruition in 1991 when armored forces crashed through Iraq's elite Republican Guard during Operation Desert Storm (see PERSIAN GULF WAR). General Frederick M. Franks Jr.'s VII Corps waged a 100-hour ground campaign that featured highly accurate targeting, long-range weapons engagement, fully integrated command and control, and precision navigation. Observers heralded the resulting victory as a revolution in warfare.

U.S. armored warfare capabilities have progressed dramatically since the early efforts of World War I. Despite impressive technical achievements, the requirement for mobility and survivability on the battlefield will continue to guide developments in armored vehicle doctrine and technology.

BIBLIOGRAPHY

Childs, David J. *A Peripheral Weapon? The Production and Employment of British Tanks in the First World War.* Westport, Conn.: Greenwood Press, 1999.

Citino, Robert M. *Armored Forces: History and Sourcebook.* Westport, Conn.: Greenwood Press, 1994.

Clancy, Tom. *Armored Cav: A Guided Tour of an Armored Cavalry Regiment.* New York: Berkley Books, 1994.

Harris, J. P., and F. H. Toase, eds. *Armoured Warfare.* New York: St. Martin's Press, 1990.

Anthony Christopher Cain

ARMORY SHOW. At the beginning of the twentieth century, a group of artists formed a loosely affiliated school of thought that centered on creating works of art that presented a realistic portrayal of everyday life. Often called "The Eight," or the ASHCAN SCHOOL, the group (George Luks, William Glackens, John Sloan, Everett Shinn, Arthur B. Davies, Maurice Prendergast, Ernest Lawson, and George Bellows) painted with a journalistic approach, portraying the grit and seedy elements of society. Critics and academics were outraged by the Ashcan School and declared the work vulgar.

Despite the negative critical response, the Ashcan artists gained a following. They held their first public exhibition in 1908, followed by a second show two years

Nude Descending a Staircase. Marcel Duchamp's avant-garde painting of motion was a major sensation of the groundbreaking and extremely controversial Armory Show of 1913. ARTISTS RIGHTS SOCIETY, INC.

later. The second exhibition caused such a sensation that riot police had to subdue the crowd. The notoriety only increased the group's popularity.

The Ashcan School reached its apex in February 1913 when, in conjunction with the Association of American Painters and Sculptors, it staged the Armory Show, by some accounts the most important exhibit ever held in the United States. More than 300 artists were represented with a collection of 1,600 paintings, sculpture, and decorative works. The Armory Show shocked the public by showcasing the outrageous styles adopted by The Eight and vanguard European artists—styles such as Symbolism, Impressionism, Post-Impressionism, Cubism, and Futurism. European participants included Pablo Picasso, Wassily Kandinsky, Paul Cezanne, and Henri Matisse, among others—many whose work was being seen for the first time in the United States. The groundbreaking show launched the term "modern art" and changed the course of American art.

Located in New York City, the Armory provided an enormous space to hold an art exhibition. Since it had no internal walls, organizers used screens covered in fireproof burlap to divide the giant space into eighteen octagonal rooms, each decorated with pine branches and live potted trees.

One of the most sensational pieces at the exhibit was Marcel Duchamp's *Nude Descending a Staircase*. Critics viewed it as the single representation of all that was wrong with avant-garde European art, particularly Cubism, Impressionism, and Futurism. Critics also denounced other French artists, particularly Matisse, for painting in a manner that seemed to defy common sense. Later, when the show traveled to Chicago, art students burned Matisse in effigy. Despite the critical turmoil, more than 500,000 people viewed the Armory Show in New York, Chicago, and Boston.

BIBLIOGRAPHY

Braider, Donald. *George Bellows and the Ashcan School of Painting.* Garden City, N.Y.: Doubleday, 1971.

Hughes, Robert. *American Visions: The Epic History of Art in America.* New York: Knopf, 1997.

Mendelowitz, Daniel M. *A History of American Art.* New York: Holt, Rinehart and Winston, 1970.

Perlman, Bennard B. *Painters of the Ashcan School: The Immortal Eight.* New York: Dover, 1988.

Shi, David E. *Facing Facts: Realism in American Thought and Culture, 1850–1920.* New York: Oxford University Press, 1995.

Bob Batchelor

See also **Art.**

ARMS RACE AND DISARMAMENT.

The term "arms race" generally refers to peacetime competitions between states for military superiority. Efforts to control or limit such competitions by mutual agreement are variously referred to as "arms control," "arms limitation," "arms reduction," or "disarmament." Though many of these expressions date to the nineteenth century, it was not until the twentieth century that they entered common usage. Examples of "arms races" are found throughout much of American history, but the largest and most important remains the one between the United States and the Soviet Union during the COLD WAR, especially as it involved nuclear weapons.

The most common explanation for the origins of arms races has to do with what political scientists call the "security dilemma." According to this theory, one state takes steps to increase its security, such as strengthening its military, which makes potential rivals feel less secure, causing them to take similar measures that in turn increase insecurity in the first (and other) states. The result is a spiraling arms race in which each side can view its actions as defensive in nature. Critics of such "action-reaction" models reject the idea that arms races are essentially "misunderstandings" and assert instead that arms races are often caused by attempts to gain military superiority for coercive purposes or are even caused for domestic political reasons. Historical debates over the nature and desirability of arms control similarly vary. Supporters of disarmament usually assert that arms races cause wars. Critics of this view contend that the fundamental problem is usually not the arms race itself but the political disagreements that underlie international tension. In this view an arms race is only a symptom, not the disease, thus arms control only becomes possible when it is no longer necessary. Needless to say the theory behind arms races and disarmament is a matter of intense debate.

Antecedents

Throughout most of its early history, the United States retained only a small peacetime military establishment. The Atlantic Ocean would shield North America from large European armies, and the militia was thought sufficient for initial protection from any British (Canadian) threats from the north, Indian threats from the west, or Spanish threats from the south. Further the ideology of the timid early Republic saw the very existence of a large professional army in peacetime as a threat to democracy. These factors combined to keep peacetime military spending low, and arms races remained rare and disarmament for the most part irrelevant. An extreme illustration of the effects of all this was the brief moment in June 1784 when the entire U.S. Army consisted of only eighty men and a handful of officers.

A series of incidents in the late eighteenth century and early nineteenth century, however, gradually led to the establishment of what today would be called a rudimentary "MILITARY-INDUSTRIAL COMPLEX." In the 1790s part-time soldiers proved embarrassingly likely to run in a series of encounters with large Indian forces, and in 1814 the rapid collapse of a militia force outside Washington, D.C., allowed British troops to burn the nation's capital. Waiting until war was imminent to create military forces proved even less tenable when it came to navies, given the long lead time associated with shipbuilding. In the 1790s the Federalists authorized the creation of a substantial force of naval frigates, and though President Thomas Jefferson at first disdained the naval force that resulted, this did not prevent him from using it against Barbary pirates in the first decade of the nineteenth century. Jefferson also tacitly recognized the need for at least a small core of professional officers with his creation in 1802 of the U.S. Military Academy at West Point. The War of 1812 made clear that the one potentially significant exception to American geographic protection from the "great powers" was the existence of British Canada. American invasions of Canada during the war failed, but the potential for more remained. In the Rush-Bagot Agreement of 1817 the United States and Britain agreed to severely limit the establishment of any future naval forces on the Great Lakes. The first major incidence of successful arms control in American history, this agreement remains among the most important, as it eventually led to a sturdy Canadian-American peace and what was at the beginning of the twenty-first century the longest undefended border in the world.

With the gradual disappearance of the British threat to the north and the increasing disparity between the population of the United States and that of the American Indians, American geographic isolation seemed as strong as ever by the mid-nineteenth century. Scattered Indian wars and even a major war with Mexico (1846–1848) occurred, but in each case the rapid mobilization of armies of volunteers, built around a small core of professional soldiers, proved sufficient. The slow growth of the peacetime military establishment proceeded, most notably with the continued expansion of the federal armories at Springfield, Massachusetts, and Harpers Ferry, Virginia (now West Virginia), and the creation in 1845 of the U.S. Naval Academy. The largest example of this nineteenth-century pattern in American history was of course the Civil War. Though some informal preparations took place in both the North and the South in the 1850s, not until the commencement of hostilities did either side begin its rapid military expansion. Demobilization swiftly followed the end of the war, and by the 1870s the American army was once again a small peacetime force, scattered for the most part among various western outposts.

American Imperialism and the World Wars, 1890–1945

By the 1890s, however, the United States developed a growing thirst for land and influence beyond the confines of North America. Advocates of expansion, such as Senator Henry Cabot Lodge and Assistant Secretary of the Navy Theodore Roosevelt, no longer feared the "great powers"—they wanted the United States to become one. The rapid pace of change in naval technology over the previous few decades had leveled the playing field by rendering old fleets of wooden sailing vessels obsolete, and spurred by the writings of "navalists" like Alfred Thayer Mahan, the United States joined wholeheartedly in the international competition for the best new "steel and steam" warships. The fate of navies who fell behind in this arms race was dramatically illustrated in Manila Bay during the brief 1898 Spanish-American War, when a fleet of newer American warships obliterated an older Spanish fleet. The American squadron was outnumbered seven to six, and the two forces exchanged fire for over two hours. Yet when the smoke cleared, not a single American sailor was dead as the result of enemy fire. Theodore Roosevelt became president in 1901, and not coincidentally by the end of the decade American naval spending had more than doubled from even 1899 levels. By the 1914 outbreak of World War I, the United States possessed the third most powerful navy in the world.

Until the Cold War the classic example of an arms race remained the intense Anglo-German naval competition that preceded World War I. This and other prewar arms races were widely blamed for the disaster that was the "Great War," and the years that followed saw a worldwide explosion of interest in arms control and even complete disarmament. Before the war even ended President Woodrow Wilson listed among his famous Fourteen Points for a "just and stable peace" the demand that "national armaments . . . be reduced to the lowest point consistent with domestic safety." At the WASHINGTON NAVAL CONFERENCE of 1921–1922 the United States, Britain, and Japan agreed to restrictions on building naval bases in the Pacific and limited the tonnage of their capital ships along the ratio of 5:5:3. The United States was signatory to numerous other interwar arms control measures, including a 1925 protocol to the Geneva Convention that outlawed the use of chemical and biological weapons and even the ambitious 1928 KELLOGG-BRIAND PACT, which at least in theory outlawed war altogether. Of course wars have occurred since 1928, and some have involved the use of chemical and biological weapons. Even successful arms control sometimes just provided an inadvertent spur to technological development, such as the diversion of funds from the battleships restricted at the 1921–1922 Washington Naval Conference to newer vessels unrestricted by treaty, such as submarines and aircraft carriers. By the mid-1930s the failure of interwar disarmament had become apparent. Japan chose not to renew its naval treaties, and Nazi Germany openly announced its intention to rearm in violation of the 1919 Treaty of Versailles. Meanwhile in the United States congressional hearings chaired by Senator Gerald Nye in 1934 succeeded in convincing many Americans of the unlikely notion that the United States had essentially been tricked into entering World War I by domestic weapons manufacturers, the so-called "merchants of death." As European armies frantically prepared for war, the U.S. Congress passed in the mid- and late 1930s a series of neutrality acts in an attempt to ensure that, when the next war came, this time the United States would remain aloof from any "foreign entanglements."

Of course given the armaments of the twentieth century, even the Atlantic and Pacific Oceans were insufficient buffers against the aggression of Nazi Germany and Japan's military dictatorship. As the populace wrestled with pacifism, President Franklin D. Roosevelt quietly prepared the nation for war. Following the Nazi occupation of France in 1940, the United States created its first ever peacetime military draft and in general embarked on a massive expansion of its land, sea, and air forces. In 1939 the defense budget accounted for approximately 1 percent of the U.S. gross national product; by 1943 that percentage had grown to over 35 percent. In the ATLANTIC CHARTER, signed by Franklin D. Roosevelt and the British prime minister Winston Churchill on 9 August 1941, both leaders paid lip service to "lighten[ing] . . . the crushing burden of armaments," but this was for appearances only. Both men were determined to achieve and maintain peace this time through military force, not any "scrap of paper." World War II also sowed the seeds for the largest arms competition in history, the Cold War nuclear arms race. The United States and Britain ignored the advice of scientists such as Niels Bohr and chose not to inform their wartime ally, the Soviet Union, of the crash Anglo-American MANHATTAN PROJECT to develop the atomic bomb. Numerous Soviet spies kept the Soviet dictator Joseph Stalin well informed throughout the war, however, and this only increased his already substantial paranoia about Western postwar intentions. Thus even before World War II was over, preparations for a possible world war III had already begun.

The Cold War: "Massive Retaliation," 1945–1962

Pressures for worldwide postwar disarmament were immediate and intense. World War II was even more destructive than World War I, and the atomic bombings of Hiroshima and Nagasaki made it plain to all that the next time around entire nations might be annihilated. Peace groups of private citizens came to the natural conclusion that the only solution was the complete prevention of all war and that this was only possible through the creation of one world government. But for a variety of reasons this was of course an impossibility in 1945. World leaders did create the UNITED NATIONS (UN), but the possession of veto power in the Security Council by both the United States and the Soviet Union meant that any dispute between the two would lead only to stalemate in the UN. Any successful international agreement to control atomic energy would require an enormous amount of mutual trust, and by 1947 trust was a scarce commodity in Soviet-American relations. Though for propaganda purposes both sides kept up the appearance of serious disarmament negotiations, neither thought it was a realistic possibility during these earliest and most intense days of the Cold War.

In 1945 the United States had yet again conducted a massive demobilization of its wartime armed forces. By default military planners were therefore forced to rely on the American monopoly on NUCLEAR WEAPONS for the deterrence of future war. Should deterrence fail and a war with the Soviet Union ensue, the plan was simple: strike at Soviet industry and morale by dropping the entire American stockpile of atomic bombs on Soviet cities. To this end the United States concentrated its military resources into the U.S. Air Force's new Strategic Air Command and proceeded to encircle the Soviet Union with bases from which to launch its medium- and long-range bombers. In August 1949 the Soviet Union tested its first atomic bomb, which thanks to Soviet espionage was a near copy of the first American plutonium bomb. This came several years before expected by the United States and only redoubled determination within the United States to continue expansion of its nuclear arsenal. Emphasis on the atomic air offensive that would take place at the outset of war increased, except now the highest priority was to preempt Soviet nuclear capabilities by striking so hard that no reply was possible, something that

came to be called a "successful first strike." In addition to the Soviet nuclear test, the world in 1949 and 1950 experienced the twin shocks of Communist victory in the Chinese civil war and the North Korean invasion of South Korea in June 1950. Later that year President Harry S. Truman reluctantly approved a massive increase in military spending, and within one year the defense budget of the richest nation in the world had tripled.

Developments in the nuclear arms race came at a dizzying rate throughout the rest of the decade. In 1950 Truman approved the construction of a hydrogen bomb, a weapon of potentially unlimited power. When the United States tested the first of this new category of "thermonuclear" weapons in November 1952, the resulting explosion was over eight hundred times as powerful as the bomb dropped on Hiroshima. By November 1955 the Soviet Union had perfected the design of its own "superbomb." American defense spending was reined in to some degree beginning in 1953 by the administration of Dwight D. Eisenhower, as it attempted to get more "bang for the buck" by relying yet again more on nuclear than on conventional forces. This policy, which came to be known as "massive retaliation," came under increasing domestic criticism by the late 1950s, however. The unexpected Soviet test of an intercontinental ballistic missile (ICBM) in August 1957 provoked fears of a "missile gap" and threatened to reduce the potential warning time of an enemy attack from hours to minutes, raising the specter of a "nuclear Pearl Harbor." By 1961 it had become apparent, however, that despite this the United States did in fact retain its substantial lead in the nuclear arms race, including in the number and quality of intermediate- and long-range missiles. In his 1961 farewell address Eisenhower cautioned the nation about the increasing influence of what he called the MILITARY-INDUSTRIAL COMPLEX. Few were in the mood to heed this warning, however, until the world came perilously close to nuclear war during the October 1962 CUBAN MISSILE CRISIS.

The Cold War: "Mutual Assured Destruction," 1962–1990

Political leaders around the world were deeply shaken by what McGeorge Bundy has called the "nuclear danger" they glimpsed during the Cuban Missile Crisis, and for the first time since the 1920s meaningful arms control seemed again a realistic possibility. A "hot line" was established to enable virtual immediate communication between the White House and the Kremlin, and in 1963 the superpowers agreed to the Limited Test Ban Treaty, banning all aboveground nuclear tests. By the mid-1960s defense intellectuals argued that the point of diminishing returns had been reached and that additional American nuclear weapons would only marginally increase the destruction that would be visited upon the Soviet Union in a general war. Secretary of Defense Robert S. McNamara announced that the American goal of "assured destruction" had been reached, and from the 1960s through the end of the Cold War the number of American ICBMs

Moscow Summit. President Richard Nixon (*left*) exchanges signed copies of the historic SALT agreement with Soviet leader Leonid Brezhnev in May 1972. © CORBIS

and submarine-launched ballistic missiles (SLBMs) remained remarkably constant (at approximately 1,000 and 650, respectively). The expansion of Soviet nuclear capabilities continued at a rapid rate, however, and by the early 1970s it had become apparent that literally tens of millions of Americans would likely die in any general nuclear exchange with the Soviet Union. The assured destruction was now mutual, leading to the apt acronym MAD.

By the 1970s both sides were looking for economic relief from over two decades of continuous arms race, and given the rough parity that finally existed, neither side thought it had much of a lead left to protect. In the 1972 STRATEGIC ARMS LIMITATION TALKS (SALT) agreement, each superpower agreed to limits on its future ICBM production. The associated Anti-Ballistic Missile (ABM) Treaty also severely restricted the deployment of and even future research on defenses against missile attack. Arms control was now a virtual Cold War obsession, with the world's attention focused on each dramatic new "summit" between Soviet and American leaders. In 1979 the two sides agreed in the SALT II agreement on a more comprehensive series of restrictions, including for the first time limits on the ability of either side to deploy multiple warheads (MIRVs) on individual missiles. In the wake of the 1979 Soviet invasion of Afghanistan, however, the U.S. Senate refused to ratify SALT II, and that year President Jimmy Carter announced a dramatic increase in American military spending.

In 1981 Ronald Reagan was elected to the presidency amid promises that the United States would "catch up" to the Soviet Union in the arms race. He publicly labeled the Soviet Union an "evil empire," and following a series of crises in 1983, the Cold War reached its most dangerous period since 1962. Nuclear freeze or "ban the bomb" movements around the world reached unprecedented levels of popularity, and fears of nuclear war soared. In 1983 Reagan called for the creation of a massive new antimissile

defense system, the STRATEGIC DEFENSE INITIATIVE. Just as the arms race seemed to be reaching a fever pitch, however, Mikhail Gorbachev became the new leader of the Soviet Union and embarked on a program to restructure the Soviet economy in what turned out to be a futile attempt to stave off economic collapse. In the Intermediate Nuclear Forces (INF) Treaty of 1987 the two sides agreed for the first time to actually reduce, as versus simply limit, nuclear armaments. Work proceeded on the more comprehensive Strategic Arms Reduction Talks (START), but before they could be completed, to the surprise of just about everyone, in November 1989 the sudden end of the Cold War was announced to the world by East and West Germans dancing together on the Berlin Wall.

The Post–Cold War World, 1990–
Meaningful arms control now appeared to be finally becoming possible just as it was no longer necessary. In the 1990s Russia and the United States agreed to massive cuts in their respective nuclear arsenals through the START and START II agreements. Even though the U.S. Senate refused to ratify the latter, unilateral and voluntary cuts by both sides threatened to make future arms control irrelevant. Attention increasingly turned to the prevention of the proliferation of "weapons of mass destruction," that is, nuclear, chemical, and biological weapons, to states beyond those that already possessed them, continuing a process begun by the 1968 NUCLEAR NONPROLIFERATION TREATY. The 1996 Comprehensive Test Ban Treaty promised to make the worldwide ban on nuclear tests complete, but in 1999 the Senate, concerned that verification might prove impossible, refused to ratify it. Following the terrorist attacks of September 2001, arms races and state-to-state arms control seemed suddenly less relevant in a world where individuals, not governments, might be the greatest threats of all.

BIBLIOGRAPHY

Bundy, McGeorge. *Danger and Survival: Choices about the Bomb in the First Fifty Years.* New York: Random House, 1988. Thoughtful combination of history and memoir.

Burns, Richard Dean, ed. *Encyclopedia of Arms Control and Disarmament.* 3 vols. New York: Scribner, 1993.

Dingman, Roger. *Power in the Pacific: The Origins of Naval Arms Limitation, 1914–1922.* Chicago: University of Chicago Press, 1976.

Evangelista, Matthew. *Innovation and the Arms Race: How the United States and the Soviet Union Develop New Military Technologies.* Ithaca, N.Y.: Cornell University Press, 1988. Political science case study focusing on tactical nuclear weapons.

Federation of American Scientists. "Weapons of Mass Destruction." Available http://www.fas.org/nuke/index.html. Detailed, heavily illustrated information on arms control and nuclear, chemical, and biological weapons.

Garthoff, Raymond L. *Détente and Confrontation: American–Soviet Relations from Nixon to Reagan.* Rev. ed. Washington, D.C.: Brookings Institution, 1994. First published in 1985.

Glynn, Patrick. *Closing Pandora's Box: Arms Races, Arms Control, and the History of the Cold War.* New York: Basic Books, 1992. Conservative perspective on arms control.

McDougall, Walter A. *The Heavens and the Earth: A Political History of the Space Age.* New York: Basic Books, 1985.

Millett, Allan R., and Peter Maslowski. *For the Common Defense: A Military History of the United States of America.* Rev. and expanded. New York: Free Press, 1994. Military policy in peace as well as war. First published in 1984.

Newhouse, John. *War and Peace in the Nuclear Age.* New York: Knopf, 1989. Politics of arms control.

Rosen, Stephen Peter. *Winning the Next War: Innovation and the Modern Military.* Ithaca, N.Y.: Cornell University Press, 1991. Twentieth-century case studies.

Wittner, Lawrence S. *The Struggle against the Bomb: A History of the World Nuclear Disarmament Movement.* 3 vols. Stanford, Calif.: Stanford University Press, 1993–.

David Rezelman

See also **Army, U.S.; Cold War; Hydrogen Bomb; Navy, U.S.; Nuclear Weapons;** *and vol. 9:* **Eisenhower's Farewell Address.**

ARMY, CONFEDERATE. On 6 March 1861 the Confederate Provisional Congress established the Army of the Confederate States of America. This army, poorly organized when the war began, was soon overshadowed by the volunteer forces known officially as the Provisional Army. On 28 February and 6 March the Confederate Congress gave the president control over military operations and the power to muster state forces and volunteers. On 8 May it authorized enlistments for the war, and on 8 August, after four more states had joined the Confederacy, it called for 400,000 volunteers to serve for either one or three years. In April 1862, congressmen passed the first conscription act, which drafted men directly into the Provisional Army.

The decentralized political structure of the Confederacy forced lawmakers to clarify its military chain of command from the start. On 16 May 1861 the Confederate congress established the rank of general to give Confederate commanders control over state troops. Under an act passed on 28 February 1861, the military gained the power to appoint major generals in the Provisional Army. Finally, in September 1862, Confederate legislators created the rank of lieutenant general in the Provisional Army.

The Confederacy faced serious challenges outfitting its troops and planning a vast military campaign throughout the Civil War. The government had little access to modern weaponry and was forced to hire privateers to run the Union blockade and purchase arms abroad. The fledgling government also faced the task of procuring shoes, clothing, and blankets for soldiers at a time when wool and leather were scarce. Furthermore, the region's dearth of railroads and canals made it difficult for the government to ship goods and to feed its troops. The South's weak infrastructure also affected Confederate military

strategy. By 1863, horses and mules were scarce, which limited the mobility of the army's cavalry, artillery, and baggage trains. These difficulties were exacerbated by a divided leadership structure that limited prompt coordination between military departments. All of these challenges dictated how Confederate generals would wage war against Union leaders, who could draw recruits from a larger population and enjoyed access to better transportation and resources.

Because of incomplete surviving records, the number of enlistments in the Confederate armies has long been in dispute. The U.S. census for 1860 indicates approximately 1,100,000 men of military age in the seceded states, but these figures are deceptive. Many sections where hostility to the Confederacy developed furnished few soldiers, while other areas of the South were overrun by Union armies. Exemptions, details for industrial work, and other evasions of service also cut down enlistments. Probably between 800,000 and 900,000 men actually enrolled in the Confederate army. Consolidated returns in the war department showed the following figures:

	Total present and absent	Total present	Total effective present for duty
31 Dec. 1862	449,439	304,015	253,208
31 Dec. 1863	464,646	277,970	233,586
31 Dec. 1864	400,787	196,016	154,910

The state militia, serving short terms, uncertain in number, and of dubious value, probably fell short of 100,000 at any given date. In April and May 1865, losses from battle, disease, capture, and desertion had so devastated the Confederate army that only 174,223 soldiers surrendered to Union forces.

BIBLIOGRAPHY

Carter, Dan T. *When the War Was Over: The Failure of Self-Reconstruction in the South, 1865–1867.* Baton Rouge: Louisiana State University Press, 1985.

Harsh, Joseph L. *Confederate Tide Rising: Robert E. Lee and the Making of Southern Strategy, 1861–1862.* Kent, Ohio: Kent State University Press, 1998.

Linderman, Gerald F. *Embattled Courage: The Experience of Combat in the American Civil War.* New York: Free Press, 1987.

Royster, Charles. *The Destructive War: William Tecumseh Sherman, Stonewall Jackson, and the Americans.* New York: Knopf, 1991.

Thomas, Emory M. *The Confederate Nation, 1861–1865.* New York: Harper and Row, 1979.

Eric J. Morser
Charles W. Ramsdell

See also **Confederate States of America; Impressment, Confederate; States' Rights in the Confederacy;** *and vol. 9:* **Robert E. Lee's Farewell to His Army.**

ARMY, UNION. When Confederate forces attacked Fort Sumter, the United States army had barely 16,000 enlisted men and officers. The resignations of Robert E. Lee and other Southern officers had also crippled the military. For the next three years, Northern states desperately passed laws to raise, equip, and train volunteers. By April 1861, state governors had offered some 300,000 such troops to the federal government. President Abraham Lincoln, however, refused to assemble Congress before 4 July. Therefore, with no new legislation to authorize an increase in the army, all of the recruiting fervor of the early spring was wasted.

The 75,000-man militia, which the government called up on 15 April, had only three-month terms of enlistment and was ill prepared when it rushed into battle at Bull Run. The crushing defeat at Bull Run aroused the federal government, and on the very next day (22 July 1861) Congress authorized the creation of a volunteer army of 500,000 men. At first, political generals chosen by the state governors and officers elected by the enlisted men commanded this army. As a result, its discipline and efficiency developed slowly. The army was further plagued by competition between the state governments and the War Department over military supply contracts, which led to graft, high prices, and shoddy products.

The United States had difficulty maintaining even a rudimentary army after the disastrous defeat at Bull Run. The first army had been so badly depleted by disease and battle that on 2 July 1862 the federal government ordered the states to call up an additional 300,000 volunteers. When volunteering proved sluggish, the United States instituted a draft. Although the draft provided just 65,000 men, federal, state, and local bounties lured enough volunteers during the next few months to boost military morale.

Early in 1863 U.S. leaders feared that the army would collapse as a result of heavy casualties, desertions, short-term enlistments, and scanty volunteering. Consequently, Congress passed the Enrollment Act of 3 March 1863 to stimulate volunteering by threat of conscription. Under the act, men of means could either pay a $300 commutation fee or hire someone to take their place. Congress later limited the commutation fee to conscientious objectors, but rich draftees could hire substitutes until the end of the war. The direct product of two years of repeated drafting was about 50,000 conscripts and 120,000 substitutes. In the same period, however, the promise of government bounties lured more than a million volunteers.

Before federal conscription began on 1 January 1863, the Union army numbered just under 700,000 troops. On 1 May 1865, at its highest point, this number reached nearly 800,000. These totals do not include about 200,000 men unfit for active service. Although the Union army was vast, it suffered from political partisanship and inefficiency. Eventually, however, the army weeded out inexperienced political appointees, eliminated regimental elections of officers, and established a greater degree of military discipline. Contract grafts also continued to undermine the army's efficiency, but to a diminishing degree

as the war raged on. Ultimately, the Union army's advantages in manpower, supplies, and access to transportation turned the tide of battle against the Confederacy.

BIBLIOGRAPHY

Linderman, Gerald F. *Embattled Courage: The Experience of Combat in the American Civil War*. New York: Free Press, 1987.

McPherson, James T. *For Cause and Comrades: Why Men Fought in the Civil War*. New York: Oxford University Press, 1997.

Paludan, Phillip S. *A People's Contest: The Union and Civil War, 1961–1865*. New York: Harper and Row, 1988.

Royster, Charles. *The Destructive War: William Tecumseh Sherman, Stonewall Jackson, and the Americans*. New York: Knopf, 1991.

Eric J. Morser
Fred A. Shannon

See also **Bull Run, First Battle of; Peninsular Campaign;** *and* vol. 9: **Letters from Widows to Lincoln Asking for Help.**

ARMY, UNITED STATES, came into being on 14 June 1775 by an act of the Second Continental Congress. The new Continental army sustained the patriot cause in the American Revolution and established several important traditions, including subordination of the army to the civilian government, reliance on citizen-soldiers (militia, volunteers, draftees, and organized reserves) to bolster the regular army in wartime, and a quick return to a small core of professional soldiers during peacetime. The pattern of American war—a sudden and massive buildup of army manpower and material after years of neglect, quickly followed by an equally rapid and sweeping demobilization with the outbreak of peace—persisted for the next 175 years. Breaking with tradition, the U.S. Army after 1945 remained large and in a high state of readiness even in peacetime due to the Cold War. Even with the disintegration of the Communist bloc in 1989 and the collapse of the Soviet Union, the U.S. Army has remained the preeminent army in the world.

Missions

Historically the U.S. Army has performed a variety of missions, among them homeland defense, expeditionary military efforts, scientific and humanitarian duties, and the restoration of domestic order.

The army's most fundamental mission is to safeguard the lives, property, and territorial rights of the United States and its citizens. The army was called to homeland defense against the forces of Great Britain in the American Revolutionary War (1775–1783) and the WAR OF 1812 (1812–1815). One might also include in this category the American CIVIL WAR (1861–1865), although the federal government led by President Abraham Lincoln never recognized the southern Confederacy as a sovereign state. However, it took nearly four years of bloody conflict before the federal Army of the Union subdued the rebellious eleven southern states and restored, in fact as well as in law, the political integrity of the nation. Following the Civil War, the increasingly close relationship between the United States and its two neighbors, Canada and Mexico, gave the nation a high degree of continental security, although the army continued to man dozens of coastal installations. The army also served a constabulary role on the expanding frontier, which frequently brought it into conflict with Native Americans.

U.S. foreign policy, especially since the late-nineteenth century, has often required the army to fulfill international missions. Expeditionary armies fought in major declared wars such as the SPANISH-AMERICAN WAR (1898), WORLD WAR I (1917–1918), and WORLD WAR II (1941–1945), as well as large-scale but undeclared wars including the KOREAN WAR (1950–1953), VIETNAM WAR (1957–1975), and PERSIAN GULF WAR OF 1991 (1991). The army has intervened to rescue American citizens (such as the BOXER REBELLION in China in 1900) and mounted campaigns to retaliate for the loss of American lives and property, including the PUNITIVE EXPEDITION INTO MEXICO in 1916–1917, an unsuccessful attempt to capture the bandit Francisco (Pancho) Villa. In the twentieth century, the army has fought counterinsurgency wars (such as in the Philippines in 1898–1899, Central America and the Caribbean between the 1910s and 1930s, and Southeast Asia in the early 1960s) and acted as a peacekeeping force in dysfunctional societies (such as Haiti in 1994 and Bosnia in 1995).

The army has promoted scientific discovery and national development. The U.S. Army academy at West Point, founded in 1802, has helped train generations of engineers and scientists. When the United States acquired the Louisiana Purchase, it was an army expedition led by two officers, Captain Meriwether Lewis and Lieutenant William Clark, which first explored the territory in an epic three-year journey (1804–1806). As the nation expanded from east to west over the next several decades, army engineers surveyed for roads, canals, and railroads and constructed bridges, public buildings, telegraph lines, and aqueducts. The most famous and complex engineering project the army oversaw was the Panama Canal, completed in 1914. Between the 1880s and 1918, the army also helped survey and administer the emerging system of national parks to promote conservation and recreation. During the Great Depression in the 1930s, the army played a central role in developing the CIVILIAN CONSERVATION CORPS, a New Deal program to give men work on conservation projects. In the Cold War era, the army contributed to the space program and researched new materials and technology that also had consumer applications.

In times of great civil disorder, the army sometimes helped civilian agencies restore public authority and safety. It dispersed the WHISKEY REBELLION of 1794 in western Pennsylvania when angry farmers rebelled against excise taxes on liquor and stills, attempted to stop a guerrilla war between pro- and antislavery forces that began

in Kansas in 1854, and mobilized to stop the violence and destruction of property during the great RAILROAD STRIKE OF 1877. Between 1863 and 1877, the army also acted as an administrator and constabulary force in the South during RECONSTRUCTION, supervising the reintegration of the confederate states into the union, distributing aid to former slaves through the Freedmen's Bureau, and enforcing (albeit with limited effect) the new rights of black citizens. Nearly a century later, when the federal government enforced the racial integration of Central High School in Little Rock, Arkansas, in 1957, paratroopers helped enact the law. In times of dire emergency, the army has contributed manpower, expertise, and equipment to cope with natural disasters such as tornadoes, floods, forest fires, and earthquakes as well as man-made disasters such as riots and terrorist attacks.

Organization

The organization of the army has changed dramatically since 1775, influenced by tactical innovations, technological improvements, and financial and political debates within the government.

During the American Revolution, the basic tactical unit was the brigade, composed of several regiments each recruited from a specific colony. Each brigade of between 1,000 and 2,500 men was either named for its commander or given a numerical designation. Most Continental soldiers were infantry, supported by a smaller number of artillery and cavalry units. Commanders relied on a few personal aides to carry out staff work, and many officers were chosen on the basis of their social standing, political connections, or financial resources. The support elements, such as quartermaster and medical details, were typically formed on an ad hoc basis with civilian laborers.

Immediately following the Revolutionary War, the army shrank to a mere 718 men because Congress saw a large standing army as inimical to democracy and ruinously expensive. However, the continued threat from hostile Indians and European powers with territorial ambitions in North America convinced Congress to gradually expand the army, while the new Constitution passed in 1789 gave the federal government more power to legislate and tax on behalf of national defense. In the years between 1792 and 1796, the army expanded to more than 5,000 men organized into a single legion, a mixed tactical formation with infantry, artillery, and cavalry. The legion proved to be unwieldy, however, and in 1796 the army adopted the regiment as its basic tactical formation, a system of organization that would persist until the twentieth century.

During the War of 1812 against Great Britain, volunteers and federalized militia supplemented regulars to form ad hoc field armies, often with minimal logistical support and widely divergent standards of discipline and drill. Although Congress authorized the army to grow to 35,000 men, with an additional 50,000 volunteers and

Winfield Scott. The supreme commander of the U.S. Army from 1841 to 1861 (*on horseback, waving his hat*) leads regulars and volunteers to victory at Contreras, Mexico, 20 August 1847, en route to his capture of Mexico City. LIBRARY OF CONGRESS

100,000 militia, the actual size of field armies was rarely more than several thousand during any campaign.

In the years between 1815 and 1846, the army retained an average strength of little more than 6,000 men, mostly occupied with Indian wars and garrison duty. With the outbreak of war against Mexico in 1846, Congress called for 50,000 volunteers rather than expand the regular army. Through the next two years of conflict, the expeditionary armies in Mexico—the largest was just 12,000 men—were a mixture of well-trained regulars and eager but unruly volunteers.

America's next conflict, the Civil War, exceeded all previous wars in size and intensity. The federal army, only 16,000 at the outbreak of war in April 1861, expanded with a massive stream of new soldiers—volunteers, mostly—and eventually surpassed one million men on active duty in May 1865. The Union organized field armies as large as 100,000 men, and most regiments were made up of soldiers from a particular state or region, often with a distinctive ethnic or racial identity (including the first African-American combat regiments).

The army shrank again quickly after the Civil War, falling to 54,302 in 1866 and then just 27,442 by 1876. When war broke out with Spain in April 1898, Congress authorized a call for 200,000 volunteers, only some of which joined the regulars to see action in Cuba (although more of the volunteers saw action against guerrillas in the Philippines).

The Spanish-American War revealed serious tactical and logistical shortcomings in the army that Secretary of War Elihu Root pledged to reform in 1903. Under his guidance, the army created a general staff—a permanent headquarters of senior-level officers—to develop doctrine and to plan for future conflicts. Although the army made great strides in training and organization over the next decade, it was still far too small for the task when the United States entered World War I in April 1917.

The wartime army drew upon three sources—an expanded regular army, the federalized National Guard, and the draftees of the National Army—to eventually reach a total of 1.3 million men. Forces were organized around a large, "square" division (28,000 men divided into two brigades with two regiments each) to compensate for the lack of officers, to maximize firepower, and to build a unit that could handle sustained combat. The army grew to sixty-four divisions during World War I, forty-three of which deployed to Europe. Airplane and tank units were added during the war, new technologies that would revolutionize the battlefield in the twentieth century.

At the conclusion of the war troop strength declined once again, and by 1922 its size was only 144,000 officers and men. The isolationist and fiscally conservative policies of the 1920s and 1930s kept the army small, but the totalitarian menace of Germany, Japan, and Italy led to its expansion once again with the Selective Training and Service Act of 1940. When the United States entered the war in December 1941, there were already 1.6 million men in the army, organized around "triangular" divisions averaging 12,000 men that offered better mobility and command efficiency than the "square" divisions of World War I. In 1943, the air services became a semi-independent branch called the U.S. Army Air Forces. During the war, the army fielded eighty-nine divisions (one light, one cavalry, five airborne, sixteen armored, and sixty-six infantry) within a total strength of 7.7 million personnel. Sixty-eight divisions fought in the European theater and twenty-one in the Pacific.

Although the army shed much of its strength following Japan's surrender in September 1945, the emergence of the Cold War halted and then reversed the decline. The number of active divisions fell from eighty-nine in 1945 to just twelve in 1947—the Air Force also became a fully independent service branch on 18 September of that year—but rising tensions with the communist world and the outbreak of the Korean War in June 1950 spurred a major rebuilding effort. The army committed eight combat divisions and formally abolished racial segregation in its units during the war. By 1953 it had grown to 1.5 million men, and even when the war ended Congress retained a force of one million on active duty.

Between 1956 and 1960, the army experimented with a "pentomic" division structure based on five battle groups designed to operate on an atomic battlefield. The formation proved unsuitable and a new, more flexible division structure was adopted in 1961. The so-called ROAD division was organized around brigade task forces adaptable to a wide range of missions, ranging from atomic to unconventional warfare.

Between 1961 and 1972, the army fought a major conflict in South Vietnam that required at its peak the equivalent of nine combat divisions and nearly 361,000 men (out of a total strength of 1.5 million), and developed a new kind of "airmobile" division based around helicopters for greater mobility. A drawdown after the war reduced manpower to 650,000 men, and the end of the draft in 1973 transformed the army into an all-volunteer force. Changing social mores and more opportunities in the army led to a growing number of women to join.

After a period of turmoil following Vietnam, the army began to rebuild in the 1980s as tensions rose again with the Soviets. When the Warsaw Pact collapsed in 1989, the army devoted more attention to the unstable Middle East region. Following Iraq's invasion and occupation of Kuwait in August 1990, the army committed

"I Want You!" Artist and illustrator James Montgomery Flagg's famous painting—created during World War I—is the model for this U.S. Army recruitment sign photographed in 1961. AP/WIDE WORLD PHOTOS

the equivalent of seven divisions and nearly 300,000 soldiers. The Persian Gulf War culminated with the retaking of Kuwait in February 1991, accomplished in fewer than 100 hours of ground combat. In the decade after the war, the army evolved into a smaller, leaner organization—471,000 personnel in 2001—but continued to fulfill a wide variety of global missions, including peacekeeping efforts, special operations training, and preparations for conventional war.

Following the terrorist attacks against the World Trade Center in New York City and the Pentagon in Washington, D.C., on 11 September 2001, the army began preparing for war against the Al Qaeda terrorist network and its state sponsors. Between October and December 2001, Army Special Forces soldiers played a key role in defeating the Taliban regime of Afghanistan, the primary state sponsor of Osama bin Laden's Al Qaeda network, by directing air strikes against the enemy and by helping to organize friendly Afghan troops. When Army conventional forces, particularly from the 101st Airborne

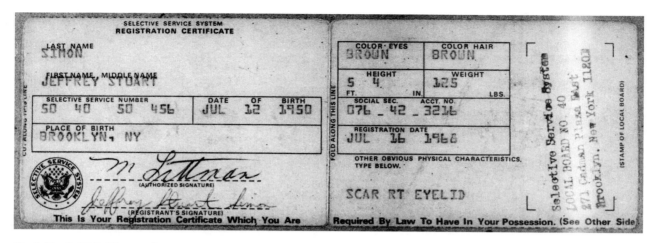

Draft Card, 1968. Heavy reliance on conscription during the Vietnam War resulted in widespread resistance to the draft—and the imprisonment of some protesters for burning their draft cards. AP/WIDE WORLD PHOTOS

and Tenth Mountain Divisions, began operating in Afghanistan, they enjoyed considerable success in damaging and disrupting the Al Qaeda network, an effort that continues and will likely last for many years.

BIBLIOGRAPHY

Hogan, David W., Jr. *225 Years of Service: The U.S. Army, 1775–2000.* Washington, D.C.: Center of Military History, United States Army, 2000.

Millett, Allan R., and Peter Maslowski. *For the Common Defense: A Military History of the United States of America.* Rev. ed. New York: Free Press, 1994.

Wilson, John B. *Maneuver and Firepower: The Evolution of Divisions and Separate Brigades.* Washington, D.C.: Center of Military History, United States Army, 1998.

Erik B. Villard

See also **Military Service and Minorities; Women in Military Service.**

ARMY OF NORTHERN VIRGINIA.

On 1 June 1862, Confederate President Jefferson Davis personally placed Robert E. Lee in command of the Confederate army and officially designated it the Army of Northern Virginia. Thereafter, until the surrender at Appomattox nearly three years later, Lee commanded this most famous and best known of Confederate armies. During this period, he established his reputation as one of the most skillful of American generals. Likewise, the Army of Northern Virginia became one of the Confederacy's most effective fighting weapons. At its largest, the army consisted of 90,000 soldiers, but by the end of the war, only 8,000 remained.

BIBLIOGRAPHY

Gallagher, Gary W. *Lee and His Generals in War and Memory.* Baton Rouge: Louisiana State University Press, 1998.

Power, J. Tracy. *Lee's Miserables: Life in the Army of Northern Virginia from the Wilderness to Appomattox.* Chapel Hill: University of North Carolina Press, 1998.

Angela Ellis
Thomas Robson Hay

See also **Army, Confederate; Army of Virginia; Civil War; Confederate States of America;** *and vol. 9:* **Robert E. Lee's Farewell to His Army.**

ARMY OF OCCUPATION.

As part of the Allied Army of Occupation, which occupied German territory between 1918 and 1923, the American Third Army crossed into Germany in December 1918 and took up station in the north sector of the Coblenz bridgehead. Units of the Third Army were stationed at various points within the American area of control and engaged in duties of the occupation, which included participation in civil administration of German territory. The Third Army was discontinued on 2 July 1919 and was eventually succeeded by the "American Forces in Germany."

Major General Edward F. McGlachlin Jr. commanded this newly designated force until 8 July 1919, when its permanent commander, Major General Henry T. Allen, arrived in Germany. From January 1920, Allen worked with the Rhineland High Commission to govern the occupied territory. At noon on 27 January 1923, Allen relinquished command, and American troops ended their occupation of Germany.

BIBLIOGRAPHY

Allen, Henry T. *The Rhineland Occupation.* Indianapolis, Ind.: Bobbs-Merrill, 1927.

Fraenkel, Ernst. *Military Occupation and Rule of Law: Occupation Government in the Rhineland, 1918–1923.* New York: Oxford University Press, 1944.

Keegan, John. *The First World War.* New York: Knopf, 1999.

Eric J. Morser
Robert S. Thomas

See also **Germany, Relations with.**

ARMY OF THE JAMES, in existence from April to December 1864, consisted of the Tenth and the Eighteenth Corps, commanded by Union general B. F. Butler. It constituted the left wing of General Ulysses S. Grant's army. Butler received instructions to occupy City Point, threaten Richmond, and await Grant's arrival in the James River region of Virginia, but Confederate troops checked his army at Drewry's Bluff and bottled it up at Bermuda Hundred. Most of his command later transferred to the Army of the Potomac and served, usually under General E. O. C. Ord, until the Confederate surrender at Appomattox.

BIBLIOGRAPHY

McPherson, James M. *Battle Cry of Freedom: The Civil War Era.* Volume 6, *Oxford History of the United States.* New York: Oxford University Press, 1988.

Thomas Robson Hay/c. w.

See also **Appomattox; Army of the Potomac; Civil War.**

ARMY OF THE POTOMAC. In 1861 the U.S. Congress created the Army of the Potomac to protect Washington, D.C., from advancing Confederate forces. The demoralization of the Union army after its defeat at the First Battle of Bull Run on 21 July left Washington undefended and might have proved disastrous had the Confederacy been able to take advantage of its opportunity to strike a fatal blow against the Union. To protect Washington, Congress authorized the Division of the Potomac on 25 July 1861 and placed General George B. McClellan in command two days later. The division's immediate purpose was to guard the approaches to the Potomac River and thus to protect the capital city from attack. McClellan fell heir to "a collection of undisciplined, ill officered, and uninstructed men," already demoralized by defeat. On 1 August there were only about 37,000 infantry in the ranks, and the terms of many regiments were expiring. Four months later, there were some 77,000 effectives available for active operations, aside from regiments on garrison and other duty. For the next year, McClellan would mold the ragtag division into a modern army.

McClellan's first job was to whip this heterogeneous mass of raw recruits into an effective fighting unit. The trainees came from all walks of life and every part of the country. Some were volunteers from foreign nations, and many could not speak English. McClellan was hampered by ineffectual generals appointed for political purposes, the officious meddling and machinations of government leaders, and his own temperament. Nevertheless, in a few months he built one of the most imposing armies in the nation's history and inspired it with a newfound spirit of loyalty.

Although McClellan was an effective military manager, his caution as field commander of the Army of the Potomac crippled the Union military effort early in the war. In April 1862 McClellan's army slowly marched into Virginia to try to capture Richmond, the Confederate capital. Yet, in the Seven Days' Battles of late June and early July, Confederate General Robert E. Lee drove McClellan's vast army into Maryland. On 17 September Lee's army fought McClellan's superior forces to a bloody standstill at the Battle of Antietam. Finally, on 5 November, President Abraham Lincoln, frustrated by McClellan's caution, relieved him of command and replaced him with General John Pope. For the next two years, Union forces were unable to subdue Lee's army in Virginia. Under the command of General George Meade, however, the Army of the Potomac defeated Lee's Confederate force at Gettysburg in July 1863 and helped turn the tide of the war in favor of the Union.

BIBLIOGRAPHY

Paludan, Phillip S. *A People's Contest: The Union and Civil War, 1861–1865.* New York: Harper and Row, 1988.

Rowland, Thomas J. *George B. McClellan and Civil War History: In the Shadow of Grant and Sherman.* Kent, Ohio: Kent State University Press, 1998.

Sears, Stephen W. *Controversies and Commanders: Dispatches from the Army of the Potomac.* Boston: Houghton Mifflin, 1999.

Eric J. Morser
Fred A. Shannon

See also **Bull Run, First Battle of; Bull Run, Second Battle of; Peninsular Campaign.**

ARMY OF VIRGINIA constituted 26 June 1862, consisted of the corps of Union generals John C. Frémont, Nathaniel P. Banks, and Irvin McDowell, with General John Pope as commander. Union strategy called for Pope to drive General Robert E. Lee out of Richmond. The Confederate army marched northward to oppose Pope. Union General George B. McClellan's Army of the Potomac came to Pope's aid. Lee's troops defeated the combined Union armies in the second Bull Run campaign, fought 29 and 30 August 1862, and forced them to retreat into Washington. Pope lost his command, and the Union broke up the Army of Virginia and dispersed it.

BIBLIOGRAPHY

Cozzens, Peter. *General John Pope: A Life for the Nation.* Urbana: University of Illinois Press, 2000.

Schutz, Wallace J. *Abandoned by Lincoln: A Military Biography of General John Pope.* Urbana: University of Illinois Press, 1990.

Angela Ellis
Thomas Robson Hay

See also **Bull Run, Second Battle of; Seven Days' Battles; Virginia, Army of Northern.**

ARMY ON THE FRONTIER. From the founding of the nation through the end of the nineteenth century, the U.S. Army played a crucial role in American westward expansion. During this time, Americans generally feared a large standing army as a potential instrument of oppression, so the regular army deliberately was kept small in relation to the total population and was divided between coastal fortifications and the frontier. Along the frontier, the zone of contact between the settled portions of the country and the uncharted territory inhabited by the various American Indian nations, the army was first and foremost an agent of expansion. One of the army's primary duties was exploration. Army expeditions, commanded by such notables as Meriwether Lewis and William Clark, Zebulon Pike, Stephen Long, and John C. Frémont, mapped and catalogued the interior of the United States and stirred up American interest in the West. The frontier army also assisted in the rapid settlement of the frontier. Soldiers built forts, constructed paths and roads, laid telegraph cables, built reservoirs and dams, guarded railroad lines, and often served as a frontier constabulary in areas where civilian law had yet to be implemented. Following the American Civil War, many of these menial tasks were assigned to black units, known as buffalo soldiers, while combat was reserved for white troops.

Yet the army's principal and most recognized task on the frontier was the prosecution of federal Indian policy. Along the eastern frontier, the army carried out Indian removal, the government's policy of forcefully removing Indians from desirable areas, as tragically epitomized by the transfer of the Five Civilized Tribes from the southeastern United States to Oklahoma Territory to make way for white settlement. By the late 1840s, the army had essentially cleared the eastern portion of the country of its original inhabitants and assumed an increasing role in the expansion of the United States beyond the Mississippi River. As increasing numbers of settlers poured into the West during the 1840s and 1850s, the army established a regional defense system along the overland trails, composed of forts located at strategic intervals to provide protection and provisions to the migrants.

This system of protected migration worked reasonably well as long as the main wave of settlers bypassed Indian territory in the continent's interior and continued on to the Pacific Coast. Following the close of the Civil War, however, settlers increasingly took an interest in the Great Plains, which brought conflict with the region's Indian inhabitants. As a result of settler-Indian conflicts in the West, the policy of Indian removal was replaced by a new federal agenda that called for the confinement of Native peoples on reservations, usually a barren or otherwise undesirable tract set aside as a permanent Indian refuge. Many Indian tribes refused to surrender their freedom and accept reservation status. They resisted the federal government's attempts to confine them to specific geographical limits, and it fell to the army to force their compliance.

From 1860 to 1886, the army waged war against the western Indians up and down the frontier, although it proved exceedingly difficult to enforce reservation treaties upon the variegated Native population of the West. The frontier army quickly learned that pacifying the Plains Indians was not an easy task. Unless the Indians had greatly superior numbers, they avoided pitched battles, preferring to hit and run, ambush detachments, and cut off stragglers. As frustrations and setbacks mounted, the army turned to a policy of total warfare along the frontier. Beginning with George Armstrong Custer's November 1868 attack on a Cheyenne camp at Washita Creek, Oklahoma, mounted cavalry columns increasingly implemented a strategy devised by General Philip Sheridan, commander of the frontier department after the Civil War, whereby the army attacked the migratory Great Plains tribes in the winter after they had established their stationary seasonal camps along a river or stream. The cavalry attacked the winter villages, killed not only the warriors but also the women and children, and destroyed the Indians' shelter, food, and livestock. Left at the mercy of the elements, most Indians surrendered and moved onto reservations.

The symbolic and literal culmination of this policy occurred on 29 December 1890 near WOUNDED KNEE Creek in South Dakota, when a division of the Seventh Cavalry killed several hundred Lakota Sioux who resisted reservation confinement. These tactics often brought frontier army commanders into conflict with civilian authorities in the nation's capital, particularly the Bureau of Indian Affairs, but the success of the army's tactics in clearing the frontier usually outdistanced concern over its methods.

BIBLIOGRAPHY

Goetzmann, William H. *Army Exploration in the American West, 1803–1863.* Austin: Texas State Historical Association, 1991.

Tate, Michael L. *The Frontier Army in the Settlement of the West.* Norman: University of Oklahoma Press, 1999.

Utley, Robert M. *Frontiersmen in Blue: The United States Army and the Indian, 1848–1865.* New York: Macmillan, 1967.

———. *Frontier Regulars: The United States Army and the Indian, 1866–1891.* New York: Macmillan, 1973.

Daniel P. Barr

See also **Army, United States; Army Posts; Black Cavalry in the West; Black Infantry in the West; Frontier; Frontier Thesis, Turner's; Indian Policy, U.S., 1775–1830; Indian Policy, U.S., 1830–1900; Indian Removal; Indian Reservations; Indian Territory; Westward Migration.**

ARMY POSTS established by the U.S. Army played an important part in the conquest and settlement of western lands by white Americans. In the older, eastern states army posts became centers for recruiting and drilling troops and guardians of the coastline at strategic points.

In contrast to these elaborate structures, forts on the frontier of white settlement were often crudely built and uncomfortable for their inhabitants. Nevertheless, these outposts served as effective tools of economic and military control. Among other things, the army posts enforced the Indian factory system, a system of production and exchange introduced by President THOMAS JEFFERSON as a means of "civilizing" Native Americans. Most importantly, the armed troops and artillery in the forts served as potent bargaining chips during negotiations with Native Americans. Using the promise of protection—or the threat of military force—army officers won important concessions of assistance and land from Native American tribes.

The army built forts slightly in advance of the line of settlement, pushing rapidly into the old NORTHWEST TERRITORY, formerly claimed by the British, after the War of 1812. As Spain and Mexico retreated to the Southwest, army posts followed. By 1845, a line of eleven forts extended from Lake Superior to the Gulf of Mexico. Indian raids during the Civil War, the extension of mail routes, and the completion of railroads to the Pacific Ocean necessitated the building of forts at strategic points.

Regular-army forts accommodated from two to six companies with artillery. They consisted of a quadrangle constructed around a parade ground, with the officers' quarters, barracks, post traders, and hospital on one side and the stables and quartermaster's supplies on the other. The ends of the quadrangle might be occupied by the guardhouse, company kitchens, and workshops, and farther back by the laundresses' quarters. Not all new forts had such elaborate equipment, however. Temporary centers, designated as camps or cantonments, were usually little more than huts or shelters suitable for a few days' stay.

Despite the lack of amenities, life at some frontier posts was pleasant, in peacetime, for younger people. Young WEST POINT men brought their wives, who maintained as far as possible the social standards of their old homes, and "post hops," riding and hunting parties, and card games were held. Gardens and farms were laid out around the posts to provide vegetables, grains, and forage. Flour mills were constructed at such posts as Snelling and Atkinson. Most garrisons had post schools, libraries, newspapers, and magazines.

Settlements grew up around the posts, and towns of the same name frequently remained after army buildings were sold and land was ceded or auctioned off. In a few cases, abandoned posts were made into national reserves.

BIBLIOGRAPHY

Prucha, Francis Paul. *A Guide to the Military Posts of the United States, 1789–1895.* Madison: State Historical Society of Wisconsin, 1964.

Roberts, Robert B. *Encyclopedia of Historic Forts: The Military, Pioneer, and Trading Posts of the United States.* New York: Macmillan, 1988.

Utley, Robert M. *Frontiersmen in Blue: The United States Army and the Indian, 1848–1865.* New York: Macmillan, 1967.

———. *Frontier Regulars: The United States Army and the Indian, 1866–1891.* New York: Macmillan, 1973.

———. *The Indian Frontier of the American West, 1846–1890.* Albuquerque: University of New Mexico Press, 1984.

Carl L. Cannon / A. R.

See also **Army on the Frontier; Frontier Defense; Hays, Fort; Snelling, Fort.**

ARNOLD'S MARCH TO QUEBEC. In the summer of 1775 Colonel Benedict Arnold went to Cambridge, Massachusetts, and laid before Commander in Chief George Washington a plan for attacking Canada. Washington was sympathetic. He assigned a classic route of attack, by way of Lake George, Lake Champlain, and the Richelieu River, to General Richard Montgomery. Washington had just heard of another passage, by way of the Kennebec and Chaudière Rivers, and he assigned this route to Arnold. The journey through the Maine wilderness was one of the most taxing treks of the American Revolution and proved Arnold's tenacity and leadership abilities. On 19 September, Arnold's command left Newburyport, Massachusetts, and went by sea to the Kennebec. There U.S. forces provided two hundred greenwood boats. These bateaux proved ill-equipped to handle the rushing waters of the Kennebec, but Arnold persisted. Arnold also persisted in his march up the Dead River, where he endured ice, snowstorms, and insufficient food and clothing. He continued the march even after one of his majors, Roger Enos, turned back with a fourth of the army. On 28 October, Arnold and his men arrived at the divide between the St. Lawrence and Atlantic watersheds. Arnold plunged ahead with an advance guard while the remainder of his troops were reduced to eating dogs and shoe leather. At Sertigan, Arnold arranged for supplies that refreshed his exhausted detachment so that they were able to go down the Chaudière and reach the St. Lawrence on 9 November 1775.

In the meantime, Montgomery had reached Montreal, but Arnold went on across the St. Lawrence and was in front of Quebec before Montgomery arrived. Guy Carleton, the British commander at Montreal, evacuated his troops and got into Quebec before Montgomery could join Arnold on 2 December. Carleton had twelve hundred men, while the combined American forces numbered scarcely one thousand. Nevertheless, in a blinding snowstorm Montgomery and Arnold assaulted Quebec on the night of 31 December 1775. The effort failed, and Montgomery was killed. Arnold was wounded and soon thereafter was promoted to brigadier general.

BIBLIOGRAPHY

Hatch, Robert McConnell. *Thrust for Canada: The American Attempt on Quebec in 1775 – 1776.* Boston: Houghton Mifflin, 1979.

Martin, James Kirby. *Benedict Arnold, Revolutionary Hero: An American Warrior Reconsidered.* New York: New York University Press, 1997.

Roberts, Kenneth, ed. *March to Quebec: Journals of the Members of Arnold's Expedition.* New York: Doubleday, Doran, 1938.

Randolph G. Adams / F. B.

See also **Burgoyne's Invasion; Ticonderoga, Capture of.**

ARNOLD'S RAID IN VIRGINIA,

actions during the American Revolution. In December 1780 Commander in Chief Sir Henry Clinton of the British armies in North America determined to send an expedition into the Tidewater region of Virginia. Clinton entrusted command of the expedition to Benedict Arnold because he admired Arnold's intrepidity and believed he could induce more Americans to desert. Arriving at Hampton Roads on 30 December, Arnold seized the small boats on the James River and pushed upstream to Westover. Sending John Simcoe's rangers ahead, Arnold moved his own forces to Richmond, which he occupied following a skirmish on 5 January 1781. After destroying the iron foundry at Westham and the American stores at Richmond, Arnold reembarked for Portsmouth, which he fortified and used as a base for raids.

In April, Arnold, now under the command of Major General William Phillips, staged another river raid on the James, this time landing at City Point and proceeding overland to Petersburg. His marauding band sunk a small American fleet at Osborn's on the James, destroyed twelve hundred hogsheads of tobacco in Manchester, and burned flour magazines and mills in Warwick. In May the force fell down to Westover, thence to Brandon. Throughout these movements the British were harassed by the inferior forces of the Marquis de Lafayette and Anthony Wayne. Phillips died at Petersburg on 13 May 1781, and the chief command momentarily devolved on Arnold. Lord Cornwallis arrived with his superior forces and joined Arnold's detachment for the campaign of the summer of 1781.

BIBLIOGRAPHY

Comtois, Pierre. "Virginia Under Threat." *Military History* 11, no. 4 (1994): 54–60.

Randall, William Sterne. *Benedict Arnold.* New York: Morrow, 1990.

Simcoe, John Graves. *A Journal of the Operations of the Queen's Rangers.* New York: New York Times, 1968.

Randolph G. Adams / A. R.

See also **Revolution, American: Military History; Virginia.**

ARNOLD'S TREASON.

Brig. Gen. Benedict Arnold of the Continental army fought for the American cause from Ticonderoga (1775) to Saratoga (1777), but by the spring of 1779 several motives led him to open up a treasonable correspondence with the British headquarters in New York. Arnold felt repeatedly slighted by Congress, he resented authorities in Pennsylvania who had court-martialed him, he needed money, and he was opposed to the French alliance of 1778.

Throughout the rest of 1779 and 1780, he transmitted military intelligence about the American army to the British. On 12 July 1780 he accepted the command at WEST POINT, New York. He demanded £20,000 if he was able to successfully betray West Point. In the event of his failure, Arnold was still assured £10,000 for his allegiance to Britain. He negotiated with Maj. John André, adjutant general of the British army. André visited Arnold on 21 September 1780. The Americans captured André on 23 September, found documents implicating Arnold, and sent them to Gen. George Washington. News of André's capture was also sent to Arnold, thus giving him time to escape down the HUDSON RIVER to the British before he could be arrested for treason. He became a brigadier general in the British army, went to England after the defeat of the British, and died there on 14 June 1801.

BIBLIOGRAPHY

Martin, James Kirby. *Benedict Arnold, Revolutionary Hero: An American Warrior Reconsidered.* New York: New York University Press, 1997.

Randall, Willard Sterne. *Benedict Arnold: Patriot and Traitor.* New York: Morrow, 1990.

Wilson, Barry K. *Benedict Arnold: A Traitor in Our Midst.* Montreal: McGill-Queen's University Press, 2001.

Randolph G. Adams / F. B.

See also **Arnold's March to Quebec; Arnold's Raid in Virginia; Spies; Ticonderoga, Capture of.**

AROOSTOOK WAR

(1838–1839), an undeclared and bloodless war occasioned by the failure of the United States and Great Britain to determine the northeast boundary between New Brunswick and what is now MAINE. After Maine became a state in 1820, the Maine legislature, jointly with Massachusetts, made grants to settlers along both branches of the Aroostook River, ignoring British claims to area in Aroostook County. In 1831, the United States and Great Britain tried to compromise on the boundary by submitting the issue to the king of the Netherlands for review. An agreement was reached, but the U.S. Senate rejected the plan in 1832. In January 1839, a posse of Americans entered the disputed area to oust Canadian lumberjacks working in the region. The Canadians arrested the posse's leader, and within two months 10,000 Maine troops were either encamped along the Aroostook River or were on their way there. At the insistence of Maine congressmen, the federal government voted to provide a force of 50,000 men and $10 million in the event of war. To prevent a clash, General Winfield

Scott was dispatched to negotiate a truce with the lieutenant governor of New Brunswick. Great Britain, convinced of the seriousness of the situation, agreed to a boundary commission, whose findings were incorporated in the Webster-Ashburton Treaty (1842), which also addressed a number of other disputed boundary issues.

BIBLIOGRAPHY

Burrage, Henry S. *Maine and the Northeastern Boundary Controversy.* Portland, Me.: Printed for the State, 1919.

Corey, Albert B. *The Crisis of 1830–1842 in Canadian-American Relations.* New York: Russell & Russell, 1970.

Scott, Geraldine Todd. *Ties of Common Blood: A History of Maine's Northeast Boundary Dispute with Great Britain, 1783–1842.* Bowie, Md.: Heritage Books, 1992.

Elizabeth Ring / h. s.

See also **Great Britain, Relations with.**

ARREST. An arrest occurs when a public officer acting under legal authority detains an individual to answer for a criminal offense. Historically, arrests were also made in connection with civil cases: a court might order a citizen apprehended to ensure that he or she fulfilled a contractual obligation. In modern times, however, a deprivation of physical liberty is usually justified only as an instrument of criminal law enforcement.

Statutes typically authorize federal and state law enforcement officers to arrest suspects and, concomitantly, set limits on that authority. In some jurisdictions, for example, the police are only empowered to make arrests for serious offenses, not for nonviolent misdemeanors or traffic offenses punishable by a fine. More often, legislatures authorize arrests in any circumstance that the Constitution allows officers to take suspects into custody.

The Fourth Amendment to the Constitution guarantees "the right of the people to be secure in their persons, houses, papers, and effects, against unreasonable searches and seizures" and bars the issuance of warrants "but upon probable cause, supported by Oath or affirmation, and particularly describing the place to be searched, and the persons or things to be seized." The meaning of that language is not self-evident. Accordingly, the Supreme Court has fashioned a body of more precise doctrines to implement the Fourth Amendment's fundamental principles. Many of these doctrines bear on police authority to make an arrest.

Although the term "arrest" does not appear in the Fourth Amendment explicitly, the Supreme Court has declined to hold, on that basis alone, that the Fourth Amendment has no application to arrests. The amendment addresses both "searches" and "seizures." The Court has interpreted "seizures" to refer both to the confiscation of property and to the apprehension of persons. An arrest, by the Court's account, is a "seizure of the person." This much of the Court's work is not controversial. The police

must have some authority to make arrests in order to enforce criminal law effectively. Yet an arrest necessarily entails an extraordinary encroachment on individual liberty. It is expected that the Constitution's demand that any arrests the police make must be reasonable restraints on citizens' freedom of movement.

The Fourth Amendment sometimes imposes the same, or similar, restrictions on the authority of the police to search, on the one hand, and their authority to arrest, on the other. For example, the police can conduct a search only if they have probable cause to believe particular evidence will be found. Similarly, the police can make an arrest only if they have probable cause to believe a person has committed or is committing a criminal offense. Yet the rules governing searches do not always apply to arrests. The general rule for searches is that the police cannot routinely rely on their own judgment regarding the existence of probable cause. Whenever there is time, they must explain to a magistrate why they think they will discover evidence in the place they wish to search. The magistrate, in turn, will issue a warrant authorizing the officers to proceed if, in his or her judgment, the facts and circumstances establish probable cause. In the case of an arrest, by contrast, the police can usually proceed on the basis of their own determination of probable cause.

Ideally, it would be better if both searches and arrests were made only after a magistrate concludes that probable cause exists and issues a warrant. Police officers are engaged in detecting crime and apprehending perpetrators. They may believe they have sufficient cause for invading a suspect's privacy or depriving him or her of liberty. But their judgment may be clouded by zeal. Judges are detached from the law enforcement mission, and comparatively neutral. Thus, their judgment may be more reliable. The reason for the distinct treatment of searches and arrests is pragmatic. In the case of a search, the Court has concluded that the value of a judicial determination of probable cause outweighs the costs of requiring police officers to postpone action until they have procured a warrant. A search can typically be delayed without undermining its purpose. The suspect is often unaware that the police intend to conduct a search, and thus, while police take their case to a magistrate, incriminating evidence would not be removed. In the case of an arrest, by contrast, the Court has concluded that delay can jeopardize public safety. The police may need to capture a suspect caught in the act or attempting to flee. If they delay action obtaining a warrant from a magistrate, the suspect may abscond. Accordingly, officers can rely on their own determination of probable cause and make an arrest without benefit of a warrant issued by a judge. This reasoning is not perfectly symmetrical. The usual rule requiring a warrant for a search is subject to exceptions for exigent circumstances. If there is no time to go to a judge before conducting a search, the police typically may proceed on the basis of their own judgment regarding probable cause. There is no mirror-image rule that the police must obtain a warrant to make an arrest when there is time to do so. In the case of an arrest, the Supreme Court has decided that police need a clear rule on which to rely, one subject to no exceptions and requiring additional judgment in the field. That they usually need an arrest warrant is a rule that serves this purpose.

Any significant interference with a person's freedom of movement is a seizure that must be justified in light of the Fourth Amendment. But not every seizure is an arrest implicating the particular Fourth Amendment standard pertaining to arrests: the requirement of probable cause. If the police only stop a person on the street for a brief period, their actions are subject to a different and less rigorous test. The police do not need probable cause to believe that a person has committed or is committing an offense. They need only reasonable suspicion that a crime is in progress. The difference between probable cause and reasonable suspicion is elusive. It is clear, however, that the latter is less demanding. It follows that police may stop a person for a short time on the basis of facts and circumstances that would not justify an arrest.

This distinction has important practical consequences. The Supreme Court has held that police may conduct searches incident to both arrests and "stops." A search incident to an arrest can be extremely thorough. The suspect is about to be transported to a police station for the initiation of a criminal prosecution. The Court has held that the additional intrusion associated with an incidental search for evidence is minimal by comparison. A search incident to an investigative stop, however, must be more limited. By hypothesis, the suspect will be in the officer's presence only temporarily. The point of a search incident to a stop is not to look for evidence that might be incriminating, but rather to safeguard the officer during the encounter. Accordingly, the officer may only "frisk" (pat down) a person's outer clothing to determine whether he or she has a weapon and may reach inside the person's clothing only if the officer feels something that could be a dangerous instrument.

The Supreme Court has held that evidence obtained by means of an invalid stop or arrest usually must be excluded if and when the person is charged and brought to trial. The rationale of the "exclusionary rule" is that police must be discouraged from disregarding Fourth Amendment limits on their authority. If they know that evidence discovered during an invalid stop or arrest will be inadmissible, they will have an incentive to behave properly (and thus to secure evidence that *can* be used to prove a suspect's guilt). Accordingly, if the police obtain incriminating evidence when they search a person they have detained, it is crucial to determine whether the original seizure of that person was a stop or an arrest. If it was a stop, the evidence will be admissible at trial as long as the police took action on the basis of reasonable suspicion. If it was an arrest, the evidence will be admissible only if the police took action on the basis of probable cause.

BIBLIOGRAPHY

LaFave, Wayne R. *Search and Seizure: A Treatise on the Fourth Amendment.* Rev. ed. St. Paul, Minn.: West, 1996.

Larry Yackle

See also **Civil Rights and Liberties; Police Power; Search and Seizure, Unreasonable.**

ARREST, ARBITRARY, DURING THE CIVIL WAR.

Freedom from arbitrary arrest, guaranteed in the writ of habeas corpus, has long been a centerpiece of American civil liberties. During the Civil War, however, President Abraham Lincoln suspended habeas corpus and arrested antiwar protesters to suppress dissent. Under presidential orders, the federal government required residents to carry passports, organized a secret service, and cooperated with local police to apprehend suspects. The government also circumvented the civil liberties of political prisoners. Although federal officials usually detained suspects for only short periods, they did so without any regular hearings.

Furthermore, the federal government sometimes used military commissions to try civilians for their crimes. Although the Supreme Court did not question the power of such commissions during the war, their use outside the war zone for the trial of civilians was declared unconstitutional after the war. High-ranking politicians were not immune from conviction; federal agents imprisoned several prominent politicians, including the mayors of Baltimore and Washington, D.C., Congressman Henry May, and former Kentucky governor Charles S. Morehead, as well as many Northern newspaper editors. Historians do not know exactly how many people the government arrested for antiwar protests during the Civil War, although estimates vary from just over 13,000 to as many as 38,000. Chief Justice Roger B. Taney and other jurists questioned Lincoln's actions and held that only Congress could suspend habeas corpus. The president, however, defended his position in a series of open letters and continued to arrest antiwar protesters, even after 3 March 1863, when federal lawmakers required the government to release or subject political prisoners to regular judicial procedure.

The Confederacy likewise made summary arrests to suppress disloyalty. The Confederacy's success was small, however, not only because political prisoners became popular martyrs but also because numerous champions of states' rights resisted Confederate policy.

BIBLIOGRAPHY

Duker, William F. *A Constitutional History of Habeas Corpus.* Westport, Conn.: Greenwood Press, 1980.

Neely, Mark E., Jr. *The Fate of Liberty: Abraham Lincoln and Civil Liberties.* New York: Oxford University Press, 1991.

Martin P. Claussen
Eric J. Morser

See also **Copperheads; Habeas Corpus, Writ of; Vallandigham Incident.**

ART

This entry includes 10 subentries:
Decorative Arts
Glass
Interior Decoration
Interior Design
Painting
Photography
Pottery and Ceramics
Sculpture
Self-Taught Artists
Stained Glass Windows

DECORATIVE ARTS

The distinction between the fine arts and the "decorative" is mostly arbitrary. It was not made until eighteenth-century Europeans decided to do so, allowing fine art to gain an aura of associated mystique. Today the distinction is a familiar one, if not a clear one. The decorative arts are viewed as more craft based, serving or alluding to a function. While the categories of decorative arts are vast, fine craftsmanship seems to be the single unifier. Craftsmanship is more than technical virtuosity. It demands a profound understanding of materials and of the tools with which those materials are fashioned.

Probably the single most important factor in the creation of the decorative arts is the maker's genuine pride in the process of production, the need to make things as well as they can be made. At a purely utilitarian level, this drive to achieve perfection might seem excessive, but it is very human. However, it may well disappear in the face of consumer demand. Often, consumer goods are not made as well as they could be, nor do they last as long as they could be made to last, but these are careful adaptations to the economics of the market. Few if any machine-made products are designed to last forever, allowing for new and improved products to be designed and built with the same purpose but a different look.

Early Colonial Style

During the early colonial period, America imported its consumer products and craftsmen from Europe, resulting in the same pieces on both sides of the Atlantic. Any products made in the colonies had very similar designs to those found in the maker's originating culture. As local manufacturers became more prominent, slight modifications on the original designs began to appear. As the wealth of the colonies increased, initially in the South, so did the demand for quality furniture. A variety of indigenous soft and hardwoods, such as pine, birch, maple, oak, hickory, and later walnut, were readily available to colonial furniture craftsmen. With each ship new furniture forms arrived, including cane-back, slat-back, and leather-back chairs, as well as the upholstered chairs better known as easy chairs. Three styles came from England: William and Mary (c. 1700–1725) is an adaptation of the Baroque; Queen Anne (c. 1725–1760) is a refined Baroque with a greater aware-

Chippendale Chest-on-Chest. A double chest of drawers made in Philadelphia from a design by the eminent English Rococo cabinetmaker Thomas Chippendale, c. 1760. © PETER HARHOLDT/CORBIS

ness of technique; and Chippendale (c. 1760–1790) is a high English variant of French Rococo.

Pottery

With the arrival of the Europeans came the potter's wheel and many types of ceramic vessels. By 1635, Philip Drinker, an English potter, had started working in Charlestown, Massachusetts, and before 1655, Dirck Claesen, a Dutch "pottmaker," was working in Manhattan. By the very nature of local needs, most British colonial pottery production was utilitarian ware called redware, modeled on English and German storage jars, jugs, bowls, and plates. It was needed and produced in quantity, formed of the same red clay from which bricks were made. When fired, the clay remained porous. The glazing and ornamentation were basic. Redware (fired at 900° C–1040° C) was usually given a clear lead glaze (using a highly toxic sulfide or oxide of lead), that emphasized the clay's red tones. Adding metal oxides such as copper, iron, or manganese pro-

Federal-Style Home. A 1995 photograph of the East Drawing Room—used as a music room—of the Edmondston-Alston House, built in 1825 on the High Battery in Charleston, S.C. © KEVIN FLEMING/CORBIS

duced various bright colors that enhanced the surface of redware.

Most potters were either immigrants or only a generation or two removed from European or English craftsman traditions. As the immigrants began to see themselves as Americans and heirs to a continent, they sought more intellectual diversity and distance from contemporary European sources, while continuing to buy European products. By 1800, the Adamesque Neo-Classicism of Britain had pervaded domestic manufacturing design, and those ancient Greek and Roman shapes took root to varying degrees in different art forms and regions of America. Across the newly expanding country the Federal Style (c. 1785–1815) was followed by the Empire Style (c. 1815–1830). Both styles were versions of the Robert Adam–inspired Classical Revival in England and the variant Biedermeier style in Austria and Germany.

Chairs, Ceramics, and Silver

While the SHAKERS, a branch of the English Quakers, were rejecting the world about them, they made ladderback chairs and sat as other Americans sat. While rockers were not a Shaker invention—the earliest-known citation is from 1741–1742 by Solomon Fussell, a Philadelphia

furniture maker—their popularity may owe much to the inventiveness of the Shaker chair makers and to their readiness to accommodate to new styles.

In ceramics, the venerable English firm of Josiah Wedgwood was the leader in pottery. Wedgwood's invention of basalt ware in 1768, followed within a decade by his exquisitely modeled jasper ware, inspired ceramists everywhere. In the early nineteenth century the Wedgwood potteries did not produce porcelain, but the Worcester, Derby, and Coalport factories did, and those who sought fashionable dishes either got them from those factories or, starting about 1825, found suitable reproductions made by some twenty skilled craftsmen from England and France employed to make porcelain for the Jersey Porcelain and Earthenware Company in Jersey City, New Jersey. Other ventures followed in Philadelphia.

At the same time, and serving many of the same customers, silversmiths were both manufacturers and retailers, their shops often doubling as a workroom and a showroom. This practice continued until about 1840, when the discovery of the technique of electroplating led to the rise of large companies that produced and sold silver plate in stores. While not eliminating individual silversmiths, it did reduce their importance. Ultimately large corporations such as the Gorham Manufacturing Company and International Silver Company largely depersonalized the industry. Those individual shops that survived specialized more in repair, chasing, and engraving than in creating products.

Industrialization and Decorative Style

The American ambivalence about industrialization helps explain the inherent ideological contradictions in the decorative arts between 1850 and 1900. Laminating rosewood, for example, required a large number of technologically sophisticated pieces of shop equipment, and it is ironic that such technical and mechanized operations produced forms that were emotional cues to the antithesis of mechanization. Besides the various European-derived revival styles, the Rococo Revival became an important stylistic force among wealthy Americans by 1850. The most influential sources for designers were the natural world, the past, and the exotic. Immensely popular in America were china patterns produced in England such as the transfer image "Ontario Lake Scenery." Mass-produced of cheap materials, the scene shows a castle, Niagara Falls, and tepees against a mountainous background. The newly powerful merchants, industrialists, and their managers bought this ware and anything else they saw at a reasonable price. The mass market was born, as was the separation of design from material reality in popular decorative arts.

Oriental Style

While China and Japan had been very important design sources for the decorative arts of elite culture before 1800, the American middle class discovered the Orient at the 1876 Philadelphia Centennial Exhibition. Everyday objects such as the inro, netsuke, and fans became decorative materials for homes or prized collections. "Oriental" was also a decorating, ceramics, and furniture style; at its extreme, oriental pieces were cast or carved to resemble bamboo, ebonized, or lacquered; paper parasols were popular, as were paper lanterns, fans, and kimonos. By the end of the century, artisans were manufacturing large numbers of items in the Oriental style expressly for use in America. By 1900 most "Made in Japan" furniture resembled forms from China. Design had succumbed to the marketplace.

But the Oriental influence also took another direction in the ceramic glazes and shapes developed by such potters as William Henry Grueby, who set up the Grueby Faience Company of Boston in 1894. Working with George Prentiss Kendrick, an established designer in brass and silverware, the shop created outstanding European-Japanese–inspired shapes and a range of delicious semi-matt glazes: blues, yellows, browns, grays, and an ivory-white crackle. His most sought-after and imitated glaze was a semi-matt green. Grueby green became an industry standard.

Grueby was an instant success at the Society of Arts & Crafts Exhibit in Boston in 1897. While already rep-

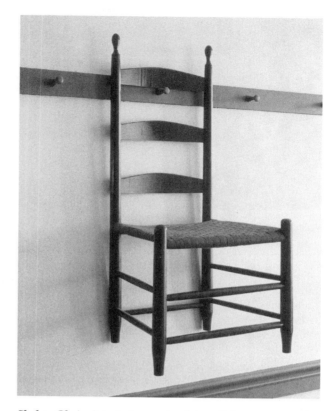

Shaker Chair. A typical example of the religious movement's simple designs, photographed in 1996 at the restored Shaker Village of Pleasant Hill in Harrodsburg, Ky. © KEVIN R. MORRIS/CORBIS

resented by Siegfried Bing (1838–1905), founder of the Gallery of Art Nouveau and Tiffany's European outlet, in 1900, Grueby was awarded one silver and two gold medals in Paris. In 1900 the pottery won a gold medal at St. Petersburg and in 1901 the Highest Award at the PAN-AMERICAN EXPOSITION in Buffalo, at which Grueby contributed to rooms designed by Gustav Stickley, a pioneer of Arts & Crafts–style furniture in America. The Highest Award followed in Turin in 1902 and the Grand Prize in St. Louis in 1904.

Art Deco Style

While the Art Deco style actually budded between 1908 and 1912, it did not bloom until after World War I. The style draws on a host of diverse and often conflicting influences—Cubism, Russian Constructivism, Italian Futurism, abstraction, distortion, and simplification. Art Deco's tenet that form must follow function remained unchallenged by all succeeding schools of design. However, its accompanying dictum that the piece should also be unique or, at most, a limited edition proved elitist in an age ruled by Modernism. The Modernists argued that the new age demanded excellent design for everyone and that quality and mass production were not mutually exclusive. The

Glassmaker. Jane Osborn-Smith sculpts a clay model of a glass design for Steuben Glass. © JAMES L. AMOS/CORBIS

future of the decorative arts did not rest with the rich; rather, an object's greatest beauty lay in its perfect adaptation to its usage. For the first time, the straight line became a source of beauty. In the late 1920s a moderated Modernism was all the fashion.

French Art Deco styling produced by Steuben (1903–) and Libbey Glass Compay (1892–) revived the American glass industry somewhat; it had suffered a decline after Art Nouveau flourished under Louis Comfort Tiffany. Steuben produced expensive, limited editions of art glass designed by its founder, the Englishman Frederick Carder (1863–1963). The Libbey Glass Company was in the vanguard of 1930s American commercial glass design. The tradition-bound American home of the 1930s was jolted by the Consolidated Lamp and Glass Company of Coraopolis, Pennsylvania, when it designed a Cubist line of glassware called Ruba Rombic, which was offered in pale hues such as gray, topaz, and amber.

The Great Depression struck a fatal blow to luxury items, and in America the Art Deco style was only reluctantly adapted to jewelry design. To accommodate the trend, Tiffany of New York created traditional objects in the new style, but without the crisp angularity found in Paris. C. D. Peacock and Spaulding-Gorham Inc. in Chicago produced jewelry in the new idiom, but again without the panache of their French counterparts. One genuinely new form appeared in American jewelry at the time: the stepped outline, which coincided with the emergence of the stepback skyscraper, the most beautiful examples of which are the Chrysler Building and the Empire State Building in New York City.

Modernism

When the American skyscraper boom of the mid-1920s started, America did not have its own Modernist style. The country was still decorating tall buildings in a Gothic style derived from the pens of Cass Gilbert or Hood and Howells' Chicago Tribune Tower. As in traditional buildings, Modernist decoration served as a transitional device

to alert the viewer to a change in contour. It was often not designed by the architect but purchased directly from companies such as Northwestern Terra Cotta in Chicago. A sumptuous combination of stone, brick, terracotta, and metal often transformed an otherwise bland structure into a source of great civic pride.

Since 1945 the decorative arts in America have served as a template for the culture of consumerism, with its attendant design functions. By the 1960s commercial television, various other advertising media, consumer magazines, and city sign systems both commercial and practical emerged as challenging and exciting new disciplines and venues in the ongoing interface between consumer and product: promising, seducing, fueling, and directing. The cultural role of the decorative arts and design was extended well beyond the need for harmony between form and function. The artisan and designer became a communicator, giving form to products not in the abstract but within a culture and for a marketplace. Never before had there been such an intensive dialogue between the "fine" and the "decorative" arts. By the 1970s Pop artists were devising their own set of rules, an antithesis to Modernism ideology yet not antagonistic. Pop was about being Modern in a different though not exclusive sense. It was the Modern of fashionable, high-impact design; a never-mind-about-tomorrow, brash, superficial Modern. All the while, decorative arts changed rapidly, embracing both functional and fully nonfunctional, both the beautiful and the ugly, limited only by the inventiveness of the craftsperson.

BIBLIOGRAPHY

Adams, Henry. *Viktor Schreckengost and Twentieth-Century Design.* Cleveland, Ohio: Cleveland Museum of Art, 2000.

Clark, Garth, and Margie Hughto. *A Century of Ceramics in the United States, 1878–1978: A Study of Its Development.* New York: Dutton, Everson Museum of Art, 1979.

Dietz, Ulysses Grant, et al., ed. *The Glitter and the Gold: Fashioning America's Jewelry.* Newark, N.J.: Newark Museum, 1997.

Kardon, Jane, ed. *Craft in the Machine Age, 1920–1945.* New York: American Craft Museum, 1995.

Rolf Achilles

See also **Art: Pottery and Ceramics; Metalwork; Pop Art.**

GLASS

Glass is created by fusing silica (sand, quartz, or flints) with alkaline fluxes (soda ash or potash) in a crucible, a fireclay pot, within a furnace. Fuel for heating is usually based on local availability. Two basic techniques dominate glassmaking: molding and blowing. All glass must also be annealed, slowly cooled to become less brittle.

Color has been an important component of the appeal of glass since the beginnings of glassmaking. Color demands a sophisticated and specialized knowledge. Some of the most popular oxide additives to molten glass are cobalt, which produces a wide range of blues; gold, the most romanticized of the additives, which produces a range of reds; antimony, which produces an opaque yellow; iron, which produces a range of colors from yellow to green to blue; copper, which produces a wide range of blues, greens, and reds, and even a glittering metal in suspension; and manganese, which can produce an amethyst color. Surface color can be quickly achieved by exposing the glass to various chemicals or gasses, thus causing iridescence similar to that found in long-buried Roman glass. Louis Comfort Tiffany became the acknowledged master of manufactured iridescence.

Early Glassmaking and Industrialization

When Jamestown Virginia was founded in 1607, glassblowers were among the settlers. Like the colony, their glassmaking venture, America's first industry, failed. Other glassmakers followed in New Amsterdam (later New York), Salem, Boston, and Philadelphia. All were short-lived ventures. But demand for glass was great in colonial America. In 1739, in the face of a British ban on manufacturing glass, a German glassmaker, Caspar Wistar, established a factory in southern New Jersey that successfully produced window glass, bottles, and tableware. Free-blown glass was also popular. Many glassmakers, mostly German, followed Wistar's example, but despite abundant fuel and sand, most failed. But failure did not deter the industry, and every decade of the eighteenth century saw production increase as the demand grew for bottles, windows, and free-blown vessels. While blowing glass into a mold was efficient, the development of mechanical glass-pressing machines in the 1820s actually industrialized the industry. American glass of seemingly ever-new colors could now be pressed into a myriad of shapes. This sudden speedup in production, the first in almost 2,000 years, was America's first great contribution to the glass industry.

For the first time identical pairs or interchangeable sets were possible. Home decorating changed forever. The New England Glass Company in East Cambridge, Massachusetts (1818–1888), became one of the glassmaking giants of the century and produced an enormous variety of wares of international importance. The Boston and Sandwich Glass Company, in Sandwich, Massachusetts (1825–1889), was a significant competitor. Others followed.

After about 1845, Bohemian-style glass, blown, cut, wheel-engraved, or machine-pressed, became the rage. Soon fine line cutting and panel cuts, deep reds and blues, marble or agate glass, and cased, flashed, and stained ware were common sights in better American homes. In 1864, William Leighton of Hobbs, Brockunier, and Company in Wheeling, West Virginia, developed a soda lime glass that looked like expensive lead glass but was much cheaper to produce. It changed the industry, especially that of luxury glass. The Philadelphia Centennial Exhibition of 1876 led the campaign for glass that was deeply cut, more elaborate, and handmade. Instantly popular, it

Feeding the Flamingoes. Glass art designed by Louis Comfort Tiffany, c. 1893. © James L. Amos/corbis

is now referred to as "brilliant," or Victorian, glass, and its production continued until about 1915. Libbey Glass Company in Toledo, Ohio, became a leader in this type of American glass.

Art Glass and Modern Styles

Paralleling brilliant glass was the very popular new taste for art glass, another continuation of Americans' desire for excess that spawned novel glass colors, finishes, and shapes, mostly for the production of decorative objects. Louis Comfort Tiffany was the uncontested master. His development of Favril glass in the late 1870s, based on existing German technologies and ideas developed by John La Farge, ushered in a new style of glass, which in 1895 was called "art nouveau." Exhibited at the 1893 Chicago World's Columbian Exhibition, Tiffany glass was immediately purchased by several European museums, internationally acclaimed, and copied. Endlessly adapting Roman, medieval, and Muslim shapes and surfaces, Tiffany's genius sprang forth in colors, patterns, and marketing. Along with "brilliant" cut glass, Tiffany glass dominated until about 1915. Brilliant cut slipped into stuffy obscurity, and Tiffany's glass was maligned, neglected, and forgotten until the early 1970s, but since then

Tiffany glass has become once again the most sought-after of all glass.

The 1920s ushered in severe changes in style. Out went ornamental, in came functional. This change proved difficult for the glass industry and its designers. The great designer Frederick Carder employed elegantly simplified forms that helped make the work of Steuben Glass Works in Corning, New York, broadly popular. In 1939–1940 Libbey Glass Company turned new streamlined designs by Edwin W. Fuerst into a line called "Modern American." American glass of the 1950s, made by such firms as Blenko Glass Company in West Virginia, was broadly popular, and by the early 1990s American glass of the 1950s had become much sought-after by collectors. Art galleries specializing in modern and 1950s glass sprang up to meet the demand.

Studio Glass

Arguably the most influential change in modern glass-making occurred in 1962, when the Toledo Museum of Art organized a hands-on glass working seminar. Led by the glass technician Dominick Labino and the ceramist and glass designer Harvey K. Littleton, both of the University of Wisconsin, the seminar's emphasis on uniting the traditional functions of craftsman and designer (separated since the early eighteenth century) led directly to a renaissance in contemporary hand-worked glass seen as a sculptural medium.

The studio-glass phenomenon attracted new glass artists who migrated from other materials and who used not only traditional hot glass methods such as blowing and casting but also warm techniques such as fusing, slumping, and enameling, as well as cold techniques such as cutting, polishing, etching, sandblasting, painting, and joining with new acrylic adhesives to achieve their designs. Glass, like other materials, became the embodiment of an "artistic gesture."

Starting in the late 1960s, Dale Chihuly, Richard Marquis, James Carpenter, Michael Nourot, William Prindle, and others (Robert Willson had been there first, in 1958) had all spent time in Murano, Italy, studying ancient glassblowing traditions with master craftsmen. In 1971, Chihuly founded Pilchuck Glass Center outside Seattle, Washington, and began to work in his signature technique based on centuries-old Venetian glass traditions, without the constraint of fifteenth- and sixteenth-century technology. The same decade saw the founding of the Penland School in North Carolina and the Haystack Mountain School in Maine. Publications such as *Craft Horizons* and *New Glass Review*, and regular exhibitions, became significant supports. The American Crafts Council has had its own museum in New York since 1987, the same year the Corning Museum in upstate New York placed part of its modern glass collection on permanent display. Since these ambitious moves, the creativity and diversity of glass artists has found appeal among countless collectors, making glass the most collected of all contemporary art media.

BIBLIOGRAPHY

Contemporary American and European Glass from the Saxe Collection. Oakland, Calif.: Oakland Museum, 1986.

Koch, Robert. *Louis Comfort Tiffany, Rebel in Glass.* New York: Crown, 1982.

McKearin, George S., and Helen McKearin. *American Glass.* 1948. Reprint, New York: Bonanza, 1989.

Memories of Murano: American Glass Artists in Venice. New York: American Craft Museum, 2000.

Warmus, William. "Steuben Forever." *Urban Glass Art Quarterly* 81 (winter 2000): 36–41.

Rolf Achilles

See also **Art: Decorative Arts, Stained Glass Windows; Collecting.**

INTERIOR DECORATION

Interior decoration is a profession that deals with the placement of furniture, with color, textiles, window treatments, lighting, finishes, and materials, and with the selection and display of collected objects. It mainly concentrates on the domestic interior and emphasizes the ornamental, applied, and decorative arts in creating ephemeral ambience utilizing the more easily transformed aspects of a room. Decorators tend to work either in private practice, store-home consulting, or furniture and material showrooms. Educational programs can be found in schools of architecture, art and design, human ecology, or human economics.

European Influences

Any survey of the history of American interior decoration must begin by acknowledging the importance of European influence. The majority of work in the field is based on the importation and revival of European styles, although there has also been some emphasis on broader global influences and contemporary American popular culture.

American interior decoration has built a design tradition that reflects the successive waves of explorers, settlers, and immigrants who have come to the United States over hundreds of years. English citizens in search of religious freedom, Spanish missions spreading Christianity, and Dutch merchants seeking wealth in the trade market all brought elements of their decorative heritage to the new land. Each wave of immigrants strove to recreate the living spaces they had left behind.

At the same time, the American homestead reflected a constant process of shaping the past to meet the demands of the present. Initially, the fundamental necessities of life determined decorative style. In the northern colonies, space and heat were high priorities, as people would eat, sleep, prepare meals, and socialize all in one-room parlors (see, for example, the Parson Capen House, Topsfield, Massachusetts, 1683). Beds were curtained off, and rugs were thrown over crude wood floors. Regional folk-art painting was used to enliven the severe, plain forms of the exposed-wood structures (see the Fraktur Room at Winterthur House, near Wilmington, Delaware, or the Pembroke Room at Beauport [the Sleeper-McCann House], Gloucester, Massachusetts, [1907–1934]). Spanish homes, with their whitewashed walls, were equally austere, though highlights of bold color added interest. In the southern colonies, interiors were somewhat more luxurious: various surviving structures in Williamsburg, Virginia, provide a complete picture of the comfortable, paneled rooms of the 1750s.

The early simplicity of interiors shaped by the necessities of survival gave way to new luxuries as plantation owners, merchants, and prosperous traders furnished their homes with furniture and decorative objects that were locally created versions of prominent styles from Paris and London (see the Washington Library, Mount Vernon, Virginia, or Gunston Hall, Lorton, Virginia, 1755). With greater prosperity came new types of spaces for dining, entertaining, and performance, all featuring European-influenced ornamentation. After the Revolutionary War (1775–1783), the typically restrained decor of the eighteenth-century interior became more expressive. Two major new styles predominated: the graceful, neoclassical Federal style, which grew out of the work done in England by American architect Robert Adam, and the American Empire style, modeled after design trends in Napoleonic France (see the Bartow-Pell Mansion, Bronx, New York, 1842, or Samuel McIntire's Derby West House, Peabody, Massachusetts, 1801). Prominent developments in furniture design included the Sheraton style (named for English designer Thomas Sheraton), the Hepplewhite style (named after British designer and cabinetmaker George Hepplewhite), the Robert Adam style (named for the American architect mentioned above, who also designed furniture while in England), and the Duncan Phyfe Adaptation (named after an American cabinetmaker who combined Empire motifs with influences from Adam, Sheraton, and Hepplewhite). These neoclassical design trends were influenced greatly by the English Regency style. Swags, husks, flutings, festoons, and rams' heads were common motifs applied to furniture.

Prosperity Leads to Modernism

At the end of the eighteenth century, continued prosperity brought to the United States treasures garnered from the expansion of trade routes throughout Europe and the Orient. Prosperous fleet owners built and embellished coastal mansions using local craftspeople and completed them with imported goods. Grand staircases, parlors, sitting rooms, verandas, dining rooms, libraries, front offices, upstairs bedrooms, and detached servant quarters completed the array of spaces necessary for commodious living. Paneling was replaced with wainscoting, while moldings, reduced in size, began featuring reeding, channeling, and a greater variety of shapes and expressions. Plaster cornices and bas-relief work complemented an increased use of color and of patterns from every historic period.

From the post-Revolution era to the antebellum period, interiors featured very tall ceilings; walls without wainscoting were edged with massive molded baseboards. The furniture of choice was mostly of Empire design with brass mounts. Tall French mirrors over mantels and between windows expanded the space, which was hung with dark damask (see the Nathaniel Russell House, Charleston, South Carolina, 1809). The next wave in decoration came during the Victorian period and involved an array of revivals of various historical styles. Extraordinary excess was the hallmark of the period, as reflected in the elaborately carved furniture, the rich fabrics, the luxurious window treatments, and the signature gilding of objects (see the Wickham-Valentine House, Richmond, Virginia, 1812). Along with the Rococo revival, other eccentric displays of Victorian taste were the Neo-Gothic and Neo-Renaissance styles. A. J. Davis's Lyndhurst Castle (1838), in Tarrytown, New York, is a premier example of the Gothic influence, with its ribbed vaulting, arched moldings, and furniture inspired by medieval churches. The Ramsey Mansion (1872) in St. Paul, Minnesota, exhibits all the trappings of the fashion for classicism. World's Fair exhibitions showcased Victorian opulence and the increasing array of domestic products. Museums began to collect and put on permanent display furniture and period objects, and began recreating interiors.

Along with the embellishment of styles derived from Europe, nineteenth-century America also saw the development of a unique design sense derived from the beliefs and practices of the Shakers. This fundamentalist community shunned elaborate expressions of wealth and opulence, and developed a style based on essential forms and a spare purity of line, reflecting their belief that form follows function. Their minimalist approach was a key component in the mix of influences that led to twentieth-century modernism. Regional craftsmen and artisans also worked outside the heroics of revivalism and created instead simple, unadorned pieces intended not for the wealthy, but for those of average income. At the same time, the factories of the new machine age made high-quality work available to more people for less money; in contrast to handcrafted furniture, they produced painted cottage furniture or slat-back chairs.

Publications, Film, and New Technology

The pre-Modernist sensibilities of nineteenth century decoration, including the Victorian era's taste for eclecticism, survived well into the twentieth century. In 1913, for example, Elsie de Wolfe, considered the first professional decorator, wrote *The House in Good Taste* to promote the use of a range of historical styles. At the same time, the new age of travel, with its ocean liners and airliners, established contemporary aesthetics that favored the streamlined and the modern.

Even as much of its aesthetic orientation remained rooted in the nineteenth century, the field of interior decoration rapidly modernized and professionalized itself. In 1897, the novelist Edith Wharton collaborated with architect Ogden Codman Jr. in writing *The Decoration of Houses*, in which the authors define interior decoration as dealing with surface treatments and interior design as encompassing the design of interior spaces. In 1904, *The Interior Decorator* began publishing; one of the earliest specialist publications, it soon set standards for the profession. Nancy McClelland established the interior decoration department of New York's Wanamaker Department Store in 1913, and in 1923 Eleanor McMillen founded McMillen, Incorporated, credited with being the country's first interior-decorating firm. Beginning in the 1930s, John Fowler, Terence Harold Robsjohn-Gibbings, and Billy Baldwin all became coveted professional decorators. The American Institute of Decorators was founded in 1931.

In the 1930s, the fantastic world of film first became the prominent influence on American interior decoration it would continue to be throughout the twentieth century. The decorative styles of the English country house, the Californian Spanish house, and the Art Deco interiors of the Jazz era were all disseminated through Hollywood set design. The stylized "Modern" look of the 1930s owed much to futuristic epics like *Metropolis* (1927), while the nostalgia for the Civil War period inspired by *Gone with the Wind* (1939) also greatly influenced decoration. Later in the century, the sensational *Cleopatra* (1963) created a resurgence in Egyptian motifs, while the futuristic sets of *2001: A Space Odyssey* (1968) helped inspire the distinctive minimalist environments of the late 1960s and 1970s. Mail-order catalogs and women's magazines, while not as glamorous as Hollywood, also exerted a strong influence on interior decoration. They featured an expanding diversity of goods and began portraying fashionable interiors.

In the second half of the century, the dominant architectural philosophy sought a reduction in ornamentation, and objects both small and large were increasingly made of synthetic materials. Technological innovations transformed interior spaces as the television and hi-fi made their way into everyone's living room during the 1950s and 1960s. During the 1990s, the widespread usage of the Internet made information readily accessible, transforming the profession of interior decoration itself. Access to any image, the availability of increasingly varied products and furniture types, and an ever-expanding and increasingly sophisticated lighting industry all expanded the decorator's palette.

Initially a luxury for society's affluent, the interior decorator at the start of the twenty-first century is a consultant to businesses and middle-class homeowners alike, helping them shape living and work environments through the use of an ever-expanding range of possibilities.

BIBLIOGRAPHY

Aguilar, Kathleen, and Michael Anderson. *Miniature Rooms: The Thorne Rooms at the Art Institute of Chicago.* New York: Abbeville, 1984.

Ball, Victoria Kloss. *Architecture and Interior Design: Europe and America from the Colonial Era to Today.* New York: John Wiley, 1980.

Friedman, Arnold, J. Pile, and F. Wilson. *Interior Design: An Introduction to Architectural Interiors.* New York: American Elsevier, 1970.

Geck, Francis J. *Interior Design and Decoration.* Dubuque, Iowa: Brown, 1971.

Pile, John F. *History of Interior Design.* London: Laurence King, 2000.

Rogers, Meyric R. *American Interior Design: The Traditions and Development of Domestic Design from Colonial Times to the Present.* New York: Norton, 1947.

Wharton, Edith, and Ogden Codman Jr. *The Decoration of Houses.* New York: Norton, 1997. Reprint of the original 1897 edition.

Whiton, Augustus Sherrill. *Interior Design and Decoration.* 4th ed. Philadelphia: Lippincott, 1974.

Linda Nelson Keane
Mark Keane

See also **Collecting; Furniture; Metalwork.**

INTERIOR DESIGN

American interior design has its roots in the traditions of interior decoration that developed in the United States during the eighteenth and nineteenth centuries. Interior decoration was primarily concerned with the surface decoration of the home, its furnishings and room arrangement. Interior design came to be conceived, following the publication in 1897 of *The Decoration of Houses*, by Edith Wharton and Ogden Codman Jr., as encompassing the design of interior spaces. Both disciplines involve the planning and organization of space, lighting, and color; surface treatments of walls, windows, floors, and ceilings; furniture selection and arrangement; and the choosing of accessories. But in the twentieth century, the growth of corporate office-space planning needs, the infusion of European design influences, the historic preservation movement, and the formation of national governing agencies for the profession altered the traditional parameters of interior design.

The history of American interior design parallels that of American interior decoration. Colonial styles took their inspiration primarily from the former European homes of Dutch, French, Spanish, and English settlers. Wealthy eighteenth-century Americans developed tastes influenced by the Georgian style popular in England (see, for example, the Governor's Palace, Williamsburg, Virginia, 1722). The third President of the United States, Thomas Jefferson, championed Palladian ideals at Monticello (1784–1809), as did Benjamin Latrobe, long considered the nation's first architect. The furniture and interior design of the Federal Style of the late eighteenth and early nineteenth centuries was a reflection of contemporary interest in the Greek world, an interest undergirded by a paralleling of the young America with the first pure democracy of Periclean Athens.

The Gothic Revival of the early nineteenth century paralleled contemporaneous English and German tastes. This reflection upon the Middle Ages led to a style known as Carpenter Gothic, which featured simple rural construction, and to more mainstream revivalisms across the expanding country. The Victorian Age that followed offered an eclectic mix of styles borrowed from any and all periods of design history, with a vital infusion supplied by the mechanized processes of the new Industrial Age. This period in history witnessed the first widespread introduction of factory-made products. The Arts and Crafts movement objected to the machine's impact on design and to the elimination of the craftsman. Out of this movement came the first generation of design that departed from European traditions and was truly American. Gustav Stickley and others were leaders in developing the Craftsman style, a proportioned plane and linear language that was expressed in architecture, furniture, and interiors. Also emerging from the latter half of the nineteenth century were the minimal and restrained design forms of the Shaker religious community. Shaker simplicity, so divergent from the elaborate ornamentation popular in the Gilded Age, helped point the way toward twentieth-century Modernism.

Louis Sullivan (Chicago Auditorium, 1889) and Frank Lloyd Wright (Robie House, Chicago, 1909) offered an American response to the international Art Nouveau movement with their nonhistorical, nature-based decorative vocabulary. Their late-nineteenth- and early-twentieth-century masterpieces were direct descendants of the Modern movement. Complementing their work in the Midwest were the California designers Greene and Greene (Gamble House, Pasadena, California, 1909) and Bernard Maybeck.

The Modern movement was built on the principles of the antihistorical Dutch group De Stijl and on the teachings of the Bauhaus—a German school of design—and can also be seen as a reaction to World War I (1914–1918). Modernism ran counter to the popular Art Deco style favored by the era's dominant academic institution, the École des Beaux Arts in Paris, at which many American architects and designers were trained. Its key proponents, the Germans Walter Gropius and Ludwig Mies van der Rohe, and the Finn Eliel Saarinen, all emigrated to the United States and landed at premier design institutions: the Harvard School of Design, the Illinois Institute of Technology, and Cranbrook Academy, respectively. Mechanization, reconceptualization of interior space, and the suspension of the barrier between interior and exterior space were key principles in this functionalist approach. Convenience and economy became paramount, and were supported by the development of electric power, temperature control, and lighting and ventilating innovations.

In the middle of the twentieth century, a shift took place in the practice of interior design. In 1958, the National Society of Interior Designers was established to complement the American Institute of Decorators. The profession of interior decoration as developed by the early pioneers in the field, Elsie de Wolfe, Nancy McClelland, and Ruby Ross Wood, expanded its scope to encompass new design programs. Commercial interior design became a new business venture. Key individuals like Florence Knoll championed the modern movement and its response to post–World War II (1939–1945) corporate America. In 1965, Art Gensler opened a firm that focused on corporate office design. Traditional architecture firms like Skidmore, Owings, and Merrill began to add services that specialized in office interiors. Office planning, facilities management, movements supporting historic preservation and adaptive reuse, and the expanding scope of the built environment all offered new horizons for the field and led to a new definition of interior design as a separate discipline. Differentiated from interior decoration and architecture, interior design attempted to claim the territory of the public interior. Beyond arrangement and selection of furnishings and finishes, interior designers concentrated on the human experience of the design environment. With this focus, interior design became a science as well as an art.

Interior design expanded to encompass telecommunications, mechanical and electrical systems, ergonomics, food and beverage service, kitchens and commercial laundries, and the educational, institutional, medical, and hospitality fields. Social science research began to be developed to identify and meet user needs. Color theory, acoustics, lighting, human behavioral studies, anthropology, and sociology began to inform the design process.

Large furniture manufacturers like Knoll, Steelcase, and Herman Miller responded to the corporate world's needs. Design and continued modification of the "workstation" transformed rooms of closed offices into open-plan multiuse corporations. Herman Miller's "Action Office," a system of freestanding panels and reconfigurable countertops and storage elements, was one of the responses to the demand for a transformed office. In the late 1940s and 1950s, Ray and Charles Eames created office interiors specifically for the people who worked in them, using only the furniture and objects necessary to work effectively and efficiently. The Eameses stressed appropriate, socially conscious, egalitarian, and ethical designs.

From producing a limited set of choices, the furniture industry expanded into use-specific and ergonomically designed offerings that have multiplied the possibilities. The science of lighting design expanded from general lighting to include task, accent, and ever-changing mood lighting. The specifications for materials superseded mere questions of color and texture, and added durability, toxicity, flammability, and impact on the environment as new variables. The development of design knowledge in academia, practice, and allied industry began to change interior design from an aesthetic process into an analytical, research-oriented endeavor that advocated change in the environment.

The field of interior design continues to develop and expand its arena of expertise. It overlaps with construction, architecture, art, design technologies, mechanical systems, lighting, and product and environmental design. In 1950, there were seventy programs focusing on interiors at various U.S. schools of design, architecture, and home economics. In 1971, the Foundation for Interior Design Education and Research (FIDER) was formed by the Interior Design Education Committee to govern the growth and direction of the emerging profession. The National Council for Interior Design Qualifications was created in 1974 by the American Society of Interior Designers to ensure professional competence. By 2000, FIDER listed 130 accredited interior design programs.

At the beginning of the twenty-first century, the interior design professional functions in three types of work environments: architectural firms that have both design and technical teams who work collaboratively on larger projects; firms in which architects oversee project management while interior designers contribute color, materials, and treatments; and the interior design firm that features the designer as "decorator."

Interior design was unregulated, but this had changed by the end of the twentieth century. New regulation requires familiarity with energy-conscious products and safety issues. Health and safety issues have led to licensing in some states, and there is a gradual trend toward licensing nationwide. Licensing examinations reflect the growing nature of the field, as applicants must now show proficiency in programming and planning, theory, contract documents, building construction, materials, professional practice, history, and design.

BIBLIOGRAPHY

Ching, Francis D. K. *Interior Design Illustrated.* New York: Van Nostrand Reinhold, 1987.

Keane, Linda, and Mark Keane. "Interior Design Education." In *Handbook on Interior Design.* Edited by Cindy Coleman. New York: McGraw-Hill, 2001.

Knackstedt, Mary, with Laura J. Haney. *Interior Design and Beyond: Art, Science, Industry.* New York: John Wiley, 1995.

Nielsen, Karla, and David Taylor. *Interiors: An Introduction.* 3d ed. New York: McGraw-Hill, 2002.

Pegler, Martin M. *The Dictionary of Interior Design.* New York: Fairchild, 1983.

Russell, Beverly. *Women of Design: Contemporary American Interiors.* New York: Rizzoli, 1992.

Linda Nelson Keane
Mark Keane

See also **Architecture; Furniture.**

PAINTING

The Colonial Era: Rising from the Formulaic

The first paintings executed in the American colonies were portraits of early settlers, mostly in Boston or New Amsterdam (later New York City), painted by artists trained in England or the Netherlands. These portraits from the second half of the seventeenth century are rudimentary in execution. There is little attempt to create convincingly modeled forms, and facial features are only broadly described. The sitters are for the most part well-to-do merchants and landowners who have about them a sense of sobriety and determination. These early artists are sometimes known as limners and they also worked as sign painters or even house painters. The names of only a few of these early artisans are known, the earliest being Henri Couturier, who in 1663 executed a portrait of Governor Peter Stuyvesant in New Amsterdam. Also active in that area at this time were Evert Duyckinck and his son Gerrit, while in Boston native-born John Foster painted portraits while also teaching school, and made the first woodcut known to be executed in the colonies.

Farther south, in Charleston, Mrs. Henrietta Johnston is the first recorded woman painter, while in Maryland, Justus Engelhardt Kühn made several crudely executed portraits of early settlers. By the mid-eighteenth century, Gustavus Hesselius had painted some portraits that have a sense of the personality of the sitter. Hesselius also worked in the more ambitious categories of religious and mythological painting, although the practical demands of establishing a new nation offered little scope for ambitious multifigure canvases. Eighteenth-century colonists preferred portraits or views of early colonial towns.

The first native-born artist of note was Robert Feke, active in the Boston area, as well as in Newport and Philadelphia. His handling of the medium of paint and his use of rich colors marks an advance over most colonial portraiture, which presents the sitter in a formulaic pose painted with a restricted, drab palette. Gustavus Hesselius's son John painted portraits of settlers along the eastern seaboard from Philadelphia to Virginia. His most striking image is *Charles Calvert and Slave* (1761), which shows one of Maryland's wealthiest landowners and one of his African chattel.

The high point of American colonial painting is attained in the work of John Singleton Copley, a native of Boston. A self-taught artist, Copley's ambitions went beyond portraiture. As a student he copied prints after the work of earlier European masters as a way of teaching himself anatomy. Copley's portraits of New England's social and political figures are notable for the acuteness with which he suggested the personality of his sitters. Copley's portraits owe their success in large part to his skill in representing the accessories of people's lives, the rich fabrics of their clothes or the gleaming surfaces of their household furnishings. Frequently, the artist used unconventional poses for his sitters, which enhanced the sense of their individuality. His double portrait, *Mr. and Mrs. Isaac Winslow* (1774), is a characteristic, masterful image of colonial painting just prior to the American Revolution. In 1774 Copley left to study in England and on the Continent; the next year he settled in London, where in addition to portraits he painted historical themes such as *Watson and the Shark* (1778). Copley was driven abroad by the absence in the colonies of any training for artists and of any public collections of art.

Charles Willson Peale moved from Maryland to Philadelphia, where he painted portraits of the city's aristocracy. His commission from the Cadwalader family in 1772 for five large portraits was unique. Peale used the conventions of fashionable contemporary British art as the basis of his work, which reflects the wealth and sophistication possible at the apex of colonial life. Peale trained his sons Raphaelle, Rubens, and Rembrandt to become painters; they not only did portraits, but Raphaelle executed meticulously observed and rendered still lifes of familiar objects such as arrangements of books or flowers and fruit.

The Early Republic: Beyond Portraiture

In 1795 Charles organized the Columbianum, a short-lived artists' association modeled on Britain's Royal Academy in London. Within the first decade of the nineteenth century, art academies were established in New York City (American Academy of Fine Arts, 1802, and National Academy of Design, 1826) and Philadelphia (Pennsylvania Academy of Fine Arts, 1805), evidence that the new republic was assured enough to recognize the fine arts as a basic part of civilized education.

In the early republic, portraiture continued to be a major area of endeavor for American painters, who looked to England for inspiration. Gilbert Stuart studied in Britain before returning to the United States in 1792, where he produced his celebrated portrait of George Washington, which exists in numerous replicas. Thomas Sully studied in London, where he was greatly impressed by the portrait style of Sir Thomas Lawrence, whose gracefully posed sitters are rendered by an easy, assured handling of paint. Sully adopted Lawrence's manner to represent the comfortable lifestyle of his patrons, whether wealthy or middle class.

As the nation grew more prosperous, some artists attempted to create large-scale paintings of historical or mythological subjects, which in European art academies were considered the most worthwhile, and most difficult, subject matter for a painter to master. John Trumbull and John Vanderlyn each studied in Europe before returning home to paint canvases in the grand manner of epochal themes. Trumbull's paintings of subjects from America's Revolutionary War were installed in the Capitol, although to severe criticism, and Vanderlyn's mythological figures such as Ariadne fared no better with the public at the time, which is generally known as the age of Romanticism. Washington Allston was the most complex individual in American art in this epoch. Educated at Harvard University, he then left to study painting in London and on the Continent. His writings on art dismissed the notion of painting as imitation of appearances and placed emphasis on the imagination and intuition. Allston's huge *Belshazzar's Feast* (begun 1817) remained unfinished and is one of America's great Romantic images.

Alongside these painters, who were laboring to create in America an art of grand achievements in European terms, existed a number of largely self-taught artists, usually active outside of America's big cities. The best known is the Quaker missionary and preacher Edward Hicks. His paintings are executed with an emphasis on outline to define objects and the simplicity of his compositions recalls the bold immediacy of sign paintings. In sympathy with his pacifist religious convictions, Hicks's work centers on the biblical theme of the Peaceable Kingdom, as with *Noah's Ark* (1846).

As the United States developed, people were curious to see the largely unexplored western territories. Landscape painting, often executed in a very idealized manner, was a response to this demand for information. North of New York City the Hudson River School comprised professional artists such as Thomas Cole, who specialized in landscapes, and as national boundaries spread beyond the Mississippi River, artists traveled westward to paint the countryside and its inhabitants. George Catlin is the best-known artist to paint the American Indians, their customs, and the rugged terrain in which they lived and hunted as he explored the Missouri River in 1832. An exhibition of these works surprised audiences in New York City, London, and Paris. The life and customs of Native Americans were also the subject of Karl Bodmer's work, while somewhat later Alfred J. Miller made more picturesque images of the people and landscape of the West. The grandeur of the western terrain, with its stretches of towering snow-capped mountains, inspired painters such as Albert Bierstadt, Thomas Moran, and Frederick E. Church to create vast panoramic canvases of views at Yellowstone and the Grand Canyon that were purchased by private collectors for huge prices.

The everyday activities of life were represented in the popular category of genre painting, while ordinary objects were represented in still-life paintings executed with crystalline realism. These paintings, known as trompe l'oeil (fool the eye) compositions, take commonplace objects and arrange them in imaginary compositions executed in an astonishingly realistic manner. William M. Harnett's *Old Cupboard Door* (1889) and John F. Peto's *Still Life with Lard-Oil Lamp* (c. 1900) are characteristic trompe l'oeil works, with things arranged in curious, unexplained juxtapositions that may imply a moral or humorous anecdote.

The Mid- and Late Nineteenth Century: Europeanists and Individualists

By mid-century many American artists still felt the need to study abroad; art academies in London, Paris, or Mu-

The Oxbow. An 1836 painting—more formally, *View from Mount Holyoke, Northampton, Massachusetts, after a Thunderstorm*—by Thomas Cole, a leader of the nineteenth-century Hudson River School. © Francis G. Mayer/corbis

nich were favored by painters in search of contact with more sophisticated training than they could find at home. John La Farge studied in Paris, where he came to know the work of old masters, contemporary artists such as Eugène Delacroix, and Oriental art, the stylized decorative qualities of which so attracted him that eventually he traveled to Japan and the South Pacific. Paris and the work of the French Impressionists attracted Mary Cassatt to the city, and eventually she settled in France, where she lived for the rest of her life. James A. McNeill Whistler first studied in Paris, and then went on to spend his mature years in London. His views of London and the river Thames at dusk or in fog, painted in a narrow, delicately modulated range of colors that he called nocturnes, became popular with American collectors; his art was well-known in the United States during his lifetime.

Another mid-century artist, William M. Chase, studied at Munich; his most attractive canvases are his landscapes painted out-of-doors with a free touch and in bright, clear colors. John Singer Sargent studied in Paris and then moved across the English Channel to London, where he became one of the most acclaimed portraitists of his time. He had an international clientele of wealthy, powerful sitters and his portraits create a record of an

epoch. Later, Sargent went to Boston, where he executed important murals (begun in 1890) commissioned by the Boston Public Library and, later, by the Museum of Fine Arts in Boston, on which he worked from 1916 until his death in 1925. In Paris, Theodore Robinson discovered the paintings of the Impressionists, and in the 1880s he was so taken with Monet's colorful, vividly executed landscapes that the American settled in Giverny, where the French painter had a studio. Childe Hassam adopted the Impressionists' painting technique to create views of the New England countryside—coastal scenes or villages with neat houses and churches.

The two greatest personalities in American art in the late nineteenth century were Winslow Homer and Thomas Eakins, neither of whom owed much to European influences. Homer was largely self-taught and his early training prepared him to work as a magazine illustrator. His interest in the American scene was a constant in his art, whether he recorded events from the Civil War or later, often working in isolation in Maine, painted the outdoors life of hunters and fishermen. Homer's preference for stretches of New England wilderness, as in *Breezing Up* (1876), stands in contrast to the growing industrialization of America's cities. Thomas Eakins studied at the Paris École des Beaux Arts but returned to Philadelphia in 1870. There he taught painting at the Pennsylvania Academy of the Fine Arts, where he insisted that students work after nude models. That resulted in his dismissal in 1886 and afterward he turned increasingly to portraiture as a means of continuing his career. Eakins's celebrated *The Concert Singer* (1890–1892) is characteristic of the introspective, sometimes plaintive character of his portrayals.

Academic Artists and Modernists

The art of these individualists stands apart from the academic work that was popular at the turn of the twentieth century. High-minded civic virtues were expressed in solidly grounded technique by painters such as Thomas W. Dewing, Edmund Charles Tarbell, and William Morris Hunt, whose scenes of polite society or allegories of political or social idealism avoided the ugly realities of urban, industrial life.

The social problems that came with the rapid growth of America's big cities became the subject matter for a group of artists who rejected academic art. These realist artists originated in Philadelphia and comprised Robert Henri, George Luks, William Glackens, John Sloan, and Everett Shinn. Later they moved to New York City, where their subject matter was the metropolis, including its tenement life, the isolation possible in its crowded environment, and the diversions of the city. These five painters were joined by Arthur B. Davies, Maurice Prendergast, and Ernest Lawson to form a group that was known as The Eight or the Ashcan School in recognition of the commonplace themes of their art. These progressives were interested in current European modernism, and Henri, Sloan, and Luks were instrumental in organizing the controversial 1913 Armory Show, the first large-scale presentation in America of such controversial art as French cubism and the work of Henri Matisse, Maurice de Vlaminck, and Georges Rouault, which was seen alongside avant-garde American works by John Marin, Marsden Hartley, Joseph Stella, and Charles Sheeler, among others.

Prior to the Armory Show it was almost impossible to see progressive European work in the United States, with the rare exception of the photographer Alfred Stieglitz's Photo-Secession Gallery in New York City, which exhibited work by Paul Cézanne, Matisse, Pablo Picasso, and Constantin Brancusi as well as American art and children's drawings. Both Marin and Stella celebrated America's engineering marvels—its skyscrapers and bridges—in paintings that use both cubist and Italian futurist devices to express the magnitude of America's urban buildings and the fast-paced life of its cities. Examples are *New York Interpreted* (1920–1922) and *The Bridge* (1922), by Stella, and Marin's *The Woolworth Building* (1912). Not all American modernists followed the lead of European painters. A case in point is Arthur Dove, whose abstract canvases often use biomorphic shapes to suggest fantasy landscapes, sometimes recalling the work of the Russian

artist Wassily Kandinsky, as in Dove's *A Walk, Poplars* (1920). Another modernist who defies categorization is Marsden Hartley, sponsored by Alfred Stieglitz and sent by him to Europe in 1912, where Hartley not only came to know the work of French modernists but those of the Russian Kandinsky and the German Expressionists. Hartley's works, including *Painting No. 4* (also called *A Black Horse*, 1915), are concerned with representing spiritual values through symbolism and are deliberately ambiguous.

Several artists continued to explore city life as the subject of their work, and in this sense they perpetuated the Ashcan School's concern with urban realities. George Bellows combined a relish for all aspects of urban existence with superb, academically oriented draftsmanship. His figure style is most evident in his prizefight subjects, as in *Stag at Sharkey's* (1907). Bellows's relish for city life was shared by other realist painters such as Jerome Meyers and Leon Kroll.

While European cubism of the 1920s had little effect on American painting, the Cubists' clarity of organization is evident in the early work of Stuart Davis, whose *Super Table* (1925) is clearly in their debt. Davis's later, large abstract compositions were influenced by American billboard paintings, with their strident colors and bold shapes. The work of the American Precisionist Movement reflects a knowledge of cubism's rigorous organization, but also of photography's clarity of representation. Charles Sheeler was both a photographer and a painter. His photographs undoubtedly nurtured his preference for clarity and sharp focus observation. Their subjects are taken from the immediate world of his rural Pennsylvania background, the factories of industrial America, or—as in *Rolling Power* (1939)—the skyscraper architecture of cities. Edward Hopper recorded with clarity and unmatched poignancy the isolation of urban life. His *Nighthawks* (1942) is a precise evocation of nighttime, when people's energies are at low ebb. Hopper's views of Victorian houses and his seacoast paintings of crashing waves and boats at sea present a more optimistic view of American life as it exists in small towns freed of urban complexities.

Georgia O'Keefe's startling close-up views of organic forms make no reference to cubism but instead concentrate on details of plants or the skulls and bones of the New Mexico desert, where she lived during the later part of her career. Vast stretches of sky suggest the isolation in which she pursued her art, as in *From the Plains* (1952–1954).

Regionalism

A reaction against European modernism developed partly in response to America's economic and political isolation after World War I. Regionalism is particularly identified with artists working in the Midwest and the Great Plains. The low horizons and towering skies of the regionalists' landscapes make a backdrop for the farmers' and ranchers' life of isolation and hard work. Thomas Hart Benton's gaunt figures sometimes approach caricature and his themes are anecdotal as well as political, as in *Cotton Pickers* (1928–1929). Other Regionalists include Grant Wood, whose *American Gothic* (1930) is an iconic image of a farming couple standing in front of their wood Gothic-looking house. John Stewart Curry also portrayed the rural Midwest with humor.

This Regionalist aspect of American art received support during the depression years of the 1930s from the federal government, whose Federal Art Project, which ran from 1935 to 1943, was administered under the Works Progress Administration. The program supported both easel painting, the graphic arts, and murals for public buildings. Regional committees administered the project's awards on a competitive basis. A bias existed in favor of representational styles and American subject matter. No outstanding artist came to prominence as a result of this support, but the program enabled many painters to continue to work who would otherwise have been forced to put aside their art and seek other employment.

Avant-Garde Art

European avant-garde art came to the United States at the outset of World War II with the arrival of a new wave of artists (including Yves Tanguy, Piet Mondrian, Max Beckmann), many of whom settled in New York City. The German painter Hans Hofmann became an important teacher and an example for the development of abstract expressionism. The German Expressionist Max Beckmann also taught, and the presence of his art in the United States made the country more aware of expressionism as an important movement. Another major teacher was Josef Albers, from the Bauhaus at Weimar, who worked and taught at Yale University, while another Bauhaus artist, László Moholy-Nagy, was instrumental in founding the New Bauhaus, later known as the Illinois Institute of Design, in Chicago, which carried on the severe aesthetic of the German institution. At first, art training in America was carried out in the master's studio; later, major art schools were attached to art museums such as the School of Fine Arts, Boston (1876), The Art Institute in Chicago (1879), and the Cleveland Institute of Art (1882). Training for artists in a university context—established at Princeton in 1831, New York University in 1832, Yale in 1866—was usually more perfunctory. Thus, the presence of an artist of Albers's stature at New Haven was a major advance in raising the caliber of instruction in a university context.

Painting and Social Justice

Alongside the arrival of European Modernists during the late 1920s and early 1940s, there coexisted artists concerned with issues of social justice. Ben Shahn created powerful images, such as the dejected couple in *Willis Avenue Bridge* (1940), while Jacob Lawrence's art dealt with the plight of African Americans and social discrimination in works such as *Migration of the Negro* (1940–1941), as did Romare Bearden's. Joseph Hirsch's paintings of urban laborers can be seen as a continuation of the Ashcan School's concerns, while Paul Cadmus presents an often bawdy view of city life, sometimes with homoerotic implications, as with *The Fleet's In!* (1934).

After 1945

In the 1950s, abstract expressionism dominated progressive American painting. The movement was centered in New York City, and the artists' large, sometimes wall-size canvases, and bold, gestural handling of paint soon caught the attention of critics and collectors. The artists' gestures became the subject matter of the work, a break with convention that soon attracted international notice. At the head of the movement was Jackson Pollock, whose celebrated "drip" paintings were created by stretching canvas on the floor and dripping skeins of paint from cans or brushes in broad rhythmic motions. Variations of this bold application of paint were created by Franz Kline, Willem de Kooning, and Robert Motherwell, among others. There also existed many important artists who stood apart, working in personal styles that they often developed away from New York City. Foremost is Mark Tobey, whose paintings of fragile interlaced lines, recalling Oriental calligraphy, were created in Seattle, although he ended his career in Switzerland. In contrast to Tobey's abstract canvases, figurative art continued to flourish, as in Fairchild Porter's scenes of a comfortably well-to-do, genteel lifestyle or Andrew Wyeth's minutely detailed rural landscapes including *Dodge's Ridge* (1947).

By the 1960s, a group of artists in Chicago were painting figurative compositions of great emotional intensity, frequently with surrealist-inspired juxtapositions of objects. Known as the Chicago Imagists, Ed Paschke and Roger Brown created raw, disturbing imagery reflecting their interest in psychoanalysis, "primitive" art, and bizarre or hallucinatory conditions, as in Paschke's *Hophead* (1970). Other figurative painters, such as Philip Pearlstein and Alice Neel, both active in New York City, observe their subjects with such intensity that their images have the sense of being isolated from the real world.

During the 1960s, color field painting arose as an alternative to the bold work of abstract expressionism. Mark Rothko's large canvases of highly saturated color retain evidence of his brushwork; this gesture reference was largely eliminated by color field artists such as Frank Stella, Kenneth Noland, and Jules Olitski, who preferred strong colors and sometimes used shaped canvases that broke with the traditional rectangle, as is evident in the work of Ellsworth Kelly. Other painters, such as Helen Frankenthaler and Morris Lewis, applied paint by staining their canvases with water soluble acrylic pigments, often pouring the medium onto the surface.

Coincident with color field painting, minimalist artists sought to create a sense of classical order in their geometric grids painted with quiet, almost monochromatic colors. Brice Marden, Robert Ryman, Agnes Martin, and Sol Le Witt are the leading names of this movement. On the West Coast, the Fetish Finish artists—including

Larry Bell and Craig Kaufmann—used industrial materials like automobile paint, plastic, and lacquer to create works, sometimes three-dimensional, that explore how light is reflected and perceived. At the same time, the dean of West Coast painters was Richard Diebenkorn, whose series of Ocean Park canvases (begun in 1967) celebrate the radiant light of Southern California.

Starting in the 1970s and 1980s, a number of artists have found the conventional limitations of easel painting too confining to express their reactions to complex social problems like pacifism, social equality, feminism, the devastation of AIDS, or ethnic identities. America's culture of materialism is deeply offensive to some artists, like Jenny Holzer and Barbara Kruger, who have taken to the streets to express their outrage through wall murals or commercial illuminated signage. The use of nontraditional materials and the rejection of the conventional museum-gallery audience gives power to the minority and often marginalized voices of these contemporary American artists. Video and computer-generated imagery give artists access to an international audience with such immediacy as to call into question the relevance of national identities.

BIBLIOGRAPHY

Battock, Gregory. *Minimal Art: A Critical Anthology.* New York: E. P. Dutton, 1968.

Beckett, Wendy. *Contemporary Women Artists.* Oxford: Phaidon, 1988.

Hunter, Sam. *American Art of the Twentieth Century.* New York: Harper and Row, 1972.

Lewis, Samella S. *Art: African American.* New York: Harcourt Brace Jovanovich, c1978.

Lippard, Lucy R. *Mixed Blessings: New Art in a Multicultural America.* New York: Pantheon Books, 1990.

Lucie-Smith, Edward. *Movements in Art since 1945.* New York: Thames and Hudson, 1995.

Novak, Barbara. *American Painting of the Nineteenth Century.* 2d ed. New York: Abrams, 1979.

Plagens, Peter. *Sunshine Muse: Contemporary Art on the West Coast.* New York: Praeger, 1974.

Wilmerding, John. *American Art.* New York: Penguin Books, 1976.

Victor Carlson

See also **Abstract Expressionism; Armory Show; Art Institute of Chicago; Ashcan School; Catlin's Indian Paintings; Cubism; Genre Painting; Hudson River School; Remington and Indian and Western Images; Romanticism; Works Progress Administration.**

PHOTOGRAPHY

Americans rapidly embraced the new medium of photography within months of Louis-Jacques-Mandé Daguerre's introduction of his process in 1839. Samuel F. B. Morse and his wife attempted to use it in the fall of 1839, and Alexander S. Wolcott and John Johnson claimed to open the first portrait studio in New York City in October 1839. Within a few years, rapid improvements and the introduction of plastic "union cases" resulted in a democratized use of daguerreotypes. In Massachusetts alone, over 403,000 daguerreotypes were recorded in the year ending 1 June 1855. Daguerreotypes were useful for art and architectural recordings. Street scenes, buildings, monuments, and human nudes were early subjects. Soon even cheaper competition emerged. Calotypes and ambrotypes were popular in the 1850s, and after that tintypes and carte de vistes flourished beyond possible calculation. While these methods greatly democratized portraiture and allowed people to gain perspectives on their appearances (mirrors were still uncommon), gradually more elite forms appeared. Mathew Brady's portrait studio on Lower Broadway in New York City became favored by the wealthy. Brady and the popular historian Charles Edwards Lester produced lavish illustrated books. In the late 1850s the first stereographs appeared, which, using two parallel images, allowed depth perception. Mounted on stereopticons, these photos of city scenes, world attractions, and major events became staples of middle-class parlors.

Early Journalistic and Documentary Photography

The next big jump came with the Civil War. Previously, photographers transferred their images into line drawings for publication in new magazines such as *Harper's Weekly*, *Leslie's Weekly*, and *Gleason's*, all of which catered to the middle classes. The demands for immediate news during the war quickly meant constant use of photography. Brady, Timothy O'Sullivan, and Alexander Gardener became famous for battlefield photographs, even if, as was later revealed, they arranged corpses for effects. The work was tedious and dangerous; Brady was nearly killed at Bull Run and was disoriented for days. Although line drawings continued in use after the war, by the late 1880s photographs dominated daily and weekly media. Photographers now roamed throughout the country looking for newsworthy and evocative images. The American West provided a fruitful source of dramatic imagery. The work of Carleton Watkins, William H. Jackson, Eadweard Muybridge, and Timothy O'Sullivan dramatically portrayed the massive natural beauty of the West.

Photography's democratic impulse expanded after the Civil War. The use of photographs in books was common. Photographers catering to African Americans, Chinese Americans, and other ethnic groups abounded. Photographers such as Edward Curtis set about recording and preserving hundreds of images of Native Americans. At the bottom of society, Inspector Thomas Byrnes's famous book of American criminals introduced the use of mug shots for identification. American usage of photographs as postcards became widespread by the end of the nineteenth century. Colorized and tinted postcards demonstrated the potential of color photography.

Publication of Jacob Riis's *How the Other Half Lives* (1890) showed the power of photography to promote so-

Pictorialism. In photographs such as this one from 1892, titled *Terminal*, as well as in his publications, gallery, and work with disciples, Alfred Stieglitz demonstrated his unwavering and extraordinarily influential belief in photography as an art form. NATIONAL ARCHIVES AND RECORDS ADMINISTRATION

cial reform. Riis's grainy images of the poor of New York City sparked calls for social justice. Lewis Hine, who illustrated sociological treatises of exploited child labor with evocative documentary photographs, improved upon his work early in the next century.

Pictorialism

In contrast to this devotion to straight photography to record social conditions was the work of Alfred Stieglitz. Oriented to photographic aesthetics and influenced by the photo salon movement in Europe, Stieglitz constantly experimented with light, paper, and subject before coming to the United States. In New York, he urged consideration of photography as an art form, something few had ever considered. His photograph of the Plaza Hotel in New York City, *Reflections, Night—New York*, is remarkable for its study of wet pavements reflecting light from streetlamps and windows. Stieglitz became the president (and dictator) of the New York Camera Club, which became noted for its extraordinary reproductions and as a clearinghouse for innovative ideas. His unabashed elitism, adherence to pictorialism, and disdain for documentary photography established photography as an art form. His publication *Camera Notes* and his organization of the Photo-Secession movement were aimed expressly at that

purpose. *Camera Notes* in its fifty issues published what it considered the best of photography and surveyed the history of the method. Within a few years, pictorial photographs graced the walls of museums and exhibitions and Stieglitz's approach was seemingly triumphant. Though the movement lapsed in 1917 with the end of the magazine and the destruction of its New York headquarters, his influence on Edward Steichen, the future photography editor of *Vanity Fair* magazine, and Paul Strand, who revived straight photography, was immense.

Pictorialism had unintended influence. It dominated the rising genre of Hollywood photography, done first on a freelance basis and then by regular studio photographers. Such cameramen as Eugene Robert Ritchie, George Hurrell, Clarence Sinclair Bull, and John Engstead used pictorialism to improve upon the attractiveness of the stars and, as they did, create new concepts of American beauty, especially in their emphasis on face, hair, shoulders, and breasts. Steichen, Horst, and Carl Van Vechten of *Vanity Fair* extended such absorption to literary and artistic personalities, creating new types of American portraiture. The democratic principal of such photography can be found in the work of Alfred Eisenstadt for *Life* magazine and in photographs found in sports magazines.

Life and its rival publication *Look* used the cooperative work of editors and staff photographers. Picture essays were planned and researched before the photographer shot the subject. Multiple images were made in the quest for the best possible moment. This method created carefully conceived and executed projects; it also made for predictability, something photographers had learned to prize about their medium. The method was best exploited by Walker Evans, who worked for *Fortune Magazine* on assignment for years. Although Evans was supposedly working with a team back in the office, in fact he was roaming around the country searching for the precise moment when his technical expertise and subject matter merged.

Varieties of Documentary Photography

Stieglitz's insistence on the photographer's control over the image influenced Evans, who started shooting images of American vernacular architecture and signs and then, during the Great Depression, concentrated on the American poor. Along with Charles Sheeler, Evans became known for the originality and evocativeness of his subject matter and for the precision of his images. Simultaneously, Berenice Abbott, who had trained in Paris under Man Ray and with Bill Brandt, and there fell under the sway of the urban documentarian Eugene Atget, returned to New York in 1929 to record the changes in the city. Though she was unable to get funding to finish her project of photographing every building and block in Manhattan, Abbott's images captured the city as it moved into world status. On the local level, the work of the Harlem photographer James Van Der Zee recorded the images of several generations of black New Yorkers. Similarly, Marvin and Morgan Smith, Gordon Parks, Robert S. Scurlock, and others sought to record the significant events of African American experiences and of the civil rights movement.

Their fascination with city people and architecture did not extend throughout photography. In the American West, Edward Weston and his son Brett, Imogen Cunningham, Ansel Adams, and Georgia O'Keefe made virtuoso photography of the natural world. Their conception was always that the photographer predetermine what the image would be and set exposure and development to gain control over nature.

Documentary photography received a large boost during the Great Depression of the 1930s. The director Roy Emerson Stryker hired a talented team of photographers for the Historical Section of the Farm Security Administration. The group included Dorothea Lange, Walker Evans, Marion Post Wolcott, Ben Shahn, Arthur Rothstein, and Russell Lee. They took over 270,000 images of American life from Maine to San Diego. There approach was catholic; anything having to do with the American people was appropriate, except Wall Street and celebrities. FSA photographers sought out ordinary citizens working in arduous times. The FSA photos are a linchpin between the natural democratic use of the pho-

tograph in the nineteenth century, the work of Riis and Hine, and the self-conscious search for Americaness found in the New York school.

Consciously learning from Hine, Evans, and other classic documentarians, the New York school of photographers used small cameras, available light, and a sense of the fleeing and the real. At times, however, they seemed more aligned with action painting or abstract expressionism. Photographers from the New York school included Diane Arbus, Richard Avedon, Alexy Brodovitch, Ted Croner, Bruce Davidson, Don Donaghy, Louis Faurer, Robert Frank, Sid Grossman, William Klein, Saul Leiter, Leon Levinstein, Helen Levitt, Lisette Model, David Vestal, and Weegee. Each of them aspired to finding what Henri Cartier-Bresson, the French master, called "the precise moment." Weegee in particular specialized in crime scenes, fires, and other human disasters. While such photography normally would have been consigned to tabloid newspapers, in time it became considered art. Weegee used flash photography to create weird lighting, unpleasant shadows, and a sensibility associated with noir films at the end of the 1940s. Weegee's sense of urban motion and bizarre subject matter influenced William Klein, Robert Frank, and especially Diane Arbus. Bruce Davidson, on the other hand, sought carefully defined long-term projects devoted to urban life, which he then made into classic books on East Harlem, the subway, and Central Park. Richard Avedon became a premier portraitist.

Although *Life* and *Look* eventually ceased publication, their method of photojournalism set the terms by which photojournalists of war conducted their work. Beginning with World War II and especially in the Vietnam War, photojournalists began to define the nature of the conflict far better than official reports. Images of the war by Robert Capa in World War II, David Douglas Duncan in the Korean War, and Larry Burrows were printed in major magazines and reprinted on posters that galvanized public opinion about Vietnam.

New Directions

The disorienting effects of Vietnam on American society pushed photography in two directions. One was to reemphasize documentary photography as found in the works of Lee Friedlander, Gary Winograd, and Joel Meyerowitz, who looked for spontaneous images in American street life. A second direction was to embrace artifice and to create a private world of photography. The instant photography of Andy Warhol, who used either subway photo booths or, later, Polaroid photography as the basis for his portraits of the glitterati of the 1970s, was influential. Warhol's open use of sexual imagery was also liberating, though the final effect was more depressing than sensual. Nan Goldin pursued this direction, combining Warhol's casual approach with the druggy subject matter of Larry Clark. Cindy Sherman aimed for total artifice in her *Untitled Film Stills* series of the late 1970s, in which she portrayed herself in Hollywood-style costumes. Rob-

Documentary Photography. Movie billboards in front of houses, photographed in 1936 by Walker Evans, the artist best known for his photos in *Let Us Now Praise Famous Men* (1941), with text by James Agee, depicting the effects of the Great Depression on ordinary people. LIBRARY OF CONGRESS

ert Mapplethorpe adopted Warhol's disdain for technique by shooting masterful and sometimes sexually bizarre images and then having them developed at the corner drugstore. Black photographers in particular embraced new technologies and approaches in the 1980s. Dawoud Bey used giant Polaroids to create portraits of unknown black teenagers. Albert Chong transposed images onto everyday objects to suggest African spiritual qualities.

The arrival of the Internet and the invention of filmless digital cameras in the late 1990s promised an even greater dissemination of photography as a democratic art. Combined with the Immigration Act of 1965, which opened wider the gate to America, global imagery and multicultural expression worked well with "virtual photography," which included images that would never be on paper. Improved color copiers also democratized photography. E-mail attachments allowed for the ability to shoot an image, save it, and then send it across the world in a matter of a minute or so. Such freedom challenges the art ideology of photography and raises again old questions about the democratic powers of transmitted images.

BIBLIOGRAPHY

Armstrong, Carol. *Scenes in a Library: Reading the Photograph in the Book, 1843–1875.* Cambridge, Mass.: MIT Press, 1998.

Foresta, Mary A. *American Photographs: The First Century.* Washington, D.C.: Smithsonian Institution Press, 1996.

Galassi, Peter. *American Photography, 1890–1965, from the Museum of Modern Art New York.* New York: Museum of Modern Art, 1995.

Livingston, Jane. *The New York School: Photographs, 1936–1963.* New York: Stewart, Tabori and Chang, 1994.

Newhall, Beaumont. *The History of Photography: From 1839 to the Present.* 5th ed. Boston: Little, Brown, 1988.

Stryker, Roy Emerson, and Nancy Wood. *In This Proud Land: America 1935–1943 as Seen in the FSA Photographs.* New York: Galahad, 1973.

Trachtenberg, Alan. *Reading American Photographs: Images as History from Mathew Brady to Walker Evans.* New York: Hill and Wang, 1989.

Westerbeck, Colin, and Joel Meyrowitz. *Bystander: A History of Street Photography.* Boston: Little, Brown, 2001.

Willis, Deborah. *Reflections in Black: A History of Black Photographers, 1840 to the Present.* New York: Norton, 2000.

Wood, John, ed. *America and the Daguerrotype.* Iowa City: University of Iowa Press, 1991.

Graham Russell Hodges

See also **Photographic Industry.**

POTTERY AND CERAMICS

Clay is an earthen substance transformed by fire. Pottery is anything made of clay. The word "ceramics" refers to all nonmetallic, inorganic materials that are transformed by firing at high temperatures to a permanent hard, brittle state. Making ceramics is one of the most ancient and widespread technologies. It is labor intensive and common to all but the most arctic cultures.

Before it is ready to use, clay requires water and usually some alkaline substances called fluxes as well as other materials. These add softness, make it stable, color it, or contribute some other refinements. This mix requires some manipulation before it becomes suitable to form. As the clay dries it shrinks and becomes brittle; firing or baking the dried clay—at 150 to 600 degrees centigrade for the most basic pottery and as high as 1400 degrees centigrade for porcelain—renders it hard enough to be useful.

Glazes seal and protect the fired clay, making the finished piece impervious to liquids while also providing various surface textures and colors. Glazes add sophistication to the otherwise earthbound pottery. There are several families of glazes. Lead glazes, made of lead oxide and lead carbonate, are among the earliest and most widespread. They fuse at about 800 degrees centigrade and give a fine range of colors when mixed with other metallic oxides. Tin glaze is composed of a lead glaze made opaque by the addition of tin oxide. Firing it produces a dense white surface that is perfect for painting on. Salt glaze is used with stoneware that is heated very high. Salt is thrown into the kiln and the heat causes the soda to combine with the silica of the clay to form a glassy surface. Feldspathic glazes are nonvitreous and made from powdered feldspar.

Native American Pottery

Throughout the Americas pottery was used daily, as seed jars, water containers, cooking pots, mugs, bowls, serving dishes, ladles, and burial vessels. New heights were reached in Peru during the Moche culture (A.D. 200–700) with the development of ceramic molds, which allowed the Moches to mass-produce ceramic forms. The stirrup handle is a feature common to Moche and other South and Central American pottery vessels that in the 1920s inspired American and European designers.

In North America, the Mississippian cultures made ceramic vessels from about A.D. 800 on and traded them throughout the eastern region of the continent until the arrival of Europeans. In the American Southwest from about 300 B.C. to about A.D. 1300, the Mogollon, Hohokam, and Anasazi cultures were very adept at making pottery vessels. These were superbly painted in geometric designs in black and white. The Anasazi also made red-on-orange ware. Women of the Anasazi culture made finely crafted earthenware jars and pots in the coil-built method around A.D. 1100–1300. Their descendents, the Hopi and Zuni, continued this technical virtuosity until the mid–nineteenth century. During the 1930s and 1940s

Pueblo ceramic artists participated in the Ceramics National Exhibitions, and their work was quickly prized and collected. Some of the most important pottery of the time was created by Maria Martinez and her husband, Julian. Around 1918, Julian discovered how to recreate a traditional blackware that had been excavated by archaeologists at San Ildefonso. Following ancient practices, Maria formed the vessels; Julian added the decoration and did the firing. These works quickly attracted attention and armies of collectors. After Julian's death in 1943, Maria continued making pottery with her daughter-in-law, Santana, and her son, Popovi. The blackware is now a highly prized Pueblo pottery made by several highly skilled artists.

Colonial Pottery and Early Mass Production

With the arrival of the Europeans came the potter's wheel and many more types of ceramic vessels. By 1635, Philip Drinker, an English potter, had started working in Charlestown, Massachusetts, and before 1655 Dirck Claesen, a Dutch "pottmaker," was working in Manhattan. Most British colonial pottery production was utilitarian ware, modeled on English and German storage jars, jugs, bowls, and plates. It is called redware and was needed and produced in quantity, individually, of red clay, the same clay from which bricks were made. When fired (at 900 to 1040 degrees centigrade) the clay remained porous. The glazing and ornament were basic. Redware was usually given a clear, lead glaze (highly toxic sulfide or oxide of lead) that emphasized the clay's red tones. Adding metal oxides such as copper, iron, or manganese produced several bright colors. Most potters were either immigrants or only a generation or two removed from European or English craft traditions. William C. Ketchum Jr. notes that of New York's "367 potters (in 1875), 30 percent were German born, 23 percent from England, and only 41 percent native" ("American Ceramics," p. 23). Once artisans had met the basic needs, some craftsmen sought out other suitable clays. At first, their find was a stoneware clay (fired at 1200 to 1280 degrees centigrade) limited to New York, New Jersey, the Carolinas, and Pennsylvania. Then clays for yellow-bodied ceramics were found in New Jersey, Pennsylvania, and Ohio. The potters of New England found no local clay deposits, but this did not deter them. They responded by importing clay and offsetting its high cost by designing better ovens that allowed higher temperatures, mechanizing production, inventing ever new shapes, and finding financial backing from outside the industry. As the advanced ceramic technologies spread westward, the individual potter soon disappeared from all but the most rural areas. For example, the yellow clays of Ohio lent themselves to casting, and by the 1830s large, efficient factories were turning out a seemingly endless supply of mixing bowls, baking pans, and other kitchen utensils to meet the demand of a fast-growing country of immigrants. Applying a brown, tortoiseshell glaze developed in England in the late eighteenth century called Rockingham, the mass-produced pottery came from Maryland and Ohio, but is most closely associated with Bennington, Vermont. This work is much sought after today.

As early as the 1770s John Bartlam of Charleston, South Carolina, used a clay found in New Jersey, the Carolinas, and Ohio that fired white to produce Queensware, a thin-bodied, cream-colored ceramic. Within eighty years this ware was successfully mass-produced. In 1738, in nearby Savannah, André Duché took the first steps toward locally produced porcelain, but it was not until 1770 that domestic porcelain production, free of European ties, was realized by Gousse Bonnin and George Anthony Morris, who founded America's first successful porcelain factory in Philadelphia. By the Centennial Exposition of 1876 in Philadelphia, porcelain helped celebrate the nation's anniversary with explicitly patriotic themes, flamboyant, even gaudy vessels, and sculptures that were mostly not well received by the public.

Art Pottery

While the dissatisfaction with industrially mass-produced ceramics was not as great in the United States as in Europe and never nurtured the likes of a William Morris, American art pottery began to flower in the 1870s with the help of Maria Nichols and Mary Louise McLaughlin of the Cincinnati School of Art, who were already well aware of Morris and the aesthetic reforms in England by 1872. The Centennial Exposition of 1876 in Philadelphia gave many Americans their first look at highly sophisticated European ceramics technology, Japanese ceramics, the new aesthetic pottery from England and Germany, and the French *barbotine*, an underglaze, slip-painting technique developed at the Haviland works. Fairs and pottery went together. The ceramics at the New Orleans Cotton Exposition in 1884 inspired Mary G. Sheerer to found the Newcomb Pottery in 1894. At the 1889 Paris World's Fair, Rookwood Pottery of Cincinnati won a gold medal. The mat glazes of Auguste Delaherche and Ernest Chaplet exhibited at the 1893 Chicago World's Columbian Exposition inspired William Grueby of Boston.

Arts and Crafts production relied on muscle and skill, not a machine, to develop a vessel. The scientific knowledge of clays and glazes and the physical stamina required for mixing the clay and throwing and firing the pots were considered masculine functions, while decoration was securely in female hands. Thus it was the male potters who won scholarships and gained individual international recognition. Exceptions were Mary Perry Stratton (1867–1961) and Adelaide Alsop Robineau (1865–1929), who achieved great fame through their art ware.

Around 1900 the United States was the world leader in art potteries, whose works were widely exhibited and are seriously collected today. Among these were Biloxi Art Pottery (Biloxi, Mississippi, c. 1882–1910), Buffalo Pottery (Buffalo, New York, 1901–1956), Dedham Pottery (Dedham, Massachusetts, 1895–1943), Fulper Pottery (Flemington, New Jersey, 1899–1955), Grueby Pottery (Boston, 1897–1921), Moravian Pottery and Tile Works (Doylestown, Pennsylvania, 1898–present), Newcomb Pottery (New Orleans, 1895–1940), Onondaga Pottery (Syracuse, New York, 1871–1966), Pewabic Pottery (Detroit, 1903–1961; reopened 1968), Rookwood Pottery (Cincinnati, 1880–1967), Roseville Pottery (Zanesville, Ohio, 1890–1954), Tiffany Pottery (Corona, New York, 1898–1920), Van Briggel Pottery (Colorado Springs, 1902–present), and Weller Pottery (Zanesville, Ohio, 1872–1949).

The eye-pleasing appeal of art pottery fed a wide public interest in ornament and clay, which by the 1920s had helped legitimize the study of ceramics at Alfred University in New York or the Art Institute of Chicago. Academic pottery studies produced beautifully formed and subtly glazed vessels and led to a renewed interest in the traditional pottery making of the Southwest, which was studied, revived, copied, and highly prized. In Cleveland there was also a strong interest in contemporary Viennese ceramics, and several American ceramists, among them Viktor Schreckengost and Edward Winter, who later married the ceramist Thelma Frazier, went to Vienna to study at the Wiener Kunstgewerbeschule.

By the mid to late 1930s several European-trained ceramic artists emigrated to the United States. Among them was Maija Grotell (1899–1973), born in Helsinki, Finland, who arrived in New York in 1927 and within a decade had established herself as one of the leading modernists, teaching at Rutgers. When Cranbrook Academy opened in Bloomfield Hills, Michigan, Grotell became head of its ceramics department. Under her directorship, Cranbrook became one of America's leading centers of ceramic studies. Another notable emigrant was Valerie Wieselthier (1895–1945), who had studied with Michael Povolny in her native Austria and had solo exhibitions in New York beginning in 1929. Wieselthier brought to the American ceramics scene a new attitude toward clay, one that valued its carefree expressive qualities, and she used colors differently. Marguerite Wildenhain (1896-1985), having studied at the Bauhaus in Germany and then run her own successful ceramics factory until 1933, settled near Oakland, California, in 1940. Through her studio at Pond Farm, she played a major role in bringing the modernist Bauhaus craft-based aesthetic to the United States.

At the commercial end of ceramic production, the American Russell Wright (1904–1976) designed many household furnishings as well as the food and fashion section at the 1939 World's Fair in New York. While these did not make him famous, his 1937 curvaceous "American Modern" dinnerware for Steubenville Pottery did. Mass-produced in various pastel and earth tones, since the late 1980s the set has been highly sought by collectors.

While traditional colored clays and popular wares have, with some notable exceptions in hands of current Arts and Crafts artists, been reduced to satisfying a nostalgic craving in contemporary table setting, various white earthenwares, such as ironstone china and porcelain, have found broad acceptance in our daily lives.

Later Studio Ceramics

In 1940 Bernard Leach (1887–1979), a British potter, published *A Potter's Book*, which rapidly became indispensable to the studio potter. After several visits to the United States in the 1950s, sometimes accompanied by the craft philosopher Soetsu Yanagi and the potter Shoji Hamada, Leach became an exceptionally influential champion of pottery, attracting many with his hip understanding of Zen Buddhist aesthetics. Leach arrived at a perfect time. American potters saw themselves as having no traditions, as naïve. They were looking for a new start. Leach and his friends had a great influence on Peter Voulkos (b. 1924), an enormously energetic potter teaching at the Otis Art Institute in Los Angeles. Voulkos was the perfect conduit for Leach's ideas, and soon attracted a group around him that would become the next generation of American potters. Not everyone followed Leach and Voulkos. With his entry of a toilet, entitled *Funk John*, into a ceramics exhibition at the Kaiser Center in Oakland, Robert Arneson (1930–1992) founded the Funk movement, a new form of American ceramic sculpture that dominated the 1970s and continues to be influential.

Since the 1980s studio ceramics, mostly faculty-based in university ceramics departments, is diverse in its aesthetic and technical approaches. While some artists use traditional approaches to clay, exploring form and finish, others are more fascinated with clay's expressive potential. Whichever the direction—a vessel's form, colors, finish, the human figure, themes of nature, social issues, or architecture—the possibilities of clay remain inexhaustible in imaginative hands.

BIBLIOGRAPHY

Bassett, Mark, and Victoria Naumann. *Cowan Pottery and the Cleveland School*. Atglen, Pa.: Schiffer, 1997.

Darling, Sharon S. *Chicago Ceramics and Glass: An Illustrated History from 1871 to 1933*. Chicago: University of Chicago Press, 1979.

Frelinghuysen, Alice Cooney. *American Porcelain: 1770–1920*. New York: Metropolitan Museum of Art, 1989.

Ketchum, William C., Jr. "American Ceramics 1700–1880." In *American Ceramics: The Collection of the Everson Museum of Art*. Edited by Barbara Perry. New York: Rizzoli, 1989.

The Ladies, God Bless 'Em: The Women's Art Movement in Cincinnati in the Nineteenth Century. Cincinnati: Cincinnati Art Museum, 1976.

Weis, Peg, ed. *Adelaide Alsop Robineau: Glory in Porcelain*. Syracuse, N.Y.: Syracuse University Press, 1981.

Rolf Achilles

See also **Arts and Crafts Movement; Art, Indian; Porcelain.**

SCULPTURE

The beginnings of American sculpture are found in the seventeenth-century gravestones of New England, produced by artisan stone carvers, with their Protestant imagery of death. Gravestone carving continued to flourish in the eighteenth century throughout the colonies, but the images became less preoccupied with death. The first statue erected in America was a sculpture by Joseph Wilson of William Pitt, a gift from England to her colonies in 1770 (erected in New York City and Charleston, South Carolina). The statue was torn down by British troops. A lead equestrian statue of George III was set up in New York City and torn down by American revolutionaries. Years before Houdon's statue of George Washington was placed in Richmond, Virginia, there was a marble statue carved in London in 1773 by Richard Hayward of Norborne Berkley, royal governor of Virginia, that was set up in Williamsburg. The increased wealth of the eighteenth century brought about a demand for fine wood carving, for elegant Chippendale furniture, and for elaborate decorative architectural carving. The Skillen family of Boston and Samuel McIntire of Salem excelled in this type of work, as did William Rush of Philadelphia. These men also carved handsome figureheads for the burgeoning American merchant fleet. Rush carried the native school of wood carving to its zenith, as may be seen in his figure *George Washington* (1814, Philadelphia Museum of Art).

After the revolutionary war, Americans turned to foreign sculptors to produce marble images of their great men, thereby downgrading the native school of carvers. The most prestigious of the foreign sculptors was the Frenchman Jean-Antoine Houdon. His marble statue *George Washington* (1788, Virginia State Capitol, Richmond) is a good example of the kind of neoclassical sculpture that influenced several generations of American sculptors. In the second quarter of the nineteenth century, America produced its own native school of sculptors, led by Horatio Greenough, Hiram Powers, and Thomas Crawford.

Greenough, a Bostonian, left in 1825 for Italy, where he spent most of his remaining life. He thereby became one of the first expatriate American sculptors. These expatriates could not find at home the art schools, models, artisan assistants, fine marble, or artistic climate that Italy offered in abundance. In Florence, Greenough created his Zeus-like marble statue, *George Washington* (1832–1841, Smithsonian Institution). Powers, a mechanic from Cincinnati, took up sculpture and went to Italy in 1837, never to return to the United States. Countless Americans visited his famous studio in Florence to have busts made of themselves in his undramatic, naturalistic style. Powers's most popular piece was the celebrated full-length, life-size marble *Greek Slave* (1843, Yale University Art Gallery); it was as famous in Europe as in the United States. Crawford began as a wood carver and tombstone cutter in New York City. He studied and continued to work in Italy. He created the sculptures for the pediment of the Senate wing of the U.S. Capitol (1855) in his studio in Rome.

Henry Kirke Brown also went to Italy, but in 1846 he returned to America, rejecting Italianate neoclassicism for a style based on naturalism, as in his bronze equestrian statue, *George Washington* (1853–1856, New York City). With Brown began the age of bronze sculpture in America. Clark Mills was a former plasterer with no formal training in sculpture. He had never created anything more ambitious than a few portrait busts when he was commissioned to make *Andrew Jackson* (1848–1853, Washington, D.C.), a tour de force in bronze equestrian statuary and an excellent example of nineteenth-century American ingenuity in technology. During the same period, in the area of Albany, New York, the former carpenter Erastus Dow Palmer produced a thoroughly American counterpart to Powers's *Greek Slave* in his marble *White Captive* (1857, Metropolitan Museum of Art). Another sculptor with little formal training was John Rogers. A former engineer, he began modeling small, naturalistic genre groups in about 1860. Thousands of these groups were cast and Rogers attained great popularity among the middle class.

Another generation followed the first to Italy, men such as the Bostonian William Wetmore Story, who gave up a career in law to create heroic marble figures. Most acclaimed was his *Cleopatra* (1858, Metropolitan Museum of Art). Story's studio was a center of the artistic and intellectual life in Rome. From Baltimore, young William Rinehart came to Rome in 1858 where he, too, created marble images of antique subjects (for example, *Clytie*, 1872, Metropolitan Museum of Art) and naturalistic portraits of prominent Americans. Randolph Rogers epitomized the romantic neoclassicism in his statue of *Nydia, the Blind Girl of Pompeii* (1853, Metropolitan Museum of Art), which was so popular that nearly one hundred replicas were commissioned in the years that followed. Rogers also produced several multifigured war memorials, which became big business for American sculptors in the years between the Civil War and World War I.

Bronze portrait statuary was created in abundance in the "era of the galvanized hero," particularly by John Quincy Adams Ward, a student of Brown. His *Henry Ward Beecher* (1891, Brooklyn, New York) and *President James A. Garfield* (1887, Washington, D.C.) possess the unromanticized, undramatic naturalism that was then in vogue. Ward became the dean of American sculptors in the last quarter of the nineteenth century, and was one of the founders of the National Sculpture Society Thomas Ball was another practitioner of this rather prosaic naturalism in portrait statuary.

With the rise of the generation led by Augustus Saint-Gaudens and Daniel Chester French, the aesthetics of naturalism were revitalized. Italy was largely rejected as a place to study; the new style, instead, came out of the École des Beaux Arts in Paris. Nowhere is this better demonstrated than at the World's Colombian Exposition in Chicago in 1893, where Saint-Gaudens, French, Olin L. Warner, Frederick W. MacMonnies, Philip Martiny,

Karl Bitter, and Hermon A. MacNeil collaborated with numerous architects to give the exposition that neobaroque exuberance which characterizes the Beaux Arts style. Saint-Gaudens and French dominated this golden age; the former is best known for his vigorous portraiture, as in his bronze *Abraham Lincoln* (1887, Chicago) and his equestrian *General William T. Sherman* (1903, New York City). His most successful attempt at symbolic imagery was the sibyl-like *Adams Memorial* (1886–1891, Washington, D.C.). But it was French who gave the era its sculptured personifications of such idealized concepts as the Republic, death, political and civic virtues, and industry. French's career began auspiciously with the bronze *Minuteman* (1874, Concord, Massachusetts) and closed half a century later with his marble, seated *Abraham Lincoln* (1922), part of the Lincoln Memorial in Washington, D.C.

In the years preceding World War I, there was a confrontation of artistic ideologies; the conservatives, represented by the academic tradition, and the advocates of the eclectic Beaux Arts style, who entrenched themselves against the aesthetic assault of those who pursued the experiments of the modern movement. Paul Manship and Paul Jennewein represented a compromise that drew on the past but incorporated some abstraction. American sculptors did not give themselves over to total annihilation of natural form the way some of their European counterparts did, and men such as Robert Laurent, William Zorach, and John B. Flannagan developed an aesthetic around the simplification and stylization of natural form plus the technique of direct carving in wood and stone.

Post–World War II

World War II caused a huge influx of European artists into America, and particularly into New York City, where they began to explore the abstract and the surreal in their art, producing "subconscious" assemblage and collage works, and later primitive totems and existential works. After World War II, American sculpture moved dramatically toward abstract and nonobjective form, influenced by such European artists as Piet Mondrian and Julio Gonzalez. David Smith introduced welded metal and Alexander Calder, who lived in France for most of his creative life, and whose father, Alexander Stirling Calder, and grandfather, Alexander Mine Calder, were a recognized Philadelphia dynasty, developed his well-known mobiles and stabiles; both men were greatly influenced by constructivism. Others owed more to abstract expressionism, including Seymour Lipton, Herbert Ferber, and Theodore Roszak, whose work may be seen at the Museum of Modern Art in New York City.

The generations of the 1960s and 1970s brought American sculpture into a direct confrontation with reality as it incorporated actual everyday objects into its art, as in George Segal's *Girl in Doorway* (1965) and Marisol's *Women With Dog* (1964), both at the Whitney Museum of American Art in New York City. "Junk sculpture," or assembled discarded objects, is represented by Louise Nevelson and Richard Stankiewicz, while "light sculptures," using neon and fluorescent tubes, have been created by Dan Flavin and Chryssa.

The late 1960s saw the rise of minimalism as the dominant art form in sculpture. Minimalism can be viewed as a logical extension and exploration of the ideas of later modernist sculpture produced by such artists as David Smith. Late modern sculpture was pushing toward a purified nonillusionistic form expressed through basic geometric structures. The pioneering minimalists Donald Judd, Robert Morris, Dan Flavin, and Carl Andre reduced their sculptures to essentials, removing the artist's touch. Judd's metallic boxes were factory fabricated according to his specifications. Andre's modular work used presized timbers and bricks. Minimalists dispensed with pedestals and bases, hoping to achieve engagement between viewer and art object without the artifice of illusion in a formal "frame." If the ends of minimalism seemed simple enough, the means were multifaceted and intellectually charged. It explored notions of time and space, measurement, mathematics, proportional systems, and perceptual psychology. Minimalists included Beverly Pepper, Richard Serra, and southern California artists Robert Irwin and Larry Bell. Minimalism achieved acceptance in the 1970s, when it influenced the International style of architecture favored by corporate America, but many artists felt constrained by the purity of minimalism. They could not ignore the social issues that were gripping the country: the Vietnam War, pollution, sexism, racism, and consumerism. Four movements followed minimalism, ushering in the postmodern era: process art, conceptual art, earth art, and performance art.

Eva Hesse, Jackie Winsor, and Hans Haacke were important process artists. Hesse created soft, organic hanging works that were rich with generative and sexual metaphor. She allowed materials and techniques to influence her sculpture and, in contrast to the minimalists, used such fragile and malleable materials as cheesecloth and latex. Winsor subjected her meticulously self-constructed cubes to fire and explosives. Haacke used the cube to create self-contained "weather boxes" that addressed the relation between nature and culture. In response to the increasing commercialism of the art world, conceptual artists focused on ideas behind their sculpture. Artists such as Sol LeWitt, Robert Morris, and Joseph Kosuth expressed their ideas through temporary installations. LeWitt's *Variations of Incomplete Open Cubes* (1974) was an investigation of the mental possibilities of permutation. Morris's *Steam Cloud* (1969) represented an attempt at deobjectification. As early as 1965, with *One and Three Chairs*, Kosuth investigated the relation between language and visual art. His text-object sculpture continues to influence artists, who often make reference to semiotics and linguistics.

Earth art is exemplified in *Spiral Jetty*, constructed in Utah's Great Salt Lake by Robert Smithson in 1970.

Prompted by environmental concerns, large-scale earthworks were created throughout the 1970s with the aid of heavy machinery and complex engineering. Walter de Maria's *Lightning Field*, completed in 1977, and Michael Hiezer's *Double Negative* (1970) are striking examples of what was accomplished by earth artists. Prominent women sculptors of earth art include Alice Aycock, Nancy Holt, and Ana Mendieta. Influenced by sacred architecture, Holt was known for her precise celestial orientations. By the late 1970s, many sculptors had turned to performance art, which used multidimensional and interdisciplinary media to more fully engage their audiences. Laurie Anderson, Chris Burden, and Bruce Nauman often used film or video. Burden, known for his masochistic performances, created such politically charged installations as *The Reason for the Neutron Bomb* (1979).

Impressive public sculptures were commissioned throughout the 1970s and 1980s. Some commissions were publicly acclaimed, such as Isamu Noguchi's 1975 design for Hart Plaza in Detroit, while others, such as minimalist Serra's site-specific *Tilted Arc* installed in Federal Plaza in New York City, met with negative criticism and was removed in 1989. Women sculptors in the 1970s came into their own, fueled by the second wave of feminism, and brought political and social themes before the public with their art, including female eroticism and objectification. Maya Lin's abstract design for the Vietnam War Memorial in Washington, D.C., dedicated in 1982, so disappointed conservative critics that a figurative sculptural grouping of three soldiers by Frederick Hart was added. "The Wall," as it came to be known, nevertheless would be recognized, over time, as the profound memorial its creator intended.

The pluralistic sculpture of the 1980s was known as new image art. Minimalism had lost momentum and sculptors returned to figurative and metaphorical subjects borrowed from art history and science, appropriating them in surprising ways. The sculpture of Nancy Graves derived from the study of taxidermy and fossils. Joel Shapiro constructed minimal stick figures from modules similar to those of Andre. Scott Burden's rock chairs seemed to be both natural rock formation and functional furniture. Jonathan Norofsky and Siah Armajani created multilayered sculptures that elude precise meaning. In the late 1980s, Duane Hanson and John De Andrea made hyperrealist sculpture. Countering it were the colorful and active neoexpressionist wall assemblages of Judy Pfaff and the brooding abstract bronzes of Julian Schnabel. The 1990s were characterized by variety, exemplified in exhibitions at New York City's Whitney Museum in which the sculpture ranged from the sardonic pop-inspired objects of Jeff Koons to the elegant abstract pieces of Martin Puryear and the socially poignant installations of Jenny Holzer.

Women Sculptors

An important part of the history of American sculpture includes a compelling body of women artists, beginning with Patience Wright (1725–1786), who started with small figures made from bread dough and natural clay. Her work, necessary to support herself and her family after she was widowed, included a Philadelphia show in the early 1770s of wax figures of prominent personages of the time that were admired for their detail and realism. She continued her work after moving to England in 1772 and received much public acclaim, most notably for her precise depiction of human physiological characteristics during an era when women were forbidden to study anatomy.

Nineteenth century. At the same time that American male sculptors were moving to Europe to study, several nineteenth-century women sculptors also made the voyage abroad for the same purpose, including Harriet Hosmer (1830–1908), Vinnie Ream (1847–1914), Anne Whitney (1821–1915), Edmonia Lewis (c. 1844–1911), Louisa Lander (1826–1923), Margaret Foley (1827–1877), and Emma Stebbins (1815–1882). In America, the National Academy of Design recognized two female sculptors for distinctive work: Frances Lupton was elected Artist of the Academy in 1827 and Mary Ann Delafield Dubois was elected an associate in 1842. Joanna Quiner exhibited her sculpted portraits at the Boston Athenaeum (1846–1848). Caroline Davis Wilson (1810–1890) created a marble statue in 1860 titled *Mary of Bethany*, for which she used her daughter as a model. Rosalie French Pelby (1793–1857) was known for her wax renditions of religious subjects and exhibited in New York, Boston, and Philadelphia between 1846 and 1851.

Turn of the twentieth century. From 1876 to 1905, when American society prospered, art and artists directly benefited by a growing demand for large-scale public sculpture and art that portrayed the American vision. Women artists flourished because of the suffrage movement, receiving formal training both at home and abroad and producing pieces that dealt with war, victory, and patriotism as well as realistic portrayals of contemporary women leaders and public figures. These women sculptors include Elisabet Ney (1833–1907), who exhibited her work at the Paris Salon in 1861 before she became an American; Blanche Nevin (1841–1925); Ella Ferris Pell (1846–1922); and Sarah Fisher Clampitt Ames (1817–1901), whose bust of Abraham Lincoln can be seen in the gallery of the U.S. Senate. The works of about sixteen other women sculptors were accepted for exhibition at the Paris Salon between 1878 and 1900. Women sculptors were showcased in the 1876 Philadelphia Centennial Exposition and the 1893 World's Columbian Exposition in Chicago. Theo Alice Ruggles Kitson (1871–1932) was a sculptor of military monuments (*The Hiker* symbolized the Spanish-American War). Julia Bracken Wendt (1870–1942) was a leading sculptor in Los Angeles, best known for her *The Three Graces: Art, Science, and History* (1914, Natural History Museum of Los Angeles County). Bessie Potter Vonnoh (1872–1955) and Carol Brooks MacNeil (1871–1944) created small bronzes depicting the life of children and mothers; Enid Yandell (1870–1934) is best known for her life-size bronze statue, *Daniel Boone* (c. 1893), commissioned for the World's Columbian Exposition in Chicago. Nellie Verne Walker (1874–1973) was a member of the communal Midway Studio in Chicago and sculpted over thirty-five public monuments over a period of forty years working out of a Chicago studio. Frances Grimes (1869–1963), Annetta Johnson St. Gaudens (1869–1943), Mary Lawrence (1868–1945), Helen Farnsworth Mears (1871–1916), Elsie Ward (1872–1923), and Caroline Peddle Ball (1869–1938) all studied with Augustus Saint-Gaudens. Katherine M. Cohen's (1859–1914) life-size statue, *The Israelite*, was accepted by the Paris Salon in 1896. She worked to convince Americans to support artists at home the way Europeans did. Adelaide Johnson (1859–1955) captured Susan B. Anthony, Elizabeth Cady Stanton, and Lucretia Mott in her 1921 marble sculpture, *Memorial to the Pioneers of the Women's Suffrage Movement*. By 1916, the works of no fewer than seventy-four women sculptors were exhibited at the Plastic Club of Philadelphia.

The twentieth century. Serious training, a sense of purpose and possibility enhanced by winning the right to vote in 1920, and an evolving sense of self within a burgeoning cosmopolitan society gave rise to a significant body of work by women artists. Janet Scudder (1869–1940) is best known for her garden sculpture; Harriet Whitney Frishmuth (1880–1980) captured the essence of liberation in her nude figures, as did Maude Sherwood (1873–1953). Others include Beatrice Fenton (1887–1983), known for her public fountains; Anna Coleman Watts Ladd (1878–1939), who organized the first outdoor sculpture exhibit in Philadelphia; Edith Barretto Stevens Parsons (1878–1956), whose specialty was babies; Mabel Viola Harris Conkling (1871–1966), president of the National Association of Women Painters and Sculptors; and animal sculptors Anna Hyatt Huntington (1876–1973), Ward Lane Weems (1899–1989), Gertrude Katherine Lathrop (1896–1986), and Lindsey Morris Sterling (1876–1931).

Several women received major commissions for large-scale public works: Evelyn Beatrice Longman (1874–1954); Malvina Hoffman (1885–1966); Gertrude Vanderbilt Whitney (1875–1942); Laura Gardin Fraser (1889–1966); Gail Sherman Corbett (1870–1952); Nancy Coonsman Hahn (1887–1976); Margaret French Cresson (1889–1973), daughter of Daniel Chester French; Meta Vaux Warrick Fuller (1877–1968); and May Howard Jackson (1877–1931), whose work focused on the culture of African Americans. Four women sculptors—Ethel Myers, Sonia Gordon Brown, Minna Harkavy, and Concetta Scaravaglione—objecting to the traditionalism of the National Association of Women Painters and Sculptors, helped found the New York Society of Women Artists in 1925, and several women became patrons and avant-garde salon leaders. A sense of social reform and empathy with the less fortunate of society surfaced in the women artists of the Ashcan School: Abastenia St. Leger Eberle (1878–

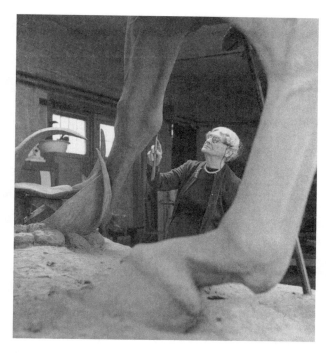

Anna Hyatt Huntington. The sculptor works on her equestrian statue of the Cuban revolutionary hero José Martí, for New York's Central Park. NATIONAL ARCHIVES AND RECORDS ADMINISTRATION

1942), Mae Ethel Klinck Myers (1881–1960), Alice Morgan Wright (1881–1975), and Adelheid Lange Roosevelt (1878–1962). Women comprised a significant portion of the membership of the Sculptors Guild in the 1930s and 1940s and women were well represented among artists who benefited from the 1935 Federal Art Project.

Prominent women sculptors in various major schools, movements, and styles include the Baroness Elsa von Freytag-Loringhoven (1874–1927) of the New York dada movement; Brenda Putnam (1890–1975), contributor to art deco and modernism; constructivists Ruth Asawa (1926–) and Sue Fuller (1914–); abstract expressionist Louis Nevelson (1899–1988); Mary Callery (1903–1977), sculptor in bronze and steel; Claire Falkenstein (1908–), contributor to cubism and topology; Lin Emery (1926–), sculptor of kinetic forms; Beverly Pepper (1924–), known for her exploration of the relationship between sculpture and landscape; political feminist Judy Chicago (1939–); absurdist Eva Hesse (1936–1970); Alice Adams (1930–), known for her work in eccentric abstraction; Vija Celmins (1939–), pop sculptor; and Lenore Tawney (1925–), devoted to woven forms.

The 1980s saw the rise of a new form of exhibition known as sculpture parks—public areas used to display works of sculpture in an outdoor setting. Different types of sculpture parks include open-air collections, such as Storm King Art Center in Mountainville, New York, and museum gardens such as Hirshhorn Museum Sculpture Garden in Washington, D.C. The oldest sculpture park,

which opened in 1932, is Brookgreen Gardens near Myrtle Beach, South Carolina. Brookgreen has the largest outdoor display of American figurative sculpture in the world, with more than 550 works by over 250 artists spread over 300 acres. The combined effect of stimulating works of art viewed in a relaxed and natural setting, especially in urban areas, is a powerful antidote to the stresses of modern life. This popularity created an extraordinary increase in the number of sculpture gardens in the country between 1987 and 1996, a trend that continues into the early twenty-first century.

BIBLIOGRAPHY

Barrie, Brooke. *Contemporary Outdoor Sculpture*. Cincinnati: Rockport Publishers, 1999.

Craven, Wayne. *Sculpture in America*. Rev. ed. New York: Cornwall Books, 1984.

Curtis, Penelope. *Sculpture 1900–1945: After Rodin*. New York: Oxford University Press, 1999.

Gates, Sarah. *From Neo-Classical and Beaux-Arts to Modernism: A Passage in American Sculpture*. Seattle, WA: University of Washington Press, 2001.

International Sculpture Center. Home page at http://www.sculpture.org.

Rubinstein, Charlotte Streifer. *American Women Sculptors: A History of Women Working in Three Dimensions*. Boston: G. K. Hall, 1990.

Salmon, Robin R., Ilene Susan Ford, and Loretta Dimmick. *American Masters: Sculpture from Brookgreen Gardens*. Murrells Inlet, SC: Brookgreen Gardens, 1996.

Shapiro, Michael Edward. *Twentieth-Century American Sculpture*. St. Louis, MO, Saint Louis Art Museum, 1986.

Taft, Loredo. *History of American Sculpture*. New York: Macmillan, 1903.

Wheeler, Daniel. *Art Since Mid-Century: 1945 to the Present*. Englewood Cliffs, N.J.: Prentice-Hall, 1991.

Christine E. Hoffman

See also **Abstract Expressionism; Pop Art; Vietnam War Memorial; War Memorials; Whitney Museum.**

SELF-TAUGHT ARTISTS

During the first half of the twentieth century, the term "folk art" was used to describe the traditional crafts and the decorative and purely artistic expressions of artists and artisans who were informed by ethnic, community, family, and religious traditions. Folk art implied its connection to a "folk" population, made by and generally for common people, outside of the realms of the academy or high culture. Traditional American folk art encompasses a broad variety of eighteenth-, nineteenth-, and early-twentieth-century objects that primarily reflect life in rural, pre-industrial America. The recognition of folk art as a significant current of American culture paralleled changes in American society, leading to the evolution of terms used to describe nonacademic art.

In the second half of the twentieth century, the rise of interest in nonacademic art, especially post-industrial expressions, stimulated a reexamination of its nature and origins. Work by artists that represented a personal artistic vision which was not demonstrably informed by ethnic, community, family, and religious traditions has been described variously as isolate, outsider, and visionary and by the widely accepted term "self-taught" art.

With the exception of traditional folk art as defined above, the boundary between "folk" and "self-taught" art has become more relaxed than distinct since the 1970s. Since its establishment in 1961, the Museum of American Folk Art—the field's most established institution—has presented a rigorous program exploring works of art from both realms under the rubric "folk art." The discussion of what defines nonacademic art and how best to name it continues to evolve as interest in the field accelerates.

Traditional American folk art forms range from functional, decorative, and purely aesthetic objects reflecting religion, faith and personal devotion, trades and commerce, and many aspects of daily life. Folk art forms include quilts and other domestic textiles, ceramic vessels, baskets, tools, furniture, weather vanes, architectural ornament, trade signs and sculpture, waterfowl and fish decoys, fraktur (Pennsylvania German hand-lettered, decorated documents), portrait and scene painting, itinerant arts, and memorial sculpture, to name some examples. Folk art reflected the variety of European cultural traditions brought by immigrants to America. Through the process of assimilation, European art and craft traditions found a new, American context. Appreciation of folk art focused on aesthetically exceptional examples that often expressed the maker's original artistic vision through a traditional form. In 1947 the Shelburne Museum, a vast collection of traditional American folk art collected from 1907 by fine art aficionado Electra Havemeyer Webb, opened in Shelburne, Vermont. The Shelburne Museum combines folk art with a collection of historic architectural structures, presenting a panorama of traditional American folk art and folk life.

In the early twentieth century European art dominated American art institutions. This Eurocentrism affected American attitudes toward its own indigenous art forms, motivating some artists and curators to look to folk and vernacular art with vigorous interest. Juliana Force, the first director of the Whitney Studio Club (formed in 1918, to become the Whitney Museum of American Art in 1930), with her patron, Gertrude Vanderbilt Whitney, embarked on a mission to recognize and validate American artists and American contemporary art. Force had a longtime interest in (and collection of) Shaker furniture and other examples of folk art and she included folk art within the scope of the Whitney Studio Club's exhibitions. The country's first exhibit of American folk art, *Early American Art*, curated by artist Henry Schnackenberg, opened at the Whitney Studio Club in 1924. The exhibit included works primarily from artists' collections, including objects from Charles Demuth and Charles Sheeler. In 1930 Holger Cahill organized *American Prim-*

itives: An Exhibit of Paintings of Nineteenth-Century Folk Artists for the Newark Museum. In 1932 *Art of the Common Man in America 1750–1900* was organized by Holger Cahill for the Museum of Modern Art. This exhibit included works from the collection of Abby Aldrich Rockefeller, whose collection later anchored the Abby Aldrich Rockefeller Folk Art Center in Williamsburg, Virginia, established in 1957.

Artists and curators recognized a modern aesthetic in folk art forms. Robert Henri and other artists at the Ogunquit colony in the 1920s collected and were influenced by examples of New England folk art. Elie Nadelman's collection of folk carvings strongly influenced his work, which contained a "folk" sensibility. The perception of a modern aesthetic in traditional folk art carried over to works by artists whose connections with folk traditions were subtle or even nonexistent. Drawings created by African American self-taught artist Bill Traylor were discovered by the formally trained artist Charles Shannon in Montgomery, Alabama, in 1939. Traylor, who had been born into slavery, began drawing after a lifetime of farm work. His large body of drawings created between 1939 and 1942 was recognized as being simultaneously "primitive" and startlingly modern. The religiously inspired stone carvings of African American self-taught artist William Edmondson were appreciated for their spare, formal beauty and were compared to works by modern sculptor Constantin Brancusi. In 1937 Edmondson became the first African American and the first self-taught artist to have a solo show at the Museum of Modern Art. In 1941 the Arts Club of Chicago included a number of paintings by Horace Pippin, an African American self-taught artist from Pennsylvania, in an exhibition that also included works by Salvador Dali and Fernand Leger. Despite these and a number of other landmark exhibitions, and the growing analysis of works by self-taught artists according to modernist, formalist criteria, self-taught art remained segregated from the realm of mainstream art.

The Recognition of Twentieth-Century Self-Taught Art

In 1961 the Museum of American Folk Art was formed in New York City and soon became a defining force in the field. It presented traditional folk art and works by twentieth-century self-taught artists, and traced the evolution of both genres as currents in American art. Founder and early curator Herbert Waide Hemphill Jr. advocated the recognition and acceptance of works by twentieth-century self-taught artists into a field that had previously focused on traditional folk art. Hemphill and Julia Weissman co-authored *Twentieth-Century Folk Art and Artists* (1974), which explored works by folk and self-taught artists, artists' environments, and vernacular yard sculpture, broadening the scope of folk and self-taught art into previously unrecognized realms. Hemphill's vision in redefining the field was paralleled by his outstanding and influential collection, which ranged from traditional folk art to contemporary self-taught art. The exhibit *American Folk Art: The Herbert Waide Hemphill Jr. Collection* opened at the Milwaukee Art Museum in 1981, and traveled to five other cities. The acquisition by gift and purchase of 378 works from the Hemphill collection by the National Museum of American Art (later the Smithsonian American Art Museum) in Washington, D.C., in 1986 further codified the acceptance of self-taught art into the folk art arena and underscored the subject's significance by its prominent inclusion in a national museum.

Self-Taught Art in Chicago and the Midwest
Chicago developed as a notable center for engendering some of the country's exceptional self-taught artists and for its rigorous acceptance of self-taught art into the art culture of the city. Beginning in the 1940s and 1950s "Monster Roster" artists Cosmo Campoli, Leon Gollub, George Cohen, June Leaf, Seymour Rosofsky, and unaffiliated artist H. C. Westermann all studied and were influenced by non-mainstream art, including works by autodidacts, institutionalized artists, and examples of non-Western art, known then as primitive art. In 1951, ten years after Horace Pippin's work was shown at the Arts Club of Chicago, Jean Dubuffet delivered there his influential lecture, "Anti-Cultural Positions." In it he introduced the European concept of the "artist outsider" and his theories of Art Brut or "raw art"—art arising completely from within the artist without connection to established cultural constructs. Dubuffet's lecture had a strong impact on artists, curators, and collectors, validating their established interest in art from beyond the mainstream and thus setting the stage for a new generation of artist-collectors.

In the 1960s a group of young artists who later became known as Chicago Imagists developed a collective interest in self-taught art. These artists studied at The School of the Art Institute of Chicago, where they were encouraged to look beyond the mainstream and to recognize art from many sources and origins. Chicago Imagist artists Roger Brown, Ray Yoshida, Jim Nutt, Gladys Nilsson, Karl Wirsum, Phil Hanson, and Christina Ramberg became known not only for the power and originality of their own works, but for the integral connection between their work and their collections. These artists assembled eclectic collections that included works by self-taught and institutionalized artists, tramp art, bottle cap sculptures, twig furniture, prison art, traditional and non-traditional folk art from many cultures, and objects from material culture.

Imagist artists accepted folk and self-taught art on an equal footing with their own works and with mainstream art in general. In the 1960s and 1970s Chicago artists, educators, dealers, and collectors eagerly embraced the works of self-taught artists working in Chicago, who have since received international acclaim. Joseph E. Yoakum, of African American and Creek-Cherokee lineage, created spiritually inspired visionary landscape drawings between 1962 and 1972. Henry Darger, whose works were discovered in 1973 just after his death, created complex and disturbingly beautiful panoramic collage-drawings to illustrate his epic novel, "The Realms of the Unreal. . . ." Drossos Skyllas, a Greek immigrant and self-taught painter, worked in a painstakingly meticulous style that challenged the assumption that folk and self-taught art were primitive or technically unsophisticated. Italian-American artist Aldo Piacenza filled his north suburban Chicago yard with birdhouse sculptures representing the churches, cathedrals, and duomos of Italy. Lee Godie was a street person who appeared on the steps of The Art Institute of Chicago in 1968, selling portraits of Chicago's Gold Coast elite. William Dawson began carving his distinct and original portraits and figural sculpture in the early 1970s.

Finding their works consistent, provocative, and highly original, Chicago Imagist artists embraced the work of these and other self-taught artists, crediting its influence on their work and its impact on their fundamental ideas about art. Chicago art dealer Phyllis Kind was an early proponent of self-taught artists and began exhibiting works of such artists from America and Europe in the early 1970s. From the 1970s to the early twenty-first century there were many exhibitions of self-taught art in the Midwest, including *Outsider Art in Chicago* at that city's Museum of Contemporary Art in 1979. Building on its commitment to folk art represented in its collections of Haitian and American folk art, the Milwaukee Art Museum in 1979 acquired the Michael and Julie Hall Collection of American Folk Art. Also in the Midwest, the John Michael Kohler Arts Center in Sheboygan, Wisconsin, exhibited works by self-taught or "grassroots" artists regularly, starting in 1978 when it mounted the exhibit *Grass Roots Art Wisconsin: Toward a Redefinition*. Since that time the center has assembled an extensive permanent collection of works by self-taught artists, as well as parts of and entire folk art environments, which are regularly exhibited.

In 1991 Intuit: The Center for Intuitive and Outsider Art (originally Society for Outsider, Intuitive, and Visionary Art) was established, solidifying Chicago as a national center for the exhibition and interpretation of self-taught art. Intuit defines intuitive and outsider art as "the work of artists who demonstrate little influence from the mainstream art world and who instead seem motivated by their unique personal visions. This definition includes what is known as art brut, nontraditional folk art, self-taught art and visionary art." By its tenth anniversary in 2001, Intuit had mounted forty-five exhibitions. Its exhibition history reflected the breadth of the organization's scope; exhibits ranged from theme shows addressing West African barber-style signboards, thrift store paintings, bottle cap art, and eccentric chairs to solo shows of works by Mose Tolliver, Emery Blagdon, Drossos Skyllas, Cora Meek, Jim Work, and Aldo Piacenza. Intuit's exhibition history is distinguished by the fact that the majority of works in most exhibitions have come from Chicago-area collections. Intuit established its American Masters gallery in 1999 to showcase a revolving roster of self-taught artists who have achieved the critical acclaim and status reserved for "master" artists. Intuit committed to a program of preservation by saving the contents of the room (home and studio) of Henry Darger for eventual reinstallation before the room itself was demolished in 2000.

Folk Art Environments

"Folk art environments," or simply "art environments," are an essential element of folk and self-taught art in America. Art environments are composite sites that include elements of art, architecture, and landscape architecture in varying combinations. They are extended artistic creations of interrelated elements, as opposed to discrete works of art, and they occupy a specific place—an exterior landscape, an interior space, or both. Their content and meaning is derived from the spatial context or relationship of components to each other, to their location, and generally to the life of the artist. Major extant American art environments include Simon Rodia's *Watts Towers* of Los Angeles; S. P. Dinsmoor's *Garden of Eden* in Lucas, Kansas; Fred Smith's *Wisconsin Concrete Park* in Phillips, Wisconsin; St. Eom's *Pasaquan* in Buena Vista, Georgia; Edward Leedskalnin's *Coral Castle* in Homestead, Florida; and Jeff McKissack's *Orange Show* in Houston, Texas.

Widespread recognition of a few major examples of art environments in the United States, such as the *Watts Towers* and the *Wisconsin Concrete Park*, stimulated some initial public interest in such sites in the 1950s and 1960s. In his photo essay, "The Grass-Roots Artist" in *Art in America* (September–October 1968), Gregg N. Blasdel presented the concept of grassroots artists and art environments—until then an art genre that had received little critical attention—to the mainstream art world. This article featured the environments of fifteen artists (including environments that are now no longer extant, by Dave Woods, Jesse "Outlaw" Howard, Clarence Schmidt, and Ed Root) and inspired a number of artists to travel around the country to visit and document art environments. The article precipitated an awareness of environments as an important aspect of self-taught art and a cognizance of the twentieth-century built environment. Blasdel's article also stimulated early efforts to preserve art environments.

In addition to Blasdel's article, the exhibition *Naives and Visionaries* at the Walker Art Center in Minneapolis, Minnesota, in 1974 contributed to the awareness and preservation of art environments. The exhibit featured the art environments of nine artist-builders, represented primarily through photographs, and augmented by a selection of objects that could be temporarily removed from sites. The exhibit introduced the genre of art environments as sites comprised of integral components that lose their integrity and full significance if dismantled, encouraging people to visit them in person. In 1974 the Kansas Grassroots Art Association (KGAA) was formed to preserve grassroots art on its original site if possible, or off

the site if necessary; to document grassroots art through photographs and documentation; and to increase public awareness and appreciation of grassroots art. The first permanent organization formed to preserve art environments, the KGAA initially rallied around art environments in Kansas and the Great Plains region, but eventually expanded its scope to include international sites. In 1978 Saving and Preserving Arts and Cultural Environments (SPACES) was formed in Los Angeles to document art environments and advocate for their preservation. The first effort to preserve an American art environment began in1959 when the Committee for Simon Rodia's Towers in Watts was formed. Consisting of local artists, writers, and educators, it began a long struggle to save the Watts Towers, now a National Historic Site. In 1977 preservation efforts began in Wisconsin, with the Kohler Foundation's purchase and preservation of Fred Smith's *Wisconsin Concrete Park*. Since that time preservation efforts have grown around the country, and a number of sites have been preserved in situ, including S. P. Dinsmoor's *Garden of Eden*; the *Orange Show*; St. Eom's *Pasaquan*; Nick Engelbert's *Grandview*, near Hollandale, Wisconsin; and Herman Rusch's *Prairie Moon Museum and Sculpture Garden*, near Cochrane, Wisconsin, to name a few.

Preserving art environments presents daunting challenges to supporters, including the purchase and maintenance of real estate, the preservation of complex sites created with nontraditional media and techniques, and exposure to the elements. Calvin and Ruby Black's *Possum Trot*, built in the Mojave Desert, is one of several environments that were dismantled and whose elements were sold as individual works of art. Preservation in situ has not always been possible, and museums have participated in the preservation of entire sites or elements of sites. The first environment to be preserved and permanently installed in an American museum was James Hampton's *The Throne of the Third Heaven of the Nations Millenium* (sic) *General Assembly*, an elaborate interior environment created by an African American janitor from Washington, D.C. Hampton's installation was acquired in its entirety by the National Museum of American Art shortly after the artist's death in 1964. Since that time some museums have acquired elements of art environments.

Folk and Self-Taught Art Organizations

The last two decades of the twentieth century saw growth in institutions dedicated to folk and self-taught art, and publications about the subject proliferated during those years. In 1987 the Folk Art Society of America was formed and its newsletter, *Folk Art Messenger*, was launched. In 1989 *Raw Vision*, the international journal of outsider art, was established and Intuit began publishing *The Outsider* (originally *In'tuit*) in 1992. In 1995 the American Visionary Art Museum was established in Baltimore, launching a program of ambitious theme shows featuring the range of nonacademic art. The Museum of American Folk Art, which publishes *Folk Art Magazine* (formerly *The Clarion*), established its Contemporary Center in 1997 to address contemporary trends in self-taught art while continuing to examine traditional American folk art. The museum officially changed its name to the American Museum of Folk Art in 2001 to reflect its international scope. Other American museums that have significant collections of self-taught art include the High Museum of Art in Atlanta, Georgia, opened in 1983, and the Menello Museum of American Folk Art in Orlando, Florida, established in 1998. Self-taught art's commercial success has been underscored by its annual trade shows, the Outsider Art Fair in New York City and Folk Fest in Atlanta.

The discussion of what to call works beyond the mainstream has not lost its vigor. The term "outsider art" gained widespread acceptance beginning in the 1980s. Some object to this designation, which implies a segregationist polarity between artists on the "inside," in an assumed position of power, and artists on the "outside," disenfranchised from the cultural mainstream. The term "post-mainstream" has been suggested but has not been widely accepted. Despite the mercurial nature of folk and self-taught art, which continues to evolve while resisting precise definition, a growing number of individuals and organizations that demonstrate an interest in and commitment to the genre is paralleled by the expanding recognition of it as a significant, recurrent, and enduring facet of the nation's artistic culture.

BIBLIOGRAPHY

American Folk Art: The Herbert Waide Hemphill Jr. Collection. Milwaukee, Wisc.: Milwaukee Art Museum, 1981. Out of print.

Beardsley, John. *Gardens of Revelation: Environments by Visionary Artists.* New York: Abbeville Press, 1995.

Blasdel, Gregg N. "The Grass-Roots Artist." *Art in America* 56, no. 5 (September–October 1968): 25–41.

Cardinal, Roger. *Outsider Art.* New York: Praeger, 1972.

Cerney, Charlene, and Suzanne Seriff. *Recycled, Re-Seen: Folk Art from the Global Scrap Heap.* New York: Harry N. Abrams, 1996.

Hall, Michael D. *Stereoscopic Perspective: Reflections on American Fine and Folk Art.* Ann Arbor, Mich.: UMI Research Press, 1988.

———, and Eugene W. Metcalf Jr., eds. *The Artist Outsider: Creativity and the Boundaries of Culture.* Washington, D.C.: Smithsonian Institution Press, 1994.

Hartigan, Lynda Roscoe, and Andrew L. Connors. *Made with Passion: The Hemphill Folk Art Collection in the National Museum of American Art.* Washington, D.C.: Smithsonian Institution Press, 1990.

Hemphill, Herbert W., Jr., and Julia Weissman. *Twentieth-Century Folk Art and Artists.* New York: E. P. Dutton, 1974.

Intuit: The First Ten Years. Chicago: Intuit: The Center for Intuitive and Outsider Art, 2001.

Livingston, Jane, and John Beardsley. *Black Folk Art in America, 1930–1980.* Jackson: University Press of Mississippi, 1982.

Milwaukee Art Museum. *Common Ground/Uncommon Vision: The Michael and Julie Hall Collection of American Folk Art in the Milwaukee Art Museum.* Milwaukee, Wisc.: The Museum, 1993. Available from the Milwaukee Art Museum and the Art Institute of Chicago.

Outsider Art: An Exploration of Chicago Collections. Chicago: City of Chicago Department of Cultural Affairs and Intuit: The Center for Intuitive and Outsider Art, 1997.

Self-Taught Artists of the 20th Century: An American Anthology. New York: Museum of American Folk Art, 1998.

Sellen, Betty-Carol. *Self-Taught, Outsider, and Folk Art: A Guide to American Artists, Locations and Resources.* Jefferson, N.C.: McFarland, 2000.

Stone, Lisa, and Jim Zanzi. *Sacred Spaces and Other Places: A Guide to Grottos and Sculptural Environments in the Upper Midwest.* Chicago: School of the Art Institute of Chicago Press, 1993.

Lisa Stone

See also **Art Institute of Chicago; Arts and Crafts Movement; Museums; Smithsonian Institution; Whitney Museum.**

STAINED GLASS WINDOWS

The American glass industry first began to prosper after the War of 1812 temporarily eliminated all European imported glass. Until the 1840s, however, there were few stylistic variations in American colored leaded windows, which generally contained numerous glass squares or diamonds with stenciled designs of floral and leafy patterns, giving the appearance of looking through a large kaleidoscope. The first American figural windows were made by the English-born brothers John and William Bolton in the mid-1840s for (St. Ann and) Holy Trinity Church in Brooklyn, New York.

The Gothic Revival movement in Europe greatly affected stained glass in America. Much figural stained glass was imported from Germany and England, and its subject matter frequently featured scenes that had their origins in paintings by the German artists Heinrich Hoffmann (1824–1911) and Bernard Plockhorst (1825–1907). At least fifteen of Hoffman's paintings were reproduced as stained glass windows, with *Christ in the Garden of Gethsemane* being the most popular, while Plockhorst's painting *The Good Shepherd* was also very widely copied. These and other themes rendered in glass by the Munich-based Mayer and Zettler studios were very influential in the United States, and are still commonly seen in new works produced by American studios.

By the 1870s, milky opalescent glass, usually found in bottles, began to appear in the work of both John La Farge and Louis Comfort Tiffany, after they discovered a process by which molten glass could have varying degrees of color and opacity "built in." Truly an American phenomenon, this painterly approach greatly reduced the use of enamels and fired-on paint for folds of clothing, foliage, and other elements. The use of opalescent glass began to decline by the early twentieth century, however, in part because of the rising popularity of such neo-Gothic architecture as New York's Cathedral of St. John the Divine. The cathedral's architect, Ralph Adams Cram, was openly hostile toward opalescent glass, and demanded that the stained glass used for St. John the Divine imitate the form, figures, and color palette found in Chartres Cathedral in France. Not long afterward, these same aesthetic prejudices began to be reflected in the productions of many American studios, including, most notably, those run by Charles Connick in Boston and William Willet in Philadelphia. A more contemporary (and iconoclastic) approach to stained glass had its origins in the work of Frank Lloyd Wright, who presented his vision for stained glass through a 1907 European exhibition and subsequent publications.

The depression of the 1930s and World War II put a damper on new building, which in turn stifled stained glass production worldwide. Postwar German artists, however, began to extend certain extraordinary reforms that had been initiated by the Bauhaus movement before the war. In new churches and public buildings alike, they created stained glass that was abstract, mostly colorless, linear, and without any paint.

In the 1960s and early 1970s, artists from the West Coast, receptive to this modern approach, began pilgrimages to Germany. They returned as revolutionaries in a field previously dominated by traditionalists, desirous of becoming "artists" in stained glass. This new movement allowed stained glass to have a venue outside of churches and to be displayed in art galleries and private homes. It also encouraged more artistic freedom and the use of new techniques and technology—flashed, opak, and opal glass; laminating bevels and jewels to plate glass; silk screening on glass; detailed sand carving; fusing and bending; and a spin-off from the space industry, dichroic glass.

BIBLIOGRAPHY

Connick, Charles. *Adventures in Light and Color: An Introduction to the Stained Glass Craft*. New York: Random House, 1937.

Hanks, David. *The Decorative Designs of Frank Lloyd Wright*. New York: Dutton, 1979.

Harrison, Martin. *Victorian Stained Glass*. London: Barrie and Jenkins, 1980.

Knapp, Stephen. *The Art of Glass: Integrating Architecture and Glass*. Glouster, Mass.: Rockport, 1998.

Moor, Andrew. *Architectural Glass: A Guide for Design Professionals*. New York: Watson-Guptill, 1989.

Weis, Helene. "Those Old Familiar Faces." *Stained Glass Quarterly* (Fall 1991): 204–207, 216–218.

Barbara Krueger

See also **Art: Glass.**

ART, INDIAN. Although day-to-day existence took precedence over artistic endeavors, Native Americans beautified even mundane objects in some manner. Artifacts found in burial mounds of the eastern Woodland tribes show that pottery vessels, made for holding liquids or storing food, were both useful and ornamental. Bowls and jars were decorated with relief, achieved by textured stamps or carved by paddles. These tribes also molded bowls into shapes of birds, fish, reptiles, or human heads, which may have had mythological significance. Carved shells were used to ornament the nose, ears, and wrists. Several frequent designs carved on this early jewelry were birds, spiders, serpents, the cross (probably directional), and the scalloped disk for the sun.

Art of the Plains Indians, who were semi-sedentary before the introduction of European horses, centered on pictographic displays painted on hides used for tipis and clothing. These flat dimensional pictures served mnemonic purposes and often depicted special events.

Indians of the northwest coast carved totem poles that towered above their longhouses. Abundant forests provided the raw material for the poles, as well as for highly decorated watertight wooden boxes and elaborately carved wooden masks, used to disguise the wearer, helping him or her to capture the spirit of supernatural beings. The totems carved on the poles and the masks depicted animals or supernatural animals, such as the thunderbird, in unconventional forms. Flat-dimensioned animal body parts were not necessarily anatomically arranged. The Indians also carved totems on bones and tusks.

In Alaska's arctic regions, long winter nights allowed the Indians to decorate their tools and clothing, and sometimes just for pleasure they made toys and games out of animal bones. Their elaborate ceremonial masks rivaled

Potter. A 1905 photograph by Edward S. Curtis of a Santa Clara woman—a member of a Pueblo tribe in southwestern New Mexico—working on her pottery. LIBRARY OF CONGRESS

those of the northwest coast Indians, and Indian women wore intricate finger masks for ceremonial dances.

The sedentary lifestyle of the southwest Indians led to their developing advanced skills in making pottery, jewelry, baskets, and woven cloth. Different tribes could be recognized by their specialized decorations. Geometric designs, spirals, dots, frets, bands, bars, zigzags, and terraced figures graced the pottery of the Pueblo tribes. The Hopis stylized birds so that individual species could not always be identified. The Zunis used triangles, open circles, coils, diamonds, arches, and scrolls. Their ceremonial masks were easily identified by rolled collars of feathers.

Following the arrival of Europeans, the Navajos borrowed weaving techniques from the Pueblos, but instead of using cotton, they used wool from recently acquired sheep, weaving from the bottom up on upright looms. Sometimes the weaver drew intricate patterns in the sand, but usually she kept the design in her memory. The Navajos were also known for their unique sand paintings using different-colored sand and gravel. Large paintings required several painters as well as an artist to grind the colors. Generally used in healing ceremonies, the sand painting was made between dawn and sunset and was destroyed after its use.

With the arrival of Europeans, Indian art gradually changed from utilitarian to commercial. Indians adopted European tools and materials. Indians in the east sold baskets made from wood splints, instead of baskets woven from thin grass fibers. The Navajos also made blankets in serape style for soldiers.

The ARTS AND CRAFTS MOVEMENT in the late nineteenth century, coupled with the growth of tourism, led to an increased interest in Indian art. In actuality though, Indians were not practicing their traditional arts, but were producing new art strictly for sale. Once consumers put Navajo blankets on floors, the Navajos adapted the idea and changed their rugs, which became their dominant product. Pueblo Indians manufactured ashtrays, candlesticks, and figurines instead of their traditional bowls and jars. California Indians adapted their basketry tradition to this modern marketplace as well. This commercialism sparked the debate about what in Indian art was valuable as fine art, what was valuable as craft, and what was valuable as ethnographic history.

Western art techniques were taught alongside traditional practices at Indian schools, especially those in Oklahoma and New Mexico. With drawings on paper and canvas, Indians made their art forms more comprehensible to non-Indians. Yet, they also incorporated elements of traditional forms.

In 1939, the Golden Gate International Exposition in San Francisco featured Indian art; in 1941, the Museum of Modern Art in New York exhibited Indian art on three floors and drew attention to Indian art. From 1946 to 1979, the Philbrook Museum in Tulsa, Oklahoma, held juried competitions for Indian art. The competitions set

Weavers. Three Navajo women work on their weaving—from wool provided by sheep like the ones nearby—in this 1914 photograph by William J. Carpenter. LIBRARY OF CONGRESS

the standard for what was considered Indian art—a flat, pictorial style.

Indian artists Oscar Howe, Joe Herrera, and Allan Houser led the way into the modern period. By exploring form and content, they captured the spirit and mythical traditions of their people through abstractions and modern mediums. A force in this development was the establishment in 1962 of the Institute of American Indian Arts in Santa Fe, New Mexico, funded by the Bureau of Indian Affairs.

In 1989, the National Museum of the American Indian was established within the Smithsonian Institution with exhibition facilities designated for New York and Washington, D.C. Other museums that feature major displays of Indian art include the Gilcrease Museum in Tulsa, Oklahoma, the Eiteljorg Museum in Indianapolis, and the Southwest Museum in Los Angeles, California.

BIBLIOGRAPHY

Berlo, Janet C., and Ruth B. Phillips. *Native North American Art.* New York: Oxford University Press, 1998.

Naylor, Maria, ed. *Authentic Indian Designs: 2,500 Illustrations from Reports of the Bureau of American Ethnology.* New York: Dover, 1975.

Taylor, Colin F., ed. *Native American Arts and Crafts.* London: Salamander Books, 1995.

Whiteford, Andrew Hunter. *North American Indian Arts.* New York: St. Martin's Press, 2001.

Veda Boyd Jones

See also **Dance, Indian; Indian Oral Literature; Music: Indian; National Museum of the American Indian; Tribes: Southwestern;** *and vol. 9:* **Land of the Spotted Eagle.**

ART INSTITUTE OF CHICAGO. Dualities have defined the history of the Art Institute of Chicago (AIC), a museum and school (The School of The Art Institute of Chicago, or SAIC) in ambivalent relationship with one another and their host community. AIC's iconic Shepley, Rutan, and Coolidge building on Michigan Avenue, erected on debris from the great fire of 1871, first served the Columbian Exposition, whose congresses it housed in 1893 before AIC occupied it at year's end. This nearly windowless structure on the edge of the frenetic central Loop served as a refuge from urban disorder. Yet like the surrounding noise, filth, and labor conflict, AIC was a by-product of railroad development, meat processing, and other forms of commerce that fueled Chicago's growth.

In 1866 sculptor Leonard W. Volk and other artists formed the Chicago Academy of Design. Partly as a result of losses caused by the fire, the academy encountered financial difficulties and solicited help from business leaders. Employing some sleight of hand, these businessmen created in 1879 a new organization, the Chicago Academy of Fine Arts, renamed The Art Institute of Chicago in 1882. Its charter provided that it be "privately administered for the public benefit by a Board of Trustees." Under the leadership of the grain merchant and banker Charles L. Hutchinson, president of that board from 1882 to 1924, AIC's art school became the nation's best enrolled and its museum, with a half-million visitors by 1899, developed the largest membership. In addition to moving AIC to its permanent home in 1893, Hutchinson attracted distinguished faculty, including sculptor Lorado Taft, and enlarged the museum's collections. Major donors included Martin A. Ryerson and Bertha Honoré Palmer, who with painter Mary Cassatt's advice acquired a superb collection of nineteenth-century French paintings.

Along with others who followed Hutchinson, museum directors Daniel Catton Rich (1938–1958) and, in the decades after 1980, James Wood, strengthened curatorial areas such as Prints and Drawings, Architecture, and African and Amerindian Art and museum education, and brought square footage to more than ten times its 1893 total. Expansion occurred in every decade except the 1930s and 1940s. Examples of growth include the Ryerson Library (1901); the Ferguson Building (1958), whose funding with monies designated for commissioning "statuary and monuments" drew legal challenges; new facilities for the SAIC (1977); and several wings and buildings over the following quarter century. The museum developed outstanding collections in numerous areas, such as Impressionism, Flemish and Italian painting, and—with

the help of the Buckingham family—prints and drawings and Asian art.

Although conservative aesthetic and social impulses guided many of the trustees, the institution helped expand definitions of what constituted significant art, as in its 1895 exhibition of works by Claude Monet and Édouard Manet, and in the 1906 purchase of *Assumption of the Virgin* (1577) by El Greco, then a largely neglected master. Amid great controversy, AIC in 1913 presented a distillation of New York City's Armory Show, which gave tens of thousands of Chicagoans their first encounter with Pablo Picasso, Marcel Duchamp, and other avant-garde artists. Only a few modernist works entered the collection in the next fifteen years. However, with gifts such as those from Frederic Clay Bartlett, which included Georges Seurat's *Sunday Afternoon on the Island of the Grand-Jatte* (1884) in 1926, Arthur Jerome Eddy's 1931 bequest of Expressionist works by Wassily Kandinsky, and others, AIC developed a major modern collection, which also included important American paintings, some by former SAIC students such as Georgia O'Keeffe, Archibald J. Motley, and Grant Wood. Appointment in the 1940s of the innovative gallery owner Katherine Kuh as a curator indicated increased commitment to exhibiting challenging contemporary work.

In 2001 the museum's ten curatorial departments included some with continuity to the founding era, and others such as Photography that reflected the broadened definition of museum-worthy art. Changes in cultural perceptions led in 1956 to formation of a Department of Primitive Art, later renamed the Department of African and Amerindian Art. Some areas diminished in importance. Plaster reproductions of classical works, considered an important aspect of the collections in the 1880s, had been removed from display by the 1950s. The museum achieved a higher level of professionalism when a comprehensive exhibition held in conjunction with the 1933–1934 Century of Progress Exposition suggested the wisdom of arranging AIC's collections in a systematic, integrated manner rather than displaying together all works given by one donor.

Although trustees assumed a less direct role in curatorial and curricular decisions as the museum became more professional, a seat on AIC's board continued to be one of the highest distinctions available to Chicago's social and economic elite. Support from large corporations such as Kraft General Foods and Ameritech became increasingly important. In 2001 the largest sources of support were gifts and endowment income and school revenues, mostly from tuition. Other sources were museum admissions and memberships; and public funds, which became available when AIC's building was erected on Chicago Park District Land in 1893 and were later supplemented by state and federal programs.

The provocations of contemporary art, in conjunction with identity politics, sparked controversies in the 1980s and 1990s that threatened but did not end this public support. As always, balancing the goals of building an international art collection and serving the needs of a local arts community presented challenges and some resentments, as when in the 1980s AIC abandoned its Chicago and Vicinity show, once a regular event. Increased emphasis in the contemporary art world on work that responded to the concerns of particular communities, some outside the traditional arts audience, created new possibilities for collaboration and conflict.

BIBLIOGRAPHY

Chicago History 8, no. 1 (spring 1979). Special issue on The Art Institute of Chicago.

Gilmore, Roger, ed. *Over a Century: A History of the School of the Art Institute of Chicago, 1866–1981.* Chicago: The School of the Art Institute of Chicago, 1982.

Horowitz, Helen Lefkowitz. *Culture and the City: Cultural Philanthropy in Chicago from the 1880s to 1917.* Chicago: University of Chicago Press, 1989.

Prince, Sue Ann. *The Old Guard and the Avant-Garde: Modernism in Chicago, 1910–1940.* Chicago: University of Chicago Press, 1990.

George H. Roeder Jr.

See also **Art: Painting, Photography; Museums.**

ARTICLES OF CONFEDERATION. Between September 1774 and June 1776, delegates to the Continental Congress devised and debated several plans for establishing an independent constitutional union among the American colonies. In July 1775, Benjamin Franklin presented Congress with the first written plan for a new national government, the Articles of Confederation and Perpetual Union. Other plans also were introduced during the following year, but it was not until 11 June 1776 that the Continental Congress appointed one committee to draft the Declaration of Independence and a second committee, composed of a single delegate from each colony, to prepare a plan of confederation. A month later, the latter committee presented Congress with a draft constitution known as the Articles of Confederation. The committee's constitution assigned broad powers to the new national government, including the authority to tax, to determine state boundaries, and to dispose of all other unsettled "Lands for the general Benefit." The draft document also placed restrictions upon the authority of the states; divided national expenses proportionally among the states according to their population; and most contentiously, granted each state delegation a single vote within a unicameral national Congress.

Despite general agreement for the Declaration of Independence and a widespread recognition of the need to provision the military resistance against Great Britain, there was no immediate constitutional consensus concerning the terms of a new national government. Rather, during the next year and one-half, state delegates discussed, debated, and periodically attempted to amend the original draft of the Articles of Confederation. A confluence of factors—including the norms of international protocol, wartime economic disruptions, the possibility of military defeat, and several critical changes in the draft constitution that weakened Congress's authority—helped secure Congress's endorsement of the Articles of Confederation on 15 November 1777. Several state legislatures quickly ratified the Articles, but others expressed strong reservations about one or more of its provisions. Indeed, about half of the states had approved the Articles of Confederation by the 10 March 1778 deadline established by Congress, yet unanimous approval was required to make the Articles effective. One of the most vocal state opponents, Maryland, objected to the lack of national control over the vast western territories and the state withheld its consent until Virginia in January 1781 agreed to a conditional cession of part of its western territorial claims. In March 1781, Maryland became the final state to ratify the Articles of Confederation.

Although the Articles remained in force until the new U.S. Constitution took effect in 1788, many provisions of this first national constitution had enduring constitutional effects. Article I, for example, identified the new union as "the United States of America." Article II determined that "each State retains its sovereignty, freedom, and independence." Article III bound the states together into a "league of friendship" for their "common defense, the security of their Liberties, and their mutual and general welfare." Article IV guaranteed free inhabitants "all privileges and immunities" of the other states, and the right to travel freely across state boundaries. Article V granted each state a single vote in Congress. Article VI prohibited the states from making treaties with or war upon other countries without the consent of Congress. Article IX empowered Congress to make war and treaties; to borrow, to coin, and to regulate the value of money; and to appoint the commander in chief of the army or navy. That Article's powers, however, required the consent of nine of the thirteen states. Finally, Article XIII determined that the Articles could be amended with the approval of Congress and the unanimous consent of the state legislatures.

BIBLIOGRAPHY

Kromkowski, Charles A. *Recreating the American Republic: Rules of Apportionment, Constitutional Change, and American Political Development, 1700–1870.* New York: Cambridge University Press, 2002.

Matson, Cathy D., and Peter S. Onuf. *A Union of Interests: Political and Economic Thought in Revolutionary America.* Lawrence: Kansas University Press, 1990.

Rakove, Jack N. *The Beginnings of National Politics: An Interpretive History of the Continental Congress.* New York: Knopf, 1979.

Charles A. Kromkowski

See also **Constitution of the United States; Continental Congress;** *and vol. 9:* **From Annapolis to Philadelphia.**

ARTIFICIAL INTELLIGENCE, a branch of computer science that seeks to create a computer system capable of sensing the world around it, understanding conversations, learning, reasoning, and reaching decisions, just as would a human. In 1950 the pioneering British mathematician Alan Turing proposed a test for artificial intelligence in which a human subject tries to talk with an unseen conversant. The tester sends questions to the machine via teletype and reads its answers; if the subject cannot discern whether the conversation is being held with another person or a machine, then the machine is deemed to have artificial intelligence. No machine has come close to passing this test, and it is unlikely that one will in the near future. Researchers, however, have made progress on specific pieces of the artificial intelligence puzzle, and some of their work has had tangible benefits.

One area of progress is the field of expert systems, or computer systems designed to reproduce the knowledge base and decision-making techniques used by experts in a given field. Such a system can train workers and assist in decision making. MYCIN, a program developed in 1976 at Stanford University, suggests possible diagnoses for patients with infectious blood diseases, proposes treatments, and explains its "reasoning" in English. Corporations have used such systems to reduce the labor costs involved in repetitive calculations. A system used by American Express since November 1988 to advise when to deny credit to a customer saves the company millions of dollars annually.

A second area of artificial intelligence research is the field of artificial perception, or computer vision. Computer vision is the ability to recognize patterns in an image and to separate objects from background as quickly as the human brain. In the 1990s military technology initially developed to analyze spy-satellite images found its way into commercial applications, including monitors for assembly lines, digital cameras, and automotive imaging systems. Another pursuit in artificial intelligence research is natural language processing, the ability to interpret and generate human languages. In this area, as in others related to artificial intelligence research, commercial applications have been delayed as improvements in hardware—the computing power of the machines themselves—have not kept pace with the increasing complexity of software.

The field of neural networks seeks to reproduce the architecture of the brain—billions of connected nerve cells—by joining a large number of computer processors through a technique known as parallel processing. Fuzzy systems is a subfield of artificial intelligence research based on the assumption that the world encountered by humans is fraught with approximate, rather than precise, information. Interest in the field has been particularly strong in Japan, where fuzzy systems have been used in disparate applications, from operating subway cars to guiding the sale of securities. Some theorists argue that the technical obstacles to artificial intelligence, while

large, are not insurmountable. A number of computer experts, philosophers, and futurists have speculated on the ethical and spiritual challenges facing society when artificially intelligent machines begin to mimic human personality traits, including memory, emotion, and consciousness.

BIBLIOGRAPHY

Kurzweil, Ray. *The Age of Spiritual Machines.* New York: Viking, 1999.

Partridge, Derek. *A New Guide to Artificial Intelligence.* Norwood, N.J.: Ablex, 1991.

Shapiro, Stuart C., ed. *Encyclopedia of Artificial Intelligence.* 2d ed. New York: Wiley, 1992.

Turbam, Efraim. *Expert Systems and Applied Artificial Intelligence.* New York: MacMillan, 1992.

Vincent Kiernan / A. R.

See also **Computers and Computer Industry; Cybernetics; Cyborgs; Robotics; Virtual Reality.**

ARTILLERY in the U.S. Army dates from the American Revolution, when Massachusetts and Rhode Island units joined in the siege of Boston. The first Continental army artillery regiment was raised in January 1776; by 1777, four Continental regiments were in operation. Artillerymen manned the country's first coast defenses in 1794, leading to a traditional classification of U.S. Army artillery into field, siege and garrison, and coast artillery.

A few units served as light artillery during the War of 1812, but most doubled as either infantry or manned coast defenses. In 1821 Congress authorized four artillery regiments of nine companies each. It increased the number of companies in each artillery regiment to twelve in 1847. Most artillery regiments in the Mexican-American War (1846–1848) fought as infantry, although a few performed well as light artillery. After the war, the batteries of artillery scattered all over the United States. By the end of the Civil War, the regular army had five artillery regiments, with a total of sixty batteries, mostly field artillery. In 1898, two additional regiments were organized, and in 1899 each regiment gained two heavy batteries, bringing the total number of batteries to ninety-eight. After a major reorganization of artillery in 1901, the coast and field artillery became full separate branches in 1907. The number of field artillery regiments greatly increased during World War I, and antiaircraft units swelled the size of coast artillery.

Increased demand in World War II for flexible, mobile, and more powerful units led to the reorganization of regiments into separate battalions, batteries, and groups of field, coast, and antiaircraft artillery. They remained separate until the advent of the Combat Arms Regimental System in 1957, which reorganized the three components as regiments. In 1968 the Air Defense Artillery became a separate branch, and the artillery branch dissolved when Field Artillery again became a separate branch in 1969.

Artillery. In this eighteenth-century illustration from *A Treatise of Artillery*, one soldier fires a cannon while another (*right*) loads a mortar.

Most American artillery has copied, improved on, or adapted the ordnance of other nations. Between 1840 and 1860, John A. Dahlgren and T. J. Rodman improved the range and weight of shot used in cast guns. During the Civil War, the Robert P. Parrott rifled muzzle-loading gun outranged its smoothbore contemporaries. From 1865 to the Spanish-American War, inventors paid a great deal of attention to fortress guns, with innovations in mounts and fire control. The proximity fuse (introduced just before World War II) carried a miniature radio set that sent a continuous impulse. As the shell approached the target, the impulse's echo duration became shorter, activating the firing mechanism at a predetermined interval. Initially most useful in antiaircraft guns, the fuse's adaptation to regular artillery had devastating effect.

American inventiveness concentrated on fire control and laying techniques. By the Spanish-American War the artillery had perfected the indirect laying method and developed overhead fire procedures. This led to the technique of using map data to fire on unseen targets, a method used widely in World War I. By World War II the United States fielded the most widely feared artillery

of the combatants. One especially effective technique was the time-on-target (TOT), whereby any number and caliber of guns within range of a target could fire so that all their shells arrived at the same time.

During the nuclear arms race of the 1950s, American artillery units developed nuclear projectiles for use with conventional 203 mm howitzers. The Soviets developed a comparable system. Since then, however, developments in artillery technology have focused on conventional munitions. In the 1970s, projectiles were developed that could emit a number of submunitions, capable of destroying a variety of targets. Later, the army developed the guided projectile—the artillery version of the "smart bomb" that debuted with such fanfare during the Persian Gulf War—which forward personnel could illuminate by laser and guide to its target.

BIBLIOGRAPHY

Downey, Fairfax Davis. *The Sound of the Guns.* New York: D. McKay, 1956.

Dupuy, R. Ernest. *The Compact History of the United States Army.* New York: Hawthorn Books, 1973.

Sawicki, James A., ed. *Field Artillery Battalions of the U.S. Army.* Dumfries, Va.: Centaur Publications, 1977.

U.S. Army Artillery School. *U.S. Army Field Artillery School Guide.* Fort Sill, Okla.: Author, 1983.

Warner Stark / C. W.; A. R.

See also **Army, United States; Munitions; Ordnance.**

ARTISTS' COLONIES are collective, nonprofit organizations that serve as creative retreats for visual and performing artists, musicians, composers, and writers. Often situated in rural areas, these colonies offer a respite from city life, a quiet place to work, and a sense of creative community, along with workshops and studio time. Museums, colleges, artists, teachers, government programs, and wealthy patrons—together or individually—provide accommodations, services, and financial resources. Artists may apply for residency, but often the most prestigious and least publicized colonies are by invitation only. Colonies generally house resident artists for several weeks to many months at a time in facilities ranging from college dormitories and rustic outdoor accommodations to the private homes of wealthy patrons.

The first American artists' colony emerged in 1877, when William Morris Hunt, Barbizon painter and colleague of Jean-François Millet, established a plein-air (outdoor) painting school in Magnolia, Massachusetts. The 1880s and 1890s represented the peak of rural colony activity in Europe, and many American artists returned to the United States to create their own communities stateside. Early American art colonies imitated the French tradition of drawing artists from urban art centers into the countryside to experiment with light and movement in outdoor painting. William Merritt Chase's art school in Long Island, New York (founded 1891) and Charles Hawthorne's Cape Cod School of Art in Provincetown, Massachusetts (founded 1896) both emulated the plein-air and Impressionist orientation of French art colonies.

Other American art colonies, however, drew their inspiration from the Arts and Crafts movement and the social reform movements of the turn of the century, perceiving artists' communities to be utopian sites for alternative cultural lifestyles, the practice of social equity, and unfettered creativity. These included the MacDowell Colony in New Hampshire (founded 1907); Yaddo in Saratoga Springs, New York (founded 1900); The Art Students' League Summer School in Woodstock, New York (founded 1906), where Robert Henri and George Bellows of the Ashcan School taught; Carmel, California, home to writers' colony founders George Sterling and Mary Austin (founded 1905); and the Mabel Dodge Luhan house in Taos, New Mexico (founded 1918), a retreat for American cultural icons such as Georgia O'Keeffe, D. H. Lawrence, and Dennis Hopper. Woodstock and Taos remained centers for countercultural art scenes throughout the 1960s and 1970s, while both the MacDowell and Yaddo colonies continue to host up to one hundred artists each year.

BIBLIOGRAPHY

Alliance of Artists' Communities. *Artists Communities: A Directory of Residencies in the United States That Offer Time and Space for Creativity.* New York: Allworth Press, 2000. Up-to-date, illustrated reference source on current American art colonies.

Bowler, Gail Hellund. *Artists and Writers Colonies: Retreats, Residencies, and Respites for the Creative Mind.* Hillsboro, Oregon: Blue Heron Publishing, Inc., 1995.

Jacobs, Michael. *The Good and Simple Life: Artist Colonies in Europe and America.* Oxford: Paidon, 1985. Classic text.

Rudnick, Lois Palken. *Utopian Vistas: The Mabel Dodge Luhan House and the American Counterculture.* Albuquerque: University of New Mexico Press, 1996.

Sarah Schrank

ARTS AND CRAFTS MOVEMENT.

Started in England in the late nineteenth century, the Arts and Crafts movement affected nearly every aspect of household design, from architecture to pottery, and continues to do so. The movement was a response to the dehumanizing effects of the Industrial Revolution and the excesses of the Victorian Age, during which the middle classes collected frilly, mass-produced knickknacks. Arts and Crafts embraced simplicity of line, good, durable materials, and the human touch. Proponents were divided over the use of machines for production.

The English poet and artist William Morris, widely considered the movement's founder, articulated its philosophy, stressing the importance of the dignity and humanity of the work of craftsmen: "everything made by

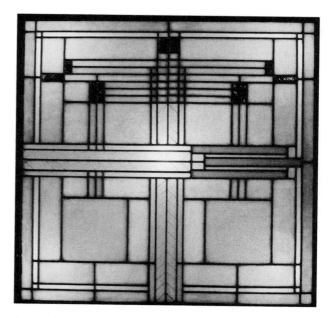

Arts and Crafts Movement. A stained-glass dining-room ceiling light with geometric patterns from the Ward Willits House in Highland Park, Ill., one of the Prairie Houses designed by Frank Lloyd Wright, 1902. © THOMAS A. HEINZ/ CORBIS

man's hands has a form, which must be either beautiful or ugly; beautiful if it is in accord with Nature, and helps her; ugly if it is discordant with Nature, and thwarts her." In America, the movement spawned a number of organizations and guilds dedicated to its ideals. In 1895, a group of artisans established "Roycroft" ("King's Craft"), in East Aurora, N.Y., a community (which is again functioning) whose mission was to evoke images of medieval craftsmanship. Other guilds included the Society of Arts and Crafts of Boston and the Chicago Arts and Crafts Society, both founded in 1897. Guild members represented almost all aspects of design, including architecture, furniture, gardens, textiles, stained glass, pottery and cast iron.

In architecture, the first major innovations appeared in Chicago and the Midwest, where Frank Lloyd Wright designed Prairie Style homes, which used horizontal lines to follow the landscape. The bungalow, a later architectural development, began in southern California; and it brought the concepts of the Prairie Style to small, middle-class homes. Built largely in the early twentieth century, bungalow houses incorporated Prairie Style features such as exposed joinery and low-hanging eaves.

Gustav Stickley led the way in furniture design. To this day, the factory he founded in upstate New York turns out Mission Style furniture, which uses strong, simple woods such as oak and clean, geometric lines with exposed joinery.

The leaders in Arts and Crafts pottery included Henry Chapman Mercer, whose Moravian Pottery and Tile Works, founded in the 1890s, used local clay and hand craftsmanship to make mosaic and story tiles. Artus van Briggle invented a matte glaze that resembled ancient Chinese pottery. His designs are still reproduced at his factory in Colorado.

BIBLIOGRAPHY

London, Neil, and Chris Wheeler. *The Arts and Crafts Legacy.* Home and Garden Television, 2001.

Morris, William. *Hopes and Fears for Art.* Boston: Roberts Brothers, 1882.

Stansky, Peter. *Redesigning the World: William Morris, the 1880s, and the Arts and Crafts.* Princeton, N.J.: Princeton University Press, 1985.

Rebekah Presson Mosby

See also **Architecture; Furniture.**

ASHCAN SCHOOL. A group of artists loosely formed a group they called "the Eight" or the Ashcan School because they could find art in the "ashcans" of dirty cities. Led by Robert Henri, the group included George Luks, William Glackens, John Sloan, Everett Shinn, Arthur B. Davies, Maurice Prendergast, and Ernest Lawson, and later it added Henri's prized student George Bellows.

Not a formal society or school, as all were fiercely independent, they shared a common look at everyday life through the lens of a journalist and the soul of a poet. Many had work experience as illustrators at magazines or newspapers, which contributed to their journalistic approach. The Ashcan artists disdained the academic pretensions of the established art world, while critics, who did not want to see such vulgarity displayed in art, called the group "the Revolutionary Black Gang."

The Eight held its first exhibition in 1908 and another in 1910. The show was so popular and sensational that riot police had to be called to subdue the crowd. The true impact of the Ashcan School did not occur until three years later with the ARMORY SHOW, by some accounts the most important exhibit ever held in the United States. The Armory Show shocked the public by showcasing the outrageous styles adopted by the Eight and by European artists, including Pablo Picasso, Paul Cezanne, and Henri Matisse. Despite the critical turmoil, more than 300,000

Dempsey and Firpo. This well-known lithograph by George Bellows, the ninth member of "the Eight," shows the moment in the legendary slugfest on 14 September 1923 when Luis Firpo punched Jack Dempsey clear out of the ring (but the champion knocked Firpo down nine times before knocking him out—in just the second round). © GEOFFREY CLEMENTS/CORBIS

Americans saw the Armory Show, which invented the term "modern art."

Henri and the other original members of the Ashcan movement took Winslow Homer as their spiritual guide and also looked to the great poet Walt Whitman for inspiration. Bellows used the gritty streets as his guide, including the illegal boxing clubs of the early 1900s. His *Stag at Sharkey's* (1909) and *Both Members of This Club* (1909) are possibly the most powerful paintings stemming from the group.

BIBLIOGRAPHY

Braider, Donald. *George Bellows and the Ashcan School of Painting.* Garden City, N.Y.: Doubleday, 1971.

Perlman, Bennard B. *Painters of the Ashcan School: The Immortal Eight.* New York: Dover, 1988.

Bob Batchelor

ASIAN AMERICANS.

The 2000 census showed Asian Americans to be the fastest-growing racial group in the United States, increasing from 3.8 million in 1980 to 6.9 million in 1990 to 10.2 million in 2000. That increase during the 1990s was slightly greater than the increase among Hispanics and was many times greater than the population increases of African Americans and whites. The rapid increase in the Asian American population was driven by an immigration made possible by the IMMIGRATION ACT OF 1965 that ended the national-origins quota system. Between 1951 and 1960 Asians accounted for a mere 6 percent of immigrants to the United States, but between 1981 and 1989 they made up 42 percent of the total. Also assisting the increase were the Indochina Migration and Assistance Act of 1975, the REFUGEE ACT OF 1980, and the Amerasian Homecoming Act of 1987. Despite the fact that in 2000 Asian Americans were the largest group in Hawaii (41.6 percent of the population, compared to 24.3 percent for whites) and the third largest in California (behind whites and Hispanics or Latinos), they represented only 3.6 percent of the population of the United States.

The term "Asian Americans" encompasses a range of people whose ancestries derive from countries in West, South, Southeast, and East Asia with widely different cultures and histories. Institutions and social relations define them as a whole, however, and Asian Americans during the 1960s sought a unifying designation while trying to preserve the cultural and historical integrity of their re-

Field Laborers. A photograph of Japanese Americans getting ready for work in 1942—during the period of widespread internment of Japanese Americans in wartime camps in the West. LIBRARY OF CONGRESS

Under Attack. People yell and hurl rocks at a wagon full of Chinese immigrants arriving in San Francisco in the 1870s, shortly before nativist hostility led to the harsh Chinese Exclusion Act of 1882. BANCROFT LIBRARY, UNIVERSITY OF CALIFORNIA

spective ethnic groups. Chinese are the largest group, followed by Filipinos, Japanese, Asian Indians, Koreans, Vietnamese, Laotians, Cambodians, Thais, and Hmongs.

Asian Americans have been widely touted as America's "model minority." The 1990 census showed the median income of Asian Americans to be $35,900, 3 percent higher than that of whites. Of Asian Americans age twenty-five and older, 40 percent had four years of college education, compared with 23 percent of whites. With low crime and juvenile delinquency rates, low divorce rates, and a strong cultural emphasis on the family, Asian Americans have been cited as indicators of successful adaptation to life in the United States and as proof that other minority groups, such as AFRICAN AMERICANS and HISPANIC AMERICANS, can pull themselves up from poverty and discrimination. Others have pointed out, however, that median income is calculated per family unit, and Asian American families have more members and income earners than whites. Despite higher levels of education, Asian Americans earn less than whites with comparable educational levels and occupy lower management positions in businesses. In addition, higher percentages of Asian Americans live in regions such as Hawaii, California, and New York and in urban areas, where a high cost of living pre-

vails. Critics of the "model minority" image question the possible motives behind propagation of a stereotype that ignores problems among Asian Americans at a time of civil unrest among African and Hispanic Americans.

In 1980 a third of Vietnamese immigrants, half of Cambodians, and two-thirds of Laotians lived in poverty; among Asian Americans together poverty was more than twice that among whites in 1988. Asian Americans also faced racism and prejudice. A 1992 report of the Commission on Civil Rights showed Asian Americans to be 20 percent of Philadelphia's victims of hate crimes while constituting only 4 percent of Philadelphia's population. A Boston Police Department analysis of civil rights violations from 1983 through 1987 found that Asian Americans suffered higher rates of racial violence than any other group in the city. In 1988 arsonists set fire to the Cambodian houses in Lynn, Massachusetts; in 1990 a Chinese church in Chandler, Arizona, and fifty-five Hindu temples nationwide were vandalized; during the 1980s Vietnamese fishermen were harassed by white fishermen in Florida and California and by the KU KLUX KLAN in Texas. In 1987 Asian American students at the University of Connecticut in Storrs were spat upon by fellow students on their way to a Christmas dance. Vincent Chin, a Chinese

Chinese Fisherman. A photograph by Floyd Lamb taken in Monterey, Calif., c. 1895; hundreds of thousands of Chinese immigrants remained in the United States despite several decades of restrictive laws and harassment.

American, was killed by two automobile factory workers in Detroit in 1982; Navroze Mody, an Asian Indian, was bludgeoned to death in 1987 by a gang of youths in Jersey City, New Jersey, where a group called the "Dotbusters" had vowed to drive out all of the city's Asian Indians; Hung Truong, a Vietnamese, was beaten to death in Houston in 1990 by two skinheads. Patrick Edward Purdy fired on and killed five Cambodian and Vietnamese children and wounded thirty others in 1989 in an elementary-school yard in Stockton, California, using an AK47 assault rifle.

Contrary to popular opinion, Asian Americans are not recent immigrants. Some of the earliest Asian communities in the United States were formed with arrival of Filipinos in Louisiana, possibly as early as 1765, and with settlement of Asian Indians in Philadelphia and Boston during the 1790s. Asians arrived in the Hawaiian kingdom about a century before the islands were annexed in 1898, and sizable Chinese communities in California and New York City developed beginning in the 1850s, followed by Japanese in 1869 in California. Chinese were introduced by planters in the South during the 1870s, when they also arrived in large numbers in the American West, where they were particularly attracted to opportunities working in western mines and on railroad construction crews until the CHINESE EXCLUSION ACT of 1882 banned Chinese immigration for a decade. Many Koreans, Filipinos, and Asian Indians arrived in California after 1900.

Early communities were unlike the urban concentrations of the late twentieth century, called "ethnic enclaves." Filipinos formed distinctive fishing villages in Louisiana, but Mexicans and Spaniards lived within those communities. Asian Indians who arrived on the East Coast during the 1790s adopted English names and probably intermarried with African Americans. New York's Chinese lived among African and Irish Americans, and substantial numbers of Chinese men married Irish women. Chinese in California lived mainly in rural towns in mining and agricultural counties of the state before nativism drove them into San Francisco and Los Angeles. Asian Indians, mainly men, who arrived in California, married Mexican women and formed a Punjabi-Mexican-American community. Increasing anti-Asian laws and practices made these porous borders of race and geography less permeable.

Asian Americans nonetheless have sought inclusion in the promise of equality for all citizens. In *Yick Wo v. Hopkins* (1886), a suit brought by Chinese Americans in San Francisco, the SUPREME COURT broadened equal protection under the Fourteenth Amendment by asking whether discrimination impinged the rights of a person or group. Because of this and other litigation brought by Asian Americans, the Court upheld the fight of Japanese-language schools in 1927, mandated bilingual education in public schools in 1974, and contributed to equal protection under the law, desegregation in schools and workplaces, and workers' and language rights. Nevertheless, discrimination against Asian Americans has also erupted intermittently across the twentieth century, from the internment of Japanese Americans during World War II to the targeting of Korean shopkeepers during the Los Angeles riots of 1992.

By the end of the century, it had become clear that the social tendency to consider Asians as a single group had an unexpected political potency. The struggle for black equality in the 1960s inspired some Asian Americans to forge a new pan-Asian identity, one that established common bonds across the many nationalities, cultures, and languages that make up the tapestry of the Asian community in America. Asian Americans ever since have worked together to assert themselves in local, state, and national politics. In 1996, for example, Gary Locke, then a Washington State county executive, was elected as the first Chinese American governor on the U.S. mainland.

BIBLIOGRAPHY

Chan, Sucheng. *Asian Americans: An Interpretive History.* Boston: Twayne, 1991.

Espiritu, Yen Le. *Asian American Panethnicity: Bridging Institutions and Identities.* Philadelphia: Temple University Press, 1992.

Takaki, Ronald T. *Strangers from a Different Shore: A History of Asian Americans.* Boston: Little, Brown, 1989.

United States Commission on Civil Rights. *Civil Rights Issues Facing Asian Americans in the 1990s.* Washington, D.C.: U.S. Commission on Civil Rights, 1992.

Zia, Helen. *Asian American Dreams: The Emergence of an American People.* New York: Farrar, Straus and Giroux, 2000.

Gary Y. Okihiro / c. w.

See also **Asian Indian Americans; Asian Religions and Sects; Chinese Americans; Education, Bilingual; Filipino Americans; Immigration; Immigration Restriction; Japanese Americans; Korean Americans; Minority Business; Southeast Asian Americans;** *and vol. 9:* **Gentlemen's Agreement; The Japanese Internment Camps, 1942; War Story.**

ASIAN INDIAN AMERICANS

ASIAN INDIAN AMERICANS have a long history in the United States. Some arrived as indentured laborers during the eighteenth century. Others came to Pennsylvania as slaves, adopted or received English names, and probably became indentured after the state passed its gradual emancipation bill in 1780. A few lived and worked in Massachusetts when America began trading with India in the 1790s.

In the late nineteenth and early twentieth centuries, some Asian Indian merchants imported silk, linen, and other goods, but, like most ASIAN AMERICANS before World War II, most came as migrant workers and were a part of the worldwide movement of labor and capital in the global marketplace. Steamship companies and employers recruited Asian Indians with stories of wealth in British Columbia. Those migrants, mainly Sikhs from Punjab, eventually crossed into Washington and Oregon, where they labored in lumber mills, and into California, where they were agricultural workers. After the 1965 Immigration Act, Asian Indian Americans numbered 50,000, but after IMMIGRATION reform, the Asian Indian American population grew to 815,447 in 1990. Early in the twenty-first century, Asian Indian Americans comprised the fourth largest Asian American group, behind Chinese, Filipino, and Japanese Americans. Like other Asian American designations, the term "Asian Indian American" encompasses a range of cultural, linguistic, and sectarian groups.

Political and economic conditions in India and in the Asian Indian global diaspora also influenced the migration of Asian Indians. Rising expectations following India's independence, especially among Indians seeking employment in government and the economy, led to a high demand for education. When India's economy was unable to absorb the educated, many chose emigration. Like Korean and Filipino Americans, the first group that emigrated after 1965 sought employment in the United States. After the 1980s, however, family reunification became their principal purpose for emigrating.

Unlike other groups, Asian Indian Americans have had a fairly even gender balance. Although the earlier population was overwhelmingly male, there has apparently been a greater number of Asian Indian female infants born in the United States. This fact, together with the death of older Asian Indian American men, has resulted in virtual gender parity. In the early 2000s, California had the largest number of Asian Indian Americans, a statistic that held for all Asian American groups, but Asian Indians were not concentrated in the West. One-third of all Asian Indians resided in the Northeast, and one-fourth lived in the South. Like most Asian Americans, Asian Indians have settled in urban centers, in such metropolitan areas as New York–Newark–Jersey City, Los Angeles–Long Beach–Anaheim, and Chicago.

BIBLIOGRAPHY

Bacon, Jean Leslie. *Life Lines: Community, Family, and Assimilation Among Asian Indian Immigrants.* New York: Oxford University Press, 1996.

Jensen, Joan M. *Passage From India: Asian Indian Immigrants in North America.* New Haven, Conn.: Yale University Press, 1988.

La Brack, Bruce. *The Sikhs of Northern California, 1904–1975.* New York: AMS Press, 1988.

Leonard, Karen Isaksen. *Making Ethnic Choices: California's Punjabi Mexican Americans.* Philadelphia: Temple University Press, 1992.

Gary Y. Okihiro / E. M.

See also **Asian Religions and Sects; Assimilation; Trade, Foreign.**

ASIAN RELIGIONS AND SECTS

ASIAN RELIGIONS AND SECTS. Asian religions, originating in India or the Far East, began flourishing in the United States after 1965, when earlier U.S. immigration quota laws were superseded by a single allocation of immigrants from all countries outside the western hemisphere. Of all religions originating in Asia, Buddhism is the most widespread in the United States, with over a thousand Buddhist centers and practice groups established since the mid-1970s. Forty percent of the Buddhist community lives in southern California, making Los Angeles the most diverse urban Buddhist community in the world.

In the United States, Japanese forms of Buddhism have the largest following among the various Buddhist groups. In 1889 Soryu Kagahi of the Jodo Shinshu lineage arrived in Honolulu to minister to Buddhists on the plantations. By the end of the nineteenth century three more Japanese lineages had arrived in Hawaii: Soto, Nichiren, and Shingon. The first Japanese Buddhist to come to the mainland United States was a Rinzai Zen monk, Soyen Shaku, who addressed the World Parliament of Religions in 1893. Thirty-five years later Sokei-an established Rinzai practice in New York City. In the 1960s and 1970s, after Daisetz Teitaro Suzuki's writings popularized Zen, Buddhist communities established monasteries in California, Hawaii, and New York State for intensive Zen meditation. Hosen Isobe began Soto Zen in Hawaii in 1916, and organized the Zenshuji Mission (now called the Soto Mission) in Los Angeles in 1922. Wealthy benefactors facilitated the spread of Zen Buddhism in the United States, for example, Chester F. Carlson, who founded the Zen Mountain Center in Tassajara Springs, California.

The two largest Japanese Buddhist groups in the United States originally branched from (1) Nichirenshu, whose members follow the teachings of Nichiren, a thirteenth-century Japanese Buddhist leader, and who believe that salvation results from chanting portions of the Lotus Sutra, and (2) Pure Land (Jodo Shinshu), whose adherents believe that individual rebirth in the Western Paradise occurs through faith in Amida Buddha. The fastest-growing branch of Buddhism in the United States is Soka Gakkai International (which claimed 500,000 members in 1994, although actual membership was closer to 100,000–200,000). Soka Gakkai was formerly the lay branch of Nichiren, whose members regard Nichiren as the Buddha of the age. One of the more popular Pure Land groups is the Buddhist Churches of America, with approximately fifty thousand members in 1994. There are over 375 Zen and other Mahayana Buddhist Centers in the United States.

In 1878 a Chinese monk brought both a Kuan Yin (the Chinese version of the Indian Buddhist bodhisattva of compassion, Avalokitesvara) and a Kuan Ti (a military hero of the third century B.C. who became a popular saint) statue to Honolulu and built a temple (joss house) to Kuan Yin. Chinese joss houses appeared in California by 1900 and are now concentrated mainly in New York City, large cities of California, and Hawaii. Hsuan-hua, a Chinese Zen Buddhist, founded the Dharma Realm Buddhist Association in 1962. Eleven years later this organization, located in Talmage, California, established the first Buddhist university in the West.

Theravada Buddhism, a form of Buddhism recognizing only the earliest Buddhist scriptures, predominates in southeast Asia, Burma, and Sri Lanka. Sri Lankan Theravadans constructed the first American Buddhist temple. During the 1970s many adherents arrived from southeast Asia, particularly Vietnam. In 1976 the Insight Meditation Society established its first lay center, in western Massachusetts. There are more than 500,000 Theravada Buddhists throughout the United States in 128 centers.

Tibetan Buddhism came to the United States in 1945 under the auspices of the American Buddhist Society and Fellowship, set up by Robert Ernest Dickhoff. The first Tibetans arriving in Howell, New Jersey, founded the Tibetan Buddhist Learning Center. Although all four Tibetan Buddhist lineages are represented in the United States, the largest group is Vajradhatu, representing the Kagyupa lineage. Their center, which was opened in Boulder, Colorado, in 1973 by Rinpoche Chogyam Trugpa, includes the Naropa Institute, an accredited college (at present this institution is nonsectarian). By the mid-1980s Caucasian practitioners of Tibetan Buddhism outnumbered their Tibetan counterparts, making Tibetan Buddhism one of the fastest growing segments of the American Buddhist community. There are 279 Tibetan centers scattered throughout the United States.

The Association of American Buddhists, founded in 1980 by Kevin R. O'Neill, stresses an American form of Buddhism integrating the universal principles of all Buddhist lineages without the divisive cultural issues that have kept Buddhist lineages apart for millennia. Many predict that this form of Buddhism will be the future of American Buddhism. In contrast to Buddhism in Asia, where the major focus is on monastic Buddhism, the majority of American Buddhists want to apply Buddhist contemplative practice in their noncelibate lives and insist on participation by the whole community, both women and men. There are 129 nonsectarian Buddhist centers in the United States.

The first Hindu guru to arrive in the United States, Protap Chunder Mozoomdar, was a guest of Ralph Waldo Emerson's widow in 1883. Twelve years later the charismatic Swami Vivekananda, a disciple of Sri Ramakrishna, brought Hinduism to prominence by founding the Vedanta Society, which emphasizes universal philosophical principles. In New York City, Pandit Acharya founded the Temple of Yoga, the Yoga Institute, and Prana Press in the early decades of the twentieth century. The most successful of these early Hindu gurus was Paramahansa Yogananda, who arrived in 1922 and founded the Yogoda Satsang, known today as the Self-Realization Fellowship. His *Autobiography of a Yogi*, published in 1946, continues to be popular.

The Indian Hindu community in the United States is remarkably diverse, although most worship one of three popular deities—Shiva, the Goddess, or Vishnu. The vast majority of Indian lay Hindus (the wealthiest religious community per capita in the United States) have been concentrating on building temples and bringing officiating priests from India to conserve their traditions for the benefit of their American-born children. It is only individual Hindu gurus who have been interested in cultivating an American following. The Vishwa Hindu Parishad, a Hindu nationalist political group, serves the Indian American community to bridge these manifold sectarian and linguistic Hindu communities. Swami Prabhupada established the International Society for Krishna Consciousness (ISKCON), popularly known as Hare Krishna, in New York City in 1966, stressing a chanting exercise as an expression of devotion to Krishna, a manifestation (avatar) of Vishnu. In 1997 there were two thousand monastic members in the United States, living in twelve centers with thirty teachers (swamis). Another significant Vaishnava group, the Swami Narayan movement (sixty thousand members in 1991), started in the late 1960s and is composed largely of Gujarati Indian Americans.

Sikhism, founded in India as a unique synthesis of Hindu and Islamic ideas and practices, began to grow in the United States from 1905 to 1913, with the arrival of thousands of Sikhs. They opened their first *gurdwara* (house of worship) in Stockton, California, in 1912. The Sikhs were one of the few major religious groups not represented in the World Parliament of Religions in 1893. By 1915 the vast majority of the seven thousand Indians in the United States were Sikhs. In 1969 Sikhs constructed the largest *gurdwara* in the world in Yuba City, California, one of the central places of worship for the roughly 250,000 Sikhs in the United States. During the 1970s Yogi Bhajan began converting non-Indian Americans and established a national organization, the Sikh Dharma, which had ten thousand members in 1992 and is headquartered in Los Angeles. In 1995 there were 139 ashrams/teaching centers scattered throughout the United States.

Taoism, based on the Chinese principles of yin-yang and chi (the flow of energy through the body), has spread considerably in the United States through tai chi (a meditation/martial arts form), chi gong (exercises to circulate chi), and feng shui (Chinese geomancy). Dozens of books beginning with "*The Tao of*" have been published in English. Much of the interest in these practices is the interconnectedness of the experience of the embodied physical practice with spiritual and emotional aspects of life. Translations of Taoist texts appeal to those who desire a nontheistic philosophy that is harmoniously anchored in the natural world. In contrast to Buddhism, there is no Taoist *sangha* (community), monastic tradition, or unified set of ritual practices that facilitate institutionalization in the West. The Chinese government has allowed a few Taoist monks to visit the United States, and there are Taoist Chinese masters in the United States, but this cannot compare to the extensive East-West activities in the Buddhist community. Up to the beginning of the twenty-first century, the message of Taoism has been transmitted to the American public largely through translations of Taoist texts, particularly the *Tao Te Ching*.

Many other religions originating in Asia are represented in the United States. Jainism, which stresses austere practices that avoid hurting any living creatures, has communities in Chicago and New York City. In 1893 Virchand Gandhi addressed the World Parliament of Religions in Chicago. He took the minority Jain position (at that time) by insisting that it was not morally incumbent to travel only by foot. There are two hundred Jains in the Chicago area, and others are scattered in urban areas around the United States. Shintoism, the indigenous religion of Japan, has many temples in Hawaii. Two Japanese new religions, Tenrikyo (in 1987 there were fifty-four churches and three thousand members) and Konko Kyo, based upon Shintoism, have spread in the United States. Seicho-No-Le, another Japanese new religion, is popular with people attracted to psychic and New Age groups.

BIBLIOGRAPHY

Clark, J. J. *The Tao of the West: Western Transformations of Taoist Thought.* London and New York: Routledge, 2000.

Fields, Rick. *How the Swans Came to the Lake: A Narrative History of Buddhism in America.* 3d ed. Boston: Shambhala, 1992.

Melton, J. Gordon. *Encyclopedia of American Religions.* 6th ed. Detroit: Gale, 1999.

Morreale, Don, ed. *The Complete Guide to Buddhist America.* Boston: Shambhala, 1998.

Richardson, E. Allen. *East Comes West: Asian Religions and Cultures in North America.* New York: Pilgrim Press, 1985.

Arthur F. Buehler

See also **Buddhism; Hinduism.**

ASSASSINATIONS, PRESIDENTIAL. Political assassinations were not supposed to happen in the United States of America. In Old World despotisms such extreme measures might be necessary to remove tyrants, but they were not necessary, so it was generally believed, in a Republic whose leaders were by definition responsive to the popular will. Consequently until 1901 American presidents were not even supplied with Secret Service protection. Their office doors were open to all comers; they freely walked the streets mingling with the people they served. When President Rutherford B. Hayes, for example, wanted to visit the Centennial Exposition in Philadelphia, he bought a railroad ticket and took the coach, just as any other American might do.

Created in the afterglow of the Enlightenment, the United States clung to that era's rationalistic, optimistic view of human nature, even after sad experiences demonstrated its limitations. William H. Seward reflected the views of a majority of Americans when he flatly declared, "Assassination is not an American practice or habit." James A. Garfield more fatalistically concluded, "Assassination can no more be guarded against than death by lightning; and it is best not to worry about either." Both Seward and Garfield later had cause to regret their tooeasy reliance on Enlightenment assumptions at the expense of the irrational, dark side of human nature.

Richard Lawrence and Andrew Jackson

The first president to become an assassin's target was ironically the first to have been elected by mass popular suffrage, Andrew Jackson. On 30 January 1835 he attended a funeral service for Congressman Warren R. Davis in the hall of the House of Representatives. Aged and frail, Jackson emerged leaning on a cane. A thirty-five-year-old, English-born housepainter named Richard Lawrence stepped out from the crowd of spectators brandishing a pistol, which he fired at the president's breast from about a dozen feet away. The weapon misfired, but the sound of the exploding percussion cap sent most of the mourning dignitaries scrambling for cover. Not so the aged hero of New Orleans, who advanced on his assailant with upraised cane. Lawrence pulled out a second pistol and fired it at point-blank range, but it too misfired. By that time the would-be assassin had been wrestled to the ground, and the angry president had to be restrained from thrashing him with his cane. "I know where this comes from," Jackson shouted, convinced that Lawrence was in league with his political enemies.

Evidence presented at the trial on 11 April 1835 did not support Jackson's suspicions. Rather than the agent of a political conspiracy, Lawrence was revealed as a delusion-obsessed loner. Lawrence believed he was the rightful king of England and hence heir to vast estates that the machinations of President Jackson had prevented him from enjoying. The trial was brief, lasting only one day, and the prosecuting attorney, Francis Scott Key of "Star Spangled Banner" fame, was inclined to leniency in view of Lawrence's clearly disturbed mental condition. After five minutes of deliberation, the jury found Lawrence not guilty by reason of insanity. He spent the remainder of his life in mental hospitals and died on 30 June 1861 at St. Elizabeth's in the District of Columbia.

John Wilkes Booth and Abraham Lincoln

Thirty years passed before the next attempted presidential assassination, which was different from its predecessor in many ways. This assault was conducted by a band of conspirators, they were rational though misguided, and above all they succeeded. Unlike the obscure misfits generally attracted by the reflected glory of murdering famous men, John Wilkes Booth was a successful member of America's most prominent family of Shakespearian actors. He was an ardent Confederate sympathizer who late in the Civil War conceived a plan to aid his cause by kidnapping President Abraham Lincoln and exchanging him for high-level Confederate prisoners of war.

The surrender of General Robert E. Lee's Confederate army at Appomattox put an end to this project, but the embittered Booth substituted another plan to strike one last blow for the South, the simultaneous murders of President Lincoln, Vice President Andrew Johnson, Secretary of State William Seward, and General Ulysses S. Grant. Through his show business connections, Booth learned that Lincoln and Grant were expected to attend a performance of the hit comedy *Our American Cousin* at Ford's Theatre on Good Friday, 14 April 1865. Using his professional access to the building, Booth tiptoed into the president's box, and at the point in the play that evoked the loudest laughter, he fatally shot Lincoln in the back of the head with a single-shot derringer pistol. General Grant had declined to attend the play at the last minute. His seat was occupied by Major Henry R. Rathbone, whose left arm Booth slashed with a dagger when he attempted to restrain the assassin. As Booth jumped onto the stage, his spurs caught in a flag, and he broke his left leg in the awkward fall. Hobbling to a waiting horse, he made good his escape.

The other conspirators were not as successful. George Atzerodt, who had been assigned to kill Vice President Johnson, got cold feet and drank himself into a stupor. Lewis Payne forced his way into Secretary Seward's home, where he wounded Seward and four other residents but killed none before he fled.

Booth escaped to Virginia, where the pain from his broken leg kept him from traveling farther. After a twelve-day manhunt, he was cornered in a tobacco barn and shot on 26 April. Atzerodt, Payne, David Herold, and Mary Surratt were tried by a military court and were hanged on

7 July 1865. Others involved, including Samuel Mudd, the doctor who set Booth's broken leg, served long prison sentences.

Charles Guiteau and James A. Garfield

The misleading label "disappointed office seeker" is invariably attached to the name of Charles Julius Guiteau, the assassin of James A. Garfield. True he did continually pester the newly elected president for a choice diplomatic position, but this was merely one of Guiteau's grandiose delusions.

Born in 1841 in Freeport, Illinois, Guiteau spent some years at John Humphrey Noyes's Perfectionist community at Oneida, New York, before pursuing a series of occupations. He dabbled in journalism, hoping to start a newspaper though he was penniless; in law, trying only one case; in theology, being hooted off the lecture stage; in literature, plagiarizing a book by Noyes; and finally in politics. He believed a speech he had prepared but never delivered was responsible for Garfield's 1880 presidential election win, and he expected a suitable reward, preferably consul general in Paris. When this hope was frustrated, he seized upon the conviction that God had chosen him to "remove" President Garfield to heal the breach with the Stalwart wing of the Republican Party. As an added bonus, the publicity might stimulate sales of Guiteau's plagiarized book.

Armed with a .44 caliber, ivory-handled pistol, Guiteau stalked his prey for six weeks, catching up with him at the Baltimore and Potomac railroad station on 2 July 1881, as the president was about to leave Washington, D.C., for a summer vacation. Declaring "I am a Stalwart of the Stalwarts," Guiteau pumped two bullets into the president's back, leaving him severely wounded. Garfield clung to life throughout the summer but died on 19 September, shortly after he was moved to the seaside resort of Elberon, New Jersey.

Guiteau turned his trial into a tasteless circus, singing and raving. Despite his antics, the jury found him both sane and guilty after deliberating for slightly over an hour. He was hanged on 30 June 1882 while reciting a childish hymn of his own composition. Subsequently Congress passed the Civil Service Reform Act, which reformers promoted by exploiting the late president's tragedy to further their own cause.

Leon Czolgosz and William McKinley

Twenty years later tragedy struck another president. Leon Czolgosz (pronounced "sholgosh") was born near Detroit in 1873, shortly after his parents emigrated from Poland. Moody, friendless, and sullen, he drifted into anarchist circles, but even they distrusted him. From his half-digested reading of anarchist tracts he concluded: "I don't believe we should have any rulers. It is right to kill them."

On 6 September 1901 President William McKinley attended the Pan American Exposition in Buffalo, New York, where he greeted the public at a reception in the

Temple of Music. Czolgosz, a drab, inoffensive-looking figure with a handkerchief wrapped around his right hand as if it were a bandage, waited in the long receiving line. The handkerchief concealed a small pistol, and when Czolgosz reached the president, he pressed the concealed weapon against McKinley's abdomen and fired twice. He was instantly wrestled to the ground, and the stunned president ordered, "Be easy with him, boys!"

For a time it seemed as if the wounded president might recover, but he died in Buffalo of complications brought on by blood poisoning early on the morning of 14 September. Czolgosz was rushed to trial nine days later. The trial lasted eight hours; the jury required thirty-four minutes to find him guilty. Shortly after midnight on 29 October the assassin was electrocuted.

Early Twentieth Century Attempts

After the death of McKinley, the third president murdered in thirty-six years, presidents were finally given protection by the Secret Service. For another sixty-two years no president was assassinated, but in that interval unsuccessful attempts were made on the lives of a former president, a president-elect, and a sitting president.

Former president Theodore Roosevelt attempted a political comeback in 1912. This break with tradition was particularly offensive to John N. Shrank, a thirty-six-year-old German who had immigrated to New York at the age of thirteen. A friendless, moody young man with literary and intellectual aspirations, Shrank became obsessed by the conviction that in seeking a third term Roosevelt was subverting the principles of the American Republic. This conviction was strengthened by Shrank's two vivid dreams, in which the ghost of President McKinley said of Roosevelt: "This is my murderer. Avenge my death."

Armed with a .38 caliber Colt pistol, Shrank stalked Roosevelt on his campaign swing for twenty-four days and two thousand miles, finally catching up with him in Milwaukee, Wisconsin, on 14 October. Leaving the Gilpatrick Hotel to deliver a speech at the Milwaukee Auditorium, the former president stood in his open car, waving to the crowd. Shrank shot him in the chest from a distance of only six feet. Fortunately for Roosevelt, the bullet struck his breast pocket and spent much of its force passing through his glasses case and the folded manuscript of his speech before lodging in his body. Roosevelt, who boasted that he was as strong as "a bull moose," insisted on delivering his scheduled address. Ruled insane, Shrank spent the rest of his life in a mental hospital near Oshkosh, Wisconsin, where he was considered a model patient. He died on 15 September 1943. During his long incarceration he never received a single letter or visitor.

Like Shrank, Giuseppe Zangara was a lonely immigrant with an obsession. Born in southern Italy in 1900, he went to work at the age of six to help his impoverished family. He attributed the stomach pains that tormented him throughout his life to that wrenching experience. Zangara vowed revenge on the capitalists and "bosses" responsible for his stomachache: "I make my idea to kill the President—kill any President, any king." While still living in Italy, Zangara unsuccessfully stalked King Victor Emmanuel III, and after immigrating to the United States in 1923, he considered murdering Presidents Calvin Coolidge and Herbert Hoover. A more convenient target appeared in February 1933, when the president-elect Franklin Roosevelt made an appearance in Miami, where Zangara was spending the winter. Hoover or Roosevelt, it made no difference, "everybody the same."

On the night of 15 February, Zangara joined the crowd gathered at Bayfront Park to observe the newly elected president. Roosevelt delivered a brief speech from the back seat of his car, which was parked in front of the amphitheater's stage. When the speech was over, he asked some dignitaries on the stage, including Chicago's visiting Mayor Anton Cermak, to come down to his car, which the crippled Roosevelt was unable to leave easily. As they chatted, Zangara jumped onto a folding chair and fired wildly. Roosevelt was not hit, but Cermak and four spectators were wounded. Cermak died on 6 March. At his two trials, one before, the other shortly after the death of Cermak, Zangara was judged sane. Sentenced to be electrocuted, he went to his death on 20 March 1933 still muttering curses against "the lousy capitalists" who had caused his stomach to ache.

The 1950 attack on President Harry Truman represented a new style in presidential assassinations—terrorist violence designed to gain publicity for a cause. The assailants, Oscar Collazo and Griselio Torresola, Puerto Ricans living in New York, were active in the island's independence movement. Whether their attack was their own initiative or the command of the organization is unclear. On the afternoon of 31 October they boarded a train for Washington, D.C., a city they had not visited previously. Their preparations were haphazard. They did not know the location of the president's residence, they were not aware of his whereabouts, and Collazo did not even know how to operate the automatic pistol he carried.

As it happened President Truman was then living in Blair House, across the street from the White House, which was undergoing repairs. On the afternoon of 1 November he was taking his customary after-lunch nap in an upstairs bedroom when Collazo and Torresola tried to storm their way through the front door of Blair House. In the flurry of gunfire that followed, Collazo and two Secret Service agents were wounded. Torresola fatally shot agent Leslie Coffelt, who managed to kill his attacker before he died. Collazo was tried and sentenced to death, but on 24 July 1952 President Truman commuted the sentence to life in prison. On 10 September 1979 President Jimmy Carter released Collazo from jail along with three Puerto Ricans who had fired shots into the House of Representatives on 1 March 1954. The would-be assassin returned to Puerto Rico, where he died on 20 February 1994 at the age of eighty, unrepentant to the end.

Lee Harvey Oswald and John F. Kennedy

Although every aspect of the assassination of John F. Kennedy has been the subject of controversy, the basic facts seem beyond dispute. At 12:30 P.M. on 22 November 1963, while riding in an open car past Dealey Plaza in Dallas, Texas, President John F. Kennedy was fatally struck by two bullets from a high-powered rifle fired from the adjacent Texas Book Depository building.

All evidence pointed to a worker in that building, Lee Harvey Oswald. A former marine, Oswald had defected to the Soviet Union, redefected, and most recently had been active on behalf of Fidel Castro's Cuba. He owned the murder weapon, had been seen smuggling a long package into the building, had fled shortly after the assassination, and had killed a policeman in panic. Furthermore he was capable of committing political murder, having recently attempted to shoot the retired general Edwin A. Walker, a prominent right-wing figure.

Nonetheless many Americans were not convinced. Perhaps unwilling to acknowledge that such an insignificant figure as Oswald could single-handedly alter the course of history, they followed conspiracy theories trumpeted by sensational books and in the tendentious motion picture *JFK* (1991). The alleged conspiracies were masterminded either by the Russians, the Cubans, the Mafia, the Central Intelligence Agency, Vice President Lyndon Johnson, or time travelers from an alternate universe. Two days after Kennedy's assassination, while Oswald was being transferred to another jail, he was killed by Jack Ruby, a Dallas strip club operator, providing more fuel for the conspiracy theories. Even in the early twenty-first century polls consistently showed that most Americans continued to believe in a conspiracy theory even though no credible evidence emerged to seriously challenge the conclusion of the WARREN COMMISSION that Oswald acted alone.

A Violent Era

The death of President Kennedy signaled the beginning of an era of violence in American public life. It was stoked by the counterculture's exaltation of sensation, including violence, and by the social upheavals generated by racial, generational, and sexual hostility, all aggravated by the unpopular Vietnam War. In addition to attacks on presidents, the era experienced the successful assassinations of Robert Kennedy, Martin Luther King, and John Lennon and unsuccessful attempts on George Wallace and Andy Warhol.

On 22 February 1974 Samuel Byck, an in-and-out mental patient whose family and business lives were crumbling, attempted a spectacular plan to avenge himself on President Richard Nixon, whom he considered the source of his problems. Intending to hijack a commercial airliner and crash it into the White House, Byck forced his way into an airplane parked on the Baltimore airport runway, killing a security guard as he stormed into the cockpit. Byck then killed the copilot and seriously

Assassination Attempt. President Ronald Reagan reacts as John Hinckley shoots at him in Washington, D.C., on 30 March 1981. AP/WIDE WORLD PHOTOS

wounded the pilot before security guards on the tarmac shot him through the plane's window. Byck then turned his gun on himself.

Nixon's successor Gerald Ford was the target of two assassination attempts, both of them made by women. Lynette "Squeaky" Fromme was a devoted follower of the cult leader Charles Manson. After Manson's imprisonment for the brutal Tate-Bianca killings, Fromme's mission in life was to spread his message. Shooting or threatening to shoot a president, she reasoned, could publicize her cause and perhaps even give Manson a worldwide forum if he testified at her trial. On the morning of 5 September 1975, as President Ford walked across the capitol grounds in Sacramento, California, Fromme stepped out from the crowd of onlookers, pulled a pistol from her flowing robes, and leveled it at the president from a distance of about two feet. Before she could fire, she was tackled by Secret Service agents and was disarmed. At her trial, where Manson was not allowed to testify, she was found guilty and was sentenced to life imprisonment.

Later that same month President Ford was the target of another California woman with ties to the counterculture, Sara Jane Moore. After five failed marriages and a botched career as an accountant, the middle-aged Moore had drifted into the radical underground, where she found an acceptance that had been lacking in her earlier middle-class life. To add to her sense of excitement and importance, she also became a Federal Bureau of Investigation (FBI) informant, spying on her new friends. Remorseful over betraying them and fearful of their revenge, she decided to reestablish her radical bona fides by shooting the president. On 22 September 1975, after dropping her son off at school, she joined the crowd behind the rope line across the street from San Francisco's St. Francis Hotel. When the president emerged at 3:30 P.M., she fired once but missed her target. She too was sentenced to life in prison.

Earlier assassins were motivated by the voice of God or by some ideological commitment, but John Hinckley exhibited a more contemporary sensibility. He wanted to attract the attention of the movie actress Jodie Foster, the star of his favorite film, *Taxi Driver* (1976), which featured a political assassination. Hinckley decided to reenact the movie by killing President Ronald Reagan, even though he had no political or personal grievance against him.

On 30 March 1981, as Reagan was leaving the Washington Hilton Hotel, Hinckley began firing wildly, seriously wounding the president, the president's press secretary James Brady, a policeman, and a Secret Service agent. The president escaped fatal injury, but Brady was left paralyzed. The grace and courage Reagan displayed following the attack did much to cement his subsequent popularity. Hinckley was found not guilty by reason of insanity and was confined to St. Elizabeth's mental hospital in Washington, D.C., the same institution that had housed Lawrence.

Conclusions

Aside from the attacks on presidents Lincoln and Truman, none of these assassination attempts were political, in the strictest sense of the term. Each of the presidential assassins was delusional to one degree or another and projected those delusions onto the figure of the president. With the exceptions of the Lincoln and Truman attacks, the assassins apparently worked alone. No conspiracy has been credibly established, though conspiracy theories surrounded all the attempts, dating to the attack on Jackson that the president himself believed was inspired by his Whig opponents. Some have maintained, on equally flimsy evidence, that Secretary of War Edwin Stanton was implicated in Lincoln's death or that Zangara's real target was Mayor Cermak, who had aroused the enmity of the Chicago mob. These theories seem to represent an attempt to find some rational meaning for what were essentially irrational deeds.

By and large the stronger the president the more likely he is to attract assassins, not because of his controversial policies but because of his commanding presence. No one tried to kill Millard Fillmore or Benjamin Harrison. It can hardly be a coincidence that assassination attempts have increased along with the twentieth century's enlargement of the so-called "imperial presidency."

If, however, President William Clinton was correct that "the era of big government is over," then perhaps the twenty-first century will see a decline in presidential assassinations as well.

BIBLIOGRAPHY

Bishop, Jim. *The Day Lincoln Was Shot.* New York: Harper and Row, 1955.

Clarke, James W. *American Assassins: The Darker Side of Politics.* Princeton, N.J.: Princeton University Press, 1982.

Donovan, Robert J. *The Assassins.* New York: Harper, 1955.

Ford, Franklin L. *Political Murder: From Tyrannicide to Terrorism.* Cambridge, Mass.: Harvard University Press, 1985. Chapter 15 deals with the United States.

Hanchett, William. *The Lincoln Murder Conspiracies.* Urbana: University of Illinois Press, 1983.

Jackson, Carlton. "Another Time, Another Place: The Attempted Assassination of President Andrew Jackson." *Tennessee Historical Quarterly* 26 (summer 1967): 184–190.

Manchester, William. *The Death of a President, November 20–November 25, 1963.* New York: Harper and Row, 1967.

McKinley, James. *Assassination in America.* New York: Harper and Row, 1977.

Peskin, Allan. *Garfield.* Kent, Ohio: Kent State University Press, 1978. Chapter 25 deals with the assassination.

Posner, Gerald L. *Case Closed: Lee Harvey Oswald and the Assassination of JFK.* New York: Random House, 1993. Refutes the various conspiracy theories.

United States. Warren Commission. *Report of the President's Commission on the Assassination of President John F. Kennedy.* Washington, D.C.: U.S. Government Printing Office, 1964. The Warren Commission report.

Allan Peskin

See also **Conspiracy; Secret Service, United States; Warren Commission.**

ASSASSINATIONS AND POLITICAL VIOLENCE, OTHER.

Statistically, the United States is one of the most violent nations of the industrialized world. While it is difficult to measure contemporary trends against earlier epochs, it may be said that the use of violence in American culture has deep historic roots. With each new generation, the means and applications of societal violence change. If one constant may be claimed about America's past concerning violence, however, it is its employment against minority groups to attain or maintain economic, social, and political controls.

As with many other arenas of American life, the Civil War was a watershed mark in the use of lethal force for political ends. Prior to the Philadelphia Riot of 1844, a clash sparked by nativism and anti-Catholicism resulting in fourteen deaths and fifty wounded, societal violence in the antebellum period normally took the form of physical assaults to intimidate and instill fear. In Kentucky on 6 August 1855, nativism was again the source of violence

Political Violence. The victim of a anarchist's bomb that exploded in Union Square, New York, during a demonstration by unemployed people, 28 March 1908. LIBRARY OF CONGRESS

when a group of German immigrants, presumably Catholic, were attacked while attempting to cast ballots in the local mayoral race. Bloody Monday resulted in the deaths of twenty "foreigners" and left hundreds wounded. Similar forms of vigilantism spread particularly to the frontier, where, paradoxically, mob violence was the recourse of law-abiding citizens for maintaining the social order.

As animosities over slavery and western expansion grew, so too did the use of violence to solve the nation's political divisions. Two celebrated incidents of violence dramatically widened the political gap between North and South. The brutal caning of Massachusetts senator Charles Sumner by South Carolina representative Preston Brooks in the Senate Chamber of the Capitol on 22 May 1856 deeply alarmed northerners, who viewed it as an example of the great lengths southerners would take to defend the institution of slavery. Three year later, on 16 October 1859, abolitionist John Brown led a raid at Harpers Ferry, Virginia (later in West Virginia), striking deep fear in the hearts of southerners, who believed abolitionists would stop at nothing to achieve their political ends.

In the aftermath of the Civil War, African Americans were the targets of violent reprisals, particularly in the South. Organizations such as the Ku Klux Klan sought to "redeem" the South's former social order through violence. By the 1880s, public lynchings were widespread throughout several regions of the South—as a means of

"law enforcement," many whites publicly claimed. The threat of such sporadic violence proved an effective tool used by whites to reconcile the problem of weak local governments while maintaining their social superiority. Two subregions of the South, the Gulf Plain area and the cotton uplands of Arkansas, Louisiana, Mississippi, and Texas, witnessed the highest lynching rates in this period.

By the twentieth century, assassinations, premeditated acts of killing—secretively or publicly, and often in a brutal manner—influenced race relations as calls for desegregation and equal rights gained national prominence. Leaders of the National Association for the Advancement of Colored People (NAACP) were often the target of white reprisals. On 7 May 1955, for example, the Reverend George Lee was assassinated by three unknown assailants while driving his car in the black section of Belzoni, Mississippi. Protests by African Americans soon followed, with the NAACP leader, Roy Wilkins, calling upon the Justice Department to investigate what was deemed the first racial murder since the U.S. Supreme Court's decision in *Brown vs. the Board of Education of Topeka* in May 1954. Other murderous acts soon followed.

On 12 June 1963 Medgar Evers, a field secretary for the NAACP, was assassinated outside his home in Jackson, Mississippi. This crime sparked numerous demonstrations throughout the nation. The continued violence against blacks, particularly in high-profile cases like that of Evers, coupled with public pressure from the movement led by Martin Luther King Jr., prompted federal officials to take stronger action in the fight for civil rights. Nearly two weeks after Evers's murder, FBI agents arrested Byron de la Beckwith, a former marine and a member of the White Citizens Council, for the crime. Following Ever's funeral, his body was transported from Jackson to Arlington National Cemetery, where it was laid to rest.

Militant whites renewed their public efforts to maintain racial segregation in the South in the fall of that same year. A little more than two weeks following the Freedom March on Washington, D.C., and King's "I Have a Dream" speech, a member of the Ku Klux Klan bombed the Sixteenth Street Baptist Church in Birmingham, Alabama, killing four young black girls. The bombing on 15 September 1963 sparked protests that let to further bloodshed in the city. In the wake of Birmingham bombings, six persons were killed and nineteen others injured.

Not all acts of violence were carried out in such a public manner, nor were blacks the sole victims. The following summer, members of the Congress of Racial Equality (CORE) traveled to Philadelphia, Mississippi, to investigate the burning of a black church. Shortly after their departure, the three-member investigating team was reported missing. Their disappearance captured headlines. Then, on 4 August 1964, the bodies of James Chaney, Michael Schwerner, and Andrew Goodman—the latter two white—were found buried in an earthen dam. While historically such covert uses of violence and murder had proven to be effective tools in maintaining the

South's racial status quo, the murder of Evers and the three CORE members exposed the South's use of political violence to maintain white racial supremacy and brought considerable external pressure to bear on the region.

BIBLIOGRAPHY

Ayers, Edward L. *Vengeance and Justice: Crime and Punishment in the 19th Century American South.* New York: Oxford University Press, 1984.

Bellesiles, Michael A., ed. *Lethal Imagination: Violence and Brutality in American History.* New York: New York University Press, 1999.

Collier-Thomas, Bettye, and V. P. Franklin, eds. *My Soul Is a Witness: A Chronology of the Civil Rights Era, 1954–1965.* New York: Holt, 2000.

Graham, Hugh Davis, and Ted Robert Gurr, eds. *The History of Violence in America: Historical and Comparative Perspectives.* New York: Praeger, 1969.

Kent A. McConnell

See also **Civil Rights Movement; Ku Klux Klan; Lynching; Philadelphia Riots; Riots; Riots, Urban; Vigilantes.**

ASSAY OFFICES. The Assay Offices of the United States are part of the United States Treasury Department. They are responsible for the testing, melting, and refining of gold and silver bullion and foreign coins and recasting them into bars, ingots, or discs. Assaying is done at all the federal mints, but special plants were established at New York in 1853, at Boise, Idaho, in 1869, at Helena, Montana, in 1874, at Deadwood, South Dakota, at St. Louis, Missouri, in 1881, at Seattle, Washington, in 1898, and at Salt Lake City, Utah, in 1909. Other than the federal mints, there is now only one assay office. It is located in San Francisco.

BIBLIOGRAPHY

Taxay, Don. *The United States Mint and Coinage: An Illustrated History from 1776 to the Present.* New York: Arco, 1966.

Watson, Jesse P. *The Bureau of the Mint: Its History, Activities, and Organization.* Baltimore, Md.: Johns Hopkins University, 1926.

Meg Greene Malvasi

See also **Treasury, Department of the.**

ASSEMBLIES, COLONIAL, were the standard for representative government. Initially, elected representatives met in joint sessions with the governor and the council, later becoming the lower house of the legislature. It took most colonies until the 1720s to develop bicameral bodies that met regularly and had sufficient internal organization and systematic record keeping. Most of an assembly's workload developed from petitions, or constituent requests to the assemblies. The assemblies increased in output and importance from 1730 to 1765. Most legislation utilized Britain's criminal and civil code that governed elite procedures and was not for the citizens at large; thus, government was kept small to minimize the tax burden.

Initially, legislation was passed simply at the behest of the governor and his council, but in the late seventeenth century, the lower houses began to assert their authority in order to counter threats to local autonomy from governors and royal appointees, reversing the balance of power that had been in place since the early 1600s. Internal proceedings concerning taxes and the budget were strengthened. As the lower houses controlled local revenue, they held the power to vote permanent incomes to executive officers, including the governor's salary.

The first colonial assembly was the Virginia House of Burgesses, created on 30 July 1619, with a governor, Sir George Yeardley, four members of the council, and two burgesses from each of the Virginia boroughs as a unicameral body enlisting the settlers' support for the decisions passed by the company headquarters in London. Not until 1628 did it have the ability to pass tax or other laws. Under the Massachusetts Bay Company, the second colonial representative body emerged in 1629, composed of all adult males who were full church members and thus freemen. In 1634, this membership was changed to two delegates from each town to attend the annual meeting, chaired by the governor and the Court of Assistants, later evolving into a representative bicameral body. Rhode Island's assembly, developed after 1663, had the dominant role in government; the elected governor had little power and the assembly made official appointments. Connecticut's assembly was similar until the middle of the eighteenth century, when it was replaced with local elections for colonial officials. In Maryland, the proprietor Cecil Calvert, Lord Baltimore, struggled with the assembly, but finally allowed it to initiate laws on the condition that it submit them to him for acceptance or rejection. Carolina's eight divergent proprietors sought to enforce the feudal Fundamental Constitutions while the settlers upheld their right to a popular elected assembly of freeholders, guaranteed by the Concessions and Agreement of 1665. From the beginning, Pennsylvania had a popularly elected assembly, which clashed frequently with the Penn family proprietors, although in 1756, six pacifist Quakers resigned from the assembly in response to the threat of oaths required by Parliament, resulting in a short period of harmony between the legislature and executive. Conflicts with the governors consistently left the assemblies in an increasingly stronger position up to the Revolution.

BIBLIOGRAPHY

Andrews, Charles McLean. *Colonial Self-government, 1652–1689.* New York: Harper and Brothers, 1904.

Bliss, Robert M. *Revolution and Empire: English Politics and the American Colonies in the Seventeenth Century.* Manchester, U.K.: Manchester University Press, 1990.

Greene, Jack P. *The Quest for Power: The Lower Houses of Assembly in the Southern Royal Colonies, 1689–1776.* Chapel Hill: University of North Carolina Press, 1963.

Sosin, Jack M. *English America and Imperial Inconstancy: The Rise of Provincial Autonomy, 1696–1715.* Lincoln: University of Nebraska Press, 1985.

Michelle M. Mormul

See also **Colonial Councils; Colonial Policy, British; House of Burgesses; Representative Government.**

ASSEMBLIES OF GOD emerged from the mass of Pentecostal sects that formed during the nineteenth century and trace their formation to the Azusa Street revival of 1906. Following early efforts by Pentecostals to organize, southern leaders called for a general conference to meet at Hot Springs, Arkansas, in 1914. Although many pastors feared the usurpation of congregational autonomy, the three hundred who did attend recognized the advantages of cooperation, fellowship, and the setting of standards of conduct and practice. Founder Eudorus N. Bell also argued the need to expand publishing, missionary, and education efforts. The new body showed great respect for congregational autonomy and did not initially adopt a statement of faith, holding the Bible to be "all sufficient rule for faith and practice." A twelve-man executive presbytery was created, and by the end of 1914, the number of ministers participating stood at 531.

Bell drafted an early summary of beliefs, which included the preaching of salvation, baptism in the Spirit, spiritual gifts, premillenialism, divine healing, and observance of baptism and communion. In 1915, however, the "Jesus Only" controversy erupted, when several pastors called for rebaptism in the name of Jesus alone. This led in 1916 to the General Council's preparation of a statement of fundamental truths, a serious matter in a movement that disdained creedal statements. Although 156 ministers left, membership continued to climb, and by 1918 ministerial membership stood at 819. In 1918, the Assemblies of God also took a firm stand that the baptism of the Holy Spirit was regularly evidenced by the initial physical sign of speaking in tongues.

After 1918, the Assemblies of God operated from Springfield, Missouri, where the Gospel Publishing House provided vital periodical support to a scattered flock. The *Word and Witness* spread the Pentecostal message, while the *Christian Evangel* serviced the Pentecostal constituency. After 1919, the *Christian Evangel*, renamed the *Pentecostal Evangel*, became the sole paper of the movement. The 1945 General Council set up a radio department, with its first broadcast in 1946, and created the half-hour *Revivaltime* in 1950. The Assemblies of God also founded the Midwest Bible School at Auburn, Nebraska, in 1920 and Central Bible Institute at Springfield in 1922. For missionary work, the General Council of 1914 created the Home and Foreign Missions Presbytery to funnel funds, offer counsel, and provide legal holding of property purchased abroad. The 1915 General Council set guidelines for making missions effective, and the Foreign Missions Department was created in 1919. In 1937, the Assemblies of God established a Home Missions Department, with special ministries to the deaf, foreign-language groups, and Native Americans.

During the 1940s, 76,000 members of the Assemblies of God served in the military and 1,093 were killed. The denomination began work among servicemen and the Servicemen's Department was set up in 1944, while thirty-four pastors became military chaplains. Closer cooperation with other denominations also took place. Representatives of the Assemblies of God attended the 1942 St. Louis meeting that formed the National Association of Evangelicals, with which the 1943 General Council voted to affiliate. The Assemblies of God also joined the World Pentecostal Conference in 1947, and participated in the Pentecostal Fellowship of North America organized in 1948, for which J. R. Flower of the Assemblies of God was appointed to draw up the constitution.

In the postwar world, the Assemblies of God faced new challenges as Pentecostalism won public acceptance. A renewed focus on evangelism and spiritual life was emphasized with the establishment of the Evangelism Committee in 1965. The Assemblies of God refined its statements on biblical inerrancy and engaged in greater cooperation with other religious groups on issues of moral and social concern. In an effort to retain its appeal to a younger generation, it created a youth department in 1940 and fostered campus ministries and the Mobilization and Placement Service, which allowed church members to use their skills in Christian service. The Teen Challenge program proved particularly effective in dealing with troubled youth, through coffee hours, drop-in centers, school and club programs, and some vocational training. In 1999, the Assemblies of God, under the leadership of general superintendent Thomas Trask, boasted a constituency of 2,574,531. It was a growing body and the largest single Pentecostal denomination, apart from the Church of God in Christ.

BIBLIOGRAPHY

Blumhofer, Edith L. *Restoring the Faith: The Assemblies of God, Pentecostalism, and American Culture.* Urbana: University of Illinois Press, 1993.

McGee, Gary B. *People of the Spirit: The Assemblies of God.* Springfield, Mo.: Gospel Publishing House, 1997.

Jeremy Bonner

See also **African American Religions and Sects; Evangelism, Evangelicalism, and Revivalism; Pentecostal Churches.**

ASSEMBLY, RIGHT OF. See **First Amendment.**

ASSEMBLY LINE. The assembly line is often described as a process that uses machines to move material from one place to another, but in practice, machines are not always needed. For instance, mass-market jewelers often use assembly lines in which materials are handed from one worker to another, without the benefit of machinery. At its most basic, an assembly line is a series of stations at which people or machines add to or assemble parts for a product. One of the values of the assembly line is its versatility: it can be simple, but it has the capacity to be very complex. An assembly line can begin as many different lines each devoted to a different component of a product, with the lines converging upon one another, becoming fewer until only one line is left for the final product. Automotive companies often have assembly lines that begin with raw materials and end five miles away with a completed automobile. A structure for a complex assembly line begins as one main line with stations along it that are fed by lines running perpendicular to it, with each of these side lines feeding components for the finished product. Although the assembly line has occasionally been considered outmoded, it has survived by repeatedly changing its form.

Foundations of the Assembly Line

The idea of the assembly line has many parents. In the scientific revolution of the eighteenth century, scientists, especially mathematicians tried to quantify what made an industry productive and tried to find ways to make industries more productive. The goal was to create an industry that functioned without human labor. The most important people of the time for the development of the assembly line were the Americans Oliver Evans and Eli Whitney and the Frenchman Gaspard Monge. Evans is known for his invention of the first motorized amphibious vehicle, but his most influential achievement was to design a flour mill. During the late eighteenth century, he used steam engines to power mills that used belt and screw conveyors, as well as moving hoppers, to move grain through the process of becoming flour and then to move the flour to where it could be packaged. While his equipment was not exactly an assembly line, all the basic components were there.

Best known for creating the cotton gin, Eli Whitney also contributed to the development of the assembly line with his invention of interchangeable parts. Whitney created machine tools that could create parts so closely resembling each other they could be substituted for one another without harm. In 1798, the United States government ordered 10,000 muskets, and in a preview of the assembly line, Whitney set his employees to work on manufacturing parts that were assembled bit by bit into muskets. A Whitney musket could be repaired in the field with spare parts.

Gaspard Monge made his contribution while in Italy during the Napoleonic era. He took the principals of descriptive geometry and applied them to machinery. By breaking a machine down into its component parts, Monge found that he could show how each part related to the others; this would evolve into technical drawing, which

Assembly Line. Frames of early automobiles move along for assembly, part by part, an innovation credited to Henry Ford. LIBRARY OF CONGRESS

allowed people to make machines they had never seen, machines that would share interchangeable parts with any other machine made with the same diagrams.

Henry Ford

Making automobiles was a hobby for many Americans, and Henry Ford began as a hobbyist, but he brought to his hobby an unsurpassed ambition. In 1899, he started his own automobile manufacturing company; he wanted to produce cars in large enough quantities to make them available to everyone. In 1908, he divided up the tasks involved in manufacturing an automobile; he broke these tasks down to the function of each autoworker, conceiving of each worker as a part of a machine that made cars. At first, he tried having chassis pulled along factory floors with towropes. Men walked alongside the chassis to stations, at each station parts were added. Manufacturing time for a single automobile decreased from twelve hours to five and one-half hours. In 1913, he installed conveyor belts in his factories. With these, workers stood at their stations, each doing the same repetitive task over and over again. Manufacturing time for one car fell to around an hour and a half. At such a pace, Ford could make a small profit on each car but could make much more money from selling the cars in the millions. By the end of 1914, his employees were the highest paid industrial workers in the world; a worker performing the simplest of tasks could, and some did, become rich.

World War II

When the United States entered World War II, its heavy industries were charged with manufacturing the matériel for the armed services. The assembly line was crucial to this production. In March 1941, Ford began building a factory and, by the end of 1942, was taking in raw materials at one end, processing them, and producing B-24 bombers. By the end of the war, Ford's factory was producing B-17 bombers at the rate of one every sixty-three minutes.

General Motors made an impressive innovation with its production of chassis for combat tanks. Despite being a big and heavy machine, a tank needed to be tight in its joints and fluid in its reactions to the men operating it. With early tanks, the impact of an enemy shell might not breach the American tank's armor but would blow bolts loose in the interior, killing the people inside. The management at General Motors was not alone in realizing that the bolts had to be replaced by welds, but it was their engineers who came up with the assembly line innovation that helped make the welds succeed. Instead of using machines to do the welding, they employed human welders as craftsmen; they created an enormous machine that could pick up a tank chassis and tilt it quickly to any angle the welders wanted. The assembly line station became a craftsman's shop, with the line responding to the workers rather than the workers just being parts of the machine. Decades later, the Japanese manufacturer Toyota would use a similar machine to weld its automobile chassis, and a similar concept for the work stations. General Motors did them both first.

The assembly line affected the lives of American women. Women fit into many assembly line jobs previously only done by men. The assembly line was successful enough at relieving workers of the tasks requiring brute strength. Historians note the millions of American women who left their jobs when American servicemen returned to civilian life; not so often noted is that women workers were so good at their tasks that aircraft manufacturers and auto makers kept many of them employed to handle tasks such as wiring.

Wounded but Still Alive
The wear and tear on workers created by relentlessly repetitive physical motions on assembly lines became increasingly public after World War II. Further, factories that relied on an assembly line seemed to have become inefficient. When Japanese automakers began to make inroads into American markets in the 1970s, American industry seemed less than up to the challenge. Toyota had introduced a concept called *kaizen*, meaning "continuous improvement." The idea was to have assembly line workers participate in the development of a product and to suggest changes even during the production process. This idea harkened back to when Ford and Chevrolet encouraged worker suggestions, back in the late 1910s and early 1920s, saving the companies millions of dollars by pointing out inefficiencies. By the 1980s, it was known as the Toyota Production System.

Although General Motors began using robots on the assembly line in the 1960s, it was not until the 1980s that robots were extensively used on the industrial assembly line. Robots could be very efficient at doing certain repetitive jobs, and Japanese manufacturers soon led the world in using them on their assembly lines. Station workers' costs were cut, because fewer workers were needed. Yet, the overall use of robots was by 1990 becoming a failure. Many people were required to maintain the robots and program the computers that directed them. In the 1990s, Ford and Chrysler developed "value engineering," a process by which the basics of a design were kept simple, allowing them to be repeated for several different products; about 70 percent of the parts for a new car would be shared with a previous design. This allowed for quick responsiveness to the public's desires, since a plant did not have to completely retool for each different car model. This development was combined with ergonomic workstations. By asking workers on the assembly line for ideas, manufacturers discovered that something as basic as moving a conveyor belt from the floor to waist height could increase productivity and decrease injuries. With robots proving not to be complete substitutes for human beings, the comfort and care of workers became ever more important. By creating work stations that were comfortable and by combining work stations into groups, communication among workers increased. Most manufacturers found this led to increased productivity and improvements in quality. The fundamental concept of the assembly line still remains the basis for the most efficient mass production of manufactured goods.

BIBLIOGRAPHY

"The Arsenals of Progress." *The Economist* (US) 330, no. 7853 (5 March 1994): M5–7.

Chow, We-Min. *Assembly Line Design: Methodology and Applications.* New York: Marcel Dekker, 1990.

De Camp, L. Sprague, and Catherine C. De Camp. *The Story of Science in America.* New York: Charles Scribner's Sons, 1967.

Hapgood, Fred. "Keeping It Simple." *Inc.* 18, no. 4 (19 March 1996): 66–70.

Nof, Shimon, W. Wilhelm, and H. Warnecke. *Industrial Assembly.* New York: Chapman & Hall, 1996.

Scholl, Armin, and A. Siedenberg, eds. *Balancing and Sequencing of Assembly Lines.* New York: Springer-Verlag, 1999.

Womack, James R., Daniel Roos, and Daniel T. Jones. *The Machine That Changed the World: The Story of Lean Production.* New York: Rawson Associates, 1990.

Kirk H. Beetz

See also **Automobile Industry; Industrial Revolution; Mass Production; Robotics.**

ASSIMILATION refers to the integration of the members of a minority group into the broader society to which they belong. According to the sociologist Milton M. Gordon, it is a seven-stage process, in which "acculturation," or the adoption by newcomers of the language, dress, and other daily customs of the host society, is the first step. "Structural assimilation," the second, involves the large-scale entrance of minorities into the cliques, clubs, and institutions of the host society, in a manner that is personal, intimate, emotionally affective, and engaging the whole personality. Once a group has achieved structural assimilation, the remaining stages "naturally follow." Those include "amalgamation" or frequent intermarriage, the development of a sense of peoplehood based solely on the host society, the disappearances of prejudiced attitudes and of discriminatory behavior toward the minority, and the absence of civic conflicts in which the competing interests of the majority and minority groups are an issue.

Assimilation is a problematic term. It can refer to the experiences of a group or of its individual members. Originating in the natural sciences, it identified a process through which one organism absorbs another; the latter then ceases to exist in recognizable form. Scholars are vague about the techniques for measuring the progress of assimilation and imprecise in defining its practical completion short of the disappearance of the minority, which rarely occurs. Some focus on socioeconomic adjustment and demographic behavior, while others emphasize changes in identity. Advocates with differing political agendas regarding national development debate whether assimilation is a desirable outcome for a society containing multiple groups.

Theorists have given names to existing, implicit models of assimilation and have proposed alternative ones. Identifying the boundaries that separate terms such as "melting pot," "pluralism," "cultural pluralism," and "multiculturalism" is not easy. The use of ancillary concepts, including "Anglo-conformity," "triple melting pot," "primordial ethnicity," "symbolic ethnicity," and "postethnicity" further complicates discussions.

The Melting Pot

In the 1780s, Hector St. Jean de Crèvecoeur offered one of the earliest descriptions of the formation of the American population as the physical melding of diverse European peoples into a new, single people. Israel Zangwill's eponymous 1908 play made "melting pot" the twentieth century's phrase for Crèvecoeur's idea. An English Jew who espoused various forms of Zionism throughout his life, Zangwill nevertheless presented, as the outcome of life in the American cauldron, the union of seemingly implacable enemies—a Russian Jewish immigrant to New York and the daughter of the tsarist official who had ordered the destruction of his village.

Although melting pot implies mutual change leading to the creation of a new alloy, most who adopted the phrase described a process, which Milton Gordon later called "Anglo-conformity," through which newcomers adapted to norms derived from an Anglo-American heritage. Alternative visions arose almost immediately. In 1915, Horace Kallen described the United States as an orchestral combination of constant European cultures. Cultural pluralism, as Kallen's outlook became known, rejected the melting pot and described ancestral roots as so determinative that Americanization had to be repeated with each generation. Writing as an opponent of U.S. involvement in World War I, Randolph Bourne critiqued the melting pot ideal as the effort of Anglophiles to place their own culture ahead of others and envisioned Americans sifting and winnowing the best from all traditions. Unlike Kallen, Bourne implied greater mutual change among the nation's constituent groups, with residual differences being of little consequence. Bourne's phrase, "trans-national America," has not survived, but the term "pluralism," or some variant of it, has captured the spirit of his ideas.

The melting pot metaphor, especially as expressed by proponents of "100-percent Americanism," held sway through World War I and after. As of the New Deal and World War II, however, concepts like "cultural democracy" and versions of cultural pluralism closer to Bourne's point of view than to Kallen's became predominant. Under the influence of thinkers like the sociologist Robert E. Park, the criteria for assimilation became political loyalty, adoption of generally accepted social customs, and conformity to national practices and aspirations.

As limited immigration changed the demographics of America's foreign stock after the 1920s, the Great Depression, World War II, cinema, radio, and eventually television spread generations of common experiences across the nation. By the 1940s, the sociologist Ruby Jo Reeves Kennedy argued that a "triple melting pot" had emerged. Clear ethnic boundaries were disappearing, as Protestants, Catholics, and Jews willingly married across nationality groups but within their religious traditions.

Religious Segmentation

Religion's potential for segmenting the population was a source of concern. Paul Blanshard accused Catholics of hostility to America's democratic and liberal traditions. Several observers noted the lagging socioeconomic status of Catholics, and Gerhard Lenski attributed the gap to values rooted in the religion. Overall, however, the triple melting pot was simply an elaborated expression of the benign pluralist model of the era. Will Herberg, in *Protestant, Catholic, Jew: An Essay in American Religious Sociology* (1955), argued that the nation's three major religions shared the political and civil values that made the United States the world's leading theistic power. Subsequent scholarship indicated that, on average, foreign-stock Euro-Americans had "caught up" by 1950. For those seeking reassurance, the election of John F. Kennedy, a Catholic, as president offered evidence that differences based in religious background had waned.

Race Succeeds Religion

The issue of race was peripheral to the assimilation debate in the first half of the century. With the rise of the civil rights movement, however, race succeeded nationality and religion as the final frontier of America's assimilation history. Drawing from works like Stanley Elkins's *Slavery: A Problem in American Institutional and Intellectual Life* (1959), liberals assumed that slavery had deracinated blacks and made them the most culturally American of all the peoples who had come to the New World. Color prejudice, therefore, was the primary obstacle to total assimilation.

This optimism waned when dismantling discriminatory legislation proved an inadequate means to achieve rapid structural assimilation for black Americans. Critics argued that the legacy of slavery and the visibility of color differences made it impossible for racial minorities to attain assimilation of the kind achieved by Americans of European origin. They denied that blacks had reached the status of an "interest group," which Nathan Glazer and Daniel Patrick Moynihan saw as the remaining function for group identity among the Irish, Italians, Jews, blacks, and Puerto Ricans of New York City. Rediscovering ties to Africa, or reinventing them, activists posited the existence of true cultural differences separating blacks from the majority in the United States. Similar developments occurred among smaller minority populations, including Native Americans, Latinos, and Asians who had experienced discrimination analogous to that suffered by blacks.

The Revival of Multiculturalism

After the 1960s, Kallen's version of cultural pluralism, which the author himself had long since abandoned, enjoyed a revival, often under the term "multiculturalism." Although some commentators used the word simply as a synonym for the view of pluralism dominant at midcentury, others offered multiculturalism as a distinct alternative. They saw ethnic and racial identities as primordial or ineradicable; accepted the existence of real and permanent cultural differences; vested the strength of the United States in its diversity, which the government, therefore, had an obligation to preserve; and stressed the importance of group as well as individual rights.

Multiculturalism did not escape criticism, especially when its proponents reduced American diversity to a split between Europeans and allied "peoples of color," and, in an era of renewed immigration, not only predicted what the future would be but also offered policy prescriptions for what it should be. Although Asian and Latino newcomers to the United States in the late twentieth century had direct or indirect ties with groups that had suffered prejudice on the basis of ascriptive characteristics, they arrived in an era when the nation had rejected discrimination based on such grounds. They constitute majorities in the minority groups to which they ethnically belong, and the empirical evidence leaves it open to debate whether their experiences are replicating the history of exclusion associated with race or the history associated with the integration of European immigrant groups.

Michael Novak, in *The Rise of the Unmeltable Ethnics: Politics and Culture in the Seventies* (1972), adopted some multicultural premises but used them to demonstrate that Europeans from quadrants outside the northwest of that continent suffered exclusions similar to those experienced by racial minorities. Arthur M. Schlesinger Jr., in *The Disuniting of America* (1991), and Nathan Glazer, in *Affir-*

mative Discrimination: Ethnic Inequality and Public Policy (1975), more thoroughly disagreed with the contentions of the multiculturalists and with the various programs they endorsed to preserve minority cultures and to promote access to education and employment for minority group members.

Moderate commentators have sought to find themes that may lead to a generally accepted interpretation of assimilation. Although cognizant of the real experiential differences between the heirs of European immigrants and descendants of African slaves, Matthew Frye Jacobson, in *Whiteness of a Different Color: European Immigrants and the Alchemy of Race* (1998), demonstrated the overlapping histories of the terms "race" and "ethnicity" and the constructed rather than substantive meanings of both. Herbert Gans has claimed that for Americans of European descent ethnicity is primarily a "symbolic" identity that they can use voluntarily and in positive ways. Ann Swidler has similarly described ethnicity as just one of the cultural tools through which persons can express their identities. David Hollinger, in *Postethnic America: Beyond Multiculturalism* (1995), argued for a future in which all persons can comfortably claim one or more ethnic identities without having their expectations or behaviors limited by those identities.

BIBLIOGRAPHY

Blanshard, Paul. *American Freedom and Catholic Power.* Boston: Beacon Press, 1949.

Bourne, Randolph. "Trans-national America." *Atlantic Monthly* 118, no. 1 (July 1916): 86–97.

Gans, Herbert J. "Symbolic Ethnicity: The Future of Ethnic Groups and Cultures in America." *Ethnic and Racial Studies* 2, no. 1 (January 1979): 1–20.

Glazer, Nathan, and Daniel Patrick Moynihan. *Beyond the Melting Pot: The Negroes, Puerto Ricans, Jews, Italians, and Irish of New York City.* Cambridge, Mass.: MIT Press, 1963.

Gordon, Milton M. *Assimilation in American Life: The Role of Race, Religion, and National Origins.* New York: Oxford University Press, 1964.

Kallen, Horace. "Democracy Versus the Melting Pot." *The Nation* (18 Feb. 1915): 190–194 and (25 Feb. 1915): 217–220.

Lenski, Gerhard E. *The Religious Factor: A Sociological Study of Religion's Impact on Politics, Economics, and Family Life.* Garden City, N.Y.: Doubleday, 1961.

Park, Robert E., and Herbert A. Miller. *Old World Traits Transplanted.* New York and London: Harper, 1921.

Swidler, Ann. "Culture in Action: Symbols and Strategies." *American Sociological Review* 51, no. 2 (April 1986): 273–286.

Thomas Archdeacon

See also **Melting Pot; Multiculturalism; Pluralism.**

ASSISTANT. According to the charter of the Massachusetts Bay Company (1629), the company would be managed by a general court comprised of an elected governor and eighteen elected assistants, later known as magistrates. But the smaller Court of Assistants (six assistants and the governor) was permitted to take care of routine business. Responding to protests about his attempts to consolidate power in the Court of Assistants, Governor John Winthrop agreed to let every town send two deputies to the general court. The deputies eventually broke off and became the lower house (1644). Connecticut's Fundamental Orders (1639) provided for a governor and six assistants, plus four deputies from each town.

BIBLIOGRAPHY

Middleton, Richard. *Colonial America: A History, 1585–1776.* Malden, Mass.: Blackwell, 1996.

Jeremy Derfner

See also **Assemblies, Colonial.**

ASSISTED SUICIDE   is the act of helping people to end their lives by providing information or means, which is self-administered. By contrast, EUTHANASIA is the intentional killing of an individual in a relatively painless way for reasons of mercy. Traditionally, the law has considered any kind of suicide one of the most heinous crimes against society. In colonial America, under common law anyone who committed suicide forfeited all his goods, leaving his family destitute in many cases. The colonies eventually abolished these harsh penalties, recognizing that the laws punished the wrong people. Lawyer Zephaniah Swift wrote in 1796 that to punish the family of an offender was the ultimate cruelty. The earliest American statute to outlaw suicide was enacted in 1828. Between 1857 and 1865 a New York commission led by Dudley Field, a New York jurist, was charged with reorganizing New York's civil and criminal law and created the first law to forbid anyone from assisting another in taking their life. By 1868 nine of thirty-seven states had adopted laws making the assisting of suicide a crime.

Individual states have reevaluated assisted-suicide laws as medicine and technology have advanced, but the laws have generally remained constant. The Uniform Determination of Death Act (1981) states that when a person's heart and lungs stop or brain functions end the person is legally dead and may be disconnected from life support. Two legal documents also addressed the issue of life support: the living will and Durable Power of Attorney for Health Care. Both documents allowed a person to have their wishes addressed in the event they became unable to speak for themselves. Some states have enacted death with dignity laws such as Oregon's 1994 law.

The most famous cases of assisted suicide involve Dr. Jack Kevorkian, a Michigan pathologist. Kevorkian allegedly helped more than 130 terminally ill people commit suicide with a machine set up to deliver a fatal solution intravenously when the patient pulls a plunger. In 1999 Kevorkian was convicted of second degree murder and use of a controlled substance and was sentenced to two terms in prison.

Arguments over the issue of assisted suicide involve emotional and deeply personal religious beliefs. On one side, proponents argue that people have a right to die with dignity when their illness or disability has become so advanced that relief is unrealistic and that doctors who help these patients are following the ill person's wishes. Meanwhile, opponents argue that suicide in any form is immoral and that the Hippocratic oath prohibits doctors from assisting in suicide.

BIBLIOGRAPHY

de Vries, Brian, ed. *End of Life Issues: Interdisciplinary and Multidimensional Perspectives.* New York: Springer, 1999.

Gorsuch, Neil M. "The Right to Assisted Suicide and Euthanasia." *Harvard Journal of Law and Public Policy* 23, no. 3 (summer 2000): 599–710.

Lisa A. Ennis

See also **Death and Dying; Health Care.**

ASSOCIATED PRESS.   *See* **Press Associations.**

ASSOCIATION OF SOUTHERN WOMEN FOR THE PREVENTION OF LYNCHING. Jessie Daniel Ames was the spark behind the formation of the Association of Southern Women for the Prevention of Lynching (ASWPL). Ames was a leader in a number of different organizations, including the Texas League of Women Voters, of which she was founding president in 1919. In 1930, she was the director of the Women's Work Committee of the Commission for Interracial Cooperation when the number of lynchings in the South spiked, although they were still lower than previous peak years.

Because of this alarming development, Ames called a conference on 1 November 1930 to explore the means for southern white women to stop lynching. Twenty-six women attended the conference and twelve formed the nucleus for the ASWPL. Most of the women were leaders in southern Protestant churches, frequently the heads of the women's missionary societies. The essential argument of the ASWPL, as articulated by Ames, was that the justification for lynching was false. Perpetrators claimed that they were defending the virtue of southern white women. Yet statistics that Ames gathered showed that only 29 percent of the 204 lynchings from 1922 to 1929 involved allegations of crimes against white women. The women's strategy was constantly to educate people about the fallacy of lynching's rationale. In addition, they engaged in action at the county level, where they enlisted existing organizations and lobbied local officeholders to prevent lynching before it happened. If a lynching did occur, they exposed the facts behind it to the wider world. The women obtained signatures on pledges to eradicate lynching. They considered county sheriffs the key to the prevention of lynching.

By 1938, the number of lynchings had fallen by 50 percent. In that year alone, sheriffs and police officers prevented forty lynchings. By 1939, 1,229 peace officers in fifteen states had signed the pledge and tens of thousands of other southerners, mostly women, had done so as well. In 1942, when Ames discontinued the organization, lynching was rare. Ames never supported a federal anti-lynching law, believing that such a statute would end local action and reduce her effectiveness.

BIBLIOGRAPHY

Ames, Jessie Daniel. "Southern Women and Lynching." *Women and Social Movements in the United States, 1775–2000.* Available from http://womhist.binghamton.edu.

Barber, Henry E. "The Association of Southern Women for the Prevention of Lynching, 1930–1942." *Phylon* 34, no. 4 (December 1973): 378–89.

Hall, Jacquelyn Dowd. *Revolt against Chivalry: Jessie Daniel Ames and the Women's Campaign against Lynching.* New York: Columbia University Press, 1979.

Bonnie L. Ford

See also **Lynching.**

ASSOCIATION ON AMERICAN INDIAN AFFAIRS,

a significant player in the history of Native American advocacy in the twentieth century. From its foundation by non-Indians in New York City in 1922 to its move to South Dakota in 1995 under a wholly Indian administration, the AAIA came to consider itself unique in advocating the Indians' own vision of their rights and welfare.

The AAIA was created in direct response to federal legislation (the infamous Bursum Bill) designed to enable non-Indians to lay claim to Pueblo land in New Mexico. This legislation occasioned the ire of non-Indian friends of the Pueblos and inspired the creation of the Eastern Association on Indian Affairs. By joining forces, the EAIA, the New Mexico Association on Indian Affairs (NAIA), and the American Indian Defense Association, led by John Collier, were instrumental in defeating the Bursum Bill. Following their victory, these groups saw that the needs of Indian people reached far beyond one piece of legislation. In 1933 Oliver La Farge, an anthropologist and Pulitzer Prize–winning novelist, became the EAIA's president; in 1939 he merged his group, the faltering NAIA, and the American Indian Defense Association into what became the American Association on Indian Affairs, with headquarters in New York.

While remaining focused on the native peoples of the Southwest, the association's concerns reached throughout the country. La Farge and the association supported the work of commissioner John Collier and opposed the federal government's attempt to terminate its involvement in the lives of Native Americans.

As the battle over termination subsided, the association turned to broader Native American concerns. In 1955 the group elected its first Native American board member, Edward Dozier, a Santa Clara Pueblo anthropologist. The organization proposed programs that would develop the social and economic potential of Native American communities without destroying indigenous cultures. In 1973 the association elected a Native American president, Alfonso Ortiz, a San Juan Pueblo professor of anthropology at Princeton. Ortiz brought the board into a balance of Indians and Anglo advocates and focused its efforts on tribal self-determination through health, education, and economic development programs. He also paid special attention to land, water, and religious rights. When Ortiz left office in 1988 the association was at the zenith of its accomplishments. In the years following his departure, difficulties raising money led its executive director, Jerry Flute, the onetime chairman of South Dakota's Sisseton-Wahpeton Sioux, to reduce the association's activities and move its offices to Sisseton, South Dakota. The Archive of the Association on American Indian Affairs is housed in the Princeton University Library.

Alfred Bush

See also **American Indian Defense Association; Termination Policy.**

ASSOCIATIONS.

An association is an organization of social equals agreeing to work for a common purpose or to promote a common cause. The twelve English colonies in North America applied this name to their organizations for boycotting British manufactured goods prior to the American Revolution. Merchants in the cities of New York, Boston, and Philadelphia each created formally named associations of nonimportation to protest the Stamp Act in the fall of 1765. These associations dissolved with the Stamp Act's repeal in March 1766, but reformed to protest the Townsend Acts in June 1767. On 18 May 1769, George Washington and George Mason introduced to the Virginia House of Burgesses legislation to establish a colonywide association for nonimportation. The Virginia Association called for the cultivation of crops other than tobacco, an expansion of local manufacturing, a boycott all British goods, and a refusal to accept new slaves into the colony. In the next two years, eight additional colonies created similar associations with locally elected committees of compliance and committees of correspondence. On 20 October 1774, the First Continental Congress established the Continental Association, with stiff penalties for nonobservance of the boycotts declared by Congress. Its committees often became ad hoc local governments during the Revolution.

Organizations for purposes other than boycotts also called themselves "associations." During the Revolution, ad hoc militias took the name to justify local looting and pillaging. In New Jersey, the moderately pro-British Association for Retaliation fought the more radical Board of Associated Loyalists between 1780 and 1783 as much as they did the rebels. "Association" later became a popular name for professional and other voluntary organizations in the United States. In 2001, 7,700 national organizations used the term "association," while only 2,700 used the nearly synonymous term "society."

BIBLIOGRAPHY

Jensen, Merrill. *The Founding of a Nation: A History of the American Revolution, 1763–1776.* New York: Oxford University Press, 1968.

Ragsdale, Bruce. *A Planters' Republic: The Search for Economic Independence in Revolutionary Virginia.* Madison, Wisc.: Madison House, 1996.

Bill Olbrich

See also **Boston Committee of Correspondence; Committees of Correspondence; Continental Congress; Virginia Resolves.**

ASTOR PLACE RIOT, in New York City on 10 May 1849, sparked by a long-standing rivalry between the American actor Edwin Forrest and the English tragedian William Charles Macready. The haughty and aristocratic Macready had already emerged as a hated figure among working-class audiences. Forrest, for his part, did little to discourage the flames of anti-British sentiment and class discontent.

On 7 May the two actors appeared simultaneously, just blocks apart, in separate productions of *Macbeth*. Forrest performed before cheering crowds, while Macready was forced from the stage of the Astor Place Opera House by a flurry of chairs thrown from the gallery. Macready prepared to leave the country, but members of the New York literati convinced him to complete his American tour.

On 10 May, the night of Macready's next performance, a pro-Forrest crowd of ten thousand gathered outside the Astor Place Opera House. The mob shelled the theater with stones and charged the entrance, only to be repelled when the state militia fired directly into the crowd, killing at least twenty-two that night; nine others died of their wounds within the next few days. Eighty-six men, mostly workingmen, were arrested. The clash outside the Astor Place Opera House symbolized the growing cultural stratification in antebellum New York. Even a cultural icon as universal as Shakespeare had become a battleground of class sentiment.

Great Riot at the Astor Place Opera House. Nathaniel Currier's lithograph depicts the unusual New York City battleground on 10 May 1849, when a theatrical rivalry led to more than thirty deaths and nearly one hundred arrests. GRANGER COLLECTION, NEW YORK.

BIBLIOGRAPHY

Buckley, Peter G. "To the Opera House: Culture and Society in New York City, 1820–1860." Ph.D. diss., State University of New York at Stony Brook, 1984.

Levine, Lawrence W. *Highbrow/Lowbrow: The Emergence of Cultural Hierarchy in America.* Cambridge, Mass.: Harvard University Press, 1988.

Moody, Richard. *The Astor Place Riot.* Bloomington, Ind.: Indiana University Press, 1958.

Stanley R. Pillsbury / A. R.

See also **Riots, Urban.**

ASTORIA. John Jacob Astor dreamed of an organized continent-wide fur trade well before American occupation of the upper Missouri country. To his AMERICAN FUR COMPANY, chartered in 1808, he added the PACIFIC FUR COMPANY, organized in 1810, and proceeded to extend his organization from Saint Louis, Missouri, to the mouth of the Columbia River in Oregon. Astor's company sent two expeditions to Oregon: one by sea, and one along the route of the LEWIS AND CLARK EXPEDITION. The seagoing party, under Capt. Jonathan Thorn, embarked 6 September 1810 in the *Tonquin* and, after a stormy voyage, reached the Columbia on 23 March 1811. Within three weeks, Astoria was established under the direction of Duncan McDougal, acting resident agent. In June, Capt. Thorn and a trading party clashed with local Indians in Nootka Sound, resulting in the death of Thorn's entire party and a number of Indians.

On 15 July 1811 a party of Canadians, sent by the rival NORTH WEST COMPANY to forestall the Americans, arrived at Astoria. In January 1812, a second party came from the North West Company post on the Spokane River. Then came the Astor Overlanders (the group traveling by land), thirty-four in number. They had left Saint Louis on 12 March 1811 under the leadership of Wilson Price Hunt and had traveled up the Missouri River and westward through the country of the Crow Indians, over the Continental Divide to the Snake River, then to the Columbia and the Pacific, where they arrived 15 February 1812. In May an Astor ship, the *Beaver,* arrived. Company representatives extended their activities inland to the mouth of the Okanagan, to the Spokane, and to the Snake rivers. Robert Stuart and a small party of eastbound Astor Overlanders set out with dispatches for Astor in New York on 29 June 1812. They ascended the Snake River to its head, became the first white men to cross the South Pass, wintered on the Platte River, and arrived in Saint Louis on 30 April 1813. They never returned to the West, for news of the War of 1812 sounded the doom of the Astor enterprise. On 23 October 1813, while Hunt was absent, McDougal and his associates, whose sympathies were with the British, sold all the Astor interests on the Columbia to the North West Company. Hunt returned to find Astoria in rival hands, the post renamed Fort George, and the British flag flying. The Treaty of Ghent restored Astoria to the United States in 1818.

BIBLIOGRAPHY

Mackie, Richard S. *Trading beyond the Mountains: The British Fur Trade on the Pacific, 1793–1843.* Vancouver, Canada: University of British Columbia Press, 1997.

Wishart, David J. *The Fur Trade of the American West, 1807–1840: A Geographical Synthesis.* Lincoln: University of Nebraska Press, 1979.

Carl P. Russell / c. w.

See also **Fur Companies; Fur Trade and Trapping; Ghent, Treaty of.**

ASTRONOMY. Colonial Americans lacked instruments and libraries. They had difficulty communicating with each other and often relied on English correspondents for news of other colonialists. During the seventeenth century, European astronomy was focused on extending Isaac Newton's mathematical description of the solar system, and a few Americans contributed their observations to the Royal Society of London. American observations served European theories.

When Venus passed in front of the sun in 1761 and 1769, transits revealed the distance of the earth from the sun. John Winthrop, professor of mathematics and natural philosophy at Harvard, organized an expedition to Newfoundland to observe the first transit. The Massachusetts Assembly assigned a ship to transport Winthrop's group and Harvard permitted him to take college instruments, provided they were insured against loss or damage. The observations were sent to Europe for analysis.

Winthrop lectured his students that determination of the distance of the earth from the sun would result in a deeper insight into God's wonderful works. Enlightenment faith in the discernable regularity of the universe also encouraged the study of astronomy in early American colleges. In its appeal to the Pennsylvania Assembly for funds to observe the 1769 transit, the American Philosophical Society, founded in Philadelphia in 1743, cited a more utilitarian goal, "the Promotion of Astronomy and Navigation, and consequently of Trade and Commerce." In a period of increasing cultural nationalism, the society also wanted to win recognition for American achievements.

Many of America's astronomers were surveyors. The self-taught American astronomer David Rittenhouse made his living as a clockmaker, but he was also a surveyor. In 1767, he constructed in Philadelphia his famous orrery, or mechanical planetarium, which represented with great precision the motions of the planets around the sun. The Pennsylvania assembly paid for it. The onset of the Revolutionary War suspended hope to build an observatory.

With political independence came a desire for cultural independence. However, little public patronage was forthcoming for astronomy in the early national period.

In 1825, President John Quincy Adams pointed out that Europe had 130 "lighthouses of the skies" but the United States none. Yet his request for funds for a national observatory was denied.

The American Academy of Arts and Sciences, founded in Boston in 1780 by John Adams, published astronomical observations by Nathaniel Bowditch, a self-educated Salem seaman. His *The New American Practical Navigator* (1800) became the most widely used nautical guide, and in 1811, he observed a solar eclipse to improve the determination of the longitude of Cambridge. The European scientific community applauded Bowditch's translation and commentary on Pierre Laplace's *Mécanique céleste*. The American Academy offered to pay for publication, but Bowditch waited until he could afford to publish it himself.

Through much of the nineteenth century, the United States was a nation in development. While some of their European brethren made observations and contributed to the advance of knowledge, American astronomers often struggled with more mundane problems, including writing textbooks, acquiring books and journals for libraries, and building, equipping, and financing observatories. Elias Loomis, a professor at Western Reserve College in Ohio, at the University of the City of New York, and at Yale University, published *An Introduction to Practical Astronomy* in 1855 and a *A Treatise on Astronomy* in 1876, both of which went through numerous editions. At both New York and Yale, Loomis arranged to receive publications from European observatories on an exchange basis. His will left funds to pay observers and publish their results.

College observatories consisted of a small building and telescope intended for the education of undergraduate students, but they could not pay researchers or provide funds for publication. The University of North Carolina built an observatory in 1831, which lasted several years. Observatories were constructed at Yale (1830s), at Williams College (1838), at Western Reserve College (1838), at the Philadelphia High School (1838), at West Point (1839), and at Georgetown (1843). In 1839, Harvard lured William Cranch Bond from his private observatory to supply his own instruments and work for no salary. The great comet of 1843 aroused public interest, which manifested itself in public support to construct and endow the Harvard College Observatory. Harvard ordered from the German firm Merz and Mahler a twin to the Russian Pulkova Observatory's fifteen-inch (lens diameter) telescope, then the largest in the world.

There were also public observatories: the Cincinnati Observatory, whose cornerstone John Quincy Adams laid in 1843, and the Dudley Observatory in Albany, built between 1852–1856. The tribulations of the Cincinnati Observatory illustrate the obstacles to practicing astronomy in mid-nineteenth-century America. Ormsby MacKnight Mitchel, a West Point graduate, moved to Cincinnati and became professor of mathematics, civil engineering, me-

chanics, and machinery at Cincinnati College. His public lectures on astronomy led to the founding of the Cincinnati Astronomical Society and the municipal Cincinnati Observatory, funded by public subscription. After five hours of teaching, Mitchel would supervise construction of the observatory in the afternoons. Cincinnati purchased an 11.25-inch telescope from Merz and Mahler, but Mitchel spent much of his time displaying the heavens to subscribers, from 4:00 to 10:00 P.M. daily. He tried publishing a journal to raise money for auxiliary instruments and for his salary, the observatory having no endowment for operating expenses, and did make money from a book on popular astronomy and from surveying a railroad route. His observations of singular phenomena, a kind of natural history of the heavens, fell short of a new professional emphasis on measurement and theory, requiring considerable mathematical competence. Economic forces discouraged sustained, structured research.

A few would-be professional astronomers received training and employment with the Coast Survey, established in 1807 in response to commercial interests of seaboard states. In legislation for the Coast Survey in 1832, Congress explicitly declared that it did not authorize construction or maintenance of a permanent astronomical observatory. A decade later, the Naval Observatory was created surreptitiously, as part of the Depot of Charts and Instruments. Not until 1866, however, would the observatory begin a program of fundamental research in astronomy. Meanwhile, the Nautical Almanac, located in Cambridge, Massachusetts, was established under the Naval Observatory budget in 1849. It reported directly to the secretary of the navy, provided training and employment for a few astronomers, and improved navigation and raised America's scientific standing with an annual astronomical almanac more accurate and theoretically advanced than the British Nautical Almanac. Simon Newcomb, one of America's best-known scientists at the end of the century, got his start at the Nautical Almanac, and also worked at the Naval Observatory. He analyzed the motions of the moon and planets.

There were also a few private observatories in America. Lewis Rutherfurd, a wealthy New Yorker and trustee of Columbia College, had a nine-inch diameter telescope, and also a small transit instrument belonging to Columbia College at his observatory at Second Avenue and Eleventh Street. The Coast Survey used this observatory in 1848 to determine the longitude of New York. Rutherfurd was a pioneer in astronomical photography. Not until late in the century, though, would individual American fortunes fund the establishment and sustenance of large observatories with systematic programs of scientific investigation carried on by full-time, paid employees.

The second half of the nineteenth century saw advances in telescope production, especially by the Boston firm of Alvan Clark & Sons. Their metal tubes were stiffer yet lighter than wooden telescopes. Larger pieces of optical glass were now available, and the Clarks figured the lens for the world's largest refracting telescope on five occasions: an 18.5-inch lens for the University of Mississippi in 1860, a 26-inch lens for the Naval Observatory in 1873 (with which Asaph Hall discovered Mars's moons in 1877), a 30-inch lens for the Pulkova Observatory in 1883, a 36-inch lens for the Lick Observatory of the University of California in 1887, and a 40-inch lens for the Yerkes Observatory of the University of Chicago in 1897. James Lick, a California land speculator during the gold rush, and Charles Yerkes, a Chicago street car magnate, put up the funds for their eponymous observatories, under university auspices, and Boston investor Percival Lowell directed his own observatory. All three observatories were far removed from cities, and Lick's and Lowell's were on mountain peaks. With the largest telescopes in the best locations, American observatories now surpassed all others.

Growing interest in astrophysics and in distant stars and nebulae encouraged the development of new observatories with large steerable reflecting (light focused by a curved mirror) telescopes suitable for photography and auxiliary instruments for the analysis of starlight. George Ellery Hale founded the *Astrophysical Journal* in 1895, the American Astronomical and Astrophysical Society in 1899, the Mount Wilson Observatory in 1904, and the International Astronomical Union in 1918. Hale was an early prototype of the high-pressure, heavy-hardware, big-spending, team-organized scientific entrepreneur. In 1902, Andrew Carnegie, rich from innovations in the American steel industry, created the Carnegie Institution of Washington to encourage investigation, research, and discovery in biology, astronomy, and the earth sciences. Its ten million dollars were more than the total of endowed funds for research in all American universities combined. Hale left the Yerkes Observatory to build, with Carnegie money, the Mount Wilson Observatory on a mountain above Los Angeles. There George Willis Ritchey, who accompanied Hale from Yerkes, made the photographic reflecting telescope the basic instrument of astronomical research, constructing a 60-inch telescope in 1908 and a 100-inch telescope in 1919. They were the largest telescopes in the world and revolutionized the study of astronomy. Harlow Shapley found that the system of stars is a hundred times larger than previous estimates and that the sun is far from the center. Edwin Hubble showed that spiral nebulae are independent island universes beyond our galaxy and that the universe is expanding. Cosmology, previously limited to philosophical speculations, joined mainstream astronomy.

The Mount Wilson Observatory depended on its relationship with physicists at the nearby California Institute of Technology for its dominance of astrophysics during the first half of the twentieth century. A scientific education was fast becoming necessary for professional astronomers, as astrophysics came to predominate, and the concerns of professionals and amateurs diverged. As late as the 1870s and 1880s, the self-educated American astronomer Edward Emerson Barnard, an observaholic with indefatigable energy and ocular acuteness, could earn positions at the Lick and Yerkes observatories with visual observations of planetary details and discoveries of comets and moons. Already, however, he was an exception and an anachronism. Soon an advanced academic degree and considerable theoretical understanding were required of professional astronomers in America.

Supposedly, only men could withstand the rigors of observing the heavens all night in unheated telescope domes. Women were first employed to examine photographs of stellar spectra and to catalog the spectra. Edward Pickering, director of the Harvard College Observatory in 1881 and an advocate of advanced study for women, was so exasperated with his male assistant's inefficiency that he declared even his cook could do a better job of copying and computing. Pickering hired her and she did do a better job, as did some twenty more females over the next several decades, recruited for their steadiness, adaptability, acuteness of vision, and willingness to work for low wages. In 1925, Cecilia Payne, a graduate student, determined the relative abundances of eighteen chemical elements found in stellar atmospheres. Her Ph.D. thesis has been lauded as the most brilliant written in astronomy. Her degree, however, was from Radcliffe College, before Harvard granted degrees to women, and in subsequent employment at Harvard she was initially budgeted as "equipment."

Radio astronomy began in America in 1933. Karl Jansky, a radio engineer with the Bell Telephone Company, detected electrical emissions from the center of our galaxy while studying sources of radio noise. Optical astronomers were not interested, nor were Jansky's practical-minded supervisors. Grote Reber, an ardent radio amateur obsessed with distance communication, was interested, and built for a few thousand dollars a 31.4-foot-diameter pointable radio antenna in his backyard in Wheaton, Illinois. In 1940, he reported the intensity of radio sources at different positions in the sky. Fundamental knowledge underlying radio astronomy techniques increased during World War II, especially with research on radar.

Advances in nuclear physics during the war made possible quantitative calculations of the formation of elements in a supposed primeval fireball. The Russian-American physicist George Gamow sought to explain the cosmic abundance of elements as the result of thermonuclear reactions in an early hot phase of an expanding universe, consisting of high-energy radiation. In 1963, unaware of Gamow's work, Arno Penzias and Robert Wilson at the Bell Telephone Laboratories detected radiation of cosmic origin. Meanwhile, Robert Dicke at Princeton University had independently thought of the cosmic background radiation and set a colleague to work calculating its strength. When Dicke learned in 1965 of Penzias and Wilson's measurement, he correctly interpreted it as Gamow's predicted radiation. A Nobel Prize went to Penzias and Wilson. Their discovery won general acceptance of the big bang theory and refuted the rival steady state theory.

World War II changed the relationship between science and the state. Radar, missiles, and the atomic bomb established state-sponsored and state-directed research and development. Furthermore, groups of scientists brought together in wartime proved effective. After the war, engineers and physicists with their instruments, techniques, training, and ways of operating moved into astronomy. Then came Sputnik in 1957, the world's first satellite. This Soviet triumph challenged American supremacy in military might and world opinion.

After Sputnik, the National Science Foundation supplied many millions of dollars for construction of the Kitt Peak National Observatory on a mountain near Tucson, Arizona. It is the largest collection of big telescopes in the Northern Hemisphere. Seventeen universities came together in AURA, the Association of Universities for Research in Astronomy, to manage the observatory.

Another response to Sputnik was the creation of the National Aeronautics and Space Administration (NASA). Among its accomplishments are automated observatories launched into space, including the Hubble Space Telescope. Its primary mirror is eight feet in diameter. Including recording instruments and guidance system, the telescope weighs twelve tons. It has been called the eighth wonder of the world, and critics say it should be, given its cost of 1.5 billion dollars! The telescope is as much a political and managerial achievement as a technological one. Approval for a large space telescope was won in a political struggle lasting from 1974 to 1977, but not until 1990 were a plethora of problems finally overcome and the telescope launched into space, only to discover that an error had occurred in the shaping of the primary mirror. One newspaper reported "Pix Nixed as Hubble Sees Double." The addition of a corrective mirror solved the problem.

NASA also funds X-ray astronomy. Captured German rockets provided the first proof of X-rays from the sun. Astronomers did not expect to find X-ray sources and were skeptical that brief and expensive rocket-borne experiments were worthwhile. NASA, however, had more money than there were imaginative scientists to spend it, and the military, even more. One imaginative and eager scientist was the Italian-born Riccardo Giacconi, who in 1960, funded by the Air Force Cambridge Research Laboratories, discovered a cosmic X-ray source, and in 1963, detected a second. NASA adjudicates questions of scientific priority and supplies money for space observatories; industry helps build them; universities or consortiums of universities design and operate them and analyze the data. NASA then funded a rocket survey program and a small satellite for X-ray astronomy and in 1978 the Einstein X-ray telescope. Unlike the relatively quiescent universe seen by earth-bound astronomers, the universe revealed to engineers and physicists observing from satellites is violently energetic.

Major changes have occurred in both the size and scope of American astronomy over the centuries, but never more rapidly nor more dramatically than at the beginning of the Space Age. There were some five hundred American astronomers in 1962 and three times that many a decade later. Only four worked on X-rays in 1962 compared to over forty times that many in 1972. Over eighty percent of them were migrants from experimental physics, with expertise in designing and building instruments to detect high-energy particles.

Astronomers now realize that important cosmological features can be explained as consequences of new theories of particle physics, and particle physics increasingly drives cosmology. Conversely, particle physicists, having exhausted the limits of particle accelerators and public funding for yet larger instruments, turn to cosmology for information regarding the behavior of matter under extreme conditions, such as those prevailing in the early universe.

The spectacular rise of American astronomy roughly parallels the remarkable evolution of the nation, itself, from British colonies to world super power. Once limited to visual observations and determining positions, astronomy now includes cosmology, the study of the structure and evolution of the universe, and analysis of the physical and chemical composition of the universe and its components. Once peripheral, now American astronomers, men and women, formally educated in a variety of fields, working in large teams, on systematic long-term projects, and enjoying government patronage, lead world advances in instrumentation, observation, and theory.

BIBLIOGRAPHY

Christianson, Gale E. *Edwin Hubble: Mariner of the Nebulae*. New York: Farrar, Stauss, Giroux, 1995.

Edmundson, Frank K. *AURA and its US National Observatories*. New York: Cambridge University Press, 1997.

Hetherington, Norriss S. *Hubble's Cosmology: A Guided Study of Selected Texts*. Tucson, Ariz.: Pachart Publishing, 1996.

Hindle, Brook. *David Rittenhouse*. New Jersey: Princeton University Press, 1964.

Hoyt, William Graves. *Lowell and Mars*. Tucson: University of Arizona, 1976.

Jones, Bessie Judith Zaban, and Lyle Gifford Boyd. *The Harvard College Observatory: The First Four Directorships, 1839–1919*. Cambridge, Mass. Belknap Press, 1971.

Lankford, John. *American Astronomy: Community, Careers, and Power, 1859–1940*. Chicago: University of Chicago Press, 1997.

Levy, David H. *Clyde Tombaugh: Discoverer of Planet Pluto*. Tucson: University of Arizona Press, 1991.

Osterbrock, Donald E. *Eye on the Sky: Lick Observatory's First Century*. Berkeley: University of California Press, 1988.

———. *Yerkes Observatory 1892–1950: The Birth, Near Death, and Resurrection of a Scientific Research Institution*. Chicago: University of Chicago, 1997.

———. *Pauper and Prince: Ritchey, Hale, & Big American Telescopes*. Tucson: University of Arizona Press, 1993.

345

Sheehan, William. *The Immortal Fire Within: The Life and Work of Edward Emerson Barnard.* New York: Cambridge University Press, 1995.

Smith, Robert W. *The Space Telescope: A Study of NASA, Science, Technology, and Politics.* New York: Cambridge, 1989.

Tucker, Wallace, and Karen Tucker. *The Cosmic Inquirers: Modern Telescopes and Their Makers.* Cambridge: Harvard University Press, 1986.

Warner, Deborah Jean. *Alvan Clark & Sons: Artists in Optics.* Richmond, Va.: Willmann-Bell, 1995.

Norriss Hetherington

See also **Coast and Geodetic Survey; Hubble Space Telescope; Observatories, Astronomical; Physics; Surveying.**

AT&T (American Telephone and Telegraph) is virtually synonymous with the TELEPHONE. It existed as a government-regulated monopoly until its court-ordered breakup in 1984. In return for its monopoly status, the company provided universal phone service at a reasonable cost. For most of the twentieth century, AT&T (or "Ma Bell") was the largest company in the world, with more than 1 million employees and $155 billion in assets. In the early 1980s, the dawn of the Information Age, political maneuvers and competition for control of the long-distance market combined to break up the Bell System.

After inventing the phone in 1876, Alexander Graham Bell founded Bell Company a year later (eventually renamed AT&T). Following years of patent battles and squeezing its competition, AT&T symbolized corporate greed, poor quality, and awful customer service. In the early twentieth century, however, under the leadership of Theodore Vail, AT&T became a model for the modern corporation. Vail centralized management, emphasized customer service, and formed BELL TELEPHONE LABORATORIES in 1925. AT&T's management training program also served as a breeding ground for generations of business leaders.

The public quickly considered the telephone an indispensable part of life. AT&T also created the distinction between local and long-distance phone calls, a staple of modern telecommunications. The separation facilitated the rise of the regional Bell Companies, the "BABY BELLS," and ultimately to the breakup of the parent company.

AT&T played a critical role in increasing American influence overseas. In addition to spreading phone service across the globe, Bell Labs invented the transistor in 1948, whose inventors—William Shockley, John Bardeen, and Walter Brattain—won the 1950 Nobel Prize for Physics. Bell Labs also developed cellular wireless technology (1947), computer modems (1957), lasers (1958), and communications satellites (1962). The electronic switching systems AT&T installed in 1965 paved the way for the Information Age and enable the Internet to exist today.

After divestiture in 1984, AT&T evolved into an integrated voice and data communications company. C. Michael Armstrong took over in 1997 and initiated a new sense of mission, direction, and urgency. Armstrong cut costs (including tens of thousands of layoffs) while increasing capital expenditures to secure AT&T's future. By mid-2000, AT&T had three rapidly evolving networks (broadband, wireless, and data) and four separate businesses (cable, wireless, business, and consumer).

In October 2000 AT&T announced a restructuring into four publicly held companies, AT&T Broadband, AT&T Wireless, AT&T Business, and AT&T Consumer, each trading as a common or tracking stock. On 9 July 2001, AT&T Wireless split off. In 2000 AT&T had revenues of nearly $66 billion, ran the world's largest communications network, and was the largest cable operator in the United States.

BIBLIOGRAPHY

Smith, George David. *The Anatomy of a Business Strategy: Bell, Western Electric, and the Origins of the American Telephone Industry.* Baltimore: Johns Hopkins University Press, 1985.

Stone, Alan. *Wrong Number: The Breakup of AT&T.* New York: Basic Books, 1989.

Temin, Peter and Louis Galambos. *The Fall of the Bell System: A Study in Prices and Politics.* Cambridge: Cambridge University Press, 1987.

Bob Batchelor

See also **AT&T Divestiture; Bell Telephone Laboratories; Telegraph.**

AT&T DIVESTITURE. American Telephone and Telegraph (AT&T) was the largest company in the world for most of the twentieth century, with $75 billion in assets and more than a million employees. Unlike other corporations, AT&T was a regulated monopoly; the government allowed it to operate without competitors in return for high-quality, universal service.

Despite the success of the Bell System, which provided the world's best telephone service, competitors, state regulators, legislators, and the federal government conspired to break it up. AT&T faced constant regulatory scrutiny, but the alliance between the company and regulators was never formal enough. Many of the relationships rested on faith and personal assurances, even after the FEDERAL COMMUNICATIONS COMMISSION (FCC) was created to regulate telecommunications. The FCC gradually permitted competition, while technology hastened the process. By the end of the 1970s, most sectors of telecom were on the way to becoming fully competitive.

Advanced technology made it impossible to adhere to the structure that shaped the industry for so long. No regulatory body could keep pace. Computer switching equipment, satellite communications, and fiber optics made it simpler and less expensive for companies to enter the market. The regulated monopoly seemed like an anachronism and an enemy of the free-market economy.

In 1974, the government filed an antitrust suit. AT&T officials believed that the antitrust actions were unfair, since the Bell System operated under regulatory statutes fundamentally incongruous with antitrust law. Essentially, AT&T resented being punished for observing its regulatory charter. The FCC clearly did not understand the forces it had set in motion. The commission attempted to make incremental changes without adequately considering the long-term impact the decisions would have.

In March 1981, *United States v. AT&T* came to trial under Assistant Attorney General William Baxter. AT&T chairman Charles L. Brown thought the company would be gutted. He realized that AT&T would lose and, in December 1981, resumed negotiations with the Justice Department. Reaching an agreement less than a month later, Brown agreed to divestiture—the best and only realistic alternative. AT&T's decision allowed it to retain its research and manufacturing arms. The decree, titled the Modification of Final Judgment, was an adjustment of the Consent Decree of 14 January 1956. Judge Harold H. Greene was given the authority over the modified decree.

The government's antitrust suit, supposedly protected from political maneuvering, turned out to be wholly political, and it was political reasons that kept President Reagan from ending the suit. Dismissing the antitrust case would have generated bad publicity and started a partisan fight between Congress and the president. Since there was simply no easy way for the Reagan administration to end the case, it did not act. The lack of Congressional control over telecom helped competitors enter the market. No single agency had authority over the entire process, so the breakup occurred, despite widespread political support.

In 1982, the U.S. government announced that AT&T would cease to exist as a monopolistic entity. On 1 January 1984, it was split into seven smaller regional companies, BellSouth, Bell Atlantic, NYNEX, American Information Technologies, Southwestern Bell, US West, and Pacific Telesis, to handle regional phone services in the U.S. AT&T retains control of its long distance services, but was no longer protected from competition.

BIBLIOGRAPHY

Cohen, Jeffrey E. *The Politics of Telecommunications Regulation: The States and the Divestiture of AT&T.* Armonk, N.Y: M.E. Sharpe, 1992.

Cole, Barry G., ed. *After the Breakup: Assessing the New Post-AT&T Divestiture Era.* New York: Columbia University Press, 1991.

Coll, Steve. *The Deal of the Century: The Breakup of AT&T.* New York: Simon and Schuster, 1988.

Henck, Fred W., and Bernard Strassburg. *A Slippery Slope: The Long Road to the Breakup of AT&T.* New York: Greenwood Press, 1988.

Kleinfield, Sonny. *The Biggest Company on Earth: A Profile of AT&T.* New York: Holt, Rinehart, and Winston, 1981.

Shooshan, Harry M., ed. *Disconnecting Bell: The Impact of the AT&T Divestiture.* New York: Pergamon Press, 1984.

Smith, George David. *The Anatomy of a Business Strategy: Bell, Western Electric, and the Origins of the American Telephone Industry.* Baltimore: Johns Hopkins University Press, 1985.

Stone, Alan. *Wrong Number: The Breakup of AT&T.* New York: Basic Books, 1989.

Tunstall, W. Brooke. *Disconnecting Parties: Managing the Bell System Break-Up, An Inside View.* New York: McGraw-Hill, 1985.

Wasserman, Neil H. *From Invention to Innovation: Long-distance Telephone Transmission at the Turn of the Century.* Baltimore: Johns Hopkins University Press, 1985.

Bob Batchelor

See also **Antitrust Laws; Government Regulation of Business; Telecommunications; Trusts.**

ATHEISM has regularly been defined as the denial of the existence of a deity. Under such a definition—one that implies a positive, dogmatic assertion of antitheism—the role of atheism in American history (and in most other histories) would be limited. It is important to note, however, the existence of some unabashedly atheistic individuals and organizations in America, such as the American Association for the Advancement of Atheism (founded in 1925). A more capacious definition of atheism is available, however, one in which the stress is on a lack of belief or even a sheer lack of philosophical interest, in God, rather than on a positive denial of God's existence. Such an atheism, grounded in Enlightenment rationalism and supported by a scientific paradigm insisting that the matter of the physical world represents reality in its entirety, was bolstered (albeit in different ways) by the nineteenth-century attempts of Feuerbach, Marx, and Nietzsche to offer naturalistic accounts of religion, and by a positivist current within twentieth-century philosophy in which any and all questions about the existence of God were dismissed as unintelligible. While these intellectual movements derived much of their energy and personnel from Europe, they have intersected dynamically with the broader tradition of American free thought. Individuals such as Clarence Darrow, John Dewey, Robert G. Ingersoll, Abner Kneeland, and Joseph Lewis (some of whom can be defined as atheists; others, not) have all helped to define the varieties of atheism, antitheism, and agnosticism. An important contribution to the history of atheism has been the recent effort, beginning with those of the American Atheists organization, founded by the late Madalyn Murray O'Hair, to comprehend and protect atheism within the terms of the First Amendment and Jefferson's wall of separation between church and state. The 1963 Supreme Court decision on school prayer in *Murray v. Curlett* marked the beginning of a strenuous effort to defend the civil rights of atheists through the court.

BIBLIOGRAPHY

Brown, Marshall G., and Gordon Stein. *Freethought in the United States: A Descriptive Bibliography.* Westport, Conn.: Greenwood Press, 1978.

Rinaldo, Peter M. *Atheists, Agnostics, and Deists in America: A Brief History.* Briarcliff Manor, N.Y.: DorPete Press, 2001.

Jon Wright

See also **Agnosticism; Deism.**

ATLANTA. Probably the only major city in the United States named after a hotel—the Atlanta, erected in 1847—after the small town had already gone through two incarnations as Terminus (1837) and Marthasville (1843), Atlanta has never relinquished its unabashed boosterism. In 1860, just two decades beyond its founding, the city already boasted ten thousand residents. Temporarily thwarted by a swath of destruction during the Civil War, the nascent railroad junction quickly rebounded as local newspaperman Henry W. Grady touted the city to any and all comers and, in the process, authored the New South Creed, a wide-ranging blueprint for economic recovery in a region devastated by the Civil War. Whatever the disappointments of these plans for the South as a whole, Atlantans embraced the main chance, and by 1900 rendered their city the primary commercial center of the Southeast and a key distribution point for the rest of the region. By that time an impressive downtown skyline was rising in an area known as Five Points, and Coca-Cola, headquartered in Atlanta, was well on its way to becoming a national drink.

The city's turn-of-the-century prosperity masked racial tensions. In the decades after the Civil War, a prosperous black middle class had evolved, but segregation, disfranchisement, and the surge in lynching during the

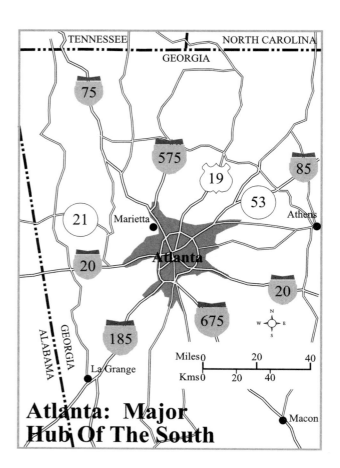

Atlanta: Major Hub Of The South

Nineteenth-Century Atlanta. A view of the booming young railroad terminus from just before or during the Civil War, when the city was devastated—but not for long. LIBRARY OF CONGRESS

1890s threatened its advances. Whites resented black prosperity and success. These tensions culminated in a vicious race riot in 1906. Despite these setbacks, a vibrant black community continued to grow in an area centered around Sweet Auburn, south and west of the city center. Here black businesses and black churches flourished, albeit within the confines of a rigid Jim Crow society. Black leaders such as the educator John Hope, the businessmen Heman Perry and Alonzo Herndon, and, later, the civil rights leader Martin Luther King Jr. emerged from this district. During the 1920s, with city planning in vogue across the nation, zoning and land use policies further divided the city into black and white areas. This was also the decade when Atlanta became national headquarters for a revived Ku Klux Klan.

Atlanta attained more positive national recognition in 1939 when Margaret Mitchell's best-selling novel, *Gone with the Wind,* was adapted for the screen and the city hosted its world premiere. The movie, along with "the world's largest painting," *Cyclorama of the Battle of Atlanta,* and the incomplete likenesses of Jefferson Davis, Thomas "Stonewall" Jackson, and Robert E. Lee etched into Stone Mountain fixed Atlanta as a Confederate shrine, a view that seemingly contradicted its New South image but in truth served to mask the more raw forms of boosterism

Early-Twentieth-Century Atlanta. A stereographic view of this prosperous but segregated city, looking west on Marietta Street from the Five Points area, c. 1929. LIBRARY OF CONGRESS

and racial intolerance. By the 1950s Atlanta was the self-styled "city too busy to hate."

"Busyness" indeed characterized Atlanta during the first half of the twentieth century. By the 1940s the city had surpassed its last major rival, Birmingham, Alabama, most particularly with the growth of what became Hartsfield International Airport. Atlanta also evolved into an important center for higher education. Atlanta University (1867) emerged as one of the key institutions of black higher education in the nation; Georgia Tech (1888), Emory University (1836, relocated to Atlanta in 1915), and Georgia State University (1955) offered a variety of educational options for an increasingly cosmopolitan region. The High Museum of Art and the Atlanta Symphony spread a cultural patina over the booster image. It was not until the 1990s, however, that the city enjoyed excellent dining. Atlanta still lags behind Dallas, Miami, and certainly New Orleans in terms of culinary imagination.

The major postwar political change occurred in 1973 with the election of Maynard Jackson, son of a prominent black family, as mayor. Jackson's election reflected the growth of the city's black population, a demographic inevitability because, unlike other southern cities, Atlanta could no longer annex whites who had fled to the suburbs. The last major annexation occurred in 1952 with the addition of predominantly white Buckhead. School desegregation eventually became an unattainable objective; by the 1990s more than 80 percent of the school population was black, and a sharp divide emerged between an increasingly black city and mostly white suburbs, reflecting the intracity divisions that had existed since late in the nineteenth century. Even the extension of the public transport system, known as MARTA, became fraught with racial overtones in the 1990s.

While Atlanta began the twentieth century seeking regional dominance, the effort at the beginning of the twenty-first century focuses on becoming a "world-class city." The "city too busy to hate" has become the rather tepid "The World's Next Great City," a boast given some credibility by its hosting of the 1996 Summer Olympic

349

Games. As world headquarters of Cable News Network (CNN), Delta Airlines, and Coca-Cola, Atlanta indeed has a global reach. At the same time many of its problems, including black poverty, traffic gridlock, air pollution, and suburban sprawl, remain intractable as city and suburban leaders find few common areas of cooperation. The city's demographic and economic profile more nearly fits the struggling, declining cities of the Rust Belt rather than the Sun Belt ideal.

BIBLIOGRAPHY

Bayor, Ronald H. *Race and the Shaping of Twentieth-Century Atlanta.* Chapel Hill: University of North Carolina Press, 1996.

Preston, Howard L. *Automobile Age Atlanta: The Making of a Southern Metropolis, 1900–1935.* Athens: University of Georgia Press, 1979.

Russell, James Michael. *Atlanta, 1847–1890: City Building in the Old South and the New.* Baton Rouge: Louisiana State University Press, 1988.

Rutheiser, Charles. *Imagineering Atlanta: The Politics of Place in the City of Dreams.* London and New York: Verso, 1996.

David Goldfield

See also **Georgia; Race Relations.**

ATLANTA CAMPAIGN.   Major General William T. Sherman's campaign in 1864 to capture Atlanta, Georgia, resulted in the loss of the Confederacy's most important railroad hub. Atlanta was also the location of important factories, foundries, munitions plants, and supply depots. The Union advance to Atlanta began on 5 May 1864, simultaneously with Lieutenant General Ulysses S. Grant's advance to Richmond. Sherman commanded a force of three armies totaling 100,000 men. He was opposed by Confederate General Joseph E. Johnston's Army of Tennessee, which numbered 65,000. Sherman's superior force

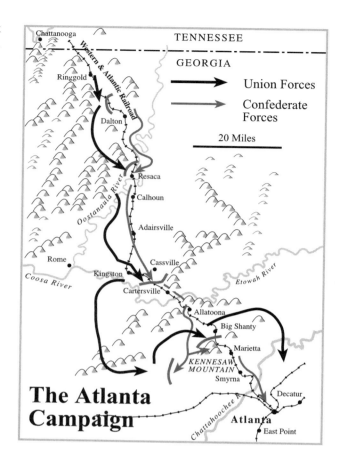

The Atlanta Campaign

Atlanta Fortifications. A view looking east from near Peachtree Street, before the fall of the city to Union forces in 1864. Photograph by studio of Matthew Brady. NATIONAL ARCHIVES AND RECORDS ADMINISTRATION

led Johnston to adopt a defensive strategy of continuous retreat, to which the mountainous topography of northern Georgia was favorable. His army could not withstand a direct battle with Sherman's. The resulting campaign was one of maneuver and little fighting. Sherman attempted an attack at Resaca, but overcautious subordinates and an overestimation of enemy strength produced only a skirmish. Johnston considered fighting Sherman at Cassville, halfway to Atlanta, but subordinates believed the risk too great and he did not attack. Sharp but indecisive fighting occurred at New Hope Church from 25 to 28 May. Both armies then settled down for several weeks of skirmishing, maneuvering, and raiding. Johnston moved skillfully and entrenched his army so well that Sherman was unable to find a weak point to attack. As the opposing armies drew closer to Atlanta, fighting became more frequent. Sherman broke the stalemate with a frontal attack against Confederate fortifications at Kenesaw Mountain on 27 June. He was bloodily repulsed, losing 3,000 men compared to Confederate losses of 442.

The size of Sherman's three armies required him to keep his forces close to railroad lines for the entire advance to Atlanta. Frequent raids on Union supply trains by Confederate cavalrymen Nathan Bedford Forrest and Joseph Wheeler slowed Sherman considerably. However, the sheer size of Sherman's armies allowed them to outflank Johnston and continue the advance despite these raids and the defeat at Kenesaw Mountain.

By 9 July, Sherman forced Johnston to move his army across the Chattahoochee River, into fortifications along Peachtree Creek, only four miles from downtown Atlanta. This threw the city into a panic as well as the Confederate government in Richmond. On 17 July, Confederate President Jefferson Davis relieved Johnston of command and replaced him with John B. Hood, who Davis believed would be more aggressive. Hood attacked Sherman on 20 July but was repulsed. He initiated the Battle of Atlanta on 22 July, but suffered another costly defeat. A third Confederate offensive on 28 July at Ezra Church again ended in a bloody repulse. These three battles cost Hood 15,000 casualties compared to Sherman's 6,000. The Union armies besieged Atlanta during August. Hood evacuated Atlanta on 1 September and moved his army south. The mayor of Atlanta surrendered the city to Sherman the next day. Sherman burned Atlanta on 15 November before setting out on his "march to the sea."

The capture of Atlanta boosted Northern war morale, weakened the peace platform of the Democratic presidential candidate George B. McClellan, and contributed to Abraham Lincoln's reelection that November. The fall of Atlanta also weakened Confederate morale. The city's importance to the Confederate military effort made it second only to the capital, Richmond, as a symbol of Southern strength and resistance.

BIBLIOGRAPHY

Hattaway, Herman, and Archer Jones. *How the North Won: A Military History of the Civil War.* Urbana: University of Illinois Press, 1983.

McPherson, James M. *Battle Cry of Freedom: The Civil War Era.* New York: Oxford University Press, 1988.

W. Scott Thomason

See also **Atlanta; Civil War; Sherman' March to the Sea.**

ATLANTIC, THE. One of the nation's most distinguished and long-lived magazines, the *Atlantic Monthly* has been publishing continuously since 1857. No journal has showcased more illustrious American writers, from Ralph Waldo Emerson and Harriet Beecher Stowe to William F. Buckley and Toni Morrison.

The *Atlantic* was originally an organ of Boston's male literary elite. Emerson, Henry Wadsworth Longfellow, and Oliver Wendell Holmes Sr. were early contributors. Its first editor was James Russell Lowell.

In the years after the Civil War, the *Atlantic*'s scope became national. The novelist William Dean Howells served as editor during the 1870s, increasing the number of writers drawn from outside New England and making the *Atlantic* into one of the most influential proponents of literary realism, publishing writers such as Mark Twain, Henry James, Edith Wharton, and Sarah Orne Jewett.

Atlantic Monthly. A cover of the magazine from 1881. THE ATLANTIC MONTHLY

The magazine distinctly fell behind the times in the 1890s. While it offered some sharp political commentary, it was not until 1909, when Ellery Sedgwick became editor, that the *Atlantic* took a new direction. Sedgwick, who remained editor until 1938, combined a feel for literary innovation and incisive political writing while maintaining the stately tone of the journal. He published Robert Frost, Ernest Hemingway, and Gertrude Stein, among others. Circulation rose significantly. Sedgwick published a range of opinion, but he himself was conservative, defending the Spanish dictator Francisco Franco in the *Atlantic* during the 1930s.

Edward A. Weeks, editor from 1938 to 1966, continued Sedgwick's editorial tradition while making the magazine's politics more liberal. The *Atlantic* hit another slump during the 1970s and was in danger of closing. In 1980, publisher Morton Zuckerman bought the magazine. He hired William Whitworth as editor, who published very high-quality political and cultural commentary. Zuckerman sold the *Atlantic* in 1999. It remains one of the more influential journals of opinion in the nation.

BIBLIOGRAPHY

Howe, M. A. De Wolfe. *The Atlantic Monthly and Its Makers.* Boston: Atlantic Monthly Press, 1919. Reprint, Westport, Conn.: Greenwood Press, 1972.

Mott, Frank Luther. *A History of American Magazines, 1850–1865.* 5 vols. Cambridge, Mass.: Harvard University Press, 1938.

Kenneth Cmiel

See also **Magazines.**

ATLANTIC, BATTLE OF THE, the 1939–1945 struggle between Allied shipping and German SUBMARINES and Luftwaffe. Although the United States was officially neutral in WORLD WAR II before November 1941, President Franklin D. Roosevelt's pledge of "all aid short of war" to the Allies had antagonized the Germans, obligating U.S. naval patrols to protect pro-Allied merchantmen plying the broad neutrality zone. After several inclusive skirmishes, a German torpedo sank the American destroyer *Reuben James* into the waters south of Iceland on 31 October 1941. Before the American declaration of war, the Axis had sunk 2,162 ships totaling 7,751,000 tons. One month after the Japanese attack on Pearl Harbor, a damaging U-boat attack in American waters convinced U.S. military planners to organize the Tenth Fleet to bring all antisubmarine activities under a single command. An interlocking convoy system gradually developed across the Atlantic, forcing German Admiral Karl Dönitz to withdraw his U-boats to mid-ocean. U-boats had great success against Russian convoys. Most destructive was the concerted air and U-boat attack on Convoy PQ-17, which lost two-thirds of its thirty-three ships in July 1942.

However, burgeoning U.S. naval strength, as well as scientific advances, operations analysis, and improved radar, soon began to thwart U-boats. The development of support groups to aid endangered CONVOYS was decisive. Shaken, Dönitz largely abandoned attacks on convoys. U.S. hunter-killer groups using "jeep" aircraft carriers had increasing success also. U-boats could never regain the initiative. Overall, U-boats destroyed 2,775 ships, at a loss of 781 of the 1,175 completed U-boats. By the last months of the war, the U-boats were nearly impotent.

BIBLIOGRAPHY

Blair, Clay. *Hitler's U-Boat War.* New York: Random House, 1996–1998.

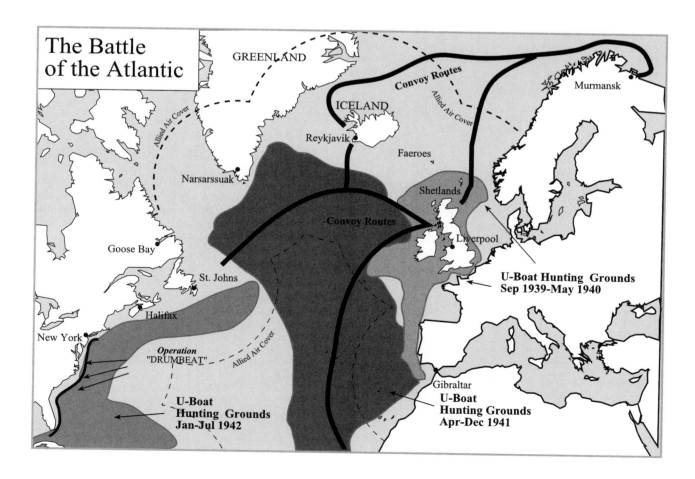

Macintyre, Donald G. F. W. *The Battle of the Atlantic*. New York: Macmillan, 1961.

Morison, Samuel E. *History of United States Naval Operations in World War II*. Volume 1: *The Battle of the Atlantic, September 1939–May 1943*. Volume 10: *The Atlantic Battle Won, May 1943–May 1945*. Boston: Little, Brown, 1947–1962.

Syrett, David. *The Defeat of the German U-Boats: The Battle of the Atlantic*. Columbia: University of South Carolina Press, 1994.

Henry H. Adams / A. R.

See also **Torpedo Warfare; World War II, Navy in.**

ATLANTIC CHARTER was signed 14 August 1941, by President FRANKLIN D. ROOSEVELT and Prime Minister Winston Churchill of Great Britain at a meeting in Argentia Bay off the coast of Newfoundland. The United States, still technically neutral in WORLD WAR II, had already taken a number of steps that brought it closer to war. The charter resembled President WOODROW WILSON'S FOURTEEN POINTS in that both declarations expressed idealistic objectives for a postwar world. The charter included the following points: the renunciation of territorial aggrandizement; opposition to territorial changes not approved by the people concerned; the right of people to choose their own form of government; equal access to trade and raw materials of the world; promotion of economic advancement, improved labor standards, and social security; freedom from fear and want; freedom of the seas; and disarmament of aggressor nations pending the establishment of a permanent system of peace.

Although only a press release as first issued, the charter was nonetheless well understood to be a pronouncement of considerable significance. It acquired further authority when, on 1 January 1942, twenty-six countries (including the United States and Great Britain) signed the UNITED NATIONS DECLARATION, which included among its provisions formal endorsement of the charter.

BIBLIOGRAPHY

Dallek, Robert. *Franklin D. Roosevelt and American Foreign Policy, 1932–1945*. New York: Oxford University Press, 1979.

Kimball, Warren F. *Forged in War: Roosevelt, Churchill, and the Second World War*. New York: Morrow, 1997.

Charles S. Campbell / A. G.

See also **Four Freedoms; Great Britain, Relations with; Treaties with Foreign Nations.**

ATLANTIC CITY, New Jersey, founded in 1854 on the Jersey Shore, soon became the nation's premier beach resort. The city's elegant hotels and simple rooming houses serviced luxury travelers as well as middle-class vacationers and day-trippers from nearby cities. Diverse tourists crowded the four-mile-long boardwalk and ocean piers, which offered such attractions as dance bands, a diving horse, and, beginning in 1921, the Miss America Pageant. Increasingly, however, wealthy travelers favored beach houses in the Hamptons or farther afield, and low-income tourists preferred newer motels and flashier boardwalks elsewhere along the Jersey Shore.

Because of the decline in tourism, the city suffered economically in the mid-twentieth century. This trend reversed after 1976, when New Jersey voters approved a referendum to allow casino gambling in Atlantic City to restore the city's prosperity and yield revenue for educational and social programs. The first casino opened in 1978. Soon afterward, Atlantic City became the eastern seaboard's gambling mecca and witnessed sharp economic growth. The city remained divided, however, between the glitz of the beachfront casinos and the poverty and high unemployment elsewhere in the city. Moreover, its future as a gambling center became uncertain as other states legalized casino and riverboat gambling or permitted Native Americans to operate casinos. Still, New Jersey committed to redeveloping Atlantic City by funding airport renovations, a new convention center, and other projects.

BIBLIOGRAPHY

Funnell, Charles E. *By the Beautiful Sea: The Rise and High Times of That Great American Resort, Atlantic City*. New York: Knopf, 1975.

Paulsson, Martin. *The Social Anxieties of Progressive Reform: Atlantic City, 1854–1920*. American Social Experience Series. New York: New York University Press, 1994.

Sternlieb, George, and James W. Hughes. *The Atlantic City Gamble*. Cambridge, Mass.: Harvard University Press, 1983.

Robert Fishman / S. B.

See also **Gambling; Miss America Pageant; Tourism.**

ATROCITIES IN WAR. The history of warfare is replete with examples of atrocities, and the American experience offers no exception. Americans have been the perpetrators as well as the victims of atrocities. Sometimes referred to as war crimes, atrocities have usually involved torture, maiming, or killing of civilians and noncombatants; destruction of nonmilitary targets; maltreatment and killing of wounded and prisoners of war; and use of weapons to cause superfluous damage or injury.

Many atrocities committed by Americans have occurred during guerrilla counterinsurgent wars, such as the American Indian wars, the PHILIPPINE INSURRECTION, and the Vietnam War. Colonial Indian wars, such as the PEQUOT WAR (1637) and KING PHILIP'S WAR (1675–1676), decimated or annihilated entire Indian societies in New England. Callous military tactics characterized the pacification of the SEMINOLE tribe in Florida and the forced removal of the Five Civilized Tribes from the southern states. Massacres such as those suffered by the CHEYENNE at Sand Creek (1864) and at Summit Spring (1868), by the Piegan Blackfoot Indians in Montana (1870), and by the SIOUX at Wounded Knee (1889) are flagrant examples of atrocities by the U.S. Army on the frontier. Neither women nor children were spared; many victims were sexually mutilated, disemboweled, and inflicted with other indignities, while the survivors were treated with indifference and their crops and herds destroyed. Revenge and retaliation for atrocities of equal brutality committed by the Indians often motivated such massacres.

Americans have, on occasion, been the victims of atrocities on home soil and abroad. Two such events—both stemming from America's westward expansion into lands belonging to others—have reached iconic status in national lore. In 1836, Mexican troops executed the Texan soldiers who survived the siege of the Alamo. Forty years later a U.S. Army regiment under the command of Col. George A. Custer was slaughtered by Sioux Indians at the Battle of Little Bighorn. A complex mythology has developed around both massacres. They have been used both as symbols of courageous American manhood and as justifications for the expansionist policies that caused them in the first place.

Revelations that American soldiers in the Philippines were murdering civilians, destroying their villages, indiscriminately killing prisoners, and using dum-dum bullets and torture such as the "water cure" to defeat the Philippine insurgents led to the court-martial of Brig. Gen. Jacob Smith and other officers in 1902. Smith was charged with "conduct prejudicial to good order and military discipline" because of his orders to kill prisoners and destroy civilian property in the course of his pacification efforts. Smith was found guilty, admonished by President Theodore Roosevelt, and forced into early retirement. Apologists for the military claimed that the unconventional tactics of the insurgents and the difficulty in distinguishing them from the native peasants justified the extraordinary measures.

American military operations in South Vietnam were characterized by conditions similar to those in the Philippines, and allegations were made of similar atrocities perpetrated by American soldiers. The majority of the allegations concerning Vietnam atrocities were proved false, and other actions, such as the use of napalm and crop destruction, have been defended on the basis of military necessity. The most publicized, proven atrocity of the Vietnam War was the killing of unarmed civilians, mostly women and children, at the village of My Lai in 1968. Several American officers were punished for participation in this massacre or for failure to investigate its occurrence. The events of the Vietnam War continued to prick the American conscience, however. In 2001 the decorated Vietnam veteran and U.S. senator Bob Kerrey sparked a new round of debate about the U.S. atrocities during the war when he admitted that his platoon had probably killed a number of women and children during a confused night raid in 1969.

The number of proven atrocities in American military history is small in relation to the large number of men who have participated in the nation's wars. This is particularly true for conventional wars. Undisciplined volunteers were responsible for massacres on several occasions during the Mexican-American War, the most infamous occurring at Guadalupe on 25 March 1847. The number of American war crimes during the two world wars was small, primarily involving individual acts of murder, sex crimes, and abuse of enemy prisoners of war. The number of such crimes was greater during the occupation after World War II than during combat.

American prisoners of war have suffered cruel and inhumane treatment during several wars. Deplorable conditions characterized the British prison ships of the American Revolution and the Confederate and Union prisons such as ANDERSONVILLE, Rock Island, ELMIRA, and Camp Chase during the CIVIL WAR. On 12 April 1864 Confederate troops killed scores of black Union army prisoners after the capture of Fort Pillow in Tennessee. During WORLD WAR II, a number of American prisoners died in the Japanese prison camps that housed the survivors of the BATAAN-CORREGIDOR CAMPAIGN. During the Battle of the Bulge in December 1944, near the town of Malmédy in the Belgian Ardennes, eighty-six American prisoners were executed by German SS Panzer troops.

Several international protocols and conventions have attempted to curb unnecessary violence and atrocities in war by prohibiting use of certain types of weapons and codifying rules of warfare pertaining to the protection of civilians, the treatment of wounded and prisoners of war, and the protection of cultural landmarks. The Nuremberg trials of German war criminals and the Japanese war crimes trials after World War II established that senior commanders are responsible for atrocities and war crimes perpetrated by subordinates. War criminals ever since have been tried at the international courts of arbitration and justice in The Hague in Holland. Human rights activists had long sought a United Nations war crimes court. Progress toward that end was stalled in 2001, however, when the U.S. government refused to ratify the International Criminal Court for fear that its military personnel would be exposed to legal risks for actions taken during the course of humanitarian, counterespionage, or antiterrorist campaigns. (Also opposing the U.N. war crimes court, ironically, were Iraq and Libya, nations identified as proterrorist states by President George W. Bush.)

The depth of the international community's unwillingness to prosecute war crimes was severely tested in the 1990s. Little action was taken when fanatically nationalistic members of the Hutu tribe in the African country of Rwanda slaughtered more than 500,000 of their Tutsi rivals. Stronger actions were taken in response to "ethnic cleansing" that took place during the ethnic conflict in Yugoslavia in the 1990s. An army led by the Bosnian Serb Radisav Krstic invaded Srebrenica in 1995—easily overrunning the token United Nations force that had prematurely declared the city a "safe haven" for war refugees—and massacred eight thousand Muslim men and boys. Elsewhere, the Serbian army and local militia groups murdered tens of thousands of Bosnian Muslims and buried them in mass graves. Krstic was later tried in The Hague for his role in the Srebrenica massacre and sentenced to forty-six years in prison.

The United States became deeply involved in the conflict in March 1999. Yugoslav President Slobodan Milosevic, a Serb, had initiated a campaign to "cleanse" the region of Kosovo of ethnic Albanians, sending hundreds of thousands of Kosovar Albanians fleeing into impoverished neighboring countries and creating a massive humanitarian crisis. After evidence of atrocities against civilians surfaced, the United States led an air strike sponsored by the North Atlantic Treaty Organization against Serbian forces in Kosovo on 25 March 1999. The strikes expanded into a full-scale bombing campaign that lasted for seventy-eight days, ruining much of Yugoslavia's industrial infrastructure and killing some civilians. Although the United States was roundly criticized for its aggressive stance, the air campaign succeeded in ousting Milosevic, who was later caught and put on trial for human rights abuses. At the time of this writing, his fate had not yet been decided.

BIBLIOGRAPHY

Brown, Dee A. *Bury My Heart at Wounded Knee: An Indian History of the American West.* New York: Holt, 2001.

Hersh, Seymour M. *My Lai 4: A Report on the Massacre and its Aftermath.* New York: Random House, 1970.

Jacobs, Wilbur R. *Dispossessing the American Indian: Indians and Whites on the Colonial Frontier.* New York: Scribner, 1972; Norman: University of Oklahoma Press, 1985.

Kerrey, Bob. *When I Was a Young Man: A Memoir.* New York: Harcourt, 2002.

Peterson, Scott. *Me Against My Brother: At War in Somalia, Sudan, and Rwanda: A Journalist Reports from the Battlefields of Africa.* New York: Routledge, 2000.

Ratner, Steven R., and Jason S. Abrams. *Accountability for Human Rights Atrocities in International Law: Beyond the Nuremberg Legacy.* New York: Oxford University Press, 2001.

Sells, Michael. *The Bridge Betrayed: Religion and Genocide in Bosnia.* Berkeley: University of California Press, 1996; 1998.

Taylor, Telford. *Nuremberg and Vietnam: An American Tragedy.* Chicago: Quadrangle Books, 1970.

Wolff, Leon. *Little Brown Brother: How the United States Purchased and Pacified the Philippine Islands at the Century's Turn.* New York: Doubleday, 1961.

Vincent H. Demma / A. R.

See also **Alamo, Siege of the; Little Bighorn, Battle of; Malmédy Massacre; My Lai Incident; Pillow, Fort, Massacre at; Vietnam War; War, Laws of; Wars with Indian Nations, Later Nineteenth Century (1840–1900); Yugoslavia, Relations with.**

ATTAINDER. In common law, attainder caused the loss of civil rights and forfeiture of estate of one who had been sentenced to death for treason or felony. Parliament enacted bills of attainder having that effect without criminal trials in ordinary course. During the American Revolution, a few colonial legislatures enacted such bills. They are now prohibited by Article 1, sections 9 and 10 of the Constitution. In *United States v. Lovett* (1946), the U.S. Supreme Court held that a statute mandating the firing of three federal employees on national-security grounds was unconstitutional as a bill of attainder.

William M. Wiecek

See also **Common Law.**

ATTICA. When Attica State Prison in New York opened in the 1930s, it promised improvements over the old "silent system," which had previously been used at New York prisons like Sing Sing. In time, however, Attica became a Spartan facility in which conditions were unusually harsh and discipline exceptionally brutal. In 1971, inmates captured control of a major part of the institution, took hostages, and issued a list of proposals for reform. The prisoners demanded better food and medical care, safeguards for religious practices, and higher wages for prison jobs. They also sought amnesty for any criminal offenses they had committed incident to the disturbance. The inmates released several guards, one of whom had been severely injured and later died of his wounds. The commissioner of corrections, Russell G. Oswald, agreed to consider the prisoners' demands and appointed a special committee of state employees, politicians, reporters, and others to facilitate negotiations. In succeeding days, the tense situation at Attica captured headlines across the nation. At one point, inmates exhibited hostages with knives to their throats. The commissioner responded favorably to some demands, but refused to guarantee amnesty.

On the morning of the fifth day, Governor Nelson Rockefeller ordered the prison retaken by force. State authorities later explained that they believed "revolutionaries" had planned the initial action and that hostages were being executed or castrated. Helicopters dropped canisters of tear gas. Hundreds of guards and riot police stormed the facility, shooting indiscriminately. They wounded more than eighty inmates and killed twenty-nine. In the chaos, they also inadvertently shot ten hostages to death. When the institution was secure, the officers forced inmates to strip naked and lie on their faces in the mud. They beat or shot inmates who raised their heads. Some officers tormented inmates with racial epithets and threats of castration. Other officers formed a gauntlet and clubbed naked prisoners as they ran through it. National television carried images of the spectacle.

State authorities charged numerous prisoners with criminal offenses allegedly committed during the five-day episode. Yet most of the charges were ultimately abandoned. In 1976, Governor Hugh Carey issued a blanket pardon for everyone and ordered the records concerning

Attica. State police and prison guards stand over inmates after the violent end to the hostage situation at the state prison in September 1971. © CORBIS CORPORATION

Attica sealed for fifty years. A congressional committee condemned the violent nature of the assault and the savage treatment of inmates that followed. A special New York commission concluded that the inmates had not planned the uprising, but had acted spontaneously out of hostility born of poor living conditions. More than a thousand inmates sued state officials over the abuse they had suffered. After years of litigation, the prisoners won an $8 million settlement.

The events at Attica left deep psychological scars. For some, Attica demonstrated the many failures of American penal policy, especially the disastrous consequences of confining large numbers of prisoners under severe discipline in primitive, crowded quarters.

BIBLIOGRAPHY

New York State Special Commission on Attica. *Attica: The Official Report of the New York State Special Commission on Attica.* New York: Bantam, 1972.

Oswald, Russell G. *Attica: My Story.* Garden City, N.Y.: Doubleday, 1972.

Wicker, Tom. *A Time to Die: The Attica Prison Revolt.* 2d ed. Lincoln: University of Nebraska Press, 1994.

Larry Yackle

See also **Prisons and Prison Reform; Riots.**

AUBURN PRISON SYSTEM. *See* **Prisons and Prison Reform.**

AUCTIONS are a method of allocating goods and services based on competitive price offerings from sellers and buyers. While auctions can take various forms, the most common form is generally called an English auction, in which the potential buyers compete for the item or set of items offered for sale by raising their bids until a single buyer remains. This process is generally overseen by an auctioneer, who recognizes the various bids as they are made and determines when the bidding is ended. In a Dutch auction, derived from its use in the Netherlands for the wholesale sale of flowers and other agricultural goods, the seller begins with a high price and then lowers it in regular increments. The first buyer to bid gets the object. Due to the split second differences in bids, bidding in these auctions is often done electronically.

There are numerous other variations. Some auctions entail simultaneous bidding from multiple buyers and sellers. This is the method used on most major international mercantile exchanges, such as the Chicago Board of Exchange, where commodity futures are bought and sold. It is commonly referred to as a Japanese auction, however, based on its use in traditional Japanese fish auctions. Other auctions, including most oil and mineral rights auctions, rely on written bids, which must be submitted by a specified time and date when they are opened. This method is also used in what are commonly called "silent auctions." Years ago, before it became common for people to wear watches, there were "candle auctions" in which the bidding ended when the candle went out.

Perhaps the oldest recorded auction is the bride auction described by Herodotus, existing as early as 500 B.C., in which once a year females of marriageable age were sold to the highest bidding suitors. Roman soldiers are recorded as auctioning off captured war booty, *sub hasta* or "under the spear," to merchants who traveled with the army. The earliest reference to the term "auction" in the *Oxford English Dictionary* is dated 1595. Auctions appear to have become significantly more common in the seventeenth century as part of the growth in international trade, particularly as a means for selling imported goods. The world famous auctioneer houses of Sotheby's and Christie's were founded in England in 1744 and 1766, respectively. While the names Sotheby's and Christie's are still closely associated with auctions, especially when it comes to the sale of very expensive antiques and art objects, in gross economic terms agricultural and financial auctions entail much larger sums of money. In the 1990s, meanwhile, the Internet became the locus for the emergence of a large number of new auctions, such as those sponsored by eBay and Yahoo.

Despite their common use, auctions have historically had a dubious reputation, in part due to the negative impact that many seventeenth-, eighteenth-, and nineteenth-century auction sales had on established businesses. This was especially true of eighteenth-century seaport auctions in which British goods were often "dumped" in American ports. Auctions were also closely associated with the infamous slave trade. This negative attitude toward auctions was not lessened when they were commonly used, especially on the frontier, in bankruptcy and delinquency sales. Auctions continue to be used in most liquidation sales. Both the positive and negative response generated by auctions relates to their primary use in allocating and pricing goods that have an ambiguous value, be it a Babylonian bride, Roman war booty, foreign goods, a repossessed farm, a newly discovered artistic masterpiece, an antique necklace, or a highly perishable agricultural commodity. While the auction process resolves what differences might exist, at least for the moment, a good number of people are likely to feel that the auction price was either too high or too low. This ambiguity also offers opportunities for more knowledgeable participants to exploit the less knowledgeable. Since different types of auctions vary in numerous ways, the rules governing them intended to ensure fairness also vary. Many auctions, including most financial and commodity auctions, are restricted to members only. Some auctions allow for reserve prices while others do not. Buyer "rings" are prohibited in some auctions and not in others.

During the last quarter of the twentieth century, as the world economy became more market oriented, auctions grew in importance. Seen as embodying free market principles in their purest form, Western capitalist governments, particularly the United States, have supported their use in allocating resources, including previously owned government resources. This greater use of auctions has also been fostered by the growth of e-commerce and the Internet, which enable otherwise separated individuals to interact directly with each other electronically. Globalization and market growth is likely to further enhance this prominence in the twenty-first century.

BIBLIOGRAPHY

Cassady, Ralph, Jr. *Auctions and Auctioneering*. Berkeley and Los Angeles: University of California Press, 1967.

Smith, Charles W. *Auctions: The Social Construction of Value*. New York: Free Press, 1989.

Vickrey, William. "Counterspeculation, Auctions, and Competitive Sealed Tenders." *Journal of Finance* 16 (1961): 8–37.

Charles W. Smith

AUDIO TECHNOLOGY INDUSTRY. In 1877, Thomas Alva Edison completed his experiments with recorded sound technology, or what would become popularly known as the phonograph. The inventor discovered that the sound vibrations of his voice were powerful enough to allow a stylus to cut a signal into a revolving sheet of tinfoil. Building upon Alexander Graham Bell's work with the telephone, Edison speculated that his "talking machine" would allow businessmen to record and preserve their conversations. Edison also believed that phonographs had significant commercial potential for entertainment, bringing great music within reach of every American. Edison's vision, which built upon the work of other inventors such as Leon Scott in Paris, paved the way for a recording industry that would earn lavish profits and alter music, popular culture, and leisure time in the twentieth century.

Edison, however, was not without competitors. Bell and Charles Tainter worked at the Volta laboratory to develop the gramophone, substituting wax for the tinfoil and using a needle to indent the sound waves. The Volta associates offered to join with Edison to exploit the phonograph commercially, but Edison refused, choosing to perfect his phonograph by having the revolving cylinder powered by an electric motor rather than the gramophone's hand crank. Nevertheless, Edison faced stiff competition, because his English patents on the phonograph lapsed in 1885.

Jesse Lippincott created the North American Phonograph Company in 1888 in order to sell Edison's phonograph and Bell's gramophone. Yet the anticipated business market failed to materialize due to the commercial dictating machines' poor sound reproduction quality. By 1891, only nineteen of Lippincott's original thirty-three franchises were still in operation, and matters worsened with the financial panic of 1893. But the entertainment potential of the talking machine was becoming increasingly evident.

The Popular Market

Popular audiences were fascinated by early sound reproduction, depositing nickels into coin-slot phonographs, which were often installed alongside kinescopes (peephole viewers) in public amusement arcades. Seeking to exploit this market, Edison contemplated a duplicating system in which a master music recording could be used to create multiple copies. Following the demise of the North American Phonograph Company, and spurred by the competition among the entrepreneur inventors Edison, Emile Berliner, and Elridge Johnson, record sales in the United States climbed from 500,000 in 1897 to almost 3 million two years later.

The record and phonograph industry was dominated by the so-called big three: Edison's National Phonograph Company; the Victor Talking Machine Company, formed by Berliner and Johnson; and Columbia, under the direction of Edward Easton, a former congressional stenographer. The big three owed their dominant market shares to patent position and large-scale manufacturing. Each of the big three made extensive use of mass advertising; maintained a line of models ranging from small $10 record players to elaborate cabinet models that sold for as much as $500; developed a chain of exclusive dealers who were expected to follow company price and maintenance standards; signed artists such as the Italian tenor Enrico Caruso to promote record sales; and sought to develop international markets, especially in Europe. According to U.S. census figures, in 1914 the recorded sound industry produced sales in excess of $27 million.

The Rise of Jazz and Radio

While World War I led to temporary market dislocations, the postwar economy witnessed a surge in consumer spending, with Edison selling phonographic merchandise worth more than $22 million in 1920. However, the vast potential profits and expiration of patents lured many new enterprises to the industry. While there were 18 recorded sound companies in 1914, this number had climbed to 166 by 1918, with sales during this period rising from $27 million to $158 million. While profit margins declined, the industry continued to be dominated by the big three, which had signed most well-known classical musicians to exclusive contracts. This monopoly of talent forced new companies to seek untapped audiences. Accordingly, the recorded sound industry introduced the general public to African American blues and jazz, although white executives rather than black musicians such as Louis Armstrong enjoyed most of these growing profits. While Edison continued to enhance the quality of recorded sound with Diamond brand disks, his company's sales sagged as the inventor stubbornly clung to classical records and failed to capitalize on the popular taste for jazz.

During the 1920s, the recorded music industry faced a new challenge: radio. The talking machine businesses initially perceived radio as a competing technology that might replace the phonograph in the American home. This potential conflict was resolved by the Western Electric scientists Joseph Maxfield and H. Harrison's development of electrical recording, making it possible for the phonograph companies to produce high quality radio sets. Rather than destructive competition, radio and the talking machine established a symbiotic relationship. Following a sales slump in 1924–1925, the recorded sound industry rebounded, taking advantage of new markets in talking films, which electrical sound reproduction had made possible.

As a pioneer in developing the talking picture, Warner Brothers acquired musical rights and record companies, such as Brunswick Records in 1930, increasing its capitalization from $10 million in 1927 to $230 million in 1930. Radio Corporation of America (RCA), led by David Sarnoff, moved into film production, forming Radio-Keith-Orpheum (RKO) in 1928. This followed its 1919 takeover of the Victor Company, the leading member of the big three. The new company was referred to as RCA Victor, a manufacturer of radio sets, radio-phonograph combination sets, and records. Columbia responded to this merger by purchasing a small radio network in 1927, obtaining air time to promote its records. This new company was called the Columbia Phonograph Broadcasting System (later CBS).

The Industry during the Depression

While the film industry was doing well in the 1925–1929 period, the recorded sound industry remained sluggish, with yearly sales of talking machines staying in the $70 million range. The electronic phonograph players were also expensive, selling for nearly $400 a set, the equivalent of a Ford Model T. And the depression had a devastating impact on the industry. On 2 November 1929, Thomas A. Edison, Incorporated, ceased manufacturing recorded sound products. In 1930, industry recording and recording machine sales fell to $46 million. The following year, sales figures slumped to $17 million, while factories and recording studios often stood vacant.

The depressed industry attracted foreign investors looking for bargains, such as England's Ted Lewis, who established an American subsidiary of Decca records in 1934. Decca produced cheaper popular records destined for the nation's jukeboxes, which contributed more than half the nation's record sales by the end of the 1930s. The radio industry weathered the depression by providing a psychological sense of comfort for troubled Americans, with a unit in more than 60 percent of homes. RCA, with the financial support of General Electric and Westinghouse, formed the National Broadcasting Company (NBC). To provide radio programming, these media conglomerates increasingly turned to prerecorded sound. Thus, the record industry rose out of the depression on the coattails of radio, which promoted its recordings. By

1938, record sales had climbed to 33 million, dominated by RCA Victor, Decca, and Columbia/ARC (American Recording Corporation). The process of consolidation in the entertainment industry was accelerated by the depression. The interlocking system of record production, filmmaking, and radio broadcasting helped foster a popular musical form, swing, in the 1930s, which provided commercial product for the media empires.

An Era of Changing Technology

World War II contributed to the pace of technological change in American life, including the recording industry, which introduced magnetic tape recording, the vinyl microgroove record, and the stereophonic reproduction of sound, in addition to the extended play or LP (for long-playing) during the 1930s. The new technology appealed to audiophiles, reflecting postwar society's fascination with technological innovation. In addition, the development of solid-state electronics and transistors brought smaller and cheaper record players within range of the growing teen market.

Technology and the youth culture combined to produce a revolutionary new music form: rock and roll. Inexpensive magnet recording made it possible for independent record labels to market the new rock music as well as specialty fields—Folkways and Vanguard Records for folk music, and Atlantic Records for rhythm and blues. Independent record labels captured American musical roots in folk, blues, and country music, while innovations in the sound studio allowed for greater collaboration between artists and engineers with the synthesizer and electronic keyboard. By 1958, the big four companies—Columbia, RCA Victor, Decca, and Capitol accounted for only 36 percent of hits on the Billboard chart of best-selling records.

Initially reluctant to embrace rock music, the major labels eventually recognized the market potential of the youth culture. The record industry in America during the 1960s was, indeed, a lucrative business, as sales reached more than $1 billion by decade's end. This market was once again dominated by major companies—by 1967, Columbia (renamed CBS Records), RCA, and Capitol accounted for market shares of 12 to 13 percent each. During the 1960s and 1970s, media conglomerates such as CBS, Warner Brothers, RCA, Capitol-EAAI, PolyGram, and MCA (Music Corporation of America) controlled the recorded sound industry. By 1979, the annual sales of audio products in the United States totaled slightly more than $4 billion.

While the conglomerates were in an excellent position to promote their music through such important venues as Music Television (MTV), the introduction of digital sound recording technology in the 1980s made Japanese and European companies predominant in the industry. While Philips negotiated an agreement with MCA to jointly introduce its laser vision system of videodiscs, in 1988 the Sony Corporation purchased CBS Rec-

ords for $2 billion. In 1990, Matsushita paid $6.59 billion for MCA. In regard to market share, Sony, Matsushita, and Philips were the modern-day equivalent of the big three. Digital technology increased corporate sales, but tensions developed between record companies and artists not to mention consumers seeking to download free music from such Web sites as Napster. Digital technology, the compact disc, the computer, and the CD-ROM replaced Edison's phonograph. Nevertheless, much of Edison's dream regarding commercial profits for the recording industry, as well as changes in the leisure habits of Americans, had been realized.

BIBLIOGRAPHY

Brady, Erika. *A Spiral Way: How the Phonograph Changed Ethnography.* Jackson: University Press of Mississippi, 1999.

Denisoff, R. Serge. *Tarnished Gold: The Record Industry Revisited.* New Brunswick, N.J.: Transaction Books, 1986.

Gelatt, Roland. *The Fabulous Phonograph, 1877–1977.* 2d ed. New York: Macmillan, 1977.

Millard, Andre. *America on Record: A History of Recorded Sound.* Cambridge, U.K.: Cambridge University Press, 1995.

Ron Briley

See also **Music Industry; Music Television; Radio; Rock and Roll.**

AUDUBON SOCIETY, a citizens' organization that has been a major force in shaping America's wildlife protection and conservation movement. The society's roots go back to the latter part of the nineteenth century, when there were virtually no effective game laws: waterfowl were being shot by the wagonload to sell to restaurants; plumed birds were being slaughtered for feathers to decorate ladies' hats; and buffalo were being hunted almost to extinction. In an early attempt to protect wildlife, an Audubon society, named in honor of the artist and naturalist John James Audubon (1785–1851), was established in 1885 by George Bird Grinnell, editor of *Forest and Stream.* The organization lived only until 1888. In 1896, however, a group of women formed the Massachusetts Audubon Society and refused to buy or wear hats or clothing that used bird plumes. They also began lobbying politicians to protect birds, and their efforts led to the formation of a number of state Audubon societies; the membership included hunters who saw that without controls game would be wiped out, as well as other individuals who were appalled by the cruelty and waste in the destruction of wildlife. During the next several years progress was made at the state level, but it also became clear that there was need for a coordinated national effort for federal regulation. In 1905 twenty-five state Audubon societies joined to form the National Association of Audubon Societies for the Protection of Wild Birds and Animals. In 1940 the organization shortened its name to the National Audubon Society.

John James Audubon. An 1861 engraving of the artist, from an earlier painting by Alonzo Chappel. © CORBIS-BETTMANN

During its first two or three decades the new national organization was concerned primarily with campaigning for bird protection laws and with direct protection of wildlife. But from its earliest days the society had broader wildlife and conservation interests. As early as the 1920s the society was actively campaigning for an international treaty to curb the menace of oil spills. In 1910 the society formed the Junior Audubon Club to educate children about the protection of birds, and in 1936 the society opened its first summer ecology camp for adults. Both efforts helped spearhead ecology instruction in the United States. In the 1960s and 1970s the Audubon Society focused its efforts on federal environmental policy. The society opened an office in Washington, D.C., in 1969 and urged passage of the Clean Air, Clean Water, Wild and Scenic Rivers, and Endangered Species Acts. In the late twentieth century the society concentrated on protecting ancient forests in the Pacific Northwest, preserving wetlands, and preventing oil drilling in the Arctic National Wildlife Refuge. By the beginning of the twenty-first century, the Audubon Society boasted 508 chapters in the Americas, a membership of 550,000, and 100 Audubon sanctuaries and nature centers.

BIBLIOGRAPHY

Graham, Frank, Jr. *The Audubon Ark*. New York: Knopf, 1990.

Orr, Oliver H., Jr. *Saving American Birds: T. Gilbert Pearson and the Founding of the Audubon Movement*. Gainesville, Fla.: University Press of Florida, 1992.

Price, Jennifer. "When Women Were Women, Men Were Men, and Birds Were Hats." In *Flight Maps: Adventures with Nature in Modern America*. New York: Basic Books, 1999.

Robert C. Boardman
Flannery Burke

See also **Conservation; Endangered Species; Environmental Protection Agency; Ornithology; Wildlife Preservation.**

AUGUSTA, TREATY OF. *See* **Indian Land Cessions and Indian Treaties.**

AURORA. Founded in 1790 as the *General Advertiser* by Benjamin Franklin's grandson, Benjamin Franklin Bache, this Philadelphia newspaper was the most important political journal of its era. After Philip Freneau's *National Gazette* folded in 1793, Bache's journal became the nation's leading outlet for criticism of the Washington administration and its policies. Adding *Aurora* to the title in November 1794, Bache defended the French Revolution and the Democratic-Republican Societies and bitterly opposed the administration's perceived pro-British slant. After publishing the leaked text of the Jay Treaty in 1795 and helping generate widespread protests against it, the *Aurora* became one of the few newspapers to extensively criticize George Washington himself, accusing the president of monarchical tendencies, financial malfeasance, and a poor military record. Losing the fight against the Jay Treaty, the *Aurora* emerged as the most important journalistic champion of Thomas Jefferson over John Adams in the elections of 1796 and 1800, becoming the hub of a Jeffersonian Republican newspaper network that spread the *Aurora*'s message into every corner of the nation. The *Aurora* was widely cited by allies and enemies alike as a key factor in Jefferson's eventual victory.

Subjected to multiple forms of legal, social, and physical harassment, the editors of the *Aurora* were considered the primary targets of the 1798 Sedition Act; Bache was arrested under the law but died of yellow fever before he could be tried. His assistant, the radical Irish refugee William Duane, took over a revived *Aurora* and made it even more effective, setting its attacks on Adams and its defenses of Jefferson in the context of a wide-ranging indictment of British imperialism, religious intolerance, and the "reign of terror," which Republicans believed Federalists were conducting to force their opponents and the general population into submission. During 1800, Duane conducted a long investigation into alleged corruption at the Treasury and War Departments, supposedly covered up by arson just after Adams was defeated. Duane suffered myriad beatings, prosecutions, and lawsuits for his trouble, including a citation of contempt of the U.S. Senate that forced him into hiding for a time in 1800.

Duane's uncompromising radicalism on issues such as banking and the judiciary increasingly estranged him from the regnant Republican establishment, elements of which set up competing newspapers that aimed to curb his power. This campaign against the alleged "tyranny of printers" took its toll by the 1810s, reducing the *Aurora* to the status of influential in-house critic, rather than semi-official voice, of the Republican Party. It nevertheless continued to publish until 1824.

BIBLIOGRAPHY

Pasley, Jeffrey L. *"The Tyranny of Printers": Newspaper Politics in the Early American Republic.* Charlottesville: University Press of Virginia, 2001.

Phillips, Kim T. *William Duane, Radical Journalist in the Age of Jefferson.* New York: Garland, 1989.

Rosenfeld, Richard. *American Aurora: A Democratic-Republican Returns.* New York: St. Martin's, 1997.

Tagg, James. *Benjamin Franklin Bache and the Philadelphia "Aurora."* Philadelphia: University of Pennsylvania Press, 1991.

Jeffrey L. Pasley

See also **Newspapers; Republicans, Jeffersonian; Sedition Acts.**

AUSTIN, founded in 1839, was named for Stephen F. Austin, the principal American colonizer of TEXAS. Austin served temporarily as the Texas capital until 1842, when legislators moved the seat of government to Houston, and later to Washington-on-the-Brazos. They returned it to Austin in 1845. Austin experienced moderate growth in the 1850s with the construction of government buildings, but growth slowed during the Civil War. Later, Austin benefited from its location near the CHISHOLM TRAIL and from the arrival of the railroad in 1871. The state legislature designated the city the permanent capital of Texas the following year.

World War II marked an important turning point in the city's history, with the location of air bases and army camps nearby. After the war, Austin profited as high-tech electronics industries relocated there. The University of Texas, founded at Austin in 1883, not only maintained its position as one of the city's major employers but also attracted a variety of research and development firms that fueled the city's growth. In addition, expanding government and a thriving tourist industry promoted Austin's development. Austin experienced explosive population growth during this time, from 22,000 in 1950, to 251,808 in 1970, to 465,622 in 1990, to 642,994 in 2000.

BIBLIOGRAPHY

Cantrell, Gregg. *Stephen F. Austin, Empresario of Texas.* New Haven, Conn.: Yale University Press, 1999.

Humphrey, David C. *Austin: A History of the Capital City.* Austin: Texas State Historical Association, 1997.

Robert B. Fairbanks / s. b.

See also **Empresario System; Mexican-American War; Railroads; Sunbelt.**

AUSTRALIA AND NEW ZEALAND, RELATIONS WITH.

Countless Americans have traveled to Australia and New Zealand. Many important commercial contacts were made in the earliest years of Australian colonization, from the first settlement of free citizens in New South Wales in the 1790s to the gold fever years in Victoria in the 1850s. Yankee sailors, whalers, and explorers made their presence known in this area of the Southwest Pacific for the next century. None was more significant, however, than the impact of the 1 million American soldiers and sailors who poured into Australia during World War II, helping to lift the despair felt in that wholly unprepared nation of 7 million people from the fall of Singapore in February 1942 to the Battle of the Coral Sea the following May. History and geography have been of vital importance to Australia and New Zealand's perception of external affairs and the usefulness of force, but in different ways. New Zealand has been relatively free of the anxieties engendered by the proximity of hostile neighbors, whereas Australia has stood almost defenseless on the doorstep of a threatening Asia. New Zealand was once noted for its staunch and compliant membership in alliances—with Britain and then with the United States. Yet since the 1980s a revulsion against nuclear weapons has stimulated a peace movement there, which is determined to keep the nation nuclear free. But Australia, with its more clearly defined perception of threat and security, forged a formal place for itself within the U.S. security systems from early in the Cold War.

Whatever their particular perspective, however, the common national security interests of Australia, New Zealand, and the United States have made their citizen-soldiers comrades in arms five times in the twentieth century. In World War I the three nations helped defeat Imperial Germany, with Australia alone losing 59,000 out of a population of 5 million. In World War II, particularly in the Pacific theater, Australia and New Zealand contributed substantial naval and air forces and the ANZACs (Australia and New Zealand Army Corps) fought ferociously in New Guinea. Australia and New Zealand both contributed, each in its own way, to the Korean War, the Vietnam War, and the Gulf War.

The heart of the modern Australian-New Zealand-American security relationship has been the ANZUS Treaty, or what is left of it after Ronald Reagan's administration pushed aside the nuclear-sensitive New Zealanders in the 1980s. The treaty was signed in San Francisco on 1 September 1951, ratified by President Harry S. Truman on 15 April 1952, and entered into force two weeks later. Conceived in connection with the conclusion of a "soft" Japanese peace treaty, and—despite charges of subservience on the side of the junior partners—the ANZUS Treaty was negotiated after much tough bargaining. Canberra and Wellington wanted strategic reassurance that America would come to their aid in their next time of troubles; Washington merely wanted cooperation, especially the opportunity to take advantage of Australia's unique geographical position and its overall political position in Southeast Asia. Neither got exactly what it wanted.

For over fifty years the primary goal of Australian foreign policy has been to have an engaged United States as the ultimate guarantor of Australian sovereignty; for Washington, Australia remains the southern anchor of America's security arrangements (with Japan as the northern anchor), standing astride both the Indian and Pacific Oceans and intermediate between California and Southeast Asia.

BIBLIOGRAPHY

Grattan, C. Hartley. *The United States and the Southwest Pacific.* Cambridge, Mass.: Harvard University Press, 1961.

Harper, Norman. *A Great and Powerful Friend.* St. Lucia, Queensland, Australia: Queensland University Press, 1987.

Siracusa, Joseph M., and Yeong-Han Cheong. *America's Australia: Australia's America.* Claremont, CA: Regina Books, 1997.

Joseph M. Siracusa

See also **World War II; World War II, Navy in.**

AUTO EMISSION TESTING AND STANDARDS.

In 1967, the United States congress passed the Air Quality Act, authorizing the Secretary of Health, Education, and Welfare to establish different air quality regions in the United States. Most of the responsibility for setting air quality standards and enforcing them was left to the individual states. Believing the act lacked enough punch for enforcement, Congress passed the Clean Air Act in 1970, which set deadlines for cleaning pollutants out of America's air. In response, President Richard Nixon created the Environmental Protection Agency (EPA), on 2 December 1970.

At the time, the EPA initiated research into testing automobile emissions for pollutants, but its powers to enforce regulations were weak. In 1973, Congress passed amendments to the Clean Air Act mandating the use of catalytic converters and the testing of converters every 50,000 miles by 1975. General Motors surprised almost everyone by having catalytic converters installed in nearly all of its new cars within one year. In 1974, Honda responded with the Compound Vortex Controlled Combustion (CVCC) engine, which burned fuel so cleanly it met emission standards without a catalytic converter.

The long battle to eliminate lead from gasoline was begun in 1973, after numerous scientific reports linking even small amounts of lead in the atmosphere to poor health, especially for children. At the time, 200,000 tons of lead were used in gasoline per year. The EPA mandated 1.7 grams per gallon by July 1, 1975, 1.2 grams by July 1, 1976, 0.9 grams by July 1, 1977, and 0.6 grams by July 1, 1978. The EPA further ordered that at least one grade of gasoline had to be lead free to protect catalytic converters. Small refineries were given an extension to 1 July 1977 to meet the lead-free gasoline requirement. In 1975, the EPA required all foreign-made automobiles to have catalytic converters.

Congress' Clean Air Act Amendments of 1977 weakened EPA standards on automobile emissions, especially for lead. New Jersey and California responded by creating their own stricter regulations for emissions. In 1978, the EPA again tried to set nationwide regulations to control lead emissions, mandating all grades of gasoline be lead free by October 1979. Gasoline manufacturers complained that the rules were too strict, and Congress weakened automobile emissions standards, even though environmental groups sued the EPA to enforce the stricter standards. In 1985, the EPA passed stricter emission standards, including a stricter standard for lead. Before the new standard, lead content was allowed to be 1.1 grams per gallon; the new regulation set a maximum of 0.1 grams per gallon and a deadline to meet the standard of 1 January 1986. This was an urgent matter, because lead ruined the ability of catalytic converters to control the emissions of ozone, nitrogen oxides, and soot.

In November 1990, Congress passed the Clean Air Act Amendments of 1990, requiring lead-free gasoline and an end to ozone and soot emissions. On 29 January 1996, the EPA announced revisions of its emission regulations in light of the Congressional mandate, declaring the use of leaded gasoline against the law. On 16 November 1999, the EPA issued a report claiming that the reduction in automobile pollution would save 23,000 lives by 2010 and had already saved the American economy four times as much as it has spent on low-emission engines and catalytic converters.

BIBLIOGRAPHY

Harrington, Winston, Margaret A. Walls, and Virginia D. McConnell. "Using Economic Incentives to Reduce Auto Pollution." *Issues in Science and Technology* 11, no. 2 (Winter 1994): 26–32.

Ingrassia, Paul, and Joseph B. White. *Comeback: The Fall and Rise of the American Automobile Industry.* New York: Simon & Schuster, 1994.

Merline, John. "Buy a New Car, Clean the Air." *Consumers' Research Magazine* 83, no. 8 (August 2000): 10.

Walsh, Campion. "The Regulatory Toll." *Wall Street Journal* (13 September 1999): R9.

Kirk H. Beetz

See also **Air Pollution; Clean Air Act; Environmental Protection Agency; Ozone Depletion.**

AUTOBIOGRAPHY OF BENJAMIN FRANKLIN,

one of the foundational texts of American literature, has undergone a variety of published incarnations since Franklin's creation of the work in 1771. In his opening paragraph, the author introduces the twofold nature of his text, commenting first that it will be a means for his son William "to know the Circumstances of my Life" but also that "my Posterity . . . may find . . . fit to be imitated" some of Franklin's means of "having emerg'd from the Poverty and Obscurity in which I was born & bred, to a State of Affluence & some Degree of Reputation in the World." More than simply a memoir, the *Autobiography* presents Franklin's conscious recognition of his place in history; more broadly, it serves as an illustration of the author's identification with the new republic—the self-made man in the land of self-made men—and his desire to share that dream and achievement with his countrymen.

In Part One of the *Autobiography*, Franklin offers the story of his own life, beginning with his family genealogy, describing his childhood as the youngest son of a harsh father, and discussing at length his youthful rebellion against both personal and social patriarchy. From his earliest youth, Franklin displayed an optimism, self-confidence, and independence of thought that at times bordered on arrogance, traits that would come to define his life. While this attitude occasionally took its toll on the young man, it overwhelmingly factored into Franklin's success as a businessman, inventor, diplomat, and statesman. Intended as an inspiration to young Americans and written in 1784 and 1788 at the request of several admirers, Parts Two and Three continue Franklin's account of his life but focus more on the public and theoretical man as opposed to the private individual. *The Autobiography of Benjamin Franklin* achieves its goal of providing a model for successive generations, due in great part to the author's careful construction of his own persona as the representative American.

BIBLIOGRAPHY

Franklin, Benjamin. *The Autobiography of Benjamin Franklin*. Edited by Louis P. Masur. Boston: Bedford, 1993.

Barbara Schwarz Wachal

AUTOBIOGRAPHY OF MALCOLM X.

The *Autobiography* is an American literary classic. On the one hand it resembles Benjamin Franklin's *Autobiography* and Horatio Alger's *Ragged Dick*, stories of innocent youths who found success by adapting to the scheming lifestyles of the American city. On the other hand it provides the most important framework for African American political discourse in the twentieth century. It shows the life then, and in some ways now, of a Negro in America. Its movement from individual alienation to spiritual and ultimately social transformation grounds it in the tradition of St. Augustine's *Confessions* and Frederick Douglass's *Autobiography*.

Malcolm X created the *Autobiography* by telling his compelling though undocumented story to Alex Haley, a journalist, via some fifty interviews that began in the spring of 1963. Many of these were recorded covertly by the FBI, which considered Malcolm X a security threat. In an epilogue to the book, Haley described how he gained Malcolm X's confidence to share his story.

Published in November 1965, the *Autobiography* gained praise by the *New York Times* as "an eloquent statement." It allowed its author's charismatic leadership example to transcend his assassination on February 21 of that year. Its impact was to make available to millions of African American street youths, inmates, and activists Malcolm X's model of self-emancipation. There were four stages in his transformation. The first was the exploited, a depression era boy who lost his father to the Ku Klux Klan. Second was the exploiter, a street hustler and criminal. Third was the self-emancipator, the devotee of the Black Muslims and preacher of black nationalism. Finally came the social liberator, the founder of the short-lived ORGANIZATION OF AFRO-AMERICAN UNITY, a group committed to interracial and pan-African efforts toward human rights. Through his record of these stages, Malcolm X became a role model of how one could transform oneself and others in the struggle for collective liberation.

BIBLIOGRAPHY

Dyson, Michael Eric. *Making Malcolm: The Myth and Meaning of Malcolm X*. New York: Oxford University Press, 1995.

Gallen, David. *Malcolm X as They Knew Him*. New York: Carroll and Graf, 1992.

Wood, Joe, ed. *Malcolm X: In Our Own Image*. New York: St. Martin's Press, 1992.

Timothy M. Roberts

See also **Nation of Islam.**

AUTOMATED TELLER MACHINES

(ATMs) are data terminals for convenient money transactions. Don Wetzel is credited as the inventor of the ATM. He created the machine while working for the Docutel Company in Dallas, Texas, during the 1960s.

ATMs are actually kiosk computers with a keypad and screen. The patron is prompted with instructions and given a choice of transactions. An optional receipt can be printed for patron records. Bank access to accounts is provided through telephone networking, a host processor, and a bank computer to verify data. Using an ATM card, a debit card, or a credit card, bank patrons can electronically access their accounts and withdraw or deposit funds, make payments, or check balances.

ATMs have eliminated the need to enter a bank for basic transactions and allow access to accounts at machines throughout the United States. Financial institutions started charging fees to use their ATMs in the mid-1990s, making the transactions very profitable for the host banks. The use of ATMs has cut service staff in traditional banks, impacting employment in the industry. As many machines are now commercially owned and leased in public venues, a technical industry for creating, leasing, and maintaining the machines has developed.

Innovation in ATMs has included machines designed for use by the blind, kiosk machines in stores, gas stations, malls, and other public places, and machines with verbal prompts.

BIBLIOGRAPHY

Fitch, Thomas P. *Dictionary of Banking Terms.* 4th ed. Hauppauge, N.Y.: Barron's Educational Series, 2000.

Shaw, Tony. "Beyond Cash and Carry: Up-and-Coming Features Make Today's ATMs More than Simple Cash Dispensers." *Independent Banker* 50, no. 2 (2000): 64.

Karen Rae Mehaffey

See also **Banking: Overview.**

AUTOMATION

Roots of Automation

"Automation" refers more to an ideal for industrial production than any one set of technologies or practices. The word was coined in 1946 by the Ford Motor Company's vice president, Dale S. Harder, who used it to describe the automatic or semiautomatic mechanical equipment then coming into use for the assembly of automobiles, the machining of automobile parts, and the stamping of sheet metal items such as fenders. While the popular press sometimes described these machines as "robots," implying a humanlike flexibility of application, the technologies Harder described were designed to perform a single task. Later, the term automation was often used to describe computer-controlled (usually programmable) machines that did include the potential to work on various different tasks. What Harder described was the culmination of the evolution of machine production underway for at least a century and was an extension of what had previously called "mechanization." This mechanization was largely a nineteenth-century phenomenon, involving the deskilling of work or the outright replacement of craft workers with machines. This movement was reaching its limits at Ford and elsewhere by 1950, just at the time when university and military researchers were investigating a new technology that combined traditional production machinery, especially machine tools, and the newly developed electronic computer. By the early 1950s, there would be a distinction in engineering circles between "Detroit automation," relying on purely mechanical means, and computer automation.

The impetus for this development was the military's desire to produce aircraft parts at a high rate of speed and with high quality control. Also, aircraft and missiles were then being developed which used parts that were extremely difficult to make, and it was believed that a machine could do a better job than even the most skilled machinist. The U.S. Air Force, working closely with engineers at MIT and elsewhere, introduced the first "numerically controlled" (NC) machine tools in the late 1940s. These machine tools used technologies derived from the computer to control the motions of the machine in accordance with a predetermined program. An NC-equipped machine tool could be conveniently reprogrammed whenever necessary, avoiding the inflexibility that was seen as the major pitfall of Detroit automation. Although the early machines did not completely eliminate human labor, they approached the ideal. Later, engineers distinguished these NC tools from so-called computer numerical control (CNC), which received instructions from a general-purpose computer, often linked to the tool by wires. CNC is the standard technology used today, although its commercial success was slow in coming. While the aircraft industry, largely because of military support, widely adopted NC and CNC machine tools by the 1960s, few other industries followed suit. Few consumer products were as profitable as aircraft parts, making NC/CNC tools too expensive to justify.

Reaction in 1950s

There was sustained resistance to the adoption of NC and CNC tools for other reasons as well. Labor unions saw these technologies as a threat and forecasted massive technological unemployment. The public's reaction to the threat of automated factories was generally unfavorable, despite attempts by industrialists to provide reassurances. One of the most influential books of the era was John Diebold's *Automation* (1952), which explained the alleged advantages of the technology to the nonexpert. Countering Diebold, Kurt Vonnegut's 1952 novel *Player Piano* was a dystopic vision of what might happen if automation succeeded. So powerful was the idea of automation that the image of the "push button factory" of the near future became a cliché in movies and the popular press in the 1950s. In the auto industry and elsewhere, unions were able to reach a compromise with managers, allowing automated equipment to be installed in factories while preserving the wages and hours of most workers. The new factories qualitatively degraded the work experience for many highly skilled machinists and greatly reduced the need for them over the long term. Other types of automated equipment did eliminate some of the simplest assembly and materials-handling tasks, leading to some loss of jobs. However, automated production machinery eventually reduced costs and improved the quality of many items.

Other Forms of Automation

Outside the automobile and aircraft industries, automation of another sort also began to emerge in the early twentieth century. Engineers in the chemical industries, where it was common to employ complex, continuously operating processes, developed a form of automation beginning in the 1930s. There large-scale reactions such as the "cracking" of petroleum were monitored and controlled from centralized control rooms. Sensors and actuators, often in the form of pneumatically operated devices, connected the control room to the plant itself. Despite great differences between the chemical and metalworking industries, engineers by the 1940s also described this as part of the same general automation movement. Similarly, the growing size and complexity of electric power plants in the post-1945 period stimulated experiments with centralized control of the boilers, steam turbines, generators, and switch gear associated with the stations. Relying on pneumatic or electrical controls, the power industry thus also developed a distinctive variety of automation. With the advent of nuclear power in the 1950s, the design of this type of centralized automation reached a high state. The control room of a nuclear plant, filled with switches and dials, became an easily recognized symbol of the industry by the 1970s, when many such plants were in operation. There were also nonindustrial applications of automation. A prime example is the sorting of mail, which was done almost entirely by hand until the 1950s. The Post Office sponsored a far-reaching program to automate sorting processes, installing its first semiautomatic mail sorter in Baltimore in 1956. By 1965, the Post Office had installed its first optical character recognition device, which allowed a machine to sort some letters according to their city, state, and ZIP code.

Robotics

An example of the eventual convergence of Detroit-style automation and electronic computing is the development of the industrial robot. Long a feature of science fiction, the first robots were merely armlike mechanical devices, specially designed to handle one particular task. Their utility was limited to applications where high temperature or other factors made it impossible or dangerous for people to perform the same tasks. However, programmable robots appeared as early as 1954, when Universal Automation offered its first product, the Unimation robot. Although General Motors installed such a robot on a production line in 1962, sales of robots were quite limited until the 1970s. During the 1960s, many universities participated in the development of robots, and although many concepts carried over into the industrial robotics field, these did not immediately result in commercial adoption.

It was Japanese companies that moved rapidly into robot utilization in the 1970s. Kawasaki Corporation purchased the Unimation robot technology, and by 1990 forty companies in Japan were manufacturing industrial robots. The shock accompanying the rapid penetration of the domestic auto market by Japanese auto companies led American corporate leaders to adopt Japanese methods, speeding up the diffusion of industrial robotics in the United States.

The Microchip's Role in the Success of Automation

A key technical and economic factor in the widespread success of various forms of automation technologies in the 1980s and 1990s was the development of the micropro-

Automation. Robotic machines like this are designed to handle a variety of dangerous or difficult tasks, or ones that require exceptionally precise maneuvering. STOCK MARKET

cessor. This tiny electronic device was invented in the United States in the late 1970s, intended for use in calculators and computers. However, its utility as an industrial process controller was almost immediately exploited. Less well known to the public than the microprocessor, a similar device called the microcontroller outsells the microprocessor today. The original applications for the microcontroller were as an electronic replacement for electromechanical devices called process controllers, such as the ones used in chemical plants. Process controllers incorporated logic circuits that were usually not programmable. They were used to regulate multistep industrial processes using a timed cycle. A familiar example of such a device is the electromechanical switch/timer used on home washing machines for many years. Process controllers using microprocessors or microcontrollers allowed convenient reprogramming, and eventually these were linked together to provide overall monitoring and control of plant activities from a remote central computer or control room.

The Electronics Industry as Automation's Prophet

At the beginning of the twenty-first century, American industries were still in the process of implementing automated production systems. The highest overall level of automation was in the manufacturing of microelectronic devices such as microprocessors and memory chips. The microelectronics industry builds devices on such a small scale and requires such high levels of cleanliness that some kind of mechanical handling is necessary if only to keep levels of contamination and breakage to a minimum. Microelectronics companies have pushed forward the development of specialized, computer-controlled equipment for manufacturing, inspecting, and handling chips.

The Institute of Radio Engineers held its first conference on the use of automated equipment in the manufacture of electronic parts in 1954. By 1960, the Western Electric Corporation had constructed a highly automated plant for assembling electrical components called resistors in North Carolina, which became a showpiece for automated production. Yet after the invention of the integrated circuit in 1958, the scale of chip production did not justify robotic handling of the chips, which were simply carried from machine to machine by hand or placed on conveyor belts. Chip manufacturers actually preferred hand labor to automated equipment until the diminishing size of the chips and the extreme level of attention paid to particulate contamination compelled them to isolate the manufacturing process inside closed "microenvironments" in the 1980s. By this time, the cost of robotic arms and similar products had dropped, and the reliability of the systems had risen from a few thousand average hours between failures to over 80,000 hours. While in the 1980s there was considerable talk about "lights out" chip fabrication facilities completely devoid of humans, that goal has proven less attractive over time, as corporations have continued to rely on some operators even in this highly automated industry.

BIBLIOGRAPHY

Adler, Paul S., and Bryan Borys. "Automation and Skill: Three Generations of Research on the NC Case." *Politics and Society* 17 (September 1989): 377–402.

Beniger, James R. *The Control Revolution: Technological and Pronomic Origins of the Information Society.* Cambridge, Mass.: Harvard University Press, 1986.

Bennett, Stuart. *A History of Control Engineering, 1930–1955.* Stevenage, U.K.: Institute of Electrical Engineers, 1993.

Noble, David F. *Forces of Production: A Social History of Industrial Automation.* New York: Knopf, 1984.

David Morton

See also **Aircraft Industry; Assembly Line; Automobile Industry; Mass Production; Robotics.**

AUTOMOBILE.

During the first half of the twentieth century, the automobile evolved from a marginal curiosity to the dominant mode of ground transportation in the United States, spawning a vast network of national interstate highways, spurring the postwar suburban sprawl, opening up unprecedented possibilities of mobility for the average Amreican, but also spawning a host of stubborn social ills: air pollution, traffic jams, road rage, and even a major contribution to global climate change.

Origins and Early Development

Although a smattering of inventors on both sides of the Atlantic worked on developing various forms of automotive technology between 1860 and 1890, German and French inventors were well ahead of their American counterparts by the 1890s in development of the gasoline-powered automobile. In Germany, Gottlieb Daimler and his assistant William Maybach had perfected a four-cycle internal-combustion engine by 1885 and had built four experimental vehicles by 1889. Karl Benz built his first

Early Automobile. The inventor Thomas Alva Edison and his wife sit in a Baker Electric car, powered by Edison-designed batteries. AMERICAN AUTOMOBILE ASSOCIATION

car in 1886 and by 1891 had developed the automobile to the stage of commercial feasibility. In France, Emile Constant Levassor created the basic mechanical arrangement of the modern motorcar in 1891 by placing the engine in front of the chassis, making it possible to accommodate larger, more powerful engines. By 1895, when Levassor drove a car over the 727-mile course of the Paris-Bordeaux-Paris race at the then incredible speed of fifteen miles per hour, automobiles regularly toured the streets of Paris.

The United States lagged well behind. Credit for the first successful American gasoline automobile is generally given to the winners of the *Times-Herald* race held on Thanksgiving Day 1895: Charles E. Duryea and J. Frank Duryea of Springfield, Mass., bicycle mechanics who built their first car in 1893 after reading a description of the Benz car in *Scientific American* in 1889. It is now known that several American inventors built experimental gasoline automobiles prior to the Duryeas, but it was the Duryeas who initiated the manufacture of motor vehicles for a commercial market in the United States in 1896. Allowing for changes of name and early failures, thirty American automobile manufacturers produced an estimated 2,500 motor vehicles in 1899, the first year for which the United States Census of Manufactures compiled separate figures for the automobile industry. The most important of these early automobile manufacturers in volume of product was the Pope Manufacturing Company of Hartford, Conn., also the nation's leading bicycle manufacturer.

After these inauspicious beginnings, the United States emerged in the first decade of the twentieth century as the world's leading car culture. The market for motorcars expanded rapidly as numerous races, tours, and tests demonstrated their strengths, and three transcontinental crossings by automobile in 1903 inaugurated informal long-distance touring by the average driver. The most important organized reliability runs were the Glidden Tours, sponsored annually between 1905 and 1913 by the American Automobile Association. Speed tests and track and road races gave manufacturers publicity for their products and contributed much to the development of automotive technology. Among the early competitions stressing speed, none excited the popular imagination more than the Vanderbilt Cup road races (1904–1916).

Despite a brief but intense reaction between 1900 and 1906 against the arrogance displayed by the owners of automobiles, many of whom sped dangerously through city neighborhoods, kicked up dust on rural roads, and seemed to delight in their ability to spook horses, many Americans displayed great enthusiasm for the motorcar from its introduction. Municipal and state regulations concerning motor vehicles developed slowly, reflected the thinking of the automobile clubs, and typically imposed lighter restrictions than those in European nations. Years before Henry Ford conceived of his universal car for the masses, few people doubted that automobiles were cleaner and safer than the old gray mare. The automobile seemed to fire the imagination of the American people, who provided a large and ready market for the nascent industry's products.

Americans had registered some 458,500 motor vehicles by 1910, making the United States the world's foremost automobile culture. Responding to an unprecedented seller's market for an expensive item, between 1900 and 1910 automobile manufacturing leaped from one hundred and fiftieth to twenty-first in value of product among American industries and became more important to the national economy than the wagon and carriage industry by all measurable economic criteria.

Automobile Manufacturing

Because the automobile was a combination of relatively standard components already being produced for other uses—stationary and marine gasoline engines, and carriage bodies and wheels, for example—early automobile manufacturers merely assembled available components to supply finished cars. The small amount of capital and the slight technical and managerial expertise needed to enter automobile manufacturing were most commonly diverted from other closely related business activities—especially from machine shops and from the bicycle, carriage, and wagon trades. Assemblers met their capital requirements mainly by shifting the burden to parts makers, distributors, and dealers. Manufacturers typically required 20 percent advance cash deposits on orders, with full payment upon delivery; and the assembly process took well less than the thirty- to ninety-day credit period that parts makers allowed. These propitious conditions attracted some 515 companies into automobile manufacturing by 1908, the year in which Henry Ford introduced the Model T and William C. Durant founded General Motors.

The Association of Licensed Automobile Manufacturers (ALAM) attempted to restrict entry into, and severely limit competition within, the automobile industry. This trade association formed in 1903 to enforce an 1895 patent on the gasoline automobile originally applied for in 1879 by George B. Selden, a Rochester, New York, patent attorney. The ALAM, which tended to emphasize higher-priced models that brought high unit profits, sued the Ford Motor Company and several other unlicensed "independents," who were more committed to the volume production of low-priced cars and who made and sold cars without paying royalties to the association. A 1911 written decision sustained the validity of the Selden patent but declared that Ford and others had not infringed upon it because the patent only covered automobiles with a narrowly defined, outdated engine type. To avoid other patent controversies, the newly formed National Automobile Chamber of Commerce (which became the Automobile Manufacturers Association in 1932 and the Motor Vehicle Manufacturers Association in 1972) instituted a cross-licensing agreement among its members in 1914. This patent-sharing arrangement proved to be an effective antimonopoly measure and prevented companies from using the patent system to develop monopoly power within the industry.

Although the pending Selden suit discouraged high-volume production before 1911, some manufacturers experimented with quantity production techniques from an early date. Ransom E. Olds initiated volume production of a low-priced car, but the surrey-influenced design of his $650, one-cylinder, curved-dash Olds (1901–1906) was soon outmoded. The $600, four-cylinder Ford Model N (1906–1907) deserves credit as the first reliable, powerful, low-priced car. The rugged Ford Model T (1908–1927), remarkably adapted to the wretched rural roads of the day, gained almost immediate popularity and caused Ford's share of the market for new cars to skyrocket to roughly 50 percent by the outbreak of World War I.

Mass production techniques—especially the moving-belt assembly line perfected at the Ford Highland Park, Mich., plant in 1913–1914—progressively reduced the price of the Model T to a low of $290 ($2,998 in 2002 dollars) for the touring car by 1927, placing reliable automobiles within reach of most middle-class Americans. Equally significantly, Ford production methods, when applied to the manufacture of many other items, spurred a shift from an economy of scarcity to one of affluence, created a new class of semiskilled industrial workers and opened new opportunities for remunerative industrial employment to unskilled workers. The five-dollar ($89.95 in 2002 dollars), eight-hour day instituted at Ford in 1914—which roughly doubled wages for a shorter workday—dramatically suggested that mass production necessitated mass consumption and mass leisure.

To compete with the Model T's progressively lower prices, the makers of moderately priced cars followed the lead of the piano industry and began extending installment credit to consumers, lowering a major bar to purchase. More than 110 automobile finance corporations existed by 1921, most notably the General Motors Acceptance Corporation, founded in 1919, and by 1926 time sales accounted for about three-fourths of all automobile sales. By the late 1920s, critics complained that this kind of buying, which became increasingly popular for other types of merchandise, too, was causing an erosion of the values of hard work, thrift, and careful saving sanctified in the Protestant ethic and so central to the socioeconomic milieu of perennial scarcity predicted by the classical economists.

Effect of the Automobile

During the 1920s and 1930s the mass adoption of the automobile in the United States left few facets of everyday life untouched, and the young technology became deeply woven into the fabric of the country's economy, mobility patterns, and culture. As cities became larger and denser, industries increasingly sought cheap land on the urban periphery where they could erect the large, horizontally configured factories that mass production techniques necessitated. Wealthier urbanites, too, dispersed into outlying suburban areas, closely trailed by retail stores seeking their patronage. Across rural America, larger trading areas hastened the death of the village general store, cut into small local banks' deposits, forced the mail-order houses to open suburban retail stores, and prompted the large-scale reorganization of both retail and wholesale trades, particularly as they fought to stay afloat during the Great Depression. Urban amenities, too, reached into formerly isolated rural areas, most notably in the form of far better medical care and consolidated schools. The Model T, the motor truck, and the motorized tractor also played a role in the reorganization of the agricultural sector as large-scale agribusiness began to replace the traditional family farm.

Large-scale use of automobiles had a tremendous effect on the cities, too. Public health benefited as horses disappeared from cities; but street life became increasingly hazardous, especially for playing children, and automobile accidents became a major cause of deaths and permanent disabilities. Modern city planning and traffic engineering arose to meet growing traffic and parking problems; and attempts to accommodate the motorcar through longer blocks, wider streets, and narrower sidewalks strained municipal budgets even as they undercut the tax base by encouraging residential dispersal. Parents complained that automobiles undercut their authority by moving courtship from the living room into the rumble seat; police complained that getaway cars made it more difficult to catch crooks. Recreational activities changed, too, as the automobile vacation to the seashore or the mountains became institutionalized and as the Sunday golf game or drive became alternatives to church attendance, the family dinner, and a neighborhood stroll.

By the mid-1920s automobile manufacturing ranked first in value of product and third in value of exports among American industries. The automobile industry had become the lifeblood of the petroleum, steel, plate glass, rubber, and lacquer industries, and the rise of many new small businesses, such as service stations and tourist accommodations, depended on the 26.7 million motor vehicles registered in the United States in 1929—one for every 4.5 persons—and the estimated 198 billion miles they traveled. Construction of streets and highways was the second largest item of governmental expenditure during the 1920s, accounting in 1929 alone for over $2.2 billion in road expenditures, financed in part by $849 million in special motor vehicle taxes, $431 million in gasoline taxes, and the steady expansion of the federal-aid road system that began dispersing funds in 1916.

Improvements in Technology

Improved roads and advances in automotive technology ended the Model T era. As the 1920s wore on, consumers came to demand much more than the Model T's low-cost basic transportation. The self-starter, which superseded the hand crank, gained rapid acceptance after 1911. Closed cars increased from 10.3 percent of production in 1919 to 82.8 percent in 1927, making automobiles year-round, all-weather vehicles. Ethyl gasoline, octane-rated fuels, and better crankshaft balancing led to the high-compression engine in the mid-1920s. By then four-wheel brakes, "balloon" tires, and wishbone front-wheel suspension provided a smoother, safer ride. Mass-produced cars of all colors became possible after quick-drying Duco lacquer made its debut in the "True Blue" of 1924 Oakland. By the mid-1920s, Chevrolet offered a larger, more powerful, and faster six-cylinder car costing only a few hundred dollars more than a Model T.

Thus, Henry Ford's phenomenally successful market strategy—a single, static model at an ever-decreasing price—became outmoded in the 1920s. In its place emerged the General Motors strategy, pioneered by Alfred P. Sloan, Jr., of blanketing the market with cars in several price ranges, constantly upgrading product through research and testing, and changing models annually. And while Henry Ford ran his company as an extension of his personality, General Motors developed the decentralized, multidivisional structure of the modern industrial corporation, becoming the prototype, widely copied after World War II, of the rational, depersonalized business organization run by a technostructure.

Competition sharpened in the late 1920s as the market approached saturation. Replacement demand outpaced demand from initial owners and multiple-car owners combined in 1927, and in 1929 total production peaked at 5.3 million motor vehicles—not again equaled until 1949. The inadequate income distribution of Coolidge prosperity meant a growing backlog of used cars on dealers' lots, and only about a third of all dealers were making money. A trend toward oligopoly in the automobile industry, observable since 1912, accelerated as economies of scale and the vertical integration of operations became more essential for survival. The number of active automobile manufacturers dropped from 108 to 44 between 1920 and 1929; Ford, General Motors, and Chrysler combined for about 80 percent of the industry's output. The 1930s depression shook out most of the remaining independents. Despite mergers among the independents that survived into the post–World War II period, in the mid-1970s only American Motors (formed from Nash-Kelvinator and Hudson in 1954) survived to challenge Detroit's Big Three. New firms, such as Kaiser-Frazer and Tucker, failed in the postwar industry.

The major innovations in modern automotive technology not yet incorporated by the late 1920s were the all-steel body, the infinitely variable automatic transmission, and drop-frame construction, which placed the passenger compartment between rather than upon the axles, lowering the car's height and center of gravity. Increasingly, since the 1930s, auto executives placed emphasis on styling, which the Chrysler "Airflow" models pioneered in the 1930s and which the 1947 Studebaker exemplified. The automatic transmission, introduced in the 1939 Oldsmobile, had by the 1970s become standard equipment along with power brakes, power steering, radios, and air conditioning. A horsepower race in the 1950s, spurred by the high-compression, overhead-cam, V-8 engine, culminated in the "muscle cars" of the late 1960s.

But mounting consumer demand throughout the 1960s for the economical Volkswagen, a number of Japanese-built compacts, and domestic models such as the Nash Rambler and the Ford Mustang reversed, at least temporarily, the industry trend toward larger, more powerful, and more expensive cars, particularly during the energy crises beginning in 1973 and 1979. The major innovations of the 1980s and 1990s grew out of new computer-aided engineering (CAE), design (CAD), and manufacturing (CAM), which helped manufacturers streamline production, reduce the cost and time required to introduce new models, and lower drag coefficients of new car designs. Engineers also made use of electronic sensors and controls, along with new technologies such as fast-burn/lean-burn engines, turbochargers, and continuously variable transmissions, to improve car and engine performance.

The Post–World War II Industry

Before the mid-1980s, the post–World War II American automobile industry could be considered a technologically stagnant industry, though it progressively refined its product and automated its assembly lines. Neither motorcars nor the methods of manufacturing them changed fundamentally over the next generation. Many of the most promising improvements in the internal-combustion engine—such as the Wankel, the stratified charge, and the split-cycle rotary engines—were pioneered abroad, as were the first significant attempts to depart from traditional assembly-line production. Common Market and Japanese producers steadily encroached upon the dominant American manufacturers, who responded to foreign competition by cutting labor costs—heightening factory regimentation, automating assembly lines, and building overseas subsidiaries. Detroit's share of the world market for cars slipped from about three-fourths in the mid-1950s to little more than a third by the mid-1970s. The market share for American manufacturers began a steady rise in the early 1980s, however, as the Big Three cut their overseas subsidiaries, improved the quality of design and manufacturing, and developed new styles of vehicles, such as the minivan and the sport utility vehicle (SUV), that built on their traditional strengths in the large-car market.

Federal legislation affecting the automobile industry proliferated from the New Deal era on. The National Labor Relations Act of 1935 encouraged the unionization of automobile workers, making the UNITED AUTOMOBILE WORKERS OF AMERICA an institution within the automobile industry. The so-called Automobile Dealer's Day in Court Act (Public Law 1026) in 1956 attempted to correct long-standing complaints about the retail selling of automobiles. The Motor Vehicle Air Pollution Act of 1965 and the National Traffic and Motor Vehicle Safety Act of 1966 regulated automotive design, and the 1970 Clean Air Act set stringent antiemission standards, leading to the universal use of catalytic converters. In 1975 the Energy Policy and Conservation Act required automakers' product lines to meet a steadily rising average fuel economy, beginning with 18 mpg in 1978 and rising to 27.5 (later reduced to 26) by 1985. Progressive governmental regulation of the post–World War II automobile industry, however, was accompanied by the massive, indirect subsidization of the Interstate Highway Act of 1956, which committed the federal government to pay, from a Highway Trust Fund, 90 percent of the construction costs for 41,000 miles (later 42,500 miles) of mostly toll-free expressways.

American reliance upon the automobile remained remarkably constant through peace and war, depression and prosperity. Although motor vehicle registrations declined slightly during the Great Depression, causing factory sales to dwindle to a low of 1.3 million units in 1932, the number of miles traveled by motor vehicle actually increased. Full recovery from the Depression was coupled with conversion of the automobile industry to meet the needs of the war effort. Production for the civilian market ceased early in 1942, with tires and gasoline severely rationed during the war. The industry converted to the manufacture of military items, contributing immeasurably to the Allied victory. After the war, pent-up demand and general affluence insured banner sales for Detroit, lasting into the late 1950s, when widespread dissatisfaction with the outcome of the automobile revolution began to become apparent.

Increasingly, in the 1960s, the automobile came to be recognized as a major social problem. Critics focused on its contributions to environmental pollution, urban sprawl, the rising cost of living, and accidental deaths and injuries. Much of the earlier romance of motoring was lost to a generation of Americans, who, reared in an automobile culture, accepted the motorcar as a mundane part of the establishment. While the automobile industry provided one out of every six jobs in the United States, its hegemony had been severely undercut over the preceding decades by proliferation of the size, power, and importance of government, which provided one out of every five jobs by 1970. With increased international involvement on the part of the United States, the rise of a nuclear warfare state, and the exploration of outer space, new industries more closely associated with the military-industrial complex—especially aerospace—became, along with the federal government, more important forces for change than the mature automobile industry.

These considerations notwithstanding, the American automobile culture continued to flourish in the 1960s. Drive-in facilities, automobile races, hot rodders, antique automobile buffs, and recreational vehicle enthusiasts all made their mark. And factory sales (over 11.2 million in 1972), registrations (more than 117 million), and the percentage of American families owning cars (83 percent) all indicated the country's reliance upon, if not necessarily its love for, automobiles. Whatever their problems, automobiles remained powerful cultural symbols of individualism, personal freedom, and mobility, even if certain realities—the industry's resistance to changing consumer demands, increasingly limited transportation alternatives, and lengthening average commutes—exposed some of the cracks in the symbol's veneer.

This phenomenal post–World War II proliferation of the U.S. automobile culture came to an abrupt halt in 1973–1974 with the onset of a worldwide energy crisis. Domestic oil reserves in mid-1973 were reported to be only 52 billion barrels, about a ten-year supply. Experts projected that crude petroleum imports would increase from 27 percent in 1972 to over 50 percent by 1980 and that all known world reserves of petroleum would be exhausted within fifty to seventy years. An embargo by the Arab oil-producing nations resulted, by 1 January 1974, in a ban on Sunday gasoline sales, a national 55-mph speed limit, five- to ten-gallon maximum limitations on gasoline purchases, and significantly higher prices at the pump. Despite short-range easing of the fuel shortage with the lifting of the Arab embargo, the crisis exposed potential limits on the further expansion of mass personal automobility.

The American auto industry was ill-prepared for the marked shift in consumer preference from large cars to smaller, more fuel-efficient alternatives, and, for the first quarter of 1974, Detroit's sales slipped drastically. Large cars piled up on storage lots and in dealers' showrooms, and massive layoffs accompanied the shifting of assembly lines to the production of smaller models. As the share of small cars in the U.S. market more than doubled from 27 percent in 1978 to 61.5 percent by 1981, the market share of imports began a slow and steady rise from 17.7 percent in 1978 to a high of 27.9 percent in 1982, with foreign imports taking over 25 percent of the U.S. market for passenger vehicles through 1990.

By the mid-1980s, however, the American automotive industry had begun a remarkable comeback, although its successes grew from its traditional strengths—big cars and cheap energy—rather than from adapting to the new paradigm that appeared inevitable in the late 1970s. Chrysler, on the verge of bankruptcy in 1979, led the turnaround. After securing a controversial $1.2 billion in federally guaranteed loans, the company promptly shed its overseas operations, modernized its management, and improved the quality of its product under the leadership of its new chief executive, Lee Iacocca. Chrysler's fuel-efficient K-car won awards, but in the long run its more successful innovation was the minivan, which found a highly profitable market niche and opened the door for the development of even larger and more-profitable "sport utility vehicles" (SUVs) in the 1990s. Ford, too, converted its more than $1 billion losses in 1980 and 1981 to profits of $1.87 billion in 1983 and $2.91 billion in 1984 by slashing payrolls, closing plants, and increasing operating efficiencies. With the rise of the SUV and the onset of recessions in Asia and the European Common Market, the percentage of foreign imports in the U.S. market dropped from 25.8 percent in 1990 to 14.9 percent in 1995, its lowest percentage since the late 1960s. And the average weight of American automobiles, which, through the use of lighter-weight materials and smaller designs, had dropped from 3,800 pounds in 1975 to 2,700 pounds in 1985, began a slow but steady march upward.

BIBLIOGRAPHY

Flink, James J. *America Adopts the Automobile, 1895–1910*. Cambridge, Mass.: MIT Press, 1970.

———. *The Car Culture*. Cambridge, Mass.: MIT Press, 1975.

Ingrassia, Paul J., and Joseph B. White. *Comeback: The Fall and Rise of the American Automobile Industry*. New York: Simon and Schuster, 1994.

McShane, Clay. *Down the Asphalt Path: The Automobile and the American City*. New York: Columbia University Press, 1994.

Rae, John Bell. *The American Automobile: A Brief History*. Chicago: University of Chicago Press, 1965.

———. *The Road and the Car in American Life*. Cambridge, Mass.: MIT Press, 1971.

Rothschild, Emma. *Paradise Lost: The Decline of the Auto-Industrial Age*. New York: Random House, 1973.

White, Lawrence J. *The Automobile Industry Since 1945*. Cambridge, Mass.: Harvard University Press, 1971.

James J. Flink
Christopher Wells

See also **Air Pollution; American Automobile Association; Automobile Industry; Automobile Racing; Automobile Safety; Clean Air Act; Gasoline Taxes; Installment Buying, Selling, and Financing; Interstate Highway System; Japan, Relations with; Mass Production; National Labor Relations Act; National Traffic and Motor Ve-**

hicle Safety Act; Oil Crises; Road Improvement Movements; Roads; Selden Patent.

AUTOMOBILE INDUSTRY became the world's largest form of manufacturing by the middle of the twentieth century, making more money and employing more people than any other industry. In the United States, the automobile industry changed how business was conducted and how Americans lived; automobiles were more popular in America than anywhere else in the world.

Origins of the Industry

It was in America that the first three important steps toward automobile manufacture were taken, two of them by Oliver Evans of Philadelphia. During the last two decades of the 1700s, he created an automated flourmill. It took in unprocessed grain and used conveyor belts and screws to transport the grain from step to step, through chaffing, grinding, and packaging, without human intervention. The mill was powered by a steam engine. Evans had not quite invented the assembly line Henry Ford would later use to change how the world manufactured almost everything, but the basic ideas were present: stations for each step in the flour-making process and machines doing the physically strenuous work.

Evans's other significant contribution was the world's first amphibious, fully functioning automobile. In 1805, he completed work on a machine that could be stored on land, driven to the shoreline, and then paddled through the water. It was a dredge for keeping waterways clear. With its steam engine chugging away, Evans' automobile made a great deal of noise as it was driven down to the docks on four large wheels. Once in the water with the paddle wheel attached, the machine could paddle about for several hours. It was the first clear demonstration that a mechanically powered transport could function for hours at a time without falling apart and do practical work.

The other important American in the history of the automobile from Evans's day was Eli Whitney of Connecticut. He developed the concept of interchangeable parts and showed that the concept could be put to practical use: in 1798, he was contracted by the United States government to produce 10,000 muskets that would be identical to each other.

In the 1830s, Charles Goodyear discovered that sulphur mixed with boiling natural rubber created a material that was not prone to melting under friction; this breakthrough would lead to the tires that automobiles would use. In 1832, Walter Hancock of Britain made a steam carriage for personal use. His ideas would quickly evolve into busses that ran regular routes in England, but the English government would outlaw most uses of mechanical power for transportation, dropping England out of the competition for producing practical automobiles.

In 1860, in France, Étienne Lenoir invented a rival to the steam engine, the first practical internal combustion engine. Its advantage over the steam engine was its compactness: it was smaller and lighter. The German engineer Nikolaus Otto refined the internal combustion engine, making it more powerful and more efficient. In 1876, he introduced his four-stroke-cycle compression engine. A compression engine mixes air and fuel, draws the mixture into a chamber, a piston compresses it, and then it is ignited by a spark.

Otto's engine would become the foundation for most internal combustion engines. Almost immediately, it was put to use in automobiles. In some, it generated electricity rather than powering a drive shaft; the electric cars needed no gearshifts and gained or lost power smoothly when in use. These electric cars would be competitive with automobiles with direct drives into the 1920s. Another German, Wilhelm Maybach, invented the carburetor that, by squirting a spray of fuel into air to form the mixture the piston would compress, made possible the use of gasoline in Otto's engine.

In 1879, New Yorker George Baldwin Selden applied for a patent for what he called a "road locomotive." It was the frame of a buckboard with a compression engine underneath the front seat, above the front axel. Selden quickly discovered that the technology of the time needed to catch up to him; the tools for manufacturing his machine were not in general use, so he delayed the patent process until he had financial backing and a market for his device. He and his backers claimed the patent rights to every motor vehicle that used a compression engine, and they made millions of dollars from the manufacturers of cars until they pushed Henry Ford too hard; he took them to court and won in January 1911, breaking their monopoly.

In 1894, the French firm Panhard and Levassor produced an automobile with a V-engine, a water-cooling system, a gearshift transmission, springs under the passengers to cushion the ride, and brakes fitted to wheel hubs. This state-of-the-art automobile was crafted piece by piece, rather than with interchangeable parts, but it is the first automobile to pull together most of the major ingredients of the modern automobile. In 1899, a visionary American, Ransom E. Olds, made the necessary leap of thought to the idea of using interchangeable parts for the purpose of producing automobiles for the masses and soon out produced every other automobile manufacturer in the world; in 1901, he produced the Oldsmobile. Elsewhere in 1899, Henry Ford helped form the Detroit Automobile company. Ford had an idea for a simple-to-maintain automobile that would appeal to farmers. His first effort was taken over by his financial backers, becoming Cadillac. In 1903, Buick Motor Company was founded in Flint, Michigan, while Ford formed the Ford Motor Company in Detroit, Michigan.

Henry Ford and Mass Production

Henry Ford did not invent the automobile, but he did coin the phrase "mass production," and he found a way to excel beyond Olds' efforts by creating a *process* whereby goods could be made so fast, and in such great quantities, that they could be sold for a tiny profit and still earn millions for their manufacturer. In 1903, he produced his first Model A (there was another in 1927). He tried new designs, working up the alphabet until he reached T in 1908. In 1908, he tried reorganizing his factory; it took twelve-and-a-half hours to produce one car, and he realized that he had just about reached the limit for speeds using old, craftsman techniques of fitting parts to automobiles. His ambition was to sell a car to every American home, and he needed to speed up the process of production. Two of his innovations began the mass-production revolution.

One had to do with small parts. At the time, automobile manufacturers used wood for many of their parts because steel was so soft it would warp when heated during the manufacturing process. It took workers many hours to hammer such parts back into shape and to file them until they fit each other. Ford took advantage of a new kind of steel that was hardened during production and therefore would not warp during the manufacturing of an automobile or while the automobile was in use. Ford combined this development with manufacturing-to-gauge: that is, he assigned an exact set of specifications for every part, and all the parts were to be made exactly to those specifications so they did not need to be hammered or filed to fit a particular car; the idea was that if the parts of cars were all mixed together, workers would be able to build the cars while randomly selecting their pieces. Ford was obsessed with manufacturing-to-gauge, and brought his zeal to the work floor of his factory.

With parts made of hardened steel that were universally interchangeable, he was able to effect his other great innovation. He had chassis of his automobiles hitched to ropes and towed the length of his factory. Workers would walk alongside the chassis to piles of parts; each pile was a *station* where the chassis would stop and the workers would add the parts. In 1908, this dropped the production time for a single automobile to under six hours, and his company became the world's largest annual producer of cars.

The Model T became popular. At a little over 900 dollars, it was within the financial reach of middle-class Americans. Even so, Ford wanted the car to be within reach of anyone earning a living wage; this meant faster production and lower overhead. In 1913, he introduced the assembly line, as it would be known even into the twenty-first century. Instead of having workers move to piles of parts, he had the parts moved to them; each station had a worker or a small team of workers who performed one function over and over throughout their long work day. The time to produce one Model T dropped to one-and-a-half hours. In 1914, the price for one Model T dropped to 490 dollars and Ford produced forty-five percent of America's automobiles.

Ford's business practices were considered insane by most manufacturers: in 1915, he shook the manufacturing

Model T. Inexpensive and enormously popular for two decades, "Tin Lizzies" are ready for delivery from the Ford plant in Detroit, 1917. LIBRARY OF CONGRESS

world. He promised customers that if he sold 300,000 Model Ts during the year he would send each purchaser a rebate; when sales exceeded 300,000 he rebated fifty dollars per car. More disturbing to other companies was his doubling the minimum wage of his workers from $2.50 a day to $5.00 a day. It became possible for a Ford worker who stayed on the job for several years to own his own home and automobile and to build a sizeable savings. Ford would go on to advocate shorter working hours and fewer work days, because, he said, mass production enabled a company to meet all of its market demands with shorter work times; in the 1930s, he advocated a thirty-hour work week. In 1917, he bought out his stockholders for $105,250,000, and then he could experiment even more.

He did what he did partly out of idealism and partly because of his memories of being young and poor. Further, he wanted to build worker loyalty; he wanted his workers to have jobs for life with his company. In addition, he wanted to build brand loyalty; he wanted his customers to remember that Ford gave them a fair deal. Not all of his efforts worked. His implementation of the assembly line changed how workers viewed their jobs. No longer craftsmen who would learn how everything in the factory worked, Ford's workers learned only about the function of their specific work stations; status came not from skill but from seniority, and status was not rewarded with increasing responsibilities for the manufacturing process but by moving to the work stations that required the least amount of physical effort. Workers became more like interchangeable parts of the manufacturing process. When Dodge began production in 1915, the lesson became clear: assembly-line workers could easily move to another factory and stand at workstations doing what they had done before. There was another dark side to Ford's achievements: while long-term workers benefited from their loyalty to Ford, on average, a worker lasted three months on the assembly line. The tedium was overwhelming; assembly lines were dangerous and losing limbs was a risk workers took; what came to be known as *repetitive motion* injuries could cripple workers. Automobile manufacturers managed to cover up many of these problems well into the 1920s, but they were a constant tax on production.

1920–1950

By 1920, the automobile industry was shaking down to a small number of competitors. A recession in 1921 caught small manufacturers without enough cash on hand to operate their factories. During the 1920s, the big two manufacturers were Ford and General Motors (GM), with a young Chrysler Motor Corporation, established in 1925, gaining ground. In 1920, the luxury carmaker Dusenberg introduced four-wheel brakes and a straight-eight engine. In 1924, Hudson introduced an enclosed sedan as a standard release, costing the same as its open car, $895.00. Further, ethylene glycol antifreeze was invented. These two innovations meant that manufacturers could produce all-weather cars that could withstand cold and shelter their drivers.

In 1925, the last strong challenge to the internal combustion engine ended when the versatile Stanley Steamer ceased being manufactured. Journalists had been predicting the "saturation" of the automobile market for over a decade, claiming automobile sales had to decline once everyone who wanted a car had a car; they had long been wrong. In 1925, Alfred P. Sloan, Jr., who ran GM, suggested that the time was coming when the saturation of the market would have to be dealt with, and he suggested what would later be called "planned obsolescence" as the solution. Change the style every year to make older styles seem out of date. By 1927, GM's Chevrolet division was outselling Ford. Meanwhile, Chrysler bought out Dodge and in 1928, launched Plymouth and De Soto.

It was in 1928 that automakers began to make planned obsolescence a reality, but in the early 1930s, the industry was hit hard by the Great Depression. From 1931 to 1932, nine thousand auto dealerships went out of business, although neither Ford nor GM lost even one. Because of its virtues of being inexpensive and durable, the Ford Model A, introduced in 1927, helped Ford retake its lead in sales in a much diminished market. In 1933, Chrysler introduced aerodynamic designing, but its futuristic offering did not fit public tastes in hard times.

Unionization hit the industry in the 1930s. Ford was outraged, viewing his workers as ungrateful, but his reaction was mild compared to the violence GM used to discourage unionization of its plants. Even so, the major automakers eventually signed collective bargaining agreements with the United Auto Workers. In 1942, the automotive industry almost came to a stop because the United States had entered World War II. The government ordered the automobile companies to produce war supplies, and this they did. The Ford Motor Company had been taken over by Henry Ford II, grandson of the founder, and he was beginning to reshape the company in 1941. During the war, Ford applied its mass production principles to manufacturing heavy bombers. By the end of the war, it was producing a B-24 bomber every sixty-three minutes. To GM fell the manufacturing of tanks. The GM management rethought their manufacturing process, introducing teams of workers who ran their work stations and a new whole chassis welding process that encouraged workers to be their own quality managers.

1950–1980

In 1945, Henry Kaiser founded Kaiser-Frazer Corporation and began manufacturing innovative automobiles. In 1954, Nash and Hudson merged to form American Motors. The big three in automobile production were GM, first, Chrysler, second, and Ford, third. At the time, about seventeen percent of American-made automobiles were sold in foreign countries. Ford was especially well positioned for sales in Europe with factories in England and elsewhere on the continent. The "Big Three" did not seem to care about what was happening in Japan during the 1950s.

The Japanese were listening to American management consultant W. Edwards Deming, who told them they should produce high-quality, durable products, and stand behind their quality with warranties in order to sell their wares internationally. Not all Japanese manufacturers believed Deming, but some invested everything they had into Deming's ideas. One such company was Toyota, who developed the "Toyota Production System." They encouraged worker suggestions for improving products as well as procedures and they created teams of workers who were responsible for the quality of their workstations' performances, which they called *kaizen*. During the 1950s and 1960s, planned obsolescence governed the American auto industry; the fiasco in 1957 of the Ford Easel came about in part because it was not at all innovative in performance or design.

Meanwhile, the world and Americans were changing fast. By the end of the 1960s, people who had never been in a coalmine were dying of black lung disease in polluted cities such as New York and Los Angeles. In the early 1970s, the United States Congress mandated cleaner-burning automobile engines and set standards for automobile safety. The Japanese were ready with cars that met the standards; the Americans were not. Then in 1973, the Organization of Petroleum Exporting Countries (OPEC) cut back steeply on exports, gasoline prices rose steeply, and Americans had to wait in long lines at gas stations because of gasoline shortages. Since the 1920s, automobile manufacturers knew that Americans preferred big cars over small ones. A forty-miles-per-gallon automobile, the Crassly Hotshot, had been produced in the 1940s but had disappeared because of poor sales. In the 1970s, Americans wanted small, gas efficient cars. The Japanese had them.

In 1977, more American automobiles were recalled because of faulty parts or construction than were actually built during the year. In 1979, Chrysler almost went bankrupt, and only earnest pleas for help from charismatic company president Lee Iacocca won the federal loan guarantees the company needed in order to continue operations.

Meeting the Japanese Challenge

In 1980, America's automakers lost 1.8 billion dollars. In 1980, Japanese automobiles outsold American automobiles worldwide for the first time. Yet, in that year, American automobile companies invested seventy billion dollars to reconstruct their plants. They were putting computers into their cars to manage fuel, the shifting of gears, and other aspects of cars, to make driving them more efficient and with less wear and tear. The Texaco Controlled-Combustion System, invented in the 1940s, allowed automobiles to burn almost any fuel efficiently, and engines that ran on methanol, coal dust, and natural gas were created.

Meanwhile, Japanese manufacturers ran into problems. The most important one was their dependence on foreign imports of raw materials. Another problem was the saturation level: they were running out of markets for their small cars, and without high volume sales, it was hard to earn profits making them. Thus, Japanese manufacturers began to shift toward making more expensive large automobiles with luxury features; they could make a higher profit per car for the large ones than for the smaller ones. Further, the Japanese yen had been strong against the American dollar for many years, helping make Japanese cars cheaper than American ones. By 1985, the yen had dropped against the dollar, adding two thousand dollars to the price of a Japanese automobile in America.

In 1987, Chrysler bought out American Motors and showed its renewed financial strength by paying back its loans early. GM showed that there was still life in the idea of worker participation in quality management by beginning, in June 1982 (but publicly announced in 1983), a new car division for the Saturn, the first of which was manufactured 15 September 1984. The car depended on its reputation for high quality to succeed in the American market. In Japan, automobile manufacturers depended heavily on robots to man their workstations, whereas American companies did not. What seemed to make economic sense in the 1980s, proved a money pit for the Japanese. They discovered that while they saved money from laying off workers who were replaced by robots, they were spending extra money on the people who maintained the robots and programmed the robots' computers. Plus, *kaizen* was disappearing as the workers who could have made constructive suggestions were laid off. The result was that by 1995, American automobile makers regained their dominant position in the marketplace.

BIBLIOGRAPHY
"The Arsenals of Progress." *The Economist* (US) 330, no. 7853 (5 March 1994): M5–7.
De Camp, L. Sprague, and Catherine C. De Camp. *The Story of Science in America.* New York: Charles Scribner's Sons, 1967.
Grove, Noel. "Swing Low, Sweet Chariot!: The Automobile and the American Way." *National Geographic* (June 1983): 2–35.
Hapgood, Fred. "Keeping It Simple." *Inc.* 18, no. 4 (19 March 1996): 66–70.
Ingrassia, Paul J., and Joseph B. White. *Comeback: The Fall and Rise of the American Automobile Industry.* New York: Simon & Schuster, 1994.
Kerson, Roger. "Ending the Bends." *Technology Review* 89 (April 1986): 6.
Showalter, Williamm Joseph. "The Automobile Industry: An American Art That Has Revolutionized Methods of Manufacturing and Transformed Transportation." *National Geographic* 44, no. 4 (October 1923): 337–414.
Sloan, Alfred P., Jr. *My Years with General Motors.* New York: Doubleday, 1972.
Smith, Philip Hillyer. *Wheels within Wheels: A Short History of American Motor Car Manufacturing.* New York: Funk & Wagnalls, 1968. By someone who actually lived the history.
"Toyota's New Bombshell." *World Press Review* 42, no. 6 (June 1995): 33.
Womack, James P., Daniel T. Jones, and Daniel Roos. *The Machine That Changed the World: How Japan's Secret Weapon in the Global Auto Wars Will Revolutionize Western Industry.* New York: Maxwell Macmillan International, 1990.

Kirk H. Beetz

See also **Air Pollution; Assembly Line; Ford Motor Company; General Motors; Mass Production; Steam Power and Engines; United Automobile Workers of America;** *and* *vol. 9:* **Ford Men Beat and Rout Lewis.**

AUTOMOBILE RACING. On 28 November 1895, the *Chicago Times Herald* sponsored the first automobile race held in the United States. Its purposes were to test American cars and promote the nascent automobile industry. The winning speed, in a Duryea car, was 7.5 miles per hour (mph). The first series of races on American soil was organized in 1900 by Gordon Bennett, the owner of the *New York Herald*, with national automobile clubs of entrant nations choosing teams of three cars to compete on open roads. With a variety of mechanical and design improvements, race speeds had increased significantly and fatal accidents were not uncommon, involving both drivers and spectators.

First U.S. Auto Race. A photograph taken in 1895, when the winning speed was 7.5 mph. AMERICAN AUTOMOBILE ASSOCIATION

The years from 1904 to 1910 saw the first Vanderbilt Cup street races on Long Island, organized by William K. Vanderbilt and held despite both legal threats and public misgivings. The first race, held on 8 October 1904 and sanctioned by the new American Automobile Association, had eighteen entrants on a 30.24-mile course mostly through Nassau County in New York. In 1906 the race attracted 250,000 spectators, but because of safety concerns it was canceled in 1907, resuming the following year after the Long Island Motor Parkway was built.

In 1908, the Savannah Automobile Club hosted the first American Grand Prize race. The original seventeen-mile course, built in 1904, was expanded to 25.13 miles. Present were sixteen thousand crowd-control marshals and thirty doctors. There were fourteen European and six American entries. The Gold Cup prize for the race was $5,000, twice that of the Vanderbilt Cup. Production cars were introduced to the American Grand Prize in 1909. Governed by the Automobile Club de France rules, the American Grand Prize was now the main American race entered by European drivers.

Also in 1909, the first closed-circuit dirt track was opened in Indianapolis, Indiana, by a group of automobile manufacturers to test the endurance of American-made automobiles, but this "stock car" testing course was later transformed into a racing speedway. The inaugural race was called the Indianapolis 500 and was run on Memorial Day in 1911. The Indy 500 continues to be run on Memorial Day every year.

In 1914, the Santa Monica speedway was established to host both the Vanderbilt Cup and the American Grand Prize. The 8.4 mile course along the Pacific shoreline included a ninety-degree left turn known as Death Curve. After a year in San Francisco, the races were again held

in Santa Monica in 1916, the last time an American Grand Prize was held on a road course until the Vanderbilt Cup was held in New York in 1936.

The first major race after World War I was the Indianapolis 500 on 30 May 1919, in which Arthur Thurman was killed and Louis LeCocq and his mechanic were burned to death when their car overturned and caught fire. The Americans Howdy Wilcox and Eddie Hearne took first and second place, respectively. In 1921, American driver Jimmy Murphy won the French Grand Prix at Le Mans with a time of 4 hours, 7 minutes, and 11.2 seconds. The total distance was 322 miles at a speed of 79.04 mph.

The first world championship race was held in 1925 at the Indianapolis 500, a contest between manufacturers rather than drivers, but escalating costs subsequently forced manufacturers to abandon racing car production for nearly a decade. In 1928, racing rules changed from a strict formula based on engine size and weight to Formula Libre rules, with drivers in partnership with such racing car specialists as Alfa Romeo, Maserati, Bugatti, and in 1930, Scuderia Ferrari.

In 1935, at the Bonneville Salt Flats in Utah, the British racer Sir Malcolm Campbell became the first driver to go faster than three hundred miles per hour. On 12 October 1936, the first three-hundred-mile Vanderbilt Cup race at the new Roosevelt Raceway was held. For the first time, the European Auto Union and Mercedes entered drivers. The race was won by the German racer Bernd Rosemeyer driving for Auto Union. The Roosevelt Raceway was a post-depression attempt to resurrect international motor racing in the United States by Eddie Rickenbacker and a group of Wall Street financiers, who established the Motor Development Corporation to create a racing circuit for the best European and American drivers and automobiles. Designer Mark Linenthal, however, failed to deliver a suitable venue. Afterward, international road racing took place primarily in Europe until 1959.

Broad public interest in stock car racing lead to the formation of the National Association for Stock Car Auto Racing (NASCAR) at Daytona Beach in 1947. Stock car racing enjoys wide popularity and is the fastest growing spectator sport in the world. The 1990s in particular saw major growth in the sport's popularity primarily due to NASCAR's proactive marketing efforts and television's hunger for ratings. With inventions such as in-car and bumper-mounted cameras, fans watching the races on television were able to feel as if they were in the middle of the action. Additionally, in a society enamored of superstars, race drivers, more so than other sports figures, are accessible to their fans, typically having come from small towns in the South and racing in venues that are far removed from Hollywood or New York City. In 2001, NASCAR had a broader television viewership than Major League Baseball, the National Basketball Association, the National Hockey League, and the Women's National

Auto Race near Washington, D.C., c. 1922. The cars are lining up on an elevated track prior to the start. © CORBIS

Basketball Association. In 2001, Fox, NBC, and TNT (Turner Television) signed a six-year, $2.4 billion deal for NASCAR's television rights. (In comparison, NASCAR received only $3 million for its television rights in 1985.) Fox's television viewership in 2001 averaged 5.2 million fans per broadcast race (a 41 percent increase over the previous year), and NBC and TNT television viewership in the same year averaged 3.9 million viewers per race (a 35 percent increase over the previous year). NASCAR conducts stock car races under the auspices of its Grand National Division. The Sports Car Club of America (SCCA), established in Westport, Connecticut, in 1945, oversees sports car racing in the United States. Additionally, the National Hot Rod Association (NHRA), founded in Los Angeles in 1951, sponsors drag racing at the Winternationals in Los Angeles, the Springnationals in Bristol, Tennessee, a national meet in Indianapolis, and a World Championship race in Tulsa, Oklahoma. The NHRA, the SCCA, NASCAR, and the United States Auto Club belong to the Automobile Competition Committee of the United States (ACCUS), which is the U.S. representative to the Federation Internationale de l'Automobile (FIA), the controlling body of automobile racing worldwide since World War II.

In 1950, the first World Championship for drivers was held based on the results of the British, Swiss, Monaco, Belgium, French, and Italian Grand Prix and the Indianapolis 500. The Indy 500 was included to promote Grand Prix racing in America.

The U.S. Grand Prix, the first American Formula One (F1) race since the American Grand Prize series from 1908 to 1916, was held at the Sebring, Florida, air base in 1959. There were nineteen entrants, including six Americans. The American Bruce McLaren was the youngest driver to win an F1 race. In 1961, the U.S. Grand Prix was relocated to Watkin's Glen, New York, one of the best U.S. tracks, comparable to Monza and Silverstone. Wat-

kin's Glen hosted Grand Prix races through 1980. The first U.S. Grand Prix West was held at Long Beach, California, in 1975. Other Grand Prix circuits included Long Island (1904–1910, birthplace of the Vanderbilt Cup); San Francisco (1915, on a 3.84-mile circuit constructed on landfill in the San Francisco Bay); Riverside, California (1960); Long Beach, California (1976–1983, considered the third best street course in the world after Monaco and Adelaide); Las Vegas (1981–1982, a "parking lot" course, that is, not a street course or circuit course built purposefully for racing, but literally a parking lot used as a race track); Detroit (three races in 1982); Dallas (1984–1985); and Phoenix (1989–1991, the last year a Grand Prix was held in the United States).

BIBLIOGRAPHY

Brown, Allan E. *The History of the American Speedway: Past and Present.* Marne, Mich.: Slideways Publications, 1984.

Macgowan, Robin, and Graham Watson. *Kings of the Road: A Portrait of Racers and Racing.* Champaign, Ill.: Leisure Press, 1987.

Christine E. Hoffman

See also **American Automobile Association; Automobile; Automobile Industry.**

AUTOMOBILE SAFETY. Until the 1950s, Americans paid little attention to the problem of automobile safety. The typical American automobile had dashboards with numerous hard protrusions, no seatbelts, poor brakes and tires, noncollapsible steering columns, doors that opened on impact, soft seats and suspension systems, and windshield glass that shattered easily. These features were the consequence of manufacturer neglect, consumer preferences, the psychology of driving, and the failure of the government to further public interest in this matter.

Not surprisingly, more than thirty thousand Americans died as a result of traffic accidents in 1950, and that number increased to more than fifty thousand two decades later. Despite obvious evidence to the contrary, industry representatives maintained that drivers and their behaviors, not automobile design features, caused accidents and injuries. Nevertheless, several forces for change converged during the late 1950s and the early 1960s. Indeed, by the end of the 1960s, the previously unassailable industry was brought to its knees by the rising tide of public opinion, regulatory legislation, and a newly created federal government bureaucracy.

One major reason for the new emphasis on auto safety came as a result of enhanced technical knowledge about the "second crash," that is, the collision of the automobile's passengers with the interior after the initial exterior impact. Wartime studies at Wright-Patterson Air Force Base and Cornell University Medical College in New York on aircraft cockpit injuries were subsequently extended to similar phenomena inside automobiles at the Cornell Aeronautical Laboratory. Evidence from these studies, coupled with the work of the Detroit plastic surgeon Claire Straith on "guest" passenger injuries, clearly suggested that relatively simple design modifications could save lives and prevent serious injuries. In 1955 and 1956 the industry was confronted with these facts and failed to respond with enthusiasm. The industry thus lost any chance to remain autonomous with regard to safety and design, and federal legislation addressing design safety passed a decade later.

The convergence of forces for change took the industry by total surprise in the months immediately after the presidential election of 1964. The willingness of the administration of Lyndon B. Johnson to sponsor social reform legislation and the appearance on the Washington scene of Ralph Nader, Abraham Ribicoff, and the American Trial Lawyers' Association are only part of the story. Additionally, widespread consumer dissatisfaction with the American automobile industry, its practices, and its increasingly defective products contributed to the realization that auto safety was a good political issue and news story.

In 1966, Congress passed the National Traffic and Motor Vehicle Safety Act, establishing the National Highway Traffic Safety Administration (NHTSA) within the Department of Commerce. This agency created standards for production vehicles that included recessed and padded dashes, dual braking systems, standard bumper heights, safety door latches, and impact-absorbing steering columns. The scope of the NHTSA was later expanded to include mandated public recall of defective vehicles, seat belt enforcement issues, and an active campaign to introduce passive restraints, including air bags. Ever at the center of controversy, the NHTSA continued in the early twenty-first century to have its detractors as well as supporters, the former arguing that enhanced safety features have in reality done little to change the incidence of automobile deaths and injuries, events that ultimately must be traced to driver judgment and behavior.

BIBLIOGRAPHY

Drew, Elizabeth Brenner. "The Politics of Auto Safety." *Atlantic Monthly* 218 (October 1966): 95–105.

Eastman, Joel W. *Styling vs. Safety: The American Automobile Industry and the Development of Automotive Safety, 1900–1966.* Lanham, Md.: University Press of America, 1984.

Flink, James J. *The Automobile Age.* Cambridge, Mass.: MIT Press, 1988.

John Heitmann

See also **Automobile Industry; Consumer Protection;** *Unsafe at Any Speed.*

AUTOMOBILE WORKERS V. JOHNSON CONTROLS, INC.,

499 U.S. 187 (1991), a Supreme Court case that found an employer's fetal protection policy to be invalid under federal antidiscrimination laws. Johnson Controls had established a protection policy excluding fertile women but not men from jobs exposing workers to lead during the manufacture of batteries. Lower federal courts ruled that the employer's concern for protecting the next generation as well as potential liability for birth defects took precedence over equal employment opportunities for women. The Supreme Court, however, held that Title VII of the Civil Rights Act of 1964 and the Pregnancy Discrimination in Employment Act of 1978 prevented this type of employment discrimination against women. Moreover, because males also faced risk to their reproductive capacities from lead exposure, the facts of the case indicated discrimination based solely on gender and childbearing ability.

Johnson Controls failed to prove that its gender discrimination was a legitimate sexually based bona fide occupational qualification for the manufacture of batteries. According to the Court, Congress intended in its legislation to let women and their families, not employers, decide for themselves as to the relative importance of economic and reproductive roles. Considering that tens of millions of industrial jobs could have been denied to women applicants if the lower-court decisions had stood, *Automobile Workers v. Johnson Controls* was widely regarded as one of the most important sex discrimination cases since 1964 and a landmark in the abortion debate over fetal rights.

BIBLIOGRAPHY

Baer, Judith A. *Women in American Law.* New York: Holmes and Meier, 1996.

Sullivan, George M., and William A. Nowlin. "Gender-Based Fetal Protection Policies: Impermissible Sex Discrimination." *Labor Law Journal* 42 (July 1991).

Gilbert J. Gall/A. R.

See also **Abortion; Discrimination: Sex; Pregnancy Discrimination Act.**

AVIATION.

See **Air Transportation and Travel; Aircraft Industry.**

AWAKENING, SECOND.

The term refers to a resurgence of religious activity from the close of the eighteenth century through the first decades of the nineteenth century. This designation covers a wide variety of religious movements and trends that defy simple categorizations.

The first indications of a religious revival in New England emerged in the 1790s in Connecticut, where Trinitarian clergy feared the nation had suffered a decline in religious values following the Revolution, as evidenced by the appearances of unitarianism and deism. Although undoubtedly exaggerated, this perception contributed to the rise of ministers such as Timothy Dwight, Asahel Nettleton, Lyman Beecher, and Nathaniel William Taylor, who at the opening of the nineteenth century commenced a series of revivals that generally sustained the Congregational Standing Order.

Timothy Dwight. President of Yale University from 1795 until his death in 1817, Congregational minister, and an early leader of the religious revival known as the Second Awakening. LIBRARY OF CONGRESS

Soon the revivals spread beyond New England and moved away from their conservative origins. The "burned-over district" of upstate New York became the center for extensive revivals that lasted through the 1830s. Led by such ministers as Charles G. Finney, revivalists not only instigated a wave of religious enthusiasm but also challenged more traditional Calvinist theology and methods. Consternation over Finney's flagrant challenges to the existing ministerial system in New York produced the acrimonious New Lebanon Conference of 1827. For a short time Finney seemed to move closer to more conventional Presbyterians and Congregationalists. His revival in Rochester during the winter of 1830–1831 was one of the most successful of the era and a model for future revivals.

In time, however, some aspects of the Second Awakening drifted even further away from traditional Calvinism. After leaving the Presbyterian community in 1835, Finney embraced a perfectionist theology, which asserted that all humans are fully capable of perfect compliance with God's laws. William Miller's predictions of the end of the earth in 1843 and 1844 found a substantial audience, especially in northern New York.

Revivals occurred concurrently within the South and Southwest. Methodism experienced a remarkable growth during the last quarter of the eighteenth century. By the beginning of the nineteenth century the Second Awakening was manifested in camp meetings. Apparently beginning with small encampments near revivals, camp meetings grew into spectacular events, culminating with the revival at Cane Ridge, Kentucky in 1801. Thereafter the religious culture of the region reflected the camp-meeting style. Denominations such as the Church of Christ, led by Barton Stone, the Disciples of Christ, led by Alexander Campbell, and the Cumberland Presbyterians, led by James McGready, entered the American religious scene at this time. The Baptists also expanded from their dissenting origins into a major denomination.

Beginning with a handful of people during postrevolutionary years, Methodism grew to approximately 250,000 communicants by 1816. The earliest growth came within the Delmarva Peninsula, where the quarterly meetings spurred religious growth even before the camp meetings affected the religious climate. With an organizational structure that encouraged rapid expansion and supported by a system of circuit riders, the Methodists proved exceptionally adapted to the growing population in the western regions. The denomination's emphasis upon human ability was suited for the climate of the Second Awakening.

Within the nation's two major Calvinist denominations, the Congregationalists and the Presbyterians, the Second Awakening produced mixed results. These denominations grew, although at a slower pace than the Methodists. Nevertheless, this growth was marred by bitter theological disputes. The New Haven or New School theology developed under the leadership of Taylor and his adherents made significant modifications to the traditional Calvinist tenets of God's sovereignty to allow for greater emphasis upon human freedom. The concerns of traditional Calvinists eventually resulted in the schism of the Presbyterian Church in 1837.

The combination of increased religious activity with a theology that emphasized human abilities also contributed to a growing number of antebellum reform movements. Missionary enterprises, Sabbath observance, religious instruction, and temperance movements were especially compatible with the religious trends of the Second Awakening. The reform impulse was powerful among the New School Congregationalists and Presbyterians. Under the leadership of such men as Beecher, Protestant ministers energetically promoted these causes through voluntary societies supplemented by political action where necessary. Later in the nineteenth century antislavery movements flourished among the same religious elements that were prominent in the Second Awakening.

Historical treatment of the Second Awakening has been as varied as the phenomenon itself. Historians who see the movement as an expression of optimism in human nature emphasize the departures from traditional Calvinist religion, particularly the perfectionist theology of Finney. Other historians have interpreted religious activity as a means of exerting social control over a rapidly changing society. For these historians Beecher and Dwight, with their emphasis upon a settled order, were more typical figures of the Second Awakening. Another interpretation of the period emphasizes the democratic trends of denominations that appealed to a wider range of social classes, especially such denominations as the Methodists or the Disciples of Christ.

The long-term effect of the Second Awakening expanded and deepened the religious foundations of the early Republic. Even as the nation grew dramatically during these years, churches demonstrated a vibrancy and an adaptability that endured throughout the nineteenth century.

BIBLIOGRAPHY

Conkin, Paul K. *The Uneasy Center: Reformed Christianity in Antebellum America*. Chapel Hill: University of North Carolina Press, 1995.

Cross, Whitney R. *The Burned-Over District: The Social and Intellectual History of Enthusiastic Religion in Western New York, 1800–1850*. Ithaca, N.Y.: Cornell University Press, 1950.

Hatch, Nathan O. *The Democratization of American Christianity*. New Haven, Conn.: Yale University Press, 1989.

Heyrman, Christine Leigh. *Southern Cross: The Beginnings of the Bible Belt*. Chapel Hill: University of North Carolina Press, 1998.

Hirrel, Leo P. *Children of Wrath: New School Calvinism and Antebellum Reform*. Lexington: University Press of Kentucky, 1998.

Hood, Fred J. *Reformed America: The Middle and Southern States, 1783–1837*. University: University of Alabama Press, 1980.

Johnson, Paul E. *A Shopkeeper's Millennium: Society and Revivals in Rochester, New York, 1815–1837*. New York: Hill and Wang, 1978.

Keller, Charles Roy. *The Second Great Awakening in Connecticut*. New Haven, Conn.: Yale University Press, 1942.

Shiels, Richard D. "The Second Great Awakening in Connecticut: A Critique of the Traditional Interpretation." *Church History* 49 (December 1980): 401–415.

Walters, Ronald G. *American Reformers, 1815–1860*. 2d ed. New York: Hill and Wang, 1997.

Wigger, John H. *Taking Heaven by Storm: Methodism and the Rise of Popular Christianity in America*. New York: Oxford University Press, 1998.

Leo P. Hirrel

See also **Evangelicalism and Revivalism; Great Awakening; Religion and Religious Affiliation.**

BABY BELLS. In response to efforts by the U.S. Department of Justice to split up the company, American Telephone and Telegraph (AT&T) signed a consent decree in 1984 divesting itself of seven regional telecommunications companies. These companies included Bell Atlantic, Bell South, NYNEX, Pacific Telesis, Southwestern Bell, Ameritech, and U.S. West, collectively known as the Baby Bells. The Baby Bells were restricted from offering long distance services, and were required to offer customers equal access to all long distance providers. Passage of the Telecommunications Act of 1996 removed these impediments. Now any company can offer local or long distance service. The breakup of AT&T is credited with reducing long-distance phone rates and fostering more competition on the local level. For the Baby Bells, the transition to long distance carriers was relatively smooth. They managed to provide relatively inexpensive service and maintain both a trained work force and a loyal customer base. Despite the inroads they made into the long distance market, estimated to yield $68 billion in annual profits, the Baby Bells encountered difficulties in the closing years of the 1990s. Through various acquisitions and mergers, four new Baby Bells emerged. Qwest was formed in 1999 by a merger of U.S. West and Qwest Communications. Verizon was formed when Bell Atlantic (which had previously merged with GTE) merged with NYNEX in 1999, a $21 billion merger, the second largest in U.S. history; this merger created the nation's second largest telecommunications company, behind only AT&T itself. SBC Communications was formed from a merger between SBC and Ameritech in 2000. This left Bell South Communications as the only original Baby Bell. Although the Baby Bells operate in a regulated industry, matters were complicated by complaints of price gouging, poor service, and refusal to work with smaller local and long distance companies. The companies have frequently resorted to lawsuits to protect their interests. An analysis of local Bell phone markets published in *U.S. News* during 1996 showed the consumer-complaint rate had climbed 20 percent since 1991 and reached a five-year high in 1995. Officials in a number of states are responding to the service problems by hitting local phone companies with fines and penalties. At one point, the Baby Bells appeared ready to jump into the long distance and data businesses with little threat to their local residential markets.

But competition for customers in local markets was so great, particularly as the Baby Bells found themselves contesting with AT&T and other broadband cable companies such as Comcast and Cox, that business suffered. During the fourth quarter of 2001, for example, the cable industry added nearly 923,000 broadband subscribers, nearly twice as many as the 540,000 customers who opted for the Bells' comparable high-speed digital subscriber line (DSL) Internet service. In addition, the Baby Bells also faced increasing competition from cable companies that now offer local telephone services. Finally, they must come to terms with the problem of wireless communications that are eroding traditional local phone service. According to a study published in 2002, approximately 3 percent of Americans have already disconnected their traditional phone service and rely entirely on cellular phones. The study predicted the use of wireless phones would nearly double by 2005. By contrast, the study forecasts that traditional wireline minutes will drop by 22 percent. The Baby Bells have tried to meet the challenge by forming their own wireless companies such as Verizon Wireless, a joint venture of Verizon and the European mobile phone company Vodafone, and Cingular, which is a partnership between SBC and BellSouth.

BIBLIOGRAPHY
Elstrom, Peter. "Will the Baby Bells Crack Too?" *Business Week* (June 18, 2001), p. 112–114.
Kushnick, Bruce A. *The Unauthorized Biography of the Baby Bells & Info-Scandal.* New York: New Networks Institute, 1998.
Stone, Alan. *Wrong Number: The Breakup of AT&T.* New York: Basic Books, 1989.

Meg Greene Malvasi

See also **AT&T; Government Regulation of Business; Telecommunications; Telecommunications Act.**

BABY BOOM. *See* **Demography and Demographic Trends.**

BACKCOUNTRY AND BACKWOODS. The term "backwoodsman" became common when pioneers began advancing the frontier into and beyond the mountains of Pennsylvania, Virginia, and the Carolinas, regions which came to be known to the coastal states as the backcountry. For generations after the great westward movement began (about 1769–1770), this backcountry, comprising the present Middle West, West Virginia, Kentucky, Tennessee, and other inland areas farther south, was predominantly forest. Until 1800 few roads fit for wheeled vehicles existed, and most people traveled by water or by mere horse trail. There were still only a few small cleared areas in southwestern Virginia (present-day Kentucky) when, in 1776, the settlers chose two agents to ask for protection of Virginia. As a result, Kentucky County was created, and in 1777 it sent two burgesses to the Virginia legislature.

During the American Revolution backwoodsmen under George Rogers Clark took Kaskaskia (July) and Vincennes (December)—both in Illinois—from the British in 1778. In Tennessee they first organized the Watauga Association and then the State of Franklin. An undisciplined but efficient army of backwoodsmen defeated Maj. Patrick Ferguson's force at the Battle of King's Mountain, in western North Carolina. Later, under their idol, Andrew Jackson, they fought the CREEK WAR and won the Battle of New Orleans. Their prowess in war bred in them a group consciousness and pride. On Jackson's inauguration as president in 1829, the backwoodsmen flocked to Washington and made the occasion, including the White House reception, so turbulent and uproarious that old Federalists and Whigs thought the era of mob rule had come. During that period the word "backwoodsman" acquired a disgraceful connotation that it never afterward lost.

BIBLIOGRAPHY

Clark, Thomas Dionysius. *Frontier America: The Story of the Westward Movement.* 2d ed. New York: Scribners, 1969.

Roosevelt, Theodore. *The Winning of the West.* In *Works.* New York: Scribners, 1923–1926.

Alvin F. Harlow / c. w.

See also **Clark's Northwest Campaign; Franklin, State of; New Orleans, Battle of; Revolution, American: Military History; Westward Migration.**

BACKLASH. In the mid-1950s the word "backlash" entered the American political lexicon. Initially, it referred to the hostile reaction of conservative Democratic southerners to the liberal stance adopted by the national party on domestic issues, particularly race relations. Passage of the CIVIL RIGHTS ACT OF 1957 increased the alienation of southern Democrats. In the 1960s the term achieved prominence, and its application spread to the North. The national Democratic Party adopted a series of reform programs, such as the Economic Opportunity Act of 1964, the CIVIL RIGHTS ACT OF 1964, the VOTING RIGHTS ACT OF 1965, and the Open Housing Act of 1968, that evoked opposition among traditional Democratic

supporters. "Backlash" came to mean the hostile response to these initiatives among blocs of rank-and-file voters considered Democrats since at least the New Deal era.

During the 1960s the term increasingly identified voters who supported the presidential candidacy of George C. Wallace. In 1964 Wallace entered several northern Democratic primaries and captured a significant minority of the vote. In his 1968 presidential bid, Wallace also benefited from the backlash of white citizens. Nevertheless, at this time "backlash" characterized not only regular Democrats' reactions against reform legislation and support for Wallace but also, more generally, resistance to reform among white citizens who felt that Afro-Americans were demanding too much, too fast, with too much violence. According to some observers, when nonviolent protest by Afro-Americans quickly gave way to massive civil disorder, backlash against these events even consisted of a change in attitudes among previously supportive white citizens, many of whom recoiled against the demands by Afro-Americans for equality of treatment in housing, education, law enforcement, and employment.

BIBLIOGRAPHY

Carter, Dan T. *The Politics of Rage: George Wallace, the Origins of the New Conservatism, and the Transformation of American Politics.* New York: Simon and Schuster, 1995.

Cohodas, Nadine. *Strom Thurmond and the Politics of Southern Change.* New York: Simon and Schuster, 1993.

Robinson, Cedric J. *Black Movements in America.* New York: Routledge, 1997.

Angela Ellis
David J. Olson

See also **Civil Rights Movement; Conservatism.**

BACON'S REBELLION was a revolt in Virginia in 1676 led by Nathaniel Bacon Jr., a young planter, against the aged royal governor, Sir William Berkeley. The revolt has usually been interpreted as an attempt at political reform directed against the allegedly oppressive rule of the governor. Bacon's Rebellion, so the argument goes, was prologue to the American Revolution. Late-twentieth-century scholarship, however, has questioned this thesis and emphasized controversy over Indian policy and class divisions within the colony as fundamental causes of the rebellion. The ensuing civil war exposed deep social rifts between the poor whites and the Anglo-American elites of the Chesapeake region.

When Indian attacks occurred on the northern and western frontiers late in 1675 and early in 1676, Bacon demanded the right to lead volunteers in retaliation against all Indians, even those living peacefully within the colony. Berkeley, fearing unjust dispossession and slaughter of the friendly Native American tribes, refused. Bacon ignored the governor's restriction and in May 1676 led volunteers to the southern frontier, where he slaughtered

The rebellion, already flagging, came to an abrupt end when Bacon died in October 1676. Berkeley, having recruited forces on the Eastern Shore, returned to the mainland, defeated the remaining rebels, and by January 1677 had reestablished his authority. Soon thereafter, eleven hundred troops, sent by Charles II to suppress the rebellion, arrived, accompanied by commissioners to investigate its causes. Berkeley's strict policy toward the defeated rebels was severely censured by the commissioners, who attempted to remove him from the governorship. Berkeley returned to England in May 1677 to justify himself, but died on 9 July before seeing the king. Charles II installed Colonel Herbert Jeffreys as governor and promised a plan of internal reform. These reforms erased much of the political autonomy built during Berkeley's regime and reasserted imperial control over Virginia.

BIBLIOGRAPHY

Frantz, John B., ed. *Bacon's Rebellion: Prologue to the Revolution?* Lexington, Mass.: Heath, 1969.

Webb, Stephen Saunders. *1676, The End of American Independence.* New York: Knopf, 1984.

Wilcomb E. Washburn / A. R.

See also **Colonial Policy, British; Indian Policy, Colonial; Insurrections, Domestic.**

BACTERIOLOGY. *See* **Microbiology.**

BADLANDS, an area in southwestern South Dakota where water and frost have carved prehistoric river sediments and volcanic ash into pinnacles and other fantastic geological formations. Arikara Indians frequented the area in the 1700s; Lakotas arrived around 1775. Frustrated French fur traders labeled the severely eroded formations "bad lands to traverse," and the term "badlands" came to describe any area with similarly eroded topography. In the 1840s, scientific societies, museums, and educational institutions began unearthing the Badlands' paleontological treasures: fossils of piglike oreodonts, rhinoceros-sized titanotheres, and prehistoric camels, horses, and tigers. By the 1890s, with the Lakotas confined to reservations (including the Pine Ridge reservation immediately to the south), ranchers—and later, farmers—occupied the Badlands, but neither thrived. In 1939 the federal government reserved part of the area as a national monument and built highways for tourists. The reserve area was enlarged in 1968 and became a national park in 1978.

BIBLIOGRAPHY

Hall, Philip S. *Reflections of the Badlands.* Vermilion: University of South Dakota Press, 1993.

Bacon's Rebellion. Nathaniel Bacon Jr. confronts Sir William Berkeley, governor of Virginia, at Jamestown, 1676. ARCHIVE PHOTOS, INC.

and plundered the friendly Occaneechee Indians. When the governor attempted to call him to account, Bacon marched to Jamestown and, at gunpoint, forced the House of Burgesses of June 1676 to grant him formal authority to fight the Indian war. The burgesses and the governor, powerless before the occupying army and eager to be rid of it, quickly acquiesced. Bacon then marched against another nonhostile tribe, the Pamunkey.

When Berkeley attempted to raise forces to reestablish his own authority, Bacon turned on the governor with his volunteers. Civil war ensued. Berkeley was driven to the eastern shore of Virginia. Jamestown, the capital, was burned. For a few months Bacon's word was law on the mainland. Bacon's rebels retained the loyalty of many indentured servants and small landholders. The colony depended heavily on supplies from England, however, and the sea captains and sailors sided with Berkeley.

In the Bad Lands. This photograph by Edward S. Curtis, first printed c. 1904 and published in 1908 in volume 3 of his classic twenty-volume photographic collection, *The North American Indian,* shows Sioux riding near Sheep Mountain in the Pine Ridge reservation in southwestern South Dakota. LIBRARY OF CONGRESS

Hauk, Joy Keve. *Badlands: Its Life and Landscape.* Interior, S. Dak.: Badlands Natural History Association, 1969.

Doane Robinson / w. p.

See also **Great Plains; Sioux.**

BAHÁ'Í. The Bahá'í religion developed out of the Bábí movement, which in turn sprang from Shi'ite Islam. Bahá'u'lláh, born in Tehran in 1817, became a Bábí in 1844 (the year the Bábí movement began) and in 1863 announced that he was the divine messenger awaited by the movement. Within a few years virtually all Bábís accepted Bahá'u'lláh's messianic claim, thereby becoming Bahá'ís. Bahá'u'lláh gave his religion shape through fifteen thousand letters and about one hundred essays and books, which form the core of Bahá'í scripture. In them he described the nature of God, revelation, humanity, and physical creation; delineated the path of individual spiritual development, involving prayer, scripture study, fasting, pilgrimage, material sacrifice, and service to humanity; defined the holy days and governing institutions of the Bahá'í community; and described a spiritual civilization in which war would be abolished, humanity would be unified, and all would have access to education, opportunity, and prosperity. Before Bahá'u'lláh died in 1892 he appointed his son, 'Abdu'l-Bahá (1844–1921), as head of the religion.

In 1892 the Bahá'í religion was brought to the United States by Middle Eastern immigrants. The first American, Thornton Chase (1847–1912), converted in 1894 in Chicago; by 1900 there were some 1,500 Bahá'ís in the United States, with the largest communities in Chicago, New York, and Kenosha, Wisconsin. The first Bahá'í temple in the Western world was built in Wilmette, a Chicago suburb, from 1912 to 1953. American Bahá'ís played a major role in taking the religion to Europe (1899), East Asia (1914), South America (1919), Australia (1920), and sub-Saharan Africa (1920). They helped organize many of the earliest Bahá'í local and national "spiritual assemblies" (governing councils); the National Spiritual Assembly of the Bahá'ís of the United States dates back to 1926, with a predecessor institution dating to 1909. The religion has seen steady membership growth in the United States, from 3,000 in 1936 to 140,000 in 2000. Worldwide in 2000 it had more than 5 million members.

BIBLIOGRAPHY

Smith, Peter. *The Bábí and Bahá'í Religions: From Messianic Shi'ism to a World Religion.* Cambridge, U.K.: Cambridge University Press, 1987.

Robert Stockman

BAIL is money or property, usually in the form of a refundable bond, that a defendant posts with a court to obtain his or her release in exchange for a guarantee of appearance later for trial. The right originated in English common law, and both the English Bill of Rights of 1689 and the Eighth Amendment to the U.S. Constitution prohibit "excessive bail," that is, an amount greater than necessary to prevent flight by the accused. In *Stack v. Boyle* (1951), the U.S. Supreme Court affirmed the importance of bail in protecting the presumption of innocence of defendants and allowing them to prepare for trial, while acknowledging that traditionally bail has been denied altogether in capital cases.

To relieve the financial burden bail places on low-income defendants, the federal Bail Reform Act of 1966 provides for releases on bases such as family and community ties and previous criminal record. The Bail Reform Act of 1984, however, permits the denial of bail to defendants deemed likely to be dangers to the community, and the Supreme Court in *United States v. Salerno* (1987) upheld the legality of such "preventive detentions." The Eighth Amendment has not yet been incorporated under the Fourteenth Amendment, though many states have similar constitutional or statutory prohibitions against excessive bail.

BIBLIOGRAPHY

Epstein, Lee, and Thomas G. Walker. "The Pretrial Period and the Right to Bail." In *Constitutional Law for a Changing America: Rights, Liberties, and Justice.* 4th ed. Washington, D.C.: Congressional Quarterly, 2001.

Renstrom, Peter G. *Constitutional Rights Sourcebook.* Santa Barbara, Calif.: ABC-CLIO, 1999.

Jeffrey T. Coster

BAKER CASE. Robert G. ("Bobby") Baker, secretary to the U.S. Senate majority at the time of his resignation under fire in 1963, was one of the most powerful congressional staff members of his time. His personal business ventures, which a Senate committee later found to involve abuse of his trusted political position, became a national scandal that briefly threw the spotlight on the sometimes unchecked power of little-known, but influential, Capitol Hill aides.

Baker rose from Senate page to top Senate assistant with the special help of Majority Leader Lyndon B. Johnson and Senator Robert S. Kerr of Oklahoma. He was indicted in January 1966 on nine charges, including grand larceny and attempted tax evasion. His conviction and prison sentence of from one to three years were based partly on evidence that he had pocketed approximately $100,000 solicited from business interests as campaign payments and that he had tried to conceal these transactions in his income tax declarations. After four years of appeals and litigation over admittedly illegal government eavesdropping, Baker entered Lewisburg Penitentiary in January 1971. Paroled in June 1972, he returned to an apparently flourishing motel enterprise, but not to politics.

BIBLIOGRAPHY

Beschloss, Michael R., ed. *Taking Charge: The Johnson White House Tapes, 1963–1964.* New York: Simon and Schuster, 1997.

Dallek, Robert. *Flawed Giant: Lyndon Johnson and His Times, 1961–1973.* New York: Oxford University Press, 1998.

John P. Mackenzie / T. G.

See also **Corruption, Political; Political Scandals.**

BAKER V. CARR 369 U.S. 186 (1962), decided on 26 March 1962, arose in Tennessee, which in violation of its own constitution had not reapportioned its general assembly for over sixty years, maintaining rural, conservative control of the state legislature and leaving its more liberal urban areas severely underrepresented. Six of eight participating justices agreed that federal courts had jurisdiction to decide the complaints that Tennessee's malapportionment violated the equal protection clause of the Fourteenth Amendment. Justice William J. Brennan wrote the opinion, which was among the Warren Court's boldest constitutional decisions.

In *Colegrove v. Green* (1946) the Court had pronounced reapportionment among the political questions that traditionally were not appropriate for judicial decision. However, such restraint was inconsistent with the Warren Court's active protection of civil and political rights and with the post–New Deal Court's general philosophy of promoting the openness of the democratic process and protecting minorities. In the years following *Baker v. Carr* the Warren Court established the principle of one person, one vote, forcing a major realignment of representation in nearly every state, most of which had apportioned at least one house of their legislatures by some standard other than numerical representation. The decision encouraged Congress to pass the Voting Rights Act of 1965, which made it illegal to discriminate against racial and other minorities in electoral districting. Subsequent Court decisions built upon both *Baker v. Carr* and the Voting Rights Act to encourage equal representation. But *Baker v. Carr* did not have the expected effect of shifting political power to more liberal urban areas. Instead it helped assure equal representation of the booming suburbs, whose representatives often joined those of rural areas to promote conservative social and economic policies.

BIBLIOGRAPHY

Cortner, Richard C. *The Apportionment Cases.* Knoxville: University of Tennessee Press, 1970.

Grofman, Bernard. *Voting Rights, Voting Wrongs: The Legacy of "Baker v. Carr."* New York: Twentieth Century Fund, 1990.

Michael Les Benedict

See also **Apportionment; Voting Rights Act of 1965.**

BAKKE V. REGENTS OF THE UNIVERSITY OF CALIFORNIA,

438 U.S. 265 (1978), a case in which the Supreme Court overturned a quota policy for admissions at the University of California at Davis, while generally approving affirmative action programs. Allan Bakke, a white male, was denied admittance to the medical school at Davis in 1973 and 1974. In both years the school admitted only one hundred students, reserving sixteen seats for minorities. Bakke sued, claiming "reverse discrimination" because some of the minorities admitted had lower grade point averages and lower scores on the Medical College Admission Test than his. Four justices wanted to end the program for violating Title VI of the CIVIL RIGHTS ACT OF 1964 without addressing the constitutionality of the medical school's affirmative action program. Four others wanted the Court to rule that the program was constitutional and that the medical school rightfully denied Bakke admittance. Justice Lewis Powell Jr. essentially split the difference, arguing that fixed racial quota programs such as the medical school's violated the Civil Rights Act, but also that a public school's admission policy "may" consider race as long as it was not the determining factor. This was constitutionally permissible under the First Amendment, he argued, because it allowed educational institutions to promote cultural diversity. The Court's decision, which affected only affirmative action programs at schools receiving federal funds, did not settle the question of reverse discrimination, because it was decided on narrow statutory grounds.

As backlash mounted against affirmative action programs in the 1990s, the decision became a lightning rod for controversy. In July 1995, for example, the University of California's Board of Regents rejected the *Bakke* standard, which allowed "race as one of many factors" in admissions decisions, voting to prohibit schools in the UC system from using "race, religion, sex, color, ethnicity or national origin" in admissions decisions. In March 1996 the U.S. Court of Appeals for the Fifth Circuit, in *Hopwood v. State of Texas*, decided in favor of four white students who had been denied admission to the University of Texas Law School. The court ruled that the students had suffered reverse discrimination and declared unconstitutional the use of race as one of several factors in admissions decisions. The Supreme Court declined to review the case, allowing it to stand as law in Texas, Mississippi, and Louisiana.

In March 2001 Judge Bernard Friedman's district court ruling on *Grutter v. Bollinger* ordered the University of Michigan Law School to cease considering race as a factor in admissions, although the Sixth Circuit Court of Appeals issued a stay of this order in April. In May 2002 the Supreme Court reversed the district court's ruling and upheld the use of race in admissions to the school.

BIBLIOGRAPHY

Carter, Stephen L. *Reflections of an Affirmative Action Baby.* New York: Basic Books, 1991.

O'Brien, David M. *Storm Center: The Supreme Court in American Politics.* New York: Norton, 1986.

Thomas G. Gress / A. R.; C. W.;

See also **Affirmative Action; California Higher Educational System; Discrimination: Race.**

BALANCE OF TRADE.

Trade balances are the financial flows that arise from trade in goods and services and unilateral transfers between countries. These financial flows constitute a portion of a country's current account. The balance of trade is measured by the dollar value of payments and receipts for goods and services.

Overview

From 1815 to 1934, U.S. governments generally enacted policies that limited imports of manufactured goods, in the interest of protecting domestic producers. Trade balances were generally negative until the United States emerged as an industrial power in the 1870s. Notwithstanding the improving competitive position of U.S. manufacturers, reflected in surging trade surpluses, high tariffs remained in place until the Smoot-Hawley tariff of 1930 brought protectionism into disrepute.

The administration of President Franklin D. Roosevelt adopted a freer trade position with the passage of the Reciprocal Trade Agreements Act in 1934. In the context of growing surpluses in the trade of merchandise goods, the United States played a leading role in liberalizing trade after World War II (1939–1945). Persistent and growing trade deficits from the 1970s on prompted successive administrations in Washington to pursue "strategic" trade policies that retreated selectively from the free trade position of the early postwar period. Despite the concessions to so-called fair trade, U.S. governments remained biased toward freer trade, despite the large and growing trade deficits of the 1980s and 1990s.

Economists generally frown on the idea that trade surpluses are better than deficits and believe that policies that suppress imports invariably reduce exports in the long run. With the growth of the trade deficit, concern over jobs and the means to service trade balances have prompted calls for policy changes that redress the imbalance among exports and imports. At the end of the twentieth century, however, public policy expressed little concern regarding the trade deficit.

From Colonialism to World War I

The thirteen American colonies ran persistent trade deficits with Great Britain from 1721 to 1772. Surpluses with other countries reduced the overall deficit somewhat. Yet from 1768 to 1772, colonial exports totaled £2.8 million, while imports equaled £3.9 million. There were significant regional differences. As of 1770, for instance, Georgia, Maryland, Virginia, and the Carolinas maintained a roughly even trade balance with Britain on the strength of staple crop exports. At the same time, the Mid-Atlantic and New England colonies ran significant deficits. They serviced them with earnings from shipping and other mercantile services, in which New York and Philadelphia excelled, and exports of primary and semi-processed products.

The new American nation maintained imports of British manufactured goods. American producers benefited from the Napoleonic Wars (1803–1815); in 1807, they were exporting three times more goods than they had exported in 1793. From 1807 to 1830, British protectionism and a growing U.S. economy produced growing trade deficits, as manufacturing imports soared, while Britain kept its markets closed to U.S. finished goods. However, British demand for cotton soared during the mid-nineteenth century, and exports of the staple crop constituted half of America's total exports in the two decades prior to the Civil War (1861–1865). From 1791 to 1850, America's merchandise trade balance was in a deficit for all but eight years. At the same time, the volume of U.S. exports increased more than sevenfold, from $19 million in 1791 to $152 million in 1850. When services are included, the trade balance was in surplus for nineteen of the sixty years between 1791 and 1850.

From 1850 through the end of World War I (1914–1918), America's trade balance moved from slightly unfavorable to enormously favorable, reflecting the nation's emergence as a world economic power and the continuation of trade protectionism. Thus, from 1850 to 1873, the merchandise trade deficit totaled $400 million, as exports grew from $152 million to $524 million. From 1874 to 1895, the trade balance turned favorable on the strength of agricultural exports and increases in shipments of manufactured goods. Volume increased steadily as well, with exports of goods and services reaching $1 billion for the first time in 1891. From 1896 to 1914, the trade balance was markedly favorable, as U.S. manufacturers competed globally for markets. Indeed, the merchandise trade balance was some $9 billion in surplus for this period. Purchases of services reduced the overall trade surplus to $6.8 billion. Spurred by the European demand for U.S. goods and services during World War I, the U.S. trade surplus soared from 1915 to 1919. Net goods and services totaled $14.3 billion for the five-year period, with exports topping $10.7 billion in 1919—an amount that was not exceeded until World War II (1939–1945). Not incidentally, America also became a creditor on its current account for the first time, on the strength of lending to wartime allies Britain and France.

From World War II to the Twenty-First Century

During the interwar period, the U.S. trade balance was consistently in surplus on greatly reduced volumes of trade, even as the merchandise trade balance turned negative from 1934 to 1940. As was the case during World War I, U.S. exports soared during World War II, peaking at $21.4 billion in 1944. Much of this volume was owed to the lend-lease program. As a result, America enjoyed an enormously favorable balance of trade, which it sustained during the early postwar period, from 1945 to 1960.

The favorable trade position of the United States at the end of World War II, underpinned by the relative strength of its manufacturing sector, contributed to the willingness of U.S. administrations to liberalize the global trading regime through the General Agreement on Tariffs and Trade and its successor, the World Trade Organization. Both Democratic and Republican administrations remained committed to a freer trade policy stance—despite many exceptions, most notably steel, autos, and semiconductor chips—even as the U.S. merchandise trade balance disappeared in the late 1960s and then turned negative in the context of growing competitiveness on the part of European and Japanese manufacturers and sharply increased prices for crude oil.

From 1984 to 2000, the merchandise trade balance topped $100 billion in all but the recession years of 1991 and 1992, even as trade volumes increased absolutely and relative to GNP. In 1997, it exceeded $200 billion, as exports nearly reached $900 billion and GNP hit $8 trillion for the first time. For the twelve months ending 31 December 2001, the merchandise trade deficit stood at $425 billion. A surplus in services, which grew from $6.1 billion in 1980 to $85.3 billion in 1997, has offset 30 to 40 percent of the deficit on goods. America has funded its trade deficit largely by attracting foreign investment, so that it runs large surpluses on its capital account. As a result, the United States became the world's largest debtor on its current account during the 1980s and remained so at the beginning of the twenty-first century.

BIBLIOGRAPHY

Balaam, David N., and Michael Veseth. *Introduction to International Political Economy.* Upper Saddle River, N.J.: Prentice Hall, 1996. See chapter 8.

Lovett, William A., Alfred E. Eckes Jr., and Richard L. Brinkman. *U.S. Trade Policy: History, Theory, and the WTO.* Armonk, N.Y.: M. E. Sharpe, 1999.

Thompson, Margaret C., ed. *Trade: U.S. Policy Since 1945.* Washington, D.C.: Congressional Quarterly, 1984.

U.S. Department of Commerce. *Historical Statistics of the United States: Colonial Times to 1970.* Washington, D.C.: General Printing Office, 1975.

Walton, Gary M., and Hugh Rockoff. *History of the American Economy.* 8th ed. New York: Harcourt, Brace, 1998.

Michael R. Adamson

See also **Debt and Investment, Foreign; Trade, Foreign.**

BALANCED BUDGET AMENDMENT, if approved by Congress and ratified by the states, would forbid Congress to appropriate more money than the federal government receives in revenues. This requirement could be waived (in wartime for example) by a three-fifths vote of Congress. The amendment would also require a three-fifths vote to raise taxes. In 1997, during the 105th Congress, the amendment failed by one vote in the Senate, just as it had in the 104th Congress, when Senator Mark Hatfield of Oregon, a Republican, voted "No," drawing the wrath of conservatives in the Senate and nationwide. The House of Representatives approved the measure by a large margin in both instances.

Proponents argue that without the Balanced Budget Amendment Congress will be unable to resist deficit spending; opponents argue that it would hamstring Congress unnecessarily, especially in times of national emergency. While it failed to send a balanced budget amendment to the states, the 105th Congress did approve the Balanced Budget Act of 1997, signed into law by President William J. Clinton on 5 August 1997, which included a host of spending initiatives and tax credits. Subsequent to the act's passage, the federal government ran budget surpluses through the remaining years of the 1990s.

R. Volney Riser

See also **Budget, Federal.**

BALKANS. *See* **Kosovo Bombing; Yugoslavia, Relations with.**

BALLADS. A ballad is a short narrative set to song. A folk ballad is generally short and simple, telling a dramatic story using dialogue and action. American folk ballads tend to rhyme and to be divided into stanzas. The ballad is an enduring musical form and often the first type of song children hear, since many lullabies are ballads. The earliest known American ballads are based on European models, some of which date to the late Middle Ages. American ballads often glorify cowboys, lumberjacks, and other working-class people as opposed to European ballads, which tend to focus on the highborn. (A recent example is singer Elton John's tribute, written upon the death of Princess Diana, "Candle in the Wind 1997.")

Many American ballads are also based on news events. There are numerous versions of "Stackalee" (or "Stagolee"), which tells about an actual murder said to have taken place in St. Louis in 1895. While all the versions tell the story somewhat differently, they have in common that "Stagalee, he was a bad man," a theme that runs through many ballads, especially those innovated in prisons, bars, and work camps. This tradition was revived in 1973 when singer-songwriter Jim Croce had a hit song with "Bad, Bad Leroy Brown." More recent ballads have used historical events to promote patriotic fervor. In

"When This Cruel War Is Over." Sheet music for a popular Civil War ballad (also called "Weeping, Sad and Lonely"), with music by Henry Tucker and lyrics by Charles C. Sawyer. LIBRARY OF CONGRESS

1966, during the Vietnam War, Staff Sergeant Barry Sadler had a top forty radio success with "Ballad of the Green Berets," and almost immediately after the 11 September 2001 terrorist attacks, country singer Alan Jackson's song, "Where Were You (When the World Stopped Turning)," went to the top of the country music charts.

Ballads often skip expository material and focus on a particular moment in time, such as the dying words of a young cowboy in "The Streets of Laredo," or in more recent times, the moment at which a woman walks down the street in Roy Orbison's "Oh, Pretty Woman" (1964).

The first collection of ballads published in America was compiled by Francis James Child in a five-volume work, *English and Scottish Popular Ballads* (1883–1898). Most early American ballads are variations on the 305 types defined by Child. The early American "Fatal Flower Garden" is based on a ballad identified by Child as "Sir Hugh." The original song, which tells of a gruesome child murder, dates as far back as 1255. Few early ballads have a definitive version because they were often sung by unlettered people who did not write them down. In their important 1934 work, *American Ballads and Folk Songs*, John A. Lomax and Alan Lomax provide twenty-five different categories of songs, many with alternative versions of a particular ballad. Their categories include "Working on the Railroad," "Songs from Southern Chain Gangs," "Negro Bad Men," "Cowboy Songs," "The Miner," "War and Soldiers," "White Spirituals," and "Negro Spirituals." In the first edition of the *Dictionary of American History* (1976), John A. Lomax wrote that American ballads tend to follow the pattern of the come-all-ye's and are peopled with working-class characters. Undoubtedly the most popular of indigenous types are the occupational ballads, the bad-man ballad, the murder ballad, and the vulgar or bawdy ballad. As the English loved Robin Hood because he took from the rich to give to the poor, so the American folksinger has commemorated Jesse James. Probably more than anyone else, the Lomaxes are responsible for recording America's folk heritage, including one of the greatest repositories of its ballads, Huddie Ledbetter, or Leadbelly. They wrote that among the ballads they recorded, beginning in 1932, were many that were too bawdy for print; thus their books often contain sanitized versions of the original work.

The singer Pete Seeger has also been a proponent of recording and singing American ballads in order to keep the songs alive. The son of a musicologist, Seeger wrote his own songs ("Turn, Turn, Turn") and popularized those of other artists (for example, Leadbelly's "Goodnight Irene").

While Seeger and the Lomaxes collected primarily folk ballads, the form has endured in nearly every category of American music including rock, pop, rhythm and blues, jazz, religious, and perhaps especially, country and western. Pop ballads have been sung by artists as diverse as Bob Dylan ("The Times They Are A'changin'") and Billy Joel ("Piano Man"). Ray Charles combined blues music with country in his influential ballads (including "I Can't Stop Loving You"). The list of country and western ballads is enormous and some of the titles are an entertainment in themselves.

Poets, including the twentieth-century Anglo-American W. H. Auden, also wrote poems in a ballad form ("If I Could Tell You," "O Where are You Going"). Some of these works were published as broadsides rather than as music.

BIBLIOGRAPHY

Lomax, John A., and Alan Lomax. *American Ballads and Folk Songs.* New York: Macmillan, 1934.

———. *Folk Song U.S.A.* New York: New American Library, 1947.

Seeger, Pete. *American Favorite Ballads: Tunes and Songs As Sung by Pete Seeger.* Edited by Irwin Silber and Ethel Raim. New York: Oak Publications, 1961.

Smith, Harry, ed. *Anthology of American Folk Music.* Smithsonian Folkways compact disks (6).

Rebekah Presson Mosby

See also **Music: Country and Western, Early American, Folk Revival.**

BALLET. The "unofficial" ballet came to America with immigrant performers and dancing masters. Performances in the colonial and early federal periods were presented in the port cities on the East Coast and inland cities connected to them by navigable rivers. The first documented ballet presented in America was *The Adventures of Harlequin and Scaramouch, with the Burgo'master Trick'd* (4 February 1735), given in Charleston by Henry Holt, a British dancing master. The next major figure was Alexander Placide, who trained at the Paris Opéra in ballet before learning tightrope with the popular Les Grands Danseurs du Roi. He brought companies of ballet and rope dancers to Santo Domingo (1788), New York (1792), and Charleston (1794–1796). The latter seasons brought the first presentations of the Paris Opéra repertory, staged by Jean-Baptiste Francisqui.

Nineteenth-Century Touring Performers

European performers from opera houses and popular theater continued to tour and immigrate to the United States throughout the nineteenth century. Augusta Maywood and Mary Ann Lee, each raised in Philadelphia theater families, are jointly considered America's first native-born ballerinas. As adolescents, they studied with Paris Opéra–trained Paul H. Hazard and performed in Philadelphia and on the Mississippi River circuit from 1837 before going to Paris for further study. Maywood remained in Europe, becoming a prima ballerina at Milan's Teatro alla Scala. Lee returned to America, where she staged and starred in *Giselle* and other Romantic ballets of Jean Coralli before retiring in 1847. The tour of Fanny Elssler in 1840 imported the cults of Romantic ballet and performer celebrity to America. She was thronged from Boston south to Havana and New Orleans. Elssler's grace and pointe work inspired poems, music, laudatory odes, and engravings.

As transatlantic travel became safer, family troupes from opera-ballet and popular theater scheduled tours of North America and Central America. The gold rush brought an expansion of American audiences and theaters, especially in the San Francisco Bay area and mining communities in Nevada and Colorado. Tours for ballet on its own or as part of extravaganzas began in New York's Niblo's Garden and moved west to the theaters owned by Thomas Maguire or his rivals in San Francisco. La Scala ballerinas Maria Bonfanti, Rita Sangalli, and Giuseppina Morlacchi presented ballet solos and pas de deux interpolated into huge extravaganzas, most notably *The Black Crook* (1867). The corps de ballets for these productions were mostly local women, trained by European émigré dancing masters.

The Impact of the Russian Ballets

Meanwhile, in Europe, ballet itself was changing. Mikhail Fokine tried to shift the emphasis of the Imperial Russian Ballet away from full-length, three- or four-act plotted ballets. He choreographed shorter works, many of them more abstract music visualizations, such as his *Les Sylphi-*

des (1907) to piano works by Chopin. This change was considered "too revolutionary" for the Imperial Ballet but was adopted by impresario Serge Diaghilev for his Ballets Russes tours of western Europe. Although some full-evening ballets, such as *Swan Lake, Coppelia,* and *The Nutcracker,* remained popular, the Fokine revolution took hold in twentieth-century ballet companies and served as the model for most ballet presentations in America.

Although Diaghilev's company did not reach the United States until 1916, many rival companies of dancers associated with the troupe brought its repertoire and designs to America, using names such as the All-Star Imperial Russian Ballet. Anna Pavlova, generally considered the greatest ballerina of the early twentieth century, presented music visualizations by (or after) Fokine on annual Western Hemisphere tours from 1910 through the 1920s. Like Elssler, she inspired America's love for Romantic ballet and had a major impact on the development of ballet schools, companies, and audiences.

A large number of Ballets Russes dancers chose to stay in America, becoming teachers, choreographers, and ballet masters for theaters, civic ballets, and opera houses across the country. Many worked in prologs (short vaudevilles that alternated with feature films in motion picture palaces of the 1920s–1940s). Among them were Theodore Kosloff, who became a popular choreographer for silent films, and Mikhail Mordkin, whose school and company were the incubators for Ballet Theatre.

Sol Hurok, an impresario based in New York, had a national network of local auditoriums and concert promoters. Hurok added the post-Diaghilev Ballets Russes de Monte Carlo to his roster in 1934 and presented it until 1939 and after 1946. The Ballets Russes de Monte Carlo and the related Original Ballet Russe toured in some manifestation until 1962. These companies brought many more fine European dancers and teachers to the United States, where they worked with opera companies, ballet schools, and universities, raising the level of technical training available in America. Hurok maintained ballet on his national roster throughout his career, becoming known in the 1950s and 1960s for his importation of the (British) Royal Ballet and the Soviet Bolshoi and Kirov companies. He was often able to place excerpts from ballet and folklore on television variety shows, such as the *Ed Sullivan Show,* greatly expanding the audience for ballet.

Americana Ballet

Choreographers and companies have intermittently pursued the idea that ballet in America should be distinctly American. Ballet Caravan, Lincoln Kirstein's small troupe, existed from 1936 to 1941. Although generally remembered as an interim step between the School of American Ballet and the NEW YORK CITY BALLET (NYCB), it also represents an unusual ballet experiment with Americana, living composers, and popular front imagery. The Americana ballets created for and by company members in-

cluded Lew Christensen's *Pocahontas* (1939, music by Elliott Carter) and *Filling Station* (1938, Virgil Thomson); William Dollar's *Yankee Clipper* (1937, Paul Bowles); and Eugene Loring's masterpiece *Billy the Kid* (1938), with a commissioned score by Aaron Copland. The Ballets Russes de Monte Carlo also occasionally experimented with Americana, commissioning *Ghost Town* (1939, choreographed by Marc Platt to music by Richard Rodgers) and *Rodeo* (1942, Agnes de Mille to Aaron Copland). That work, like De Mille's *Fall River Legend* (1948, to Morton Gould) and *Billy the Kid,* remains in the active repertory of the AMERICAN BALLET THEATRE (ABT). The short-lived Jerome Robbins' Ballets: USA, in the mid-1950s, experimented with American movement vocabularies, jazz music, and silence. One of the few companies independent of ABT and NYCB was the Joffrey Ballet (founded 1956), which became the City Center Joffrey Ballet (NYC) in 1966 and later relocated to Chicago. Joffrey and fellow choreographer Gerald Arpino created ballet works inspired by 1960s American counterculture.

Civic, Regional, and Professional Companies

Major professional ballet companies have been established and maintained across the country. Among the best regarded are the San Francisco Ballet, associated with long-term director Lew Christensen, and Utah's Ballet West, directed by his brother Willam. There have been major companies in Chicago since the rival troupes of Ballets Russes dancers Adolf Bolm and Andreas Pavley and Serge Oukrainsky. Bolm protégée choreographer Ruth Page ran the Chicago Lyric Opera Ballet for much of the latter twentieth century.

Former NYCB dancers directed companies across the country, among them the Christensens, Kent Stowell's Pacific Northwest Ballet, Arthur Mitchell's Dance Theatre of Harlem, and Edward Villella's Miami City Ballet. In the mid-1970s, two of ABT's dancers who had been experimenting with choreography left to form companies—Eliot Feld remained in New York with the Eliot Feld Ballet (later Ballet Tech), while Dennis Nahat established the San Jose Cleveland Ballet.

The schools that had been thriving since the Pavlova tours began to convert from annual recitals to established civic or regional ballet companies. Many had only two seasons per year—a Christmas presentation of *The Nutcracker* and a late spring "graduation" performance. But some companies became major cultural forces, performing regularly scheduled seasons with live music and professional dancers. The first Regional Ballet Festival was held in Atlanta in 1956. The National Association for Regional Ballet mounts festivals and seminars on choreography, teaching, and nonprofit management across the country. *The Nutcracker* is still the most popular presentation, giving American audiences a taste of ballet's history.

BIBLIOGRAPHY

Barker, Barbara. *Ballet or Ballyhoo: The American Careers of Maria Bonfanti, Rita Sangalli, and Giuseppina Morlacchi.* New York: Dance Horizons, 1984.

Barzel, Ann. "European Dance Teachers in the United States." *Dance Index* III, no. 4–6 (April–June, 1944).

Delarue, Allison, ed. *Fanny Elssler in America.* Brooklyn: Dance Horizons, 1976. Anthology includes her memoir of the American tour as well as verses about her.

Hudson, Alice C., and Barbara Cohen-Stratyner. *Heading West, Touring West: Mapmakers, Performing Artists, and the American Frontier.* New York: New York Public Library, 2001.

MacDonald, Nesta. *Diaghilev Observed by Critics in England and the United States, 1911–1929.* New York: Dance Horizons, 1975.

Magriel, Paul, ed. *Chronicles of the American Dance: From the Shakers to Martha Graham.* New York: Da Capo Press, 1978. Anthology originally published in 1948.

Moore, Lillian. *Echoes of American Ballet: A Collection of Seventeen Articles.* New York: Dance Horizons, 1976. Anthology of historical articles from *American Dancer, Dance Index, Dance Magazine, Dancing Times,* and *Etude.*

Barbara Cohen-Stratyner

See also **Alvin Ailey Dance Theater; Dance.**

BALLINGER-PINCHOT CONTROVERSY.

When William H. Taft became president of the United States in 1909, his administration canceled an order of former president Theodore Roosevelt that had withdrawn from sale certain public lands containing WATERPOWER sites in Montana and Wyoming. Gifford Pinchot, chief of the U.S. FOREST SERVICE, protested and publicly charged Secretary of the Interior Richard A. Ballinger with favoritism toward corporations seeking waterpower sites. Pinchot also defended a Land Office investigator who was dismissed for accusing Ballinger of being a tool of private interests that desired access to Alaskan mineral lands. Taft fired Pinchot, and a joint congressional investigating committee exonerated Ballinger. Nevertheless, public outcry over the controversy forced Ballinger to resign in March 1911, and the controversy widened the split between conservative (Taft) and progressive (Roosevelt) Republicans.

BIBLIOGRAPHY

Anderson, Donald F. *William Howard Taft: A Conservative's Conception of the Presidency.* Ithaca, N.Y.: Cornell University Press, 1973.

Coletta, Paolo E. *William Howard Taft: A Bibliography.* Westport, Conn.: Meckler, 1989.

Penick, James L., Jr. *Progressive Politics and Conservation: The Ballinger-Pinchot Affair.* Chicago: University of Chicago Press, 1968.

Glenn H. Benton / A. G.

See also **Environmental Business; Interior, Department of the; Marine Sanctuaries; Waterways, Inland.**

BALLOONS. The advent and use of balloons spans the history of the United States and has made substantial contributions to science, military technology, and entertainment.

The notion of ballooning gained acceptance in the seventeenth century, but it was not until the late eighteenth century that the first designs were successfully tested. In France in 1783 the Robert brothers built the first hydrogen balloon, designed by Jacques Charles. Later in the year, the Montgolfier brothers demonstrated their own designs, one of which lifted two noblemen, Jean-François Pilâtre de Rozier and François d'Arlandes, on the first human flight.

News of such experiments reached the United States, and several projects were tested in Philadelphia. One of these projects, that of Peter Carnes, was a tethered balloon that successfully lifted thirteen-year-old Edward Warren in Baltimore on 24 June 1784. The experiment also suggests that Carnes had successfully solved most of the problems associated with early ballooning without access to information about the French designs. But it was not until January 1793 that an American untethered manned balloon flight took place, when the Frenchman Jean-Pierre Blanchard traveled from Philadelphia to Gloucester County, New Jersey.

During the Civil War both the Union and the Confederacy made use of ballooning for observation purposes. In the North, Thaddeus Lowe distinguished himself through his enthusiasm and his capacity for convincing authority figures, including President Lincoln, who authorized him to organize what Lowe would later call "the Aeronautic Corp." Lowe had seven balloons built (another three may have been added to the inventory later on) and enlisted the help of several fellow balloonists. His team provided valuable intelligence. Both the army and navy would make use of ballooning units until World War II.

Ballooning also found an application in the realm of science. In the late nineteenth century, atmospheric measurements were undertaken to further meteorological knowledge, and the practice was carried on through the use of unmanned sounding balloons.

In the twentieth century new balloon models set altitude records. Travel into the stratosphere was first achieved in 1931 by the Swiss scientist Auguste Piccard aboard a Belgian-funded balloon, and U.S. balloonists soon followed suit at the "Century of Progress" exhibit in Chicago in 1933. Two years later two army aeronauts aboard *Explorer II*, a helium-filled balloon, set an altitude record by reaching 72,395 feet and sent radio broadcasts from their pressurized gondola. In 1962 high altitude ballooning enabled the highest parachute jump ever, from

113,739.9 feet. NASA was also involved in the use of high-altitude balloons. In 1966, for example, it worked with the Air Force Cambridge Research Laboratories to launch a mylar crib balloon to an altitude of 139,800 feet before deflating it to test a parachute recovery for a possible landing on Mars.

By far the biggest application for balloons today is the recreational use of hot-air balloons. In the early twentieth century, aerial races such as the Gordon Bennett Cup captivated the general public, but the sport remained an expensive and dangerous undertaking. Tests of various plastics after World War II yielded promising results (partly because they are cheaper to produce and can be sealed easily), and in 1955 Ed Yost built a thirty-nine-foot-diameter polyethylene balloon in his backyard and added a multiple-burner propane heater to inflate it. In 1960 he completed the first successful modern hot-air balloon flight, ascending to 9,300 feet before landing three hours and fifteen minutes later. His design included a "rip panel" that allows quick deflation for rapid descent, first imagined in 1859 by John Wise. In the early 1950s Don Piccard, Robert McNair, and Peter Wood formed the Balloon Club of America, which became part of the new Balloon Federation of America in 1961. The largest balloon gathering is the annual World Hot Air Balloon Championship.

Though much more expensive, some helium balloons have been used for long-range flights. Several such flights have set new records and received wide publicity. Among them were the first Atlantic crossing, in 1978 aboard *Double Eagle II*; the first Pacific crossing, in 1981 aboard *Double Eagle V*; Joe Kittinger's solo transatlantic flight in 1984; and Steve Fossett's round-the-world flight in 2002.

BIBLIOGRAPHY

Baldwin, Munson. *With Brass and Gas: An Illustrated and Embellished Chronicle of Ballooning in Mid-Nineteenth-Century America*. Boston: Beacon, 1967.

Crouch, Tom D. *The Eagle Aloft: Two Centuries of the Balloon in America*. Washington, D.C.: Smithsonian Institution Press, 1983.

Devorkin, David H. *Race to the Stratosphere: Manned Scientific Ballooning in America*. New York: Springer-Verlag, 1989.

Jackson, Donald Dale. *The Aeronauts*. Alexandria, Va.: Time-Life, 1980.

Guillaume de Syon

BALLOT, a method of voting by way of a form that lists the voter's options. The ballot was preceded in early America by other methods of VOTING, such as by vocal statement or by letting corn or beans designate votes cast. During the early national period, the paper ballot emerged as the dominant voting method, and many states allowed the voter to make up his own ballot in the privacy of his home. Almost immediately, however, the POLITICAL PAR-

TIES, motivated by a desire to influence the vote, started to print ballots as substitutes for handwritten ones, a practice that was constitutionally upheld by a Massachusetts Supreme Court decision in 1829. These "party strip" ballots listed only the candidates of a single party and were peddled to the voters on or before election day. Voting by such ballots was almost always done in public—contrary to the notion of a secret vote cherished today. The system of party ballots led to widespread intimidation and corruption, which were not corrected until the ballot reform period of the 1890s.

Between 1888 and 1896, civic groups and "good government" supporters convinced over 90 percent of the states to adopt a new ballot patterned after one introduced in Australia in the 1850s to eliminate vote corruption in that country. The Australian ballot was the exact opposite of the earlier party ballots. It was prepared and distributed by the government rather than by the political parties, it placed the candidates of both major parties on the same ballot instead of on separate ballots, and it was secret. Still in use in all states at the end of the twentieth century, this type of ballot successfully eliminated much of the partisan intimidation and vote fraud that once existed; it also facilitated split-ticket voting.

During the 2000 presidential election, however, ballot irregularities and inconsistencies, particularly in the state of Florida, illustrated that significant flaws still remained in the American ballot system. Reforms, including the use of computerized ballots, were under review in many states after the Florida controversy touched off a national debate over which ballots should be used for national elections.

BIBLIOGRAPHY

Evans, Eldon Cobb. *A History of the Australian Ballot System in the United States*. Chicago: University of Chicago Press, 1917.

Fredman, Lionel E. *The Australian Ballot: The Story of an American Reform*. East Lansing: Michigan State University Press, 1968.

Jerrold G. Rusk / A. G.

See also **Blocs; Canvass; Election Laws; Elections; Massachusetts Ballot; Voter Registration.**

BALTIMORE, the largest city in Maryland, was founded as a port city in 1729 and then incorporated as a city in 1796. Baltimore takes its name from Charles Calvert, Lord Baltimore. Due to its vast natural harbor, the city served as a shipbuilding and transportation hub for the Middle Atlantic states throughout the nineteenth and twentieth centuries. During the growth of railroads in the 1830s, Baltimore served as a headquarters for the Baltimore and Ohio railroad and the Baldwin Locomotive Works, the largest in North America. The city continued to compete vigorously with Philadelphia and New York into the twentieth century, gaining Bethlehem Steel's main shipyards and maintaining large port facilities. Heavy industry's movement away from major cities in the 1950s and 1960s contributed to Baltimore's sharp economic decline. Beginning in the 1950s, city leaders attempted to reverse its fortunes.

The city's renewal efforts rank among the most ambitious in the United States. William Schaefer, the city's outspoken mayor from 1971 to 1986, managed construction of the Inner Harbor Project, the National Aquarium, the Maryland Science Center, as well as a convention center and two waterfront malls. Neighborhoods, however, lagged, and lost business to the harbor area, but Schaefer obtained federal money for housing improvement loans and neighborhood pride projects. Despite these efforts neighborhoods continued to decline and the drug trade flourished in the 1970s and 1980s, blighting neighborhoods even further.

Baltimore's African American population increased from 24 percent in 1950 to more than 60 percent in 1994, and in 1987 the city elected Kurt Schmoke its first black mayor. After his reelection in 1991, the stimulus of urban reconstruction was almost over, federal and state funds had dried up, and the tourist boom had leveled off. Schmoke and Schaefer, the latter was elected governor in 1987, persuaded the Maryland legislature to expand the city's transportation system; to assume certain expenses from its community college, libraries, zoo, and jail; and to build a stadium, Camden Yards, beside the Inner Harbor for the Baltimore Orioles baseball team. Even as the city declined in population and wealth, it was merging with its suburbs and surrounding area. In 1993, the U.S. Census Bureau recognized a combined Washington-Washington-Baltimore Consolidated Statistical Area. The city's population dropped from 950,000 in 1950 to 736,000 in 1990 and then to 651,154 in 2000. Despite a booming economy, the population drop in Baltimore was among the largest in U.S. cities during the 1990s. The 2000 mayoral election emphasized the crisis of Baltimore's neighborhoods as the city's social network continues to struggle.

BIBLIOGRAPHY

Callcott, George H. *Maryland and America, 1940 to 1980.* Baltimore: Johns Hopkins University Press, 1985.

Fee, Elizabeth. et al., eds. *The Baltimore Book: New Views of Local History.* Philadelphia: Temple University Press, 1991.

Olson, Sherry H. *Baltimore: The Building of an American City.* Baltimore: Johns Hopkins University Press, 1997.

Orser, W. Edward. *Blockbusting in Baltimore: The Edmondson Village Story.* Lexington: University Press of Kentucky, 1994.

George H. Callcott
Matthew L. Daley

See also **Baltimore Riot; Maryland; Railroads.**

BALTIMORE BELL TEAMS were named for the small bells suspended in metal arches over the curved wooden supports (called hames) to which the lines of a draft horse's harness were attached. The bells served to speed the horses and sound warnings on narrow, crooked roads. These teams hauled farm produce to Baltimore, Maryland, and returned with goods for homes and local merchants. Such teams made regular trips from points as far southwest as Knoxville, Tennessee, and operated until 1850 or later, when they were replaced by canals and railroads.

BIBLIOGRAPHY

Raitz, Karl, ed. *The National Road.* Baltimore: Johns Hopkins University Press, 1996.

John W. Wayland/A. R.

See also **Pack Trains; Wagoners of the Alleghenies.**

BALTIMORE RIOT (19 April 1861). An attack by pro-Southern Baltimoreans on Pennsylvania and Massachusetts militia en route to Washington. Since the railroad was not continuous through Baltimore, horses were normally required to draw the cars from one terminal to the other. With the arrival of Union forces, protesters blocked the connecting tracks with anchors and other obstacles, forcing later Union contingents to march on foot. The crowd pursued the Union men with stones, bricks, and a few pistol shots, forcing the militia to return fire and break into a run. Baltimore's mayor appealed for calm, and finally, near the Washington terminal, the police succeeded in holding the people back until the troops entrained. Four militiamen and twelve civilians were killed and an unknown number wounded. To quell any further defiance, President Abraham Lincoln sent federal troops to Maryland and suspended the writ of habeas corpus.

BIBLIOGRAPHY

Ellenberg, Matthew. "Whigs in the Streets?" *Maryland Historical Magazine* 86, no. 1 (spring 1991): 23–38.

Towers, Frank. "'A Vociferous Army of Howling Wolves': Baltimore's Civil War Riot of April 19, 1861." *Maryland Historian* 23, no. 2 (fall/winter 1992): 1–27.

George Frederick Ashworth/A. R.

See also **Arrest, Arbitrary, during the Civil War; Habeas Corpus, Writ of.**

BANK FOR INTERNATIONAL SETTLEMENTS. The Bank for International Settlements (BIS), based in Basel, Switzerland, is the oldest international financial institution in the world and the principal center for international central bank cooperation. Known as the "central bankers' central bank," where more than one hundred central banks from around the world have deposits, the BIS is an important financial intermediary. Unlike a central bank, however, the BIS cannot issue notes, accept bills of exchange, lend money to governments, or hold a majority interest in any business. Its holdings are also immune from appropriation by any government. The BIS was established as the result of the Hague Agreement of 20 January 1930, which dealt with the issue of reparation payments imposed upon Germany in the Treaty of Versailles (1919). The bank opened on 17 May 1930 with an authorized capital of 1,500 million Swiss gold francs, or approximately $26,835,000. One of the first duties of the new bank was to oversee the reparations payments. In addition, the BIS was to promote cooperation among central banks throughout the world. Six countries originally helped start the bank: Belgium, France, Germany, United Kingdom, Italy, and Japan (which sold its interests in 1952). Although the United States has never been formally represented on the Board of Directors of the BIS, Americans have served as presidents of the Bank and in other key administrative posts. Today, the central banks of all Western European nations are members of the BIS. As of 31 March 2000, the total deposits placed with the BIS amounted to $128 billion, representing approximately 7 percent of world exchange reserves. At the same time, the balance sheet for the BIS stood at 76,054 million gold francs, a record for the end of a financial year. In fact, the balance of the BIS would have been larger by some 3.2 billion gold francs were it not for the appreciation of the U.S. dollar between the beginning and the end of the financial year.

Over the last seventy years, the BIS has undertaken a number of important duties, including acting as a forum for central bank cooperation. Through regular meetings, the BIS facilitated the exchange of information among central banks throughout the world, even though during the Bretton Woods Conference of 1944 it was suggested that the BIS be liquidated. The BIS managed capital flows following the two oil crises and the international debt crisis of the 1980s. More recently, the bank has worked hard to promote financial stability in the wake of economic integration and globalization and, when needed, to offer emergency financing in support of the international monetary system. The BIS was instrumental in aiding the transition of western European nations from national currencies to the Euro, adopted in 2002. The BIS also conducts research that contributes to international monetary and financial stability, and collects and publishes statistical data on international finance. Using committees of national experts the BIS regularly makes recommendations to the international financial community that will strengthen the international financial and monetary system.

BIBLIOGRAPHY

Baker, James C. *The Bank for International Settlements: Evolution and Evaluation.* Westport, Conn.: Greenwood Publishing, 2002.

Bank for International Settlement. *BIS 71st Annual Report.* Basel: Bank for International Settlements Press, Information and Library Services, June 2001.

Meg Greene Malvasi

See also **Bretton Woods Conference; International Monetary Fund; Versailles, Treaty of.**

BANK OF AMERICA. Under the leadership of its founder, A. P. Giannini, Bank of America played a fundamental role in the development of the West Coast. The bank not only transformed the way banks operated but also financed many important public works and private enterprises across California. These ingenious deals fueled the development of the West, enabling California to become the nation's symbol of hope and inspiration for generations.

Born in 1870 in San Jose to immigrant parents, Giannini's business career began in San Francisco at age twelve, working for his stepfather's wholesale business, handling produce, fruits, and dairy products. The young man traveled the length of the state, making contacts and building a strong reputation. Working directly with farmers, small merchants, and peddlers gave Giannini a lifelong respect for the working class.

On 17 October 1904, after resigning from the board of a San Francisco bank over its policy of ignoring working-class customers, Giannini opened Bank of Italy (later renamed Bank of America) in a remodeled saloon. His employees went door-to-door soliciting business from workers, immigrants, and others ignored by most banks.

Bank of America was transformed from a new bank to a revered institution after its actions during the 1906 San Francisco earthquake and fire, which ravaged the city. Realizing customers needed immediate assistance, Giannini set up an outdoor desk (a wooden plank atop two barrels) and gave people money to rebuild although they had little collateral in return. He recognized the power banks could play in helping transform people's lives and rededicated himself to banking.

Bank of America was the first bank in the United States to open a statewide system of branch banks. By 1920, it expanded to New York and added an overseas branch in Italy. Focusing on community development, the bank financed bonds for hundreds of local governments to build housing, libraries, and roads. Soon it moved into other areas of the nation, including Boston, Chicago, and Dallas. The bank also pioneered new methods of financing California's agricultural industries.

Bank of America funded other extraordinary projects, including the Golden Gate Bridge, Hollywood production companies, and Disneyland. In the 1950s, after Giannini's death in 1949, it was the first bank to use computers and introduced the first nationwide credit card.

In 1998, NationsBank, based in Charlotte, North Carolina, acquired Bank of America. The new organization retained the Bank of America name but kept its headquarters in Charlotte. Three years later it ranked as one of the largest corporations in the world, reporting revenues of nearly $53 billion and profits of $6.8 billion.

BIBLIOGRAPHY

Bonadio, Felice A. *A. P. Giannini: Banker of America*. Berkeley: University of California Press, 1994.

James, Marquis, and Bessie Rowland James. *Biography of a Bank: The Story of Bank of America*. New York: Harper, 1954. Reprint, Westport, Conn.: Greenwood Press, 1971.

Johnston, Moira. *Roller Coaster: The Bank of America and the Future of American Banking*. New York: Ticknor and Fields, 1990.

Bob Batchelor

See also **Banking; Credit; Credit Cards.**

BANK OF AUGUSTA V. EARLE,

13 Peters 519 (1839), involved the right of a Georgia bank to recover on a bill of exchange purchased in Alabama. The Supreme Court, speaking through Chief Justice Roger B. Taney, affirmed the principle of interstate comity, in which corporations chartered in one state were entitled to make contracts and do business in another state. It denied, however, that a corporation possessed the same rights as a naturalized citizen and recognized the right of a state to exclude foreign corporations, should it wish to do so. Taney's opinion became the leading authority on the law of foreign corporations.

BIBLIOGRAPHY

Finkelman, Paul. *An Imperfect Union: Slavery, Federalism, and Comity*. Chapel Hill: University of North Carolina Press, 1981.

Lewis, H. H. Walker. *Without Fear or Favor: A Biography of Chief Justice Roger Brooke Taney*. Boston: Houghton Mifflin, 1965.

Charles Fairman / A. R.

See also **Commerce Clause; Interstate Compacts.**

BANK OF NORTH AMERICA,

America's first government-incorporated bank. In response to a severe depreciation of Continentals, bills of credit that had been used to finance the American Revolution, the Continental Congress appointed Robert Morris superintendent of a new department of finance in 1781. Morris opened a national bank that commenced operations in Philadelphia on 7 January 1782. The bank supplied vital financial aid to the government during the closing months of the American Revolution. Original depositors and stockholders included Thomas Jefferson, Alexander Hamilton, Benjamin Franklin, John Paul Jones, James Monroe, John Jay, and Stephen Decatur.

BIBLIOGRAPHY

Rappaport, George D. *Stability and Change in Revolutionary Pennsylvania*. University Park: Pennsylvania State University Press, 1996.

Ver Steeg, Clarence L. *Robert Morris*. Philadelphia: University of Pennsylvania Press, 1954. Reprint, New York: Hippocrene Books, 1970.

A. W. Whittlesey / F. B.

See also **Banking; Revolution, American: Financial Aspects.**

BANK OF THE UNITED STATES.

Secretary of the Treasury Alexander Hamilton's concept of a central bank grew out of his belief that the government needed a repository for federal funds and an entity to act as its fiscal agent. In 1791, President George Washington signed into law an act creating the Bank of the United States over the objections of Secretary of State Thomas Jefferson. Jefferson and his backers believed this to be an unconstitutional use of federal power and felt it favored commercial and industrial ventures over agrarian interests. They also feared it would promote paper currency over the use of specie, gold and silver coin. However, debt from the Revolutionary War and the differing currencies utilized by each state caused Congress to grant the bank a twenty-year charter.

The bank, based in Philadelphia with branches in eight cities, was empowered to carry on a commercial banking business. It was authorized to issue circulating notes up to $10 million, the amount of its capital. The bank was not permitted to deal in commodities or real estate. It was essentially a private, for-profit institution competing with state banks for deposits and loan customers. At the same time, the Bank of the United States was the Treasury fund depository. Thus, state banks joined the opposition, arguing that the Bank of the United States set the rules and then competed in the marketplace.

During its first eight years of operation, the bank operated conservatively and made few loans. This fiscal conservancy caused state banks and entrepreneurs to complain that economic development was being hampered. By 1811, 70 percent of the bank's stock was held by foreign interests, which would have sent millions in specie overseas had the charter been renewed. That fact, plus opposition from the state banks and agrarians as well as the question of the bank's constitutionality, prevented the charter from being renewed, and the bank ceased operations in 1811.

Debt from the War of 1812 brought about renewed interest in a central bank, particularly as inflation surged from the increasing number of notes issued by private banks, now unrestricted by a federal bank. A twenty-year charter established the Second Bank of the United States in 1816. Congress expected the bank to restore currency soundness through deposits of mass quantities of bank notes by the government. As a large creditor of state banks, the Bank of the United States demanded specie payments for those notes, forcing the state banks to limit the amount of notes and loans they issued. This restriction of credit, which occurred while the population and economy were expanding, led to the same complaints that had plagued the first Bank of the United States.

In 1833, President Andrew Jackson, who had been battling the bank's existence since 1829, removed all federal funds from the bank, placing them in "pet banks." Due to the actions of President Jackson, as well as continuing opposition from state banks and agrarians, the charter was not renewed in 1836. The Second Bank of the United States ceased existing as a national institution.

BIBLIOGRAPHY

Hammond, Bray. *Banks and Politics in America from the Revolution to the Civil War.* Princeton, N.J.: Princeton University Press, 1957.

Knox, John Jay. *A History of Banking in the United States.* New York: Bradford, Rhodes, 1900.

Remini, Robert V. *Andrew Jackson.* New York: Twayne, 1966.

T. L. Livermore
Terri Livermore

See also **Banking: Overview; Hamilton's Economic Policies; Pet Banks; Removal of Deposits.**

BANKHEAD COTTON ACT, approved 21 April 1934, was designed to supplement the cotton-production control provisions of the Agricultural Adjustment Act of 1933. While not actually placing limits on the growing of cotton by individual farmers, the act established a national quota and levied a prohibitive tax of 50 percent of the central market price (but not less than five cents per pound) on cotton ginned in excess of the individual quota. This tax was the essence of the act. The Kerr-Smith Tobacco Control Act of 1934 used a similar taxation strategy to limit tobacco production. Following the *United States v. Butler* (1936) decision of the Supreme Court invalidating the Agricultural Adjustment Act, Congress repealed the Bankhead Act (10 February 1936). Nineteen days later, Congress passed the Soil Conservation and Domestic Allotment Act, which limited production by paying farmers not to plant soil-depleting crops.

BIBLIOGRAPHY

Heacock, Walter J. "William B. Bankhead and the New Deal." *Journal of Southern History* 21 (August 1955): 347–359.

Saloutos, Theodore. *The American Farmer and the New Deal.* Ames: Iowa State University Press, 1982.

R. P. Brooks/T. M.

See also **Agriculture; New Deal.**

BANKING

This entry includes 9 subentries:
Overview
Bank Failures
Banking Acts of 1933 and 1935
Banking Crisis of 1933
Export-Import Banks
Investment Banks
Private Banks
Savings Banks
State Banks

OVERVIEW

The fundamental functions of a commercial bank during the past two centuries have been making loans, receiving deposits, and lending credit either in the form of bank notes or of "created" deposits. The banks in which people keep their checking accounts are commercial banks.

There were no commercial banks in colonial times, although there were loan offices or land banks that made loans on real estate security with limited issues of legal tender notes. In 1781 Robert Morris founded the first commercial bank in the United States—the Bank of North America. It greatly assisted the financing of the closing stages of the American Revolution. By 1800, there were twenty-eight state-chartered banks, and by 1811 there were eighty-eight.

Alexander Hamilton's financial program included a central bank to serve as a financial agent of the treasury, provide a depository for public money, and act as a regulator of the currency. Accordingly, the first Bank of the United States was founded 25 February 1791. Its $10 million capital and favored relationship with the government aroused much anxiety, especially among Jeffersonians. The bank's sound but unpopular policy of promptly returning bank notes for redemption in specie (money in coin) and refusing those of non-specie-paying banks—together with a political feud—was largely responsible for the narrow defeat of a bill to recharter it in 1811. Between 1811 and 1816, both people and government were dependent on state banks. Nearly all but the New England banks suspended specie payments in September 1814 because of the War of 1812 and their own unregulated credit expansion.

The country soon recognized the need for a new central bank, and Congress established the second Bank of the United States on 10 April 1816. Its $35 million capitalization and favored relationship with the Treasury likewise aroused anxiety. Instead of repairing the overexpanded credit situation that it inherited, it aggravated it by generous lending policies, which precipitated the panic of 1819, in which it barely saved itself and generated widespread ill will.

Thereafter, under Nicholas Biddle, the central bank was well run. As had its predecessor, it required other banks to redeem their notes in specie, but most of the banks had come to accept that policy, for they appreciated the services and the stability provided by the second bank. The bank's downfall grew out of President Andrew Jackson's prejudice against banks and monopolies, the memory of the bank's role in the 1819 panic, and most of all, Biddle's decision to let rechartering be a main issue in the 1832 presidential election. Many persons otherwise friendly to the bank, faced with a choice of Jackson or the bank, chose Jackson. He vetoed the recharter. After 26 September 1833, the government placed all its deposits with politically selected state banks until it set up the Independent Treasury System in the 1840s. Between 1830 and 1837, the number of banks, bank note circulation, and bank loans all about tripled. Without the second bank to regulate them, the banks overextended themselves in lending to speculators in land. The panic of 1837 resulted in a suspension of specie payments, many failures, and a depression that lasted until 1844.

Between 1833 and 1863, the country was without an adequate regulator of bank currency. In some states, the laws were very strict or forbade banking, whereas in others the rules were lax. Banks made many long-term loans and resorted to many subterfuges to avoid redeeming their notes in specie. Almost everywhere, bank tellers and merchants had to consult weekly publications known as Bank Note Reporters for the current discount on bank notes, and turn to the latest Bank Note Detectors to distinguish the hundreds of counterfeits and notes of failed banks. This situation constituted an added business risk and necessitated somewhat higher markups on merchandise. In this bleak era of banking, however, there were some bright spots. These were the SUFFOLK BANKING SYSTEM of Massachusetts (1819–1863); the moderately successful SAFETY FUND system (1829–1866) and Free Banking (1838–1866) systems of New York; the Indiana (1834–1865), Ohio (1845–1866), and Iowa (1858–1865) systems; and the Louisiana Banking System (1842–1862). Inefficient and corrupt as some of the banking was before the Civil War, the nation's expanding economy found it an improvement over the system on which the eighteenth-century economy had depended.

Secretary of the Treasury Salmon P. Chase began agitating for an improved banking system in 1861. On 25 February 1863, Congress passed the National Banking Act, which created the National Banking System. Its head officer was the comptroller of currency. It was based on several recent reforms, especially the Free Banking System's principle of bond-backed notes. Nonetheless, the reserve requirements for bank notes were high, and the law forbade real estate loans and branch banking, had stiff organization requirements, and imposed burdensome taxes. State banks at first saw little reason to join, but, in 1865, Congress levied a prohibitive 10 percent tax on their bank notes, which drove most of these banks into the new system. The use of checks had been increasing in popularity in the more settled regions long before the Civil War, and, by 1853, the total of bank deposits exceeded that of bank notes. After 1865 the desire of both state and national banks to avoid the various new restrictions on bank notes doubtless speeded up the shift to this more convenient form of bank credit. Since state banks were less restricted, their number increased again until it passed that of national banks in 1894. Most large banks were national, however.

The National Banking System constituted a substantial improvement over the pre–Civil War hodgepodge of banking systems. Still, it had three major faults. The first was the perverse elasticity of the bond-secured bank notes, the supply of which did not vary in accordance with the needs of business. The second was the decentralization of bank deposit reserves. There were three classes of national banks: the lesser ones kept part of their reserves in their own vaults and deposited the rest at interest with the larger national banks. These national banks in turn lent a considerable part of the funds on the call money market to finance stock speculation. In times of uncertainty, the lesser banks demanded their outside reserves, call money rates soared, security prices tobogganed, and runs on deposits ruined many banks. The third major fault was that there was no central bank to take measures to forestall such crises or to lend to deserving banks in times of distress.

In 1873, 1884, 1893, and 1907, panics highlighted the faults of the National Banking System. Improvised use of clearinghouse certificates in interbank settlements somewhat relieved money shortages in the first three cases, whereas "voluntary" bank assessments collected and lent by a committee headed by J. P. Morgan gave relief in 1907. In 1908 Congress passed the ALDRICH-VREELAND ACT to investigate foreign central banking systems and suggest reforms, and to permit emergency bank note issues. The Owen-Glass Act of 1913 superimposed a central banking system on the existing national banking system. It required all national banks to "join" the new system, which meant to buy stock in it immediately equal to 3 percent of their capital and surplus, thus providing the funds with which to set up the Federal Reserve System. State banks might also join by meeting specified requirements, but, by the end of 1916, only thirty-four had done so. A majority of the nation's banks have always remained outside the Federal Reserve System, although the larger banks have usually been members. The Federal Reserve System largely corrected the faults to which the National Banking System had fallen prey. Admittedly, the Federal Reserve had its faults and did not live up to expectations. Nevertheless, the nation's commercial banks had a policy-directing head and a refuge in distress to a greater degree than they had ever had before. Thus ended the need for the Independent Treasury System, which finally wound up its affairs in 1921.

Only a few national banks gave up their charters for state ones in order to avoid joining the Federal Reserve System. However, during WORLD WAR I, many state banks became members of the system. All banks helped sell Liberty bonds and bought short-term Treasuries between bond drives, which was one reason for a more than doubling of the money supply and also of the price level from 1914 to 1920. A major contributing factor for these doublings was the sharp reduction in reserves required under the new Federal Reserve System as compared with the pre-1914 National Banking System.

By 1921 there were 31,076 banks, the all-time peak. Every year, local crop failures, other disasters, or simply bad management wiped out several hundred banks. By 1929 the number of banks had declined to 25,568. Admittedly, mergers eliminated a few names, and the growth of branch, group, or chain banking provided stability in some areas. Nevertheless, the 1920s are most notable for stock market speculation. Several large banks had a part in this speculation, chiefly through their investment affiliates. The role of investment adviser gave banks great prestige until the panic of 1929, when widespread disillusionment from losses and scandals brought them discredit.

The 1930s witnessed many reforms growing out of the more than 9,000 bank failures between 1930 and 1933 and capped by the nationwide bank moratorium of 6–9 March 1933. To reform the commercial and central banking systems, as well as to restore confidence in them, Congress passed two major banking laws between 1933 and 1935. These laws gave the Federal Reserve System firmer control over the banking system. They also set up the Federal Deposit Insurance Corporation to insure bank deposits, and soon all but a few hundred small banks belonged to it. That move greatly reduced the number of bank failures. Other changes included banning investment affiliates, prohibiting banks from paying interest on demand deposits, loosening restrictions against national banks' having branches and making real estate loans, and giving the Federal Reserve Board the authority to raise member bank legal reserve requirements against deposits. As a result of the Depression, the supply of commercial loans dwindled, and interest rates fell sharply. Consequently, banks invested more in federal government obligations, built up excess reserves, and imposed service charges on checking accounts. The 1933–1934 devaluation of the dollar, which stimulated large imports of gold, was another cause of those excess reserves.

During WORLD WAR II, the banks again helped sell war bonds. They also converted their excess reserves into government obligations and dramatically increased their own holdings of these. Demand deposits more than doubled. Owing to bank holdings of government obligations and to Federal Reserve commitments to the treasury, the Federal Reserve had lost its power to curb bank-credit expansion. Price levels nearly doubled during the 1940s.

In the Federal Reserve-treasury "accord" of March 1951, the Federal Reserve System regained its freedom to curb credit expansion, and thereafter interest rates crept upward. That development improved bank profits and led banks to reduce somewhat their holdings of federal government obligations. Term loans to industry and real es-

tate loans increased. Banks also encountered stiff competition from rapidly growing rivals, such as savings and loan associations and personal finance companies. On 28 July 1959, Congress eliminated the difference between reserve city banks and central reserve city banks for member banks. The new law kept the same reserve requirements against demand deposits, but it permitted banks to count cash in their vaults as part of their legal reserves.

Interest rates rose spectacularly all during the 1960s and then dropped sharply in 1971, only to rise once more to 12 percent in mid-1974. Whereas consumer prices had gone up 23 percent during the 1950s, they rose 31 percent during the 1960s—especially toward the end of the decade as budget deficits mounted—and climbed another 24 percent by mid-1974. Money supply figures played a major role in determining Federal Reserve credit policy from 1960 on.

Money once consisted largely of hard coin. With the coming of commercial banks, it came also to include bank notes and demand deposits. The difference, however, between these and various forms of "near money"—time deposits, savings and loan association deposits, and federal government E and H bonds—is slight. Credit cards carry the confusion a step further. How does one add up the buying power of money, near money, and credit cards? As new forms of credit became more like money, it was increasingly difficult for the Federal Reserve to regulate the supply of credit and prevent booms.

Since 1970 banking and finance have undergone nothing less than a revolution. The structure of the industry in the mid-1990s bore little resemblance to that established in the 1930s in the aftermath of the bank failures of the Great Depression. In the 1970s and 1980s, what had been a fractured system by design became a single market, domestically and internationally. New Deal banking legislation of the Depression era stemmed from the belief that integration of the banking system had allowed problems in one geographical area or part of the financial system to spread to the entire system. Regulators sought, therefore, to prevent money from flowing between different geographical areas and between different functional segments. These measures ruled out many of the traditional techniques of risk management through diversification and pooling. As a substitute, the government guaranteed bank deposits through the Federal Deposit Insurance Corporation and the Federal Savings and Loan Insurance Corporation.

In retrospect, it is easy to see why the segmented system broke down. It was inevitable that the price of money would vary across different segments of the system. It was also inevitable that borrowers in a high-interest area would seek access to a neighboring low-interest area—and vice versa for lenders. The only question is why it took so long for the pursuit of self-interest to break down regulatory barriers. Price divergence by itself perhaps was not a strong enough incentive. Rationing of credit during tight credit periods probably was the cause of most innovation.

Necessity, not profit alone, seems to have been the cause of financial innovation.

Once communication between segments of the system opened, mere price divergence was sufficient to cause flows of funds. The microelectronics revolution enhanced flows, as it became easier to identify and exploit profit opportunities. Technological advances sped up the process of market unification by lowering transaction costs and widening opportunities. The most important consequence of the unification of segmented credit markets was a diminished role for banks. Premium borrowers found they could tap the national money market directly by issuing commercial paper, thus obtaining funds more cheaply than banks could provide. In 1972 money-market mutual funds began offering shares in a pool of money-market assets as a substitute for bank deposits. Thus, banks faced competition in both lending and deposit-taking—competition generally not subject to the myriad regulatory controls facing banks.

Consolidation of banking became inevitable as its functions eroded. The crisis of the savings and loan industry was the most visible symptom of this erosion. Savings and loans associations (S&Ls) had emerged to funnel household savings to residential mortgages, which they did until the high interest rates of the inflationary 1970s caused massive capital losses on long-term mortgages and rendered many S&Ls insolvent by 1980. Attempts to regain solvency by lending cash from the sale of existing mortgages to borrowers willing to pay high interest only worsened the crisis, because high-yield loans turned out to be high risk. The mechanisms invented to facilitate mortgage sales undermined S&Ls in the longer term as it became possible for specialized mortgage bankers to make mortgage loans and sell them without any need for the expensive deposit side of the traditional S&L business.

Throughout the 1970s and 1980s, regulators met each evasion of a regulatory obstacle with further relaxation of the rules. The Depository Institutions Deregulation and Monetary Control Act (1980) recognized the array of competitors for bank business by expanding the authority of the Federal Reserve System over the new entrants and relaxing regulation of banks. Pressed by a borrowers' lobby seeking access to low-cost funds and a depositors' lobby seeking access to high money-market returns, regulators saw little choice but capitulation. Mistakes occurred, notably the provision in the 1980 act that extended deposit insurance coverage to $100,000, a provision that greatly increased the cost of the eventual S&L bailout. The provision found its justification in the need to attract money to banks. The mistake was in not recognizing that the world had changed and that the entire raison d'être of the industry was disappearing.

Long-term corporate finance underwent a revolution comparable to that in banking. During the prosperous 1950s and 1960s, corporations shied away from debt and preferred to keep debt-equity ratios low and to rely on ample internal funds for investment. The high cost of issuing bonds—a consequence of the uncompetitive system of investment banking—reinforced this preference. Usually, financial intermediaries held the bonds that corporations did issue. Individual owners, not institutions, mainly held corporate equities. In the 1970s and 1980s, corporations came to rely on external funds, so that debt-equity ratios rose substantially and interest payments absorbed a much greater part of earnings. The increased importance of external finance was itself a source of innovation as corporations sought ways to reduce the cost of debt service. Equally important was increased reliance on institutional investors as purchasers of securities. When private individuals were the main holders of equities, the brokerage business was uncompetitive and fees were high, but institutional investors used their clout to reduce the costs of buying and selling. Market forces became much more important in finance, just as in banking.

Institutional investors shifted portfolio strategies toward equities, in part to enhance returns to meet pension liabilities after the Employment Retirement Income Security Act (1974) required full funding of future liabilities. Giving new attention to maximizing investment returns, the institutional investors became students of the new theories of rational investment decision championed by academic economists. The capital asset pricing model developed in the 1960s became the framework that institutional investors most used to make asset allocations.

The microelectronics revolution was even more important for finance than for banking. Indeed, it would have been impossible to implement the pricing model without high-speed, inexpensive computation to calculate optimal portfolio weightings across the thousands of traded equities. One may argue that computational technology did not really cause the transformation of finance and that increased attention of institutional investors was bound to cause a transformation in any event. Both the speed and extent of transformation would have been impossible, however, without advances in computational and communications technologies.

BIBLIOGRAPHY

Bodenhorn, Howard N. *A History of Banking in Antebellum America: Financial Markets and Economic Development in an Era of Nation-Building.* Cambridge: Cambridge University Press, 2000.

Gilbart, James William. *The History of Banking in America.* London: Routledge/Thoemmes Press, 1996.

Hoffmann, Susan. *Politics and Banking: Ideas, Public Policy, and the Creation of Financial Institutions.* Baltimore: Johns Hopkins University Press, 2001.

Mehrling, Perry. *The Money Interest and the Public Interest: American Monetary Thought, 1920–1970.* Cambridge, Mass.: Harvard University Press, 1997.

Timberlake, Richard H. *Monetary Policy in the United States: An Intellectual and Institutional History.* Chicago: University of Chicago Press, 1993.

Timberlake, Richard H. *The Origins of Central Banking in the United States.* Cambridge, Mass.: Harvard University Press, 1978.

Wicker, Elmus. *Banking Panics of the Gilded Age.* Cambridge, Mass: Cambridge University Press, 2000.

Wright, Robert E. *Origins of Commercial Banking in America, 1750–1800.* Lanham, Md.: Rowman and Littlefield, 2001.

Donald L. Kemmerer
Perry G. Mehrling / A. E.

See also **Bank of America; Bank of the United States; Clearinghouses; Credit Cards; Credit Unions; Federal Reserve System; Financial Panics; Financial Services Industry; Savings and Loan Associations.**

BANK FAILURES

American financial history to 1934 was characterized by numerous bank failures, because the majority of banks were local enterprises, not regional or national institutions with numerous branches. Lax state government regulations and inadequate examinations permitted many banks to pursue unsound practices. With most financial eggs in local economic baskets, it took only a serious crop failure or a business recession to precipitate dozens or even hundreds of bank failures. On the whole, state-chartered banks had a particularly poor record.

Early Bank Failures

Early-nineteenth-century banks were troubled by a currency shortage and the resulting inability to redeem their notes in specie. States later imposed penalties in those circumstances, but such an inability did not automatically signify failure. The first bank to fail was the Farmers' Exchange Bank of Glocester, R.I., in 1809. The statistics of bank failures between 1789 and 1863 are inadequate, but the losses were unquestionably large. John Jay Knox estimated that the losses to noteholders were 5 percent per annum, and bank notes were the chief money used by the general public. Not until after 1853 did banks' deposit liabilities exceed their note liabilities. Between 1830 and 1860, weekly news sheets called bank note reporters gave the latest discount quoted on the notes of weak and closed banks. All businesses had to allow for worthless bank notes. Although some states—such as New York in 1829 and 1838, Louisiana in 1842, and Indiana in 1834—established sound banking systems, banking as a whole was characterized by frequent failures.

The establishment of the National Banking System in 1863 introduced needed regulations for national (i.e., nationally chartered) banks. These were larger and more numerous than state banks until 1894, but even their record left much to be desired. Between 1864 and 1913—a period that saw the number of banks rise from 1,532 to 26,664—515 national banks were suspended, and only two years passed without at least one suspension. State banks suffered 2,491 collapses during the same period.

The worst year was the panic year of 1893, with almost five hundred bank failures. The establishment of the FEDERAL RESERVE SYSTEM in 1913 did little to improve the record of national banks. Although all banks were required to join the new system, 825 banks failed between 1914 and 1929, and an additional 1,947 failed by the end of 1933. During the same twenty years there were 12,714 state bank failures. By 1933 there were 14,771 banks in the United States, half as many as in 1920, and most of that half had disappeared by the failure route. During the 1920s, Canada, employing a branch banking system, had only one failure. Half a dozen states had experimented with deposit insurance plans without success. Apparently the situation needed the attention of the federal government.

FDIC Established

The bank holocaust of the early 1930s—9,106 bank failures in four years, 1,947 of them national banks—culminating in President Franklin D. Roosevelt's executive order declaring a nationwide bank moratorium in March 1933, at last produced the needed drastic reforms. In 1933 Congress passed the GLASS-STEAGALL ACT, which forbade Federal Reserve member banks to pay interest on demand deposits, and founded the Federal Deposit Insurance Corporation (FDIC). In an effort to protect bank deposits from rapid swings in the market, the Glass-Steagall Banking Act of 1933 forced banks to decide between deposit safeholding and investment. Executives of security firms, for example, were prohibited from sitting as trustees of commercial banks.

The FDIC raised its initial capital by selling two kinds of stock. Class A stock (paying dividends) came from assessing every insured bank 0.5 percent of its total deposits—half paid in full, half subject to call. All member banks of the Federal Reserve System had to be insured. Federal Reserve Banks had to buy Class B stock (paying no dividends) with 0.5 percent of their surplus—half payable immediately, half subject to call. In addition, any bank desiring to be insured paid .083 percent of its average deposits annually. The FDIC first insured each depositor in a bank up to $2,500; in mid-1934 Congress put the figure at $5,000; on 21 September 1950, the maximum became $10,000; on 16 October 1966, the limit went to $15,000; on 23 December 1969, to $20,000; and on 27 November 1974, to $40,000. At the end of 1971 the FDIC was insuring 98.6 percent of all commercial banks and fully protecting 99 percent of all depositors. However, it was protecting only about 64 percent of all deposits, with savings deposits protected at a high percentage but business deposits at only about 55 percent. By the mid-1970s the FDIC was examining more than 50 percent of the banks in the nation, which accounted for about 20 percent of banking assets. It did not usually examine member banks of the Federal Reserve System, which were the larger banks. There was a degree of rivalry between the large and small banks, and the FDIC was viewed as the friend of the smaller banks.

Whereas in the 1920s banks failed at an average rate of about six hundred a year, during the first nine years of the FDIC (1934–1942) there were 487 bank closings because of financial difficulties, mostly of insured banks; 387 of these received disbursements from the FDIC. During the years from 1943 to 1972, the average number of closings dropped to five per year. From 1934 to 1971 the corporation made disbursements in 496 cases involving 1.8 million accounts, representing $1.215 billion in total deposits. The FDIC in 1973 had $5.4 billion in assets. Through this protection, people were spared that traumatic experience of past generations, a "run on the bank" and the loss of a large part of their savings. For example, in 1974 the $5 billion Franklin National Bank of New York, twentieth in size in the nation, failed. It was the largest failure in American banking history. The FDIC, the Federal Reserve, and the comptroller of the currency arranged the sale of most of the bank's holdings, and no depositor lost a cent.

The 1980s and the Savings and Loan Debacle

The widespread bank failures of the 1980s—more than sixteen hundred FDIC-insured banks were closed or received financial assistance between 1980 and 1994—revealed major weaknesses in the federal deposit insurance system. In the 1970s, mounting defense and social welfare costs, rising oil prices, and the collapse of American manufacturing vitality in certain key industries (especially steel and electronics) produced spiraling inflation and a depressed securities market. Securities investments proved central to the economic recovery of the 1980s, as corporations cut costs through mergers, takeovers, and leveraged buyouts. The shifting corporate terrain created new opportunities for high-risk, high-yield investments known as "junk bonds." The managers of the newly deregulated savings and loan (S&L) institutions, eager for better returns, invested heavily in these and other investments—in particular, a booming commercial real estate market. When the real estate bubble burst, followed by a series of insider-trading indictments of Wall Street financiers and revelations of corruption at the highest levels of the S&L industry, hundreds of the S&Ls collapsed. In 1988 the Federal Home Loan Bank Board began the process of selling off the defunct remains of 222 saving and loans. Congress passed sweeping legislation the following year that authorized a massive government bailout and imposed strict new regulatory laws on the S&L industry. The cost of the cleanup to U.S. taxpayers was $132 billion.

In addition to the S&L crisis, the overall trend within the banking industry during the 1980s was toward weaker performance ratios, declining profitability, and a quick increase in loan charge-offs, all of which placed an unusual strain on banks. Seeking stability in increased size, the banking industry responded with a wave of consolidations and mergers. This was possible in large part because Congress relaxed restrictions on branch banking in an effort to give the industry flexibility in its attempts to adjust to the changing economy. Deregulation also made it easier for banks to engage in risky behavior, however, contributing to a steep increase in bank failures when loans and investments went bad in the volatile economic climate. Legislators found themselves torn among the need to deregulate banks, the need to prevent failures, and the need to recapitalize deposit insurance funds, which had suffered a huge loss during the decade. In general, they responded by giving stronger tools to regulators but narrowly circumscribing the discretion of regulators to use those tools.

During the 1990s, the globalization of the banking industry meant that instability abroad would have rapid repercussions in American financial markets; this, along with banks' growing reliance on computer systems, presented uncertain challenges to the stability of domestic banks in the final years of the twentieth century. As the economy boomed in the second half of the decade, however, the performance of the banking industry improved remarkably, and the number of bank failures rapidly declined. Although it was unclear whether the industry had entered a new period of stability or was merely benefiting from the improved economic context, the unsettling rise in bank failures of the 1980s seemed to have been contained.

BIBLIOGRAPHY

Benston, George J. *The Separation of Commercial and Investment Banking: The Glass-Steagall Act Revisited and Reconsidered.* New York: Oxford University Press, 1990.

Calavita, Kitty, Henry N. Pontell, and Robert H. Tillman. *Big Money Crime: Fraud and Politics in the Savings and Loan Crisis.* Berkeley: University of California Press, 1997.

Dillistin, William H. *Bank Note Reporters and Counterfeit Detectors, 1826–1866.* New York: American Numismatic Society, 1949.

Lee, Alston, Wayne Grove, and David Wheelock. "Why Do Banks Fail? Evidence from the 1920s." *Explorations in Economic History* (October 1994): 409–431.

Thies, Clifford, and Daniel Gerlowski. "Bank Capital and Bank Failure, 1921–1932: Testing the White Hypothesis." *Journal of Economic History* (1993): 908–914.

Walton, Gary M., ed. *Regulatory Change in an Atmosphere of Crisis: Current Implications of the Roosevelt Years.* New York: Academic Press, 1979.

Donald L. Kemmerer / A. R.; C. W.

See also **Business Cycles; Savings and Loan Associations; Specie Payments, Suspension and Resumption of.**

BANKING ACTS OF 1933 AND 1935

The Banking Act of 1933, approved on 16 June and known also as the GLASS-STEAGALL ACT, contained three groups of provisions designed to restore stability to and confidence in the banking system. The first group of provisions increased the power of the Federal Reserve Board to control credit. The second group separated commercial and investment banking functions by prohibiting commercial banks from operating investment affiliates and by prohibiting investment banking houses from carrying on a deposit banking business. (These provisions were repealed by the Gramm-Leach-Bliley Act of 1999, also known as the Banking Modernization Bill.) The third group of provisions dealt with commercial banks and included a provision providing for the insurance of bank deposits under the supervision of the Federal Deposit Insurance Corporation (FDIC). (Creation of the FDIC is one of the New Deal's most important legacies and probably prevented a large-scale banking collapse in the early 1980s.)

The Banking Act of 1935, approved on 23 August, further increased government control over currency and credit. Title I amended the deposit insurance provisions of the Banking Act of 1933, and Title III contained a series of technical amendments to the banking laws governing the operations of the commercial banks. The most important of the act's three titles was Title II, which drastically reorganized the Federal Reserve Board and centralized control of the money market in its hands. The act authorized the president to appoint the seven members of the newly named "Board of Governors of the Federal Reserve System" for fourteen-year terms. It also increased and centralized the board's powers over discount and open market operations of the Reserve banks and materially broadened the discount base.

BIBLIOGRAPHY

Dawley, Alan. *Struggles for Justice: Social Responsibility and the Liberal State.* Cambridge, Mass.: Harvard University Press, 1991.

Leuchtenburg, William E. *Franklin D. Roosevelt and the New Deal, 1932–1940.* New York: Harper and Row, 1963.

McElvaine, Robert S. *The Great Depression: America 1929–1941.* Rev. ed. New York: Times Books, 1993.

Frederick A. Bradford / C. P.

See also **New Deal.**

BANKING CRISIS OF 1933

The outcome of both the large number of bank failures during 1931–1932 and the wave of hoarding which swept the country in response, markedly weakened the banking structure. Attempts by the RECONSTRUCTION FINANCE CORPORATION to avoid disaster were in large measure nullified by the publication of the names of banks that had borrowed from it, a procedure not calculated to restore confidence to frightened depositors.

Banking difficulties in Michigan finally caused Governor William A. Comstock to declare a bank "holiday" in that state on 14 February 1933. Alarm quickly spread to neighboring states. Banking moratoria were declared in four other states by the end of February and in seventeen additional states during the first three days of March. Finally, on 4 March 1933, on his first day in office,

President Franklin D. Roosevelt closed banks in the remaining states.

The situation was serious, and prompt action was imperative. Congress, called in special session by the president, passed the Emergency Banking Relief Act of 1933 on 9 March, thus providing machinery for reopening the banks. Under this act, only sound banks were to be reopened, while those of questionable soundness were to be placed in the hands of conservators and opened later if conditions permitted. The national bank moratorium was extended a few days to permit the provisions of the act to be put into effect. Sound banks reopened on 13–15 March. By the latter date, banks controlling about 90 percent of the banking resources of the country were again in operation, and the banking crisis of 1933 was at an end.

BIBLIOGRAPHY

Dawley, Alan. *Struggles for Justice: Social Responsibility and the Liberal State.* Cambridge, Mass.: Harvard University Press, 1991.

Kennedy, Susan Estabrook. *The Banking Crisis of 1933.* Lexington: University Press of Kentucky, 1973.

McElvaine, Robert S. *The Great Depression: America, 1929–1941.* Rev. ed. New York: Times Books, 1993.

Frederick A. Bradford / C. P.

See also **Glass-Steagall Act;** *and vol. 9:* **Fireside Chat on the Bank Crisis.**

EXPORT-IMPORT BANKS

The Export-Import Bank of the United States (Ex-Im Bank) is the official export credit agency (ECA) of the United States. Its purpose is to match officially supported foreign competition and to address export financing needs that are unmet by the private sector in order to maximize American exports. Currently, Ex-Im Bank performs this function through direct loans or guarantees of commercial loans to foreign buyers of American exports, working capital guarantees for United States exporters, and export credit insurance. In 2001 it made $871 million in direct loans, $6.1 billion in loan guarantees, and $2.3 billion in export credit insurance.

Franklin D. Roosevelt established the first Ex-Im Bank by executive order. It was chartered on 12 February 1934 as an instrument of his foreign policy and to promote economic recovery from the Great Depression by providing financing for moribund foreign trade. The bank's initial purpose was to facilitate trade with the Soviet Union after the United States extended diplomatic recognition. A second Ex-Im Bank was chartered in March to facilitate trade with a new government in Cuba, but its charter was quickly changed to allow it to finance trade with all countries except the Soviet Union. In June 1935, when it became apparent that government-supported trade with the Soviet Union would not materialize, the two banks were merged. Until 1945 Ex-Im Bank financed its operations by the sale of Reconstruction Finance Corporation stock to the Treasury Department. It primarily financed the foreign purchase of American exports of transportation equipment and agricultural products to Latin America. Ex-Im Bank also supported American exports used in infrastructure projects in strategic nations such as Haiti and Brazil, where Nazi influence was increasing, or in China, which was at war with Japan. These activities led Congress in 1939 to impose a dollar limit on the total loans the agency could have outstanding at any given time. Such congressional limits remain a feature of the bank's operations. The limit as of 2002 was $75 billion.

During World War II Ex-Im Bank's activities were largely confined to Latin America and financing American exports for projects that related to infrastructure and production of strategic materials. Subsequently, Congress passed the Export-Import Bank Act of 1945. It established Ex-Im Bank as an independent agency, with a bipartisan, appointed board of directors, including a chair, confirmed by the Senate. Capital was $1 billion in stock purchased by the Treasury, and Ex-Im Bank had authority to borrow up to $2.5 billion from the Treasury to finance its operations. In 1947 Congress required periodic rechartering of all federal corporations, including Ex-Im Bank. Since that time, Congress has used the process periodically to increase the bank's outstanding loan ceiling. Finally, the 1945 act mandated that Ex-Im Bank not compete with the private sector and that it make only those loans with a "reasonable assurance of repayment," principles that had already become part of the bank's institutional culture.

Immediately after the end of World War II and the termination of the lend-lease program that provided strategic materials to Allied countries, Ex-Im Bank made over $2 billion in loans to Western European nations for purchases of American exports. This pre–Marshall Plan assistance was crucial to European recovery. However, the generous repayment terms dictated by foreign policy considerations were a matter of consternation to many at Ex-Im Bank. After the start-up of the Marshall Plan, the bank was again able to focus on its traditional customers in Latin America. During the 1950s, loans to finance the purchase of American exports by Asian governments increased.

From the end of the 1950s through the early 1970s, the United States incurred substantial international balance-of-payment and budget deficits. Exporter and government pressure on Ex-Im Bank to enhance its assistance to American exporters increased as foreign ECAs became more aggressive supporters of their exporters. By 1971 Congress mandated that Ex-Im Bank's assistance to American exporters and foreign purchasers of American exports be competitive with those of other ECAs. After 1961 the bank increasingly leveraged its assistance to exporters by creating and expanding partnerships with the private sector. It guaranteed loans made by private institutions and underwrote export credit insurance in conjunction with an expansion of its traditional direct loan program. These operations increasingly financed the foreign purchase of new American technologies such as jet aircraft, nuclear power, and communications equipment. Beginning in 1963 Congress specifically authorized annual limits on Ex-Im Bank loan and guarantee activity in addition to its traditional approval of its annual administrative budget.

Increasing federal deficits, the oil price rise, and the end to fixed exchange rates in 1973 brought major changes to Ex-Im Bank's environment. Some critics thought that the end to fixed rates undermined the rationale for Ex-Im Bank's promotional activities. Critics from a variety of political perspectives noted that assistance to exporters was overwhelmingly bestowed on a few firms that exported large capital goods such as aircraft, power generation equipment, and construction machinery. In a period of tight federal budgets, critics also wondered just how effective were Ex-Im Bank's increasing subsidies in creating new export sales.

The high interest rates of the 1970s and intensified competition from foreign ECAs created major financial problems for Ex-Im Bank by the early 1980s. The "spread" between its high cost of borrowing from the Treasury and the lower rates it had to give foreign purchasers of American exports to keep U.S. exports competitive created huge losses and undermined the bank's balance sheet. By the early 1980s the debt crisis in the developing world dramatically reduced demand for foreign trade finance but increased the amount of underperforming or nonperforming loans or guarantees on Ex-Im Bank's books.

Ex-Im Bank's and the Treasury Department's response to the bank's worsening finances was slow in developing, but by the 1990s it had achieved success. Beginning in 1978, a series of increasingly stringent understandings about the terms of international export finance and their enforcement were developed through the Organization for Economic Cooperation and Development. The long-term impact has been to reduce export subsidies in international trade. During the 1980s Ex-Im Bank improved its risk assessment mechanisms and adjusted its fee structure. In 1989 the bank established a nonspecific loss reserve for nonperforming assets in its loan portfolio. Legislation enacted by Congress in 1990 provided a continuing appropriation for nonperforming assets, and by 2000 Ex-Im Bank received an annual appropriation of approximately $1 billion to cover the assessed risk of its ongoing activities. During the 1990s the privatization of state enterprises worldwide, the capital needs of the former Soviet Bloc, and the continued reluctance of private institutions to commit to export finance in many such markets led to dramatic increases in Ex-Im Bank loan guarantee activity.

BIBLIOGRAPHY

Adams, Frederick C. *Economic Diplomacy: The Export-Import Bank and American Foreign Policy, 1934–1939*. Columbia: University of Missouri Press, 1976.

Becker, William H., and William M. McClenahan. *The Market, the State, and the Export-Import Bank of the United States, 1934–2000.* New York: Cambridge University Press, 2003.

Hufbauer, Gary Clyde, and Rita M. Rodriguez, eds. *The Ex-Im Bank in the Twenty-first Century: A New Approach.* Washington, D.C.: Institute for International Economics, 2001.

Hillman, Jordan Jay. *The Export-Import Bank at Work: Promotional Financing in the Public Sector.* Westport, Conn.: Quorum Books, 1982.

Rodriguez, Rita M., ed. *The Export-Import Bank at Fifty: The International Environment and the Institution's Role.* Lexington, Mass: Lexington Books, 1987.

William M. McClenahan Jr.

See also **Banking: Overview; Export Taxes; Organization for Economic Cooperation and Development; Trade, Foreign.**

INVESTMENT BANKS

Investment banks are not banks in the strictest sense of the term. Unlike financial intermediaries (of which commercial banks are the most well-known), investment banks do not themselves acquire funds from savers (lenders) in order to provide those funds to investors (borrowers). Instead, these institutions facilitate the flows of funds from savers to corporations (or government agencies) that wish to raise capital. (This function should be distinguished from the resale of existing securities, a process that is simplified by the existence of organized secondary markets such as the New York Stock Exchange.)

Practices

Investment banks work through a process called underwriting. Usually acting in a group or syndicate, the bankers first advise the borrower on what sort of security to use to raise the required funds, the options being equity (stocks) or debt (bonds). Next, the underwriting syndicate itself purchases the new issue from the firm or the government borrower. Finally, networks of agents (brokers) associated with the investment banks sell the bonds or stocks to the ultimate lenders, who might be either individuals or large institutional investors such as life insurance companies and pension funds. If the syndicate has correctly judged the market for these new financial instruments, it will profit from the spread between the price it paid for the new issue and the price at which the syndicate was able to sell the issue. This is the investment banker's return for assuming the risk of marketing the borrower's securities.

Investment banks thus help provide capital for large borrowers, most of whom do not have the necessary expertise to negotiate and market their own financial liabilities. The history and evolution of investment banking in the United States is one of the interplay of three factors: need (the demand for large amounts of capital); opportunity (the supply of available funds); and constraints (the limitations placed on investment bankers by regulators). Despite years of change in environment and practice,

however, many of the names of twenty-first century investment banks include those of the proprietors or partners of private investment banks in the nineteenth century. Among these are Morgan, Kidder Peabody, Goldman Sachs, and Kuhn Loeb.

Early Institutions

Investment banks were rare in the pre–Civil War period. American business and government had not yet put large capital demands on the economy, so that the small, short-term loans typical of commercial banks sufficed for most enterprises. The few large borrowers called upon loan contractors, who—using personal wealth—bought up securities to resell them at a profit. Stephen Girard and John Jacob Astor acted as loan contractors in the early 1800s, but most American borrowers relied upon the experience of European firms such as London's Rothschild family and the Baring Brothers. Later, as bigger commercial banks were formed in the 1830s, some (such as the United States Bank of Philadelphia, headed by Nicholas Biddle) became involved in buying up new securities for resale to the public.

Civil War Finance

It was not until 1860 that investment banking began its rise to prominence in American financial markets. Between the Civil War and World War I, the supply of funds changed. Instead of a few very wealthy Americans, savings were more widely distributed among individuals at home and abroad. More importantly, demand for funds shifted away from relatively small, commerce-based firms and toward government, public utilities, and industry, whose capital requirements far outstripped the ability of commercial banks to meet them. These changes put investment banks at the forefront of financing the large projects that transformed the American economy in the latter part of the nineteenth century.

Unable to sell all of the federal government's Civil War–generated bond issue in 1861, Secretary of the Treasury Salmon Chase called upon Jay Cooke, who earlier that year had had some success organizing the first syndicate of banks for the purpose of underwriting a large Pennsylvania state bond issue. Cooke, relying upon a far-flung domestic network of commission salesmen, distributed the issue and in 1870 formed a syndicate to refinance the $1.5 billion federal debt. (These two innovations—the distribution network and the syndicate—have characterized much of investment banking ever since.) Other early investment banking houses were involved in distributing the federal debt, including Kuhn Loeb and Goldman Sachs.

The House of Morgan

Cooke was also involved, although less successfully, in financing the other great borrower at the time, the railroads. The scope of railroad building in the 1860s and 1870s—stretching from the Midwest to the Pacific Coast—required vast new amounts of capital. Much of it was raised in Europe, where more funds were available. It was in this arena that the Morgans, arguably the best-known banking family in the country, got their start. Junius Morgan began the dynasty as an agent of the George Peabody Company, selling American railroad securities in London before the Civil War. In 1880, his son, J. P. (Pierpont) Morgan, organized a syndicate that sold a $40 million bond issue for the Northern Pacific Railroad, the largest American railroad bond transaction up to that time.

The activities of Morgan and his son, J. P. (Jack) Morgan, reflect the development of investment banking in the twentieth century. As the railroads forged an increasingly competitive national market, some manufacturing businesses saw the key to profitability in merging into larger, consolidated enterprises; other firms concluded that the key to survival was to reorganize and restructure. The result was a merger wave at the turn of the century, with both consolidation and reorganization (or, in modern terms, mergers and acquisitions) becoming a primary activity of investment banking. In 1892, for example, J. P. Morgan Company (along with another Yankee firm, Lee Higginson) negotiated and financed the merger of Edison General Electric and Thomson-Houston into the General Electric Company. In 1906, Goldman Sachs underwrote both the consolidation of the United Cigar Company and the expansion of Sears, Roebuck and Company. (The latter was the first instance of an investment bank underwriting the securities of a retail firm—a business that, unlike railroads or manufacturing, had few large physical assets that creditors could liquidate in the event of bankruptcy.)

At about the same time, the United States began exporting capital, particularly to countries needing to fund wars. American investment bankers underwrote the British National War Loan of 1900 (for the Boer War) and Japanese bonds used to finance the Russo-Japanese War of 1904 and 1905. Funding for the allied effort in World War I came from the $500 million Anglo-French loan of 1915, which J. P. Morgan marketed.

Regulation

While the U.S. government seemed to approve of investment bankers' international role, those bankers' domestic reputation was not as favorable. As a result of their intimate knowledge of industrial structure, many investment bankers in the early 1900s became directors of the corporations whose financial needs they had serviced. This intersection of industry and finance gave rise to worries that economic power was being centralized in what was called a "money trust." After an investigation in 1912 by the Pujo Committee of the U.S. House of Representatives, numerous recommendations were made for federal laws to limit the influence, and increase the federal oversight, of large private investment banking houses such as J. P. Morgan, Kuhn Loeb, and Kidder Peabody. Although none of these recommendations were adopted, the committee's hearings were a warning to the investment banking community that it no longer could expect to function outside regulatory purview.

Nineteenth-century regulation had already limited commercial banks' ability to engage in investment banking. Underwriting was a risky venture, and many regulators believed that an institution that held the public's deposits should not be allowed to use those deposits in what were considered highly speculative activities. Consequently, the National Banking Act of 1864 strictly limited the ability of federally chartered banks to deal in securities other than some government bonds (such as the popular Liberty Bonds issued in World War I). But during the 1920s, profits available from underwriting ran as high as 20 percent as the stock market boom raised both the demand for capital and the supply of small investors' funds. Commercial bankers knew that their established base of borrowers (firms) and savers (depositors) put them in a unique position to deal in securities and regain some of their market share. Thus, banks circumvented federal regulations by establishing state-chartered affiliates that could legally engage in all types of investment banking. Several large commercial bank–investment bank combinations were formed before the Great Depression, including National City Bank–National City Company and Chase National Bank–Chase Securities Company.

By 1930, commercial banks were underwriting half of all new securities issues, but the stock market crash of 1929 (and the bank failures that followed) put the regulatory spotlight back on this activity. Although modern economic research has found no connection between commercial bank failures and the securities business of those banks, Congress passed the Banking Act of 1933 (Glass-Steagall Act) that, in effect, put a fire wall between commercial and investment banks. Commercial banks were required to sever all ties to securities affiliates, and private bankers were forced to choose between engaging in commercial banking or in investment banking. A number of banks soon sheared off their investment banking activities into wholly separate firms. Thus, at the beginning of the twenty-first century, there were investment banks with names like Morgan Stanley, the progeny of J. P. Morgan, and First Boston Corporation, an offshoot of First National Bank of Boston. (In an interesting replay of the Pujo hearings, an antitrust suit was brought in 1947 against seventeen of these investment banks. *United States v. Morgan* was concluded in 1953, when Judge Harold Medina ruled that these investment banks were not engaged in anticompetitive behavior.)

As part of the financial shake-up of the 1930s, regulation of investment banks increased. Probably the most powerful regulatory measure was the Securities Act of 1933, which required that investment bankers practice "due diligence" and make full disclosure before publicly marketing any security. Such oversight was lessened, however, if new issues were distributed in a "private placement" with a large investor who, it was thought, could

405

assess the risks of a new issue itself. The number of these placements rose rapidly in the late 1930s, but it cannot be determined whether this was the result of investment bankers' attempts to circumvent disclosure laws or the natural outcome of the rise in large institutional investors such as life insurance companies and pension plans.

Modern Investment Banking

Fifty years after the New Deal, some of the financial structures built in response to the Great Depression began to be dismantled. This was, in part, the result of rapid innovation in financial markets (including the money market mutual fund) and unusual variations in inflation and interest rates. At the same time, scholars questioned the received 1930s wisdom that investment and commercial banking should never be mixed, and experts in international finance claimed that universal banking (as practiced in countries such as Germany) seemed to be an efficient and relatively safe way to mobilize capital. As a result, new laws passed in the 1980s blurred the distinctions between commercial banks and savings and loan banks and between commercial banks and investment banks.

At the turn of the twenty-first century, Glass-Steagall still technically reserves securities underwriting to the investment bankers. But commercial bankers were testing this fire wall, and some predicted that the separation of American investment and commercial banks would soon be a thing of the past, perhaps returning, full circle, to the world of late-nineteenth-century financial capitalism.

BIBLIOGRAPHY

Benston, George J. *The Separation of Commercial and Investment Banking: The Glass-Steagall Act Revisited and Reconsidered.* New York: Oxford University Press, 1990.

Calomiris, Charles W. *U.S. Bank Regulation in Historical Perspective.* New York: Cambridge University Press, 2000.

Carosso, Vincent P. *Investment Banking in America: A History.* Cambridge, Mass.: Harvard University Press, 1970.

Chernow, Ron. *The House of Morgan: An American Banking Dynasty and the Rise of Modern Finance.* New York: Atlantic Monthly Press, 1990.

Endlich, Lisa. *Goldman Sachs: The Culture of Success.* New York: Knopf, 1999.

Hayes, Samuel L., III, and Philip M. Hubbard. *Investment Banking: A Tale of Three Cities.* Boston: Harvard Business School Press, 1990.

Peach, W. Nelson. *The Security Affiliates of National Banks.* Baltimore: Johns Hopkins University Press, 1941.

Redlich, Fritz. *The Molding of American Banking.* New York: Johnson Reprint, 1968.

Sobel, Robert. *The Life and Times of Dillon Read.* New York: Dutton, 1991.

White, Eugene Nelson. *The Regulation and Reform of the American Banking System, 1900–1929.* Princeton, N.J.: Princeton University Press, 1983.

Kerry A. Odell

PRIVATE BANKS

The term "private banks" is misleading in American financial history. Virtually all of the banks in the United States were privately owned—even the First and Second Banks of the United States, the nation's "national" banks, sold 80 percent of their stock to private individuals. Apart from a few state-chartered banks owned exclusively by the state governments (the Bank of the State of Alabama and the Bank of the State of Arkansas, for example), all of the financial institutions in the United States were privately held. The confusion arose in the chartering process. If states chartered the banks, they were usually referred to as "state banks," even though they were not owned by the states. Alongside these chartered banks, however, existed another set of privately owned banks called "private banks." The chief difference between the two lay not in ownership, but in the authority to issue bank notes, which was a prerogative strictly reserved for those banks receiving state charters.

Private bankers ranged from large-scale semibanks to individual lenders. The numbers of known private bankers only scratch the surface of the large number of businesses engaging in the banking trade. Some of the larger nonchartered banks even established early branches, called "agencies," across state lines. They provided an important contribution to the chartered banks by lending on personal character and by possessing information about local borrowers that would not be available to more formal businesses. Private bankers also escaped regulation imposed on traditional banks, largely because they did not deal with note issue—the issue that most greatly concerned the public about banks until, perhaps, the 1850s. "Private banking" continued well into the early twentieth century.

BIBLIOGRAPHY

Helderman, Leonard C. *National and State Banks.* Boston: Houghton Mifflin, 1931.

Schweikart, Larry. "Private Bankers in the Antebellum South." *Southern Studies* 25 (Summer 1986): 125–134.

———. "U.S. Commercial Banking: A Historiographical Survey," *Business History Review* 65 (Autumn 1991): 606–661.

Smith, Alice E. *George Smith's Money: A Scottish Investor in America.* Madison: State Historical Society of Wisconsin, 1966.

Sylla, Richard. "Forgotten Men of Money: Private Bankers in Early U.S. History." *Journal of Economic History* 29 (March 1969): 173–188.

Larry Schweikart

SAVINGS BANKS

The broad category of savings institutions is made up of several types of legal structures, including savings banks, building and loan associations, and savings and loan associations. Two of the most distinctive features of savings institutions are their mutual ownership structures and operation as cooperative credit institutions, which exempt them from income taxes paid by commercial banks and other for-profit financial intermediaries.

Savings banks originated in Europe. The first ones in the Western Hemisphere were the Philadelphia Saving Fund Society (opened 1816, chartered 1819) and the Provident Institution for Savings in Boston (chartered 1816). The concept of savings banks originated in the philanthropic motives of the wealthy, who wished to loan funds to creditworthy poor who exhibited the discipline of thrift through their savings behavior. Although savings banks provided a safe haven for small accounts, it is doubtful that these banks made many loans to the poor.

Rapid Expansion in the Nineteenth Century

Early savings banks were immediately popular. During their first twenty years of development in the United States, savings bank deposits grew to some $11 million. The popularity of savings banks resulted in part from their reputation for safety. They avoided runs by enforcing bylaws that restricted payments to depositors for up to sixty days. As a result of these provisions, no savings banks failed in the panic of 1819. Around nine hundred commercial banks failed in the panic of 1837, but only a handful of savings banks met that fate.

Most savings banks also survived the subsequent panics of the nineteenth century. In the panic of 1873, some eighteen out of more than five hundred savings banks in existence suspended operations nationwide. Losses to savings bank depositors are thought to have been relatively insignificant across most of the nineteenth century. Between 1819 and 1854 no savings banks failed in the state of New York. Between 1816 and 1874, a period that includes the panic of 1873, total losses to savings bank customers in Massachusetts totaled only $75,000 on a savings bank deposit base of $750 million. As a result of their safety, savings banks' popularity surged and by 1890, 4.3 million depositors held $1.5 billion in savings banks across the nation.

The panic of 1893, however, slowed savings bank growth. Through the latter half of the nineteenth century, the class of acceptable investments for savings banks was broadened. By 1890, savings banks were invested in a wide array of assets, including government and state securities and corporate equities and bonds. Moreover, some savings banks began establishing themselves as joint-stock rather than mutual institutions. The combination of these two developments began to blur the distinction between investments of savings banks and commercial banks. Again, in 1893 most savings banks avoided failure by enforcing bylaws that restricted payments to depositors. But consumer and business confidence was low and the economic disruption long. As a result, savings bank growth fell off considerably during and after the 1893 panic, although they soon recovered.

Competition, Federal Regulation, and the Democratization of Credit

In 1903 the comptroller of the currency ruled that national banks could hold savings balances. Hence, following the panic of 1907 concern for depositor safety grew in all sectors of the financial services industry. This concern, along with substantial heterogeneity in savings institutions in general and savings bank investments and operations in particular, led to the establishment of the postal savings system in 1910 as a direct competitor to existing savings institutions.

The postal savings system provided a safe haven for commercial bank depositors during the Great Depression. However, savings bank depositors experienced far fewer losses than commercial bank depositors during this period because of their diversification and their bylaws allowing the restriction of payments.

New Deal legislation contained many provisions for depositor safety, including an expansion of federal authority over savings banks and building and loan associations. Prior to the 1930s, all savings banks were chartered and regulated by the states in which they operated. The New Deal established federal authority under the Federal Home Loan Bank Board for chartering and regulating savings banks and savings and loans. The creation of the Federal Deposit Insurance Corporation (FDIC) in 1933 and the expansion of the network of savings institutions are undoubtedly related to the demise of the postal savings system in the 1950s.

Savings banks and related institutions are thought to have contributed substantially to the democratization of credit in the United States during the twentieth century. Mortgage lending by these institutions led to widespread home and property ownership. Moreover, nonmortgage savings bank lending was the basis for the development of Morris Plan lending, an early form of consumer finance. Pioneered by Morris Plan Company in 1914, small, short-term (less than one year) loans were made to individuals who repaid them in fifty weekly installments. The loans became extremely popular, and by 1917 Morris Plan loans totaled more than $14.5 million to over 115,000 borrowers.

Although savings banks and savings and loans (and their predecessors, building and loan associations) were cooperative credit institutions, historically the institutions differed in some important ways. Savings and loans (and building and loan associations) concentrated primarily on residential mortgages, while savings banks operated as more diversified institutions. In the twenty years following World War II mortgages were favorable investments, so the difference between savings bank and savings and loan operations was insignificant. However, during late 1966 and 1967 savings banks were able to invest in corporate securities in the absence of mortgage loan demand, while savings and loans were not.

Decline and Resurgence

Many savings banks converted from mutual to joint-stock ownership during the 1980s. Facing new profit pressures from shareholders, the newly converted savings banks adopted portfolios similar to those of savings and loans. When sharply increased interest rates and the fundamental maturity mismatch between short-term deposits and long-term mortgages led to protracted difficulties in the savings and loan industry, many of these newly converted savings banks failed. Although lax supervision led to the replacement of the regulator of both savings and loans and savings banks (the Federal Home Loan Bank Board) with a completely new regulator (the Office of Thrift Supervision), savings bank deposits were insured by the FDIC and thus were not affected by the failure of the Federal Savings and Loan Insurance Corporation.

Although the popularity of savings institutions (including savings banks) waned in comparison with commercial banks following the crisis of the 1980s, savings institutions experienced a resurgence during the 1990s because of competitive loan and deposit rates, their mutual ownership structure and resulting tax advantages, and the broad array of financial services they may offer under contemporary banking law.

BIBLIOGRAPHY

Alter, George, Claudia Goldin, and Elyce Rotella. "The Savings of Ordinary Americans: The Philadelphia Saving Fund Society in the Mid-Nineteenth Century." *Journal of Economic History* 54 (1994): 753–767.

Davis, Lance Edwin, and Peter Lester Payne. "From Benevolence to Business: The Story of Two Savings Banks." *Business History Review* 32 (1958): 386–406.

Olmstead, Alan L. "Investment Constraints and New York City Mutual Savings Bank Financing of Antebellum Development." *Journal of Economic History* 32 (1972): 811–840.

Sherman, Franklin J. *Modern Story of Mutual Savings Banks: A Narrative of Their Growth and Development from the Inception to the Present Day.* New York: J. J. Little and Ives, 1934.

Welfling, Weldon. *Mutual Savings Banks: The Evolution of a Financial Intermediary.* Cleveland, Ohio: Press of Case Western Reserve University, 1968.

White, Lawrence J. *The S&L Debacle: Public Policy Lessons for Bank and Thrift Regulation.* New York: Oxford University Press, 1991.

Joseph Mason

See also **Financial Panics; Savings and Loan Associations.**

STATE BANKS

State investment in banks was common before the panic of 1837. The idea behind it was that bank profits would lead to the abolition of taxes. This idea had its roots in the early eighteenth century, when colonies used the interest earned from loans made through loan offices and land banks as revenue to pay the expenses (chiefly administrative salaries) of the provincial governments. For example, between about 1724 and 1754, such income paid most of the cost of New Jersey's government.

In the nineteenth century the state was sometimes the sole owner of a bank, as in South Carolina, but more commonly it was a partial owner, as in Indiana. In some cases the ventures were profitable; in others they were disastrous. In Illinois, where the state owned $3.6 million in stock, the bank's failure forced the state to divorce its interests in 1843. In Mississippi, Arkansas, and Florida, where the investment was nearly $12 million, the result was repudiation of a debt that was never paid. In Louisiana, where the bonds issued to aid banks amounted to $19 million, there was a collapse followed by reform under the Specie Reserve System of 1842.

Among the successful state-owned banks, the State Bank of Missouri was the most important. It continued operation through the panics of 1837 and 1857, and in 1862, when it entered the national system as a private bank, the state sold its stock for a premium. The State Bank of Indiana survived the panics and emerged in 1857, when its charter expired, with a net profit to the state of more than $2 million. The Bank of the State of South Carolina also withstood the panics and continued through the Civil War as one of the strongest financial institutions in the nation.

In the aftermath of the public distrust of banks after the panic of 1819, the political struggle with Andrew Jackson over renewing the charter of the second BANK OF THE UNITED STATES, and especially after the panic of 1837, states were presented with three banking options. Some chose to forbid banking altogether—seven of thirty-one states exercised this option in 1852. Others, such as Indiana, Missouri, and Ohio, made banking a state monopoly, or at least set up a state-owned bank. Some indecisive states tried one solution, then another; Iowa, for example, went from prohibition to state banking. The majority—including New York, Michigan, and Louisiana—elected to regulate banking more closely.

With the passage of the July 1865 amendment to the National Banking Act, which imposed a 10 percent tax on state bank notes after 1 July 1866 to force all state banks to join the national banking system, state-owned banks disappeared. State-chartered banks found a way around the law by encouraging borrowers to use check currency.

BIBLIOGRAPHY

Cable, John Ray. *The Bank of the State of Missouri.* New York: Columbia University, 1923.

Hammond, Bray. *Banks and Politics in America, from the Revolution to the Civil War.* Princeton, N.J.: Princeton University Press, 1957.

Helderman, Leonard C. *National and State Banks: A Study of Their Origins.* Boston: Houghton Mifflin, 1931.

Sylla, Richard, John B. Legler, and John Joseph Wallis. "Banks and State Public Finance in the New Republic: The United

States, 1790–1860." *Journal of Economic History* (June 1987): 391–403.

Donald L. Kemmerer / A. R.; C. W.

See also **Federal Reserve System; Financial Panics; National Bank Notes; Specie Payments, Suspension and Resumption of;** *and vol. 9:* **Fireside Chat on the Bank Crisis.**

BANKRUPTCY LAWS.

Any economic system that rewards success has to provide as well for failure. The major industrial nations have long had bankruptcy systems, though they differ dramatically in philosophy and in practice, to liquidate or revive failing businesses and to settle consumer debts when individuals become overwhelmed economically. Countries in transition from planned to free market economies have recognized that a bankruptcy structure is indispensable.

Article I, section 8, of the Constitution gives Congress the power "to establish . . . uniform laws on the subject of bankruptcies throughout the United States." Antecedents to that provision are found in eighteenth-century British common law and even in Roman law. Philosophically and politically, however, the genesis of the American bankruptcy system is found in the debtors' prisons of England and the colonies, where punishment and disgrace rather than repayment and economic rehabilitation were the principal focus.

For more than one hundred years, U.S. bankruptcy law has reflected a different approach. The U.S. Bankruptcy Code attempts to balance the rights of debtors with the rights of their creditors and, among creditors, balance their competing rights based on the security they hold for the debt and the nature of the underlying obligation. The Code determines which creditors will be paid in full, which paid in part, and which paid not at all.

The law also declares that some personal obligations are "nondischargeable" and must be paid regardless of bankruptcy. For individual debtors, these include tax obligations, criminal fines and penalties, alimony and child support, and student loans; corporations must pay administrative expenses, including some wage and benefit obligations to employees, if the company is to be permitted the chance to reorganize.

The U.S. Bankruptcy Code contains separate chapters and, often, separate procedures to handle financial failure. Chapter 7, which governs the liquidation of a debtor's assets, is chosen by about 70 percent of all individuals and half of all businesses filing for bankruptcy. The remaining chapters of the Code provide for reorganization—the readjustment of the debt, its full or partial payment, and the economic survival of the debtor in some form. For individuals who do not choose Chapter 7, economic reorganization is available in Chapter 13. Corporations and partnerships reorganize in Chapter 11, family farms in Chapter 12, and an occasional municipality or utility district in Chapter 9. By law, certain businesses are ineligible for bankruptcy protection—banks, insurance companies, and railroads, for example. When they become insolvent, they turn to state law or other federal statutes to resolve their obligations.

State law plays an important role even in a "uniform" federal bankruptcy system because state law most often defines contractual and commercial relationships. States also have their own legal procedures for business insolvencies that a debtor can elect although the state procedures are often less defined, less flexible, and less sophisticated than the federal bankruptcy system.

Bankruptcy Courts and Code

The Constitution establishes a federal judiciary in Article III. The federal bankruptcy courts are established under Article I, which limits the authority of the nation's more than 250 bankruptcy judges, and they are considered adjunct to the Article III federal district courts. Bankruptcy courts, which have broad authority under the Bankruptcy Code, are adjunct to the federal district courts and their judges serve fourteen-year terms. (Unlike the life tenure of federal judges.) Judges are appointed by the U.S. Courts of Appeals without confirmation by the U.S. Senate.

The Bankruptcy Code is complex. A business that hopes to reorganize under Chapter 11 must propose a plan of reorganization that, with rare exceptions, its creditors must vote to accept. In a Chapter 11 reorganization, the company will still be operated by the same management but will have creditor and court oversight and public disclosure of business results. In business insolvencies, secured creditors retain their security interests and the promise of a payment at least equal to the value of their collateral. Unsecured creditors generally receive a pro rata distribution that, by law, cannot be less than what they would have received had the company been liquidated.

Most Chapter 11 bankruptcies leave the equity holders—in a public company, the shareholders—without any payment or dividend. In establishing payment priorities, the bankruptcy law dictates that equity holders be paid last and only if all of the other creditors are paid first and in full. Despite its complexity, a Chapter 11 reorganization can save jobs, provide at least a partial payment to creditors, and possibly maintain the business.

The current business bankruptcy provisions were largely fashioned in 1978 when Congress last enacted a comprehensive revision of the bankruptcy law. Perhaps the single most important part of the Code, unique to American bankruptcy, is the "automatic stay," a provision that automatically stops all pending litigation or legal proceedings against a company in Chapter 11. It brings all of those cases, in effect, into the bankruptcy court where all of a company's assets and its liabilities are consolidated and the claims against the company resolved to determine if it can survive.

Chapter 11 of the Bankruptcy Code has been a legal and economic success. Under the law's protection, major department stores, steel companies, airlines, and energy companies have restored themselves and are productive businesses today. Other countries are assessing their bankruptcy procedures, and some are moving from the automatic liquidation approach—which characterizes British business law, for example—to the American approach with its emphasis on saving the company and the jobs that it provides.

Consumer Bankruptcy

Since the revision of the bankruptcy code in 1978, consumer bankruptcy law has become more complex and, for more and more American families and their creditors, more important. In 1980, there were 288,000 consumer bankruptcies; by 2002, the number had exceeded 1.5 million. Debate continues about the "cause" of this dramatic increase; however, it has paralleled the rise in consumer debt and, in particular, credit card debt. Congress changed some of the consumer bankruptcy provisions of the Code in 1984 and 1994, largely to the benefit of unsecured creditors. The framework for consumer bankruptcy, however, remains as it was in 1938 when Congress, in the wake of the Great Depression, passed the Chandler Act. That law gave consumers a procedural choice for personal bankruptcy. Chapter 7 is a relatively quick process in which the debtor's assets are liquidated (with some exemptions) and the proceeds distributed to creditors pro-rata. The debtor emerges with most, but not all, unsecured debts discharged (except taxes, student loans, and marital and child support obligations) and either surrenders the collateral for a secured debt (a house, a car) or arranges to continue to make current payments. While supervised by the bankruptcy court, the process is largely administrative. In more than 95 percent of the Chapter 7 cases, the debtor has no assets to distribute to creditors.

When individuals declare bankruptcy, federal law permits retention of some assets as "exemptions" because stripping a debtor of everything, leaving no assets for a fresh start, would be neither humane nor economically efficient. The bankruptcy code recognizes a homestead exemption and modest exemptions for household goods, medical devices, and a car. Federal law also permits the individual states to give debtors only the exemptions permitted by state law. The use of state exemptions, for example, permits residents in some states to shelter an unlimited amount of assets in a home, leaving their creditors empty handed. Other states provide no homestead exemption.

The alternative to Chapter 7 for consumer debtors is Chapter 13. Only about three in ten consumer debtors choose Chapter 13. Chapter 13 also has the debtor and creditors agree on a plan for installment payments of all or part of the debt. The debtor obtains a discharge of the unpaid debts only on the successful completion of the plan. Chapter 13 provides some unique incentives for consumers that, in most cases, make it easier to retain ownership of a home or a car. The debtor still must pay all of nondischargeable debts.

Maintaining the Balance

In the century that followed the 1898 Bankruptcy Act, the first comprehensive code, Congress has made significant changes four times. Each time, Congress attempted to maintain a balance between creditor rights and debtor rights. The goal, stated or not, of each change was to maintain the ability of the debtor, whether business or consumer, to make a "fresh start."

Since the 1960s, the consumer credit industry has crusaded for significant changes in the bankruptcy law to alter the balance between debtor rights and creditor rights, and the industry convinced Congress to change the Code to its advantage. In 2000, Congress adopted major changes in the law that would have made it more pro-creditor, but President Bill Clinton exercised his veto. Creditors want a "means test" that would eliminate the choice between Chapter 7 and Chapter 13. Creditors want consumers to be obliged to use Chapter 13 on the theory that at least some consumers could pay at least some of their debts.

The explosion of consumer debt in the 1990s has changed the profile of the American family in bankruptcy. With about 1.5 million families a year filing for protection under Chapter 7 or Chapter 13, it has become a "safety net" largely for middle-class families hit by unexpected illness, job layoff or downsizing, divorce, or another economic calamity beyond their control. Because the law always has been based on a code (like the tax and social security laws of the country), because it is a law that affects more families than most other federal laws, proposals will always be before Congress to change its terms. Always at stake will be the balance between debtor rights and creditor rights recognized when the framers adopted the Constitution in 1789.

BIBLIOGRAPHY

Jackson, Thomas. *The Logic and Limits of Bankruptcy Law*. Cambridge, Mass.: Harvard University Press, 1986.

Mann, Bruce H. *Republic of Debtors: Bankruptcy in the Age of American Independence*. Cambridge, Mass.: Harvard University Press, 2002.

National Bankruptcy Review Commission. *Bankruptcy: The Next Twenty Years*. Final Report. Washington, D.C.; Government Printing Office, 1997.

Skeel, David A. *Debt's Dominion: A History of Bankruptcy Law in America*. Princeton, N.J.: Princeton University Press, 2001.

Sullivan, Teresa, Elizabeth Warren, and Jay Lawrence Westbrook. *The Fragile Middle Class: Americans in Debt*. New Haven, Conn.: Yale University Press, 2000.

Tabb, Charles Jordan. *The Law of Bankruptcy*. New York: Foundation Press, 1997.

Warren, Elizabeth. *Business Bankruptcy.* Washington, D.C.: Federal Judicial Center, 1993.

Brady C. Williamson

See also **Credit; Credit Cards; Frazier-Lemke Farm Bankruptcy Act.**

BAPTIST CHURCHES.

The distinguishing feature of Baptist churches is their belief that a true church is a local community of faithful believers. This belief led the Baptist founders to reject infant baptism, for which they found no biblical warrant, and to insist that local congregations were subject to no supra-local ecclesiastical agency.

Origins

Baptists originated in the puritan reforming movements in the seventeenth-century Church of England that attempted to restore the primitive worship and organization of the churches described in the New Testament. A few of these reformers withdrew into small independent congregations, and in 1608 the English separatist John Smyth led one of them to Amsterdam, where he soon decided that the Bible offered no precedent for the baptism of infants and that infant baptism contradicted a true view of the church as a community of the faithful. In conversation with Dutch Anabaptists, whose origins could be traced to similar efforts at restoration in sixteenth-century Switzerland, Smyth's group also made known its dislike of the Calvinist theology held by many of its allies in reform. In 1612 some in the congregation, under Thomas Helwys, returned to England, where their anti-Calvinist belief that Christ died for all persons (a "general" atonement) gave them the name General Baptists. In 1638, however, defectors from an independent Southwark (London) separatist congregation initiated, under the leadership of John Spilsbury, a Calvinistic Baptist church. Because of their belief that Christ died only for the elect, they became known as Particular Baptists.

Both traditions found supporters in colonial America. The Baptist congregations established by Roger Williams in 1639 in Providence, Rhode Island, and John Clarke between 1638 and 1648 in Newport, Rhode Island, adhered to a Calvinist theology. By 1652, however, General Baptist theology had a foothold in Rhode Island, and by the end of the century it had spread to the South. Often subjected to restriction and persecution by colonial authorities, both strands of the movement expanded slowly, with only about thirty-five congregations between them in 1700. In 1707, however, five Calvinist churches in New Jersey, Delaware, and Pennsylvania formed the

Roger Williams (d. 1683) Departing from Salem. CORBIS/BETTMANN

Philadelphia Baptist Association to help coordinate the spread of the Baptist message. In 1751, Oliver Hart led the formation of a second association in Charleston, South Carolina, and others soon followed in New England and Virginia.

In 1742 the Philadelphia Association adopted what became known as the Philadelphia Confession, a statement of belief modeled after the Calvinist London Confession of 1689, which affirmed that a sovereign God granted the gift of faith and salvation only to the elect, who were foreordained to eternal life. While many Baptists objected to creeds, insisting on the sole sufficiency of Scripture, these confessional statements influenced local congregations and associations throughout the colonies.

After a surge of religious revivals that began around 1738, a Baptist theology of the church attracted adherents among former Congregationalists whose insistence on the necessity for an experience of conversion or "rebirth" led them to separate from less demanding Congregational churches. When some of these Separate Baptists migrated from New England, they carried their revivalist form of Calvinist piety into the Middle Colonies and the South. After 1755, led especially by Shubael Stearns in North Carolina, they gradually began to outnumber earlier Calvinistic Baptists, who adopted the name Regular Baptists to distinguish themselves. A smaller number of anti-Calvinist, or "free-will," Baptists established themselves in North Carolina in 1727 through the leadership of Paul Palmer and in northern New England through the preaching of the lay exhorter Benjamin Randall, who inspired the formation in New Hampshire of a Free Will Baptist Association in 1782. By 1780 the various Baptist groups had formed around 450 churches, a number exceeded only by Congregationalists with about 750 and Presbyterians with some 490.

Vigorously opposed to the colonial church establishments, eighteenth-century Baptists struggled for the separation of church and state. Prominent Baptists like John Leland in Virginia spoke out for religious freedom and "soul liberty," a term derived from Roger Williams to designate the rights of individual conscience. The gradual collapse of state religious establishments after ratification of the U.S. Constitution in 1789 served Baptist purposes, and by 1800 they had become for a while the largest denomination in the nation, with almost twice as many adherents as the second-ranked Congregationalists.

Diversity

In his *Fifty Years Among the Baptists* (1860), the denominational historian David Benedict recalled that in 1800 the Baptists remained a "poor and despised" people, "denounced" by more fashionable churches as "the dregs of Christendom," but that the denomination also had its share of educated leaders, who supported the creation of colleges, seminaries, tract societies, and missionary agencies. Educated leaders provided the impetus for the crea-

tion in 1814 of a General Missionary Convention, soon called the Triennial Convention, to sponsor home and foreign missions. Before long, it had allied itself with other agencies to promote publication and education.

Other Baptists, often expressing cultural resentment of the educated, opposed this organized missionary movement on the grounds that it lacked biblical warrants and that God would save the elect without the aid of human agencies. These critics had coalesced by 1832 into the Primitive (or Hard-Shell, or Anti-Missionary) Baptist movement, but their numbers remained small. Most of the Calvinistic Baptist churches preferred a moderate Calvinism of the sort promoted in the New Hampshire Confession (1833), emphasizing that belief in God's sovereignty and the doctrine of election was compatible with a proper understanding of human free agency. The majority gave strong encouragement to home and foreign missions while also supporting colleges like Brown (1764), Furman (1826), and Baylor (1845) and theological seminaries including Newton (1825) and Southern Baptist (1859).

Far more serious were divisions over slavery, racial difference, and region. When the Executive Board of the Home Mission Society of the Triennial Convention refused to appoint slaveholding missionaries, southerners created the Southern Baptist Convention in 1845. White discrimination had long intensified the desire of African Americans to form their own congregations—like the church at Silver Bluff across the Savannah River from Augusta, Georgia, founded around 1773—and by 1865 black Baptists had created more than 200 churches. After an influx of new members following the Civil War, the black churches organized the Foreign Mission Baptist Convention in 1880 and the National Baptist Convention in 1895. In 1907, moreover, the predominantly white churches of the North combined several independent agencies to form the Northern Baptist Convention (renamed in 1973 as the American Baptist Churches in the U.S.A.). These divisions endured into the twenty-first century.

One further nineteenth-century division helped shape the ethos of Baptist churches in the South. In 1851, James R. Graves in Tennessee began to argue that Baptists represented an unbroken succession of visible churches since the time of John the Baptist and Christ, that they were the only true churches, that they alone administered baptism properly, and that their members could not join in church fellowship with other Christians, including other Baptists who did not accept these truths. This Landmark Baptist movement (so named from the title of a book promoting it) influenced many local churches in the South and helped give rise in 1905 to the Baptist General Association, enlarged and reorganized in 1924 into a group that became known as the American Baptist Association, which also represented a protest by several church leaders in the Southwest against the authority of the Southern Baptist Convention.

Abyssinian Baptist Church. New York City, 1958. AP/WIDE
WORLD PHOTOS

National Baptist Convention to the social activism of the
Baptist minister Martin Luther King Jr. led in 1961 to
the formation of a separate Progressive National Baptist
Convention.

Despite the internal ferment, Baptists remained the
largest Protestant grouping in the nation. By 2001, the
twenty-seven largest Baptist denominations reported an
approximate membership of 28 million, but by then Baptists had organized themselves into more than sixty supra-
local entities and close to 95,000 independent congregations, so the total membership was undoubtedly larger.
The largest group was the Southern Baptist Convention,
which claimed more than 15 million members and set
much of the tone for southern Protestantism. As a whole,
however, Baptists represent a diversity of theological and
social views. Few generalizations can apply to all of them.
They generally prefer simplicity in worship, with no fixed
ritual formularies. They insist on the authority of Scripture as the source of their norms, and most do not regard
the historic confessional statements as compulsory. And
although in practice they grant considerable authority to
centralized agencies, including the state and national convention organizations, they continue to affirm an ideal of
the church as a local autonomous congregation of faithful
Christians.

BIBLIOGRAPHY

Benedict, David. *Fifty Years Among the Baptists.* New York: Sheldon, 1860.

Brackney, William Henry. *The Baptists.* New York: Greenwood
Press, 1988.

Leonard, Bill J. *God's Last and Only Hope: The Fragmentation of
the Southern Baptist Convention.* Grand Rapids, Mich.: Eerd-
mans, 1990.

Lumpkin, William L., ed. *Baptist Confessions of Faith.* Valley
Forge, Pa.: Judson Press, 1959. Contains documents and
commentary.

McBeth, H. Leon, ed. *The Baptist Heritage: Four Centuries of Baptist Witness.* Nashville, Tenn.: Broadman Press, 1987.

McLoughlin, William G. *New England Dissent, 1630–1833: The
Baptists and the Separation of Church and State.* Cambridge,
Mass.: Harvard University Press, 1971.

Sobel, Mechal. *Trabelin' On: The Slave Journey to an Afro-Baptist
Faith.* Princeton, N.J.: Princeton University Press, 1979.

Wyatt-Brown, Bertram. "The Antimission Movement in the
Jacksonian South: A Study in Regional Folk Culture." *Journal of Southern History* 36 (1970): 501–529.

E. Brooks Holifield

See also **African American Religions and Sects; Creationism;
Fundamentalism; Religion and Religious Affiliation;
Social Gospel.**

By the early twentieth century, however, influential
Baptists in the North, like William Newton Clarke at
Colgate Theological Seminary, joined in the effort to re-
state Protestant theology in the light of modern thought,
while others, like Walter Rauschenbusch of Rochester
Theological Seminary, promoted a "social gospel" that
called for justice for the poor. These revisionist currents
gradually influenced some of the churches of the Northern Baptist Convention, but they also evoked reactions by
fundamentalists, who formed such counter organizations
as the General Association of Regular Baptist Churches
(1932) and the Conservative Baptist Association (1947),
along with thousands of independent Baptist congregations. The mood of reaction eventually shook even the
conservative Southern Baptist Convention when fundamentalists, claiming to find liberalism in Baptist colleges,
seminaries, and agencies, and also disturbed by the ordination of women, began in 1979 a successful takeover of
the convention, which had led by 1987 to a gradual withdrawal of many moderates.

Although few in the Baptist churches accepted the
social gospel, by 1908 Baptist denominations began to
create new agencies and commissions to address public
affairs. The effort proved divisive. Baptists could agree
about the evils of alcohol abuse, gambling, and other
vices, but they moved in different directions on social
policies. When the Christian Life Commission (CLC) of
the Southern Baptist Convention affirmed the Supreme
Court's rulings on racial integration and school prayer,
southern social conservatives objected, and when the
CLC refused to condemn the Court's 1973 ruling on
abortion, the conservatives organized a movement that by
1987 had transformed the CLC into an agency dedicated
to a legal ban on all abortion. The civil rights movement
also divided Baptists, even in the black churches, which
provided strong lay and clerical leadership in the battle
for racial equality. The opposition of the leaders of the

BARBADOS. The easternmost of the Caribbean's
Windward Islands, Barbados is known as much for its
tropical breezes as for its sugarcane fields. The earliest
inhabitants were the Amaraks, Amerindians from Vene-

Barbados. Children walk past a mural in Boscobel, St. Peter Parish. © TONY ARRUZA/CORBIS

zuela who are believed to have arrived around 1623 B.C. In 1200, the cannibalistic Caribs conquered the Amaraks. They, in turn, were conquered, enslaved, and finally decimated by smallpox when the Spanish arrived in the Caribbean in 1492. But Spain failed to colonize the island, leaving the British to settle Barbados in 1627 and introduce sugarcane as a major crop.

The American colonies had close ties to Barbados for a number of reasons, including the fact that in 1649, the Barbadian Society of Gentlemen Adventurers settled what became known as the Carolinas. Many Carolinians (North and South) still trace their roots to Barbados.

Barbados's climate also gained renown and in 1751 a young George Washington went there on his only trip abroad. He brought his ailing half brother to the island in search of a miracle tropical cure.

In the seventeenth and eighteenth centuries, Barbados was a frequent exporter of sugar, ginger, molasses, and cotton to the American colonies. Those crops took a terrible toll on Barbados's West African slaves, brought there by Dutch merchants. (Many other slaves died en route to the island's plantations.) In 1834, slavery was technically abolished on Barbados; after the slaves served a mandatory four-year "apprenticeship," some seventy thousand

newly free islanders of African descent celebrated their true emancipation in 1838.

British rule ended in 1966, when the island was finally granted full independence. Its bicameral parliament, however, remains British in style, with a Senate appointed by the governor general, who represents the British monarchy, and a House of Assembly elected by the voters.

The U.S.-Barbadian relations have always been strong. From 1956 to 1978, the U.S. operated a naval base there, and the two nations also signed a mutual legal assistance treaty (MLAT) in 1996. The U.S. also supports Barbadian economic development and provides aid to combat narcotics trafficking.

While sugarcane is still a mainstay crop (Barbados's fifteen hundred small farms produce some sixty thousand tons of sugar annually), tourism is the island's leading industry. With the development in the 1990s of the Port Charles Marina in Speightstown and the opening of additional tourist facilities around the island, Barbados has a sunny future as a popular destination.

BIBLIOGRAPHY

Beckles, Hilary McD. *A History of Barbados: From Amerindian Settlement to Nation-State.* Cambridge, U.K.: Cambridge University Press, 1990.

———. *Natural Rebels: A Social History of Slave Women in Barbados, 1627–1715.* New Brunswick, N.J.: Rutgers University Press, 1989.

Broberg, Merle. *Barbados.* Broomall, Pa.: Chelsea House, 1999.

Puckrein, Gary A. *Little England: Plantation Society and Anglo-Barbadian Politics, 1627–1700.* New York: New York University Press, 1984.

Vaitilingham, Adam. *The Mini "Rough Guide" Barbados.* New York: Rough Guides, 2001.

The World Factbook. Washington, D.C.: Central Intelligence Agency, 2001.

Laura A. Bergheim

See also **West Indies, British and French.**

BARBARY WARS, a series of mostly naval conflicts between the United States and the Barbary states (Morocco, Algiers, Tripoli, and Tunis), along the coast of North Africa. The Barbary nations had long plagued American and European shipping in the Mediterranean Sea through acts of piracy, taking advantage of the United States's lack of naval vessels. The war broke out with Tripoli and, later, Algiers only after the United States realized the need for a navy and began to acquire the ships and ports to support this enterprise.

The Tripolitan War occurred between 1801 and 1805. After the American Revolution, the United States, following the example of European nations, made annual payments to the Barbary states for unmolested passage along North Africa's Barbary Coast. Constant difficulties ensued in spite of this arrangement. In 1801 Tripoli declared war and seized several Americans and their vessels. The largely naval war that followed was feebly executed until Commodore Edward Preble arrived in 1803 with the USS *Constitution*, the USS *Philadelphia*, and several brigs and schooners. His arrival galvanized the entire force into vigorous action. In a naval demonstration before Tangiers, Preble set up a blockade of Tripoli. On 31 October 1803 the *Philadelphia* ran aground on a reef just outside the harbor and was captured by the Tripolitans, who later floated it and anchored it under the guns of the citadel. On 16 February 1804 Lieutenant Stephen Decatur and eighty officers and men recaptured and burned the *Philadelphia* in a daring night attack. During August and September 1804, Preble, in addition to blockading, harassed the Tripolitan shipping and fortifications with frequent attacks. Small gunboats fearlessly entered the harbor, enabling the crews to board and capture piratical craft while the larger ships kept up a protective fire on batteries. Such activity backfired on 4 September, when the USS *Intrepid*, with a cargo of gunpowder and explosive shells, maneuvered into the harbor at night. An explosion occurred prematurely, killing all the participants but doing little damage to Tripolitan shipping.

Preble was relieved by Commodore Samuel Barron, and Barron was relieved the following spring by Commodore John Rodgers. At this point, the bey (ruler) of Tripoli was ready to conclude peace, compelled partly by the success of the Derna land expedition, in which U.S. marines had captured the coastal city and were threatening to march on Tripoli. The treaty, hastily concluded on 4 June 1805, abolished all annual payments but provided for $60,000 ransom to be paid to Tripoli for the release of the officers and crew of the *Philadelphia*.

Although annual payments were maintained to the other Barbary states, Algiers continued to seize American merchantmen such as the *Mary Ann*, for which $18,000 was paid, and to threaten others such as the *Allegheny*, for which increased payments were demanded and secured. As a result, the United States declared war on Algiers in 1815. Immediately afterward, Decatur (promoted to commodore) and William Bainbridge were ordered to the Mediterranean with an overwhelming force. Within forty days after his June 1815 departure from New York, Decatur achieved his immediate mission. He captured the Algerian flagship *Mashuda* in a running fight. Appearing off the coast of Algiers, he demanded and secured a treaty humiliating to the once proud piratical state. His demands required no future payments, restoration of all American property, the emancipation of all Christian slaves escaping to U.S. men-of-war ships, civilized treatment of prisoners of war, and $10,000 for a merchantman recently seized. Tunis and Tripoli were forced to equally hard terms, and a U.S. squadron remained in the Mediterranean, ensuring the safety of American commerce.

BIBLIOGRAPHY

Chidsey, Donald Barr. *The Wars in Barbary: Arab Piracy and the Birth of the United States Navy.* New York: Crown, 1971.

Kitzen, Michael L. S. *Tripoli and the United States at War: A History of American Relations with the Barbary States: 1785–1805.* Jefferson, N.C.: McFarland, 1993.

Nash, Howard Pervear. *The Forgotten Wars: The Role of the U.S. Navy in the Quasi War with France and the Barbary Wars 1798–1805.* South Brunswick, N.J.: A. S. Barnes, 1968.

Tucker, Glenn. *Dawn Like Thunder: The Barbary Wars and the Birth of the U.S. Navy.* Indianapolis, Ind.: Bobbs-Merrill, 1963.

Walter B. Norris / H. S.

See also **Constitution; Decatur's Cruise to Algiers; Piracy.**

BARBECUE. Barbecue, a method of cooking meat over outdoor, open pits of coals, comes from the Spanish word "barbacoa." Barbecue entered the United States through Virginia and South Carolina in the late seventeenth century by way of slaves imported from the West Indies. The barbecue as a social event became very popular during the 1890s, when the United States began building its national park system, and Americans began socializing outdoors. However, the barbecue as a site for political campaigning dates back to George Washington. Candidates often held barbecues on the grounds of the county courthouse, offering free food in return for an opportunity to share their political platform with the dining public. Although initially associated with poorer citizens, barbecue, as both a method of cooking and recreation, spread to the middle and upper classes by the middle of the twentieth century and continues to dominate the southern United States's cultural landscape today.

BIBLIOGRAPHY

Edge, John T. *A Gracious Plenty: Recipes and Recollections from the American South.* New York: G. P. Putnam's Sons, 1999.

Elie, Lolis Eric. *Smokestack Lightning: Adventures in the Heart of Barbecue Country.* New York: North Point Press, 1996.

Neal, Bill. *Bill Neal's Southern Cooking.* Chapel Hill: The University of North Carolina Press, 1985.

Perl, Lila. *Red-Flannel Hash and Shoo-Fly Pie: American Regional Foods and Festivals.* Cleveland: The World Publishing Company, 1965.

Root, Waverley, and Richard de Rochemont. *Eating in America: A History.* New York: William Morrow and Company, Inc., 1976.

Kimberly Little

Barbed Wire. Coils of steel rods are stacked up before being converted into barbed wire at the Pittsburg Steel Company, Monessen, Pa. LIBRARY OF CONGRESS

BARBED WIRE is fencing contrived of two longitudinal wires twisted together into a cable with wire barbs wound around them at consistent intervals. It was first developed in the United States as a means of controlling and protecting the once open range. Range practices began to change in the 1860s as grass and water rights became issues of contention between the increasing population and ranchers who sought ways to protect their crops and livestock.

Traditional fencing materials were scarce on the prairie, expensive to transport, and frequently not suited to the environment. Smooth wire was experimented with but found inadequate for deterring livestock. Stockmen began to experiment by adding points, or barbs, to smooth wire. Several attempts were made at creating a functional barbed wire, and one was patented in 1867. The barbed wire that is commonly used today, however, may be credited to Joseph Glidden of De Kalb, Illinois, who invented his wire in 1873. Glidden improved on earlier attempts by attaching barbs at regular intervals to a smooth wire and then using a second wire to hold them in place. In 1874, Glidden secured a patent for his wire, invented a practical machine for its manufacture, and, in 1875, opened the Barb Fence Company with his partner Isaac Ellwood. Use of the invention spread quickly and soon demand was high. In 1876, Glidden sold his interests to a Massachusetts manufacturing company.

Washburn and Moen Manufacturing Company aggressively sought to limit competition by buying or claiming patents on all aspects of the industry. Several innovative farmers contested their attempts, but legal disputes were largely settled by an 1880 court decision that supported the company's monopoly.

Barbed wire, while immediately popular with many ranchers, was also controversial. Livestock suffered when they encountered barbed wire. Their discomfort aroused public protest, and earned barbed wire the title "The Devil's Rope." Animals were not the only victims of barbed wire and the newly parceled range. Free-range grazers felt their livelihood threatened, and trail drivers suffered the new obstruction of settler's fences. Some barbed wire opponents cut the wire fences, and the act was made illegal in some states. Wire cutting was such a problem in Texas, where some ranchers claimed territory illegally and used barbed wire to protect land, that the 1870s and 1880s were marked by what were known as the wire-cutting "wars." By 1890, the use of barbed wire had transformed the open ranges of the American West and Southwest into fenced pastureland.

Originally intended to control pasturage on the range, barbed wire became an effective deterrent to human beings as well. Barbed wire was used as a military obstacle across Europe during both world wars. Concentration camps constructed during World War II were surrounded with barbed wire, and many prisons and other high-security environments are still protected by barbed wire.

BIBLIOGRAPHY

McCallum, Henry D., and Frances T. McCallum. *The Wire That Fenced the West.* Norman: University of Oklahoma Press, 1965.

Starrs, Paul F. *Let the Cowboy Ride: Cattle Ranching in the American West.* Baltimore: Johns Hopkins University Press, 1998.

Deirdre Sheets

See also **Livestock Industry; West, American.**

BARBIE DOLL. Perhaps the most famous name in doll-making history, Barbie has delighted children since 1959, and has become a magnet for doll collectors. The brainchild of Ruth and Elliot Handler, Barbie was modeled after a German doll, Lilli, a shapely, pretty fashion doll first made in 1955. Made of molded plastic with her hair pulled back into a ponytail, she was available in either 11.5-inch or 7-inch heights.

The idea for Barbie originated when Ruth Handler, part owner of the Mattel company with her husband Elliot and family friend Harold Mattson, noticed that her daughter, Barbara, enjoyed playing with adult female dolls more than with baby dolls. She decided, therefore, to create a doll that would allow young girls to envision what they might become as they grew older.

Her creation, named in honor of daughter Barbara and backed by Mattel, debuted at the American Toy Fair in New York City in 1959. Although Mattel had been hesitant to risk producing the Barbie doll, Barbie set a new sales record for Mattel after the first year on the market. At a cost of three dollars each, Mattel sold 351,000 dolls during the first year of production, and within ten years, the public had purchased $500 million worth of Barbie products.

The first Barbie featured a ponytail hairstyle, black and white zebra-striped bathing suit, open-toed shoes, sunglasses, and earrings, and also featured various accessories and clothing styles created by the fashion designer Charlotte Johnson. Over the years, Barbie has been joined by family and friends, beginning with boyfriend Ken, named after the Handler's son, Kenneth, in 1961; sister Skipper in 1965; and Becky, Barbie's friend, in a wheelchair, in 1997.

Over the years, Barbie has undergone various cosmetic alterations, including a change to reflect criticism that Barbie reinforced sexism by representing a young woman with questionable intelligence and a sculpted physique. Over the years, Barbie has appeared as a doctor, UNICEF volunteer, athlete, and businesswoman, and has enjoyed universal appeal as a collector's item.

BIBLIOGRAPHY

Melillo, Marcie. *The Ultimate Barbie Doll Book.* Iola, Wis.: Krause Publications, 1996.

Valenti, Keni. *Barbie Dolls.* Philadelphia: Running Press, 1999.

Jennifer Harrison

See also **Toys and Games.**

BARGEMEN was a term used interchangeably with "keelboatmen," "bargers," and "keelers." It applied to men who operated riverboats that traveled upstream (as distinct from flatboats). Often wearing the traditional red shirt of their profession, most full-time bargemen worked on the lower Mississippi and on the Ohio River and its tributaries. After 1820 this occupation gradually disappeared as the steamboat, turnpike, and railroad took over transportation.

The bargemen were traditionally thought of as the roughest element in the West, celebrated as prodigious drinkers, fighters, gamblers, pranksters, and workers. A number of them were famous in their day, notably Mike Fink, who became a popular character in several folktales.

BIBLIOGRAPHY

Baldwin, Leland D. *The Keelboat Age on Western Waters.* Pittsburgh: University of Pittsburgh Press, 1941.

Blair, Walter, and Franklin J. Meine, eds. *Half Horse, Half Alligator: The Growth of the Mike Fink Legend.* Chicago: University of Chicago Press, 1956.

Mahoney, Tomothy R. *River Towns in the Great West: The Structure of Provincial Urbanization in the American Midwest, 1820–1870.* New York: Cambridge University Press, 1990.

Leland D. Baldwin / T. D.

See also **Flatboatmen; Natchez Trace; River Navigation.**

BARGES. See **Towboats and Barges.**

BARN RAISING, a colonial American building practice in which as many as one hundred people from neighboring farms would volunteer to help a family construct the frame and rafters of their barn in a single day, using pre-cut lumber. The event had practical significance, in that every new farm bolstered the prosperity of the frontier, yet it also became a social celebration that strengthened families' bonds with the community; women prepared food and men held competitions of speed and strength. Barn raisings were also held to rebuild barns after fires or other disasters. Occasionally still held in the Midwest and other rural areas, they are a cherished tradition among the Amish.

BIBLIOGRAPHY

Weyer, Jim, and Dick Roberts. *Red Walls, Black Hats: An Amish Barn Raising.* Toledo, Ohio: Weyer International, 1988.

Connie Ann Kirk

See also **Bees.**

BARNBURNERS was the nickname of a progressive faction of the New York State Democratic Party in the 1840s. The name "Barnburner" came from the story of the Dutch farmer who was willing to burn his barn to get rid of the rats. In direct opposition to the southern wing of the Democratic Party, Barnburners supported the Wilmot Proviso, which proposed to ban slavery from the territories captured in the Mexican War. In 1848 the Barnburners bolted from the Democrats and nominated the Free Soil candidate, Martin Van Buren, for president.

The Barnburners' defection ensured the defeat of the Democratic nominee, Lewis Cass. In the 1850s most of the Barnburners joined the newly founded Republican Party.

BIBLIOGRAPHY

Potter, David M. *The Impending Crisis, 1848–1861.* Edited and completed by Don E. Fehrenbacher. New York: Harper and Row, 1976.

Rayback, Joseph G. *Free Soil: The Election of 1848.* Lexington, Ky.: University Press of Kentucky, 1970.

Augustus H. Shearer / A. G.

See also **Free Soil Party; Wilmot Proviso.**

BARNSTORMING. Originally, the term "barnstorming" applied to traveling theater companies bringing plays to the nineteenth-century American frontier because company members frequently performed and slept in barns. Subsequently, the term was more commonly used to describe itinerant flyers (also called gypsies) in the half decade immediately following World War I who buzzed the countryside performing stunts or taking people on their first airplane ride.

When World War I ended, the men trained to be military pilots quickly bought surpluses of military aircraft. The barnstormers took to the air, seeking to find fame and fortune and to introduce the airplane and its potential to America. The pilots cut dashing figures and their daring stunts captured the American imagination. As more people became familiar with airplanes, the barnstormers had to become more innovative (or reckless) to keep the public's attention. Critics felt the spectacular crashes and resulting fatalities did more harm than good to the image of flying. Notable barnstormers included Walter H. Beech, African American Bessie Coleman, and Charles A. Lindbergh. "Barnstorming" is also used to describe the numerous road games outside the regular league schedule played by baseball's Negro league teams during the Jim Crow era. These games occasionally included some white teams during the off-season.

BIBLIOGRAPHY

Brady, Tim, ed. *The American Aviation Experience: A History.* Carbondale: Southern Illinois University Press, 2000.

Gorn, Elliott J., and Warren Goldstein. *A Brief History of American Sports.* New York: Hill and Wang, 1993.

Joel D. Kitchens

See also **Sports; Theater.**

BARNUM'S AMERICAN MUSEUM. Located at Ann Street and Broadway in Lower Manhattan and owned by P. T. Barnum from 1841 until it burned down in 1865, the American Museum housed a diverse collection of exhibits, ranging from such oddities as a huge hair-

P. T. Barnum. The showman and later circus owner's famous New York City museum was a conglomeration of more or less scientific displays, exhibits of outright oddities, zoo, aquarium, and theater. LIBRARY OF CONGRESS

ball extracted from the belly of a swine to those of a scientific or quasi-scientific nature, such as aggregations of insects, shells, and butterflies. It was the site of America's first public aquarium, where visitors could observe both commonplace and exotic creatures. Among the latter were a number of beluga whales, whose saltwater requisites were pumped in from New York Bay. The museum also included a menagerie of the familiar, such as tigers, bears, lions, primates, and the obscure, including a giraffe, a rhinoceros, and a hippopotamus. The last-mentioned animal was reputedly the first of its kind displayed in the United States. Theatrical productions were staged in the museum's Lecture Room, including an adaptation of Harriet Beecher Stowe's *Uncle Tom's Cabin* (1852) and the temperance drama *Ten Nights in a Barroom.* In the twenty-three and one-half years that Barnum owned the museum, ticket sales approached 38 million. Distinguished visitors included Henry David Thoreau, Walt Whitman, and the Prince of Wales.

BIBLIOGRAPHY

Saxon, A. H. *P. T. Barnum: The Legend and the Man.* New York: Columbia University Press, 1989.

William F. O'Connor

See also **Museums; Science Museums; Theater; Zoological Parks.**

BARRON V. BALTIMORE,

BARRON V. BALTIMORE, 7 Pet. 32 U.S. 243 (1833), 7–0. Barron claimed that the Fifth Amendment to the U.S. Constitution forbade the taking of his property by Baltimore without just compensation. When Baltimore refused to pay, Barron brought suit. Chief Justice John Marshall's opinion held that the Bill of Rights (the first ten amendments) was intended only to restrain the federal government. The holding in effect was overturned by decisions of the Court in the twentieth century that the Fourteenth Amendment was intended to "incorporate" various provisions of the Bill of Rights to prevent any state or locality from denying its citizens due process or the equal protection of the laws.

BIBLIOGRAPHY

Amar, Akhil Reed. *The Bill of Rights: Creation and Reconstruction.* New Haven, Conn.: Yale University Press, 1998.

Presser, Stephen B. *Recapturing the Constitution: Race, Religion, and Abortion Reconsidered.* Washington, D.C.: Regnery, 1994.

Stephen B. Presser

See also **Due Process of Law; Equal Protection of the Law.**

BARTLETT'S FAMILIAR QUOTATIONS.

BARTLETT'S FAMILIAR QUOTATIONS. First published in 1855 by Cambridge, Massachusetts, bookseller John Bartlett as *A Collection of Familiar Quotations,* this reference guide has enjoyed continuous commercial success while registering the changing shape of American public culture. Early editions comprised widely cited passages from the Bible, Shakespeare, and Anglo-American sentimental poetry. The ninth (1891) and tenth (1914) editions added ancient and early modern sources and the American favorites Thoreau and Whitman. Editors of the eleventh edition (1937) reconstructed the canon to stress literary prowess, with extensive material from recent modernists such as Joyce and Fitzgerald and such earlier innovators as Blake, Dickinson, Hawthorne, and Melville. Editions since 1948 have steadily expanded to include quotes from political leaders, academic intellectuals, world literature, women and other underrepresented voices, sports figures, movies, and popular musicians.

BIBLIOGRAPHY

Cochrane, Kerry L. " 'The Most Famous Book of Its Kind': *Bartlett's Familiar Quotations.*" In *Distinguished Classics of Reference Publishing.* Edited by James Rettig. Phoenix, Ariz.: Oryx Press, 1992.

Katz, Bill. *Cuneiform to Computer: A History of Reference Sources.* Lanham, Md.: Scarecrow Press, 1998.

Rubin, Joan Shelley. *The Making of Middlebrow Culture.* Chapel Hill: University of North Carolina Press, 1992. A good introduction to American literary history with bibliography.

Andrew Jewett

BASEBALL.

BASEBALL. Contrary to the myth that Abner Doubleday originated the sport in 1839 in Cooperstown, New York, a form of baseball was played in the 1820s, if not before. The sport probably originated in England from games like cricket and rounders, in which players struck a ball with a stick and ran to a base. In 1748, an English woman recorded that the family of the Prince of Wales played baseball. George Washington's army at Valley Forge played a game of "base." By the 1840s, different types of baseball had developed in Pennsylvania, New York, and New England. In 1845, Alexander Cartwright, a New York bank teller, proposed rules borrowed from these various forms to organize the sport for middle-class gentlemen. Unlike today, pitchers threw underhand, the winning team had to score twenty-one runs, and batters were out if hit by a thrown ball or when a hit was caught on one bounce. But Cartwright's rules did require play on a diamond-shaped field with bases ninety feet apart, nine players on the field, and three outs to an inning.

By the Civil War, baseball was a popular sport with men from both the middle and working classes and had spread to the Midwest and California. Newspapers already reported on it regularly. In fact, one newspaper in 1856 described baseball as "the national pastime," a claim that soon became true and remained so at the beginning of the twenty-first century, no matter how clichéd the phrase itself has become. Henry Chadwick, an English immigrant and sportswriter, did much to popularize baseball by creating the box score in 1860, by calculating batting averages, and by promoting the game as an enjoyable sport to play and to watch. From the start, as Chadwick discerned and generations since have discovered, baseball's statistics have proved to be a subject of debate and fascination, more so than in any other sport.

After the Civil War, baseball's popularity spread to the South, and growing numbers of fans throughout the country encouraged more intense competition and brought money into the sport. The first professional team was the Cincinnati Red Stockings, founded in 1869. While the quality of play steadily increased and amateurs rarely won against professionals, disputes over salaries, gambling, alcohol abuse, and rowdy fans also began to plague professional baseball by the early 1870s.

Players organized the first professional league in 1871 but it collapsed in 1875. A year later, William Hulbert, owner of the Chicago White Stockings, helped create the National League with teams from other cities in the Midwest and East. While this league also saw many franchises fail over the years, it did survive. The rival American Association was formed late in 1881. By 1887, at a time when the country accepted the practice of Jim

The First World Series. The Boston Pilgrims (renamed the Red Sox in 1907) of the upstart American League play—and beat—the veteran National League's Pittsburgh Pirates in 1903; an overhead view of the Boston ballpark, on Huntington Avenue. AP/WIDE WORLD PHOTOS

Crow segregation, players and owners agreed not to employ African Americans in baseball. The owners also agreed to the reserve clause, which at first limited the number of players eligible to switch teams. By 1889, the reserve clause blacklisted any player who broke his contract, thus keeping players' salaries low and ensuring the owners' survival. It also prevented players from marketing their talents freely. A century later, the reserve clause would be broken and players' salaries would explode.

By the late 1880s, baseball resembled the modern game. Baseball parks began to be built, and the two leagues played a series to determine the world champion. The distance between the mound and home plate lengthened to fifty feet; overhand pitching became the norm; four balls, not seven, made a walk; a strike zone was defined; and most players wore gloves, thus reducing errors. Players like Cap Anson and King Kelly had become stars, popular culture celebrated the sport in poems such as "Casey at the Bat," and periodicals devoted exclusively to baseball, such as *The Sporting News*, appeared. In 1890, players rebelled against the salaries imposed by the owners and formed a union and a new league. However, the players' league lasted only one year and helped kill the American Association.

Lack of competition in the twelve-team league, the dominance of pitching, and the poor reputation of players like John McGraw hurt baseball in the 1890s and attendance declined. But in 1893 the distance between home plate and the pitcher was increased to its present sixty feet six inches and as a result hitting improved. In 1899, Ban Johnson, a former sports editor who influenced baseball until the 1920s, transformed a minor league into the American League. It won acceptance as an equal from the National League in 1902, creating a rivalry that has endured. The first modern World Series was held in 1903. Major stars, such as shortstop Honus Wagner of the Pirates, and superlative teams—like those managed by Mc-Graw in New York and Connie Mack in Philadelphia—arose. After 1909, ten ballparks were either built or remodeled, replacing wooden structures prone to fire with steel, and were located near public transit stations to attract the growing urban middle class. Wrigley Field and Fenway Park, for example, were built during this period. In 1910, in a reflection of the importance of baseball, President William Howard Taft threw out the first ball of the season, establishing a tradition that has continued ever since.

Despite the play of stars like Ty Cobb, Christy Mathewson, Grover Alexander, and Walter Johnson, attendance began to decline in 1909, for no clear reason. Even so, baseball continued to attract wealthy investors, and in 1914 the Federal League was founded. Although the new league lasted only two years, it lured away many players from the other two leagues, doubled many players' salaries, and hurt most owners. Attendance revived in 1916, but World War I reduced baseball's appeal and more than two hundred players went into the service. The 1919 season might have been cancelled had the war continued. Baseball rebounded well from the war and doubled the attendance of the previous year as the nation embraced a return to normalcy. In addition to enjoying fine pennant races, baseball audiences were thrilled by Babe Ruth, a superb pitcher for the Red Sox, who, after being moved to the outfield, hit twenty-nine homers, a record that had stood since 1884.

Yet in retrospect, 1919 proved to be a disastrous year for baseball when in 1920 it was found that eight White Sox players had conspired with gamblers to lose the 1919 World Series to the underdog Cincinnati Reds. Rumors of a fix appeared even before the series began, but White Sox owner Charles Comiskey, who underpaid his talented players, ignored them. Five of the eight players were clearly guilty of throwing the series. The newly appointed baseball commissioner, Judge Kenesaw Mountain Landis, banned all eight for life. The ban included Shoeless Joe Jackson, a marvelous hitter, who was probably not involved. Landis's autocratic rule, which lasted into World War II, helped save baseball, as did the outlawing of trick pitches like the spitball.

Another factor that restored popularity to the game was Babe Ruth's superlative performance as a New York Yankee during the 1920s. The slugger, from a Baltimore home for wayward boys, hit fifty-four home runs in 1920 and transformed the game. While he also hit .376, it was Ruth's power and personality that attracted millions of fans. His personal home run total was greater than the team totals of all but one of the fifteen other teams and his slugging percentage was the best ever until Barry Bonds broke his record in 2001. The next year, he hit fifty-nine homers. It was not until the 1970s that Henry "Hank" Aaron broke his home run total record. The Yankees became the first team ever to draw one million fans in a season and did so six more times in the 1920s, allowing them to build Yankee Stadium in 1922. More generally, baseball's new emphasis on the home run, as opposed to a dependency on pitching and defense, changed the game dramatically. Pitchers won thirty or more games seventeen times between 1900 and 1920, but not once in the 1920s. In addition to homers, eight players hit over .400 between 1920 and 1930. Only Ted Williams, in 1941, has done so since.

The era from 1920 through 1930 was a great one for baseball. The Yankees began one of their many dynasties, the Philadelphia Athletics under Connie Mack may have been the best team ever, and Branch Rickey, through his invention of the farm system, made the Cardinals a strong franchise despite not having much money. There were also many stars besides Ruth, including Lou Gehrig, Al Simmons, George Sisler, Hack Wilson, and Rogers Hornsby, probably the greatest right-handed hitter ever.

Not surprisingly, the Great Depression and World War II hurt baseball severely. Attendance declined so much that many teams faced collapse, often selling off good players just to survive, while many stars had to serve in the war. Hard times, however, bred innovation to maintain fan interest. The All-Star game, the Hall of Fame, and the Most Valuable Player award were invented in the 1930s. Night baseball, pushed by Larry MacPhail, and radio broadcasts, especially with Red Barber in Cincinnati, became popular. Among the great players of the 1930s, Hank Greenberg, a Jew, and Joe DiMaggio, an Italian American, illustrate the important role minorities have played in baseball. African Americans, however, were conspicuous by their absence.

Blacks, of course, had continued to play baseball at all levels after whites barred them from organized baseball in the 1880s. But none of the black leagues lasted very long until the 1920s, when Andrew "Rube" Foster, formerly a great pitcher, helped establish the Negro National League with teams in the Midwest and East. A rival league survived for only five years. As with the majors, black teams did well in the 1920s but only a few prospered in the 1930s. By World War II, the idea of integration had surfaced, largely from a desire to exploit black talent and interest in baseball. While most African Americans wanted baseball to integrate, many realized it would kill the Negro leagues, an integral part of their society. In 1945, Branch Rickey, now of the Brooklyn Dodgers, signed the twenty-six-year-old Jackie Robinson to a contract with the minor-league Montreal Royals, thus breaking the color barrier. In 1947, Robinson played for the Dodgers and won the Rookie of the Year award. Later in the same year, Larry Doby of the Indians integrated the American League, but it lagged behind the senior circuit in signing black players until the 1960s.

The end of World War II, the return of baseball's stars, and good pennant races increased attendance dramatically up through 1949. To exploit this success, the Mexican League tried to lure players away with large salaries in 1946 but the effort failed. Prompted by talk of a players' union, the owners established a minimum salary and a pension plan in 1946, halting unionization for another twenty years. Baseball faced other problems by the late 1940s, however. The Dodgers, Giants, and Yankees, with stars like Robinson, Mickey Mantle, and Willie Mays, proved too dominant up through 1956 for the sport's health. Television hurt attendance, particularly in the minor leagues, and owners feared using it to broadcast games. And baseball had not followed the population flow into the South, West, and the suburbs; franchises had not moved out of the East and Midwest for almost a century.

In 1952, the Boston Braves decided to move to Milwaukee, thus beginning a shift of franchises that has consistently annoyed the cities, such as Boston and then Milwaukee, which were abandoned, enthralled those that got teams, and led to a dilution of talent. Soon the St. Louis Browns became the Baltimore Orioles, the Athletics moved to Kansas City and then to Oakland, and the Dodgers went to Los Angeles and the Giants to San Francisco. In the early 1960s, expansion occurred in Washington, D.C., Los Angeles, New York, and Houston, followed in 1969 by the first international team, the Montreal Expos, then eight years later by the Toronto Blue Jays. Having more teams prompted baseball to divide the league into divisions in 1969, with playoffs to determine World Series opponents.

Sports became a phenomenal business in the 1960s. Baseball's attendance increased by more than 60 percent during the decade, even as basketball and football grew tremendously, competing for both athletes and customers. The influx of great black athletes into baseball began to slow in the 1960s, partly replaced by an expansion in the number of Hispanic players, such as Roberto Clemente, Orlando Cepeda, Juan Marichal, and Tony Oliva. Baseball itself also changed after the pitcher's mound was raised in 1962; defense, pitching, and speed came to dominate, with players like Maury Wills, Sandy Koufax, Bob Gibson, Denny McLain, and Lou Brock replacing the sluggers as heroes. In addition, relief pitching became more important, further weakening the offense. In 1973, to increase run production and attendance, the American League introduced the controversial designated hitter, who could replace the pitcher as a batter.

Money proved the most significant problem for baseball, however. After World War II, the owners controlled both baseball and the commissioner. In 1966, the players' association hired Marvin Miller, formerly of the United Steel Workers of America, to help them bargain. Often helped by weak commissioners and inept owners, Miller and the players changed labor relations dramatically. After a brief strike in 1972, their pension plan greatly improved and they won the right to arbitration in disputes with the owners. In 1975, five years after the Cardinals' Curt Flood unsuccessfully challenged the reserve clause, two players, with Miller's counsel, successfully evaded the clause by letting their contracts lapse. Thereafter, players could become free agents and bargain for higher salaries, which they quickly did. In 1981, another strike occurred as owners tried but failed to regain their control of baseball.

Regardless of labor difficulties, baseball enjoyed great success from the late 1970s into the 1990s, with competitive races and great players like Reggie Jackson, Mike Schmidt, Tom Seaver, George Brett, Nolan Ryan, Tony Gwynn, Wade Boggs, and Cal Ripken Jr., who broke Gehrig's consecutive game record. Until later in the decade, when the Yankees prevailed, no team dominated. As attendance rose, with increased leisure time, expansion continued even as franchises became incredibly expensive. Strikeouts increased dramatically as more players tried for home runs and the importance of relief pitching increased. In 1955, only three players struck out 100 times; in 1998, seventy-three players matched that total. But home runs also increased and spectacularly so in 1998 and 1999, when Mark McGuire hit 70 and 65 and Sammy Sosa 66 and 63 to shatter Roger Maris's mark of 61 in 1961. In 2001, Barry Bonds surpassed McGuire's record

by hitting 73. For his part, Sosa hit over 60 for the third time, becoming the first player ever to achieve such a feat.

Labor troubles also remained part of baseball with another strike in August of the 1994 season. It was a bitter struggle that wiped out the World Series and only ended at the start of the 1995 season, with both sides far apart and the public angry. Attendance dropped by 20 million from 1993 and was regained only by 2000. The appeal of baseball remained, however, as enthusiasm for minor league teams revived and new parks in Baltimore, Seattle, Chicago, San Francisco, and Cleveland renewed interest. But baseball faced serious problems, such as increased competition for the entertainment dollar, high ticket prices, excessively long games, declining television audiences, the weakness of small market teams with poor finances, and the need to import more and more talent, now from Japan, to play the national pastime.

BIBLIOGRAPHY

Rogosin, Donn. *Invisible Men: Life in Baseball's Negro Leagues.* New York: Atheneum, 1983.

Rossi, John P. *The National Game: Baseball and American Culture.* Chicago: Ivan Dee, 2000.

Seymour, Harold. *Baseball: The Early Years.* New York: Oxford University Press, 1960.

———. *Baseball: The Golden Age.* New York: Oxford University Press, 1971.

Solomon, Burt. *The Baseball Timeline.* Rev. and updated ed. London and New York: Dorling Kindersley, 2001.

Thorn, John, Pete Palmer, and Michael Gershman, eds. *Total Baseball.* 7th ed. Kingston, N.Y.: Total Sports Publishing, 2001.

Tygiel, Jules. *Past Time: Baseball as History.* New York: Oxford University Press, 2000.

Voigt, David. *American Baseball.* 3 vols. University Park: Pennsylvania State University Press, 1983.

White, G. Edward. *Creating the National Pastime: Baseball Transforms Itself, 1903–1953.* Princeton, N.J.: Princeton University Press, 1996.

Zimbalist, Andrew. *Baseball and Billions: A Probing Look Inside the Big Business of Our National Pastime.* New York: Basic Books, 1992.

John Syrett

See also **Black Sox Scandal; College Athletics; Sports.**

BASEBALL UNION. For almost a century, baseball's reserve system bound players to their clubs for life or until the club decided to trade or release them. In the decade following April 1966, the Major League Baseball Players Association changed that, altering the economic structure of baseball in a way that would have an impact on all professional team sports. The start of the process was the decision of the players to hire Marvin J. Miller, an executive with the United Steelworkers of America, as their first full-time executive director. The defining moment for the future of the union was the solidarity that allowed it to prevail during its first strike in 1972.

The basis for all of the union's future success was in 1968, when it negotiated a collective bargaining agreement with the owners that included an impartial grievance procedure. In 1970, Curt Flood sued to overturn the reserve system on antitrust grounds but lost at trial and before the Supreme Court in 1972. In 1975, two players challenged the contractual basis of the reserve system. The arbitrator, Peter Seitz, upheld their grievance, declaring them to be free agents. The impact was both immediate and far-reaching. In 1966, the minimum salary was $6,000, and the average was $19,000. By 1981 these figures were $32,500 and $185,651, and by 2000, $200,000 and $1,398,830.

Salary increases were not the only consequences. There were work stoppages in 1972, 1976, 1981, 1985, 1990, and 1994–1995. Free agent movement, length of contracts, and the size of salaries became as important as the statistics normally associated with the sport. The attitude of the public toward athletes and sports was altered forever. And every other professional team sport had to create systems to deal with the new aspirations of their players to emulate the success of the major league baseball players.

BIBLIOGRAPHY

Burk, Robert F. *Much More Than a Game: Players, Owners and Baseball Since 1921.* Chapel Hill: University of North Carolina Press, 2001.

Koppett, Leonard. *Koppett's Concise History of Major League Baseball.* Philadelphia: Temple University Press, 1998.

Korr, Charles. *The End of Baseball As We Knew It: The Players Union, 1960–1981.* With Foreword by Bob Costas. Urbana and Chicago: University of Illinois Press, 2002.

Lowenfish, Lee. *The Imperfect Diamond: A History of Baseball's Labor Wars.* Rev. ed. New York: De Capo Press, 1991.

Miller, Marvin. *A Whole Different Ball Game: The Sport and the Business of Baseball.* New York: Birch Lane Press, 1991.

Charles P. Korr

BASKETBALL. James Naismith, originally from Almonte, Ontario, invented basketball at the International YMCA Training School in Springfield, Massachusetts, in 1891. The game was first played with peach baskets (hence the name) and a soccer ball and was intended to provide indoor exercise for football players. As a result, it was originally a rough sport. Although ten of Naismith's original thirteen rules remain, the game soon changed considerably, and the founder had little to do with its evolution.

The first intercollegiate game was played in Minnesota in 1895, with nine players to a side and a final score of nine to three. A year later, the first five-man teams played at the University of Chicago. Baskets were now constructed of twine nets but it was not until 1906 that the bottom of the nets were open. In 1897, the dribble was first used, field goals became two points, foul shots one point, and the first professional game was played. A year later, the first professional league was started, in the East, while in 1900, the first intercollegiate league began. In 1910, in order to limit rough play, it was agreed that four fouls would disqualify players, and glass backboards were used for the first time. Nonetheless, many rules still differed, depending upon where the games were played and whether professionals, collegians, or YMCA players were involved.

College basketball was played from Texas to Wisconsin and throughout the East through the 1920s, but most teams played only in their own regions, which prevented a national game or audience from developing. Professional basketball was played almost exclusively in the East before the 1920s, except when a team would "barnstorm" into the Midwest to play local teams, often after a league had folded. Before the 1930s very few games, either professional or amateur, were played in facilities suitable for basketball or with a perfectly round ball. Some were played in arenas with chicken wire separating the players from fans, thus the word "cagers," others with posts in the middle of the floor and often with balconies overhanging the corners, limiting the areas from which shots could be taken. Until the late 1930s, all players used the two-hand set shot, and scores remained low.

Basketball in the 1920s and 1930s became both more organized and more popular, although it still lagged far behind both baseball and college football. In the pros, five urban, ethnic teams excelled and played with almost no college graduates. They were the New York Original Celtics; the Cleveland Rosenblums, owned by Max Rosenblum; Eddie Gottlieb's Philadelphia SPHAs (South Philadelphia Hebrew Association); and two great black teams, the New York Renaissance Five and Abe Saperstein's Harlem Globetrotters, which was actually from Chicago. While these teams had some notable players, no superstars, such as Babe Ruth, Jack Dempsey, or Red Grange, emerged to capture the public's attention as they did in other sports of the period. The same was true in college basketball up until the late 1930s, with coaches dominating the game and its development. Walter "Doc" Meanwell at Wisconsin, Forrest "Phog" Allen at Kansas, Ward "Piggy" Lambert at Purdue, and Henry "Doc" Carlson at Pittsburgh all made significant contributions to the game's development: zone defenses, the weave, the passing game, and the fast break.

In the decade preceding World War II, five events changed college basketball and allowed it to become a major spectator sport. In 1929, the rules committee reversed a decision that would have outlawed dribbling and slowed the game considerably. Five years later, promoter Edward "Ned" Irish staged the first intersectional twin bill in Madison Square Garden in New York City and attracted more than 16,000 fans. He demonstrated the appeal of major college ball and made New York its center. In December 1936, Hank Luisetti of Stanford revealed the virtues of the one-handed shot to an amazed Garden audience and became the first major collegiate star. Soon thereafter, Luisetti scored an incredible fifty points against Duquesne, thus ending the East's devotion to the set shot and encouraging a more open game. In consecutive years the center jump was eliminated after free throws and then after field goals, thus speeding up the game and allowing for more scoring. In 1938, Irish created the National Invitation Tournament (NIT) in the Garden to determine a national champion. Although postseason tournaments had occurred before, the NIT was the first with major colleges from different regions and proved to be a great financial success. The National Collegiate Athletic Association (NCAA) created its own postseason tournament in 1939 but did not rival the NIT in prestige for some time.

The 1940s saw significant changes for college basketball. Players began using the jump shot after Kenny Sailors of Wyoming wowed the East with it in 1943. The behind-the-back dribble and pass also appeared, as did exceptional big men. Bob Kurland at Oklahoma A&M was almost seven feet tall and George Mikan at DePaul was six feet ten inches. While Kurland had perhaps the better college career and played in two Olympics, he chose not to play professional ball, whereas Mikan became the first dominant star in the pros. Their defensive play inspired the rule against goal tending (blocking a shot on its downward flight). Adolph Rupp, who played under Phog Allen, also coached the first of his many talented teams at Kentucky in that decade. However, in 1951, Rupp and six other coaches suffered through a point-shaving scandal that involved thirty-two players at seven colleges and seriously injured college basketball, particularly in New York, where four of the seven schools were located. While the game survived, the NCAA moved its tournament away from Madison Square Garden to different cities each year and the NIT's prestige began to decline.

Professional basketball remained a disorganized and stodgy sport up until the late 1940s, with barnstorming still central to the game and most players still using the set shot. In 1946, however, hockey owners, led by Maurice Podoloff, created the Basketball Association of America (BAA) in the East to fill their arenas, but few fans came, even after Joe Fulks of Philadelphia introduced the jump shot. The BAA's rival, the National Basketball League, had existed since the 1930s, had better players, like Mikan of the Minneapolis Lakers, Bob Davies of the Rochester Royals, and Dolph Shayes of the Syracuse Nationals, but operated in much worse facilities and did not do much better at attracting audiences. In 1948, Podoloff lured the Lakers, Royals, and two other teams to the BAA and proposed a merger of the two leagues for the 1949–1950 season. The result was the National Basketball Association

(NBA), with Podoloff its first commissioner. The seventeen-team league struggled at first but soon reduced its size and gained stability, in large part because of Mikan's appeal and Podoloff's skills.

Despite the point-shaving scandal, college ball thrived in the 1950s, largely because it had prolific scorers and more great players than in any previous decade. Frank Selvy of Furman and Paul Arizin of Villanova both averaged over forty points early in the decade, while Clarence "Bevo" Francis of tiny Rio Grande College in Ohio amazed fans by scoring 116 points in one game while averaging 50 per game for a season. The decade also witnessed some of the most talented and complete players ever. Tom Gola at LaSalle, Bill Russell at San Francisco, Wilt Chamberlain at Kansas, Elgin Baylor at Seattle, Jerry West at West Virginia, and Oscar Robertson at Cincinnati, all had phenomenal skills that have since been the measure of other players. And in 1960 one of the best teams ever, Ohio State, won the NCAA title led by Jerry Lucas and John Havlicek.

Professional basketball underwent major changes in the 1950s that helped increase its popularity. In 1950, Earl Lloyd, from West Virginia, played for the Washington Capitols and became the first African American to play in the NBA. In 1954, Danny Biasone, owner of the Syracuse Nationals, persuaded the NBA to institute the twenty-four-second shot clock, requiring a team to shoot within that time. This eliminated the slow pace that had long prevailed in the pros and made the NBA more exciting. Teams now scored one hundred points a game regularly. The league also now awarded foul shots when the other team received more than five personal fouls a period, greatly reducing the rough play that had hurt the pro game. In 1956, Red Auerbach of the Boston Celtics made the best deal in NBA history when he acquired the draft rights to Bill Russell, the defensive player and rebounder he needed to complement Bob Cousy and Bill Sharman in the backcourt.

With the addition of Russell, the Celtics became the best pro team ever, winning eleven of the next thirteen championship titles before expansion diluted the talent in the NBA. The St. Louis Hawks, with Bob Pettit, beat the Celtics in 1958, and the Philadelphia 76ers, with Chamberlain, beat them in 1967. But Russell, a player-coach for two titles, and his teammates formed the greatest dynasty in pro ball. Even the Los Angeles Lakers, who had moved from Minneapolis in 1960, with West and Baylor, were no match for the Celtics over these years. While West, Baylor, Chamberlain—who averaged over fifty points a game in 1962—and Oscar Robertson—who in the same year averaged a triple double per game in points, assists, and rebounds—were superior to any individual Celtic, no other team could consistently play defense, rebound, and run with the Celtics.

College basketball also experienced tremendous growth and increasing racial diversity during the 1960s. While Russell, Chamberlain, Baylor, and Robertson were

Oscar Robertson. "The Big O," playing for the University of Cincinnati, grabs a rebound in midair during a game against Kansas State University in March 1959, a year before his spectacular professional career began. The University of Cincinnati

proof of the integration of college ball in most of the country, many teams from the South would still not play against black players. That changed in the 1960s. In 1963, Loyola College of Chicago, on its way to the NCAA title with four black starters, beat Mississippi State, which had refused to play against a team with a black player the year before. Three years later, Texas Western, with five black starters, beat Adolph Rupp's heavily favored all-white Kentucky team for the NCAA title. Thereafter, black players began to dominate basketball, a trend that has since become steadily more pronounced. While pro and college basketball have hired more black coaches and executives than any other sport, their numbers do not begin to match black players' contribution to the game.

The 1960s and 1970s also witnessed the amazing success of John Wooden's UCLA Bruins. In twelve years from 1964 on, the Bruins won ten NCAA titles. While five titles resulted from the dominance of Lew Alcindor (later Kareem Abdul-Jabbar) and then Bill Walton at center, Wooden won the other five with speed, a full court zone defense, and talented guards and forwards. Other coaches have also compiled excellent NCAA tournament records: Rupp at Kentucky; Dean Smith, another Phog Allen protégé, at North Carolina; Bobby Knight at Indiana; Denny Crum at Louisville; and Mike Krzyzewski at Duke. But Wooden and his Bruins remain unique. They also helped create the excitement that now surrounds the NCAA finals.

With the end of the Celtic dynasty, the NBA fell on relatively hard times in the 1970s. There were great players, of course, like Alcindor with the Milwaukee Bucks, Walton with the Portland Trailblazers, Elvin Hayes with the Washington Bullets, Dave Cowens with the Celtics, Rick Barry with the Golden State Warriors, Willis Reed with the New York Knicks, and West and Chamberlain with the Lakers. But no new transcendent stars emerged. In addition, a number of players with drug problems hurt the league's image. Many felt that the rival American Basketball Association—which started in 1968 and had stars like Connie Hawkins, George Gervin, and the amazing Julius Irving—played a more exciting game. The ABA used a red, white, and blue-colored ball, allowed the three-point shot, and had a helter-skelter style. However, it folded in 1976, after which four of its teams joined the NBA.

College basketball, as usual, provided exciting players to revitalize the pros. In the late 1970s, Larry Bird, a marvelous shooter, passer, and rebounder, starred for Indiana State. In 1979, he played and lost in the NCAA finals to another superb player, Earvin "Magic" Johnson, a six foot nine inch guard for Michigan State. The next year, Johnson went to the Lakers and Bird to the Celtics, where they, with talented teammates, created a rivalry that reinvigorated pro basketball. Of equal importance was David Stern, who became commissioner in 1984. He facilitated a compromise between labor and management and helped the NBA become a global success.

Women's basketball also attracted a larger audience beginning in the 1970s with Anne Meyers of UCLA and Nancy Lieberman of Old Dominion as the first big stars. In the early 1980s, Cheryl Miller at USC and Lynette Woodard at Kansas, the first black stars, along with Carol Blazejowski at Montclair State, demonstrated the scoring and athleticism previously associated with men's ball. In

1982, the first NCAA women's tournament was held as the sport grew in popularity. In 1996, the American Basketball League began and the next year the WNBA, sponsored by the NBA, started. In late 1998, the ABL folded with some teams becoming part of the WNBA. The Houston Comets, with its superstar Cynthia Cooper, dominated the league.

College basketball has been very competitive and hugely successful since the Wooden era. Eighteen different teams won the NCAA tournament from 1976 to 2002, although most have been from the major conferences. Since then, the dunk, banned in 1968 to limit Alcindor, has been restored; the shot clock was introduced along with the three-point field goal; first-year students became eligible to play; and recruiting became more competitive among the big conferences. As with the pros, television has made college basketball available on many channels, all season long, with more money involved every year. Many fine teams have arisen: North Carolina, Kansas, Indiana, Georgetown, Duke, Louisville, Michigan, Kentucky, and the University of Nevada at Las Vegas. Increasingly, however, stars have turned pro after one or two years of eligibility and many high school standouts have begun forgoing college altogether. While this has precluded dynasties from developing, it has hurt continuity, hurt the quality of play, and may discourage enthusiasm for the college game.

The pro game enjoyed tremendous success up through the 1990s, thanks to players like Jabbar, Bird, Johnson, Isiah Thomas, Reggie Miller, Charles Barkley, Karl Malone, Patrick Ewing, and Hakeem Olajuwon—and, of course, the magnificent Michael Jordan. Jordan turned pro in 1984, leaving North Carolina early, and became an incredible scorer and a superlative defender for the Chicago Bulls, though it was not until 1991, with Scottie Pippen and Coach Phil Jackson, that the Bulls won a title. They then won five more titles in seven years to rank them near the Celtics. In the process, Jordan became the planet's most famous athlete and the NBA became a marketing phenomenon. Jordan retired in 1998, then returned in 2001, saying he had an "itch that needed to be scratched." Nonetheless, his playing seemed to have lost much of its luster, and despite the emergence of new stars, like Kobe Bryant, Vince Carter, Grant Hill, Allen Iverson, and Shaquille O'Neal, it remained unclear how popular the NBA will be in the years to come.

BIBLIOGRAPHY

Axthelm, Pete. *The City Game: Basketball from the Garden to the Playgrounds.* New York: Harpers Magazine Press, 1970.

Bjarkman, Peter C. *The History of the NBA.* New York: Crescent Books, 1992.

———. *Hoopla: A Century of College Basketball, 1896–1996.* Indianapolis: Masters Press, 1996.

———. *The Biographical History of Basketball.* Lincolnwood, Ill.: Masters Press, 2000.

George, Nelson. *Elevating the Game: The History and Aesthetics of Black Men in Basketball.* New York: Simon and Schuster, 1992.

Gutman, Bill. *The History of NCAA Basketball.* New York: Crescent Books, 1993.

Ham, Eldon L. *The Playmasters: From Sellouts to Lockouts—An Unauthorized History of the NBA.* Chicago: Contemporary Books, 2000.

Isaacs, Neil D. *Vintage NBA—The Pioneer Era, 1946–1956.* Indianapolis: Masters Press, 1996.

Peterson, Robert W. *Cages to Jump Shots: Pro Basketball's Early Years.* New York: Oxford University Press, 1990.

Sachare, Alex. *One Hundred Greatest Basketball Players of All Time.* New York: Simon and Schuster, 1997.

John Syrett

See also **College Athletics; Sports.**

BASTOGNE, a town in the Belgian Ardennes, scene of an epic defense by American troops during the Battle of the Bulge in World War II. Controlling a vital road network, Bastogne was an obvious goal when German armies on 16 December 1944 launched a surprise counteroffensive. The Allied commander, General Dwight D. Eisenhower, rushed infantry divisions to the area to ensure that the Tenth Armored Division's tanks would reach Bastogne ahead of the Germans. Contingents of the Fifth Panzer Army encircled Bastogne the night of 20 December, but because the main German objective was to cross the Meuse River to the west, all-out attack was delayed. When the Germans on 22 December demanded surrender, the American commander, Brigadier General Anthony C. McAuliffe, responded with derision: "Nuts!" That same day, the U.S. Third Army began to drive to Bastogne's aid, and clearing weather on 23 December enabled American planes to drop supplies. Although the Germans attacked strongly on Christmas Day, the defenses held, and on 26 December tanks of the Fourth Armored Division broke the siege. Heavy fighting nevertheless continued as the Germans for another week tried desperately to take the town. Reinforced by more troops of the Third Amy, the defenses held, so that on 3 January 1945 the Third Army was able to begin an offensive aimed at eliminating the "bulge" the Germans had created in American lines. After the war the Belgians erected a monument *(Le Madrillon)* at Bastogne in tribute to the American stand there and elsewhere in the Battle of the Bulge.

BIBLIOGRAPHY

Cole, Hugh M. *The Ardennes: Battle of the Bulge.* Washington, D.C.: Center of Military History, U.S. Army, 1965. Reprint, 1994.

Elstob, Peter. *Bastogne: The Road Block.* New York: Ballantine Books, 1968.

Marshall, S. L. A. *Bastogne: The Story of the First Eight Days.* Washington, D.C.: Infantry Journal Press, 1946. Reprint,

Washington, D.C.: Center of Military History, U.S. Army, 1988.

Charles B. MacDonald / A. R.

See also **Bulge, Battle of the.**

BATAAN-CORREGIDOR CAMPAIGN.

A few hours after the surprise attack on Pearl Harbor (7 December 1941), Japanese air units from Taiwan attacked Clark Field to destroy the backbone of American air power in the Philippines. Major landings by Lieutenant General Masaharu Homma's Fourteenth Army on Manila on 22 and 24 December caught defending forces under General Douglas MacArthur in a trap, forcing a retreat to the Bataan peninsula. When the Japanese attacked on 7 January 1942, MacArthur's largely Filipino reservist army, backed up by a division of American and Filipino Scout regulars, retreated to a secondary line and then held, inflicting heavy losses.

By February, MacArthur's men were gravely short of food, quinine to combat malaria, and supplies of all sorts. A tight Japanese blockade had isolated the Philippines. In early March, at President Franklin D. Roosevelt's order, MacArthur slipped through the blockade by PT boat to escape to Australia. Homma attacked again on 3 April and quickly cut through the starving defenders. On 9 April 1942 Bataan surrendered; 79,500 men laid down their arms; and many hundreds perished afterward from weakness and brutal treatment by guards on the infamous death march to prison camps in central Luzon.

Corregidor, a fortress island in Manila Bay, held out for three weeks more under MacArthur's former subor-dinate, General Jonathan M. Wainwright. Japanese artillery and aircraft bombarded the island, forcing thousands to take shelter in tunnels, including the famous Malinta Tunnel, which contained the headquarters, hospital, and nurses' quarters. The Japanese Fourth Division troops broke through on 5 May, inducing Wainwright to surrender the 16,000 defenders the next day. After the war Homma was tried as a war criminal in Manila and executed.

BIBLIOGRAPHY

Belote, James H., and William M. Belote. *Corregidor: The Saga of a Fortress*. New York: Harper and Row, 1967.

Falk, Stanley. *Bataan: The March of Death*. New York: Norton, 1962.

Knox, Donald. *Death March: The Survivors of Bataan*. New York: Harcourt Brace Jovanovich, 1981.

Morris, Eric. *Corregidor: The End of the Line*. New York: Stein and Day, 1981.

James H. Belote
William M. Belote

See also **Atrocities in War; Philippines.**

BATHTUBS AND BATHING.

For most of history, bathing was a luxury associated with trips to spas and resorts. Even wealthy people did not routinely bathe with soap. They occasionally cleaned themselves using only a basin and washcloth. The desire to bathe became common during the nineteenth century, when greater wealth allowed more people to eliminate dirt from their houses, clothes, and bodies. However, at midcentury, only wealthy

American Prisoners in the Philippines. NATIONAL ARCHIVES

Americans had bathrooms with running water. Typical families purchased washstands as furniture for their bedrooms and provided space for a basin, pitcher, and chamber pot. Most bathtubs were metal, portable objects that could be stored inconspicuously until needed. Because they were filled by hand with buckets of water, families still bathed infrequently, often in the kitchen, without bothering to change the bath water after each bather.

Once bathing became routine among the middle classes, they adopted new standards of cleanliness. Persons who wished to prosper bathed in order to advance socially and economically. By the 1870s, middle-class mothers had indoctrinated their children with modern standards and habits. A wealth of prescriptive literature encouraged their efforts, including advice from medical experts, who now considered bathing healthful. These new attitudes led schoolteachers and urban middle-class reformers to campaign actively to change the behaviors of an increasingly immigrant working class, whose lack of hygiene was seen as a threat to society. Since private baths remained prohibitively expensive, the reformers championed public facilities.

Modern bathrooms with tubs, sinks, toilets, and running water did not become common until the twentieth century, so business interests were slow to promote the ideal of cleanliness among the general population. A few corporations, such as Procter and Gamble, aggressively advertised soaps for the masses, but manufacturers of cast iron sinks and bathtubs did not sell products directly to consumers. They sold to jobbers—middlemen who linked manufacturers with the plumbers who installed products. Before 1920, even highly successful manufacturers of tubs and sinks did not produce toilets, which demanded a vitreous finish produced by potters rather than metal workers. Consequently, the plumbing industry remained decentralized, without an integrated leader who could promote hygiene aggressively.

In anticipation of the housing boom of the 1920s, dramatic changes occurred. Mail-order firms, especially Sears Roebuck, began marketing suites of low-cost toilets, sinks, and bathtubs. Recognizing the potential market, large plumbing firms such as American Standard, Crane, and Kohler consolidated holdings and adopted capital-intensive methods of manufacture. During the boom, they produced a great volume of moderately priced plumbing goods for the common bathroom. By 1940, roughly three of four urban families had residences with modern bathrooms. Within a decade, bathing had become a habitual activity for most Americans.

For two generations, Americans preferred less expensive, utilitarian plumbing, making it impossible for manufacturers to transform fixtures into luxury items. Families were most concerned with cost, especially as they began to add second and even third bathrooms to their houses. Later in the twentieth century, however, consumers began to purchase fiberglass spas and hot tubs. Often

elaborate, these new fixtures reintroduced the concept of bathing as a luxury for the middle class.

BIBLIOGRAPHY

Bigott, Joseph C. *From Cottage to Bungalow: Houses and the Working Class in Metropolitan Chicago, 1869–1929*. Chicago: University of Chicago Press, 2001.

Blaszcyk, Regina Lee. *Imagining Consumers: Design and Innovation from Wedgwood to Corning*. Baltimore: Johns Hopkins University Press, 2000.

Bushman, Richard L., and Claudia L. Bushman. "The Early History of Cleanliness in America." *Journal of American History* 74 (1988):1213–1238.

Joseph C. Bigott

See also **Hygiene.**

BATTERY, ELECTRIC. *See* **Electricity and Electronics.**

BATTLE FLEET CRUISE AROUND THE WORLD was ordered by President Theodore Roosevelt in response to recommendations from the Navy Department that the Atlantic Fleet be transferred to the Pacific. On 16 December 1907, the fleet, consisting of sixteen battleships, sailed from Hampton Roads, Virginia, under the command of Rear Admiral Robley D. Evans. It was bound for San Francisco by way of the Strait of Magellan. The cruise served as an exercise in naval training and planning should relations with Japan degenerate because of Japanese aggressive actions in Manchuria and issues of Japanese immigration to the West Coast. Roosevelt, however, recognized that the cruise could also generate support for the navy among the American people and demonstrate American power to the world. Thus the arrangements for the return voyage represented an exercise in naval diplomacy.

From San Francisco the fleet, now commanded by Rear Admiral Charles S. Sperry, sailed to Hawaii, then New Zealand, Australia, the Philippines, China, and Japan. It returned home, via the Suez Canal and the Mediterranean, to Hampton Roads on 22 February 1909. Naval greetings were exchanged with fourteen countries, and the fleet was welcomed everywhere it went with huge celebrations. The cruise demonstrated America's new global reach, but its real significance lies in the effect it had on the navy itself, which became more organized, professional, and efficient.

BIBLIOGRAPHY

Hart, Robert A. *The Great White Fleet: Its Voyage Around the World, 1907–09*. Boston: Little, Brown, 1965.

Reckner, James R. *Teddy Roosevelt's Great White Fleet*. Annapolis: Naval Institute Press, 1988.

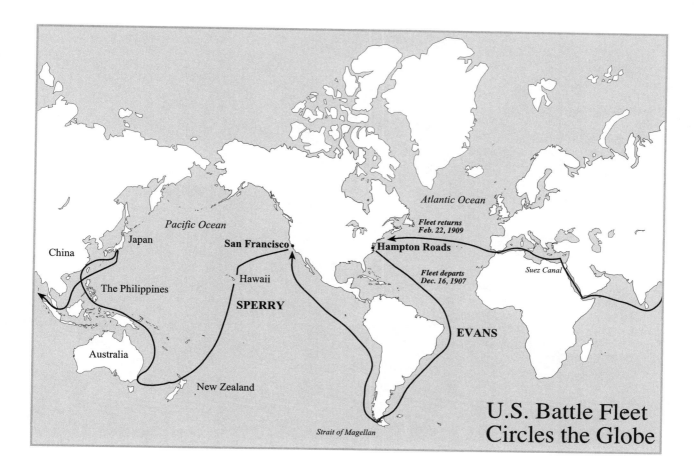

Pacific Ocean

China
Japan
The Philippines
Australia
New Zealand
Hawaii
San Francisco
SPERRY
Strait of Magellan

Atlantic Ocean
*Fleet returns
Feb. 22, 1909*
Hampton Roads
*Fleet departs
Dec. 16, 1907*
EVANS
Suez Canal

U.S. Battle Fleet
Circles the Globe

Wimmel, Kenneth. *Theodore Roosevelt and the Great White Fleet: American Sea Power Comes of Age.* London: Brassey's, 1998.

Erin Black

See also **Navy, United States.**

"THE BATTLE HYMN OF THE REPUBLIC."

Poet Julia Ward Howe wrote the words to "The Battle Hymn of the Republic," the great Civil War song that became an American anthem of righteousness and power, in November of 1861. Composed in a flash of inspiration to the tune of the marching song "John Brown's Body," the poem was published in *The Atlantic Monthly* in February 1862. However, "Battle Hymn" was popularized as a song by Union chaplain Charles Cardwell McCabe, who often included it in his lectures and sang it on important occasions. The hymn was also a favorite of Abraham Lincoln and Theodore Roosevelt, and remains a staple of American patriotic and religious music.

In 1862, Howe journeyed to Washington, D.C., in company of her abolitionist husband, Samuel Gridley Howe. Although slow to embrace abolitionism, Howe was caught up in the drama of John Brown's martyrdom for his failed attack on Harpers Ferry. Her powerful Biblical imagery linking the Old Testament prophesy of vengeance and redemption ("I have trodden the wine press alone . . . and trampled them in my wrath . . . For the day of vengeance was in my heart, / and my year of redemption has come." [Isaiah 63:1–6]) with God's mercy and Christ's sacrifice framed the Civil War as a Christian crusade. The music to "John Brown's Body" and "Battle Hymn" is based on an old Methodist hymn.

BIBLIOGRAPHY

Grant, Mary H. *Private Woman, Public Person: An Account of the Life of Julia Ward Howe from 1819 to 1868.* Brooklyn, N.Y.: Carlson Publishing, 1994.

Ream, Debbie Williams. "Mine Eyes Have Seen the Glory." *American History Illustrated* 27 (January/February 1973): 60–64. Abstract.

Ross, William E. "The Singing Chaplain: Bishop Charles Cardwell McCabe and the Popularization of the 'Battle Hymn of the Republic.'" *Methodist History* 29, no 1 (1989): 22–32. Abstract, *America: History and Life*.

Williams, Gary. *Hungry Heart: The Literary Emergence of Julia Ward Howe.* Amherst: University of Massachusetts Press, 1999.

Perry Frank

Captured Members of Assault Brigade 2506. © AFP/CORBIS

BAY OF PIGS INVASION (17 April 1961), the abortive attempt by Cuban exiles—organized, financed, and led by the U.S. Central Intelligence Agency (CIA)—to overthrow the revolutionary regime of Premier Fidel Castro in Havana. The landing by the 1,453 men of Brigade 2506 on the swampy southwestern coast of Cuba turned within seventy-two hours into a complete disaster as the Castro forces captured 1,179 of the invaders and killed the remaining 274. For the United States and for President John F. Kennedy, who had authorized the operation in his third month in the White House, the Bay of Pigs became a bitter political defeat as well as a monumental failure in a large-scale intelligence enterprise. The invasion led to an increase in Soviet aid to Cuba that climaxed with the installation of nuclear warheads in Cuba in 1962. The Cuban missile crisis that followed was one of the most dangerous moments in post–World War II relations between the United States and the Soviet Union.

The plans for the Bay of Pigs were conceived by the CIA during 1960, toward the end of the Eisenhower administration, on the theory—proved by events to have been totally erroneous—that a landing by the exiles' brigade would touch off a nationwide uprising against Castro. Kennedy's administration shared the Eisenhower ad-

ministration's fear of Castro's leftward leanings, and Kennedy authorized the plan shortly after Soviet Premier Nikita Khrushchev publicly described conflicts in Vietnam and Cuba as "wars of national liberation" that merited Soviet support.

From the mistaken assumption that Cuba would rise against Castro to its poorly managed execution, the entire venture was marked by miscalculation. To prepare for the invasion, the CIA trained the force in secret camps in Guatemala for nearly six months. But long before the landing, it was widely known in the Cuban community in Florida (and, presumably, the information was also available to Castro agents) that such a landing was in the offing. Finally, the invasion failed because Kennedy refused to provide U.S. air support for the brigade. Castro's aircraft easily disposed of the exiles' tiny air force and proceeded to sink the invasion ships and cut down the men holding the Bay of Pigs beachhead. Twenty months later, in December 1962, Castro released the 1,179 Bay of Pigs prisoners in exchange for $53 million worth of medical supplies and other goods raised by private individuals and groups in the United States.

Kennedy came under criticism both from those who believed the invasion never should have taken place and from Cuban exiles, most notably José Miró Cardona, president of the U.S.-based National Revolutionary Council, who blamed the invasion's failure on Kennedy's refusal to authorize air support. The invasion forced the resignation of the CIA director, Allen Dulles, embarrassed the Kennedy administration, and contributed to decades of tension between the United States and Cuba.

BIBLIOGRAPHY

Higgins, Trumbull. *The Perfect Failure: Kennedy, Eisenhower, and the CIA at the Bay of Pigs*. New York: Norton, 1987.

Johnson, Haynes B. *The Bay of Pigs*. New York: Norton, 1964.

Szulc, Tad, and Karl E. Meyer. *The Cuban Invasion*. New York: Praeger, 1962.

Flannery Burke
Tad Szulc

See also **Central Intelligence Agency; Cuba, Relations with; Cuban Americans; Cuban Missile Crisis.**

BAY PSALM BOOK. The *Bay Psalm Book*, formally titled *The Whole Book of Psalmes Faithfully Translated into English Metre* (1640), was the first book printed on Anglo-American soil. The Puritan divines of the Massachusetts Bay Colony set out to produce a translation from the Hebrew that was reflective of their unique brand of Calvinism and more literal than the most popular Psalter of the day. Although approximately thirty clergymen contributed to the book, Richard Mather, John Eliot, and Thomas Welde were its primary authors. Scholars have disputed the authorship of the preface, some attributing it to Mather and others to John Cotton.

The use of the *Bay Psalm Book* in both public services and private devotions underscores the central place of song in Puritan religious life. The book's cultural significance was originally underestimated by modern scholars because of its awkward poetic style, but recent interpreters point out that the authors' primary aim was to translate the Scriptures as literally as possible into musical form. Furthermore, they stress that the book is an artifact of a society that defined itself through oral communication, and that its unsophisticated rhymes and phrasing facilitated memorization in an age when many could not read. The *Bay Psalm Book* went through twenty-seven editions, the last of which appeared in 1762.

BIBLIOGRAPHY

Amory, Hugh, and David D. Hall, eds. *The Colonial Book in the Atlantic World*. New York: Cambridge University Press, 2000.

Hambrick-Stowe, Charles E. *The Practice of Piety: Puritan Devotional Disciplines in Seventeenth-Century New England*. Chapel Hill: University of North Carolina Press, 1982.

Haraszti, Zoltán. *The Enigma of the Bay Psalm Book*. Chicago: University of Chicago Press, 1956.

K. Healan Gaston

See also **Puritans and Puritanism.**

BAYARD V. SINGLETON, North Carolina Superior Court (1787), the first reported decision overruling a law as unconstitutional. The defendant moved for dismissal of the case according to an act of the legislature that required the courts to dismiss, upon affidavit, suits against persons holding forfeited Tory (enemy alien) estates. The court overruled the motion and declared that the constitution of the state gives every man a right to a decision concerning property by jury trial.

BIBLIOGRAPHY

Adams, Willi Paul. *The First American Constitutions*. Chapel Hill: University of North Carolina Press, 1980.

Lutz, Donald S. *Popular Consent and Popular Control*. Baton Rouge: Louisiana State University Press, 1980.

Robert W. Winston / A. R.

See also **Holmes v. Walton; Judicial Review; Judiciary Act of 1789; Marbury v. Madison; Vanhorne's Lessee v. Dorrance.**

BAYARD-CHAMBERLAIN TREATY was drafted in February 1888 by Great Britain and the United States to resolve a protracted fisheries dispute in the waters of Newfoundland and the adjacent provinces. It provided for a joint commission to define American rights in Canadian waters, recognized exclusive Canadian jurisdiction in bays whose outlets were less than six miles in width, and promised further concessions should the United States remove tariff duties on Canadian fish. The U.S. Senate rejected the treaty, but more than twenty years later, the substance of several of its provisions appeared in the award that an arbitration tribunal at The Hague rendered against American claims.

BIBLIOGRAPHY

LaFeber, Walter. *The New Empire: An Interpretation of American Expansion, 1860–1898*. Ithaca, N.Y.: Cornell University Press, 1963. 35th Anniversary Edition, 1998.

Welch, Richard E., Jr. *The Presidencies of Grover Cleveland*. American Presidency Series. Lawrence: University Press of Kansas, 1988.

W. A. Robinson / A. G.

See also **Canada, Relations with; Canadian-American Reciprocity; Treaties with Foreign Nations.**

BAYNTON, WHARTON, AND MORGAN was a Philadelphia mercantile firm that virtually monopolized the Western trade at the close of the French and Indian

War. Through contacts in North America and London, these merchants exploited the West in one of the most significant commercial enterprises of the day. Before the legal opening of Indian trade, the firm sent the first cargo of goods westward (1765). This premature attempt to capture Indian trade provoked protests from frontier settlers, but the firm soon had 600 pack horses and wagons on the road between Philadelphia and Pittsburgh and some 300 boatmen on the Ohio River.

The firm's fortunes declined during 1767, due to its unscrupulous business methods, British restrictions on colonial contact with Indians, French interference with Anglo-Indian trade, and competition from other firms. The company soon entered into voluntary receivership and joined with another firm—Simon, Trent, Levy, and Franks—to organize the Indiana Company to secure land grants for losses incurred through Indian attacks. Sir William Johnson negotiated a treaty for this company at Fort Stanwix in 1768 in which the Six Nations ceded 2.5 million acres of land. Immediate objections arose, the crown withheld confirmation, and representatives of the firm went to London to negotiate for the Indiana Company. Here competing claims of other groups brought about the formation of the Grand Ohio Company, or Walpole Company, in which the Indiana land grant was merged in 1769. The outbreak of the Revolution led to this project's collapse, and the firm withdrew completely from the Illinois trading venture in 1772.

BIBLIOGRAPHY

Cayton, Andrew R. L. *Frontier Indiana.* Bloomington: Indiana University Press, 1996.

Merrell, James H. *Into the American Woods: Negotiators on the Pennsylvania Frontier.* New York: Norton, 1999.

Sosin, Jack M. *Agents and Merchants.* Lincoln: University of Nebraska Press, 1965.

Julian P. Boyd / s. b.

See also **Colonial Commerce; Fur Trade and Trapping; Indian Land Cessions; Indiana Company; Trading Companies; Vandalia Colony.**

BAYOU, a term used throughout the South, may refer to bays, creeks, sloughs, or irrigation canals for rice fields. However, in the Mississippi River Delta region of Louisiana and Mississippi, it chiefly refers to the sluggish offshoots of rivers that meander through marshes and alluvial lowlands in the flat delta. During floods, the river may break through its curving banks to forge a more direct channel. The old channel, having lost the principal flow, becomes a sluggish stretch of brown water called a bayou. Some larger examples, such as Bayou Lafourche, are remnants of belts the Mississippi once followed to the Gulf of Mexico. Five times in the last five thousand years, the Mississippi has shifted to an entirely new course. In 1963 the Army Corps of Engineers installed a dam to try to prevent the Mississippi from diverting into the Atchafa-

Fishing in a Bayou. In this 1940 photo, two boys fish in a bayou in Schriever, La. © CORBIS

laya River, a diversion that could leave New Orleans on a bayou.

The term "bayou" most likely came from the Choctaw *bayuk* ("small sluggish stream"), although some sources insist it is derived from the French *boyau* ("gut" or "channel"). When boats were virtually the only means of transportation in the delta region, much human activity focused on bayous. Legendary pirate Jean Laffite used Bayou Barataria in southeastern Louisiana as his headquarters in the early 1800s. Bayou Pierre, southwest of Jackson, Mississippi, was an obstacle well known to travelers on the Natchez Trace. Antebellum planters romanticized the bayous' beauty, building colonnaded mansions among moss-draped live oaks on the shores. During the Civil War, Confederates used bayous flowing into the Gulf to run weapons, medical supplies, and other contraband past the Union blockade. Today bayous are used for flood control, fishing, and even recreation. Louisiana has incorporated several bayous into its state parks.

BIBLIOGRAPHY

Balée, William, ed. *Advances in Historical Ecology.* New York: Columbia University Press, 1998.

Kane, Harnett T. *The Bayous of Louisiana.* New York: Morrow, 1943.

McPhee, John. *The Control of Nature.* New York: Farrar, Straus, Giroux, 1989.

Robert W. Twyman / w. p.

See also **Acadia; Houma; Mississippi River.**

BEAR FLAG REVOLT. In the last four years of Mexican rule in California, hundreds of Americans settled in the Sacramento Valley. Tensions rose between the

United States and Mexico, and by the winter of 1845–1846 war seemed inevitable but remote. Spurring conflict was John Charles Frémont, a U.S. Army mapmaker on an official mission to map California, with a band of ninety well-armed men, a considerable army in thinly settled California.

Ordered to leave by Mexican authorities, Frémont fortified a hilltop east of Monterey and raised the American flag. Although the adventuresome mapmaker quickly backed down and withdrew north, the Mexican provincial government issued a proclamation ordering all foreigners out of California, meaning the settlers as well. The American settlers turned to Frémont for help, but he refused to act, even though the MEXICAN-AMERICAN WAR had now begun further east. The settlers then took the initiative. They seized a herd of horses going south for use by the Mexican army; then, at dawn on 14 June 1846, they captured Sonoma, the only important Mexican stronghold north of San Francisco Bay.

General Mariano Guadalupe Vallejo, the dominant Mexican figure in Sonoma, favored American acquisition of California, and helped the Americans draw up the surrender. The rebels raised their banner, the Bear Flag, and proclaimed the Bear Flag Republic, an independent California. On 7 July, a U.S. fleet captured Monterey, California's capital. Now Fremont finally stepped in, taking command at Sonoma, and on 9 July the Bear Flag came down in favor of the Stars and Stripes. The original Bear Flag was destroyed in the San Francisco fire of 1906. A version of it remains the state flag.

BIBLIOGRAPHY

Ide, William Brown, and Simeon Ide. *Who Conquered California?* 1880. Reprint, Glorieta, N.M.: Rio Grande Press, 1967. A firsthand account by California's first and only president, William Ide.

Walker, Dale L. *Bear Flag Rising: The Conquest of California, 1846.* New York: Forge, 1999.

Cecelia Holland

See also **California**.

BEAT GENERATION. The beats emerged in and around Columbia University in New York City in the 1940s. Picking up the word "beat" from their friend Herbert Huncke, the original beat writers, William Burroughs, Allen Ginsberg, and Jack Kerouac, used it to describe their free-form, improvisational style of writing and their unconventional, spontaneous way of life. Joined by writers such as Lawrence Ferlinghetti, Gary Snyder, Michael McClure, and Gregory Corso, the movement flowered in California in the mid-1950s and influenced much of the cultural rebellion of the 1960s.

At the Six Gallery in San Francisco on 7 October 1955 Ginsberg gave the first public reading of "Howl," a poem characteristically full of vivid imagery, confessional candor, and unbridled self-expression that authorities subsequently labeled vulgar. Ferlinghetti, the director of San Francisco's City Lights Books, was in the audience, and he offered to publish Ginsberg's work. The resulting *Howl and Other Poems* (1956) gave rise to a censorship trial that brought the beats into the public eye for the first time and cast them as literary rebels prepared to test the limits of censorship and social convention.

The most famous beat novel, Kerouac's *On the Road*, was written in 1951 but was not published until 1957. Based on his adventures with Neal Cassady in the late 1940s, the book reportedly encouraged countless others to seek personal fulfillment through the pursuit of an existential lifestyle. The success of *On the Road* thrust Kerouac into the spotlight, where he was acclaimed the "avatar" of the beat generation. Unprepared for fame and ill-equipped to deal with the critical backlash that followed, Kerouac withdrew from the media glare, dropped his beat friends, and distanced himself from the actions and ideals of those who claimed him as an inspiration. When Ginsberg became an important player in the activism of the 1960s, Kerouac denounced his former friend as "anti-American."

Originally derided by most serious critics and lampooned as "beatniks" by the popular media, the beats were rehabilitated in the 1970s. Their work, the basis of numerous academic courses and the subject of hundreds of books, significantly changed American literary conventions and values, and their lifestyle inspired restless souls and cultural rebels of all stripes. In June 2001 the manuscript of *On the Road* sold at auction for $2.43 million.

BIBLIOGRAPHY

Charters, Ann, ed. *The Portable Beat Reader.* New York: Penguin, 1992.

George-Warren, Holly, ed. *The Rolling Stone Book of the Beats: The Beat Generation in American Culture.* New York: Hyperion, 1999.

Tytell, John. *Naked Angels.* New York: Grove Press, 1976.

Watson, Steven. *The Birth of the Beat Generation: Visionaries, Rebels, and Hipsters, 1944–1960.* New York: Pantheon, 1995.

Rick Dodgson

See also **Hippies; Literature**.

BEAUTY CONTESTS evolved from early-twentieth-century bathing-beauty contests, where women participated in swimsuit competitions in beach resort cities. The Miss America pageant, which became the standard for American beauty contests, began in 1921 in Atlantic City, New Jersey, as a promotional gimmick by the hotelier H. Conrad Eckholm. Early beauty pageants, and the unmarried, made-up, and swimsuit-wearing women who competed in them, were often viewed as morally suspect and criticized by women's church groups and conservative politicians. Pageants became more respectable and legit-

Miss America. Phyllis George walks down the runway in Atlantic City after being named Miss America in 1970. AP/WIDE WORLD PHOTOS

imate in the 1940s, when women's roles were changing, largely as a result of their work experiences during both world wars, and when pageant winners sold war bonds and won college scholarships.

By the 1950s pageants had become widely accepted. The first Miss World competition took place in 1951, followed by pageants of every sort. Pageant winners, or beauty queens, represent commodities, ethnic identities, festivals and fairs, sports, and geographic regions. There are also beauty contests for babies, children, mothers, grandmothers, and, occasionally, men. Despite their variety, contests typically include judges, talent shows, prizes, and bathing-suit competitions. Beauty contests became newly controversial in the 1960s as a target of feminist groups.

BIBLIOGRAPHY

Cohen, Colleen Ballerino, Richard Wilk, and Beverly Stoeltje, eds. *Beauty Queens on the Global Stage: Gender, Contests, and Power.* New York: Routledge, 1996.

Savage, Candace. *Beauty Queens: A Playful History.* New York: Abbeville Press, 1998.

Deirdre Sheets

See also **Miss America Pageant.**

BEAVER. Found throughout most of the United States and Canada, the beaver (*Castor canadensis*) is the largest rodent in North America. From thirty to forty inches long and weighing as much as sixty pounds, the beaver is unique among rodents in possessing webbed rear feet and a broad, flat tail. Historically, it was eaten as a delicacy by many Native American tribes, a custom adopted by colonial Americans and early frontier residents. Water and wood dependent, the beaver is herbaceous, preferring the bark of deciduous trees along with a variety of aquatic plants and grasses. Its propagation is guaranteed by pond-building activity associated with damming of streams in the process of creating lodges. Once described by naturalist Enos A. Mills as "the original conservationist," beaver-engineered dams and diversion ponds serve to prevent floods and loss of surface soils during spring thaws and summer rainstorms.

Since the sixteenth century, the beaver has been the target of Indians and European immigrants alike for its luxurious pelt. Also, its underwool—prized for its suppleness and water resistance—has been commercially valuable in the felting industry for the making of hats. (See BEAVER HATS.) The earliest European efforts to settle colonies along the St. Lawrence River and in New England were funded by a beaver trade that soon spread into the interior of North America, generating intense intertribal and international rivalries among competing groups. French, English, Dutch, Swedish, Russian, and Spanish fur trading companies were organized to tap the wealth that beaver skins afforded on the European fur market based in London and Leipzig. Two types of pelts were sought. One was coat beaver, or castor gras—pelts that had been worn by Indians for at least one winter, so that the outer or "guard" hairs were loosened for easier processing by felters. The other was parchment beaver or castor sec—those pelts trapped, skinned, and flattened for easy storage and shipment in bales.

In 1638, King Charles II decreed that all fur hats manufactured in England be made of North American beaver, fueling a series of beaver wars between the Iroquois and their English allies and the French and their Indian allies. Many towns such as Albany (1624), Montreal (1642), Detroit (1701), New Orleans (1718), and St. Louis (1764) were established as fur trade entrepôts, servicing large hinterlands. The French dominated the fur trade until 1763, with beaver replacing cod as New France's primary staple export. After the fall of New France, the fur industry was dominated by the London-based Hudson's Bay Company, chartered in 1670 with the exclusive right to trade and trap the lands that drain into

Hudson Bay. However, from its founding in 1779 to its merger in 1821 with the H.B.C., the Montreal-based North West Company outproduced the Bay Company, sending to market an annual average of 130,000 pelts, three times that of its archrival. After the merger in 1821 the numbers harvested continued to rise despite fluctuations in wholesale prices.

By 1900, beaver numbers had declined and the animal had almost been exterminated in many parts of North America as a result of overhunting by Indians and whites alike. American mountain men operating out of St. Louis and Santa Fe, as well as brigades of Canadian trappers, scoured the western streams, glutting the European market by the mid-1830s. Simultaneously, hatters substituted the South American nutria and silk for headgear. This allowed a restoration of beaver populations in once-decimated areas and an expansion of their numbers in areas where climax forests had been cleared, encouraging succession species to thrive, especially aspen, one of the beaver's favorite foods. Ironically, more beaver have been trapped annually since the 1950s than at any other time in North American history, with nearly 670,000 pelts recorded in 1980. Beaver trapping continues in the early twenty-first century in Canada's far north and is a highly regulated source of subsistence income in Alaska and parts of the lower forty-eight states.

BIBLIOGRAPHY

Chittenden, Hiram Martin. *The American Fur Trade of the Far West*. 3 vols. New York: F. P. Harper, 1902.

Innis, Harold A. *The Fur Trade in Canada*. Toronto: Oxford University Press, 1927.

Mills, Enos A. *In Beaver World*. Boston: Houghton Mifflin, 1913.

Novak, Milan, et al., eds. *Wild Furbearer Management and Conservation in North America*. Toronto: Ohio Ministry of Natural Resources, 1987.

William R. Swagerty

See also **Fur Trade and Trapping; Hudson's Bay Company; North West Company.**

BEAVER HATS became popular menswear during the colonial period as a result of the expanding fur trade between North America and Europe. America produced quantities of beaver fur from hunting areas in the Great Lakes region, but European manufacturers produced men's beaver hats, which Americans imported until about the mid-seventeenth century. Virginia's colonial government sought to stimulate hat manufacturing in 1662 by offering a subsidy of ten pounds of tobacco for every good hat produced from native fur or wool. After the implementation of this policy, hat manufacturing in America grew rapidly and spread beyond Virginia to the Middle and New England colonies.

By 1731, London's hatmakers were complaining to Parliament that manufacturers in New England and New York were producing ten thousand hats annually and exporting them not only to British possessions but to Spain, Portugal, and the West Indies, thereby encroaching on the English hatmakers' market. In 1732, Parliament responded to these complaints by forbidding American producers to export hats, even to other American colonies. New restrictions also stipulated seven years' apprenticeship for all hatmakers, and no African Americans were permitted to work at the trade. Although Parliament intended these regulations to impede American hat production and trade, manufacturers tended to ignore or evade the law, which remained in force until the American Revolution. Beaver hats remained popular through the early decades of the nineteenth century, until the manufacture of silk hats expanded and fashion began to favor silk over beaver for men's headwear.

BIBLIOGRAPHY

Carson, Cary, Ronald Hoffman, and Peter J. Albert, eds. *Of Consuming Interests: The Style of Life in the Eighteenth Century*. Charlottesville: University Press of Virginia, 1994.

Kammen, Michael G. *Empire and Interest: The American Colonies and the Politics of Mercantilism*. Philadelphia: Lippincott, 1970.

Alvin F. Farlow / s. b.

See also **Clothing and Fashion; Colonial Commerce; Fur Trade and Trapping; Mercantilism.**

BEECHER'S BIBLES, the Sharps rifles given to settlers during the Kansas struggle between the free-state and the proslavery elements. In March 1856, in New Haven, Connecticut, Henry Ward Beecher addressed a meeting at which the attendees donated funds to equip a company of free-state emigrants to Kansas. Beecher said that for Kansas slaveholders, a Sharps rifle was a greater moral argument than a Bible. Benjamin Silliman of the Yale College faculty pledged a contribution for the first rifle, and the pastor of the church in which the meeting took place pledged the second. Beecher pledged the last twenty-five for his congregation, the Plymouth Church of Brooklyn.

BIBLIOGRAPHY

Fehrenbacher, Don Edward. *Sectional Crisis and Southern Constitutionalism*. Baton Rouge: Louisiana State University Press, 1995.

SenGupta, Gunja. *For God and Mammon: Evangelicals and Entrepreneurs, Masters and Slaves in Territorial Kansas, 1854–1860*. Athens: University of Georgia Press, 1996.

James Elliott Walmsley / A. E.

See also **Antislavery; Kansas Free-State Party.**

BEEF TRUST CASES. In 1902 three large meat packers—Swift, Armour, and Morris—formed the National Packing Company, securing control of packing houses in three cities and prompting a federal antitrust indictment. In 1905 the Supreme Court in *Swift and Company v. United States* (196 U.S. 375) upheld the government charges for the most part, but failed to order dissolution of the National Packing Company. Government efforts to break the monopoly did not succeed until 1920, when the packers agreed to dispose of their stockyard interests, their retail meat markets, and the wholesaling of lines not directly related to meat packing.

BIBLIOGRAPHY

Himmelberg, Robert F. *The Monopoly Issue and Antitrust, 1900–1917.* New York: Garland, 1994.

McCraw, Thomas K., ed. *Regulation in Perspective.* Cambridge, Mass.: Harvard University Press, 1982.

R. E. Westmeyer/A. R.

See also **Antitrust Laws; Interests; Meatpacking; Packers' Agreement; Sherman Antitrust Act; Trust-Busting; Trusts.**

BEEKEEPING. The honeybee, *Apis mellifera*, is not native to North America. The common black bees of Europe were imported to Virginia in 1621, followed by the Italian, Egyptian, Cyprian, Tunisian, Carniolan, and Caucasian strains. Honeybees spread slowly throughout the United States, not reaching Florida until 1763 or California until 1856. As postal and railway systems expanded near the end of the nineteenth century, honeybees spread more rapidly as entrepreneurs developed new procedures for shipping live swarms of bees in packages without combs.

The Reverend Lorenzo L. Langstroth, of Andover, Massachusetts, is known as the father of American beekeeping. He developed the movable-frame hive in 1852, which, with minor modifications, was still being used in the early 2000s. Langstroth was also noted for his book *Langstroth on the Hive and the Honey-Bee: A Bee Keeper's Manual.* His contemporary Moses Quinby wrote *Mysteries of Beekeeping Explained.* The publication of these two books in 1853 marked the real beginning of beekeeping in the United States. Both Langstroth and Quinby made major contributions to practical beekeeping that led ultimately to a new industry. The development of the movable-frame hive, the wax foundation, the bee smoker, the honey extractor, package bee shipments, and techniques of queen production revolutionized beekeeping. In the same period, two enduring beekeeping trade journals made their first appearance: *The American Bee Journal* (1861) and *Gleanings in Bee Culture* (1873). The American Bee Association, formed in 1860, was the first national organization of beekeepers.

Much of the progress of the industry in the twentieth century can be attributed to earlier research in apiculture conducted by state and federal scientists. For example, the development of instrumental insemination of queens by Lloyd R. Watson made controlled bee breeding possible. This technique, subsequently improved by others, enabled bee breeders to develop and maintain stocks for specific purposes, such as gathering more nectar, efficiently pollinating specific crops, or adapting to specific environmental conditions. Research in the United States also led to the discovery of the pathogenic agent of American foulbrood disease, the use of chemotherapeutic agents for the control of bee diseases, and improved bee management and technology. These breakthroughs resulted in larger honey yields, more efficient methods of harvesting and processing honey, and more efficient use of bees for pollination.

In 1899 the beekeeping industry produced 30,983 tons of honey and 882 tons of beeswax. By 1970, 4.6 million colonies produced 117,395 tons of honey and 2,324 tons of beeswax, which were valued at $40.8 million and $2.8 million, respectively. By the turn of the twenty-first century, however, production in the United States averaged only some 100,000 tons of honey annually. A variety of factors explained the declining production: the loss of agricultural land to highways and subdivisions; the spread of parasitic tracheal and varroa mites after the mid-1980s; a steady decline in the number of beekeepers, from 212,000 in 1976 to 125,000 in 1992; and stiff competition from foreign producers, first in Latin America and later in China.

BIBLIOGRAPHY

Crane, Eva. *The World History of Beekeeping and Honey Hunting.* New York: Routledge, 1999.

H. Shimanuki/C. W.

See also **Epidemics and Public Health; Railroads.**

BEES were social gatherings that combined work with pleasure and often competition. They were named specifically for the task around which they centered. Appleparing, corn-husking, quilting, wool-picking, houseraising, log-rolling, and other sorts of bees served to ease the labor of the individual.

Cooperative work for productivity and pleasure was an English custom that came across the Atlantic with early settlers. In the New England and middle colonies and on the early frontiers, various communal activities formed an important exception to the ordinarily isolated lives of American farm families. The motivation was both economic and social. Log rollings and BARN RAISINGS necessitated collective effort; corn-husking and threshing were most efficiently done by common endeavor. Quilting, sewing, and canning bees afforded women the opportunity to discuss family, friends, and community while they worked collectively. The cooperative nature of bees served as a basis for socialization. Bees roused the competitive spirit, making a sport of work. And the feasting, music, dancing, and games that followed the work itself provided courting opportunities for young people.

Machinery and specialized labor largely ended these practices. Some, such as the threshing ring, survive where farms are not large and farming is diversified.

BIBLIOGRAPHY

Earle, Alice Morse. *Home Life in Colonial Days.* 1898. Stockbridge, Mass.: Berkshire Traveller Press, 1974.

Hawke, David Freeman. *Everyday Life in Early America.* New York: Harper and Row, 1988.

Deirdre Sheets

See also **Toys and Games; Work.**

BEHAVIORISM. Since the early twentieth century behaviorism has offered the public and the field of PSYCHOLOGY a mix of applied technology and philosophical iconoclasm. In 1913 John B. Watson proclaimed himself a "behaviorist" and announced a new theoretical tendency within psychology. "Behaviorism," he promised, would be a "purely objective experimental branch of natural science," dedicated to the "prediction and control of behavior." Consciousness, thoughts, and feelings would no longer be studied, he explained, just the behavior of animals—including humans. Purged of its metaphysical baggage, Watson claimed, psychology could be applied to various human problems created by industrialization and rapid social change. To businessmen he promised to "show how the individual may be molded (forced to put on new habits) to fit the environment." To parents he promised methods for rearing fearless children who could learn any trade or profession. Such techniques would be based on Pavlovian conditioning of involuntary behavior and the extinction of existing responses that were maladaptive (e.g., fear of harmless animals).

Forced to leave academe for a career in advertising, Watson never developed the techniques that would deliver on his promises. Nevertheless, by the 1930s the field of psychology had moved close enough to Watson's concepts that observers spoke of it undergoing "an intellectual revolution." Psychologists' methods became more objective and their data became more behavioral. At the same time, the psychology of learning became dominated by neobehaviorists, whose theories readmitted internalist concepts like "drive" that were anathema to Watson.

Skinner's Behaviorism

In the second half of the twentieth century, B. F. Skinner's radical behaviorism revived Watson's call for a practical psychology of behavioral control. This was coupled with a radical empiricist epistemology in which drives, motives, and awareness play no role. Skinner's theory of motivation calls voluntary acts "free operants"; these are controlled by positive and negative reinforcers (similar to what others would call rewards and punishments). Key to Skinner's operant conditioning is the narrow specification of a behavior, whose repetitions are counted by an observer or mechanical device. The paradigmatic research

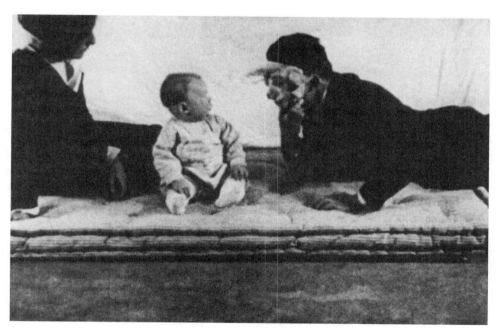

"Little Albert." The pioneer behaviorist John B. Watson (with Rosalie Rayner, his research assistant and later his wife) wears a Santa Claus mask to test the reaction of an infant he called Albert, in an experiment in conditioning published in 1920.

apparatus is a "Skinner box," which holds a white rat (or sometimes a pigeon); the rat is taught to press a small lever and given reinforcement in the form of food pellets. This methodology provided Skinner with the basic data he used to construct his "laws of learning." Those laws, to Skinnerians, have universal applicability, explaining everything from lion-taming to human social events and what others would call moral development.

Like Watson, Skinner was a tireless popularizer who never shied from controversy. His blueprint for a utopian community, *Walden Two* (1948), found a receptive audience in the counterculture of the 1960s and inspired a number of experiments in communal living. In *Beyond Freedom and Dignity* (1971), he argued that social problems were best solved by behaviorists rather than philosophers, religious thinkers, or a political democracy.

Within psychology the influence of Skinner's radical behaviorism reached its peak in the 1960s, losing credibility in subsequent years as researchers found types of learning (e.g., language acquisition) that violate Skinnerian assumptions. Consequently, psychology has turned toward neobehavioral explanations, at the same time that cognitive and evolutionary schools of thought have become popular. As a behavioral methodology, operant conditioning has proven essential to fields as varied as psychopharmacology, neuroscience, and mental retardation. Versions of behaviorism have also appeared in other academic disciplines including philosophy and economics.

To the public, behaviorism has been notable for its environmentalist view of man and its promise of behavioral control. In 1923–1924, Watson advanced progressivist themes against the instinctivist social psychology of Harvard's William McDougall. In the pages of the *New Republic*, lectures at the New School, and in a public debate with McDougall in Washington D.C., Watson promoted his views, becoming an influential figure who promised a new man built on behaviorist principles.

By mid-century, many had come to see this promise of behavioral transformation as sinister and antihumanist. In his dystopia *A Clockwork Orange* (1963), Anthony Burgess portrayed an authoritarian government that exerts control using liberal rhetoric as well as Pavlovian conditioning and traditional punishments. *The Manchurian Candidate* (1959) expressed Cold War fears that foreign communists had perfected a neo-Pavlovian form of mind control.

In the Vietnam War era, the behaviorism of Skinner came under attack, in part because of Skinner's outspoken social philosophy. In 1971, *Beyond Freedom and Dignity* earned him a place on the cover of *Time* magazine and criticism from the political right and left. Vice President Spiro Agnew denounced him as a dangerous social engineer with a freedom-denying, anti-family agenda. To Noam Chomsky and the New Left, behaviorism was the technology of an incipient totalitarianism, with "gas ovens smoking in the distance."

In the late twentieth and early twenty-first centuries, with post-Skinner behaviorists less visible and less philosophically radical, their image has become that of just another research specialty. Their reduced circumstance can be seen in *The Hitchhiker's Guide to the Galaxy* (1990), where we learn that the masters of the universe are not behaviorists but the rats pretending to run through their mazes.

BIBLIOGRAPHY

Bjork, Daniel W. *B.F. Skinner: A Life*. New York: Basic Books, 1993.

Buckley, Kerry W. *Mechanical Man: John Broadus Watson and the Beginnings of Behaviorism*. New York: Guilford Press, 1989.

Harris, Benjamin. "'Give Me a Dozen Healthy Infants . . .': John B. Watson's Popular Advice on Childrearing, Women, and the Family." In *In the Shadow of the Past: Psychology Portrays the Sexes*, edited by Miriam Lewin. New York: Columbia University Press, 1984.

Kallen, Horace M. "Behaviorism." In *Encyclopedia of the Social Sciences*, edited by Edwin R. A. Seligman, Vol. 2. New York: Macmillan, 1930.

O'Donnell, John M. *The Origins of Behaviorism: American Psychology, 1870–1920*. New York: New York University Press, 1985.

Smith, Laurence D. "Situating B. F. Skinner and Behaviorism in American Culture." In *B. F. Skinner and Behaviorism in American Culture*, edited by Laurence D. Smith and William R. Woodward. Bethlehem, Pa.: Lehigh University Press, 1996.

Ben Harris

See also **Psychology**.

BEIRUT BOMBING (23 October 1983). Arguably the greatest foreign policy disaster of President Ronald Reagan's administration occurred when a truck loaded with explosives crashed into U.S. marine barracks at Lebanon's Beirut International Airport, killing 241 U.S. marines and sailors and wounding over 100 others. Eight years of sectarian strife, complicated by competing Syrian, Israeli, and Palestinian interests within Lebanon, had transformed the country into a beleaguered armed camp. Four months of U.S.-brokered negotiations in 1983 failed to find a settlement and coincided with a suicide car bombing of the U.S. embassy in Beirut on 18 April that killed sixty-three people. When Israel redeployed forces south of Beirut on September 3 and 4, heavy fighting exposed U.S. marines to enemy fire. The simultaneous suicide bombings by Muslim militants of U.S. and French peacekeeping headquarters on October 23 renewed Reagan's public determination to stay in Lebanon rather than risk losing American credibility. The collapse of Lebanon's Christian-led coalition government on 5 February 1984, and the routing of West Beirut's Christian militia two days later, forced Reagan to reconsider. By the time U.S. marines had been redeployed offshore on that date, a total of 257 service personnel had been pointlessly killed, according to Reagan administration critics. Even administration supporters admitted that U.S. peacekeeping forces had failed to appreciate the intractable character of Lebanon's bloody civil war.

BIBLIOGRAPHY

Hourani, Albert, and Nadim Shehadi, eds. *The Lebanese in the World.* London: Centre for Lebanese Studies, 1991.

Mackey, Sandra. *Lebanon: Death of a Nation.* Chicago: Congdon and Weed, 1989.

Rabinovich, Itamar. *The War for Lebanon, 1970–1983.* Ithaca, N.Y.: Cornell University Press, 1984.

Bruce J. Evensen / c. w.

See also **Arab Nations, Relations with; Israel, Relations with; Peacekeeping Missions.**

BELGIAN RELIEF was organized by Herbert Hoover during the Allied blockade of the European mainland in World War I. The Commission for Relief in Belgium (CRB) was created in October 1914 by a group of Americans to supply German-occupied Belgium with direly needed food. Heading the CRB, Hoover was able to persuade the Allies that the food would not be used by the German army, and he convinced the Germans to allow the Belgians to distribute the food locally. From 1915 until the United States entered the war in 1917, Hoover collected almost one billion dollars in voluntary donations and government grants to finance the operations. Despite many setbacks, with the government's approval the Commission members were able to pass more than 5.1 million tons of provisions and supplies into Belgium and into northern France through neutral channels. Operating factories, mills, ships, and railroads, the CRB helped to feed eleven million people. Hoover was particularly proud that he was able to provide millions of children in that region with an adequate diet, and that the administration of the relief effort, costing less than one-half of one percent of the total amount he had collected, was most efficient. Highly praised, Hoover became administrator of the American wartime Food Administration until 1920.

BIBLIOGRAPHY

Hoover, Herbert. *Memoirs of Herbert Hoover.* Vol I. New York: Macmillan, 1951.

Nash, George H. *The Life of Herbert Hoover.* New York: Norton, 1983.

Michael Wala

See also **World War I, U.S. Relief in.**

BELIZE, RELATIONS WITH. Never colonized by the Spanish, Belize (formerly British Honduras) remains a Central American anomaly. In the sixteenth and seventeenth centuries, English pirates and loggers settled the Caribbean coast on sparsely populated lands once claimed by the Mayan empire. In 1862, the British settlement became a colony, reflecting the ascendance of British power in the Western Hemisphere. The United States protested under the 1850 CLAYTON-BULWER TREATY that closed Central America to colonizing powers, but unable to force the British out, it acquiesced. By the 1930s, the United States quietly endorsed the stability and order of British colonialism.

In the twentieth century, cooperative relations with the British in the Caribbean assured U.S. objectives: promoting stability and investment, defending national security, and protecting Panama Canal trade routes. Pervasive U.S. economic and cultural influences challenged British political control. The small elite of colonial administrators and civil servants shared prestige with a growing business and merchant class dependent on U.S. trade. Since 1894, American Catholic missionaries, headed by Missouri Province Jesuits, operated and taught in most of the colony's denominational schools, including the prestigious St. John's College. In the 1940s and 1950s, Jesuits promoted grassroots cooperatives and credit unions that became the focal point of colonial development.

Following British currency devaluation on 31 December 1949, the country's first broad-based nationalist movement emerged under the Peoples' United Party (PUP). Nearly all the nationalist leaders were Jesuit-educated Catholics, including PUP leader George C. Price, who had studied for the priesthood in the United States. Strong American ties, compounded by the predominance of American movies, media, and literature, resonated with most Belizeans. Despite PUP's pro-American, pro–free enterprise, anticommunist, and anticolonial orientation, the United States refused to recognize the movement, preferring slow British decolonization to sudden and uncertain independence. After 1959, the Price government's refusal to support anti-Castro efforts and U.S. desire to improve relations with Guatemala reinforced the United States' reluctance to accept United Nations petitions for Belizean independence, which was eventually granted in 1981.

BIBLIOGRAPHY

Barry, Tom, with Dylan Vernon. *Inside Belize.* Albuquerque, N.M.: Resource Center Press, 1995.

Bolland, O. Nigel. *The Formation of a Colonial Society: Belize, from Conquest to Crown Colony.* Baltimore: Johns Hopkins University Press, 1977.

————. *Belize, a New Nation in Central America.* Boulder, Colo.: Westview Press, 1986.

Shoman, Assad. *Thirteen Chapters of a History of Belize.* Belize City: Angelus Press, 1994.

Dominic Cerri

See also **Caribbean Policy.**

BELKNAP SCANDAL, one of the series of scandals that marked President Ulysses S. Grant's second administration. Carrie Tomlinson Belknap, second wife of Secretary of War William W. Belknap, secured a lucrative post tradership at Fort Sill for John S. Evans. Mrs. Belknap reportedly received $6,000 per year for this service. After her death in 1870 it was alleged that the money was paid directly to Secretary Belknap. A subsequent congressional investigation revealed that Secretary Belknap continued to receive payments from Evans even after Mrs. Belknap's death. On 2 March 1876 the House of Representatives voted unanimously to impeach the secretary. Belknap resigned the same day, and Grant, a personal friend of the Belknap family, immediately accepted his resignation. Grant's quick acceptance of the resignation proved critical in Belknap's subsequent trial. The impeachment trial, held in April and May, resulted in acquittal; twenty-two of the twenty-five members voting for acquittal declared that the Senate had no jurisdiction over a resigned officer.

The Belknap scandal came at a particularly inopportune moment for the Grant administration. In 1874 the Democrats had won control of the House of Representatives and placed the administration under close scrutiny through a series of congressional investigations, including the Crédit Mobilier affair and the WHISKEY RING. Grant himself had not profited from any of the scandals that took place during his administration, but the resulting outcry placed the end of his second term under a cloud of corruption from which he would never fully emerge.

BIBLIOGRAPHY

McFeely, William S. *Grant: A Biography*. Newtown, Conn.: American Political Biography Press, 1996. The original edition was published in 1981.

Simpson, Brooks D. *The Reconstruction Presidents*. Lawrence: University Press of Kansas, 1998.

Anthony Gaughan
W. B. Hesseltine

See also **Crédit Mobilier of America; Political Scandals.**

BELL TELEPHONE COMPANY. *See* **AT&T.**

BELL TELEPHONE LABORATORIES. Serving as one of the world's premier private research and development companies, Bell Labs funds scientific and communication research involving 30,000 engineers and scientists located in thirty countries. Bell Labs has generated over 40,000 inventions, including such innovations as the radio, the transistor, the television, the laser, the remote control, Telstar satellites, the VCR, stereo, the CD player, and the computer.

However, its beginnings were much less auspicious: In 1876, Elisha Gray lost the race to file the first patent for the telephone, having submitted his claim just hours after Alexander Graham Bell. Nonetheless, Gray's prior years of research in electronics paid off, and his business went on to become Western Electric. By 1880, Gray's firm was the largest electrical manufacturing company in the United States, producing such electrical products as the first commercial typewriter as well as telegraph equipment. A year later, as a growing telephone network began to take hold, American Bell (later to become AT&T) bought controlling interest in Western Electric and used the business exclusively to develop and manufacture the Bell Telephone Company's equipment.

In 1925, AT&T and Western Electric created Bell Labs to combine the two companies' research and engineering resources. During World War II, Bell Labs turned its research toward support of the war effort and provided communications and command equipment for the U.S. military, significantly in the development of radar systems. Postwar decades saw Bell advances in communications and information systems that included electronic switching, the UNIX operating system, and packet data switching.

Litigation triggered by U.S. Justice Department antitrust suits, begun in 1949 but revisited in 1956 and settled in 1974, resulted in AT&T's agreement to divest its local telephone companies. The parent company developed a new charter to manufacture and sell consumer products, network systems, technology systems, and information systems. Increasingly, the company developed worldwide affiliates, and Bell Labs accordingly expanded its scope to support research in an information age at a global level. In 1996, AT&T separated its systems and technology enterprises to create Lucent Technologies, which utilizes Bell Labs as its central tool for research and development.

Through the years, eleven researchers have shared six Nobel Prizes in physics for work done while they worked at Bell Labs, and nine Bell scientists have received the National Medal of Science. Significant recognition of Bell researchers began in 1937, when Dr. Clinton J. Davisson received a Nobel Prize for experimental work confirming the wave nature of electrons. In 1956, John Bardeen, Walter H. Brattain, and William Shockley collaboratively received a Nobel Prize for their 1947 invention of the transistor. Philip W. Anderson shared a Nobel Prize in 1977 for research that led to a greater understanding of solid-state electronics. A year later, Arno A. Penzias and Robert W. Wilson jointly accepted a Nobel Prize for their discovery of the cosmic microwave background, the radiation remaining from the "big bang" explosion that gave birth to the universe billions of years ago. Steven Chu, now at Stanford University, shared a Nobel Prize in 1997 for developing methods to cool and trap atoms with laser light. In 1998, Horst Störmer, Robert Laughlin, now at Stanford University, and Daniel Tsui, now at Princeton University, were awarded a Nobel Prize for the discovery and explanation of the fractional quantum Hall effect.

BIBLIOGRAPHY
Bell Labs Web Site. http://www.bell-labs.com.

"Seventy-fifth Anniversary: 1925–2000 Commemorative Issue." *Bell Labs Technical Journal* 5, no. 1 (January-March 2000).

Mark Todd

See also **AT&T; Laboratories.**

BELLEAU WOOD, BATTLE OF. The German Seventh Army, under General Max von Boehn, driving southward from the Chemin des Dames toward Paris on 31 May 1918, approached the Marne at Château-Thierry. To the west, the American Second Division, under the command of Major General Omar Bundy, hastened in support of the French Twenty-first Corps, the left corps of the French Sixth Army. Forcing back minor French units, by 3 June the Germans uncovered the American front line, which stood fast and stopped them. On 6 June the Americans assumed the offensive. Against bitter resistance the Fourth Marine Brigade, commanded by Brigadier General James Harbord, recaptured Bouresches and the southern edge of Belleau Wood, while on its right the Third Infantry Brigade advanced nearly to Vaux.

Continuing their local offensive, the Americans took most of Belleau Wood on 8–11 June, and despite desperate counterattacks completed its capture on 21 June. On 1 July, following an intense artillery preparation, the Third Infantry Brigade stormed Vaux and La Roche Wood. The division front, everywhere established on favorable ground, was turned over to the American Twenty-sixth Division on 9 July, the Second Division retiring to a support position.

American losses were severe—nearly eight thousand killed, wounded, or missing. Approximately sixteen hundred German prisoners were taken. In 1923 the site was made a permanent memorial to the Americans who died during the battle, and by order of the French government the site was renamed Bois de la Brigade Marine.

BIBLIOGRAPHY
Asprey, Robert B. *At Belleau Wood.* New York: Putnam, 1965.

Mackin, Elton E. *"Suddenly We Didn't Want to Die."* Novato, Calif.: Presidio Press, 1993.

Joseph Mills Hanson/A. R.

See also **Aisne-Marne Operation; Champagne-Marne Operation; Château-Thierry Bridge, Americans at.**

BENEFIT CONCERTS were a popular form of nonviolent protest and activism throughout the twentieth century as artists donated their talents to raise awareness and funds for social and environmental causes, poverty relief, cultural organizations, healthcare, and human rights efforts. During the 1930s and 1940s artists like

Farm Aid V. Willie Nelson performs at a 1992 concert in Irving, Tex., to benefit family farmers. AP/WIDE WORLD PHOTOS

Woody Guthrie, Leadbelly, and later, the Weavers, raised funds for political movements and labor organizations. Clara Ward, the Clark Sisters, and other gospel artists raised funds for religious organizations and charities. In later years benefit concerts evolved into large, organized events featuring popular artists and raising tremendous sums of money. The first was the 1971 Concert for Bangladesh, featuring George Harrison and Bob Dylan, which raised nearly $250,000 for relief in that country. Unfortunately, the organization failed to set up tax-exempt conduits and the money remained in an Internal Revenue Service escrow account for years. The concert and its affiliated recording, products, and promotions, however, suggested that musical activism could be used on a large scale.

In 1979 Bonnie Raitt and fellow performers formed MUSE, Musicians United for Safe Energy, and held a five-night No More Nukes concert in Madison Square Garden. In 1979 the international human rights organization Amnesty International held its first benefit concert in London and has continued to host benefit concerts, which has greatly increased its budget as well as awareness of human rights abuses. In 1985 USA for Africa, the creation of musician Bob Geldof and promoter Bill Graham, which brought together a group of recording stars for the hit song and video "We Are the World," and the internationally televised concert Live Aid, raised $67 million for African relief. This was followed later that year by the first of a series of Farm Aid concerts. This brainchild of Willie Nelson and John Mellencamp raised over $7 million for America's family farmers and continued annual concerts into the twenty-first century.

In 2001, following the September 11 attacks on the Pentagon and the twin towers of the World Trade Center, numerous benefit concerts were held to raise funds for families of victims and rescue workers, as well as relief for the city of New York. Among these was the "Concert for New York City," held at Madison Square Garden and featuring an impressive roster of performers, the "United We Stand" music festival held at RFK Stadium in Washington, D.C., and the two-night "Alliance of Neighbors" concert at the Count Basie Theatre in Red Bank, New Jersey. The September 11 attacks spawned numerous other benefit concerts as well as long-term relief efforts that continued to use benefit concerts as a form of fundraising.

BIBLIOGRAPHY

Crosby, David, and David Bender. *Stand and Be Counted: Making Music, Making History: The Dramatic Story of the Artists and Causes that Changed America.* San Francisco: Harper, 2000.

Ward, Ed, Geoffrey Stokes, and Ken Tucker. *Rock of Ages: The Rolling Stone History of Rock and Roll.* New York: Rolling Stone Press, 1986.

Deirdre Sheets

See also **Charity Organization Movement; Music Industry.**

BENIGN NEGLECT

BENIGN NEGLECT is a national race policy whereby the federal government does nothing more than allow the massive civil rights progress of the 1960s to take effect. The future Democratic U.S. senator from New York, Daniel Patrick Moynihan, in his role as domestic adviser to Republican president Richard Nixon, is widely credited with making the phrase a political buzzword in 1969. The phrase began to define the controversy over whether to accept the status quo in government race policy. As a result, in New York State and elsewhere, Senator Moynihan lost much political support among African Americans, who wanted the government to pursue a more aggressive policy to correct racial inequalities.

BIBLIOGRAPHY

Barker, Lucius Jefferson, Mack H. Jones, and Katherine Tate. *African Americans and the American Political System.* 4th ed. Upper Saddle River, N.J.: Prentice Hall, 1998.

Parent, F. Dale, and Wayne Parent. "Benign Neglect: The Realpolitic of Race and Ethnicity." In *An American Quarter Century: U.S. Politics from Vietnam to Clinton,* edited by Philip John Davies. New York: Manchester University Press, 1995.

Wayne Parent

See also **Discrimination: Race.**

BENNING, FORT

BENNING, FORT. Camp Benning (redesignated as Fort Benning in 1922), named for the Confederate general Henry L. Benning, was established near Columbus, Georgia, during World War I. By consolidation of three smaller military training schools in Kansas, California, and Oklahoma, a model infantry school was established

at Benning in 1920. In 1941 the alleged lynching of Private Felix Hall at Fort Benning raised troubling questions about race relations in a segregated military. By the 1950s Fort Benning had emerged as the nation's foremost infantry training center. In the early 2000s it housed a number of active regiments, the National Infantry Museum, and the U.S. Army Infantry School, where soldiers learn everything from basic combat training to high-tech surveillance. The base also housed the controversial School of the Americas, dedicated to inter-American military cooperation.

BIBLIOGRAPHY

Bridges, Connie, Richard Brill, Terry Ray, and Jennifer St. Onge. *The History of Fort Benning: Diamond Jubilee, 1918–1993.* Columbus, Ga.: The Advertiser Company, 1994.

Robert S. Thomas/A. R.

See also **Army, United States; Military Service and Minorities: African Americans; Rangers.**

BENNINGTON, BATTLE OF

BENNINGTON, BATTLE OF (16 August 1777). In mid-August 1777 the British general John Burgoyne planned a raid on the American stores at Bennington, Vermont. His purpose was fourfold: to encourage the Loyalists, frighten New England, replenish his stock of provisions, and mount a regiment of heavily equipped German dragoons. Accordingly, these dragoons, lumbering along on foot in their enormous jackboots and stiff leather breeches, were made the nucleus of a raiding force of about 800 Tories, Canadians, Indians, and English under the command of the German colonel Frederich Baum. Nearing Bennington, Baum learned that the American general John Stark had assembled about 1,500 troops at Bennington to oppose him, and he sent to Burgoyne for reinforcements. Colonel Heinrich von Breyman, with about 500 men, was sent to his aid.

In the meantime, Stark, hearing of Baum's advance, marched to meet him. His attack on the afternoon of 16 August exposed severe weaknesses in the English lines: Baum's command was too widely dispersed; his auxiliaries were scattered; and his regulars, hastily entrenched on a hill overlooking the Walloomsac River, were surrounded and most of them captured. Meanwhile, Breyman, ignorant of the battle, approached. Stark, now reinforced by Colonel Seth Warner with 350 men, re-formed and attacked. The Germans retreated and were pursued until dark. The Americans took about 700 prisoners. The victory did much to improve the morale of the American forces.

BIBLIOGRAPHY

Bird, Harrison. *March to Saratoga.* New York: Oxford University Press, 1963.

Ketchum, Richard M. "Bennington." *The Quarterly Journal of Military History* 10, no. 1 (1997): 98–111.

Shalhope, Robert H. *Bennington and the Green Mountain Boys.* Baltimore: Johns Hopkins University Press, 1996.

A. C. Flick/A. R.

See also **Burgoyne's Invasion; German Mercenaries; Green Mountain Boys.**

BEREA COLLEGE V. KENTUCKY, 211 U.S. 45
(1908). Kentucky law forbade the teaching of black and white students in the same classroom, and the state supreme court upheld the statute. The U.S. Supreme Court dodged the issue of interracial education and upheld the Kentucky law on the narrow grounds involving the right of the state to change or amend the charter of a corporation. The decision reinforced and expanded the 1896 PLESSY V. FERGUSON ("separate but equal") doctrine.

BIBLIOGRAPHY

Beth, Loren P. *The Development of the American Constitution, 1877–1917.* New York: Harper and Row, 1971.

Hardin, John A. "Hope versus Reality: Black Higher Education in Kentucky, 1904–1954." Ph.D. diss., University of Michigan, 1989.

Henry N. Drewry/A. R.

See also **Jim Crow Laws; Segregation.**

BERLIN, TREATY OF. After the U.S. Senate rejected the Treaty of Versailles in March 1920, the United States and Germany remained technically in a state of war. After taking power in March 1921, the Warren G. Harding administration conducted direct negotiations with Germany to arrive at a separate peace treaty. In August the two nations agreed to a formal peace treaty, which they signed in Berlin. The Treaty of Berlin was unique because, as an index treaty, it had no distinct provisions of its own. Rather, it comprised a scaled-down version of the Treaty of Versailles, including its provisions with respect to colonies, disarmament, reparations, and responsibility for the war. The most important features of the Treaty of Versailles that the Berlin treaty excluded were the LEAGUE OF NATIONS, the INTERNATIONAL LABOR ORGANIZATION, and the boundaries provisions. Approximately two-thirds of the Treaty of Versailles, including its harshest provisions, was accepted by the United States through the Treaty of Berlin.

BIBLIOGRAPHY

Hoff, Joan. *American Business and Foreign Policy, 1920–1933.* Boston: Beacon Press, 1973.

Clarence A. Berdahl/A. G.

See also **Germany, Relations with; Versailles, Treaty of; World War I.**

Berlin Airlift. Flour rations are unloaded from a line of C-54s on 26 July 1948—a tiny fraction of the yearlong, around-the-clock delivery of supplies to the people of Berlin's Western sectors. AP/WIDE WORLD PHOTOS

BERLIN AIRLIFT. The Berlin Blockade of 1948 to 1949 became one of the earliest tests of the U.S. Cold War policy of containment of the Soviet Union. The U.S. response to the challenge, history's largest exclusively aerial supply effort in the form of the Berlin Airlift, was initially designed as a temporary measure but became symbolic of American ingenuity and resolve.

The crisis had its origins in World War II–era agreements on the occupation of postwar Germany that placed a jointly occupied Berlin approximately 110 miles within Soviet-occupied territory. Between 1945 and 1948 relations between the international forces stationed in Germany deteriorated, with the growing conflict coming to a head in mid-1948. Protesting the merging of the British, French, and American occupation zones, Soviet officials in Germany walked out of the Allied Control Council, the quadripartite governing body, and the West implemented currency reform in the Western zones. In response, the Soviets announced that they were taking steps to preserve the economic integrity of the Soviet occupation zone and that effective 24 June "technical difficulties" would prevent land access between the Western zones of Germany and Berlin.

Once it became clear that the Soviets had in fact blockaded Berlin, President Harry Truman responded with a firm decision that the United States would maintain its right to be in Berlin even at the risk of war. As a temporary effort to maintain the small Western military garrisons in the city, British and American forces implemented a small-scale airlift. Flying along air corridors established under separate agreements with the Soviets, the airlift was gradually built up to sustain the population of 2.5 million civilians in the Western sectors of the city, an effort code-named Operation Vittles and directed by U.S. Military Governor General Lucius D. Clay.

Mounting an airlift on such a scale proved an enormous logistical challenge, particularly in light of U.S. postwar demobilization. During the airlift over a quarter of a million flights supplied the city with basic needs, including food and coal, at a rate of a plane landing every two to three minutes around the clock. Although Soviet forces harassed some flights, they never did so to the extent of interfering seriously with the airlift. Inclement weather and fatigue ultimately proved more dangerous, and the operation cost thirty-one American, thirty-nine British, and nine German lives. The impasse was finally resolved through informal talks between the American and Soviet representatives to the United Nations, and the blockade was lifted on 12 May 1949. Beginning 1 August 1949, the airlift was gradually phased out over a three-month period.

BIBLIOGRAPHY

Collier, Richard. *Bridge Across the Sky: The Berlin Blockade and Air Lift, 1948–1949.* London: MacMillan, 1978.

Shlaim, Avi. *The United States and the Berlin Blockade, 1948–1949.* Berkeley: University of California Press, 1983.

Tusa, Ann, and John Tusa. *The Berlin Blockade.* London: Hodder and Stoughton, 1988.

David G. Coleman

See also **Cold War.**

BERLIN WALL. A product of the prolonged Berlin crisis period from 1958 to 1962, the Berlin Wall came to symbolize the Cold War division of Germany and the world between the communist and noncommunist blocs.

Having repeatedly threatened since November 1958 to end Western rights in West Berlin, the Soviet premier Nikita Khrushchev and the East German leader Walter Ulbricht sought a way to stabilize the East German economy, which was being undermined by a growing flow of refugees leaving through West Berlin. Just after midnight on 13 August 1961 Soviet and East German troops sealed the border between East and West Berlin. Within weeks, the initial barbed wire was replaced with a concrete wall. In response, President John F. Kennedy judged that so long as Western rights in West Berlin were not being directly challenged the United States could not interfere, a decision that led to widespread criticism of American inaction.

The wall itself—constructed of concrete, seven and a half miles long, and twelve feet high—was part of a 102-mile system of fortifications encircling West Berlin. The fortifications were built in stages and included military watchtowers, tripwires, and minefields. A constant stream of escape attempts highlighted the repression of the Communist regime. When West German protesters breached the wall on 9 November 1989, it provided the Cold War's symbolic end. Few remnants remain of this once sinister symbol of the Cold War.

Berlin Wall. A U.S. Army checkpoint, West Berlin, 1961. LIBRARY OF CONGRESS

BIBLIOGRAPHY

Gelb, Norman. *The Berlin Wall.* London: M. Joseph, 1986.

Wyden, Peter. *Wall: The Inside Story of Divided Berlin.* New York: Simon and Schuster, 1989.

David G. Coleman

See also **Cold War; Germany, Relations with.**

BERMUDA CONFERENCES. During the twentieth century, officials from the United States and Great Britain met several times on the British-owned Atlantic island of Bermuda to discuss diplomatic issues. The first and most notorious Bermuda conference was held from 19 to 29 April 1943, when pressure from the news media, politicians, and religious leaders in both countries led the British and American governments to try to work out a common response to the Nazi murder of European Jews. The two governments selected Bermuda for a conference on refugees because wartime regulations restricted access to the island, assuring that no demonstrations or unwanted lobbying would take place. Rather than agreeing to take urgent measures to provide havens for Jewish refugees, the mid-level diplomats in attendance agreed that great difficulties would be presented if Nazi Germany released large numbers of Jews to the Allies. They avoided discussion of bringing pressure to bear upon countries allied with Germany, delivering food parcels, opening Palestine to additional Jewish immigration, or other rescue and relief efforts. Instead, each side made a point of touting its own actions taken on behalf of needy civilians; the United States even listed its incarceration of more than 110,000 Japanese and Japanese Americans as evidence of steps taken to shelter refugees.

The main outcome of the Bermuda conference was to arrange the evacuation of two thousand Jewish refugees from Spain—and to dash hopes that the Allies might undertake more ambitious efforts. In despair at the paucity of results, a Jewish member of the Polish government-in-exile in London, Szmul Zygielbojm, committed suicide. Scholars generally share the assessment of Rabbi Israel Goldstein, who said: "The job of the Bermuda Conference apparently was not to rescue victims of Nazi terror, but to rescue our State Department and the British Foreign Office."

On 11 February 1946, American and British officials signed an agreement at Bermuda governing aviation between the two countries. International rules establishing pilot licensing standards, aircraft standards, aircraft safety, and territorial overflight regulations had been established during a meeting of representatives from fifty-three nations in Chicago two years earlier, but specific questions of access to national markets for individual carriers, routes, and capacity were left to bilateral negotiation. The 1946 agreement, known as Bermuda I, was the first such bilateral agreement; its principles of restricting service to protect flag carriers served as a model for other countries to follow until they were replaced by open skies policies in the 1990s in many markets. Air travel between the United States and the United Kingdom, however, remained tightly regulated through the end of the twentieth century.

From 4 to 8 December 1953, President Dwight D. Eisenhower, Secretary of State John Foster Dulles, British prime minister Winston Churchill, French premier Joseph Laniel, and French foreign minister Georges Bidault met at Bermuda to discuss issues relating to international security. The American officials urged their French counterparts not to oppose the incorporation of West Germany into the western alliance. Other topics under discussion included British control of the Suez Canal, the Vietnamese revolt against French rule in Indochina, and the end of the Korean War, but no major agreements were signed.

In January 1957, President Eisenhower invited British prime minister Harold Macmillan to a meeting designed to improve relations recently strained over U.S. criticism of the British role in the Suez Crisis. From 20 to 24 March, the two leaders met at Bermuda to demonstrate publicly their friendship—they had served together in North Africa during World War II—and to discuss privately their differences over Middle East issues.

Eisenhower pressed Macmillan to set aside British bitterness toward Egypt's president Gamal Abdel Nasser and recognize that restoring close relations with Egypt while working to isolate Nasser internationally would be more likely than outright hostility to serve Anglo-American interests in the region. Eisenhower and Dulles also urged the British to consider Saudi Arabia's King Saud as a potential rival to Nasser. The British, not prepared to give up their claims against Egypt, demurred and the distance between the two countries' positions was made clear a year later when the Eisenhower Doctrine established a unilateral role for the United States in defending its interests in the Middle East. Macmillan and Eisenhower did, however, reach an accord on security issues, agreeing that sixty American Thor missiles would be based in Great Britain, within range of the Soviet Union and under joint Anglo-American control.

BIBLIOGRAPHY

Ashton, Nigel John. *Eisenhower, Macmillan, and the Problem of Nasser: Anglo-American Relations and Arab Nationalism, 1955–59.* New York: St. Martins' Press, 1996.

London, Louise. *Whitehall and the Jews, 1933–1948: British Immigration Policy, Jewish Refugees, and the Holocaust.* Cambridge, U.K.: Cambridge University Press, 2000.

Wyman, David S. *The Abandonment of the Jews: America and the Holocaust, 1941–1945.* New York: New Press, 1984.

Max Paul Friedman

See also **Eisenhower Doctrine; Great Britain, Relations with; Suez Crisis.**

BERMUDA ISLANDS, roughly 300 small coral islands, twenty of which are inhabited, are in the Atlantic Ocean east of North Carolina. Bermuda is a reference point of the Bermuda Triangle, an area of the Atlantic Ocean in which ships and airplanes have disappeared under supposedly mysterious circumstances that scientists attribute to weather and currents.

Discovered by the Spanish captain Juan de Bermúdez in 1503, Bermuda was first settled in 1609 by a hundred shipwrecked English colonists, including Sir Thomas Gates, Sir George Somers, and William Strachey. In 1612 Bermuda, called Somers Islands, was colonized by the Virginia Company. It became an autonomous company in 1615 and subsequently a British Crown colony. Bermuda records first mention slaves in 1617. In 1620, under probably the first conservation laws in the New World, Bermuda provided limited protection for turtles.

In 1946 the civil rights advocate E. F. Gordon delivered to London a petition protesting the political and racial conditions in Bermuda. In 1959 blacks boycotted hotels and theaters, forcing integration of those facilities. Black voting rights (1963), universal adult suffrage (1968), and school integration followed (1971).

In 2000 Bermuda had a population of 62,275 and 98 percent literacy. Reflecting its history of immigration, shipwrecks, and slavery, it is 59 percent blacks, 36 percent whites, and 6 percent others.

Because only 6 percent of Bermuda's land is arable, the islands survived by supplying ships, smuggling rum during U.S. prohibition, and providing services. From 1940 to 1995 the United States leased land for naval and air bases, which were important during World War II. Bermuda's economy is approximately 1 percent agriculture, 10 percent industry, and 89 percent services.

The islands' subtropical climate attracts tourists, especially from the United States, a major source of income, revenue, and employment. Bermuda is a major international offshore financial services and banking center, where transnational corporations shelter their assets and profits under permissive tax and banking laws.

Bermuda is a British territory with an appointed governor. Citizens elect a parliament, and the governor appoints the prime minister, the leader of the largest parliamentary party. A referendum on independence was defeated in 1995. In November 1998 the Progressive Labor Party won the general election, ending the United Bermuda Party's thirty-five years of control, and Stanley Lowe became the first black speaker of the House of Assembly. Opinion surveys in the late 1990s showed Bermudians increasingly inclined toward independence from Britain.

BIBLIOGRAPHY

Ahiakpor, James C. W. *The Economic Consequences of Political Independence: The Case of Bermuda.* Vancouver, British Columbia, Canada: Fraser Institute, 1990.

Boultbee, Paul G., and David F. Raine, comps. *Bermuda.* Oxford and Santa Barbara, Calif.: Clio Press, 1998.

Steffen W. Schmidt

See also **Rum Trade; Slave Trade.**

BERMUDA TRIANGLE, the best-known of a variety of folk names given to a triangular region of the Atlantic Ocean whose apexes are Miami, Florida; San Juan, Puerto Rico; and the island of Bermuda. Numerous ships and aircraft have disappeared in the area, the most famous being a flight of five U.S. Navy Avenger torpedo bombers that failed to return from a routine training mission in December 1945. Other losses range from small pleasure boats to the 542-foot U.S. Navy collier *Cyclops*, lost with all hands in 1918. Since the 1960s, some commentators have attributed these disappearances to powerful, mysterious forces that include UFOs, time warps, and the "lost continent" of Atlantis. Scientific and maritime authorities have consistently rejected these explanations in favor of naturalistic ones such as turbulent seas, rapidly changing weather conditions, and the errors of inexperienced sailors and pilots.

The name "Bermuda Triangle" first appeared in a 1964 *Argosy Magazine* article by Vincent Gaddis. A widely reprinted 1967 National Geographic Society press release gave it national prominence. Charles Berlitz's sensationalistic book *The Bermuda Triangle* (1974) and Steven Spielberg's references to the Avengers' Flight 19 in his film *Close Encounters of the Third Kind* (1977) bracketed the peak of the legend's popularity.

BIBLIOGRAPHY

Kusche, Larry. *The Bermuda Triangle Mystery—Solved.* New York: Harper and Row, 1975. Buffalo, N.Y.: Prometheus Books, 1995. Debunks the legend in detail.

A. Bowdoin Van Riper

See also **Unidentified Flying Objects.**

BEVERAGE INDUSTRY. *See* **Brewing; Soft Drink Industry; Wine and Spirits Industry.**

BEYOND THE MELTING POT (Glazer and Moynihan). In this 1963 work, subtitled *The Negroes, Puerto Ricans, Jews, Italians, and Irish of New York City*, the sociologists Nathan Glazer and Daniel Patrick Moynihan sought to explain the persistence of ethnic affiliation in New York City, and by implication the United States, long after "distinctive language, customs, and culture" had been lost (p. 17). What impeded the absorption of ethnic groups into "a homogeneous American mass" (p. 20)? Material necessity wed to sentimental attachment, Glazer and Moynihan maintained—a combination of "history, family and feeling, interest, [and] formal organizational life" (p. 19).

In its day the book was praised for denying the inevitability and desirability of cultural homogenization and for regarding ethnicity as a historical, hence a changing, artifact—staples of contemporary multiculturalism. The book was criticized for allegedly elevating ethnicity over class, for conflating ethnicity and race, and for maligning the African American family. Glazer and Moynihan had anticipated, if inadequately, the first two objections. The last raised the vexing problem of fact and value. Were the authors describing or evaluating African American institutions? Thus inadvertently *Beyond the Melting Pot* helped transform a subtle discussion about ethnic distinctions into a bald discourse about racial differences. As a result an undeniably progressive book became tainted with an aura of reaction.

BIBLIOGRAPHY

Glazer, Nathan. *We Are All Multiculturalists Now.* Cambridge, Mass.: Harvard University Press, 1997.

Glazer, Nathan, and Daniel Patrick Moynihan. *Beyond the Melting Pot: The Negroes, Puerto Ricans, Jews, Italians, and Irish of New York City.* 2d ed. Cambridge, Mass.: MIT Press, 1970. This second edition includes a noteworthy introduction written by Glazer ten years after he initially undertook the project.

Sollors, Werner, ed. *Theories of Ethnicity: A Classical Reader.* New York: New York University Press, 1996.

Jonathan M. Hansen

See also **African American Studies; New York City; Sociology.**

BIBLE. No book has influenced American history and culture more than the Bible. For legions of American Protestants, who inherited the Reformation's slogan of "Scripture alone," the English Bible functioned not only as a working text but as the icon of a word-centered piety that supposedly transcended superstition and built religion on solid empirical foundations. To the extent that Protestants once dominated American religious culture, this veneration of vernacular Scripture influenced other groups, including Roman Catholics and Jews, who published their own biblical translations partly as a statement of their American identity. Indeed, for Americans of many denominations, the Bible was long the wellspring of national mythology, although the prevailing biblical stories and imagery changed with time and circumstance.

Colonial America

The Puritan colonies of seventeenth-century New England were arguably the most biblically saturated culture America has ever known. America in Puritan eyes was the New Israel, although this Old Testament image always coexisted with the New Testament image of the primitive, gathered church, uncorrupted by the accretions of "invented" human traditions. Puritan emphasis on Scripture as the antidote to Catholic "superstition" led to much higher rates of literacy in the New England colonies than in any other part of British America or most of England. Probate records reveal that Puritan families who could afford only a few books invariably owned a copy of the Scriptures, either the Geneva Bible (a copiously annotated version begun during the reign of Mary Tudor and published in 1560, or the King James, or Authorized, Bible (a new translation published in 1611 that preserved the verse-numbering system introduced by the Geneva version but eliminated the heavily Calvinist doctrinal glosses).

Even outside of New England, the Bible's influence in the American colonies was considerable. Biblical passages against adultery, blasphemy, sodomy, witchcraft, and other practices influenced legal codes across the American colonies. European settlers also tended to draw on the Bible in the encounter with the Native Americans, whom they variously interpreted as existing in a state of Edenic innocence or as resembling the Canaanites who had to be driven out of the Promised Land.

New Nation

The first complete Bible printed in America originated in the English encounter with Native Americans. John El-

iot's Indian Bible (1663), a translation into the Massachusett language, was one of a number of non-English Bibles published during the colonial period, including several editions of Luther's German translation, printed in Germantown, Pennsylvania, in the 1740s. The English Bible was not printed in America until 1777, when the war with England, which curtailed international trade and halted importation of British Bibles, prompted Robert Aitken of Philadelphia to print an American edition of the King James New Testament.

The Bible market in the early republic would soon include other English versions as well. After Aitken published the entire King James Bible in 1782, the Irish Catholic printer Mathew Carey printed the Catholic Douay Bible in Philadelphia in 1790. Most Protestant Bibles lacked the Apocrypha, or Deuterocanonical books, which Catholics regarded as authoritative, and Carey's edition filled this void. The Protestant King James Version, however, continued to be required reading in many public schools, leading to periodic conflicts between Catholics and Protestants, especially during the 1840s when large numbers of Catholic immigrants arrived in Boston, New York City, Philadelphia, and other cities. Riots in Philadelphia in 1844 over which Bible to use in the public schools left thirteen people dead and whole blocks of Irish homes in ruins.

Yet the presence of Catholics, and Catholic Bibles, did not deter antebellum American Protestants, who entertained sweeping visions of a Protestant America founded on the rock of Holy Writ. The American Bible Society, founded in 1816 by the consolidation of over one hundred local societies, distributed millions of Bibles in successive campaigns to put a copy of the King James Bible in every American home. Scores of other antebellum reform societies invoked the Scriptures to combat perceived ills such as intemperance and Sabbath breaking. Meanwhile, the Bible was a touchstone for a variety of antebellum religious prophets, from Latter-day Saints founder Joseph Smith, who penned *The Book of Mormon* (1830) in the familiar idiom of the King James Version, to the lay preacher William Miller, who calculated from biblical evidence that the Second Coming of Christ would occur in 1843.

The Civil War

Perhaps nowhere did the Bible loom larger in the nineteenth century than in the debate over slavery, which revealed as never before the difficulties of forging a universally acceptable civil religion based on Scripture. As President Abraham Lincoln said of North and South in his second inaugural address, "Both read the same Bible, and pray to the same God; and each invokes His aid against the other." For its opponents, slavery called into question the old Puritan identification of America as the New Israel. America instead appeared as Egypt, the land of bondage, which could only be escaped by crossing the "Red Sea of war," as the prominent Brooklyn preacher,

Bible. President Harry S. Truman is presented with the first copy of the *Revised Standard Version* of the Bible; with him is Luther A. Weigle, the Lutheran minister who headed the committee that produced the controversial translation. AP/WIDE WORLD PHOTOS

Henry Ward Beecher, put it in a famous 1861 sermon. African American Christians used the biblical Exodus motif extensively in preaching, political oratory, and spirituals, even as Southern white supporters of slavery appealed to the "curse of Ham" (Genesis 9:25) as a divine warrant for keeping dark-skinned peoples in perpetual servitude. The New Testament also admitted of conflicting interpretations on the slavery question. Slavery's opponents frequently invoked Paul's declaration that "there is neither bond nor free . . . for ye are all one in Jesus Christ" (Galatians 3:28), while slavery's supporters cited Paul's admonition to servants to "obey in all things your masters" (Colossians 3:22).

The exegetical impasse over slavery contributed indirectly to future ideological divisions among American Protestants. On the one hand, it hastened the advent of modern Protestant liberalism, which tended to relativize biblical texts that were not amenable to a progressive ethic. This liberal theology, in turn, provoked a reaction within Protestant denominations from conservative parties determined to uphold the authority of Scripture as a timeless moral and doctrinal standard.

The Bible and Modern Scholarship

The greatest challenge to traditional biblical authority, however, would come from American colleges and theological seminaries, where a generation of antebellum scholars had pioneered critical biblical studies in America. These antebellum scholars included the Unitarians Andrews Norton and George Rapall Noyes and the Congregationalists Edward Robinson and Moses Stuart. After the Civil War, as American scholars looked to the German model of the research university, American biblical studies developed rapidly on two fronts, known popularly as higher and lower criticism.

Higher or historical critics tended to question the accuracy of biblical history as well as traditional assumptions about biblical authorship (for example, that Moses wrote the Pentateuch). Among the most celebrated higher critics was Charles Augustus Briggs, who was suspended from the Presbyterian Church in 1893 but retained on the faculty of Union Theological Seminary in New York City, which severed its Presbyterian ties because of the affair. Historical criticism also influenced the female authors of *The Woman's Bible* (1895–1898), an early feminist

Bible commentary whose chief contributor, the woman suffragist Elizabeth Cady Stanton, argued that the Scriptures "bear the impress of fallible man." Meanwhile, opponents of higher criticism, including the Princeton Seminary professors Archibald Alexander Hodge and Benjamin Breckinridge Warfield, were constructing elaborate defenses of biblical infallibility and inerrancy, arguing that apparent historical, geographic, or scientific errors in Scripture stemmed from incomplete knowledge or misunderstandings on the part of interpreters.

Lower or textual critics were concerned with the most accurate reconstruction of the biblical text from the immense array of surviving manuscript variants. Their work assisted Bible translators, who drew on new manuscript discoveries to improve the English text of Scripture. The *Revised Version* (1881–1885), a British American translation and the first major new English Bible since 1611, was a transatlantic publishing sensation that provoked criticism from Americans still committed to the cherished language of the King James Bible. Opposition to modern translations reached a climax with the *Revised Standard Version* (1952), which many fundamentalist Protestants vilified as a symbol of the liberal church establishment. By the latter half of the twentieth century, however, the American publishing market was awash in Bibles of every denominational and ideological stripe, even as polls showed relatively low levels of biblical literacy among Americans. The Catholic *New American Bible* (1970), the evangelical Protestant *New International Version* (1978), and the Jewish Publication Society *Tanakh* (1985) were among dozens of translations and annotated editions in print.

The Bible's continuing influence in twentieth-century American culture was particularly evident in American politics. In crafting his philosophy of nonviolent resistance during the civil rights movement, Martin Luther King Jr. drew on themes of social justice in the Hebrew prophets as well as Jesus' radical demands for love in the Sermon on the Mount. Meanwhile, the U.S. Supreme Court in 1963 outlawed Bible reading in the opening exercises of public schools. This was one of a series of legal cases that helped galvanize political conservatives, who accused liberals of seeking to dethrone Scripture as the standard of American morality. By the 1980s, a powerful new religious right, led by Baptist preacher Jerry Falwell, Christian broadcaster Pat Robertson, and other advocates of biblical norms in public and private morality, helped Ronald Reagan win two terms as president. The Bible remained a presence in politics at the turn of the twenty-first century, particularly in battles over gay and lesbian rights, with conservatives citing Leviticus 20:13 and Romans 1:24–32 to condemn homosexuality, and liberals echoing biblical refrains about justice and the equality of all persons in Christ.

BIBLIOGRAPHY

Armory, Hugh, and David D. Hall, eds. *A History of the Book in America*. Volume 1: *The Colonial Book in the Atlantic World*. Cambridge, U.K.: Cambridge University Press, 2000.

Barlow, Philip L. *Mormons and the Bible: The Place of the Latter-day Saints in American Religion*. New York: Oxford University Press, 1991.

Brown, Jerry Wayne. *The Rise of Biblical Criticism in America, 1800–1870: The New England Scholars*. Middletown, Conn.: Wesleyan University Press, 1969.

Fogarty, Gerald P. *American Catholic Biblical Scholarship: A History from the Early Republic to Vatican II*. San Francisco: Harper and Row, 1989.

Gaustad, Edwin S., and Walter Harrelson, eds. *The Bible in American Culture*. 6 vols. Philadelphia: Fortress Press, 1982–1985.

Gutjahr, Paul C. *An American Bible: A History of the Good Book in the United States, 1777–1880*. Stanford, Calif.: Stanford University Press, 1999.

Hatch, Nathan O., and Mark A. Noll, eds. *The Bible in America: Essays in Cultural History*. New York: Oxford University Press, 1982.

Noll, Mark A. *Between Faith and Criticism: Evangelicals, Scholarship, and the Bible in America*. San Francisco: Harper and Row, 1986.

———. "The Bible and Slavery." In *Religion and the American Civil War*. Edited by Randall M. Miller, Harry S. Stout, and Charles Reagan Wilson. New York: Oxford University Press, 1998.

Thuesen, Peter J. *In Discordance with the Scriptures: American Protestant Battles over Translating the Bible*. New York: Oxford University Press, 1999.

Wimbush, Vincent L., ed. *African Americans and the Bible: Sacred Texts and Social Textures*. New York: Continuum, 2000.

Wosh, Peter J. *Spreading the Word: The Bible Business in Nineteenth-Century America*. Ithaca, N.Y.: Cornell University Press, 1994.

Peter J. Thuesen

See also **American Bible Society; Antislavery; Denominationalism; Fundamentalism; Modernists, Protestant; Protestantism; Puritans and Puritanism; Radical Right.**

BIBLE COMMONWEALTH is a Christian theocratic political economy such as those of the Puritan colonies of Massachusetts Bay and New Haven, Connecticut. There, laws intended for the common good were based on the Bible and the right to vote was limited to church members. In a Bible commonwealth, civic officials wrote into law their interpretations of Bible commands; the economy subsidized Christian public education, printed materials, and ministers; and official religious and political duties often overlapped. An attempt to establish a Bible commonwealth is represented by the New Haven colony's use of *An Abstract of the Lawes of New England* (1641)—a code prepared by Massachusetts Bay minister John Cotton—as the basis of its government.

BIBLIOGRAPHY

Heyrman, Christine Leigh. *Commerce and Culture: The Maritime Communities of Colonial Massachusetts, 1690–1750*. New York: Norton, 1984.

Peterson, Mark A. *The Price of Redemption: The Spiritual Economy of Puritan New England.* Stanford, Calif.: Stanford University Press, 1997.

Deirdre Sheets

See also **Massachusetts Bay Colony; New England Colonies; New Haven Colony.**

BICAMERALISM. *See* **Legislatures.**

BICENTENNIAL. The 200th anniversary of the signing of the Declaration of Independence was the country's most broadly celebrated anniversary. Like the 1876 centennial, it followed a period of social tension that created an ominous backdrop for the event. The bicentennial represented, in the words of the poet Archibald Mac-Leish, "a noble past and an ignoble present brought face to face."

Planning for the celebration began early. In 1966, Congress established the American Revolutionary Bicentennial Commission (ARBC). Boosters envisioned the celebration as a showcase of American achievements and called for a world's fair. As with other recent commemorations, they hoped to invigorate democratic community with pageantry and patriotic lore.

Not everyone agreed with the genial, patriotic consensus of the bicentennial's national sponsors. Women's groups, Native Americans, African Americans, Hispanics, and young people worried about efforts to instill "artificial homogeneity" and called for inclusion. A New Left–inspired organization, the People's Bicentennial Commission (PBC), combined hostility to corporations into pleas for a second revolution. When reenactors threw crates of leaves into the harbor to commemorate the Boston Tea Party, the PBC staged its own theater, tossing used oil drums into the water. In Philadelphia, neighborhoods fought to keep a world's fair out of their backyard. Local protests and a lack of funding forced planners to abandon the project. Voters in Colorado followed a similar path and vetoed hosting the Olympic Games. Meanwhile, various ARBC documents surfaced in 1972, revealing partisan ties between the agency and the administration of Richard M. Nixon. Several studies recommended replacing the ungainly commission; Congress responded by establishing the American Revolution Bicentennial Administration (ARBA) in 1973, with generally improved results.

Without a grand bicentennial event, the national committee focused on supporting local celebrations, as in other recent commemorations. Communities registered their projects, which, if approved, could display the official tricolored star logo. Promoters also committed to advancing multicultural campaigns, often expanding the accepted revolutionary narrative to recognize the contributions of ethnic groups. Eventually, the ARBA catalogued over 66,000 events. Corporate sponsorship made possible two American Freedom Trains containing precious cargo of American history, a covered-wagon train, parts of which made stops in all fifty states, and 732 televised "Bicentennial Minute" vignettes. Critics decried the commercial entanglement, along with the ubiquitous sale of souvenirs such as ashtrays, belt buckles, and teddy bears that recited the Pledge of Allegiance, as creating a "Buy-centennial." The ARBA responded that these things were out of its control.

The national celebrations culminated during the Fourth of July weekend in 1976. Sixteen tall-masted ships traveled to New York Harbor for a naval review, creating the most enduring bicentennial memory. Thousands lined the waterway and millions viewed nationally televised specials. Most Americans, however, held local commemorations. In Washington, D.C., celebrants ate from the world's largest birthday cake. Others held parades, rang bells, and covered innumerable water towers and fire hydrants with red, white, and blue. Bicentennial events continued after the Fourth (and even after 1976). World leaders and royalty visited the United States and gave impressive bicentennial gifts. Backers saw the bicentennial as a peaceful ending to the upheavals of the previous decade. President Gerald R. Ford also considered it a high point in his presidency. Speaking at the Old North Church in Boston, he urged Americans to remember, "We kept the faith, liberty flourished, freedom lived."

BIBLIOGRAPHY

American Revolution Bicentennial Administration. *The Bicentennial of the United States of America: A Final Report to the People.* 5 vols. Washington, D.C.: U.S. Government Printing Office, 1977.

Bodnar, John. *Remaking America: Public Memory, Commemoration, and Patriotism in the Twentieth Century.* Princeton, N.J.: Princeton University Press, 1992.

Fried, Richard M. *The Russians Are Coming! The Russians Are Coming!: Pageantry and Patriotism in Cold-War America.* New York: Oxford University Press, 1998.

Klein, Milton M. "Commemorating the American Revolution: The Bicentennial and Its Predecessors." *New York History* 58 (July 1977): 257–276.

David W. Veenstra

See also **Declaration of Independence.**

BICYCLING. Primitive, bicycle-like machines appeared in early nineteenth-century Europe. Draisines, celefires, celeripedes, and velocipedes preceded the development in England of bicycles, known as penny farthings or ordinaries, with large front wheels attached to small rear wheels by backbones. Colonel Albert A. Pope saw them exhibited at the Centennial Exposition in Philadelphia in 1876. Intrigued, he imported English bicycles before creating in 1878 the Pope Manufacturing Company. In the mid-1880s the introduction of the "safety" bicycle, with smaller, similar-sized wheels connected by a dia-

Bicycling. Four women take part in a race on early bicycles, with wheels of unequal size.

mond frame and with pneumatic tires, expanded the popularity of bicycling to women and older men. By the mid-1890s, 2.5 million American men, women, and children rode. Four hundred American manufacturers produced some 2 million bicycles in 1897. Major cities had riding schools, and newspapers devoted weekly columns to bicycling news, which covered both the sporting and the touring aspects of this new phenomenon. Numerous manuals appeared with information on choosing a bicycle, learning to ride, maintenance, and tips for tourists.

Thomas Stevens became the first person to ride across North America when he rode and walked his high wheeler from San Francisco to Boston in 1884. Sponsored by one of America's leading sporting magazines, *Outing,* he became the first person to ride around the world, completing his circuit in San Francisco in January 1887. He inspired several other Americans, one of whom was murdered in the Middle East, to follow in his wheel tracks. Magazines and newspapers sponsored others who rode around the perimeter of the United States, through each state and its capital, and around the world. While the majority who rode were men, the bicycle had a significant impact on women as well.

The bicycle provided individual freedom and mobility, giving young men and women a newfound opportunity to be alone. They could now court individuals from other towns and villages without having a chaperone along. Because women's dresses went down to their feet with petticoats and yards of material, it was difficult for

them to ride. The bicycle encouraged women to change to a skirt to the knees with modified bloomers covering the rest of their legs. By encouraging the rational dress movement, the bicycle allowed women greater mobility and freedom to engage in other activities. Despite early articles that claimed bicycling was unhealthy and immoral for women, physicians soon supported this form of exercise.

Bicycles worked best on good roads, but few roads were paved. Consequently the League of American Wheelmen, founded in 1880, began a "good roads movement" that continued with the automobile. As more people traveled further and further, road signs appeared, as did inns and other establishments for the aid of the bicycle traveler.

In addition, bicycle racing became popular in the United States, and people collected trading cards of the some six hundred professional racers. In 1899 one of them, Charles M. Murphy, became the first to ride a bicycle one mile in less than one minute. Another standout was Major Taylor, one of the most successful bicycle racers and an African American. Velodromes saw all kinds of races, from sprints to the grueling six-day races that drew sell-out crowds, but by the 1930s bicycle racing in the United States was coming to an end.

With the development of the automobile, the bicycle's place in the United States was relegated to that of a child's toy. While adults continued to ride bicycles, most gave them up when they became old enough to drive. The 1960s, however, saw a resurgence of interest in bicycles, with increasing numbers of baby boomers riding. Bicycle clubs began sponsoring tours for their members and the general public, and the League of American Wheelmen (now the League of American Bicyclists), which had been languishing for decades, experienced rising membership. *Bicycling*, which began as a mimeographed newsletter, quickly expanded into a widely read magazine. In the 1970s another bicycle organization, Bikecentennial (now Adventure Cycling), developed cross-country routes for bicyclists. The U.S. Cycling Federation continued to certify races, mostly at the local level. Only a few, the Tour Dupont, Boston-Montreal-Boston (based on Paris-Brest-Paris), and the Race across America (RAAM), achieved any sort of national attention.

Mountain bicycles developed in the 1980s and quickly became the most popular style, forcing bicycle manufacturers to scale back dramatically their production of road bicycles. Furthering interest in bicycling, Greg LeMond became the first American to win the Tour de France in 1986. He won again in 1989 and 1990, becoming one of only a handful of riders to win the tour three times. In 1999 Lance Armstrong became the first to win the Tour de France as a member of an American team. He won again in 2000, 2001, and 2002.

BIBLIOGRAPHY

Harmond, Richard. "Progress and Flight: An Interpretation of the American Bicycle Craze of the 1890's." *Journal of Social History* 5 (winter 1971–1972): 235–257.

Nye, Peter. *Hearts of Lions.* New York: Norton, 1988.

Ritchie, Andrew. *King of the Road: An Illustrated History of Cycling.* London: Wildwood House, 1975.

Smith, Robert A. *A Social History of the Bicycle, Its Early Life and Times in America.* New York: American Heritage Press, 1972.

Stevens, Thomas. *Around the World on a Bicycle.* Volume 2: *From Teheran to Yokohama.* New York: Scribner, 1988.

Tobin, Gary Allan. "The Bicycle Boom of the 1890's: The Development of Private Transportation and the Birth of the Modern Tourist." *Journal of Popular Culture* 7, no. 4 (spring 1974): 838–847.

Duncan R. Jamieson

See also **Recreation; Roads; Sports.**

BIG BROTHER MOVEMENT began in Cincinnati in 1903 when a small group of men led by stockbroker Irvin F. Westheimer agreed to mentor fatherless boys in that city. The movement was formalized in New York City a year later by Ernest K. Coulter, clerk of the children's court. Big Brothers of America, a national body, was formed in 1947. That organization merged with Big Sisters in 1977 to form Big Brothers and Big Sisters of America, with headquarters in Philadelphia. By 2000 the organization operated more than five hundred programs, all of which mentored children living in single-parent families. Big Brothers Big Sisters International was formed in 1998.

BIBLIOGRAPHY

Beiswinger, George L. *One to One: The Story of Big Brothers/Big Sisters Movement in America.* Philadelphia: Big Brothers/Big Sisters of America, 1985.

Raymond J. Hoffman / T. D.

See also **Family; Juvenile Courts; Volunteerism.**

BIG HORN MOUNTAINS, a range of the Rocky Mountains that lies mainly in north central Wyoming, but also extends into southern Montana. American fur traders frequented the mountains, and, in 1811, Wilson Price Hunt crossed the Big Horns in the overland Astoria ex-

Big Horn Mountain Country. The Bighorn River runs north through the Bighorn Canyon National Recreation Area from Wyoming into Montana, just southwest of the site of the Battle of Little Bighorn. Wyoming Division of Tourism

pedition. The Fetterman Massacre took place in the Big Horns near Fort Phil Kearny, Wyoming, in 1866. In 1876, the Battle of Little Bighorn between the Sioux and Northern Cheyenne against the Seventh Cavalry under George Custer became an important landmark in relations between the U.S. Government and the Indians of the Great Plains.

BIBLIOGRAPHY

Fox, Richard Allan, Jr. *Archaeology, History, and Custer's Last Battle: The Little Big Horn Reexamined.* Norman: University of Oklahoma Press, 1993.

Freed, Elaine. *Preserving the Great Plains and Rocky Mountains.* Albuquerque: University of New Mexico Press, 1992.

Smith, Duane A. *Rocky Mountain West: Colorado, Wyoming, and Montana, 1859–1915.* Albuquerque: University of New Mexico Press, 1992.

Dan E. Clark / H. S.

See also **Little Bighorn, Battle of; Wyoming.**

BIG SISTERS, an organization dedicated to providing female mentorship for underprivileged and single-parent children, was founded in New York in 1908. The organization was created to help combat growing juvenile delinquency and deal with the problem of youth poverty by assigning a volunteer woman to a needy boy under the age of ten or girl under the age of sixteen. Big Sisters grew rapidly, soon becoming a conglomerate of autonomous local chapters, collectively called Big Sisters International, Inc. In 1977 they merged with Big Brothers of America to form Big Brothers Big Sisters of America.

BIBLIOGRAPHY

Beiswinger, George L. *One to One: The Story of the Big Brothers/ Big Sisters Movement in America.* Philadelphia: Big Brothers/ Big Sisters of America, 1985.

"Big Brothers/Big Sisters." *Encyclopedia Americana.* Danbury: Grolier, 1999 ed.

Eli Moses Diner

See also **Big Brother Movement.**

BILINGUALISM. *See* **Education, Bilingual.**

BILL OF RIGHTS IN STATE CONSTITUTIONS. Each of the states has its own constitution, and each state constitution has a bill of rights, sometimes called a declaration of rights. A bill of rights is composed of provisions protecting individual liberties, such as free speech, the right to assemble, and the free exercise of religion, and protecting an accused in a criminal prosecution by ensuring, for example, the accused an impartial jury and the right to confront witnesses.

Bills of rights were part of colonial charters and early state constitutions. They inspired the text of the first ten amendments to the U.S. Constitution, generally referred to as the federal Bill of Rights. The federal Bill of Rights and state bills of rights in turn influenced the text of later state constitutions.

Thus many rights set forth in state constitutions parallel those in the federal Bill of Rights. In addition, several state constitutions recognize individual rights that are not explicitly expressed in the federal Constitution or in sister state constitutions. For example, about ten state constitutions expressly recognize the right that every person shall be secure against unreasonable invasions of privacy, a right not explicitly mentioned in the federal Constitution.

From the beginning of the country's history until 1925, the United States Supreme Court interpreted the federal Bill of Rights as limiting the conduct of the federal government but not protecting against abuses by the states. Thus during this time the state bills of rights were the primary protectors of individual rights against state government. For example, in the nineteenth century criminal defendants were entitled to the assistance of counsel under some state constitutions but not under the federal Bill of Rights.

Beginning in 1925 with *Gitlow v. New York*, the United States Supreme Court began interpreting the due process clause of the Fourteenth Amendment to the Constitution as incorporating provisions of the federal Bill of Rights to restrain state governments. The process of applying certain provisions of the federal Bill of Rights to state action is referred to as selective incorporation. Selective incorporation increased significantly after 1960, when the United States Supreme Court required state courts to accord a criminally accused many federal constitutional protections, including for example, the assistance of counsel. As a result of the selective incorporation process, at the end of the twentieth century many provisions in the federal Bill of Rights restricted the conduct of state governments as well as the federal government. Although individuals had the protection of both the federal and state constitutions, the importance of the state bills of rights waned as federal and state courts and claimants relied primarily on the federal Bill of Rights rather than on state bills of rights to protect individuals against abusive state government action.

A renewed interest in and emphasis on state bills of rights began in the last quarter of the twentieth century with the growth of a legal movement called "new federalism." Proponents of new federalism urged litigants and state courts to base civil liberty claims solely on state bills of rights or in addition to the federal Bill of Rights. They argued that reliance on state constitutional law would strengthen the role of states in the federal system, would enable states to ensure greater protection to their people than granted under the federal Constitution, and would protect state court decisions from federal court review and reversal.

The federal Constitution defines the minimum level of individual rights and leaves each state free to provide greater rights for its people through its state constitution, statutes, or rules. Thus a state court could construe state constitutional protections to give persons greater protection than the United States Supreme Court does when applying the Fourteenth Amendment to the federal Bill of Rights.

In interpreting the federal Constitution, a state court applies federal case law, and its decision may be reviewed and reversed by the United States Supreme Court. In contrast, in interpreting its state constitution a state court applies state law, and its decision is generally not reviewable by the United States Supreme Court, so long as the state decision rests on independent and adequate state grounds and does not authorize action that is prohibited by the federal Constitution.

A state court's interpretation of the state constitution can differ from an interpretation of an overlapping federally protected right. The variance may arise from a number of circumstances, including textual differences, different legislative histories, and disagreement among courts about the correct interpretation of constitutional language. For some, independent state interpretation of state bills of rights has the benefit of allowing states to be laboratories of experimentation for new or different legal doctrines. Moreover, a state court may be better able to provide stability and clarity of law than a distant federal court.

Although no one disputes the right of a state court to interpret its state constitution independent of federal case law interpreting the federal Constitution, some criticize new federalism as destroying national uniformity; undermining the authority of the United States Supreme Court; requiring additional education and training of professionals such as lawyers and law enforcement officers; generating uncertainty and confusion for the public; creating pressure to amend state constitutions to overcome judicial interpretations; and placing state courts at the center of controversial issues and putting pressure on state judges, many of whom are elected, to decide cases on the basis of public opinion, rather than legal principles.

Considering the arguments of the proponents and opponents of new federalism, state courts have, in the last quarter of the twentieth century, issued hundreds of opinions declaring that state constitutions grant individuals more protection than do analogous provisions of the federal Constitution. In many more cases, however, state courts have taken a "lockstep" approach in interpreting their state constitutions—that is, they adopt the United States Supreme Court case law in interpreting their analogous state constitutional provisions.

State bills of rights will continue to play a significant role in the changing concepts of individual liberties and federalism in the twenty-first century. United States Supreme Court Justice William H. Brennan Jr., the intellec-

tual leader of new federalism, characterized new federalism as "an important and highly significant development for our constitutional jurisprudence and for our concept of federalism."

BIBLIOGRAPHY

Abrahamson, Shirley S. "State Constitutional Law." In *Encyclopedia of the American Judicial System*. Edited by Robert J. Janosik. New York: Scribners, 1987.

Brennan, William J., Jr. "State Constitutions and the Protection of Individual Rights." *Harvard Law Review* 90 (1977): 489–504.

Friesen, Jennifer. *State Constitutional Law*. 3d ed. Charlottesville, Va.: Michie Law Publishing, 2000.

Gitlow v. New York, 268 U.S. 652 (1925).

Shirley S. Abrahamson

See also **Colonial Charters; Constitution of the United States; Declaration of Rights; Virginia Declaration of Rights.**

BILL OF RIGHTS IN U.S. CONSTITUTION.

When the American colonists separated from Britain in 1776, most of the states wrote new constitutions to replace their defunct colonial governments. Many, although not all, of these new constitutions were accompanied by declarations or bills of rights. These documents recognized a combination of natural rights and essential civil liberties derived from Anglo-American common law jurisprudence and representative government. They also contained language that stated fundamental principles of republican government. Prior to the adoption of the Massachusetts constitution of 1780, these declarations of rights were not formally incorporated in the actual constitutions. Rather, they were companion documents that reminded Americans what their rights were; their legal authority remained uncertain.

Campaign for a Bill of Rights

When the Federal Convention met in 1787, only a handful of delegates expressed any interest in including a comprehensive list of rights in the new constitution of national government they were drafting. On 12 September 1787, five days before the convention was to adjourn, two of the three delegates still present raised the issue of including a bill of rights in the Constitution; these delegates indicated that they would refuse to sign the completed Constitution without such inclusion. George Mason, one of the two, apparently thought that the convention could simply imitate the influential VIRGINIA DECLARATION OF RIGHTS that he had drafted in 1776. The convention dismissed the idea after perfunctory debate.

Once the Constitution was published, the omission of a bill of rights quickly became a rallying point for its Antifederalist opponents. Their concern deepened after James Wilson, a leading framer and Federalist from Pennsylvania, gave a speech maintaining that the inclusion of a bill of rights would have threatened liberty by implying that the new government possessed powers it had not been granted. The adoption of clauses protecting freedom of press or religion, Wilson asserted, would suggest that Congress had the authority to infringe those rights. In response, the Antifederalists noted that the Constitution did explicitly protect some rights and asked why including a clause prohibiting the suspension of habeas corpus was necessary, for example, if the power to infringe the "great writ" had never been delegated?

ANTIFEDERALISTS did not necessarily regard a bill of rights as a legally enforceable set of claims that individuals could invoke; rather, they thought of it as a statement of principles that would enable the people to judge the legitimacy of acts of government. Without such a document, the people could not determine whether or when government was abusing its power. No one in 1776 would have argued that such declarations created the rights they protected; they merely recognized the existence of rights whose authority was derived from other sources. But by asserting that rights would be insecure if they were not explicitly incorporated in the text of a written constitution, Antifederalists were moving toward the modern positivist conception of law that requires rights and other legal enactments to be grounded upon some explicit act of duly constituted authority. Without a strong textual foundation, rights would eventually be lost. Federalists did not initially take Antifederalist objections seriously, but as the ratification campaign progressed, they began to rethink their position. In states where the two sides were closely balanced, Federalists declared willingness to recommend various lists of amendments for the consideration of the new Congress to be elected after the Constitution was ratified. (Note that these amendments were only recommended, not required; Federalists successfully insisted amendments must follow ratification, not become a condition of it.) Many of the amendments that Antifederalists sought were structural, but others consisted of the kinds of articles that could also be found in the declarations of rights of various states.

Thomas Jefferson, the American minister to France, endorsed the inclusion of a bill of rights. Jefferson let it be known that he hoped that after the necessary nine states had ratified the Constitution, the remaining four would withhold their assent until agreement was reached on the adoption of a bill of rights. Jefferson expressed his support for a bill of rights in letters to James Madison. "A bill of rights is what the people are entitled to against every government on earth," he observed in December 1787. He was equally direct in dismissing the Federalist argument that the enumeration of particular rights would impair the authority of others left unstated. "Half a loaf is better than no bread," he wrote Madison in January 1789. "If we cannot secure all our rights, let us secure what we can."

Madison was not convinced. Like Wilson, he doubted the value of a federal bill of rights, but for other reasons. Madison was strongly committed to the protection of freedom of conscience, rights of property, and basic civil liberties. He thought the real danger to rights came from state governments, not national government. The best way to protect rights, Madison believed, would be to give the national government veto power over state laws, which it could use to guard individuals and minorities against the unjust laws that Madison believed the state legislatures were too prone to pass. The fact that many of the states had adopted declarations of rights only proved how ineffective they were. In Madison's view, such declarations were only "parchment barriers" that could never withstand the popular interests and passions that were the real source of too much state legislation. Madison had felt no qualms when the Federal Convention ignored Mason's plea for a bill of rights, and Antifederalist arguments in favor of a bill of rights left him unconvinced.

Nevertheless, as the leading advocate for the Constitution at the closely divided Virginia ratification convention, Madison found himself in the same position as Federalists elsewhere. To assure ratification, he reluctantly agreed that the convention could recommend amendments to the future federal Congress. In an equally difficult race against James Monroe for election to the first House of Representatives, he had to declare his public support for a bill of rights. Once elected, Madison took this campaign pledge seriously. At the same time, he continued to doubt that a federal bill of rights would do much good—unless it could somehow be extended to apply against the states. In Madison's thinking, its main value would be to quiet lingering Antifederalist reservations about the Constitution. If the First Congress acted quickly, he believed, it could address the lingering reservations of those well-meaning (if misguided) Antifederalists who found the omission of a bill of rights so troubling.

Madison's Proposals

In preparing his amendments, Madison reviewed all the proposals of the state conventions. Many of these amendments were structural, proposing alterations to the institutions of government and the powers these institutions would exercise. Neither Madison nor any of the Federalists who dominated the First Congress intended to consider such recommendations. Indeed, a majority of members in both houses probably believed that considering any amendments in any form was unnecessary. With the Constitution safely ratified and its supporters the clear victors in the first federal elections, they were inclined to deny that any firm bargain had been struck in the course of ratification. The new government had far more urgent matters to take up. The few Antifederalists elected to Congress were not great supporters of amendments. Because they knew the structural changes they desired had no chance of success, they saw little value in debating a bill of rights that would leave the new government in possession of all its powers.

Madison remained committed to his campaign promise, however. Structural amendments were unacceptable, but the addition of new articles protective of rights could still be useful. In drafting his amendments, Madison was also mindful of the defects of the states' declarations of rights. He did not want to draft a traditional bill of rights—supplemental articles or a distinct document standing apart from the main constitutional text. His preference was to insert the new provisions directly into those sections of the existing Constitution where they would be most relevant, principally Article I, Section 9. That section of the Constitution was devoted to limitations on the legislative authority of Congress. In his analyses of state constitutions and republican government more generally, Madison had repeatedly argued that the legislature was the most dangerous branch of government—an "impetuous vortex," as he called it in *Federalist* No. 48—and accordingly the task of protecting rights first and foremost required imposing limits on the legislative power of government. Moreover, by substituting the mandatory verb "shall" for the hortatory "ought" preferred by the state declarations, Madison further indicated that his articles were to be interpreted as legal commands rather than moral injunctions.

It was not only the legislative power of Congress that Madison wanted to limit, however. He still believed that the greater danger to rights was likely to arise not from the national government but from the individual states. He accordingly included in his original list of amendments another article providing that "No state shall violate the equal rights of conscience, or the freedom of the press, or the trial by jury in criminal cases"; this to be inserted in Article I, Section 10, which dealt with prohibitions on the powers of the states. Although this proposal fell short of the federal veto on state laws that he had championed at the Federal Convention, it represented one last effort to enable the national government to become a protector of rights within the individual states.

This article did not survive the eventual scrutiny of the Senate, but most of the other clauses Madison introduced on 8 June formed the foundation of the articles that Congress ultimately endorsed. For Madison, however, the introduction of these amendments was only the first step in an uphill struggle—"the nauseous project of amendments," he called it in August—to get his colleagues to take his proposals seriously. Congress had more pressing business, and neither Federalist nor Antifederalist members felt the same urgency as did Madison. It took the House six weeks to appoint a committee to consider Madison's amendments, and several more weeks passed before the House was ready to take up the committee's report.

The House made two substantial changes in Madison's proposals. In addition to articles protecting specific rights, Madison had also proposed adding language to the preamble to the Constitution. These clauses were more reminiscent of the state declarations of rights; they would have affirmed the basic principles that government derives its authority from the people; that it exists to secure to the people the benefits of their fundamental natural

rights; and that the people retain the right "to reform or change their government" whenever it was proved "adverse or inadequate" to these ends. On 19 August, the House deleted these provisions, evidently on the grounds that including such general statements in the Constitution was redundant.

On that same day, the House made a second and arguably more momentous change in Madison's proposed amendments. Rather than "interweave" these articles separately into the original text of the Constitution, at the point where they seemed most salient, the House now agreed to treat these proposals as supplemental or additional articles. The impetus for this change came from Roger Sherman of Connecticut, an elder statesman of the Revolution. Sherman had proposed his own version of a bill of rights, much closer in form and substance to the state declarations. Sherman's articles generated little interest, but after two rebuffs, he at last persuaded a majority of the representatives that Congress had no right to tamper with the original Constitution as proposed and ratified. The amendments were to be treated as a postscript. Arguably one effect of this change was to make less clear which institutions of government were deemed most dangerous to rights or most responsible for their enforcement.

On 24 August 1789, the House approved seventeen amendments and submitted these to the Senate. Unlike the House, the upper chamber met behind closed doors, and the records of its debates are largely lost to history. The Senate made a number of editorial changes in the House amendments. It rejected Madison's article protecting freedom of conscience, freedom of speech, and trial by jury against state infringement, and another article affirming the principle of separation of powers. It bundled together the separate House articles on freedom of religion and the freedom of speech and press, and the right of petition, into one article, implying a strong link between freedom of religion and political rights. It also seemingly narrowed the House provision stating that "Congress shall make no law establishing religion" by stating instead that "Congress shall make no laws establishing articles of faith, or a mode of worship," implying that it might "establish" religion in other ways. It made several noteworthy changes in the article protecting "the right of the people, to keep and bear arms." As that article came from the House, it read: "A well regulated militia, composed of the body of the People, being the best security of a free State, the right of the People to keep and bear arms, shall not be infringed, but no person religiously scrupulous of bearing arms, shall be compelled to render military service in person." The Senate deleted this last clause as well as the qualifying definition of the militia as "composed of the body of the People," thereby strongly implying that it would remain in the power of Congress to determine the composition of the militia.

The Senate returned twelve articles to the House, and these then went to a conference committee on which

Madison sat for the lower chamber. The committee made one key change in the religion clause of the third article, replacing the Senate's narrow prohibition of laws "establishing articles of faith, or modes of worship," with the broader if more ambiguous phrase, "respecting an establishment of religion." On 28 September 1789, the completed set of amendments was submitted to the state legislatures for ratification.

Ratification and Impact

The first two amendments proposed did not address issues of rights. The first, which failed of ratification, related to the apportionment of representatives in the House. The second, requiring a new election of representatives to occur before congressional pay raises take effect, was also rejected (it eventually became the 27th Amendment, ratified in 1992). The remaining articles became the first ten amendments to the Constitution following their ratification by Virginia in December 1791. The provisions protect the following rights: freedom of religion, speech, press, and assembly and petition (First Amendment); a right "to keep and bear arms," most likely conceived as a reminder that a republic should maintain organized state militias as an alternative to a national standing army (Second Amendment); a now unimportant restriction on quartering soldiers in civilian homes (Third Amendment); a guarantee against unreasonable searches and seizures (Fourth Amendment); essential civil liberties relating primarily to the rights of individuals accused of crimes or otherwise involved in legal proceedings (Fifth, Sixth, and Seventh Amendments); and prohibitions on excessive bail and cruel and unusual punishments (Eighth Amendment). The Ninth Amendment restates the Federalist concern that a positive enumeration of rights carried with it the risk of relegating other rights, potentially of equal value, to an inferior status simply by virtue of their omission; it suggests that the eight previous articles do not establish a comprehensive list of constitutional rights. The Tenth Amendment similarly echoes Wilson's original argument against a bill of rights by suggesting that all powers not vested in the national government by the Constitution remain with the states or the people.

Following its ratification, the Bill of Rights (as it gradually came to be known) had little noticeable effect on the development of the Constitution. An early test of its potential use came in 1798, when Congress adopted the Sedition Act to enable the administration of President John Adams to punish critics of its foreign and domestic policies. Neither the free speech nor free press clauses of the First Amendment nor the Tenth Amendment's affirmation of the limited powers of the national government proved effective against this controversial act. In an important decision of 1833, the Supreme Court held (in *Barron v. Baltimore*) that the Bill of Rights acted as a restraint only on the national government, not the states; and because the national government played only a minimal role in the lives of most Americans, the original amendments had little practical effect.

A generation later, many of the Republican congressmen who drafted the Fourteenth Amendment in 1866 thought that its critical first section could be read to repudiate the result in *Barron*, and thereby make the Bill of Rights judicially and legislatively enforceable against the states. That interpretation did not prove persuasive to the Supreme Court in subsequent decades. Only after World War I did the justices gradually began to apply the Bill of Rights against the states, first in the realm of freedom of speech and religion, then more extensively in other areas. Under the so-called incorporation doctrine, the Fourteenth Amendment was reinterpreted to protect the wide array of civil rights recognized in the original amendments against the authority of state and local governments—and by implication, the national government. The climax of this reinterpretation of the meaning and impact of the Bill of Rights came during the 1960s, under Chief Justice Earl Warren, making the original amendments proposed by Madison in 1789 the most controversial elements of the Constitution.

BIBLIOGRAPHY

Amar, Akhil Reed. *The Bill of Rights: Creation and Reconstruction.* New Haven, Conn.: Yale University Press, 1996.

Bodenhamer, David J., and James W. Ely, Jr., eds. *The Bill of Rights in Modern America: After 200 Years.* Bloomington: Indiana University Press, 1993.

Cogan, Neil H., ed., *The Complete Bill of Rights.* New York: Oxford University Press, 1997.

Levy, Leonard. *Origins of the Bill of Rights.* New Haven, Conn.: Yale University Press, 1999.

Rakove, Jack N. *Declaring Rights: A Brief History with Documents.* Boston: Bedford Books, 1998.

Rutland, Robert A. *The Birth of the Bill of Rights, 1776–1791.* Boston: Northeastern University Press, 1983.

Jack Rakove

See also **Constitution of the United States; Federalist Party; and vol. 9: The Call for Amendments; Virginia Declaration of Rights.**

BILLETING, the quartering of military troops at public expense, was a British practice that infuriated American colonists and fueled calls for revolution. Billeting became a contentious issue, particularly in New York and Philadelphia, as Great Britain sent more and more soldiers to fight the French during the Seven Years' War (1756–1763). To offset the cost of maintaining a modern army in North America, the British parliament passed the Mutiny Act of 1765, more commonly known as the Quartering Act. This new act required colonial governments to billet troops in taverns, barns, and uninhabited houses and to furnish them with provisions when barracks were not available. As "a common resort of arbitrary princes," billeting aroused resistance in Charleston in 1764, New York in 1766, and Boston in 1768, largely owing to aversion to higher taxes and to anger over the British military's willingness to enforce the act. This resistance fed on the traditional British opposition to standing armies. The colonies eventually agreed to quarter the British army. Billeting aggravated tensions between American colonists and British soldiers, however, and led directly to the Boston Massacre in 1770. Although Parliament passed the Quartering Act of 1774 to permit billeting within Boston, this new legislation did little to stem the tide of revolution in North America. Billeting not only sparked calls for independence but also conditioned how Americans would view standing armies. As a result of Parliament's attempt to force the American colonies to quarter British troops, Congress prohibited billeting in the Third Amendment of the Bill of Rights.

BIBLIOGRAPHY

Maier, Pauline. *From Resistance to Revolution.* New York: Knopf, 1972.

Wood, Gordon S. *The Radicalism of the American Revolution.* New York: Knopf, 1992.

Young, Alfred F. *The Shoemaker and the Tea Party.* Boston: Beacon Press, 1999.

Zobel, Hiller B. *The Boston Massacre.* New York: Norton, 1970.

Elbridge Colby
Eric J. Morser

See also **Boston Massacre; Coercive Acts; Mutiny Act; Quartering Acts.**

BILLINGS. Located in MONTANA on the Yellowstone River, Billings was founded in 1882 and was incorporated in 1885. The city was built by the Northern Pacific Railroad and was named after its president, Frederick K. Billings. It became the communications and trading center for southern Montana and northern Wyoming. At the end of the twentieth century Billings had a population of approximately sixty-seven thousand.

Between 1885 and 1890 the population of Billings decreased sharply, and it appeared the city was fated to become a minor railroad town if not a ghost town. However, civic leadership and the reorganization of the American railroad system after the depression of 1893 revitalized it. Billings became the meeting point of three railroads, the Northern Pacific, the Great Northern, and the Burlington. By 1900 Billings had three thousand residents and was on its way to becoming the most important city in the Yellowstone Valley in the twentieth century. Important industries centered there are coal mining, meatpacking, oil and sugar refining, and flour milling.

BIBLIOGRAPHY

Phillips, Charles, and Alan Axelrod, eds. *The Encyclopedia of the American West.* New York: Macmillan, 1996.

West, Carroll Van. *Capitalism on the Frontier: Billings and the Yellowstone Valley in the Nineteenth Century.* Lincoln: University of Nebraska Press, 1993.

Henry E. Fritz

BILLS OF CREDIT are non-interest-bearing government obligations that circulate as money. In the mid-eighteenth century, the term was commonly used to describe issues by the colonies and, later, by the Continental Congress and states during the Revolutionary War. Since the establishment of the national government, such issues have been known as treasury notes or United States notes.

Bills of credit in the colonies began with an issue of £7,000 (shortly increased to £40,000) in Massachusetts in 1690. This was followed by similar actions by New Hampshire, Rhode Island, Connecticut, New York, South Carolina, and New Jersey before 1711, North Carolina in 1712, Pennsylvania in 1723, Maryland in 1733, Delaware in 1739, Virginia in 1755, and Georgia in 1760. In most cases the bills were issued to excess and depreciated sharply in value. Parliament finally prohibited such paper currency in New England in 1751 and in the other colonies in 1764.

As soon as the colonies broke away from England, they again began to emit bills of credit in large amounts. The Continental Congress, unable to obtain necessary funds from other sources, authorized $241,552,780 of bills from 1775 to 1779, while the various states put out $209,524,776 of bills during the same period.

BIBLIOGRAPHY

Ferguson, E. James. *The Power of the Purse: A History of American Public Finance, 1776–1790.* Chapel Hill: University of North Carolina Press, 1961.

Hall, Arthur P. "State-Issued Bills of Credit and the United States Constitution." Ph.D. diss., University of Georgia, 1991.

Frederick A. Bradford / A. R.

See also **Debts, Revolutionary War; Legal Tender; Revolution, American: Financial Aspects.**

BIMETALLISM. In 1791, most of the world's leading nations were on a bimetallic standard in which both gold and silver served as the basis for coinage (known as "specie"). Following the recommendations of Alexander Hamilton and Thomas Jefferson, the U.S. Congress passed the Coinage Act of 1792, in which a gold eagle ($10) gold piece of 247.50 grains, 100 percent fine, a silver dollar of 371.25 grains, and subsidiary silver coins including half-dollars, quarters, and dimes of proportional weight became the money standard for the new nation.

The American silver dollar circulated at face ("par") value in Latin America even though it weighed less than the Latin American dollar. Consequently most of the coins that were minted were exported and did not circulate internally to any significant extent. In 1806, President Jefferson suspended the coinage of silver dollars.

The mint ratio of silver to gold (15 to 1) undervalued gold. An owner of gold could sell it to the mint at the government-set price of $19.40 per ounce, but in the market, where prices were set by supply and demand, the same owner could obtain nearly $20 per ounce. The undervalued metal in a dual system such as this tends to cease circulation once the disparity between the mint and market ratios becomes large enough to yield a profit after transaction costs are paid—a phenomenon known to economists as "Gresham's law" ("good money drives out bad"). Until the Napoleonic wars, the disparity between the prices in gold and silver still did not grow far enough to induce many people to take advantage of the price differential (a process known as "arbitrage"). But in 1821, England adopted the gold standard, which raised the demand for gold and raised its price beyond the level needed to initiate Gresham's law. Gold all but disappeared from circulation.

By the early 1820s, many proposals were made to devalue gold, but the scarcity of the metal argued against devaluation. After gold was discovered in the Appalachians, however, Congress in 1834 reduced the gold content of the eagle to 232 grains. Three years later, the weight was increased to 232.2 grains, making the mint ratio of silver to gold 15.988 to 1. Gold was overvalued at the mint, but it took until 1844 for all the silver coins to disappear from circulation. To bring back silver for daily transactions, Congress in 1853 reduced the halfdollar from 206.25 grains, 90 percent fine, to 192 grains, and reduced other coins proportionately.

Civil War inflation drove all specie out of circulation. The country was on an irredeemable paper standard from 1861 to 1879. In light of the fact that the silver dollar had not circulated for thirty years, the coinage laws were rewritten: the act of February 1873 dropped the silver dollar and made the gold dollar the monetary standard, evoking a howl of protest from agrarian groups and miners who wanted to inflate the currency. They referred to this as the "Crime of '73."

A series of events in the early 1870s reduced the demand for silver. In 1871–1873, Germany went on the gold standard, demonetizing silver; several Latin American countries closed their silver coinage production; Scandinavia adopted the gold standard; and Russia, in 1876, suspended its silver coinage. Meanwhile, new discoveries of silver in Nevada, combined with the continued productivity of the Comstock Lode, increased U.S. silver production by about 20 percent.

The price of silver fell sharply, and, combined with a worldwide gradual deflation, many Americans saw the declining price levels as a conspiracy or plot by lenders to maintain deflation. "Silverites" (who began to meld into the newly forming Populist Party) clamored for "free and unlimited silver at 16 to 1." In 1878, pressure from silver interests led to passage of the BLAND-ALLISON ACT, which required the U.S. Treasury to purchase $2.5 million worth of silver every month for coinage into silver dollars at the rate of 412.5 ounces, 90 percent fine. The catch was that the Treasury was to pay market prices, not "16 to 1." Thus the anticipated inflation that would have ensued had the silverites' program been adhered to did not materialize.

Silver forces relentlessly pressed their program. In June 1890, Congress passed the SHERMAN SILVER PURCHASE ACT, which required the purchase of 4.5 million ounces of silver per month at slightly higher than market prices of approximately 16.5 to 1. This had the disastrous effect of draining gold out of the country at precipitous rates. By the time Grover Cleveland was reelected president in 1892, the nation teetered on the edge of bankruptcy. Congress repealed the act in November 1893, but not in time to stop the panic of 1893. Worse, the gold drain on the government's vaults had continued: in 1892 the government had $84 million in gold, but by 1894 the reserves had fallen to $69 million and continued to drop. Finally Cleveland worked with the banker J. P. Morgan to arrange a massive syndicate to lend the U.S. government gold totaling more than $65 million, which stabilized the markets. In 1896, the bimetallism issue was politically ended with the election of the Republican William McKinley, who favored a gold standard, over the Democratic silverite William Jennings Bryan, who had won the nomination with his famous CROSS OF GOLD SPEECH.

The Great Depression brought new calls to add silver back to the monetary mix. On 5 April 1933, President Franklin D. Roosevelt suspended the gold standard. The Thomas Amendment to the Agricultural Adjustment Act (May 1933) authorized the president to devalue the gold dollar up to 50 percent, accept up to $200 million in silver at 50 cents an ounce in payment for war debts, and to restore bimetallism. By the GOLD RESERVE ACT of January 1934, the weight of the gold dollar was reduced from 23.22 to 13.71 grains, making gold worth $35 an ounce instead of $20.67. The government also bought more domestically mined silver during the depression.

During the 1960s, the United States abandoned all but the symbolism of a metallic standard. In acts of 1965 and 1968, Congress eliminated the gold reserve requirement for Federal Reserve bank deposits and Federal Reserve notes. In 1965 the government quit minting standard silver coins and in 1971 temporarily suspended the right to convert dollars into gold. In 1972, the dollar was devalued, raising the price of gold to $38 per ounce; a year later, the dollar was devalued again, forcing the price up to $42. It was hopeless for the government to try to peg the price of the dollar to gold, or vice versa, and soon the dollar (as did all currencies) "floated" against the value of gold and all other currencies. During the oil crisis of the mid-1970s, the market gold price soared to as much as $900 an ounce, although once oil prices stabilized, the price of gold fell back to around $300, where (with a few exceptions) it has remained.

BIBLIOGRAPHY

Friedman, Milton. "Bimetallism Revisited." *Journal of Economic Perspectives* 4 (1990): 95–104.

Friedman, Milton, and Anna J. Schwartz. *A Monetary History of the United States, 1867–1960*. Princeton, N.J.: Princeton University Press, 1967.

Krooss, Herman E. *Documentary History of Banking and Currency in the United States*. New York: Chelsea House, 1969.

Laughlin, J. L. *History of Bimetallism in the United States*. Princeton, N.J.: Princeton University Press, 1963.

Larry Schweikart

See also **Currency and Coinage; Federal Reserve System.**

BIOCHEMISTRY, the chemical investigation and explanation of biological processes. American biochemistry acquired its institutional base as a result of the medical reform movement during the Progressive Era and was characterized until World War II by its emphasis on applied research and close association with medicine. American biochemists have been involved in the testing of foods and drugs, the development of diagnostic tests and medical treatments, and the production of consumer goods ranging from synthetic fibers and biological detergents to vitamin supplements and the contraceptive pill. Since the 1970s, biochemists have been actively engaged in biotechnological enterprises.

Biochemistry's antecedents lie in nineteenth-century Europe, where the rise of organic chemistry and experimental physiology generated much investigation into the chemical constituents of living organisms and the chemical changes associated with physiological functions. The many American scientists who trained in European laboratories imported these practices into the United States, where research in animal chemistry, agricultural chemistry, medical chemistry, and physiological chemistry gained a firm foothold in agricultural research stations, hospitals, colleges, and universities.

In the early 1900s, investigators in Europe and America sought to unite the diverse fields dealing with the chemistry of life under name of "biochemistry" or "biological chemistry" (then the preferred term in the United States). Among the first journals expressing this aim was the *Journal of Biological Chemistry*, founded in the United States in 1905. The American Society of Biological Chemists was constituted in 1906. In the same decade, many American medical schools, newly under university control, began to teach biochemistry as part of a nationwide reorganization of preclinical education. By 1920, most American medical schools had established departments of biochemistry where research had a predominantly clinical orientation.

Early American biochemists led in the development of new analytical methods for determining chemicals in the body that were used to diagnose specific diseases and monitor physiological states. Otto Folin at Harvard, Donald D. Van Slyke at the Rockefeller Institute Hospital in New York, and Stanley Benedict at Cornell acquired international renown. The widespread use of techniques they developed led simultaneously to redefinitions and reclassifications of diseases in chemical terms.

A second prominent stream of American biochemistry, that of nutritional investigation, built on established strengths in agricultural research, especially at experimental stations in Connecticut and Wisconsin. Recognition of the importance for health of vitamins stimulated much American research into the distribution of vitamins in foods, their chemical properties, and their role in metabolism. Diseases identified as resulting from vitamin deficiencies in the diet, such as rickets, scurvy, and pellagra, were cured and prevented by specific dietary changes. Commercially produced vitamin preparations and vitamin-fortified foods were widely promoted among the public from the 1920s and became an important source of profit for the American food and pharmaceutical industries.

In the 1930s, some American centers began to develop biochemistry as a broad, fundamental biological science, after the model of leading German, English, and Scandinavian schools. A similar vision was promoted by Warren Weaver, who, as manager of its Natural Sciences Division, turned the Rockefeller Foundation into the major international funding body for basic research in biochemistry and biophysics. In this decade, the biochemistry department at Columbia University in New York, headed by Hans T. Clarke, became the largest and most influential American school of basic biochemical research.

Clarke gave place in his department to an exceptionally high number of biochemists who had escaped national socialist regimes in Europe and who brought their distinctive research styles with them. Among them was Rudolf Schoenheimer, who, at Columbia, was responsible for a milestone in twentieth-century biochemistry: he introduced the use of isotopes as labels that allow biochemists to follow in detail how, and at what rate, specific molecules undergo change in metabolic reactions. His research with David Rittenberg and Sarah Ratner not only heralded the use of what has since become an indispensable tool in the life sciences but showed that all cell constituents are in constant flux: molecules are continuously being broken down and rebuilt from the foods organisms ingest.

During World War II, biochemists participated in the war effort in major ways. For example, American biochemists were involved in the large-scale production of penicillin, other antibacterial drugs, and blood fractionation products for use in transfusion. These war-related projects involved complex translations between basic and applied research, managed through close collaborations between scientists, government, and industry. The blood fractionation project, organized by Edwin Cohn of the physical chemistry department at Harvard, was one of the wartime successes that stimulated a massive expansion of public funding for basic biochemical research in postwar America.

One manifestation of this new focus was the foundation of institutes dedicated to basic biochemistry, the first being the Enzyme Institute at the University of Wisconsin, opened in 1950. By the 1960s, fundamental biochemical research was firmly entrenched institutionally, and American biochemists were making ever more internationally renowned contributions to all areas of biochemistry. Indicative of this trend is the rapid increase in Nobel laureates among American biochemists.

Between 1901 and 1950, only three Nobel Prizes were awarded for American biochemical research: the 1946 chemistry prize awarded to James B. Sumner, John H. Northrop, and Wendell M. Stanley for work on enzymes and virus proteins; and two prizes in physiology or medicine (shared with others abroad), awarded to Edward A. Doisy in 1943 for work on vitamin K, and to Carl F. Cori and Gerty Radnitz Cori in 1947 for work on glycogen metabolism. (Gerty Cori was the third woman, and the first woman biochemist, to win a Nobel Prize.) In the second half of the twentieth century, by contrast, approximately forty Nobel Prizes were awarded for American research with a biochemical dimension, to some seventy American laureates.

In this later period, biochemistry became increasingly intertwined with molecular biology and cell biology, partly through the development of new chemical, physical, and morphological techniques used in all three fields and through much traffic of biochemists across the boundaries between them. For biochemistry, these new developments made it possible to locate particular biochemical reactions in specific structures of the cell. Moreover, its institutional strength and practical flexibility enabled biochemistry to withstand challenges to its status as a fundamental science of life when these were issued in the 1950s and 1960s by molecular biologists seeking autonomy for their own science. In practice, there has been continuous overlap, and in 1987 the American Society of Biological Chemists renamed itself the American Society for Biochemistry and Molecular Biology.

BIBLIOGRAPHY

Apple, Rima D. *Vitamania: Vitamins in American Culture.* New Brunswick: Rutgers University Press, 1996.

Bud, Robert. *The Uses of Life: A History of Biotechnology.* New York: Cambridge University Press, 1993.

De Chadarevian, Soraya, and Harmke Kamminga, eds. *Molecularizing Biology and Medicine: New Practices and Alliances, 1910s–1970s.* Amsterdam: Harwood Academic Publishers, 1998.

Kohler, Robert E. *From Medical Chemistry to Biochemistry: The Making of a Biomedical Discipline.* Cambridge, U.K.: Cambridge University Press, 1982.

Harmke Kamminga

See also **Chemistry; Medical Research; Microbiology; Molecular Biology; Nutrition and Vitamins.**

BIOETHICS addresses the moral and ethical issues arising from clinical practice, medical and biological research, resource allocation, and access to biomedical technology. Van Rensselaer Potter at the University of Wisconsin and Andre Hellegers at the Kennedy Institute of Ethics independently coined the term "bioethics" in the early 1970s to describe different concepts, and its exact definition remains contested today. However, it is nonetheless possible to discern the growth of a professional bioethics industry and discipline intimately tied to cultural mores and new advances in biomedical technology and techniques. Indeed, the field of bioethics underwent explosive growth and institutionalization in the 1970s as challenging issues such as euthanasia, in vitro fertilization, organ transplantation, and genetic engineering attracted the public's attention and concern. Because questions over appropriate science and social policies exist at the crossroads of legal, political, and moral disputes, the history of American bioethics is one of contentious debate, government regulation, and continuing growth.

The history of medical ethics dates to antiquity, and the Hippocratic Oath to "do no harm" remains at the core of modern medical ethics. The American Medical Association (AMA) established a code of ethics in 1846 to regulate medical practice; a hundred years later, revelations about Nazi medical experimentation led to the Nuremberg Code, requiring "informed consent" from human subjects involved in research. In the 1960s the introduction of dialysis machines, and the resulting "God committees" to decide who would receive the life-saving treatments, strained the medical community's ethical consensus. At the same time, a cultural emphasis on individual rights merged with growing concerns over medical and biological advances to require government intervention. For example, the definition of "brain death," the ethics of organ transplantation, and the potential for prenatal genetic discrimination led to the first Senate hearings on bioethics in 1968. These issues also led to the establishment of the Institute of Society, Ethics, and the Life Sciences (also known as the Hastings Center) in 1969; the National Science Foundation's Ethics and Human Values Implications of Science and Technology (EHVIST) program in 1971; and the Joseph and Rose Kennedy Center for the Study of Human Reproduction and Bioethics (later the Kennedy Institute of Ethics) in 1971.

Throughout the 1970s a professional bioethics industry developed in response to numerous ethical and medical dilemmas. The wide assortment of issues attracted attention from diverse groups. Many religious communities felt genetic screening might increase abortions of "defective" babies, while the *Roe v. Wade* decision and questions regarding fetal research ensured the active participation of women's groups. The disclosure of improper medical conduct and a lack of informed consent in the Tuskegee, Alabama, syphilis study heightened awareness about the regulation and control of research, as the public questioned whether researchers could be trusted with ethical responsibilities. These questions resurfaced in disputes over the morality of "gene splicing" throughout the decade, while the Karen Ann Quinlan case thrust the "right to die" movement into the spotlight. The birth of Louise Brown, the first "test-tube" baby, also ignited public interest, as the government and the public struggled to address the plethora of issues. By 1980, many medical schools had established programs and journals to discuss the challenging new issues and prepare students for their future careers; the first *Encyclopedia of Bioethics* appeared in 1978.

In 1974 the United States Congress, led by Massachusetts Senator Edward Kennedy, established the National Commission for the Protection of Human Subjects of Biomedical and Behavioral Research. The commission released a series of reports over the next four years that provided the "official" positions necessary to create uniformity in American policies on the various complex legal and ethical issues. Given the religiously pluralistic fabric of American society, the committee's primary position, as outlined in *The Belmont Report*, relied on the three principles of beneficence, justice, and autonomy as acceptable, and secular, bioethical guidelines. Early treatises on medical ethics, such as Joseph Fletcher's *Morals and Medicine* (1954) or Paul Ramsey's *The Patient as Person* (1970), had often combined Christian theology with a liberal philosophy to help reconsider the doctor-patient relationship in light of the latest medical developments. Indeed, some observers credit the rise of bioethics with revitalizing philosophical ethics, as the new challenges demanded a fresh approach and a resolution.

However, the guidelines failed to quell public uneasiness and led many groups to question the official principles throughout the 1970s and 1980s. Christian fundamentalists and Christian Scientists were especially vocal and litigious in challenging the emphasis on individual autonomy. Critics often charged that the *Belmont Report's* principles downplayed the importance of community and family and argued against the autonomy of children and mentally handicapped patients in making decisions regarding abortion, euthanasia, or life-saving medical treatments. Similar disagreement followed the 1982 release of the President's Commission for the Study of Ethical Problems in Medicine and Biomedical and Behavioral Research (est. 1980) report *Splicing Life* because it advocated the patenting of genetically-altered organisms and stated that future debates on biological research could rely on professional bioethicists, rather than theologians, for moral and ethical perspectives.

By the early 2000s bioethics was internationally recognized and interdisciplinary, drawing participants and perspectives from philosophy, medicine, biology, theology, and history. By 1990, over 100 organizations and institutions dedicated to bioethics had been established, many of them in the United States, an acknowledged leader in the field. Indeed, responding to ethical concerns over human gene therapy and experimentation with human subjects, President Bill Clinton established the National Bioethics Advisory Commission in 1996. Chaired by Harold Shapiro, former president of Princeton University, the commission produced the influential report *Cloning Human Beings*, which outlined the ethical issues related to the emerging technology. The commission's charter expired in October 2001, leaving empty that critical nexus where specialists in medical, clinical, or research ethics could address the latest bioethical developments, from reproductive techniques and access to artificial organs to cloning, stem cell research, and genetic privacy and discrimination. As the sophistication of medical technology and biological research increases, the field of bioethics continues to grow, preparing to meet the unforeseen challenges of the twenty-first century.

BIBLIOGRAPHY

Engelhardt, H. T. *The Foundations of Bioethics.* Oxford: Oxford University Press, 1986.

Jonsen, Albert R. *The Birth of Bioethics.* New York: Oxford University Press, 1998.

Reich, Warren, ed. *The Encyclopedia of Bioethics.* New York: Simon and Schuster, 1995.

Stevens, M. L. *Bioethics in America: Origins and Cultural Politics.* Baltimore, Md.: Johns Hopkins University Press, 2000.

J. G. Whitesides

See also **Clinical Research; Euthanasia; Medical Research.**

BIOLOGICAL CONTAINMENT, an effort to investigate the hazards of, and develop containment standards for, genetic engineering research. In 1975, three years after the first successful in vitro transfer of bacterial genes into a mammalian virus ushered in the age of recombinant DNA, scientists gathered at an international meeting at the Asilomar Conference Center in Pacific Grove, California, to explore the implications of the discovery. What has become known as the recombinant DNA (rDNA) controversy arose soon after in Cambridge, Massachusetts, when the city established a citizen review board to assess whether the guidelines issued in 1976 by the NATIONAL INSTITUTES OF HEALTH (NIH) were sufficient to protect public health. The city established a moratorium on certain classes of rDNA research during the period its board investigated the new research techniques. As an outgrowth of the panel's findings, Cambridge in 1977 passed the first ordinance regulating genetics research in the United States. It set up a municipal biohazard committee to oversee rDNA activities, made NIH guidelines mandatory for all research and development in the city, whether publicly or privately funded, and established procedures for laboratory surveillance of biological hazards.

Between 1976 and 1980 the NIH relaxed its guidelines significantly. Public concern shifted from laboratory safety to the containment and safety standards of commercially developed genetically modified organisms, primarily in the form of genetically modified plants and microorganisms for agriculture, food production, mining, and bioremediation. Without new legislation for products of biotechnology, Congress urged federal agencies to use existing statutes, mostly dedicated to regulation of chemical products. Agencies began developing rules for large-scale fermentation, field tests, and the intentional release of transgenic organisms into the environment.

The U.S. Department of Agriculture is responsible for rules governing the introduction of genetically modified plant species into the environment to minimize the creation of new plant pests or dissemination of weeds. Since 1985, hundreds of transgenic plant species have been approved for field tests. The ENVIRONMENTAL PROTECTION AGENCY (EPA) is responsible for regulating biological pesticides under the Federal Insecticide, Fungicide, and Rodenticide Act (1972), as well as all other releases of bioengineered products other than plants under the Toxic Substances Control Act (1976). The first bioengineered microorganism approved for field testing by the EPA, on 5 December 1985, was ice minus, a genetically modified strain of a soil bacterium, *Pseudomonas syringae*, which reduces frost damage on certain crops.

Safety requirements for releasing genetically modified organisms (GMOs) into the environment must take into consideration whether the GMOs will spread beyond designated areas, whether they will transfer genes to other organisms, and whether they will turn safe organisms into plant pests or into organisms that overwhelm indigenous species. Much of the scientific debate over bioengineered organisms and their containment has centered on the relevance to risk of how an organism is modified, the analogy between the release of nonindigenous species and bioengineered organisms, and whether ecological assessment can lessen the hazards of environmental releases of GMOs. Much of the social protest related to GMOs, particularly in the 1990s, centered around such issues as requiring the labeling of genetically modified foods, replacing voluntary safety testing of new products by the industries producing them with mandatory safety testing by independent research groups, and developing liability standards for contamination and unforeseen damage to public health or the environment.

BIBLIOGRAPHY

Grobstein, Clifford. *A Double Image of the Double Helix: The Recombinant-DNA Debate.* San Francisco: W. H. Freeman, 1979.

Krimsky, Sheldon. *Genetic Alchemy: The Social History of the Recombinant DNA Controversy.* Cambridge, Mass.: MIT Press, 1982.

———. *Biotechnics and Society: The Rise of Industrial Genetics.* New York: Praeger, 1991.

National Research Council (U.S.). *Field Testing Genetically Modified Organisms: Framework for Decisions.* Washington, D.C.: National Academy Press, 1989.

Sheldon Krimsky/c. w.

See also **Biochemistry; Genetic Engineering; Microbiology.**

BIOLOGICAL WARFARE. *See* **Chemical and Biological Warfare.**

BIONICS, broadly defined, is the application of the understanding of biological functions to solving engineering problems. Studies of how birds fly, for example, have been used to design aircraft. Research in bionics led to the development of functional aids for humans. In 1928 Philip Drinker and Louis A. Shaw of the Harvard School of Public Health designed the iron lung to allow poliomyelitis patients to breathe. Denton Cooley in 1969 and Robert Jarvik in 1982 and 1984 devised artificial hearts for temporary use. Bionics also contributed to the designs of prostheses. The 1961 Nobel Prize winner for physiology or medicine, Georg von Békésy, discovered the mechanisms of stimulation of the inner ear, which enabled the Minnesota Mining and Manufacturing Company to develop the cochlear implant in 1973, bringing varying degrees of hearing to the totally deaf. In the late 1980s, U.S. scientists studied the neural systems in order to aid paralysis victims, persons with artificial limbs, and the blind. Kendall D. Wise and David J. Edell experimented with devices that could detect neural commands and transform them into electronic commands to produce movement in paralyzed limbs. In the early 1990s Robert Birge of Syracuse University experimented with protein extracted from a saltwater bacterium to develop an artificial eye, and Carver Mead at the California Institute of Technology worked on producing an all-electronic silicon retina. Research on mechanical prostheses continued in the late 1990s, despite advances in the discovery of cloning, which focused scientific attention on the genetic replication of human organs.

BIBLIOGRAPHY

Flam, Faye. "Getting an Eyeful of Biomolecules." *Science* 255, no. 5042 (17 January 1992): 289.

Souhrada, Laura. "Bionic Prostheses Restore Neurological Activity." *Hospitals* (5 July 1989).

Zorpette, Glenn, and Carol Ezzell, eds. "Your Bionic Future." *Scientific American* 10, no. 3 (September 1999). Special issue.

Ruth Roy Harris/A. R.

See also **Heart Implants; Medicine and Surgery; Robotics; Transplants and Organ Donation.**

BIOREGIONALISM, as much a movement as a philosophy, is a North American response to the modern environmental crisis. The term comes from the Greek root *bio* (life) and the Latin *regio* (place). As a philosophy, bioregionalism refers to the fullness of all earthly life existing in mutuality and synergy. Regions are defined not by legislation, with dotted lines and borders, but by nature, with a commonality of climate, geology, hydrology, species, and earth forms. Islands and deserts are defined as bioregions. Usually, however, the term applies to a watershed, an area defined by a network of runoffs into a central river that forms a kind of organizing spine. It is along such spines that all natural species, including humans, have situated themselves. Bioregionalism posits that human societies must learn to honor these networks if they are to be ecologically sound. The philosophy also argues that nations, empires, and large political economies of any kind are antiecological, claiming that the bigger they are, the more threatening to nature they become. It is only at the natural scale of the bioregion that people can learn the complete systems and species of nature and thus know how to satisfy their basic needs and create social institutions that do not do violence to that ecosystem.

As a movement, bioregionalism began in the late 1970s in the San Francisco Bay Area and slowly spread through the West and into the Ozarks, Appalachia, and the Hudson River area. The first continent-wide gathering was held in the tall-grass prairie near Kansas City in 1984. Since then, congresses have been held at sites from the Squamish bioregion of British Columbia to the Gulf of Maine bioregion on the Atlantic. Over the years these meetings have established a bioregional "platform," with position papers on subjects ranging from agriculture and forestry to art, economics, and community. By 1994 there were more than one hundred active bioregional groups throughout North America, or what bioregionalists call (following Native American tradition) Turtle Island. Movements have also taken root in Europe and Australia. In the United States, bioregionalism groups do local ecological work, especially restoration and environmental education. Other groups concentrate on forming networks and "green pages," environmentally focused directories, within their regions, often with newsletters and magazines. Other bioregionalist groups work to link like-minded organizations into alliances on specific issues, such as water conservation, organic farming, and tree planting. Movements within the larger bioregionalism movement focus on practices such as permaculture (short for permanent agriculture) and asset-based community development, which are attempts to make communities more self-sufficient by mapping and utilizing local assets. Communities were mapping such local assets through the late 1990s. Other concerns include bioremediation, which aims to clean up polluted land, water, and air using organic means.

BIBLIOGRAPHY

McGinnis, Michael Vincent, ed. *Bioregionalism*. New York: Routledge, 1999.

Plant, Christopher, and Judith Plant. *Turtle Talk: Voices for a Sustainable Future*. Philadelphia: New Society, 1990.

Sale, Kirkpatrick. *Dwellers in the Land: The Bioregional Vision*. San Francisco: Sierra Club Books, 1985.

Kirkpatrick Sale / H. S.

See also **Conservation; Organic Farming.**

BIOSPHERE 2. Constructed of steel-framed glass, this 1.28-hectare structure near Oracle, Arizona, is intended to replicate ecological environments on earth (that is, Biosphere 1) under closed conditions. In addition to agricultural and living areas for its human occupants, Biosphere 2 houses tropical rain forest, desert, savannah, and cloud forest ecosystems as well as a coral reef within a miniature ocean. The original purpose of Biosphere 2 was to provide baseline data for designing structures for long-term habitation by humans in space. The underlying philosophy was that biological systems were self-organizing and self-regulating on a global scale, a notion that met with considerable skepticism in the scientific community. In an exercise described by some as more showmanship than science, four men and four women sealed themselves within Biosphere 2 in September 1991. Over a two-year period, oxygen was depleted and had to be replenished, and failed crops resulted in the restriction of the occupants' diets to 1,750 calories per day. Supporters maintained that results of serious scientific interest were obtained, including data on nutrient dynamics and waste-recycling technology. Critics pointed out that Biosphere 2 was privately funded (by the Texas oil billionaire and self-described "ecopreneur" Edward Bass), freeing it from the strict, objective evaluation required of publicly funded research. A second, seven-person team inhabited Biosphere 2 between March and September of 1994. During that period, in an effort to rehabilitate the project's credibility, a new administration established a consortium to conduct future research with scientists from Columbia University's Lamont-Doherty Earth Observatory.

BIBLIOGRAPHY

Vergano, Dan. "Brave New World of Biosphere 2." *Science News* 150, no. 20 (16 November 1996): 312–313.

Susan Andrew / A. R.

See also **Environmental Movement.**

BIOTERRORISM, the deliberate, private use of biological agents to harm and frighten the people of a state or society, is related to the military use of biological, chemical, and nuclear weapons. Formally the use of such weapons by one state to threaten or attack another state is warfare, although such warfare may violate the laws of war, and any use of such weapons by private individuals is terrorism.

The use of biological weapons for terror is ancient. Assyrian politicians (c. 650 B.C.) dumped fungus from rye into their opponents' wells, giving them fatal ergot poisoning. Armies besieging a town relied on increased disease among the defending populace and threw dead animals into water supplies to encourage it. Fourteenth-century Tatars spread bubonic plague by catapulting diseased corpses into towns.

With the advent of the germ theory of disease, greater knowledge of microbiology, and military bioengineering, the potential devastation due to biological weapons grew exponentially. In 1876, the German biologist Robert Koch first proved that anthrax is caused by bacteria. In World War I (1914–1918), biological weapons developed by the United States and Germany were perhaps used to contaminate animal fodder, and the Germans used *Burkholderia mallei* to cause glanders in enemy support animals. During World War II renewed concern over "germ warfare" fueled both sides' research regarding biological weapons, but there is no record of their being used. The height of the development of "weaponized" biological agents was the Cold War (1946–1991), in which both the United States and the Soviet Union created arsenals of biological agents for use both in battle and against civilian populations. This research led to propagandist charges of using such weapons; during the Korean War (1950–1953), North Korea accused the United States of dropping bombs containing diseased flies. Since the 1975 ratification of the Biological Weapons Convention, the United States, Russia, and most states have publicly claimed that they have destroyed their stockpiles and now research biological warfare only to defend against it. Even so, during the Persian Gulf War of 1991, Iraq equipped, but did not fire, rocket warheads containing anthrax.

The danger of the use of biological weapons by terrorists has grown as knowledge of such weapons and the military technology for them has become more widely available following the end of the Cold War. Acts of bioterrorism have increased in frequency and severity since then. In 1984, the pseudo-Buddhist Rajneeshee cult distributed salmonella in restaurants and a grocery store in The Dalles, Oregon, attempting to poison civic leaders to gain control of local government; 751 people developed gastroenteritis. Aum Shinrikyo, a Japanese cult, killed twelve people and injured thousands in the Tokyo subway through a sarin gas attack in 1995 and has made further, but unsuccessful, attempts to release airborne biological agents in the subways.

In 2001, letters containing anthrax spores were mailed to television news anchor Tom Brokaw, U.S. Senator Tom Daschle, and others, leading to the deaths of five people and the hospitalization of at least twelve others, although the targeted individuals were unhurt. The attacks coincided with the attacks by the Islamic terrorist group Al Qaeda on New York City and Washington, D.C., although at this writing their perpetrator remains unknown.

BIBLIOGRAPHY

Falkenrath, Richard A., Robert D. Newman, and Bradley A. Thayer. *America's Achilles' Heel: Nuclear, Biological, and Chemical Terrorism and Covert Attack.* Cambridge, Mass.: MIT Press, 1998.

Laqueur, Walter. *The New Terrorism: Fanaticism and the Arms of Mass Destruction.* New York: Oxford University Press, 1999.

Miller, Judith, Stephen Engelberg, and William J. Broad. *Germs: Biological Weapons and America's Secret War.* New York: Simon and Schuster, 2001.

Zilinskas, Raymond A. "Rethinking Bioterrorism." *Current History* 100 (2001): 438–443.

Stephen M. Sheppard

See also **Chemical and Biological Warfare; Terrorism.**

BIRDS. *See* **Ornithology.**

BIRDS OF PASSAGE is a term used to describe temporary migrants who move so they can fill jobs that are often viewed as beneath native-born laborers. The term was used in the United States as early as the 1840s to refer to British immigrants and remained in use through the late twentieth century to refer to Asian, European, and Latin American immigrants. The phenomenon of temporary or return migration can be traced back to the early decades of industrialization. Improvements in technology had an impact on the number of birds of passage moving to the United States and other countries that welcomed immigrants. In particular, in the latter half of the nineteenth century, the steamship made travel easier and moving back and forth all the more possible. Industrial expansion, economic opportunities, and the possibility of returning to their homelands motivated birds of passage. Statistics vary depending on national origin and era; return rates could be as low as 10 percent or as high as 80 percent. Birds of passage were a crucial part of the U.S. economy during the height of mass immigration (1880–1920), when more than 20 million immigrants arrived in the United States. Before the passage of the Johnson-Reed Act in 1924, which limited the number of immigrants allowed to enter the United States, the phenomenon of birds of passage was used by both sides to argue for and against restricting immigration.

BIBLIOGRAPHY

Bodnar, John. *The Transplanted: A History of Immigrants in Urban America.* Bloomington: Indiana University Press, 1985.

Piore, Michael J. *Birds of Passage: Migrant Labor in Industrial Societies.* New York: Cambridge University Press, 1979.

Wyman, Mark. *Round-Trip to America: The Immigrants Return to Europe, 1880–1930.* Ithaca, N.Y.: Cornell University Press, 1993.

Caroline Waldron Merithew

See also **Immigration; Immigration Restriction.**

BIRMINGHAM, the largest city in ALABAMA, was first settled in 1813 as the town of Elyton. During the CIVIL WAR, it was the site of a Confederate blast furnace because of its rich iron ore and other mineral deposits. The modern city was laid out in 1870 at the intersection of two railroads and was incorporated in 1871. Steel was first manufactured in the city in 1899, and Birmingham grew rapidly as an industrial center. During the second half of the twentieth century, however, Birmingham suffered in the same shadow of deindustrialization as the cities of the Midwest. In 1949, the IRON AND STEEL INDUSTRY provided 20 percent of employment within the metropolitan area; by 1968 that employment had dropped to 10 percent. By 1980, four out of five of the largest employers were service-related industries.

No other city has been more synonymous with civil rights history than Birmingham, where in the 1960s, fire hoses, dogs, and police were vivid symbols of troubled race relations in the United States. Birmingham was the scene of several violent incidents during the CIVIL RIGHTS MOVEMENT. In 1961, white segregationists assaulted FREEDOM RIDERS in the city, and the bombing of an African American church killed four young girls in 1963, sparking race riots. INTEGRATION came to Birmingham along with other southern cities in 1964, and the city slowly moved toward acceptance. In 1979, Birmingham elected its first black mayor. In 1992 the city opened an institute that documents its role in the struggle for civil rights.

BIBLIOGRAPHY

Garrow, David J., ed. *Birmingham, Alabama, 1956–1963: The Black Struggle for Civil Rights.* Vol. 8, *Martin Luther King, Jr. and the Civil Rights Movement.* Brooklyn, N.Y.: Carlson Pub., 1989.

Lamonte, Edward Shannon. *Politics and Welfare in Birmingham, 1900–1975.* Tuscaloosa: University of Alabama Press, 1995.

Lewis, W. David. *Sloss Furnaces and the Rise of the Birmingham District: An Industrial Epic.* Tuscaloosa: University of Alabama Press, 1994.

McWhorter, Diane. *Carry Me Home: Birmingham, Alabama: The Climactic Battle of the Civil Rights Revolution.* New York: Simon and Schuster, 2001.

Bobby M. Wilson / C. P.

See also **Rustbelt.**

BIRTH CONTROL. The term "birth control" was coined by Margaret Sanger in 1921, when she founded the American Birth Control League (later Planned Parenthood). She believed that women should have control over their own bodies and their own pregnancies. Though she recognized birth control in larger social and political contexts and was criticized for working too closely with the eugenics movement, she saw it clearly as a health issue for women. Sanger worked as a nurse in New York City's "Hell's Kitchen" and saw women's health suffering as the result of many pregnancies. Her own mother died of tuberculosis after bearing eleven children.

Sanger had promoted the use of birth control in the decade before 1921 as a means to less restrictive sexuality for women. But such claims were considered far too radical and would not facilitate legalizing contraceptives. Contraceptives had become illegal in the United States in 1873 in a Victorian purity crusade led by Anthony Comstock. For centuries, couples had used a variety of methods of birth control—animal skin condoms, vaginal sponges, douches, abstinence, abortion—but nineteenth-century technology brought rubber condoms into mass production and the mass market. The Comstock laws prohibited all contraceptives and contraceptive information, categorizing them as obscenity. The movement to make them legal again would gain momentum with the aid of the American Medical Association, which promoted birth control as a public health issue.

More permissive attitudes toward sexual behavior developed in the twentieth century—flappers of the 1920s flaunted apparent promiscuity, and by the 1940s the automobile allowed for more privacy in dating, and vending machines were dispensing condoms. Still, numbers of unmarried women having sexual intercourse remained comparatively low until the 1960s. Contraceptives were generally intended for, and used by, married couples. The sexual revolution and the introduction of the birth control pill in the 1960s would change that. The United States Supreme Court ruled against a Connecticut law prohibiting the dispensing of contraceptives to married couples in *Griswold v. Connecticut* (1965), a move that paralleled changing attitudes toward birth control in American society. The women's movement embraced reproductive rights as fundamental to progress for women in the workplace, education, and politics, as they could more easily limit their family size.

The birth control pill was promoted as liberating for women as it did not interfere in the act of sexual intercourse, and it was nearly 100 percent effective. In turn, it was embraced by men, as women became less inhibited in sex because the fear of pregnancy was removed. Other forms of contraceptives such as intrauterine devices and Norplant were marketed in subsequent decades, and while each involved risks, women readily accepted them.

BIBLIOGRAPHY

Gordon, Linda. *The Moral Property of Women: A History of Birth Control Politics in America.* 3rd ed. Chicago: University of Illinois Press, 2002.

Tone, Andrea. *Devices and Desires: A History of Contraceptives in America.* New York: Hill and Wang, 2001.

Kathleen A. Tobin

See also **Griswold v. Connecticut.**

BIRTH CONTROL MOVEMENT. A birth control movement did not exist in the United States in the nineteenth century; still, the birth rate steadily declined from 1800. Women prevented conception by a number of different methods—abstinence, breastfeeding for long periods, male withdrawal before ejaculation, douching with common ingredients, abortifacients such as pennyroyal, condoms made from linen or animal intestines, and homemade sponges.

Reformers advocated various forms of birth control beginning in the 1830s. The 1830s and 1840s were a period when Americans were receptive to experimental ideas. In 1831 Robert Dale Owen, son of utopian socialist Robert Owen, wrote the first major American book on birth control, *Moral Physiology; or, A Brief and Plain Treatise on the Population Question.* In this book he reviewed available birth control methods—the condom, the vaginal sponge, and coitus interruptus. He recommended the latter as the best choice. This work led Charles Knowlton, a physician, to write in 1832 a more thoroughgoing tract on birth control, *Fruits of Philosophy; or, The Private Companion of Young Married People.* Not satisfied with Owen's choice, he worked diligently to find another, more realistic method of birth control. After some thought on the subject, he advocated that women douche with a spermicidal solution after intercourse. Both books were also philosophical treatises on the benefits to society of family planning.

Birth control was revolutionized by the vulcanization of rubber in 1837. After it had been refined to a thinner more flexible product, innovations began to emerge in the 1850s and 1860s which made use of this new medium—condoms, male caps (which covered only the tip of the penis), douching devices, and womb veils or diaphragms. All were available from commercial sources. Edward Bliss Foote, a physician, advocated the womb veil in his 1864 edition of *Medical Common Sense.*

The ready availability of contraceptive devices on the commercial market led Anthony Comstock, a moral crusader, to try to curb the trade. In 1873, at the behest of Comstock, Congress included clauses in a postal act defining obscene materials barred from the mail. Included in the definition of obscenity was any drug or device that prevented conception or produced abortion, or any literature that discussed birth control or abortion. The Comstock Act provided punishment of fines from $100 to $5,000 and/or imprisonment at hard labor from one to ten years for those who put obscene materials in the mails. Commercial birth control purveyors disguised their products with words that conveyed safety and security for married men and women, enabling a healthy market in birth control to grow during the Comstock era. Because of a lack of postal agents to enforce the law, most of this trade went unpunished. Little Comstock laws—state laws such as one in New York—made it illegal to give away or sell contraceptive information or products. In this atmosphere the early birth control movement arose. The Comstock law had made birth control a criminal enter-

prise. Abortion was also made illegal in most states by 1870.

By the 1870s feminists such as Elizabeth Cady Stanton were espousing voluntary motherhood. They were not advocating contraception, but rather abstinence or a woman's right to refuse sexual relations with her husband. In the early 1900s radical socialists and anarchists, especially Emma Goldman, addressed the birth control issue. Goldman, an immigrant and anarchist from Russia, was the most active spokesperson for birth control during this period. She wrote about contraception in her publication, *Mother Earth,* as early as 1906 and gave lectures on the subject in 1910. She smuggled contraceptives into the U.S. from Europe, and printed up birth control pamphlets. Though active on the subject of birth control, she had many other interests and never devoted herself exclusively to that cause. She became the mentor of Margaret Sanger, who became the foremost leader of the birth control movement in the United States. Women and men in radical groups, which formed birth control leagues all over the country, supported Sanger.

Margaret Sanger and the Comstock Act

In 1911 Margaret Sanger, newly married and educated as a nurse, moved to New York City and joined the Socialist Party, which was then enjoying its greatest popularity in U.S. history. There she met the leading radicals of the period and began to write articles for the *New York Call* on sex education. One of her columns on venereal disease caused issues of the *Call* to be seized by the postal department in 1912. Sanger's mother had borne eleven children and had died of tuberculosis at age 49. Sanger was attracted to the birth control issue because of her mother's death, her work with poor women on the Lower East Side of New York, and her belief that women's sexual experience was diminished by the fear of unwanted pregnancy.

Sanger went to Europe in 1913 and began investigating birth control methods. She found that in France birth control was perfectly acceptable. Upon her return to the United States, Sanger published a periodical called *The Woman Rebel,* in which she first used the term birth control. The postal authorities subsequently suppressed the publication. Indicted for violation of the postal code, Sanger left for Europe. She left 100,000 copies of a pamphlet called *Family Limitation,* which described condoms, douches, and cervical caps, to be distributed when she signaled. The news of her indictment caused local birth control groups to form all over the country during 1914 and 1915.

While she was in Europe, she visited the Netherlands; there she found birth control centers where doctors individually fitted women with advanced spring-type diaphragms, which were more reliable and better-fitting than the womb veil. This provided her with a model for her work in the United States when she returned in 1915.

The government dropped the charges against Sanger in 1916 because of extensive publicity surrounding the case. This development allowed her to open a birth control clinic in Brooklyn on 16 October 1916. She and her sister, Ethel Byrne, ran the clinic and dispensed birth control information and devices. The police closed down the clinic under the New York law after only ten days. Her trial and imprisonment for this act made her renowned. The appeal of her case led to a breakthrough for the birth control movement. In 1918 Judge Frederick Crane of the Court of Appeals of New York stated in his decision that doctors could prescribe birth control to women for the cure and prevention of disease. Sanger took this as a mandate to open birth control clinics staffed by physicians. Condom manufacturers saw it as the chance to sell condoms. Their business thrived to the dismay of Sanger, who wanted woman-controlled birth control.

Sanger forged ahead with the loophole granted her by the judge's decision, but she was opposed by Mary Ware Dennett, a birth control reformer in her own right and founder of the National Birth Control League, later the Voluntary Parenthood League. Dennett was striving for complete abolition of the laws against the dispensing of birth control devices and information. She considered Sanger's strategy a capitulation to the moral crusaders; birth control should be freely dispensed, not controlled exclusively by the medical establishment.

The American Birth Control League and the growth of clinics.
In 1921 Sanger organized the American Birth Control League (ABCL). Soon she began to cultivate wealthy people to back birth control clinics. Her second marriage to J. Noah Slee, president of the Three-in-One Oil Company, took place in 1922. He became the major contributor to the ABCL. In 1923 Sanger opened the Clinical Research Bureau in New York City, later the Birth Control Clinical Research Bureau (BCCRB), the first legal clinic in the United States to be staffed by a physician. Slee funded a manufacturer, Holland-Rantos Company, to make diaphragms to Sanger's specifications for dispensing by private physicians and by those at ABCL clinics.

Other events indicated that there was a major shift in the country's attitude toward birth control. The courts finally reversed the Comstock Act's definition of birth control as obscenity in *United States v. One Package* (1936). This opened the way for contraceptive materials to be mailed to physicians. In 1937 the American Medical Association agreed that birth control should be taught in medical schools, and by 1938 ABCL had opened three hundred birth control clinics across the nation. In 1942 Sanger founded Planned Parenthood, the successor to the ABCL, and she had a role in the 1952 founding of International Planned Parenthood.

Development of the Pill
Still Sanger was not satisfied. Clinics were reaching only a small percentage of the population and most people relied on commercial products for birth control. In 1946 she began to think about the development of a pill that,

unlike the diaphragm, would separate sex from birth control. In 1917 Sanger had befriended Katharine Dexter McCormick, one of the first two women to graduate from the Massachusetts Institute of Technology with science degrees. She was the widow of Stanley McCormick, heir to the International Harvester Company fortune. Katharine McCormick had smuggled contraceptives into the United States from Europe for Sanger's clinics for many years. She had written to Sanger in 1950 asking where she could best put her fortune to use. Her interest in biology and birth control motivated her to donate $2 million to the effort to develop the pill.

With this financial backing, Sanger commissioned Dr. Gregory Pincus to develop the pill in 1951. Pincus had developed the first test-tube rabbit embryo, which so scandalized Harvard University that they denied him tenure. He founded his own independent biological laboratory in 1944 and sought grants to keep it funded. For this reason, one of the most brilliant scientists of sexual physiology was available for Sanger's project. His team included John Rock and Min-Chueh Chang. They were aided in their quest by chemists Carl Djerassi and Frank Colton, who synthesized progesterone potent enough to be effective in a pill.

In May 1960 the Food and Drug Administration approved the pill, called Enovid, for use as a contraceptive. The pill quickly became the most popular form of birth control in the United States because of its ease of use, its reliability, and its control by women. Sanger's dream of a woman-controlled pill prescribed by a doctor had come true.

Still there were barriers to its use. Some state laws modeled on the Comstock law were still in force. In Connecticut a state law outlawed the prescription of contraception by a doctor. Planned Parenthood opened a clinic, distributed the pill and challenged the law. The Supreme Court case GRISWOLD V. CONNECTICUT (1965) held that married people had a constitutional right to privacy in the bedroom—and therefore the right to use birth control. Not until 1972 were unmarried people allowed the same privacy rights by *Eisenstadt v. Baird*. Comstockery was finally dead.

Advancement of Birth Control
The pill had been tested on a relatively small sample. When it became widely used, problems emerged, such as blood-clotting disorders that could lead to death. By 1970 when Senator Gaylord Nelson was holding hearings on the safety of the pill, the new women's health movement was advancing. Feminists wanted birth control, but they wanted it to be safe. Two women's health groups had been formed in 1969, the Boston Women's Health Collective and the National Abortion and Reproductive Rights Action League. The hearings were well attended. Women resented the fact that birth control decisions were being made by an all-male group of politicians. Manufacturers lowered the dosage of the pill and, because of the protest

and subsequent regulations, included inserts in the pill's package describing its side effects.

Meanwhile a new doctor-prescribed birth control product was being developed; the IUD (Intrauterine Device) came in a number of different forms such as the Lippes Loop and the DALKON SHIELD. Problems began to arise with these devices as well—especially the Dalkon Shield. Because the FDA only tested drugs, there was no government testing of IUDs. Some of the data presented to the FDA before the Dalkon Shield was marketed was untrue. Eventually it was withdrawn from the market after it had caused hundreds of thousands of injuries and millions of dollars had been awarded in court cases. Other IUDs lost their sheen in the face of the Dalkon Shield publicity.

New birth control methods were developed in the 1980s and 1990s, which separated birth control from sex even more completely than did the pill. Depo-Provera is a hormonal contraceptive injected every three months, while Norplant silicone implants periodically emitted hormones into a woman's system for five years. Norplant was controversial, because silicone was suspected of causing breast cancer in women with silicone breast implants. Though these products were effective, their semipermanency caused concern that they would be used to suppress pregnancy in poor women, just as sterilization laws had once been used. Starting in 1907 states had passed involuntary eugenic sterilization laws, which were not repealed until the 1960s. Under these laws many disabled and poor women had been sterilized.

In the 1990s new hormone regimens were developed—the morning-after pill and Mifepristone, or RU-486. The morning-after pill delivered a high dosage of hormones to delay ovulation and act on cervical mucous to prevent conception. In the early 2000s feminists were working to make this pill available at pharmacies without a prescription so that women could take it within 72 hours of unprotected intercourse, the only time it could be effective.

Mifepristone, an orally ingested hormone for use by prescription in the first three months of pregnancy, caused the lining of the uterus to be shed. Feminists saw these two new drugs as a means of avoiding surgical abortion, which antiabortion groups have made harder to obtain.

The birth control movement made great headway in the twentieth century. From the complete ban on birth control devices at the beginning of the century to the availability of a wide array of products by the end of the century, birth control had revolutionized sexual relations and marriage. In 2000, 80 percent of women had used the pill at some time in their lives. Still, the United States had a greater unwanted pregnancy rate than most industrialized countries and many were still dissatisfied with the methods at their disposal. Many women were tired of birth control responsibility and wanted reliable birth control for men to become a reality.

BIBLIOGRAPHY

The Boston Women's Health Book Collective. *The New Our Bodies, Ourselves: A Book by and for Women*. New York: Simon and Schuster, 1992.

Chen, Constance M. *"The Sex Side of Life": Mary Ware Dennett's Pioneering Battle for Birth Control and Sex Education*. New York: New Press, 1996.

Chesler, Ellen. *Woman of Valor: Margaret Sanger and the Birth Control Movement in America*. New York: Simon and Schuster, 1992.

Gordon, Linda. *Woman's Body, Woman's Right: A Social History of Birth Control*. New York: Grossman, 1976.

Reed, James. *From Private Vice to Public Virtue: The Birth Control Movement and American Society since 1830*. New York: Basic Books, 1978.

Tone, Andrea. *Devices and Desires: A History of Contraceptives in America*. New York: Hill and Wang, 2001.

Watkins, Elizabeth Siegel. *On the Pill: A Social History of Oral Contraceptives 1950–1970*. Baltimore, Md.: Johns Hopkins University Press, 1998.

Bonnie L. Ford

See also **Pro-Choice Movement; Women's Health; Women's Rights Movement.**

BIRTH OF A NATION, THE. The first feature-length film, *The Birth of a Nation* was made in 1915 and concerns the struggles of a southern family during the Civil War and Reconstruction. Directed by David Wark Griffith, *Birth* is as renowned for its technical innovations as it is notorious for its racial stereotypes and violence. Griffith and cameraman G. W. "Billy" Bitzer innovated

The Birth of a Nation. The "heroic" Ku Klux Klan attacks villainous blacks to save white honor in this 1915 melodrama; combining exceptional early filmmaking with some extreme historical distortions, it was reviled by African Americans and others, though southern-born President Woodrow Wilson likened it to "writing history in lightning." THE KOBAL COLLECTION

close-ups, fade-outs, and cross-cutting techniques that revolutionized motion picture production. Griffith based his screenplay on Thomas Dixon Jr.'s best-selling novels *The Leopard's Spots* (1902) and *The Clansman* (1905) and their subsequent adaptation as a touring stage production. After the Civil War, the former Confederate colonel Ben Cameron (Henry B. Walthall) watches as the radical policies of politician Austin Stoneman (Ralph Lewis) allow carpetbaggers and black freedmen to overrun his South Carolina town. A black soldier (Walter Long) assaults Ben's little sister (Mae Marsh), and a mulatto politician (George Seigmann) demands to marry Ben's love interest (Lillian Gish). In response, Ben organizes the Ku Klux Klan, restoring control of the South to southern white men. While *Birth* is remarkably accurate in many historical details, its portrayal of race relations is obscured and exaggerated to justify whites' violent repression of blacks. The film was nevertheless a box-office hit and played in theaters for nearly fifty years, despite persistent controversy and protest.

BIBLIOGRAPHY

Aitken, Roy E. *The Birth of a Nation Story*. As told to Al P. Nelson. Middleburg, Va.: William W. Denlinger, 1965.

Rogin, Michael. " 'The Sword Became a Flashing Vision': D. W. Griffith's *The Birth of a Nation*." In *The New American Studies: Essays from Representations*, edited by Philip Fisher. Berkeley: University of California Press, 1991.

Silva, Fred, ed. *Focus on* The Birth of a Nation. Englewood Cliffs, N.J.: Prentice Hall, 1971.

Kristen L. Rouse

See also **Film Industry.**

BISMARCK ARCHIPELAGO CAMPAIGN

of World War II was fought in Douglas MacArthur's Southwest Pacific area from late 1943 to early 1944. Located just north of New Guinea, these islands were situated along the Allied advance toward the Philippines. The formidable Japanese bastion at Rabaul, on the northern edge of New Britain, presented a serious threat to Allied forces. Thus the campaign had the two objectives of isolating Rabaul and securing bases for further advances toward the Philippines.

The first assaults began in December 1943 with landings on the southern edge of New Britain and concurrent Australian and American advances over the northern coast of New Guinea. In February 1944 MacArthur ordered a hazardous assault on the Admiralty Islands to the north and west of Rabaul. Despite unexpectedly strong Japanese resistance, soldiers of the First Cavalry Division captured the islands, and the excellent anchorage of the Admiralty Islands provided the necessary logistical base for further Allied advances. At the same time Allied possession of these islands isolated and neutralized the Japanese stronghold at Rabaul, thus accomplishing the objectives of this campaign. Operations in these jungle islands were ex-

tremely difficult for soldiers from both sides, as the harsh environment caused diseases, especially malaria and psychological stress. Subsequent scholarship has pointed to the enormous advantage the Americans obtained by breaking Japanese codes.

BIBLIOGRAPHY

Drea, Edward J. *MacArthur's ULTRA: Codebreaking and the War against Japan, 1942–1945*. Lawrence: University Press of Kansas, 1992.

Miller, John. *Cartwheel: The Reduction of Rabaul*. Washington, D.C.: Office of the Chief of Military History, Department of the Army, 1959.

Morison, Samuel Eliot. *History of United States Naval Operations in World War II*. Volume 6: *Breaking the Bismarcks Barrier, 22 July 1942–1 May 1944*. Boston: Little, Brown, 1960.

Leo P. Hirrel

See also **World War II.**

BISMARCK SEA, BATTLE OF

(2–4 March 1943). To reinforce the Japanese garrison at Lae, New Guinea, eight Japanese transports carrying seven thousand troops, escorted by eight destroyers, left Rabaul, New Britain, about midnight on 28 February 1943. Hidden initially by bad weather, the convoy was spotted in the Bismarck Sea by Allied patrol planes on 1 March. Heavy bombers struck the ships on 2 March, but the biggest attack came the following day as the convoy entered Huon Gulf. Brushing aside feeble Japanese air cover, at about 10 A.M. more than three hundred American and Australian bombers and fighters unleashed a devastating attack. Some of the medium bombers used a new "skip bombing" technique, coming in at very low levels, in the manner of torpedo planes, and dropping delay-fuse bombs that bounced from the water to explode against the sides of Japanese ships. These attacks on 3 and 4 March and a quick strike by American motor torpedo boats sank all eight transports as well as four destroyers, at a cost of only four Allied planes. More than half of the Japanese troops were killed, the rest being rescued by Japanese destroyers and submarines. The Japanese never again sent convoys to Lae; subsequent attempts at reinforcement were made only by individual high-speed ships or small coastal craft.

BIBLIOGRAPHY

McAulay, Lex. *Battle of the Bismarck Sea*. New York: St. Martin's, 1991.

Morison, Samuel Eliot. *History of United States Naval Operations in World War II*. Vol. 6, *Breaking the Bismarcks Barrier, 22 July 1942–1 May 1944*. Boston: Little, Brown, 1962.

Null, Gary. *The U.S. Army Air Forces in World War II: Weapon of Denial: Air Power and the Battle for New Guinea*. Washington, D.C.: U.S. Government Printing Office, 1995.

Stanley L. Falk / A. R.

See also **World War II, Air War against Japan.**

BITBURG CONTROVERSY. At the request of West German chancellor Helmut Kohl, President Ronald Reagan visited a military cemetery, Bitburg, in West Germany on 6 May 1985 to honor the war dead buried there and as an expression of reconciliation between wartime enemies. But Reagan's planned appearance stirred up considerable protest and outrage when the public discovered that among the German soldiers buried there were forty-nine members of the notorious SS, the organization that had actively participated in the genocidal policies of Adolf Hitler's Third Reich. Nevertheless Reagan felt obligated to accept Kohl's invitation because Kohl had allowed the placement of American missiles in West Germany in 1983.

After presenting a wreath to the war dead at Bitburg, Reagan later that same day journeyed to the Bergen-Belsen concentration camp. There he delivered a moving speech denouncing Hitler's extermination policies.

BIBLIOGRAPHY

Cannon, Lou. *President Reagan: The Role of a Lifetime.* New York: Simon and Schuster, 1991.

William C. Berman

See also **Germany, Relations with.**

BLACK BELT, a crescent-shaped prairie named for its unusual black soil, extending mostly along the Alabama River in Alabama but also up the Tombigbee River in northeastern Mississippi. Decomposed limestone underlies the belt, causing it to lie lower than the surrounding country and making it more fertile.

Whites entered the Alabama Black Belt after the Creek cession of 1816, but their suspicion of the dark soil kept them from settling the region until the Jacksonian migration of the 1830s. Then whites entered the Mississippi portion as well, replacing indigenous Choctaws and Chickasaws, who had been forced west of the Mississippi. Fertile soil and access to the port at Mobile situated the Black Belt to become a major cotton plantation region. From 1830 to 1860, it was Alabama's most prosperous area, was home to the most slaves, and produced the most cotton. It was also the bulwark of the Whig Party and boasted three of Alabama's five capitals—Cahaba, Tuscaloosa, and Montgomery.

During the Civil War, the Black Belt supplied food to Confederate soldiers. Having almost no railroad connections with the West or North, it remained practically untouched by Northern armies. After the war, it again became the South's leading cotton region, a distinction it lost to Texas by 1880. By the early twentieth century, boll weevil infestations had forced many Black Belt farmers to convert to food crops. Even then, the Black Belt remained the principal cotton region east of the Mississippi.

Today the term "Black Belt" sometimes refers to parts of the South that were dominated by plantation agriculture before the Civil War and thus were home to large numbers of slaves. In Chicago the "Black Belt" was a South Side neighborhood that became heavily African American during the Great Migration of the 1910s and 1920s.

BIBLIOGRAPHY

Fite, Gilbert C. *Cotton Fields No More: Southern Agriculture, 1865–1980.* Lexington: University of Kentucky Press, 1984.

Rogers, William Warren, et al. *Alabama: The History of a Deep South State.* Tuscaloosa: University of Alabama Press, 1994.

R. S. Cotterill / w. p.

See also **Boll Weevil; Cotton; Plantation System of the South.**

BLACK CAUCUS, CONGRESSIONAL (CBC), was formed in 1971 by African American members of the U.S. House of Representatives, with the specific aim of challenging President Richard Nixon's conservative civil rights and social welfare policies. Dominated through 2002 by liberal Democrats from inner-city districts, the CBC annually issued an "alternative budget" that called for increased domestic spending and military cuts. The Caucus lobbied for aid to Africa, sanctions against South Africa under its apartheid regime, as well as expansion of economic opportunities for African Americans. The CBC formed a nonprofit foundation in 1976 to carry out public policy research as well to hold conferences on issues related to the cause of black equality. In the early 2000s, the CBC was criticized for its lack of ideological diversity as well as its inability to work closely with moderate Democrats.

BIBLIOGRAPHY

Singh, Robert. *The Congressional Black Caucus: Racial Politics in the U.S. Congress.* Thousand Oaks, Calif.: Sage Publications, 1988.

Richard M. Flanagan

BLACK CAVALRY IN THE WEST. Established by an act of Congress in 1866, the African American cavalry serving the American West consisted of the Ninth and Tenth Cavalry regiments. Their service covered the expanses of Kansas, Texas, Indian Territory, Nebraska, New Mexico, Arizona, Colorado, and the frigid plains of the Dakotas. Twenty-one Medals of Honor decorated the uniforms of black cavalrymen, and many commendations for valor were conferred upon individual soldiers. As a title of respect, these troopers were called "Buffalo Soldiers" by the Indians, supposedly because they saw a similarity between the hair of the black troopers and that of the buffalo, their sacred animal of the plains.

During their twenty-five years of service, the black cavalrymen fought Indians, bandits, horse thieves, and Mexican revolutionaries. The Ninth Cavalry was ordered into Texas in 1867, where it spent eight years along the Rio Grande housed in run-down posts and serving under the most trying of conditions. In 1881 the Ninth was assigned to duty in Kansas and in Indian Territory. Its task was to keep the "Boomer" settlers out of Indian country. After four years, the Ninth was transferred to Nebraska, Wyoming, and Utah. It participated in the Pine Ridge campaign, helping to quell the last major Indian uprising.

The Tenth Cavalry was assigned to Texas in 1875, after the Ninth received orders to go to New Mexico. It remained along the Rio Grande, taking an active role in running the Apache warrior Victorio back into Mexico. Ten years later, in 1885, the regiment was sent to Arizona to participate in the campaign against Geronimo. Its final achievement was the capture of the Apache chief Mangas Coloradas.

BIBLIOGRAPHY

Kenner, Charles L. *Buffalo Soldiers and Officers of the Ninth Cavalry, 1867–1898: Black and White Together.* Norman: University of Oklahoma Press, 1999.

Kinevan, Marcos E. *Frontier Cavalryman: Lieutenant John Bigelow with the Buffalo Soldiers in Texas.* El Paso: Texas Western Press, 1998.

Schubert, Frank N. *Black Valor: Buffalo Soldiers and the Medal of Honor, 1870–1898.* Wilmington, Del.: Scholarly Resources, 1997.

Arlen L. Fowler
Honor Sachs

See also **African Americans; Army, United States; Black Infantry in the West.**

BLACK CODES were the acts of legislation enacted in the Confederate states in 1865 and 1866 to limit the freedom of recently freed blacks. Some apply the term to Southern antebellum legislation that restricted the action and movements of slaves, although such laws are more frequently referred to as slave codes. Persons using the term "black codes" to include all such laws see the codes as originating in the seventeenth century, continuing until the Civil War, and being reenacted in slightly modified form immediately after the war.

The laws passed in 1865–1866 by the several states did extend some civil and legal rights to freed persons—permitting them to acquire and own property, marry, make contracts, sue and be sued, and testify in court cases involving persons of their own color. But the main purpose of the legislation was to stabilize the black workforce by compelling African Americans to work and by limiting their economic options. The codes typically had provisions for declaring blacks to be vagrants if they were unemployed and without permanent residence. As vagrants, they were subject to being arrested, fined, and bound out for a term of labor if unable to pay the fine. The codes also imposed penalties for refusing to complete a term of labor as well as for breaking an agreement to work when

it was entered into voluntarily. Those who encouraged African Americans to refuse to abide by these restrictive laws were themselves subject to penalties. In like manner, black orphans could be apprenticed to work for a number of years. In many of these cases the whites to whom blacks were assigned turned out to be their former owners. The codes barred African Americans from testifying in court cases involving whites, often prohibited them from bearing firearms, and forbade intermarriage between the races. Of the states with the most restrictive legislation, Mississippi limited the types of property blacks could own, and South Carolina excluded blacks from certain businesses and from skilled trades.

Being strikingly similar to the antebellum slave codes, the black codes were, at the very least, not intended to protect the rights to which African Americans were entitled as free persons. The laws aimed to replace the social controls of slavery, which had been legally swept away by the EMANCIPATION PROCLAMATION and the Thirteenth Amendment, and to reinstate the substance of the slave system without the legal form.

Enactment of black codes in the Southern states was a factor in the conflict within the federal government between the executive and legislative branches for control of the process of RECONSTRUCTION. More than any other single factor, it demonstrated what African Americans could expect from state governments controlled by those who had actively supported the Confederate cause. Northern reaction to the codes helped to produce Radical Reconstruction and the Fourteenth and Fifteenth Amendments, which temporarily removed such legislation from the books. Following Reconstruction, many of the provisions of the black codes were reenacted in the Jim Crow laws that continued in effect until the Civil Rights Act of 1964.

BIBLIOGRAPHY

Foner, Eric. *Reconstruction: America's Unfinished Revolution, 1863–1877.* New York: Harper and Row, 1988.

Franklin, John Hope, and Alfred A. Moss Jr. *From Slavery to Freedom: A History of African Americans.* 7th ed. New York: McGraw-Hill, 1994.

Litwack, Leon F. *Been In the Storm So Long: The Aftermath of Slavery.* New York: Knopf, 1979.

Wilson, Theodore B. *The Black Codes of the South.* Birmingham: University of Alabama Press, 1965.

Henry N. Drewry/c. p.

See also **Code Noir; Jim Crow Laws;** *and vol. 9:* **Black Code of Mississippi; Police Regulations of Saint Landry Parish.**

BLACK FRIDAY (24 September 1869) was the climactic day of an effort by the financiers Jay Gould and James Fisk Jr., with the help of President Ulysses S. Grant's brother-in-law Abel Rathbone Corbin and one or two associates, to corner the ready gold supply of the United States. Because the nation was then on a paper money basis, gold was dealt in as a speculative commodity on the New York exchange. On 2 September Gould began buying gold on a large scale; on 15 September, Fisk also began buying heavily and soon forced the price from $135 to $140. The movement excited much suspicion and fear, and the *New York Tribune* argued that the Treasury had the "plain and imperative" duty to sell gold and break up the conspiracy. Secretary of the Treasury George S. Boutwell visited New York but decided not to act. Meanwhile, Grant had gone to Washington, Pennsylvania, and was out of touch until he returned to Washington, D.C., on 22 September. On 23 September, with gold at $144, the New York panic grew serious.

On 24 September, as the price rose to $160, Secretary Boutwell urged the sale of $3 million of the federal government's gold reserve. Grant suggested $5 million, and Boutwell telegraphed an order to sell $4 million. Gould, perhaps forewarned by the head of the New York subtreasury, had already begun selling, and gold sank rapidly to $135. Fisk immediately found means to repudiate his contracts. The episode ruined scores of investors, caused heavy indirect losses to business, and placed an ugly smirch on the Grant administration. Gould and Fisk made an $11 million profit.

BIBLIOGRAPHY

Ackerman, Kenneth D. *The Gold Ring: Jim Fisk, Jay Gould, and Black Friday, 1869.* New York: Dodd, Mead, 1988.

Boutwell, George S. *Reminiscences of Sixty Years in Public Affairs.* New York: McClure, Phillips and Co., 1902.

Brands, H. W. *Masters of Enterprise: Giants of American Business from John Jacob Astor and J. P. Morgan to Bill Gates and Oprah Winfrey.* New York: Free Press, 1999.

McFeely, William S. *Grant: A Biography.* Newtown, Conn.: American Political Biography Press, 1996. The original edition was published in 1981.

Allan Nevins/c. p.

See also **Gold Exchange; Political Scandals; Treasury, Department of the.**

BLACK HAWK WAR

BLACK HAWK WAR (1832), a conflict between the United States and a faction of Sauk (or Sac) and Fox Indians, waged mainly in Illinois and Wisconsin. The leader of the Sauk and Fox was an aging chief named Black Hawk, who was the rival of Keokuk, another Sauk chief. Keokuk had been receptive to ceding land to the whites and with his faction of the Sauk and Fox had moved across the Mississippi River to Iowa in 1823. Black Hawk, who had fought on the side of the British in the War of 1812, declined to evacuate his village at Rock Island, Illinois.

At issue was a treaty made at St. Louis in 1804, under the terms of which the Sauk and Fox supposedly agreed to cede all their lands on the eastern side of the Mississippi River and in return remain undisturbed until the country should be opened to settlement. Black Hawk vehemently denied the validity of the 1804 treaty, maintaining that the party of Sauk and Fox who had signed the treaty had had no authority to do so and had been deceived while intoxicated. In 1829, under pressure from Indian agents, a band of Sauk under the leadership of Keokuk moved to the western side of the Mississippi and established a village on the Iowa River. Black Hawk tried to organize the discontented Sauk east of the Mississippi into a confederacy to resist further incursions by the Americans. He believed strongly that the British would back them against American aggression, although support never materialized.

Intertribal conflicts and clashes with settlers came to a head in 1831 when settlers preempted the site of Black Hawk's village at present-day Rock Island, Illinois. Hostilities with the Indians were narrowly averted that year when an army of regulars and Illinois militiamen assembled. Black Hawk yielded to this threat of force and withdrew west across the Mississippi.

Early in 1832, despite the opposition of Keokuk, Black Hawk crossed back into Illinois and moved toward Rock Island with four hundred warriors and their families. The militia ordered Black Hawk to return to Iowa. War erupted after a peaceful emissary sent by Black Hawk was murdered. After Black Hawk won a bloody skirmish, the poorly trained American troops regrouped and strengthened. Battles raged for fifteen weeks and moved up the Rock River into southern Wisconsin. Black Hawk was finally overtaken by a force of American volunteers and defeated on 28 July in a crushing battle in which sixty-eight Indian warriors were killed and many more wounded. The remnant of Black Hawk's forces pushed across southern Wisconsin to the mouth of the Bad Axe River, where on 2 August they were massacred as they attempted to escape across the Mississippi into Iowa. Black Hawk himself escaped but was later captured by the Winnebagos, who turned him over to American troops for the reward.

Under the terms of the peace settlement, signed on 21 September 1832, the Sauk and Fox agreed to cede 6 million acres of land in eastern Iowa, and a tract of 400 square miles was reserved along the western bank of the Mississippi for Keokuk and his followers, who had refrained from hostilities during the war. Nine Sauk and twenty-four Fox signed the treaty. As punishment, Black Hawk was briefly incarcerated in Virginia; he then returned west to Iowa and was placed under the supervision of Keokuk.

BIBLIOGRAPHY

Hagan, William Thomas. *The Sac and Fox Indians.* Norman: University of Oklahoma Press, 1988.

Jackson, Donald, ed. *Black Hawk: An Autobiography.* Chicago: University of Illinois Press, 1964.

Nichols, Roger. *Black Hawk and the Warrior's Path.* Wheeling, Ill.: Harlan Davidson, 1992.

Wallace, Anthony F. *Prelude to Disaster: The Course of Indian-White Relations Which Led to the Black Hawk War of 1832.* Springfield: Illinois State Historical Society, 1970.

Kenneth M. Stewart/ H. S.

See also **Warfare, Indian; Mesquakie; Wars with Indian Nations: Early Nineteenth Century (1783–1840);** *and vol.* 9: **Life of Ma-ka-tai-me-she-kai-kiak.**

BLACK HILLS, a group of mountains in western South Dakota and northeastern Wyoming. The hills were formed by an upthrust of rock dating to the Archean geologic eon through the overlying strata to a maximum height of 7,242 feet above sea level. Harney Peak, the highest point, is the granite core of the upthrust. From the surrounding prairie through the foothills to Harney Peak, each stratum rises in regular order, from shales to gypsum, sandstone, schists, limestones, and granite. As they fold back, these layers afford an unusual opportunity to study the geological formations underlying the region.

The major rivers in the area include the Belle Fourche and the Cheyenne. Most of the forest and timberlands in South Dakota cover the Black Hills region and lie within the Black Hills National Forest. In addition, the area contains one of the nation's largest bison herds. The Black Hills region produces a number of minerals, including gold, silver, lead, copper, iron ore, tin, petroleum, salt, coal, mica, and gypsum.

The Black Hills became part of the Great Sioux Reservation by terms defined in the Laramie Treaty of 1868. However, gold was discovered in the hills in 1874 by miners accompanying General George Custer's expedition. The federal government sought to protect Indian rights to the Black Hills until a new treaty could withdraw those rights. When the Sioux refused to give up the Black Hills, the United States opened the region to gold miners, who rushed to Sioux land seeking the precious metal. The miners first assembled at Custer, South Dakota, where fifteen thousand passed the winter of 1875 to 1876. When gold was found in Deadwood Gulch, there was a stampede from Custer to the new diggings early in 1876, and Deadwood quickly became the most exciting and picturesque gold camp on the continent. The diggings at that time were entirely in placer gravel, but before autumn the Homestake gold mine had been established at Lead and had passed into the hands of San Francisco capitalists. The Homestake mine was developed and for over one hundred years yielded fabulous sums.

The invasion of gold miners led to the Black Hills War, the high point of which was the destruction of Custer's army by the Sioux and Cheyenne on the banks of the Little Bighorn River in June 1876. The Indians lost the war, however, and in 1877 the U.S. government forced a treaty of relinquishment and established a civil government in the region.

In 1925 the Black Hills were chosen as the site for the Mount Rushmore National Memorial. This $1 million enterprise was a massive sculpture carved into granite on the southeast-facing side of Mount Rushmore, northeast of Harney Peak. The memorial depicts the heads of U.S. presidents George Washington, Thomas Jefferson, Theodore Roosevelt, and Abraham Lincoln. It stands five hundred feet above the valley floor, and each president's head stands sixty feet tall. The region is also the site of Wind Cave National Park and Jewel Cave and Devils Tower National Monuments.

The Black Hills remain an area of conflict today. The Sioux continue to fight to regain lands taken by the United States in the 1870s. In 1973 a group of Oglala Sioux and American Indian Movement (AIM) activists seized the town of Wounded Knee and demanded that the U.S. Senate investigate reservation living conditions and honor treaties made in the past. In 1980 the U.S. Supreme Court ordered that the Sioux be paid about $106 million compensation for the seizing of their Black Hills lands. This has complicated the issue for the Sioux, many of whom reject the reparations because they want the Black Hills returned to them.

BIBLIOGRAPHY

Geores, Martha. *Common Ground: The Struggle for Ownership of the Black Hills National Forest.* Lanham, Md.: Rowman and Littlefield, 1996.

Lee, Robert. *Fort Meade and the Black Hills.* Lincoln: University of Nebraska Press, 1991.

Parker, Watson. *Gold in the Black Hills.* Norman: University of Oklahoma Press, 1966.

Peattie, Roderick. *The Black Hills.* American Mountain Series. New York: Vanguard Press, 1952.

Doane Robinson
Honor Sachs

See also **Mount Rushmore; Sioux; South Dakota.**

BLACK HILLS WAR. The Black Hills of western South Dakota and adjacent northeastern Wyoming were hunting grounds, as well as sacred territory, for the western bands of the Sioux, or Dakota, Indians. Under the terms of the Laramie Treaty of 1868, the Black Hills were recognized as part of the Great Sioux Reservation. Although whites were to be excluded from the reservation, persistent rumors of mineral wealth attracted gold seekers. In 1874, yielding to the demands of the prospectors, the U.S. government dispatched troops into the Black Hills under General George Armstrong Custer to establish sites for army posts.

After the Sioux threatened war over the intrusions, the government offered to purchase the land, but the Indians refused to sell. In November 1875 all Indians who had been roaming off the reservation hunting buffalo were ordered to report to their agents, but few of them complied. In March 1876 General George Crook headed north from the Platte River to round up the absentee bands.

In June the military mounted a three-pronged invasion of the Indian country, with Crook leading the attack. Crook was stopped on Rosebud Creek in south central Montana by Oglala Sioux under the war leader Crazy Horse. Crazy Horse joined a large encampment of Northern Cheyenne on the Little Bighorn River, in Montana, where they defeated Custer and his troops on 25 June 1876.

After their victory at the Little Bighorn, the Indians dispersed and were unable to organize against renewed military offensives. Under the terms of a treaty in 1877, the Sioux were obliged to cede the Black Hills for a fraction of their value, and the area was opened to the gold miners.

BIBLIOGRAPHY

Lazarus, Edward. *Black Hills/White Justice: The Sioux Nation Versus the United States: 1775 to the Present.* New York: HarperCollins, 1991.

Robinson, Charles M. *A Good Year to Die: The Story of the Great Sioux War.* New York: Random House, 1995.

Sajna, Mike. *Crazy Horse: The Life behind the Legend.* New York: Wiley, 2000.

Kenneth M. Stewart/H. S.

See also **Laramie, Fort, Treaty of (1868); Little Bighorn, Battle of; Sioux.**

BLACK HORSE CAVALRY

BLACK HORSE CAVALRY was the name applied to a bipartisan group of corrupt legislators in the New York State Assembly in Albany. During the last quarter of the nineteenth century, they gained notoriety by extorting campaign funds and bribes from corporations and other institutions that did business with state government. They usually used blackmail by introducing bills damaging to the business of corporations, bills that would be killed if sufficient payments were forthcoming. Theodore Roosevelt was appalled by the rampant corruption when he entered the state assembly in January 1882, an experience that helped place him on the path of progressive reform.

BIBLIOGRAPHY

Brands, H. W. *T. R.: The Last Romantic.* New York: Basic Books, 1997.

Moscow, Warren. *Politics in the Empire State.* New York: Knopf, 1948.

Harold Zink/A. G.

See also **Corruption, Political; Government Regulation of Business.**

BLACK INFANTRY IN THE WEST

BLACK INFANTRY IN THE WEST. In 1866 Congress authorized six regiments of African American troops (each regiment to consist of ten, sixty-six-man companies) to be included in the regular army. Two of the regiments were designated cavalry and four, infantry. The infantry units were activated as the Thirty-eighth, Thirty-ninth, Fortieth, and Forty-first Infantry regiments. The Thirty-ninth and Fortieth Infantries, which were later consolidated into the Twenty-fifth, were assigned to the South. The Thirty-eighth and Forty-first, which later became the Twenty-fourth Infantry, were sent to the West.

In 1870 the black regiments moved out onto the Texas frontier and began a tour of duty along the Rio Grande that was to last a decade. They participated in many of the army forays into Mexico and contributed to the defeat of the Apache warrior Victorio and to the general pacification of the Texas frontier.

The two regiments separated in 1880, with the Twenty-fourth Infantry moving to Indian Territory and the Twenty-fifth Infantry to Dakota Territory. The Twenty-fourth Infantry remained in Indian Territory for eight years before being assigned to Arizona and New Mexico Territories, where it would finish out the period of Indian wars. While in Arizona, a noncommissioned officer of the Twenty-fourth Infantry won the Medal of Honor for his heroic part in defense of an army paymaster during a robbery attempt.

In Dakota Territory, some Twenty-fifth Infantry units were assigned the task of guarding the Sioux chief Sitting Bull and his people at Fort Randall. The infantry remained in Dakota Territory until the summer of 1888, when it was moved to Montana Territory.

BIBLIOGRAPHY

Fowler, Arlen L. *The Black Infantry in the West, 1869–1891.* Contributions in Afro-American and African Studies Series, no. 6. Westport, Conn.: Greenwood Press, 1971.

Schubert, Frank N. *Black Valor: Buffalo Soldiers and the Medal of Honor, 1870–1898.* Wilmington, Del.: Scholarly Resources, 1997.

Arlen L. Fowler/H. S.

See also **Black Cavalry in the West; Dakota Territory;** *and picture (overleaf).*

BLACK LAWS

BLACK LAWS. Slavery was not legal in Ohio, but the state legislature tried to discourage settlement of free blacks in the state through "black laws," which imposed constraints on black residents. Ohio enacted laws in 1804 and 1807 compelling registration of all African Americans in the state, requiring that they show proof of freedom, forbidding any free black to remain without giving $500 bond against his becoming a public charge, and denying validity to an African American's testimony in trials where whites were involved. The legislature imposed even more restrictions in the 1830s. However, in the legislative session of 1848–1849, a coalition led by the Free Soil Party repealed most of the restrictions.

Black Infantry. Company B of the Twenty-fifth Infantry Regiment, Captain Charles Bentzoni commanding, assembles at Fort Randall, Dakota Territory, in 1882. NATIONAL ARCHIVES AND RECORDS ADMINISTRATION

BIBLIOGRAPHY

Finkelman, Paul. *An Imperfect Union: Slavery, Federalism, and Comity.* Chapel Hill: University of North Carolina Press, 1981.

Horton, James Oliver, and Lois E. Horton. *In Hope of Liberty: Culture, Community, and Protest among Northern Free Blacks, 1700–1860.* New York: Oxford University Press, 1997.

Alvin F. Harlow / C. P.

See also **Free Soil Party.**

BLACK MONDAY STOCK MARKET CRASH

(19 October 1987), a record 508-point plunge of the Dow Jones Industrial Average index of leading stocks that pro- voked fears of a 1929-size depression. The crash abruptly ended a five-year bull market and led to a 17 percent col- lapse of stock values worldwide. Soaring federal and trade deficits, pressure on interest rates, and lack of liquidity in the stock market were blamed for the plunge in share prices. The crisis led to reforms in computerized trading programs and a budget compromise between President and Congress that was designed to reassure investors. The incident reaffirmed the importance of psychology in the stock market's performance.

BIBLIOGRAPHY

Fadiman, Mark. *Rebuilding Wall Street: After the Crash of '87, Fifty Insiders Tell About Putting Wall Street Together Again.* Englewood Cliffs, N.J.: Prentice Hall, 1992.

Metz, Tim. *Black Monday: The Catastrophe of October 19, 1987, and Beyond.* New York: Morrow, 1988.

Bruce J. Evensen / c. p.

See also **Business Cycles; Stock Market; Wall Street.**

BLACK MUSLIMS. *See* **Nation of Islam.**

BLACK NATIONALISM.

The idea that black people should establish a nation-state that would manifest their social and cultural aspirations can be located in the thought of African Americans in the seventeenth and eighteenth centuries. While the particulars of the nationalist idea have changed with shifts in the political and social climate, four elements consistently surface in dialogue about the proposition: assumptions about racial traits and black identity, the prospect of a territorial homeland, the self-help emphasis, and antiwhite ideology.

As white hostility toward free blacks increased throughout the North during the first half of the nineteenth century, black communities launched many self-help institutions such as churches, schools, and benevolent associations. But as political steps taken to disenfranchise free blacks in Northern states spread rapidly, many blacks abandoned the hope of meaningful freedom in the United States and turned their attention to the possibility of migration to Africa, Canada, or other countries.

Expressions of nationalism in this period were grounded in the contemporary ideas about "race" and "nation." Proponents of emigration and a sovereign state assumed that certain inherent values, abilities, and temperaments of black people would provide the cultural and social cohesion necessary to mold a new and just nation. From the perspective of the theories about racial traits characteristic of Western social thought at the time, the goal of a sovereign state seemed logical, if not practical. But leaders like Frederick Douglass rejected the claim that there were inherent differences between blacks and whites and questioned the notion of a nation organized around racial group membership. Douglass conceded the need for blacks to act collectively and aggressively against racial oppression, but he held forth for racial justice on American soil.

The annual Negro Conventions that met from 1830 to 1861 thoroughly debated the merits of colonization and racial separatism. Blacks in several Northern cities launched programs to relocate blacks outside of the United States. In 1816 an ideologically eclectic group of whites formed the AMERICAN COLONIZATION SOCIETY (ACS) to promote and orchestrate colonization of the free black population in Africa. The ACS could claim limited success when, in 1821, despite strong opposition in urban black communities, 17,000 blacks voluntarily migrated to Liberia on the west coast of Africa.

Marcus Garvey in 1922. ASSOCIATED PRESS/WORLD WIDE PHOTOS

Through the abolitionist 1850s, few blacks opted to seek well-being abroad. Yet some of the best-educated blacks, including Edward Wilmot Blyden, Alexander Crummel, and Martin Delaney, continued to press for a black nation on African soil. Emancipation and the defeat of the slaveholding South produced a surge of optimism in black America. A significant number of blacks elected to acquire land in the Midwest and establish all-black towns, under the rubric of state and regional authorities. But as political and economic conditions worsened for blacks at the end of the nineteenth century in the North and South, the ideological seed of racial nationalism found an effective host in Marcus Garvey.

Garvey, born in Jamaica, was an activist for workers' rights and racial justice in his native land and later in London. He formed the Universal Negro Improvement Association (UNIA) in 1914 in Jamaica to promote black self-help programs in the West Indies, Africa, and in the United States, to which he moved in 1916.

Garvey found a receptive audience for his race pride and self-help message. The virulent racism of the first decades of the twentieth century heightened the racial consciousness of the urban black masses. Many Southern blacks had migrated to the industrial North seeking economic gains, yet found themselves relegated to low-paying and irregular employment. Black soldiers returned from World War I and the European theater only to again confront racial hostility. The contrast between the degree of liberty black soldiers enjoyed in Europe and the social climate they were expected to weather in the United

States was dramatic. The agendas of mainstream black organizations like the National Association for the Advancement of Colored People (NAACP) reflected priorities of the nascent black middle class, rather than the concerns of laboring black masses. The UNIA spoke to these needs. It became the largest black mass organization in American history.

Garvey confronted the "race"/"nation" conundrum in an interesting way. He urged that blacks everywhere consider themselves part of a black nation and take aggressive steps to build institutions and enterprises to enhance the well-being of blacks. This formulation dodged the question of a sovereign territory, yet encouraged a "race-first" or Pan-Africanist development. Garvey's foray into territorial separatism led to his downfall. A project to organize a steamship line to build trade with Africa and relocate blacks in Africa ran into management difficulties. Garvey's foes—black and white—pressed to remove him from the political equation in America. He was convicted for mail fraud and served three years in federal prison before receiving a pardon from President Calvin Coolidge and agreeing to leave the country. When the charismatic Garvey was deported, the UNIA declined in both membership and impact

The next forceful expression of racial nationalism came from the NATION OF ISLAM (NOI) under Elijah Muhammad. The NOI (whose members are often referred to as Black Muslims) blended key elements of the Garvey self-help program and demanded land in the South on which to found a black nation. They considered the requested land as reparation for the economic and social subjugation of blacks during slavery. Unlike Garvey, Muhammad's nationalism was religiously grounded in Islam and contained a robust strain of antiwhite ideology that appealed to poor urban blacks. Buoyed by the potential of racial self-sufficiency, the NOI created farms, fisheries, and other businesses designed to break links of dependency with "the white devils." Elijah Muhammad's protégé Malcolm X emerged in 1962 as a militant and charismatic voice for NOI-style nationalism.

In the mid-1960s, the optimism of the Southern civil rights movement collapsed in the face of white indifference. Youthful black-consciousness advocates steered many blacks and intellectuals away from the integrationist ideals of Martin Luther King Jr. and the civil rights campaigns. The term "black nationalism" quickly made its way into the American lexicon, but unlike the earlier land-based nationalism, the term spread into literature, music, and the arts. Paralleling the pan-racial vision of Garvey, cultural nationalists like Amiri Baraka spoke about the "oneness" of African people wherever they were. Arguments about the existence of a black aesthetic leavened the social and cultural thought of the period.

At the start of the twenty-first century, black nationalists had all but abandoned hope for a sovereign state. Yet blacks from across the political spectrum endorse the idea of group self-help even as they debate the govern-

ment's obligation to ameliorate black disadvantage. Continuing patterns of racial inequality and oppression guarantee that a significant number of black people will remain estranged from white society. The national dialogue has now shifted away from polarizing approaches to "blackness" and its meaning, but racial pride and consciousness have veered toward nationalism in times of sharp social conflict. The future of black nationalism is uncertain.

BIBLIOGRAPHY

Evanzz, Karl. *The Messenger: The Rise and Fall of Elijah Muhammad*. New York: Pantheon, 1999.

Franklin, Vincent P. *Black Self-Determination: A Cultural History of the Faith of the Fathers*. Westport, Conn.: Lawrence Hill and Company, 1984.

Fredrickson, George M. Black *Liberation: A Comparative History of Black Ideologies in the United States and South Africa*. New York: Oxford University Press, 1995.

McCartney, John. *Black Power Ideologies: An Essay in African-American Political Thought*. Philadelphia: Temple University Press, 1992

Moses, Wilson Jeremiah, ed. *Classical Black Nationalism: The American Revolution to Marcus Garvey*. New York: New York University Press, 1996.

Vincent, Theodore G. *Black Power and the Garvey Movement*. Rev. ed. Berkeley, Calif.: Ramparts Press, 1972.

William M. Banks

See also **Africa, Relations with; Black Panthers; Black Power; Emigration; Pan-Africanism;** *and vol. 9:* **Black Power Speech.**

BLACK PANTHERS. Organized in Oakland, California, in October 1966 by Huey P. Newton and Bobby Seale, the Black Panther Party for Self-Defense incorporated Marxist ideology into its platform to include demands for health care, housing, employment, and education reforms. A militant stance against police brutality, however, drew most of its media attention, particularly after the group staged an armed protest at the California General Assembly on 2 May 1967 against a proposed ban on concealed weapons. In contrast to separatist groups, the Black Panthers advocated a cross-racial coalition that emphasized both class and racial inequities. Although it failed to become a true mass movement—never growing beyond an estimated five thousand members in thirty-five cities—the Black Panther Party was the target of numerous federal and local police investigations designed to discredit its leadership and weaken its influence.

A short-lived alliance in 1968 with the Student Nonviolent Coordinating Committee was one of many internal tensions that marked the Black Panthers. In February 1971, the Panthers' minister of information, Eldridge Cleaver, already in exile to avoid a prison term, was expelled over ideological differences within the group. Seale faced charges of conspiring to incite a riot at the 1968

Bobby Seale. A founder of the Black Panthers, and a leader of the militant organization until he left in 1974. ARCHIVE PHOTOS, INC.

Democratic National Convention; after his acquittal as part of the Chicago Seven, he ran unsuccessfully for mayor of Oakland in 1973 and left the Black Panthers in 1974. Newton, facing criticism for corruption and an indictment for murder, left in November 1974.

Under the leadership of Elaine Brown, the Black Panthers revived many of their community programs. The group also turned to electoral politics; Brown vied unsuccessfully for a seat on the Oakland City Council in 1973 and 1975 and served as a delegate for candidate Jerry Brown at the 1976 Democratic National Convention. The Black Panthers dissolved in 1982.

BIBLIOGRAPHY

Brown, Elaine. *A Taste of Power: A Black Woman's Story.* New York: Pantheon, 1992.

Foner, Philip S., ed. *The Black Panthers Speak.* Philadelphia: Lippincott, 1970.

Seale, Bobby. *Seize the Time: The Story of the Black Panther Party and Huey P. Newton.* New York: Random House, 1970.

Van Deburg, William L. *Black Camelot: African-American Culture Heroes in Their Times, 1960–1980.* Chicago: University of Chicago Press, 1997.

Timothy G. Borden

See also **Chicago Seven; Student Nonviolent Coordinating Committee.**

BLACK POWER encompasses a political belief in self-determination, anti-racism, and racial consciousness among African Americans. The term became prominently known when, in June 1966 during a protest march in the South, Stokely Carmichael (later Kwame Turé) and Willie Ricks of the STUDENT NONVIOLENT COORDINATING COMMITTEE used the phrase as a rallying cry. The ambiguity of the term led to many different interpretations. The media and some mainstream civil rights organizations saw Black Power as negative because of its perceived anti-white and separatist tone. But others, ranging from black intellectuals to political activists, saw Black Power as a positive expression of cultural nationalism. Over time, it became another means by which black Americans united themselves to achieve equality, freedom, and dignity.

BIBLIOGRAPHY

Carmichael, Stokely, and Charles V. Hamilton. *Black Power: The Politics of Liberation in America.* London: Cape, 1968.

Gates, Henry Louis, Jr., and Kwame Anthony Appiah, eds. "Black Power." In *Africana: The Encyclopedia of the African and African American Experience.* New York: Basic Civitas Books, 1999.

Charles Pete Banner-Haley

See also **African Americans; Radicals and Radicalism;** *and* vol. 9: **Black Power Speech;** *and picture (overleaf).*

BLACK SOX SCANDAL. The Black Sox scandal began with the World Series of October 1919, when eight members of the Chicago White Sox baseball team allegedly conspired to lose to the Cincinnati Reds. The Reds won five games to three at a time when the series could go to nine games. The scandal did not become public until almost a year later, however. In August 1921, a jury found the accused conspirators innocent. Nonetheless, the day after their acquittal the newly appointed commissioner of major league baseball, Judge Kenesaw Mountain Landis, banned them from professional baseball for the rest of their lives.

Gambling had been a presence in baseball long before the Black Sox scandal, and the major league team owners had done little to limit its influence. Rumors of a fix circulated before, during, and after the 1919 series, but the White Sox owner, Charles Comiskey, chose not to investigate them. Prompted by concerns of several jour-

Black Power. Stokely Carmichael, who popularized the phrase, speaks at a 1966 rally in California. AP/WIDE WORLD PHOTOS

nalists and baseball executives, a grand jury investigated allegations over a fixed 1920 season game, which eventually led to investigation of the 1919 series and the indictment of the eight players. None of the gamblers, such as the notorious Arnold Rothstein, who organized the fix, were charged with a crime, however, partly because documents were stolen and bribes paid.

Five of the players—infielders Arnold "Chick" Gandil and Charles "Swede" Risberg, outfielder Oscar "Happy" Felsch, and pitchers Ed Cicotte and Claude "Lefty" Williams—were guilty of throwing the five games. Fred McMullin only batted twice in the series, and infielder Buck Weaver's only crime was remaining silent about the fix. The part played by the great hitter "Shoeless Joe" Jackson, who was illiterate, has been debated ever since.

Baseball survived the Black Sox scandal mostly because gambling's influence declined and Babe Ruth, beginning his Yankee career in 1920, transformed the game.

BIBLIOGRAPHY

Asinof, Eliot. *Eight Men Out: The Black Sox and the 1919 World Series.* New York: Holt, Rinehart, and Winston, 1963.

Seymour, Harold. *Baseball: The Golden Age.* New York: Oxford University Press, 1971.

White, G. Edward. *Creating the National Pastime: Baseball Transforms Itself, 1903–1953.* Princeton, N.J.: Princeton University Press, 1996.

John Syrett

See also **Baseball; Gambling;** *and picture (facing page).*

BLACK SWAMP, a term once applied to much of northwestern Ohio but more accurately to an area lying chiefly in the drainage basin of the Maumee River, including all or parts of a dozen present-day counties. Glacial Lake Maumee once covered this area, leaving behind a level and poorly drained landscape. Drainage difficulties, malarial diseases, and general inaccessibility discouraged whites from settling here long after they had moved into surrounding areas. However, the swamp underwent rapid development after 1850 when German immigrant farmers began draining and settling the land. Today the former Black Swamp constitutes one of the richest farming areas in the state.

BIBLIOGRAPHY

Jones, Robert Leslie. *History of Agriculture in Ohio to 1880.* Kent, Ohio: Kent State University Press, 1983.

Eugene H. Roseboom / w. p.

See also **Defiance, Fort; Wetlands.**

North America. The Blackfeet believe that within the earth, the water, and the sky reside a great variety of natural and supernatural beings. Within Blackfeet territory live not only the Niitsitapi—the original people—but also the Suwitapi, the underwater people and the Spomitapi, the sky people.

The Amskapi Pikuni divided themselves into dozens of bands of related families who lived together. Buffalo played a central role in the religious life of the Blackfeet as well as being their major source of food, clothing, shelter, and tools. In addition to the buffalo, the Blackfeet relied on plant roots and berries for subsistence and medicinal plants. Although often described as nomadic, their travels throughout their territory were strategic. The Blackfeet had extensive knowledge of the land and its uses.

The introduction of the horse (roughly 1725–1750) allowed the Blackfeet to travel greater distances, access a wider range of trading partners, and accumulate more food and material goods. Horses also enabled the Blackfeet to become more effective in controlling access within their territory. The earliest recorded contact between non-Natives and the Blackfeet is by David Thompson, an explorer who spent the winter of 1787 to 1788 with the Piegan in southern Alberta. He recorded that the Piegan had guns, metal pots, and other European objects for at least fifty years before his arrival. After initial contacts with traders, the Blackfeet attempted to control European access to their territory, in order to limit their enemies' access to guns, and to ensure they did not become overly dependent on Europeans themselves.

From the sixteenth century through the nineteenth century, European diseases such as smallpox and consumption wreaked havoc with the Blackfeet and diminished their ability to control their territory. Up to 18,000 Blackfeet died from smallpox during the 1836–1837 pandemic. Throughout this time the Blackfeet attempted to live autonomously and to pray for *missaamipaitapiisin*, a long life.

The Fort Laramie treaty of 1851 and Lame Bull's treaty with the United States (1855) began to define on paper Blackfeet territory. About thirty years later, the buffalo disappeared from the Great Plains. The loss of buffalo destroyed Blackfeet independence. They suffered a debilitating winter in 1883 and 1884 during which many Blackfeet died of starvation. The Blackfeet were forced to sell land on their eastern and western boundaries in 1888 and 1896 for food and moved onto what remained of their homeland.

As the twentieth century began, the Blackfeet needed to find a new livelihood and began to worry about their future, something they had never done before. The buffalo, the key element of their history, religion, and subsistence, were gone. The Blackfeet attempted to cooperate with the U.S. government but consistently struggled for control over their land and themselves. The govern-

"Shoeless Joe" Jackson. One of the best hitters in baseball history—but permanently barred from the Hall of Fame. Though he later confessed to receiving a payoff, his statistics in the 1919 World Series were exemplary.

BLACKFEET. The Blackfeet live on what remains of their ancestral homeland: one reservation in northern Montana and three reserves in southern Alberta, Canada. This Blackfoot Confederacy is made up of three distinct nations who share a common language and a common history: the Kainai or Blood, the Siksika or Blackfoot, and the Northern and Southern Pikuni or Piegan. The Amskapi Pikuni or Southern Piegan live on their reservation in the United States and are known as the Blackfeet.

Blackfeet ancestral territory extends along the east side of the Rocky Mountains from the Yellowstone River in southern Montana, north to the North Saskatchewan River in Canada. Anthropologists believe that the Blackfeet originated in the northeast and migrated to their present location only a few centuries ago, while archaeologists think that their residence reaches back thousands of years. The Blackfeet believe they have always lived in their present location, and their complex mythology speaks of their origin and continued intimacy in this area of

Blackfeet Camp. A view of several tipis on the northern prairie. NATIONAL ARCHIVES AND RECORDS ADMINISTRATION

ment wanted the Blackfeet to convert to Christianity and outlawed many Blackfeet religious practices. The government also started numerous agricultural programs on the reservation. These were paid for by the Blackfeet and over the years either failed or had limited success. The government forced Blackfeet children to attend American schools either on or off the reservation. These institutions suppressed the use of the Blackfeet language and lifeways.

In 1915, the Blackfeet Tribal Business Council (BTBC) was created. The BTBC had limited authority and jurisdiction over the reservation but struggled to be heard in federal decision making. In 1934, the Blackfeet voted to accept the Indian Reorganization Act (IRA), which empowered the BTBC to incorporate and manage tribal property and income. Although the IRA system gave the Blackfeet more authority, it also introduced a foreign government structure into Blackfeet society.

The Blackfeet of the early 2000s are dramatically different from their ancestors. The Blackfeet continue to be extremely religious people, but the majority of Blackfeet are Christian, with most belonging to the Catholic Church. A small minority of Blackfeet join Blackfeet religious societies. English is the first and only language of most Blackfeet; less than 3 percent are fluent in the Blackfeet language.

Despite these changes, many Blackfeet values remain the same. Blackfeet are strongly connected to their homeland and revere their family bonds. The most important value in Blackfeet society, though, remains generosity. Generous people are held in high esteem and individuals are ridiculed if they accumulate wealth without the intention of sharing their good fortune. Blackfeet people continue to pray for good fortune and a long life, not for themselves, but to share with those around them.

Omaq-kat-tsa. A portrait of a chief of the Blackfeet, wearing a feathered headdress. LIBRARY OF CONGRESS

BIBLIOGRAPHY

Duvall, D.C., and Clark Wissler. *Mythology of the Blackfeet Indians.* Lincoln: University of Nebraska Press, 1995. Originally published in 1908 by the American Museum of Natural History.

Ewers, John C. *The Horse in Blackfeet Culture: With Comparative Material from Other Western Tribes.* Washington, D.C.: Smithsonian Institution Press.

Farr, William E. *The Reservation Blackfeet, 1882–1945: A Photographic History of Cultural Survival.* Seattle: University of Washington Press, 1984.

Grinnell, George Bird. *Blackfoot Lodge Tales: The Story of A Prairie People.* Williamstown, Mass.: Corner House Publishers, 1972. Originally published in 1892 by Charles Scribner's Sons.

Holterman, Jack, et al. *A Blackfoot Language Study.* Browning, Mont.: Piegan Institute, 1996.

McClintock, Walter. *The Old North Trail; or Life, Legends and Religion of the Blackfeet Indians.* Lincoln: University of Nebraska, 1968. Originally published in 1910 in England.

Rosier, Paul. *Rebirth of the Blackfeet Nation, 1912–1954.* Lincoln: University of Nebraska Press, 2001.

Rosalyn LaPier

See also vol. 9: **Fort Laramie Treaty of 1851.**

BLACKLISTING, an employer practice of excluding politically "undesirable" individuals from the job market. Originating in the 1830s, blacklisting, along with use of agents provocateurs and injunctions, was a widely popular anti-union weapon. Employers usually provided blacklists upon request and sometimes circulated lists through employers associations. Blacklists continued to be used following the Civil War, especially as violence between labor and business escalated in the late nineteenth century. Despite attempts to curb blacklisting, employers could easily communicate with one another in secret, making blacklists a fact of life before the 1930s. In 1935 the NATIONAL LABOR RELATIONS ACT, or Wagner Act, brought a measure of effective control by establishing the right to collective bargaining.

The COLD WAR added a new dimension to blacklists. Investigations into Communist activities in America resulted in the expulsion of Communists from trade unions and of Communist-dominated unions from national labor organizations. The most glaring example of blacklisting resulted from congressional investigations, the most celebrated of which was that of the so-called Hollywood Ten, who went to jail rather than answer questions concerning their political affiliations. In the subsequent exhaustive probe into the entertainment world, uncooperative individuals were placed on a blacklist and barred from employment in motion pictures, television, and radio for the next decade. Although blacklisted writers managed to continue working under assumed names, most blacklisted actors left the country or found other employment. Some found work in the theater because legitimate theater organizations, such as the Actors' Equity Association and the League of New York Theatres, were able to enforce a mutually agreed-upon antiblacklisting resolution.

BIBLIOGRAPHY

Ceplair, Larry, and Steven Englund. *The Inquisition in Hollywood.* Garden City, N.Y.: Anchor, 1980.

Meltzer, Milton. *Bread—And Roses: The Struggle of American Labor, 1865–1915.* New York: Facts on File, 1991.

Vaughn, Robert. *Only Victims: A Study of Show Business Blacklisting.* New York: Putnam, 1972.

Joseph A. Dowling/c. w.

See also **Injunctions, Labor; Labor Legislation and Administration; Subversion, Communist.**

BLACKSMITHING. In colonial times, the blacksmith was an important part of the community. In 1607 the first colony at Jamestown brought over a blacksmith.

Blacksmithing. A blacksmith—to some extent a forerunner of the modern ironworker—and his helper work in front of the Clinch River at the site of Norris Dam in Tennessee. The dam was the first project of the Tennessee Valley Authority and was completed in 1936. NATIONAL ARCHIVES AND RECORDS ADMINISTRATION

In 1810 Pennsylvania reported 2,562 blacksmith shops doing $1,572,627 worth of work. In 1850 the United States had 100,000 blacksmiths and whitesmiths, in addition to gunsmiths and machinists.

The basic equipment of the blacksmith shop was forge and bellows, anvil and slack tup, hammer and tongs, swage and cutter, chisel and punch, and file and drill. The blacksmith not only made shoes for horses and oxen and applied them but also made such hardware as latches, hinges, andirons, farm tools, nails, hammers, axes, chisels, and carving tools. In horse-drawn society he was the mainstay of transportation. He welded and fitted wagon tires and hub rings and made and fitted all metal parts of wagons, carriages, and sleighs. Moreover, he was the single source of decorative ironwork for fine houses. Most skilled of all blacksmiths were those who shaped iron to the precise and intricate needs of ships. Warships and whaling vessels usually carried their own blacksmiths to repair fittings and guns at sea and to make grappling hooks and harpoons.

In the latter part of the twentieth century, blacksmiths had all but disappeared from the American scene. A few dressed picks and mattocks, air drills, stone chisels, and various knives used in industry. Others, known as farriers, worked in rural areas caring for racing and riding horses, though these were more in demand for their veterinary practices than for their knowledge of ironworking.

BIBLIOGRAPHY

Bayly, E. Marks. "Skilled Blacks in Antebellum St. Mary's County, Maryland." *Journal of Southern History* 53 (1987): 537–564.

Bezis-Selfa, John. "A Tale of Two Ironworks: Slavery, Free Labor, Work, and Resistance in the Early Republic." *William and Mary Quarterly* 56 (1999): 677–700.

Daniels, Christine. "Wanted: A Blacksmith Who Understands Plantation Work: Artisans in Maryland, 1700–1810." *William and Mary Quarterly* 50 (1993): 743–767.

Herbert Manchester / A. E.

See also **Hardware Trade; Industries, Colonial; Iron and Steel Industry; Metalwork; Wagon Manufacture.**

BLAND-ALLISON ACT, the first of several U.S. government subsidies to silver producers in depression periods. The five-year depression following the panic of 1873 caused cheap-money advocates (led by Representative R. P. Bland of Missouri) to join with silver-producing interests in urging a return to BIMETALLISM, the use of both silver and gold as a monetary standard. The controversial mint reform act of 1873 eliminated the coinage of silver at a time when increased supplies from newly discovered Western mines were lowering prices. Silver advocates, decrying the so-called Crime of '73, demanded restoration of free coinage of silver at a ratio to gold of 16 to 1, approximately $1.29 an ounce.

Free coinage, as the symbol of justice for the poor, was seized upon by others determined to prevent resumption of specie payments (the redemption, in metallic coin, of U.S. paper money by banks or the Treasury) and desirous of plentiful inflationary currency. Bland's bill for free coinage, passed by the House on 5 November 1877, jeopardized Secretary of the Treasury John Sherman's plans for resuming specie payments. Sherman, through a Senate amendment sponsored by Senator W. B. Allison of Iowa, was able to substitute less inflationary limited purchases for free coinage. Silver producers accepted the arrangement as likely to restore silver to $1.29.

The law, passed 28 February 1878 over President Rutherford B. Hayes's veto, required government purchases, at market prices, of $2 million to $4 million worth of silver bullion monthly, and coinage into legal tender 16-to-1 dollars, exchangeable for $10 silver certificates. The president was directed to arrange an international bimetallic conference to meet within six months. These provisions signified victory for producers over inflationists.

BIBLIOGRAPHY

Nugent, Walter T. K. *Money and American Society, 1865–1880.* New York: Free Press, 1968.

Unger, Irwin. *The Greenback Era: A Social and Political History of American Finance, 1865–1879.* Princeton, N.J.: Princeton University Press, 1964.

Weinstein, Allen. *Prelude to Populism: Origins of the Silver Issue, 1867–1878.* New Haven, Conn.: Yale University Press, 1970.

Jeannette P. Nichols / T. M.

See also **Free Silver; Resumption Act; Sherman Silver Purchase Act; Silver Legislation.**

BLAST FURNACES, EARLY.

Blast furnaces use fuel to smelt iron ore, often with a flux to facilitate the process. The molten ore, separated from impurities, is poured into forms. Though sometimes formed into final cast products, more typically early blast furnace molten ore was cooled into ingots or "pigs." Foundries used the pigs as input for molten iron, then cast the iron into final products. Though using more fuel, this two-step heating process further refined the iron. In forges, ingots were heated, then beaten into shapes, producing wrought or bar iron that could then be processed into final products. The intermittent heating and beating further removed impurities and strengthened the product. Blast furnaces therefore produced primarily intermediate goods, pig and bar iron, that were further refined in forges and foundries.

Eighteenth-century consumers used a growing array of iron and steel products including stoves, fireplaces, nails, scythes, irons, hoes, axes, saws and other tools, pots, pans, and ships' hardware. Warfare created demand for iron armaments and ammunition. Refinement of iron bars required heavy iron hammers and anvils. With application of steam power to production and transportation, demand increased for iron machinery, steamboat parts, and, later, locomotives, train car parts, and rails. By the latter part of the nineteenth century, more sophisticated blast furnaces produced vast amounts of iron and steel for railroad transportation and for such urban uses as structures and pipes.

The product of blast furnaces weighed less than the raw material inputs, so that furnace location tended to be near raw materials rather than consumers. Depending on time and place, production varied by the fuel used, the quality of ore and fuel, the product produced, and the degree of vertical integration. Early colonial blast furnaces used charcoal as fuel, giving land-abundant America an advantage over deforested Europe. American charcoal iron producers integrated fuel and iron production, often on plantations of extensive acreage. Early blast furnaces were strong in local markets, but national industrial concentration was low. Early furnaces were tied to ore deposits, which were relatively abundant especially in Pennsylvania, Virginia, and the bogs of New Jersey. Secretary of the Treasury Albert Gallatin's 1810 report on manufactures counted 530 furnaces and forges and noted that iron ore was found in every state.

England shifted to coal as fuel for its iron production in the late eighteenth century, but the American colonies continued to rely on charcoal because eastern coal was difficult-to-ignite anthracite. The more combustible Appalachian bituminous coal deposits were to the west. By 1840, technological change had led to furnaces that could generate sufficient heat to burn anthracite coals. Charcoal plantation iron production gave way to anthracite and then, with westward movement, also bituminous coal production. Producers could control the purity of charcoal better than that of coal, which allowed continued production with charcoal until high-quality coke could be produced. Iron production shifted both technologically and in terms of location to coal sources; output and scale increased.

Eighteenth- and nineteenth-century ironmasters did not know the science that underlay the considerable variation in chemical composition of iron ore deposits. Experience taught expert ironmasters which combinations of ore, fuel, and flux produced the best intermediate iron for different final products. Steel, an alloy of iron and carbon, could only be produced in small quantities with antebellum technology. The development of Bessemer and open-hearth furnaces in the 1870s permitted production of large quantities of steel, concentrated both geographically and industrially.

BIBLIOGRAPHY

Clark, Victor S. *History of Manufactures in the United States.* 3 vols. New York: McGraw-Hill for the Carnegie Institution of Washington, 1929. Reprint, New York: Peter Smith, 1949.

Hogan, William Thomas. *Economic History of the Iron and Steel Industry in the United States.* 5 vols. Lexington, Mass: Heath, 1971.

Temin, Peter. *Iron and Steel in Nineteenth-Century America: An Economic Inquiry.* Cambridge, Mass.: MIT Press, 1964.

Ann Harper Fender

BLIZZARDS

are defined by the National Weather Service as winter storms with sustained or gusting winds of 35 mph that produce blowing or drifting snow that reduces visibility to one-quarter mile or less for over three hours. While this is the technical definition of the word, for most people any sustained snowstorm accompanied by fierce winds is considered a blizzard. Blizzards are often, but not always, accompanied by extremely cold temperatures. They are most common in the Great Plains, the Great Lakes states, and the northeastern states along the coast, and less common in the Pacific Northwest.

The earliest European settlers in the colonies were stunned by the ferocity of North American blizzards. In 1717 a blizzard hit the eastern seaboard and was known as the "Great Snow" for more than a century. During this storm three to four feet of snow fell and harsh winds whipped it into twenty-five-foot drifts.

By the nineteenth century settlement had stretched westward, and settlers there were exposed to the howling winds and heavy snows of the prairie and plains areas. Railroads were frequently stalled by heavy snows. Food and fuel shortages could develop over time if a blizzard persisted for days on end. Fires were also a hazard in blizzards as stoves were overworked and water lines froze, preventing effective fire suppression. Telegraph, electric, and phone lines could be toppled. And the new suspension bridges could collapse under the heavy load of snow and ice.

January in Ketchikan. Snowbanks partially obscure buildings in this Alaskan town. NATIONAL ARCHIVES AND RECORDS ADMINISTRATION

Major blizzards racked the nation during the nineteenth century. In October of 1846 a blizzard struck northern California. Over eight days, heavy snows resulted in forty-foot drifts over Truckee Pass. The DONNER PARTY of eighty-seven was trapped on the mountain, and when spring finally came in April of that year only forty-seven made their way back down. Cannibalism was reported here and elsewhere during blizzards in isolated western regions. In 1873 a major blizzard struck the northern Great Plains, leaving at least seventy people dead and paralyzing the railroad system for much of the winter.

In January of 1888 a blizzard struck the Great Plains, with deep snow and rapidly falling temperatures. The thermometer dropped sixty degrees in eighteen hours. Many of the 200 dead were children trying to make their way home from school. Later that year came the "Blizzard of '88." This storm still warrants inclusion in many history books for its sheer size and ferocity. From the Chesapeake Bay to Nantucket nearly 200 ships were damaged or destroyed. Then, from 10 to 14 March, the eastern seaboard was pummeled. From two to four feet of snow fell over three days across much of the region. Freezing temperatures were accompanied by wind gusts of over 70 mph across New York City. The snow drifted more than twenty feet deep, covering vehicles and even the first floors of some New York City structures. People in the city were trapped in elevated cars, stores, trains, and offices. In Connecticut and Massachusetts, forty to fifty inches of snow fell and formed drifts up to fifty feet deep. Entire houses and trains were buried. At the end of the storm more than 400 people had died.

By the twentieth century new technologies helped people deal with the consequences of blizzards. Massive plows could be attached to locomotives or trucks. Telegraphs and phones could be used to report approaching blizzard conditions. And by later in the century, sophisticated weather tracking and warning systems were in place. In Washington, D.C., from 27 to 29 January 1922, a winter storm buffeted the city, leaving nearly two feet of snow. It became known as the "Knickerbocker Storm" because the roof of the Knickerbocker Theater collapsed, killing nearly 100 inside. In 1941, March started out warm in the upper Midwest, and duck hunters took to the lakes when the season opened. But on 15 March a sudden blizzard whipped up and more than seventy died in the Dakotas, Minnesota, Wisconsin, and Michigan. A famous blizzard struck Chicago in 1967 when a series of strong storms struck at the western edge of Lake Michigan. It began on 26 January, and by the next day two feet of snow covered the city. It took two weeks to clear the snow; during that time sixty people died and the city experienced heavy looting.

In the late twentieth century two major storm periods racked the nation. The "Superstorm of 1993" (some called it the "Blizzard of the Century") arrived in March of that year involving nearly two-thirds of the entire nation and setting snowfall records across the eastern seaboard. Blizzard conditions existed from Alabama to Massachusetts, where some termed the storm a "white hurricane." To the west lay a vast track of thunderstorms, tornadoes, and floods. At least ninety-two died in the series of storms. In 1996 came another "Blizzard of the Century," blasting the snowfall records set in 1993. The storm came in three major parts, again affecting nearly two-thirds of the continental United States. It began in the southeast, striking from 6 to 8 January. As it moved north, it left more than four feet of snow in places like Virginia, a record snowfall. Nearly three feet of snow fell in Pennsylvania and two feet in parts of New York and New Jersey. Nine states were virtually paralyzed, and more than 100 people died. A week later, 11–13 January, another storm rocked the northeast. The following week, 17–18 January, a major blizzard struck the central and northern plains.

Yet another season of major winter storms and blizzards arrived the next November, beginning with massive ice storms. Blizzards struck some areas of the Great Plains and Great Lakes two times a week in a repeated pattern that left record snow amounts of two to three feet per blizzard. Winter temperatures reached minus eighty degrees with wind chills. Total snowfall in some Great Plains and Great Lakes areas exceeded 100 inches. The fall and

Blizzard in New York. Street-cleaning efforts following a severe winter snowstorm, 1899. LIBRARY OF CONGRESS

winter storms left a season of disastrous flooding from the Red River of the north to parts of the Upper Mississippi.

BIBLIOGRAPHY

Cable, Mary. *The Blizzard of '88*. New York: Atheneum, 1988.

Polly Fry

See also **Disasters; Weather Service, National.**

BLOCKADE, the closing by sea of the coasts and ports of an enemy in such a manner as to cut off entirely the enemy's maritime communications. Naval blockades have played a prominent role in U.S. diplomacy since the Revolutionary era. At that time, the United States had a small navy and a large merchant marine and therefore sought to limit the scope and uses of blockades. In 1784 the Continental Congress argued that a blockade was legitimate only if a nation closely patrolled an enemy's coast and ports. During the Napoleonic wars, however, Britain and France went far beyond this definition in order to cripple each other. In May 1806 Britain declared a blockade around the entire European coast, from the Elbe River to the port of Brest, although the British had far too few ships to patrol such a vast area. Napoleon responded by closing all European ports under his control to British shipping and to neutral vessels that had either traded at a British port or been searched by British cruisers. The United States protested that these declarations went far beyond the traditional practice of blockade. In his 1812 war message to Congress, President James Madison named Britain's "mock blockade" as one of the chief grievances of the United States against the British.

Ultimately, the American limited definition of blockades prevailed. The Declaration of Paris (1856) stipulated that a blockade was binding only if the nation involved maintained "a force sufficient really to prevent access to the coast of the enemy." Ironically, the United States did not sign the declaration, because it objected to another provision in the agreement outlawing privateers, and large-scale blockades became central to American military strategy. At the onset of the Civil War, President Abraham Lincoln proclaimed a blockade of the Confederate coast, which proved vital to the Union's victory. After the Civil War the United States became a naval power and moved away from its limited definition of blockades. American forces, for example, often relied on the expansive doctrine of "continuous voyage," which held that a nation could seize foreign ships destined for neutral countries if it could prove that their cargo would eventually reach a blockaded port.

By the time of World War I the development of submarines, mines, and long-range artillery made traditional "close" blockades almost impossible. During the war Britain rejected the Declaration of Paris and used minefields and cruiser patrols to establish a "far" blockade around Germany. Although the United States protested this action, German naval strategy soon outraged Americans even more. In 1915 the Germans exacerbated tensions with the United States when they announced a policy of unrestricted submarine warfare in the waters surrounding Great Britain. This "blockade," which many Americans construed as a flagrant violation of traditional warfare, eventually brought the United States into the war on the side of the Allies. In World War II, submarines and aircraft again altered the nature of blockades. During the conflict the United States and Britain employed a long-range air and naval blockade against Germany, while the Germans used unrestricted submarine warfare against the Allies. Blockades also shaped the course of the Cold War. In 1962 the United States imposed a "quarantine" of Cuba to stop the Soviet Union from shipping offensive weapons to Cuba and to force the Soviets to dismantle missiles already on the island.

BIBLIOGRAPHY

Bess, H. David, and Martin T. Farris. *U.S. Maritime Policy*. Westport, Conn.: Greenwood Press, 1981.

Freedman, Lawrence. *Kennedy's Wars*. New York: Oxford University Press, 2002.

Hickey, Donald R. *The War of 1812*. Urbana: University of Illinois Press, 1995.

LaFeber, Walter. *The American Age*. New York: Norton, 1994.

Spivak, Burton. *Jefferson's English Crisis, 1803–1809*. Charlottesville: University Press of Virginia, 1979.

Ronald Spector / E. M.

See also **Contraband of War; Neutral Rights; Neutrality; Trade with the Enemy Acts.**

BLOCKADE RUNNERS, CONFEDERATE. On 16 April 1861, during the American Civil War, President

Abraham Lincoln proclaimed a naval blockade of the Confederacy's 3,500 miles of coastline. The effectiveness of the blockade increased after early Union victories along the coast, elevating the risk of capture from an average of one in ten in 1861 to one in three by 1864. The trade with other countries by running the blockade proved highly lucrative. The value to the Confederacy is told in the record of 1.25 million bales of cotton run out as well as in 600,000 small arms and other munitions, endless supplies of provisions, clothing, hospital stores, manufactures, and luxuries run in. The estimated value of the goods entering the Confederacy is $200 million.

Had it not been for the blockade runners, the Confederate armies more than once would have been on the verge of starvation. Except for the increasing stringency of the blockade, the runners might have enabled the South to win its independence by keeping a federal squadron of six hundred vessels occupied. Furthermore, runners afforded the one means of outside communication.

Blockade running had its disadvantages, however. The traffic drained away the gold supply, contributing to depreciation of Confederate currency. It drew attention to the ports, probably precipitating attacks on their defenses. The yellow fever scourge in Wilmington, Delaware, had its source in a blockade runner. The traffic also stimulated a hunger for speculation and the riotous living of the blockade-running gentry, demoralizing many citizens.

BIBLIOGRAPHY

Browning, Robert M. *From Cape Charles to Cape Fear: The North Atlantic Blockading Squadron during the Civil War.* Tuscaloosa: University of Alabama Press, 1993.

Carse, Robert. *Blockade: The Civil War at Sea.* New York: Rinehart, 1958.

Wise, Stephen R. *Lifeline of the Confederacy: Blockade Running during the Civil War.* Columbia: University of South Carolina Press, 1988.

Ella Lonn / C. W.

See also **Blockade; Civil War; King Cotton;** *and vol. 9:* **A Confederate Blockade Runner.**

BLOCS, a name given to organized voting groups in American legislative bodies, and more loosely, to associations of pressure groups attempting to lobby in American legislatures. In either case, the purpose of organizing a bloc is to create a group of legislators who will vote together consistently on certain issues. Blocs are highly organized, are based on closely shared interests, and command a high degree of loyalty from their members. A farm bloc, a protectionist bloc, a wet bloc, a dry bloc, a progressive bloc, and a veterans' bloc were all active in Congress during the early to middle twentieth century. After World War II the veterans' bloc and the protectionist bloc lost considerable influence. A labor bloc and a civil rights

bloc rose to prominence in their place, but neither had an organization in Congress.

The rise of political action committees (PACs) in the late twentieth century supplanted blocs, making PACs the major lobbyists in Congress. The intensification of congressional partisanship during the 1990s weakened the power of bipartisan blocs, but it simultaneously strengthened the hand of ideological blocs within the two major parties. By 2002 virtually every bloc drew on PACs for fund-raising and congressional lobbying.

BIBLIOGRAPHY

Gais, Thomas. *Improper Influence: Campaign Finance Law, Political Interest Groups, and the Problem of Equality.* Ann Arbor: University of Michigan Press, 1996.

Ness, Immanuel. *Encyclopedia of Interest Groups and Lobbyists in the United States.* Armonk, N.Y.: Sharpe, 2000.

Sheppard, Burton D. *Rethinking Congressional Reform: The Reform Roots of the Special Interest Congress.* Cambridge, Mass.: Schenkman Books, 1985.

Robert Eyestone / A. G.

See also **Caucus; Lobbies; Subsidies.**

BLOODY SHIRT was part of the expression "waving the bloody shirt," referring to a political ploy used in campaigns during the RECONSTRUCTION period, following the CIVIL WAR. This term described the attempts made by radical northern Republicans to defeat southern Democrats by using impassioned oratory about bloody sacrifice designed to keep alive the hatreds and prejudices of the Civil War period. During the most vehement attacks, in the campaigns of 1872 and 1876, orators would literally wave a bloody shirt to remind audiences of the Civil War casualties.

BIBLIOGRAPHY

Foner, Eric. *Reconstruction: America's Unfinished Revolution, 1863–1877.* New York: Harper and Row, 1988.

Hirshson, Stanley P. *Farewell to the Bloody Shirt: Northern Republicans and the Southern Negro, 1877–1893.* Bloomington: Indiana University Press, 1962.

Hallie Farmer / H. S.

See also **Elections, Presidential; Radical Republicans.**

BLOOMERS was the term given to a woman's garment credited to Elizabeth Smith Miller that involved baggy, pantaloon-style pants cinched at the ankle and a matching overblouse that came down to the knees. Miller had purchased the garment in Switzerland, where it was made for women to wear while hiking at health resorts. In 1851 she brought it with her on a visit to her cousin Elizabeth Cady Stanton in Seneca Falls, New York. Stanton made others like it, which she wore around town to

Bloomers. An illustration showing women in the clothing that became the rage—but to many others, were just outrageous—in the 1850s thanks to women's rights advocate Amelia Bloomer. Cleveland Antiquarian Books

the embarrassment of her father, Judge Cady, and her son. Stanton showed it to Amelia Bloomer, who was then editor of *The Lily*, a woman's journal. Like Stanton, Bloomer embraced the idea that it freed women to wear looser clothing than the corsets, petticoats, and long dresses they were enduring at the time. She featured a picture of it in *The Lily*, and hundreds of women wrote in asking for patterns on how to make it. Newspaper reporters gave the term "bloomers" to the garment after Amelia Bloomer who had popularized it.

Bloomers not only brought new physical freedom and comfort in daily life for women in the mid-nineteenth century, but they also served as a vehicle for opening discussion of other women's issues such as suffrage and property rights. Subscriptions to *The Lily* increased, and activists such as Elizabeth Stanton and Susan B. Anthony wore the new garment on their lecture tours. Despite their popularity, bloomers outraged many men and women at the time, who thought them vulgar and unladylike.

BIBLIOGRAPHY

Bloomer, Amelia Jenks. *Hear Me Patiently: The Reform Speeches of Amelia Jenks Bloomer.* Westport, Conn.: Greenwood Press, 1994.

Connie Ann Kirk

BLOUNT CONSPIRACY takes its name from William Blount, U.S. senator from Tennessee in 1796–1797. The conspiracy was connected with the Yazoo land frauds of 1796, and its main purpose seems to have been to raise the value of western lands by driving the Spaniards out of Louisiana and Florida. This was to be accomplished by a land force of western frontiersmen and Indians with the aid of a British fleet. The British minister in the United States, Robert Liston, gave the conspirators some encouragement and sent one of them to London. The conspiracy was exposed when an incriminating letter written by Blount to one of his agents fell into the hands of the administration and was transmitted by President John Adams to the Senate (3 July 1797). Blount was promptly expelled from that body. Impeachment proceedings against him were considered but dropped because of his expulsion. Exposure of the conspiracy had repercussions in the domestic politics and foreign relations of the United States. After Jay's Treaty of 1795, relations between the United States and Great Britain had seemed to be improving, but the Blount Conspiracy scandal set the two nations at odds once again. In particular, the Jeffersonian opposition to the Adams administration cited the conspiracy as evidence that Great Britain still desired to meddle in the internal affairs of the United States. Spain's presence on the nation's southern frontier would also re-

THE AMERICAN ANTI-SUNDAY LAW CONVENTION OF 1848

The right of every man to worship God according to the dictates of his own conscience is inherent, inalienable, self-evident. Yet it is notorious that, in all the states, excepting Louisiana, there are laws enforcing religious observance of the first day of the week as the Sabbath, and punishing as criminals such as attempt to pursue their usual avocations on that day,—avocations that even Sabbatarians recognize as innocent and laudable on all other days. . . . There is, therefore, no liberty of conscience allowed to the people of this country, *under the laws thereof,* in regard to the observance of a Sabbath day. . . .

SOURCE: From William Lloyd Garrison, "An Appeal to the Friends of Civil and Religious Liberty."

main a major political issue until 1819, when the United States formally purchased Florida from Madrid.

BIBLIOGRAPHY

Brown, Ralph Adams. *The Presidency of John Adams.* Lawrence: University Press of Kansas, 1975.

Arthur P. Whitaker / A. G.

See also **Conspiracy; Great Britain, Relations with; Spain, Relations with.**

BLUE AND GRAY, familiar names for the armies of the North and the South, respectively, during the CIVIL WAR, derived from the fact that the Union Army wore blue uniforms, while the Confederates wore gray. As sectional hatred died, these terms superseded some of the more derogatory names of the nineteenth century.

BIBLIOGRAPHY

McPherson, James M. *Battle Cry of Freedom: The Civil War Era.* Vol. 6 of *The Oxford History of the United States.* New York: Oxford University Press, 1988.

Fred B. Joyner / F. B.

See also **Army, Confederate; Army, Union.**

BLUE EAGLE EMBLEM. On 20 July 1933, Hugh S. Johnson, the head of the NATIONAL RECOVERY ADMINISTRATION, proclaimed the Blue Eagle emblem, a blue-colored representation of the American Indian thunderbird with outspread wings, the symbol of U.S. industrial recovery. All who accepted President Franklin D. Roo-

sevelt's reemployment agreement or the special CODE OF FAIR COMPETITION could display a poster that reproduced the blue eagle with the motto "Member N.R.A. We Do Our Part." The invalidation of the compulsory code system on 5 September 1935 led to the abolition of the emblem and the prohibition of its future use as a symbol.

BIBLIOGRAPHY

Brand, Donald Robert. *Corporatism and the Rule of Law: A Study of the National Recovery Administration.* Ithaca, N.Y.: Cornell University Press, 1988.

Himmelberg, Robert F. *The Origins of the National Recovery Administration: Business, Government, and the Trade Association Issue, 1921–1933.* 2d ed. New York: Fordham University Press, 1993.

Erik McKinley Eriksson / A. E.

See also **Government Regulation of Business; Great Depression; New Deal.**

BLUE LAWS. Also known as Sabbath or Sunday Laws, Blue Laws prohibit secular activities on Sunday, and may also compel church attendance. The term comes from the use of blue paper to publish the regulations of New Haven colony. Blue Laws were incorporated into American law from the English common law. The first regulation was enacted in 1610 by Sir Thomas Gates, deputy governor of Virginia, as part of the colony's laws. Most seventeenth- and eighteenth-century versions resembled the 1676 Sunday law of Charles II, prohibiting "worldly labour" and "ordinary callings" such as travel, recreation, and trade. Traditionally, penalties were pecuniary, though provisions for corporal punishment were not uncommon.

American courts have considered these laws to be part of the state and local police power to promote health, safety, and morality. As such, they have generally been upheld against constitutional challenges, be they charges of "class legislation" or state establishment. Sabbatarian politics, however, have always been bitterly contested.

Blue Laws were originally motivated by religious goals. Although religion continued to drive sabbatarian politics after the founding (especially among evangelical Protestants during the Second Great Awakening), Blue Laws were increasingly supported to promote secular goods (such as temperance, labor efficiency, and public order) after the 1840s. Enforcement has veered from concerted to indifferent. After the Civil War, Blue Laws were regularly violated and unenforced, and through the twentieth century they proved no match for the pressures of commercialization. They remain relevant, in truncated form, on a regionally varying basis.

BIBLIOGRAPHY

Blakely, William Addison, ed. *American State Papers Bearing on Sunday Legislation.* 1911. Reprint, New York: Da Capo, 1970.

King, Andrew J. "Sunday Law in the Nineteenth Century." *Albany Law Review* 64 (2000): 675.

Novak, William J. *The People's Welfare: Law and Regulation in Nineteenth Century America.* Chapel Hill: University of North Carolina Press, 1996.

Raucher, Alan. "Sunday Business and the Decline of Sunday Closing Laws: A Historical Overview." *Journal of Church and State* 36 (1994): 13–33.

Kimberly A. Hendrickson

See also **Church and State, Separation of; Police Power; Temperance Movement.**

BLUE SKY LAWS are state laws designed to prevent fraud in the sale of corporate securities. These laws preceded federal regulation of securities, which began in 1933. Kansas enacted the first statute in 1911, and by the end of 1923, forty-five of the forty-eight states had followed suit. The term "blue sky" arose when the U.S. Supreme Court stated in *Hall v. Geiger-Jones Co.* (1917) that the laws were intended to prevent speculative schemes based on nothing more than "so many feet of 'blue sky.'" The requirements of blue sky laws vary from state to state, but generally stipulate that securities offerings and brokers be registered.

BIBLIOGRAPHY
Hazan, Thomas Lee. *The Law of Securities Regulation.* 3d ed. St. Paul, Minn.: West Publishing, 1998.

Ratner, David L. *Securities Regulation in a Nutshell.* St. Paul, Minn.: West Publishing, 1992.

Katherine M. Jones

See also **Stock Market.**

BLUEGRASS COUNTRY, a region of about 8,000 square miles in north central Kentucky, is named for its nutritious grass. European settlement, coming from Virginia, Maryland, and the Carolinas, started in the mid-1770s, and the region was well settled by 1800. The fertile soil, especially around Lexington, attracted many of the old agrarian gentry who were granted or bought large tracts of land, created estates, usually with slaves, and continued their former way of life. Smaller farmers occupied interstices between large farms as well as the less-fertile outlying areas. The region produced tobacco, hemp, and grains, and bred livestock, especially horses. The undulating countryside, with meadows, trees, rock fences, and elegant buildings, presents a patrician landscape, much like that of an English park. A similar region with a similar history is located in middle Tennessee.

BIBLIOGRAPHY
Alvey, R. Gerald. *Kentucky Bluegrass Country.* Jackson: University of Mississippi Press, 1992.

Bluegrass Country. This 1940 photograph shows tobacco growing, and a barn where it is stored, near Lexington, Ky. LIBRARY OF CONGRESS

Aron, Stephen. *How the West Was Lost: The Transformation of Kentucky from Daniel Boone to Henry Clay.* Baltimore: Johns Hopkins University Press, 1996.

Davis, Darrel H. *The Geography of the Blue Grass Region of Kentucky.* Frankfort: Kentucky Geological Survey, 1927.

Raitz, Karl B. *The Kentucky Bluegrass: A Regional Profile and Guide.* Chapel Hill: University of North Carolina, Department of Geography, 1980.

———. "Rock Fences and Preadaptation." *Geographical Review* 85, no.1 (1995): 50–62.

Trimble, Stanley W. "Ante-Bellum Domestic Architecture in Middle Tennessee." In *The American South*, vol. 25 of *Geoscience and Man*, edited by R. L. Nostrand and S. B. Hilliard. Baton Rouge: Department of Geography and Anthropology, Louisiana State University, 1988: 97–117.

Stanley W. Trimble

See also **Kentucky.**

BLUES as a musical term can describe an oral tradition of African American poetry set to music using blues form (typically three-line stanzas with the first two lines being similar, set to a twelve-bar harmonic framework called a blues progression); the form of the poetry and/or the music; and an aesthetic that remains an ideal for JAZZ performance in general.

Blues originated as an expression of the individual and interactive social tradition of a displaced African American population. It began with the African American agrarian working class of the Mississippi Delta and combined African American and European American traditions, particularly hollers (field work songs) and British ballads. It was established by the late 1800s as primarily a vocal and improvisatory genre, often with instrumental accompaniment. Later it became a purely instrumental genre as well, and other blues regions developed—each with its own localized style. Until about 1930 there was a distinction between the earthier style of country blues and the smoother urban blues. Only after blues was well established did it broaden to include the white middle class and function as a form of entertainment.

Often using SLANG, blues texts address life's troubles, freedom, and gender roles and relationships, and are often explicit about sex. The recognizable style of the blues may include call and response, a constant rhythmic pulse, blue notes (lowered third and seventh scale degrees), and gritty timbres.

Publications (from about 1912) and recordings (from about 1920) came after blues had long been an established oral practice. The leading performers to popularize classic blues with early recordings were Mamie Smith, Ma Rainey, and Bessie Smith. Blind Lemon Jefferson, Robert Johnson, Big Bill Broonzy, Muddy Waters, and B. B. King exemplify styles after 1930.

Many small and large jazz ensembles still play blues titles, use blues form, and borrow its manner of expression. Blues has influenced many substyles of jazz and instigated numerous pop genres, including ROCK AND ROLL. The participation of different races and nationalities in the production and consumption of blues today make it a global phenomenon.

BIBLIOGRAPHY

Erlewine, Michael, et al., eds. *All Music Guide to the Blues: The Experts' Guide to the Best Blues Recordings*. 2d ed. San Francisco: Miller Freeman, 1999.

Murray, Albert. *Stomping the Blues*. New York: Da Capo, 1989. The original edition was published in 1976.

Oliver, Paul. *Yonder Come the Blues: The Evolution of a Genre*. Cambridge, U.K., and New York: Cambridge University Press, 2001.

Christina Linsenmeyer–van Schalkwyk

See also **Music: African American.**

BOARD OF INDIAN COMMISSIONERS,

established by Congress on 10 April 1869, was authorized to give advice on the conduct of federal policy regarding Native Americans and to inspect supplies delivered to Indian agencies in fulfillment of treaty obligations. Originally consisting of ten Protestant, male members, it was the kind of group that had been recommended by humanitarian reformers for years.

The immediate result of the board's efforts was Ulysses S. Grant's "peace policy," which, among other things, involved the nomination of agents by Protestant and Catholic churches. The strategy was to force peaceable Indians onto reservations, where Christian agents and missionaries would prepare them for assimilation into the mainstream of society. Indians who refused to move to reservations would be treated as hostile and would be pur-

sued by the army until they acquiesced or were killed. During the late nineteenth century the board was a powerful force in determining federal policy, advocating citizenship for Indians and their assimilation into the mainstream of American life through education, enactment of laws, and the allotment of reservation land in severalty.

By 1900 the board had declined, but it soon revived as old members died and new ones were appointed. Two Catholics were members in the twentieth century, and two women were appointed in the 1920s. In 1909 Warren K. Moorehead discovered fraud in the sale of white pine timber at White Earth in Minnesota, and he made other members of the board aware of serious health problems among reservation residents. With the board's encouragement, Commissioner of Indian Affairs Charles Burke began a health drive in 1923, and the board was instrumental in initiating the Meriam survey of conditions on Indian reservations in 1926 and 1927.

Many recommendations of the board from the late Progressive Era through the 1920s reached fruition during the Indian New Deal and beyond. Congress authorized a $600,000 revolving fund in 1914, and the Wheeler-Howard Act of 1924 increased the fund to $10 million. Tribal ownership of cattle herds and the timber industry began in 1916. In the 1920s the board recommended the assignment of doctors from the U.S. Public Health Service to the Indian Health Service, the decentralization of the Indian service, and the Court of Indian Claims. These reforms were accomplished by 1954. Despite these areas of agreement, however, New Deal reformers believed the Board of Indian Commissioners had outlived its usefulness. When John Collier became commissioner of Indian Affairs in 1933, he immediately terminated the board by executive order.

BIBLIOGRAPHY

Fritz, Henry E. *The Movement for Indian Assimilation, 1860–1890*. Philadelphia: University of Pennsylvania Press, 1963.

———. "The Board of Indian Commissioners and Ethnocentric Reform, 1878–1893." In *Indian White Relations: A Persistent Paradox*. Edited by Jane F. Smith and Robert M. Kvasnicka. Washington, D.C.: Howard University Press, 1976.

———. "The Last Hurrah of Christian Humanitarian Indian Reform: The Board of Indian Commissioners, 1909–1918." *Western Historical Quarterly* 16, no. 4 (1985): 147–162.

Fritz, Henry E., ed. "The Board of Indian Commissioners and the Reform of Indian Affairs from the Late Progressive Era to the New Deal." In *Making United States Indian Policy, 1829–1933*. Norman: University of Oklahoma Press, forthcoming.

McDonnell, Janet A. *The Dispossession of the American Indian, 1887–1934*. Bloomington: Indiana University Press, 1991.

Prucha, Francis Paul. *American Indian Policy in Crisis: Christian Reformers and the Indian, 1865–1900*. Norman: University of Oklahoma Press, 1976.

Henry E. Fritz

See also **Indian Policy, U.S.; Meriam Report.**

Boeing. During World War II, the company supplied the military with such important weapons as the B-17 and B-29 bombers. © BETTMANN/CORBIS

BOARD OF TRADE AND PLANTATIONS was created out of a committee of the Privy Council as the main British colonial office to oversee colonial affairs on 15 May 1696, replacing the Lords of Trade and Plantations. It was a paid board of eight members, plus the chief officers of the state as ex officio members. They made sure that the colonial laws were not contrary to English common law or British interests, issued commissions for royal governors, organized the consular service, oversaw colonial commercial relations with other nations, enforced the trade and navigation acts, heard and investigated complaints of merchants, recommended imperial legislation, supervised the negotiation of treaties, and controlled the poor relief in England. Additional transformations made in the eighteenth century included developing plans to strengthen the position of the royal governors, make judges dependent upon the Crown and the leaders for their salaries and terms of office, and moderate between the agents of the Crown and the leaders of the colonial legislatures.

The board was part of the regular political system, and the members changed with shifts within the government. Permanent administrative positions of the board were the permanent secretaries, who were the best-informed administrators on colonial affairs in England; the solicitor and clerk of reports, who prepared all formal information, assembled information for board use, and represented the Board of Trade before other departments of the govern-

ment; and the attorney, who examined the validity of all colonial laws within English law.

BIBLIOGRAPHY

Andrews, Charles M. *British Committees, Commissions, and Councils of Trade and Plantations, 1622–1675.* 1908. Reprint, New York: Kraus Reprint, 1970.

Christie, Ian R. *Crisis of Empire: Great Britain and the American Colonies, 1754–1783.* New York: Norton, 1966.

Dickerson, Oliver Morton. *American Colonial Government, 1696–1765: A Study of the British Board of Trade in Its Relation to the American Colonies, Political, Industrial, Administrative.* Reprint. New York: Russell and Russell, 1962.

Steele, Ian Kenneth. *Politics of Colonial Policy: The Board of Trade in Colonial Administration, 1696–1720.* Oxford: Clarendon Press, 1968.

Michelle M. Mormul

See also **Lords of Trade and Plantation; Privy Council.**

BOEING COMPANY. In 1917, one year after forming Pacific Aero Products in Seattle, William E. Boeing changed his young firm's name to Boeing Airplane Company. During World War I, Boeing Airplane supplied American military forces with planes and assisted in training pilots. In 1929, Boeing Airplane joined several other firms, including United Air Lines, to form the United Aircraft and Transportation Company. Frustrated with a government investigation into the formation of this and other aircraft holding companies, Boeing retired in 1933 and Philip Johnson became the company's new president, a position he held until his death in September 1944.

Upon U.S. entry into World War II, Boeing began supplying planes to the military. Boeing's initial involvement was rather inauspicious: it supplied only 255 small trainers and 38 bombers out of the military's first order of 6,000 aircraft. Yet Boeing's B-17 bomber, nicknamed the Flying Fortress, proved tremendously effective and the military ordered large numbers of the plane. During its peak production period in the middle of 1944, Boeing produced a new B-17 every ninety minutes. To handle this demand, Boeing enlarged the workforce at its Seattle factories from under 2,000 workers in 1938 to nearly 45,000 in 1945.

Although the B-17 was a tremendous success, the military needed an even bigger plane. Boeing began designing one in 1942, an effort that culminated in the B-29 bomber, nicknamed the Superfortress. A very complicated aircraft, the B-29 became the second most expensive weapons project of the war, trailing only the development of the atomic bomb. These two projects were ultimately united when it was decided to use B-29s to drop the atomic bombs on Hiroshima and Nagasaki in August 1945.

After the war, Boeing again began to produce civilian aircraft. In 1953 William Allen, who had replaced Phil Johnson as the company's president, convinced government officials to allow Boeing to use government-owned facilities to develop a new civilian-military jet. In May 1954, Boeing introduced the B-707, a commercial jet that proved immediately popular. During the 1960s, Boeing introduced two new jet models, the 727 and the 737. Its next significant contribution was the introduction of the first jumbo jet, the 747, which was capable of carrying twice as many passengers as the next biggest aircraft. Boeing delivered the first 747s in 1969, and this model helped secure its place in the competitive commercial aircraft market. By the 1990s, only two commercial aircraft makers were left: Boeing and Airbus, a European consortium led by France and Germany.

BIBLIOGRAPHY

McCraw, Thomas K. *American Business, 1920–2000: How It Worked.* Wheeling, Ill.: Harlan Davidson, 2000.

Rodgers, Eugene. *Flying High: The Story of Boeing and the Rise of the Jetliner Industry.* New York: Atlantic Monthly Press, 1996.

Sell, T. M. *Wings of Power: Boeing and the Politics of Growth in the Northwest.* Seattle: University of Washington Press, 2001.

Martin H. Stack

See also **Air Transportation and Travel; Aircraft, Bomber; Aircraft Industry; World War II, Air War against Germany; World War II, Air War against Japan.**

BOERNE V. FLORES, 521 U.S. 507 (1997), reaffirmed *Marbury v. Madison*'s doctrines concerning judicial review and the separation of powers, while limiting congressional authority under section 5 of the Fourteenth Amendment.

In *Employment Division v. Smith*, 494 U.S. 872 (1990), the U.S. Supreme Court sustained a state's power to deny members of the Native American Church unemployment benefits after being fired for ingesting peyote sacramentally. Justice Antonin Scalia's 5–4 majority opinion declined to apply the then prevailing standard that required government to demonstrate a compelling interest when it impinged on First Amendment religious liberties. Instead, Scalia reverted to the doctrine of *Reynolds v. United States*, 98 U.S. 145 (1878), which held that a state need not make an exception from otherwise valid, generally applicable laws for conduct motivated by religious belief. Scalia acknowledged that his holding would "place [religious minorities] at a relative disadvantage."

Troubled by the Scalia opinion's indifference to the burden on the religious practices of some racial minorities, Congress enacted the Religious Freedom Restoration Act (RFRA) in 1993, restoring the compelling-interest test in free-exercise cases, in effect "overruling" *Employment Division v. Smith*.

In *Boerne*, which involved a dispute between Boerne, Texas, and Archbishop P. F. Flores over Flores's wish to remodel a church incompatible with city zoning laws, the court split 6–3 to hold RFRA unconstitutional. Justice Anthony Kennedy held that Congress lacked power to enact RFRA under section 5 of the Fourteenth Amendment. He stated that section 5 permits Congress to enact only remedial measures enforcing constitutional rights, not to create new substantive rights inconsistent with a previous Supreme Court interpretation. In *Boerne*, the Supreme Court continued to exalt its powers at the expense of congressional authority.

BIBLIOGRAPHY

Engel, Steven A. "The McCulloch Theory of the Fourteenth Amendment: *City of Boerne v. Flores* and the Original Understanding of Section 5." *Yale Law Journal* 109 (1999): 115–154.

McConnell, Michael W. "Institutions and Interpretations: A Critique of *City of Boerne v. Flores.*" *Harvard Law Review* 111 (1997): 153–195.

Symposium: "State and Federal Religious Liberty Legislation: Is It Necessary? Is It Constitutional? Is It Good Policy?" *Cardozo Law Review* 21 (1999): 415–806.

William M. Wiecek

See also **Marbury v. Madison; Reynolds v. United States.**

BOLAND AMENDMENTS. *See* **Iran-Contra Affair.**

BOLL WEEVIL, a quarter-inch-long beetle that eats the buds and young bolls of cotton plants, resulting in damage that reduces the fiber output of the plants. Boll weevils produce several generations each year between spring and fall before hibernating over the winter. A native insect of Mexico and Central America, the boll weevil first crossed into south Texas about 1892. Over the next three decades, it advanced north and east through almost the entire Cotton Belt of the South, reaching the Atlantic coast by the 1920s. The damage was estimated to be in the tens of millions of dollars annually.

The arrival of the boll weevil triggered an examination of cotton planting, harvesting, and field-clearing practices by farmers, scientists, and government officials in attempts to decrease areas where the pests could live. They also searched for and developed weevil-resistant cotton varieties that could be planted earlier and grow faster, which reduced the time plants were susceptible to boll weevils. Even though cotton agriculture changed radically as a result of the boll weevil invasion, the changes resulted only in controlling and limiting the damage caused by the boll weevil, but not in its extermination.

Since the 1970s the boll weevil has made new advances into parts of western Texas, New Mexico, and Arizona. This pest continues to cause $300 million in damage annually, mostly in Texas and the mid-South. Its total impact has been estimated at over $15 billion during the twentieth century. The boll weevil is the target of ongoing eradication efforts in regional programs throughout the United States and northern Mexico. The National Boll Weevil Eradication Program, established in the late 1970s, has certified California, Arizona, and from Alabama eastward as now being weevil-free.

In 1919 residents of Enterprise, Alabama, erected a larger-than-life statue of the boll weevil as a monument "in profound appreciation" of being forced to diversify its economy from cotton into other crops because of the pest's arrival a few years earlier.

BIBLIOGRAPHY

Hunter, W. D., and W. D. Pierce. *The Mexican Cotton-Boll Weevil.* U.S. Department of Agriculture Bureau of Entomology Bulletin No. 114. Washington, D.C.: Bureau of Entomology, 1912. A detailed history and scientific description.

Dickerson, Willard A., et al., eds. *Boll Weevil Eradication in the United States through 1999.* Memphis, Tenn.: Cotton Foundation, 2001. A comprehensive history of boll weevil eradication in the United States and each state.

Cameron L. Saffell

BOMBING. By the end of World War I, aerial bombing remained in the primitive stages. There were German raids on London and American pilots saw action, but the conflict ended before bombing reached its full potential. However, the seeds had been sown for decades of postwar controversy over the role of air power. Central figures were the Italian Air Force officer Giulio Douhet, author of *The Command of the Air* (1921); Sir Hugh Trenchard, the commander of the first independent air service, Britain's Royal Air Force (RAF) from 1919 to 1929; and the American brigadier general Billy Mitchell, whose unbridled advocacy of air power, although it led to a court-martial, would be tragically vindicated at Pearl Harbor on 7 December 1941.

Great advances in aircraft design occurred in the 1930s, with increases in speed, range, ceiling, and load-carrying capacity. By 1939, both the U.S. Army Air Corps (USAAC) and the U.S. Navy had conceptualized the means by which they would employ aircraft in future bombing roles. The USAAC's principal emphasis was on long-range strategic bombing—bombing of an enemy's industry, transportation, fuel, and power as opposed to its military. They also recognized the need for tactical bombing—close-in support of ground forces on the battlefield. The U.S. Navy's interest lay primarily in dive-bombing in support of landing operations, striking targets protected by terrain from the low trajectory of naval artillery.

The shocking success of the German Luftwaffe early in World War II caught the world's attention, as did the daring Japanese attack on Pearl Harbor. Becoming the U.S. Army Air Forces (USAAF) in February 1942, the former USAAC rapidly grew to unprecedented size. The U.S. and British Combined Chiefs of Staff recognized that several years would pass before Adolf Hitler's vaunted "Fortress Europe" could be struck by any other means than through the air. Prime Minister Winston Churchill famously commented that Fortress Europe lacked a roof, so it could be bombed by the Allies "around the clock." Beginning in August 1942 the USAAF joined RAF Bomber Command in attacks on Germany and occupied Europe almost until V-E Day (8 May 1945). Controversy surrounds these campaigns concerning their military effectiveness and moral appropriateness.

In the Pacific theater, USAAF and U.S. Navy bombing prior to late 1944 focused on supporting landing operations and destroying Japanese shipping. Continual bombing of mainland Japan began in November 1944 from bases in the Mariana Islands. These greatly intensified after March 1945 and culminated in the dropping of two atomic bombs on 6 and 9 August 1945, by B-29 Superfortresses. The lasting controversy of this event was exemplified by the National Air and Space Museum "Enola Gay" exhibit fiasco of 1995, in which revisionist historians attempting to politicize and criticize the bombings, minimizing Japan's guilt in World War II, met a firestorm of criticism from the general public and veterans. Japan's surrender prior to the planned invasion proved the effectiveness of these attacks, occurring, as they did, concurrently with a tight naval blockade.

Bombing. During the Vietnam War, U.S. Air Force pilots drop their bombs over a target in southern North Vietnam. NATIONAL ARCHIVES AND RECORDS ADMINISTRATION

With the National Security Act of 1947, the wartime USAAF finally became the independent service that air prophets like Billy Mitchell had long fought for. The U.S. Air Force (USAF) exemplified the then widely-held assumption that wars of the future would be won by nations capable of conducting atomic (later nuclear) warfare most efficiently on short notice. This assumption lay behind the subsequent buildup of the USAF's Strategic Air Command (SAC) into the most powerful air striking force in the world, armed with both bombers and intercontinental ballistic missiles (ICBM's). SAC and its B-52 Stratofortresses would epitomize the Cold War for decades.

These assumptions about future conflicts also caused the tendency to look on the Korean War (1950–1953) as an aberration, not to be taken seriously as a portent of things to come. During the Vietnam War, the bombing in Indochina was conducted under a series of tactical and strategic restrictions that frustrated the airmen assigned to the task but that they nonetheless honored, often to their considerable peril.

With the rise of terrorism as an instrument of state policy, bombing proved adaptable to smaller conflicts. In April 1986, President Ronald Reagan ordered England-based F-111 bombers to attack Libya in response to a terrorist bombing tied to Libyan intelligence. The raid

subdued Libyan dictator Muammar Qaddafi, deterring him from further attacks on U.S. interests and servicemen.

The remarkable F-117 Nighthawk stealth fighter was first flown in 1981, in total secrecy, and became operational in 1983. Its existence was not confirmed by the American government until 1988. First used operationally in the U.S. invasion of Panama in 1989, by the Persian Gulf War of 1991, dramatic television footage appeared of F-117s dropping laser-guided bombs on Iraqi targets with pinpoint accuracy. The success of the Northrop B-2 Spirit "Stealth Bomber"—the most expensive warplane in history—remains to be seen in future operations.

Developments in the 1990s and After
In the Persian Gulf War (1991), bombing was aided by electronic suppression systems and airborne radar. These not only gave the United States extensive knowledge of the enemy opposition, but denied the Iraqis knowledge of, and communication with, their own forces, resulting in a remarkable victory for air power. While the state-of-the-art F-117 was the darling of the American media, the old Cold War and Vietnam-era warhorse, the B-52 Stratofortress, also performed very well. On January 16, 1991, B-52G bombers flying from Barksdale AFB, Louisiana to the Persian Gulf and back completed the longest bombing mission in history—a fifteen-hour flight. They attacked high-priority Iraqi targets in Iraq and Kuwait with air-launched cruise missiles packing a 1,000-pound conventional warhead. The next day, air strikes using B-52–launched cruise missiles and F-117s, attacking deep in Iraq, achieved total air superiority before the beginning of the coalition ground campaign.

The dissolution of the Warsaw Pact and the breakup of the Soviet Union in 1991 heralded a remarkable American victory in the Cold War. In September 1991, the U.S. Air Force's Strategic Air Command, long a symbol of superpower tension, stood down from its decades-long, around-the-clock vigil. But the B-52, an abiding symbol of the Cold War, would soldier on, modified and updated. Although they were to be replaced by the Rockwell B-1 Lancer, which has become the mainstay of the U.S. long-range bomber fleet, B-52s continued to be used as of the early 2000s, bombing terrorist targets in Afghanistan.

August 1995 saw a NATO bombing campaign against Bosnian Serbs. Far more dramatic was the 1999 NATO aerial bombing campaign in Kosovo, in the former Yugoslavia. Initially, to supporters of air power, this appeared to be, at last, the long-prophesied decisive military campaign won entirely by air power, without the insertion of major ground troops. But enforcing the 1995 Dayton peace accords required American troops on the ground. After the terrorist attack on the United States on 11 September 2001, American bombers struck military targets of the Al Qaeda network in Afghanistan. The results there, like those in Kosovo, were unusually successful, but it remains to be seen whether the victory of American and

NATO air power was a result of unique circumstances—third-rate powers (Serbia and Afghanistan) versus the state-of-the-art precision bombing technology of most of the Free World—or the total victory of air power long prophesied by Douhet, Trenchard, Mitchell, and their supporters.

BIBLIOGRAPHY

Atkinson, Rick. *Crusade: The Untold Story of the Persian Gulf War.* Boston: Houghton Mifflin Company, 1993.

Boyne, Walter J. Beyond the Wild Blue: *A History of the United States Air Force, 1947–1997.* New York: St. Martin's Press, 1997.

Cate, James L. and Wesley F. Craven, eds., *The Army Air Forces in World War II.* Washington, D.C.: Office of Air Force History, 1983.

Leyden, Andrew. *Gulf War Debriefing Book.* Grants Pass, Oreg.: Hellgate Press, 1997.

Sherry, Michael. *The Rise of American Air Power: The Creation of Armageddon.* New Haven, Conn.: Yale University Press, 1987.

Christian Mark DeJohn
David MacIsaac

BONANZA KINGS, John W. Mackay, James G. Fair, James C. Flood, and William S. O'Brien, organized the Consolidated Virginia Silver Mine in 1871 near Virginia City, Nevada, from a number of smaller claims on the Comstock Lode. The term "bonanza" was applied to the large ore body that lay in a vertical rift of the hanging wall of the Comstock Lode. For three years after large ore bodies were uncovered in 1874, the mines produced $3 million per month. Production began to fall off in 1879, but in twenty-two years of operation the mines yielded $150 million in silver and gold and paid more than $78 million in dividends.

BIBLIOGRAPHY

Greever, William S. *The Bonanza West: The Story of the Western Mining Rushes, 1848–1900.* Norman: University of Oklahoma Press, 1963.

Peterson, Richard H. *The Bonanza Kings: The Social Origins and Business Behavior of Western Mining Entrepreneurs, 1870–1900.* Lincoln: University of Nebraska Press, 1977.

Carl L. Cannon/h. s.

See also **Comstock Lode; Silver Prospecting and Mining; Virginia City.**

BONHOMME RICHARD–SERAPIS ENCOUNTER (23 September 1779), one of the most notable victories in American naval history. John Paul Jones's flagship, the *Bonhomme Richard,* an Indian merchantman that had been renamed in honor of Benjamin Franklin, was proceeding with Jones's tiny fleet up the east coast of England in quest of English cargoes. Although worn-out and

John Paul Jones Capturing the *Serapis.* Nineteenth-century engraving by Alonzo Chappel. NATIONAL ARCHIVES AND RECORDS ADMINISTRATION

unseaworthy, it carried forty-two guns. At about noon, Jones sighted two enemy ships of war, the *Serapis* and the *Countess of Scarborough,* convoying ships loaded with naval stores. Jones maneuvered his ship close to the *Serapis,* and both ships opened broadside fire. Jones had placed some of his guns below, and two of the larger ones on the lower deck burst, killing and wounding several men. This catastrophe necessitated using only the lighter guns and musketry. The slaughter on both sides was terrible, and the American ship leaked badly. After an hour of fighting, Jones answered the British challenge to surrender, saying, "I have not yet begun to fight." The two vessels became locked together, and the battle raged for more than two hours longer. Jones was hampered by the treachery of a captain in his own fleet, but using British prisoners to work the pumps, he kept his ship afloat and wore down the enemy to the point of exhaustion and surrender.

BIBLIOGRAPHY

Boudriot, Jean. *John Paul Jones and the "Bonhomme Richard."* Translated by David H. Roberts. Annapolis, Md.: Naval Institute Press, 1987.

Dean, Nicholas. "John Paul Jones Came Awfully Close to Being a Loser." *Smithsonian* 11, no. 9 (September 1980): 139–154.

Jones, John Paul. *Battle Between the "Bon Homme Richard" and the "Serapis."* Boston: Directors of the Old South Work, 1904.

Arthur R. Blessing / A. R.

See also **Warships.**

BONUS ARMY. In May 1932 thousands of World War I veterans began gathering in Washington, D.C., in order to pressure Congress to pass the Patman Bonus Bill. The legislation called for the immediate payment of war bonuses for World War I veterans. Under legislation passed with the approval of veterans groups in 1924, payments had been deferred, with interest, until 1945. But with the economic hardship of the depression, veterans clamored for immediate assistance.

The official response to the encampments (some including the mens' families) was initially benign. Washington, D.C., Police Superintendent Pelham Glassford, a veteran himself who was sympathetic toward the movement, set aside building space and campgrounds. At the height of the Bonus Army, between seventeen and twenty thousand veterans were encamped near the Washington Mall and at a site on the Anacostia River, forming the largest of the nation's Hoovervilles.

Although the House passed the Patman Veterans Bill, the Senate rejected its version on 17 June. When veterans protested by marching on Pennsylvania Avenue, police responded violently, resulting in the deaths of two veterans and two policemen. On 28 July President Hoover ordered the Secretary of War to disperse the protesters. In the late afternoon, cavalry, infantry, tanks, and a mounted machine gun pushed the Bonusers out of Washington. Although under orders from Hoover to show restraint, the troops injured more than one hundred veterans. General Douglas MacArthur sent troops into the Anacostia camp, directly disobeying Hoover's orders. A fire of unknown origin, although suspected of being started by the troops, burnt down most of the veterans' tents and other structures.

Hoover's public image suffered greatly as a result of the troops' actions, which helped Franklin Roosevelt win the presidential election a few months later. Although Roosevelt scored political points because of Hoover's missteps, he showed little sympathy for the veterans once in office. Congress passed, over his veto, a bill that paid out the bonuses in 1936, at a cost of $2.5 billion.

BIBLIOGRAPHY

Lisio, Donald J. *The President and Protest: Hoover, MacArthur, and the Bonus Riot.* New York: Fordham University Press, 1994.

Waters, Walter. W. *B. E. F.: The Whole Story of the Bonus Army.* New York: The John Day Company, 1933.

Richard M. Flanagan

See also **Great Depression.**

BONUS BILL OF 1816 was intended to direct profits from the second national bank to fund internal improvements. On 16 December 1816 John C. Calhoun recommended that the House of Representatives appoint a committee to investigate such an application of federal profits. Calhoun, as chairman of the committee, introduced a bill on 23 December 1816 to set apart as a permanent fund for internal improvements the $1.5 million bonus exacted from the bank as a price of its charter and the profits from the $7 million of bank stock owned by the United States. Although the House passed the bill, President James Madison vetoed it on 3 March 1817 on the grounds that it was unconstitutional. Madison suggested that an amendment to the Constitution would remove all doubts on the subject.

BIBLIOGRAPHY

Dangerfield, George. *The Awakening of American Nationalism, 1815–1828.* New York: Harper and Row, 1965.

Larson, John Lauritz. " 'Bind the Republic Together': The National Union and the Struggle for a System of Internal Improvements." *Journal of American History* 74 (September 1987): 363–387.

George D. Harmon / T. M.

See also **Bank of the United States; Banking.**

BONUSES, MILITARY, gratuities or benefits, usually paid in a lump sum, to veterans of military service. They should be distinguished from pensions, which are a continuing compensation paid to disabled veterans or their dependents. Until World War II, bonuses paid to veterans in the United States took the form of both cash payments and land grants. The practice began in 1776, when the Continental Congress voted to reward men of the Continental army with grants of land that ranged in size from 100 acres for noncommissioned officers and privates to 1,100 acres for a major general. Public lands in Ohio (U.S. Military District) were reserved for location of the bounties, and warrants totaling more than 2 million acres were eventually issued. In 1778, acting on a suggestion by George Washington, the Congress voted to give, at the end of the war, an additional five years' pay to commissioned officers and a sum of about eighty dollars to all others as a bonus.

During the first half of the nineteenth century, bonuses took the exclusive form of land grants. An act of 1811 extended to veteran noncommissioned officers and privates, with five years of service, a grant of 160 acres of the public domain. In 1846 Congress awarded 160 acres of land to noncommissioned officers and privates who had served in the War with Mexico. In 1850 an act granted eighty acres to any veteran of the War of 1812 excluded under the act of 1811, to commissioned officers of the Mexican War, and to any person who had served in an Indian war since 1790. Finally, in 1855, Congress raised the minimum land grant for all previous laws to 160 acres and lowered all previous eligibility requirements to fourteen days service or participation in one battle. Although warrants for more than 65 million acres were issued under these various laws, very little of the land was actually taken up by veterans, since the warrants could be sold to other persons or exchanged for interest-bearing or Treasury scrip. A large market for the warrants developed, and most of the bonus lands fell into the hands of speculators.

Civil War veterans of the Union Army received bonuses adjusted to the length of service, a maximum of $100 being paid to those who had served three years. In 1875 President Ulysses S. Grant vetoed a congressional measure that would have equalized the bonus payments of all Union soldiers. The veterans of the Spanish-American War were not given a bonus, and the issue was not raised again until after World War I.

Although servicemen received a mustering-out bonus of sixty dollars at the end of World War I, the American Legion led a movement for an additional bonus. At its fall convention in 1919 the legion took the position that former servicemen were entitled to "adjusted compensation"—that is, the difference between the money they actually received while in the service and the larger amount they could have earned had they remained at home. A bill to grant such a bonus was passed over President Calvin Coolidge's veto in 1924. More than 3.5 million interest-bearing adjusted compensation certificates were issued, with a total value of $3.5 billion, actual payment being in the form of paid-up twenty-year endowment insurance policies, deferred until 1945. With the coming of the Great Depression and massive unemployment, the American Legion demanded immediate cash payment of the certificates. In 1931 Congress passed over President Herbert Hoover's veto a compromise bill under which veterans could borrow 50 percent of the cash value of their certificates at 4.5 percent interest. That measure did not quiet the veterans, however, and subsequent demands for full and immediate payment were highlighted by the Bonus Army incident in the summer of 1932, when between 12,000 and 15,000 veterans assembled in Washington to demand cash payment of their certificates. The issue was finally resolved in January 1936, when Congress, over President Franklin Roosevelt's veto, passed a bill authorizing immediate payment of the certificates.

While the United States was still involved in World War II, Congress passed the Servicemen's Readjustment Act of 1944, popularly called the GI Bill of Rights. The act provided a comprehensive program of veterans' benefits, including unemployment compensation, education, and job training, and guaranteed housing and business loans. Through the date of its termination in July 1949, the unemployment compensation program paid almost $4 billion in "readjustment allowances" to nearly 9 million veterans. The education and job-training program, which terminated in July 1956, provided educational benefits at the secondary and college level and on-the-job training to almost 10 million veterans at a cost exceeding $13 billion. The insured-loan program came to an end for most veterans in July 1962, and by that date more than 5 million applicants had obtained loans totaling more than $50 billion.

In July 1952 Congress passed the Veterans Readjustment Act, which extended the benefits of the earlier measure to veterans of the Korean conflict. Congress passed still another GI bill, the Veterans Readjustment Benefits Act of 1966. In addition to extending benefits of the previous measures to veterans of the military conflict in Vietnam, it also applied retroactively to those who had served for more than 180 days after 31 January 1955, the date after which veterans became ineligible under the 1952 act. Thus the act of 1966 seemed to commit the nation for the first time to the idea that peacetime veterans were entitled to receive the same benefits as wartime veterans. In December 1974 Congress passed, over President Gerald Ford's veto, the Vietnam Era Veterans Readjustment Act. The main provisions of the act extended the period of educational benefits from thirty-six to forty-five months and increased the monthly payments to veterans enrolled in college by 23 percent. In 1976 Congress passed the Post-Vietnam Era Veterans' Educational Assistance Program. It was the first program that required a contribution from the enlisted individual for participation. The program allowed for the voluntary contribution of between $25 and $100 a month, which the government would match two-to-one. In 1984 Congress passed the Montgomery GI Bill. This bill also required a voluntary contribution for participation in the amount of $100 a month for the first twelve months of service. The government paid up to $400 a month for thirty-six months for tuition and educational expenses for those who elected to participate in the program.

BIBLIOGRAPHY

Asch, Beth J., and James N. Dertouzas. *Educational Benefits versus Enlistment Bonuses: A Comparison of Recruiting Options.* Santa Monica, Calif.: Rand, 1994.

Gates, Paul W. *History of Public Land Law Development.* Washington, D.C.: William W. Gaunt, 1987.

Lewis, Elmer E., ed. *Laws Relating to Veterans, 1914–1941.* Washington, D.C.: U.S. Government Printing Office, 1945.

Ross, Davis R. B. *Preparing for Ulysses.* New York: Columbia University Press, 1969.

Seddie Cogswell

See also **GI Bill of Rights; Pensions, Military and Naval.**

BOOBY TRAPS, devices that explode when a hidden or apparently harmless object is disturbed and detonate before the victim can recognize and react to the danger. Traps executed in warfare have existed since antiquity, but the modern booby trap did not appear until World War I.

The Germans and the Japanese used booby traps extensively during World War II, usually as defensive weapons. The Korean War also saw wide use of booby traps by the Chinese and the North Koreans. In the Vietnam War, booby traps became a major weapon, their employment by the Vietcong and the North Vietnamese being so common that they had the practical effect of serving as offensive as well as defensive weapons. Soldiers in these armies extensively booby trapped their supply caches, known routes of communications, and approaches to hidden base camps. The Vietcong used nonexplosive traps as well, especially sharpened stakes hidden in vegetation at likely helicopter landing zones. U.S. troops seldom used booby traps in World War II and the Korean War but did so frequently in Vietnam, where Americans employed the "mechanical ambush" using a pellet-firing mine activated by a hidden trip wire.

BIBLIOGRAPHY

Convention on Prohibitions or Restrictions on the Use of Certain Conventional Weapons. Washington, D.C.: U.S. Government Printing Office, 1995.

Sullivan, George E. *Suicidal Booby Traps.* Washington, D.C.: G. E. Sullivan, 1949.

John Albright / c. w.

See also **Guerrilla Warfare; War Casualties; Wars, Laws of.**

BOOK BANNING has existed in America since colonial times, when legislatures and royal governors enacted laws against blasphemy and seditious libel. Legislatures in the early American republic passed laws against obscenity. Though freedom of the press has grown significantly over the course of the twentieth century, book banning and related forms of censorship have persisted due to cyclical concerns about affronts to cultural, political, moral, and religious orthodoxy.

Books can be restricted by an outright ban or through less overt forms of social or political pressure. One formal method is a legislative prohibition of certain subjects and texts being taught in schools, including Tennessee's 1925 law proscribing the teaching of evolution in schools (which led to the Scopes "Monkey Trial"). In *Epperson v. Arkansas* (1968), the Supreme Court invalidated a similar law in Arkansas. Informal banning, which John Stuart Mill considered even more pernicious to liberty, also occurs. During the McCarthy era, many college instructors dropped communist and socialist books from courses due to informal pressures.

Another method of book banning occurs through postal and customs restrictions. The federal government has prohibited the importation and interstate shipment of obscene works since the middle of the nineteenth century, most famously by the so-called Comstock Act (1873), which is still in effect in modified form. Since 1960, literary works dealing with sexual themes have enjoyed strong First Amendment protection, but before this time the U.S. Post and Customs Offices banned classic works such as *Ulysses, Leaves of Grass, Tropic of Cancer,* and *God's Little Acre.* Only after a federal court extended First Amendment protection to D. H. Lawrence's *Lady Chatterley's Lover* in *Grove Press v. Christenberry* (1959) have works with literary merit been assured of escaping federal censorship.

Book banning also prominently takes the form of removing books from libraries or other sources. During the 1950s, the banning of liberal and left-wing books was widespread. In the last decade, censors have targeted such allegedly "politically incorrect" books as *Huckleberry Finn* and *Lolita.* Traditional moralists have continued to single out books dealing with controversial social and sexual subjects, including teenage sexual exploration, such as in Judy Blume's *Forever,* homosexuality in Michael Willhoite's *Daddy's Roommate,* and racial tensions, such as in Maya Angelou's *I Know Why the Caged Bird Sings.* In 1982, the Supreme Court heard a case where a school board removed *Slaughterhouse-Five, The Naked Ape,* and *Soul on Ice* from the school library for being "anti-American, anti-Christian, anti-Semitic, and just plain filthy." The Court ruled in *Board of Education Island Trees Union Free School District v. Pico* that books may not be removed if the decision to do so is motivated by disapproval of the viewpoint expressed in the book.

Donald A. Downs
Martin J. Sweet

See also **Censorship, Press and Artistic; First Amendment.**

BOOK-OF-THE-MONTH CLUB. Harry Scherman, a former advertising copywriter, launched the Book-of-the-Month Club in 1926. Among the club's business innovations was the "negative option": while subscribers could select alternates to the main selection, they had to accept a book, which ensured a steady business. The club was a quick success, reaching a membership of 110,000 in 1929, and its standard monthly order format was imitated by other mail-order businesses.

The Book-of-the-Month Club is a prime example of the growth in the early twentieth century of middlebrow culture, which mixed the values of an expanding consumer economy with those of traditional high culture. Like advertisements for other contemporary products, those for the club promised convenience and addressed the anxiety of the "average intelligent reader" who wished to remain au courant. Yet the club took seriously its mission to provide readers with "the best new books published each month." In order to ensure the literary quality of its books, a panel of expert judges from the world of letters made the monthly selections.

Some intellectuals criticized the club for introducing commercial values into the literary world and standardizing the reading tastes of the American public. Supporters of the club, however, argued that it democratized access to literary works. Although the club eliminated its panel of judges in 1994, it continued to distribute hundreds of thousands of books monthly at the end of the century.

BIBLIOGRAPHY

Radway, Janice. *A Feeling for Books: The Book-of-the-Month Club, Literary Taste, and Middle-Class Desire.* Chapel Hill: University of North Carolina Press, 1997.

Rubin, Joan Shelley. *The Making of Middlebrow Culture.* Chapel Hill: University of North Carolina Press, 1992.

Daniel Geary

See also **Mail-Order Houses; Middlebrow Culture.**

BOOMER MOVEMENT, a term applied to attempts of white settlers to occupy an area in Indian Territory from 1879 to 1885. The so-called Five Civilized Tribes of American Indians, driven from the Southeast in the 1830s, had settled on a reservation extending to the boundaries of the present state of Oklahoma, excluding the Panhandle (see CIMARRON, PROPOSED TERRITORY OF).

Elias C. Boudinot. His newspaper article eventually led to white settlement of part of Indian Territory. LIBRARY OF CONGRESS

In 1866, as punishment for having participated in the Civil War on the side of the South, they were compelled to cede the western half of their domain to the United States as a home for Indians of other tribes. During the next ten years several tribes were given reservations on these lands, but a fertile region of some 2 million acres near the center of Indian Territory was not assigned to any tribe and came to be known as the "unassigned lands" or Old Oklahoma.

Early in 1879 Elias C. Boudinot, a railway attorney of Cherokee descent, published a newspaper article stating that this was public land and so open to homestead entry. Widely reprinted, this article created great excitement. Later in the same year, a colony of home seekers under the leadership of Charles C. Carpenter sought to enter Indian Territory and occupy this area but were prevented by federal troops under General John Pope.

In 1880 David L. Payne organized the "Boomer" movement and charged a small fee for membership in his "Oklahoma colony." During the next four years he and his followers made eight attempts to settle the region, but in each case they were ejected by soldiers. Upon Payne's death at Wellington, Kansas, in 1884, his lieutenant, W. L. Couch, led an expedition to the forbidden area that was promptly removed by the military. The struggle was then transferred to the national capital, and on 22 April 1889 the unassigned lands were opened to settlement under the provisions of an act of Congress. Some white settlers, called "Sooners," had already entered the territory illegally and had established farms. At noon on 22 April thousands of white men, women, and children on horseback, in wagons, and sometimes on foot rushed into the interior of the former Indian Territory to stake out their homesteads.

BIBLIOGRAPHY

Joyce, Davis D., ed. *"An Oklahoma I Had Never Seen Before": Alternative Views of Oklahoma History.* Norman, Okla.: University of Oklahoma Press, 1994.

Morgan, H. Wayne, and Anne Hodges Morgan. *Oklahoma.* New York: Norton, 1977.

Edward Everett Dale / A. R.

See also **Civilized Tribes, Five; Indian Territory; Sooners.**

BOOMTOWNS, settlements that sprang up or grew rapidly as the result of some economic or political development. Rochester, New York, for example, grew rapidly after 1825 as the result of the completion of the ERIE CANAL and the harnessing of the Genesee River's waterpower. San Francisco boomed during the California gold rush of 1849–1851, while in the 1860s gold strikes in Idaho, Montana, and Colorado attracted thousands of settlers into hastily built towns. Most of those towns were ephemeral, but Helena, Montana, and Denver, Colorado, were permanent. Gold brought Deadwood, South Da-

Leadville. This Colorado silver-mining camp flourished from 1878 to 1893; this photograph was taken in 1919 by F. E. Colburn.
© CORBIS

kota, into existence in 1876. Two cities built on silver evolved swiftly in 1878. TOMBSTONE, Arizona, gained a new foundation, and the population of Leadville, Colorado, leaped from three hundred to thirty-five thousand in two years. Oil City, Pennsylvania, in 1859 was the first in a long series of petroleum boomtowns that later continued into Ohio, Indiana, Oklahoma, and Texas. The opening of a portion of Indian Territory to colonization in 1889 created Guthrie and Oklahoma City almost overnight. Hopewell, Virginia, was a typical creation of a World War I munitions plant, and war production during World War II dramatically expanded a number of western towns and cities. Beginning in 1956, Cape Canaveral, Florida, developed into a prosperous town with more than thirty-five thousand inhabitants employed in the U.S. space program. Construction of the Alaska pipeline began in 1974, and boomtowns sprang up along the pipeline's route as work progressed.

Boomtowns have been susceptible to the environmental, economic, and political forces that created them. For example, cutbacks in space research in the 1970s brought severe economic stress to the Cape Canaveral area. As the mineral and manufacturing economies declined in many regions of the country in the late twentieth century, the challenges facing former boomtowns became acute.

BIBLIOGRAPHY

Holliday, J. S. *Rush for Riches: Gold Fever and the Making of California.* Oakland, Calif.: Oakland Museum of California, 1999.

Nash, Gerald D. *World War II and the West.* Lincoln: University of Nebraska Press, 1990.

Alvin F. Harlow / A. R.

See also **Gold Rush; Mining Towns.**

BOOT AND SHOE MANUFACTURING. Bootmakers and shoemakers arrived early in the history of each of the colonies to provide the settlers with much-needed products. After acquiring leather from nearby tanneries, cobblers, who frequently worked at home, used hand tools and centuries-old techniques to cut out the various parts, to sew together the pieces to make the upper, and to attach the upper to the sole, shaping each shoe over a wooden last or form. A nascent industry developed in eastern Massachusetts by the end of the colonial era. Lynn had become a leading center after John Adam Dagyr and other immigrants introduced the most recent European hand processes, permitting colonists to make products that competed successfully with foreign imports.

In order to supply the demands of a growing population after the Revolutionary War, merchant capitalists slowly reorganized the trade. They purchased leather from both American and foreign markets, cut the materials, hired craftsmen to make the shoes in their homes or small shops, and sold the finished products. This domestic, or putting-out, system of manufacture meant the cobbler worked for the merchant. Two kinds of specialization emerged: shoemakers in a region would specialize in a particular type of shoe, while craftsmen would specialize in only one step in the MANUFACTURING process. Improving transportation networks and growing financial resources permitted shoe manufacturers in Massachusetts and the Middle Atlantic states to exploit southern and western markets.

Factories and mechanization came to this large industry after 1850, as entrepreneurs gradually recognized the usefulness of consolidating the various processes at one location, where better supervision of the increasingly specialized steps could occur. Within these central shops, or factories, machines were perfected that imitated specific hand processes. Of the more than five thousand American patents issued before 1900 for improvements in shoemaking, three developments proved most significant: the adaptation of the Howe sewing machine to stitching uppers; the invention by Lyman R. Blake, a black mechanic, of a device for sewing the upper to the sole (the machine bears the name of Col. Gordon McKay, who improved and marketed it during the Civil War); and the perfection, by Charles Goodyear, Jr., by 1875 of Auguste Deystouy's welt-stitching machine for joining the upper and sole. The advantages of machines, especially those that were power driven, encouraged the further subdivision of processes that led, by the end of the century, to a process with more than 170 steps. Mechanization reduced the time required to make a shoe by more than 80 percent.

With the creation of large, integrated factories, employees turned toward trade unionism. In 1895, in the wake of several other more radical labor associations, workers formed the International Boot and Shoe Workers Union. In 1899 the principal producers of shoemaking machinery formed the United Shoe Machinery Company, which still controlled this industry in the mid-1970s. In 1905 the shoe manufacturers formed the National Boot and Shoe Manufacturers Association.

Although New England and the Atlantic seaboard dominated shoemaking, before World War I other centers of manufacture emerged in western New York, the Midwest, and the upper South, using materials from throughout the world. Consolidation reduced the number of firms to 1,449 in 1919, but these companies had 211,000 employees and an output of 331 million pairs of shoes. Americans exported almost $75 million worth of leather footwear per year.

After World War I the shoemaking industry experienced difficulties. Although Americans refined techniques, foreign machinery manufacturers competed successfully. Imported shoes and a trend toward canvas and rubber shoes eroded the domestic market. Synthetic leather materials forced firms to adopt costly new technology. A more affluent society encouraged companies to design new styles, which then presented inventory problems. As competition and the size of the required capital investment rose, many firms either closed or consolidated.

Many of the most successful American firms in subsequent decades produced sneakers and athletic shoes.

Athletic shoes were first marketed in the 1910s and 1920s as necessary components of such new popular sports as tennis and baseball. Only in the 1930s, however, did most firms add traction to the soles of shoes and sell different models for different sports. The market expanded somewhat in the 1950s, but sneaker production did not become big business until the 1970s. The popularity of running and more relaxed dress codes in schools and workplaces led to a boom in the market for athletic shoeware. Manufacturers introduced sophisticated marketing techniques to launch state-of-the-art advertising campaigns, funded extensive research to develop high-tech shoe soles, and paid famous athletes to wear and promote their shoes. Athletic shoes became fashion statements, subject to yearly model changes and very high markups.

Although many American firms profited from sales of these shoes, they were rarely manufactured in the United States. Only Converse, New Balance, and Hyde Athletics (makers of Saucony) maintained some manufacturing operations in the United States by 1997; domestically manufactured sneakers accounted for only 10 percent of the total sold in 1995. Most firms shifted production to overseas factories, often working through Asian subcontractors. One reason for the move was technological; Korea and Taiwan had fully developed networks of parts producers that could satisfy the need for constantly changing equipment and technologically advanced shoes. But economics also played a role. Wages, especially in poorer countries like Indonesia, were dramatically lower than those in the United States. Working conditions were also generally much harsher and more repressive. Manufacturers were subject to intensifying public scrutiny over charges of exploitation of overseas workers. These complaints resulted in increased oversight of American firms' overseas suppliers and antisweatshop activism on many college campuses. Athletic shoes nonetheless remained extraordinarily popular; by 1997 these shoes had more than twice the market share of dress or casual shoes.

BIBLIOGRAPHY

Blewett, Mary H. *Men, Women, and Work: Class, Gender, and Protest in the New England Shoe Industry, 1780–1910.* Urbana: University of Illinois Press, 1988.

Dawley, Alan. *Class and Community: The Industrial Revolution in Lynn.* Cambridge, Mass.: Harvard University Press, 1976.

Hazard, Blanche Evans. *The Organization of the Boot and Shoe Industry in Massachusetts Before 1875.* Cambridge, Mass.: Harvard University Press, 1921.

Vanderbilt, Tom. *The Sneaker Book: Anatomy of an Industry and an Icon.* New York: New Press, 1998.

Lucius F. Ellsworth / T. D.

See also **Basketball; Clothing Industry; Labor; Massachusetts; Rubber.**

BOOTLEGGING. In January 1920, the Eighteenth Amendment became law, banning the manufacture, transportation, importation, and sale of intoxicating liquors in the United States. Known as Prohibition, the amendment was the culmination of more than a century of attempts to remove alcohol from society by various temperance organizations. Many large cities and states actually went dry in 1918. Americans could no longer legally drink or buy alcohol. The people who illegally made, imported, or sold alcohol during this time were called bootleggers.

In contrast to its original intent, Prohibition, a tenet of the "Jazz Age" of the 1920s, caused a permanent change in the way the nation viewed authority, the court system, and wealth and class. Particularly damning was the lack of enforcement, which led to the rise of the mob and notorious criminals such as Al Capone. As a result, bootlegging became big business in the era, often as immigrants took hold of power in urban centers.

Despite enforcement efforts by federal, state, and local officers, Prohibition actually instigated a national drinking spree that persisted until Americans repealed the law thirteen years later. The effects on the American national psyche, however, were long lasting, ushering in a general cynicism and distrust. Many cities proudly proclaimed that they were the nation's wettest. In the early 1920s, Chicago had more than 7,000 drinking parlors, or speak-easies, so named because patrons had to whisper code-words to enter. Physicians nationwide dispensed prescriptions for medicinal alcohol, while pharmacies applied for liquor licenses. Alcohol was available for a price and delivered with a wink and wry smile.

Given the pervasive lawlessness during Prohibition, bootlegging was omnipresent. The operations varied in size, from an intricate network of bootlegging middlemen and local suppliers, right up to America's bootlegging king, George Remus, who operated from Cincinnati, lived a lavish lifestyle, and amassed a $5 million fortune. To escape prosecution, men like Remus used bribery, heavily armed guards, and medicinal licenses to circumvent the law. More ruthless gangsters, such as Capone, did not stop at crime, intimidation, and murder.

Under those conditions, the nation's cities were ripe for crime. In cities like Pittsburgh and Cleveland, numerous ethnic gangs fought to control the local bootlegging activities. In Chicago, 800 gangsters were killed in gang warfare during Prohibition, primarily due to the fight over alcohol sales.

Bootleggers counterfeited prescriptions and liquor licenses to gain access to alcohol. The most common practice was to import liquor from other countries aboard ships. The river between Detroit and Canada was a thriving entry point, as was the overland method on the long border between the two countries. Bootleggers also evaded authorities by building secret breweries with intricate security systems and lookouts. In addition to eluding the police, bootleggers had to fend off other bootleggers who would steal the precious cargo for their own sale. Bootleggers began a national controversy by selling adulter-

ated liquor, which resulted in countless fatalities and poisonings.

Bootlegging grew into a vast illegal empire, in part, because of widespread bribery. Many enforcement agents received monthly retainers (some receiving $300,000 a month) to look the other way. Critics said that Prohibition Bureau agents had a license to make money through bribes from bootleggers. The corruption among agents was so prevalent that President Warren G. Harding commented on it in his State of the Union address in 1922.

Countless books and movies, including F. Scott Fitzgerald's *The Great Gatsby* and the hit film *The Untouchables*, have chronicled the period. As a result of Prohibition and the illegal bootlegging culture, popular culture examines both the Roaring 1920s and the darker aspects of the period, which play an important role in creating the American mythos.

BIBLIOGRAPHY
Behr, Edward. *Prohibition: Thirteen Years that Changed America.* New York: Arcade, 1996.
Coffey, Thomas M. *The Long Thirst: Prohibition in America, 1920–1933.* New York: W.W. Norton, 1975.
Kobler, John. *Ardent Spirits: The Rise and Fall of Prohibition.* New York: Putnam, 1973.
Pegram, Thomas R. *Battling Demon Rum: The Struggle for a Dry America, 1800–1933.* Chicago: Ivan R. Dee, 1998.

Bob Batchelor

See also **Crime, Organized; Prohibition; Speakeasy.**

BORAX (sodium tetraborate) became important in the European Middle Ages as a flux for soldering—that is, for cleaning the surfaces of metal pieces to be joined by being melted together. Native European sources were unknown, and the nature and origin of this mysterious material was long a puzzle to chemists. Borax was ultimately traced to Tibet—almost the only source known until the discovery (1776) and exploitation (1820) of Italian springs of boric acid (hydrogen tetraborate), which could be converted by the addition of soda (sodium carbonate) into borax. Italy became the principal source of borax until the 1860s, when desert areas now in Chile began to supply borax.

The key figure in the discovery of borax in North America was John A. Veatch, who found it in California in 1856, first in springs at the north end of the Sacramento Valley (Tehama County) and then in larger quantities in a cutoff bay of Clear Lake (Lake County). Veatch himself stated that the discovery was accidental, sparked by the presence in the region of an Englishman who had formerly worked for a London borax company. The California Borax Company was organized to exploit this source, and the company struggled for a decade to extract and purify a material encrusted on the bottom of an isolated wilderness lake. In 1857 Veatch's explorations took him to southern California, where he found borax in the waters of mud volcanoes in the Colorado desert. Within the next decade, borax was found in surface encrustations in more convenient locations in Nevada and southern California. In 1871 the *Mining and Scientific Press* of San Francisco reported borax to be "all the rage," with production in progress at Columbus, Fish, and Teal marshes in Esmeralda County, Nevada. In 1880 production began in Death Valley, California, where the famous twenty-mule-team wagons carried it out of this below-sea-level depression to the railroad junction at Mojave, 160 miles away.

These surface deposits of borax were largely sodium calcium tetraborate (ulexite), known from their appearance as cotton balls. Their conversion to true borax was chemically simple but difficult in practice. American producers mastered the conversion process by the mid-1880s and supplied the domestic and international markets. However, they drove the price down to a level that caused most producers to fail. The principal survivor, Francis "Borax" Smith, employed Stephen Mather to promote borax in 1896, starting with a pamphlet advertising two hundred "recipes" for borax. This successful advertising campaign greatly expanded the demand for borax, which had become relatively inexpensive, especially in washing powders, glass, and ceramic glazes.

Although Smith controlled nearly all American sources of borax, financial troubles with his other investments forced him to merge with the English borax company Redwood and Sons in 1896 to form a company known in the early 2000s as U.S. Borax. Exploitation of shallow deposits terminated once drilling began in the Mojave Desert, at a site marked by the company town, Boron. In the 1970s production there and at Searles Lake, California, exceeded one million tons per year and satisfied the borax demands of the United States, western Europe, Japan, and many other parts of the world.

BIBLIOGRAPHY

Coolidge, Dane. *Death Valley Prospectors.* Morongo Valley, Calif.: Sagebrush Press, 1985.

Spears, John R. *Illustrated Sketches of Death Valley and Other Borax Deserts of the Pacific Coast.* Morongo Valley, Calif.: Sagebrush Press, 1977.

Travis, Norman J., and E. J. Cocks. *The Tincal Trail: A History of Borax.* London: Harrap, 1984.

Robert P. Multhauf/h. s.

See also **Death Valley; Soap and Detergent Industry.**

BORDER RUFFIANS, citizens of western Missouri who endeavored to establish slavery in Kansas Territory. Following passage of the Kansas-Nebraska Act in 1854, which allowed local voters to decide whether Kansas would be a free or a slave state, pro- and antislavery groups battled for control of Kansas Territory. The term "border ruffians" originated in 1855 with Gen. B. F. Stringfellow's assault upon A. H. Reeder, governor of the territory, and was first used by the *New York Tribune.* Missourians readily adopted the name, and border ruffian stores, hotels, and riverboats capitalized upon it. Antislavery presses and orators soon expanded the term to include all proslavery southerners in Kansas, from carousing criminals to elite individuals like Senator David R. Atchison. Some slavery opponents even used the term to raise contributions for antislavery emigrant aid societies. Border ruffians voted illegally in Kansas elections, stole horses, and raided several towns including Lawrence on 21 May 1856. Antislavery Kansans responded in kind, most famously in John Brown's massacre of five proslavery settlers on Pottawatomie Creek. A spirit of lawlessness prompted both groups to use extreme measures, and conflicts between border ruffians and their antislavery foes soon prompted the name "Bleeding Kansas" for the territory. Violence between various groups did not decline until 1859, and tensions remained high through the outbreak of the Civil War. During that conflict, Missourians used the terms "border ruffians" and "bushwackers" interchangeably.

BIBLIOGRAPHY

Johannsen, Robert W. *The Frontier, the Union, and Stephen A. Douglas.* Urbana: University of Illinois Press, 1989.

Morrison, Michael A. *Slavery and the American West.* Chapel Hill: University of North Carolina Press, 1997.

Rawley, James. *Race & Politics: "Bleeding Kansas" and the Coming of the Civil War.* Philadelphia: Lippincott, 1969.

Wendell H. Stephenson/f. h.

See also **Border War; Emigrant Aid Movement; Harpers Ferry Raid; Jayhawkers; Kansas-Nebraska Act; Lawrence, Sack of.**

BORDER SLAVE STATE CONVENTION, also known as the Peace Convention and Peace Conference, took place at Willard's Hotel in Washington, D.C., from 4 to 27 February in 1861. Initiated by Virginia's legislature, the convention hoped to avert war and reunite seceded Southern states with the Union, but the seven states from the deep South, along with Arkansas, Wisconsin, Minnesota, California, and Oregon, refused to send delegates. The convention president and former U.S. President John Tyler said the convention's goal was "to bring back the cotton states and thereby restore the Constitution and the Union of the States." Three days after the convention commenced, the seceding states adopted a provisional constitution for the Confederate States of America. The convention, however, continued its efforts to modify the Crittenden Compromise, which had failed as a proposed constitutional amendment in the preceding January session of the House of Representatives. Though attempts at modification of the proposed amendment failed to fully satisfy Peace Convention attendees, the group submitted its resolution for recommendations to

Congress on 27 February 1816. The recommendations arrived thirty-six days before the South fired its first shot at Fort Sumter and marked the territory's last attempt at reconciliation regarding slavery.

BIBLIOGRAPHY
Kirwan, A. D. *John J. Crittenden: The Struggle for the Union.* Lexington: University of Kentucky Press, 1962.

Randall, J. G. *The Civil War and Reconstruction.* 2d ed. Boston: Little, Brown, 1969.

James T. Scott

See also **Crittenden Compromise; Secession.**

BORDER WAR

BORDER WAR (1854–1859). The KANSAS-NEBRASKA ACT of 1854, which allowed local voters to decide whether Kansas would be a slave state or a free state, prompted emigration from the Northeast of antislavery groups, the arrival of squatters and speculators, and the presence of an adventurous element recruited from both North and South. Ideological differences over slavery and recurring personal altercations led proslavery and free-state groups to organize regulating associations and guerrilla bands. Lynching, horse stealing, pillaging, and pitched battles marked the years from 1854 to 1859 and inspired the name "Bleeding Kansas" for the territory. The first eighteen months of settlement witnessed sporadic shootings, killings, and robberies, including the Wakarusa War (December 1855), which brought over one thousand BORDER RUFFIANS into the territory. The sack of Lawrence (21 May 1856) by a posse of border ruffians and John Brown's massacre of five proslavery men at POTTAWATOMIE three days later started a four-month reign of terror. Free-state men won victories at Black Jack, Franklin, Fort Saunders, Fort Titus, Slough Creek, and Hickory Point; their opponents pillaged and later burned Osawatomie (30 August 1856), but official intervention prevented them from further destroying Lawrence. A semblance of order restored by Governor John W. Geary in the fall was of brief duration. The Marais des Cygnes massacre of nine free-state men on 19 May 1858 was the last wholesale slaughter. Major conflict terminated in 1859, albeit sporadic disorders continued until the CIVIL WAR. Anticipating a congressional appropriation that did not materialize, territorial commissioners approved claims for losses resulting from border trouble totaling over $400,000, which, though exaggerated, give some notion of the extent of property damage.

BIBLIOGRAPHY
Johannsen, Robert W. *The Frontier, the Union, and Stephen A. Douglas.* Urbana: University of Illinois Press, 1989.

Morrison, Michael A. *Slavery and the American West: The Eclipse of Manifest Destiny and the Coming of the Civil War.* Chapel Hill: University of North Carolina Press, 1997.

Rawley, James A. *Race & Politics: "Bleeding Kansas" and the Coming of the Civil War.* Philadelphia: Lippincott, 1969.

Wendell H. Stephenson

See also **Emigrant Aid Movement; Harpers Ferry Raid; Jayhawkers; Lawrence, Sack of.**

BORDERLANDS. *See* **Spanish Borderlands.**

BORK CONFIRMATION HEARINGS. President Ronald Reagan, long a critic of liberal and activist judges who "made law" rather than simply applying the original intentions of the founders, repeatedly expressed his hope for placing conservative and self-restrained justices on the Supreme Court. When Lewis Powell, a moderate conservative, announced his retirement, Reagan sent forward a nomination fully embodying this hope. Sixty-year-old Robert Heron Bork had a distinguished career as a law professor at Yale (1962–1973, 1977–1981), as U.S. solicitor general (1973–1977), and as a federal appeals judge

Robert Bork. The highly controversial nominee to the Supreme Court, whose defeat in 1987 embittered his supporters. CORBIS-BETTMANN

for the District of Columbia (1982–1988). During the Watergate hearings, Bork's two superiors decided to resign rather than carry out President Richard Nixon's order to fire special prosecutor Archibald Cox. Bork, however, earned some notoriety for his willingness to carry out the president's order.

The televised confirmation hearings were bitter, spirited, and harsh. Bork's supporters pointed to his record of service and his brilliance as a theorist, writer, and judge. Opponents, quoting his judicial opinions and other writings, insisted that his elevation would endanger civil rights, the right to privacy, the legality of abortion, and the constitutional protections of nonpolitical speech. On 27 October, the Senate defeated the nomination on a largely party-line vote (Democrats, 52 to 2 against; Republicans, 40 to 6 for). The nominee's angry supporters coined a new verb: to be "borked" is to be unfairly treated, to have one's views misrepresented. In 1988, Bork resigned his judgeship to become a scholar-in-residence at the conservative American Enterprise Institute.

BIBLIOGRAPHY

Bork, Robert H. *The Tempting of America: The Political Seduction of the Law.* New York, Free Press, 1990.

Bronner, Ethan. *Battle for Justice: How the Bork Nomination Shook America.* New York: Norton, 1989.

David W. Levy

See also **Confirmation by the Senate; Supreme Court; Thomas Confirmation Hearings.**

BOROUGH, the English trading community that featured corporate organization and limited self-government, provided the model for many colonial towns. A colonial borough typically received its charter from the governor, who appointed a mayor and a recorder to sit on a common council with aldermen whom the freemen elected. These officials passed bylaws to regulate commerce and labor, to indenture orphans, to supervise relief for the poor, to fix bread prices, and to admit freemen, who in early days enjoyed a monopoly on retail trade. Sitting as a mayor's court or sessions court, these officials handled civil and criminal law. After the American Revolution state legislatures granted borough charters that frequently widened suffrage and allowed popular mayoral elections and greater self-rule.

BIBLIOGRAPHY

Hartog, Hendrik. *Public Property and Private Power.* Ithaca, N.Y.: Cornell University Press, 1989.

New York (City) Mayor's Court. *Select Cases of the Mayor's Court of New York City, 1678–1784.* Washington, D.C.: American Historical Association, 1935.

Richard B. Morris / s. b.

See also **Local Government.**

BOSNIA-HERZEGOVINA. *See* **Yugoslavia, Relations with.**

BOSSES AND BOSSISM, POLITICAL. A pejorative typically applied to leaders who control the selection of their political party's candidates for elected office and dispense patronage without regard for the public interest. The power of a boss turns on his ability to select single-handedly the candidates who will win an election. Indebted elected representatives then turn the reigns of government over to the boss, who makes policy decisions and uses government jobs and revenue to employ party loyalists and fund party functions.

The strongest bosses augmented their power as political party leader with an elected post. Among the most famous political bosses were the Chicago mayor and head of the Cook County Democratic Party, Richard J. Daley (1955–1976); Frank Hauge, mayor of Jersey City, New Jersey (1917–1947); and Edward Crump, mayor of Memphis (1910–1916) and congressman from Tennessee (1931–1935). Many other bosses maintained power without holding any official office, including the New Yorker William Marcy Tweed, head of the Tammany Hall political club in the 1860s, and Tom Pendergast, who ran the Jackson County Democratic Club and bossed Kansas City, Missouri, from 1911 until his incarceration for tax fraud in 1939.

Bossism is most closely associated with big cities, but bosses have also controlled political party organizations at the state level as well as in suburban and rural counties. Harry Flood Byrd, for example, dominated the Democratic Party in Virginia from the 1920s to the 1940s. Boss power has occasionally been exercised in presidential politics, too. A group of big city bosses helped secure the nomination of Harry Truman for vice president at the 1944 Democratic convention, and Richard Daley's support was considered critical to John F. Kennedy's election in the close 1960 presidential race.

The conditions for bossism were most widely present from the 1860s until World War II, with the waves of immigration that marked that period. Political machines and their bosses provided immigrants with jobs, small favors, and a sense of ethnic solidarity, forging personal relationships with new voters. In exchange, voters loyally supported machine candidates. At the turn of the twentieth century, Progressive reformers and many newspapers successfully attacked the inefficiency and immorality of the big city bosses. Civil service legislation forced bosses either to reform or have their candidates turned out of office.

The decline in machine strength after World War II has been attributed to changes in immigration policy and big city demography, the spread of federal social welfare programs, and the decline in voter loyalty to party organizations. In addition, the rise of media such as television and radio allowed individual candidates to reach voters

Tweed Ring. One of Thomas Nast's many political cartoons attacking William Marcy Tweed and his henchmen, this one—published in *Harper's Weekly* on 23 September 1871—includes the caption "A group of vultures waiting for the storm to 'blow over'—'Let us prey.'" LIBRARY OF CONGRESS

BIBLIOGRAPHY

Erie, Steven P. *Rainbow's End: Irish Americans and the Dilemmas of Urban Machine Politics, 1840–1985.* Berkeley: University of California Press, 1988.

Richard M. Flanagan
J. Leiper Freeman

See also **Corruption, Political; Immigration; Machine, Political; Tweed Ring.**

BOSTON. The capital and largest city of MASSACHUSETTS, Boston is a port of approximately forty-six square miles and the center of a metropolitan area of approximately 5.8 million people. According to the 2000 Census, Boston, with a population of 589,141, ranks as the twentieth largest city in the nation. This figure marks a 2.6 percent increase over 1990, when the population was 574,283.

Among the country's oldest cities, Boston is most famous for its role in the American Revolution; for its leading part in the nation's literary life; and as a center of social reform, education, and cultural accomplishment. The Boston area is the hub of New England's cultural and economic life and has a remarkable collection of educational institutions, including HARVARD UNIVERSITY, the MASSACHUSETTS INSTITUTE OF TECHNOLOGY, Boston College, Tufts University, Boston University, the University of Massachusetts at Boston, and Northeastern University.

The Boston area is the birthplace of U.S. presidents John Adams (Quincy), John Quincy Adams (Quincy), John F. Kennedy (Brookline), and George H. W. Bush (Milton). Historic sites are dedicated to the first three, and the John F. Kennedy Library and Museum is in the Dorchester neighborhood of Boston.

Boston's rich history is evident throughout the city. The Boston African American National Historic Site offers the Black Heritage Trail on Beacon Hill. The Freedom Trail connects such historic sites as the BOSTON COMMON, the Charles Bulfinch–designed State House atop Beacon Hill, the Old State House, the Old Corner Bookstore, the Old South Meeting House, FANEUIL HALL, the Paul Revere House, and OLD NORTH CHURCH. Walkers may follow the trail over to Charlestown to see the USS *Constitution*, where Old Ironsides resides in the old Navy Yard.

Colonial Era

Boston was founded in 1630 by English Puritans led by John Winthrop and named after the hometown of many of their band. These early settlers sought to create a "godly commonwealth" but their stress on conformity meant banishment for Anne Hutchinson, Roger Williams, and others who failed to accept Puritan ways. Williams moved on to establish a separate, successful colony in Rhode Island.

directly, thereby undercutting the need for political clubs and other boss-controlled institutions to "deliver the vote" in a primary election.

Academic evaluation of the phenomenon of bossism is riddled with ambivalence. In the early twentieth century, the academy heaped scorn on bosses and big city political machines for perpetuating corruption and inefficiency, and called for civil service and electoral reform that would drive bosses out of power. As the power of the more prominent city bosses began to wane in the 1950s, revisionist historians pointed to the class bias and nativism of the reformers as a counterbalance to the admitted faults of the bosses. In the late twentieth century, scholarship focused on such matters as the widespread machine practice of electoral exclusion of minorities, the collusion between machines and the economic elite, and the stalled economic mobility of ethnic groups closely associated with political machines.

Others seeking economic opportunities and land also left the town to settle elsewhere in New England, yet Boston continued to thrive. Boston's early economy was based on shipbuilding, fishing, and the coastal and West Indian trade, all of which resulted in the town becoming England's largest North American settlement.

Boston's fame as a literary and cultural center dates from its earliest years and stemmed from the Puritan attention to education. In 1635 Bostonians established the Boston Latin School, the first free public school in the colonies that would become the United States, while in 1636 they chartered Harvard College in Cambridge.

In the 1690s the MASSACHUSETTS BAY COLONY received a royal charter under England's new sovereigns, William and Mary, which placed the theretofore largely independent enterprise under closer British control. Because Boston's economy and standing were already in decline in the eighteenth century, British imperial reorganization following the French and Indian War was especially harmful to the town. In the 1760s the British government tightened its control over its colonies, leading directly to the American Revolution.

Creating a Nation

Boston's Faneuil Hall is called the "cradle of liberty" because of the stirring orations in opposition to British colonial government given there, but Bostonians' claim to birthing American independence rests largely with Samuel Adams. In the 1760s Adams organized the Sons of Liberty and aroused Bostonians to the dangers of British taxes. He fostered anti-British sentiment in 1770 by devising the term "BOSTON MASSACRE" to characterize how British troops shot and killed five Bostonians, including Crispus Attucks, a runaway slave.

The Adams-organized BOSTON TEA PARTY on the night of 16 December 1773 did even more to separate the colonies from Britain. Adams organized protests against imperial taxes on tea, and Bostonians masquerading as Indians boarded the ships carrying the offending cargo and dumped it into the harbor. In response, British officials closed the port of Boston and imposed martial law. Adams organized colonial opposition to these so-called Intolerable Acts and attended the First Continental Congress in Philadelphia in 1774 with his cousin, John Adams.

Searching for military supplies, British troops were met on 19 April 1775 outside of Boston at Lexington and Concord by local militia or "minutemen" who had been warned by Paul Revere and others. The famous "shot heard 'round the world" began the American Revolution. The hostilities continued as British forces attacked rebels who were in Charlestown, across the river from Boston, on 17 June 1775. The British won the famous conflict known as the Battle of BUNKER HILL only after suffering heavy losses. (Although the actual fighting took place on neighboring Breed's Hill, the name Bunker Hill stuck and is commemorated by a 221-foot granite obelisk, known as the BUNKER HILL MONUMENT.) George Washington

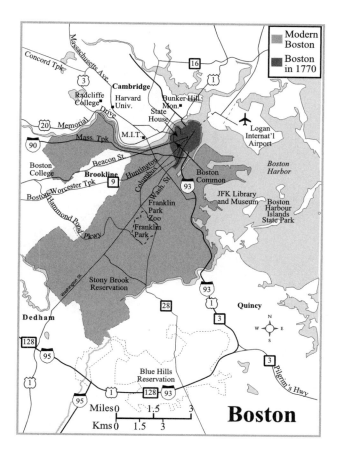

arrived soon after the battle to take charge of the newly formed Continental Army, and in March 1776 succeeded in banishing the British from Boston by strategically placing cannons on a hillside overlooking the town. Thus ended Boston's part in the fighting.

The Nineteenth Century

In the 1790s the famous China trade established Boston's economic base for the nineteenth century. Boston capitalists built textile mills in the early nineteenth century, but later in the century Boston declined economically relative to New York City. Boston changed in the early nineteenth century through its incorporation as a city in 1822 and as a result of landfill operations that created the new Back Bay and the South End neighborhoods. By the 1840s Boston had become a famous literary and cultural center, boasting such writers as Ralph Waldo Emerson, Henry David Thoreau, Margaret Fuller, and Nathaniel Hawthorne. At the same time Dr. Samuel Gridley Howe's stewardship of the Perkins Institution for the Blind in Boston pioneered new methods of education. Similarly, the Boston schoolteacher Dorothea Dix led the way in improving the care of mentally ill people throughout the state and nation.

Boston, Old and New. Soaring over the Romanesque Trinity Church in Copley Square, the windows of the modern John Hancock Tower reflect the previous John Hancock building in this 1973 photograph by Ernst Halberstadt. NATIONAL ARCHIVES AND RECORDS ADMINISTRATION

William Lloyd Garrison's uncompromising, radical abolitionism firmly established Boston's reputation as a hotbed of reform and a center of moral leadership for the nation in the Civil War era. During that war, Boston's Robert Gould Shaw, a young white officer, led the nation's first all-black regiment, the 54th Massachusetts, into battle and everlasting fame in the tragic 1863 assault on South Carolina's Fort Wagner.

In the decades after the Civil War, so-called Boston Brahmin families controlled the city's economy and supported cultural institutions such as the Museum of Fine Arts, the Massachusetts General Hospital, the Boston Symphony Orchestra, and Harvard University. During this period the fashionable Back Bay area was completed along with Copley Square, graced by architect Henry H. Richardson's masterpiece, Trinity Church, and its impressive neighbor, the Boston Public Library.

Immigrants and Change

Boston's demographics changed the city in the second half of the nineteenth century. The population rose as large numbers of New Englanders and European immigrants crowded into the city. In the 1860s and 1870s, Boston annexed the adjacent streetcar suburbs of Roxbury, Dorchester, West Roxbury, and Brighton. The Irish predominated among the immigrants and, with the election of mayors John F. Fitzgerald ("Honey Fitz," grandfather of John F. Kennedy) in 1905 and James Michael Curley in 1914, seemed destined to control Boston's politics.

Winning four mayoralty elections in the years between 1914 and 1945, Curley also served several terms in Congress as well as one stint as governor of the state. Despite considerable accomplishments in public works projects, he is most renowned for his chronic corruption, two jail sentences, and his willingness to "do it for a friend." Many of the friends that Curley assisted were Irish, but countless others were Italian and Jewish.

The Late Twentieth Century

The harmful effects of the Great Depression and the long decline of the New England textile industry lasted into the 1950s in Boston. At mid-century the city was close to fiscal and political bankruptcy. Fortuitously, however, economic and political circumstances in the second half of the twentieth century created the New Boston. The dazzling rise of the computer industry, largely resulting from the presence of the Massachusetts Institute of Technology in neighboring Cambridge, allowed Boston to make a remarkable economic recovery. In the last decades of the century, the emergence of a knowledge-based economy made Boston the envy of many cities.

In the 1960s Mayor John F. Collins and Edward J. Logue, director of the Boston Redevelopment Authority, created a new City Hall and Government Center. During the mayoralty of Kevin H. White, who succeeded Collins in 1969, Boston's skyline was drastically changed as skyscrapers began to rise above the modest heights of older buildings.

During those same years, however, racial conflict overshadowed the emergence of a revitalized downtown. As fearful, racially biased groups of citizens reacted violently to court-ordered desegregation of the city's public schools in the 1970s, Boston drew national attention and scorn. The city's long-standing African American population increased dramatically in the second half of the twentieth century and grew beyond its old geographical borders. Raymond L. Flynn succeeded Kevin White as mayor in 1984 by drawing some of the city's ethnic and racial groups together. Thomas M. Menino, Flynn's successor, became the city's first Italian American mayor in 1993; he was reelected in 1997 and 2001.

The most famous Boston politician of the late twentieth century was Thomas P. "Tip" O'Neill, speaker of the U.S. House of Representatives. O'Neill, known for popularizing the adage that "all politics is local," won fed-

Siege of Boston. British warships in Boston Harbor fire shells at American positions in Charlestown. LIBRARY OF CONGRESS

eral funding for Boston's Big Dig, the most ambitious public works project in American urban history. This Central Artery/Tunnel Project to place interstate highways underground is opening up acres of surface space downtown for parks and buildings.

Long claiming moral and intellectual distinction as the Athens of America, Boston has left behind much of its widely celebrated provincialism. It remains, however, a charming city that is also now counted among the most exciting in America.

BIBLIOGRAPHY

Handlin, Oscar. *Boston's Immigrants, 1790–1880: A Study in Acculturation.* Rev. ed. Cambridge, Mass.: Harvard University Press, 1991.

Kennedy, Lawrence W. *Planning the City upon a Hill: Boston since 1630.* Amherst: University of Massachusetts Press, 1994.

O'Connell, Shaun. *Imagining Boston: A Literary Landscape.* Boston: Beacon Press, 1990.

O'Connor, Thomas H. *The Hub: Boston Past and Present.* Boston: Northeastern University Press, 2001.

Warner, Sam Bass, Jr. *Streetcar Suburbs: The Process of Growth in Boston, 1870–1900.* 2d ed. Cambridge, Mass.: Harvard University Press, 1978.

Whitehill, Walter Muir, and Lawrence W. Kennedy. *Boston: A Topographical History.* 3rd ed. Cambridge, Mass.: Harvard University Press, 2000.

Lawrence W. Kennedy

See also **Antislavery; Boston, Siege of; Busing; Immigration; Puritans and Puritanism; Revere's Ride; Transcendentalism; Urban Redevelopment; Urbanization.**

BOSTON, SIEGE OF, the military operations during which George Washington liberated the city from the British during the American Revolution. One day after the Battle of Lexington (19 April 1775), the Massachusetts Committee of Safety called out the militia. On 22 April the Massachusetts Provincial Congress resolved to build an army of thirty thousand men, half furnished by Massachusetts and the rest by the other New England colonies. Progress was slow. The old militia regiments could not be held together, and new ones had to be raised. The British victory at the Battle of Bunker Hill on 17 June confirmed the military obstacles facing the rebels.

George Washington, chosen as commander in chief by the Continental Congress, assumed command on 3 July. The British held Bunker Hill and Boston Neck, and the Americans faced them, their left in Somerville, their right in Roxbury, and their center in Cambridge. Because the patchwork of provincial militias around Boston was clearly inadequate, Washington resolved to organize a Continental army. During the winter no serious operations were undertaken. The Americans, lacking artillery and ammunition, focused their energies on military organization and command. The British commanders could see no advantage in starting a campaign that they could not press to a finish.

The guns the Americans had captured at Ticonderoga on 10 May 1775 reached Cambridge in January 1776. On 4 March, Washington seized Dorchester Heights, from which his guns commanded the city and the harbor. The British forces were now in an untenable position, and on 17 January they embarked for Halifax. The Americans immediately occupied the city, and the siege of Boston was over.

BIBLIOGRAPHY

French, Allen. *The Siege of Boston, and of the Battles of Lexington, Concord, and Bunker Hill.* New York: Macmillan, 1911.

Frothingham, Richard. *History of the Siege of Boston.* Boston: Little and Brown, 1851.

Ketchum, Richard M. *The Battle for Bunker Hill.* Garden City, N.Y.: Doubleday, 1962.

Oliver Lyman Spaulding / A. R.

See also **Bunker Hill; Lexington and Concord; Ticonderoga, Capture of.**

BOSTON COMMITTEE OF CORRESPONDENCE.

The American colonies inherited a tradition of forming citizen committees to deal with various common problems. Such committees were most often organized as committees of "safety," "correspondence," and sometimes "inquiry." They were usually formed when the official organs of government either were not functioning, were perceived to be inadequate, or were functioning in opposition to local public will. In the American colonies, officials that were supposed to be provided by the British government were often not available or responsive, and so lacking other legal structures, colonists would elect committees of safety as local provisional governing bodies, and committees of correspondence to inform one another of common threats, such as movements of enemy forces during the French and Indian War (1756–1763). As tensions between the colonies and British government intensified during the 1760s and 1770s, these informal bodies became much more important. A committee of correspondence would focus on investigation, communication with other areas, and publication of information for the public. The Boston Committee of Correspondence was appointed by a town meeting on 2 November 1772, upon the motion of Samuel Adams. It consisted of twenty-one men headed by James Otis. The committee gathered and shaped public opinion and communicated Boston's position on colonists' rights and abuses by British officials, first to other Massachusetts cities, then to other colonies. It requested that similar committees, and committees of safety, be set up in all the colonies. Within a few months, eighty committees had been organized in Massachusetts alone.

Such committees had in the past tended to be temporary organizations that were dissolved shortly after their usefulness was exhausted. But Rhode Island's *Gaspee* affair, in which a British customs schooner was burned, led Richard Henry Lee and his Raleigh Tavern associates in Virginia to suggest the establishment of an intercolonial standing Committee of Correspondence. On 12 March 1773, Dabney Carr, a close friend of Thomas Jefferson, introduced a resolution for the establishment of a standing Committee of Correspondence and Inquiry. This committee was to contact the legislatures of each colony so that they could join Virginia and offer concerted opposition to British encroachments on colonial rights. The resolution was passed unanimously, and eleven were appointed to serve on the committee. Virginia thus formed the opposite pole to Massachusetts, but also bridged New England and the southern colonies. Within a year, all the colonies had formed committees of correspondence, most within a few months.

BIBLIOGRAPHY

Brown, Richard D. *Revolutionary Politics in Massachusetts: The Boston Committee of Correspondence and the Towns, 1772–1774.* Cambridge, Mass.: Harvard University Press, 1970.

Wells, William V. *The Life and Public Services of Samuel Adams.* 3 vols. Boston: Little, Brown, 1866.

Jon Roland

See also **Committees of Correspondence; Committees of Safety.**

BOSTON COMMON

is to Boston what Hyde Park is to London—that is to say it is a place where free speech abounds. Carved out in the 1630s within the infant town's borders, Boston Common was where the militia drilled, merchants and their families strolled its 45 acres, workingmen bowled and played sports, and lovers found shelter. It was also a rallying point where the Liberty Pole was erected before the Revolution, and along its borders stand the city's most symbolic monuments: that to the Battle of Bunker Hill, and Robert Gould Shaw's statue, commemorating his leadership of the first all-black regiment in the Civil War.

BIBLIOGRAPHY

Bailyn, Bernard. *The Ordeal of Thomas Hutchinson.* Cambridge, Mass.: Harvard University Press, 1974.

Carl E. Prince

BOSTON MASSACRE.

As discontent over Britain's taxation policies mounted in the 1760s, violence in the seaport cities escalated. In June 1768, British customs officials in Boston attempting to seize John Hancock's sloop *Liberty* for tax violations were attacked by a mob and beaten. To subdue the spreading revolt, British regulars arrived to take control of the city on 1 October 1768. Many Bostonians resented the British practice of billeting troops in private homes. Skirmishes between troops and civilians ensued. On the evening of 5 March 1770, a grenadier of the Twenty-ninth Regiment was on duty at the customhouse when he was beset by a taunting crowd of civilians. Captain Thomas Preston, with seven men, marched to the customhouse. Unable to quell the crowd, Preston loudly ordered his men, "Don't fire!" while the mob was shouting, "Fire and be damned!" The soldiers fired, killing three men instantly; two died later. Patriot

Boston Common. This lithograph shows people enjoying a "Water Celebration" in October 1848. NATIONAL ARCHIVES AND RECORDS ADMINISTRATION

leaders promptly decried the "massacre" and aroused mass meetings in protest. Lieutenant Governor Thomas Hutchinson, fearing an even bloodier reprisal, pulled his troops back to an island in the Boston harbor. The repeal of most of the offending import duties further demonstrated the weakness of imperial power when faced with a well-organized local resistance movement.

In October 1770 Preston, defended by John Adams and Robert Auchmuty, assisted by Josiah Quincy Jr., was tried for murder and acquitted by a Boston jury. The soldiers—defended by Adams, Quincy, and Sampson Salter Blowers—won acquittals a month later. Four civilians, accused of firing from the customhouse windows, were tried in December 1770; all were acquitted.

BIBLIOGRAPHY

Nash, Gary B. *The Urban Crucible: The Northern Seaports and the Origins of the American Revolution.* Abridged ed., Cambridge, Mass.: Harvard University Press, 1986. The original edition was published in 1979.

Zobel, Hiller B. *The Boston Massacre.* New York: Norton, 1970.

Hiller B. Zobel / A. R.

See also **Billeting; Colonial Policy, British;** *and vol. 9:* **Eyewitness Account of the Boston Massacre; Slave Andrew's Testimony in the Boston Massacre Trial;** *and picture (overleaf).*

BOSTON POLICE STRIKE. About three-quarters of the Boston, Massachusetts police force went on strike 9 September 1919, when the police commissioner refused to recognize the officers' right to affiliate with the American Federation of Labor. To prevent the strike, Mayor Andrew J. Peters and a citizens' committee made compromise proposals relating to pay and working conditions, but the police commissioner rejected them. The resulting strike left Boston virtually unprotected, and disorder, robberies, and riots ensued.

At the time of the strike, Boston's police commissioner was appointed, not by the mayor of the city, but by the governor of the state. Before the strike occurred, Calvin Coolidge, then governor, was urged by the mayor and the citizens' committee to intervene, but he refused to act. When the rioting occurred, Peters called out the Boston companies of the militia, restored order, and broke the strike. With the city already under control, Coolidge ordered the police commissioner again to take charge of the police and called out the entire Massachusetts militia, declaring, "There is no right to strike against the public safety by anybody, anywhere, any time." This action gave Coolidge a reputation as a courageous defender of law and order, which led to his nomination for U.S. vice president (1920) and his eventual election (1924) to the presidency.

Boston Massacre. LIBRARY OF CONGRESS

BIBLIOGRAPHY

Russell, Francis. A *City in Terror: 1919, The Boston Police Strike*. New York: Viking, 1975.

Sobel, Robert. *Coolidge: An American Enigma*. Washington, D.C.: Regnery, 1998.

Clarence A. Berdahl / A. G.

See also **American Federation of Labor–Congress of Industrial Organizations; Boston; Conciliation and Mediation, Labor; Labor; Massachusetts; Police; Trade Unions.**

BOSTON TEA PARTY. The British East India Company, facing severe financial reverses, convinced Parliament to allow them to sell tea in the American colonies at a price that would undercut even smuggled Dutch tea, and raise revenue while clearing their warehouses of a huge surplus. Unfortunately, this tea would still carry the despised three-pence per pound tax, which had remained as a token duty, and would be sold through only a handful of dealers in America. This high-handed policy united small merchants, left out of the deal, with patriot organizations that protested the tax. The arrival of the tea ships *Eleanor*, *Dartmouth* and *Beaver* sparked public protest in Boston, including public meetings, fliers and ha-

rassment of the consignees, who took shelter in Castle William to avoid the crowds.

The Sons of Liberty, led by Samuel Adams, decided on 13 December 1773 that the tea must not be unloaded, nor could it remain onboard twenty days and thus be seized for sale by customs officials. On 16 December, the night the Sons of Liberty planned their raid, a public protest at the Old South Meeting House turned rowdy after someone suggested dumping the tea in the harbor. As protesters stormed out of the meetinghouse, they met Sons of Liberty, costumed as Narragansett Indians, on their way to do the same thing. With a crowd of perhaps 1,000 Bostonians following, the "Indians" and volunteers stormed the three ships and in a three-hour fracas, broke open all 342 of the tea chests and dumped them into the harbor, which was at low tide.

The attackers were conscientious, and they damaged no ship or other cargo. Only one man was injured, knocked unconscious by a collapsing winch. However, they had ruined 18,000 pounds worth of tea and infuriated the British government, particularly the king. Despite arresting a barber named Francis Eckley, who had been caught bragging about his participation, the Boston authorities were unable to find anyone who could identify

Boston Tea Party. This lithograph by Sarony and Major depicts the Sons of Liberty's innovative, destructive, and provocative tax protest, which helped cause the American Revolution sixteen months later. NATIONAL ARCHIVES AND RECORDS ADMINISTRATION

the protestors. Patriots tarred and feathered Eckley's accuser in retaliation. George III specifically noted the Tea Party in his address to Parliament, and he and Prime Minister Lord North pushed through the Coercive Acts by April 1774. The Coercive Acts were designed to punish Boston and the colony of Massachusetts. They sparked further protests and eventually, war between Britain and her American colonies.

Although usually considered by itself, the Boston Tea Party was a natural growth of other protests against the British administration in Boston, centered on royal governor Thomas Hutchinson and his subordinates. Until the publication of Thomas Paine's *Common Sense* in 1776, these protests were notable in their careful avoidance of blaming George III, instead focusing on his council or colonial administrators. The costumes and violence of the Tea Party were also an outgrowth of regular crowd demonstrations in Boston, including burning Catholic figures in effigy, vandalizing administrator's homes or intimidating customs and tax inspectors. Even when not politically motivated, the apprentices and laborers of Boston also engaged in highly charged territorial contests that often ended in injuries and rowdy outbursts, and were led by men who took pains to hide their appearance using symbolic disguises. In all these respects, it was not the Tea Party itself that was unusual, but the British reaction to it.

BIBLIOGRAPHY

Griswold, Wesley S. *The Night the Revolution Began.* Brattleboro, Vt.: The Stephen Green Press, 1972.

Labarre, Benjamin Woods. *The Boston Tea Party.* New York: Oxford University Press, 1964.

Shaw, Peter. *American Patriots and the Rituals of Revolution.* Cambridge: Harvard University Press, 1981.

Margaret D. Sankey

See also **Sons of Liberty (American Revolution); Townshend Acts.**

BOTANICAL GARDENS. Botanical, or botanic, gardens are tracts of land set aside for the cultivation of a diversity of plant species, grown not as cash crops—although botanical gardens may have commercial purposes—but rather for study and pleasure. Botanical gardens, including arboretums (tree collections), have served a variety of purposes throughout American history: research, education, conservation, plant development, and entertainment. Botanical gardens may specialize in local flora or present plants from around the world, within the limits of the local soil and climate unless the plants are placed in a greenhouse.

The arrangement of the botanical garden must balance an aesthetic presentation with educational purposes and spaces open to visitors, and yet useful for botanists and conservationists, although most botanical field research is carried out in environments other than public botanical gardens. Botanical gardens are often home to experiments with hybridization and the development of new plant species (cultivars).

In the eighteenth century, it became fashionable to construct gardens around Carl Linnaeus's classification system, which made comparisons within plant families easier. Moreover, the distinctions between more rustic English gardens and more geometric and orderly French gardens have also influenced American designers of botanical gardens. In addition, American gardens presenting species from around the world often group them by origin, sometimes fashioning each section to look like the native area. Alternately, plants are sometimes grouped by the geological features where they are found. However, American botanical gardens, especially those further north, must account for seasonal changes in planning their design, sometimes closing during the winter.

European Gardens

European botanical gardens originated in the Renaissance during the sixteenth century. During the Middle Ages, botanical investigations had been greatly hampered by the inability of manuscripts to depict plants accurately, as each copy was made anew. The invention of printing in the 1450s, combined with the recovery of ancient botanical texts, allowed the study of botany to flourish in the late fifteenth and sixteenth centuries.

It is believed that Luca Ghini created the first botanical garden in Pisa in 1543, but such gardens quickly spread throughout Italy and beyond into Europe, often connected to schools of medicine and focusing on medicinal herbals. Early medicinal gardens in America were modeled on these, most famously and perhaps first, a garden founded in 1694 outside Philadelphia by German Pietists.

Gardens of the Eighteenth and Nineteenth Centuries

Philadelphia was also the first center for public botanical gardens in the American colonies. Botanist John Bartram initiated the Philadelphia Botanical Garden just outside the city in 1728. The five-acre garden featured both native and exotic plants and Bartram traveled around America looking for worthy additions, some of which he sent to European gardens. The garden closed during the American Revolution.

Colonial powers often used botanical gardens to grow spices and exotic goods, but because of colonial America's relatively cold climate, gardens designed for overseas trade never became as prevalent as in India, Malaysia, or the West Indies. However, throughout American history botanical gardens have stimulated American agriculture by providing seeds for many commercial plants. The distinction between a garden and a nursery has never been absolute, as evidenced by the nursery founded in 1737 by Robert Prince in Flushing, New York. The nursery cultivated exotic trees and plants to sell to Americans and one famous patron was George Washington. In 1793, William Prince expanded the holdings and named it the Linnaean Botanic Garden. Many plants gathered during the explorations of Lewis and Clark were sent there. The garden thrived until the Civil War, collapsing in 1865.

Other nursery gardens, however, were spectacular failures, notably the Elgin Botanical Garden founded in Manhattan by physician David Hosack in 1801. This garden, which included greenhouses and hothouses to allow for the cultivation of species from warmer climates, was an early influence on the young John Torrey, an influential botanist. Hosack planted thousands of species on the twenty acres of land for medicinal, educational, and commercial purposes and spent vast sums on importing, growing, researching, and displaying plants from around the world. Bankrupted by the expense, however, Hosack had to sell the garden in 1810 at a net loss to New York State, which gave the land to Columbia College. The garden, on which Rockefeller Center stands, was quickly terminated.

The idea for a national botanic garden was first suggested in 1816 and one was established in Washington, D.C., in 1842, after a more modest attempt failed in 1837. The United States Botanic Garden, which, expanding, shifted locations in 1850 and 1933, became the receiver of plants collected on expeditions, which were then cultivated, studied, displayed, and dispersed. The garden today has over twenty-six-thousand plants, including ones that are rare, of historic value, are medicinally important, or are the subject of study. Meanwhile, the U.S. National Arboretum, also in Washington, D.C., was founded in 1927. Almost 450 acres are devoted to the display and study of trees and other flora. It is supervised by the Agricultural Research Service of the Department of Agriculture and has hybridized and introduced 650 new plant species to the American landscape.

Although other short-lived attempts to establish botanical gardens were made in the nineteenth century, it was not until 1859 that another (and the longest-running) public, non-governmental botanical garden was successfully opened in America. The Missouri Botanical Garden, which was begun in 1859 by Henry Shaw, an English merchant motivated to create a garden on his lands in St. Louis by a trip to London in 1851, including a visit to the renowned Royal Botanic Gardens at Kew. The Missouri Botanical Garden, operating into the twenty-first century, serves as the home for the Center for Plant Conservation, a coalition of over thirty botanical gardens nationwide that attempts to preserve endangered native American plants.

The Proliferation of Botanical Gardens

The late nineteenth and early twentieth century saw a marked increase in the number of public botanical gardens, many of them affiliated with universities or other research centers. Some were bequeathed to the public by devoted amateurs. Notable among the botanical gardens begun in this period include the Arnold Arboretum (1872), the New York Botanical Garden (1891), The Smith College Botanic Garden (1893–94), the Brooklyn Botanic Garden (1911), the Huntington Botanical Gardens (1912), Longwood Gardens (1921), and the University of California Botanical Garden in Berkeley (1928).

The Arnold Arboretum is affiliated with Harvard University, which had begun the much smaller Harvard Botanic Garden in connection with the Botanic research facilities in 1805, but the Arboretum estate was bequeathed by James Arnold for an open-air collection of both local and exotic woody plants. The Arboretum consists of 265 acres in Jamaica Plain, Massachusetts. It was created by Frederick Law Olmsted and its first director, Charles Sprague Sargent. Although suffering great damage in a 1938 hurricane, it remains one of the outstanding American gardens, known for its scientific research, plant development, extensive herbarium, and East Asian collections.

The New York Botanical Garden has 250 acres in The Bronx, and is a National Historic Landmark, along with the Missouri Botanical Garden and the recreation-only Boston Public Gardens. Many botanical gardens produce journals of their research, but the New York Botanical Garden has its own press, producing journals and books. In 2002, the garden opened the International Plant Science Center for its herbarium and library, both of which are among the largest in the world. The garden is renowned for its scientific research; climate change, molecular biology, plant diseases, and biodiversity are studied.

Smith College, which has a strong tradition in the botanical sciences, considers its entire campus, as reworked in 1893 by Frederick Law Olmsted, to be an arboretum, in addition to the botanical garden, which was officially begun in 1894. Today there are a variety of botanical resources at Smith College, including an herbarium and smaller gardens, that supplement the study of botany.

The Brooklyn Botanic Garden has fifty-two acres in the middle of New York City. As a small, urban garden, much of the scientific research focuses on plants native to the New York area and on the recent Center for Urban Restoration initiative with Rutgers University, which studies ways to ameliorate the environmental impact of urban development. Historically, a key element of the Brooklyn Botanic Garden's popularity has been its success in introducing botany to and encouraging horticulture among people living in the largest American city.

The Huntington Botanical Gardens in San Marino, California, were initially part of the estate of Henry Huntington, who began working on his botanical gardens in 1903 and officially founded the gardens in 1912. On the 150 acres there are several specialized gardens demonstrating landscapes from around the world, including subtropical and jungle. The garden is especially known for cultivating exotic succulents.

The Longwood Gardens in Pennsylvania offer 1,050 acres dedicated mostly to display and education, although there is also a center for research. Prior to the founding of the gardens, the estate—known as Peirce Farm—had a remarkable tree collection, which Pierre du Pont bought. In the early twentieth century, he began converting it into a public garden known for its beauty and extravagance. It was largely based on Italian and French models, but included display gardens exhibiting species from around the world.

The University of California Botanical Garden in Berkeley was originally established in 1890 as a garden specializing in native species. Upon being moved to a different campus location in 1928, the collection began to expand to include exotic species. Although the garden is only thirty-four acres, the collection is known for the diversity and depth of its holdings.

Also notable is the Desert Botanical Garden in Phoenix, Arizona, one of the largest desert gardens in the world. Founded in 1937, the southwestern climate allows the garden to cultivate and display in a natural setting plants that could not survive elsewhere in America.

Toward the end of the nineteenth century, botanical classifications and research became oriented toward physiology rather than morphology. This increased the amount of scientific equipment necessary for a botanical garden and encouraged a move away from Linnaean displays.

Botanical Gardens and Conservation

The suburbanization of the American landscape in the twentieth century has threatened the prominence and viability of public botanical gardens, especially those in cities. Urban renewal projects of the 1970s and 1980s, when combined with economic growth, perhaps resulted in an urban revival of the 1990s, in which botanical gardens again began to flourish.

Although botanical gardens remain significant for recreation and education, the most important trend in botanical gardens worldwide during the twentieth century has been an increasing awareness of the their potential to assist in conservation efforts. Industrialization, pollution, urbanization, suburbanization, the destruction of rainforests, climate change, and the spread of invasive species as a result of globalization are all currently threatening biodiversity, with plant species going extinct every day.

Botanical gardens can offer *ex situ* conservation from species that are being ousted from their original habitats.

The first attempt to involve botanical gardens around the world in coordinated conservation efforts was made in 1987 with the founding of the Botanic Gardens Conservation Secretariat. At the start of the twenty-first century, the Center for Plant Conservation houses 580 rare native American species. But according to its statistics, 730 of the 20,000 American native plant species are now officially endangered, while about 4,000 are considered threatened. It seems that conservation has become the most important research function of botanical gardens today.

BIBLIOGRAPHY

Correll, Philip G. *Botanical Gardens and Arboreta of North America: An Organizational Survey.* Los Angeles: American Association of Botanical Gardens and Arboreta, 1980.

Directory of Gardens of North America. Kennett Square, Pa.: American Association of Botanical Gardens and Arboreta, 1998.

Hill, Arthur W. "The History and Function of Botanic Gardens." *Annals of the Missouri Botanical Garden* 2 (February–April 1915): 185–240.

Hyams, Edward. *Great Botanical Gardens of the World.* New York: Macmillan, 1969.

MacPhail, Ian, comp. Hortus Botanicus: *The Botanic Garden and the Book.* Chicago: Morton Arboretum, 1972.

Mulligan, William C. *The Complete Guide to North American Gardens.* Boston: Little Brown, 1991.

O'Malley, Therese. "Your Garden Must Be a Museum to You." In *Art and Science in America.* Edited by Amy R. W. Meyers. San Marino, Calif.: Huntington Library, 1998.

Piacentini, Richard. *The Plant Collections Directory: Canada and the United States.* Kennett Square, Pa.: American Association of Botanical Gardens and Arboreta, 1996.

Caroline R. Sherman

See also **Gardening.**

BOTANY. The history of botany in America has several themes: the identification and study of new species discovered in the New World; the transformation of the field away from classification based on morphology, or shape, and toward interest in physiology and, later, genetics; the concomitant specialization and professionalization of botany, a subject that was originally relatively open to amateur practitioners, including women; and the development of American botanical research to rival the initially dominant European centers in England, France, and Germany. The European Renaissance had seen a revival of interest in botany and in ancient botanical works that was aided by the invention of the printing press in 1453, which allowed for a uniformity of plant depictions that hand-drawn manuscripts could not ensure.

Discoveries in the New World

The exploration of the New World, beginning with Columbus's voyage of 1492, was marked by the discovery of new flora and fauna, enthusiastically documented and de-

scribed by travelers. It was not uncommon for those who wrote about the Americas to describe the plants and animals they had seen in terms of familiar European species, and, indeed, sometimes to mistakenly identify American species as being the same as European species. However, since plants do not move—unlike animals that might offer colonial settlers and travelers only a glimpse before disappearing—many American plants were quickly identified to be distinct from similar species in the Old World. Although Native Americans had developed their own classifications of North American flora, and although Native Americans were often a source of knowledge for colonists learning about the uses of new plants, Europeans tended to impose their own classifications onto the plants of the New World.

At the time, the discovery of new species posed a theological problem for European Christians, as the description of Noah's Ark insisted that Noah had gathered every kind of plant, while the New World contained many plants not part of the European and Asian ecosystems. Questions quickly arose as to whether there had once been a land bridge between the Americas and Eurasia and, even prior to Darwin, whether American plant species were modified variations on European species.

Moreover, some plants from the Americas became quite profitable crops for Europeans, most notably tobacco and chocolate, and many Europeans came over to explore and study the new plants. The first notable publication on the flora of the Americas was by Nicolás Monardes, who never traveled to the New World but wrote on its plants in his 1574 *Historia Medicinal,* which was translated into English by John Frampton as *Joyfull Newes out of the Newe Founde Worlde* (1577). The work was primarily concerned with the medicinal benefits of the plants and herbs in the Americas, and, indeed, many of the practitioners of botany in the sixteenth, seventeenth, eighteenth, and even into the nineteenth centuries were also trained in medicine and were interested in the possible new cures available in undocumented American plants.

However, amateurs also made important contributions to the study of American botanicals, examining the plants in local areas, presenting their findings at botanical societies, swapping samples with other botanists and sending plants back to Europe, and cultivating herbaria and arboreta. From colonial times until the mid-nineteenth century, the work of amateurs in finding, studying, and documenting new species was important to the study of botany as a whole. A primary example is Jane Colden (1724–1766), the daughter of the botanist Cadwallader Colden. Tutored only by her father, Jane Colden studied and drew the plants of New York, classifying hundreds of plants, including the gardenia, which she discovered.

Jane Colden was especially renowned for understanding and using the Linnaean classification scheme. Carl Linnaeus (1707–1778), a Swedish doctor and botanist, developed his hierarchy throughout his life, his most notable publications including the *Systema Naturae* (1735), *Genera*

Plantarum (1737), and *Species Plantarum* (1753). The Linnaean system, which has since been greatly revised, divided animals and plants into kingdoms, classes, orders, genera, and species, all written in Latin. Each species was given a two-part (binomial) name of genus and species.

Classification

Linnaeus's classification system greatly influenced eighteenth-century botany in America. Some of his students came over to categorize the species of the New World, most significantly Pehr Kalm, who traveled through the Great Lakes, the Mid-Atlantic colonies, and Canada, bringing back samples. Meanwhile, colonial settlers like John Bartram (1699–1777), Cadwallader Colden (1688–1776), Humphry Marshall (1722–1801), and others worked to incorporate the local flora into the work of Linnaeus, which provided a new sense of order for those working on studying the plants and animals of the overwhelmingly diverse and novel New World.

But although the Linnaean system was helpful, it could not survive the strain of the thousands of new discoveries in the Americas and Asia. Plant classifications based on reproduction resulted in categories that contained obviously widely diverging plants. In particular, Linnaeus was challenged by French botanists who emphasized grouping plants by shape (morphology). Antoine Laurent de Jussieu's (1748–1836) 1789 *Genera Plantarum* prompted the reorganizing of classification by appearance and added levels to the taxonomy.

The Jussieu modifications quickly, but not uncontroversially, became added to botanical literature, although the Linnaean system continued to be used in many prominent American publications through the early nineteenth century. Meanwhile, French botanists made other contributions to the study of North American plants. André Michaux (1746–1802) and his son, François André (1770–1855), traveled through much of eastern North America, from Canada to the Bahamas, observing and collecting. The end result of their massive researches was the 1803 *Flora Boreali-Americana*, the first large-scale compilation of North American plants. The work of the Michaux drew, not uncritically, on the reforms of Jussieu.

Nineteenth-Century American Botanists

The Michaux volumes encouraged revisions, the first coming in 1814 with the *Flora Americae Septentrionalis* of Frederick Pursh (1774–1820), which incorporated findings from the Lewis and Clark Expedition and thus contained information about western America. Pursh's contemporary, Thomas Nuttall (1786–1859), was born and died in England, but his interest, education, and work in botany were conducted primarily in America, where he explored the south and west, collecting and publishing his findings. Although he is known for his extensive discoveries, Nuttall also wrote the 1818 *Genera of the North American Plants* and 1827 *Introduction to Systematic and Physiological Botany*. His work is symbolic of a turn from

European-dominated study of North American plants toward American specialists in native species. Although Americans had always played important roles in the discovery, cataloging, and study of local plants, the early and mid-nineteenth century saw the burgeoning of work by American botanists, both amateur and professional. Meanwhile, the American government sponsored expeditions to find and collect plant species in the less studied areas of the south and west of America.

Among the American botanists of the early nineteenth century, the most famous are Jacob Bigelow (1786–1879), Amos Eaton (1776–1842), John Torrey (1796–1873), and Thomas Nuttall (1786–1859). Bigelow, who was trained as a doctor, was primarily interested in the medicinal uses of plants, but he also surveyed the flora of Boston for his *Florula Bostoniensis* (1814). Additionally, he did work in physiology, which was already a topic of considerable interest in the first decades of the century and would come to dominate morphology in botanical concerns by the end of the nineteenth century.

Amos Eaton gained his reputation primarily through his *Manual of Botany* (first published in 1817, but revised and enlarged through many editions), which became the basic botanical teaching text of the first half of the nineteenth century. Eaton, who also worked in geology and chemistry, encouraged the participation of women in science, although indeed women were already quite well represented in botany, which he noted. In part this botanical activity by women was due to the fact that contemporary botany required little laboratory equipment: discoveries could be made by anyone who was diligent and well read in botany, and so graduate degrees or access to laboratories—both largely denied at the time to women—were unnecessary to botanical work. However, although Eaton emphasized field work, the most accessible kind of botanical study, he was also part of a trend toward including laboratory experiments.

Eaton's teaching and text were very influential, perhaps most importantly in botany upon John Torrey, whom Eaton met while serving a prison sentence for forgery—a charge he denied. Torrey was the son of a man who worked for the State Prison of New York, and Eaton gave the young Torrey lessons in a variety of scientific subjects, including botany. While Torrey went on to have a career that included work in medicine, geology, mineralogy, and chemistry, he is primarily remembered for his botanical work, cataloging New York flora, collaborating with Asa Gray, creating a renowned herbarium, promoting government-financed expeditions, utilizing—albeit inconsistently—the classification work of John Lindley, and serving as the first president of the Torrey Botanical Society, a group of prominent amateur and professional botanists in New York. The *Bulletin of the Torrey Botanical Society*, which began publication in 1870, is the oldest American botanical journal.

Although Bigelow, Eaton, Torrey, Nuttall, and others did much to encourage and expand knowledge of native plants, it is Asa Gray (1810–1888) who takes center stage in the history of American botany in the nineteenth century. Gray published *A Flora of North America* (1838–1843) with Torrey, which drew on the Lindley classification system, which was a development from Jussieu's "natural system." Gray's textbooks replaced those of Eaton, and the botanical research center he set up at Harvard cultivated many of the next generation of botanists and encouraged work in anatomy, cellular structure, and physiology, realms that were dominated by German botanists. Interested in East Asian flora as well as that of North America, Gray quickly supported Charles Darwin's evolutionary theory as expounded in the 1859 *Origin of Species* because he had noticed regional variation himself. This drew him into conflict with another Harvard professor, the zoologist Louis Agassiz, who was a prominent anti-Darwinian. However, evolution soon became a guiding principle in botanical study.

Theoretical Research

The twentieth century saw the rise of American research devoted to the theoretical aspects of botany, areas in which America had typically lagged behind Europe, as American botanists became more involved in experiments, physiology, anatomy, molecular biology, biochemistry, and genetics, and less involved in the discovery of new species. While Darwin could not provide an explanation for the origins of variation and the inheritance of characteristics, Gregor Mendel (1822–1884), a Moravian monk, offered hereditary principles based on experiments with pea plants in his *Versuche über Pflanzenhybriden* (Experiments in plant hybridization; 1865, 1869). Although Mendel's research went unacknowledged until 1900, when rediscovered it was profoundly influential in turning the research edge of botany, which was already moving from morphology to physiology, toward genetics as well. In addition, during the first half of the twentieth century, ecological research, which tied together the plants and animals of a habitat, began to thrive, as evidenced by the work of Henry Chandler Cowles (1869–1939) and others. Mathematics was put to use in the study of plant and animal populations, and in 1942 Raymond Lindeman (1915–1942) demonstrated the "trophic-dynamic aspect" of ecology to show how energy moves from individual to individual through a local environment.

Since the 1960s, plant physiology has looked more to understanding the relationship between plants and their surrounding environment: studying plant reactions to environmental change, both with a look to the evolutionary mechanisms involved and concerning the ongoing degradation of the global environment.

Moreover, the introduction of genetic research has prompted yet another change in taxonomy, with the rise of phylogenetics, in which variation is traced to the genetic level, allowing botanists to reorganize classification by evolutionary relatedness, replacing previous categories. Relatedly, work on population genetics, genetic engineering, and genomics (the study of all of the genes in a DNA sequence) has blossomed since the 1960s, a notable recent achievement being the completion of the *Arabadopsis thaliana* genome—the first plant genome completely sequenced—in 2000. Although some of the work was completed by American researchers and partly funded by the American government, the project represents the prominent international collaborations that are shaping botany today, with aid also provided by the European Union and the Japanese government and research carried out in America, Great Britain, France, Germany, and Japan.

BIBLIOGRAPHY

Evans, Howard Ensign. *Pioneer Naturalists: The Discovery and Naming of North American Plants and Animals.* New York: Henry Holt, 1993.

Greene, Edward Lee. *Landmarks of Botanical History.* Edited by Frank N. Egerton. Stanford: Stanford University Press, 1983.

Humphrey, Harry Baker. *Makers of North American Botany.* New York: Ronald Press, 1961.

Keeney, Elizabeth B. *The Botanizers: Amateur Scientists in Nineteenth-Century America.* Chapel Hill: University of North Carolina Press, 1992.

Mauseth, James D. *Botany: An Introduction to Plant Biology.* 2d ed. Boston: Jones and Bartlett, 1998.

Morton, A. G. *History of Botanical Science: An Account of the Development of Botany from Ancient Times to the Present Day.* New York: Academic Press, 1981.

Reveal, James L. *Gentle Conquest: The Botanical Discovery of North America with Illustrations from the Library of Congress.* Washington, D.C.: Starwood, 1992.

Stuckey, Ronald L., ed. *Development of Botany in Selected Regions of North America before 1900.* New York: Arno Press, 1978.

Caroline R. Sherman

See also **Botanical Gardens.**

BOUGAINVILLE, site of U.S. landing in Pacific during World War II. With the objective of gaining airfields for a strike on New Britain Island, Lieutenant General A. A. Vandegrift's First U.S. Marine Amphibious Corps landed on the western coast of Bougainville, the largest of the Solomon Islands, on 1 November 1943. The marines faced a scarcity of amphibious shipping, a swampy terrain, and worthless naval gunfire support. Nevertheless, this was at the time the best-planned and best-executed amphibious operation of World War II. By 13 November 33,861 marines had been put ashore to face a Japanese contingent of approximately 58,000. By 15 December the American perimeter was defended by a well-anchored defense. The objective had been achieved at a cost to the U.S. Marines of 423 killed and 1,418 wounded; 2,500 Japanese were killed.

Attacking a Pillbox on Bougainville. Flame-throwers were often needed to dislodge tenacious Japanese defenders in the Pacific. NATIONAL ARCHIVES AND RECORDS ADMINISTRATION

BIBLIOGRAPHY

Dyer, George Carroll. *The Amphibians Came to Conquer.* Washington, D.C.: U.S. Marine Corps, 1991.

Gailey, Harry A. *Bougainville, 1943–1945.* Lexington: University Press of Kentucky, 1991.

W. M. Darden / A. R.

See also **Guadalcanal Campaign.**

BOUNDARY DISPUTES BETWEEN STATES.

At the time of the adoption of the CONSTITUTION OF THE UNITED STATES, apparently only Pennsylvania and Maryland, of the original thirteen states, had no pending question as to the correctness of their boundaries. They had resolved their dispute in 1769 with the ratification of the Mason-Dixon line as their common boundary. Pennsylvania had also resolved colonial disputes with Virginia and Connecticut. Since the formation of the nation, however, more than half of the states have been involved in some kind of boundary disagreement with one or more neighboring states. These disputes have been mostly minor and have been settled by common agreement—with or without the consent of Congress, by congressional action alone, or by the Supreme Court. In large measure, the disputes over boundaries have developed because of the interpretation of colonial grants or charters, of treaties, or of general international law. A few controversies have arisen about boundaries established by Congress either before or at the time of the admission of new states.

Of the disputes having their origin in colonial arrangements, probably the first to be settled was that between North Carolina and South Carolina. This dispute was ended by a survey in 1815 that extended the 1772 line to the corner of Georgia. The Massachusetts–Rhode Island dispute originated in the Plymouth colony grant of 1630 and the Rhode Island charter of 1663. In spite of an 1846 Supreme Court case that Rhode Island lost, the dispute was not settled until the two states later agreed on a boundary line, an agreement to which Congress assented in 1858. The states revised the compact in 1899 by mutual consent and established a line that could be more readily marked. The boundary dispute between Connecticut and New York, which began before 1650, was settled by the two states in 1880; Congress approved their action in 1881. The Massachusetts–New Hampshire boundary controversy, which originated in the Massachusetts charter of 1629, was settled in 1895 by an agreement on the gen-

Boundary Disputes

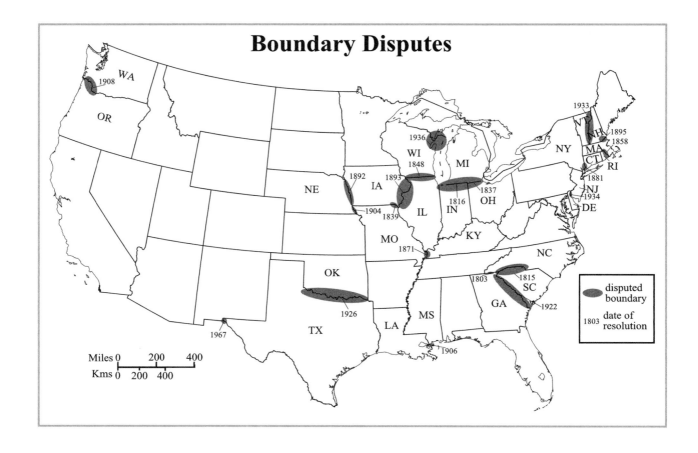

erally recognized boundary of the time. Cases decided by the Supreme Court concerning boundaries of colonial origin include *Rhode Island v. Massachusetts* (1846), *Georgia v. South Carolina* (1922), *Vermont v. New Hampshire* (1933), and *New Jersey v. Delaware* (1934).

The disputes that have been settled by congressional action alone have related chiefly to boundaries originally established between territories by acts of Congress. Notable among these controversies are those involving the boundaries of Michigan. Congress moved the Michigan-Indiana boundary north by the 1816 act admitting Indiana to statehood, in order to give that state an outlet on Lake Michigan. The act admitting Michigan to the Union in 1837 ended the serious and long-running dispute with Ohio by moving the Michigan-Ohio boundary north to put the Toledo area in Ohio. As recompense for its loss of the disputed territory, Michigan was given what is now the upper peninsula of that state. A protracted Illinois-Wisconsin dispute was settled with the admission of Wisconsin into the Union in 1848.

The Supreme Court has settled many boundary disputes between states. Where specific treaties have been involved, these have been interpreted and followed by the Court. This was true in the dispute between Missouri and Kentucky; the Court ruled that, since the treaty signed by

France, Spain, and England in 1763 set the Mississippi River as the boundary, the boundary "has remained . . . as they settled it" (*Missouri v. Kentucky* [1871]). The 1783 Peace of Paris that ended the war with Great Britain set the western boundary of the United States, and its terms were followed in setting all or part of the boundaries of the states along the Mississippi River. This same treaty also determined the northern boundary of Florida and set the Chattahoochee River as part of the Alabama-Georgia boundary. The 1819 treaty with Spain defined the Oklahoma-Texas boundary (except the Panhandle portion) and the southern boundaries of Oregon and Idaho. The Rio Grande portion of the New Mexico–Texas boundary was a heritage from the Treaty of Guadalupe Hidalgo of 1848.

In the determination of boundary questions between states not involving specific treaties, the Supreme Court has applied the principles of international law. In the many disputes involving water boundaries in rivers and bays, the Court has held that the doctrine of the thalweg (that is, that the main—and deepest—channel of navigation is the middle of a river rather than a line equidistant between the two banks) is applicable between states unless the boundary has been fixed in some other way, such as by agreement, practical location, or prescription. The

Court used this principle in its determination of the boundary between New Jersey and Delaware on the Delaware River in 1934. Along the unstable Missouri River, the Court has applied the rules of international law concerning river change by avulsion or accretion—for example, in *Nebraska v. Iowa* (1892). The Court followed still another rule of international law to determine the Ohio River boundary. According to the rule regarding cession of territory on a river boundary, the boundary set by this river is the north, or far, bank at low water. The Supreme Court held that when Virginia ceded to the United States territory to the northwest of the Ohio River (the territory involved now makes up Kentucky and West Virginia), Virginia must have intended to retain the river (*Handly's Lessee v. Anthony* [1820], *Indiana v. Kentucky* [1890]).

In several controversies, the riches lying in the water or underneath the land motivated the rival parties. Oyster beds were at least partly the cause of disputes decided by the Supreme Court in *Louisiana v. Mississippi* (1906), which concerned the boundary from the mouth of the Pearl River to the high sea. The same issue was involved in *Smith v. Maryland* (1855). Fishing rights were among the questions involved in Supreme Court decisions in 1926 and 1935 on the Michigan-Wisconsin boundary in Green Bay and Lake Michigan (*Michigan v. Wisconsin* [1926] and *Wisconsin v. Michigan* [1936]). Oil wells in the bed of the Red River made the precise location of the Oklahoma-Texas boundary very important, and the Court decided this matter in *Oklahoma v. Texas* (1926).

While disputes over boundaries between states have been somewhat heated in a few instances—as in the Georgia–North Carolina dispute over Walton County in 1803, the Ohio-Michigan dispute of 1818–1837, and the Iowa-Missouri controversy in 1839—in general, boundary questions, as distinct from regional disputes, have not had a disrupting effect.

BIBLIOGRAPHY

Danson, Edwin. *Drawing the Line: How Mason and Dixon Surveyed the Most Famous Border in America.* New York: Wiley, 2001.

De Vorsey, Louis, Jr. *The Georgia–South Carolina Boundary: A Problem in Historical Geography.* Athens: University of Georgia Press, 1982

Nathan, Roger E. *East of the Mason-Dixon Line: A History of the Delaware Boundaries.* Wilmington: Delaware Heritage Press, 2000.

Onuf, Peter S. *The Origins of the Federal Republic: Jurisdictional Controversies in the United States, 1775–1787.* Philadelphia: University of Pennsylvania Press, 1983.

Scott, James Brown. *Judicial Settlement of Controversies Between States of the American Union.* Oxford: Clarendon Press, 1919.

Skaggs, Marvin L. *North Carolina Boundary Disputes Involving Her Southern Line.* Chapel Hill: University of North Carolina Press, 1941.

Van Zandt, Franklin K. *Boundaries of the United States and the Several States.* Washington, D.C.: United States Government Printing Office, 1976.

Paul C. Bartholomew / C. P.

See also **International Law; Mason-Dixon Line; Michigan; Ohio; Pennsylvania; Rivers; Supreme Court; Territories of the United States; Treaties with Foreign Nations.**

BOUNTIES, COMMERCIAL, played an important role throughout the history of economic development in the United States. During the colonial period, Great Britain paid bounties to its American colonies that exported hemp, flax, tar, potash, indigo, and a number of other commodities. Such bounties stimulated colonial production of the commodities and diminished Britain's dependence on foreign nations for these items. North Carolina and South Carolina profited the most from these bounties. The production of NAVAL STORES (products from pine trees, such as pitch, turpentine, and rosin, used in shipbuilding) and indigo became, with rice cultivation, a cornerstone of the Carolinian economy. The loss of these bounties after the American Revolution brought disaster to those who depended on them, particularly those engaged in the production of naval stores and indigo. The colonial governments also offered bounties to encourage the manufacture of such goods as linen, woolens, iron, glass, brick, and salt, and after 1775 they redoubled their efforts to build up domestic manufactures by combining cash bounties, financial subsidies, and TARIFF protection.

Following the Revolution, the states continued to give bounties for wheat, flax, and even corn and for the manufacture of hemp, glass, and sailcoth. At least six states offered bounties for the production of silk. The federal government offered direct bounties for various commercial purposes. It achieved the same result indirectly by requiring the navy to buy only rope made from American hemp and by sending scientists abroad to find better strains of sugarcane and other plants that might be adapted to American growing conditions. On the eve of the CIVIL WAR, the Southern states, which felt that bounties, tariff protection, and subsidies to internal improvements had chiefly benefited other sections, incorporated a provision in the Confederate constitution forbidding them.

In 1890 the United States offered a bounty of two cents per pound on sugar produced within the nation. Individual states likewise gave bounties to the beet sugar industry. Such bounties, coupled with high tariff protection and huge subsidies in the far West for irrigation projects, have been responsible for the growth of the U.S. sugar beet industry.

In the twentieth century individual states continued to use bounties to rid the land of wolves and other carnivorous animals. The federal government, on the other hand, discarded bounties in favor of tariffs and quotas as its method of stimulating and protecting American industry.

BIBLIOGRAPHY

Beer, George Louis. *British Colonial Policy, 1754–1765*. Gloucester, Mass.: Peter Smith, 1958. The original edition was published New York: Macmillan, 1907.

Handlin, Oscar, and Mary Flug Handlin. *Commonwealth: A Study of the Role of Government in the American Economy: Massachusetts, 1774–1861*. Cambridge, Mass.: Belknap Press of Harvard University Press, 1969.

Larson, John Lauritz. *Internal Improvement: National Public Works and the Promise of Popular Government in the Early United States*. Chapel Hill: University of North Carolina Press, 2001.

Paul Wallace Gates / c. w.

See also **Colonial Commerce; Indigo Culture; Rice Culture and Trade.**

BOUNTIES, MILITARY, a method of stimulating military enlistments with inducements of land or money. For Indian and French campaigns, colonies offered cash inducements for both enlistments and supplies. During the Revolution, the states and Congress often bid against one another for recruits. Sums mounted and bounty jumping and reenlisting were prevalent.

With the peace, bounties shrank to $6 in 1791 for Indian campaigns, but climbed after the WHISKEY REBELLION to $16 and 160 acres. During the WAR OF 1812 offers increased to $124 and 320 acres. Though abolished in 1833, the Mexican-American War revived bounties in 1847. CIVIL WAR bounties repeated revolutionary history, with the exception of land grants—although servicemen did enjoy a favored position under the Homestead Act. Since July 1861, Congress had allowed a $100 bounty for three-year men. The passage of the Militia Draft Act in July 1862 provided $25 for nine-month and $50 for twelve-month volunteers. In March 1863, Congress legalized $100 bounties for conscripts and substitutes and supplemented the monthly pay of three- and five-year enlistees.

A worse system prevailed for state bounties. To avoid the disgrace of resorting to a draft, communities filled their quotas by offering bounties. Richer districts thus enticed volunteers from poorer localities, easily filling their quotas and leaving low-bounty regions depleted of manpower and overtaxed by the federal draft. Bounty jumpers and dishonest bounty brokers greatly aggravated the problem.

In four years, the federal government paid more than $300 million in bounties, and the states and localities paid roughly $1 billion. Bounties disappeared after Appomattox, and recruiting bounties were expressly forbidden by the Selective Service Act of 1917.

BIBLIOGRAPHY

Murdock, Eugene Converse. *Patriotism Limited*. Kent, Ohio: Kent State University Press, 1967.

Oberly, James Warren. *Sixty Million Acres: American Veterans and the Public Lands Before the Civil War*. Kent, Ohio: Kent State University Press, 1990.

Shannon, Fred A. *The Organization and Administration of the Union Army*. Cleveland: Arthur H. Clark, 1928.

Elbridge Colby
Fred A. Shannon / c. w.

See also **Conscription and Recruitment.**

BOUNTY JUMPER, a Civil War deserter. The system of military bounties paid during the Civil War to encourage enlistment in the U.S. military produced bounty jumpers. Aided and abetted by bounty brokers, a man would enlist, collect the bounty, desert, and then reenlist elsewhere. He would repeat this process until authorities finally caught him. One especially devious deserter received a sentence of four years in prison after confessing to jumping bounties thirty-two times. The large initial bounty payments were a major cause of desertion from the ranks of the Union army. More than 268,000 soldiers deserted from the Union forces during the Civil War.

BIBLIOGRAPHY

Welcher, Frank J. *The Union Army, 1861–1865: Organization and Operations*. Bloomington: Indiana University Press, 1989.

Fred A. Shannon / A. E.

See also **Desertion; Substitutes, Civil War.**

BOURBONS, the term originally applied to the faction within the southern Democratic-Conservative party that, during Reconstruction, opposed the party's New Departure policy. It was derived from the name of the post-Napoleonic French royal family and connoted intransigence to social and political change. Whereas New Departurists advocated soliciting the black vote and cooperating with dissident Republicans as the means to regain political control from the northern-supported Republicans, Bourbons rejected black suffrage and argued that Democrats should maintain their principles, including states' rights and free trade. They also tended to represent the economic interests of the white agricultural elite, a position that, despite their political majority among white voters, later placed them at odds with advocates of the New South and the southern populists.

BIBLIOGRAPHY

Perman, Michael. *The Road to Redemption: Southern Politics, 1869–1979*. Chapel Hill: University of North Carolina Press, 1984.

Woodward, C. Vann. *Origins of the New South, 1877–1913*. Baton Rouge: Louisiana State University Press, 1951.

C. Wyatt Evans

See also **Reconstruction.**

BOWERY. The Bowery is a neighborhood in lower Manhattan most often associated with the poor and the homeless. The modern street bearing that name begins at Chatham Square in Chinatown and continues north to Coopers Square where it merges into Third Avenue. The street's origins date back to the seventeenth century, when it was named *Bouwerie* (farm) Lane because it was a primary route of egress from the Dutch-controlled city of New Amsterdam to the farm of its governor, Peter Stuyvesant. In 1673, a mail route using this road was established between New York City and Boston. At the end of the American Revolution, on 25 November 1783 (long celebrated as "Evacuation Day"), the Bowery provided the main route by which the last of the occupying British army marched down to the East River wharves and departed. By the mid-nineteenth century, the Bowery neighborhood had become a center for popular entertainment and was home to an assortment of theaters, saloons, brothels, and dance halls. At the same time, it became the center of the "b'hoy" movement, in which multiethnic, working-class young men affected a new image by wearing loud clothing, greasing back their hair, and frequenting the cruder nightlife centered around the Bowery. Petty crime and prostitution followed in their wake, and by the early twentieth century, most respectable businesses and entertainment had fled the area. Throughout most of the 1900s, the word "Bowery" was synonymous with the homeless and indigent. However, beginning in the 1990s, significant changes came to the Bowery. The once-squalid area became home to a new generation of artists, clothing designers, trendy cafes, restaurants, and boutiques.

BIBLIOGRAPHY

Burrows, Edwin G., and Mike Wallace. *Gotham: A History of New York City to 1898.* New York: Oxford University Press, 1999.

Harlow, Alvin F. *Old Bowery Days: The Chronicles of a Famous Street.* New York: D. Appleton, 1931.

Faren R. Siminoff

BOWIE KNIFE. Devised by either Rezin P. Bowie or his brother James, who died in the siege of the Alamo, the Bowie knife achieved fame in the Sandbar duel in 1827, when Jim Bowie killed a man. It has since become the subject of a cycle of heroic folktales. Although supplanted by the COLT SIX-SHOOTER, it was standard equipment for frontiersmen and backwoodsmen for four decades. MOUNTAIN MEN used a modified form of the Bowie knife, TEXAS RANGERS rode with it, and Mississippi River pirates disemboweled their victims with it. With a strong, well-guarded blade that could be thrown as well as wielded, it was both economical and practical for skinning, cutting meat, eating, fighting duels, hammering, and performing other functions.

BIBLIOGRAPHY

Davis, William C. *Three Roads to the Alamo: The Lives and Fortunes of David Crockett, James Bowie, and William Barret Travis.* New York: HarperCollins, 1998.

J. Frank Dobie/C. W.

See also **Alamo, Siege of the; Frontier.**

BOWLES'S FILIBUSTERING EXPEDITIONS. In the early 1780s William Augustus Bowles traveled to the Bahamas, where he became the agent of the trading house of Miller, Bonnamy, and Company, reinforced with the benevolent and probable financial interest of Lord Dunmore, governor of the islands. In this capacity, Bowles sought to secure the trade of the Creek Indians in FLORIDA, which another English firm, Panton, Leslie, and Company, held rather securely.

Bowles appeared in western Florida in 1788 with a cargo of goods, which he liberally distributed among the Indians without arousing suspicion. Bowles probably intended to attack the Spaniards through Indian allies, but he left after some of his men deserted. In 1791, the year after the Creek chief Alexander McGillivray made the Treaty of New York with the United States, Bowles returned to Florida with the idea of supplanting McGillivray in Creek leadership, being aided by the unpopularity of that agreement. He plundered the Panton, Leslie storehouse at Saint Marks, but after being tricked by the Spanish spent the next few years as a prisoner in Havana, Madrid, Cádiz, and the Philippines. He escaped and returned to Nassau in 1799, and soon embarked for Florida on his third and last FILIBUSTERING expedition. In 1800 he seized the Spanish fort at Saint Marks and held it for a few months before being forced out. At the suggestion of the United States, the Spaniards offered a reward of $4,500 for his capture and in May 1803 he was seized on American soil. He died two years later in Morro Castle, Havana.

BIBLIOGRAPHY

Saunt, Claudio. *A New Order of Things: Property, Power, and the Transformation of the Creek Indians, 1733–1816.* Cambridge, U.K.: Cambridge University Press, 1999.

E. Merton Coulter
Christopher Wells

See also **Creeks; Indian Treaties; Spain, Relations with.**

BOWLING. According to archaeological evidence, ancient Egyptians played a game similar to bowling in 3200 B.C. The game was popular in medieval Europe, and American colonists bowled in the streets of Jamestown, but the modern tenpin game developed with the German immigrant community in America in the mid-nineteenth century. Most bowling alleys were located in saloon basements, and the game's association with drunkenness,

Bowling. Floretta D. McCutcheon, a professional champion who spent nearly thirty years going on numerous exhibition tours and teaching the sport, gives a lesson to fans in 1932. © CORBIS

violence, and gambling quickly earned it an unsavory reputation.

PROHIBITION severed the direct connection between saloons and bowling, but the game still struggled with its image problem. The "pin boys" who cleared and reset pins and returned balls after each roll were a public-relations disaster. The dangerous and demanding work paid very little, and in general, only vagrants and young teenagers would take the job. Child welfare advocates condemned bowling alleys as SWEATSHOPS teeming with immoral influences.

The invention of the automatic pinsetter in 1951 had a great impact on the game. No longer reliant on unpredictable labor, alley proprietors saw an opportunity to expand their market beyond league bowlers, and they advertised the game as good clean family fun. Glitzy recreation centers with cheerful names such as "Bowl-O-Drome" and "Victory Bowling" opened in shopping plazas throughout the country. Many featured Laundromats and nurseries to serve the family needs of suburban consumers, and a few even banned alcohol to encourage parents to think of the lanes as a safe place for their kids. Now packaged as "the people's country clubs," bowling alleys grew increasingly extravagant. Chicago's Holiday Bowl Recreation maintained sixty-four lanes, an Olympic-size swimming pool, and tennis courts. In 1958, the Professional Bowlers Association, which organizes about twenty tournaments each year, was created to capitalize on the success of television broadcasts. By the late 1960s, however, the bowling boom was over.

Still, the game remains one of America's most popular pastimes, and it has become a powerful if contested cultural symbol. Many artists and writers use bowling, especially the sweat-stained embroidered bowling shirt, to represent suburban conservatism and provincialism. But Robert Putnam's influential book *Bowling Alone*, which laments the decline of "social capital" in the United States, employs bowling as a metaphor for a less crassly individualistic era.

BIBLIOGRAPHY

Hurley, Andrew. *Diners, Bowling Alleys, and Trailer Parks: Chasing the American Dream in the Postwar Consumer Culture.* New York: Basic Books, 2001.

Luby, Mort Jr. "The History of Bowling." *Bowlers Journal* 70, no. 11 (1983): 102–159.

Putnam, Robert D. *Bowling Alone: The Collapse and Revival of American Community.* New York: Simon and Schuster, 2000.

Jeremy Derfner

See also **Recreation; Sports.**

BOXER REBELLION, an antiforeign uprising in China by members of a secret society beginning in June 1900. The society, originally called the Boxers United in Righteousness, drew their name from their martial rites. Over the course of the uprising, a force of some 140,000 Boxers killed thousands of Chinese Christians and a total of 231 foreigners, including Germany's ambassador. On 17 June 1900, the Boxers began a siege of the legations in Peking. The United States joined Great Britain, Russia, Germany, France, and Japan in a military expedition for the relief of the legations, sending 5,000 troops for this purpose. The international relief expedition marched

Boxer Rebellion. Captured members of the militant Chinese secret society are held in a camp. © CORBIS

from Taku to Tientsin and thence to Peking, raising the siege on 14 August. Believing that an intact China would further U.S. trade interests in Asia, Secretary of State John Hay chose the opportunity to reiterate the "Open Door" policy of the United States and issued a circular note identifying the U.S. goal to "preserve Chinese territorial and administrative entity." In addition, the United States did not join a punitive expedition under German Commander in Chief Count von Waldersee, and, during the Peking Congress (5 February–7 September 1901), the United States opposed the demand for a punitive indemnity, which might have led to the dismemberment of China. The Boxer protocol finally fixed the indemnity at $333 million, provided for the punishment of guilty Chinese officials, and permitted the major nations to maintain legation guards at Peking and between the capital and the sea. The U.S. share of the indemnity, originally set at $24.5 million but reduced to $12 million, was paid by 1924.

BIBLIOGRAPHY

Esherick, Joseph. *The Origins of the Boxer Uprising.* Berkeley: University of California Press, 1987.

Schaller, Michael. *The United States and China in the Twentieth Century.* New York: Oxford University Press, 1979.

Kenneth Colegrove
Flannery Haug

See also **China, Relations with; Indemnities; Open Door Policy.**

BOY SCOUTS OF AMERICA is based on the ideals of Robert Baden-Powell (1857–1941), a British hero of the Boer War who founded the Boy Scouts in England in 1908. Inspired by Baden-Powell's scouts, the Chicago publisher William Boyce incorporated the Boy Scouts of America on 8 February 1910. Other similar American groups already existed, including the Woodcraft Indians organized by the naturalist and writer Ernest Thompson Seton. Congress granted a charter to the Boy Scouts on 15 June 1916.

Scouting is an educational program that aims to build character, promote citizenship, and develop personal fitness among boys and young men. The Boy Scouts emphasizes outdoor activities such as hiking, canoeing, and camping, as well as first aid and civic service. The scout motto is "Be Prepared," and under scout law, members promise to be trustworthy, loyal, helpful, friendly, courteous, kind, obedient, cheerful, thrifty, brave, clean, and reverent.

Scouting is divided into three main age groups: Cub Scouts for boys seven to ten, Boy Scouts for boys eleven to seventeen, and Venturers for young men and women ages fourteen to twenty. Over the years, many other subdivisions have been created, including Sea Scouts, Varsity Scouts, and a division for the very young called Tiger Cubs. The Venturers (known until 1998 as Explorers) is scouting's only coed division.

Boy Scouts gather in local groups known as troops, with each troop led by adult volunteers. Merit badges are awarded to scouts who master disciplines ranging from forestry and horsemanship to space exploration, American cultures, and dentistry. Older scouts who earn a prescribed set of merit badges and demonstrate exceptional leadership can qualify for scouting's highest rank, that of Eagle Scout.

Scouts wear a military-style uniform but have no affiliation with the military or the U.S. government. While open to boys of all faiths, the Scout Oath requires members to affirm a "duty to God." In the 1980s and 1990s the organization endured considerable public controversy over its determination to exclude atheists as well as homosexuals from membership.

James Dale, a former assistant scoutmaster in New Jersey, filed a 1992 complaint against the Scouts after his membership was revoked due to his open homosexuality. On 28 June 2000, the U.S. Supreme Court ruled 5 to 4 in favor of the Boy Scouts, saying that the organization had a First Amendment right to exclude leaders who openly disagreed with its principles. Writing for the majority, Chief Justice William Rehnquist opined that "the Boy Scouts is an expressive association and that the forced inclusion of Dale would significantly affect its expression."

Though autonomous, the Boy Scouts of America maintains ties to scouting programs in more than 100 other countries worldwide. (The Boy Scouts is not affiliated with the Girl Scouts of the U.S.A., a separate organization also based in part on Baden-Powell's ideals.) National and international Boy Scout conferences, called jamborees, are held every four years. Basic scouting tenets and skills are explained in the official *Boy Scout Handbook*, and an official monthly magazine, *Boys' Life*, has been published since 1911.

By 2000, the organization claimed a membership of 3.3 million youths, along with 1.2 million adult leaders. The same year the organization named Mario Castro, a twelve-year-old from Brooklyn, as the 100 millionth member in Boy Scout history.

BIBLIOGRAPHY

Boy Scouts of America. *Boy Scout Handbook.* 10th ed. Irving, Tex.: Boy Scouts of America, 1990.

Mechling, Jay. *On My Honor: Boy Scouts and the Making of American Youth.* Chicago: University of Chicago Press, 2001.

Rosenthal, Michael. *The Character Factory: Baden-Powell and the Origins of the Boy Scout Movement.* New York: Pantheon, 1986.

Ryan F. Holznagel

See also **Girl Scouts of the United States of America.**

Boycotting. Marchers in Los Angeles call on all Americans to join the Jewish American boycott of products from Nazi Germany, 1938. © CORBIS

BOYCOTTING is the organized refusal to purchase goods or services in protest of the policies of the firm or country that produces it. Boycotting has been a popular strategy since before the American Revolution and continues to be a significant tactic of resistance among groups at all points on the political spectrum.

Although the term "boycott" did not come into popular usage in the United States until about 1880, its tactics were in use as early as the mid-eighteenth century. Over the course of the 1760s and 1770s, groups like the Sons of Liberty oversaw a series of boycotts in which both merchants and individual consumers refused to purchase British-made goods. Patriots celebrated "homespun" cloth produced in the colonies from fiber produced in the colonies. These boycotts were successful on many levels, embarrassing Parliament, raising concerns among British and Loyalist merchants, and according to historian T. H. Breen, providing a basis for a common cultural identity and experience among the diverse group of colonists.

Americans continued to practice boycotts in the antebellum era, albeit on a smaller scale. Many abolitionist families made a point of avoiding goods that had been produced by the labor of enslaved people. Similarly, some Southerners boycotted northern-made goods in response to abolitionist efforts to inundate the south with anti-slavery tracts. These antebellum boycotts, however, seem to have been neither widespread nor terribly effective.

Boycotting became a tactic in the burgeoning labor movement of the late nineteenth century. The Knights of Labor (KOL), one of the largest unions of this era, made boycotting a central strategy. Terrence Powderly, the leader of the KOL, explicitly preferred boycotts to mass walkouts or strikes. Boycotts were also often an effective weapon. Unions used publicity, personal contact, and blacklists to prevent small businesses and shoppers from doing business with firms that purchased goods or services from nonunion or antilabor businesses. For example, New York City carpenters refused to use wood trim or nails that had been produced by nonunion labor. Judges in both criminal and civil cases often ruled that such "secondary" or "material" boycotts were illegal. By the first decades of the twentieth century, both the broad-based organizing strategy of unions like the KOL and the heavy reliance on secondary boycotts had all but disappeared.

Boycotts led by individuals frustrated with rising prices achieved prominence in the first decades of the twentieth century. In New York, Missouri, Massachusetts, and towns and cities across the country, local organizations publicly attacked retailers and suppliers for raising prices faster than wages had increased. Boycotters proved especially angry over rising costs of beef, for which they blamed collusion among beef processors. These protests became violent at times, with angry shoppers threatening to attack retailers, suppliers, and violators of the boycott. Women were particularly important in the neighborhood-organizing strategies of these boycotts.

Individuals seeking social or political change organized the largest boycotts of the twentieth century. These boycotts achieved new prominence in the 1930s, a highpoint of consumer activism. In 1933, Jewish Americans began a nine-year-long boycott of German-made products. Japan's 1931 and 1937 invasions of Manchuria spurred Chinese people and Chinese Americans to lead a boycott of Japanese goods. Chinese Americans won the support of many liberal groups and movie star celebrities. American imports of Japanese silk were 47 percent lower in the first six months of 1938 than they had been for the corresponding period a year earlier.

Finally, throughout the late 1920s and 1930s, African Americans across the country led "Don't Buy Where You Can't Work" campaigns—boycotts of stores that refused either to hire or to promote African Americans. Begun in Chicago in 1929, these boycotts proved successful in New York, Cleveland, Baltimore, Washington, D.C., and other cities. Pickets and reprisals against violators sometimes became violent, and businesses often sought relief through court injunctions. Nonetheless, protestors successfully won African Americans hundreds of jobs at a variety of chain and locally owned stores, even in the midst of the Great Depression.

African American boycotting in Montgomery, Alabama, launched the modern civil rights movement. African Americans had begun organized boycotts of segregated public school systems since before the civil war and had been protesting segregated public transportation as early as 1905. Companies were generally able to survive African Americans' refusal to ride in public streetcars. In 1955, however, seamstress and civil rights activist Rosa Parks challenged a bus driver in Montgomery who demanded that she move to the back of the bus. Her actions led to a yearlong near-total boycott of public transportation by African Americans. Instead of using public transportation, African Americans in Montgomery walked or car-pooled. Not only did activists cause steep losses to the local bus company, they mounted and won a court case

forcing the city to desegregate public transportation. The Montgomery bus boycott catalyzed civil rights activism in other southern cities and brought movement leader Martin Luther King Jr. to national prominence.

From the 1960s through the 1990s, boycotts brought attention to a variety of causes. The United Farm Workers, an organization of migrant workers, led a national boycott, first of particular California grape growers and then of all California table grapes from 1965 to 1970. Later boycotts of grapes and lettuce followed, though none were as effective at lowering sales or forcing concessions from growers. Many Americans also boycotted meat during the rapid rise in food prices of the early 1970s. In 1997, the Southern Baptist Convention announced a nationwide boycott of Disneyland, Disney World, and Disney subsidiaries in protest of what they termed Disney's "anti-family" and "anti-Christian" direction. The World Council of Churches, along with numerous liberal organizations, organized a boycott of Nestlé products in protest of Nestlé's refusal to stop extensive marketing of infant formula in impoverished third world nations. With the exception of the grape boycott, few of these boycotts have caused serious financial damage to firms, but most have resulted in embarrassment and some, as in the case of Nestlé, in occasional policy changes.

Neither the growth of multinational corporations, nor the changing political landscape, seem to have undermined the use of boycotts. Indeed, if anything, the growth of a consumer society has only made the boycott a more accessible and meaningful tactic for many Americans. Barring court injunctions, Americans continue to boycott as a method of registering their alarm and disapproval, particularly when governmental solutions are difficult to obtain.

BIBLIOGRAPHY

Breen, T.H. "Narrative of Commercial Life: Consumption, Ideology, and Community on the Eve of the American Revolution." *William and Mary Quarterly* 50 (1993): 471–501.

Ernst, Daniel R. *Lawyers Against Labor: From Individual Rights to Corporate Liberalism.* Urbana: University of Illinois Press, 1995.

Fink, Leon. *Workingmen's Democracy: the Knights of Labor and American Politics.* Urbana: University of Illinois Press, 1983.

Frank, Dana. *Buy American: The Untold Story of Economic Nationalism.* Boston: Beacon Press, 1999.

Friedman, Monroe. *Consumer Boycotts: Effecting Change through the Marketplace and the Media.* New York: Routledge, 1999.

Hyman, Paula. "Immigrant Women and Consumer Protest: The New York City Kosher Meat Boycott of 1902." *American Jewish History.* 70 (1980): 91–105.

Meier, August, and Elliott M. Rudwick, "The Boycott Movement against Jim Crow Streetcars in the South, 1900–1906." *Journal of American History* 55 (1969): 756–775.

Tracey Deutsch

See also **Civil Rights Movement; Free Trade; Sons of Liberty (American Revolution); United Farm Workers Union of America.**

BRADDOCK'S EXPEDITION,

unsucessful British attempt to capture Fort Duquesne (Pittsburgh, Pennsylvania) during the French and Indian War. On 14 April 1755 General Edward Braddock, the commander of all British forces in America, was dispatched with two regiments. The first objective was Fort Duquesne. The regulars, the colonials, and a small contingent of Indian allies rendezvoused at Fort Cumberland to start for Fort Duquesne by the route later called Braddock's Road. The army, 2,200 men strong, started west on 7 June but had advanced only to Little Meadows (near Grantsville, Maryland) by 16 June. On the advice of Lieutenant Colonel George Washington, his aide-de-camp, Braddock left his heavier supplies behind and pushed on rapidly with some 1,200 men and a minimum of artillery.

Meanwhile, from Fort Duquesne, Captain Daniel Beaujeu led some 250 French soldiers and 600 Indians to oppose Braddock. When the two parties met unexpectedly on 9 July, the British opened fire, putting most of the French to flight and killing Beaujeu. Beaujeu's subordinate rallied the Indians to seize an unoccupied hill and to surround the British line. The van of the English, falling back, became entangled with the main body, and order was lost. The British stood under a galling fire for three hours before Braddock ordered a retreat. The general and many of the officers were killed, and the retreat became a rout.

Colonel William Dunbar, now in command, retreated to Fort Cumberland. Refusing the request of Virginia and Pennsylvania to build a fort at Raystown (Bedford, Pennsylvania) and defend the frontier, he marched to Philadelphia in August and left the border to suffer Indian raids. Although Braddock's expedition failed, it demonstrated that an army could march over the Alleghenies, it taught the troops something of Indian fighting, and its very mistakes contributed to the success of the Forbes Expedition in 1758.

BIBLIOGRAPHY

Cohen, Sheldon S. "Major William Sparke along the Monongahela." *Pennsylvania History* 62, no. 4 (1995): 546–556.

Kopperman, Paul E. *Braddock at the Monongahela.* Pittsburgh, Pa.: University of Pittsburgh Press, 1976.

Pargellis, Stanley. "Braddock's Defeat." *American Historical Review* 41, no. 2 (January 1936): 253–269.

Solon J. Buck / A. R.

See also **Allegheny Mountains, Routes Across; Duquesne, Fort; Monongahela, Battle of the.**

BRADY BILL,

officially the Brady Handgun Violence Prevention Act of 1993, established a national five-day waiting period for retail handgun purchases. The bill was named for James Brady, the White House press secretary wounded in John Hinckley's attempt to assassinate President Ronald Reagan in 1981. The waiting period was intended to provide time for police to undertake criminal-records checks of prospective handgun purchasers. Supporters widely hailed passage of the act as a major defeat for the National Rifle Association, the powerful progun lobby that successfully opposed other types of gun controls.

BIBLIOGRAPHY

Anderson, Jack. *Inside the NRA: Armed and Dangerous: An Expose.* Beverly Hills, Calif.: Dove Books, 1996.

James D. Wright / c. w.

See also **Gun Control; National Rifle Association.**

BRADY PHOTOGRAPHS,

collection of photographs taken by Mathew B. Brady and his associates during the Civil War. In addition to portraits of military commanders, they document scenes of the battlefield and daily life in the camp along with houses, hospitals, ships, and railroads. Brady was the first photographer to extensively chronicle historical events and to advance photography beyond the art of portraiture.

Born in 1823 or 1824 in Warren County, New York, and trained as a portrait painter, Brady became interested

Ravages of War. This photograph credited to Mathew Brady (but which, like many others, may have been taken by an assistant) shows a scene in war-torn Charleston, S.C. © BETTMANN/CORBIS

Alexander Gardner. Standing next to a photographic supply wagon is Mathew Brady's employee, then rival, who took many of the Civil War photographs credited to Brady. © Bettmann/corbis

in daguerreotypy in 1839. He opened a studio in New York five years later and in 1850 published portraits and biographical sketches of eminent American citizens in his first book, *The Gallery of Illustrious Americans.* He opened his National Photographic Art Gallery in Washington, D.C., in 1858 and a couple of years later a National Portrait Gallery in New York City. Brady specialized in *carte-de-visite* portraits of national leaders, politicians, and foreign dignitaries. Among them were Abraham Lincoln, Jefferson Davis, and Edward Albert, prince of Wales.

When the Civil War began in 1861, Brady was at the peak of his success as a portrait photographer. He later claimed to have had a calling to chronicle the Civil War and tried unsuccessfully to photograph the Battle of Bull Run. Brady organized his efforts on a grand scale: employing a large number of photographers, he provided equipment, planned assignments, supervised their activities, and collected and preserved the fragile photographic plates and negatives. He also bought a large number of photographs from freelance battlefield photographers to ensure that his collection would cover all aspects of the war. All of these pictures were published as "Photograph by Brady," which led to frictions with a number of his photographers.

The nearly $100,000 he invested in this project never paid off, although some of his photographs were pub-lished in the weeklies *Leslie's* and *Harper's,* particularly after Alexander Gardner's photographs of the carnage at Antietam exhibited at Brady's New York gallery attracted large crowds. This was the first time a sizable number of people not involved in the fighting received a visual impression of the terrible reality of battle. The photographic supply firm of E. and H. T. Anthony Company published and sold some of the photographs in exchange for financing his venture, but at the end of the war Brady had to hand over some of his negatives to the company as payment for his debt. These photographs, together with about 2,000 of Gardner's, served as the basis for the ten-volume *Photographic History of the Civil War,* first published in 1896. This collection was purchased by the Library of Congress in 1943, published in 1961 as the microfilm publication *Civil War Photographs, 1861–1865,* and in 1991 included in the library's digital online "American Memory." Brady even had to auction his Washington, D.C., studio before the War Department purchased more than 6,000 of his photographs in 1874–1875 for $25,000. They are now located in the National Archives and have been accessible as digital copies since 1998. Another 5,000 negatives were sold by the Anthony Company to a British collector at the turn of the century, a collection that the National Portrait Gallery acquired for the Smithsonian Institution in 1981.

BIBLIOGRAPHY

Panzer, Mary. *Mathew Brady and the Image of History*. Washington, D.C.: Smithsonian Institution Press for the National Portrait Gallery, 1997.

———. *Mathew Brady*. London and New York: Phaidon, 2001.

Michael Wala

See also **Photography, Military.**

BRAIN TRUST.

BRAIN TRUST. Before his 1932 nomination as the Democratic presidential candidate, FRANKLIN D. ROOSEVELT brought together RAYMOND MOLEY, Rexford G. Tugwell, and Adolph A. Berle, Jr. as close advisers. These three continued to aid Roosevelt during his campaign for election. After his inauguration, they became prominent in the councils of the chief executive and received salaried offices in Washington. They and the group of economists, lawyers, and scholars who subsequently joined the administration earned the name "the brain trust," whether or not they were close to the president or truly responsible for any novel programs or policies. Thus, the expression "brain trust" became a symbol for all NEW DEAL experimentation.

BIBLIOGRAPHY

Reagan, Patrick D. *Designing a New America: The Origins of New Deal Planning, 1890–1943*. Amherst: University of Massachusetts Press, 2000.

Rosenof, Theodore. *Economics in the Long Run: New Deal Theorists and Their Legacies, 1933–1993*. Chapel Hill: University of North Carolina Press, 1997.

Erik McKinley Eriksson / A. E.

See also **Great Depression; President, U.S.**

BRANDEIS CONFIRMATION HEARINGS.

BRANDEIS CONFIRMATION HEARINGS. On 28 January 1916, President Woodrow Wilson electrified the nation by nominating Louis D. Brandeis to replace the deceased Joseph R. Lamar as an Associate Justice of the Supreme Court. Brandeis, a Boston attorney, was a nationally known progressive reformer and the first Jew ever nominated to the Court. Wilson, who had come to rely on Brandeis's advice on domestic issues, was willing to face the inevitable political storm. He also recognized that Brandeis's appointment would help win two important constituencies in the approaching presidential election: Jewish voters and progressives who had voted in 1912 for Theodore Roosevelt.

Conservative leaders and newspapers exploded. They claimed that Brandeis was a radical and an unprofessional self-promoter who lacked a "judicial temperament." The religious issue was not emphasized publicly, but it probably influenced some to oppose the nomination. Progressives were jubilant at Wilson's announcement. For more than a decade, Brandeis had been in the forefront of crusades on behalf of labor, conservation, the antitrust movement, and consumer rights, earning the respect and admiration of many Americans sympathetic to progressive reform.

A subcommittee of the Senate Judiciary Committee began hearings on 9 February, and every aspect of Brandeis's career was scrutinized by numerous friendly and unfriendly witnesses. The culmination of what can be seen as a symbolic struggle between conservative and progressive elements in American society came with the subcommittee voting for confirmation by 3 to 2 along party lines (1 April), and the full Judiciary Committee voting for Brandeis 10 to 8, again along strict party lines (24 May). In the Senate, on 1 June, after five months of vigorous debate, the nominee was confirmed by a vote of 47 to 22; only one Democrat voted against Brandeis, while three progressive Republicans voted with the majority. Brandeis began his twenty-three years of distinguished service on the Court by taking the oath of office on 5 June.

BIBLIOGRAPHY

Strum, Philippa. *Louis D. Brandeis: Justice for the People*. Cambridge: Harvard University Press, 1984.

Todd, A. L. *Justice on Trial: The Case of Louis D. Brandeis*. New York: McGraw-Hill, 1964.

United States Senate. *Hearings before the Sub-Committee of the Committee of the Judiciary . . . on the Nomination of Louis D. Brandeis to be an Associate Justice of the Supreme Court of the United States*. 64th Congress, 1st Session. 2 vols. Washington, D.C.: Government Printing Office, 1916.

David W. Levy

See also **Anti-Semitism; Progressive Movement.**

BRANDYWINE CREEK, BATTLE OF

BRANDYWINE CREEK, BATTLE OF (11 September 1777), was fought in Chester County, Pennsylvania, ten miles northwest of Wilmington, Delaware. The British and Hessian troops commanded by the generals Sir William Howe, Lord Cornwallis, and Baron Wilhelm von Knyphausen composed a force of nineteen thousand. The American army under General George Washington numbered eleven thousand. The British crossed the east side of the creek at Jeffrie's Ford, continued southward, and suddenly attacked General John Sullivan's troops near Birmingham Meetinghouse. The outnumbered Americans suffered one thousand casualties and were compelled to retire. At night Washington withdrew his army toward Philadelphia.

BIBLIOGRAPHY

Canby, Henry Seidel. *The Brandywine*. New York: Farrar and Rinehart, 1941.

Townsend, Joseph. *The Battle of Brandywine*. New York: New York Times, 1969.

Charles W. Heathcote / A. R.

See also **German Mercenaries.**

BRANNAN PLAN, a farm price support plan using direct payments to the farmer under certain conditions as a substitute for other price supports. Among the initiatives of President Harry Truman's Fair Deal, this plan was first proposed by Secretary of Agriculture Charles Brannan in April 1949. The proposal aroused considerable opposition. Its opponents characterized it as unsound and fantastically expensive. In the 1952 presidential campaign, Republicans argued that the Brannan plan was an example of Democratic profligacy. Supporters of the plan countered that it was a rational approach to income protection for agriculture and a more effective and less costly way than price supports to subsidize the farmer when assistance is needed. Although advocated in Congress a number of times, usually in amended form, the plan was never approved.

BIBLIOGRAPHY

Christensen, Reo Millard. *The Brannan Plan.* Ann Arbor: University of Michigan Press, 1959.

Dean, Virgil W. "Why Not the Brannan Plan?" *Agricultural History* 70 (Spring 1996).

Thomas Robson Hay / T. M.

See also **Agriculture; Fair Deal.**

BREAST IMPLANTS. Although the practice was decried by most physicians, some surgeons pioneered breast reconstruction and augmentation by injecting paraffin, implanting skin and fat grafts, and using subcutaneous glass-ball prostheses between 1895 and 1945. New plastics developed during World War II revolutionized breast implant technology. Along with shaped plastic sponges, silicone—a synthetic polymer known for its flexibility and chemical stability—seemed to offer an ideal material. Liquid silicone was originally an engine lubricant, but by 1946 Japanese doctors were injecting it into women's breasts to increase their size. Reports of complications from silicone injections prompted the Food and Drug Administration (FDA) to regulate liquid silicone in 1965, and in 1971 physicians began abandoning silicone injections. In 1963, however, Texas plastic surgeons Thomas Cronin and Frank Gerow, working with Dow Corning, unveiled a "natural feel" implant, a silicone rubber capsule filled with silicone gel they named Silastic. An estimated 2 million American women had received silicone implants by the late 1980s.

Silastic also presented complications, however. A tissue capsule tended to surround the implant, sometimes causing hardening. Some women developed inflammation; others exhibited symptoms that mimicked rheumatoid arthritis and immune system disorders. The discovery that Silastic implants often leaked precipitated a crisis. Between 1990 and 1992, Congress and the FDA held hearings on the safety of silicone implants. Implant advocates blamed complications on poor surgical technique, not silicone. Satisfied recipients argued that women, as part of their ability to control their own bodies, had a right to choose implants. Opponents argued that women had been misled, exposed to unnecessary health risks, and sacrificed for corporate profits. The FDA began regulating silicone implants in 1992. Thousands of lawsuits against implant manufacturers ended in multi-billion-dollar settlements between 1995 and 1998. Controversy continued because numerous scientific studies after 1995 disputed the links between silicone implants and disease. Silicone gel implants remained restricted, however, and most women preferred implants filled with saline. While breast augmentations dropped dramatically to 30,000 per year in 1992, by 1997 they had rebounded to more than 120,000, with many women using illegally obtained silicone gel implants.

BIBLIOGRAPHY

Coco, Linda. "Silicone Breast Implants in America: A Choice of the 'Official Breast.'" In *Essays on Controlling Processes.* Edited by Laura Nader. Berkeley, Calif.: Kroeber Anthropological Society, 1994.

Jacobson, Nora. *Cleavage: Technology, Controversy, and the Ironies of the Man-Made Breast.* New Brunswick, N.J.: Rutgers University Press, 2000. Comprehensive, fascinating, and brilliant.

Parker, Lisa S. "Social Justice, Federal Paternalism, and Feminism: Breast Implants in the Cultural Context of Female Beauty." *Kennedy Institute of Ethics Journal* 3 (1993): 57–76.

Gregory Michael Dorr

See also **Cosmetic Surgery; Medicine and Surgery.**

BRETHREN (often nicknamed Dunkers) originated in central Germany in 1708. They were former Reformed and Lutheran Pietists (largely from the Palatinate), dissatisfied with state-linked churches. Pietism sought to complete the reformation of doctrine with a reformation of life. Earnest Christians gathered in small groups to search the Scriptures for guidance. Those who participated often suffered expulsion from their homes.

These religious refugees found temporary haven after 1700 in the county of Wittgenstein. As they continued their Bible studies, they became aware of passages that called for resolution of difficulties by appeal to the church. At that point having no such organization, five men and three women considered how to proceed. They were influenced by Anabaptism (rebaptism), a radical movement of the sixteenth century. Anabaptists differed from larger Protestant bodies by their concerns for a covenanted church formed through the baptism of adult believers, religious liberty, and pacifism. The Wittgenstein settlers were attracted to these beliefs because they understood them to be biblical. However, they did not wish to join contemporary Anabaptists known as Mennonites, because (in their view) after long decades of persecution, these Anabaptists had lost their original vitality.

REVOLUTIONARY WAR STATEMENT

A short and sincere Declaration, To our *Honorable Assembly,* and all others in high or low Station of *Administration,* and to all Friends and Inhabitants of this Country, to whose Sight this may come, be they EN-GLISH or GERMAN. . . .

Further, we find ourselves indebted to be thankful to our late worthy Assembly, for their giving so good an Advice in these trouble-some Times to all Ranks of People in *Pennsylvania,* particularly in allowing those, who, by the Doctrine of our Saviour Jesus Christ are persuaded in their Conscience to love their Enemies and not to resist Evil, to enjoy the Liberty of their Conscience, for which, as also for all the good Things we enjoyed under their Care, we heartily thank that worthy Body of Assembly, and all high and low in Office who have advised to such a peacefull Measure. . . .

The Advice to those who do not find Freedom of Conscience to take up Arms, that they ought to be helpfull to those who are in Need and distressed Circumstances, we receive with Cheerfulness toward all Men of what Station they may be—it being our Principle to feed the Hungry and give the Thirsty drink;—we have dedicated ourselves to serve all Men in every Thing that can be helpful to the Preservation of Men's Lives, but we find no Freedom in giving, or doing, or assisting in any Thing by which Men's Lives are destroyed or hurt. We beg the Patience of all those who believe we err in this Point. . . .

This Testimony we lay down before our worthy Assembly, and all other Persons in Government, letting them know, that we are thankfull as above-mentioned, and that we are not at Liberty in Conscience to take up Arms to conquer our Enemies, but rather to pray to God, who has Power in Heaven and on Earth, for *US* and *THEM.* . . .

> The above Declaration, signed by a Number of Elders and Teachers of the Society of Mennonists, and Some of the German Baptists, presented to the Honorable House of Assembly on the 7th day of November, 1775, was most graciously received.

SOURCE: Donald F. Durnbaugh, ed. *The Brethren in Colonial America.* Elgin, Ill.: Brethren Press, 1967, pp. 362–365.

The original group of eight therefore proceeded to organize themselves as an Anabaptist congregation, choosing a former miller, Alexander Mack Sr. (1679–1735), as their minister. The Brethren were so evangelistic that from this modest start their numbers increased within twelve years to about five hundred adult members. They initiated daughter congregations in Wetteravia, the Palatinate, Switzerland, Hamburg-Altona, and the lower Rhine region.

Emigration and Expansion

This expansion drew opposition. The Wetteravian body was expelled in 1715, finding refuge in Krefeld on the lower Rhine. However, when these members continued to evangelize, they again were prosecuted. The first band of Brethren emigrated from the lower Rhine area to Pennsylvania in 1719. After settling there, they reorganized in 1723 in Germantown, near Philadelphia. Once again they reached out to baptize others, soon founding new congregations in Pennsylvania and New Jersey. The original congregation in Wittgenstein, some two hundred in number, relocated in 1720 in Friesland but moved on as a body to Pennsylvania in 1729, led by Alexander Mack. By 1740 there was no organized Brethren activity left in Europe.

Upon arrival in Pennsylvania, Mack found that all was not well with the Brethren in America. A charismatic mystic named Conrad Beissel (1691–1768) drew many Brethren (and others) into the Ephrata Cloister. Its artistic and musical achievements won international fame. Despite this schism, by 1770 there were some 1,500 adult members, with congregations in New Jersey, Pennsylvania, Maryland, Virginia, and the Carolinas.

During the national period, Brethren moved westward with the expansion of the frontier, among the earliest settlers in Kentucky, Missouri, Ohio, Indiana, and Kansas. The first Brethren reached the West Coast by 1850. Unity was preserved by traveling elders and an annual meeting that brought large numbers to a central location for joint worship and business meetings. Most Brethren were farmers and sought fertile lands where they settled in rather isolated, German-speaking enclaves. By the end of the eighteenth century, Brethren had adopted a uniformly styled plain dress, with beards and broad-brim hats for men and form-concealing dark dresses and bonnets for women. This plain style persisted, despite increasing resistance, until 1911, when congregations were allowed to relax these guidelines. By 2000, only a few congregations in southeastern Pennsylvania and Maryland persisted with this costume.

Division

After 1850 new methods of church work began to make inroads, with resultant tensions within the church, now known as the German Baptist Brethren. These included periodicals, Sunday schools, higher education, revival meetings, and financial support for ministers (who were self-supporting). Conservative leaders opposed these innovations and also the growing calls for sending missionaries to isolated rural areas and cities (home missions) and to other nations (foreign missions). They (correctly) predicted that the latter programs would result in more rationalized organization to raise funds, recruit personnel, and administer overseas projects.

These tensions led to a three-way split in the early 1880s. The most conservative took the name Old German Baptist Brethren, the most progressive, the Brethren Church, each numbering about five thousand. The much larger middle grouping (about 50,000) retained the name German Baptist Brethren until 1908, when it was changed to the present Church of the Brethren. In 1926 a small number of conservative members branched off to form the Dunkard Brethren. In 1939 the Brethren Church divided with the formation of the Fellowship of Grace Churches, which in turn split with the emergence of the Conservative Grace Brethren Churches by 1991.

Outreach and Organization

The Church of the Brethren began in the 1940s to become increasingly ecumenical, with active membership in national and world councils of churches. As one of the Historic Peace Churches (along with Mennonites and Friends), Brethren wish to work positively for peace. During World War II, the church began large-scale social-action projects on an international basis, sponsored by the Brethren Service Commission. Several of these are well known, such as the Heifer Project International and the Christian Rural Overseas Program (CROP). Brethren helped to create the International Voluntary Service program, a direct forerunner of the Peace Corps. The Brethren Volunteer Service program has placed thousands of younger Brethren and others in social projects in the United States and abroad since 1948.

In polity, Brethren have balanced congregational independence with a strong connectionalism. The final authority in matters of church doctrine and practice is the Annual Conference, a delegated body meeting in late June and early July with sites rotated around the nation. Delegates elect a general board of twenty, who employ staff to execute the programs of the church; they are largely based at offices in Elgin, Illinois, and New Windsor, Maryland, but are increasingly dispersed. Agencies related to the Annual Conference are the Association of Brethren Caregivers, Bethany Theological Seminary, Brethren Benefit Trust, and On Earth Peace Assembly. The approximately 1,030 congregations are organized into twenty-three districts.

Although noncreedal, Brethren share basic Protestant convictions, and their worship services are similar to those of other Protestant churches. The central liturgical observance is the "love feast," consisting of an examination service, foot washing, fellowship meal, and commemorative bread-and-cup Eucharist. A distinguishing feature is the manner of baptism of professing converts, a threefold forward immersion in the name of the Trinity.

In 2001 the Church of the Brethren numbered 137,000, the Brethren Church 11,000, the Fellowship of Grace Brethren Churches 34,000, the Conservative Grace Brethren Churches 2,500, the Old German Baptist Church 6,000, and the Dunkard Brethren 1,050.

EXCERPT FROM THE DIARY OF JOHN KLINE (1797–1864), A VIRGINIA ELDER ASSASSINATED BY CONFEDERATE IRREGULARS DURING THE CIVIL WAR

Thursday, February 22 [1849]

Hear the distant report of cannon in commemoration of the birth of George Washington, which is said to have occurred on the twenty-second day of February, 1732. It is presumable that those who find pleasure in public demonstrations of this sort are moved by what they regard as patriotic feelings and principles. Let their motives and enjoyments spring from what they may, they have a lawful right to celebrate the anniversary of his birth in any civil way they may choose. But I have a somewhat higher conception of true patriotism than can be represented by the firing of guns which give forth nothing but meaningless sound. I am glad, however, that these guns report harmless sound, and nothing more. If some public speakers would do the same, it might be better for them and their hearers.

My highest conception of patriotism is found in the man who loves the Lord his God with all his heart and his neighbor as himself. Out of these affections spring the subordinate love for one's country; love truly virtuous for one's companions and children, relatives and friends; and in its most comprehensive sense takes in the whole human family. Were this love universal, the word *patriotism,* in its specific sense, meaning such a love for one's country as makes its possessors ready and willing to take up arms in its defense, might be appropriately expunged from every national vocabulary.

SOURCE: Benjamin Funk, ed. *Life and Labors of Elder John Kline, The Martyr Missionary, Collated from His Diary.* Elgin, Ill.: Brethren Publishing House, 1900, p. 246.

BIBLIOGRAPHY

Bowman, Carl F. *Brethren Society: The Cultural Transformation of a "Peculiar People."* Baltimore: Johns Hopkins University Press, 1995. A sociological study.

Durnbaugh, Donald F. *Fruit of the Vine: A History of the Brethren, 1708–1995.* Elgin, Ill.: Brethren Press, 1997. A social history.

Durnbaugh, Donald F., ed. *The Brethren Encyclopedia.* 3 vols. Philadelphia: Brethren Encyclopedia, 1983–1984.

Kraybill, Donald B., and C. Nelson Hostetter. *Anabaptist World USA.* Scottdale, Pa.: Herald Press, 2001. Contains statistics.

Donald F. Durnbaugh

See also **Pietism.**

BRETTON WOODS CONFERENCE, also known as the United Nations Monetary and Financial Conference, held in New Hampshire in July 1944, was attended by forty-four nations. The conference was held to make plans for post–World War II international economic cooperation similar to the groundwork for political cooperation laid by the ATLANTIC CHARTER. The delegates reached agreement on an International Monetary Fund to promote exchange stability and expansion of international trade and on an International Bank for Reconstruction and Development, which became the World Bank. Four of the nations attending, Haiti, Liberia, New Zealand, and the Soviet Union, did not sign.

BIBLIOGRAPHY

Dam, Kenneth W. *The Rules of the Game: Reform and Evolution in the International Monetary System.* Chicago: University of Chicago Press, 1982.

Kunz, Diane B. *Butter and Guns: America's Cold War Economic Diplomacy.* New York: Free Press, 1997.

Charles S. Campbell / A. G.

See also **International Monetary Fund.**

BREWING. Like wine making, brewing has existed for millennia as an art; only in the twentieth century have its practitioners attempted to transform it into an applied science. The earliest settlers brought beer from England with them to America. At that time, brewing was a household industry, carried on primarily by farmers and tavern keepers, but commercial breweries soon emerged, selling to local areas they could reach by horse and wagon. William Penn established such a business in Pennsbury in 1683, not only to make a profit but also to encourage the drinking of beer rather than hard liquor, in the interest of temperance.

The early process of brewing began by heating and soaking barley to force germination. Producers then mixed the end product, called malt, with water and boiled it to form what brewers called the wort. They then added hops to the boiling liquid to give it a pleasantly bitter taste and a distinctive aroma. After straining the liquid, brewers added yeast and allowed the wort to ferment for a few days. Until the twentieth century, brewers governed the proportions of the ingredients and the exact timing of the process by age-old recipes or simply by rule of thumb. The reputation of a commercial brewery depended greatly on the skill of its brewmaster rather than on any particular technology or equipment.

Early American beer was similar to English beer, which was fermented with yeast that floated on top of the wort. Near the middle of the nineteenth century, the many German immigrants to the United States brought a different type of beer. Following German brewing traditions, they used a yeast that stayed at the bottom of the wort during fermentation. Then, after its removal, they

Brewery. A view of the interior of the Schlitz Brewing Company, Milwaukee, Wis., c. 1900. LIBRARY OF CONGRESS

allowed the fermented wort to age at low temperatures for some weeks. The milder and more aromatic German lager soon captured most of the beer market, and the English type of fermentation became confined to ale.

From about 1875, technological and scientific changes took place in brewing that made it very difficult for the amateur or small-scale operator to compete with the up-to-date, large brewery. The railroad made it possible for breweries with limited local markets, such as those in Milwaukee, Wis., to seek nationwide distribution—which, in turn, required beer able to withstand temperature changes, bumping, and the lapse of time. From the 1880s, pasteurization checked bacterial growth, chemical additives were eliminated (this was enforced by law in 1907), bottling became mechanized, and brewers devised new methods to artificially control carbonation levels. In addition to changing their product, commercial brewers infiltrated the territory of local brewers by devising new business tactics to influence local sellers, ranging from discounts and credits to purchases of saloon properties.

The brewing industry that revived after the years of PROHIBITION (1919–1933) had most of the same large producers but operated in a quite different environment from the old one. Because Prohibition had accustomed people to drinking hard liquor, it took a dozen years to build the market for beer back to its pre–World War I size. As late as 1970, domestic consumption of beer still remained slightly less per capita than it had been in 1914. Meanwhile, the motor truck, cans, and a more exact understanding of the chemistry of brewing aided the competitive position of the larger breweries relative to would-be small-scale producers. There were only 150 brewers in 1970, compared to 1,400 in 1914, and fewer than a dozen sold their product throughout the nation. Since all these companies could make reliable beer with many desirable qualities and were forbidden by federal law from controlling outlets, competition was chiefly in marketing and rapid adjustment to changes in public taste.

In 1976, however, the federal government legalized home brewing, and in the late 1970s and 1980s a number of small-scale "craft" brewers emerged to capture loyal local, regional, and eventually national followings. Craft beer sales began to grow exponentially in the 1990s, as sales from larger commercial brewers flattened out, causing some to declare a "Beer Rennaissance" in the United States and leading many larger brewers to begin marketing their own versions of the stronger, darker beers that regional breweries and microbreweries had so successfully popularized.

BIBLIOGRAPHY

Baron, Stanley Wade. *Brewed in America: A History of Beer and Ale in the United States.* Boston: Little, Brown, 1962.

Cochran, Thomas C. *The Pabst Brewing Company: The History of an American Business.* New York: New York University Press, 1948.

Thomas C. Cochran / c. w.

See also **German Americans; Taverns and Saloons.**

BRICKER AMENDMENT to the U.S. Constitution was introduced in January 1953 by Senator John W. Bricker of Ohio, a former governor of his state and the Republican vice presidential nominee in 1944. According to the original bill, no part of any treaty that overrode the Constitution would be binding upon Americans, treaties would become law only "through legislation which would be valid in the absence of a treaty," and Congress would have the same restrictions upon presidential executive agreements that it did upon treaties. Cosponsored by some sixty-four senators, the amendment reflected their abhorrence over Franklin Roosevelt's foreign policy, the possible prerogatives of the United Nations, and fears that U.S. armed forces overseas could be tried in foreign courts. Frank E. Holman, president of the American Bar Association in 1948 and 1949 and a Seattle attorney, drafted the legislation.

In the course of a year the amendment underwent several versions, with Senators Arthur Watkins (Republican from Utah) and Walter George (Democrat from Georgia) offering drafts favored by the more isolationist faction and Senators William F. Knowland (Republican from California) and Homer Ferguson (Republican from Michigan) offering renderings endorsed by the administration of Dwight D. Eisenhower. In February 1954 the Senate defeated the amendment by one vote. It was never resubmitted, and after Bricker failed to be reelected in 1958, the issue was dropped.

BIBLIOGRAPHY

Koo, Youngnok. "Dissenters from American Involvement in World Affairs: A Political Analysis of the Bricker Amendment." Ph.D. diss., University of Michigan, 1966.

Tananbaum, Duane. *The Bricker Amendment Controversy: A Test of Eisenhower's Political Leadership.* Ithaca, N.Y.: Cornell University Press, 1988.

Justus D. Doenecke

See also **Isolationism; Treaties, Negotiation and Ratification of.**

BRIDGER, FORT, on Black's Fork, Uinta County, Wyoming, was a frontier trading post and later a U.S. Army fort. In 1843, James Bridger and his partner, Louis Vasquez, built it and operated it for a number of years. Bridger's post gained its greatest fame as a way station and supply point for western emigrants. Around 1855, Mormon colonists from Utah took over the post and in 1857 burned it on the approach of U.S. troops. In 1858 the U.S. Army rebuilt it as a military post and in 1890 finally abandoned it. It is now a state park.

BIBLIOGRAPHY

Janin, Hunt. *Fort Bridger, Wyoming: Trading Post for Indians, Mountain Men, and Westward Migrants.* Jefferson, N.C.: McFarland, 2001.

Rupert N. Richardson

See also **Mormon Expedition; Trading Posts, Frontier.**

BRIDGES. Bridges have been essential to America's growth, and countless types were devised to carry highways, railroads, and even canals. Location, materials, cost, traffic, and the ingenuity and creativity of bridge engineers all have influenced the evolution of American bridge technology.

The Colonies and the Early Republic

Large-span bridge building in North America began with the Charles River Bridge at Cambridge, Massachusetts, in 1662. Its pile and beam construction was not unlike that used for centuries in Europe. The design placed heavy timber beams across piles that were hand driven into the riverbed. Side members were then tied together by cross beams, and wood decking was attached to stringers running parallel to the sides. Spans built this way were limited by the length of available timber and the depth of the water.

A more versatile bridge form, the truss, first came into use in the United States during the late eighteenth century. Trusses composed of a series of triangles were assembled from short lengths of timber that, depending upon their location, resisted the forces of either compression or tension. Because of the way in which it was assembled, the truss bridge could be lengthened to span distances far greater than the simple pile and beam bridge. Structural integrity in these bridges came from a balance of the opposing forces inherent in their construction. Because these spans were not self-supporting during con-

Covered Bridges. Bridges of the type shown here were common in the United States in the early nineteenth century. The wooden roof and walls were necessary to protect the wooden trusses that supported the bridge; left unprotected, the trusses would be damaged by the weather and put the bridge in danger of collapsing. © FIELD MARK PUBLICATIONS

struction, however, they were built on false work or framing that was later removed. As with all bridges regardless of type, they had to be designed to support their own weight or dead load, as well as the moving weight or live load that passed over them.

During the first two decades of the nineteenth century, Theodore Burr of Connecticut was one of the best-known American bridge builders. His 1817 patent for a combination arch and truss design was widely used in covered bridges. He had erected some forty-five highway spans in New York, New Jersey, and Pennsylvania by the time of his death in 1822. The wooden walls and roofs that were typical of covered bridges were necessary to protect the truss's countless wooden joints from the ravages of the weather.

By far the most lasting bridges built in the eighteenth and early nineteenth centuries were those made of masonry, but masonry construction was expensive and a shortage of qualified masons in the early Republic limited the number that were constructed. Those bridges were most often built in the form of an arch and assembly proceeded on timber falsework, for these bridges were self-supporting only after the last stone was put in place. When America's first railroads began laying out their routes in the 1820s and 1830s, their bridges were apt to be of stone, since once erected such bridges required little attention and were highly durable. As the pace of railroad expansion quickened toward the mid-nineteenth century, however, the need for bridges burgeoned and permanency was abandoned for expediency. The prevailing attitude was that quickly assembled and even temporary timber bridges and trestles could be replaced at some later date with more lasting structures once a rail line was producing revenue. The railroads' need for quickly constructed spans spurred the development of the truss bridge, constructed primarily of wood, throughout the first half of the nineteenth century.

The Expanding Nation

Individual types of truss bridges can be identified by the way their members were assembled. A large number of designs were patented during the nineteenth century. Some trusses were of no practical value, while others were over-engineered or too expensive to build. Those popular during the nineteenth century did not necessarily find similar acceptance in the twentieth century. In time, the broad range of trusses was gradually reduced to a few basic types that proved to be the strongest and most economical to build. By the early twentieth century, the Pratt and Warren were the most commonly used trusses and into the 1920s the truss was the most common bridge type in America.

As the railroads used ever heavier and faster rolling stock, it was necessary to replace wooden bridges with heavier and sturdier construction. Beginning in the 1840s, cast and wrought iron were being substituted for wood members in some bridges and during the 1850s railroads began turning to bridges made entirely of iron. During the 1870s, steel production increased greatly and the price fell to levels that made it reasonable for use in bridges. By 1930, the expansion of American railroads was over and their influence on the structural development of bridges was at an end.

Two significant advances in bridge technology took place in the late 1860s and early 1870s with the construction of the long-span metal arch bridge across the Mississippi River at St. Louis. First, not only was this bridge the first major spanning of North America's largest river, but engineer James B. Eads specified the use of steel in the bridge's arch members. The three tubular arches rested on masonry piers built on wooden caissons sunk in the riverbed. Second, this was the initial use in the United States of the technique in which excavation work inside a caisson took place in an atmosphere of compressed air. Prior to that workers had labored under water or in areas where water was diverted in some way. Air pressure within the caisson equaled the force exerted by the river water outside and the shell did not flood as excavation work inside progressed down toward bedrock. This technology was crucial in the successful execution of all subsequent subaqueous foundation work.

Limitations imposed by location have forced bridge builders to be innovative. It would be impractical, if not impossible, to erect a bridge across wide, deep ravines if the bridge required the support of extensive false work during construction. As a result, a method evolved that avoided the use of staging. In October 1876, engineer Charles Shaler Smith embarked on the construction of the first modern cantilever railroad span to bridge the 1,200-foot-wide and 275-foot-deep valley of the Kentucky River. Smith refined a bridge-building technique little used outside of ancient China. Cantilever construction employed counterbalancing forces so that completed segments supported ongoing work as it progressed inward toward the span's midpoint.

Although the suspension bridge was not new in 1842, its future form was forecast when Charles Ellet's Philadelphia wire suspension bridge was opened to highway traffic that year. Suspension bridges in which the roadway or deck was suspended from heavy wrought iron chains had been built for years. For the first time in a major American span, the deck was suspended from relatively lightweight wire cables. Ellet used a European cable-making technique in which cables were composed of a number of small-diameter parallel wires. The shape of each cable was maintained and its interior protected when the bundle's exterior was wrapped with additional wire. The scale of the bridges that followed increased tremendously, but the basic technology for cable making remained the same.

Civil engineer John A. Roebling was the preeminent suspension bridge designer of the nineteenth century. His career began with a suspension canal aqueduct at Pittsburgh in the 1840s, and each of his following projects reflected a growing skill and daring. His combined railroad and highway-carrying suspension bridge across the Niagara River gorge was completed in 1855. In it a suspended double-deck wooden truss carried the two roadbeds. Although other types of bridges would be built to carry highway and urban rail systems, this was the lone example of a suspension bridge constructed to carry both. The overall design and appearance of his Ohio River suspension bridge at Cincinnati in 1867 foretold of his plans for New York City's even larger and monumental Brooklyn Bridge of 1883. The extensive use of steel throughout the bridge, and especially for its cables, was a watershed in bridge technology.

The Early Twentieth Century

A number of large suspension bridges were built during the first half of the twentieth century. They were ideal for spanning the broad waterways that seemed to stand in the way of the growth of modern America. Neither their construction nor their final form posed an impediment to the nation's busy waterways. During the first four decades of the century, New York City was the focus of much of that construction. The city's boroughs were joined by the Williamsburg (1903), Manhattan (1909), Triborough (1936), and Bronx-Whitestone (1939) suspension bridges. However, none compared in size to the magnificent George Washington Bridge, completed in 1931. It was the first bridge linking Manhattan and New Jersey, and represented a remarkable leap forward in scale. Its 3,500-foot-long suspended span was double the length of the next largest. The bridge's four massive suspension cables passed over towers soaring more than 600 feet high and its roadway was suspended 250 feet above the Hudson River. It was never truly completed, as the masonry facing

called for on each of its steel towers was omitted because of the Great Depression.

The federal government responded to the depression by funding many massive public works projects. Partially as a form of unemployment relief, San Francisco undertook the construction of two great suspension bridges. They spanned greater distances than any previously built bridges. Strong Pacific Ocean currents and the depth of the water in San Francisco Bay made the construction of both the San Francisco–Oakland Bridge (1936) and the Golden Gate Bridge (1937) particularly challenging, and no part of the project required more technical expertise than building the subaqueous tower piers.

Triumphs in bridge building have been tempered by failures and perhaps no span has received more notoriety because of its collapse than did the Tacoma Narrows Suspension Bridge across Puget Sound in Washington State. Beginning in the late 1930s, its construction progressed uneventfully until the bridge was completed in July 1940. The valley in which the bridge was built was subject to strong winds and gusts that set the bridge in motion even while it was under construction. These wind-induced undulations increased in frequency as the bridge neared completion. So noticeable were the span's movements that they earned the bridge the sobriquet Galloping Gertie. Several months after its opening, the bridge was subjected to a period of intense high winds, during which it literally tore itself apart. The rising, falling, and twisting of the deck was so violent that it broke loose from its suspender cables and crashed into the sound. It was later determined that the failure resulted from the bridge being too flexible. The narrow deck and the shallow profile of the steel girders supporting the deck provided little resistance to aerodynamic action. The bridge's collapse prompted a reevaluation of suspension bridge design and resulted in a move away from flexible designs toward much stiffer and wind-resistant construction. A redesigned span across Puget Sound was completed in 1950.

Of the few suspension spans built in the United States after the middle of the twentieth century, one of the more remarkable was the Verrazano-Narrows Bridge, which opened in November 1964. The bridge, situated across the entrance to New York Harbor, connected Staten Island to Brooklyn. It was designed by engineer Othmar H. Ammann, who during his career designed a number of New York City's bridges, including the George Washington Bridge. While no new techniques were introduced in its construction, the bridge is remembered for it huge overall dimensions and the unprecedented size of its individual parts as well as the speed—five years—with which it was erected.

The Late Twentieth Century

Although the first cable stay bridges appeared in seventeenth-century Europe, this type of bridge emerged in a rationalized form only during the 1950s. Their configuration may vary in appearance and in the complexity of the tower or towers as well as in the symmetry and placement of the cables. The most recognizable spans are characterized by a single tower or mast and multiple diagonal cables that, if arranged in a single vertical plane, pass over the tower and are affixed at opposite points along the center line of the deck. Decks can be assembled in cantilever fashion from sections of pre-cast, pre-stressed concrete. They offer many of the advantages of suspension bridges, yet require neither the lengthy and costly process of cable spinning nor large cable anchorages. Their overall load-bearing capacity is less than the more complex suspension bridge. One of the most notable American examples is the Sunshine Skyway Bridge completed across Tampa Bay, Florida, in 1987.

With the expansion of American railroads nearing its end, highways became a major factor in bridge design and construction during the 1920s. As a result, the majority of spans constructed during the remainder of the twentieth century were relatively light, reinforced, and pre-stressed concrete highway bridges. Reinforced concrete bridge construction, in which steel imbedded in the concrete controls the forces of tension, was introduced in the United States in the late nineteenth century. Eventually, a variety of reinforcing systems were patented. The interstate highway system's rapid growth during the 1950s and 1960s fostered the widespread use of pre-stressed concrete beam bridges. Beams fabricated in this way were strengthened by built-in compressive forces. These bridges became the most common type of span in late-twentieth-century America.

BIBLIOGRAPHY

Condit, Carl W. *American Building Art: The Nineteenth Century.* New York: Oxford University Press, 1960.

———. *American Building Art: The Twentieth Century.* New York: Oxford University Press, 1961.

Jackson, Donald C. *Great American Bridges and Dams.* Washington, D.C.: Preservation Press, 1988.

McCullough, David. *The Great Bridge.* New York: Simon and Schuster, 1972.

Petroski, Henry. *Engineers of Dreams: Great Bridge Builders and the Spanning of America.* New York: Knopf, 1995.

Scott, Quinta, and Howard S. Miller. *The Eads Bridge.* Columbia: University of Missouri Press, 1979.

Van der Zee, John. *The Gate: The True Story of the Design and Construction of the Golden Gate Bridge.* New York: Simon and Schuster, 1986.

Wittfoht, Hans. *Building Bridges: History, Technology, Construction.* Dusseldorf, Germany: Beton-Verlag, 1984.

William E. Worthington Jr.

See also **Brooklyn Bridge; Eads Bridge; George Washington Bridge; Golden Gate Bridge; Toll Bridges and Roads; Verrazano-Narrows Bridge.**

BRISCOE V. BANK OF THE COMMONWEALTH OF KENTUCKY, 11 Peters 257 (1837). Article 1, sec-

tion 10, of the Constitution of the United States forbids states from emitting coin money or bills of credit. Repudiating *Craig v. State of Missouri*, the Supreme Court ruled that the Bank of Kentucky, although entirely owned by the state and managed by state-appointed officers, could legally issue bank notes. The Supreme Court found the notes to be backed by the resources of the bank, not the credit of the state, and the bank to be a separate entity capable of suing and being sued. Therefore, such notes were not bills of credit in the prohibited sense.

BIBLIOGRAPHY

White, G. Edward, with Gerald Gunther. *The Marshall Court and Cultural Change, 1815–35.* New York: Macmillan, 1988.

Harvey Pinney / A. R.

See also **Bills of Credit;** *Craig v. State of Missouri.*

BRITISH DEBTS.

At the time of the American Revolution (1775–1783), merchants and planters in the thirteen colonies owed British creditors some £5 million. Virginia planters held the greatest portion, owing £2.3 million. Overall, retail credit constituted the bulk of the debt. As a result, the matter involved many small claims in amounts of less than £500, and hundreds of creditors and debtors. During the revolution, payment on these debts all but ceased. From the creditors' point of view, interest on the debts nevertheless continued to accumulate. Resolution of the principal and interest on these debts was a key issue in the 1782 negotiations that led to the Treaty of Paris (1783), and remained a protracted issue of foreign relations until a convention in 1802 settled the matter.

These private debts were part of a general indebtedness accumulated by the colonies and individuals under the British imperial system. Colonial borrowing from 1703 to 1775 for the purposes of generating revenue for current expenses, establishing loan funds, and injecting paper money into the economy created substantial debts that were denominated in local currencies, rather than specie. That is, colonial money was not convertible into sterling. Colonial governments retired their debts through inflation, benefiting holders of private debts and harming their creditors. British merchants, officials, and other lenders constituted the chief losers. American debtors, principally farmers, planters, and politically connected individuals, profited. They remained interested in low taxes and new money issues. Thus the fiscal and monetary practices of individual colonies helped to create a class and political consciousness among colonists.

During the American Revolution, all of the newly declared states enacted laws that impaired the position of creditors. Some laws confiscated the property of Loyalists, which adversely affected any credits the latter held. Others sequestered the debts, paying them into respective state treasuries. Still others barred or restricted the ability of creditors and their representatives to collect debts.

The Treaty of Paris

Debts emerged as a prominent issue in the negotiation of the Treaty of Paris. Once the British government abandoned hope of reunion with America, it was interested in making a generous peace with a truly independent nation, that is, one not linked or dominated by another European power. To this end, the British cabinet initially adopted a lax position on both impaired debts and the confiscated property of Loyalists. The government counted on international norms and opinion to persuade America to make a just debt settlement, and therefore gave its negotiator ample leeway on the issue. For their part, neither John Jay nor Benjamin Franklin, the American negotiators, were interested in making debts part of a settlement. Indeed, the initial draft of the treaty, which Jay offered, made no mention of debts.

Persuaded by creditors and other interests, the British cabinet rejected Jay's draft and insisted that the Americans address debt collection and other economic issues. The elevation of these issues to matters of top priority threatened to derail the negotiations. However, John Adams, who joined Jay and Franklin in October, argued—without consulting his colleagues—for the inclusion of debts, stating in the course of negotiations: "I have no notion of cheating anybody." Article Four of the treaty provided that Congress would see to it that the states open their courts to the recovery of bona fide debts.

Soon after America and Britain ratified the Treaty of Paris the states resumed their harassment of creditors. Their tactics included closing their courts to debt cases, denying admission to creditors and their agents, disallowing the accumulation of interest during the war, and terminating debts. The states also failed to restore the confiscated property of Loyalists, as Article Five of the treaty prescribed. The British responded by keeping their troops at their posts to the north and west of the thirteen states, encouraging Native American tribes to attack settlers, refusing to move forward with a trade treaty, and seizing American merchant vessels. The British government justified its actions on the grounds that America was failing to uphold the 1783 treaty. After 1787, however, this claim constituted little more than an excuse. Once the U.S. constitution established a Supreme Court and declared treaties to be the law of the land, federal courts began to adjudicate debt cases in accordance with the Treaty of Paris. Nonetheless, the deterioration of relations was especially acute from 1792 to 1793, which prompted the negotiation of Jay's Treaty. For the purposes of avoiding war and improving commercial relations, the treaty addressed the collection of private debts.

Jay's Treaty

As chief justice of a Supreme Court that upheld the Treaty of Paris and the leading American negotiator with the British, Jay was eager to resolve the debt issue. Article Six of Jay's Treaty, which Congress narrowly ratified in 1795, provided for the recovery of debts "with interest thereupon from the time of being contracted." The treaty also provided for the arbitration of debt disputes. Stripping the U.S. Supreme Court of its jurisdiction, Jay's Treaty set up a joint, five-person commission to hear the appeals of creditors from American courts. The British and U.S. governments each selected two delegates, and a fifth commissioner was chosen by lot.

The commission, which sat in Philadelphia from May 1797 through July 1799, did not resolve the debt issue. It adopted, by a three-to-two margin, the British position on such matters as jurisdiction, the nature of legal impediments, the solvency of debtors, and amounts of wartime interest. The two American commissioners eventually resigned from the body. As a result, the debt issue again became a matter of bilateral foreign relations.

Resolution

In January 1802, the Jefferson administration agreed to pay the British government £600,000 to settle outstanding British claims. The paltriness of the amount, much less than U.S. liability under Jay's Treaty, reflected the lack of documentation for many debts and the recognition of only those debts that amounted to £500 or more. On receiving this payment, the British government established a commission to assess the claims of creditors. It sanctioned about one quarter of the claims it heard and paid out on about 45 percent of the approved claims.

BIBLIOGRAPHY

Bemis, Samuel Flagg. *Jay's Treaty: A Study in Commerce and Diplomacy.* 2d. ed. New Haven, Conn.: Yale University Press, 1962. A detailed political and legal analysis of the treaty. The original edition was published in 1923.

Hoffman, Ronald, and Peter J. Albert, eds. *Peace and the Peacemakers: The Treaty of 1783.* Charlottesville: University Press of Virginia for the U.S. Capitol Historical Society, 1985. Several essays discuss debts within the context of treaty negotiations.

Moore, John Bassett, ed. *International Adjudications, Ancient and Modern.* Volume 3. Reprint, Buffalo, N.Y.: W. S. Hein, 1996. A thorough legal study of the topic, with documents. The original edition was published in 1931.

Nash, Gary B. *The Urban Crucible: The Northern Seaports and the Origins of the American Revolution.* Abridged ed. Cambridge, Mass.: Harvard University Press, 1986. Puts debts into economic, social, and political context.

Ratchford, B. U. *American State Debts.* Durham, N.C.: Duke University Press, 1941. Provides a valuable survey of the public finance practices of colonial governments.

Michael R. Adamson

See also **Paris, Treaty of (1783).**

BRITISH EMPIRE, CONCEPT OF. The concept of the British Empire holds more coherence for historians than it did for eighteenth-century Americans. The idea of empire was not clearly thought out by Americans or Britons until the intensification of British-colonial relations between 1763 and 1776 and the subsequent onset of the revolutionary war. The idea of empire initially connoted mercantilism, a nexus of political, military, and economic considerations directed toward the creation of a self-sufficient imperium where the colony would supply the mother country with raw materials, and the mother country would provide for the military defense of the colony. This relationship was codified through the various Navigation Acts passed between 1651 and 1696, as well as by numerous laws passed in the eighteenth century that tied the thirteen colonies to Britain as a dependent economic market. The concomitant political implication was that the thirteen colonies were subordinate to the imperial Parliament in London, a parliament in which they were not represented.

In practice, though, the imperial relationship was not always so rigorous. The colonial assemblies were granted a great degree of autonomy, and London often did not support its royal governors in disputes with local bodies. Two serious tremors destroyed the imperial relationship: the Seven Years' War (1756–1763), and the passage of the so-called Intolerable, or Townshend, Acts (1767). The Seven Years' War (the French and Indian War as it was known to the colonists) was a contest between France and Britain for supremacy in North America and set off conflict around the globe. Colonists fought the French and their Indian allies alongside their British cousins, and indeed the imperial relationship remained a strong bond after the Treaty of Paris (implemented 10 February 1763). Nevertheless, the spirit of autonomy that had developed throughout the century led many colonists to conceive of empire as pluralistic, rather than a British imperium. As colonial desire for autonomy increased, the British Parliament exacerbated tensions by trying to reassert its hegemony through a series of acts, including the Stamp Act (1765), the Declaratory Act (1766), the Tea Act (1773), and finally the Quebec Act (1774). These measures were viewed by the colonists as punitive and provoked sporadic

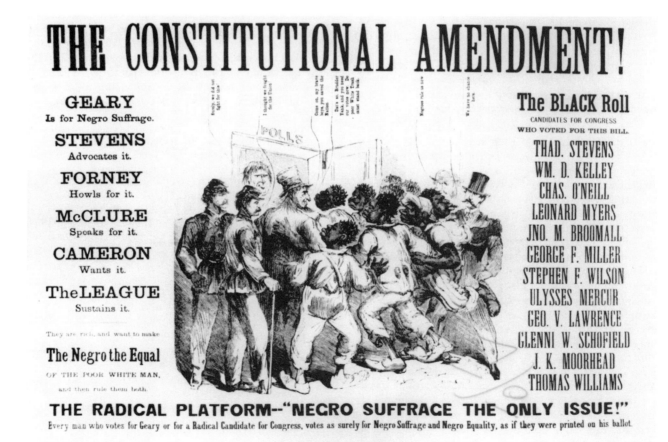

Broadside: "The Constitutional Amendment." Woodcut, c. 1866. A political broadside on black suffrage and the gubernatorial race in Pennsylvania (won by antislavery Republican John White Geary). The Fifteenth Amendment, granting African Americans the right to vote, was ratified in 1870 but was widely ineffective before the Voting Rights Act of 1965. LIBRARY OF CONGRESS

A Chorus Line. "One" is the rousing finale to one of the longest-running musicals in Broadway theater history (6,137 performances from 1975 to 1990 at the Shubert Theatre). ARCHIVE PHOTOS, INC.

violence, including the infamous Boston Massacre in 1770. Pontiac's War in 1763 further destabilized British rule in North America. Many colonial subjects, though, still wished to maintain the imperial tie, with their protests reflecting a desire to redefine the parameters of power rather than a call for independence.

More significantly for the dissolution of the imperial relationship, colonial voices such as Thomas Jefferson, Benjamin Franklin, and John Adams propagated the position that colonial assemblies enjoyed the same sovereignty as their British counterparts. This view was put to the Continental Congress, convened at Philadelphia in September 1774, and marked the ideological end of British imperialism in what was to become the United States. The outbreak of open hostilities at Lexington, Massachusetts, on 19 April 1775 permanently severed America from the British Empire. The concept of the British Empire was thus consciously rejected in America after the revolutionary war, with the United States assuming in the main an isolationist stance in world affairs.

BIBLIOGRAPHY

Anderson, Fred. *Crucible of War: The Seven Years' War and the Fate of Empire in North America, 1754–1766.* New York: Knopf, 2000.

James, Lawrence. *The Rise and Fall of the British Empire.* Rev. ed. London: Abacus, 1998.

Marshall, Peter, and Glyn Williams, eds. *The British Atlantic Empire before the American Revolution.* London: Frank Cass, 1980.

Daniel Gorman

See also **Colonial Assemblies; Colonial Policy, British; French and Indian War; Imperialism.**

BROADSIDES were sheets of paper printed on one side only that colonial Americans used for poetical effusions, news items, and propaganda. Revolutionary partisans used them for political purposes, and patriot broadsides were often reprinted in newspapers. Later, reformers used broadsides in political, antislavery, and temperance campaigns. During the Civil War they were distributed as song sheets and parodies. They also have been used for memorials and obituaries, accounts of trials and executions, crude poetry, official proclamations, and posters. Newspaper carriers used them for New Year's offerings.

BIBLIOGRAPHY

Berger, Carl. *Broadsides and Bayonets.* San Rafael, Calif.: Presidio Press, 1976.

Bradley, Patricia. *Slavery, Propaganda, and the American Revolution.* Jackson: University Press of Mississippi, 1998.

Augustus H. Shearer / s. b.

See also **Propaganda;** *and picture (facing page).*

BROADWAY, a street in NEW YORK CITY running the length of Manhattan. Most of the lower course of Broadway is said to follow the routes of old Indian trails, and farther north it generally follows the line of the Bloomingdale Road to 207th Street. Beyond the Harlem River it becomes a part of the highway to Albany.

In New Amsterdam (now New York City) its first quarter mile was originally called the Heerewegh or Heere Straat. The name was anglicized to Broadway about 1668. George Washington lived at 39 Broadway for a time during his presidency. In 1852 a cable-car line gained a franchise on Broadway, then the city's chief residential street. The line, fought in the courts for more than thirty years, was finally built in 1885, but by then the street had become the city's main business thoroughfare. The first subway line under Broadway was begun in 1900.

In the late nineteenth century, theaters clustered along Broadway, first below and then above Longacre (now Times) Square, so that its name became synonymous with the American theater. The first arc electric streetlights in New York were placed on Broadway in 1880, and the brilliant LIGHTING in the early twentieth century earned it the nickname "the Great White Way."

BIBLIOGRAPHY

Burrows, Edwin G., and Mike Wallace. *Gotham: A History of New York City to 1898.* New York: Oxford University Press, 1999.

Jackson, Kenneth T., ed. *The Encyclopedia of New York City.* New Haven, Conn.: Yale University Press, 1995.

Alvin F. Harlow/c. w.

See also **Railways, Urban, and Rapid Transit; Theater.**

BROKERS date back to the colonial period. The colony of Massachusetts, in the throes of a price inflation in 1748, adopted a tabular standard made up of an assortment of goods, in specified quantities, to be used as a test of the value of money. All money payments had to be made according to the changes in the value of money as reflected by this goods assortment. The astronomer Simon Newcomb suggested the need for managing money to achieve a stable price level in an article in the *North American Review* (September 1879). In 1911 the economist Irving Fisher outlined a plan for stabilizing the dollar in his *Purchasing Power of Money* and again in 1920 in his *Stabilizing the Dollar.* Fisher's system presupposed no gold coins in circulation. To correct the trend of the price level, he would increase or decrease the amount of gold representing a dollar, such dollars being disbursed in ingots and chiefly in international payments. In 1922 he wrote *The Making of Index Numbers*, explaining how to measure the price level scientifically. Americans were particularly conscious of price level changes at this time. In the previous sixty years wholesale prices had undergone wild fluctuations, more than doubling during the Civil War, falling by two-thirds between 1865 and 1896, rising moderately until 1913, more than doubling between 1914 and 1920, and plummeting 40 percent in one year, mid-1920 to mid-1921. All these changes had political repercussions, some of them severe.

Many prominent economists, who felt there must be some way to improve the situation, helped Fisher organize the Stable Money League in 1921. Because some league members differed with Fisher as to the appropriate solution, the organization changed its name that autumn to the National Monetary Association. Dissension among its members killed the association in early 1924. The next year Fisher promoted a new group called the Stable Money Association, whose avowed goal was educational instead of legislative. It nevertheless gave thinly veiled support to other bills by Goldsborough and by Rep. James G. Strong of Kansas. The organization died in 1932.

Meanwhile, a Cornell University agricultural economist, George F. Warren, also concluded that decreasing the gold content of the dollar was the way to raise the general price level. In early 1933 farm prices were only 59 percent of what they had been in "normal" 1926, and he felt that the way to restore prosperity, especially agricultural prosperity, was to raise the price level to that 1926 level. Warren influenced then Under Secretary of the Treasury Henry Morgenthau, Jr., his former student, who had the ear of President Franklin D. Roosevelt. The United States temporarily abandoned the gold standard in March 1933 and called in all gold coins. In a 22 October radio address, Roosevelt, discussing his gold purchase plan (to drive up the price of gold), said, "We are thus continuing to move toward a managed currency." On 30 January 1934, Congress passed the Gold Reserve Act and the next day, acting on its authority, the president created a new gold dollar (never coined) of 13.71 grains, 59 percent the size of the old gold dollar. There were other managed money bills introduced in the 1930s, especially by Rep. Wright Patman of Texas, who thought himself a modern "populist," but nothing came of them.

In the early 1960s a school of economists, soon known as monetarists, headed by Milton Friedman of the University of Chicago, achieved prominence. They believed that the quantity of money in circulation, measured in a sophisticated manner, greatly affected both the severity of business cycles and the general price level. Their solution was to increase the money supply by a steady 4 percent a year, the country's annual average rate of economic growth.

In the 1980s President Reagan appointed one of Friedman's allies, Alan Greenspan, as chairman of the Federal Reserve Board. The Fed's successful battle against inflation in the 1980s and 1990s, and the rapid growth of the American economy in those years, turned Greenspan into a national icon of prosperity and increased public confidence in the efficacy of monetarist policies. But the rapid increase in consumer debt and the proliferation of credit-card borrowing remain major challenges to efforts to manage the money supply.

BIBLIOGRAPHY

Friedman, Milton. *A Program for Monetary Stability.* New York: Fordham University Press, 1960.

Greider, William. *Secrets of the Temple: How the Federal Reserve Runs the Country.* New York: Simon and Schuster, 1989.

Woodward, Bob. *Maestro: Greenspan's Fed and the American Boom.* New York: Simon and Schuster, 2000.

Donald L. Kemmerer / T. G.

See also **Bimetallism; Business Cycles; Consumer Purchasing Power; Economic Indicators; Federal Reserve System; Gold Reserve Act; Great Depression; Keynesianism; Money; Reaganomics.**

BRONSON V. RODES, 7 Wallace 229 (1868), an action on a New York executor's bond of 1851 to repay a loan "in gold or silver coin." In 1865 the obligor tendered payment in U.S. notes, which Congress had declared "lawful money and a legal tender in payment of debts." The tender was refused, and the obligor sued to cancel a mortgage securing the bond. Decrees in his favor by two state courts were reversed by the U.S. Supreme Court, which held that "express contracts to pay coined dollars are not debts which may be satisfied by the tender of U.S. Notes."

Shira Diner
C. Sumner Lobingier

BROOK FARM. Founded in 1841 on 183 acres of land purchased from Charles Ellis in West Roxbury, Massachusetts, the Brook Farm Institute of Agriculture and Education was a utopian community organized by the Unitarian-turned-transcendentalist reverend George Ripley. The community, which was founded to promote equality and education through the union of physical labor and personal self-improvement, drew support from influential transcendentalists like Ralph Waldo Emerson and Nathaniel Hawthorne (who based *The Blithedale Romance* on his time at Brook Farm), and began a well-regarded school that taught students ranging from children to young men being tutored for Harvard. The community was governed by voting, based on the shares purchased by members, whose contributions funded the undertaking, including a newspaper, *The Harbinger*, as a joint-stock company.

The introduction of the ideas of Charles Fourier in 1845, as well as a frustration on the part of members who believed others were not contributing labor fairly, led to strict enforcement of community rules, which alienated many early members. Also, the growth of the community strained its ability to sell any of Brook Farm's produce, which was largely consumed by the members. Although a great success intellectually, the community suffered a financial blow when its central building burned down in 1846, during celebrations commemorating its completion, and it failed to pay its investors dividends. Forced to disband, the community continued the publication of *The Harbinger* until 1849 in New York City, and it remains a model of mid-nineteenth-century utopianism.

BIBLIOGRAPHY
Curtis, Edith Roelker. *A Season in Utopia: The Story of Brook Farm.* New York: Thomas Nelson, 1961.

Francis, Richard. *Transcendental Utopias: Individual and Community at Brook Farm, Fruitlands, and Walden.* Ithaca, N.Y.: Cornell University Press, 1997.

Myerson, Joel. *Brook Farm: An Annotated Bibliography and Resources Guide.* New York: Garland, 1978.

Margaret D. Sankey

See also **Transcendentalism; Utopian Communities.**

BROOKINGS INSTITUTION, a pioneer nonpartisan research foundation concerned with economic, social, defense, and international public policies. Founded in 1916 as the Institute for Government Research (IGR), the Brookings Institution is considered the first "think tank" in America. The IGR was established by a group of wealthy businessmen and educators to promote the idea of "economy and efficiency" in government through an executive federal budget system, which was finally enacted as the Budget and Accounting Act in 1921. In these early years they undertook studies in state and national government reorganization, as well as establishing a graduate program in government and economics in conjunction with Washington University, St. Louis, and the Institute for Economic Research.

In 1927, the IGR was reorganized as the Brookings Institution, supported by an endowment created by Robert S. Brookings, a St. Louis philanthropist. Under its first president, Harold G. Moulton, the Brookings Institution undertook major economic studies and evaluations of NEW DEAL programs. Following the Second World War, the Brookings Institution gained a reputation as a liberal research organization. With renewed foundation support primarily from the Ford Foundation, it emerged as the preeminent think tank in Washington, D.C., in the 1960s becoming a major center for policy innovation in welfare, health care, education, housing, and taxation policy, as well as defense, international economic policy, and foreign affairs. Although challenged by the emergence of other think tanks, most notably the American Enterprise Institute (AEI) and the Heritage Foundation (HF) on the right, and the Institute for Policy Research (IPR) on the left, the Brookings Institution maintained its reputation for analytically authoritative public policy research. The institution also has become a holding area for public officials and experts temporarily out of government. Although closely associated with the Democratic party, the Brookings Institution has cooperated in joint research projects with conservative think tanks such as the AEI and the HF, especially concerning free trade.

BIBLIOGRAPHY

Critchlow, Donald T. *The Brookings Institution, 1916–1952: Expertise and the Public Interest in a Democratic Society.* DeKalb: Northern Illinois University Press, 1985.

Dixon, Paul. *Think Tanks.* New York: Atheneum, 1971.

Ricci, David. *The Transformation of American Politics: The New Washington and the Rise of Think Tanks.* New Haven, Conn.: Yale University Press, 1993.

Smith, James Allen. *The Idea Brokers: Think Tanks and the Rise of the New Policy Elite.* New York: Free Press, 1991.

Donald T. Critchlow

See also **Foundations, Endowed; Think Tanks.**

BROOKLYN, known as "Meryckawick" (sandy place) by its original Algonquin inhabitants, is one of the five boroughs of New York City. It is located at the southwestern end of Long Island, adjacent to but separated from Manhattan Island by the East River. The first European settlers in the region were the Dutch, who, through a total of some two hundred purchases, began settling Brooklyn in 1636. The flat, relatively low-lying lands of Brooklyn proved attractive to these settlers. Under Dutch rule, six mostly agricultural towns were settled. One of

Coney Island. One of the best-known sections of Brooklyn, enormously popular—especially in the early twentieth century—for its amusement parks (at one time, three of them), boardwalk, and beach. AP/WIDE WORLD PHOTOS

these, Gravesend, was founded in 1643 by the controversial Lady Deborah Moody, who had been exiled from the Massachusetts Bay Colony. In 1664, the British challenged the Dutch for supremacy over their North American holdings and, by 1674, Brooklyn, along with the rest of what had been New Netherland, passed definitively into English hands and became part of the colony of New York.

Brooklyn long resisted consolidation with New York City. It was a slow but probably inevitable event. In 1834, Brooklyn was granted city status, over the opposition of New York City. But in 1857, the state combined Brooklyn's and New York City's basic health and safety services into joint boards. Through a series of charters dating from the late seventeenth century, Manhattan gained dominance over the region's waterways at Brooklyn's expense. Over the course of the nineteenth century, an extensive network of transportation links between the two areas was put into place. A Manhattan farmer began the first ferry service linking Brooklyn to Manhattan in 1642. In 1814, the introduction of the steamboat ferry provided the first regular and rapid transportation between Manhattan and Brooklyn; the trip took fifteen minutes. Bridges and tunnels were added, and, finally, the first subway line reached Brooklyn in 1908. Most significant to the consolidation process was the completion of the Brooklyn Bridge in 1883. On 1 January 1898, Brooklyn officially became one of the five boroughs comprising New York City.

Brooklyn's population has always been diverse. By the nineteenth century, Holland, Germany, France, and England were all well represented. In addition, there were significant numbers of both free and enslaved African Americans, as illustrated by the incorporation of Brooklyn's first black church in 1794. By 1855, almost half the population was foreign-born, and, by 1860, Brooklyn was the third-largest city in the United States (behind New York and Philadelphia). Its shift to manufacturing began in 1825 with the opening of the Erie Canal and encouraged a new wave of immigration, most notably by the Irish. However, soon after the end of the Civil War (1861–1865) and into the first quarter of the twentieth century, large numbers of Italians and Jews, among others, settled in Brooklyn to live and work.

From the 1950s through the 1970s, Brooklyn's fortunes and population declined as manufacturing plants deserted the area and the borough lost residents to nearby suburbs. However, new waves of immigrants, most notably from the West Indies, South America, and Asia, helped bring about a population resurgence. In addition, after the 1980s, many of Brooklyn's brownstone neighborhoods again became popular and were gentrified.

Brooklyn has produced numerous well-known artists, writers, singers, actors, and politicians. Among them are poet Walt Whitman, writers Bernard Malamud and Arthur Miller, politician Shirley Chisholm, and singers Barbra Streisand and Richie Havens. It is also home to such important entertainment and cultural institutions as the Coney Island amusement park, the Brooklyn Academy of Music, and the Brooklyn Museum. Brooklyn was home to the much beloved Brooklyn Dodgers, established as a major league baseball team in 1884. From 9 April 1913 until the Dodgers abandoned Brooklyn for Los Angeles in 1957, the team played at the now-defunct Ebbets Field. In 1947, the Dodgers made history by signing on Jackie Robinson, the first African American to play in the major leagues.

BIBLIOGRAPHY

Burrows, Edwin G., and Mike Wallace. *Gotham: A History of New York City to 1898.* New York: Oxford University Press, 1999.

Glueck, Grace, and Paul Gardner. *Brooklyn: People and Places, Past and Present.* New York: Abrams, 1991.

Snyder-Grenier, Ellen M. *Brooklyn: An Illustrated History.* Philadelphia: Temple University Press, 1996.

Stiles, Henry Reed. *A History of the City of Brooklyn.* Reprint, Bowie, Md.: Heritage Books, 1993.

Weld, Ralph Foster. *Brooklyn Village, 1816–1834.* New York: Columbia University Press, 1938.

Faren R. Siminoff

BROOKLYN BRIDGE.

This steel-cable and stone-tower suspension bridge was the outstanding American engineering achievement of the late nineteenth century for three reasons: its towers were based on foundations built up from underwater caisson excavations, it made novel use of steel cables, and its main span was 1,595 feet in length. Built between 1869 and 1883 from a design by John Roebling and his son Washington, and costing $15 million, it served as the first bridge across the East River and connected Brooklyn and New York. An accident took John Roebling's life early during construction, and Washington was severely crippled subsequently. The beauty and utility of the bridge make it one of New York's enduring symbols.

BIBLIOGRAPHY

Brooklyn Museum. *The Great East River Bridge, 1883–1983.* Brooklyn, N.Y.: Brooklyn Museum, 1983.

McCullough, David G. *The Great Bridge: The Epic Story of the Building of the Brooklyn Bridge.* New York: Simon and Schuster, 2001.

Trachtenberg, Alan. *Brooklyn Bridge: Fact and Symbol.* 2d edition. Chicago: University of Chicago Press, 1979.

Michael Carew

See also **Bridges.**

BROTHERHOOD OF SLEEPING CAR PORTERS.

A labor union founded by A. Philip Randolph in August 1925, the Brotherhood of Sleeping Car Porters (BSCP) represented African American porters and maids who served the white patrons of Pullman sleeping and

Brooklyn Bridge. An engineering marvel and an aesthetic inspiration to poets and painters, for a time this was the tallest man-made structure in New York and the longest suspension bridge in the world. FRANCES LOEB LIBRARY, GRADUATE SCHOOL OF DESIGN, HARVARD UNIVERSITY

dining railroad cars. Threatened by the union, the Pullman Company delayed negotiations until 1935, when the Great Depression and President Franklin Roosevelt's New Deal legislation helped force employers into collective bargaining. In 1937 the BSCP settled the first contract between a major U.S. company and a black union.

The BSCP also helped improve conditions for all African Americans. In June 1941, Randolph convinced President Roosevelt to sign Executive Order 8802, banning discrimination in government-related employment, and

Brotherhood of Sleeping Car Porters. Members of the African American union display the American flag and a banner reading "Fight or be Slaves" in 1955. © CORBIS

to establish the Fair Employment Practices Committee. Randolph also helped persuade President Harry Truman to sign Executive Order 9981, barring discrimination in the military, in July 1948. BSCP member E. D. Nixon organized the Montgomery, Alabama, bus boycott in 1955, while Randolph led the August 1963 March on Washington for Jobs and Freedom.

Because airplanes had replaced railroads for luxury travel, in 1978 the BSCP merged with the Brotherhood of Railway and Airline Clerks and ceased to exist as an independent organization. Randolph, who had retired as president of the BSCP in 1968, died in 1979 at the age of ninety.

BIBLIOGRAPHY

Pfeffer, Paula F. *A. Philip Randolph, Pioneer of the Civil Rights Movement.* Baton Rouge: Louisiana State University Press, 1990.

Santino, Jack. *Miles of Smiles, Years of Struggle: Stories of Black Pullman Porters.* Urbana: University of Illinois Press, 1989.

John Cashman

BROWN UNIVERSITY, the seventh oldest institution of higher learning in the United States, was founded in 1764 in Warren, Rhode Island, as Rhode Island College. Established by Baptist clergy, the college set forth a liberal outlook in its charter, emphasizing nonsectarian principles in admissions policy and curricula. The college opened in 1765 and held its first commencement ceremony four years later, under its first president, James Manning. In 1770 the school relocated to its present campus in Providence, Rhode Island. During the American Revolution the college closed, and its University Hall became a barracks and hospital for American and French troops.

In 1804 the college was renamed Brown University in honor of Nicholas Brown, a generous benefactor. Francis Wayland, chosen as Brown's fourth president in 1827, introduced electives and a new curriculum emphasizing applied science and engineering. The university introduced intercollegiate sports after the Civil War; it awarded its first master of arts degree in 1888, followed in 1889 by its first Ph.D. degree. Under the administration of Elisha Benjamin Andrews, chosen as Brown's eighth president in 1889, nine new academic departments were created, and undergraduate enrollment and faculty size greatly increased. In 1891 Pembroke College, a coordinate undergraduate school for women, was established. During William Herbert Perry Faunce's presidency (1899–1929) the university enlarged its curriculum, inaugurated honors programs, and formally established the graduate school.

Henry Merritt Wriston, university president from 1937 to 1955, raised Brown's status from that of a regional school to that of one of the outstanding universities of the United States. Wriston brought in many outstanding fac-

ulty members, instituted important changes in the curriculum, and made the college more residential.

Like many other universities, in the late 1960s Brown found itself swept up in student activism. When Ray L. Heffner became president in 1966, he became embroiled in controversies over the university's in loco parentis policies, the role of minorities at the school, the presence of a RESERVE OFFICERS' TRAINING CORPS (ROTC) program on campus, the dearth of tenured female faculty members, and calls for curricular reform. After a tumultuous tenure, Heffner resigned in 1969. Shortly thereafter, the faculty adopted the liberal "New Curriculum," which eliminated "core" courses and distribution requirements, made letter grades optional, and encouraged cross-disciplinary study.

When Donald F. Hornig succeeded Heffner in 1970, he too faced a number of contentious issues and challenging changes: the absorption of Pembroke College in 1971, the establishment of a medical school in 1972, and an operating deficit exceeding $4 million. Hornig's austerity plan raised hackles but shored up the school's finances before he stepped down in 1976.

During the presidencies of Howard R. Swearer (1977–1988) and Vartan Gregorian (1989–1997), Brown became one of the nation's truly elite universities. Two capital drives (1979–1984 and 1993–1998) pushed the school's endowment over $800 million, enabling it to create new programs and institutes, offer better financial aid packages, and improve its facilities. Brown became a "hot" school in the early 1980s, its applications rising quickly, and in 1987 it was ranked among the top ten U.S. universities in *U.S. News & World Report.* After E. Gordon Gee's brief presidency (1998–2000), Brown named Ruth J. Simmons to the position, making her the first African American president of an Ivy League university.

BIBLIOGRAPHY

Fleming, Donald. *Science and Technology in Providence, 1760–1914: An Essay in the History of Brown University in the Metropolitan Community.* Providence, R.I.: Brown University, 1952.

Gerold, William. *College Hill: A Photographic Study of Brown University in Its Two Hundredth Year.* Providence, R.I.: Brown University Press, 1965.

Guild, Reuben Aldridge. *Early History of Brown University.* New York: Arno Press, 1980.

Kaufman, Polly Welts, ed. *The Search for Equity: Women at Brown University, 1891–1991.* Providence, R.I.: Brown University Press; Hanover, N.H.: Distributed by University Press of New England, 1991.

Mary Greenberg / A. R.; C. W.

See also **Education; Higher: Colleges and Universities; Curriculum; Ivy League.**

BROWN V. BOARD OF EDUCATION OF TOPEKA, 347 U.S. 483 (1954), decision on remedy, 349

U.S. 294 (1955), was the leading case of the five decided by the Supreme Court finding that segregation in public education violated the Constitution's guarantee of equal protection of the laws. The constitutionality of state laws requiring segregated schools seemed to be established by *Plessy v. Ferguson* (1896), which upheld a Louisiana law requiring "separate but equal" accommodations on railroads. Lawyers for the National Association for the Advancement of Colored People (NAACP), led by Charles Hamilton Houston and Thurgood Marshall, prepared the groundwork for the *Brown* decision in a series of cases in which the Supreme Court invalidated segregated education in graduate and professional schools because the segregated programs did not provide an equal education. Extending those precedents to secondary and elementary schools was a large step, because the justices believed maintaining segregated education was a central feature of the southern system of segregation as a whole.

Oliver Brown sued the Topeka, Kansas, school board because his daughter was denied admission to the school closest to the Brown home. The NAACP developed similar cases in Virginia, South Carolina, Delaware, and the District of Columbia, all of which the Supreme Court considered along with *Brown*. The lawyers for the African American plaintiffs and the school boards argued the cases twice before the Court reached its unanimous decision invalidating segregated education and casting doubt on *Plessy v. Ferguson*, which seemed to allow segregation in any public facility. Chief Justice Earl Warren's opinion said that the Court could not "turn the clock back" to 1868, when the equal protection clause was adopted, or to 1896; that segregation could "affect the hearts and minds" of African American children "in a way unlikely ever to be undone"; and that schools segregated by law could never be equal.

The Court then asked the lawyers to argue the cases a third time to determine what the proper remedy for the unconstitutional system should be. Rejecting the NAACP's arguments for immediate desegregation, the Court, again unanimously, directed the lower courts to supervise desegregation plans that would begin the process immediately and then proceed "with all deliberate speed." Some school boards, particularly in the border states, complied with court orders rather quickly, but desegregation faced resistance in the Deep South. Not until after the adoption of the Civil Rights Act of 1964 did the Deep South implement substantial desegregation.

BIBLIOGRAPHY

Patterson, James T. *"Brown v. Board of Education": A Civil Rights Milestone and Its Troubled Legacy.* New York: Oxford University Press, 2001.

Tushnet, Mark V. *Making Civil Rights Law: Thurgood Marshall and the Supreme Court, 1936–1961.* New York: Oxford University Press, 1994.

Mark V. Tushnet

See also **Civil Rights Act of 1964; Desegregation;** *Plessy v. Ferguson.*

BROWN V. MARYLAND, 12 Wheaton 419 (1827), a case on the right of a state to control the sale of imported merchandise. It afforded Justice John Marshall an opportunity to supplement his first opinion on the meaning of the commerce clause of the Constitution as originally stated in *Gibbons v. Ogden.* Marshall ruled that the Constitution prohibited a state from levying imposts or duties on imports or exports, except what may be "absolutely necessary for executing its inspection laws." The principle, broadly stated so that it would apply to foreign as well as interstate commerce, formed the basis of future opinions on the subject of commerce. (*See also* ORIGINAL PACKAGE DOCTRINE.)

BIBLIOGRAPHY

Corwin, Edward S. *The Commerce Power Versus States Rights.* Gloucester, Mass.: Peter Smith, 1962. The original edition was published in 1936.

Kelly, Alfred H., Winfred A. Harbison, and Herman Belz. *The American Constitution.* New York: Norton, 1991. The original edition was published in 1948.

Thomas Robson Hay / A. R.

See also **Cooley v. Board of Wardens of Port of Philadelphia; Commerce Clause;** *Gibbons v. Ogden.*

BROWNISTS, groups in England (c. 1580–1660) that openly separated from the established church. The term was derived from Robert Browne, author of *Reformation without Tarrying for Anie* (1583). Browne advocated an essentially Congregational polity, a church made up only of the visible elect, who were to choose and install their own officers. Later SEPARATISTS, including the PILGRIMS at Plymouth, probably owed much to Browne, as did the settlers of the Massachusetts Bay Colony, although the latter always insisted that they had never separated from the Church of England.

BIBLIOGRAPHY

Miller, Perry. *Orthodoxy in Massachusetts, 1630–1650.* Boston: Beacon Press, 1959.

Perry Miller / A. R.

See also **Church of England in the Colonies; Puritans and Puritanism.**

BROWNSVILLE AFFAIR. African American troops have a symbiotic relationship to African Americans in the larger society. Racism and its fallout have been ever present throughout U.S. history. In 1906 the Brownsville affair demonstrated how racial stereotyping governed the unspoken assumptions of those in the army and in the federal government.

After the Civil War, black troops had a distinguished record as "Buffalo Soldiers," and their role in the Spanish-American War drew praise. Despite the heroism of the B, C, and D companies of the First Battalion, Twenty-fifth Infantry, the United States Army, reflecting larger societal attitudes, worried about where to station them. The army chose Brownsville, Texas, a small town on the border with Mexico.

The established facts of what happened in Brownsville were few but clear. How the military and political authorities used those facts and their questionable conclusions would mark the changing ethnic and racial relations in the nation's history. For about ten minutes, close to midnight on 13 August 1906, armed men fired indiscriminately near Fort Brown. A policeman was wounded and one local man was dead. The identity of the shooters was never discovered. Civilians and many of the white officers thought the black troops had gone on a rampage. The evidence was highly circumstantial. Eyewitnesses were few and lacked credibility. Over the next few years several military investigations and a grand jury inquiry followed with inconclusive results. None of the accused was allowed to cross-examine witnesses, and even with less-than-adequate defense no one was found guilty.

The troops were immediately relocated to Fort Reno, Oklahoma, where on 4 October 1906 President Theodore Roosevelt issued an ultimatum that they would be dishonorably discharged if the guilty did not step forward. None did. The men were innocent but Roosevelt and others in a tragic rush to judgment "discovered" a "conspiracy of silence." All 167 black men were dishonorably discharged; over half of the men had spent five years or more in the army and ten of them had over fifteen years of service.

Senator Joseph B. Foraker (R-Ohio), as chairman of the Senate Committee on Military Affairs, opened hearings on the matter. The result only increased doubt about the fairness of Roosevelt's actions. Without a public explanation a military panel announced that 14 men from the original 167 were eligible to reenlist in January 1909. There the situation remained for over sixty-five years.

In March 1971, Representative Augustus F. Hawkins (D-Calif.) introduced legislation to change the dishonorable discharge to honorable on the military records. The secretary of the army, Robert F. Froehlke, so ordered on 22 September 1972. After a national search two men appeared out of the shadows. Edward Warfield, eighty-two, was one of the fourteen men allowed to reenlist, and Dorsie Willis spent over sixty years shining shoes in a Minneapolis barber shop. The issue of compensation took several turns. Meanwhile Warfield died on 14 November 1973, and after complex congressional maneuvers, Willis received $25,000 and ten widows received $10,000 each. Willis died 24 August 1977 at the age of

ninety-one. Near death he was quoted as saying, "Some people feel the world owes them a living. I never thought that, but I figured the world owed me an opportunity to earn a living. They took that away from me. That dishonorable discharge kept me from improving my station. Only God knows what it done to the others." Indeed. The Brownsville affair was ended, and the nation had traveled a long way since that midnight incident in a small Texas border town.

BIBLIOGRAPHY

Adams, William L. *Portrait of a Border City: Brownsville, Texas.* Austin, Tex.: Eakin Press, 1997.

Christian, Garna L. *Black Soldiers in Jim Crow Texas, 1899–1917.* College Station: Texas A&M University Press, 1995. A splendid account.

Fletcher, Marvin. *The Black Soldier and Officer in the United States Army, 1891–1917.* Columbia: University of Missouri Press, 1974. A key source.

Fletcher, Marvin. *The Peacetime Army, 1900–1941: A Research Guide.* New York: Greenwood Press, 1988. Solid material.

Weaver, John D. *The Senator and the Sharecropper's Son: Exoneration of the Brownsville Soldiers.* College Station: Texas A&M University Press, 1997. A moving account of the consequences of the event and how "history" dealt with it.

Donald K. Pickens

See also **Black Cavalry in the West; Black Infantry in the West; Military Service and Minorities: African Americans.**

BRYAN-CHAMORRO TREATY, a treaty between the United States and Nicaragua, signed by Secretary of State William Jennings Bryan and Nicaragua's Washington minister, Emiliano Chamorro, on 5 August 1914. It granted to the United States in perpetuity the exclusive right to build an interoceanic canal in Nicaragua, subject to a subsequent agreement regarding details of construction and operation. It also gave the United States a ninety-nine-year lease of Great and Little Corn islands and a right to establish a naval base in the Gulf of Fonseca. Nicaragua received $3 million. The United States had already constructed an interoceanic canal in Panama but saw the Bryan-Chamorro treaty as a means to ensure that no rival nation could build a similar canal.

Costa Rica and El Salvador protested against the treaty. Costa Rica claimed that an arbitral award by President GROVER CLEVELAND in 1888 had bound Nicaragua not to make grants for canal purposes without consulting Costa Rica because of its interest in the San Juan River. El Salvador asserted that the waters of the Gulf of Fonseca belonged jointly to El Salvador, Nicaragua, and Honduras. Both appealed to the Central American Court, which decided that Nicaragua had violated its neighbors' rights and should take steps to restore the legal status existing before the treaty. It did not declare the treaty itself invalid, because it had no jurisdiction over the United States. Nicaragua refused to accept the decision, and the treaty remained in force. The proposed naval base was never established, and the Corn Islands remained under Nicaraguan jurisdiction, except for a small area used by the United States for a lighthouse.

BIBLIOGRAPHY

Karnes, Thomas L. *Tropical Enterprise: The Standard Fruit and Steamship Company in Latin America.* Baton Rouge: Louisiana State University Press, 1978.

LaFeber, Walter. *Inevitable Revolutions: The United States in Central America.* 2d ed. New York: Norton, 1993.

Dana G. Munro/A. G.

See also **Latin America, Relations with; Nicaragua, Relations with; Nicaraguan Canal Project; Panama Canal.**

BUCCANEERS were a distinct group of pirates who operated in the Caribbean from the late sixteenth century until the first quarter of the eighteenth century. The name originally applied to a group of men who occupied the western half of Haiti. They hunted wild cattle and pigs and traded with the Spanish, but the relationship turned bitter after the Spanish attacked them. Either English or French in origin and Protestant in religion, the buccaneers waged terror against all resistance and soon developed a fearful reputation, which they used to their advantage. Sir Henry Morgan (1635–1688) led the buccaneers from their base in Jamaica. They were freebooters—seeking only treasure and freedom from all authority. The promise of wealth and adventure attracted people from all nationalities. The French called them *boucaniers*, which was later anglicized as "buccaneers."

The tale of Edward Teach (1680–1718), known as "Blackbeard," is an example of how people combined fact, fiction, and fear to create legends about the buccaneers. Among the buccaneers were such women pirates as Mary Read, who sailed with Captain Jack Rackham off Jamaica in 1720, and Anne Bonny. The buccaneers' freewheeling nature made them colorful characters in popular culture. As nations took action against them, they ceased to be a threat and became memorialized in such novels as *Treasure Island* (first published 1881–1882) by Robert Louis Stevenson.

The eighteenth century was the golden age of pirates until the end of the American Revolution (1775–1783). During this time, they contributed a key maritime function as they helped America fight the British. In 1697, the Treaty of Ryswick, which ended the War of the League of Augsburg (1689–1697), partly suppressed buccaneering. With the growth of the nation-state and its steam-powered navy, pirates, privateers, and buccaneers lost their power. The Declaration of Paris (1856), which ended the Crimean War (1853–1856), outlawed the groups. In modern times, very little piracy existed except in Southeast Asia and the backwaters of the Caribbean.

Blackbeard. A fanciful depiction of the notorious pirate Edward Teach, whose life became heavily fictionalized legend. © CORBIS

BIBLIOGRAPHY

Besson, Maurice. *The Scourge of the Indies: Buccaneers, Corsairs, and Filibusters, from Original Texts and Contemporary Engravings.* New York: Random House, 1929. Enlightening and entertaining material.

Cordingly, David. *Pirates: Fact & Fiction.* London: Collins & Brown, 1992. An informative but naive treatment of the subject.

Gosse, Philip. *The History of Piracy.* London: Longmans, Green, 1932. Reprint, Glorieta, N.M.: Rio Grande Press, 1990. An old but very useful narrative.

Donald K. Pickens

BUCKBOARDS. In the 1500s, the coach—a carriage with an enclosed cab—was developed for the well off. The early-sixteenth-century buggy, a "poor man's coach," had a roof but no sides. By the mid-1800s, Americans had developed the versatile buckboard. It had four wheels and two axles, mounted by a board of flexible wood. Its front seat could hold two people and it was drawn by one or two horses. On western farms, the almost ubiquitous buckboard was used to haul supplies. Some had sides; they rarely had roofs. Most were single-seaters for two, but some were two-seaters for four people. In 1879, American

Buckboard. Charlton Heston (*left*) drives and Gregory Peck rides along in the 1958 movie *The Big Country.* THE KOBAL COLLECTION

George B. Seldon developed a buckboard with a motor. The basic design later evolved into the pickup truck.

BIBLIOGRAPHY

"Carriage." In *The Columbia Encyclopedia.* 6th ed. New York: Columbia University Press, 2000.

Smith, Philip Hillyer. *Wheels Within Wheels: A Short History of American Motor Car Manufacturing.* New York: Funk & Wagnalls, 1968.

Kirk H. Beetz

See also **Carriage Making; Transportation and Travel.**

BUDDHISM. By 2002 Buddhism had become highly visible in many countries outside of Asia. Although it never became nearly as popular as in Asia, by the 1990s Buddhism's influence on America was visible in the arts, in the steadily increasing number of converts and Buddhist institutions, and in the growing recognition of Buddhist groups as participants in the multireligious composition of U.S. society. In each Asian culture, it generally took many centuries for Buddhism to acculturate. In contrast, in the West, attempts to create adapted, regionalized forms of Buddhism occurred at a much faster pace. New schools and lineages additionally pluralized the spectrum of Buddhist traditions present in Western countries.

History

The origin of Buddhism in America can be traced to Chinese immigrants who began to appear on the West Coast in the 1840s. By 1852, around 20,000 Chinese were present in California, and within a decade, nearly one-tenth of the state's population was Chinese.

Japanese Buddhism developed more slowly in America than the Chinese form, but had much greater impact. By 1890, the Japanese population in the United States was barely 2,000. The World Parliament of Religion, held in 1893, radically changed the landscape for Japanese Buddhism in America. Among the participants was a Rinzai Zen monk, Shaku Sōen, who returned to America in 1905, lecturing in several cities, and establishing a basic ground for the entry of Zen. Upon his return to Japan in 1906, three of his students were selected to promote Rinzai in America: Nyōgen Senzaki, Shaku Sōkatsu, and Daisetz Teitaro Suzuki.

Rinzai was one of several Zen traditions to develop in America. Sōtō Zen began to appear in America in the 1950s, and by the mid-1950s, Soyu Matsuoka Rōshi had established the Chicago Buddhist Temple. Shunryu Suzuki Rōshi arrived in San Francisco in 1959, founding the San Francisco Zen Center shortly thereafter. His (mostly Western) successors continued the Sōtō lineage. Another form of Zen that took root in America attempts to harmonize the major doctrines and practices of each school into a unified whole. Proponents of this approach include Taizan Maezumi Rōshi (who arrived in 1956), Hakuun Yasutani Rōshi (who first visited the United States in 1962), and Philip Kapleau. Also significant are Robert Aitken Rōshi, who founded the Diamond Sangha in Hawaii in 1959, Eidō Shimano Rōshi, who first came to the United States as a translator for Yasutani Rōshi, and Joshu Sasaki Rōshi, who founded the Cimarron Zen Center in Los Angeles in 1968 and the Mt. Baldy Zen Center three years later.

Zen was not the only Japanese Buddhist tradition to make an appearance in America before the turn of the twentieth century. In 1899 two Japanese missionaries were sent to San Francisco to establish the Buddhist Mission of North America, an organization associated with the Pure Land school of Japanese Buddhism. Reincorporated in 1944 as the Buddhist Churches of America, it remains one of the most stable Buddhist communities in North America.

In the 1960s, another form of Japanese Buddhism, now known as Sōka Gakkai International-USA, appeared on the American landscape, and by 1974 it boasted over 200,000 members. This group grew out of the Sōka Gakkai movement in Japan, a nonmeditative form of Buddhism that based its teachings on the thirteenth century figure Nichiren (1222–1282). Although the group splintered in the late twentieth century, it remained a formidable Buddhist presence in America, having become extremely attractive to European American and African American Buddhists.

At the same time the Chinese were once again making their presence visible in American Buddhism. One notable addition was a largely monastic group known as the Dharma Realm Buddhist Association, created by a venerable monk named Hsüan-Hua. Of even larger size was the Hsi-Lai Temple outside Los Angeles, founded in

1978, and eventually offering a wide variety of Buddhist teachings and services. By 2002 Chinese Buddhist groups could be found in virtually every major metropolitan area.

The Buddhist culture to enter America most recently is the Tibetan. Although a few Tibetan Buddhist groups appeared in the West prior to 1960, the majority came after China's invasion and occupation of their country. Communities from each of the four major Tibetan sects can now be found in America. The Tibetan groups were the most colorful of all the Buddhist groups prospering in late twentieth century America, possessing a rich tradition of Buddhist art and a powerful psychological approach to mental health. In the early 2000s they continued to grow rapidly.

The final sectarian tradition to be considered is that of the Theravāda. Most recently, groups from Laos, Cambodia, Thailand, and Myanmar migrated to the United States to escape the economic and political uncertainty of their native countries. Theravāda temples sprang up in the Southeast Asian enclaves of major cities. The Theravāda-based Vipassanā movement became the most attractive form of this tradition among Euro-Americans.

Institutional Issues

Five areas of institutional concern can be outlined in the American Buddhist tradition: ethnicity, practice, democratization, engagement, and adaptation. Two questions help to contextualize these mutually influencing issues: first, how Buddhist identity is determined, and finally, the degree to which ecumenicity might play a role in providing a unifying instrument for the exceedingly diverse spectrum of Buddhist traditions in North America.

Who is a Buddhist? Identifying and quantifying American Buddhists has been an important issue. By the mid-1990s, scholars estimated the American Buddhist population to be four to five million. Although there were many possible methods of determining Buddhist identity in America, the most accepted approach was that of self identification. This approach allowed each group to be counted regardless of how they interpreted and practiced Buddhism.

Ethnicity. One late twentieth century attempt to quantify the American Buddhist population estimated that of the total Buddhist population in the United States, perhaps 800,000 were Euro-American convert Buddhists. This suggested that the vast majority of Buddhists in America were Asian immigrants. The relationship between Asian American Buddhists and converted Buddhists was tenuous.

Practice. There was no disagreement among researchers that Asian immigrant Buddhist communities and American convert communities engaged in significantly different expressions of Buddhist practice. The general consensus was that American converts gravitate toward the various meditation traditions, while Asian immigrants

Buddhism in Wartime. This 1942 photograph by Francis Stewart shows a Buddhist church at camp two of the Gila River Relocation Center in Rivers, Ariz., an internment camp for Japanese Americans during World War II. NATIONAL ARCHIVES AND RECORDS ADMINISTRATION

maintain practices consistent with ritual activity or Pure Land observance.

Democratization. While Asian Buddhism was, for the most part, primarily hierarchical and highly authoritarian, the forms of American Buddhism that developed in the late twentieth century underwent a process of democratization. It could be observed in changing patterns of authority in the various Buddhist *sanghas*, or communities, highlighted by a reevaluation of the relationship between the monastic and lay communities. Second, democratization could be witnessed in changing gender roles in American Buddhism, especially in the prominence of women. Finally, it could be seen in the manner in which individuals pursuing a nontraditional lifestyle, particularly with regard to sexual preferences, found a meaningful role in American Buddhist communities.

Engagement. "Socially engaged Buddhism" has application to a wide variety of general human rights issues, such as antiviolence and environmental concerns, but also to the lives of individual Buddhists. The greatest challenge for socially engaged Buddhism in the West is organizational. In the early 2000s, it was far less developed in its organizational patterns and strategies than its Christian or Jewish counterparts. Nonetheless, an exciting array of activities could be documented in the records of the individual American Buddhist communities.

Adaptation. Perhaps the one issue that dominated the early comprehensive books on American Buddhism was adaptation or acculturation. As one early researcher asked, "Is there a characteristically American style of Buddhism?" Some North American Buddhists were concerned about the implications of altering the Buddhist tradition in the name of adaptation. American Buddhism has created, in addition to its distinct practices, a series of enterprises that Asian Buddhism never imagined: residential communities, businesses, farms, hospices, publishing companies, meditation products, cottage industries, and the like. Critics worried that these innovations represented a distraction from the purpose of Buddhist practice.

Ecumenicism. In each of the issues cited above, it is possible to discern the need for cooperative discussions between American Buddhists of all traditions. In July 1987, a conference on world Buddhism in North America was sponsored by the Zen Lotus Society in Ann Arbor, Michigan. It included a wide variety of talks, panel discussions, and meetings in an effort to bring together representatives of the Buddhist traditions in America to work together toward common goals. In the end, they sought to create a protective umbrella under which the issues of ethnicity, practice, democratization, engagement, and adaptation could be addressed productively, ushering in a successful future for the Buddhist movement in America.

BIBLIOGRAPHY

Morreale, Don, ed. *The Complete Guide to Buddhist America.* Boston: Shambhala, 1998.

Prebish, Charles S. *Luminous Passage: The Practice and Study of Buddhism in America.* Berkeley: University of California Press, 1999.

Prebish, Charles S. and Kenneth K. Tanaka, eds. *The Faces of Buddhism in America.* Berkeley: The University of California Press, 1998.

Seager, Richard. *Buddhism in America.* New York: Columbia University Press, 1999.

Williams, Duncan Ryūken and Christopher S. Queen, eds. *American Buddhism: Methods and Findings in Recent Scholarship.* Surrey, U.K.: Curzon Press, 1999.

Charles Prebish

See also **Religion and Religious Affiliation.**

BUDGET, FEDERAL. The federal budget, and the budgetary process, is a social contract between a people and its government. Despite its complexity, it is a document that shows our societal preferences (for example, guns versus butter) and demonstrates that we do not live in a consensus political economy—interest group and class politics are alive and well.

What Is the Budget?

According to Aaron Wildavsky, "The budget is a representation in monetary terms of government activity. If politics is regarded in part as conflict over whose prefer-

ences shall prevail in the determination of policy, then the budget records the outcomes of this struggle."

Federal financial authority comes from the U.S. Constitution. Article 1, Section 8 states: "the Congress shall have the power to levy and collect Taxes, Duties, Imposts and Excises, to pay the Debts and provide for the Common Defense and General Welfare of the United States." Federal taxing authority and the broad responsibility for the country's defense and general welfare is at the heart of the budget. "General welfare" has been broadly interpreted and serves as the justification for programs as different as space exploration, transfer payments to low-income citizens, road building, and wildlife preservation.

The federal budget is one of many tools available to the government to accomplish its goals; in addition, there is the tax system, loans and loan guarantees, monetary policy, regulation, the courts, and government-sponsored enterprises such as the mortgage lender FNMA (Federal National Mortgage Association), or Fannie Mae.

The federal budget also works with state and local government budgets. Certain government obligations are exclusively federal, such as national defense. Most education and transportation funding comes from states. Fire and police departments are paid for at the local level. Income and payroll taxes provide most federal revenue. States rely on sales taxes, and many also levy an income tax. Local services are mostly funded from property taxes.

The budgetary process is massive and involves the president and the executive departments, the Congress, outside interest groups, and the courts. To take a snapshot from 1988, the federal budget spending equaled one-fourth of national income, involved over 5 million civilian and military personnel, and was tracked in nearly 2,000 separate accounts. Even in a society that extols the virtue of free enterprise, the federal government is still the largest borrower, the largest spender, and the largest income receiver in the economy.

Key Terms and Concepts

Authorization, appropriation, and outlays. Before any federal entity can spend money, it needs both authorization—an approved guideline that explains the goals of a program and sets a spending limit—and appropriation. Appropriation is a separate legislative act that allows a program or department to make a spending commitment, such as hiring an employee or buying a jet fighter. Appropriations are not supposed to exceed budget authority. Finally, the money spent is budget outlay. In any given year, there is a significant amount of budget authority from prior years that obligates outlays in the current year.

Entitlements. A large portion of the budget is used to pay for obligations that do not require budget authority. The Social Security Act, for example, outlines who is eligible for a social security pension. The amount of money spent each year on this program, the outlay, does not de-

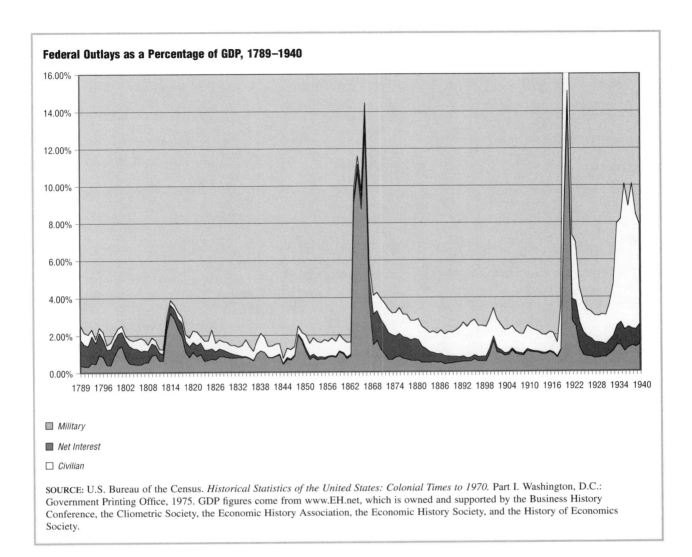

Federal Outlays as a Percentage of GDP, 1789–1940

☐ Military

■ Net Interest

☐ Civilian

SOURCE: U.S. Bureau of the Census. *Historical Statistics of the United States: Colonial Times to 1970.* Part I. Washington, D.C.: Government Printing Office, 1975. GDP figures come from www.EH.net, which is owned and supported by the Business History Conference, the Cliometric Society, the Economic History Association, the Economic History Society, and the History of Economics Society.

pend on budget authority or appropriations; it is driven by how many people are eligible under the current law. Other programs in this category include food stamps, Medicare, and veterans' pensions. Because of prior budget appropriations and formula-driven programs such as entitlements, as little as 25 to 30 percent of a given year's budget is discretionary.

Economic assumptions. Perhaps the most confusing part of any budget debate is predictions on the future performance of the economy. Both the president's OFFICE OF MANAGEMENT AND BUDGET (OMB) and the Congressional Budget Office (CBO) make economic forecasts. Often they do not agree. Even a slight discrepancy in economic growth or inflation can result in very different pictures of the future budget.

Baselines. A baseline is an estimate of what a certain program at current service levels will cost into the future. For example, many federal programs are indexed to inflation. Government payments of medical care for elderly and low-income citizens depend on the number of people who are eligible and the increase in medical costs. If medical costs are rising and/or more people are eligible for government-paid care, then the future budget baseline will be higher than the current one. In budget terms, this is neither an increase nor a cut. A decision to cut or increase funding is applied to the new baseline. Like economic projections, baseline calculations also are a source of controversy.

Off budget. Not all federal spending is reflected in the federal budget. Sometimes a particular program is funded by a special tax and therefore is not part of the budget deliberation, and some items are taken off budget as an accounting trick.

Budget effort. Measuring the budget is more difficult than it might first appear. Different indicators tell contradictory stories. In 1962, for example, the federal budget was about $107 billion. In 1984 it was nearly $852 billion. On its face, this looks like a spectacular increase

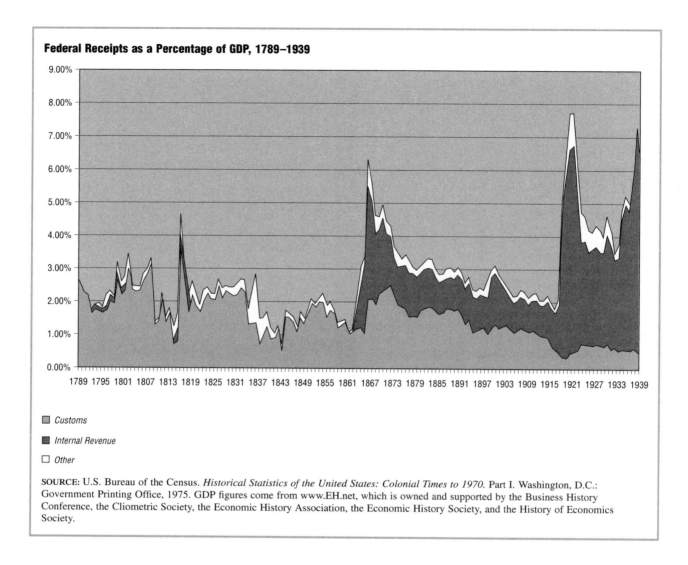

Federal Receipts as a Percentage of GDP, 1789–1939

- Customs
- Internal Revenue
- Other

SOURCE: U.S. Bureau of the Census. *Historical Statistics of the United States: Colonial Times to 1970.* Part I. Washington, D.C.: Government Printing Office, 1975. GDP figures come from www.EH.net, which is owned and supported by the Business History Conference, the Cliometric Society, the Economic History Association, the Economic History Society, and the History of Economics Society.

in spending and the growth of government. The problem with this comparison is that it does not adjust for inflation (a dollar in 1962 was "worth" more than one in 1984) or for the growth in the economy, which is typically measured as gross national product (GNP) or gross domestic product (GDP). The federal budget in 1962 amounted to 18.8 percent of GDP; in 1984, it was 22.2 percent. This suggests a rather gradual increase in government spending.

Goals of the Federal Budget

Public finance professors Peggy and Richard Musgrave argue that the federal budget has three goals: (1) to provide social goods, (2) redistribute income, and (3) manage the economy. Social goods are the things that we as a community can enjoy but that the market does not provide—including national parks, battleships, and interstate highways. The budget also redistributes income. This may take the form of transfer payments—money to low-income citizens—and subsidizing services and products used by low-income people, such as housing, medical

care, and food. Finally, the budget tries to cushion the swings in the business cycle. Since the Great Depression of the 1930s, the federal government has tried to manage the economy. The federal budget pursues this goal through automatic mechanisms and deliberate action. For example, the government automatically pumps buying power back into a community when workers are laid off through unemployment insurance payments to individuals. In addition, Congress may enact a fiscal stimulus package where the government tries to spend money with the goal of increasing economic demand and creating jobs.

The Budgetary Process

The revenue side of the budget is managed through periodic changes to the tax code. The appropriations side of the budget, however, is prepared annually to allow for regular reviews of policies and programs. Since the Budget Reform Act of 1974, the federal fiscal budget year runs from 1 October to 30 September and is known by the

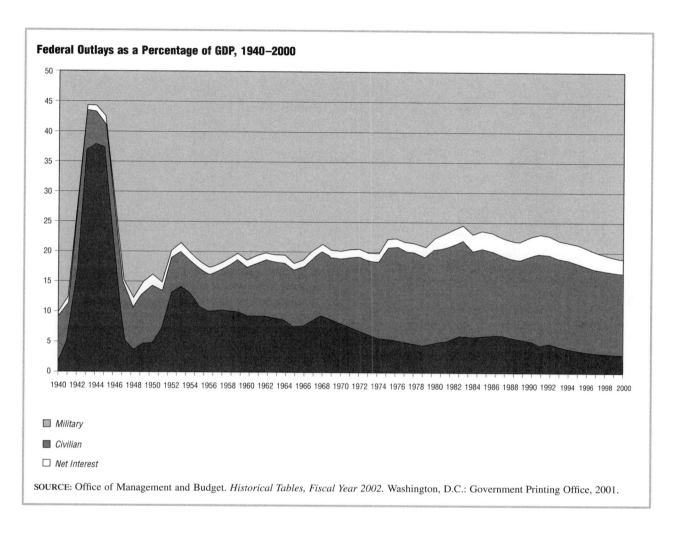

Federal Outlays as a Percentage of GDP, 1940–2000

Military

Civilian

Net Interest

SOURCE: Office of Management and Budget. *Historical Tables, Fiscal Year 2002.* Washington, D.C.: Government Printing Office, 2001.

year in which the budget ends (for example, Fiscal Year 2002 ended on 30 September 2002).

Although we often think of Congress as having the "powers of the purse," the federal budget requires the president and Congress to work together. The president presents a budget to Congress in early February. Although the budget is a single document, it is funded through thirteen separate bills. The House of Representatives and the Senate, through their committees, analyze and debate the budget and usually pass the modified funding bills between April and mid-September. If there are differences between the House and Senate versions, the bills go to the conference committee. Once both houses pass the final versions, they send them to the president for a signature. The power of a presidential veto is great since a single party rarely has the two-thirds majority vote necessary for a veto override.

At the end of the year there are two types of audits. One attempts to make sure that the money was handled honestly—a check on possible graft and corruption. The other is a performance audit that analyzes the effectiveness of different programs in an effort to enhance pro-

gram outcomes while minimizing costs. These outcomes are often measured as ratios or other numerical relationships of cost to services or product. For example, tax collecting agencies will monitor their performance as "cents to collect a dollar of taxes." This type of measurement has become increasingly important in recent years as the federal government moves in the direction of "performance-based budgeting."

Tools for Achieving Compromise

Since claims always exceed available resources, the budget is an effort to negotiate multiple claims from competing interest groups, regions of the country, and economic classes. Even when there is broad agreement, for example, on the need for a fiscal stimulus package during the recession of 2001, there are disagreements over the specifics. To combat the recession, the Republicans wanted to create jobs by giving tax breaks to corporations and derided the Democrats as giving into class warfare. The Democrats, in turn, wanted to boost consumer demand through workers spending their unemployment checks and claimed that the Republican plan was simply a pay-

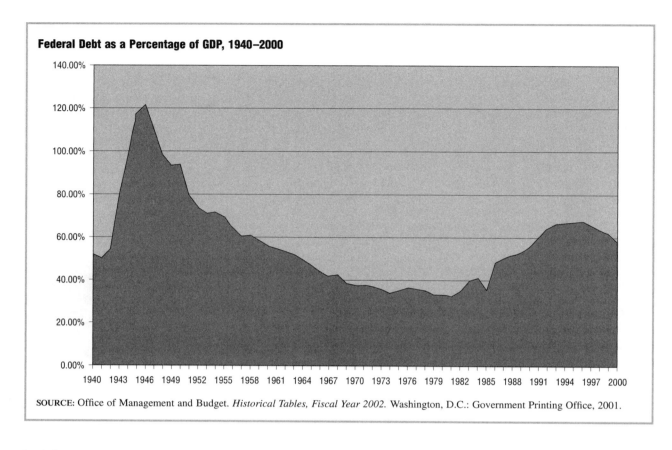

Federal Debt as a Percentage of GDP, 1940–2000

SOURCE: Office of Management and Budget. *Historical Tables, Fiscal Year 2002.* Washington, D.C.: Government Printing Office, 2001.

back for corporate campaign contributors. With this kind of rancor, how does a budget ever get passed?

There are a number of techniques that help achieve compromise. One is a concept known as "incrementalism," where there is a base funding amount that is deemed acceptable by all parties for a particular program. The budget debate focuses on the increment—increase or decrease—for next year's funding. Another technique is "decentralization," where Congress debates lump sums of funding rather than the specific programs funded by those sums. These lump sums can go to a federal bureaucracy or state or local government, where specific spending decisions are made. Finally, there is a great push to compromise because taking extreme positions often brings the government to a standstill, with serious political consequences for whomever the voting public blames for the breakdown. And when compromise is very difficult to forge, for example, during the late 1980s, the federal government has resorted to "budget summits," where the congressional leadership and the president hammer out a compromise behind closed doors. The ultimate product is usually enough of a compromise by all parties that the leadership can take the budget back to Congress for approval.

The History of the Federal Budget
The United States was born in debt. Alexander Hamilton, the nation's first secretary of the treasury, successfully lob-

bied for the federal government to assume the debt from the states for fighting the Revolutionary War. The states' debt combined with the federal debts owed to both foreign and domestic lenders totaled nearly $100 million. The early federal budget and budgetary process reflected the new nation's fear of strong executive power, entrusting most budgetary power in the legislature. During the eighteenth century and much of the nineteenth century, the departments of government made direct requests for funding to legislative committees.

Until the Republican Party began to create a stronger federal government during and after the Civil War, the federal budget was very small. In fact, even into the twentieth century, the total amount spent by city governments was greater than all the state and federal budgets combined.

The most dramatic tax story before 1940 was the dethroning of the TARIFF and the creation of an income tax as the primary source of revenue. Most of the federal government's revenue in the eighteenth and nineteenth centuries came from duties on imported goods. Other sources were the sale of public lands and excise taxes on consumer goods, such as tobacco and alcohol. Although the federal government flirted with an income tax to help pay off the North's Civil War costs, there were doubts about its constitutionality. Progressive reformers ended that debate with the Sixteenth Amendment in 1913. Since then, taxes on income—individual and corporate—have been the federal government's largest source of revenue.

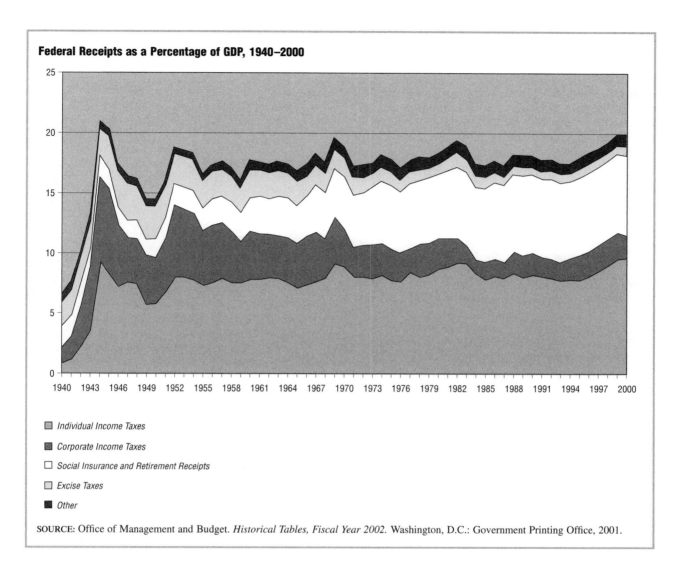

Federal Receipts as a Percentage of GDP, 1940–2000

- ☐ Individual Income Taxes
- ■ Corporate Income Taxes
- ☐ Social Insurance and Retirement Receipts
- ☐ Excise Taxes
- ■ Other

SOURCE: Office of Management and Budget. *Historical Tables, Fiscal Year 2002.* Washington, D.C.: Government Printing Office, 2001.

The federal budget has tended to accumulate large deficits in times of war and run surpluses in peacetime, which helped to pay the increased interest expenses in subsequent years. After the Civil War, however, civilian spending increased, primarily for pensions to Union veterans and their dependents. The most dramatic increase in civilian spending, however, came in the 1930s during the Great Depression when the federal government started experimenting with ways to reenergize a failing economy and quell the growing unrest of millions of citizens.

Graft, corruption, kickbacks, and rigged contracts are problems as old as government itself. Controlling these problems was a major emphasis of the Progressive Movement reforms of the late nineteenth and early twentieth centuries. Many of the budget reforms that would be incorporated in the federal budget were first tried in the private sector and by local governments. The Budget and Accounting Act of 1921 borrowed many of these ideas, modernized the budget process, and began the cur-

rent system whereby the president prepares a comprehensive budget for all government spending on an annual basis. It also created the GENERAL ACCOUNTING OFFICE (GAO) as an independent agency that would facilitate Congress's role in the audit and review of the executive branch.

For over fifty years, the president had more power over the budget than Congress. In the wake of the Watergate scandal, however, Congress reasserted some of its historic budget prerogatives. In 1974, it passed the Budget and Impoundment of Control Act, which among other things gave the Congress more oversight of the president's budget, including the creation of the CBO.

World War II made many permanent changes to the nature of the federal budget. The federal government spent and collected much more money. Federal revenue from individual income tax rose from 17 to 49 percent during the 1940s, and the corporate income tax rose more modestly from 20 to 27 percent of federal revenue. The federal government also began to take a bigger bite out of national income. The ratio of federal tax revenue to GDP doubled in the 1940s. Rising post-war wages also transformed the income tax from something that only rich people paid to a mass tax. The number of people paying income tax rose from 7 million in 1939 to 50 million in 1945. By the end of the twentieth century, nearly 100 million people paid income taxes.

At the middle of the twentieth century, the height of the Cold War, the amount of military spending reached 14 percent of GDP and then steadily dropped into the 4 to 6 percent range until the 1990s, when it hovered around 3 percent. Civilian spending, on the other hand, seems to be a mirror of that trend. It was 6 to 8 percent through the 1950s and into the 1960s, when it began to climb to its high, in 1991, of 15.8 percent. The rise in civilian spending is almost entirely due to increased spending on social security (including hospital insurance). The last important category is net interest on the national debt, which grew rapidly during the budget deficits of the 1980s.

The shortfall between revenue and outlays in any given year is the annual *deficit*. The accumulated deficits contribute to the national *debt*. Budget deficits in the 1980s and early 1990s were massive (averaging $223 billion from 1982 to 1993). That trend subsided in the mid-1990s. There were three consecutive surplus years ending in 2000, an achievement not seen since 1949. However, the U.S. government continues to hold a large debt, nearly $5.6 trillion in 2000.

Three congressional acts were created to reign in runaway deficits in the 1980s and early 1990s. They were the Budget and Emergency Control Act of 1985 (also known as the GRAMM-RUDMAN-HOLLINGS ACT), the Gramm-Rudman-Hollings Reaffirmation Act of 1987, and the summit-negotiated Budget Enforcement Act of 1990.

An important trend that gained momentum under Richard Nixon is a decentralization of the federal budget, known as "fiscal federalism," which provides state and local governments with block grants from Washington. An extension of this decentralization is evident in the increasing use of tax incentives, rather than budget spending, to achieve public policy goals. For example, in the 2000 campaign for president, both candidates discussed plans to cut taxes to provide incentives for everything from education to energy efficient cars; they did not propose new budget authority for these programs.

BIBLIOGRAPHY

Meyers, Roy T., ed. *Handbook of Government Budgeting*. San Francisco: Jossey-Bass, 1999.

Musgrave, Richard A., and Musgrave, Peggy B. *Public Finance in Theory and Practice*s. 5th ed. New York: McGraw-Hill Book Co., 1989.

Schick, Allen. *The Federal Budget: Politics, Policy, Process*. Rev. ed. Washington, D.C.: Brookings Institution Press, 2000.

U.S. Office of Management and Budget. *Budget of the U.S. Government*. Washington, D.C.: Government Printing Office Budgets from Fiscal Year 1997 forward are available online at www.access.gpo.gov.

Wildavsky, Aaron B., and Naomi Caiden. *The New Politics of the Budgetary Process*. 4th ed. New York: Addison Wesley/Longman, 2001.

David J. Erickson

See also **Debt, Public; Expenditures, Federal; Revenue, Public; Revolution, American: Financial Aspects; Surplus, Federal; Taxation.**

BUENA VISTA, BATTLE OF (22–23 February 1847). During the Mexican War General Zachary Taylor had advanced his army of about five thousand men southwestward from Monterrey in northeastern Mexico to a mountain pass south of Saltillo. Near the hacienda of Buena Vista he encountered a Mexican force three times the size of his own led by General Antonio López de Santa Anna. Although the Americans lost ground the first day, they won a brilliant victory on the second, and the Mexicans withdrew. Taylor gained a reputation that aided him in his bid for the presidency, but the further conquest of Mexico was entrusted to General Winfield Scott.

BIBLIOGRAPHY

Eisenhower, John S. D. *So Far from God: The U.S. War with Mexico, 1846–47*. New York: Random House, 1989.

Lavender, David S. *Climax at Buena Vista: The American Campaigns in Northeastern Mexico, 1846–47*. Philadelphia: Lippincott, 1966.

L. W. Newton / A. R.

See also **Mexican-American War; Monterrey, Battles of.**

BUENOS AIRES PEACE CONFERENCE. President Franklin D. Roosevelt's concern over the rise of fascism in Europe prompted him in early 1936 to suggest a meeting of the American republics to discuss the maintenance of peace in the Western Hemisphere. Such a meeting would allow Roosevelt to promote his "Good Neighbor Policy" toward Latin America, which drastically limited U.S. definitions of intervention. Latin American leaders agreed to a conference, and they placed neutrality, arms limitations, and foreign intervention high on the meeting's agenda.

Argentina's Minister of Foreign Affairs and Nobel Peace Prize winner Carlos Saavedra Lamas presided over the Inter-American Conference for the Maintenance of Peace, which met at Buenos Aires from 1 to 23 December 1936. U.S. Secretary of State Cordell Hull led the American delegation. As a show of good faith, the United States gave up some of its intervention rights. The American republics agreed to a policy of nonintervention toward one another, and to collaborate on responses to disagreements. Lamas, however, clashed with Hull when the United States attempted to form a block of nations opposed to European fascism. Unlike the isolationist United States, Argentina had crafted a foreign and economic policy tied to Europe. The nations reached no agreement on the American initiative.

BIBLIOGRAPHY

Connell-Smith, Gordon. *The United States and Latin America: An Historical Analysis of Inter-American Relations.* London: Heinemann Educational, 1974.

Schoultz, Lars. *Beneath the United States: A History of U.S. Policy Toward Latin America.* Cambridge, Mass.: Harvard University Press, 1998.

R. Steven Jones
A. Curtis Wilgus

See also **Good Neighbor Policy; Latin America, Relations with.**

BUFFALO. The city of Buffalo, New York, lies at the northeast end of Lake Erie where it flows into the Niagara River, and then into Lake Ontario. Because of its strategic position, Buffalo became a shipping and transportation hub in the nineteenth and early twentieth centuries.

Buffalo was established in 1804 as part of the speculative land development of the American West. In the War of 1812, it was seized and burned by British forces from Canada. Buffalo, as a gateway to the Great Lakes, was selected as the western terminus of the Erie Canal when it was constructed in the 1820s. With the opening of the canal in 1827, Buffalo became the storage and transshipment center for the flow of grains and raw material out of the American Midwest, and for the flow of manufactured goods into that burgeoning region.

By 1840, Buffalo's population had grown to 18,000, making it the largest city west of the Appalachians. The railroads arrived in the 1840s, enhancing Buffalo's role as a transportation center and gateway to the Midwest. By the mid-nineteenth century, the need for iron and steel for both ship construction and the railroads prompted the beginnings of heavy industry at Buffalo.

The combination of Lake Superior iron ore from the Mesabi Range in Minnesota and proximate coking coal from Pennsylvania, both cheaply moved by lake steamers, made Buffalo an ideal location for steel foundries and fabricators. By 1900, Buffalo was the second largest producer of steel in the country. With strong shipping, commercial, and industrial activity, Buffalo's financial and service sectors also expanded. This strong economic growth attracted waves of immigrants both from the American countryside and from Europe. These workers became increasingly militant, creating a strong union movement.

The twentieth century opened with bright prospects for further expansion of the heavily industrialized Buffalo, particularly with the opening of automobile factories and

related industry. Indeed, the period during the two World Wars saw strong employment and prosperity in the city. But the Great Depression of the 1930s showed the fragility of industrial concentration, and the city of Buffalo defaulted on its debts and went bankrupt. Further, the rise of national corporations took local control away from Buffalo. Finally, with the opening of the Saint Lawrence Seaway in 1959, ships were able to move directly from the Midwest to the Atlantic Ocean, and Buffalo's commercial and shipping activities contracted sharply. The attendant economic difficulties and labor unrest precipitated the flight of manufacturers, which further aggravated the decline of the Buffalo economy.

Buffalo's urban problems and "white flight" led to population declines from 530,000 in 1950 to barely 300,000 in the 1990s. New York State attempted to ease the city's social and economic difficulties by funding public work projects and rebuilding the State University of New York at Buffalo. At the end of the twentieth century, Buffalo—as part of the Great Lakes RUST BELT—continued to struggle with the decline of manufacturing urban centers throughout the American Midwest.

BIBLIOGRAPHY

Brown, Richard Carl. *Buffalo, Lake City in Niagara Land: An Illustrated History.* Woodland Hills, Calif.: Windsor, 1981.

Goldman, Mark. *High Hopes: The Rise and Decline of Buffalo, New York.* Albany: State University of New York Press, 1983.

———. *City on the Lake: The Challenge of Change in Buffalo, New York.* Buffalo, N.Y.: Prometheus, 1990.

Larned, Josephus Nelson. *A History of Buffalo, Delineating the Evolution of the City.* New York: Progress of the Empire State Company, 1911.

Michael Carew

BUFFALO (BISON). Until the end of the last Ice Age, bison were a minor species in North America. As a warming climate destroyed much of the forage upon which Ice Age megafauna such as mammoths and mastodons relied, and as human hunters destroyed those megafauna who remained, bison emerged as the dominant species of the Great Plains. The grasslands may have supported as many as 30 million bison, but changing ecological factors such as drought, blizzards, wolf predation, and the competition of other grazing animals probably caused the bison population to fluctuate considerably.

For thousands of years, Native Americans hunted bison from foot. They surrounded herds, setting fire to the grasses to enclose the animals for the kill. In other instances, they drove herds into corrals or over cliffs. Such techniques demanded the cooperation of large communities. Success was unpredictable, however, and most pedestrian bison hunters combined their pursuit of the herds with other subsistence strategies such as planting or gathering.

American Bison. Commonly but incorrectly called "buffalo," they had nearly been wiped out by 1906, when this photograph of a small herd was taken. LIBRARY OF CONGRESS

The arrival of horses to the plains transformed the relationship between hunters and the bison. Spanish colonists introduced horses to North America in the sixteenth century; the animals diffused into the Great Plains in the early eighteenth century. By the end of the century, several Native American groups, among them the SIOUX, CHEYENNES, and CROWS, had abandoned their former resource strategies and reinvented themselves as nomadic, equestrian bison hunters. That strategy sustained the nomads until the 1830s, when steamboats began to ascend the Missouri River, inaugurating a trade in bison robes that lasted until the late 1860s. Nomadic hunters supplied Euro-American traders with tens of thousands of robes annually, significantly depleting the bison population in the Great Plains.

In the 1870s, Euro-American hunters, in combination with drought and the arrival of millions of domestic livestock to the grasslands, nearly exterminated the remaining bison. While the United States government neither organized nor prosecuted the destruction of the bison, certain of its representatives endorsed it. Congressional efforts to put a stop to the slaughter in the mid-1870s were stymied by Interior Department officials who anticipated that the destruction of the bison would force the Sioux, Cheyennes, and other Native American groups to submit to the reservation system. The species was reduced to a few thousand by 1883.

In the early twentieth century, the American Bison Society, an organization made up largely of wealthy and influential easterners, managed to install a small number of bison on federal preserves as part of a nostalgic and nationalist project of frontier and wilderness preservation. A larger number of bison survived on ranches that raised them as profitable novelties. By the end of the twentieth century there were roughly 250,000 bison in North America descended from the few survivors of the nineteenth century, and bison meat had gained favor as an alternative to beef.

BIBLIOGRAPHY

Isenberg, Andrew C. *The Destruction of the Bison: An Environmental History, 1750–1920.* New York: Cambridge University Press, 2000.

Andrew C. Isenberg

See also **Great Plains; Indians and the Horse; Tribes: Great Plains.**

BUFFALO TRAILS. The first thoroughfares of North America were the traces made by buffalo and deer in seasonal migration as they searched for feeding grounds and salt licks. Before hunting reduced their populations, as many as 50 million buffalo roamed the GREAT PLAINS in sprawling herds. Many early migration routes were initially hammered by the hooves of countless buffalo that instinctively followed watersheds and the crests of ridges to avoid summer muck and winter snowdrifts. Buffalo also helped to define the geography of the midwestern grasslands by forging large areas of short-clipped grass that kept forests from growing and provided homes for prairie dogs and other plains wildlife.

Indians followed buffalo trails as courses to hunting grounds and as warriors' paths. Hunters, and later settlers, followed these trails over the southern Appalachian Mountains in the eighteenth and early nineteenth centuries. They provided easier passage and led the way to salt springs. Traders used these trails in the nineteenth century to cross the plains, and settlers followed them south along the MISSISSIPPI RIVER to the Southeast and to TEXAS. Buffalo traces characteristically ran north and south, as does the famous NATCHEZ TRACE. A few east-west trails proved to be vital routes, such as those through the CUMBERLAND GAP, along the New York watershed, through the Allegheny divide to the Ohio headwaters, and through the Blue Ridge Mountains. These trails helped to define the routes of American settlement and commerce.

BIBLIOGRAPHY

Belue, Ted Franklin. *The Long Hunt: Death of the Buffalo East of the Mississippi.* Mechanicsburg, Pa.: Stackpole Books, 1996.

Isenberg, Andrew C. *The Destruction of the Bison: An Environmental History, 1750–1920.* Cambridge, U.K.: Cambridge University Press, 2000.

E. Douglas Branch / H. S.

See also **Buffalo (Bison); Prairie; Roads; Salt.**

BUILDING AND LOAN ASSOCIATIONS. Prior to the New Deal reforms of the early 1930s, most home mortgages were for five years, after which time they had to be repaid in one lump-sum payment. Building and loan associations, first organized in Pennsylvania in 1831, developed in response to this situation, which effectively limited home ownership to the wealthy. Workers pooled their savings and then chose, often by lottery, who would be able to finance a home.

Upon this foundation the New Deal built an institutional structure that allowed over two-thirds of American households to own a home. The Federal Home Loan

Bank Board was established to regulate the building and loan associations; the Federal Savings and Loan Insurance Corporation (FSLIC) was established to insure their deposits, and interest rate ceilings were implemented to keep banks from bidding away their deposits.

The 1950s were the halcyon days of the building and loan associations' 3-6-3 policy. Their senior officers paid 3 percent for deposits, made 6 percent on thirty-year mortgages with monthly amortization payments, and played golf every day at three o'clock. The 3-6-3 policy was possible because banks met new-loan demand by selling the government bonds they had purchased to finance World War II. It began to unravel in the early 1960s, when banks had reduced their bond portfolios to the minimum required to meet pledging requirements against public deposits, and began to obtain the funds needed to meet new-loan demand by issuing three-month negotiable certificates of deposit (CDs). The Federal Reserve accommodated the banks by increasing, then eliminating, the interest rate ceiling on CDs. Consequently, people shifted their savings from the building and loan associations to the banks' higher-yielding CDs.

The building and loan associations tried to compete with the banks by raising rates on both deposits and new mortgages. As a result, by the late 1970s, with balance sheets weighed down by the 6 percent thirty-year mortgages issued in the 1950s, their average cost of funds was greater than the average return on their outstanding mortgages. They were bankrupt.

The government's initial response, the 1980 Garn-St. Germain Act, was to allow the building and loan associations to purchase assets other than mortgages, while leaving in place the insurance that insulated depositors from the riskiness of those assets. The result was a speculative mania, with investment bankers at Drexel, Burnham and Lambert in particular cold-calling the presidents of building and loan associations to peddle fantasies of greater than 15 percent returns on junk bonds, which justified raising funds by offering more than 10 percent for deposits.

The October 1987 stock market crash also devastated the junk bond market and thus the building and loan associations. In a $200 billion taxpayer-financed bailout, the 1989 Financial Institutions Reform, Recovery, and Enforcement Act (FIRREA) established the Resolution Trust Corporation to strip the building and loan associations of their worthless assets and sell off the remainder to the banks. FIRREA also abolished the FSLIC. In its place, it established the Savings Association Insurance Fund as a part of the Federal Deposit Insurance Corporation (which insures bank deposits).

BIBLIOGRAPHY

Isenberg, Dorene, and Vince Valvano. "No Expense Too Great: A History of the Savings and Loan Bailout." In *Real World Banking*. Edited by Marc Breslow, et al. 4th ed. Somerville, Mass.: Dollars and Sense, 2001.

Keith, Nathaniel S. *Politics and the Housing Crisis Since 1930*. New York: Universe Books, 1973.

Edwin Dickens

See also **Banks, Savings; Savings and Loan Associations.**

BUILDING MATERIALS. The Indian peoples of North America had developed mature building techniques suitable to Neolithic cultures long before Europeans established their first settlements on the continent. In the eastern area of America, forests covered most of the land, and building accordingly consisted of gabled, domed, or vaulted frames built up of branches or light trunks and covered with bark, thatch, or wattle and daub. On the prairies the collapsible tent of nomadic tribes was constructed of a conical framework of saplings covered with skins. Permanent structures in the northern areas were circular, framed in substantial timbers, and covered with a thick layer of mud and grass for insulation against the cold and for protection against snow and wind. In the Sierras, where snow was the chief problem, steeply pitched frames of trunks and branches were covered with heavy slabs of wood rudely shaped from trunks split by wind. Variations on these structures, built with larger openings and covered with thatch, appeared in the warmer coastal areas.

In the deserts of the Southwest, where wood was scarce and heat insulation a necessity, the large communal structures known as pueblos were constructed in tiered series of rectangular apartments. They had thick walls of adobe (sun-dried brick) and roofs composed of branches laid on transverse log beams and covered in turn with a heavy blanket of clay. In the canyons of what is now northern New Mexico and southern Colorado, clays suitable for brick were scarce, but there were extensive outcroppings of sandstone that could be easily broken off into building stones. The Indians who penetrated the canyons constructed their pueblos of thin sandstone tablets laid either on the alluvial floor or on shelves and notches eroded in the canyon walls.

The Europeans who established the North American colonies in the seventeenth century brought their knowledge of materials and techniques from their native lands, but during the first few years of settlement they were often compelled to adopt Indian techniques. The English, Dutch, German, and French who settled the seaboard and Gulf coast areas brought variations on framing in sawn timbers. Frames were usually covered with clapboard siding for walls and shingles for roofs—the latter gradually giving way to slate and tile in the more elegant houses, especially those built by the Dutch. Construction in thick wooden planks set vertically came to be common in parts of the Connecticut Valley, while construction of solid walls built up of horizontally laid logs was introduced by Swedish settlers in the Delaware Valley. The only stone in these early structures was confined to foundations and chimneys. Joints were originally the mortise-and-tenon form secured by wooden pegs, but handwrought nails began to be used early in the seventeenth century and machine-made varieties in the late eighteenth century.

In the more costly forms of buildings, brick laid up in lime mortar slowly replaced timber construction in the English-speaking areas, but expensive stone masonry was confined largely to the Dutch settlements of the New York area. The domed and vaulted construction of eighteenth-century mission churches required kiln-baked, stucco-covered brick, which was stronger and more manageable than the adobe brick, widely used in the Spanish Southwest. All of the traditional European building materials were used throughout the nineteenth century, although with some innovation. Heavy power-sawed timbers were used as posts, sills, girders, rafters, joists, and braces in buildings and truss bridges; deep laminated timbers of bolted planks were developed early in the nineteenth century for the arch ribs of bridges; thinner lumber, like the two-by-four, which was soon to become universal, became the basis of the light balloon frame invented in 1833. As the nation expanded, carefully dressed masonry work of both stone and brick began to appear in large and elegant forms.

Iron

The most far-reaching revolution in the building arts came with the introduction of iron as a primary building material. Although it was first used as early as 1770 in England, it did not appear in the United States until about 1810, and then only in the form of wrought-iron braces and ties for timber arch-and-truss bridges. Cast-iron columns were first used in Philadelphia in 1822, and the cast-iron building front combined with interior cast-iron columns was well developed by 1848. The first cast-iron arch bridge was erected in 1836–1839, exactly sixty years after the English prototype. The first iron truss, again composed entirely of the cast metal, was introduced in 1840. Cast iron, however, is relatively weak in tension and therefore had to be replaced by wrought iron for beams and other horizontal elements as buildings and bridges grew larger and the loads upon them increased. The wrought-iron roof truss was introduced in 1837 and the combination cast- and wrought-iron bridge truss in 1845, both in the Philadelphia area. Wrought-iron floor beams of a depth adequate to the new commercial structures appeared almost simultaneously in three New York buildings in 1854. The first, although unsuccessful, application of metal wire to the suspension bridge was made in Philadelphia in 1816, but this practice was not common until 1842, when a second wire-cable suspension bridge was completed over the Schuylkill River in Pennsylvania.

Steel and Concrete

The rise of the new industrial nation following the Civil War was marked by two fundamental innovations in building construction: the use of steel and concrete as primary materials. The first appeared initially in two bridges erected almost simultaneously: the steel arch structure of EAD's BRIDGE, built by James B. Ead at St. Louis (1868–1874), and the steel cables suspending the deck of John A. Roebling's BROOKLYN BRIDGE (1869–1883). The history of steel in buildings is more complex. The first elevator buildings of New York and Chicago were constructed with masonry-bearing walls and internal iron columns. The iron frame was expanded and elaborated during the 1870s and early 1880s until all internal loads were carried on cast-iron columns and wrought-iron floor beams. The decisive steps in skeletal or skyscraper construction came in Chicago: the first steel girders were introduced in the Home Insurance Building (1884–1885), and the first all-steel frame came with the second Rand McNally Building (1889–1890). Certain of these pivotal innovations in framed construction were anticipated in the Produce Exchange of New York (1881–1884).

Hydraulic concrete, originally a Roman invention, was revived in the late eighteenth century. Composed of lime (as a cementing agent), water, sand, and gravel or broken stone aggregate, it is virtually unlimited in use because in its plastic, pre-set state it can be cast in any structural shape. The hydraulic property comes from the presence of clayey materials in the lime, and before the technique of artificially producing the proper mixture was developed, builders had to depend on a supply of natural cement rock from which the hydraulic lime could be made. The regular use of concrete in the United States began in 1818, when deposits of cement rock were discovered in New York during construction of the ERIE CANAL. The first poured concrete house was constructed in 1835, and the first of precast block in 1837, both in the immediate area of New York City. The American manufacture of artificial cement was established in 1871; the use of mass concrete in walls, footings, jetties, dams, and arch bridges spread rapidly during the remainder of the century.

Plain concrete must be reinforced with iron or steel rods in order to sustain tensile and shearing stresses. Although the first experiments in this novel technique were carried out in England, France, and Germany, the first reinforced concrete structure was a house built in Port Chester, New York, in 1871–1876. The leading American pioneer in large-scale commercial and industrial building was Ernest Ransome, who built the first reinforced concrete bridge in 1889 and developed mature forms of reinforced concrete framing during the 1890s.

Few entirely new structural materials were introduced after 1900, but ferrous metals emerged in various chemical and mechanical alterations. The twentieth century saw the revival of chromium steel for the skyscrapers of the 1920s and the adaptation of self-weathering steel to structural uses in 1962. The major innovation in methods of joining members came with the application of electric arc welding to steel framing in 1920. Aluminum made its initial appearance as a structural material in 1933, when it was used for the floor framing of a bridge at Pittsburgh, Pennsylvania. Its role expanded to the primary structural elements of a bridge at Massena, New York, in 1946. The use of stressed-skin construction, with aluminum as a sheathing material, came with an experimental house of 1946, although similar construction in thin steel plate had been introduced in 1928.

The materials of reinforced concrete remained unchanged but were used in novel ways with the coming of shells (1934) and prestressed members (1938). Wood returned to large buildings in the form of heavy glue-laminated ribs and beams, appearing in the United States in 1937. Tubular forms of steel and aluminum came with the first GEODESIC DOME in 1947. PLASTICS as a sheathing material were introduced in two conservatory buildings in St. Louis in 1962, but their use as a structural material came only in the 1970s.

BIBLIOGRAPHY

Condit, Carl W. *American Building: Materials and Techniques from the First Colonial Settlements to the Present.* 2d ed. Chicago: University of Chicago Press, 1982. The original edition was published in 1968.

Friedman, Donald. *Historical Building Construction: Design, Materials, and Technology.* New York: Norton, 1995.

Simpson, Pamela H. *Cheap, Quick, & Easy: Imitative Architectural Materials, 1870–1930.* Knoxville: University of Tennessee Press, 1999.

Carl W. Condit / T. D.

See also **Adobe; Aluminum; Architecture; Bridges; Cement; Ferrous Metals; Fortifications; Housing; Nonferrous Metals; Skyscrapers; Tunnels.**

BULGE, BATTLE OF THE, a German counteroffensive in World War II, named for the forty-mile-wide and sixty-mile-deep bulge created in American lines. As German armies retreated from France in late summer 1944, Adolf Hitler planned to regain the initiative by a winter counteroffensive in the semimountainous Ardennes region of Belgium and Luxembourg, scene of German triumphs in 1914 and 1940. Over objections of his field commanders, who deemed resources inadequate for such a plan, Hitler aimed his thrust at the Belgian port of Antwerp, intending thereby to cut off to the north the British Twenty-first Army Group and the U.S. First and Ninth Armies; these forces eliminated, he hoped to gain a negotiated peace on the western front.

Through the autumn of 1944, the German commander, Field Marshal Gerd von Rundstedt, secretly massed more than 200,000 men and 1,200 tanks in the wooded Eifel region opposite the Ardennes. On 16 December three German armies struck along a sixty-mile front against seven American divisions of the First Army's Fifth and Eighth Corps. Surprise was total, but only at one point, north of Saint Vith, did the Germans achieve the swift breakthroughs they expected.

Battle of the Bulge. One of hundreds of tanks destroyed—along with more than 180,000 total casualties—in the last major German counteroffensive of World War II, in the Ardennes region of Belgium and Luxembourg from December 1944 to January 1945. © CORBIS

Allied lines held in the north against the onslaught of two Panzer armies. In the center the Twenty-eighth Infantry Division slowed a German drive across northern Luxembourg to the Belgian road center of Bastogne. In the south the Fourth Division and part of the Ninth Armored Division blocked the southern shoulder of the penetration. The German drive was thus contained at both shoulders and constricted by lack of roads.

On the second day, 17 December, the supreme Allied commander, General Dwight D. Eisenhower, and the Twelfth Army Group commander, Lieutenant General Omar N. Bradley, rushed reinforcements to the southern shoulder, in part to relieve the besieged U.S. forces in Bastogne. Other units began to build a line westward from the Elsenborn Ridge lest the Germans turn north toward supply depots around Liège. By the fourth day, 19 December, the Germans had severed communications between the southern and northern armies. This prompted Eisenhower to put Bradley's two northern armies under the Twenty-first Army Group commander, Field Marshal Bernard L. Montgomery. American commanders would later take the opinion that Montgomery claimed undue credit for the German defeat.

Hitler hoped to anchor his south flank on Bastogne and drive north to encircle American troops near Aachen.

Thus, the Germans surrounded the American forces at Bastogne on 20 December and laid siege to the town. On the twenty-third, the weather cleared, enabling Allied planes to attack German columns and drop supplies. Severe fighting continued at Bastogne, even after the Fourth Armored Division broke the siege on the twenty-sixth. The First and Third Armies, nevertheless, began to counterattack on 3 January 1945. The First Army came from the north; the Third Army from the south. On the sixteenth they converged on Houffalize, a juncture north of Bastogne, and precipitated a slow German withdrawal. The last of the "bulge" was eliminated on the twenty-eighth.

The Americans incurred about 80,000 casualties—19,000 killed and 15,000 captured; British casualties totaled 1,400. German losses totaled approximately 100,000. Each side lost 700 tanks. The counteroffensive delayed a final Allied offensive against Germany for six weeks, but in expending his last reserves, Hitler had crippled the defense of Germany on both eastern and western fronts.

BIBLIOGRAPHY

Cole, Hugh M. *The Ardennes: Battle of the Bulge.* Washington, D.C.: Office of the Chief of Military History, Department of the Army, 1994. The original edition was published in 1965.

Dupuy, Trevor N., David L. Bongard, and Richard C. Anderson. *Hitler's Last Gamble: The Battle of the Bulge, December 1944–January 1945.* New York: HarperCollins, 1994.

MacDonald, Charles B. *The Battle of the Bulge.* London: Weidenfeld and Nicolson, 1984.

Whiting, Charles. *The Last Assault: 1944, The Battle of the Bulge Reassessed.* New York: Sarpedon, 1994.

Charles B. MacDonald / A. R.

See also **Aachen; Bastogne; Malmédy Massacre; Siegfried Line.**

BULL MOOSE PARTY, the nickname given by newspapers to the Progressive Party, founded in June 1912 by progressive Republicans who bolted the GOP convention to protest the regular party's "standpatism" and the usurpation of progressive presidential electors by incumbent William Howard Taft. The "Bull Moose" tag was an obvious reference to Theodore Roosevelt, the party's leader and presidential candidate, who sometimes identified himself with the male gender of the North American ruminant. When shot by a would-be assassin only weeks before the 1912 election, Roosevelt insisted on immediately filling a speaking engagement, saying "it takes more than that to kill a bull moose."

The 1912 Progressive platform supported measures including a minimum wage, workers' compensation, and women's suffrage. It advocated "a contract with the people," with government acting to improve social and eco-

Bull Moose. This 1916 political cartoon by McKee Barclay shows the symbol of the Progressive Party—by then propped up by boards despite the third party's impressive second-place showing in the 1912 presidential election—nuzzling Theodore Roosevelt, the former president; he declined the party's nomination this time, and it collapsed. LIBRARY OF CONGRESS

nomic conditions. Many people considered the party's aims socialistic. Despite an electrifying campaign, during which Roosevelt trumpeted his New Nationalism, his candidacy split the Republican vote and arguably contributed to Woodrow Wilson's victory. Roosevelt placed second, polling 27.4 percent of the popular vote, the highest percentage ever by a third-party candidate Over the next two years, party leaders worked to build their organization, but the midterm elections proved disappointing. Wilson had stolen much of the Progressive Party's thunder, and voters were tiring of reform. In 1916, the party was largely reabsorbed into the Republican fold. During its short lifetime, however, the Bull Moose Party was a center for progressive political thinking and is credited with influencing the enactment of Wilson's own reform agenda.

BIBLIOGRAPHY

Blum, John Morton. *The Republican Roosevelt.* Cambridge, Mass.: Harvard University Press, 1954.

Cooper, John Milton, Jr. *The Warrior and the Priest: Woodrow Wilson and Theodore Roosevelt.* Cambridge, Mass.: Belknap Press, 1983.

Gable, John Allen. *The Bull Moose Years: Theodore Roosevelt and the Progressive Party.* Port Washington, N.Y.: Kennikat Press, 1978.

C. Wyatt Evans

See also **Third Parties.**

BULL RUN, FIRST BATTLE OF (21 July 1861), the first major engagement of the Civil War, known in the Confederacy as the First Battle of Manassas. The principal Union army of some 30,000 men, under General Irvin McDowell, was mobilized around Washington. Union General Robert Patterson, with a smaller army, was sent to hold Confederate General Joseph E. Johnston in the Shenandoah Valley. General Pierre G. T. Beauregard's Southern army occupied the line of Bull Run Creek, a shallow, meandering stream that runs across the main highways south of Washington.

Public opinion compelled President Abraham Lincoln to order McDowell to advance. The Union attack on 17 July forced an advance force under General M. L. Bonham back to Centreville. The next morning, Bonham rejoined the main Southern force, in a line extending about eight miles behind Bull Run. McDowell and Beauregard planned to turn each other's flank. General Richard S. Ewell, on the Confederate right, was to cross Bull Run at daylight on 21 July, with the other brigades to follow. But Beauregard's order did not reach Ewell. General James Longstreet, after crossing, waited in vain for word of his attack. By 7 A.M., Union forces were attacking the Confederate left at Stone Bridge. Johnston sent General T. J. Jackson to support the troops at Stone Bridge, and other regiments soon followed. Fierce fighting raged along Bull Run; and it is here that Jackson won the nickname "Stonewall."

The arrival of another portion of Johnston's army turned the tide in favor of the Confederates. The disorderly Union retreat across Bull Run soon became a rout as troops fled back to Washington. Afterward, bitter controversy ensued between Jefferson Davis, Johnston, and Beauregard as to the responsibility for not pursuing the defeated Federal troops into Washington. From some 13,000 men engaged, the Union tallied about 500 killed, 1,000 wounded, and 1,200 missing; the Confederates, with about 11,000 engaged, counted about 400 killed, 1,600 wounded, and 13 missing.

BIBLIOGRAPHY

Davis, William C. *Battle at Bull Run: A History of the First Major Campaign of the Civil War.* Garden City, N.Y.: Doubleday, 1977.

Johnson, Robert M. *Bull Run: Its Strategy and Tactics.* New York: Houghton Mifflin, 1913.

McDonald, JoAnna M. *We Shall Meet Again: The First Battle of Manassas (Bull Run), July 18–21, 1861.* Shippensburg, Pa.: White Mane, 1999.

Milledge L. Bonham, Jr. / A. R.

See also **Davis–Johnston Controversy.**

Union Prisoners. Soldiers from Colonel Michael Corcoran's Sixty-ninth New York State Militia, captured at the First Battle of Bull Run, are held in Castle Pinckney, Charleston, S.C. © CORBIS

BULL RUN, SECOND BATTLE OF, also known as the Second Battle of Manassas, was initiated by the decision of General Robert E. Lee, on 24 August 1862 at Jeffersonton, Virginia, to send the 23,000 troops of General T. J. ("Stonewall") Jackson to break the communications of Major General John Pope's Army of Virginia, entrenched along the Rappahannock River in Virginia. Jackson reached Bristoe Station on the twenty-sixth, plundered Pope's base at Manassas Junction the next day, and then proceeded to Groveton Heights, where he attacked a division under General Rufus King on the twenty-eighth. On the twenty-ninth, Pope in turn attacked Jackson, who with difficulty beat off repeated assaults. Lee, meantime, had brought up the remainder of his army, 32,000 men led by General James Longstreet, and formed them on Jackson's right. By nightfall of the twenty-ninth, Lee's line formed an obtuse angle, with Longstreet's troops running from north to south and Jackson's southwest to northeast. Pope, reinforced by a large part of the Army of the Potomac, renewed the attack on Jackson on the thirtieth but failed to confront Longstreet with sufficient force. Lee accordingly ordered a general attack, which swept Pope from his positions. Heavy rain on the thirty-first delayed pursuit and made it possible for Pope to retreat behind the Washington defenses.

Pope blamed his defeat on General FitzJohn Porter, who Pope believed had failed to carry out orders. Porter was cashiered and was not vindicated until 1886, but Pope himself was not again trusted with field command. Pope's losses, from 16 August to 2 September, were 1,747 killed, 8,452 wounded, and 4,263 missing or captured; those of Lee were 1,553 killed, 7,812 wounded, and 109 missing.

BIBLIOGRAPHY

Hennessy, John J. *Return to Bull Run: The Campaign and Battle of Second Manassas.* New York: Simon and Schuster, 1993.

Kelly, Dennis. "Confederates Turn Tables on a Yankee Threat: The Second Battle of Manassas," *Civil War Times Illustrated* 22, no. 3 (May 1983): 8–44.

Douglas Southall Freeman / A. R.

BULLBOATS. When HUDSON'S BAY COMPANY traders first visited the Mandan Indians in 1790, they found that the tribe possessed tublike boats with frameworks of willow poles, covered with raw buffalo hides. Later, frontiersmen who ascended the MISSOURI RIVER noted this light, shallow-draft boat. From 1810 to 1830, American fur traders on the tributaries of the Missouri regularly built boats eighteen to thirty feet long, using the methods

Derailment. Damaged by Confederate cavalrymen, the engine *Commodore* lies alongside the track of the Orange and Alexandria Railroad, a key Union supply route running through Manassas Junction in northern Virginia. NATIONAL ARCHIVES

of construction employed by the Indians in making their circular boats. These elongated "bullboats" were capable of transporting two tons of fur down the shallow waters of the Platte River.

BIBLIOGRAPHY

Meyer, Roy W. *The Village Indians of the Upper Missouri: The Mandans, Hidatsas, and Arikaras.* Lincoln: University of Nebraska Press, 1977.

Carl P. Russell / A. R.

See also **Fur Trade and Trapping; Indian Art; Indian Technology.**

BUNDLING was a mode of courtship during the colonial period. According to this practice, a young couple would go to bed together, either fully dressed or partially dressed, with a "bundling board," or long wooden slab, between them. Sometimes the woman's legs were bound in a tightly fitting "bundling stocking." This custom, inherited from Europe, apparently originated as a matter of convenience and necessity where space and heat were lacking. It became most prevalent in New England, where Puritan parents tried to provide young couples opportunities to court freely while still supervising their conduct. Bundling seems to have declined in the late eighteenth century.

BIBLIOGRAPHY

Fischer, David Hackett. *Albion's Seed: Four British Folkways in America.* New York: Oxford University Press, 1989.

Thompson, Roger. *Sex in Middlesex: Popular Mores in a Massachusetts County, 1649–1699.* Amherst: University of Massachusetts Press, 1986.

Hugh T. Lefler / s. b.

See also **Family; Marriage; Sexuality.**

BUNGEE JUMPING originated on the Pacific island of Pentecoste, where for centuries the Venuatuan natives tested their manhood by leaping from bamboo towers with vines tied to their ankles. Documented by *National Geographic* photographer Kal Muller in 1970, the phenomenon came to the United States in 1979, when four members of the Oxford University Dangerous Sports Club jumped from the Golden Gate Bridge on elastic, latex cords. Following A. J. Hackett's infamous jump from the Eiffel Tower in 1987, professionally operated bungee jumping facilities have flourished both in America and abroad. Today bungee jumping attracts thousands of American thrill-seekers each year.

BIBLIOGRAPHY

Frase, Nancy. *Bungee Jumping for Fun and Profit.* Merrilville, Ind.: ICS Books, 1992.

John M. Kinder

Bungee Jumping. A thrill-seeker plunges toward the water, a stunt that is perfectly safe—if the cord is exactly the right length and does not break. AP/WIDE WORLD PHOTOS

BUNKER HILL, BATTLE OF. To force the British from Boston, on the night of 16 June 1775 the American militia besieging the town sent 1,200 men to seize Bunker Hill, on the peninsula of Charlestown. The detachment instead decided to build a small redoubt on Breed's Hill, which was closer to Boston but easily flanked. At daybreak, the British warships that were anchored in the Boston harbor opened an ineffective fire. To strengthen his left flank, Colonel William Prescott, commanding in the redoubt, built a rail fence stuffed with hay and manned the line with 2,000 men under Major General Israel Putnam. Meanwhile, under the command of Major General Sir William Howe, some 2,000 British infantry, with a few field guns, landed below the redoubt.

Early in the afternoon, Howe, along with Brigadier General Robert Pigot, led a simultaneous attack on the redoubt and the rail fence, which was bloodily repulsed by the provincials, chiefly New Hampshire men under Colonel John Stark. After another failed attempt to take these breastworks, Howe's third assault feinted against the fence and for the first time attacked the redoubt with bayonets. Prescott's troops, out of ammunition, were forced to retreat. The defenders of the fence covered the American retreat. After an engagement lasting less than two hours, the British were masters of the peninsula, but this victory came with heavy casualties. The British lost 1,054 men, while the Americans lost, in killed, wounded,

Bunker Hill. An illustration, published in 1792, of the British naval bombardment preceding the successful but costly attack on American positions in Charlestown. © BETTMANN/CORBIS

and captured, but 441. Although the engagement took place on Breed's Hill, it has come to be known as the Battle of Bunker Hill. At first regarded by the Americans as a defeat, Bunker Hill, because of the way the militia resisted regulars, came to be regarded as a moral victory.

BIBLIOGRAPHY

Higginbotham, Don. *The War of American Independence: Military Attitudes, Policies, and Practice, 1763–1789.* New York: Macmillan, 1971. Rev. ed., Boston: Northeastern University Press, 1983.

Ketchum, Richard M. *The Battle for Bunker Hill.* Garden City, N.Y.: Doubleday, 1962.

Allen French / A. R.

See also **Boston, Siege of; "Don't Fire Till You See the White of Their Eyes."**

BUREAU OF INDIAN AFFAIRS. The Bureau of Indian Affairs (BIA) essentially has two major responsibilities: protecting Indian legal rights and providing services to Native Americans. The legal basis for federal authority rests on the power of Congress "To regulate Commerce with . . . the Indian tribes" and federal laws, treaties, and judicial decisions.

Precursors to the Bureau
In 1789, Indian affairs were assigned to the Department of War. The secretary of war headed the "Indian Department," assisted by a chief clerk and an assistant clerk. From the first, federal administration of Indian affairs

usually had a central office, various district headquarters, and the local agencies, which had direct contact with the Indians. Originally, territorial governors served as district superintendents. This created an immediate conflict of interest because the government's main concern was to promote settlement and statehood. It had little interest in advocating for the Indians and continuously pushed them further west. In 1806, Congress created a superintendent of Indian trade to supervise government trading posts. Secretaries of war often consulted with this official. After Congress abolished the government trading posts in 1824, Secretary of War John C. Calhoun appointed Thomas L. McKenny, the final superintendent of trade, as an unofficial commissioner of Indian affairs. Congress officially created the post of commissioner in 1832, and established the BIA two years later.

Transfer to the Department of Interior
After 1815, many observers questioned whether Indian affairs belonged in the Department of War, and Congress finally ordered a transfer in 1849, when it established the Department of Interior. The new department also contained the General Land Office, the Patent Office, and the Pension Office. The Department of Interior's main responsibility has been to oversee the public domain, a role that often places it in conflict with its responsibility to safeguard Indians' interests. The transfer touched off a long and bitter feud over whether military or civilian officials should handle Indian affairs.

Creation of Reservations
During the 1850s, the attempt to create reservations in California led BIA officials to extend this practice to other

areas. Administering reservations imposed new burdens on the undermanned BIA. Agents and their staffs now lived in direct contact with Indians and tried to educate their children, persuade adults to farm, and force residents to remain on their reservation. The lack of central supervision allowed for inefficiency and graft within the service.

President Ulysses S. Grant's Peace Policy

In 1869, President Grant ordered that religious organizations begin nominating field workers as a way to bring honesty to the BIA. Grant also established an all-volunteer Board of Indian Commissioners, the main responsibility of which was to oversee the purchase of BIA supplies and eliminate fraud. Neither reform worked particularly well. In 1871, the Indian Appropriation Act ended the practice of dealing with the tribes by treaty, thereby threatening tribal authority and making Indians individual wards of the federal government.

Centralization of the Bureau

As late as 1877, the Washington office did not appoint field workers, exercise much control over local agencies, or possess operational regulations; but around this time, supervisors and special agents began to inspect agencies. Regional superintendents gradually disappeared, and agents reported directly to Washington. Regulations for BIA operations became increasingly specific. After 1891 most BIA field workers came under Civil Service hiring regulations.

Congress made its first direct appropriation for education in 1871, for the sum of $100,000. In expanding its operations after 1877, the BIA emphasized education and by 1892 funding had risen to $2,277,557. In 1883, Congress authorized a superintendent of Indian schools, and in 1890 Commissioner Thomas J. Morgan (1889–1893), a professional educator, developed the first plan of study.

The Progressive Era and World War I

Progressive reforms did not alter the basic BIA goals of assimilation and land allotment, but Commissioners Francis E. Leupp (1905–1909) and Robert G. Valentine (1909–1912) stressed scientific administration. Leupp established the first real health services in 1908. The Omnibus Act of 1910 updated and expanded the BIA's responsibilities, particularly in probate, irrigation, forestry, and land allotment. Attempts were also made to achieve self-support through agriculture by giving agency superintendents greater control.

During World War I, the BIA shifted its attention to increasing food production and encouraging young Indians to enter the military. Commissioner Cato Sells (1913–1921) saw the war as a means to assimilate Indians. Unfortunately, the war sharply curtailed services, especially in health and education.

The 1920s Reform Crusade

During the 1920s, the BIA came under very sharp attacks led by social reformer John Collier. Unlike earlier critics, Collier questioned the bureau's basic assimilation philosophy and land allotment. In 1926 and 1927 a panel of ten experts, the Meriam Commission, carried out an investigation of BIA field administration. The commission's report, while generally moderate, strongly condemned land allotment, health services, and education. Modest improvements followed during the Herbert Hoover administration.

The Indian New Deal

The BIA entered perhaps its most dynamic period when John Collier became commissioner in 1933. The Indian Reorganization Act of 1934 highlighted the new administration's reforms. The legislation, among other things, allowed tribes to form governments that acted as federal municipalities. Collier also espoused cultural pluralism and tried to make the BIA into an advisory agency rather than a director of Indian affairs.

One of the Indian New Deal's strongest features was cooperative agreements with emergency agencies such as the Public Works Administration and the Civilian Conservation Corps. These arrangements greatly increased BIA funding and expertise, especially for construction and conservation.

Collier also added many Indian employees within the BIA. In 1933, Indians held a few hundred minor positions. By 1940, 4,682 Indians served in the agency, not including emergency programs. In 1980, Indians and Alaskan natives held 78% of BIA jobs, including all the major posts.

World War II

The BIA's problems in World War II repeated many of those incurred in World War I. Shortages of personnel, especially in health care and education, disrupted social services. Morale suffered when the Washington office was removed to Chicago. Finally, the urgency of the war and high rates of employment pushed the BIA into the background.

Termination

The conservative postwar mood led to renewed demands to phase out the BIA and to have its programs assumed by other federal or state agencies. Commissioner Dillon S. Myers (1950–1953) established a Division of Program to plan for withdrawal of services on reservations. The Eisenhower administration pursued the same goals through legislation terminating individual tribes. Although relatively few Indians were affected, widespread hostility and fear resulted. The BIA's relocation and industrialization programs after 1953 complemented the termination policy.

The Recent History

After 1961, the BIA assumed a very different role. Federal programs, especially President Lyndon B. Johnson's War on Poverty, allowed tribal leaders to apply to federal agencies for grants and to administer programs themselves. This shift in policy broke the BIA's monopoly on funding for tribal programs, and enabled the tribes to develop ties with a wide range of federal agencies. In 1975, Congress approved a major investigation of the BIA known as the American Policy Review Commission. Largely staffed by Indians and headed by Ernest L. Stevens, a Wisconsin Oneida, eleven task forces investigated such topics as trust responsibilities, tribal government, federal administration, health care, and education. An overriding theme in the *Final Report* was greater recognition of tribal sovereignty, a goal that BIA now fully endorses. Congress met another recommendation in 1977 when it elevated the commissionership to an assistant secretary of interior. The change gave the head of the BIA a voice in policy decisions.

The BIA has operated as a government within the federal government. Throughout its history it has suffered from serious conflicts of interest as it attempted to represent a constituency that has little influence on national politics. In 2000, the head of the BIA, Pawnee attorney Kevin Gover, issued a formal apology for the agency's past misdeeds.

BIBLIOGRAPHY

Prucha, Francis Paul. *American Indian Policy in the Formative Years: Indian Trade and Intercourse Acts, 1790–1834.* Cambridge: Harvard University Press, 1962.

———. *The Great Father: The United States Government and the American Indians.* 2 vols. Lincoln: University of Nebraska Press, 1984.

Schmeckebier, Laurence F. *The Office of Indian Affairs: Its History, Activities, and Organization.* Baltimore: Johns Hopkins University Press, 1927.

Stuart, Paul. *The Indian Office: Growth and Development of an American Institution, 1865–1900.* Ann Arbor, Mich.: University Microfilms International, 1978.

Viola, Herman J. *Thomas L. McKenney: Architect of America's Early Indian Policy, 1816–1830.* Chicago: Sage Books, 1974.

Donald L. Parman

See also **Board of Indian Commissioners; Indian Reservations; Interior, Department of the; Meriam Report.**

BUREAUCRACY. At the beginning of the twenty-first century, the federal bureaucracy consisted of 2.8 million people; almost 19 million Americans work for governments of some type, from federal to local units. In a famous lecture given in 1918, the great sociologist Max Weber predicted that the twentieth century would be an era in which governments would be dominated by professional politicians and professional bureaucrats. In most advanced industrialized democracies, Weber's prediction was born out fully. In the United States, however, the bureaucracy has not attained the degree of power or influence that Weber anticipated. The reasons for this relate to the special history of the bureaucracy in the United States.

Most advanced, industrialized democracies developed a professional, permanent bureaucracy around the middle of the nineteenth century. European reformers argued that the expanding role of government in a more urbanized and industrialized society required professional bureaucrats to make government work. Bureaucracies should consist, particularly at their highest levels, of highly educated and trained people organized rationally, not of people who were selected on the basis of whom they knew or had supported in the previous election. Such arguments were made forcefully in the United States as well, particularly later in the nineteenth century by Progressive reformers. However, the shift from patronage to a professionalized, merit-based bureaucracy ran into problems in the United States. First, the notion that making government work required special skills, talents, or education had been rejected by the Jacksonians as incompatible with American values of equality and participation. In the Federalist era, the United States had taken some limited steps along the road toward the creation of a bureaucracy composed of socially superior and educated men. Andrew Jackson reversed these trends, firmly establishing the notion that any (white) man could run government. Second, government jobs were crucial to the workings of American political parties until well into the twentieth century; "to the victor the spoils" was a key principle of party organization. Supporters expected to be rewarded with, among other things, government jobs if their party won. Parties were naturally unwilling to hand over as crucial an element in securing power as government jobs to a merit-based bureaucracy.

In spite of these problems, reformers did ultimately secure the creation of a merit-based system. The assassination of President James A. Garfield by a disappointed job seeker also highlighted the difficulties of operating a patronage system. The triumph of the Progressive reformers seemed to be completed by the New Deal, which resulted in a vast expansion in the number of government agencies and jobs. The practical problems of staffing the much-expanded government machine with political appointees, and the scale of political power that such vast opportunities for patronage could produce, were compelling reasons for completing the transition to a bureaucracy recruited and promoted on the basis of merit. From the New Deal onward, the majority of government jobs were awarded on the basis of merit, not patronage.

Yet the special factors inhibiting the growth of a professional bureaucracy in the United States insured that the reformers' triumph was never total. American government remained distinctive compared with other advanced industrialized democracies in retaining a thick layer of political appointees at the top of government departments. For much of the twentieth century, it seemed as though this layer of political appointees would gradually diminish in the face of practical problems and pressures from reformers. However, in the last few decades of the twentieth century, the number of political appointees began to increase again. In contrast to the situation in other advanced, industrialized democracies, the permanent bureaucracy was largely excluded from participation in policy making and was relegated to mere policy implementation.

Although American political parties no longer depended on patronage for their support as heavily as in the past, several trends emerged that discouraged reliance on the permanent bureaucracy. First, presidents, particularly Republican presidents, believed that the bureaucracy was ideologically predisposed against them and their policies. There is evidence that this belief had some empirical foundations in the Nixon era, though by the end of the twentieth century, bureaucrats had become noticeably more conservative and less Democratic in their personal politics. Second, all presidents found that the vast federal bureaucracy had become a "fourth branch of government" that was difficult to control. The bureaucracy had its own opinions on what constituted good policy and its own political alliances with interest groups and Congressional committees. Third, new styles of thinking, derived from microeconomics, emerged after World War II. In these "rational choice" perspectives, bureaucrats were not the selfless servants of the public good that Progressive reformers had intended but rather selfish maximizers of the size of their staffs and budgets. Writers in this school, such as William Niskanen, were particularly influential with Republican politicians. It followed that the power of bureaucrats should be reduced. Wherever possible, government work should be privatized or "contracted out" to privately owned firms. Senior bureaucrats should be limited in the role they played in developing policy and subordinated to political appointees whose loyalty to the administration was likely to be greater. However, it was a Democratic president, Jimmy Carter, who pushed through legislation that addressed these concerns by moving the most senior bureaucrats into a Senior Executive Service. With this, the president had far more control in the ability to reassign officials than over the rest of the civil service. Carter's reforms were invaluable in helping President Reagan impose radically conservative perspectives on the bureaucracy.

The distinctive history of the bureaucracy in the United States has had both advantages and disadvantages. Advantages have included the facilitated participation in government by large numbers of people from business, academic life, and other backgrounds who have served as political appointees in Washington. Political appointees have brought with them fresh perspectives and attitudes that a permanent bureaucracy may not provide. Most obvious among the system's disadvantages is the continued appointment of people to government service whose qualifications only include the payment of the large sums of money or services to the victorious presidential candidate. Additional disadvantages include the length of

time it takes to appoint and secure Senate approval for the thousands of political appointees who arrive with a new administration, which complicates the smooth running of government. Although bureaucracies can be self-interested and slow to change, they can also provide politicians with much-needed advice and perspectives; good governance may result from the effective combination of the perspectives of bureaucrats and politicians.

BIBLIOGRAPHY

Aberbach, Joel D., and Bert A. Rockman. *In the Web of Politics.* Washington, D.C.: Brookings Institution, 2001.

Light, Paul C. *Thickening Government: Federal Hierarchy and the Diffusion of Accountability.* Washington, D.C.: Brookings Institution, 1995.

Skowronek, Stephen. *Building a New American State: The Expansion of National Administrative Capacities, 1876–1922.* Cambridge and New York: Cambridge University Press, 1982.

Graham K. Wilson

See also **Civil Service; Jacksonian Democracy; New Deal.**

BURGHERS, as Dutch citizens of incorporated cities, enjoyed the economic and political rights of freemen. In NEW AMSTERDAM, burghers gained control of the municipal government in 1652, after the previous administration's reckless economic and Indian policies threatened the city's prosperity. Five years later, the Dutch government granted burgher rights, which conferred political privileges and a commercial monopoly on their recipients. In New Amsterdam, only those whom the city magistrates had classified as burghers could do business as merchants or artisans. Later, English law entitled burghers to the designation of freemen by birth or admission by the magistrates.

BIBLIOGRAPHY

Rink, Oliver A. *Holland on the Hudson: An Economic and Social History of Dutch New York.* Ithaca, N.Y.: Cornell University Press, 1986.

Shelby Balik
A. C. Flick

See also **New Netherland; Petition and Remonstrance of New Netherland; Suffrage, Colonial.**

BURGOYNE'S INVASION. In the late spring of 1777, General John Burgoyne prepared to invade New York from Canada by the Lake Champlain–Hudson River route. Lieutenant Colonel Barry St. Leger was given command of a small expedition that was to ascend the St. Lawrence River, cross Lake Ontario, and advance on Albany by the Mohawk Valley. Burgoyne's army was made up of 3,700 British regulars, 3,000 German troops, 250 American Tories and Canadians, and 400 Indians. With his well-equipped force he proceeded up Lake Champlain

General John Burgoyne. The British formed alliances with many Indian leaders during the Revolution, but most of Burgoyne's Indian allies abandoned him along the invasion route before his defeat at Saratoga. © BETTMANN/CORBIS

in late June and on 1 July was within four miles of Ticonderoga, forcing the Continentals to abandon it four days later. The taking of Ticonderoga increased the confidence of the British and was at first a severe shock to the patriots; later, it proved a stimulus to resistance.

Burgoyne's progress was retarded by his extensive baggage and because the transportation of his artillery up Lake George required all available boats, while his army proceeded overland. A force of some 2,000 Americans under General Philip Schuyler, later enlarged to 3,700, retreated before Burgoyne's slow advance, felling trees across the roads and encouraging the country people to burn their standing crops and drive off their cattle. Meanwhile, Howe, believing that the rebellion was nearly crushed and that Burgoyne did not require his help, went to Philadelphia, leaving Sir Henry Clinton at New York to make a sortie up the Hudson with such troops as could be spared from the garrison.

Fortune now began to turn against Burgoyne. A raiding force dispatched to secure patriot stores at Bennington, Vermont, was overwhelmed on 16 August by General John Stark's New Hampshire militia and Seth Warner's small force. St. Leger, besieging Fort Stanwix, managed to repulse a relieving body of militia under General Nicholas Herkimer at Oriskany, but his Indian allies dispersed before the arrival of a patriot force under Benedict Arnold, and he abandoned his campaign.

General Horatio Gates, now in command of the American army near the mouth of the Mohawk, had about 6,000 effective troops. Reinforced by General Daniel Morgan's Virginia riflemen, he moved northward and entrenched at Bemis Heights, about nine miles south of the hamlet of Saratoga (now Schuylerville). Burgoyne was close upon the American army before he realized its presence. The first Battle of Freeman's Farm was fought on 19 September. Both armies remained in position, and

Burgoyne waited, hoping for news of Clinton's advance up the Hudson, but Clinton got no farther than the highlands of the Hudson. Meanwhile, Gates's numbers were increasing, more New England militia were gathering at Burgoyne's rear, and the British supplies were running dangerously low. Burgoyne retreated to Saratoga. He was surrounded there on 17 October by more than 17,000 regulars and militia. With fewer than 3,500 infantry ready for duty, he surrendered his army to Gates.

BIBLIOGRAPHY

Billias, George A., ed. *George Washington's Opponents.* New York: Morrow, 1969.

Bird, Harrison. *March to Saratoga: General Burgoyne and the American Campaign, 1777.* New York: Oxford University Press, 1963.

Hargrove, Richard J. *General John Burgoyne.* Newark: University of Delaware Press, 1983.

Mintz, Max M. *The Generals of Saratoga: John Burgoyne and Horatio Gates.* New Haven, Conn.: Yale University Press, 1990.

Ralph Foster Weld / A. R.

See also **Oriskany, Battle of; Saratoga Campaign; Ticonderoga, Capture of.**

BURKE ACT. The Burke Act of 1906 amended the DAWES GENERAL ALLOTMENT ACT of 1887 by changing the time when Indians would be enfranchised as citizens and become subject to the civil and criminal jurisdictions of the states in which they resided. Under the Dawes Act Indians became a citizen immediately upon receipt of a "trust patent" for their allotments. A "trust patent" prevented land from being sold (and taxed) for twenty-five years. Politicians argued that many Indians at that time were unprepared for citizenship, and had been exploited in connection with their voting rights. The Burke Act intended to remedy this situation by providing that Indians would become a citizen only at the end of the twenty-five-year trust period, when they became the unrestricted owners of their land. The secretary of the interior was given the right to abbreviate the probationary period for Indians judged competent to manage their own affairs. Competent Indians received fee-simple titles, which made land subject to taxation and removed all restrictions on its lease or sale. Competency commissions were established in various parts of the country to pass on the qualifications of Indian applicants. In some cases, commissions unilaterally declared Indians who had not applied for citizenship to be competent. The net effect of the Burke Act was to accelerate the alienation of Indian lands.

BIBLIOGRAPHY

McDonnell, Janet A. *The Dispossession of the American Indian, 1887–1934.* Bloomington: Indiana University Press, 1991.

Frank Rzeczkowski

See also **Bureau of Indian Affairs.**

BURLESQUE, a popular dramatic and literary form in which parody, coarseness, mockery, and innuendo provide many of the laughs, has a long history. Literary burlesque may be traced back to Greece, where dramas presented at festivals were sometimes satiric and received with joviality. Some of the earliest burlesques were *Batrachomyomachia* (The Battle of the Frogs and Mice), an anonymous burlesque of Homer, and the comedies of Aristophanes (fifth and fourth centuries B.C.). Burlesque evolved throughout Europe, always relying on satire and parody. Fifteenth-century Italian burlesque mocked chivalry, while seventeenth-century French burlesque portrayed the clash between the "moderns" and the "ancients." English burlesque was primarily dramatic, although it included some notable burlesque poems and prose. In the nineteenth century, English burlesque began to rely on pun as much as parody and it was this new, pun-filled burlesque, influenced by a rich history of satire and staging conventions, that was brought to America.

Burlesque, sometimes called "burleycue," came to the United States from England shortly after the Civil War in the form of variety shows that included dirty jokes, parody, and chorus girls performing "leg shows." One of the first, Lydia Thompson's British Blondes, sponsored by P. T. Barnum, toured the United States parodying, or burlesquing, current events and popular plays. Another popular show of the time was the High Rollers troupe's parody of Ben Hur, titled "Bend Her" and featuring female performers suggestively costumed as Roman warriors. In saloons, especially in the western territories, chorus girls who offered bawdy dance performances were sometimes known as "honky-tonk girls."

Many burlesque performers, especially comedians, moved into the similar but more respected form of entertainment known as vaudeville. Others went on to the films of Hollywood or the stages of Broadway. Al Jolson, Fanny Brice, Sophie Tucker, Bert Lahr, W. C. Fields, Mae West, Jackie Gleason, Bobby Clark, Phil Silvers, and Bob Hope began their careers in burlesque. Some burlesque striptease artists also graduated to stardom, most notably fan dancer Sally Rand and stripper Gypsy Rose Lee.

Although burlesque was always risqué, it was not originally merely striptease. In the 1920s, as new competition such as nightclubs and movies grew, the popularity of burlesque declined. In an effort to remain in business, burlesque houses evolved into soft-pornography strip shows. In 1937 Mayor Fiorello LaGuardia closed New York City's burlesque houses.

In 1979 the tradition and spirit of burlesque was honored on Broadway with the show *Sugar Babies*. The lavish production, starring Mickey Rooney and Ann Miller, featured chorus girls, classic songs, and the traditional risqué humor of burlesque.

Gypsy Rose Lee. The early life of this famous stripper was the basis for the Broadway musical *Gypsy*. ARCHIVE PHOTOS, INC.

BIBLIOGRAPHY

Allen, Robert C. *Horrible Prettiness: Burlesque and American Culture.* Chapel Hill: University of North Carolina Press, 1991.

Goldman, Herbert G. *Fanny Brice: The Original Funny Girl.* New York: Oxford University Press, 1992.

Lee, Gypsy Rose. *Gypsy: A Memoir.* Berkeley, Calif.: Frog, 1999.

Rothe, Len. *The Bare Truth: Stars of Burlesque of the '40s and '50s.* Altgen, Pa.: Schiffer, 1998.

Deirdre Sheets

See also **Vaudeville.**

BURLINGAME TREATY, signed on 28 July 1868 in Washington, D.C., negotiated by Anson Burlingame, a former U.S. minister to China. China's government hoped that through personal persuasion and winning popular sympathy, Burlingame could preempt new demands for more rights in China. The treaty contained eight articles. It reaffirmed prior U.S. commercial rights, but left decisions on future trade privileges to the discretion of the Chinese government. The United States disavowed any desire to interfere in China's internal affairs, and the Chinese granted unlimited immunity and privileges of travel, visit, residence, and immigration to U.S. citizens. A provision for reciprocal most-favored-nation status brought criticism because it seemed to guarantee Chinese immigration to the United States, requiring negotiation of the 1880 Angell Treaty, in which China agreed that the U.S. government could suspend but not prohibit immigration. The treaty helped create the myth that the United States was China's preeminent friend and defender.

BIBLIOGRAPHY

Anderson, David L. *Imperialism and Idealism: American Diplomats in China, 1861–1898.* Bloomington: Indiana University Press, 1985.

Hunt, Michael H. *The Making of a Special Relationship: The United States and China to 1914.* New York: Columbia University Press, 1983.

Williams, Frederick Wells. *Anson Burlingame and the First Chinese Mission to Foreign Powers.* New York: Russell and Russell, 1972.

James I. Matray

See also **China, Relations with.**

BURLINGTON STRIKE. On 27 February 1888 locomotive enginemen of the Burlington Railway, members of the Brotherhood of Locomotive Engineers, struck for higher wages and abandonment of the system of classification. The strike was supported by the KNIGHTS OF LABOR. As it dragged on, violence flared, trains were wrecked, men were shot, and property was burned or otherwise destroyed. The brotherhood finally gave in, but the railway damage was enormous. By 1 February 1889 train operations were normal. The Burlington strike hastened the end of the Knights of Labor's brief reign as an effective organizer of railroad labor in the middle to late 1880s.

BIBLIOGRAPHY

McMurry, Donald L. *The Great Burlington Strike of 1888: A Case History in Labor Relations.* Cambridge, Mass: Harvard University Press, 1956.

Thomas Robson Hay / A. R.

See also **Railroad Brotherhoods.**

BURMA ROAD AND LEDO ROAD. One of the largest engineering projects of World War II was the construction of a 400-mile military highway, the Ledo Road, that ran from Ledo, India, to Muse, Burma. There it joined an existing 717-mile highway, the Burma Road, that ran from Lashio, Burma to K'un-ming, China. In 1937 the Chinese started a crash project to build a pass-

Labor Unrest. Chicago, Burlington, and Quincy Railroad workers in Chicago hurl bricks and stones at strikebreakers during the violence-ridden Burlington strike of 1888. LIBRARY OF CONGRESS

able military road between K'un-ming, the capital of Yunnan Province, and Lashio, a railhead on a railway to Rangoon. There were difficulties, however. Bullied by Japan, the British closed their 117-mile Burma sector in 1940 for a short time. Japanese air power endangered growing traffic; the Chinese in 1941 countered with protective American Air Volunteers, famed as "Flying Tigers." Finally, Japan's conquest of Burma in 1942 blocked China's land route to Rangoon.

When Lashio fell, a Chinese division fled to India. In June 1942 General Joseph W. Stilwell, American theater commander in China, Burma, and India, conceived a project to use this Chinese army in India to retake north Burma and build a 400-mile highway to link up with the Burma Road at Muse. The Ledo Road project started in October 1942, but it made little progress during 1943. After Chinese troops under Stilwell captured Myitkyina, Burma, on 3 August 1944, the Ledo and Burma Roads could be joined. Opened 27 January 1945, the combined highways were officially named the Stilwell Road.

Built by seventeen thousand Americans, Ledo Road cost 1,133 fatalities, 625 from combat. Controversy plagued Ledo Road from its beginning, and it was a contributing factor in Stilwell's recall. Nevertheless, the new Ledo Road revived China's interest in modernizing its Burma Road. Sufficient lend-lease supplies arrived on them to equip thirty Chinese divisions in 1945 for a successful stand against an eleven-division Japanese drive in East China.

BIBLIOGRAPHY

Allen, Louis. *Burma: The Longest War, 1941–1945.* London: Dent, 1984.

Anders, Leslie. *The Ledo Road: General Jospeh W. Stilwell's Highway to China.* Norman: University of Oklahoma Press, 1965.

Ford, Daniel. *Flying Tigers: Claire Chennault and the American Volunteer Group.* Washington, D.C.: Smithsonian Institution Press, 1991.

Ogburn, Charlton, Jr. *The Marauders.* New York: Harper and Row, 1959.

Charles F. Romanus/A. R.

See also **China, U.S. Armed Forces in; Flying Tigers; Lend-Lease; Merrill's Marauders; Roads, Military.**

BURNS FUGITIVE SLAVE CASE. The Burns Fugitive Slave Case of 1854 was one of three famous fugitive slave cases arising in Boston after the enactment of the Fugitive Slave Law of 1850. In 1854 Anthony Burns successfully fled bondage in Alexandria, VIRGINIA, and settled in Boston, MASSACHUSETTS. Within a few months, however, his owner, Col. Charles F. Suttle, arrived in Boston to reclaim him. In response, part of the Boston Vigilance Committee, a group of lawyers committed to protecting the rights of fugitive slaves, planned to rescue Burns from an upper room of the courthouse. On the night of 26 May, they battered in a door of the building, entered, and one of them shot and killed a U.S. marshal. Despite the committee's efforts, which included an attempt to purchase and then free Burns, U.S. Commissioner Edward G. Loring remanded Burns to his owner. On 2 June throngs witnessed the slave's departure. Violent riots in protest of his return shook BOSTON, and the federal government had to send in troops to quell the disturbance. In 1855 several rich citizens paid $1,300 for Burns's freedom, and he returned to Massachusetts. Following the Burns case enforcement of the Fugitive Slave Law declined.

BIBLIOGRAPHY

Campbell, Stanley W. *The Slave Catchers: Enforcement of the Fugitive Slave Law, 1850–1860.* Chapel Hill: University of North Carolina Press, 1970.

Von Frank, Albert J. *The Trials of Anthony Burns: Freedom and Slavery in Emerson's Boston.* Cambridge, Mass.: Harvard University Press, 1998.

Wilbur H. Siebert/A. E.

See also **Antislavery; Fugitive Slave Acts; Personal Liberty Laws; Slavery.**

BURR-HAMILTON DUEL. Dueling, used as a means of settling questions of honor, received national attention on 11 July 1804 in Weehawken, New Jersey, with the duel between Alexander Hamilton and Aaron Burr. The confrontation between Burr and Hamilton began in the early 1780s with their competition at the New York state bar and continued during the presidential election of 1800, in which Burr ran for vice president as a Republican. He tied with presidential candidate Thomas Jefferson; however, the Federalist votes in the House of Representatives kept the election in a deadlock until Hamilton's influence gave the presidency to Jefferson, and the vice presidency to Burr, thereby allowing Hamilton to thwart any of Burr's ambitions for further political office.

When Burr failed to get the Republican nomination for the governorship of New York in 1804, he solicited Federalist aid, causing Hamilton to denounce Burr as "a man of irregular and unsatiable ambition . . . who ought not to be trusted with the reins of the government." An agitated Burr challenged Hamilton to a duel, to which Hamilton agreed, although he issued a letter stating that

Aaron Burr. An engraving of the ambitious politician who nearly became president; killed his nemesis, Alexander Hamilton, in a duel while serving as vice president; and later was disgraced after being accused—though subsequently acquitted—of treason involving ambiguous land schemes. LIBRARY OF CONGRESS

compliance with the duel would prevent him from seeking further political involvement, an ironic publication since Hamilton was mortally wounded in the duel. One of the seconds reported that Hamilton had not intended to fire any shots, although both pistols discharged and Hamilton fell. Burr remained a fugitive from the law in both New York and New Jersey, becoming involved in various land schemes, before being acquitted of treason in 1807.

BIBLIOGRAPHY

Fleming, Thomas. *Duel: Alexander Hamilton, Aaron Burr, and the Future of America.* New York: Basic Books, 1999.

Kennedy, Roger G. *Burr, Hamilton, and Jefferson: A Study in Character.* New York: Oxford University Press, 2000.

Jennifer Harrison

See also **Dueling.**

BUS INDUSTRY. *See* **Transportation and Travel.**

BUSH V. GORE, 121 S. Ct. 525 (2000), the Supreme Court decision that ended the 2000 presidential election by ruling that no further recounting of the votes in Florida could occur. The 5 to 4 decision, issued at 10:00 P.M. on 12 December 2000 in the form of an unsigned per curiam opinion, left George W. Bush the certified winner of Florida's twenty-five electoral votes. Those electoral votes in turn provided the Texas governor's margin of 271 to 266 over Vice President Al Gore when the electoral college met six days later.

Destined to be one of the most disputed Supreme Court decisions in history, *Bush v. Gore* was the culmination of a thirty-four-day postelection period that began on the morning after the 7 November election with the simultaneous realization that the outcome in Florida would decide the presidency and that the result there was a statistical dead heat. Bush, the Republican candidate, apparently was ahead by fewer than two thousand votes out of nearly 6 million votes cast.

The Arguments

Amid reports of voter confusion and uncounted ballots, the strategy for both camps quickly became clear. For Gore, the Democratic candidate, it was imperative to seek recounts, and Florida's complex election law appeared to offer tools accomplishing this. For Bush the goal was to freeze in place his evanescent lead, and the Florida law's tight deadline for certifying the vote by one week after the election offered the prospect of accomplishing this. Teams of lawyers for both sides quickly assembled. Ultimately some two dozen lawsuits were filed in state and federal courts, raising a variety of claims. Two cases reached the U.S. Supreme Court, both brought by Bush as appeals of rulings by the Florida Supreme Court. Although the first case, *Bush v. Palm Beach County Canvassing*

Board, 121 S. Ct. 471 (2000), decided by a unanimous per curiam opinion on 4 December, appeared to end inconclusively by instructing the state court to clarify its actions, it occupied a significant position in the legal trajectory that produced *Bush v. Gore.*

To bring *Bush v. Palm Beach County Canvassing Board* to the Supreme Court, the Bush team had first to persuade the justices that the case raised federal questions. The Florida Supreme Court had ruled on 21 November that the secretary of state should continue to accept returns from counties conducting recounts until 5:00 P.M. on 26 November, twelve days after the statutory deadline.

In their petition for certiorari filed at the Supreme Court the next day, the Bush lawyers asserted that the ruling raised three federal questions: that the "arbitrary, standardless, and selective manual recounts" violated the constitutional guarantees of equal protection and due process; that the extension of the deadline violated an 1887 federal law, the Electoral Count Act, 3 U.S.C. Sec. 5; and that the Florida Supreme Court had supplanted the state legislature's special role, set out in Article II of the Constitution, to determine the method for choosing electors.

Two days later, on 24 November, the U.S. Supreme Court accepted the case, limited to the latter two questions. The statute provided that a state's electors chosen according to procedures in effect before election day, with any disputes resolved by six days before the date for the meeting of the electoral college, would not be subject to challenge in Congress. The Bush lawyers argued that by extending the certification deadline, the state court had set new rules, thereby denying Florida's eventual electors the law's protection. The argument under Article II, which provides that states shall appoint electors "in such manner as the legislature thereof may direct," was that the state court's interpretation of Florida law had infringed upon the legislature's unique constitutional role.

The Gore lawyers strongly disputed both these arguments, but in *Bush v. Palm Beach County Canvassing Board,* the Supreme Court did not resolve the debate. Rather, the unsigned opinion vacated the Florida court's decision on the ground that "there is considerable uncertainty as to the precise grounds for the decision" and instructed the state court to clarify whether and how it had taken the federal provisions into account.

The Final Word

No immediate response was forthcoming from the Florida justices, who instead turned almost immediately to a separate case, Gore's challenge under the state election law's "contest" provision to the certified election result that had left Bush 537 votes ahead. On 8 December, by a 4 to 3 vote, the Florida Supreme Court ordered a statewide manual recount of the thousands of "undervotes," ballots that when counted by machine had shown no vote for president. Reprising his earlier arguments, Bush appealed immediately to the U.S. Supreme Court, which the next afternoon issued an emergency stay of the recounts that had just begun and set the appeal for argument on 11 December.

For the first time the division within the Court was clear. Four justices, John Paul Stevens, David H. Souter, Ruth Bader Ginsburg, and Stephen G. Breyer publicly dissented from the stay in an opinion by Stevens, which prompted Antonin Scalia to defend the action on the ground that "the counting of votes that are of questionable legality" would cast a cloud on what Bush "claims to be the legitimacy of his election."

The divide proved unbridgeable. Five members of the court, Scalia along with Chief Justice William H. Rehnquist and Justices Clarence Thomas, Sandra Day O'Connor, and Anthony M. Kennedy, joined the unsigned opinion that was apparently written by Kennedy and O'Connor. It held that in the absence of standards for determining when a ballot validly indicated the intent of the voter, the recount as ordered by the Florida Supreme Court violated the constitutional guarantees of equal protection and due process by making it likely that similarly marked ballots would be accepted in some counties but rejected in others. As if in recognition of the unsettling nature of this conclusion in a country where no uniform rule governs the counting of ballots in the more than three thousand counties, the majority limited the holding to "present circumstances," effectively denying *Bush v. Gore* precedential value for other cases. A concurring opinion by Rehnquist, joined by Scalia and Thomas, argued that the recount also violated Article II and the Electoral Count Act.

Among the four dissenters, Stevens and Ginsburg said the recount raised no constitutional concern. Souter and Breyer said they were willing to accept the conclusion that the terms of the Florida recount violated due process or equal protection, although both justices emphatically insisted that the Court should never have accepted the appeal in the first place. Their acceptance of the majority's analysis was therefore highly conditional. In any event, they said the answer to any constitutional problem with the recount was to remand the case to the Florida Supreme Court for continued counting under uniform standards up to the 18 December date for the meeting of the electoral college if Florida so chose. However, the majority replied that no time existed for further counting because, it asserted, the Florida Supreme Court had indicated the state's desire to take advantage of the Electoral Count Act's "safe harbor," which would expire under the terms of that statute in two hours. The 2000 election was over. Gore conceded to Bush the next day.

BIBLIOGRAPHY

Ackerman, Bruce, ed. *Bush v. Gore: The Question of Legitimacy.* New Haven: Yale University Press, 2002. Academic essays on the decision, mostly critical.

Balkin, Jack M. "*Bush v. Gore* and the Boundary between Law and Politics." *Yale Law Journal* 110 (June 2001): 1407–1458. A strongly reasoned protest from an academic dissenter.

Correspondents of the *New York Times. 36 Days: The Complete Chronicle of the 2000 Presidential Election Crisis.* New York: Times Books, 2001. A collection of news articles and commentary as they appeared in the newspaper.

Dionne, E. J., Jr., and William Kristol, eds. "*Bush v. Gore*": The Court Cases and the Commentary.* Washington, D.C.: Brookings Institution Press, 2001. A useful documentary collection.

Gillman, Howard. *The Votes That Counted: How the Court Decided the 2000 Presidential Election.* Chicago: University of Chicago Press, 2001. Strong analysis and criticism.

Greene, Abner. *Understanding the 2000 Election: A Guide to the Legal Battles That Decided the Presidency.* New York: New York University Press, 2001. A usefully linear and neutral account of the litigation.

Kaplan, David A. *The Accidental President: How 413 Lawyers, 9 Supreme Court Justices, and 5,963,110 (Give or Take a Few) Floridians Landed George W. Bush in the White House.* New York: William Morrow, 2001.

Political Staff of the *Washington Post. Deadlock: The Inside Story of America's Closest Election.* New York: Public Affairs Press, 2001. A journalistic reconstruction.

Posner, Richard A. *Breaking the Deadlock: The 2000 Election, the Constitution, and the Courts.* Princeton, N.J.: Princeton University Press, 2001. A leading federal judge defends the Supreme Court's role.

Rakove, Jack N., ed. *The Unfinished Election of 2000.* New York: Basic Books, 2001. Essays by law professors on the decision.

Sunstein, Cass R., and Richard A. Epstein, eds. *The Vote: Bush, Gore, and the Supreme Court.* Chicago: University of Chicago Press, 2001. Essays by law professors.

Toobin, Jeffrey. *Too Close to Call: The Thirty-Six–Day Battle to Decide the 2000 Election.* New York: Random House, 2001.

Linda Greenhouse

See also **Election Laws; Elections, Contested; Elections, Presidential: 2000; Electoral College.**

BUSINESS, BIG. When used in the context of American economic development, the term "big business" refers to the concentration of industrial and financial power that began in the second half of the nineteenth century and continued through the end of the twentieth. The concentration of economic power began with the transformation of the United States in the nineteenth century from an agrarian, handicraft economy to an industrial, factory economy. By 1900, the United States had become the largest industrial nation in the world. This growth was due to factors including a pro-business political climate; a burst of inventions such as the telephone, the electric light, and the automobile; the availability of vast natural resources; a growing population; and improved production methods, including the division of production into discrete steps, each performed by a separate worker.

This economic growth in part depended on, and in part created, aggregations of wealth among a few individuals and the companies and banks they controlled. Andrew Carnegie, a steel magnate, became one of the world's richest men. J. P. Morgan gained extraordinary wealth in banking and finance, as did John D. Rockefeller in oil, James B. Duke in tobacco, and Cornelius Vanderbilt in steamships, railroads, banking, and manufacturing. Because the government did little to regulate business during the nineteenth century, these and other "robber barons" were able to gain monopoly or near-monopoly power in their respective industries. This was accomplished through several means, including mergers with competing businesses and the formation of trusts, where a group of managers controlled rival companies without formal ownership of the businesses. This concentration of economic power in a few giant corporations made it possible to take advantage of the efficiencies and stability that come with large-scale production, but it also gave corporations the ability to manipulate prices and government policy.

Big business thrived also because of the absence of any meaningful counterweight to its influence. Unions were very weak. Many states restricted union activity, companies routinely terminated union members, and federal or state troops often helped companies break strikes. Courts were also very supportive of corporate power. In 1886, the Supreme Court held that corporations were "persons" for the purposes of constitutional protections, such as equal protection. In 1905, in LOCHNER v. NEW YORK, the Court struck down a New York state law limiting the number of work hours for bakers, saying that such laws were contrary to the freedom of contract implicit in the Constitution. Employers thereafter used *Lochner* to strike down minimum-wage laws.

Meanwhile, states competed among themselves to be the place where companies chose to incorporate, because of the large fees thus generated. Earlier, states routinely placed restrictions on the size, life span, and activities of corporations, as well as their ability to hold stock in other companies. In 1889, New Jersey adopted a statute that released corporations from such regulation, and so many businesses rushed to incorporate in New Jersey that the entire expenses of the state were eventually paid out of incorporation fees. Other states, seeking to stem the flow of businesses to New Jersey, were forced to remove many of their own restraints on corporations. This came to be known as "the race to the bottom."

Public outcry against the power of corporations led the federal government to adopt the SHERMAN ANTITRUST ACT in 1890, which outlawed any contract, combination, or conspiracy in restraint of trade and prohibited market monopolies. The act had little meaningful effect. Other than bringing about the breakup of a few large conglomerates, such as Rockefeller's Standard Oil Company, the act did little to alter the balance of economic power. Instead, courts often applied the act against unions, saying

that strikes and other labor organizing efforts interfered with commerce.

The Great Depression, which began in 1929, began to have some effect on the power of big business. After business could not pull the nation out of depression, many people lost faith in business executives and began to look to the government and the labor movement for help. The Supreme Court overturned *Lochner*, empowering the government to enact economic regulation to limit the power of business, protect the rights of unions to organize, and secure minimum wages and reasonable hours for workers.

The framework of governmental regulation and trade union representation provided some measure of balance to the economic power of business during the middle of the twentieth century. The efforts to regulate business and the market gained energy again in the 1960s and 1970s, when the federal government passed a host of regulatory initiatives to assist workers and to control the power of big business. These initiatives included the OCCUPATIONAL HEALTH AND SAFETY ACT, anti-discrimination initiatives, increases in the minimum wage, and a host of environmental laws including the CLEAN AIR ACT and the CLEAN WATER ACT. Throughout the post–New Deal period until the early 1970s, average weekly wages (in real terms) rose, and income inequality fell.

During the last two decades of the twentieth century, business interests regained much of the influence they had lost during the middle of the century. Beginning with the strongly pro-business Reagan and Bush administrations, and continued by the Clinton administration, the federal government took a less strict attitude toward controlling monopolies and limiting the power of businesses. Bolstered further by a strong stock market, particularly in the 1990s, businesses merged at an unprecedented rate. The total dollar volume of mergers increased throughout the 1990s, setting new records in each year from 1994 to 1999 (see MERGERS AND ACQUISITIONS). Many companies became globalized, diversifying their manufacturing and sales internationally. Spurred by major technological advances, technology, computer, software, and media conglomerates became some of the most powerful companies in the United States. By late 1999, the size and economic power of some companies rivaled that of nations. The total value of the stock of International Business Machines (IBM) was roughly equal to the gross domestic product (GDP) of Colombia, Microsoft's capitalization was equal to the GDP of Spain, and American Express's capitalization equaled the GDP of New Zealand.

Meanwhile, wages for working people stagnated, and inequality between the rich and poor became worse than at any time since the 1940s. Compensation for corporate chief executive officers rose almost 600 percent during the 1990s, but average weekly wages for the working class were lower than in the early 1970s. In 1998, the CEO of the software giant Microsoft, William H. Gates 3d, had personal wealth of $50 billion, more than the combined net worth of the poorest 40 percent of the U.S. population. Union membership declined sharply, and stood at historically low levels. Some analysts argued that the power of business at the end of the twentieth century rivaled that at the end of the nineteenth.

BIBLIOGRAPHY

Beatty, Jack. *Colossus: How the Corporation Changed America*. New York: Broadway Books, 2001.

Derber, Charles. *Corporation Nation: How Corporations Are Taking Over Our Lives and What We Can Do About It*. New York: St. Martin's Press, 1998.

Prechel, Harland. *Big Business and the State: Historical Transitions and Corporate Transformation, 1880s–1990s*. Albany: State University of New York Press, 2000.

Zinn, Howard. *A People's History of the United States*. New York: Harper and Row, 1980, pp. 247–289.

Kent Greenfield

See also **Corporations; Labor.**

BUSINESS, MINORITY. The term "minority business" refers to businesses owned by members of racial or ethnic minority groups. Through the middle of the twentieth century, such enterprises were typically small businesses with relatively small amounts of working capital that served the minority community itself. As a result of the civil rights movement of the 1960s, the federal government began programs to encourage minority enterprise. In 1965, the Small Business Administration began to channel loans to minority businesses. In 1969, the Office of Minority Business Enterprise (from 1979 the Minority Business Development Agency) was created within the Department of Commerce to coordinate public and private initiatives in the development of minority businesses. The law establishing the Office designated African Americans, Latinos, Native Americans, Asians, Aleut, and Eskimos as minority groups eligible for assistance in business development. These efforts appeared to have an impact. Two 1981 surveys found that fifty-six of the top one hundred African American firms at that time had been formed between 1969 and 1976 and that forty-five of the top one hundred Latino businesses had been formed during the same time period.

During the 1970s and 1980s, while most minority enterprises continued to be small retail businesses, minority businesses were also established or expanded in construction, engineering, and business and professional services. Beginning with the administration of President Richard Nixon (1969–1974), their efforts were aided by set-aside programs of local, state, and federal governments that mandated a certain percentage of public contracts for minority firms. These set-asides were justified in part as ways to overcome past racial discrimination and in part on the grounds of breaking down barriers to business development suffered by minority-owned firms. A 1997 study by the Urban Institute identified several obstacles faced by minority firms: lack of financial capital; limited access to informal business networks; lower human capital; and limited access to nonminority markets.

Government set-asides were controversial on both political and legal grounds. They were politically divisive because some people saw them as essential to redress a long tradition of discrimination in the United States, while others saw them as unfairly reserving government contracts to businesses that did not have to compete on the same terms as others. Legally, these set-asides were controversial because they raised difficult issues about whether the government could use race as an explicit criteria in the distribution of government benefits.

Several U.S. Supreme Court cases considered this latter question. The two most important were *Richmond v. J. A. Croson Company* (1989) and *Adarand Constructors v. Pena* (1995). In *Croson*, the Court held that state and local set-aside programs would be subject to the Court's rigorous strict scrutiny standard under the equal protection clause. Under this standard of review, government programs using race as a criteria are upheld only if the racial classifications serve a "compelling interest" and are "narrowly tailored" to serve that interest. *Croson* has been interpreted to mean that state and local set-asides will be upheld only if they are intended to redress specific discrimination in a specific industry. The programs will not be upheld if they are justified as attempting to redress general societal discrimination.

In *Adarand*, the Court applied the strict scrutiny standard to a set-aside program of the federal government even though it had implied in *Croson* that the Fourteenth Amendment gave the federal government greater power than state and local governments to redress the effects of past discrimination. Thus, after *Adarand*, set-aside programs, and indeed all government affirmative action programs, had to be justified by a compelling interest and be narrowly tailored. Nevertheless, the Court left open the question of what, if any, government interest would be deemed compelling. *Adarand* and *Croson* made it much more difficult to justify government set-aside programs as a legal matter, but they did not end them entirely.

Notwithstanding the trend away from government assistance through set-asides, minority businesses were, according to a 1999 study by Small Business Administration, a fast-growing segment of the U.S. economy. By 1997, there were an estimated 3.25 million minority-owned businesses in the United States, generating nearly $500 billion in revenues and employing almost four million workers. Between 1987 and 1997, the number of minority businesses increased 168 percent, while revenues grew 343 percent and employment climbed 362 percent.

BIBLIOGRAPHY

Enchautegui, Maria E., et al. *Do Minority-Owned Firms Get a Fair Share of Government Contracts?* Washington, D.C.: Urban Institute, 1997. A comprehensive report on the status of minority-firm government contracting.

Office of Advocacy. U.S. Small Business Administration. *Minorities in Business*. Washington, D.C.: n. p., 1999. Also available at http://www.sba.gov/advo.

Rotunda, Ronald D., and John E. Nowak. *Treatise on Constitutional Law: Substance and Procedure*. 3d ed. Vol. 3. St. Paul, Minn.: West, 1999. A comprehensive treatise on constitutional law including the issue of affirmative action.

Kent Greenfield

See also **Equal Protection of the Law; *Richmond v. J. A. Croson Company*.**

BUSINESS, REGULATION OF. *See* Government Regulation of Business.

BUSINESS CYCLES

are the irregular fluctuations in aggregate economic activity observed in all developed market economies. Aggregate economic activity is measured by real gross domestic product (GDP), the sum weighted by market prices, of all goods and services produced in an economy. Comparisons of real GDP across years are adjusted for changes in the average price level (inflation). A business cycle contraction or recession is commonly defined as at least two successive three-month periods (quarters) in which real GDP falls. A business cycle then contains some period in which real GDP grows followed by at least half a year in which real GDP falls. Some business cycles are longer than others. As Table 1 shows, most contractions last for less than a year, with real GDP falling by 1 to 6 percent. Expansions are more variable, though most last from two to six years.

Business cycles date from at least colonial times. The data for the colonial period are limited; thus, it is more difficult to date cycles precisely. When the United States was primarily agricultural, fluctuations in climate exerted a strong influence on economic cycles. While business cycles are defined in terms of GDP, a number of other economic variables tend to move in concert with GDP. Aggregate consumption expenditures rise and fall with GDP. Investment does too, but it tends to rise much faster than GDP during expansions and to fall much faster in recessions. The trade balance increases as GDP falls and vice versa, and imports in particular tend to rise during expansions and fall during contractions. Interest rates, notably short-term interest rates, tend to rise in expansions and fall in contractions. The aggregate price level often moves up and down with GDP, as do profits.

Aggregate employment also rises during expansions and falls during contractions, usually fluctuating less than GDP. The unemployment rate rarely rises by more than 4 percent in a recession, in part because the average hours worked per worker rises and falls with the cycle. Also, firms tend to "hoard" some workers during recessions to obviate the need to rehire as the expansion begins. Consequently, output per worker falls during recessions.

Other economic variables sometimes move in concert with GDP. The "leading indicators," which tend to precede changes in GDP, include capacity utilization by industry, construction starts or construction plans, orders received for capital equipment, new business formation, new bond and equity issues, and business expectations. Studying these along with the aggregate variables, analysts attempt to forecast cycles, which is especially difficult when predicting the timing of turning points between expansion and contraction. While severe contractions affect every sector of the economy, milder contractions are observed only in some sectors, and employment continues to rise in about a quarter of industries.

Different Types of Cycles

Scholars in the early post–World War II period often distinguished "growth cycles," in which contractions were defined as a decline in the rate of GDP growth, from the less frequent business cycles, in which contractions were defined as decreases in GDP. Some held out hope that the business cycle could be replaced with less severe growth cycles.

While the chronology of business cycles produced by the National Bureau of Economic Research (NBER) (Table 1) is widely accepted, different definitions of the term "contraction" could easily combine or subdivide particular cycles. Indeed, the NBER does not adhere strictly to the definition of a recession as two successive quarters of GDP decline. Instead, a committee determines, by looking at movements in variables, when turning points have occurred. Some scholars have criticized this committee's decisions.

Economists from time to time have hypothesized the existence of at least three other economic cycles, including a shorter Kitchin or inventory cycle, identified by Joseph Kitchin in 1923, of about forty months in length; a Kuznets cycle, suggested by Simon Kuznets in 1958, of fifteen to twenty-five years in duration; and a Kondratiev or Long Wave cycle, popularized by Nikolai Kondratiev in 1922, of fifty to sixty years in duration. However, none of these is accepted as widely as the business cycle, which bears a strong similarity to the cycle identified by Clément Juglar in the 1860s.

Debate regarding Long Waves has been intense. If these exist, only a handful would have occurred in the modern era, and the major wars complicate interpretation of the historical record. Moreover, explaining fairly regular fluctuations of a half-century duration is arguably a more difficult theoretical task than explaining business cycles. Analyzing the same variables, most scholars of Long Waves emphasize the interplay among technological and economic phenomena. While the existence of fairly regular Long Waves is disputed both empirically and theoretically, the historical record clearly shows periods of more than one business cycle in length in which economic growth and employment were high, such as the 1950s and 1960s, and other periods of more than a business cycle in

TABLE 1

U.S. Business Cycle Expansions and Contractions

Reference Dates		Duration in Months			
		Contraction	Expansion	Cycle	
Trough	Peak	Trough from Previous Peak	Trough to Peak	Trough from Previous Trough	Peak from Previous Peak
December 1854	June 1857	–	30	–	–
December 1858	October 1860	18	22	48	40
June 1861	April 1865	8	46	30	54
December 1867	June 1869	32	18	78	50
December 1870	October 1873	18	34	36	52
March 1879	March 1882	65	36	99	101
May 1885	March 1887	38	22	74	60
April 1888	July 1890	13	27	35	40
May 1891	January 1893	10	20	37	30
June 1894	December 1895	17	18	37	35
June 1897	June 1899	18	24	36	42
December 1900	September 1902	18	21	42	39
August 1904	May 1907	23	33	44	56
June 1908	January 1910	13	19	46	32
January 1912	January 1913	24	12	43	36
December 1914	August 1918	23	44	35	67
March 1919	January 1920	7	10	51	17
July 1921	May 1923	18	22	28	40
July 1924	October 1926	14	27	36	41
November 1927	August 1929	13	21	40	34
March 1933	May 1937	43	50	64	93
June 1938	February 1945	13	80	63	93
October 1945	November 1948	8	37	88	45
October 1949	July 1953	11	45	48	56
May 1954	August 1957	10	39	55	49
April 1958	April 1960	8	24	47	32
February 1961	December 1969	10	106	34	116
November 1970	November 1973	11	36	117	47
March 1975	January 1980	16	58	52	74
July 1980	July 1981	6	12	64	18
November 1982	July 1990	16	92	28	108
March 1991	March 2001	8	120	100	128
Average					
1854–1991 (31 cycles)		18	35	53	53*
1854–1919 (16 cycles)		22	27	48	49**
1919–1945 (6 cycles)		18	35	53	53
1945–1991 (9 cycles)		11	50	61	61

*30 cycles
**15 cycles

SOURCE: National Bureau of Economic Research Website (http://www.nber.org/cycles.html)

length in which economic growth was sluggish at best and unemployment was high, such as the 1930s or the 1970s and 1980s. Such periods likely require a different type of explanation. An understanding of the causes of economic growth in general should in turn inform the understanding of business cycles, because fluctuations would not likely be seen in a world without growth.

The fact that growth rates are higher in some periods than others poses difficulties for the empirical evaluation of business cycles. Ascertaining the severity of the business cycle requires knowing the growth rate around which cyclical fluctuations occur. But observation of a change in GDP from one year to the next conflates the effect of the trend growth rate and the effect of the cycle. Thus, analysts use complex and controversial statistical techniques to distinguish trends from cycles. This task would increase in complexity if economists accepted the existence of more than one type of cycle.

The existence of natural seasonal fluctuations in economic activity, associated with climatic changes and the bunching of purchases around holidays such as Christmas, adds another complication. Economists prefer to look at "seasonally adjusted" figures when evaluating economic performance. Has the change from month to month been greater or less than is usually observed between those two months? But as the economy evolves, so does the desirable seasonal adjustment.

Causes of Business Cycles

Economists have long debated the causes of business cycles, especially since the Great Depression. At that time, macroeconomics, the study of aggregate economic activity, emerged. Economists increasingly have recognized, however, that an understanding of business cycles requires microeconomic foundations, that is, an understanding of how the interaction of individuals and firms in the markets for goods and services, finance, and labor generates business cycles.

Theories of business cycles can be divided into two broad categories. The first argues that cycles are exogenous or due to a variety of shocks. These shocks stimulate either economic expansion or contraction. The second argues that cycles are endogenous or self-generated by the market economy. Theoretical debates often have an ideological tinge influenced by scholarly attitudes toward the market economy and the desirability of government interference. Nevertheless, after decades of often heated debate, economists widely recognize that one right answer is not likely. Different forces have differential impacts on different cycles, and both exogenous and endogenous arguments have some explanatory power.

Exogenous theories emphasize a variety of shocks. Some speak of political shocks; for instance, politicians may encourage economic expansion just before elections. Shocks to the prices of important raw materials, such as oil, are often mentioned at least with respect to particular cycles.

More commonly, scholars argue that increases in the money supply encourage expansions and that central banks, fearing inflation, then restrict the money supply and trigger a contraction. To be sure, the supply of money does tend to rise and fall through cycles, but the debate concerns whether this is in large part a result of or a cause of cycles. Central banks, such as the Federal Reserve Bank, are not the sole influences on the money supply, which is affected also by the level of economic activity and the behavior of individual banks.

During the Great Depression and again later, some economists pointed to technological shocks. If, as seems to be the case, innovation does not occur evenly through time, then investment, consumption, and employment decisions would be expected to vary through time as a result. One problem that plagues this analysis is the difficulty of measuring innovation. Moreover, different innovations likely have different effects on different sectors.

The development of new products likely has a positive effect on employment, while the development of better ways of producing existing products likely has a negative effect on employment.

Theories of business cycles must grapple with two opposing questions: Why is economic activity not stable, and how is complete chaos avoided (why do both contractions and expansions always end)? The common presupposition is that equilibrating mechanisms take the economy back toward the trend growth rate but are sluggish in operation. Examples of equilibrating mechanisms include the tendency of firms to increase production as inventories fall, the tendency of people to buy more as prices fall, or the tendency of firms to hire more as wages fall. Another rarely discussed possibility is that shocks of opposing effects may hit the economy. Most of the time these shocks are roughly balanced, and thus cycles are not too severe. Occasionally, as during the Great Depression, shocks are unbalanced and produce lengthy expansions or contractions.

Exogenous theories need only posit some set of shocks and usually some imperfect equilibrating mechanisms. Endogenous theories must argue both for equilibrating mechanisms and for nonequilibrating mechanisms that take the economy away from its trend growth rate. One early example was the general theory of John Maynard Keynes in 1936. Keynes noted that any expenditure has a multiplier effect, as the person receiving the money in turn spends it and so on. He also recognized an accelerator effect in that any attempt to increase output would require a much greater increase in the rate of investment. The multiplier-accelerator mechanism would cause any positive or negative growth impulse to be magnified and the economy to move further away from the trend growth rate. Writing during the Great Depression, Keynes was skeptical that any equilibrating mechanisms were strong enough always to reverse a contraction. Subsequently, the followers of Keynes stressed that inflexibility in wages and prices can cause an economy to move away from the trend growth rate.

A variety of other endogenous approaches is possible. Banks may naturally increase and decrease credit through time. Businesses may habitually overinvest as they fight for market share and then cut back in the face of overcapacity. Businesses may also saturate markets for consumer durables and inevitably experience a sudden drop in demand for such goods, which in turn induces them to reduce production.

Theories of business cycles strive to explain not only movements in GDP but in those variables that tend to move in concert with GDP. Some theories posit that unemployment is largely voluntary. Workers adjust work decisions in response to changes in real wages, or perhaps only to perceptions of such changes if they are fooled by changes in price levels. Other theories stress the involuntary nature of unemployment. During contractions many individuals cannot find work, at least not at anything approaching previously available wage rates. The evidence from unemployed individuals seems to support the latter position, though unemployment rates are constructed on surveys that tend not to ask the unemployed what sort of wage offer they seek.

All theories of business cycles face the problem of the role of expectations. No doubt expectations influence important economic variables, notably business investment and consumer durable purchase decisions. But how are expectations formed? Do they respond primarily to movements in economic variables, and if so, do they respond in a predictable fashion?

Effects of Business Cycles

As noted, business cycles affect variables such as employment, profits, hours of work, and often prices and wages. They thus have a significant impact on people's lives. In severe contractions a sizable proportion of the population loses its income. This was especially true before the creation of unemployment insurance and welfare, when the unemployed depended on charity. Unemployment in turn can affect a variety of noneconomic variables, including decisions regarding marriage and having children; mental health; attitudes toward the wider society, including the potential for civil disorder; and voting patterns, giving politicians a greater chance of reelection during times of economic expansion.

With the advantage of hindsight, economists know that all contractions end, and most end fairly quickly. It is thus all too easy to downplay the effects of cycles. Families may be unable to either borrow or save enough in advance to avoid serious hardship during a contraction, and fears of a future recession may cause families to forgo investments in houses and cars. Moreover, individuals who come of age during a serious recession may find their entire lives affected, as during the next expansion prospective employers may eschew those who have been long unemployed.

Changes in Business Cycles

Since business cycles involve an interaction among several economic and likely several noneconomic variables, some changes in the character of business cycles, including average duration, severity of fluctuations, or impact upon different sectors of the economy, should occur as an economy develops. Some have argued for the existence of a "new economy," in which the application of information technology would lessen the severity of cycles, yet most economists have been skeptical.

Considerable debate has focused on this question: Have business cycle fluctuations become less severe than they were before World War I? The debate has hinged primarily on the estimation of movements in GDP before such statistics were collected by the government. Most economists accept that business cycles involve longer expansions and shorter and shallower recessions than did those before World War I.

Most scholars attribute the longer expansions and shorter recessions primarily to government initiatives. The establishment of automatic stabilizers, such as unemployment insurance, have ensured that workers do not lose their entire incomes and thus their ability to spend when they lose their jobs in a recession. In addition, the government and the Federal Reserve have striven to adjust spending, taxation, and the money supply to reduce the severity of cycles. By putting more or less money in people's hands, they aim to increase or decrease the level of economic activity. Some economists worry that the government, due to a limited ability to predict cycles plus the time required to actually adjust spending or tax decisions, as often as not worsens cycles by, say, increasing spending after a contraction has already ended. Another concern is that taxpayers, faced with an increase in government debt, may reduce their own spending to save in anticipation of future tax increases. Nevertheless, substantial empirical evidence indicates that changes in government spending and taxation do affect the level of economic activity.

Other possible explanations of increased economic stability include the lesser incidence of financial panics, which were an important component of nineteenth-century recessions, due in large part to deposit insurance, introduced in 1934; increased flexibility of wages and prices, important for equilibrating mechanisms; management of inventories so firms do not build them up at the start of a downturn, then slash production to compensate; increased importance of the service sector, which tends to be less volatile than industry because many goods are purchased irregularly; and increased business confidence that downturns will be short.

Analysis of Particular Cycles

The discussion above suggests that different theoretical approaches have different explanatory power with respect to particular cycles. No approach should be ignored in studying any cycle. An obvious danger is to ignore endogenous arguments in favor of unique exogenous shocks when analyzing a particular cycle. It is possible though that exogenous shocks loom larger in the more severe cycles that attract most historical attention.

Banking panics were a common characteristic of recessions as late as the Great Depression. The resulting bank failures surely exacerbated contractionary tendencies, for people could not spend money they had lost. The question is how great this contractionary tendency was relative to the size of particular recessions. Likewise, stock market crashes can have a contractionary impact; these dramatic events may receive more attention than warranted by their economic impact. More generally, changes in interest rates and money supply often are associated with cycles and are attributed an important causal role. The 1929 crash has often been blamed for inducing the Great Depression, although the crash of 1987 was not associated with a serious economic downturn.

Sudden increases in raw material prices, such as occurred with copper during the early days of electrification in 1907 or oil in the 1970s, likely played some role in inducing recessions. Electrification, the assembly line, the automobile, and the television are among a number of major technological innovations that almost certainly had some impact on the level of economic activity and employment. As prices of many products rose, consumers and investors reduced their purchases. Saturated markets for houses, cars, and other durables have been observed during contractions in the 1930s and the 1970s. New products usually, but not always, cause increased investment and employment, while new production processes generally cause employment to fall.

Since the Great Depression, governments have taken an active role in trying to affect economic activity by adjusting the level of taxes and spending. Central banks too have tried to affect economic activity through adjustments to the money supply or interest rates. Even before the Great Depression, major government expenditures, such as during war or for the development of transport infrastructure, would have had some expansionary effect. As noted above, economists debate whether governments thus alleviate cycles or instead make these worse by increasing spending during expansions or reducing spending in recessions.

BIBLIOGRAPHY

Berry, Brian J. L. *Long-Wave Rhythms in Economic Development and Political Behavior.* Baltimore: Johns Hopkins University Press, 1991.

Burns, Arthur F., and Wesley C. Mitchell. *Measuring Business Cycles.* New York: National Bureau of Economic Research, 1946. A classic work by two leading scholars of business cycles of the time.

Diebold, Francis X., and Glenn D. Rudebusch. *Business Cycles: Durations, Dynamics, and Forecasting.* Princeton, N.J.: Princeton University Press, 1999. Discusses the statistical analysis of business cycles, and compares pre–World War I and post–World War II cycles.

Friedman, Milton, and Anna J. Schwartz. *A Monetary History of the United States, 1867–1960.* Princeton, N.J.: Princeton University Press, 1963. Classic argument for the importance of changes in monetary variables in generating cycles; unusually relies on examinations of particular cycles rather than on statistical analysis across several cycles.

Goldstein, Joshua S. *Long Cycles: Prosperity and War in the Modern Age.* New Haven, Conn.: Yale University Press, 1988.

Hall, Thomas E. *Business Cycles: The Nature and Causes of Economic Fluctuations.* New York: Praeger, 1990. A rare combination of a theoretical survey and application to selected twentieth-century cycles.

Keynes, John Maynard. *The General Theory of Employment, Interest, and Money.* London: Macmillan, 1936. Generally recognized as having spawned the field of macroeconomics.

National Bureau of Economic Research. "U.S. Business Cycle Expansions and Contractions." Available at http://www.nber.org/cycles.html.

Ralf, Kirsten. *Business Cycles: Market Structure and Market Interaction.* New York: Physica-Verlag, 2000. Surveys modern theories, with an emphasis on microeconomic foundations.

Schumpeter, Joseph A. *Business Cycles.* New York: McGraw-Hill, 1939. Classic argument for the existence of four cycles of differing average durations.

Solomou, Solomos. *Phases of Economic Growth, 1850–1973: Kondratieff Waves and Kuznets Swings.* New York: Cambridge University Press, 1987. Argues for the existence of Kuznets cycles.

Zarnowitz, Victor. *Business Cycles: Theory, History, Indicators, and Forecasting.* Chicago: University of Chicago Press, 1992. Discussion of the evolution of the measurement of business cycles by a scholar long connected with the NBER.

Rick Szostak

See also **Banking; Economic Indicators; Economics; Federal Reserve System; Financial Panics; Great Depression; Keynesianism; National Bureau of Economic Research; Unemployment.**

BUSINESS FORECASTING is an estimate or prediction of future developments in business such as sales, expenditures, and profits. Given the wide swings in economic activity and the drastic effects these fluctuations can have on profit margins, it is not surprising that business forecasting has emerged as one of the most important aspects of corporate planning. Forecasting has become an invaluable tool for businesspeople to anticipate economic trends and prepare themselves either to benefit from or to counteract them. If, for instance, businesspeople envision an economic downturn, they can cut back on their inventories, production quotas, and hirings. If, on the contrary, an economic boom seems probable, those same businesspeople can take necessary measures to attain the maximum benefit from it. Good business forecasts can help business owners and managers adapt to a changing economy.

At a minimum, businesses now need annual forecasts. One reason business planners prefer the annual averages is that sudden changes in the economic climate can play havoc with the quarter-to-quarter measurements. For instance, during the first half of 1984, a sudden growth spurt in the economy upset most business forecasts. Spurred to expansiveness by a surging cash flow, businesses added to their stock of plant and equipment at the fastest rate in five years. Government spending also went up faster than expected, as did business inventories. That set the stage for the sharp second-half slowdown that included an increased demand for credit and, consequently, higher interest rates. At the time, few had foreseen the short-term trend.

Many experts agree that precise business forecasting is as much an art as a science. Because business cycles are not repetitious, a good forecast results as much from experience, sound instincts, and good judgement as from an established formula. Business forecasters can be, and have often been, completely off the mark in their predictions. If nothing else, business forecasts can be used as blueprint to better understand the nature and causes of economic fluctuations.

Creating the Business Forecast

When twentieth-century business forecasting began, economists looked at a variety of factors, from money to box-car holdings to steel production. Sometimes the factors were added together to create an index of leading economic indicators that acted as a barometer of future economic conditions.

Modern forecasting got its impetus from the Great Depression of the 1930s. The effort to understand and correct the worldwide economic disaster led to the development of a vastly greater compilation of statistics as well as the evolution of techniques needed to analyze them. Business organizations manifested more concern with anticipating the future, and a number of highly successful consulting firms emerged to provide forecasting help for governments and businesses.

Forecasting for a business begins with a survey of the industry or industries in which it is involved. Beyond that initial review, the analyst determines the degree to which the company's share of each market may vary during the forecasting period. Today, business forecasting is done with the help of computers and special programs designed to model the economic future. Many of these programs are based on macroeconomic models, particularly those of Lawrence Klein of the Wharton School of Business, winner of the 1980 Nobel Prize for his work in economic modeling. Over a period of thirty years, Klein constructed a number of forecasting systems. Two of these systems, the econometric unit of the Chase Manhattan Bank and the Data Resources Inc. (DRI) model, are among the most widely used forecasting programs.

Forecasting programs are often put together and run as a system of mathematical equations. Early models were composed of a dozen or more different equations. The larger systems of today, however, have anywhere from a few hundred to approximately 10,000 variables that can be used to create a forecast. Forecasters also examine certain external variables such as population, government spending, taxation, and monetary policy to calculate how each will influence future trends and developments. They may conduct a "naive forecast" in which they assume that the next year's rate of growth will be equal to the growth rate of the present year. Taking these factors into account, forecasters create their model to provide a business forecast for the following week, month, year, or decade.

Numerical forecasts of the main national accounts, national economic indicators, industry time series, and firm accounting statements are regularly prepared. The forecasting of business trends takes place on three levels: at the national level, at the industry or market level, and at the level of the individual firm. It has become popular to combine forecasts for one, two, or three years ahead and to include quarterly forecasts spanning the same time horizon. Some firms need monthly or weekly forecasts, whereas others use forecasts that look forward two or three decades in order to make their decisions. Among the companies that commonly use long-range forecasting are life insurance corporations, public utility companies, and firms involved in long-term construction or manufacturing projects.

The Accuracy of Business Forecasts

Although businesses and governments pay millions of dollars for forecasts, those forecasts are not always on target, particularly during turbulent economic times. Perhaps one of the worst years on record for business forecasters was 1982. Experts generally believe that business forecasters, caught up in the excitement of President Reagan's supply-side economic programs, simply stopped paying attention to what was really happening. As a result, the 1982 forecasts are among the worst in economic history.

Making accurate business forecasts is most difficult for companies that produce durable goods such as automobiles or appliances, as well as for companies that supply the basic materials to these industries. Problems arise because sales of such goods are subject to extreme variations. During the early 1970s, annual sales of automobiles in the United States increased by 22 percent in one year and declined by 22.5 percent in another. Consequently, the durable goods industries in general, and automobile companies in particular, have developed especially complex and sophisticated forecasting techniques. In addition to careful analysis of income trends (based on a general economic forecast), automobile companies, which are acutely sensitive to competition from imports, underwrite a number of studies of consumer attitudes and surveys of intentions to purchase automobiles.

The Future of Business Forecasting

Today, many executives are unhappy with the economic forecasts they receive. As a result, they have fired economists and are paying less attention to macroeconomic forecasts, arguing that these forecasts cost too much and reveal too little. Instead they are now leaning more heavily on their own rough-and-ready indicators of what is likely to happen to their businesses and industries. When they do consult economists, they increasingly send them into the field with line managers to forecast the particulars that really matter.

Executives are now exploring other means of forecasting the business future. Some watch the growth of the Gross National Product (GNP). Disposable personal income is another broad measure that suffices, particularly in retailing. By observing whether economic indicators rise or fall, executives can more accurately predict their retail sales picture in six months or a year.

For many companies, however, no single indicator works to predict the future. Some might use the monthly consumer confidence index or study the stock market with regard to certain companies. Depending on the circumstances, interest rates may have a bearing on the future. High or low rates may determine whether the consumer will be in the market to buy or just keep looking at certain products such as cars, boats, houses, and other big-ticket items. Many companies are taking one or more basic indicators and building them into economic models tailor-made for specific industries and markets.

Scenario Planning versus Business Forecasting

In the 1990s, economists developed new methods of business forecasting that rest more on hard data and less on theoretical assumptions. They acknowledge that the economy is dynamic and volatile, and have tried to keep in mind that all forecasts, however sophisticated, are greatly simplified representations of reality that will likely be incorrect in some respects.

One of the newer forecasting techniques is called "scenario forecasting." More businesses are using the scenario method to devise their "strategic direction." In scenario forecasting, companies develop scenarios to identify major changes that could happen in the world and determine the possible effects those changes will have on their operations. They then map out ways in which to react if those occurrences come to pass, hoping that the hypothetical exercise will make them better prepared to take action when a real economic crisis takes place.

One of the biggest reasons to use the scenario method is that traditional forecasting does not keep up with the lightning-quick pace at which modern business moves. Where change could once be anticipated over a period of time, the advent of sophisticated technology, which by itself is ever changing, has shown businesspeople that they need a new way of looking at and thinking about the economic future.

BIBLIOGRAPHY

Fost, Dan, and Brad Edmonston. "How to Think about the Future." *American Demographics* 20 (February 1998): 6–12.

Gunther, Robert E., and Paul J.H. Schoemaker. *Profiting from Uncertainty: Strategies for Succeeding No Matter What the Future Brings.* New York: Free Press, 2002.

Hutchins, Dexter. "And Now, the Home-Brewed Forecast." *Fortune,* 20 January 1986, 53–54.

Pindyck, Robert S., and Daniel L. Rubinfield. *Econometric Models and Economic Forecasts.* Boston: McGraw Hill, 1998.

Meg Greene Malvasi

See also **Business Cycles; Economic Indicators; Economics.**

BUSINESS MACHINES.

The history of business machines includes a vast array of devices, most invented during or after the early nineteenth century. Many of the basic technologies were invented early in the industrial revolution but not fully implemented until workers could

Chester F. Carlson. The inventor of the "xerography" process, with the result: the first Xerox copier. © CORBIS-BETTMANN

be compelled to use them. The typewriter, for example, was first patented in 1714 by Henry Mill but rarely used until the twentieth century, when low-wage female workers replaced men in clerical positions. Similarly, one of the first mechanical calculators was invented by Blaise Pascal in 1642, and while desk calculators became common in accounting offices by the nineteenth century, their operators lost their status as high-skill workers when women replaced men in the age of electronic keypunch equipment, accounting machines, and computers. In addition to their implications for male-female power struggles, many classes of business machines, such as the cash register (1879) and the dictation machine (1888), are also part of the larger story of the mechanization of white collar jobs. Many office machines were invented as part of an ongoing search for ways to improve business communication. This category includes the telegraph (1841), telephone (1876), pneumatic tube messaging systems (1865), and a succession of document facsimile or copying systems. Today, many of the functions of traditional office technologies have been incorporated into the personal computer, which has become nearly universal in the business environment.

David Morton

See also **Fax Machine; Office Technology; Telephone; Typewriter.**

BUSINESS UNIONISM. A term commonly used by scholars to characterize the historical role and strategic outlook of organized labor in the United States. Business unionism first became prominent in the 1880s, when trade union leaders organized the American Federation of Labor and explicitly emphasized improvements in wages, hours, and working conditions. Business unionism—literally, the union as a business that sells labor—stressed "pure and simple" goals in contrast to "social" unionism, which emphasized the welfare of the working class as a whole, the election of sympathetic officials, and the control of government. Business unionism had other implications. Focusing on improving wages, hours, and working conditions, these unions left other business decisions to employers; they did not attempt to influence managerial behavior except when employment levels, wages, or related matters were at stake. Business unionism also created biases in favor of workers who were the most competitive in the marketplace and an internal union structure that mimicked the structure of industry in order to facilitate collective bargaining and grievance settlements.

Business unionism received official recognition in the 1920s and 1930s with the adoption of federal and state policies (notably the Wagner Act of 1935) that encouraged union representation and collective bargaining within relatively narrow bounds. Over the last half century there has been a gradual decline of private sector unionism and a growth of public sector unionism.

BIBLIOGRAPHY

Commons, John R. et. al. *History of Labour in the United States.* New York: A.M. Kelley, 1966. The classic historical account.

Kochan, Thomas A., Harry C. Katz, and Robert B. McKersie. *The Transformation of American Industrial Relations.* Ithaca, N.Y.: ILR Press, 1994. An informed analysis that combines historical perspectives and discussions of contemporary issues.

Daniel Nelson

See also **American Federation of Labor–Congress of Industrial Organizations; Labor.**

BUSING is the transporting of children to school by bus to achieve DESEGREGATION or racial balance. Until the late 1960s, the yellow school bus had largely been viewed as a symbol of progress representing the nation's transition from the one-room schoolhouse to the comprehensive consolidated school. In some cases, the spread of the school bus actually served to preserve racial SEGREGATION instead of reducing it, but those cases were the exception. By 1970, 43 percent of the nation's 42 million children rode buses to school.

The SUPREME COURT began the process of school desegregation in 1954 with its decision in *Brown v. Board of Education of Topeka.* In many cities and towns, the immediate response to *Brown* was resistance, but the CIVIL RIGHTS ACT OF 1964, with its threat to cut off funding to schools that engaged in discrimination, prompted many southern school districts to eliminate race-conscious pupil assignments. The result was a substantial increase by the end of the decade in the percentage of African American students attending desegregated schools in the South. Nevertheless, residential segregaton and continuing resistance to integration impeded desegregation efforts in many areas. In 1971, in *Swann v. Charlotte-Mecklenburg Board of Education,* a unanimous Supreme Court held that busing children outside their immediate neighborhood was a legitimate tool for promoting school integration. Within a year of the decision, more than forty judges had entered orders directing the use of busing to eliminate school desegregation.

Busing generated intense opposition. In some places, parents resorted to protests, civil disobedience, and violence to resist efforts to bus their children away from, or to bus other children to, neighborhood schools. Many white families fled to districts not subject to busing orders. A 1971 Gallup poll found that 77 percent of respondents opposed busing, with African Americans almost evenly split. When lower federal courts, as early as 1970, began ordering busing to eliminate racial segregation in such nonsouthern cities as Denver and Detroit, members of Congress from northern and western states joined their southern colleagues in seeking antibusing legislation. They did this even though the U.S. Office of Education estimated that only 2 to 3 percent of all busing was for desegregation purposes. In March 1972, President Richard M. Nixon proposed a package of antibusing measures, including a moratorium act, and hinted at support for a constitutional amendment. In June, Congress passed the Higher Education Act, with compromise antibusing provisions, including the Broomfield amendment, which delayed implementation of court busing orders until appeals had been exhausted.

Federal judges transformed the school bus into a tool for desegregation. However, two important developments in school desegregation jurisprudence hampered the effectiveness of this tool over the last quarter of the twentieth century. The first development was a limit the Supreme Court put on interdistrict remedies for segregation. Many southern urban school districts encompassed both majority-black inner-city schools and majority-white suburban schools, so desegregation could be promoted with intradistrict remedies. In the north, on the other hand, many urban school districts contained only majority-black schools and could not be desegregated without crossing school district lines. In May 1973, the Supreme Court upheld an appeals court ruling that barred Richmond, Virginia, from merging its predominantly black city schools with predominantly white suburban schools by busing across school district lines. In a landmark decision in July 1974, the Court ruled by a vote of 5 to 4 that the federal district and appeals courts in a Detroit case, *Milliken v. Bradley*, had erred in requiring busing among suburban and city schools for purposes of desegregation, because there was no showing that the school districts had taken action that contributed to interdistrict segregation. Although some districts did use interdistrict desegregation measures after *Milliken*, either voluntarily or under court order, the case undermined the effectiveness of busing as a tool to end segregation in many urban school districts.

The second important development leading to a decline in busing for desegregation purposes was the increasing tendency of federal courts to find that the effects of past intentional segregation had been eradicated. During the 1980s, courts allowed several school districts to end court-ordered busing and return to neighborhood schools because the continuing racial isolation was due to residential segregation and not actions of the school district. In its first effort to address how to determine whether a school district had transformed itself from a dual school system to a unitary system, the Supreme Court held that a school district could be freed of court supervision if it had "complied in good faith with the desegregation decree since it was entered" and had eliminated "the vestiges of past discrimination . . . to the extent practicable." In that case, *Board of Education of Oklahoma City v. Dowell* (1991), the Court said that once a school district had achieved unitary status, it could alter its pupil assignment decisions without court supervision so long as it observed the mandate of the Fourteenth Amendment. In other words, the district could adopt a plan that exacerbated racial imbalance so long as legitimate educational concerns rather than an intent to discriminate motivated the district. By the end of the twentieth century, forty-two desegregation orders affecting forty-five school districts had been lifted. In those school districts that jettisoned busing plans and returned to neighborhood schools, school segregation usually increased.

Despite these judicial decisions, the use of busing to achieve integration had not ended by the early 2000s. Many school districts had not sought modification or termination of court-ordered desegregation plans. Furthermore, some districts had tried new desegregation strategies, such as MAGNET SCHOOLS and controlled choice plans, which allow parents to choose the schools their children will attend but which also require large-scale busing. Nevertheless, the effect of Supreme Court decisions of the 1980s and 1990s was to shift the debate over school desegregation and the desirability of busing from the federal courts to state legislatures, school boards, and parents.

BIBLIOGRAPHY

Armor, David J. *Forced Justice: School Desegregation and the Law.* New York: Oxford University Press, 1995.

Dimond, Paul R. *Beyond Busing: Inside the Challenge to Urban Segregation.* Ann Arbor: University of Michigan Press, 1985.

Formisano, Ronald P. *Boston Against Busing: Race, Class, and Ethnicity in the 1960s and 1970s.* Chapel Hill: University of North Carolina Press, 1991.

Gaillard, Frye. *The Dream Long Deferred.* Chapel Hill: University of North Carolina Press, 1988.

Orfield, Gary, Susan E. Eaton, and the Harvard Project on School Desegregation. *Dismantling Desegregation: The Quiet Reversal of Brown v. Board of Education.* New York: The New Press, 1996.

Patterson, James T. *Brown v. Board of Education: A Civil Rights Milestone and Its Troubled Legacy.* New York: Oxford University Press, 2001.

Schwartz, Bernard. *Swann's Way: The School Busing Case and the Supreme Court.* New York: Oxford University Press, 1986.

Hugh Davis Graham
Cynthia R. Poe

See also **Boston; Charlotte; Education; Education, Parental Choice in.**

BUTLER'S ORDER NO. 28. General Benjamin F. Butler became military commander of New Orleans on 1 May 1862, following the fall of the city to Union troops. Many residents were openly hostile to the federal government, and troops were especially angered by the women civilians who hurled insults at them. On 15 May, Butler ordered that any woman insulting or showing contempt for any U.S. officer or soldier should "be treated as a woman of the town plying her avocation." The order evoked a storm of protest at home and abroad and led to Butler's removal from command of New Orleans on 16 December 1862.

BIBLIOGRAPHY

Capers, Gerald Mortimer. *Occupied City: New Orleans under the Federals, 1862–1865.* Lexington: University of Kentucky Press, 1965.

Hearn, Chester G. *When the Devil Came Down to Dixie: Ben Butler in New Orleans.* Baton Rouge: Louisiana State University Press, 1997.

James E. Winston

See also **Civil War; Prostitution.**

ISBN 0-684-80523-5